EXERCISE–COGNITION
INTERACTION

EXERCISE– COGNITION INTERACTION

NEUROSCIENCE PERSPECTIVES

TERRY MCMORRIS

*Department of Sport and Exercise Science, University of
Chichester, Chichester, West Sussex, UK*

AMSTERDAM • BOSTON • HEIDELBERG • LONDON
NEW YORK • OXFORD • PARIS • SAN DIEGO
SAN FRANCISCO • SINGAPORE • SYDNEY • TOKYO

Academic Press is an imprint of Elsevier

Academic Press is an imprint of Elsevier
125 London Wall, London EC2Y 5AS, UK
525 B Street, Suite 1800, San Diego, CA 92101-4495, USA
225 Wyman Street, Waltham, MA 02451, USA
The Boulevard, Langford Lane, Kidlington, Oxford OX5 1GB, UK

Notices
Knowledge and best practice in this field are constantly changing. As new research and experience broaden our understanding, changes in research methods, professional practices, or medical treatment may become necessary.

Practitioners and researchers must always rely on their own experience and knowledge in evaluating and using any information, methods, compounds, or experiments described herein. In using such information or methods they should be mindful of their own safety and the safety of others, including parties for whom they have a professional responsibility.

To the fullest extent of the law, neither the Publisher nor the authors, contributors, or editors, assume any liability for any injury and/or damage to persons or property as a matter of products liability, negligence or otherwise, or from any use or operation of any methods, products, instructions, or ideas contained in the material herein.

ISBN: 978-0-12-800778-5

British Library Cataloguing-in-Publication Data
A catalogue record for this book is available from the British Library

Library of Congress Cataloging-in-Publication Data
A catalog record for this book is available from the Library of Congress

For information on all Academic Press publications
visit our website at http://store.elsevier.com/

Working together
to grow libraries in
developing countries

www.elsevier.com • www.bookaid.org

Publisher: Mara Conner
Acquisition Editor: April Farr
Editorial Project Manager: Timothy Bennett
Production Project Manager: Chris Wortley
Designer: Mark Rogers

Typeset by TNQ Books and Journals
www.tnq.co.in

Printed and bound in the United States of America

Contents

13. Acute Exercise and Cognition in Children and Adolescents: The Roles of Testosterone and Cortisol

FLORA KOUTSANDRÉOU, CLAUDIA NIEMANN,
MIRKO WEGNER AND HENNING BUDDE

14. The Chronic Exercise–Cognition Interaction in Older Adults

CLAUDIA VOELCKER-REHAGE, CLAUDIA NIEMANN
AND BEN GODDE

15. The Chronic Exercise–Cognition Interaction and Parkinson Disease

MADELEINE E. HACKNEY, JOE R. NOCERA,
DAWN BOWERS, LORI J.P. ALTMANN AND
CHRIS J. HASS

16. The Chronic Exercise–Cognition Interaction and Dementia and Alzheimer's Disease

FLÁVIA GOMES DE MELO COELHO, THAYS MARTINS
VITAL, RUTH FERREIRA SANTOS-GALDURÓZ AND
SEBASTIÃO GOBBI

17. The Chronic Exercise–Cognition Interaction and Diabetes

MARIA PEDERSEN AND JESPER KROGH

18. The Exercise–Cognition Interaction and ADHD

SARAH C. O'NEILL, OLGA G. BERWID AND
ANNE-CLAUDE V. BÉDARD

Contributors

Lori J.P. Altmann Department of Speech, Language and Hearing Sciences, University of Florida, Gainesville, FL, USA

Soichi Ando Graduate School of Informatics and Engineering, University of Electro-Communications, Chofu, Tokyo, Japan

Michel Audiffren Research Institute on Cognition and Learning (UMR CNRS 7295), Sport Sciences Faculty, University of Poitiers, Poitiers, France

Anne-Claude V. Bédard Department of Applied Psychology and Human Development, Ontario Institute for Studies in Education, University of Toronto, Toronto, Ontario, Canada

Tal Dotan Ben-Soussan Research Institute for Neuroscience, Education and Didactics, Patrizio Paoletti Foundation for Development and Communication, Assisi, Italy; Bar-Ilan University, Ramat-Gan, Israel

Olga G. Berwid Department of Behavioral Sciences, York College of the City University of New York, Jamaica, NY, USA

Dawn Bowers Department of Clinical & Health Psychology, University of Florida, Gainesville, FL, USA

Henning Budde Medical School Hamburg, Faculty of Human Sciences, Department of Pedagogy, Hamburg, Germany; Reykjavik University, School of Science and Engineering, Department of Sport Science, Reykjavik, Iceland

Eduardo E. Bustamante Georgia Prevention Institute, Medical College of Georgia, Department of Pediatrics, Georgia Regents University, Augusta, GA, USA

Yu-Kai Chang Graduate Institute of Athletics and Coaching Science, National Taiwan Sport University, Guishan Township, Taoyuan County, Taiwan (R.O.C.)

Jo Corbett Department of Sport and Exercise Science, Faculty of Science, University of Portsmouth, Portsmouth, UK

Flávia Gomes de Melo Coelho Institute of Biosciences, UNESP, Univ. Estadual Paulista, Physical Activity and Aging Lab (LAFE), Rio Claro, São Paulo, Brazil; Department of Sports Sciences, UFTM, Univ. Federal do Triângulo Mineiro, Uberaba, Minas Gerais, Brazil

Catherine L. Davis Georgia Prevention Institute, Medical College of Georgia, Department of Pediatrics, Georgia Regents University, Augusta, GA, USA

Jennifer L. Etnier Department of Kinesiology, University of North Carolina at Greensboro, Greensboro, NC, USA

Sebastião Gobbi Institute of Biosciences, UNESP, Univ. Estadual Paulista, Physical Activity and Aging Lab (LAFE), Rio Claro, São Paulo, Brazil

Ben Godde Jacobs Center on Lifelong Learning and Institutional Development, Jacobs University, Bremen, Germany

John Gunstad Department of Psychological Sciences, Kent State University, Kent, OH, USA

Madeleine E. Hackney Atlanta VA Center for Visual and Neurocognitive Rehabilitation, Division of General Medicine and Geriatrics, Department of Medicine, Emory University School of Medicine, Decatur, GA, USA

Beverley J. Hale Department of Sport and Exercise Science, University of Chichester, Chichester, West Sussex, UK

G.F. Hamilton Department of Psychology, The Beckman Institute, University of Illinois at Urbana-Champaign, Urbana, IL, USA

Chris J. Hass Department of Applied Physiology and Kinesiology, University of Florida, Gainesville, FL, USA

Keita Kamijo Faculty of Sport Sciences, Waseda University, Mikajima, Tokorozawa, Saitama, Japan

Flora Koutsandréou Medical School Hamburg, Faculty of Human Sciences, Department of Pedagogy, Hamburg, Germany; University of Bern, Institute of Sport Science, Bern, Switzerland

Cynthia E. Krafft MIND Institute, Department of Psychiatry and Behavioral Sciences, University of California Davis, Sacramento, CA, USA

Jesper Krogh Department of Medicine, Center of Endocrinology and Metabolism, Copenhagen University Hospital Herlev, Herlev, Denmark

Michael J. Mackenzie Department of Behavioral Health & Nutrition, University of Delaware, Newark, DE, USA

Edward McAuley Department of Kinesiology & Community Health, University of Illinois at Urbana-Champaign, Urbana, IL, USA

Jennifer E. McDowell Department of Neuroscience, University of Georgia, Athens, GA, USA

Terry McMorris Department of Sport and Exercise Science, University of Chichester, Chichester, West Sussex, UK

Lindsay Miller Department of Psychiatry and Human Behavior, Warren Alpert Medical School of Brown University, Providence, RI, USA

Claudia Niemann Institute of Human Movement Science and Health, Technische Universitaet Chemnitz, Chemnitz, Germany; Jacobs Center on Lifelong Learning and Institutional Development, Jacobs University, Bremen, Germany

Joe R. Nocera Atlanta VA Center for Visual and Neurocognitive Rehabilitation, Department of Neurology, Emory University School of Medicine, Decatur, GA, USA

Sarah C. O'Neill Department of Psychology, City College of the City University of New York, New York, NY, USA; Department of Psychology, Graduate Center of the City University of New York, New York, NY, USA

Maria Pedersen Department of Clinical Physiology and Nuclear Medicine, Copenhagen University Hospital Herlev, Herlev, Denmark

Caterina Pesce Department of Movement, Human and Health Sciences, Italian University Sport and Movement "Foro Italico", Rome, Italy

Aaron T. Piepmeier Department of Kinesiology, University of North Carolina at Greensboro, Greensboro, NC, USA

J.S. Rhodes Department of Psychology, The Beckman Institute, University of Illinois at Urbana-Champaign, Urbana, IL, USA

Ruth Ferreira Santos-Galduróz Institute of Biosciences, UNESP, Univ. Estadual Paulista, Physical Activity and Aging Lab (LAFE), Rio Claro, São Paulo, Brazil; Center of Mathematics, Computing and Cognition, UFABC, Univ. Federal of ABC, Santo André, São Paulo, Brazil

David J. Schaeffer Department of Neuroscience, University of Georgia, Athens, GA, USA

Chia-Hao Shih Department of Kinesiology, University of North Carolina at Greensboro, Greensboro, NC, USA

John Sproule Institute of Sport, PE and Health Sciences, University of Edinburgh, Edinburgh, Scotland, UK

Anthony Turner Institute of Sport, PE and Health Sciences, University of Edinburgh, Edinburgh, Scotland, UK

Thays Martins Vital Institute of Biosciences, UNESP, Univ. Estadual Paulista, Physical Activity and Aging Lab (LAFE), Rio Claro, São Paulo, Brazil; Instituto Federal Goiano - Campus Morrinhos, Morrinhos, GO, Brazil

Claudia Voelcker-Rehage Institute of Human Movement Science and Health, Technische Universitaet Chemnitz, Chemnitz, Germany; Jacobs Center on Lifelong Learning and Institutional Development, Jacobs University, Bremen, Germany

Michelle W. Voss Department of Psychological and Brain Sciences, Aging Mind and Brain Initiative (AMBI), The University of Iowa, Iowa City, IA, USA

Mirko Wegner University of Bern, Institute of Sport Science, Bern, Switzerland

Krystle E. Zuniga Nutrition & Foods, Texas State University, San Marcos, TX, USA

History of Research into the Acute Exercise–Cognition Interaction: A Cognitive Psychology Approach

Terry McMorris

Department of Sport and Exercise Science, University of Chichester, Chichester, West Sussex, UK

INTRODUCTION

In this chapter, we examine the development of theoretical underpinnings for an acute exercise effect on cognition, from the earliest research until the emergence of recent neuroscientific research. We also examine the extent to which empirical research supported the behavioral and cognitive rationales and how failure to provide strong support led to a revision of these theoretical underpinnings. The overall aim of writing this chapter is to provide the reader with an outline of the background of theory and research, which has led to the current study of the acute exercise–cognition interaction from a neuroscientific perspective.

Development of Theoretical Rationales

The earliest research was atheoretical (e.g., Gutin & Di Gennaro, 1968a; McAdam & Wang, 1967; Meyers, Zimmerli, Farr, & Baschnagel, 1969). It appears to have simply been down to the whims of the researchers. The first to provide a theoretical underpinning for hypothesizing that acute exercise would have an effect on cognition was Davey (1973). He saw exercise as being a stressor, which could affect arousal in the same way as other stressors, such as anxiety, temperature, and white noise. Davey, therefore, turned to Yerkes and Dodson's (1908) arousal–performance theory to develop his hypotheses. Yerkes and Dodson claimed that when arousal is low, performance will be poor but, as arousal rises to a moderate level, performance will become optimal. However, if arousal continues to rise, performance will return to a level equal to that shown during low levels of arousal. When plotted graphically, performance demonstrates an inverted-U curve and, as a result, Yerkes and Dodson's theory became known as inverted-U theory. Based on this, Davey claimed that at rest and during low-intensity exercise, cognitive performance would be poor. When exercise intensity rose to a moderate level, performance would be optimal, but further increases in exercise intensity would mean a return to a poor level of performance.

Yerkes and Dodson (1908) showed empirically, with mice, that task complexity acted as a moderator with regard to the purity of the inverted-U curve. They found that if a task was easy, the curve was skewed toward the higher end of the arousal continuum, but if the task was complex, it was skewed the other way. In other words, easy tasks require comparatively high levels of arousal for optimal performance, whereas complex tasks require comparatively low levels of arousal.

Inverted-U theory continues to play a major role as an underlying theory with regard to acute exercise–cognition research, but most cognitive psychologists also include adaptations of Yerkes and Dodson's (1908) theory. Several (e.g., Allard, Brawley, Deakin, & Elliott, 1989; Fleury, Bard, & Carrière, 1981; Isaacs & Pohlman, 1991) have drawn on Easterbrook's (1959) cue utilization theory. Easterbrook felt that Yerkes and Dodson's theory failed to provide a rationale for how arousal would affect performance in an inverted-U fashion. Following a number of experiments into effects of arousal on dual task performance, Easterbrook claimed that increases in arousal from low to high levels results in a narrowing of focus of attention. He stated that when arousal level is low, the individual has too broad an attentional focus and attends to both relevant and irrelevant information; as a result performance is poor. As arousal rises, however, attention reaches an optimal level, when only task relevant cues are processed. This corresponds to the top of the inverted-U curve in Yerkes and Dodson's theory. If arousal continues to rise, however, attention will narrow further and even relevant cues will be missed, hence a deterioration in performance.

Yerkes and Dodson's (1908) and Easterbrook's (1959) theories remained the most popular theories for researchers to use as the theoretical underpinnings for their hypotheses until the 1990s. At this time, first the Poitiers group (e.g., Arcelin, Delignières, & Brisswalter, 1998; Brisswalter, Arcelin, Audiffren, & Delignières, 1997; Collardeau, Brisswalter, & Audiffren, 2001; Delignières, Brisswalter, & Legros, 1994) and later ourselves (McMorris & Graydon, 1996a, 1996b, 1997; McMorris & Keen, 1994) turned to what some call allocatable resources theories but others call cognitive–energetical theories (Kahneman, 1973; Sanders, 1983). These theories still predict an inverted-U effect on performance but the theories are multidimensional and as such are better able to explain interactions between the stressor and the task.

Kahneman (1973) believed that individuals have a limited amount of resources. The amount is not fixed but flexible. He claimed that as arousal rises, the number of resources available, within the brain, increases. Like Yerkes and Dodson, he argued that this increase is beneficial for performance up to a certain point, after which there will be a return to baseline levels. It is here that Kahneman disagrees with Yerkes and Dodson. To Kahneman, increases in arousal are not the only factor affecting performance. The increase in the number of resources, as arousal increases to a moderate level, will only result in improvements in performance if the person allocates the resources to the task in hand.

The allocation of resources to task relevant information is said to be undertaken by cognitive effort (more often just referred to as effort) and depends on the individual's allocation policy. Kahneman believed that there are four factors affecting this policy, what he termed enduring dispositions, momentary intentions, evaluation of task demands, and the effects of arousal. Enduring dispositions are the rules of involuntary attention, e.g., familiar and novel stimuli will be attended to automatically. Momentary intentions refer to the instructions given to the individual for that particular task at that moment in time. Perhaps of greatest importance is the evaluation of task demands. According to Kahneman, the person decides whether or not they have sufficient capacity, at that moment, to be able to do what is required of them. Finally, the effects of arousal refers to the available channel capacity at that moment in time.

Kahneman (1973) believed that during moderate levels of arousal, effort can easily allocate resources to the task. This does not differ from Yerkes and Dodson (1908) or Easterbrook (1959); however, during high levels of arousal, Kahneman believed that the individual would not be able to allocate resources to the task. In these circumstances, evaluation of task demands will tend to lead to the perception that the task cannot be successfully completed, while enduring dispositions may lead to the individual focusing on their feelings of distress or excitement.

Sanders (1983) took a similar approach to Kahneman (1973) but there were some differences. Sanders argued that the different stages of cognitive processing needed to be energized by different energetical mechanisms. He termed these arousal, activation, the evaluation mechanism, and effort. Arousal was seen as a readiness to process input and activation as a motor readiness to respond. The role of the evaluation mechanism is to provide effort with information concerning performance outcome and, perhaps more importantly, the physiological states of the arousal and activation mechanisms. This is vital because effort is responsible for energizing response choice but also has the job of controlling and coordinating arousal and activation. Sander's model draws a great deal from the model proposed by Pribram and McGuinness (1975), which could be described as a cognitive neuroscience model.

Pribram and McGuinness (1975), after examining the neuropsychological evidence for arousal, decided that it was more accurate to divide what Kahneman (1973) had called arousal into three distinct but interacting systems, which they called arousal, activation, and effort. Arousal was defined as being "phasic physiological responses to input" (p. 115), e.g., when a batter in baseball or cricket is facing a pitcher or bowler, their alertness and attention increase. Activation was seen as "a tonic physiological readiness to respond" (p. 115), e.g., the batter readies her/himself to hit the ball. Effort was described as the coordinating activity of the arousal and activation systems.

Audiffren (2009) and Audiffren, Tomporowski, and Zagrodnik (2009) saw Hockey's (1997) cognitive–energetical theory, sometimes called compensatory control theory, as being particularly useful in explaining the acute exercise–cognition interaction. Hockey's model is mostly concerned with how the individual performs under stress. He claimed that we have two performance regulation loops, the effortful control loop and the automatic control loop. The role of the automatic control mechanism, which functions without effort, is to undertake the regulation of well-learned skills. It includes a mechanism called the action monitor, which compares target outcomes with actual outcomes. If a discrepancy is detected, adjustments in resource allocation are made. However, even with well-learned skills, when under stress task demands can affect performance. The role of the effortful control loop is to maintain performance despite interference from stressors. Hockey saw this loop as containing a mechanism similar to that of Sanders' evaluation mechanism, which he called the effort monitor mechanism. It is assumed to be sensitive to the demands placed on the automatic control mechanism and whether or not it is coping. This information is passed to the supervisory controller, which decides on the compensatory action to be taken in order to solve the problem. This can be by increasing effort, if that is deemed possible, or by adjusting the individual's goals downwards, if the goal demands are perceived as being unobtainable.

Although individual researchers differed in their choice of theory or model, almost all followed an inverted-U approach. Moreover, few voiced any objections to the notion that acute exercise is a stressor; therefore, it will affect cognition in the same way as any other stressor. My colleague Peter Keen and I (McMorris & Keen, 1994) did suggest caution when equating exercise-induced arousal with emotionally induced arousal. We argued that when physiological changes are the result of exercise, they "are induced and mediated by the activated musculature and are responding to exercise load, i.e., attempting to maintain homeostasis. Somatic arousal rising from emotions, however, is induced by the brain and destroys homeostasis" (p. 129). We accepted that exercise is a stressor and were quite happy with the idea that moderate intensity exercise would induce optimal performance but we were not convinced that heavy exercise would necessarily be perceived as being distressful by the individual. Our argument was that someone with a heart rate of 180 bpm, who was exercising maximally, was still in a state of homeostasis. As long as the individual did not perceive the task demands as being beyond his/her capabilities, they would not demonstrate very high levels of arousal and therefore cognitive performance may not return to a level equal to that during low-intensity exercise.

Although we (McMorris & Keen, 1994) questioned equating even maximal intensity exercise with very high levels of emotionally induced arousal, we did believe that an inverted-U effect would be demonstrated but it would possibly need the individual to attempt to undertake supramaximal intensity exercise for it to manifest itself.

Later, my colleague Jan Graydon and I (McMorris & Graydon, 1996b) questioned whether inverted-U theory provided an effective underpinning for hypotheses formation in acute exercise–cognition interaction studies. We claimed that drive theory (Hull, 1943; Spence, 1958) might provide a more valid rationale. According to drive theory, increases in arousal will result in an improvement in performance if habit strength is high. If habit strength is low, increases in arousal will either have no effect or will result in a breakdown in performance. Hull and Spence asserted that the equation is further complicated by the incentive value of completing the task. They stated that there will be an interaction between arousal, habit strength, and incentive value. This interaction could be explained by the formula, $P = D \times H \times I$, where P is performance, D is drive or arousal, H is habit strength, and I is incentive value. Habit strength refers to the level of automaticity of the skill. Given this theory, performance of well-learned skills may actually improve as arousal rises. However, if habit strength is low, the profile might show no effect or demonstrate a deterioration at high levels of arousal (see Figure 1).

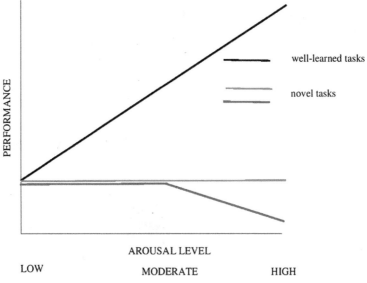

FIGURE 1 Arousal–performance interaction according to drive theory.

McMorris and Graydon (1996b) also pointed to Douchamps' (1988) theory of operational performance as a possible theoretical underpinning for an acute exercise–cognition interaction. Douchamps claimed that arousal was tridimensional in nature and he argued that there are energetic, computational, and emotional dimensions. He believed that the central nervous system (CNS) gives priority to the dimension that is most highly aroused at the expense of the other dimensions. According to Douchamps, energetic arousal is a readiness to act physically and, therefore, only positively affects motor acts. Thus, acute exercise would have a negative effect on cognition. Douchamps' argument is based on the notion of limited CNS resources; therefore, if one dimension is allocated more resources, it must be at the expense of other dimensions. This has similarities to reticular formation hypofrontality theory (Dietrich & Audiffren, 2011) (see Chapter 7). Douchamps' theory is probably only relevant when exercise is heavy, similar to transient hypofrontality theory (Dietrich, 2003), the forerunner of reticular formation hypofrontality theory.

Adam, Teeken, Ypelaar, Verstappen, and Paas (1997) also moved away from the inverted-U theories, choosing Humphreys and Revelle's (1984) theory as the underpinning for their study. Humphreys and Revelle saw arousal as being a state of "alertness, vigor, peppiness, and activation" (p. 157) and effort as being a "motivational state commonly understood to mean trying hard or being involved in a task" (p. 158). They described allocation of resources to a task as "on-task effort" (p. 158). Humphreys and Revelle did not believe in the pure inverted-U relationship between arousal and performance. They saw increases in arousal as being beneficial to what they termed "sustained information transfer tasks" (p. 154), but detrimental to short-term memory tasks. By sustained information transfer tasks, they meant tasks that primarily require attention and alertness. They believed that both increases in arousal and on-task effort would facilitate performance. Hence,

a linear improvement in performance would be demonstrated. This is similar to Hull's (1943) claims for well-learned tasks (see Figure 1). Tasks that require holding information in short-term memory would, however, be negatively affected by high levels of arousal but not moderate levels. For these tasks, they hypothesized a deterioration during higher levels of arousal. Tasks demanding both sustained information transfer and short-term memory could show an inverted-U effect. The sustained information transfer factor would be facilitated by increased arousal and on-task effort, so there would be an improvement in performance at moderate levels of arousal. However, during high levels of arousal, the negative effects on the short-term memory processes would be inhibited, thus negating the positive effects on sustained information transfer. Hence, there would be a return to baseline levels of performance.

Summary

All of the theories were devised to explain the effects of arousal and/or stress on performance in general, including cognition. No theory is based on exercise alone. Authors using these theories to underpin their hypotheses in acute exercise–cognition interaction studies assumed that exercise is a stressor and will affect cognition in the same way as other stressors. Most are inverted-U theories but demonstrate some differences to one another. Kahneman (1973) saw arousal as being unidimensional; however, Sanders (1983) divided it into arousal and activation. Both, however, believed that effort is the key in allocating resources to the task. Kahneman (1973), Sanders (1983), and Hockey (1997) claimed that there are evaluation processes that provide effort (the supervisory controller in Hockey's model) with the necessary information to aid allocation policy. Thus, we can say that these theories have many similarities. Although drive theory differs in many areas, it too involves an evaluation process of sorts, with its determination of the incentive value.

EMPIRICAL RESEARCH

A literature search using the computer databases PsycARTICLES, PsycINFO, PubMed, SPORTDiscus, and Web of Knowledge was undertaken. Key words used in the searches were combinations of "acute," "exercise," "cognition," "cognitive function," "cognitive performance," "reaction time," "response time," "accuracy," "error," "working memory," "short-term memory," "long-term memory," "memory," "recall," "executive function," "central executive," "oddball," "visual search," "attention," "anticipation," "coincidence anticipation," "decision making," "flanker task," "Simon task," "Sternberg test," "Wisconsin card sorting task," "Tower of London," and "Tower of Hanoi." In addition, reference lists from empirical reports and reviews were examined. Studies were included if they were performed on healthy individuals; the exercise intervention required the activation of large muscle groups; repeated measures, within-subject design, were used; data were provided showing the intensity of the exercise with reference to a maximum or threshold; exercise intensity was based on objective measures; the range of measures for a specific intensity was not >10% maximum volume of oxygen uptake ($\dot{V}O_{2MAX}$) or equivalent; and the dependent variables were objective. Studies including pharmacological treatments were not included.

Before examining the findings of these studies it is important to look at two issues with the design of the research, which will aid our understanding of the results, namely the exercise protocols used, especially the exercise intensities, and the types of task used.

Exercise Protocols

Early research was not only atheoretical but the nature of the exercise protocols left much to be desired. Gutin and Di Gennaro (1968a) had subjects undertake 1 min of step-ups, using the Harvard Step Test protocol. Meyers et al. (1969) used a similar step-up protocol but had subjects work for 5 min. McAdam and Wang's (1967) subjects carried out a run–jog–walk protocol for 10 min. According to the authors, this was "designed to work up a mild sweat, but not to fatigue" (p. 209). It is easy to criticize such protocols but we should remember that exercise physiology, as we know it today, was only in its infancy. In fact, in most countries it was nonexistent. The situation was to change for the better following Tomporowski and Ellis' (1986) seminal review. Tomporowski and Ellis criticized unscientific protocols and the lack of a theoretical framework behind most studies. While we have looked at developments in the latter in the previous section, here we will examine changes in research designs that have occurred since Tomporowski and Ellis' review.

Some research following Tomporowski and Ellis' (1986) paper displayed the same exercise protocol weakness as the early research, e.g., Lawless (1988) had participants run on the spot for 120 s prior to cognitive testing, while Beh (1989) had her participants do 60 s of step-ups before testing. These designs are obviously lacking in control, we simply have no idea about the intensity of exercise. However, Tomporowski and Ellis' main criticism was concerned with a failure to take account of individual differences in capacity. For example, Davey (1973) had all participants work at 420 kg/m over 15 s; 840 kg/m over 30 s; 2800 kg/m over 2 min; 4200 kg/m over 5 min; and 7000 kg/m over 10 min, regardless of their own level of fitness. He failed to take into account the fact that individuals' maximum workloads differ, therefore although these absolute workloads are identical, they are at different percentages of each individual's maximum. Hence, the relative intensities are not identical.

Some studies prior to Tomporowski and Ellis' (1986) review had probably inadvertently taken into consideration individual differences with regard to fatigue. The authors of these studies had participants exercise incrementally until voluntary exhaustion (e.g., Bard & Fleury, 1978) or had the participants exercise until they could no longer maintain a given workload (e.g., Dickinson, Medhurst, & Whittingham, 1979; Gutin & Di Gennaro, 1968b; Hanson & Lofthus, 1978). The latter is in line with Edwards (1983) definition of fatigue. Both designs are still in common use despite concerns with regard to the lack of objectivity concerning voluntary exhaustion. However, Tomporowski and Ellis' main criticism regarding individual differences was concerned with submaximal intensities used in studies. We have already seen that Davey (1973) used absolute workloads, as did Bard and Fleury (1978), Williams, Pottinger, and Shapcott (1985), Sjöberg (1975), and Weingarten and Alexander (1970). However, several did utilize relative measures (e.g., Ewing, Scott, Mendez, & McBride, 1984; Hancock & McNaughton, 1986) but the definition of these intensities as low, moderate, or heavy left much to be desired.

Defining Exercise Intensities

Determining what constitutes low, moderate, and heavy intensity exercise is not a simple process. For the early researchers, a lack of understanding of the interaction between the aerobic and the anaerobic systems did not help matters. Choices of intensities even when relative to the individual's $\dot{V}O_{2MAX}$, maximum power output ($\dot{W}_{MAX}$), or maximal heart rate (HR_{MAX}) appear to be somewhat arbitrary. To exercise physiologists, it is more important to describe the physiological and biochemical processes being undertaken rather than putting intensities into nice little boxes. However, this has become the norm in acute exercise–cognition interaction research, and broad descriptions such as low, moderate, and heavy are widely used in the literature. Therefore, we need to know what authors mean when they state low, moderate, and heavy. From reviewing the literature, specifically for this chapter and for previous reviews that I have undertaken, I think that it is fair to say that the

majority of authors have determined low as being ≤30% $\dot{V}O_{2MAX}$ (e.g., Féry, Ferry, Vom Hofe, & Rieu, 1997; Kamijo et al., 2009), although some have said ≤40% (e.g., Ando, Kokubu, Yamada, & Kimura, 2011; Fontana, Mazzardo, Mokgothu, Furtado, & Gallagher, 2009). Moderate intensity exercise has generally been claimed to be from 40% or 50% $\dot{V}O_{2MAX}$ to 79% $\dot{V}O_{2MAX}$ (e.g., Coles & Tomporowski, 2008; Fontana et al., 2009). As you will have already worked out, heavy exercise is seen as being ≥80% $\dot{V}O_{2MAX}$. Although most authors do not provide any reasoning for their choices, there is actually some support from the exercise endocrinology literature to validate the use of these intensities.

The ranges generally chosen to represent low, moderate, and heavy are very close to those identified by the exercise endocrinologist Katerina Borer (2003). She saw low-intensity as being <50% $\dot{V}O_{2MAX}$, moderate intensity (she used the term intermediate) as between 50% and 75% $\dot{V}O_{2MAX}$ and heavy as being above that. Borer's determination of what was low, moderate, and heavy was based on several endocrinological factors. For those of us studying the acute exercise–cognition interaction, probably the most important issue is effects of differing exercise intensities on central and peripheral concentrations of catecholamines and hypothalamic–pituitary–adrenal (HPA) axis hormones. Borer pointed to increases in plasma concentrations of catecholamines and the HPA axis hormone, cortisol, postexercise at 50% $\dot{V}O_{2MAX}$, as evidence of increases in exercise intensity. However, Chmura, Nazar, and Kaciuba-Uścilko (1994) believed that the step-up in intensity occurred at a specific moment during exercise, what Wasserman and McIlroy (1964) had called the anaerobic or lactate threshold (LT). This phenomenon had been discovered by Hollmann in the late 1950s (see Hollmann, 1985). He found that when exercising incrementally, there comes a point at which pulmonary ventilation increases at a greater rate than volume of oxygen uptake. He also discovered that this point coincided with significant increases in blood lactate concentrations. More importantly, with regard to the acute exercise–cognition interaction, it is also highly correlated with the plasma adrenaline (epinephrine) and noradrenaline (norepinephrine) thresholds (Podolin, Munger, & Mazzeo, 1991). For most individuals, this does not occur until ~75% $\dot{V}O_{2MAX}$ (Podolin et al., 1991), although there are large interindividual variations (Urhausen, Weiler, Coen, & Kindermann, 1994). This, however, is when exercise is incremental. Hodgetts, Coppack, Frayn, and Hockaday (1991) showed that plasma lactate and catecholamines concentrations began to rise ~20–30 min into the exercise, when the intensity was as low as 50% $\dot{V}O_{2MAX}$. However, at 30% $\dot{V}O_{2MAX}$ even 2 h of exercise did not have a significant effect. Therefore, Borer's low and moderate or intermediate categories are useful as long as duration and type of exercise, incremental versus steady state, is taken into account.

Measures of lactate and catecholamines during exercise ≥80% $\dot{V}O_{2MAX}$ of any duration show that concentrations are very high. I would argue that 80% $\dot{V}O_{2MAX}$ is a safer measure of the lower end of heavy exercise than Borer's (2003) 75% $\dot{V}O_{2MAX}$ because, during incremental exercise, it is at 80% $\dot{V}O_{2MAX}$ that significant increases in the HPA axis hormones, adrenocorticotropin hormone (ACTH), and cortisol are seen (De Vries, Bernards, De Rooij, & Koppeschaar, 2000; Hill et al., 2008; McMorris, Davranche, Jones, Hall, & Minter, 2009). During steady state exercise at <80% $\dot{V}O_{2MAX}$, it takes at least 45 min before significant increases in plasma and salivary concentrations of ACTH and cortisol are induced (Bridge, Weller, Rayson, & Jones, 2003; Jacks, Sowash, Anning, McGloughlin, & Andres, 2002; Shojaei, Farajov, & Jafari, 2011).

Anyone who has undertaken any research into responses to exercise will know that while it is necessary for practical purposes to delineate between intensities, individual differences in biochemical responses are great. For that reason, several authors have determined moderate intensity exercise as being >LT or the catecholamines thresholds (e.g., Chmura et al., 1994; Hyodo et al., 2012; Kashihara & Nakahara, 2005). Several have determined heavy exercise as being equal to 100% $\dot{V}O_{2MAX}$ or equivalent (e.g., Féry et al., 1997; Griffin et al., 2011; McMorris & Graydon, 1996a, 1996b). This solves any problems with validity of choices of intensity. If, however, we are to make sense of past research, we need to include reference to studies using the terms low, moderate, and heavy. In the rest of this chapter, we will follow McMorris and Hale's (2012) variation on Borer's (2003) categories, i.e., low is <40% $\dot{V}O_{2MAX}$, moderate is ≥40% $\dot{V}O_{2MAX}$ but <80% $\dot{V}O_{2MAX}$, and heavy is ≥80% $\dot{V}O_{2MAX}$.

Task-Type Effects

Most narrative reviews (e.g., Best, 2010; McMorris & Graydon, 2000; Tomporowski, 2003) and meta-analyses (Chang, Labban, Gapin, & Etnier, 2012; Etnier et al., 1997; Lambourne & Tomporowski, 2010; McMorris & Hale, 2012) have claimed that task type was a moderating variable; however, their task-type categories and descriptions differ from one another. Therefore, it is important to clearly define and describe the categories that we are using in this review. I have divided the tasks into attention/perception, working memory, autonomous, and learning/long-term memory tasks. Below I outline the nature of these tasks with special attention to working memory tasks, as the nature of these tasks is the most contentious (Miyake & Shah, 1999).

Attention/Perception Tasks

Pre-2000, the types of task used by researchers were mainly attention/perception tasks or what Humphreys and Revelle (1984) called sustained information transfer tasks, i.e., tasks that primarily require attention and alertness. In fact, the majority were either simple (Brisswalter et al., 1997; McMorris & Keen, 1994) or choice (Chmura et al., 1994; Côté, Salmela, & Papathanasopoulu,

1992; Delignières et al., 1994; Levitt & Gutin, 1971; Meyers et al., 1969; Reynolds, 1976; Salmela & Ndoye, 1986; Travlos & Marisi, 1995; Williams et al., 1985) reaction time tests. In reality these tests should be described as "visual response time" tests. In the simple version, participants respond by pressing the relevant button or key on a computer keyboard when the stimulus is displayed. In the choice versions, there are several, normally two or four, stimuli and the participant must press a button or key that corresponds to the illuminated stimulus. It is a response rather than a reaction because reaction time is the period of time from the presentation of a stimulus to the initiation of an overt response. Actually pressing the key is a full response.

Reaction time tests had become popular since the development of information processing theory. Many saw reaction time as being indicative of the full information processing system. Information processing models, such as Welford's (1968) model, show a process moving from presentation of the stimulus through sensation, perception, decision making, and efferent organization to action, but with an interaction between short- and long-term memory influencing perception and decision making. Many theorists, like Welford, believed that reaction time was indicative of the efficiency of the individual's ability to process information. In reality, however, several aspects of the information processing model are redundant in even a choice reaction time task. It undoubtedly requires perception to identify the stimulus and efferent organization, albeit not very demanding organization, to prepare the response. It does not, however, require short- or long-term memory or decision making. The decision is made pre-presentation. Thus, we can say that simple and choice reaction time tasks are simple tasks. It is important to remember that the term "reaction time" is also used by authors when reporting speed of response in much more complex tasks like the flanker (Eriksen & Eriksen, 1974) and Simon (1969) tasks, which are described later.

The other common types of attention/perception tasks that have been used are coincidence anticipation (Bard & Fleury, 1978; Fleury & Bard, 1990; Fleury, Bard, & Carrière, 1981; Isaacs & Pohlman, 1991), and visual search/signal detection (Allard et al., 1989; Bard & Fleury, 1978; Fleury & Bard, 1990; Fleury, Bard, Jobin, & Carrière, 1981). In the coincidence anticipation time test, the participant sees a series of light-emitting diodes illuminated and extinguished in rapid succession to give the impression of a light moving along a display board, the Bassin anticipation timer. The participant has to press a button when he/she thinks that the light has "reached" the end of the runway. Speed of the stimulus can be changed after each trial but not within trials. This is undoubtedly a test of perception and arguably requires some use of decision making. In the visual search/signal detection tasks, the participant has to search a display for a given stimulus—undoubtedly a perpetual task but with little or no memory component or decision making.

Working Memory Tasks

The notion of working memory was developed by Alan Baddeley (Baddeley, 1966, 1986; Baddeley, Emslie, Kolodny, & Duncan, 1998) to explain how we can integrate perceptual information from a variety of senses, and use that information, along with information recalled from long-term memory, to solve problems, make decisions, plan ahead, and even be creative. He saw working memory as the interactive functioning of three separate but interdependent parts, the central executive mechanism, and two short-term memory systems, which he termed the phonological loop and the visuospatial sketch pad. The phonological loop is responsible for the encoding of acoustic and verbal information. The visuospatial sketchpad has the same role as the phonological loop except that it processes visual and visuospatial information. The role of the central executive is to oversee and control the whole process. Later attempts to refine Baddeley's theory have led to some confusion in the literature as to the processes and mechanisms involved. Miyake and Shah (1999) pointed out that it is generally accepted that working memory involves executive control and that short- and long-term memory play major roles. However, they claimed that the two memory systems are really only part of working memory when their function is to provide information for completion of a more complex task, one that requires central executive control. When the aim of a short- or long-term memory task is simply to recall information, this is not a working memory task. Miyake and Shah probably felt the need to highlight this issue because often we see recall paradigms described as working memory tasks. This simply leads to confusion in the literature.

Miyake and associates (Miyake, Friedman, Emerson, Witzki, & Howerter, 2000) attempted to provide more detail concerning what constitutes a central executive task. They described the process as involving several functions including shifting between tasks or mental sets, updating and monitoring working memory representations, inhibition of prepotent responses, planning, and the coordination of multiple tasks. Leh, Petrides, and Strafella (2010) provided other examples, abstract thinking, cognitive flexibility, and selecting relevant sensory information. Shifting between tasks or mental sets can vary in complexity. When the individual has to respond to a change in stimulus by switching from one stimulus–response set to another, it is called an "attentional set shifting task." However, when the person has to reconfigure both stimulus and response sets, it is called a "task-set switching task" (see Sawada et al., 2012). An example of an everyday attentional set shifting task would be a driver changing from observing the color of traffic lights in order to know whether to stop or go, to looking at the car in front to determine whether or not to overtake. There is no need to reconfigure either stimulus–response set. An example of a task switching situation would

be a soccer player, whose team has possession of the ball and who is marked by an opponent. He/she is looking to lose her/his marker. When their team loses possession of the ball, however, the player must now mark their opponent and ensure that they do not lose contact. Thus, the stimulus–response set must be reconfigured. Updating and monitoring working memory representations involves the removal of redundant information and replacing it with new, relevant information. It requires the person to recall similar past experiences but also be aware of differences between that situation and the present one, i.e., knowing that past representations no longer apply and that new ones must be taken into account. A traffic police person controlling a busy intersection has this problem. Inhibition of prepotent responses is self-evident given its name. A defender, in any sport, who refuses to respond to a fake or "dummy" by an attacker provides a good example of inhibition. Planning and the coordination of multiple tasks are also self-evident given their names, while selecting relevant sensory information is no different to selective attention. These processes are included in most people's everyday tasks. Abstract thinking and cognitive flexibility are probably not part of everyone's normal activities but are probably necessary for creativity and innovation. The very meaning of the words creative and innovative shows that they are not the norm.

A number of cognitive tests have been devised by psychologists to test one or more of the processes outlined above. Below are descriptions of the most commonly used tasks in the acute exercise–cognition interaction studies.

Flanker Task

Developed by Eriksen and Eriksen (1974), the flanker task measures inhibition of prepotent responses. There are several variations but the most commonly used follows a similar pattern to that described below. The participants have to respond to a target stimulus, an arrow head (> or <), by pressing a button with their left index finger if the stimulus is pointing left (<) or with their right index finger if it is pointing right (>). The target stimulus is always the center stimulus in a display of five stimuli. The flanker stimuli will be congruent with the target stimulus, i.e., pointing the same way, e.g., < < < < <, or incongruent, i.e., pointing the opposite way, e.g., < < > < <. Four conditions, left congruent (< < < < <), right congruent (> > > > >), left incongruent (> > < > >), and right incongruent (< < > < <), are normally presented. The dependent variables are normally response speed and accuracy. Most authors analyze the data using an exercise intensity × congruency repeated measures analysis of variance. The task was mainly concerned with speed of response, as it was seen that this would be indicative of efficiency of response. As a result there are often very few errors in accuracy, although this is often measured as a dependent variable.

Simon Task

The Simon task (Simon, 1969; Simon & Rudell, 1967) involves the processes of inhibition and selecting relevant sensory information. Participants face a computer screen and are presented with one of two colored circles (e.g., red or green). The circle may appear to the right or left of the screen. Participants are asked to respond, as quickly and accurately as possible, by pressing the appropriate computer key with the right or the left index finger according to the color of a circle, e.g., by a left press when the circle is red and by a right press when it is green, but regardless of the location of the stimulus. In half of the trials the button to be pressed is on the same side as the stimulus, these are the congruent trials. In the other half of the trials, the button to be pressed is on the opposite side to the stimulus, the incongruent trials. The dependent variables are accuracy and response time, although most authors call it reaction time. The independent variables are exercise intensity and congruency. If there is an interaction effect, it can be shown that the Simon effect (mean response time in

congruent trials versus mean response time in incongruent trials) has been affected.

Stroop Color Task

The Stroop color test (Stroop, 1935) requires inhibition of prepotent responses and selecting relevant sensory information. It has several variations. Sibley, Etnier, and Le Masurier (2006) provided a good example of a fairly common version of the task. In the first condition, the color naming condition, participants were presented with a string of the letter "X" (e.g., XXXXX) written in red, blue, yellow, or green ink. Participants were required to, as quickly as possible, verbally state the ink color in which the letter was written. In a second condition, the color-word interference condition, participants were shown the words "red," "blue," "yellow," or "green" but the words were written in ink that was different in color to the word. The participants were told to state the color of the ink as quickly and accurately as possible. In a third condition, the negative priming condition, the ink color of each word was the same as the color word stimulus on the previous item. For example, if the color word on the previous item was "blue," the ink color of the current item would be blue. The color-word interference condition, although measuring inhibition to some extent as it is more common to read the word than state the ink color, is more a test of the individual's ability to select the relevant sensory stimuli. As a result one often sees the Stroop test described as a test of selective attention. The negative priming condition requires the same selective attention as the color-word interference condition but places an extra burden on inhibitory processes, as the correct response to the new stimulus is the color that the person has just inhibited in the previous answer. Speed and accuracy are the normal dependent variables.

Go/No Go Task

The go/no go task was developed from the work of Donders in the late nineteenth century (see Donders, 1969). It is a test of response inhibition. Participants are instructed to respond to one stimulus but to withhold the response when a different, but normally similar, stimulus is presented. For example, Lowe, Hall, Vincent, and Luu (2014) instructed participants to press a button as quickly as possible whenever a lower case letter was presented on a computer screen, and withhold their response whenever an upper case letter appeared.

Stop Signal Task

Developed from the work of Logan and Cowan (1984), the stop signal task is a test of inhibition of prepotent responses. It requires the participant to respond as quickly as possible to a predetermined stimulus, the go trial, but to abort any response when a subsequently presented stop signal is displayed. Speed and accuracy on the go trials are measured and the stop signal reaction time (SSRT), a measure of inhibition, is estimated based on Logan and Cowan's notion of a race between a go process, which is triggered by the presentation of the go stimulus, and a stop process, which is triggered by the presentation of the stop signal. When the stop process finishes before the go process, the response is inhibited, but when the go process finishes before the stop process, the response is activated. Logan and Cowan claimed that we can assume that the stop process begins when the stop signal is presented. The time between presentation of the go stimulus and presentation of the stop signal is termed the "stop signal delay" (SSD). The point at which the stop process finishes can be estimated from the observed reaction times distribution on go trials and the observed probability of having to respond to a stop signal. SSRT can be calculated by subtracting SSD from the finishing time (see Verbrugggen & Logan, 2008).

Random Number Generation Task

Baddeley's early work (Baddeley, 1966) led to the development of the random number generation task, which involves inhibition and updating and monitoring of working memory processes. Participants are told to give a number from one to nine at a constant rate (normally every second) so that a string of numbers, which are in an order that is as random as possible, will be produced. The randomness of the sequence of numbers, generally comprised 100 numbers, can be measured by different indices (Towse & Neil, 1998). Care must be taken when choosing which indices one wishes to use. Several of these indices have been analyzed using principal component analysis (e.g., Towse & McLachlan, 1999; Towse & Neil, 1998) and results show different weightings on each index for inhibition and updating. Turning Point, Adjacency, and Runs indices are the most commonly used measures of inhibition, whereas Redundancy index, Mean repetition gap, and Coupon are the most common measures of updating function.

Wisconsin Card Sorting Task

The Wisconsin card sorting task (Berg, 1948) tests the ability to shift mental sets, and update and monitor working memory representations. It can be presented manually or in computer version. The participant is given cards to sort based on color, form, or number, but the participant is not told which of the three criteria to use. The participant is told whether a trial is correct or not. Based on this, the individual deduces which criterion is being used. However, the criteria change without warning, thus the participant must alter her/his mental set and update mental representations. There are several dependent variables based on accuracy, which include perseverative errors.

Tower of London Task

The Tower of London (TOL) task (Shallice, 1982) is a planning and problem-solving task. To perform TOL well, the individual must generate and maintain goal and subgoal representations (Polk, Simen, Lewis, & Freedman, 2002), and conduct higher-level programming, selecting, executing, and evaluating actions (Dehaene &

Changeux, 1997). Thus, it is probably the most complex of the tasks used in acute exercise–cognition interaction studies.

TOL can be completed using a computer program or manually. There are several versions on computer or requiring apparatus. Here I describe the manual Drexel version (TOL^{DX}) (Culbertson & Zillmer, 2005). The TOL^{DX} apparatus consists of two identical wooden boards ($30 \times 7 \times 10$ cm), one for the participant and one for the examiner, and two sets of three beans (blue, green, and red). Each board consists of three vertical pegs of different heights. Peg 1 can hold three beans, Peg 2 two beans and Peg 3 one bean. A board is given to the participant with a standard start configuration, Peg 1 has two beans (red on top of green) and Peg 2 has the blue bean. A second board is controlled by the examiner, who chooses the bean configurations that he/she wishes the participant to achieve by moving the beans, one at time, from one peg to another. Participants are instructed to plan their moves before starting to move the beans. The normal dependent variables are total move score, total correct score, planning time (time from presentation of the goal configuration to making the first move), total execution or solving time (time from first move to completion), and total planning–solving time (Culbertson & Zillmer, 2005).

Operation Span and Reading Span Tasks

Operation span (OSPAN) (Turner & Engle, 1989) and reading span (RSPAN) (Daneman & Carpenter, 1980) tests require updating and monitoring of working memory representations. In the OSPAN task, the participants must solve a series of arithmetic equations while attempting to remember a list of unrelated words. Individuals are presented with one equation–word string at a time (e.g., $(3 \times 4) - 2 = 10$? CAT) on a computer and asked to verify aloud whether the equation is correct (hence the question mark). Individuals then read the word aloud. At the end of the series, they write down the sequence of words. The RSPAN involves reading a series

of sentence–letter strings (e.g., "Walking in the park is a very enjoyable activity." (Does this make sense?) M). In the RSPAN, individuals read the sentence aloud and are asked to verify whether the sentence makes sense. Individuals then read the letter aloud. At the end of the series, they write down the sequence of letters. In both the OSPAN and the RSPAN, each series consists of a random number of strings between two and five. Individuals are tested on three series of each length (12 in total). For both OSPAN and RSPAN, the dependent variable is the total number of words/letters correctly recalled.

Trail Making Test

The Trail Making Test (TMT) (see Reitan, 1958) has two parts and the times taken to complete each part are used to measure central executive functioning. In Part A (TMT-A), the participant must draw a line to connect consecutive numbers, from 1 to 25. In Part B (TMT-B), the participant connects numbers and letters in an alternating progressive sequence, 1 to A, A to 2, 2 to B, and so on. In order to measure central executive functioning, the difference in time taken to complete TMT-B, which stresses central executive processes of task-set inhibition, cognitive flexibility, and the ability to maintain a response set (Arbuthnott & Frank, 2000; Kortte, Horner, & Windhan, 2002), and the time to complete TMT-A, which has little executive input, is calculated. The ratio of TMT-B to TMT-A can also be used (Arbuthnott & Frank, 2000; Salthouse, Atkinson, & Berish, 2003).

n-Back Test

The n-back test (Kirchner, 1958) requires the ability to update and monitor working memory representations. The experimenter decides on the value of n. When say n = 2, participants are verbally presented with lists of numbers or, more normally, letters, and they have to indicate if the number or word is the same as the one that was presented two numbers/words earlier. n can be set at any number. In some versions pictures are presented rather than numbers or words.

Automatic Tasks

We generally think of automaticity as referring to motor skills, probably because motor learning theorists such as Fitts and Posner (1967) and Adams (1971) saw automaticity as the final goal of skill acquisition. Automaticity can occur in cognitive skills as well. Skills learned implicitly are performed autonomously or automatically (Masters, Poolton, Maxwell, & Raab, 2008). Some cognitive skills are learned implicitly, i.e., with no recourse to conscious processing. Frensch (1998) defined implicit learning as the "non-intentional automatic acquisition of knowledge about structural relations between objects or events" (p. 76). It is generally accepted that with some stimuli, repeated exposure can lead to sensitization, an increase in the readiness to respond to the stimulus. This is known as nonassociative learning. (We should note that desensitization, a decrease in readiness to respond, can also occur.) Sports coaches, the military, and firefighters use repeated exposure to situations to hopefully induce sensitization. Nonassociative memory is part of nondeclarative, long-term memory. The other components of nondeclarative, long-term memory that are of particular relevance to the acute exercise–cognition interaction research are the perceptual representation system (PRS) and procedural memory. The latter refers to memory for a vast amount of subconsciously acquired information, both cognitive and motor. Elsewhere (McMorris, 2014, p. 149), I have argued that in sport, cognitive, procedural memory is demonstrated when performers make decisions or perceive situations accurately without any explicit knowledge of what they are doing. Of course, this does not only apply to sport, it can apply to any situation in which a person makes a decision without explicit knowledge. It is, however, the PRS that can best explain some of the research findings in the acute exercise–cognition interaction studies.

The PRS is primed by experience to identify and respond, quickly and consistently, to situations of which it has a great deal of experience. It could be argued that it is similar to what Ericsson and Kintsch (1995) called long-term working memory (LTWM). Ericsson and Kintsch claimed that through repeated exposure and learning, be it explicit or implicit, the expert holds the situation plus response, termed the situation–response interaction, as one unit or bit in LTWM. Perception of the situation and retrieval of the answer are simultaneous and automatic (Mulligan, McCracken, & Hodges, 2012). Thus, well-learned, explicitly or implicitly, tasks, even if they appear to be central executive tasks such as decision making or problem solving, may well not be affected by acute exercise in the same way as comparatively novel, central executive tasks or even attention/perception tasks. Stressors other than acute exercise have been shown to affect well-learned, automatic tasks differently to nonautomatic tasks (Ehrlenspiel, Wei, & Stemad, 2010). Neuroscientific research provides the best explanations for this fact (see Chapter 4 for neurochemical explanations), but the cognitive psychologists also accepted differences between novel and well-learned skills, as is evidenced by drive theory.

In the acute exercise–cognition interaction literature, probably the best examples of automaticity of cognitive tasks are the soccer decision-making studies undertaken in our laboratory (McMorris & Graydon, 1996a, 1996b, 1997; McMorris et al., 1999) and that carried out by Fontana et al. (2009). In our studies, we aimed to devise a working memory test that required the use of planning and cognitive flexibility. However, closer inspection of the data from the test led us to believe that the participants, who were experienced soccer players, were responding in an autonomous manner. They were not thinking through the problem as we had anticipated but responding as they would in a game (see McMorris, 2009; for a more detailed review). This was supported when we compared experienced players and nonplayers, and saw that the two groups behaved differently (McMorris & Graydon, 1996a). Fontana et al., who used similarly experienced soccer players, showed the same pattern of results. To be fair to them, they never claimed to examine working memory.

We had a similar experience with a noncompatible response time test (McMorris et al., 2003). In this test, we had participants facing a display board on which there were four lights numbered 1–4, and beneath each light there was a button also numbered 1–4. Button 1 was below light 1, button 2 below light 2, and so on. When light 1 was illuminated the participant had to press button 3, when light 2 was illuminated they pressed button 4, light 3 required a press of button 1, and light 4 needed a press of button 2. This requires inhibition of the prepotent response to press the button directly beneath the light and the need to hold the information concerning the rules in short-term memory. As such it could be classed as a working memory task. However, before taking the test, each participant had 160 trials on the task. A pilot study had shown this to be sufficient to ensure a plateauing effect in performance. We did this to limit a learning effect but, in fact, we defeated our own aim of using a working memory task, as the noncompatible task was now autonomous. As the great Scottish poet Rabbie Burns said, "The best laid schemes o' mice an' men gang aft a-gley" (Burns, 1786, p. 138).

Learning/Long-Term Memory Tasks

Very few studies have examined the effects of acute exercise on learning/long-term memory and most of these fall into the neuroscience literature. The nature of the tasks differ from one another but follow the obvious pattern of exposure to the information to be learned/remembered followed by a period of no rehearsal and then a recall/retention test.

Research Results

Research Examining the Inverted-U Effect

Much of the research from Davey's (1973) paper to 2000 examined the possibility of an inverted-U effect of acute exercise on cognition. Research from 2000 onwards has tended to focus on the effects of moderate intensity exercise only but there have been some attempts to examine an inverted-U effect. There would appear to be very little support for an inverted-U effect. Chmura et al. (1994) and Chmura and Nazar (2010) showed inverted-U effects on a choice reaction time task, while Brisswalter et al. (1997), examining effects on simple reaction time, demonstrated the effect with unfit participants but not with fit ones. No other authors supported inverted-U at all. Sjöberg (1980) found no significant effects of acute exercise on a short-term memory task, while Guizani et al. (2006) found no significant effect on choice reaction time for a sedentary group but facilitation at both 60% and 80% $\dot{V}O_{2MAX}$ for a group of fencers. For simple reaction time, both groups demonstrated no significant effect. McMorris and Graydon (1996a, 1996b, 1997; McMorris et al., 1999) and Fontana et al. (2009) demonstrated no significant effects on accuracy of a soccer-specific, decision-making test but significant positive effects for speed of decision making. In all four of the McMorris and Graydon studies, decision making was significantly faster during heavy exercise than at rest, except for inexperienced soccer players in the McMorris and Graydon (1996a) study, who showed no significant effect. Speed of decision during moderate intensity exercise did not differ significantly from at rest or during heavy exercise. Fontana et al. found that speeds of decision making during exercise at 60% and 80% $\dot{V}O_{2MAX}$ were both significantly faster than at rest. However, McMorris and Graydon (1997) showed that visual search during maximal intensity exercise was significantly faster than at rest and during exercise at 70% $\dot{W}_{MAX}$.

McGlynn and associates (McGlynn, Laughlin, & Bender, 1977; McGlynn, Laughlin, & Rowe, 1979) also showed no significant effect on accuracy of a perceptual judgment task but faster performance during exercise at HR_{MAX}. Draper, McMorris, and Parker (2010) demonstrated a positive linear effect on choice reaction time but no significant effect on simple reaction time. On the other hand, McMorris, Sproule, Draper, and Child (2000) and McMorris et al. (2003) showed no significant effect of exercise on a soccer-specific, response time task and a noncompatible reaction time test, respectively; while McMorris, Collard, Corbett, Dicks, and Swain (2008) found no effect on a random number generation task but an inhibitory effect on a choice reaction time test at 80% $\dot{W}_{MAX}$. Isaacs and Pohlman (1991), McMorris and Keen (1994), and McMorris et al. (2009) have also shown significant negative effects for exercise at maximum on tests of coincidence anticipation, simple reaction time, and the flanker task, respectively. It should be noted that in the McMorris and Keen study, the participants were sedentary individuals.

Meta-analyses also fail to support an inverted-U effect (Chang et al., 2012; Lambourne & Tomporowski, 2010; McMorris & Hale, 2012) although at first glance McMorris and Hale appear to do so. They showed significant differences between mean effect sizes during low, moderate, and heavy exercise with moderate intensity demonstrating a low to moderate effect size ($g = 0.30$) while low and heavy showed nonsignificant effect sizes very close to zero. However, as the authors pointed out, observation of the effect sizes for individual studies during heavy exercise show almost equivocal numbers demonstrating positive, negative, and nonsignificant effect sizes. This has the resultant effect of the mean effect size regressing to almost zero.

While the research reviewed above suggests no inverted-U effect, we need to examine research that has compared performance in the at-rest condition with moderate exercise only or with heavy exercise only in order to increase the sample size before making any definitive conclusions.

Results of Studies Comparing Performance at Rest to Those at Moderate Intensity Exercise Only

Results of studies comparing performance at rest to those at moderate intensity exercise only are given in Table 1. Observation of Table 1 and

results for the inverted-U effect studies outlined above show that for accuracy 72.22% of experiments found no significant effect, 22.22% demonstrated a significant facilitative effect, while 5.56% showed a significant inhibitory effect. When speed was the dependent variable, there were 40.00% of studies with nonsignificant results, while 58.33% showed significant facilitation, and only 1.67% demonstrated significant inhibition. These results appear to be regardless of duration, although the situation for very long duration exercise may be different. For example, Grego et al. (2004) demonstrated negative effects following moderate intensity exercise at 2 and 3h. They also appear to be regardless of task type but meta-analyses suggest that there may be an effect of task type (Chang et al., 2012; Lambourne & Tomporowski, 2010; McMorris & Hale, 2012; McMorris, Sproule, Turner, & Hale, 2011). For example, McMorris and Hale (2012) showed a mean effect size of $g = 0.77$ for central executive tasks but only $g = 0.31$ for attention/ perception tasks.

Results Comparing Performance at Rest to Those during and following Heavy Exercise Only

Results comparing performance at rest to those during and following heavy exercise only are provided in Table 2. Observation of Table 2 and results for the inverted-U effect studies outlined earlier show that with accuracy as the dependent variable, 66.67% were nonsignificant, 9.52% demonstrated significant facilitation, while 23.81% showed a significant inhibitory effect. For speed of performance, 43.59% were nonsignificant, while significant facilitative effects were shown by 28.21% of the studies. There were 28.21% of the studies demonstrating significant inhibitory effects. Autonomic tasks showed 100% facilitation when speed was the dependent variable and tended not to show any effects at all when accuracy was the dependent variable. Attention/perception tasks tended to show either no significant effect

TABLE 1   Studies[a] that have examined the effects, compared to baseline, of exercise ≥40% but <80% maximum volume of oxygen uptake ($\dot{V}O_{2MAX}$) or equivalent

Author(s)	N	Exercise intensity and duration	Cognitive task	Result(s) accuracy	Result(s) speed
Joyce, Graydon, McMorris, and Davranche (2009)	10	40% MAP 30 min	Stop signal[f]	NS effect	Facilitation[b]
Yanagisawa et al. (2010)	20	50% $\dot{V}O_{2MAX}$ 10 min	Stroop test[f]	Not applicable	Facilitation[b]
Pesce, Cereatti et al. (2007)	25	60% HR_{RES} See note[c]	Visual attention switching[f]	Not applicable	Facilitation[b]
Pesce, Capranica, Tessitore, and Figura (2003)	16	60% $\dot{V}O_{2MAX}$ See note[e]	Visual attention switching[f]	Not applicable	Facilitation[b]
Hogervorst, Riedel, Jeukendrup, and Jolies (1996)	15	75% $\dot{W}_{MAX}$ 1 h	SRT[g]: CRT[g]: NC-CRT[g]: Stroop task[f]	Not applicable	SRT, NC-CRT, Stroop task facilitation[b]
Cereatti, Casella, Manganelli, and Pesce (2009)	24	60% HR_{RES} See note[e]	Visual attention switching[f]	NS effect	Facilitation[b]
Pesce, Tessitore et al. (2007)	48	60% HR_{RES} See note[h]	Visual attention switching[f]	Not applicable	Facilitation[b]
Pesce, Capranica, Tessitore, and Figura (2002)	16	60% $\dot{V}O_{2MAX}$ See note[c]	Visual attention switching[f]	Not applicable	Facilitation[b]
Davranche, Burle, Audiffren, and Hasbroucq (2005)	12	50% MAP See note[d]	CRT[g]	NS effect	Facilitation[b]
Davranche, Hall, and McMorris (2009)	14	50% MAP 20 min	Flanker task[f]	NS effect	Facilitation[b]
Kamijo et al. (2009)	24	50% $\dot{V}O_{2MAX}$ 20 min	Flanker task[f]	Not applicable	Facilitation[b]
Davranche, Audiffren, and Denjean (2006)	11	90% VT 17 min	CRT[g]	NS effect	Facilitation[b]
Ozyemisci-Taskiran, Gunendi, Bolukbasi, and Beyazova (2008)	11	70% HR_{MAX} 20 min	EMG RT[g]	Not applicable	Facilitation[b]
Pesce and Audiffren (2011)	100	60% HR_{RES} 20–24 min	CRT[g]	Not applicable	Facilitation[b]
McMorris et al. (2009)	24	50% MAP 15 min	Flanker task[f]	NS effect	NS effect
Arcelin and Brisswalter (1999)	19	60% MAP 10 min	CRT[g]	Not applicable	Facilitation[b]
Endo et al. (2013)	13	40%, 60% $\dot{W}_{MAX}$ 5 min	Stroop task[f]	NS effect	40% facilitation[b] 60% NS effect
Nanda, Balde, and Manjunatha (2013)	10	70% HR_{RES} 30 min	Memory[i] Reasoning[f] Concentration[g] Planning[f]	Facilitation[b] except for concentration	Facilitation[b] for total time

Continued

TABLE 1   Studies[a] that have examined the effects, compared to baseline, of exercise $\geq 40\%$ but $<80\%$ maximum volume of oxygen uptake ($\dot{V}O_{2MAX}$) or equivalent—cont'd

Author(s)	N	Exercise intensity and duration	Cognitive task	Result(s) accuracy	Result(s) speed
Hogan, Matta, and Carstensen (2013)	71	50% HR$_{RES}$ 15 min	n-back task[f]	NS effect	Facilitation[b]
Tsai et al. (2014)	40	60% $\dot{V}O_{2MAX}$ 30 min	Visuospatial attention[g]	Not applicable	Facilitation[b]
Audiffren et al. (2009)	19	90% VT 35 min	Random number generation[f]	Facilitation[b]	Not applicable
Hung, Tsai, Chen, Wang, and Chang (2013)	20	60–70% HR$_{RES}$ 20 min	Tower of London[f]	Facilitation[b]	NS effect
Travlos (2009)	12	55% $\dot{V}O_{2MAX}$ 1 h	Random number generation[f]	Facilitation[b]	Not applicable
Moore, Romine, O'Conner, and Tomporowski (2012)	15	90% VT 1 h	Central executive tasks[f]	Inhibition[b]	Inhibition[b]
Davranche and Audiffren (2004)	16	50% MAP 20 min	Attention/ discrimination task[g]	Not applicable	Facilitation[b]
Chang et al. (2011)	20	60% HR$_{RES}$ 20 min	Tower of London[f]	Facilitation[b]	Facilitation[b]
Davranche and McMorris (2009)	12	Ventilatory threshold	Simon task[f]	NS effect	Facilitation[b]
Kashihara and Nakahara (2005)	6	Lactate threshold	CRT[g]	NS effect	Facilitation[b]
Collardeau et al. (2001)	11	Ventilatory threshold	SRT[g]	Not applicable	Facilitation[b]
McMorris, Swain, Lauder, Smith, and Kelly (2006)	12	Lactate threshold	CRT[g]	NS effect	NS effect
Hyodo et al. (2012)	16	Ventilatory threshold	Stroop task[f]	NS effect	Facilitation[b]
Del Giorno et al. (2010)	13	Ventilatory threshold	Wisconsin card sorting[f]	Inhibition[b] ($p<0.05$)	Not applicable

NS, nonsignificant ($p>0.05$); MAP, maximum aerobic power; $\dot{V}O_{2MAX}$, maximum volume of oxygen uptake; HR$_{RES}$, heart rate reserve; $\dot{W}_{MAX}$, maximum power output; HR$_{MAX}$, maximum heart rate; VT, ventilatory threshold; T$_{LA}$, lactate threshold; SRT, simple reaction time; CRT, choice reaction time; NC-CRT, noncompatible choice reaction time; EMG, electromyographic.

[a] *Studies were included if they were performed on healthy individuals; the exercise intervention required the activation of large muscle groups; repeated measures, within-subject design, was used; data were provided showing the intensity of the exercise with reference to a maximum or threshold; exercise intensity was based on objective measures; the range of measures for a specific intensity was not $\geq 10\%$ $\dot{W}_{MAX}$ or equivalent; and the dependent variables were behavioral and objective. Studies including pharmacological treatments were not included.*

[b] *$p<0.05$.*

[c] *Incremental warm-up to target heart rate followed by 3–4 min at target (total time $\cong 14$ min).*

[d] *3×14–15 min sets with 10 min rest between sets.*

[e] *Incremental warm-up to target resistance followed by ~2 min at target (total time ~12 min).*

[f] *Working memory task.*

[g] *Attention/perception task.*

[h] *Autonomic task.*

[i] *Memory/learning task.*

TABLE 2 Studies that have examined the effects, compared to baseline only, of exercise >80% maximum volume of oxygen uptake ($\dot{V}O_{2MAX}$) or equivalent

Authors	N	Exercise measure	Test(s)	Results
Bard and Fleury (1978)	16	Fatigue	VS[b] CA[b]	RT NS Accuracy NS
Coco, Di Corrado, Calogero, Perciavalle, and Maci (2009)	17	Fatigue	ACT[b]	RT inhibition[a]
Delignières et al. (1994)	40	80% $\dot{V}O_{2MAX}$	CRT[b]	Expert fencers (n = 20) RT NS nonexperts (n = 20) RT inhibition[a]
Féry et al. (1997)	13	Fatigue	Recognition task[b]	RT inhibition[a]
Griffin et al. (2011)	30	100% $\dot{V}O_{2MAX}$	SCT[c] Learning/memory	Accuracy NS RT NS Accuracy facilitation[a]
Isaacs and Pohlman (1991)	12	100% $\dot{V}O_{2MAX}$	CA[b]	Accuracy inhibition[a]
Kamijo, Nishihira, Hatta, Kaneda, Wasaka et al. (2004)	12	Fatigue	No go/go[c]	EMG-RT NS
Kamijo, Nishihira, Hatta, Kaneda, Kida et al. (2004)	12	Fatigue	SRT[b]	EMG-RT NS
Thomson, Watt, and Liukkonen (2009)	16	100% $\dot{V}O_{2MAX}$	Speed discrimination[b]	RT NS Accuracy inhibition[a]

NS, nonsignificant (p > 0.05); MAP, maximum aerobic power: $\dot{V}O_{2MAX}$, maximum volume of oxygen uptake; W_{MAX}, maximum power output; VS, visual search; CA, coincidence anticipation; SRT, simple reaction time; CRT, choice reaction time; ACT, attention and concentration task; SDM, soccer decision making; SCT, Stroop color test; NC, noncompatible; STM, short-term memory; NS, nonsignificant; RT, reaction time; Sed, sedentary; EMG, electromyographic.
[a] $p < 0.05$.
[b] Attention/perception task.
[c] Working memory task.

or inhibition. Unfortunately, there were too few working memory tasks to comment on any trends. The two learning/long-term memory tasks (Griffin et al., 2011; Winter et al., 2007) both demonstrated facilitative effects but, as with the working memory tasks, there are really too few to comment on a trend.

Summary

There appears to be no real support for the inverted-U effect but moderate intensity exercise tends to show a small to moderate facilitative effect, certainly for speed of performance.

The situation for accuracy is far less clear. Heavy exercise appears to induce somewhat equivocal results except for autonomic tasks, which appear to be facilitated when speed is the dependent variable. Heavy exercise would appear to have little effect on accuracy of any type of task.

DISCUSSION

In this section, we examine how well cognitive psychology can explain the research results concerning an acute exercise–cognition interaction.

We look at key factors such as the strength of the theories in predicting performance effects, the effects of differing exercise intensities and duration, and the moderating influence of task types and complexity.

The fact that there is very little support for an inverted-U effect of acute exercise on cognition may surprise many. Davey's (1973) idea that acute exercise is a stressor, therefore it will affect cognition in an inverted-U fashion in the same way as most other stressors, has intuitive appeal. Although Tomporowski and Ellis (1986) showed that the empirical literature did not support an inverted-U effect, they believed that this was due to design issues and not a problem with Davey's reasoning or the efficacy of Yerkes and Dodson's (1908) theory when exercise is the stressor. From the results of studies that directly examined the inverted-U effect, there is undoubtedly a lack of support. However, none of the theories predicted an inverted-U effect without some form of caveat. Even the earliest theory, Yerkes and Dodson (1908), claimed that simple and complex tasks would be affected differently to one another. However, the results from those studies examining the inverted-U effect do not support the idea that for optimal performance to be elicited, simple tasks require high levels of arousal (i.e., heavy exercise) while complex tasks need low levels (i.e., low intensity). However, the differences between results and expectations may be due to the unique nature of exercise as a stressor. To equate low, moderate, and heavy exercise with low, moderate, and high arousal levels may be a little too simplistic. Given that exercise intensity increases exponentially rather than in a neat bell-curve shape, we may need to rethink the strength of the relationship between exercise intensity and arousal levels. Moreover, intensity is not the only factor that affects arousal. As we saw earlier, it is an interaction between intensity and duration. Therefore, given the small number of studies that have directly tested the inverted-U hypothesis, the failure to supply any real support for

the theory despite its intuitive appeal, and the possible moderating effects of exercise intensity × duration factors and task types, it is necessary to look at research in which cognitive performance at rest was compared to that during moderate intensity exercise only and heavy exercise only, if we are to make sense of the findings and show the extent to which cognitive psychology theories can explain these data.

Exercise Issues

Much of what has been written about the acute exercise–cognition interaction has been negatively affected by a failure to have a uniform idea of what constitutes low, moderate, and heavy exercise. This is particularly the case with moderate intensity exercise. We examined this in some detail in the second section of this chapter and have attempted to control it, at least to some extent, by strictly defining what we mean by low (<40% $\dot{V}O_{2MAX}$), moderate (>40–79% $\dot{V}O_{2MAX}$), and heavy (≥80% $\dot{V}O_{2MAX}$) exercise. This allows for uniformity when discussing results but is limited in approach. Even the cognitive psychologists were aware that increases in arousal level were affected by exercise-induced biochemical and neurochemical changes, particularly in catecholamines. Researchers simply claimed that these changes were happening as exercise intensity increased but our knowledge of how they changed and how peripheral changes affected central changes was limited. Nevertheless, the argument that increases in exercise intensity induce increased arousal levels was valid, so one would expect to see acute exercise affect cognition in the same way as other stressors. However, the empirical research does not support this even when we control intensities carefully.

Task Type × Intensity Effects

Yerkes and Dodson (1908) found that although their mice behaved in an inverted-U fashion when electric shocks were increased from low to high, task complexity was a moderating variable. As we saw in the first part of this section, task complexity does not interact with exercise intensity in the way that Yerkes and Dodson's theory would predict. The evidence that attention/perception, working memory, and autonomous tasks would be affected differently by differing exercise intensities is limited. Before examining this, however, we need to look at an anomaly that is affecting how we interpret the acute exercise–cognition interaction literature, namely that the dependent variable, accuracy versus speed, affects results.

In two meta-analyses (McMorris & Hale, 2012; McMorris, Sproule, Turner, & Hale, 2011), my colleagues and I showed that results, when accuracy was the dependent variable, were significantly different to those when speed was the dependent variable. This factor, I believe, can account for some differences between meta-analyses results found by different authors. As far as I know, we are the only authors to have separated accuracy and speed results. In the McMorris and Hale study, we found an overall effect size, with both accuracy and speed-dependent variables included, which was significant as measured by probability ($Z = 2.80$, $p < 0.01$) but which was very small ($g = 0.14$). According to Orwin (1983), an effect size as low as this should be treated as being nonsignificant. However, the effect size for speed of response was $g = 0.30$ ($Z = 3.75$, $p < 0.001$), while for accuracy the effect size ($g = 0.04$) was almost zero.

Observation of the studies analyzed by McMorris and Hale (2012) and McMorris et al. (2011), and those reviewed in this study, shows that there are not many in which accuracy was the most important measure. In most of the studies in which accuracy was measured, there were very few errors. This is because most of these studies utilized tasks such as the flanker, Simon, go/no go tasks, and noncompatible reaction time tests, which were designed to measure speed of processing, which was seen as being indicative of processing efficiency. Much more research is required using tasks that were designed to measure accuracy only. I suspect that when such tasks are used sufficiently to be able to examine effect sizes in a meta-analysis, we will get similar results to those for the speed of processing results found at the present time.

Moderate Intensity Exercise

Observation of Table 1 shows that with accuracy as the dependent variable, there appears to be little or no effect of moderate intensity exercise. This is, of course, using probability as the criterion for significance but it is in agreement with the meta-analysis of McMorris and Hale (2012), which used effect sizes as the criterion for significance. With speed of response as the dependent variable, the situation is different. With probability as the criterion, there is a definite tendency for studies, regardless of task type, to show a positive, significant effect, although McMorris and Hale (2012) showed that effect sizes for central executive tasks were significantly higher than those for attention/perception, short-term memory, and autonomous tasks ($g = 0.77$ versus $g = 0.46$). McMorris et al. demonstrated a high effect size ($g = 1.41$) for working memory tasks, i.e., including both central executive and short-term memory tasks. These results are as would be predicated by the allocatable resource theories (Hockey, 1997; Kahneman, 1973; Pribram & McGuinness, 1975; Sanders, 1983). Optimal arousal would result in increased resources and effort would have little or no difficulty in allocating these resources. Drive theory would also predict an improvement if the task were well learned. However, according to Yerkes and Dodson's (1908) theory, one might expect that moderate intensity was too high for optimal performance with the more difficult working memory tasks and possibly not high enough with the other, more simple, tasks. This may account for the lower effect sizes for attention/perception and autonomous tasks found by McMorris and Hale.

Heavy Exercise

While the overall results concerning moderate intensity exercise may be similar to those that would be predicted by the cognitive psychology theories, the situation for heavy exercise is much more complicated. Accuracy results tend to show no significant effects but not unequivocally. However, for speed of decision, results are fairly equivocal. Autonomous tasks demonstrate positive effects, which would be predicted by drive theory, but there does not appear to be any differences between attention/perception and working memory tasks, although this might be due to the small number of working memory studies that were included in the review.

These results are not as predicted from the allocatable resources theories (Hockey, 1997; Kahneman, 1973; Pribram & McGuinness, 1975; Sanders, 1983). All of these predict inhibition, as the authors saw it as impossible for effort to allocate sufficient resources to the task at such high levels of arousal. According to Hockey's theory, the action monitor would probably adjust the individual's goals downwards, as the goal demands would be perceived as being unobtainable. So in an experiment, the person would not be able to successfully undertake the task while exercising. In a real life situation, they would probably simply stop exercising. Neither do the results support Humphreys and Revelle's (1984) claims that simple, sustained information tasks would be facilitated while short-term memory tasks would be inhibited. Results for autonomous tasks are more in line with allocatable resources theories and certainly predicted by drive theory.

Learning/Long-Term Memory

So far we have ignored the effect of acute exercise on learning/long-term memory tasks. This is not because there are so few, although that makes it very difficult to draw any conclusions from the results, but because the results of these tasks cannot be predicted by any of the cognitive psychology theories. The two learning/long-term memory studies (Griffin et al., 2011; Winter et al., 2007) both showed positive effects of heavy exercise. This is the opposite of what would be predicted using the cognitive psychology theories. Neuroscience-based theories, however, do predict these findings (see Chapter 4).

CONCLUSION

Currently, it is probably safe to say that there is little support for an inverted-U effect of acute exercise on cognition. Moderate intensity, acute exercise appears to have a positive effect on speed of undertaking cognitive tasks and, moreover, this appears to be true regardless of task type. However, there is some evidence to show a greater effect on working memory tasks. This would be as predicted by cognitive–energetic, arousal–performance theories. However, results for cognition during heavy exercise are fairly equivocal, although speed of undertaking autonomous tasks is facilitated. Drive theory would predict this latter finding but the equivocal results, for heavy exercise effects on attention/perception and working memory tasks, cannot be explained by cognitive–energetic, arousal–performance theories. This may be due to the link between exercise intensity and increases in stress level being too simplistic and limitations in the interpretation of how stress affects cognition; hence, the necessity to examine the acute exercise–cognition interaction from neuroscientific perspectives as well as cognitive psychology.

References

Adams, J. A. (1971). A closed-loop theory of motor learning. *Journal of Motor Behavior, 3*, 111–149.

Adam, J. J., Teeken, J. C., Ypelaar, P. J. C., Verstappen, F. T. J., & Paas, F. G. W. (1997). Exercise-induced arousal and information processing. *International Journal of Sports Psychology, 26*, 2217–2220.

Allard, F., Brawley, L. R., Deakin, J., & Elliott, D. (1989). The effect of exercise on visual attention performance. *Human Performance, 2*, 131–145.

Ando, S., Kokubu, M., Yamada, Y., & Kimura, M. (2011). Does cerebral oxygenation affect cognitive function during exercise? *European Journal of Applied Physiology, 111,* 1973–1982.

Arbuthnott, K., & Frank, J. (2000). Trail making test, part B as a measure of executive control: validation using a set-switching paradigm. *Journal of Clinical and Experimental Neuropsychology, 22,* 518–528.

Arcelin, R., & Brisswalter, J. (1999). Performance stability in simultaneous tasks of pedalling and reaction time. *Perceptual and Motor Skills, 88,* 1193–1199.

Arcelin, R., Delignières, D., & Brisswalter, J. (1998). Effects of physical exercise on choice reaction processes. *Perceptual and Motor Skills, 87,* 175–185.

Audiffren, M. (2009). Acute exercise and psychological functions: a cognitive-energetics approach. In T. McMorris, P. D. Tomporowski, & M. Audiffren (Eds.), *Exercise and cognitive function* (pp. 3–39). Chichester: Wiley-Blackwell.

Audiffren, M., Tomporowski, P. D., & Zagrodnik, J. (2009). Acute exercise and information processing: modulation of executive control in a Random Number Generation task. *Acta Psychologica, 132,* 85–95.

Baddeley, A. D. (1966). The capacity for generating information by randomization. *Quarterly Journal of Experimental Psychology, 18,* 119–129.

Baddeley, A. D. (1986). *Working memory.* New York: Oxford University Press.

Baddeley, A. D., Emslie, H., Kolodny, J., & Duncan, J. (1998). Random generation and the central executive of working memory. *Quarterly Journal of Experimental Psychology A, 51,* 819–852.

Bard, C., & Fleury, M. (1978). Influence of imposed metabolic fatigue on visual capacity components. *Perceptual and Motor Skills, 47,* 1283–1287.

Beh, H. C. (1989). Mental performance following exercise. *Perceptual and Motor Skills, 69,* 42.

Berg, E. A. (1948). A simple objective technique for measuring flexibility in thinking. *Journal of General Psychology, 39,* 15–22.

Best, J. R. (2010). Effects of physical activity on children's executive function: contributions of experimental research on aerobic exercise. *Developmental Review, 30,* 331–551.

Borer, K. T. (2003). *Exercise endocrinology.* Champaign, IL: Human Kinetics.

Bridge, M. W., Weller, A. S., Rayson, M., & Jones, D. A. (2003). Ambient temperature and the pituitary hormone responses to exercise in humans. *Experimental Physiology, 88,* 627–635.

Brisswalter, J., Arcelin, R., Audiffren, M., & Delignières, D. (1997). Influence of physical exercise on simple reaction time: effect of physical fitness. *Perceptual and Motor Skills, 85,* 1019–1027.

Burns, R. (1786). *Poems, Chiefly in the scottish Dialect.* Kilmarnock: John Wilson.

Cereatti, L., Casella, R., Manganelli, M., & Pesce, C. (2009). Visual attention in adolescents: facilitating effects of sport expertise and acute physical exercise. *Psychology of Sport and Exercise, 10,* 136–145.

Chang, Y. K., Labban, J. D., Gapin, J. I., & Etnier, J. L. (2012). The effects of acute exercise on cognitive performance: a meta-analysis. *Brain Research, 1453,* 87–101.

Chang, Y.-K., Tsai, C.-L., Hung, T.-M., So, E. C., Chen, F.-T., & Etnier, J. L. (2011). Effects of acute exercise on executive function: a study with a Tower of London task. *Journal of Sport and Exercise Psychology, 33,* 847–865.

Chmura, J., & Nazar, K. (2010). Parallel changes in the onset of blood lactate accumulation (OBLA) and threshold of psychomotor performance deterioration during incremental exercise after training in athletes. *International Journal of Psychophysiology, 75,* 287–290.

Chmura, J., Nazar, H., & Kaciuba-Uścilko, H. (1994). Choice reaction time during graded exercise in relation to blood lactate and plasma catecholamine thresholds. *International Journal of Sports Medicine, 15,* 172–176.

Coco, M., Di Corrado, D., Calogero, R. A., Perciavalle, V., & Maci, T. (2009). Attentional processes and blood lactate levels. *Brain Research, 1302,* 205–211.

Coles, K., & Tomporowski, P. D. (2008). Effects of acute exercise on executive processing, short-term memory and long-term memory. *Journal of Sports Science, 26,* 333–344.

Collardeau, M., Brisswalter, J., & Audiffren, M. (2001). Effects of a prolonged run on simple reaction time of well trained runners. *Perceptual and Motor Skills, 93,* 679–689.

Côté, J., Salmela, J., & Papathanasopoulu, P. (1992). Effects of progressive exercise on attentional focus. *Perceptual and Motor Skills, 75,* 351–354.

Culbertson, W. C., & Zillmer, E. A. (2005). *Tower of London Drexel University: 2nd Edition (TOLDx).* North Tonawanda, NY: Multi-Health Systems, Inc.

Daneman, M., & Carpenter, P. A. (1980). Individual differences in working memory and reading. *Journal of Verbal Learning and Verbal Behavior, 19,* 450–466.

Davey, C. P. (1973). Physical exertion and mental performance. *Ergonomics, 16,* 595–599.

Davranche, K., & Audiffren, M. (2004). Facilitating effects of exercise on information processing. *Journal of Sports Science, 22,* 419–428.

Davranche, K., Audiffren, M., & Denjean, A. (2006). A distributional analysis of physical exercise on a choice reaction time task. *Journal of Sport Science, 24,* 323–329.

Davranche, K., Burle, B., Audiffren, M., & Hasbroucq, T. (2005). Information processing during physical exercise: a chronometric and electromyographic study. *Experimental Brain Research, 165,* 532–540.

Davranche, K., Hall, B., & McMorris, T. (2009). Effect of acute exercise on cognitive control required during an Eriksen flanker task. *Journal of Sport and Exercise Psychology, 31,* 628–639.

Davranche, K., & McMorris, T. (2009). Specific effects of acute moderate exercise on cognitive control. *Brain and Cognition, 69*, 565–570.

De Vries, W. R., Bernards, N. T. M., De Rooij, M. H., & Koppeschaar, H. P. F. (2000). Dynamic exercise discloses different time-related responses in stress hormones. *Psychosomatic Medicine, 62*, 866–872.

Dehaene, S., & Changeux, J. P. (1997). A hierarchical neuronal network for planning behavior. *Proceedings of the National Academy of Sciences of the United States of America, 94*, 13293–13298.

Del Giorno, J. M., Hall, E. E., O'Leary, K. C., Bixby, W. R., & Miller, P. C. (2010). Cognitive function during acute exercise: a test of the transient hypofrontality theory. *Journal of Sport and Exercise Psychology, 32*, 312–323.

Delignières, D., Brisswalter, J., & Legros, P. (1994). Influence of physical exercise on choice reaction time in sports experts: the mediating role of resources allocation. *Journal of Human Movement Studies, 27*, 173–188.

Dickinson, J., Medhurst, C., & Whittingham, N. (1979). warm-up and fatigue in skill acquisition and performance. *Journal of Motor Behaviour, 11*, 81–86.

Dietrich, A. (2003). Functional neuroanatomy of altered states of consciousness: the transient hypofrontality hypothesis. *Consciousness and Cognition, 12*, 231–256.

Dietrich, A., & Audiffren, M. (2011). The reticular-activating hypofrontality (RAH) model of acute exercise. *Neuroscience & Biobehavioral Reviews, 35*, 1305–1325.

Donders, F. C. (1969). On the speed of mental processes. *Acta Psychologica, 30*, 412–431.

Douchamps, J. (1988). A metatheoretical approach of operational performance. In J. P. Leonard (Ed.), *Vigilance: Methods, models and regulation* (pp. 23–34). Frankfurt: Long.

Draper, S., McMorris, T., & Parker, J. K. (2010). Effect of acute exercise of differing intensities on simple and choice reaction and movement times. *Psychology of Sport and Exercise, 11*, 536–541.

Easterbrook, J. A. (1959). The effect of emotion cue utilization and the organization of behavior. *Psychological Review, 66*, 183–201.

Edwards, R. H. T. (1983). Biochemical bases of fatigue in exercise performance: catastrophe theory of muscular fatigue. In H. Knuttgen, J. Vogel, & J. Poortmans (Eds.), *International series on sports sciences Biochemistry of exercise: Vol. 13.* (pp. 3–28). Champaign, Il: Human Kinetics.

Ehrlenspiel, F., Wei, K., & Stemad, D. (2010). Open-loop, closed-loop and compensatory control: performance improvement under pressure in a rhythmic task. *Experimental Brain Research, 201*, 729–741.

Endo, K., Matsukawa, K., Liang, N., Nakatsuka, C., Tsuchimochi, H., Okamura, H., et al. (2013). Dynamic exercise improves cognitive function in association with increased prefrontal oxygenation. *Journal of Physiological Sciences, 63*, 287–298.

Ericsson, K. A., & Kintsch, W. (1995). Long-term working memory. *Psychological Review, 102*, 211–245.

Eriksen, B. A., & Eriksen, C. W. (1974). Effects of noise letters upon the identification of a target letter in a nonsearch task. *Perception & Psychophysics, 16*, 143–149.

Etnier, J. L., Salazar, W., Landers, D. M., Petruzzello, S. J., Han, M., & Nowell, P. (1997). The influence of physical fitness and exercise upon cognitive functioning: a meta-analysis. *Journal of Sport and Exercise Psychology, 19*, 249–277.

Ewing, J. H., Scott, D. G., Mendez, A. A., & McBride, T. J. (1984). Effects of aerobic exercise on affect and cognition. *Perceptual and Motor Skills, 59*, 407–414.

Féry, Y.-A., Ferry, A., Vom Hofe, A., & Rieu, M. (1997). Effect of physical exhaustion on cognitive functioning. *Perceptual and Motor Skills, 84*, 291–298.

Fitts, P. M., & Posner, M. I. (1967). *Human performance.* Belmont, CA: Brooks/Cole.

Fleury, M., & Bard, C. (1990). Fatigue métabolique et performance de tâches visuelle (Metabolic fatigue and performance of visual tasks). *Canadian Journal of Sports Science, 15*, 43–50.

Fleury, M., Bard, C., & Carrière, L. (1981). Effects of physical or perceptual workloads on a coincidence/anticipation task. *Perceptual and Motor Skills, 53*, 723–730.

Fleury, M., Bard, C., Jobin, J., & Carrière, L. (1981). Influence of different types of physical fatigue on a visual detection task. *Perceptual and Motor Skills, 53*, 723–730.

Fontana, F. E., Mazzardo, O., Mokgothu, C., Furtado, O., & Gallagher, J. D. (2009). Influence of exercise intensity on the decision-making performance of experienced and inexperienced soccer players. *Journal of Sport and Exercise Psychology, 31*, 135–151.

Frensch, P. A. (1998). One concept, multiple meanings: on how to define the concept of implicit learning. In M. A. Stadler, & P. A. Frensch (Eds.), *Handbook of implicit learning* (pp. 47–104). London: Sage.

Grego, F., Vallier, J. M., Collardeau, M., Bermon, S., Ferrari, P., Candito, M., et al. (2004). Effects of long duration exercise on cognitive function, blood glucose, and counterregulatory hormones in male cyclists. *Neuroscience Letters, 364*, 76–80.

Griffin, É. W., Mullally, S., Foley, C., Warmington, S. A., O'Mara, S. M., & Kelly, Á. M. (2011). Aerobic exercise improves hippocampal function and increases BDNF in the serum of young adult males. *Physiology & Behavior, 104*, 934–941.

Guizani, S. M., Bouzaouach, I., Tenenbaum, G., Ben Kheder, A., Feki, Y., & Bouaziz, M. (2006). Simple and choice reaction times under varying levels of physical load in high skilled fencers. *Journal of Sports Medicine and Physical Fitness, 46*, 344–351.

Gutin, B., & Di Gennaro, J. (1968a). Effect of one-minute step-ups on performance of simple addition. *Research Quarterly for Exercise and Sport, 39*, 81–85.

Gutin, B., & Di Gennaro, J. (1968b). Effect of a treadmill run to exhaustion on performance of long addition. *Research Quarterly for Exercise and Sport, 39*, 958–964.

Hancock, S., & McNaughton, L. (1986). Effects of fatigue on ability to process visual information by experienced orienteers. *Perceptual and Motor Skills*, 62, 491–498.

Hanson, C., & Lofthus, G. K. (1978). Effects of fatigue and laterality on fractionated reaction time. *Journal of Motor Behavior*, 10, 177–184.

Hill, E. E., Zack, E., Battaglini, C., Viru, M., Viru, A., & Hackney, A. C. (2008). Exercise and circulating cortisol levels: the intensity threshold effect. *Journal of Endocrinology Investigation*, 31, 587–591.

Hockey, G. R. (1997). Compensatory control in the regulation of human performance under stress and high workload: a cognitive-energetical framework. *Biological Psychology*, 45, 73–93.

Hodgetts, V., Coppack, S. W., Frayn, K. N., & Hockaday, T. D. R. (1991). Factors controlling fat mobilization from human subcutaneous adipose-tissue during exercise. *Journal of Applied Physiology*, 71, 445–451.

Hogan, C. L., Matta, J., & Carstensen, L. L. (2013). Exercise holds immediate benefits for affect and cognition in younger and older adults. *Psychology of Aging*, 28, 587–594.

Hogervorst, E., Riedel, W. J., Jeukendrup, A., & Jolies, J. (1996). Cognitive performance after strenuous physical exercise. *Perceptual and Motor Skills*, 83, 479–488.

Hollmann, W. (1985). Historical remarks on the development of the aerobic-anaerobic threshold up to 1966. *International Journal of Sports Medicine*, 6, 109–116.

Hull, C. L. (1943). *Principles of behavior*. New York: Appleton.

Humphreys, M. S., & Revelle, W. (1984). Personality, motivation, and performance. A theory of the relationship between individual differences and information processing. *Psychological Review*, 91, 153–184.

Hung, T.-M., Tsai, C.-L., Chen, F.-T., Wang, C.-C., & Chang, Y.-K. (2013). The immediate and sustained effects of acute exercise on planning aspect of executive function. *Psychology of Sport and Exercise*, 14, 728–736.

Hyodo, K., Dan, I., Suwabe, K., Kyutoku, Y., Yamada, Y., Akahori, M., et al. (2012). Acute moderate exercise enhances compensatory brain activation in older adults. *Neurobiology of Aging*, 33, 2621–2632.

Isaacs, L. D., & Pohlman, R. L. (1991). Effects of exercise intensity on an accompanying timing task. *Journal of Human Movement Studies*, 20, 123–131.

Jacks, D. E., Sowash, J., Anning, J., McGloughlin, T., & Andres, F. (2002). Effect of exercise at three exercise intensities on salivary cortisol. *Journal of Strength and Conditioning Research*, 16, 286–289.

Joyce, J., Graydon, J., McMorris, T., & Davranche, K. (2009). The time course effect of moderate intensity exercise on response execution and response inhibition. *Brain and Cognition*, 71, 14–19.

Kahneman, D. (1973). *Attention and effort*. Englewood Cliffs, NJ: Prentice Hall.

Kamijo, K., Hayashi, Y., Sakai, T., Yahiro, T., Tanaka, K., & Nishihira, Y. (2009). Acute effects of aerobic exercise on cognitive function in older adults. *Journal of Gerontology B-Psychology*, 64, 356–363.

Kamijo, K., Nishihira, Y., Hatta, A., Kaneda, T., Kida, T., Higashiura, T., et al. (2004). Changes in arousal level by differential exercise intensity. *Clinical Neurophysiology*, 115, 2693–2698.

Kamijo, K., Nishihira, Y., Hatta, A., Kaneda, K., Wasaka, T., Kida, T., et al. (2004). Differential influences of exercise intensity on information processing in the central nervous system. *European Journal of Applied Physiology*, 92, 305–311.

Kashihara, K., & Nakahara, Y. (2005). Short-term effect of physical exercise at lactate threshold on choice reaction time. *Perceptual and Motor Skills*, 100, 275–291.

Kirchner, W. K. (1958). Age difference in short-term retention of rapidly changing information. *Journal of Experimental Psychology*, 55, 352–358.

Kortte, K. B., Horner, M. B., & Windhan, W. K. (2002). The trail making test, part B: cognitive flexibility or ability to maintain set. *Applied Neuropsychology*, 9, 106–109.

Lambourne, K., & Tomporowski, P. D. (2010). The effect of acute exercise on cognitive task performance: a meta-regression analysis. *Brain Research*, 1341, 12–24.

Lawless, W. F. (1988). Effect of arousal on mathematic scores. *Perceptual and Motor Skills*, 67, 318.

Leh, S. E., Petrides, M., & Strafella, A. P. (2010). The neural circuitry of executive functions in healthy subjects and Parkinson's disease. *Neuropsychopharmacology*, 35, 70–85.

Levitt, S., & Gutin, B. (1971). Multiple choice reaction time and movement time during physical exertion. *Research Quartelry for Exercise and Sport*, 42, 405–410.

Logan, G. D., & Cowan, W. B. (1984). On the ability to inhibit thought and action: a theory of an act of control. *Psychological Review*, 91, 295–327.

Lowe, C. J., Hall, P. A., Vincent, C. M., & Luu, K. (2014). The effects of acute aerobic activity on cognition and cross-domain transfer to eating behavior. *Frontiers in Human Neuroscience*, 8, 267. http://dx.doi.org/10.3389/fnhum.2014.00267.

Masters, R. S. W., Poolton, J. M., Maxwell, J. P., & Raab, M. (2008). Implicit motor learning and complex decision making in time-constrained environments. *Journal of Motor Behavior*, 40, 71–79.

McAdam, R. E., & Wang, Y. K. (1967). Performance of a simple mental task following various treatments. *Research Quartelry for Exercise and Sport*, 38, 208–212.

McGlynn, G. H., Laughlin, N. T., & Bender, V. L. (1977). Effect of strenuous to exhaustive exercise on a discrimination task. *Perceptual and Motor Skills*, 44, 1139–1147.

McGlynn, G. H., Laughlin, N. T., & Rowe, V. (1979). The effects of increasing levels of exercise on mental performance. *Ergonomics*, 22, 407–414.

McMorris, T. (2009). Exercise and decision making in team games. In T. McMorris, P. D. Tomporowski, & M. Audiffren (Eds.), *Exercise and cognitive function* (pp. 180–192). Chichester: Wiley-Blackwell.

McMorris, T. (2014). *Acquisition and performance of sports skills* (2nd ed.). Chichester: Wiley-Blackwell.

McMorris, T., Collard, K., Corbett, J., Dicks, M., & Swain, J. P. (2008). A test of the catecholamines hypothesis for an acute exercise–cognition interaction. *Pharmacology Biochemistry & Behavior, 89*, 106–115.

McMorris, T., Davranche, K., Jones, G., Hall, B., & Minter, C. (2009). Acute incremental exercise, performance of a central executive task, and sympathoadrenal system and hypothalamic-pituitary-adrenal axis activity. *International Journal of Psychophysiology, 73*, 334–340.

McMorris, T., & Graydon, J. (1996a). The effect of exercise on the decision-making performance of experienced and inexperienced soccer players. *Research Quarterly for Exercise and Sport, 67*, 109–114.

McMorris, T., & Graydon, J. (1996b). Effect of exercise on soccer decision-making tasks of differing complexities. *Journal of Human Movement Studies, 30*, 177–193.

McMorris, T., & Graydon, J. (1997). The effect of exercise on cognitive performance in soccer-specific tests. *Journal of Sports Science, 15*, 459–468.

McMorris, T., & Graydon, J. (2000). The effect of incremental exercise on cognitive performance. *International Journal of Sport Psychology, 31*, 66–81.

McMorris, T., & Hale, B. J. (2012). Differential effects of differing intensities of acute exercise on speed and accuracy of cognition: a meta-analytical investigation. *Brain and Cognition, 80*, 338–351.

McMorris, T., & Keen, P. (1994). Effect of exercise on simple reaction times of recreational athletes. *Perceptual and Motor Skills, 78*, 123–130.

McMorris, T., Myers, S., MacGillivary, W. W., Sexsmith, J. R., Fallowfield, J., Graydon, J., et al. (1999). Exercise, plasma catecholamine concentration and decision-making performance of soccer players on a soccer-specific test. *Journal of Sports Science, 17*, 667–676.

McMorris, T., Sproule, J., Draper, S., & Child, R. (2000). Performance of a psychomotor skill following rest, exercise at the plasma epinephrine threshold and maximal intensity exercise. *Perceptual and Motor Skills, 91*, 553–562.

McMorris, T., Sproule, J., Turner, A., & Hale, B. J. (2011). Acute, intermediate intensity exercise, and speed and accuracy in working memory tasks: a meta-analytical comparison of effects. *Physiology & Behavior, 102*, 421–428.

McMorris, T., Swain, J., Lauder, M., Smith, N., & Kelly, J. (2006). Warm-up prior to undertaking a dynamic psychomotor task: does it aid performance? *Journal of Sports Medicine and Physical Fitness, 46*, 328–334.

McMorris, T., Tallon, M., Williams, C., Sproule, J., Potter, J., Swain, J., et al. (2003). Incremental exercise, plasma concentrations of catecholamines, reaction time, and motor time during performance of a noncompatible choice response time task. *Perceptual and Motor Skills, 97*, 590–604.

Meyers, C. A., Zimmerli, W., Farr, S. D., & Baschnagel, N. A. (1969). Effect of strenuous physical activity upon reaction time. *Research Quarterly for Exercise and Sport, 40*, 333–337.

Miyake, A., Friedman, N. P., Emerson, M. J., Witzki, A. H., & Howerter, A. (2000). The unity and diversity of executive functions and their contributions to complex "frontal lobe" tasks: a latent variable analysis. *Cognitive Psychology, 41*, 49–100.

Miyake, A., & Shah, P. (1999). Toward unified theories of working memory: emerging general consensus, unresolved theoretical issues, and future research directions. In A. Miyake, & P. Shah (Eds.), *Models of working memory* (pp. 442–481). New York: Cambridge University Press.

Moore, R. D., Romine, M. W., O'Conner, P. J., & Tomporowski, P. D. (2012). The influence of exercise-induced fatigue on cognitive function. *Journal of Sports Science, 30*, 841–850.

Mulligan, D., McCracken, J., & Hodges, N. J. (2012). Situational familiarity and its relation to decision quality in ice-hockey. *International Journal of Sport and Exercise Psychology, 10*, 198–210.

Nanda, B., Balde, J. S., & Manjunatha, S. (2013). The acute effects of a single bout of moderate-intensity aerobic exercise on cognitive functions in healthy adult males. *Journal of Clinical and Diagnostic Research, 7*, 1883–1885.

Orwin, R. G. (1983). A fail-safe N for effect size in meta-analysis. *Journal of Educational Statistics, 8*, 157–159.

Ozyemisci-Taskiran, O., Gunendi, Z., Bolukbasi, N., & Beyazova, M. (2008). The effect of a single session submaximal aerobic exercise on premotor fraction of reaction time: an electromyographic study. *Clinical Biomechanics, 23*, 231–235.

Pesce, C., & Audiffren, M. (2011). Does acute exercise switch off switch costs? A study with younger and older athletes. *Journal of Sport and Exercise Psychology, 33*, 609–626.

Pesce, C., Capranica, L., Tessitore, A., & Figura, F. (2002). Orienting and focusing of visual attention under submaximal physical load. *Journal of Human Movement Studies, 42*, 401–420.

Pesce, C., Capranica, L., Tessitore, A., & Figura, F. (2003). Focusing of visual attention under submaximal physical load. *International Journal of Sport and Exercise Psychology, 1*, 275–292.

Pesce, C., Cereatti, L., Casella, R., Caldari, C., & Capranica, L. (2007). Preservation of visual attention in older expert orienteers at rest and under physical effort. *Journal of Sport and Exercise Psychology, 29*, 78–99.

Pesce, C., Tessitore, A., Casella, R., Pirritano, M., & Capranica, L. (2007). Focusing of visual attention at rest and during physical exercise in soccer players. *Journal of Sports Science, 25*, 1259–1270.

Podolin, D. A., Munger, P. A., & Mazzeo, R. S. (1991). Plasma-catecholamine and lactate response during graded-exercise with varied glycogen conditions. *Journal of Applied Physiology, 71*, 1427–1433.

Polk, T. A., Simen, P., Lewis, R. L., & Freedman, E. (2002). A computational approach to control in complex cognition. *Cognitive Brain Research, 15*(1), 71–83.

Pribram, K. H., & McGuinness, D. (1975). Arousal, activation and effort in the control of attention. *Psychological Review, 82*, 116–149.

Reitan, R. M. (1958). Validity of the trail making test as an indicator of organic brain damage. *Perceptual and Motor Skills, 8*, 271–276.

Reynolds, H. L. (1976). The effect of augmented levels of stress on reaction time in the peripheral visual field. *Research Quarterly for Exercise and Sport, 47*, 768–775.

Salmela, J., & Ndoye, O. D. (1986). Cognitive distortions during progressive exercise. *Perceptual and Motor Skills, 63*, 1067–1072.

Salthouse, T. A., Atkinson, T. M., & Berish, D. E. (2003). Executive functioning as a potential mediator of age-related cognitive: decline in normal adults. *Journal of Experimental Psychology, 132*, 566–594.

Sanders, A. F. (1983). Towards a model of stress and human performance. *Acta Psychologica, 53*, 61–97.

Sawada, Y., Nishio, Y., Suzuki, K., Hirayama, K., Takeda, A., Hosakai, Y., et al. (2012). Attentional set-shifting deficit in Parkinson's disease is associated with prefrontal dysfunction: an FDG-PET study. *PLoS One, 7*, e38498. http://dx.doi.org/10.1371/journal.pone.0038498.

Shallice, T. (1982). Specific impairments of planning. *Philosophical Transactions of the Royal Society B, 298*, 199–209.

Shojaei, E. A., Farajov, A., & Jafari, A. (2011). Effect of moderate aerobic cycling on some systemic inflammatory markers in healthy active collegiate men. *International Journal of General Medicine, 4*, 79–84.

Sibley, B. A., Etnier, J. L., & Le Masurier, G. C. (2006). Effects of an acute bout of exercise on cognitive aspects of Stroop performance. *Journal of Sport & Exercise Psychology, 28*, 285–299.

Simon, J. R. (1969). Reactions towards the source of stimulation. *Journal of Experimental Psychology, 81*, 174–176.

Simon, J. R., & Rudell, A. P. (1967). Auditory S–R compatibility: the effect of an irrelevant cue on information processing. *Journal of Applied Psychology, 51*, 300–304.

Sjöberg, H. (1975). Relations between heart rate, reaction speed, and subjective effort at different workloads on a bicycle ergometer. *Journal of Human Stress, 1*, 21–27.

Sjöberg, H. (1980). Physical fitness and mental performance during and after work. *Ergonomics, 23*, 977–985.

Spence. (1958). A theory of emotionally based drive (d) and its relation to performance in simple learning situations. *American Psychologist, 13*, 131–141.

Stroop, J. R. (1935). Studies of interference in serial verbal reactions. *Journal of Experimental Psychology, 18*, 643–662.

Thomson, K., Watt, A., & Liukkonen, J. (2009). Differences in ball sports athletes speed discrimination skills before and after exercise induced fatigue. *Journal of Sports Science and Medicine, 8*, 259–264.

Tomporowski, P. D. (2003). Effects of acute bouts of exercise on cognition. *Acta Psychologica, 112*, 297–324.

Tomporowski, P. D., & Ellis, N. R. (1986). Effects of exercise on cognitive processes: a review. *Psychological Bulletin, 99*, 338–346.

Towse, J. N., & McLachlan, A. (1999). An exploration of random generation among children. *British Journal of Developmental Psychology, 17*, 363–380.

Towse, J. N., & Neil, D. (1998). Analyzing human random generation behavior: a review of methods used and a computer program for describing performance. *Behavior Research Methods, Instruments and Computers, 30*(4), 582–591.

Travlos, A. K. (2009). Effect of submaximal steady-state aerobic exercise and fitness in random number generation test. *Biology of Exercise, 5*, 41–50.

Travlos, A. K., & Marisi, D. Q. (1995). Information processing and concentration as a function of fitness level and exercise induced activation to exhaustion. *Perceptual and Motor Skills, 80*, 15–26.

Tsai, C.-L., Chen, F.-C., Pan, C.-Y., Wang, C.-H., Huang, T.-H., & Chen, T.-C. (2014). Impact of acute aerobic exercise and cardiorespiratory fitness on visuospatial attention performance and serum BDNF levels. *Psychoneuroendocrinology, 41*, 121–131.

Turner, M. L., & Engle, R. W. (1989). Is working memory capacity task dependent? *Journal of Memory & Language, 28*, 127–154.

Urhausen, A., Weiler, B., Coen, B., & Kindermann, W. (1994). Plasma catecholamines during endurance exercise of different intensities as related to the individual anaerobic threshold. *European Journal of Applied Physiology, 69*, 16–20.

Verbruggen, F., & Logan, G. D. (2008). Response inhibition in the stop-signal paradigm. *Trends in Cognitive Sciences, 12*, 418–424.

Wasserman, K., & McIlroy, M. B. (1964). Detecting the threshold of anaerobic metabolism in cardiac patients during exercise. *American Journal of Cardiology, 14*, 844–852.

Weingarten, G., & Alexander, J. F. (1970). Effects of physical exertion on mental performance of college males of different physical fitness levels. *Perceptual and Motor Skills, 31*, 371–378.

Welford, A. T. (1968). *Fundamentals of skill*. London: Methuen.

Williams, L. R. T., Pottinger, P. R., & Shapcott, D. G. (1985). Effects of exercise on choice reaction latency and movement speed. *Perceptual and Motor Skills, 60*, 67–71.

Winter, B., Breitenstein, C., Mooren, F.C., Voelker, K., Fobker, M., Lechtermann, A., et al. (2007). High impact running improves learning. *Neurobiology of Learning and Memory, 87*, 597–609.

Yanagisawa, H., Dan, I., Tsuzuki, D., Kato, M., Okamoto, M., Kyutoku, Y., et al. (2010). Acute moderate exercise elicits increased dorsolateral prefrontal activation and improves cognitive performance with Stroop test. *NeuroImage, 50*, 1702–1710.

Yerkes, R. M., & Dodson, J. D. (1908). The relation of strength of stimulus to the rapidity of habit formation. *Journal of Comparative Neurology and Psychology, 18*, 459–482.

The History of Research on Chronic Physical Activity and Cognitive Performance

Jennifer L. Etnier, Chia-Hao Shih, Aaron T. Piepmeier

Department of Kinesiology, University of North Carolina at Greensboro, Greensboro, NC, USA

INTRODUCTION

The notion that regular (also called chronic) exercise benefits cognitive performance goes back to Greek and Roman times. However, the provision of scientific evidence supporting the relationship between chronic exercise and cognitive performance is a much more modern phenomenon with published studies beginning to appear in the 1950s (Baer, Gersten, Robertson, & Dinken, 1955; Oliver, 1958; Pierson, 1956; Slater-Hamel, 1955; Weber, 1953; Youngen, 1959). The interest in the relationship between exercise and cognition remained relatively modest through the remainder of the twentieth century, but during the early part of the twenty-first century, we have seen a rapid increase in the number of publications on this topic (see Figure 1).

The first decade of research was focused on exploring the potential benefits of chronic exercise for children and young adults with cross-sectional studies typically comparing athletes and nonathletes on measures of reaction time[1] and correlational studies typically testing relationships between fitness and academic achievement. Subsequently, researchers continued to use cross-sectional designs, but expanded beyond children and adults to also explore the potential benefits of regular physical activity for older adults. For example, Spirduso (1975) conducted a seminal study in which she compared reaction time and movement time between younger and older men who were either relatively inactive or who regularly participated in racket sports. Results indicated that physical activity participation did not significantly influence the results for the younger men, but did significantly benefit reaction time and movement time for the older men. Importantly, physically active older men showed similar performance on simple reaction time,

---

[1] See Hall et al. (2001) for a discussion of the extent to which measures of reaction time are indicative of cognitive performance versus motor performance.

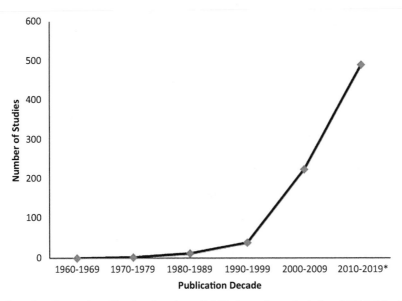

FIGURE 1　Number of studies retrieved by decade using a PubMed search conducted on 10.31.2014 with the terms (exercise or physical activity or fitness) and (cognition or cognitive performance or cognitive function or academic or executive function or memory) as the search terms joined with a Boolean "and." *=note that there were still 2 months remaining in 2014 when the search was conducted and an additional 5 years in this decade (2015–2019), hence this value of 491 might more reasonably be estimated at 1016 publications for the 2010–2019 decade.

discrimination reaction time, and movement time as younger men suggesting that physical activity could ameliorate normal age-related declines in cognitive performance. Although the cross-sectional design of this study clearly limits the inferences that can be drawn, this study paved the way for an expanded interest in the potential benefits of chronic physical activity for older adults.

The 1980s and 1990s saw a noticeable increase in the number of chronic exercise intervention studies being conducted. In 1997, Etnier et al. published the first meta-analysis of the literature on exercise and cognitive performance and an examination of the studies included in this meta-analysis provide an indication of the nature of the literature at that time. Meta-analysis is a statistical method that allows researchers to combine results from different studies and compute an overall effect size. The effect size expresses the overall

strength of a treatment effect or of an association between two variables and hence conveys the results of a body of literature. One benefit of a meta-analysis is that effects are averaged across studies meaning that the sample sizes of the studies are essentially combined, which then results in an increase in statistical power. A second benefit of a meta-analysis is that by testing for moderators of the effects (i.e., independent variables that differ between studies), we can identify aspects of the experimental designs that significantly influence the size of the effects. In this meta-analysis, Etnier et al. identified 176 studies that had examined the relationship between exercise and cognitive performance. Of those, 134 had sufficient data for the calculation of effect sizes and 45 had used a chronic exercise intervention to test the effects of regular physical activity participation on cognitive performance. Of these 45 chronic exercise studies, 4 were published in

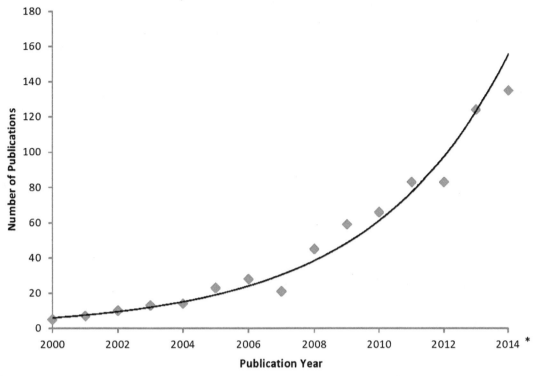

FIGURE 2 Number of studies retrieved by year using a PubMed search conducted on 10.31.2014 with the terms (exercise or physical activity or fitness) and (cognition or cognitive performance or cognitive function or academic or executive function or memory) as the search terms joined with a Boolean "and." * = note that there were still 2 months remaining in 2014 when the search was conducted, hence this value of 135 might more reasonably be estimated at 162 publications for 2014.

the 1950s, 5 in the 1960s, 9 in the 1970s, and 22 in the 1980s[2] demonstrating the increasing interest in this area of research. Interestingly, of the studies published in the 1980s and 1990s (n = 27), those that were focused on a single age range (n = 14) consisted of only a handful of studies focused on children (n = 1) or young adults (n = 2) compared to a relatively large number of studies focused exclusively on older adults (n = 11). There were also several studies designed to compare the effects of chronic physical activity between younger and older adults (n = 7).

In the 2000s, we continue to see an exponential increase in the number of publications focused on the effects of exercise on cognitive performance (see Figure 2). Although early research was dominated by a focus on demonstrating that chronic physical activity had the potential to benefit cognitive performance, scientists now are confident in that effect and are shifting their attention to trying to understand how the effect occurs as research is increasingly focused on understanding mechanisms of the effects. This is important as we move toward understanding which populations of individuals stand to

---

[2] Because the meta-analysis was published in 1997, the total number of chronic intervention studies published in the 1990s cannot accurately be determined from this review.

benefit the most from physical activity participation, how to prescribe physical activity to benefit cognitive performance or to protect against declines in cognitive performance, and how to combine physical activity with other potentially advantageous interventions (e.g., antioxidant diet and cognitive training) to maximally benefit cognitive performance.

RESEARCH WITH OLDER ADULTS

Research exploring the effects of chronic physical activity for older adults continues to increase, which reflects an interest in understanding the potential value of physical activity in the mitigation of age-related decline and the amelioration of clinical cognitive impairments. Numerous prospective studies have been conducted to examine the benefits of physical activity for cognitive performance. In prospective cohort studies, researchers assess physical activity levels (or fitness levels) in cognitively normal older adults at baseline and then measure cognitive performance again at a subsequent time point that is typically several years in the future. Differences in baseline physical activity (or fitness) are then used to predict the changes in cognitive performance that are observed over time. Prospective studies have been meta-analytically reviewed on several occasions with results indicating that physical activity reduces the risk of Alzheimer's disease (AD) by 28–45% (Daviglus et al., 2011; Hamer & Chida, 2009), of dementia by 28% (Hamer & Chida, 2009), and of general cognitive decline by 34–38% (Sofi et al., 2011). Hence, there is a robust literature demonstrating that physical activity is protective against age-related cognitive decline and suggesting that physical activity could be causally related to cognitive performance.

With older adults, many randomized controlled trials (RCTs) have also been conducted. In RCTs, participants are randomly assigned

to different conditions (i.e., an exercise group and a control group), potentially confounding variables (variables that might influence cognitive performance) are controlled either through design (e.g., matching for depression before randomly assigning to groups), through instructions (e.g., asking participants not to change their diet during the intervention), or through statistical analyses (e.g., using age as a statistical covariate), and cognitive performance is assessed at the end of the intervention. Importantly, RCTs allow researchers to establish causality, which makes RCTs the most powerful research design. RCTs with older adults have been reviewed meta-analytically in three reviews with conclusions consistently supporting small-to-moderate positive effects (Angevaren, Aufdemkampe, Verhaar, Aleman, & Vanhees, 2008; Colcombe & Kramer, 2003; Smith et al., 2010) of chronic physical activity on cognitive performance. Hence, there is also a robust literature supporting that physical activity is causally related to cognitive performance in older adults.

RESEARCH WITH CHILDREN

While age-related declines in cognitive performance have prompted an increase in research with older adults, the increase in research with children may be attributed to age-related increases in brain volume (Hedman, van Haren, Schnack, Kahn, & Hulshoff Pol, 2012; Giedd et al., 1999) as well as interests in improving academic achievement. Childhood is a developmental period of sustained brain growth, which may mean that the neural environment is more amenable to the beneficial effects from chronic physical activity. Hence, researchers may view this population as one that has great potential to benefit from physical activity participation. Coupled with this is an interest in identifying ways to improve academic achievement. Given the emphasis on academic performance resulting from the No Child Left Behind Act and the obvious need to ensure that children have every opportunity to maximize their cognitive development, the potential benefits of physical activity with regards to cognitive performance by children are intriguing.

In the literature with children, the majority of the research has used cross-sectional designs and results of these studies typically support a positive relationship between regular physical activity and cognitive performance. Only a small number of RCTs (n = 3) have been conducted to examine the causal effect of physical activity participation on cognitive performance in children. Of these, two trials had satisfactory statistical power and the results supported significant beneficial effects for measures of executive control (Davis et al., 2011; Hillman et al., 2014). Findings from the third RCT (the SMART trial) have not yet been published for the full sample, but reports from smaller subsets, which are likely underpowered, have not reached statistical significance (Krafft, Schaeffer, et al., 2014; Krafft, Schwarz, et al., 2014). An additional handful of studies have examined the effects of regular physical activity for children using designs that do not meet all the criteria of an RCT, but which approach the use of a true experimental design (Chaya, Nagendra, Selvam, Kurpad, & Srinivasan, 2012; Fredericks, Kokot, & Krog, 2006; Reed et al., 2010). The results of these studies also support beneficial effects of physical activity on academic achievement with results demonstrating significant improvements in social studies, reading, and math, as well as improvements in neuropsychological assessments of fluid intelligence and spatial development. While Chaya et al. (2012) observed nonsignificant differences in the magnitude of the improvements observed for the physical activity group and the control group, it is important to point out that the control group in this study participated in a yoga intervention. Hence, it is possible that this failure to

observe significant differences resulted from benefits that the children received from the yoga intervention. Overall, results from RCTs with children are limited in number, but results are promising and future research in this area is clearly warranted.

RESEARCH WITH YOUNG ADULTS

It is important to point out that very little research has been conducted with young or middle-aged healthy adults. In fact, to our knowledge there is only one RCT that has been conducted with healthy younger adults in isolation to examine the potential benefits of exercise on cognitive performance for this age group (Stroth, Hille, Spitzer, & Reinhardt, 2009). In this study, young adults (n = 28, 17–29 yrs) were randomly assigned to a running group (30 min/day, 5 days/week) or a no-treatment control group for 6 weeks. Results showed that participants in the running group significantly improved visuospatial memory performance, but not verbal memory or concentration, in comparison to the control group.

The dearth of research exploring benefits of exercise for young adults may be logical from the perspective that this group of individuals would not be expected to benefit as much from physical activity as children, who are experiencing rapid cognitive development, or older adults, who are experiencing cognitive decline. However, given evidence that young and middle-aged adults who are at genetic risk for AD show evidence of preclinical decrements in cerebral structure (Alexander et al., 2012; Caselli et al., 2009; Ghebremedhin, Schultz, Braak, & Braak, 1998; Morishima-Kawashima et al., 2000), that cross-sectional evidence shows that age-related cognitive decline begins in young adulthood (Salthouse, 2009), and that there is strong support for cognitive benefits as a result of physical activity in other age groups and limited support for benefits for young adults, it is important that future research also considers potential benefits for young adults.

THEORETICAL APPROACHES

Research in the area of chronic physical activity and cognitive performance has adopted various theoretical approaches and has begun to test numerous possible mechanisms of the effects. Early research focused explicitly or implicitly on the cardiovascular fitness hypothesis, which proposes that the increases in cardiovascular fitness that occur in response to physical activity are responsible for the changes in cognitive performance observed. In early cross-sectional studies, cognitive performance was compared between groups that differed on measures of aerobic fitness (Chodzko-Zajko, Schuler, Solomon, Heinl, & Ellis, 1992; Dustman et al., 1990; van Boxtel et al., 1997). In studies in which exercise was manipulated through intervention, exercise programs were designed specifically to improve aerobic fitness and gains in aerobic fitness were presented as evidence of the effectiveness of the intervention (e.g., Blumenthal et al., 1991; Dustman et al., 1984; Emery, Schein, Hauck, & MacIntyre, 1998). In an effort to clarify the extent to which changes in fitness were a mediator of the effects of regular exercise on cognitive performance, Etnier, Nowell, Landers, and Sibley (2006) used meta-regression techniques to specifically test the cardiovascular fitness hypothesis. Results did not support the cardiovascular fitness hypothesis; hence, the authors concluded that researchers should consider that aerobic fitness gains were neither necessary nor sufficient to achieve cognitive performance gains as a result of exercise programs.

Recently, the cognitive reserve hypothesis has been proposed to explain the benefits of exercise for cognitive performance particularly as related to older adults. According to the cognitive reserve

hypothesis, individuals who have a greater cognitive reserve are able to maintain their cognitive abilities better with advancing age and have a lower risk of dementia (Fratiglioni, Paillard-Borg, & Winblad, 2004; Scarmeas & Stern, 2003; Whalley, Deary, Appleton, & Starr, 2004). Greater cognitive reserves are acquired through several different lifestyle variables including formal education, occupational challenges, and physical activity (Whalley et al., 2004). At a mechanistic level, the underlying variables that are thought to contribute to cognitive reserves include brain volume, brain metabolic activity, and cerebral pathology (Stern, Alexander, Prohovnik, & Mayeux, 1992; Whalley et al., 2004). Although several reviews discuss the potential for cognitive reserves to explain the cognitive benefits of exercise (Esiri & Chance, 2012; Fick, Kolanowski, Beattie, & McCrow, 2009; Galvan & Bredesen, 2007; Henderson, 2014; Studenski et al., 2006), because of the lack of clarity in operationalizing cognitive reserves, empirical studies have not been conducted specifically to assess the role of cognitive reserves as a mediator of the effects of chronic physical activity on cognitive performance.

The frontal lobe (or executive control) hypothesis has also been forwarded as a viable explanation of the beneficial effects of exercise for cognitive performance particularly for older adults (Hall, Smith, & Keele, 2001). The frontal lobe hypothesis posits that age-related cognitive decline is largely reflective of decrements in frontal lobe functioning (West, 1996). As applied to the exercise literature, the hypothesis then suggests that the benefits of exercise should be most evident in frontally dependent tasks. When this hypothesis has been explored in the exercise literature, the focus has been almost exclusively on executive control tasks while effects on frontally dependent memory tests and in comparison to nonfrontally dependent memory tasks have not been examined (see West, 1996). Kramer et al. (1999) were the first to empirically test this hypothesis in an exercise paradigm. They randomly assigned participants to a 6-month walking group or to a stretching and toning control group. Results of their study supported the hypothesis in that the walking group experienced significant gains in executive control tasks that were not observed for the control group and were also not evident in tasks that did not require executive control. Evidence of larger effects for executive control tasks is also provided by a meta-analytic review in which larger effects were reported for executive control tasks (g=0.68) than for other cognitive tasks (controlled tasks: g=0.43; spatial tasks: g=0.43; speed tasks: g=0.27) (Colcombe & Kramer, 2003). Although continued research exploring the benefits of physical activity for executive control is certainly warranted, two important caveats should be noted. First, it is important that researchers recognize that within the cognitive domain of executive control there are several specific types of cognitive function (Miyake et al., 2000) and each of these may be differentially affected by exercise (Etnier & Chang, 2009). Further, there is evidence that when reviewed meta-analytically across adulthood (Smith et al., 2010), the effects of physical activity on cognitive performance are similar for measures of attention and processing speed, executive control, and memory, thus arguing against an exclusive focus on executive control tasks.

MECHANISMS AND MEDIATORS

Various biological mechanisms and psychological mediators have been considered as potentially explaining the benefits of chronic physical activity for cognitive performance. The purpose of research exploring mediators is to advance our understanding of *how* physical activity exerts beneficial effects on cognitive performance. It is important to point out that although these potential mechanisms are typically studied in isolation or in pairs, it is likely that these putative intervening variables actually represent only a portion of more complex micromediational and multimediational chains of events (Etnier, 2008), which then impact brain health and cognitive performance in myriad ways. Micromediational chains explain how a sequence of mechanistic events occurs along the same causal line to ultimately link the independent variable (in this case, chronic exercise) to the dependent variable (in this case, cognitive performance). Multimediational chains are suggestive of multiple mechanisms that link the independent variable to the dependent variable along discrete causal lines. The most proximal mechanisms relevant to the effects of chronic exercise on cognitive performance are likely those related to changes in cerebral structure and changes in cerebral function. These effects have been demonstrated in several RCTs, which have been conducted with both older adults and children.

In terms of cerebral structure, the first study to demonstrate differences in structure as a function of fitness was conducted by Colcombe et al. (2003) using a cross-sectional study with older adults. Results of this study indicated that decreases in tissue density related to older age were evident in frontal, parietal, and temporal areas of the brain. Importantly, these were the same brain regions where tissue loss was lower for individuals who had higher fitness levels. Hence, the authors concluded that aerobic exercise had the potential to reduce age-related structural degradation of brain tissue. Additional cross-sectional evidence continues to support that there are positive relationships between aerobic fitness and cerebral structure for older adults (Erickson et al., 2009; Honea et al., 2009). In addition, several studies have been conducted using RCT designs to attempt to establish a causal relationship between chronic exercise and brain structure. Results of these studies have been quite consistent in that older adults randomly assigned to a physical activity program have been shown to experience gains in white matter and gray matter at both the whole brain level (Colcombe et al., 2006) and at the level of more specific structures such as the hippocampus (Erickson et al., 2011). In the literature with children, evidence from two cross-sectional studies support that fitness is associated with differences in cerebral structure (Chaddock, Erickson, Prakash, Kim, et al., 2010; Chaddock, Erickson, Prakash, VanPatter, et al., 2010) and there is some evidence that these differences mediate the beneficial relationship between fitness and cognitive performance (Chaddock, Erickson, Prakash, Kim, et al., 2010). There is also evidence from the SMART trial indicating that children who were randomly assigned to a physical activity program experience changes in measures of structural integrity not evident in those assigned to a control condition (Krafft, Schaeffer, et al., 2014; Schaeffer et al., 2014).

Relative to cerebral function, the first study that focused on the effects of chronic physical activity on cerebral function was conducted by Dustman et al. (1990). In this study, the authors measured brain function (using spectral measures of brain activity and event-related potentials), aerobic fitness, and cognition in young (20–31 yrs) and older (50–62 yrs) adults. Results showed differences in cognitive performance and brain function between young and older adults, which the authors attributed to age-related declines in inhibition abilities. Results also demonstrated fitness differences on most of these same measures with fit individuals demonstrating better inhibition abilities. Since then, studies using RCT designs have demonstrated that this is a causal effect for older adults and for children. With older adults, RCTs have shown that participation in exercise results in brain activation changes during resting state (Voss et al., 2010) and during cognitive tasks (Colcombe et al., 2004; Erickson & Kramer, 2009). These findings support that aerobic exercise training is beneficial to neural plasticity in the aging brain. With children, the evidence of an association between fitness and brain function

and of changes in brain function in response to exercise is relatively substantial. Using event-related potentials, researchers have shown that characteristics of the P300 component, which are known to be related to cognitive performance, are associated with levels of fitness (Hillman, Buck, Themanson, Pontifex, & Castelli, 2009; Hillman, Castelli, & Buck, 2005; Pontifex et al., 2011). In addition, evidence from the FITKids trial (Hillman et al., 2014; Kamijo et al., 2011) and from a soccer intervention with kindergarten children (Chang, Tsai, Chen, & Hung, 2013) supports that exercise results in changes in brain function as assessed using ERPs. This causal effect has also been demonstrated in RCTs assessing brain function using functional magnetic resonance imaging such that participation in exercise has been shown to result in beneficial patterns of brain function (Chaddock-Heyman et al., 2013; Davis et al., 2011; Krafft et al., 2013).

More distal mechanisms may include changes in neurotransmitters or changes in neurotrophic factors that ultimately impact brain health. Evidence supporting the role of these mechanisms is predominantly from nonhuman animal studies (Neeper, Gomez-Pinilla, Choi, & Cotman, 1996; Vaynman, Ying, & Gomez-Pinilla, 2004), but some evidence is beginning to emerge from RCTs with humans. In particular, Erickson et al. (2011) explored the relationships between chronic aerobic physical activity, peripherally assessed concentrations of brain-derived neurotrophic factor (BDNF), hippocampal volume, aerobic fitness ($\dot{V}O_2max$), and cognitive performance (spatial memory) in a 1-year RCT with older adults. Findings from this study demonstrated that changes in aerobic fitness from pretest to posttest were positively correlated with changes in hippocampal volume, and the increase in hippocampal volume experienced in the physical activity group was positively correlated with better spatial memory performance and greater change in BDNF concentration. As part of the same 1-year chronic physical activity intervention, Voss et al. (2013) explored the relationship between chronic physical activity, BDNF, vascular endothelial growth factor (VEGF), insulin-like growth factor type 1 (IGF-1), and functional brain connectivity. The results indicated that while changes in BDNF and VEGF concentrations did not reach significance, concentrations of IGF-1 significantly reduced from pretest to posttest. In addition, changes in BDNF, IGF-1, and VEGF concentrations from pretest to posttest were correlated with increased functional connectivity for those in the physical activity group. While neither Erickson et al. (2011) nor Voss et al. (2013) applied the necessary statistical techniques to ascertain whether or not changes in neurotrophic factors actually mediate the relationship between chronic exercise and cognitive performance, these results certainly provide initial support for these mechanisms and warrant additional exploration.

In addition to biological mechanisms, it is also plausible that physical activity benefits cognitive performance through impacts on psychological mediators such as sleep and depression. This is not, of course, to suggest that these mediators work in the absence of biological mechanisms, but rather to propose that these mediators may then work through different biological mechanisms than previously discussed. As one example, provocative research relative to AD suggests that sleep deprivation results in increased amyloid deposition in rodent models for AD (see Ju, Lucey, & Holtzman, 2014 for review). Because there is evidence that exercise benefits sleep quality (Chennaoui, Arnal, Sauvet, & Leger, 2014; Yang, Ho, Chen, & Chien, 2012), it is plausible that exercise indirectly affects cognitive performance through its influence on sleep.

MODERATORS

Research in the area of physical activity and cognitive performance has also considered the potential role of moderators of the effects.

The goal of these studies is to further our understanding of *who* is expected to benefit the most from physical activity participation. As previously mentioned, early researchers were interested in whether or not the benefits of physical activity differed for various age groups. When the entire literature was reviewed meta-analytically, Etnier et al. (1997) found that age was a significant moderator of the effects for chronic exercise studies. Interestingly, the largest effects were observed with older adults (45–60 yrs) and college-aged adults (18–30 yrs). Age has also been shown to moderate the effects within specific age ranges. In a meta-analytic review of RCTs conducted with older adults, Colcombe and Kramer (2003) reported that effects were largest for the mid-old (66–70 yrs), next for the old–old (71–80 yrs), and smallest for the young–old (55–65 yrs). In a review of studies conducted with children, Sibley and Etnier (2003) found that effects were largest for middle school children as compared to all other age groups. Hence, age is clearly a variable that must be considered when attempting to understand the benefits of physical activity for cognitive performance.

In more recent research, additional potentially relevant moderators have been explored. For example, several studies provide data relative to the moderating role of gender and ApoE (apolipoprotein E) genotype (a susceptibility gene for AD) when examining the effects of chronic physical activity on cognitive performance by older adults. Evidence that gender moderates the effects comes from meta-analytic reviews. Colcombe and Kramer (2003) found that effects were highest for RCTs with a larger percentage of female participants (>50% female) than for RCTs with a larger percentage of male participants (≥50% male). With regards to ApoE genotype, two cross-sectional studies (Deeny et al., 2008; Etnier et al., 2007) and several prospective studies (Niti, Yap, Kua, Tan, & Ng, 2008; Podewils et al., 2005; Rovio et al., 2005; Schuit, Feskens, Launer, & Kromhout, 2001) have shown that the relationship between physical activity (or aerobic fitness) and cognitive performance (or the clinical diagnosis of dementia) is moderated by ApoE genotype. Overall, these findings suggest that the greatest benefit of physical activity may be obtained by those at greatest genetic risk of AD.

In addition to exercise potentially having greater benefits for women and for those at genetic risk for AD, there is also a growing interest in exploring the potential of exercise for children with attention deficit hyperactivity disorder (ADHD). The relative paucity of research to date is surprising given that deficits in frontal lobe function are thought to underlie cognitive challenges faced by children with ADHD (Castellanos & Tannock, 2002; Durston, 2003) and the aforementioned frontal lobe hypothesis for the benefits of exercise. Until recently, only one cross-sectional study on chronic exercise and ADHD had been published (Gapin & Etnier, 2010) and that study demonstrated significant positive relationships between physical activity (assessed using an accelerometer) and cognitive performance on a planning task. Recently, several RCTs have been conducted with children with ADHD to determine whether or not exercise has benefits on cognition. Verret, Guay, Berthiaume, Gardiner, and Beliveau (2012) found that ADHD children randomly assigned to exercise 45 min/day, 3 days/week for 10 weeks performed better at the posttest on measures of information processing and sustained attention as compared to the control group. Chang, Hung, Huang, Hatfield, and Hung (2014) reported that improvements in inhibition were observed in ADHD children who exercised 90 min/day, 2 days/week for 8 weeks as compared to a wait-list control group. Importantly, although both of these studies have demonstrated benefits for children with ADHD, the magnitude of these benefits was not compared to that which might have been achieved by children without ADHD. Hence, we do not know from these studies how the benefits for ADHD children compare with the benefits for non-ADHD children.

Hoza et al. (2015) recently completed a study exploring the effects of chronic physical activity for elementary school children who were either at-risk for ADHD or were typically developing children. Participants were randomly assigned to either an exercise condition or a classroom-based art condition. Both groups met for 31 min/day, 5 days/week for 12 weeks. Although cognitive performance was not measured directly in this study, results indicated that parent ratings of ADHD symptoms improved significantly as a function of the treatment for both typically developing and at-risk children. By contrast, teachers only reported significant improvements in ADHD symptoms in children who were at risk for ADHD and did not report significant changes for typically developing children. This study makes an important contribution to the literature because of the attempt to compare benefits of physical activity as a function of ADHD status. That being said, clearly this is an area of research that is worthy of further exploration as we attempt to understand whether or not physical activity may be a viable adjunctive therapy for children with ADHD.

CONCLUSIONS

There is a long history of interest in the possible benefits of chronic physical activity for cognitive performance, and early research fueled this interest by providing evidence in support of relational effects. Based upon this foundational evidence, researchers have increasingly taken advantage of stronger experimental designs (e.g., prospective studies, RCTs) to foster our understanding of the extent to which this is a causal effect. Again, the evidence is promising with meta-analytic reviews demonstrating protective effects of physical activity against age-related cognitive decline and supporting small-to-moderate causal effects for older adults and for children. Given this evidence, the most recent work in this area has focused on exploring theoretical and mechanistic explanations of the positive effects and on identifying moderators of the effects. This research exploring theoretical and mechanistic explanations is designed to answer questions about *how* physical activity benefits cognitive performance. This is a critical direction for research if we hope to move toward a day when we can prescribe physical activity specifically to benefit cognitive performance. In other words, and to put this in practical terms, when we tell people that exercise benefits cognitive performance, the logical question that they invariably ask is "how much exercise, for what intensity, and for how long?" At this point, we do not have a clear answer to this question in part because we do not fully understand *how* the benefits occur and this obviously limits our ability to prescribe exercise for cognitive benefits. Researchers identifying moderators of the effects are also conducting important work as they help to identify *who* receives the greatest benefits from physical activity. This is also an important direction for research because of the possibility that physical activity may actually provide the greatest benefits for those who stand to gain the most. In other words, for example, if experimental research confirms the findings of prospective and correlational studies showing the greatest benefits of physical activity for those at greatest genetic risk of AD, this would have important public health implications.

The number of research publications describing research on exercise and cognitive performance continues to increase exponentially and recent findings are beginning to elucidate mechanisms and moderators of the effects. As this body of literature continues to grow, it is possible that an individualized medicine approach may be applied whereby exercise is specifically prescribed to individuals expected to benefit the most from its associated cognitive benefits. This will be an important direction for future research.

References

Alexander, G. E., Bergfield, K. L., Chen, K., Reiman, E. M., Hanson, K. D., Lin, L., et al. (2012). Gray matter network associated with risk for Alzheimer's disease in young to middle-aged adults. *Neurobiology of Aging, 33,* 2723–2732.

Angevaren, M., Aufdemkampe, G., Verhaar, H. J., Aleman, A., & Vanhees, L. (2008). Physical activity and enhanced fitness to improve cognitive function in older people without known cognitive impairment. *Cochrane Database of Systematic Reviews, 3,* CD005381. http://dx.doi.org/10.1002/14651858.CD005381.pub2.

Baer, A. D., Gersten, J. W., Robertson, B. M., & Dinken, H. (1955). Effect of various exercise programs on isometric tension, endurance and reaction time in the human. *Archives of Physical Medicine and Rehabilitation, 36,* 495–502.

Blumenthal, J. A., Emery, C. F., Madden, D. J., Schniebolk, S., Walsh-Riddle, M., George, L. K., et al. (1991). Long-term effects of exercise on psychological functioning in older men and women. *Journals of Gerontology, 46,* P352–P361.

van Boxtel, M. P., Paas, F. G., Houx, P. J., Adam, J. J., Teeken, J. C., & Jolles, J. (1997). Aerobic capacity and cognitive performance in a cross-sectional aging study. *Medicine & Science in Sports & Exercise, 29,* 1357–1365.

Caselli, R. J., Dueck, A. C., Osborne, D., Sabbagh, M. N., Connor, D. J., Ahern, G. L., et al. (2009). Longitudinal modeling of age-related memory decline and the APOE epsilon4 effect. *New England Journal of Medicine, 361,* 255–263.

Castellanos, F. X., & Tannock, R. (2002). Neuroscience of attention-deficit/hyperactivity disorder: the search for endophenotypes. *Nature Reviews Neuroscience, 3,* 617–628.

Chaddock-Heyman, L., Erickson, K. I., Voss, M. W., Knecht, A. M., Pontifex, M. B., Castelli, D. M., et al. (2013). The effects of physical activity on functional MRI activation associated with cognitive control in children: a randomized controlled intervention. *Frontiers in Human Neuroscience, 7,* 72. http://dx.doi.org/10.3389/fnhum.2013.00072; 10.3389/fnhum.2013.00072.

Chaddock, L., Erickson, K. I., Prakash, R. S., Kim, J. S., Voss, M. W., VanPatter, M., et al. (2010). A neuroimaging investigation of the association between aerobic fitness, hippocampal volume, and memory performance in preadolescent children. *Brain Research, 1358,* 172–183.

Chaddock, L., Erickson, K. I., Prakash, R. S., VanPatter, M., Voss, M. W., Pontifex, M. B., et al. (2010). Basal ganglia volume is associated with aerobic fitness in preadolescent children. *Developmental Neuroscience, 32,* 249–256.

Chang, Y. K., Hung, C. L., Huang, C. J., Hatfield, B. D., & Hung, T. M. (2014). Effects of an aquatic exercise program on inhibitory control in children with ADHD: a preliminary study. *Archives of Clinical Neuropsychology, 29,* 217–223.

Chang, Y. K., Tsai, Y. J., Chen, T. T., & Hung, T. M. (2013). The impacts of coordinative exercise on executive function in kindergarten children: an ERP study. *Experimental Brain Research, 225,* 187–196.

Chaya, M. S., Nagendra, H., Selvam, S., Kurpad, A., & Srinivasan, K. (2012). Effect of yoga on cognitive abilities in schoolchildren from a socioeconomically disadvantaged background: a randomized controlled study. *Journal of Alternative and Complementary Medicine, 18,* 1161–1167.

Chennaoui, M., Arnal, P. J., Sauvet, F., & Leger, D. (2014). Sleep and exercise: a reciprocal issue? *Sleep Medicine Reviews, 20,* 59–72. http://dx.doi.org/10.1016/j.smrv.2014.06.008.

Chodzko-Zajko, W. J., Schuler, P., Solomon, J., Heinl, B., & Ellis, N. R. (1992). The influence of physical fitness on automatic and effortful memory changes in aging. *The International Journal of Aging and Human Development, 35,* 265–285.

Colcombe, S. J., Erickson, K. I., Raz, N., Webb, A. G., Cohen, N. J., McAuley, E., et al. (2003). Aerobic fitness reduces brain tissue loss in aging humans. *The Journals of Gerontology, Series A: Biological Sciences and Medical Sciences, 58,* 176–180.

Colcombe, S. J., Erickson, K. I., Scalf, P. E., Kim, J. S., Prakash, R., McAuley, E., et al. (2006). Aerobic exercise training increases brain volume in aging humans. *The Journals of Gerontology, Series A: Biological Sciences and Medical Sciences, 61,* 1166–1170.

Colcombe, S. J., & Kramer, A. F. (2003). Fitness effects on the cognitive function of older adults: a meta-analytic study. *Psychological Science, 14,* 125–130.

Colcombe, S. J., Kramer, A. F., Erickson, K. I., Scalf, P., McAuley, E., Cohen, N. J., et al. (2004). Cardiovascular fitness, cortical plasticity, and aging. *Proceedings of the National Academy of Sciences of the United States of America, 101,* 3316–3321.

Daviglus, M. L., Plassman, B. L., Pirzada, A., Bell, C. C., Bowen, P. E., Burke, J. R., et al. (2011). Risk factors and preventive interventions for Alzheimer disease: state of the science. *Archives of Neurology, 68,* 1185–1190.

Davis, C. L., Tomporowski, P. D., McDowell, J. E., Austin, B. P., Miller, P. H., Yanasak, N. E., et al. (2011). Exercise improves executive function and achievement and alters brain activation in overweight children: a randomized, controlled trial. *Health Psychology, 30,* 91–98.

Deeny, S. P., Poeppel, D., Zimmerman, J. B., Roth, S. M., Brandauer, J., Witkowski, S., et al. (2008). Exercise, APOE, and working memory: MEG and behavioral evidence for benefit of exercise in epsilon4 carriers. *Biological Psychology, 78,* 179–187.

Durston, S. (2003). A review of the biological bases of ADHD: what have we learned from imaging studies? *Mental Retardation and Developmental Disabilities Research Reviews, 9,* 184–195.

Dustman, R. E., Emmerson, R. Y., Ruhling, R. O., Shearer, D. E., Steinhaus, L. A., Johnson, S. C., et al. (1990). Age and fitness effects on EEG, ERPs, visual sensitivity, and cognition. *Neurobiology of Aging, 11,* 193–200.

Dustman, R. E., Ruhling, R. O., Russell, E. M., Shearer, D. E., Bonekat, H. W., Shigeoka, J. W., et al. (1984). Aerobic exercise training and improved neuropsychological function of older individuals. *Neurobiology of Aging, 5,* 35–42.

Emery, C. F., Schein, R. L., Hauck, E. R., & MacIntyre, N. R. (1998). Psychological and cognitive outcomes of a randomized trial of exercise among patients with chronic obstructive pulmonary disease. *Health Psychology, 17,* 232–240.

Erickson, K. I., & Kramer, A. F. (2009). Aerobic exercise effects on cognitive and neural plasticity in older adults. *British Journal of Sports Medicine, 43,* 22–24.

Erickson, K. I., Prakash, R. S., Voss, M. W., Chaddock, L., Hu, L., Morris, K. S., et al. (2009). Aerobic fitness is associated with hippocampal volume in elderly humans. *Hippocampus, 19,* 1030–1039.

Erickson, K. I., Voss, M. W., Prakash, R. S., Basak, C., Szabo, A., Chaddock, L., et al. (2011). Exercise training increases size of hippocampus and improves memory. *Proceedings of the National Academy of Sciences of the United States of America, 108,* 3017–3022.

Esiri, M. M., & Chance, S. A. (2012). Cognitive reserve, cortical plasticity and resistance to Alzheimer's disease. *Alzheimer's Research & Therapy, 4,* 7. http://dx.doi.org/10.1186/alzrt105.

Etnier, J. L. (2008). Interrelationships of exercise, mediator variables, and cognition. In W. W. Spirduso, W. Chodzko-Zajko, & L. W. Poon (Eds.), *Aging, exercise and cognition series: Vol. 2. Exercise and its mediating effects on cognition* (pp. 13–32). Urbana-Champaign, IL: Human Kinetics.

Etnier, J. L., Caselli, R. J., Reiman, E. M., Alexander, G. E., Sibley, B. A., Tessier, D., et al. (2007). Cognitive performance in older women relative to ApoE-epsilon4 genotype and aerobic fitness. *Medicine & Science in Sports & Exercise, 39,* 199–207.

Etnier, J. L., & Chang, Y. K. (2009). The effect of physical activity on executive function: a brief commentary on definitions, measurement issues, and the current state of the literature. *Journal of Sport and Exercise Psychology, 31,* 469–483.

Etnier, J. L., Salazar, W., Landers, D. M., Petruzzello, S. J., Han, M., & Nowell, P. (1997). The influence of physical fitness and exercise upon cognitive functioning: a meta-analysis. *Journal of Sport and Exercise Psychology, 19,* 249–277.

Etnier, J. L., Nowell, P. M., Landers, D. M., & Sibley, B. A. (2006). A meta-regression to examine the relationship between aerobic fitness and cognitive performance. *Brain Research Reviews, 52,* 119–130.

Fick, D. M., Kolanowski, A., Beattie, E., & McCrow, J. (2009). Delirium in early-stage Alzheimer's disease: enhancing cognitive reserve as a possible preventive measure. *Journal of Gerontological Nursing, 35,* 30–38.

Fratiglioni, L., Paillard-Borg, S., & Winblad, B. (2004). An active and socially integrated lifestyle in late life might protect against dementia. *The Lancet Neurology, 3,* 343–353.

Fredericks, C. R., Kokot, S. J., & Krog, S. (2006). Using a developmental movement programme to enhance academic skills in grade 1 learners. *South African Journal for Research in Sport, Physical Education and Recreation, 28,* 29–42.

Galvan, V., & Bredesen, D. E. (2007). Neurogenesis in the adult brain: implications for Alzheimer's disease. *CNS & Neurological Disorders-Drug Targets, 6,* 303–310.

Gapin, J. I., & Etnier, J. L. (2010). The relationship between physical activity and executive function performance in children with attention deficit hyperactivity disorder. *Journal of Sport and Exercise Psychology, 32,* 753–763.

Ghebremedhin, E., Schultz, C., Braak, E., & Braak, H. (1998). High frequency of apolipoprotein E epsilon4 allele in young individuals with very mild Alzheimer's disease-related neurofibrillary changes. *Experimental Neurology, 153,* 152–155.

Giedd, J. N., Blumenthal, J., Jeffries, N. O., Castellanos, F. X., Liu, H., Zijdenbos, A., et al. (1999). Brain development during childhood and adolescence: A longitudinal MRI study. *Nature Neuroscience, 2*(10), 861–863.

Hall, C. D., Smith, A. L., & Keele, S. W. (2001). The impact of aerobic activity on cognitive function in older adults: a new synthesis based on the concept of executive control. *European Journal of Cognitive Psychology, 13,* 279–300.

Hamer, M., & Chida, Y. (2009). Physical activity and risk of neurodegenerative disease: a systematic review of prospective evidence. *Psychological Medicine, 39,* 3–11.

Hedman, A. M., van Haren, N. E., Schnack, H. G., Kahn, R. S., & Hulshoff Pol, H. E., (2012). Human brain changes across the life span: A review of 56 longitudinal magnetic resonance imaging studies. *Human Brain Mapping, 33*(8), 1987–2002.

Henderson, V. W. (2014). Three midlife strategies to prevent cognitive impairment due to Alzheimer's disease. *Climacteric, 17*(Suppl. 2), 38–46.

Hillman, C. H., Buck, S. M., Themanson, J. R., Pontifex, M. B., & Castelli, D. M. (2009). Aerobic fitness and cognitive development: event-related brain potential and task performance indices of executive control in preadolescent children. *Developmental Psychology, 45,* 114–129.

Hillman, C. H., Castelli, D. M., & Buck, S. M. (2005). Aerobic fitness and neurocognitive function in healthy preadolescent children. *Medicine & Science in Sports & Exercise, 37,* 1967–1974.

Hillman, C. H., Pontifex, M. B., Castelli, D. M., Khan, N. A., Raine, L. B., Scudder, M. R., et al. (2014). Effects of the FITKids randomized controlled trial on executive control and brain function in children. *Pediatrics, 134*(4), e1063–e1071.

Honea, R. A., Thomas, G. P., Harsha, A., Anderson, H. S., Donnelly, J. E., Brooks, W. M., et al. (2009). Cardiorespiratory fitness and preserved medial temporal lobe volume in Alzheimer disease. *Alzheimer's Disease and Associated Disorders, 23,* 188–197.

Hoza, B., Smith, A. L., Shoulberg, E. K., Linnea, K. S., Dorsch, T. E., Blazo, J. A., et al. (2015). A randomized trial examining the effects of aerobic physical activity on attention-deficit/hyperactivity disorder symptoms in young children. *Journal of Abnormal Child Psychology, 43,* 655–667

Ju, Y. E., Lucey, B. P., & Holtzman, D. M. (2014). Sleep and Alzheimer disease pathology–a bidirectional relationship. *Nature Reviews Neurology, 10,* 115–119.

Kamijo, K., Pontifex, M. B., O'Leary, K. C., Scudder, M. R., Wu, C.-T., Castelli, D. M., et al. (2011). The effects of an afterschool physical activity program on working memory in preadolescent children. *Developmental Science, 14,* 1046–1058.

Krafft, C. E., Pierce, J. E., Schwarz, N. F., Chi, L., Weinberger, A. L., Schaeffer, D. J., et al. (2013). An eight month randomized controlled exercise intervention alters resting state synchrony in overweight children. *Neuroscience, 256,* 445–455.

Krafft, C. E., Schaeffer, D. J., Schwarz, N. F., Chi, L., Weinberger, A. L., Pierce, J. E., et al. (2014). Improved frontoparietal white matter integrity in overweight children is associated with attendance at an after-school exercise program. *Developmental Neuroscience, 36,* 1–9.

Krafft, C. E., Schwarz, N. F., Chi, L., Weinberger, A. L., Schaeffer, D. J., Pierce, J. E., et al. (2014). An 8-month randomized controlled exercise trial alters brain activation during cognitive tasks in overweight children. *Obesity, 22,* 232–242.

Kramer, A. F., Hahn, S., Cohen, N. J., Banich, M. T., McAuley, E., Harrison, C. R., et al. (1999). Ageing, fitness and neurocognitive function. *Nature, 400,* 418–419.

Miyake, A., Friedman, N. P., Emerson, M. J., Witzki, A. H., Howerter, A., & Wager, T. D. (2000). The unity and diversity of executive functions and their contributions to complex "Frontal Lobe" tasks: a latent variable analysis. *Cognitive Psychology, 41,* 49–100.

Morishima-Kawashima, M., Oshima, N., Ogata, H., Yamaguchi, H., Yoshimura, M., Sugihara, S., et al. (2000). Effect of *Apolipoprotein E* allele ε4 on the initial phase of amyloid β-protein accumulation in the human brain. *American Journal of Pathology, 157,* 2093–2099.

Neeper, S. A., Gomez-Pinilla, F., Choi, J., & Cotman, C. W. (1996). Physical activity increases mRNA for brain-derived neurotrophic factor and nerve growth factor in rat brain. *Brain Research, 726,* 49–56.

Niti, M., Yap, K. B., Kua, E. H., Tan, C. H., & Ng, T. P. (2008). Physical, social and productive leisure activities, cognitive decline and interaction with APOE-epsilon 4 genotype in Chinese older adults. *International Psychogeriatrics, 20*, 237–251.

Oliver, J. N. (1958). The effects of physical conditioning exercises and activities on the mental characteristics of educationally sub-normal boys. *British Journal of Educational Psychology, 28*, 155–165.

Pierson, W. R. (1956). Comparison of fencers and nonfencers by psychomotor, space perception, and anthropometric measures. *Research Quarterly, 27*, 90–96.

Podewils, L. J., Guallar, E., Kuller, L. H., Fried, L. P., Lopez, O. L., Carlson, M., et al. (2005). Physical activity, APOE genotype, and dementia risk: findings from the Cardiovascular Health Cognition Study. *American Journal of Epidemiology, 161*, 639–651.

Pontifex, M. B., Raine, L. B., Johnson, C. R., Chaddock, L., Voss, M. W., Cohen, N. J., et al. (2011). Cardiorespiratory fitness and the flexible modulation of cognitive control in preadolescent children. *Journal of Cognitive Neuroscience, 23*, 1332–1345.

Reed, J. A., Einstein, G., Hahn, E., Hooker, S. P., Gross, V. P., & Kravitz, J. (2010). Examining the impact of integrating physical activity on fluid intelligence and academic performance in an elementary school setting: a preliminary investigation. *Journal of Physical Activity & Health, 7*, 343–351.

Rovio, S., Kareholt, I., Helkala, E. L., Viitanen, M., Winblad, B., Tuomilehto, J., et al. (2005). Leisure-time physical activity at midlife and the risk of dementia and Alzheimer's disease. *The Lancet Neurology, 4*, 705–711.

Salthouse, T. A. (2009). When does age-related cognitive decline begin? *Neurobiology of Aging, 30*, 507–514.

Scarmeas, N., & Stern, Y. (2003). Cognitive reserve and lifestyle. *Journal of Clinical and Experimental Neuropsychology, 25*, 625–633.

Schaeffer, D. J., Krafft, C. E., Schwarz, N. F., Chi, L., Rodrigue, A. L., Pierce, J. E., et al. (2014). An 8-month exercise intervention alters frontotemporal white matter integrity in overweight children. *Psychophysiology, 51*, 728–733.

Schuit, A. J., Feskens, E. J., Launer, L. J., & Kromhout, D. (2001). Physical activity and cognitive decline, the role of the apolipoprotein e4 allele. *Medicine & Science in Sports & Exercise, 33*, 772–777.

Sibley, B. A., & Etnier, J. L. (2003). The relationship between physical activity and cognition in children: a meta-analysis. *Pediatric Exercise Science, 15*, 243–256.

Slater-Hamel, A. T. (1955). Comparisons of reaction-time measures to a visual stimulus and arm movement. *Research Quarterly, 26*, 470–479.

Smith, P. J., Blumenthal, J. A., Hoffman, B. M., Cooper, H., Strauman, T. A., Welsh-Bohmer, K., et al. (2010). Aerobic exercise and neurocognitive performance: a meta-analytic review of randomized controlled trials. *Psychosomatic Medicine, 72*, 239–252.

Sofi, F., Valecchi, D., Bacci, D., Abbate, R., Gensini, G. F., Casini, A., et al. (2011). Physical activity and risk of cognitive decline: a meta-analysis of prospective studies. *Journal of International Medicine, 269*, 107–117.

Spirduso, W. W. (1975). Reaction and movement time as a function of age and physical activity level. *Journals of Gerontology, 30*, 435–440.

Stern, Y., Alexander, G. E., Prohovnik, I., & Mayeux, R. (1992). Inverse relationship between education and parietotemporal perfusion deficit in Alzheimer's disease. *Annals of Neurology, 32*, 371–375.

Stroth, S., Hille, K., Spitzer, M., & Reinhardt, R. (2009). Aerobic endurance exercise benefits memory and affect in young adults. *Neuropsychological Rehabilitation, 19*, 223–243.

Studenski, S., Carlson, M. C., Fillit, H., Greenough, W. T., Kramer, A., & Rebok, G. W. (2006). From bedside to bench: does mental and physical activity promote cognitive vitality in late life? *Science of Aging Knowledge Environment, 10*, pe21. http://dx.doi.org/10.1126/sageke.2006.10.pe21.

Vaynman, S., Ying, Z., & Gomez-Pinilla, F. (2004). Hippocampal BDNF mediates the efficacy of exercise on synaptic plasticity and cognition. *European Journal of Neuroscience, 20*, 2580–2590.

Verret, C., Guay, M.-C., Berthiaume, C., Gardiner, P., & Beliveau, L. (2012). A physical activity program improves behaviour and cognitive functions in children with ADHD: an exploratory study. *Journal of Attention Disorders, 16*, 71–80.

Voss, M. W., Erickson, K. I., Prakash, R. S., Chaddock, L., Kim, J. S., Alves, H., et al. (2013). Neurobiological markers of exercise-related brain plasticity in older adults. *Brain, Behavior, and Immunity, 28*, 90–99.

Voss, M. W., Prakash, R. S., Erickson, K. I., Basak, C., Chaddock, L., Kim, J. S., et al. (2010). Plasticity of brain networks in a randomized intervention trial of exercise training in older adults. *Frontiers in Aging Neuroscience, 2*. http://dx.doi.org/10.3389/fnagi.2010.00032.

Weber, R. J. (1953). Relationship of physical fitness to success in college and to personality. *Research Quarterly, 24*, 471–474.

West, R. L. (1996). An application of prefrontal cortex function theory to cognitive aging. *Psychological Bulletin, 120*, 272–292.

Whalley, L. J., Deary, I. J., Appleton, C. L., & Starr, J. M. (2004). Cognitive reserve and the neurobiology of cognitive aging. *Ageing Research Review, 3*, 369–382.

Yang, P. Y., Ho, K. H., Chen, H. C., & Chien, M. Y. (2012). Exercise training improves sleep quality in middle-aged and older adults with sleep problems: a systematic review. *Journal of Physiotherapy, 58*, 157–163.

Youngen, L. (1959). A comparison of reaction time and movement times of women athletes and nonathletes. *Research Quarterly, 30*, 349–355.

3

Animal Models of Exercise–Brain Interactions

G.F. Hamilton, J.S. Rhodes

Department of Psychology, The Beckman Institute, University of Illinois at Urbana-Champaign, Urbana, IL, USA

INTRODUCTION

It has long been known that exercise strengthens muscles and bones, and that keeping physically active maintains a healthy cardiovascular system and a slim physique. However, only recently have both the scientific community and the public realized that regular exercise is also critical for maintaining cognitive health. Particularly as you age, it is now established that keeping physically active protects your brain from otherwise inevitable decay (Churchill et al., 2002; Erickson & Kramer, 2009; Erickson et al., 2011). Moreover, the effects of physical exercise on cognition are broad, crossing multiple domains related to learning, memory, attention, processing speed, and overall performance (Churchill et al., 2002; Colcombe & Kramer, 2003; Cotman & Berchtold, 2002; Erickson & Kramer, 2009; Erickson et al., 2011).

The effect size and broad benefits to cognition from exercise are particularly impressive. Unlike exercise, other ways known to improve cognitive performance, such as cognitive training (i.e., training subjects on crossword puzzles, memory tasks, problem solving, or other cognitively challenging computer games), typically do not produce cognitive benefits across broad domains. Rather, they improve performance on the task they were specifically practicing (Lee et al., 2012; Redick et al., 2013). Differences between the effects of exercise and cognitive training on the brain have major clinical significance, given that clinicians want to find a strategy that will transfer to other tasks. For example, if grandma does crossword puzzles she will be good at crossword puzzles, but it might not help her navigate around the neighborhood. In contrast, as will be demonstrated in this chapter, exercise will transfer to other tasks. Thus, exercise does something to the brain that is different to when you are cognitively challenged or learning something new.

Recent studies in aged or elderly humans have established that aerobic exercise enhances cognitive performance across multiple domains of cognition. For example, regularly engaging in fast walking for 45 min, three times a day for

6 months, a form of moderate intensity aerobic exercise that increases the efficiency and endurance of the cardiovascular system, enhances spatial learning, processing speed, reaction time, and executive function (Colcombe & Kramer, 2003), and also increases the volume of a specific part of the brain, known as the hippocampus (Erickson et al., 2011). In addition, strength training (four sets on the leg-press and leg-extension machines, three sets on chest press, lat pulldown, pec-dec, and vertical row machine) performed twice per week, under personal supervision, for a 24-week period improved cognitive performance on a variety of tasks (e.g., episodic memory, working memory and attention, processing speed, and executive function), many of which require hippocampus activation (van de Rest et al., 2014). Strength training or lifting weights represents anaerobic exercise, which strengthens muscles but does not necessarily enhance cardiovascular endurance. The fact that the hippocampus is the most responsive to both aerobic and anaerobic exercise and literally grows in size in response to exercise (Erickson et al., 2011) is fascinating because of the critical role that the hippocampus plays in learning and memory, stress coping, motivation, and emotion (Andersen, 2007).

Although the hippocampus is established as the center for effects of exercise in the brain, the mechanisms by which exercise enlarges the hippocampus and improves cognitive function are still unclear. This is where animal models become exceedingly useful. In the next section we will discuss three different animal models for studying effects of both aerobic and anaerobic exercise on the brain. These include two forms of aerobic exercise: voluntary wheel running, forced treadmill running, and one form of anaerobic exercise: strength training. Following a description of the animal models, we will review some recent discoveries of specific neurological mechanisms underlying procognitive effects of exercise.

RODENT EXERCISE MODELS

Voluntary Wheel Running

Voluntary wheel running is very commonly used as a way to exercise rodents in studies of the effects of exercise on the brain. The procedure is very simple. A running wheel is usually included in the cage or attached to the cage, and an automatic counter records wheel revolutions. Typically, wheel running distances are reported in km/day by multiplying the circumference of the wheel times the number of revolutions over a 24-h period. Depending on the strain, mice typically run between 2 and 10 km/day (Clark, Kohman et al., 2011). We have estimated that approximately 30% of revolutions occur without the animal actually running in the wheel (Girard, McAleer, Rhodes, & Garland, 2001). This estimate is likely to vary greatly depending on the size and resistance of the wheel. The 30% estimate occurs with mice running on rat-size wheels approximately 1 m in circumference, with very low resistance, and high momentum. Hence, the wheel continues to rotate when the mouse leaves the wheel, a very frequent occurrence. Mice run intermittently, i.e., short bouts of fast running separated by short breaks where they drink some water, eat some food, or just move around the cage a bit. We have also seen mice hold onto the wheel and ride it as it rotates (Girard et al., 2001). Hence, the equivalent horizontal distance that the mice would travel if they were walking/running on the ground is more difficult to judge. We believe it is best to think of voluntary wheel running as analogous to riding a bike rather than running on a flat surface. Nevertheless, 2–10 km is still quite a lot of exercise for a mouse. If you consider that mice move around in their standard shoe box cages between 0.1 and 0.5 km/day (Clark, Kohman et al., 2011), then by giving the animals access to a wheel, they roughly increased their level of physical activity by an order of magnitude.

Consistent with the idea that access to a running wheel constitutes a significant elevation in physical activity relative to a standard cage is that several weeks of running increase standard measures of aerobic fitness. These include increased aerobic capacity (Swallow, Garland, Carter, Zhan, & Sieck, 1998), decreased fat mass (Swallow, Koteja, Carter, & Garland, 2001), increased mitochondria in the muscles (Rowe, El-Khoury, Patten, Rustin, & Arany, 2012), and decreased oxidative stress (Alessio et al., 2005).

Advantages of the model:

1. Simple to employ.
2. Completely voluntary and hence devoid of stress from forcing the animal to do something it does not want to do.
3. Extremely reliable, meaning that knowing how much an individual animal ran on one day, greatly predicts how much the animal will run the next day. Pearson's correlation for day-to-day variation in wheel running is usually above 80% (Rhodes, Garland, & Gammie, 2003). This is useful for establishing correlations between individual differences in levels of exercise with physiological outcomes.

Disadvantages:

1. The investigator has no control over how much the animals will run. Animals may run at levels not desired by the investigators. Within-group variation in levels of running should be expected.
2. It is difficult to study high-intensity exercise such as would only occur if the animals were forced, or had extremely high motivation.
3. Humans do not normally run for hours a day, whereas mice spend most of their dark cycle intermittently running on running wheels (Girard et al., 2001).

Forced Treadmill Running

Forcing animals to run on a treadmill is often used in exercise–physiological studies where the goal is to study traits such as aerobic capacity, muscle adaptations, or immune responses (Woods, Davis, Mayer, Ghaffar, & Pate, 1994). However, it is less often used in studies of effects of exercise on the brain for a few different reasons. First, it is quite time-consuming, because the animals must be trained, usually over weeks, to cooperate and run steadily on a treadmill without stopping or getting caught in the apparatus behind the wheel. Given that rodents are intermittent runners, as mentioned previously, it is not natural for them to run continuously in place, and therefore takes time to adapt. In our experience, they never really get used to it, because it is so unnatural for them to run in this way. This induces a psychological type of stress in the animals, which can complicate interpretation of the brain outcomes, because they could be due to the psychological stress of the forced running rather than the exercise per se. It is notable to mention here that usually the animals need to be constantly prodded to run continuously on a treadmill. This is usually done using an electric grid or foam pad behind the treadmill so if the animals stop running and are pushed back they either land on an electric grid, or get pushed against a foam pad. Some individuals never cooperate. One of the authors of this chapter (Rhodes) used to measure maximum oxygen consumption in mice by forcing them to run as fast as they could on a treadmill while simultaneously measuring oxygen utilization and carbon dioxide expiration (Kelly et al., 2014). This involved getting mice to run in a small box placed over the treadmill. Rhodes observed some of the mice doing a split with each hind paw touching either side of a box to avoid running. Second, typically the treadmills are used at slow speeds, less than 0.5 km/h, which even for a mouse is a walk rather than a run. This is not because of any limitations of the treadmills, but rather because at higher speeds, there are more problems getting the mice to cooperate. Typically, mice are run on a treadmill for 20 min. So at a rate of 0.5 km/h, less than 0.2 km is added to their daily movement, which at most is a doubling of their normal levels of activity in a cage. This is in comparison to wheel running, where the mice move an order of magnitude more than they do in their cages. On the other hand, the treadmill method of exercise training appears, at face value, more similar to how humans would train, only 20–40min/day, 3days/week. But the problem with this argument for the treadmill model is that mice are not humans and must be considered within the appropriate ecological context or realms of their natural behaviors. As we mentioned, mice run in short bursts, taking frequent breaks over most of the night. They do not take a break from work at the factory to take a jog.

Advantages of the model:

1. The investigator can control the amount of exercise on a treadmill. All animals in a group can experience a similar amount of work.
2. The investigator can match the pattern of aerobic exercise typically performed by humans, constant exercise over a period of 20–40min a few times per week.

Disadvantages:

1. Because it is forced and unnatural for mice to run on a treadmill, even after extensive training, forced treadmill running induces a type of psychological stress in the animals each time it is administered (Cook et al., 2013), which confounds interpretation of brain measures as a result of exercise per se.
2. The animals can only be run at a slow speed, and the total increase in distance traveled as compared to movement in the home cage is marginal.
3. The animals can get hurt in the treadmill. For example, tails and feet can get caught, and the animals may need substantial prodding at least at the beginning of training. Some animals may never cooperate and have to be removed from the study entirely.

Strength Training

Resistance-based strength training regimens are more difficult to implement in rodents than in humans, because in their natural environment rodents do not typically lift heavy weights or carry heavy loads. Nonetheless, some clever solutions have been implemented to get rodents to lift weights. In one paradigm, rats stand upright restrained in an apparatus and do squats with different weights placed on their back inside a backpack (Seo et al., 2014; Tamaki, Uchiyama, & Nakano, 1992). In another paradigm, a rat pulls a weight on a treadmill (Aparicio et al., 2011). In a third paradigm, rats are trained to climb on a ladder with weights attached to their tails (Cassilhas et al., 2013). However, most studies published to date using these techniques were focused on exercise physiological changes in the muscles, not on cognitive or neurological outcomes (but see Cassilhas, Lee, Fernandes et al., 2012; Cassilhas, Lee, Venancio et al., 2012). Hence, to the best of our knowledge this is an area in the exercise–cognition field that desperately needs additional studies.

Advantages of the model:

1. The investigator can control the amount of weight an animal can carry and increase the load temporally.
2. The models have established similar exercise physiological adaptations, in the muscles of animals performing the tasks, as are seen in humans conducting strength training routines (Cassilhas et al., 2013; Tamaki et al., 1992).

Disadvantages:

1. In the squatting paradigm, the rats are restrained and forced to stand upright and squat with weights on their backs. Similarly, in the treadmill paradigm, animals are forced to pull weights. Hence, as mentioned above for the aerobic version of the forced treadmill running, psychological stress related to the restraint or punishment needed to force the animals to perform the behavior can confound interpretation of neurological results as they pertain to impacts of exercise per se.

2. These models are labor intensive because they require a great deal of training before the animal can appropriately carry out the behaviors.

Some animals may react differently than others or not perform well on the tasks, and therefore will have to be removed from the study.

3. Rats have been used primarily for the squatting paradigm and treadmill running with weights. The ladder task appears to be a good choice for mice, since it takes advantage of their natural incline to want to climb up if placed on a vertical grid.

NEUROLOGICAL EFFECTS OF EXERCISE

Exercise has both acute and chronic neurological effects. The acute effects refer to the immediate effects of exercise on brain function soon after an individual stops exercising. Acute effects wane within a few hours. For example, right after you stop exercising, your blood pressure is still elevated, your heart rate is still increased, and your blood adrenaline is still elevated. It takes time for all the residual hormonal and biochemical changes in response to the exercise to wane. These factors can improve cognitive performance and enhance the function of cells in the brain but the short-term influences of exercise are far less interesting and useful clinically than the chronic effects. After multiple bouts of exercise over a period of weeks and months, the brain accumulates substantial changes in brain morphology and physiology. These changes take a long time to go away after exercise is stopped.

The chronic effects of exercise on the brain have substantial clinical significance. For example, chronic exercise increases the total number of granule neurons in the dentate gyrus (DG) of the hippocampus (van Praag, Christie, Sejnowski, & Gage, 1999; van Praag, Kempermann, & Gage, 1999), as will be described in more detail below. The DG is exactly the area first hit by Alzheimer's disease (Rodriguez & Verkhratsky, 2011; Varela-Nallar, Aranguiz, Abbott, Slater, & Inestrosa, 2010), and it is a common area where epileptic seizures occur (Masukawa et al., 1997; Ribak & Dashtipour, 2002; Sloviter, 1994). If we can understand how to grow new neurons in this region, then we may be able to treat neurodegenerative disease, stroke, and brain trauma.

Chronic exercise broadly enhances performance across multiple domains of cognition, and on multiple different learning and memory tasks in humans and rodent models. In humans, exercise has been shown to enhance spatial learning, pattern separation, executive function, working memory, and processing speed, among others (Colcombe & Kramer, 2003; Voss, Vivar, Kramer, & van Praag, 2013). For example, in elderly subjects, 6 months of aerobic training mitigated age-related decline in both verbal and spatial memory (Ten Brinke et al., 2014) and a low activity, 8-week yoga intervention significantly improved performance on working memory (Gothe, Kramer, & McAuley, 2014). Further, in aged adults, a resistance-type exercise program of two sessions per week improved attention and working memory on a variety of tasks (van de Rest et al., 2014). In rodents, exercise has been found to enhance spatial learning and memory on the Morris water maze, eight-arm radial maze, Barnes maze, contextual fear conditioning, extinction of conditioned place preference for drugs, passive avoidance, and pattern separation, among others (Anderson et al., 2000; Creer, Romberg, Saksida, van Praag, & Bussey, 2010; Greenwood, Strong, Foley, & Fleshner., 2009; Jacotte-Simancas, Costa-Miserachs, Torras-Garcia, Coll-Andreu, & Portell-Cortes, 2013; van Praag, Christie et al., 1999; Samorajski et al., 1985; Thanos et al., 2010; Van der Borght, Havekes, Bos, Eggen, & Van der Zee, 2007).

Exercise is known to impact the physiology and morphology of multiple brain regions, which could account for the broad enhancements from exercise observed on multiple cognitive domains. Moderate aerobic exercise training increases hippocampal and prefrontal cortical volume (Erickson & Kramer, 2009). For example, Erickson et al. (2011) designed a randomized control trial wherein older adults were assigned to either a stretching control or an aerobic exercise group in which they walked for 40 min a day, once a week for 6 months. Aerobic exercise resulted in a 2% increase in hippocampal volume, effectively reversing the age-related decline.

In rodent models, voluntary wheel running increases the total number of neurons, synapses, dendritic complexity, and number of spines on neurons in the hippocampus, which could account for the volume differences observed in humans (Eadie, Redila, & Christie, 2005; Redila & Christie, 2006). Voluntary wheel running increases the concentration of several different growth and trophic factors in the hippocampus that likely support the morphological changes occurring in this region in response to exercise, including fibroblast growth factor 2 (Gomez-Pinilla, Dao, & So, 1997), insulin-like growth factor 1 (Ding, Vaynman, Akhavan, Ying, & Gomez-Pinilla, 2006), brain-derived neurotrophic factor (Neeper, Gomez-Pinilla, Choi, & Cotman, 1996), and vascular endothelial growth factor (Uysal et al., 2015), among others. It is currently debated as to whether these molecules are being secreted locally by neurons and glia or whether they are coming from the blood via the muscles (Fabel et al., 2003; Trejo, Carro, & Torres-Aleman, 2001; Wrann et al., 2013).

Rodent models have revealed that aerobic exercise impacts all the different cell types of the brain including microglia, oligodendrocytes, astrocytes, and neurons in multiple different brain regions. For example, voluntary wheel running decreases the proliferation and proinflammatory status of microglia in the hippocampus of aged mice. Moreover, running increases the proportion of microglia expressing a neuroprotective phenotype (Kohman, Bhattacharya, Wojcik, & Rhodes, 2013; Kohman, DeYoung, Bhattacharya, Peterson, & Rhodes, 2012; Kohman & Rhodes, 2013). In addition, voluntary running increases the density of blood vessels in brain regions involved in the voluntary control of movement, such as the dorsal striatum (Clark, Brzezinska, Puchalski, Krone, & Rhodes, 2009), cerebellum (Black, Isaacs, Anderson, Alcantara, & Greenough, 1990; Isaacs, Anderson, Alcantara, Black, & Greenough, 1992), and hippocampus (Clark et al., 2009). Similarly, forced treadmill running in rats increases the proliferation of astrocytes in the striatum and frontal cortex, a result likely related to increased vascular density in these regions given the role of astrocytes in connecting blood vessels to neurons (Li et al., 2005). Recently, it was discovered that running on a complex wheel (with irregularly spaced rungs) increases the formation of new oligodendrocytes in the brain (McKenzie et al., 2014). The above-mentioned biochemical, cellular, physiological, and morphological changes illustrate the breadth of the changes induced from exercise in the brain, but certainly are not meant to represent an exhaustive list.

Of all the brain regions that change their physiology and morphology from exercise, the hippocampus is by far the brain region most impacted. This is another explanation for the far-reaching impacts of exercise on cognition, because the hippocampus plays a pivotal role in cognitive performance, and improvement in this one structure could impact many different cognitive domains (Andersen, 2007). Hence, the remainder of this chapter will focus on the impact of exercise on the hippocampus.

EXERCISE AND THE HIPPOCAMPUS

It is truly intriguing that the hippocampus, of all the areas of the brain, is the one most involved in exercise. The hippocampus is the first region where all sensory modalities merge together to form unique representations and memories that bind stimuli together and, thus, it plays a critical role in learning and memory (Andersen, 2007). One of the most influential case studies ever in the history of neuroscience research that illustrates well the critical role of the hippocampus in memory is the famous case of H.M. In order to cure his epilepsy, H.M. underwent a bilateral medial temporal lobectomy, which resulted in severe anterograde amnesia and he was unable to commit new events to his explicit memory. Still, over the years, H.M. retained his short-term working memory and intellect, and he was left with residual learning capabilities (Augustinack et al., 2014). For example, he could still perform many types of motor learning tasks, though he could not remember learning them. Similarly, in rodents, hippocampal lesions impair many different forms of learning and memory (Broadbent, Gaskin, Squire, & Clark, 2010; Chen, Kim, Thompson, & Tonegawa, 1996; Cho, Friedman, & Silva, 1999; Cohen et al., 2013; Farr, Banks, La Scola, Flood, & Morley, 2000; Logue, Paylor, & Wehner, 1997). Hence, it is strange and intriguing that exercise, which presumably does not involve huge amounts of learning and memory, acutely activates the hippocampus, and results in such profound neuroanatomical, biochemical, and physiological changes in response to chronic exercise.

Anatomy of the Hippocampus

The hippocampus is located in the medial temporal lobe of the brain (Figure 1(A)). A cross-section of the brain of a macaque monkey, stained to visualize cell bodies, illustrates a key feature of the mammalian hippocampus. The mammalian hippocampus can be distinguished as a zone where the cortex narrows into a single layer of densely packed neurons, which curl into a tight U shape (Figure 1(B)). A drawing of the major cell types and their connections (Figure 1(C)) illustrates the unique circuitry, anatomy, and cellular morphological phenotypes of

the hippocampus. The hippocampal circuit is unique in that its connections are unidirectional. The major cortical input to the hippocampus comes from Layers II and III of the entorhinal cortex (EC) through excitatory glutamatergic fibers, which form the perforant pathway. The perforant pathway projects mainly to the granule cells in the DG. The axons of dentate granule cells form excitatory glutaminergic mossy fibers, which then project to the proximal (closer to cell body) apical dendrites of CA3 pyramidal cells. CA3 pyramidal cells then form the glutamatergic Schaffer collaterals, which connect to both ipsilateral and contralateral CA1 neurons. Finally, axons of CA1 cells send projections to the subiculum (Sub) as well as to deep Layer V of the EC (Andersen, 2007).

Acute Effect of Exercise on Neuronal Activation of the Hippocampus

Neuronal activity in the hippocampus is tightly correlated with the speed of running or intensity of muscular contractions, such as needed for a rat to jump to different heights (Oddie & Bland, 1998). The type or pattern of neuronal activity in the hippocampus, associated with the intensity of the movements, is very different from what occurs when an animal is learning a task. Hence, there may be two separate functions for the hippocampus, one in learning and memory and another related to generating or sensing intense movements. When animals are running, large numbers of neurons in the granule layer of the DG fire in synchrony, producing rhythmic electrical activity that can be detected using electrodes placed near the region (Ahmed & Mehta, 2012; Kuo, Li, Chen, & Yang, 2011; McNaughton, Barnes, & O'Keefe, 1983; Oddie & Bland, 1998) or using immunohistochemical techniques after the animal is euthanized (Clark, Bhattacharya et al., 2011; Clark et al., 2010; Rhodes et al., 2003). When measured using electrodes placed in the brain or outside the brain, the rhythmic activity of large numbers

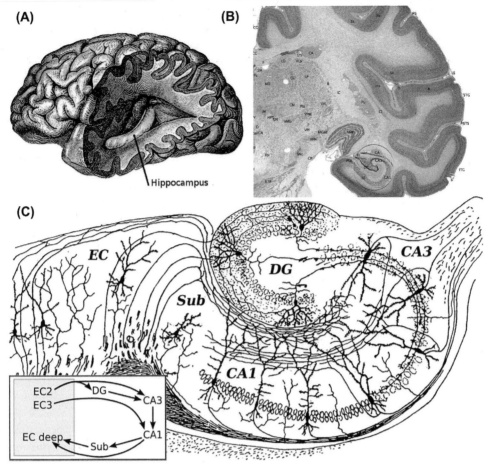

FIGURE 1   Anatomy of the hippocampus. (A) The hippocampus is located in the medial temporal lobe of the brain. (B) A Nissl-stained coronal section of a macaque monkey. The hippocampus is circled. *(This work is licensed under a Creative Commons Attribution 3.0 Unported License. Source:* brainmaps.org.*)* (C) A drawn representation of the hippocampal circuitry by Ramon y Cajal. Note the simplified circuit diagram in the bottom left-hand corner. DG, dentate gyrus; EC, entorhinal cortex; Sub, subiculum.

of cells firing in synchrony in the hippocampus produce theta and gamma oscillations. Both the amplitude and frequency of these rhythms are closely correlated with the speed of running on a treadmill in rats (Ahmed & Mehta, 2012; Kuo et al., 2011; McNaughton et al., 1983; Oddie & Bland, 1998; Vanderwolf, 1969). In addition, the force parameters exerted during a jump to different heights are closely correlated with the amplitude and frequency of theta (Oddie &

Bland, 1998). These changes in theta and gamma can be explained by larger or smaller numbers of cells firing in synchrony together in a faster or slower rhythm.

The large increase in neuronal activation of the hippocampus, titrated closely to the speed or intensity of the movement, can also be observed using immunohistochemistry. When the animals are euthanized, immediately after they have been running on their running wheels, sections of their brains can be stained to identify neurons that were recently activated. We typically stain the brain sections for a protein called c-Fos, but many other neuronal activation markers can work (Clark, Bhattacharya et al., 2011; Clark et al., 2010). C-Fos is a transcription factor, meaning it binds to other proteins that together bind to DNA and cause the transcription of many other genes. Hence, the presence of c-Fos means that the cell has recently been stimulated and is undergoing genomic changes (e.g., new proteins are being expressed because the cell is extending a process, building or removing synapses, or recycling receptors). This has been referred to as the genomic action potential (Clayton, 2000). Just as an action potential in a neuron is short lived, so is the genomic action potential, but with a slightly longer time frame. For c-Fos, concentrations reach peak concentrations within 90 min after the neuron was stimulated. As it turns out, levels of c-Fos are strongly, positively correlated with running levels within 90 min of euthanasia taken from voluntary running wheels (Clark et al., 2010) or forced treadmills (Oladehin & Waters, 2001). Although animals in sedentary cages fail to exhibit a similar correlation between distance traveled and c-Fos expression (Clark, Bhattacharya et al., 2011), the correlation reappears in animals selectively bred for high levels of physical activity that move around in their cages at distances normal animals run on running wheels (Majdak et al., 2014). Taken together, these data suggest a threshold of intensity of movement is necessary to activate the hippocampus, and that the number of neurons that are activated from exercise is strongly correlated with the intensity of the exercise.

The correlation between neuronal activation of the hippocampus and intensity of movements is incredibly strong, but that does not imply anything about causality. The leading idea in the current literature is that the hippocampus is acting as a sensory organ, integrating sensory information about the intensity of movements (Bland, 1986; Hartley, Lever, Burgess, & O'Keefe, 2014; Kuo et al., 2011). For example, the animal runs, and then the hippocampus responds to the sensory feedback from the running. However, an alternative idea is that neuronal activity in the hippocampus is the origin of the motivation required to deliver the electrical stimulation, from the motor cortex and spinal cord neurons, necessary for large rhythmic contractions of muscles (Oddie & Bland, 1998). In other words, the hippocampus controls the motor circuit at the highest level, giving it the capability to deliver the electrical activation originating from the brain, necessary to execute intense muscular contractions with the capability for doing large amounts of work. If the hippocampus is at the top of the hierarchy rather than a sensory organ, then several observations would be predicted. First is that without a hippocampus, animals should be impaired in their ability or motivation for engaging in intense physical exercise. Second, the correlation between neuronal activity in the hippocampus and movement should not occur when the level or intensity of the movement is low, such as when the animal is walking around, eating, etc. Most of these predictions appear to be true. H.M. was incredibly inactive (personal communication with Neal Cohen, Professor at the University of Illinois, who worked for several years with H.M.). Rats with their hippocampus removed can move around but they cannot run quickly or jump high (Oddie & Bland, 1998). We were only able to detect a correlation between c-Fos and distance traveled when levels of activity were high, above normal ambulation in the cage such as observed in hyperactive mice or normal mice with access to a running wheel (Clark, Bhattacharya et al., 2011; Majdak et al., 2014). Therefore, we favor the hypothesis that states that the hippocampus functions as a movement intensity generator.

Chronic Effects of Exercise on Adult Hippocampal Neurogenesis

One of the consequences of repeated activation of the hippocampus, in close association with the intensity of the exercise, is increased numbers of new granule neurons in the DG of the hippocampus. In rodents, it is clear that these new neurons add to the granule layer and make it larger (Clark et al., 2009; van Praag, Christie et al., 1999; van Praag, Kempermann et al., 1999). Human studies have confirmed that the DG grows in volume in response to exercise training in randomized controlled trials (Erickson et al., 2011). While an increase in volume could come from many changes not just increase in numbers of cells (e.g., growth of preexisting cells), the fact that neurogenesis increases in rodent models in correlation with increased dentate volume is compelling evidence of convergence across humans and rodents regarding the underlying mechanism. Hence, before we continue with a discussion of the possible functional significance of increased neurogenesis and increased volume of the granule layer of the hippocampus in response to exercise, it is necessary first to review the discovery of adult neurogenesis and its regulation by exercise.

Over 50 years ago, Joseph Altman and colleagues (Altman, 1962, 1963, 1969a,b; Altman & Das, 1965, 1966) first reported that adult neurogenesis, the continuous generation of new neurons to the adult central nervous system, occurs in the mammalian brain. However, it was not until the 1990s when new techniques to visualize new neurons became available that adult neurogenesis became a widely recognized phenomenon. Adult neurogenesis is now established to occur continuously in two regions of the mammalian brain: the subventricular zone of the anterior lateral ventricles (the site of origin for olfactory bulb neurons) and the subgranular zone of the hippocampal DG (Figure 2).

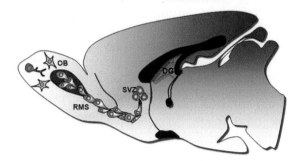

FIGURE 2   Adult mammalian neurogenesis. A schematic diagram of a rodent brain showing the two areas where adult neurogenesis occurs: the subventricular zone and the subgranular zone of the dentate gyrus. OB, olfactory bulb; RMS, rostral migratory stream; SVZ, subventricular zone; DG, dentate gyrus. *(This work is licensed under a Creative Commons Attribution 2.0 Unported License. Source: 2008 Arias-Carrión.)*

Stages of Adult Hippocampal Neurogenesis

Hippocampal adult neurogenesis is a process confined to the DG, which begins with the proliferation of a precursor progenitor cell and ends with the integration of a functional cell into the preexisting hippocampal network (Figure 3). Overall, the rodent DG consists of about one million granule cells (Rapp & Gallagher, 1996; West, Slomianka, & Gundersen, 1991), which are continuously being generated throughout the lifespan. It has been estimated that young adult rats have approximately 9000 new proliferating cells a day (Cameron & McKay, 2001); while older adult rats have approximately 4000 new proliferating cells a day (Rao & Shetty, 2004).

The process of hippocampal adult neurogenesis begins in the subgranular zone. It is here that progenitor cells proliferate. Progenitor cells are similar to stem cells, in that they divide, producing one cell that retains the self-renewing properties and a daughter cell that terminally differentiates into one of a variety of cell types. However, unlike true stem cells, the progenitor cells in the granule layer have limited self-renewing properties, and eventually

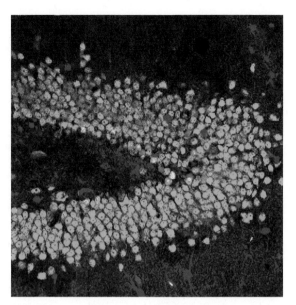

FIGURE 3 Adult hippocampal neurogenesis. A microscopic image of the dentate gyrus in cross-section showing the granule neurons of the dentate gyrus (labeled green), 1-month old cells (labeled red), and astrocytes (labeled blue). Notice that the red cells are primarily in the inner portion of the dentate gyrus (closest to the subgranular zone) and appear orange because they also express the green mature granule neuron marker, indicating that they are newly formed granule neurons.

will differentiate as an astrocyte (Kriegstein & Alvarez-Buylla, 2009). Moreover, the daughter cells that go on to differentiate into a specific cell type are restricted to a cell fate of either a neuron, an astrocyte, or an oligodendrocyte. Approximately 60% of the newly born daughter cells will die (Dayer, Ford, Cleaver, Yassaee, & Cameron, 2003), while the remaining cells will exit the cell cycle and differentiate into immature cells. It is during this phase that cells commit to a neuronal lineage and begin to express immature neuronal markers. Approximately 80–90% of adult-born neurons differentiate into mature neurons, while a low percentage (approximately 5%) will differentiate into astrocytes and a rare percentage (less than 5%) will become oligodendrocytes (Abrous, Koehl, & Le Moal, 2005;

Steiner et al., 2004). Following the cell differentiation, cells begin to migrate out of the subgranular zone into the inner granule cell layer of the DG. Immature granule cells have limited dendritic branches and are driven by inhibitory GABA interneurons. As such, they exhibit characteristics of immature neurons: hyperexcitability and enhanced synaptic plasticity (Ge, Sailor, Ming, & Song, 2008). As the neurons mature, they begin to respond solely to excitatory glutamatergic input. In addition, they form connections with inputs from the EC and send outputs to the CA3 region. Approximately 2 months after birth, adult-born neurons exhibit similar basic electrophysiological properties as mature neurons (Mongiat & Schinder, 2011), yet they do not reach a mature morphology (soma size, total dendritic length, dendritic branching, and spine density) until 4 months after their birth (Abrous et al., 2005; Song, Stevens, & Gage, 2002).

Modulation of Adult Neurogenesis from Exercise

Theoretically, exercise could increase adult neurogenesis by increasing the proliferation of progenitor cells (either by increasing the rate of cell division or by the number of cells that are dividing at a time) or by increasing the survival and neuronal differentiation of cells that have already proliferated. In 1999, Henriette van Praag hypothesized that exercise increased levels of adult neurogenesis mainly by increasing the number of proliferating cells in the DG. In fact, it was further hypothesized that exercise increased levels of adult neurogenesis through enhanced proliferation, while environmental enrichment (e.g., learning and sensory stimulation) increased levels of adult neurogenesis by supporting cell survival (Olson, Eadie, Ernst, & Christie, 2006; van Praag, Christie et al., 1999; van Praag, Kempermann et al., 1999). More recently, however, research has demonstrated that exercise increases neurogenesis mainly by increasing cell survival rather than proliferation (Clark et al., 2010; Fuss et al., 2010; Kronenberg et al., 2006; Snyder, Glover, Sanzone, Kamhi, & Cameron, 2009; Wu et al., 2008). For example, in perhaps the clearest demonstration, C57BL/6J mice were injected with BrdU (to label dividing cells) before being placed on running wheels and showed the same doubling in neurogenesis typically observed with this strain (Snyder et al., 2009). Because the BrdU was administered before exercise, the increased neurogenesis can only be attributed to increased survival or differentiation of cells that had proliferated before the exercise began. It is important to note that in the original van Praag, Kempermann et al. (1999) study that discovered exercise-induced levels of neurogenesis, proliferation was measured by labeling cells across a 12-day period. Thus, total number of cells on day 13 reflected both proliferation and survival of cells labeled on the initial days.

Exercise has been consistently proven to increase levels of neurogenesis in a variety of strains. In CD1 mice, 6 weeks' access to a running wheel produced a two- to threefold increase in newly born neurons (Bednarczyk, Aumont, Decary, Bergeron, & Fernandes, 2009). Further, Thuret, Toni, Aigner, Yeo, and Gage (2009) found that MRL/MpJ mice produce 75% fewer new neurons than do C57BL/6 mice; however, when given unlimited access to a running wheel this difference is abolished. Recently, our lab examined the exercise-enhanced levels of adult hippocampal neurogenesis in 12 different genetically divergent mouse strains (Clark, Kohman et al., 2011). Significant differences in levels of adult neurogenesis, across species, were apparent. Interestingly, the magnitude of exercise-induced neurogenesis was most significant in AKR/J mice and not in C57BL6/J, the most commonly used mouse strain in studies of effects of exercise on neurological outcomes. Strain-based differences are also evident in the number of surviving cells, as 129S1/SvlmJ mice had the lowest, while both B6129SF1/J and AKR/J mice

had the highest number of surviving cells. Interestingly, AKR/J mice only ran approximately 4 km/day, despite having the highest number of surviving cells. Still, it is important to acknowledge that although levels of adult neurogenesis vary in different mouse strains, all strains show a significant increase in levels of adult neurogenesis as a result of exercise exposure.

In addition, the distance that an animal runs impacts the levels of exercise-induced neurogenesis. This is evident in the previously mentioned study by Clark, Kohman et al. (2011), wherein significant differences in 12 different strains were found. It is important to recognize that in this study, the strains varied greatly with respect to running levels. For example, 129S1/SvlmJ mice ran approximately 2 km/day, whereas B6129SF1/J mice ran approximately 10 km/day. As a result, B6129SF1/J mice had a greater-fold increase in levels of adult neurogenesis than did 129S1/SvlmJ mice. In addition, it has recently been shown that the levels of neurogenesis may be influenced by individual differences in response to a complex environment (i.e., how much an animal is moving around an environmental enrichment cage), as genetically identical mice living in a nominally identical environment exhibited differing levels of adult neurogenesis that were positively correlated with their exploration of the environment (Freund et al., 2013). Thus, a large proportion of individual variation in levels of adult hippocampal neurogenesis can be explained by differential individual levels of physical activity.

The fact that levels of adult neurogenesis are strongly correlated with distance traveled on running wheels, both among individuals within a strain and across mouse strains, strongly suggests that it is the exercise per se that increases neurogenesis as opposed to the environmental enrichment component of wheel running. Nonetheless, it has been argued that increased neurogenesis in animals housed on running wheels relative to animals housed in cages without running wheels is actually a demonstration of environmental deprivation in the rats without wheels. This is because allowing an animal to move is more natural than constraining them to live in a cage without any other stimulation (Lavenex, Lavenex, & Clayton, 2001). One way to determine whether adding the running wheel provides a type of enrichment aside from the exercise that enhances neurogenesis is to include a group that is highly enriched but unable to exercise. We and others have performed such a study where animals were reared under four different environmental conditions, standard housing, wheel running only, environmental complexity (with the addition of toys or social groups), and the combination of environmental complexity with running wheels. The observation is that only running significantly increases neurogenesis, and that adding environmental complexity does nothing further to increase neurogenesis beyond the effects of exercise (Kobilo et al., 2011; Mustroph et al., 2012). Another possibility is that mice gain enjoyment from the exercise and it is this enjoyment that drives neurogenesis. However, if this were the case then we would not expect to see increased levels of neurogenesis in the forced treadmill studies, but we do (Kim et al., 2014; Li et al., 2013; Nam et al., 2013; Shin et al., 2013). Therefore, it appears that it is the actual physical motion of running that increases levels of adult neurogenesis.

FUNCTIONAL SIGNIFICANCE OF EXERCISE-INDUCED ADULT NEUROGENESIS

Despite the fact that exercise increases hippocampal neurogenesis in every strain of rat or mouse that has been investigated using either voluntary wheel running or treadmill running paradigms, and the observation in human studies of increased volume of the DG from exercise training, the functional significance remains a mystery. Why does the hippocampus become so activated from exercise, and why does this repeated activation result in increased neurogenesis and volume of the entire structure? Our hypothesis is that the increased neurogenesis and growth of the hippocampus serves a function related to the role of the hippocampus in regulating the intensity of movement. However, ironically we have little data directly testing this hypothesis. Instead, most of our work and the work of others has focused on the hypothesis that exercise-induced neurogenesis serves a function in learning and memory (Clark et al., 2008; Gibbons et al., 2014; Luo et al., 2007; Marlatt, Potter, Lucassen, & van Praag, 2012; Merritt & Rhodes, 2015; Mustroph et al., 2012). This is because of the dominant literature on the role of the hippocampus in learning and memory as compared to regulating the intensity of movement, and also the intuitive idea that the addition of new neurons in an area of the brain critical for learning and memory might enhance learning and memory. New neurons have not yet integrated into the circuitry, and therefore are hypothesized to be more moldable to experiences than older neurons that already have most of their processes integrated in the circuitry. Also, exercise has been proven not only to promote brain plasticity but also to enhance cognitive and spatial performance on a variety of tasks (Clark et al., 2008; van Praag, Christie et al., 1999; Van der Borght et al., 2007). Whether the exercise-induced levels of adult neurogenesis play a functional role in the enhanced learning and memory performance in exercising animals remains unclear. Over the past two decades research has examined the functional significance of exercise-generated neurons by experimentally manipulating the numbers of new neurons that an animal is capable of producing. The idea behind this approach is to reduce neurogenesis in order to see what impact the lesion has on behavior. Recently, several different techniques have been developed to reduce neurogenesis in the hippocampus, such as focal irradiation, transgenic mouse models, and optogenetics. Hence, it is likely that in the near future, we will have a better understanding of the functional role of new neurons in behavior using these new technologies.

Role of Exercise-Induced Adult Neurogenesis in Learning and Memory

Exercise consistently increases levels of hippocampal adult neurogenesis and also improves performance on a variety of learning and memory tasks in rodents. One of the most well-established improvements in function from exercise is enhanced spatial learning and memory, the ability to remember the location of an object relative to other objects in the environment (Clark et al., 2012; van Praag, Christie et al., 1999; Van der Borght et al., 2007). For example, rats exposed to prenatal noise stress, given an intervention of 30 min of treadmill running per day, exhibited significantly enhanced levels of neurogenesis and they completed the radial arm maze with significantly fewer errors than did their littermates not receiving the intervention (Kim et al., 2013). Further, in both young and aged mice, access to a running wheel improved performance on the Morris water maze and increased levels of adult neurogenesis when compared to aged-matched controls (Gibbons et al., 2014; Marlatt et.al., 2012; van Praag, Shubert, Zhao, & Gage, 2005). Running, when administered as an intervention to corticosterone administration, increases levels of adult neurogenesis and enhances Morris water maze performance in adult male Sprague–Dawley rats (Yau et al., 2011). Recently, we found that voluntary wheel running enhanced performance on the multistrain adapted plus version of the water maze in five different mouse strains (Merritt & Rhodes, 2015). Together, these studies suggest that exercise-enhanced levels of adult neurogenesis occur in parallel with improved performance on spatial learning and memory tasks. However, they do not speak to whether the two are causally related. Improved rotarod performance is consistently correlated with

increased levels of adult neurogenesis, resulting from exercise exposure (Clark et al., 2008; Marlatt et al., 2012), but no one has ever suggested that exercise-induced neurogenesis functions to support rotarod behavior. Additional work is needed to establish causality.

Several different approaches have been used to eliminate neurogenesis to see what effect that has on learning and memory tasks. Results are mixed, and the function remains unclear. When levels of adult neurogenesis are ablated through focal irradiation, the procognitive effects of exercise are no longer present on Morris water maze performance in C57BL/6J mice (Clark et al., 2008). On the one hand, these data might suggest that new neurons are required for the procognitive effects. However, on the other hand, irradiation induces inflammation, which could contribute to the impairment on the water maze observed in this study independent of whether new neurons were ablated or not. Recent studies, using transgenic methods that quite specifically reduce adult neurogenesis, have found no influence of reducing neurogenesis on learning and memory performance on a variety of tasks (for review see Groves et al., 2013). While these studies did not examine exercise-induced neurogenesis per se, the results are important because they indicate a potential limitation of the neurogenesis lesion method when studying the functional significance of new neurons. If new neurons are removed or killed, it is possible that the remaining older neurons of the granule layer can compensate for this loss by, for example, adding additional synapses, growing additional spines, or extending dendrites. Therefore, it is possible that new neurons, if present, would be preferentially recruited while an animal was learning a particular task, but if they are not present (because they are eliminated using some experimental method), then there are redundant mechanisms in the brain to compensate for their loss.

We recently obtained evidence that new neurons, in fact, are preferentially activated in the hippocampus when mice are engaged in multiple different behavioral tasks. We used a combination of the BrdU method for labeling newly divided cells and the c-Fos method for determining whether the cells were activated or not after the animal was performing a certain task (e.g., running on a wheel, navigating a water maze, or exploring an open field) (Clark et al., 2012). What we found was that new neurons were twice as likely as older neurons to display c-Fos regardless of the task. Even though each task activated the hippocampus to a different degree, e.g., running activated the hippocampus the greatest, followed by swimming in the water maze, and lastly normal cage activity, in each case new neurons were twice as likely to be activated as older mature neurons. Taken together, these results suggest that new neurons generated from exercise are broadly recruited into multiple functions of the hippocampus.

It is important to note here that the hypothesis that new neurons are broadly recruited into all functions of the DG is not necessarily consistent with recent studies that suggest new neurons in the DG function specifically in pattern separation (Clelland et al., 2009; Sahay et al., 2011). Pattern separation refers to the ability to distinguish and uniquely encode two very similar stimuli (e.g., patterns, objects, faces, scenes, experiences, etc.). Computational models suggest that new neurons in the DG could play a critical role in pattern separation (Aimone, Deng, & Gage, 2011). However, we are not certain how useful the concept of pattern separation is to the debate about the functional significance of adult hippocampal neurogenesis. We see no reason why it is necessary to pin a specific function to a neuron or a brain region. Rather we believe that new neurons are part of the development, function, and maintenance of a critical brain region that serves multiple brain functions including pattern separation.

One way to directly determine the extent to which new neurons play a specific role in behavior is to manipulate the activation of the cells after they are incorporated into the circuit. This could be done through an optogenetic method that would allow researchers, in theory, to inactivate cohorts of new neurons immediately while the animal is performing a task. This technology has promise for discovering the potential functional significance of new neurons in learning and memory because the new neurons can remain intact until the very moment researchers are interested in testing their function, leaving no time for compensatory mechanisms to interfere with the interpretation of their role in behavior. Previous studies, which delivered light-sensitive proteins using viral vectors to the granule cell layer, found that when the cells were inactivated, the animals displayed impaired learning and memory (Gu et al., 2012; Liu et al., 2012; Liu, Ramirez, & Tonegawa, 2014). The major limitation of these studies is that the viral vector delivery method cannot infect the entire granule cell layer. Hence, the method can only inactivate a portion of the new neurons in the hippocampus. If the new cells can be labeled using a genetic method instead of injecting viral vectors, the method may have real promise for uncovering the functional significance of exercise-induced adult hippocampal neurogenesis.

CONCLUSIONS

It is established that exercise is good for the brain and can enhance cognitive performance, both acutely and chronically, and regardless of the form (forced or voluntary or strength), though the precise differences in the neurological outcomes between the different forms of exercise still need to be worked out. One of the most robust effects of exercise in the brain is the growth of the hippocampus. This is striking because of the prominent role that the hippocampus plays in learning and memory. Why rhythmic activation of the hippocampus occurs from exercise and why this results in growth of the region is not known. The leading ideas in the literature point to a role of new neurons in learning and memory. However, the numbers of cells in the hippocampus involved in learning and memory are sparse in comparison to the large numbers of cells that are activated when the animal is running at high speeds. When an animal is learning a task, specific cells in the DG sparsely encode a unique representation. When the animal is running, large numbers of cells fire in synchrony, with large amounts of electrical activity that can resonate throughout the entire brain. To us, this suggests the hippocampus has multiple functions, one in learning and memory and another in regulating the intensity of movements. Rhythmic activation of the hippocampus may be required to "ramp up" the motor areas of the brain in a way that is needed to generate large rhythmic muscle contractions required for intense movements. To us, it follows then that the growth of the hippocampus is related to the increased demand from this region due to being regularly engaged for motivating the behavior. Our movement intensity hypothesis for the functional significance of exercise-induced neurogenesis is perfectly consistent with a role for the new neurons in supporting learning and memory. We believe the new neurons generated from running support both the function of the hippocampus in regulating the intensity of movement and also whatever else the hippocampus does including learning and memory, motivation, stress, etc.

The bottom line is that exercise clearly can be used as a means to promote enhanced cognitive function and brain plasticity. Still, it remains unclear how exactly exercise exerts its procognitive effects. It is likely that the hippocampus plays a role, and that exercise-induced neurogenesis and growth of the hippocampus contributes to the procognitive effects observed. New optogenetic technologies that allow precise control over the activation of new neurons may shed light on the important question of how exercise broadly enhances cognition throughout the lifespan.

References

Abrous, D. N., Koehl, M., & Le Moal, M. (2005). Adult neurogenesis: from precursors to network and physiology. *Physiological Review, 85*, 523–569.

Ahmed, O. J., & Mehta, M. R. (2012). Running speed alters the frequency of hippocampal gamma oscillations. *Journal of Neuroscience, 32*, 7373–7383.

Aimone, J. B., Deng, W., & Gage, F. H. (2011). Resolving new memories: a critical look at the dentate gyrus, adult neurogenesis, and pattern separation. *Neuron, 70*, 589–596.

Alessio, H. M., Hagerman, A. E., Nagy, S., Philip, B., Byrnes, R. N., Woodward, J. L., et al. (2005). Exercise improves biomarkers of health and stress in animals fed ad libitum. *Physiology and Behavior, 84*, 65–72.

Altman, J. (1962). Are new neurons formed in the brains of adult mammals? *Science, 135*, 1127–1128.

Altman, J. (1963). Autoradiographic investigation of cell proliferation in the brains of rats and cats. *The Anatomical Record, 145*, 573–591.

Altman, J. (1969a). Autoradiographic and histological studies of postnatal neurogenesis. 3. Dating the time of production and onset of differentiation of cerebellar microneurons in rats. *Journal of Comparative Neurology, 136*, 269–293.

Altman, J. (1969b). Autoradiographic and histological studies of postnatal neurogenesis. IV. Cell proliferation and migration in the anterior forebrain, with special reference to persisting neurogenesis in the olfactory bulb. *Journal of Comparative Neurology, 137*, 433–457.

Altman, J., & Das, G. D. (1965). Autoradiographic and histological evidence of postnatal hippocampal neurogenesis in rats. *Journal of Comparative Neurology, 124*, 319–335.

Altman, J., & Das, G. D. (1966). Autoradiographic and histological studies of postnatal neurogenesis. I. A longitudinal investigation of the kinetics, migration and transformation of cells incorporating tritiated thymidine in neonate rats, with special reference to postnatal neurogenesis in some brain regions. *Journal of Comparative Neurology, 126*, 337–389.

Andersen, P. (2007). *The hippocampus book*. Oxford, NY: Oxford University Press.

Anderson, B. J., Rapp, D. N., Baek, D. H., McCloskey, D. P., Coburn-Litvak, P. S., & Robinson, J. K. (2000). Exercise influences spatial learning in the radial arm maze. *Physiology and Behavior, 70*, 425–429.

Aparicio, V. A., Nebot, E., Porres, J. M., Ortega, F. B., Heredia, J. M., Lopez-Jurado, M., et al. (2011). Effects of high-whey-protein intake and resistance training on renal, bone and metabolic parameters in rats. *British Journal of Nutrition, 105*, 836–845.

Augustinack, J. C., van der Kouwe, A. J., Salat, D. H., Benner, T., Stevens, A. A., Annese, J., et al. (2014). H.M.'s contributions to neuroscience: a review and autopsy studies. *Hippocampus, 24*, 1267–1286.

Bednarczyk, M. R., Aumont, A., Decary, S., Bergeron, R., & Fernandes, K. J. (2009). Prolonged voluntary wheel-running stimulates neural precursors in the hippocampus and forebrain of adult CD1 mice. *Hippocampus, 19,* 913–927.

Black, J. E., Isaacs, K. R., Anderson, B. J., Alcantara, A. A., & Greenough, W. T. (1990). Learning causes synaptogenesis, whereas motor activity causes angiogenesis, in cerebellar cortex of adult rats. *Proceedings of the National Academy of Sciences of the United States of America, 87,* 5568–5572.

Bland, B. H. (1986). The physiology and pharmacology of hippocampal formation theta rhythms. *Progress in Neurobiology, 26,* 1–54.

Broadbent, N. J., Gaskin, S., Squire, L. R., & Clark, R. E. (2010). Object recognition memory and the rodent hippocampus. *Learning and Memory, 17,* 5–11.

Cameron, H. A., & McKay, R. D. (2001). Adult neurogenesis produces a large pool of new granule cells in the dentate gyrus. *Journal of Comparative Neurology, 435,* 406–417.

Cassilhas, R. C., Lee, K. S., Fernandes, J., Oliveira, M. G., Tufik, S., Meeusen, R., et al. (2012). Spatial memory is improved by aerobic and resistance exercise through divergent molecular mechanisms. *Neuroscience, 202,* 309–317.

Cassilhas, R. C., Lee, K. S., Venancio, D. P., Oliveira, M. G., Tufik, S., & de Mello, M. T. (2012). Resistance exercise improves hippocampus-dependent memory. *Brazilian Journal of Medical and Biological Research, 45,* 1215–1220.

Cassilhas, R. C., Reis, I. T., Venancio, D., Fernandes, J., Tufik, S., & de Mello, M. T. (2013). Animal model for progressive resistance exercise: a detailed description of model and its implications for basic research in exercise. *Motriz-Revista De Educacao Fisica, 19,* 178–184.

Chen, C., Kim, J. J., Thompson, R. F., & Tonegawa, S. (1996). Hippocampal lesions impair contextual fear conditioning in two strains of mice. *Behavioral Neuroscience, 110,* 1177–1180.

Cho, Y. H., Friedman, E., & Silva, A. J. (1999). Ibotenate lesions of the hippocampus impair spatial learning but not contextual fear conditioning in mice. *Behavioural Brain Research, 98,* 77–87.

Churchill, J. D., Galvez, R., Colcombe, S., Swain, R. A., Kramer, A. F., & Greenough, W. T. (2002). Exercise, experience and the aging brain. *Neurobiology of Aging, 23,* 941–955.

Clark, P. J., Bhattacharya, T. K., Miller, D. S., Kohman, R. A., DeYoung, E. K., & Rhodes, J. S. (2012). New neurons generated from running are broadly recruited into neuronal activation associated with three different hippocampus-involved tasks. *Hippocampus, 22,* 1860–1867.

Clark, P. J., Bhattacharya, T. K., Miller, D. S., & Rhodes, J. S. (2011). Induction of c-Fos, Zif268, and Arc from acute bouts of voluntary wheel running in new and pre-existing adult mouse hippocampal granule neurons. *Neuroscience, 184,* 16–27.

Clark, P. J., Brzezinska, W. J., Puchalski, E. K., Krone, D. A., & Rhodes, J. S. (2009). Functional analysis of neurovascular adaptations to exercise in the dentate gyrus of young adult mice associated with cognitive gain. *Hippocampus, 19,* 937–950.

Clark, P. J., Brzezinska, W. J., Thomas, M. W., Ryzhenko, N. A., Toshkov, S. A., & Rhodes, J. S. (2008). Intact neurogenesis is required for benefits of exercise on spatial memory but not motor performance or contextual fear conditioning in C57BL/6J mice. *Neuroscience, 155,* 1048–1058.

Clark, P. J., Kohman, R. A., Miller, D. S., Bhattacharya, T. K., Brzezinska, W. J., & Rhodes, J. S. (2011). Genetic influences on exercise-induced adult hippocampal neurogenesis across 12 divergent mouse strains. *Genes, Brain and Behavior, 10,* 345–353.

Clark, P. J., Kohman, R. A., Miller, D. S., Bhattacharya, T. K., Haferkamp, E. H., & Rhodes, J. S. (2010). Adult hippocampal neurogenesis and c-Fos induction during escalation of voluntary wheel running in C57BL/6J mice. *Behavioural Brain Research, 213,* 246–252.

Clayton, D. F. (2000). The genomic action potential. *Neurobiology of Learning and Memory, 74,* 185–216.

Clelland, C. D., Choi, M., Romberg, C., Clemenson, G. D., Jr., Fragniere, A., Tyers, P., et al. (2009). A functional role for adult hippocampal neurogenesis in spatial pattern separation. *Science, 325,* 210–213.

Cohen, S. J., Munchow, A. H., Rios, L. M., Zhang, G., Asgeirsdottir, H. N., & Stackman, R. W., Jr. (2013). The rodent hippocampus is essential for nonspatial object memory. *Current Biology, 23,* 1685–1690.

Colcombe, S., & Kramer, A. F. (2003). Fitness effects on the cognitive function of older adults: a meta-analytic study. *Psychological Science, 14,* 125–130.

Cook, M. D., Martin, S. A., Williams, C., Whitlock, K., Wallig, M. A., Pence, B. D., et al. (2013). Forced treadmill exercise training exacerbates inflammation and causes mortality while voluntary wheel training is protective in a mouse model of colitis. *Brain, Behavior, and Immunity, 33,* 46–56.

Cotman, C. W., & Berchtold, N. C. (2002). Exercise: a behavioral intervention to enhance brain health and plasticity. *Trends in Neurosciences, 25,* 295–301.

Creer, D. J., Romberg, C., Saksida, L. M., van Praag, H., & Bussey, T. J. (2010). Running enhances spatial pattern separation in mice. *Proceedings of the National Academy of Sciences of the United States of America, 107,* 2367–2372.

Dayer, A. G., Ford, A. A., Cleaver, K. M., Yassaee, M., & Cameron, H. A. (2003). Short-term and long-term survival of new neurons in the rat dentate gyrus. *Journal of Comparative Neurology, 460,* 563–572.

Ding, Q., Vaynman, S., Akhavan, M., Ying, Z., & Gomez-Pinilla, F. (2006). Insulin-like growth factor I interfaces with brain-derived neurotrophic factor-mediated synaptic plasticity to modulate aspects of exercise-induced cognitive function. *Neuroscience, 140,* 823–833.

Eadie, B. D., Redila, V. A., & Christie, B. R. (2005). Voluntary exercise alters the cytoarchitecture of the adult dentate gyrus by increasing cellular proliferation, dendritic complexity, and spine density. *Journal of Comparative Neurology*, *486*, 39–47.

Erickson, K. I., & Kramer, A. F. (2009). Aerobic exercise effects on cognitive and neural plasticity in older adults. *British Journal of Sports Medicine*, *43*, 22–24.

Erickson, K. I., Voss, M. W., Prakash, R. S., Basak, C., Szabo, A., Chaddock, L., et al. (2011). Exercise training increases size of hippocampus and improves memory. *Proceedings of the National Academy of Sciences of the United States of America*, *108*, 3017–3022.

Fabel, K., Tam, B., Kaufer, D., Baiker, A., Simmons, N., Kuo, C. J., et al. (2003). VEGF is necessary for exercise-induced adult hippocampal neurogenesis. *European Journal of Neuroscience*, *18*, 2803–2812.

Farr, S. A., Banks, W. A., La Scola, M. E., Flood, J. F., & Morley, J. E. (2000). Permanent and temporary inactivation of the hippocampus impairs T-maze footshock avoidance acquisition and retention. *Brain Research*, *872*, 242–249.

Freund, J., Brandmaier, A. M., Lewejohann, L., Kirste, I., Kritzler, M., Kruger, A., et al. (2013). Emergence of individuality in genetically identical mice. *Science*, *340*, 756–759.

Fuss, J., Ben Abdallah, N. M., Vogt, M. A., Touma, C., Pacifici, P. G., Palme, R., et al. (2010). Voluntary exercise induces anxiety-like behavior in adult C57BL/6J mice correlating with hippocampal neurogenesis. *Hippocampus*, *20*, 364–376.

Ge, S., Sailor, K. A., Ming, G. L., & Song, H. (2008). Synaptic integration and plasticity of new neurons in the adult hippocampus. *Journal of Physiology*, *586*, 3759–3765.

Gibbons, T. E., Pence, B. D., Petr, G., Ossyra, J. M., Mach, H. C., Bhattacharya, T. K., et al. (2014). Voluntary wheel running, but not a diet containing (-)-epigallocatechin-3-gallate and beta-alanine, improves learning, memory and hippocampal neurogenesis in aged mice. *Behavioural Brain Research*, *272*, 131–140.

Girard, I., McAleer, M. W., Rhodes, J. S., & Garland, T., Jr. (2001). Selection for high voluntary wheel-running increases speed and intermittency in house mice (Mus domesticus). *Journal of Experimental Biology*, *204*, 4311–4320.

Gomez-Pinilla, F., Dao, L., & So, V. (1997). Physical exercise induces FGF-2 and its mRNA in the hippocampus. *Brain Research*, *764*, 1–8.

Gothe, N. P., Kramer, A. F., & McAuley, E. (2014). The effects of an 8-week Hatha yoga intervention on executive function in older adults. *The Journals of Gerontology Series A*, *69*, 1109–1116.

Greenwood, B. N., Strong, P. V., Foley, T. E., & Fleshner, M. (2009). A behavioral analysis of the impact of voluntary physical activity on hippocampus-dependent contextual conditioning. *Hippocampus*, *19*, 988–1001.

Groves, J. O., Leslie, I., Huang, G. J., McHugh, S. B., Taylor, A., Mott, R., et al. (2013). Ablating adult neurogenesis in the rat has no effect on spatial processing: evidence from a novel pharmacogenetic model. *PLoS Genetics*, *9*, e1003718. http://dx.doi.org/10.1371/journal.pgen.1003718.

Gu, Y., Arruda-Carvalho, M., Wang, J., Janoschka, S. R., Josselyn, S. A., Frankland, P. W., et al. (2012). Optical controlling reveals time-dependent roles for adult-born dentate granule cells. *Nature Neuroscience*, *15*, 1700–1706.

Hartley, T., Lever, C., Burgess, N., & O'Keefe, J. (2014). Space in the brain: how the hippocampal formation supports spatial cognition. *Philosophical Transaction of the Royal Society of London. Series B. Biological Science*, *369*, 20120510. http://dx.doi.org/10.1098/rstb.2012.0510.

Isaacs, K. R., Anderson, B. J., Alcantara, A. A., Black, J. E., & Greenough, W. T. (1992). Exercise and the brain: angiogenesis in the adult rat cerebellum after vigorous physical activity and motor skill learning. *Journal of Cerebral Blood Flow and Metabolism*, *12*, 110–119.

Jacotte-Simancas, A., Costa-Miserachs, D., Torras-Garcia, M., Coll-Andreu, M., & Portell-Cortes, I. (2013). Effect of voluntary physical exercise and post-training epinephrine on acquisition of a spatial task in the barnes maze. *Behavioural Brain Research*, *247*, 178–181.

Kelly, S. A., Rezende, E. L., Chappell, M. A., Gomes, F. R., Kolb, E. M., Malisch, J. L., et al. (2014). Exercise training effects on hypoxic and hypercapnic ventilatory responses in mice selected for increased voluntary wheel running. *Experimental Physiology*, *99*, 403–413.

Kim, B. K., Shin, M. S., Kim, C. J., Baek, S. B., Ko, Y. C., & Kim, Y. P. (2014). Treadmill exercise improves short-term memory by enhancing neurogenesis in amyloid beta-induced Alzheimer disease rats. *Journal of Exercise Rehabilitation*, *10*, 2–8.

Kim, T. W., Shin, M. S., Park, J. K., Shin, M. A., Lee, H. H., & Lee, S. J. (2013). Treadmill exercise alleviates prenatal noise stress-induced impairment of spatial learning ability through enhancing hippocampal neurogenesis in rat pups. *Journal of Exercise Rehabilitation*, *9*, 451–456.

Kobilo, T., Liu, Q. R., Gandhi, K., Mughal, M., Shaham, Y., & van Praag, H. (2011). Running is the neurogenic and neurotrophic stimulus in environmental enrichment. *Learning and Memory*, *18*, 605–609.

Kohman, R. A., Bhattacharya, T. K., Wojcik, E., & Rhodes, J. S. (2013). Exercise reduces activation of microglia isolated from hippocampus and brain of aged mice. *Journal of Neuroinflammation*, *10*, 114. http://dx.doi.org/10.1186/1742-2094-10-114.

Kohman, R. A., DeYoung, E. K., Bhattacharya, T. K., Peterson, L. N., & Rhodes, J. S. (2012). Wheel running attenuates microglia proliferation and increases expression of a proneurogenic phenotype in the hippocampus of aged mice. *Brain, Behavior, and Immunity*, *26*, 803–810.

Kohman, R. A., & Rhodes, J. S. (2013). Neurogenesis, inflammation and behavior. *Brain, Behavior, and Immunity, 27,* 22–32.

Kriegstein, A., & Alvarez-Buylla, A. (2009). The glial nature of embryonic and adult neural stem cells. *Annual Review of Neuroscience, 32,* 149–184.

Kronenberg, G., Bick-Sander, A., Bunk, E., Wolf, C., Ehninger, D., & Kempermann, G. (2006). Physical exercise prevents age-related decline in precursor cell activity in the mouse dentate gyrus. *Neurobiology of Aging, 27,* 1505–1513.

Kuo, T. B., Li, J. Y., Chen, C. Y., & Yang, C. C. (2011). Changes in hippocampal theta activity during initiation and maintenance of running in the rat. *Neuroscience, 194,* 27–35.

Lavenex, P. B., Lavenex, P., & Clayton, N. S. (2001). Comparative studies of postnatal neurogenesis and learning: a critical review. *Avian and Poultry Biological Reviews, 12,* 103–125.

Lee, H., Boot, W. R., Basak, C., Voss, M. W., Prakash, R. S., Neider, M., et al. (2012). Performance gains from directed training do not transfer to untrained tasks. *Acta Psychologica, 139,* 146–158.

Li, J., Ding, Y. H., Rafols, J. A., Lai, Q., McAllister, J. P., 2nd, & Ding, Y. (2005). Increased astrocyte proliferation in rats after running exercise. *Neuroscience Letters, 386,* 160–164.

Li, H., Liang, A., Guan, F., Fan, R., Chi, L., & Yang, B. (2013). Regular treadmill running improves spatial learning and memory performance in young mice through increased hippocampal neurogenesis and decreased stress. *Brain Research, 1531,* 1–8.

Liu, X., Ramirez, S., Pang, P. T., Puryear, C. B., Govindarajan, A., Deisseroth, K., et al. (2012). Optogenetic stimulation of a hippocampal engram activates fear memory recall. *Nature, 484,* 381–385.

Liu, X., Ramirez, S., & Tonegawa, S. (2014). Inception of a false memory by optogenetic manipulation of a hippocampal memory engram. *Philosophical Transactions of the Royal Society B: Biological Science, 369.* http://dx.doi.org/10.1098/rstb.20130142.

Logue, S. F., Paylor, R., & Wehner, J. M. (1997). Hippocampal lesions cause learning deficits in inbred mice in the Morris water maze and conditioned-fear task. *Behavioral Neuroscience, 111,* 104–113.

Luo, C. X., Jiang, J., Zhou, Q. G., Zhu, X. J., Wang, W., Zhang, Z. J., et al. (2007). Voluntary exercise-induced neurogenesis in the postischemic dentate gyrus is associated with spatial memory recovery from stroke. *Journal of Neuroscience Research, 85,* 1637–1646.

Majdak, P., Bucko, P. J., Holloway, A. L., Bhattacharya, T. K., DeYoung, E. K., Kilby, C. N., et al. (2014). Behavioral and pharmacological evaluation of a selectively bred mouse model of home cage hyperactivity. *Behavior Genetics, 44,* 516–534.

Marlatt, M. W., Potter, M. C., Lucassen, P. J., & van Praag, H. (2012). Running throughout middle-age improves memory function, hippocampal neurogenesis, and BDNF levels in female C57BL/6J mice. *Developmental Neurobiology, 72,* 943–952.

Masukawa, L. M., O'Connor, W. M., Burdette, L. J., McGonigle, P., Sperling, M. R., O'Connor, M. J., et al. (1997). Mossy fiber reorganization and its possible physiological consequences in the dentate gyrus of epileptic humans. *Advances in Neurology, 72,* 53–68.

McKenzie, I. A., Ohayon, D., Li, H., de Faria, J. P., Emery, B., et al. (2014). Motor skill learning requires active central myelination. *Science, 346,* 318–322.

McNaughton, B. L., Barnes, C. A., & O'Keefe, J. (1983). The contributions of position, direction, and velocity to single unit activity in the hippocampus of freely-moving rats. *Experimental Brain Research, 52,* 41–49.

Merritt, J., & Rhodes, J. S. (2015). Mouse genetic differences in voluntary wheel running, adult hippocampal neurogenesis and learning on the multi-strain-adapted plus water maze. *Behavioural Brain Research, 280,* 62–71.

Mongiat, L. A., & Schinder, A. F. (2011). Adult neurogenesis and the plasticity of the dentate gyrus network. *European Journal of Neuroscience, 33,* 1055–1061.

Mustroph, M. L., Chen, S., Desai, S. C., Cay, E. B., DeYoung, E. K., & Rhodes, J. S. (2012). Aerobic exercise is the critical variable in an enriched environment that increases hippocampal neurogenesis and water maze learning in male C57BL/6J mice. *Neuroscience, 219,* 62–71.

Nam, S. M., Kim, J. W., Yoo, D. Y., Kim, W., Kim, W., Jung, H. Y., et al. (2013). Effects of treadmill exercise on neural stem cells, cell proliferation, and neuroblast differentiation in the subgranular zone of the dentate gyrus in cyclooxygenase-2 knockout mice. *Neurochemical Research, 38,* 2559–2569.

Neeper, S. A., Gomez-Pinilla, F., Choi, J., & Cotman, C. W. (1996). Physical activity increases mRNA for brain-derived neurotrophic factor and nerve growth factor in rat brain. *Brain Research, 726,* 49–56.

Oddie, S. D., & Bland, B. H. (1998). Hippocampal formation theta activity and movement selection. *Neuroscience and Biobehavioral Reviews, 22,* 221–231.

Oladehin, A., & Waters, R. S. (2001). Location and distribution of Fos protein expression in rat hippocampus following acute moderate aerobic exercise. *Experimental Brain Research, 137,* 26–35.

Olson, A. K., Eadie, B. D., Ernst, C., & Christie, B. R. (2006). Environmental enrichment and voluntary exercise massively increase neurogenesis in the adult hippocampus via dissociable pathways. *Hippocampus, 16,* 250–260.

van Praag, H., Christie, B. R., Sejnowski, T. J., & Gage, F. H. (1999). Running enhances neurogenesis, learning, and long-term potentiation in mice. *Proceedings of the National Academy of Sciences of the United States of America, 96,* 13427–13431.

van Praag, H., Kempermann, G., & Gage, F. H. (1999). Running increases cell proliferation and neurogenesis in the adult mouse dentate gyrus. *Nature Neuroscience, 2*, 266–270.

van Praag, H., Shubert, T., Zhao, C., & Gage, F. H. (2005). Exercise enhances learning and hippocampal neurogenesis in aged mice. *Journal of Neuroscience, 25*, 8680–8685.

Rao, M. S., & Shetty, A. K. (2004). Efficacy of doublecortin as a marker to analyse the absolute number and dendritic growth of newly generated neurons in the adult dentate gyrus. *European Journal of Neuroscience, 19*, 234–246.

Rapp, P. R., & Gallagher, M. (1996). Preserved neuron number in the hippocampus of aged rats with spatial learning deficits. *Proceedings of the National Academy of Sciences of the United States of America, 93*, 9926–9930.

Redick, T. S., Shipstead, Z., Harrison, T. L., Hicks, K. L., Fried, D. E., Hambrick, D. Z., et al. (2013). No evidence of intelligence improvement after working memory training: a randomized, placebo-controlled study. *Journal of Experimental Psychology: General, 142*, 359–379.

Redila, V. A., & Christie, B. R. (2006). Exercise-induced changes in dendritic structure and complexity in the adult hippocampal dentate gyrus. *Neuroscience, 137*, 1299–1307.

van de Rest, O., van der Zwaluw, N. L., Tieland, M., Adam, J. J., Hiddink, G. J., van Loon, L. J., et al. (2014). Effect of resistance-type exercise training with or without protein supplementation on cognitive functioning in frail and pre-frail elderly: secondary analysis of a randomized, double-blind, placebo-controlled trial. *Mechanisms of Ageing and Development, 136–137*, 85–93.

Rhodes, J. S., Garland, T., Jr., & Gammie, S. C. (2003). Patterns of brain activity associated with variation in voluntary wheel-running behavior. *Behavioral Neuroscience, 117*, 1243–1256.

Ribak, C. E., & Dashtipour, K. (2002). Neuroplasticity in the damaged dentate gyrus of the epileptic brain. *Progress in Brain Research, 136*, 319–328.

Rodriguez, J. J., & Verkhratsky, A. (2011). Neurogenesis in Alzheimer's disease. *Journal of Anatomy, 219*, 78–89.

Rowe, G. C., El-Khoury, R., Patten, I. S., Rustin, P., & Arany, Z. (2012). PGC-1alpha is dispensable for exercise-induced mitochondrial biogenesis in skeletal muscle. *PLoS One, 7*, e41817. http://dx.doi.org/10.1371/journal.pone.0041817.

Sahay, A., Scobie, K. N., Hill, A. S., O'Carroll, C. M., Kheirbek, M. A., Burghardt, N. S., et al. (2011). Increasing adult hippocampal neurogenesis is sufficient to improve pattern separation. *Nature, 472*, 66–70.

Samorajski, T., Delaney, C., Durham, L., Ordy, J. M., Johnson, J. A., & Dunlap, W. P. (1985). Effect of exercise on longevity, body weight, locomotor performance, and passive-avoidance memory of C57BL/6J mice. *Neurobiological Ageing, 6*, 17–24.

Seo, D. Y., Lee, S. R., Kim, N., Ko, K. S., Rhee, B. D., & Han, J. (2014). Humanized animal exercise model for clinical implication. *Pflugers Archiv: European Journal of Physiology, 466*, 1673–1687.

Shin, M. S., Ko, I. G., Kim, S. E., Kim, B. K., Kim, T. S., Lee, S. H., et al. (2013). Treadmill exercise ameliorates symptoms of methimazole-induced hypothyroidism through enhancing neurogenesis and suppressing apoptosis in the hippocampus of rat pups. *International Journal of Developmental Neuroscience, 31*, 214–223.

Sloviter, R. S. (1994). The functional organization of the hippocampal dentate gyrus and its relevance to the pathogenesis of temporal lobe epilepsy. *Annals of Neurology, 35*, 640–654.

Snyder, J. S., Glover, L. R., Sanzone, K. M., Kamhi, J. F., & Cameron, H. A. (2009). The effects of exercise and stress on the survival and maturation of adult-generated granule cells. *Hippocampus, 19*, 898–906.

Song, H. J., Stevens, C. F., & Gage, F. H. (2002). Neural stem cells from adult hippocampus develop essential properties of functional CNS neurons. *Nature Neuroscience, 5*, 438–445.

Steiner, B., Kronenberg, G., Jessberger, S., Brandt, M. D., Reuter, K., & Kempermann, G. (2004). Differential regulation of gliogenesis in the context of adult hippocampal neurogenesis in mice. *Glia, 46*, 41–52.

Swallow, J. G., Garland, T., Jr., Carter, P. A., Zhan, W. Z., & Sieck, G. C. (1998). Effects of voluntary activity and genetic selection on aerobic capacity in house mice (Mus domesticus). *Journal of Applied Physiology, 84*, 69–76.

Swallow, J. G., Koteja, P., Carter, P. A., & Garland, T., Jr. (2001). Food consumption and body composition in mice selected for high wheel-running activity. *Journal of Comparative Physiology. B, Biochemical, Systemic and Environmental Physiology, 171*, 651–659.

Tamaki, T., Uchiyama, S., & Nakano, S. (1992). A weight-lifting exercise model for inducing hypertrophy in the hindlimb muscles of rats. *Medicine and Science in Sports and Exercise, 24*, 881–886.

Ten Brinke, L. F., Bolandzadeh, N., Nagamatsu, L. S., Hsu, C. L., Davis, J. C., & Miran-Khan, K. (2015). Aerobic exercise increases hippocampal volume in older women with probable mild cognitive impairment: a 6-month randomised controlled trial. *British Journal of Sports Medicine, 49*, 248–254.

Thanos, P. K., Tucci, A., Stamos, J., Robison, L., Wang, G. J., Anderson, B. J., et al. (2010). Chronic forced exercise during adolescence decreases cocaine conditioned place preference in Lewis rats. *Behavioural Brain Research, 215*, 77–82.

Thuret, S., Toni, N., Aigner, S., Yeo, G. W., & Gage, F. H. (2009). Hippocampus-dependent learning is associated with adult neurogenesis in MRL/MpJ mice. *Hippocampus, 19*, 658–669.

Trejo, J. L., Carro, E., & Torres-Aleman, I. (2001). Circulating insulin-like growth factor I mediates exercise-induced increases in the number of new neurons in the adult hippocampus. *Journal of Neuroscience, 21*, 1628–1634.

Uysal, N., Kiray, M., Sisman, A., Camsari, U., Gencoglu, C., Baykara, B., et al. (2015). Effects of voluntary and involuntary exercise on cognitive functions, and VEGF and BDNF levels in adolescent rats. *Biotechnic and Histochemistry, 90*, 55–68.

Van der Borght, K., Havekes, R., Bos, T., Eggen, B. J., & Van der Zee, E. A. (2007). Exercise improves memory acquisition and retrieval in the Y-maze task: relationship with hippocampal neurogenesis. *Behavioral Neuroscience, 121*, 324–334.

Vanderwolf, C. H. (1969). Hippocampal electrical activity and voluntary movement in the rat. *Electroencephalography and Clinical Neurophysiology, 26*, 407–418.

Varela-Nallar, L., Aranguiz, F. C., Abbott, A. C., Slater, P. G., & Inestrosa, N. C. (2010). Adult hippocampal neurogenesis in aging and Alzheimer's disease. *Birth Defects Research Part C, 90*, 284–296.

Voss, M. W., Vivar, C., Kramer, A. F., & van Praag, H. (2013). Bridging animal and human models of exercise-induced brain plasticity. *Trends in Cognitive Sciences, 17*, 525–544.

West, M. J., Slomianka, L., & Gundersen, H. J. G. (1991). Unbiased stereological estimation of the total number of neurons in the subdivisions of the rat hippocampus using the optical fractionator. *The Anatomical Record, 231*, 482–497.

Woods, J. A., Davis, J. M., Mayer, E. P., Ghaffar, A., & Pate, R. R. (1994). Effects of exercise on macrophage activation for antitumor cytotoxicity. *Journal of Applied Physiology, 76*, b2177–2185.

Wrann, C. D., White, J. P., Salogiannnis, J., Laznik-Bogoslavski, D., Wu, J., Ma, D., et al. (2013). Exercise induces hippocampal BDNF through a PGC-1alpha/FNDC5 pathway. *Cell Metabolism, 18*, 649–659.

Wu, C. W., Chang, Y. T., Yu, L., Chen, H. I., Jen, C. J., Wu, S. Y., et al. (2008). Exercise enhances the proliferation of neural stem cells and neurite growth and survival of neuronal progenitor cells in dentate gyrus of middle-aged mice. *Journal of Applied Physiology, 105*, 1585–1594.

Yau, S. Y., Lau, B. W., Tong, J. B., Wong, R., Ching, Y. P., Qiu, G., et al. (2011). Hippocampal neurogenesis and dendritic plasticity support running-improved spatial learning and depression-like behaviour in stressed rats. *PLoS One, 6*, e24263. http://dx.doi.org/10.1371/journal.pone.0024263.

Beyond the Catecholamines Hypothesis for an Acute Exercise–Cognition Interaction: A Neurochemical Perspective

Terry McMorris[1], Anthony Turner[2], Beverley J. Hale[1], John Sproule[2]

[1]Department of Sport and Exercise Science, University of Chichester, Chichester, West Sussex, UK;
[2]Institute of Sport, PE and Health Sciences, University of Edinburgh, Edinburgh, Scotland, UK

INTRODUCTION

As we saw in Chapter 1, early research into the effect of acute exercise on cognition was atheoretical. The first to propose a theoretical underpinning was Colin Davey (1973). Davey argued that exercise was a stressor and, as such, would have the same effect on cognition as other stressors, namely an inverted-U effect, as suggested by Yerkes and Dodson's (1908) arousal–performance theory. Although Davey's hypothesis was based in cognitive psychology, he was aware that the exercise-induced changes in arousal were due to a body–brain interaction, which could be best explained by neuroscience (C.P. Davey, personal communication, August, 1994). Davey's research report in *Ergonomics* (1973, Vol. 16) was accompanied by a theoretical paper by Cooper (1973), a neuropsychologist. In this paper, Cooper proposed what we might term the "catecholamines hypothesis," in which he argued that circulating peripheral plasma catecholamines induced increases in concentrations of the neurotransmitters dopamine and noradrenaline in the brain. In turn, the brain catecholamines were responsible for increases in arousal by activating the reticular formation. In this chapter, we begin by outlining Cooper's hypothesis, followed by examination of the current theoretical rationale for the catecholamines hypothesis and whether or not the empirical evidence provides much support for the hypothesis. Then we look at the possible contributions of other neurochemicals, especially the hypothalamic–pituitary–adrenal cortex (HPA) axis hormones and brain-derived neurotrophic factor

(BDNF). We finish by examining the extent to which empirical evidence supports the hypothesis that there is an interaction between acute exercise–neurochemicals and cognition.

Cooper's (1973) Original Catecholamines Hypothesis for an Acute Exercise–Cognition Interaction

Cooper (1973) claimed that acute exercise resulted in activation of the reticular formation, which at the time was also known as the "isodendritic core." Although research into the role of the reticular formation was limited in 1973, Cooper provided sound evidence to show that increased activation induced increases in arousal. He then went on to develop an argument hypothesizing an interrelationship between acute exercise and activation of the reticular formation.

Cooper (1973) presented evidence from animal studies (Gordon, Spector, Sjoerdsma, & Udenfriend, 1966; Reis & Fuxe, 1968, 1969) to show that arousal was related to increases in brain concentrations of noradrenaline, which activates the reticular formation (Kasamatsu, 1970; Podvoll & Goodman, 1967). He also pointed to evidence of increased peripheral concentrations of noradrenaline during exercise (Vendsalu, 1960). He argued that, although catecholamines do not readily cross the blood–brain barrier, if circulating concentrations were high, the blood–brain barrier would be compromised. This argument was supported by the research, with mice, of Samorajaski and Marks (1962), who found that high concentrations of catecholamines were able to cross the blood–brain barrier in the median eminence at the base of the hypothalamus and in the anterior pituitary gland. Moreover, based on the work of Rushmer, Smith, and Lasher (1960), he stated that feedforward, due to anticipation of undertaking exercise, led to the initiation of the sympathoadrenal system (SAS) by the hypothalamus, which would also induce increased activation of the reticular formation and hence higher levels of arousal.

Cooper (1973) ended his theoretical review by positing hypotheses for the inverted-U effect of acute exercise on cognitive functioning. According to Cooper, at low levels of arousal, brain activity is limited because the appropriate sequence of neuronal activation cannot be obtained as a result of neurons being at such a low level of excitation that they cannot be stimulated to an adequate level of summation. Hence, cognitive performance is poor. Moderate intensity exercise and the resultant increase in arousal means that excitation levels are such that summation is facilitated and the appropriate sequence occurs. However, as arousal rises still further, neurons which are not part of the pattern are also activated, producing neural "noise" and hence poor cognitive performance.

CATECHOLAMINES AND THE ACUTE EXERCISE–COGNITION INTERACTION

Figure 1 provides an outline of the process whereby catecholamines are synthesized. The precursor of catecholamines synthesis is the aromatic amino acid tyrosine, which is either taken directly from food or is formed in the liver by the hydroxylation of phenylalanine. Thus, it is readily available peripherally and is transported across the blood–brain barrier by the facilitative transporter L1 (Hawkins, O'Kane, Simpson, & Viña, 2006). It should be noted that tyrosine hydroxylase is the rate-limiting enzyme in the whole process (Fernstrom & Fernstrom, 2007).

Plasma Catecholamines Responses to Exercise: Effects of Intensity and Duration

Given that the catecholamines hypothesis for an interaction between acute exercise and cognition is dependent on the interaction between peripheral plasma concentrations of catecholamines and the brain, it is necessary first to examine how different intensities and durations of exercise affect plasma concentrations. During

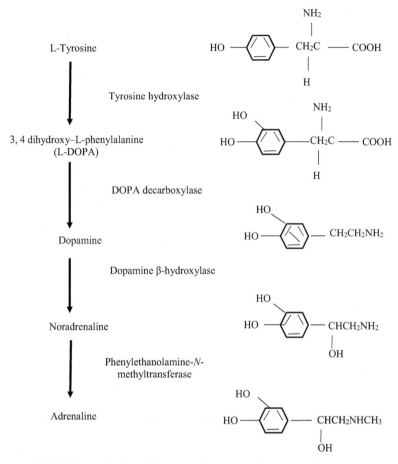

FIGURE 1   Outline of the process for the synthesis of catecholamines.

and even immediately before exercise, the hypothalamus and brainstem initiate activation of the SAS, which is part of the autonomic nervous system (ANS). This results in the release of catecholamines at the postganglionic cells of those neurons that require activating or inhibiting. Increases in plasma catecholamines are often seen pre-exercise (Mason et al., 1973). This pre-exercise increase in plasma concentrations will probably be due partially to feedforward preparing the organism for action.

Incremental Exercise to Exhaustion

Incremental exercise to exhaustion is used in tests of maximal volume of oxygen uptake ($\dot{V}O_{2MAX}$), maximum power output ($\dot{W}_{MAX}$), and maximum aerobic power (MAP). Typically, participants begin cycling on an ergometer or running on a treadmill at a low resistance. The resistance is increased at selected time intervals. Increments are decided pretest and maximum is deemed to be reached when the individual cannot maintain the workload or, in the case of $\dot{V}O_{2MAX}$, when oxygen uptake remains steady despite increases in workload. The actual duration will depend on the fitness of the participant and the increments chosen, but to reach maximum normally takes <15 min.

Peripherally, during low-intensity exercise, plasma catecholamines concentrations remain low and show only small, nonsignificant increases. However, in incremental exercise, when we plot plasma concentrations of adrenaline and noradrenaline against exercise intensity, concentrations rise exponentially (Green, Hughson, Orr, & Ranney, 1983). Green et al. termed the points at which there is a significant rise in concentrations, the adrenaline threshold (T_A) and noradrenaline threshold (T_{NA}). T_{NA} occurs when the intensity induces hypoglycemia, while T_A is triggered by a decline in hepatic glucose concentrations. T_A and T_{NA} generally show moderate to high correlations (Podolin, Munger, & Mazzeo, 1991), therefore we will call them the catecholamines thresholds (T_{CATS}) for brevity. It is generally thought that intensity needs to be ~75% $\dot{V}O_{2MAX}$ (Podolin et al., 1991), which according to Arts and Kuipers (1994) equates to ~65% $\dot{W}_{MAX}$, but there are large interindividual variations (Urhausen, Weiler, Coen, & Kindermann, 1994). Moreover, blood lactate concentrations follow a similar exponential profile and the lactate threshold (T_{LA}) also shows moderate to high correlations with T_{NA} and T_A (Podolin et al., 1991). If exercise intensity increases beyond the threshold, plasma catecholamines concentrations continue to rise and soon reach very high levels. At these suprathreshold levels the individual is said to be undertaking heavy exercise. Borer (2003) determined heavy exercise as being >80% $\dot{V}O_{2MAX}$. This choice of 80% $\dot{V}O_{2MAX}$ by Borer is based on endocrinological changes in the periphery.

Moderate to Long Duration, Low and Moderate Intensity Exercise

As we saw above, when exercise intensity is low (<40% $\dot{V}O_{2MAX}$) and for a short duration, there is very little effect on plasma concentrations of catecholamines. Hodgetts, Coppack, Frayn, and Hockaday (1991) showed that for exercise at 30% $\dot{V}O_{2MAX}$, if the duration is >60 min, there can be a small rise in catecholamines concentrations but even after 240 min concentrations are unlikely to be as high as those at T_{CATS}. However, when moderate intensity exercise is below T_{CATS},

but the duration is ≥30 min, concentrations can rise above those at T_{CATS} (Hodgetts et al., 1991).

Acute Exercise and Increases in Brain Catecholamines Concentrations

Earlier, we examined Cooper's (1973) rationale for an interaction between plasma and brain concentrations of catecholamines. Cooper believed that although catecholamines do not readily cross the blood–brain barrier, if circulating concentrations were high, the blood–brain barrier could be compromised. However, it is now generally accepted that circulating adrenaline and noradrenaline activate β-adrenoreceptors on the afferent vagus nerve, which runs from the abdomen through the chest, neck, and head, and terminates in the nucleus tractus solitarii (NTS) within the blood–brain barrier. The excitatory neurotransmitter glutamate mediates synaptic communication between the vagal afferents and the NTS, allowing noradrenergic cells in the NTS, which project into the locus coeruleus, to stimulate noradrenaline synthesis and release to other parts of the brain (McGaugh, Cahill, & Roozendaal, 1996; Miyashita & Williams, 2006). This probably also affects brain dopamine concentrations, as Devoto, Flore, Saba, Fà, and Gessa (2005) showed that electrical stimulation of the rat locus coeruleus resulted in increased concentrations of dopamine and one of its metabolites, 3,4-dihydroxyphenylacetic acid (DOPAC). Moreover, Grenhoff and associates (Grenhoff, Nisell, Ferré, Aston-Jones, & Svensson, 1993; Grenhoff & Svensson, 1993) have shown that stimulation of the α_1-adrenoreceptor by noradrenaline release from the locus coeruleus potentiates the firing of dopamine neurons in the ventral tegmental area. Velásquez-Martinez, Vázquez-Torres, and Jiménez-Riveira (2012) claimed that this was probably due to α_1-adrenoreceptor activation inducing enhanced glutamate release, which affects the excitability of dopamine neurons.

While the activation of the vagal/NTS pathway appears to be a sound explanation for acute exercise-induced increases in brain concentrations of catecholamines coming directly from the periphery, Cooper's (1973) arguments concerning indirect stimulation of increased synthesis and release of catecholamines appear to have some merit. Feedback via the ANS to the hypothalamus via the thalamus, reticular formation and limbic system, concerning stress on the cardiorespiratory system, pain and glycogen depletion probably triggers a response by the hypothalamus, which results in increased synthesis and release of catecholamines centrally. Release centrally may well also be due to the individual perceiving the situation as being unpredictable and/or one in which he/she is not in control (Mason, 1975a, 1975b), which has been shown to induce the release of catecholamines in plasma in humans (Sothmann, Hart, Horn, & Gustafson, 1991) and in the brain in animals (Wann, Audet, & Anisman, 2010). In other words, undertaking exercise has the same effect as other stressors as well as the extra dimension of vagal/NTS pathway activation. Moreover, stress causes activation of the HPA axis, which interacts with the SAS resulting in further synthesis of catecholamines (van Stegeren, Roozenddaal, Kindt, Wolf, & Joëls, 2010).

Empirical Evidence for an Acute Exercise-Induced Increase in Brain Concentrations of Dopamine and Noradrenaline

Research into the effect of acute exercise on brain concentrations of catecholamines has been largely in animal studies. The reliance on animal studies is unavoidable due to the presence of the blood–brain barrier. Catecholamines do not readily cross the blood–brain barrier (Cornford, Braun, Oldendorf, & Hill, 1982), therefore plasma concentrations of catecholamines are almost entirely the result of peripheral activity only. At best they are only capable of indicating that similar changes in concentrations may have taken place in the brain. Obviously, it is not possible to directly test brain concentrations in humans. However, in animals, microdialysis has been widely used and provides good data (see Meeusen, Piacentini, & De Meirleir, 2001, for a description of the microdialysis process).

Animal studies provide some evidence for increased brain concentrations of noradrenaline and dopamine as well as their metabolites during and immediately following exercise. For both noradrenaline and dopamine, however, results have been far from unequivocal. The effect of acute exercise on whole brain concentrations of noradrenaline in animals has shown either a decrease in concentrations or no significant effect (see Meeusen & De Meirleir, 1995; Meeusen et al., 2001). More recently, Kitaoka et al. (2010) demonstrated increased noradrenaline concentrations in the hypothalamus, but Goekint et al. (2012) found no significant effect on noradrenaline concentrations in the hippocampus. There appears to be some consistency for dopamine results. Research has demonstrated increased dopamine concentrations particularly in the brainstem and hypothalamus during and immediately following acute exercise (see Meeusen et al., 2001; Meeusen & De Meirleir, 1995, for reviews). However, Hattori, Naoi, and Nishino (1994) found that this only occurred when intensity increased to a moderate level. Recently, Kitaoka et al. (2010) supported previous findings by showing increased dopamine concentrations in the hypothalamus, while Goekint et al. (2012) found increased dopamine concentrations in the hippocampus. It should be noted that dopamine concentrations at fatigue have been shown to be similar to those at rest (Bailey, Davis, & Ahlborn, 1993a). Davis, Alderson, and Welsh (2000) claimed that this was due to an interaction with 5-hydroxytryptamine (5-HT), which shows high concentrations at fatigue, particularly following long-duration exercise (Bailey, Davis, & Ahlborn, 1993b). The decarboxylation of 3,4-dihydroxy-L-phenylalanine (L-DOPA) to dopamine requires the presence of aromatic amino acid decarboxylase

(AADC); however, AADC is also involved in the conversion of 5-hydroxytryptophan (5-HTP) into 5-HT. Whether AADC acts on 5-HTP or L-DOPA depends on a variety of factors including pH optima, the presence of cofactors, and substrate concentrations (Frazer & Hensler, 1999). It would appear that following heavy exercise particularly of a long duration, conditions favor the decarboxylation of 5-HTP.

Animal studies have also shown increases in brain concentrations of the noradrenaline metabolite 3-methoxy-4-hydroxyphenylglycol (MHPG) and the dopamine metabolites DOPAC and 4-hydroxy-3-methoxyphenylacetic acid, also known as homovanillic acid (HVA), suggesting increased turnover of dopamine and noradrenaline during exercise. Increased concentrations of MHPG have been found in most brain regions (Meeusen et al., 2001), while increased concentrations of DOPAC and HVA have been shown, particularly in the brainstem and hypothalamus (Hasegawa, Yazawa, Yasumatsu, Otokawa, & Aihara, 2000; Meeusen et al., 1997).

Only two studies have been attempted with humans. Wang et al. (2000) examined the effect of treadmill running on striatal dopamine release in human brain. Pre- and postexercising on a treadmill at an intensity >85% estimated maximum heart rate, participants underwent an intravenous injection of the radiotracer [11C] raclopride and positron emission tomography scans of the putamen and cerebellum were made. The authors expected to see a small but significant decrease in [11C]raclopride binding following exercise, as raclopride's low affinity for dopaminergic D_2 receptors means that increases in synaptic dopamine release affect [11C]raclopride binding. No significant effect was shown. The authors argued that this was probably due to the positron emission tomography protocol not being robust enough to highlight small changes in [11C]raclopride binding.

Dalsgaard et al. (2004) examined noradrenaline and adrenaline concentrations in cerebrospinal fluid (CSF) by lumbar puncture and the arterial to internal jugular venous difference (a-v diff) following exercise to exhaustion. Arterial concentrations of noradrenaline and adrenaline showed large increases but the a-v diff was not affected significantly, suggesting that there was no uptake by the brain. Exercise increased the CSF concentrations of noradrenaline only. The authors argued that the CSF increase in noradrenaline concentrations was probably due to activity in the locus coeruleus. This study provides some support for acute exercise inducing increased central nervous system (CNS) concentrations of noradrenaline in humans as a result of vagal/NTS activity.

From the evidence outlined in this section, it would appear that there is support for acute exercise increasing brain concentrations of noradrenaline and dopamine. Results are not unequivocal, which is not surprising as exercise intensities and durations varied greatly.

Catecholamines and Cognition at Rest and during Exercise

Noradrenaline, dopamine, and, to a much lesser extent, adrenaline act as neurotransmitters in the brain. Once synthesized they are held in vesicles and, when released, innervate what have been termed the noradrenergic and dopaminergic pathways. The dopaminergic pathway, which uses dopamine as the neurotransmitter, in fact consists of several pathways: we will focus on those that are the most important with regard to our review. Dopamine neurons in the zona compacta of the substantia nigra send axons to the caudate nucleus and putamen of the corpus striatum, which is part of the basal ganglia. In fact, 80% of the brain's dopamine is found in the corpus striatum. Neurons in the ventral tegmental area serve the frontal cortex, cingulate cortex, septum, nucleus acumbens, and olfactory tubercle (see Figure 2(A)). The noradrenergic pathway uses both noradrenaline and adrenaline as neurotransmitters. Noradrenaline neurons are mainly found in the locus coeruleus and lateral tegmental field. Cell bodies in

(A)

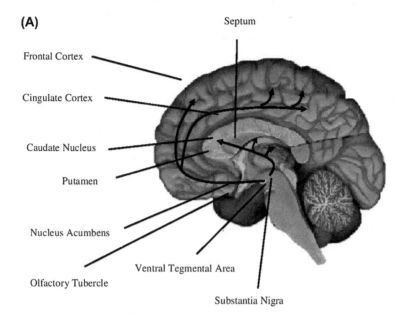

Septum

Frontal Cortex

Cingulate Cortex

Caudate Nucleus

Putamen

Nucleus Acumbens

Ventral Tegmental Area

Olfactory Tubercle

Substantia Nigra

(B)

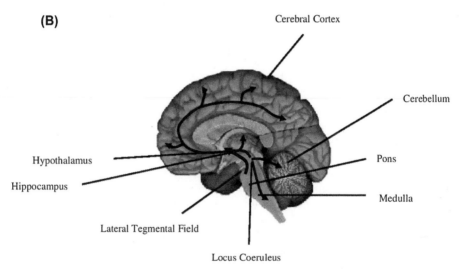

Cerebral Cortex

Cerebellum

Hypothalamus

Pons

Hippocampus

Medulla

Lateral Tegmental Field

Locus Coeruleus

FIGURE 2 (A) Schematic representation of the dopaminergic pathway. (B) Schematic representation of the noradrenergic pathway.

the locus coeruleus serve the dorsal bundle and have axons ending in the spinal cord, cerebellum, entire cerebral cortex, and hippocampus. Neurons in the lateral tegmental field are part of the ventral bundle and serve the brainstem and hypothalamus. The adrenaline cell bodies found in the pons and medulla also serve the brainstem and hypothalamus (see Figure 2(B)).

Once the neurotransmitters have been released by exocytosis, they are taken up by receptors. There are two families of dopamine receptors, D_1-like receptors (D_1 and D_5) and

D_2-like receptors (D_2, D_3, and D_4). D_1-like receptors couple to G_s and G_{olf} guanosine triphosphate (GTP)-binding proteins and stimulate cyclic adenosine monophosphate (cAMP) activation, which amplifies the effects of neuronal activity. However, D_2-like receptors inhibit cAMP activity by coupling with G_i/G_o GTP-binding proteins (El-Ghundi, O'Dowd, & George, 2007). The main receptors for noradrenaline are α_1-adrenergic (α_{1A}, α_{1B}, α_{1D}), α_2-adrenergic (α_{2A}, α_{2B}, α_{2C}), and β-adrenergic (β_1, β_2, β_3) receptors. Take-up by the β-receptors stimulates the action of the enzyme adenyl cyclase, which is necessary for the synthesis of cAMP and amplifies the effects of neuronal activity. However, take-up by the α_1-receptors results in reduced neuronal firing by phosphatidylinositol-protein kinase C intracellular signaling pathway activation. Furthermore, take-up by α_2-receptors inhibits cAMP activation in the same way as with D_2-like receptors.

Catecholamines, Stress Level, Task Type, and Cognition

Dopamine and noradrenaline work together to control cognition but their efficiency is affected by stress levels. When stress levels are low, performance is comparatively poor because, as Cooper (1973) pointed out, at low levels of arousal the appropriate sequence of neuronal activation cannot be obtained as neurons cannot be stimulated to an adequate level of summation. This would be the case when at rest and during low intensity exercise (<40% $\dot{V}O_{2MAX}$). When stress rises to a moderate level, brain catecholamines concentrations rise and there is increased firing of the high affinity α_{2A}-receptors by noradrenaline (Roth, Tam, Ida, Yang, & Deutch, 1988), which increases the strength of neural signaling in the preferred direction by inhibiting cAMP activation (Deutch & Roth, 1990). Similarly, the high-affinity D_1-receptors are activated by dopamine, which dampens the "noise" by inhibiting firing to nonpreferred stimuli (Finlay, Zigmond, & Abercrombie, 1995). So dopamine and noradrenaline working together improve the signal to "noise" ratio. This is what we would expect during moderate intensity exercise and should lead to optimal performance but this may be moderated by task type. The tasks used in acute exercise–catecholamines–cognition interaction research can be divided into three different types, working memory, attention/perception, and long-term memory tasks. Elsewhere, we have shown significant differences in how acute exercise affects these types of tasks differently and, perhaps more importantly, how an exercise intensity × duration × task-type interaction also has a moderating effect (McMorris & Hale, 2012; McMorris, Sproule, Turner, & Hale, 2011). Below, we will highlight some of the ways in which this happens.

WORKING MEMORY TASKS

According to Baddeley (1986), working memory consists of three separate but interdependent parts, the central executive mechanism, and two short-term memory systems, the phonological loop and the visuospatial sketchpad (Baddeley, 1986). The phonological loop is responsible for the encoding of acoustic and verbal information. The visuospatial sketchpad has the same role as the phonological loop except that it processes visual and visuospatial information. The role of the central executive is to oversee and control the whole process. It ensures that there is integration of perceptual input and comparison of the present situation (held in short-term memory) with recalled information from long-term memory. Short-term memory is only a subsystem of working memory when its aim is to provide information for completion of a more complex task, one which requires central executive control (Miyake & Shah, 1999).

Miyake, Friedman, Emerson, Witzki, and Howerter (2000) described the central executive process as involving several functions, which include shifting between tasks or mental sets; updating and monitoring working memory representations, which involves the removal of redundant information and replacing it with new, relevant information; inhibition of prepotent responses; planning; and the coordination of multiple tasks. Leh, Petrides, and Strafella (2010) provided other examples, for example, abstract thinking, cognitive flexibility, and selecting relevant sensory information. From a neuroscience perspective, of more importance is the fact that evidence of working memory activity is provided by positron emission tomography and functional magnetic resonance imaging research, which has identified specific neural pathways in the brain for the different processes involved in working memory. The phonological loop involves the lateral frontal and inferior parietal lobes of the left hemisphere. The visuospatial sketchpad seems to be situated in the parieto-occipital region of both hemispheres, although it is more active in the right hemisphere (Barbas, 2000; Leh et al., 2010). These two pathways are particularly important in short-memory retention and recall. Central executive tasks primarily activate the prefrontal cortex but also draw on information recalled from other parts of the brain (see Barbas, 2000; Leh et al., 2010, for reviews).

Animal studies have shown that working memory tasks are facilitated by increased α_{2A}-adrenoreceptor and D_1-receptor activation during moderate levels of stress (Arnsten, 2009, 2011). Given the nature of the processes involved in working memory tasks, which require perception of the signal among a great deal of noise, this is not surprising. However, these tasks have also been shown to be the most susceptible to the negative effects of high levels of stress. When stress levels are high, noradrenaline and dopamine concentrations become excessive. The excess noradrenaline activates the lower affinity α_1- and β-adrenoreceptors (Roth et al., 1988). Activation of α_1-adrenoreceptors results in reduced neuronal firing in the prefrontal cortex, while excessive stimulation of D_1-receptors and β-adrenoreceptors induces excess activity of the secondary messenger cAMP, which dampens all neuronal activity, thus weakening the signal to "noise" ratio (Arnsten, 2011). Hence, during heavy exercise, we expect to see cognitive performance of working memory tasks inhibited.

However, as Arnsten pointed out, some working memory processes are actually enhanced by high levels of stress.

Eagle et al. (2010, as cited by Arnsten, 2011), showed that performance of the stop signal task by rats was facilitated by increased activation of β-receptors, while attentional set shifting has been found to benefit from activation of α_1-receptors (Bondi, Jett, & Morilak, 2010; Robbins & Roberts, 2007). The stop signal task requires stopping an ongoing movement, when a predetermined stimulus appears, and is thought to be primarily controlled by the basal ganglia in the right hemisphere (Aron, 2011). In an attentional set shifting task, the participant must switch between stimulus–response sets when the stimulus changes (Sawada et al., 2012). The key brain areas involved appear to be the dorsolateral prefrontal cortex and the posterior parietal cortex (Wager, Reading, & Jonides, 2004). Both of these tasks require the participant to abort the ongoing response and change to a predetermined response. They appear to be affected differently by stress than central executive tasks, which involve competition from other stimuli and responses (Aron, 2011; Cools, Barker, Sahakian, & Robbins, 2001). Caution must be taken when applying findings from stressors other than exercise to the effects of heavy exercise because during heavy exercise brain concentrations of HPA axis hormones are also greatly increased and appear to interact with catecholamines to affect cognition.

ATTENTION/PERCEPTION TASKS

By attention/perception tasks we mean tasks that require focusing on and/or identifying relevant stimuli then carrying out a comparatively simple, predetermined response. These are tasks such as simple and choice reaction time, visual search, and coincidence anticipation. In general the first stage of such tasks requires activation of the specific sensory region or regions involved. Information extracted from the sensory cortices is passed to the prefrontal cortex where it is integrated and interpreted. The level of integration and interpretation varies between tasks but does not include any of the processes involved in working memory tasks. As such these tasks are generally thought of as being more simple than working memory tasks.

As we have already seen, moderate levels of stress are thought to improve attention via noradrenaline stimulation of the reticular formation, while activation of α_{2A}-adrenoreceptors and D_1-receptors improves prefrontal cortex activity. Therefore, one would expect to see facilitation of performance of attention/perception tasks during and immediately following moderate intensity exercise. However, high concentrations of noradrenaline activating α_1- and β-adrenoreceptors actually increase the signal to "noise" ratio in the primary sensory cortices (Waterhouse, Moises, & Woodward, 1980, 1981) and Waterhouse, Moises, and Woodward (1998) argued that increased noradrenaline concentrations in sensory neurons enabled greater precision of the encoding of sensory information. Thus, heavy exercise may, in fact, stimulate a further improvement from moderate intensity exercise. Instead of an inverted-U effect there may be a linear improvement. However, as with working memory tasks, during heavy exercise we must be aware of the possible effects of the HPA axis hormones.

LEARNING/LONG-TERM MEMORY TASKS

The effects of acute exercise on learning, and the encoding and consolidation of long-term memory have received little attention. This is especially true of studies that have also measured catecholamines concentrations. In fact, we have only been able to find one (Winter et al., 2007). This is a little surprising since animal studies have shown that stress-induced high levels of noradrenaline, acting at β-receptors, enhance memory consolidation in the hippocampus (Hopkins & Johnston, 1988; Hu et al., 2007), as well as inducing long-term potentiation (Gelinas & Nguyen, 2005; Straube, Korz Balschun, & Frey, 2003). Moreover, Wickens, Horvitz, Costa,

and Killcross (2007) found that high concentrations of dopamine release aid the promotion of habit formation in the basal ganglia. Thus, we would expect heavy exercise to aid learning and long-term memory formation.

Summary

From the literature that we have examined so far, we can safely say that animal studies provide strong evidence for increased dopamine and noradrenaline concentrations during exercise. Research examining vagal/NTS pathway activation also demonstrates increased brain catecholamines concentrations, which explains how acute exercise-induced increases in circulating noradrenaline and adrenaline might result in increased brain concentrations despite the presence of the blood–brain barrier. Moreover, research examining the interaction between dopamine and noradrenaline, and their receptors at low, moderate, and high levels of stress also provides a strong theoretical rationale for acute exercise inducing an intensity-dependent effect on working memory tasks, a possible linear facilitation effect on attention/perception tasks, and for heavy exercise aiding learning and long-term memory consolidation. The intensity-dependent effect on working memory tasks is not likely to demonstrate an inverted-U effect but rather an inverted-J, as heavy exercise should inhibit performance compared to at rest, as well as compared to moderate intensity exercise.

HPA AXIS HORMONES AND THE EXERCISE–COGNITION INTERACTION

In this section, we examine the roles of the HPA axis hormones in the acute exercise–cognition interaction. HPA axis hormones are synthesized and released in response to stress. Stress can be physiological, for example, exercise, cold, heat, and/or psychological, like taking an examination or undertaking public speaking. Regardless of the nature of the stressor, stress results in feedback to the hypothalamus from within the brain, if the stress is purely psychological, and/or from the periphery, when the stress is solely physiological or has a physiological component. The hypothalamus initiates the synthesis of corticotropin releasing factor (CRF), often called corticotropin releasing hormone, from the prepro-*CRF* gene, a process that takes place in the paraventricular neurons (PVNs) of the hypothalamus (Vale & Rivier, 1977). CRF is secreted into the hypophyseal vessels in the median eminence, where it stimulates the synthesis and release by exocytosis of adrenocorticotropin hormone (ACTH) from its precursor preproopiomelanocortin. The nonapeptide, arginine vasopressin (AVP), also known as antidiuretic hormone, also acts as a stimulator of ACTH synthesis and release. It is primarily released from its preprohormone in response to feedback concerning osmolality of body fluids, although it is also secreted as the result of other physiological responses. AVP is synthesized by cells in the supraoptic and PVN of the hypothalamus then transported to hypophyseal vessels in the median eminence.

Following synthesis, ACTH passes into the zona fasciculata of the adrenal cortex where it stimulates the synthesis and secretion of cortisol in humans and corticosterone in rodents. The precursor of cortisol is cholesterol. In the adrenals, stored, esterified cholesterol is hydrolyzed and free cholesterol is transported from storage vacuoles to the outer mitochondria. Steroidogenic acute regulatory protein mediates transfer to the inner mitochondrial membrane. Cholesterol is then converted to Δ^5-pregnenolone catalyzed by the enzyme P-450$_{SCC}$. Within the endoplasmic reticulum, Δ^5-pregnenolone is converted to 11-deoxycortisol catalyzed by 17-hydroxylase, 3β-ol-dehydrogenase, and 21-hydroxylase. 11-Deoxycortisol is transferred

back to the mitochondria and hydroxylated by 11-hydroxylase to cortisol, which diffuses from the cell (Brandenberger et al., 1980).

Brain HPA Axis Hormones during Exercise

During exercise, in the periphery, cortisol plays major roles in glucose production from proteins, the facilitation of fat metabolism and muscle function, and the maintenance of blood pressure (Deuster et al., 1989). ACTH, which is synthesized in the gastrointestinal tract as well as in the pituitary, also plays a role in lipolysis (Borer, 2003). Research examining exercise-induced changes in plasma and salivary ACTH and cortisol concentrations strongly suggests that, although the HPA axis hormones undergo circadian rhythms, normal concentrations are sufficient for efficient performance unless the exercise is heavy or of moderate intensity but carried out for long periods. Generally speaking, exercise needs to be ≥80% $\dot{V}O_{2MAX}$ for it to induce increases in plasma and salivary concentrations of ACTH and cortisol (De Vries, Bernards, De Rooij, & Koppeschaar, 2000; Hill et al., 2008). While exercise of <80% $\dot{V}O_{2MAX}$ has needed to be of at least 45 min in duration to affect plasma and salivary concentrations of ACTH and cortisol (Bridge, Weller, Rayson, & Jones, 2003; Shojaei, Farajov, & Jafari, 2011).

Centrally, rodent studies have shown evidence of increases in CRF messenger ribonucleic acid (mRNA) expression in the PVN immediately following exercise (Jiang et al., 2004; Kawashima et al., 2004; Yanagita, Amemiya, Suzuki, & Kita, 2007). Thus, the synthesis of CRF, in the brain, would be facilitated. The situation with ACTH is more complex because researchers have focused on plasma ACTH concentrations. However, ACTH does not cross the blood–CSF barrier and CSF concentrations have been shown not to correlate with plasma concentrations (Allen, Kendall, McGilvra, & Vancura, 2011). While plasma ACTH concentrations may not correlate with CSF concentrations and hence are not directly indicative of CNS activity, studies examining the effect of nonphysical, psychological stress on plasma ACTH concentrations have demonstrated significant increases (Kudielka, Buske-Kirschbaum, Hellhammer, & Kirschbaum, 2004; Weinstein et al., 2010). Thus, some interaction must be taking place. The situation with plasma cortisol concentrations is different because cortisol does cross the blood–brain barrier, hence increased peripheral cortisol concentrations mean that there is increased cortisol availability in the brain.

So far we have focused on HPA axis responses due to peripheral requirements induced by exercise. Davis, Gass, and Bassett (1981) found that during exercise, changes in plasma cortisol concentrations had no correlation to changes in physiological demands. These authors proposed that some of the increases in cortisol concentrations are due to HPA axis activity resulting from the individual's perception of the exercise as being stressful. Moreover, evidence from animal studies that have compared plasma concentrations of corticosterone in rodents, undertaking forced compared to voluntary exercise, have found that rodents undertaking forced exercise show higher concentrations of plasma corticosterone than when undertaking voluntary exercise, even when exercise intensity and duration are comparable (Droste et al., 2003; Ke, Yip, Li, Zheng, & Tong, 2011; Yanagita et al., 2007). This suggests a central, psychologically driven stress effect.

Rodent studies examining extracellular corticosterone concentrations in the brain support the peripheral plasma results (e.g., Droste, Chandramohan, Hill, Linthorst, & Reul, 2007; Droste, Collins, Lightman, Linthorst, & Reul, 2009; Droste et al., 2008). Droste et al. (2008) demonstrated significant increases in extracellular corticosterone concentrations in the hippocampus following a severe stressor, a forced swim, and a mild stressor, being placed in a novel environment. The increase as a result of the mild stress was much less than that induced by the forced swim. Interestingly, extracellular corticosterone concentrations in the brain peaked 20 min after plasma concentrations but returned to normal at the same time as plasma concentrations. Under normal conditions hippocampal, extracellular corticosterone and plasma corticosterone concentrations change synchronously due to circadian rhythms.

HPA Axis Hormones and Cognition

Researchers examining the interaction between HPA axis hormones, acute exercise, and cognition have generally based their rationales for such an interaction on the role of these hormones during periods of stress (Grego et al., 2004; McMorris, Davranche, Jones, Hall, & Minter, 2009). As we have seen earlier, feedback to the hypothalamus concerning physiological and/or psychological stress initiates the synthesis and release of CRF, ACTH, and cortisol. However, cortisol can decrease the synthesis of CRF and ACTH by inhibiting the transcription of proopiomelanocortin and blocking the release of CRF from the hypothalamus. Activation of type I corticosteroid, or mineralocorticoid receptors (MRs), and type II, or glucocorticoid receptors (GRs), in the brain, inhibit the release of CRF (Herman, Watson, Chao, Coirini, & McEwen, 1993). This allows the maintenance of homeostasis ensuring that the individual is optimally aroused. Corticosteroid receptors in the hypothalamus and hippocampus, their amount and their uptake of cortisol play a major part in this process. When these receptors are saturated or reduced in amount, plasma ACTH and cortisol concentrations increase. Moreover, during intense exercise, especially when dehydration takes place, AVP is synthesized in the median eminence and hypersecretion of AVP into the pituitary takes place. Within the pituitary, AVP acts synergistically with CRF resulting in the hypersecretion of ACTH into the adrenals (Borer, 2003; Schmidt, Binnekade, Janszen, & Tilders, 1996). This stress-induced hypersecretion of ACTH can override negative feedback from cortisol (Genuth, 2004). When this occurs, one would expect overarousal and disruption of cognitive functioning.

Since Selye's (1956) early work, it has been widely accepted that HPA axis activity can have an effect on all kinds of performance including cognitive. The areas of the brain most likely to be affected by HPA axis hormones are those in which GR, MR, ACTH, and CRF receptors are most widely found. GR and MR are found throughout the brain but are particularly dense in the limbic system (hippocampus, septum, amygdala), hypothalamic PVN, and brainstem (De Kloet et al., 2000). ACTH receptors are also widely spread but are more dense in the hippocampus, hypothalamus, amygdala, and brainstem (Hnatowich, Queen, Stein, & LaBella, 1989). CRF receptors are also widely distributed but found particularly in the PVN, brainstem, locus coeruleus, raphe nuclei, and somatosensory cortex (Austin, Janosky, & Murphy, 2003). Given the role of the limbic system in control of arousal and emotions in general, it is not surprising to find that CRF, ACTH, and cortisol have been widely shown to have an effect on attention (Otte et al., 2007) and alertness (Vgontzas et al., 2007). The most widely studied area has, however, been the hippocampus and several studies have shown negative effects of high concentrations of cortisol on memory consolidation and recall (e.g., Abercrombie, Kalin, Thurow, Rosenkranz, & Davidson, 2003; Lupien, Gillin, & Hauger, 1999; Wolf et al., 2001). MR activation is necessary for encoding, while GR activation is required for consolidation (De Kloet, Joëls, & Holsboer, 2005).

HPA axis hormones affect cognitive functioning mostly by interacting with the SAS. In the locus coeruleus, CRF neurons innervate noradrenergic neurons and noradrenaline is released (Asbach, Schulz, & Lehnert, 2001). The effect is reciprocal, as CRF synthesis and release in the locus coeruleus can be initiated by noradrenergic neurons (Valentino, Page, & Curtis, 1991). Increased CRF concentrations will lead to increased ACTH and cortisol concentrations and several authors have shown relationships between brain release of noradrenaline and increased plasma ACTH and corticosterone concentrations in rodents (Höglund, Balm, & Winberg, 2000; Wieczorek & Dunn, 2006). Similarly, there is strong evidence for an interaction between corticosterone concentrations and dopamine release (Pruessner, Champagne, Meaney, & Dagher, 2004; Wand et al., 2007). As a result of these interactions, one would expect that heavy exercise, inducing large increases in catecholamines and HPA axis hormones concentrations in the brain, would result in overarousal and negative cognitive functioning. Moreover, given that moderate increases in HPA axis hormones have been shown to induce improvements in cognitive performance (Abercrombie et al., 2003; Lupien, Maheu, Tu, Fiocco, & Schramek, 2007), one would expect moderate intensity exercise to result in improved cognition. However, as we noted earlier, moderate intensity exercise, unless it is long duration, does not appear to affect HPA axis activity, certainly as measured by plasma concentrations of ACTH and cortisol. However, centrally there may be increases in brain CRF mRNA expression and possibly CSF ACTH concentrations, which are sufficient to induce increased noradrenaline and dopamine release. This, however, is pure conjecture and needs to be tested empirically.

Summary

Evidence from human studies shows that acute exercise induces increased plasma and salivary concentrations of cortisol, as long as the exercise is of a high intensity and/or of long duration. Given that cortisol crosses the blood–brain barrier this would mean that there would be increased cortisol concentrations in the brain. Rodent studies provide direct support for increases in corticosterone (e.g., Droste et al., 2007, 2009) in the brain during acute exercise as well as increased CRF mRNA expression (Yanagita et al., 2007).

Thus, theoretically one would expect negative effects on cognition immediately following and during heavy exercise or moderate intensity exercise of a long duration.

BRAIN-DERIVED NEUROTROPHIC FACTOR

As BDNF is covered in detail in Chapter 8, here we will merely provide an outline of its synthesis, release, and properties. BDNF is a protein and a member of the neurotrophic family. It is widely distributed throughout the CNS but is particularly well represented in the hippocampus, neocortex, cerebellum, striatum, and amygdala (Binder & Scharfman, 2004). It is also found peripherally in sensory neurons and glial cells (Knaeppen, Goekint, Heyman, & Meeusen, 2010; Matthews et al., 2009). BDNF is initially encoded by the BDNF gene to pro-BDNF, which is either proteolytically cleaved intracellularly by proconvertases and secreted as mature BDNF or secreted as pro-BDNF and then cleaved by extracellular proteases to mature BDNF (see Lessmann, Gottmann, & Malcangio, 2003, for a review). The effects of BDNF on neurogenesis and synaptic transmission, and hence learning and memory, are triggered when it binds with one of its receptors, the high-affinity tropomyosin-related kinase-B. This leads to the initiation of a number of intracellular signaling cascades, including calcium/calmodulin kinase II (CaMKII) and mitogen-activated protein kinase (MAPK), resulting in the phosphorylation of cAMP-response element binding protein (CREB) (Binder & Scharfman, 2004; Waterhouse & Xu, 2009). Activation of these signaling pathways is essential for neurogenesis and neuroplasticity, and hence learning and memory.

BDNF, Acute Exercise and Cognition

It would appear that increased synthesis and release of BDNF during exercise begins as part of the hypothalamic response to undertaking exercise, particularly in its role in regulating peripheral energy metabolism (Rothman, Griffioen, Wan, & Mattson, 2012; Wisse & Schwartz, 2003). BDNF is also involved in ANS control of cardiovascular function probably via signaling in central autonomic nuclei of the brainstem (Neeper, Gomez-Pinilla, Choi, & Cotman, 1995). While the exact mechanisms are still in question, there is little doubt that acute exercise results in increased serum and plasma concentrations of BDNF in humans. With healthy human participants, several studies have shown that bouts of acute exercise have induced significant increases in serum or plasma BDNF concentrations (Ferris, Williams, & Shen, 2007; Goekint et al., 2008; Griffin et al., 2011; Rasmussen et al., 2009; Rojas Vega et al., 2006; Tang, Chu, Hui, Helmeste, & Law, 2008; Winter et al., 2007). However, nonsignificant effects were shown by other authors (Laske et al., 2010; Ströhle et al., 2010; Zoladz et al., 2008). The possibility that intensity may have an effect cannot be ruled out. Ferris et al. (2007) demonstrated that 30 min cycling at 20% below the ventilatory threshold (VT), which is closely correlated to T_{CATS}, had no significant effect on serum BDNF concentrations; however, 30 min at 10% above VT induced increased concentrations. They also showed a significant correlation (r = 0.57, p < 0.05) between Δ BDNF serum concentrations and Δ blood lactate levels. Moreover, rodent studies provide very strong evidence that acute exercise induces increased BDNF and/or BDNF mRNA expression in the brain, in particular in the hippocampus (e.g., Berchtold, Castello, & Cotman, 2010; Cotman & Berchtold, 2002; Gomez-Pinilla, Vaynman, & Ying, 2008; Griesbach, Hovda, & Gomez-Pinilla, 2009; Huang et al., 2006; Liu et al., 2009; Neeper, Gomez-Pinilla, Choi, & Cotman, 1995). These increases were transient.

Rasmussen et al. (2009) examined the effect of a single bout of acute exercise on BDNF concentrations in humans, measuring a-v diff. They showed that both arterial and internal jugular venous BDNF concentrations increased significantly during 4 h of rowing at ~85–90% T_{LA}. The a-v diff at rest and after 4 h demonstrated an increase in release of BDNF from the brain. It should be noted that after 2 h there were no significant effects of exercise. After 1 h of recovery, release of BDNF from the brain had returned to resting levels. Moreover, Rasmussen et al. showed that ~70% of resting plasma and serum BDNF originates from the brain and during exercise there is little or no change in this percentage. Gomez-Pinilla et al. (2008) claimed that increased brain BDNF expression is probably due to the fact that the intracellular signaling cascades that it initiates, CaMKII, MAPK, and CREB, are activated during exercise (Calegari et al., 2011; Egan et al., 2010).

Empirical Evidence for the Roles of Neurochemicals in the Acute Exercise–Cognition Interaction

In this section, we examine the empirical evidence directly concerning the roles of neurochemicals during the acute exercise–cognition interaction in humans, the evidence from animal studies, and "indirect" evidence from human studies. By "indirect" evidence we mean findings from studies in which there were no direct measures of neurochemicals but in which the exercise intensities and duration were such that they allow us to make reasonable assumptions concerning, at least, peripheral concentrations of neurochemicals.

The Acute Exercise–Neurochemicals–Cognition Interaction and the Inverted-U Hypothesis

Despite the fact that evidence from animal studies strongly suggests that acute exercise increases brain concentrations of catecholamines and HPA axis hormones, and the claims that these increases will result in an inverted-U effect on cognitive functioning, few researchers have actually tested these assumptions. In fact, we were only able to find six such studies and five of these are from our laboratory (see Table 1). Only

Chmura, Nazar, and Kaciuba-Uścilko (1994) demonstrated an inverted-U effect. It is safe to say from observation of Table 1 that results are somewhat equivocal. Moreover, correlational analyses were carried out in four of the studies but results add little to the picture. Chmura et al. (1994), when comparing concentrations and performance every 2 min over a period of ~18 min, demonstrated curvilinear regression correlations between plasma noradrenaline concentrations and choice reaction time ($r = 0.94$), and plasma adrenaline and choice reaction time ($r = 0.93$). McMorris et al. (2003), using multiple regression analyses, found no significant correlations between performance on a noncompatible, choice response time task, and plasma adrenaline and noradrenaline concentrations during exercise at workloads eliciting 70% and 100% W_{MAX}. Given that the task was not significantly affected by acute exercise, this is not surprising. McMorris, Collard, Corbett, Dicks, and Swain (2008) found that Δ MHPG and Δ HVA combined were good predictors of Δ performance on the random number generation task ($R^2 \geq 0.42$) and Δ choice response time ($R^2 \geq 0.44$). Unfortunately, McMorris and colleagues did not carry out any curvilinear regressions, which would have given us more information concerning an inverted-U effect.

If we widen our review by including studies in which the inverted-U hypothesis was examined but in which there were no measures of any neurochemicals (see Chapter 1), the situation is none the clearer. However, when we isolate moderate and heavy intensity exercise, and include studies in which only moderate or heavy exercise was undertaken, the picture becomes much clearer. Furthermore, given the theory discussed earlier concerning the effects of task type on the acute exercise–neurochemicals–cognition interaction, we would not expect an inverted-U effect to be demonstrated but rather an inverted-J effect for working memory tasks, a linear improvement for attention/perception tasks, and for heavy exercise to affect memory positively.

TABLE 1   Studies examining the inverted-U hypothesis and including measures of plasma catecholamines and/or catecholamines metabolites

Authors	N	Cognitive task	Moderate intensity	Heavy intensity	Result accuracy	Result speed
Chmura et al. (1994)	22	CRT	T_{CATS}	100% $\dot{V}O_{2MAX}$	Not applicable	Inverted-U effect
McMorris et al. (1999)	9	SDM	T_A	100% $\dot{W}_{MAX}$	Nonsignificant	Mod and heavy, faster than at rest
McMorris et al. (2000)	12	SDM	T_A	100% $\dot{W}_{MAX}$	Not applicable	Nonsignificant
McMorris et al. (2003)	9	NC-CRT	70% $\dot{W}_{MAX}$	100% $\dot{W}_{MAX}$	Not applicable	Nonsignificant
McMorris et al. (2008)[a]	12	RNG	40% $\dot{W}_{MAX}$	80% $\dot{W}_{MAX}$	Not applicable	Nonsignificant
McMorris et al. (2008)[a]	12	CRT	40% $\dot{W}_{MAX}$	80% $\dot{W}_{MAX}$	Not applicable	Heavy, slower than other conditions
McMorris et al. (2009)	24	Flanker task	50% MAP	100% MAP	Heavy, less accurate than other conditions	Heavy, slower than other conditions

CRT, choice reaction time; SDM, soccer decision making; NC-CRT, noncompatible choice reaction time; RNG, random number generation; T_{CATS}, catecholamines threshold; T_A, adrenaline threshold; $\dot{W}_{MAX}$, maximum power output; MAP, maximum aerobic power; $\dot{V}O_{2MAX}$, maximum volume of oxygen uptake.
[a] Noradrenaline metabolite 3-methoxy-4-hydroxyphenylglycol and dopamine metabolite 4-hydroxyl-3-methoxyphenylacetic acid were measured.

The Acute Exercise–Neurochemicals–Cognition Interaction: Effects of Moderate Intensity Exercise

Examining the results for moderate intensity exercise outlined in Table 1, we see that only two studies (Chmura et al., 1994; McMorris et al., 1999) showed significant improvements in cognitive performance from rest. Interestingly, in both of these studies moderate intensity was classed as being at or immediately following T_{CATS}. However, McMorris, Sproule, Draper, and Child (2000) failed to demonstrate any significant effect following exercise at T_A. The response in this study included whole-body movement and this has been shown to demonstrate different results to that for purely cognitive tasks or psychomotor tasks in which movement is limited in nature (McMorris et al., 2009, 2005). In

the other studies, it is distinctly probable that the exercise intensity was below T_{CATS}, which would mean that circulating adrenaline and noradrenaline were too low to stimulate vagal/NTS pathway activity. However, given that T_{CATS} correlates highly with T_{LA} (Podolin et al., 1991) and VT (Yamamoto et al., 1991), which is the point at which ventilatory carbon dioxide shows a greater increase than ventilatory oxygen (Beaver, Wasserman, & Whipp, 1986), examination of research using these biomarkers can be useful. It will help us determine whether or not T_{CATS} is the trigger point for acute exercise-induced increases in catecholamines to significantly affect cognition.

Table 2 outlines the studies that have examined the effects of T_{LA} or VT on cognition. With speed of performance as the dependent variable, five studies out of seven (71.43%) showed

TABLE 2 Studies that have examined the effects, compared to baseline, of the lactate and ventilatory thresholds on cognition

Author(s)	N	Threshold type	Cognitive test	Result accuracy	Result speed
Davranche and McMorris (2009)	12	Ventilatory	Simon task[b]	No effect (p > 0.05)	Facilitation (p < 0.05)
Kashihara and Nakahara (2005)	6	Lactate	Choice reaction time[c]	No effect (p > 0.05)	Facilitation (p < 0.05)
Collardeau, Brisswalter, and Audiffren (2001)	11	Ventilatory	Simple reaction time[c]	Not applicable	Facilitation (p < 0.05)
McMorris, Swain, Lauder, Smith, and Kelly (2006)	12	Lactate	Choice reaction time[c]	No effect (p > 0.05)	No effect (p > 0.05)
Hyodo et al. (2012)	16	Ventilatory	Stroop task[b]	No effect (p > 0.05)	Facilitation (p < 0.05)
Chmura and Nazar (2010)	13	OBLA[a] 4 mmol/l	Choice reaction time[c]	Not applicable	Facilitation (p < 0.05)
Del Giorno et al. (2010)	13	Ventilatory	Wisconsin Card Sorting[b]	Inhibition (p < 0.05)	Not applicable

[a] OBLA, onset of blood lactate.
[b] Working memory task.
[c] Attention/perception task.

significant improvements in performance. Moreover, Chmura and Nazar (2010) showed a significant correlation of $r = 0.97$ between workload eliciting T_{LA} and the shortest reaction time. With accuracy as the dependent variable, one study demonstrated inhibition while the others showed no significant effect. Elsewhere, we (McMorris & Hale, 2012; McMorris et al., 2011) have shown that accuracy does not appear to be significantly affected by moderate intensity exercise, while speed is significantly improved.

McMorris and Hale (2012) claimed that the differences in results for accuracy and speed were due to the nature of the tasks used to measure accuracy effects. They argued that accuracy results showed a ceiling effect. Furthermore, they stated that tasks like the flanker task, the Simon task, Stroop color test, choice reaction time, and the auditory oddball test were designed to measure performance through speed of processing, which is seen as being indicative of efficiency of processing. The accuracy measures are only there to ensure that the participants remain honest and continue to process the problem fully. Basically it is to safeguard against a speed–accuracy tradeoff. It could be argued that if we wish to really test the effect of acute exercise on accuracy of cognition, we need to use different cognitive measures. This is similar to claims made by Etnier and Chang (2009), who felt that the tasks, which have been commonly used in research, are not complex enough. It could be argued that in order to examine effects on accuracy, we need to use complex, central executive tasks concerned with planning, abstract thinking, cognitive flexibility, or selecting relevant sensory information. In fact, Hung, Tsai, Chen, Wang, and Chang (2013) showed facilitative effects of 20 min exercise at 60–70% heart rate reserve on performance of the Tower of London task, a central executive task of planning.

For speed of response time, the above discussion would suggest that exercise needs to be at or above T_{CATS} in order to induce improved performance. However, when McMorris and Hale (2015) compared the mean effect size for studies at T_{CATS}, T_{LA}, and VT with those where the exercise intensity was ≥40% $\dot{V}O_{2MAX}$ but <80% $\dot{V}O_{2MAX}$, which was below the thresholds or where the thresholds had not been measured, they found no significant difference (g=0.58, SE=0.20 vs g=0.54, SE=0.11). To explain this, they pointed to the fact that during exercise at subthreshold intensities, plasma catecholamines concentrations begin to rise after ~30 min (Hodgetts et al., 1991).

In fact, Chmura, Kristztofiak, Ziemba, Nazar, and Kaciuba-Uścilko (1998) actually showed a significant increase in plasma catecholamines at 20 min for a group who exercised at 75% T_{LA}.

While the above explanation may account for subthreshold exercise of >30 min inducing improved speed of cognition, it does not explain how speed was increased in those studies in which the duration was only 10–20 min (see Table 3). To account for this, McMorris and Hale (2015), in line with Cooper's (1973) original theory, argued that feedforward and feedback would affect brain catecholamines concentrations. They pointed to the fact that pre-exercise, one often

TABLE 3   Studies[a] that have examined the effects, compared to baseline, of exercise ≥40% but <80% maximum volume of oxygen uptake ($\dot{V}O_{2MAX}$) or equivalent, and in which no measures of catecholamines, lactate or ventilatory thresholds were taken or which were at subthresholds levels

Author(s)	N	Exercise intensity and duration	Cognitive task	Result(s) accuracy	Result(s) speed
Joyce, Graydon, McMorris, and Davranche (2009)	10	40% MAP 30 min	Stop signal[f]	NS effect	Facilitation[b]
Yanagisawa et al. (2010)	20	50% $\dot{V}O_{2MAX}$ 10 min	Stroop test[f]	Not applicable	Facilitation[b]
Pesce, Cereatti et al. (2007) and Pesce, Tessitore et al. (2007)	25	60% HR_{RES} See note[c]	Visual attention switching[f]	Not applicable	Facilitation[b]
Pesce, Capranica, Tessitore, and Figura (2003)	16	60% $\dot{V}O_{2MAX}$ See note[a]	Visual attention switching[f]	Not applicable	Facilitation[b]
Hogervorst, Riedel, Jeukendrup, and Jolies (1996)	15	75% $\dot{W}_{MAX}$ 1 h	SRT[g]: CRT[g]: NC-CRT[g]: Stroop task[f]	Not applicable	SRT, NC-CRT, Stroop task facilitation[b]
Cereatti, Casella, Manganelli, and Pesce (2009)	24	60% HR_{RES} See note[a]	Visual attention switching[f]	NS effect	Facilitation[b]
Pesce, Cereatti et al. (2007) and Pesce, Tessitore et al. (2007)	48	60% HR_{RES} See note[a]	Visual attention switching[f]	Not applicable	Facilitation[b]
Pesce, Capranica, Tessitore, and Figura (2002)	16	60% $\dot{V}O_{2MAX}$ See note[c]	Visual attention switching[f]	Not applicable	Facilitation[b]

TABLE 3 Studies[a] that have examined the effects, compared to baseline, of exercise ≥40% but <80% maximum volume of oxygen uptake ($\dot{V}O_{2MAX}$) or equivalent, and in which no measures of catecholamines, lactate or ventilatory thresholds were taken or which were at subthresholds levels—cont'd

Author(s)	N	Exercise intensity and duration	Cognitive task	Result(s) accuracy	Result(s) speed
Davranche, Burle, Audiffren, and Hasbroucq (2005)	12	50% MAP See note[d]	CRT[g]	NS effect	Facilitation[b]
Davranche, Hall, and McMorris (2009)	14	50% MAP 20 min	Flanker task[f]	NS effect	Facilitation[b]
Kamijo et al. (2009)	24	50% $\dot{V}O_{2MAX}$ 20 min	Flanker task[f]	Not applicable	Facilitation[b]
Davranche, Audiffren, and Denjean (2006)	11	90% VT 17 min	CRT[g]	NS effect	Facilitation[b]
Ozymesci-Taskiran et al. (2008)	11	70% HR$_{MAX}$ 20 min	EMG RT[g]	Not applicable	Facilitation[b]
McMorris et al. (2003)	9	70% $\dot{W}_{MAX}$ See note[e]	NC-CRT[g]	Not applicable	NS effect
McMorris and Keen (1994)	12	70% $\dot{W}_{MAX}$ See note[e]	SRT[g]	Not applicable	NS effect
Pesce and Audiffren (2011)	100	60% HR$_{RES}$ 20–24 min	CRT[g]	Not applicable	Facilitation[b]
McMorris et al. (2009)	24	50% MAP 15 min	Flanker task[f]	NS effect	NS effect
Arcelin and Brisswalter (1999)	19	60% MAP 10 min	CRT[g]	Not applicable	Facilitation[b]
McMorris and Graydon (1996a)	20	70 $\dot{W}_{MAX}$ See note[e]	Soccer decision making[h]	NS effect	Facilitation[b]
McMorris and Graydon (1997) Exp 1	12	70% $\dot{W}_{MAX}$ See note[e]	Visual search[g]	Not applicable	NS effect
McMorris and Graydon (1997) Exp 2	12	70% $\dot{W}_{MAX}$ See note[e]	Soccer decision making[h]	NS effect	Facilitation[b]
McMorris and Graydon (1996b) Exp 1	10	70% $\dot{W}_{MAX}$ See note[e]	Soccer decision making[h]	NS effect	NS effect

Continued

TABLE 3　Studies[a] that have examined the effects, compared to baseline, of exercise ≥40% but <80% maximum volume of oxygen uptake ($\dot{V}O_{2MAX}$) or equivalent, and in which no measures of catecholamines, lactate or ventilatory thresholds were taken or which were at subthresholds levels—cont'd

Author(s)	N	Exercise intensity and duration	Cognitive task	Result(s) accuracy	Result(s) speed
McMorris and Graydon (1996b) Exp 2	20	70% $\dot{W}_{MAX}$ See note[e]	Soccer decision making[h]	NS effect	NS effect
Guizani et al. (2006)	12	40%, 60% $\dot{V}O_{2MAX}$ 6 min	SRT[g] CRT[g]	NS effect	40% NS effect 60% facilitation[b]
Fontana et al. (2009)	32	40%, 60% $\dot{V}O_{2MAX}$ Not reported	Soccer decision making[h]	NS effect	60% facilitation[b]
Endo et al. (2013)	13	40%, 60% $\dot{W}_{MAX}$ 15 min	Stroop task[f]	NS effect	40% facilitation[b] 60% NS effect
Nanda, Balde, and Manjunatha (2013)	10	70% HR_{RES} 30 min	Memory[f] Reasoning[f] Concentration[g] Planning[f]	Facilitation[b] except for concentration	Facilitation[b] for total time
Hogan, Matta, and Carstensen (2013)	71	50% HR_{RES} 15 min	n-back task[f]	NS effect	Facilitation[b]
Tsai et al. (2014)	40	60% $\dot{V}O_{2MAX}$ 30 min	Visuospatial attention[g]	Not applicable	Facilitation[b]
Audiffren et al. (2009)	19	90% VT 35 min	Random number generation[f]	Facilitation[b]	Not applicable
Draper, McMorris, and Parker (2010)	12	80% VT Not reported	SRT[g] CRT[g]	Not applicable	Simple RT NS effect Choice RT facilitation[b]
Hung et al. (2013)	20	60–70% HR_{RES} 20 min	Tower of London[f]	Facilitation[b]	NS effect
Travlos (2009)	12	55% $\dot{V}O_{2MAX}$ 1 h	Random number generation[f]	Facilitation[b]	Not applicable
Moore, Romine, O'Conner, and Tomporowski (2012)	15	90% VT 1 h	Central executive tasks[f]	Inhibition[b]	Inhibition[b]

TABLE 3 Studies[a] that have examined the effects, compared to baseline, of exercise ≥40% but <80% maximum volume of oxygen uptake ($\dot{V}O_{2MAX}$) or equivalent, and in which no measures of catecholamines, lactate or ventilatory thresholds were taken or which were at subthresholds levels—cont'd

Author(s)	N	Exercise intensity and duration	Cognitive task	Result(s) accuracy	Result(s) speed
Davranche and Audiffren (2004)	16	50% MAP 20 min	Attention/ discrimination task[g]	Not applicable	Facilitation[b]
Chang et al. (2011)	20	60% HR$_{RES}$ 20 min	Tower of London[f]	Facilitation[b]	Facilitation[b]
McMorris et al. (2008)	12	40% $\dot{W}_{MAX}$	Random number generation[f]	NS effect	Not applicable
		6 min	CRT[g]	Not applicable	NS effect

NS, nonsignificant (p > 0.05); MAP, maximum aerobic power; $\dot{V}O_{2MAX}$, maximum volume of oxygen uptake; HR$_{RES}$, heart rate reserve; $\dot{W}_{MAX}$, maximum power output; HR$_{MAX}$, maximum heart rate; VT, ventilatory threshold; T$_{LA}$, lactate threshold; SRT, simple reaction time; CRT, choice reaction time; NC-CRT, noncompatible choice reaction time; EMG, electromyographic.

[a] Studies were included if they were performed on healthy individuals; the exercise intervention required the activation of large muscle groups; repeated measures, within-subject design, was used; data were provided showing the intensity of the exercise with reference to a maximum or threshold; exercise intensity was based on objective measures; the range of measures for a specific intensity was not ≥10% $\dot{W}_{MAX}$ or equivalent; and the dependent variables were behavioral and objective. Studies including pharmacological treatments were not included.

[b] p < 0.05.

[c] Incremental warm-up to target heart rate followed by 3–4 min at target (total time ≈ 14 min).

[d] 3 × 14–15 min sets with 10 min rest between sets.

[e] Incremental warm-up to target resistance followed by ~2 min at target (total time ~12 min).

[f] Working memory task.

[g] Attention/perception task.

[h] Autonomic task.

sees increases in plasma catecholamines concentrations (Mason et al., 1973). This pre-exercise increase in plasma concentrations will probably be due partially to feedforward preparing the organism for action. However, within the brain there is also likely to be increased catecholamines synthesis and release due to increased reticular formation and limbic system activity as a result of anticipation of the exercise inducing stress. This is in line with Mason's (1975a, 1975b) argument that stress is induced when the individual perceives the situation as being unpredictable and/or one in which he/she is not in control. Furthermore, research using National Aeronautics and Space Administration-Task Load Index (Hart & Staveland, 1988) has demonstrated increased perceptions of stress as exercise intensity increased from rest to moderate intensities during acute exercise–cognition interaction studies (McMorris et al., 2003; Tomporowski & Ganio, 2006). Similarly, several studies (e.g., Audiffren, Tomporowski, & Zagrodnik, 2009; Del Giorno, Hall, O'Leary, Bixby, & Miller, 2010; Hyodo et al., 2012; Kamijo et al., 2009) have shown increases in rate of perceived exertion, as measured by the Borg (1973) scale. If there are increases in catecholamines concentrations due to central release as a result of perception of stress, this could result in improved cognitive functioning.

Role of BDNF

Before leaving the intensity × duration of exercise moderating variable, we should note that Ferris et al. (2007) examined the effects of 20 min of cycling at 10% > VT and 20% < VT on performance of the Stroop color test, and included measures of serum BDNF concentrations. Cycling at 20% < VT had no significant effects on cognition but 10% > VT induced improved performance. However, there were no significant correlations between BDNF concentrations and Stroop performance.

Moderating Effects of Task Type

Empirical evidence for positive effects of short to moderate duration, moderate intensity exercise on speed of cognitive functioning appear to apply to both working memory as well as attention/perception tasks (see Tables 2 and 3). This is as one would expect from the theory described earlier, with this intensity and duration inducing improved performance. However, McMorris and Hale (2012) found that the mean effect size for central executive tasks, during or immediately following moderate intensity exercise ($g = 0.77$, $SE = 0.16$), was significantly ($p < 0.01$) larger than those for attention/perception and short-term memory tasks ($g = 0.46$, $SE = 0.17$). This is not totally unexpected. Both working memory and most attention/perception tasks are facilitated by increased α_{2A}-adrenoreceptor and D_1-receptor activation in the prefrontal cortex (Arnsten, 2009, 2011) and moderate levels of stress are thought to improve attention via noradrenaline stimulation of the reticular formation (Aston-Jones, Chiang, & Alexinsky, 1991; Castro-Alamancos & Calcagnotto, 2001), which would also facilitate both types of task. The lack of activation of β- and α_1-adrenoreceptors during exercise of this intensity and duration, however, would mean that the attention/perception tasks are not optimally served by the neurotransmitters, as activation of these receptors has been shown to be beneficial for such tasks (Waterhouse et al., 1980, 1981).

MODERATE AND LONG DURATION, MODERATE INTENSITY EXERCISE

Unfortunately only a few studies have examined the effect of moderate and long duration (>30 min), moderate intensity exercise on cognition. As we saw above, during moderate intensity, sub-T_{CATS} exercise, after ~30 min, plasma

catecholamines concentrations begin to rise (Hodgetts et al., 1991). Moreover, following ~45 min duration there appears to be increased plasma and salivary cortisol and ACTH concentrations (Bridge et al., 2003; Shojaei et al., 2011), which increase catecholamines synthesis and release in the brain as shown in animal studies (Höglund et al., 2000; Pruessner et al., 2004; Wand et al., 2007; Wieczorek & Dunn, 2006). Thus, the effect of this duration of moderate intensity exercise may differ to that for the shorter duration, moderate intensity exercise discussed so far.

As well as the studies, in which duration was >30 min, outlined in Table 3, three studies of this duration and intensity, in which neurochemicals were measured, have been undertaken. Peyrin, Pequignot, Lacour, and Fourcade (1987) compared urinary concentrations of noradrenaline, adrenaline, dopamine, an adrenaline metabolite (metanephrine) and selected metabolites of noradrenaline (normetanephrine, and sulfate, glucuronide and total MHPG) following cognitive performance at rest and after cycling for 1 h at ~75% $\dot{V}O_{2MAX}$. Participants showed improved performance during exercise on a word discrimination test but not an arithmetical calculation task. The authors thought that the arithmetic test had demonstrated a ceiling effect. Linear regression analyses showed significant correlations between performance on the word discrimination test, on which participants showed improved performance during exercise, and Δ adrenaline plus Δ metanephrine ($r = 0.61$), and Δ MHPG sulfate ($r = 0.63$) concentrations. Grego et al. (2004) examined the effect of long duration, moderate exercise, 3 h cycling at ~66% $\dot{V}O_{2MAX}$, on performance of an auditory oddball task, using electroencephalographic measures of P300 latency and amplitude as dependent variables. P300 latency refers to the speed of information processing, while P300 amplitude is a measure of the amount of processing. Participants also undertook a control condition when the same procedure was carried out except without cycling. Exercise induced significant increases in both P300 amplitude and latency after 2 h of cycling. These changes coincided with the time periods for significant increases in plasma adrenaline and noradrenaline concentrations, and serum concentrations of cortisol. However, correlations between the neurochemicals, and P300 latency and amplitude were nonsignificant.

The results found by Grego et al. (2004) are what one would expect for a central executive task, with high concentrations of catecholamines and cortisol inhibiting performance. However, in the Peyrin et al. (1987) study, one would have expected 1 h of cycling at 75% $\dot{V}O_{2MAX}$ to result in very high concentrations of catecholamines and cortisol, thus also inhibiting performance. That the word discrimination test showed a significant improvement is therefore surprising. According to the authors, the task required the holding of information in short-term memory and "extracting and evoking true words from an uncoherent (sic) text background" (Peyrin et al., 1987, p. 189). Furthermore, according to the authors, learning and recalling the words was "easy but the mental constraint was due to the limited timing" (p. 189). Thus, it appears that this was more of a memory task than a central executive task. As we saw earlier, memory and learning tasks benefit from high concentrations of noradrenaline and dopamine (Hopkins & Johnston, 1988; Hu et al., 2007).

More recently, Tsai et al. (2014) examined the effect of 30 min exercise at 60% $\dot{V}O_{2MAX}$ on performance of an attention/perception task. Reaction times and central contingent negative variation area, a measure of response preparation and evaluation, were facilitated for all participants. Fit participants also showed increased P300 amplitude. Serum BDNF concentrations were increased but were not correlated to any performance variables. Given the nature of the task, improved performance would be expected as both moderate and heavy exercise should facilitate attention/perception tasks. That there were no significant correlations between performance variables and BDNF concentrations is not surprising as peripheral BDNF is merely indicative of central concentrations. Moreover, the real effects of BDNF on cognition are downstream of synthesis and release.

Possible Effects of 5-Hydroxytryptamine

So far, we have commented only on the effect on cognition of interactions between moderate and long duration, moderate intensity exercise, and catecholamines, cortisol, and BDNF. However, this intensity and duration of exercise also induces increases in 5-HT, also known as serotonin. The reason for this is because, as far as we are aware, no study has examined the interaction between acute exercise, 5-HT, and cognition. This is surprising given that 5-HT activates the serotonergic neural pathway, which is heavily involved in cognition (Fernstrom, 2005; González-Burgos & Feria-Velasco, 2008). Moreover, exercise is thought by some to be a particularly good inducer of 5-HT synthesis (Blomstrand, 2006). Tryptophan, the precursor of 5-HT, is found in plasma either bound to albumin or unbound. Unbound tryptophan readily crosses the blood–brain barrier. According to Blomstrand, during exercise, free fatty acids displace tryptophan from binding with albumin, therefore there is an increase in unbound tryptophan. This crosses into the brain and forms 5-HT (Blomstrand, 2006; Hawkins et al., 2006). Some albumin-bound tryptophan also crosses the blood–brain barrier probably due to a dissociation mechanism that takes place at the surface of the brain capillary endothelium (Pardridge, 1998). However, Fernstrom and Fernstrom (2006) questioned the role of free fatty acids and unbinding of tryptophan from albumin as the cause for exercise-induced increases in 5-HT concentrations, but they did agree that exercise induces increased brain concentrations of 5-HT. It may be that the increase is centrally mediated in the same way that exercise-induced perceptions of stress result in increased catecholamines synthesis and release.

Having crossed the blood–brain barrier, tryptophan is hydroxylated to 5-HTP, under the influence of tryptophan hydroxylase. It is further broken down by AADC into 5-HT. This process takes place mainly in the raphe nuclei of the brain. This is the only place that 5-HTP is found. 5-HT is stored in vesicles, mainly the parafollicular cells of the thyroid (Lefebvre et al., 2001). Tryptophan hydroxylase is the rate-limiting enzyme for 5-HT synthesis and is not fully saturated under normal conditions, therefore increases in brain concentrations of tryptophan will facilitate 5-HT synthesis.

Given that exercise facilitates the crossing of the blood–brain barrier by tryptophan; the fact that the serotonergic system innervates most of the brain, particularly the hippocampus, hypothalamus, striatum, frontal cortex, amygdala, and substantia nigra (Frazer & Hensler, 1999; Meeusen & De Meirleir, 1995); and that tryptophan hydroxylase is not saturated, it is not surprising to find strong evidence of acute exercise-induced increases in brain concentrations of 5-HT in animal studies (Caperuto, dos Santos, Mello, & Costa Rosa, 2009; Chen et al., 2008; Chennaoui et al., 2001; see Meeusen et al., 2001; Meeusen & De Meirleir, 1995, for reviews). Moreover, Blomstrand, Møller, Secher, and Nybo (2005) examined the brain uptake of tryptophan during prolonged exercise (3 h at 200 ± 7 W, on a cycle ergometer) in humans by calculating the a-v diff multiplied by plasma flow. They found large increases in cerebral uptake. It is important to note that the exercise duration was long. The authors claimed that the increases in cerebral uptake were a direct result of the action of unbinding tryptophan from albumin as a result of the organism's use of fat as the main energy supply, thus easing the crossing of the blood–brain barrier for tryptophan. Fat rather than carbohydrates is recruited mostly in submaximal, long-duration exercise. In shorter intensity, heavy exercise, lactate restricts the transport of free fatty acids in the blood (Bülow, Madsen, Astrup, & Christensen, 1985) as does

α-adrenergic action (Gullestad, Hallén, & Sejersted, 1993), therefore there is no available free fatty acids to unbind tryptophan from albumin.

The fact that 5-HT plays a role in cognition is undisputed, but how exactly it does so is less clear. The consensus of opinion appears to be that 5-HT probably acts as a neuromodulator affecting the excitability of the nervous system (Frazer & Hensler, 1999; González-Burgos & Feria-Velasco, 2008). In the brain, 5-HT can have a detrimental effect on dopaminergic activity as a result of competition for interaction with AADC in the synthesis process of both neurotransmitters (Luciana, Collins, & Depue, 1998; Olvera-Cortés, Anguiano-Rodriguez, López-Vázquez, & Alfaro, 2008). During long-duration, moderate intensity exercise, it would appear that conditions favor the synthesis of 5-HT. Moreover, in the locus coeruleus, 5-HT_{1A} and 5-HT_{2A} receptors induce an inhibitory effect on noradrenergic neuron activity (Mongeau, Blier, & de Montigny, 1997). Also, increased stimulation of the receptors 5-HT_{1A} and 5-HT_2 induce increased plasma ACTH and cortisol (Sakaue et al., 2000). All of these effects would suggest inhibition of cognitive functioning.

The Acute Exercise–Neurochemicals–Cognition Interaction: Effects of Heavy Exercise

Examination of the results for incremental exercise to exhaustion, in the studies testing the inverted-U effect (Table 1), shows that results were somewhat equivocal. As with moderate intensity exercise, we can probably supplement our direct measures of the heavy exercise–catecholamines interaction on cognition by examining studies where individuals exercised to exhaustion but in which no catecholamines measures were undertaken. We know that catecholamines concentrations in such conditions must be very high indeed (Chmura et al., 1994; McMorris et al., 2009, 1999), therefore examination of the results for such studies can add to our understanding of the heavy exercise–catecholamines–cognition interaction.

Studies in which the effect of heavy exercise (>80% $\dot{V}O_{2MAX}$ or equivalent) on cognition has been examined, but in which catecholamines were not measured, are shown in Table 4. There are differences in results depending on the dependent variable, speed, or accuracy. Observation of accuracy data shows no significant effect for seven variables, inhibition for two, and facilitation for two. Reaction time and speed of response data are equivocal, with seven showing facilitation, six inhibition, and ten no significant effect. These results are similar to those shown by McMorris and Hale (2012), who found that the equivocal nature of the results, from individual studies, resulted in very low, nonsignificant, mean effect sizes for both speed and accuracy.

That these results are somewhat equivocal is not surprising. As we saw earlier, during heavy exercise, plasma catecholamines concentrations of dopamine and noradrenaline can be excessive. The excess noradrenaline activates the lower affinity α_1- and β-adrenoreceptors (Roth et al., 1988). Moreover, when exercise reaches an intensity ≥80% $\dot{V}O_{2MAX}$ increased plasma concentrations of cortisol are demonstrated (De Vries et al., 2000; Hill et al., 2008; McMorris et al., 2009). Such an increase in plasma cortisol will lead to increased brain cortisol, CRF, and ACTH concentrations. The effect of the latter is to further increase the synthesis and release of dopamine and noradrenaline in the brain. As the activation of α_1- and β-adrenoreceptors has different effects on working memory, attention/perception, and long-term memory/learning tasks, we need to examine results for each of these tasks separately.

Working Memory Tasks

Unfortunately, few studies examining the effects of heavy exercise on working memory have been undertaken. When comparisons between performance at rest and during/following heavy exercise, with speed of performance as the dependent variable, were undertaken, McMorris et al. (2009) showed a significant deterioration but other studies demonstrated no significant effect (Griffin et al., 2011; Kamijo Nishihira, Hatta, Kaneda, Wasaka, et al., 2004; McMorris et al., 2000, 2008). For accuracy, inhibition was shown in one study (McMorris et al., 2009) but the other studies measuring this variable (Griffin et al., 2011; McMorris et al., 2008, 2000; Sjöberg, 1980) found no significant effects. In line with inverted-U theory, no significant difference should have been found between at rest and during/following heavy exercise. However, we hypothesized a deterioration during heavy exercise or an inverted-J effect. To examine the inverted-J effect is difficult as studies comparing performance during heavy exercise with that during moderate intensity exercise are limited in number. McMorris et al. (2009) showed significant deteriorations in performance for both accuracy and speed from 50% to 80% MAP. However, McMorris et al. (2008) demonstrated no significant difference on a random number generation task between exercise at 40% and 80% $\dot{W}_{MAX}$. Furthermore, we were unable to find any studies that have measured the effect of heavy exercise on those working memory tasks, which have been shown to benefit from α_1-adrenoreceptor activation, for example, attentional set shifting (Robbins & Roberts, 2007; Bondi et al., 2010), or β-adrenoreceptor activation, for example, the stop signal task (Arnsten, 2011).

Before moving on to the attention/perception tasks, we should comment on the regression data found by McMorris et al. (2009). They showed that during exercise at 80% MAP, Δ adrenaline and Δ ACTH combined significantly predicted Δ response time on the flanker task. However, observation of the standardized β-coefficients showed that for both variables, the relationship was inverse, that is, smaller increases in ACTH and adrenaline concentrations indicated larger increases in reaction time, while larger increases indicated smaller increases in response time. If

TABLE 4 Studies that have examined the effects, compared to baseline, of exercise >80% maximum volume of oxygen uptake ($\dot{V}O_{2MAX}$) or equivalent, and in which no measures of catecholamines were taken

Authors	N	Exercise measure	Test(s)	Results
Bard and Fleury (1978)	16	Fatigue	VS[b]	RT NS
			CA[b]	Accuracy NS
Brisswalter, Arcelin, Audiffren, and Delignières (1997)	20	80% MAP	SRT[b]	RT inhibition[a]
Chmura and Nazar (2010)	13	100% $\dot{V}O_{2MAX}$	CRT[b]	RT inhibition[a]
Coco, Di Corrado, Calogero, Perciavalle, and Maci (2009)	17	Fatigue	ACT[b]	RT inhibition[a]
Delignières, Brisswalter, and Legros (1994)	40	80% $\dot{V}O_{2MAX}$	CRT[b]	Expert fencers (n = 20)
				RT NS
				Nonexperts (n = 20)
				RT inhibition[a]
Féry, Ferry, Vom Hofe, and Rieu (1997)	13	Fatigue	Recognition task[b]	RT inhibition[a]
Fontana et al. (2009)	32	80% $\dot{V}O_{2MAX}$	SDM[c]	Accuracy NS
				RT facilitation[a]
Griffin et al. (2011)	30	100% $\dot{V}O_{2MAX}$	SCT[d]	Accuracy NS
				RT NS
			Learning/memory[e]	Accuracy facilitation[a]
Guizani et al. (2006)	24	80% $\dot{V}O_{2MAX}$	CRT[b]	Fencers (n = 12)
			SRT[b]	RT facilitation[a]
				Sed group (n = 12)
				RT NS
				NS both groups
Isaacs and Pohlman (1991)	12	100% $\dot{V}O_{2MAX}$	CA[b]	Accuracy inhibition[a]
Kamijo, Nishihira, Hatta, Kaneda, Wasaka et al. (2004)	12	Fatigue	No go/go[d]	EMG-RT NS
Kamijo, Nishihira, Hatta, Kaneda, Kida et al. (2004)	12	Fatigue	SRT[b]	EMG-RT NS
McMorris and Graydon (1996a)	20	100% $\dot{W}_{MAX}$	SDM[c]	Accuracy NS
				RT facilitation[a]
McMorris and Graydon (1996b) Exp 1	10	100% $\dot{W}_{MAX}$	SDM[c]	Accuracy NS
				RT facilitation[a]

TABLE 4   Studies that have examined the effects, compared to baseline, of exercise >80% maximum volume of oxygen uptake ($\dot{V}O_{2MAX}$) or equivalent, and in which no measures of catecholamines were taken—cont'd

Authors	N	Exercise measure	Test(s)	Results
McMorris and Graydon (1996b) Exp 2	20	100% $\dot{W}_{MAX}$	SDM[c]	Accuracy NS
				RT facilitation[a]
McMorris and Graydon (1997) Exp 1	12	100% $\dot{W}_{MAX}$	VS[b]	RT facilitation[a]
McMorris and Graydon (1997) Exp 2	12	100% $\dot{W}_{MAX}$	SDM[c]	Accuracy facilitation[a]
				RT facilitation[a]
McMorris and Keen (1994)	12	100% $\dot{W}_{MAX}$	SRT[b]	RT inhibition[a]
McMorris et al. (2005)	9	100% $\dot{W}_{MAX}$	NC-CRT[b]	RT NS
Sjöberg (1980)	48	100% $\dot{W}_{MAX}$	STM[e]	Accuracy NS
Thomson et al. (2009)	163	100% $\dot{V}O_{2MAX}$	Speed discrimination[b]	RT NS
				Accuracy inhibition[a]

NS, nonsignificant ($p > 0.05$); MAP, maximum aerobic power; $\dot{V}O_{2MAX}$, maximum volume of oxygen uptake; $\dot{W}_{MAX}$, maximum power output; VS, visual search; CA, coincidence anticipation; SRT, simple reaction time; CRT, choice reaction time; ACT, attention and concentration task; SDM, soccer decision making; SCT, Stroop color test; NC, noncompatible; STM, short-term memory; NS, nonsignificant; RT, reaction time; EMG, electromyographic.

[a] $p < 0.05$.
[b] Attention/perception task.
[c] Autonomous task.
[d] Working memory task.
[e] Memory/learning task.

increases in ACTH and adrenaline plasma concentrations are indicative of increases in stress and arousal, one would have expected greater increases in adrenaline and ACTH concentrations to be related to poorer performance.

The authors presented a possible explanation for these data. According to them, the answer lies in the nature of the protocol for the flanker test. The task is a central executive one, therefore one would expect greater increases in adrenaline and ACTH to be related to slower information processing and hence indicate higher Δ response times. However, the response, pressing a button, is motoric in nature and previous research has shown decreases in movement time during heavy exercise (McMorris et al., 2009, 2005). As a result, even if central processing is slower during exercise at 80% MAP, this will be offset by faster motor time, resulting in a smaller increase

in response time. Participants who had a relatively smaller increase in adrenaline and ACTH combined would have a weaker or no positive effect on motor time, hence larger Δ response times. In other words, the slower processing would not be offset by faster motor time.

Attention/Perception Tasks

Observation of the attention/perception and autonomous tasks in Table 4 shows that with accuracy as the dependent variable, there appears to be little or no significant effect. However, with speed, results are equivocal. We need to look more carefully at the exact nature of these tasks before coming to any conclusions. McMorris and colleagues (McMorris & Graydon, 1996a, 1996b, 1997; McMorris et al., 1999, 2000) and Fontana, Mazzardo, Mokgothu, Furtado, and Gallagher (2009) tested participants on soccer-specific tests, in which the participants were well habituated. They showed that accuracy was unaffected with one exception, in which accuracy was facilitated (McMorris & Graydon, 1997). Speed of response was significantly improved in all of these studies except one (McMorris et al., 2000). McMorris (2009) described this latter study as being more like a soccer-specific choice reaction time task, with a predetermined response to each stimulus. In the other tests, the participant had to make a decision based on comparison of the present situation with past experience recalled from long-term memory. At least this was our intention. However, closer inspection of the data from the tests led us to believe that the participants who were experienced soccer players, except for one group in one study (McMorris & Graydon, 1996a), were responding in an autonomous manner. They were not thinking through the problem as we had anticipated but responding as they would in a game when under time pressure (see McMorris, 2009, for a more detailed review). This was supported when we compared experienced players and nonplayers, and saw that the two groups behaved differently (McMorris & Graydon, 1996a). Therefore, we concluded that these tasks were almost certainly autonomous to the soccer-playing participants. The results are in line with research into the effect of other stressors on automatic skills (Ehrlenspiel, Wei, & Stemad, 2010). It would appear that when tasks become automatic, there is less prefrontal cortex input (Jimura, Cazalis, Stover, & Poldrack, 2014; Poldrack et al., 2005), while activation of the sensory cortices and sensorimotor striatum triggers a predetermined response (Ashby, Turner, & Horvitz, 2010; Poldrack & Gabrieli, 2001). As a result, during heavy exercise, activation of the α_1- and β-adrenoreceptors will improve the signal to noise ratio in the sensory cortices, which in turn means that the task will be executed more quickly.

No really clear picture emerges for the results of research examining the other attention/perception tasks. Observation of Table 4 shows that only

three studies examined accuracy. Two examined coincidence anticipation, one (Bard & Fleury, 1978) found no significant effect, and the other (Isaacs & Pohlman, 1991) showed inhibition. The third study (Thomson, Watt, & Liukkonen, 2009) measured speed discrimination and found inhibition. With speed of response as the dependent variable, there was inhibition in seven studies, no significant effect in eight and facilitation in two. Given that these are comparisons with performance at rest, one would expect no significant effect according to inverted-U theory; however, given that these tasks require comparatively little prefrontal activity, based on our review of theory, we would have expected a facilitation in performance for similar reasons to that shown for automatic skills. One can understand the nonsignificance due to a ceiling effect in such simple tasks, but the inhibition is difficult to explain. There are, however, habituation effects in most of these tasks and this has not always been taken into account when designing studies (see Chapter 22).

Learning/Memory Tasks

Two studies have examined long-term memory or learning (Griffin et al., 2011; Winter et al., 2007). In both of these studies facilitation was demonstrated. The results for these studies, which required consolidation of information by the hippocampus, were as one would expect from catecholamines and BDNF perspectives. Increased activation of β-adrenergic receptors aids long-term potentiation (Gelinas & Nguyen, 2005; Straube, Korz, Balschun, & Frey, 2003) and consolidation (Hopkins & Johnston, 1988; Hu et al., 2007), while increased BDNF concentrations are essential for neurogenesis and neuroplasticity (Binder & Scharfman, 2004; Yang et al., 2014). Winter et al. demonstrated high plasma concentrations of noradrenaline and adrenaline, and high serum concentrations of BDNF during consolidation. While Griffin et al. did not measure catecholamines concentrations, they showed high serum concentrations of BDNF. However, at these intensities, one would also expect cortisol concentrations to be high and high concentrations of cortisol have been shown to impair learning (Abercrombie et al., 2003; Lupien et al., 1999; Wolf et al., 2001). However, as van Ast et al. (2013) pointed out, while the inverted-U effect of cortisol on memory applies to situations in which the stressor is emotional and the information to be learned is linked to the emotions, it is not the same with neutral information and a stressor such as exercise. Coccoz, Maldonado, and Delorenzi (2011) and Marin, Pilgrim, and Lupien (2010) demonstrated this with neutral information and psychosocial and physical stress, respectively. Indeed, with exercise as the stressor, a different perspective might be taken. In most learning research with humans, the stressor is social, for example, the Trier test, so increased BDNF expression is not induced. However, with exercise, there are increased serum BDNF concentrations and animal studies also show increased brain concentrations of BDNF. The resultant neuroplasticity may be the most important issue with regard to exercise-induced improvements in memory.

Studies Comparing Neurochemical Concentrations during Exercise, while Undertaking Cognitive Tests, with Those in an Exercise-Only Condition

Peyrin et al. (1987) compared urinary concentrations of catecholamines and selected catecholamines metabolites during exercise, while carrying out cognitive tests, with concentrations in an exercise-only condition. There were significantly greater concentrations of adrenaline plus metanephrine, and MHPG sulfate in the exercise with cognitive testing condition, suggesting that the increases were due to undertaking the cognitive tests. Webb et al. (2008) provided some support for Peyrin et al. These authors demonstrated elevated plasma noradrenaline but not adrenaline concentrations, while undertaking an exercise plus cognition task compared to exercise alone. Exercise intensity was 60% $\dot{V}O_{2MAX}$ and lasted for

37 min. Unfortunately, they did not report cognitive performance scores. However, McMorris et al. (2008) examining plasma concentrations of MHPG and HVA, found no significant differences at either 40% or 80% MAP in an exercise plus cognitive test condition compared to exercise only.

Differences in the findings of Peyrin et al. (1987) and McMorris et al. (2008) could be due to the use of urinary MHPG versus plasma concentrations. There is some disagreement over which is the better measure with regard to brain activity. Following a review of the literature, Eisenhofer, Kopin, and Goldstein (2004) argued that neither urine nor plasma concentrations of MHPG were good indicators of brain dopamine and noradrenaline activity. They claimed that contributions from brain activity could be as low as 3% and no higher than 20%. The use of plasma HVA concentrations is less contentious. Several authors have demonstrated significant correlations between plasma HVA concentrations and cognitive performance (e.g., Di Rocco et al., 2000) and plasma HVA concentrations have been shown to change in response to pharmacologically and surgically induced changes in brain concentrations in animals (Konicki, Owen, Litman, & Pickar, 1991). Kopin, Bankiewicz, and Harvey-White (1988) showed that ~25% of plasma HVA was from central dopamine turnover, while Amin et al. (1995) demonstrated figures of ~30%. Eisenhofer et al. (2004) claimed that only 12% of plasma concentrations of HVA were from brain activity.

Neither Peyrin et al. (1987) nor McMorris et al. (2008) claimed that their measurements were indicative of central activity only. However, they argued that as the only differences between the exercise-only and the exercise plus cognition conditions were the inclusion of the cognitive tasks, one would expect any differences in concentrations to be due to cognitive activity. Peyrin et al. would appear to have shown this with regard to urinary sulfate MHPG measures. While McMorris et al.'s (2008) failure to show significant differences in plasma concentrations between the exercise-only and exercise plus cognition conditions may be due to the use of plasma measures rather than urinary, they may also be because only small changes in cognition were demonstrated by these authors. Peyrin et al. (1987) found a large effect size of d = 1.50 on a word discrimination test, while the highest effect size shown by McMorris et al. (2008) was a moderate one of d = 0.50. This may mean that changes in the brain's contribution to the plasma measure may have been small and therefore masked by noise from peripheral contributions, as has been suggested by Amin et al. (1995).

CONCLUSION

Biochemical research, with humans and animals, shows that acute exercise induces increases in plasma catecholamines concentrations. The circulating adrenaline and noradrenaline stimulate the vagal/NTS pathway, which in turn induces the synthesis and release of noradrenaline and, indirectly, dopamine in the brain. Brain concentrations of catecholamines are also probably increased due to feedforward from the hypothalamus, preparing the person for action, and feedback from the brainstem concerning the stress of undertaking the task. Moderate increases in catecholamines concentrations facilitate performance of most cognitive tasks. Most tasks benefit from increased reticular formation activation aiding attention and vigilance, while prefrontal cortex tasks are also aided by increased activation of α_{2A}-adrenoreceptors. However, biochemical research also shows that long duration, moderate intensity exercise and heavy exercise induce excessive concentrations of catecholamines, as well as resulting in increased concentrations of HPA axis hormones and BDNF. During long duration, moderate intensity exercise, 5-HT concentrations are also elevated. High concentrations of HPA axis hormones and 5-HT interact with catecholamines to inhibit cognition. Heavy exercise has a beneficial effect on memory due to activation of β-adrenoreceptors in the hippocampus (Hopkins & Johnston, 1988; Hu

et al., 2007) and increased BDNF concentrations aiding neurogenesis and neuroplasticity (Binder & Scharfman, 2004; Yang et al., 2014). Heavy exercise also facilitates performance of autonomous tasks, probably due to activation of α_1- and β-adrenoreceptors. With attention/perception tasks, the picture is less clear with results being somewhat equivocal, although theoretically activation of α_1- and β-adrenoreceptors should also aid the performance of these tasks. There is at this moment insufficient studies to comment on effects on working memory tasks; however, theoretically activation of α_1- and β-adrenoreceptors should inhibit the performance of these tasks.

References

Abercrombie, H. C., Kalin, N. H., Thurow, M. E., Rosenkranz, M. A., & Davidson, R. J. (2003). Cortisol variation in humans affects memory for emotionally laden and neutral information. *Behavioral Neuroscience, 117,* 505–516.

Allen, J. P., Kendall, J. W., McGilvra, R., & Vancura, C. (2011). Immunoreactive ACTH in cerebrospinal fluid. *Journal of Clinical Endocrinology and Metabolism, 38,* 586–593.

Amin, F., Davidson, M., Kahn, R. S., Schmeidler, J., Stern, R., Knott, P. J., et al. (1995). Assessment of the central dopaminergic index of plasma HVA in schizophrenia. *Schizophrenia Bulletin, 21,* 53–66.

Arcelin, R., & Brisswalter, J. (1999). Performance stability in simultaneous tasks of pedalling and reaction time. *Perceptual and Motor Skills, 88,* 1193–1199.

Arnsten, A. F. T. (2009). Stress signalling pathways that impair prefrontal cortex structure and function. *Nature Reviews Neuroscience, 10,* 410–422.

Arnsten, A. F. T. (2011). Catecholamine influences on dorsolateral prefrontal cortical networks. *Biological Psychiatry, 69,* e89–e99. http://dx.doi.org/10.1016/j.biopsych.2011.01.027.

Aron, A. R. (2011). From reactive to proactive and selective control: developing a richer model for stopping inappropriate responses. *Biological Psychiatry, 69,* e55–e68. http://dx.doi.org/10.1016/j.biopsych.2010.07.024.

Arts, F. J. P., & Kuipers, H. (1994). The relation between power output, oxygen uptake and heart rate in male athletes. *International Journal of Sports Medicine, 15,* 228–231.

Asbach, S., Schulz, C., & Lehnert, H. (2001). Effects of corticotropin-releasing hormone on locus coeruleus neurons in vivo: a microdialysis study using a novel bilateral approach. *European Journal of Endocrinology, 145,* 359–363.

Ashby, F. G., Turner, B. O., & Horvitz, J. C. (2010). Cortical and basal ganglia contributions to habit learning and automaticity. *Trends in Cognitive Sciences, 14,* 208–215.

van Ast, V. A., Cornelisse, S., Marin, M.-F., Ackermann, S., Garfinkel, S. N., & Abercrombie, H. C. (2013). Modulatory mechanisms of cortisol effects on emotional learning and memory: novel perspectives. *Psychoneuroendocrinology, 38,* 1874–1882.

Aston-Jones, G., Chiang, C., & Alexinsky, T. (1991). Discharge of noradrenergic locus coeruleus neurons in behaving rats and monkeys suggests a role in vigilance. *Progress in Brain Research, 88,* 501–520.

Audiffren, M., Tomporowski, P. D., & Zagrodnik, J. (2009). Acute exercise and information processing: modulation of executive control in a Random Number Generation task. *Acta Psychologica, 132,* 85–95.

Austin, M. C., Janosky, J. E., & Murphy, H. A. (2003). Increased corticotropin-releasing hormone immunoreactivity in monoamine-containing pontine nuclei of depressed suicide men. *Molecular Psychiatry, 8,* 324–332.

Baddeley, A. D. (1986). *Working memory.* New York: Oxford University Press.

Bailey, S. P., Davis, J. M., & Ahlborn, E. N. (1993a). Serotonergic agonists and antagonists affect endurance performance in the rat. *International Journal of Sports Medicine, 14,* 330–333.

Bailey, S. P., Davis, J. M., & Ahlborn, E. N. (1993b). Neuroendocrine and substrate responses to altered brain 5-HT activity during prolonged exercise to fatigue. *Journal of Applied Physiology, 74,* 3006–3012.

Barbas, H. (2000). Connections underlying the synthesis of cognition, memory, and emotion in primate prefrontal cortices. *Brain Research Bulletin, 52,* 319–330.

Bard, C., & Fleury, M. (1978). Influence of imposed metabolic fatigue on visual capacity components. *Perceptual and Motor Skills, 47,* 1283–1287.

Beaver, W. L., Wasserman, K., & Whipp, B. J. (1986). Improved detection of lactate threshold during exercise using a log-log transformation. *Journal of Applied Physiology, 59,* 1936–1940.

Berchtold, N. C., Castello, N., & Cotman, C. W. (2010). Exercise and time-dependent benefits to learning and memory. *Neuroscience, 167,* 588–597.

Binder, D. K., & Scharfman, H. E. (2004). Brain-derived neurotrophic factor. *Growth Factors, 22,* 123–131.

Blomstrand, E. (2006). A role for branched-chain amino acids in reducing central fatigue. *Journal of Nutrition, 136,* 544S–547S.

Blomstrand, E., Møller, K., Secher, N. H., & Nybo, L. (2005). Effect of carbohydrate ingestion on brain exchange of amino acids during sustained exercise in human subjects. *Acta Physiologica Scandinavica, 185,* 203–209.

Bondi, C. O., Jett, J. D., & Morilak, D. A. (2010). Beneficial effects of desipramine on cognitive function of chronically stressed rats are mediated by alpha$_1$-adrenergic receptors in medial prefrontal cortex. *Progress in Neuropsychopharmacology Biological Psychiatry, 34,* 913–923.

Borer, K. T. (2003). *Exercise endocrinology.* Champaign, IL: Human Kinetics.

Borg, G. (1973). Perceived exertion: a note on history and methods. *Medicine and Science in Sports and Exercise, 5,* 90–93.

Brandenberger, G., Follenius, M., Wittersheim, G., Salame, P., Simeoni, M., & Reinhardt, B. (1980). Plasma-catecholamines and pituitary-adrenal hormones related to mental task demand under quiet and noise conditions. *Biological Psychology, 10,* 239–252.

Bridge, M. W., Weller, A. S., Rayson, M., & Jones, D. A. (2003). Ambient temperature and the pituitary hormone responses to exercise in humans. *Experimental Physiology, 88,* 627–635.

Brisswalter, J., Arcelin, R., Audiffren, M., & Delignières, D. (1997). Influence of physical exercise on simple reaction time: effect of physical fitness. *Perceptual and Motor Skills, 85,* 1019–1027.

Bülow, J., Madsen, J., Astrup, A., & Christensen, N. J. (1985). Vasoconstrictor effect of high FFA/albumin ratios in adipose tissue in vivo. *Acta Physiologica Scandinavica, 125,* 661–667.

Calegari, V. C., Zoppi, C. C., Bezende, L. F., Silveira, L. R., Carneiro, E. M., & Boschero, B. C. (2011). Endurance training activates AMP-activated protein kinase, increases expression of uncoupling protein 2 and reduces insulin secretion from rat pancreatic islets. *Journal of Endocrinology, 208,* 257–284.

Caperuto, E. C., dos Santos, R. V., Mello, M. T., & Costa Rosa, L. F. (2009). Effect of endurance training on hypothalamic serotonin concentration and performance. *Clinical and Experimental Pharmacology and Physiology, 36,* 189–191.

Castro-Alamancos, M. A., & Calcagnotto, M. E. (2001). High-pass filtering of corticothalamic activity by neuromodulators released in the thalamus during arousal: in vitro and in vivo. *Journal of Neurophysiology, 85,* 1489–1497.

Cereatti, L., Casella, R., Manganelli, M., & Pesce, C. (2009). Visual attention in adolescents: facilitating effects of sport expertise and acute physical exercise. *Psychololy of Sport and Exercise, 10,* 136–145.

Chang, Y.-K., Tsai, C.-L., Hung, T.-M., So, E. C., Chen, F.-T., & Etnier, J. L. (2011). Effects of acute exercise on executive function: a study with a Tower of London task. *Journal of Sport and Exercise Psychology, 33,* 847–865.

Chen, H. I., Lin, L. C., Yu, L., Liu, Y. F., Kuo, Y. M., Huang, A. M., et al. (2008). Treadmill exercise enhances avoidance learning in rates: the role of down-regulated serotonin system ion the limbic system. *Neurobiology of Learning and Memory, 89,* 489–496.

Chennaoui, M., Drogou, C., Gomez-Merino, D., Grimaldi, B., Fillion, G., & Guezennec, C. Y. (2001). Endurance training effects on 5-HT(1B) receptors mRNA expression in cerebellum, striatum, frontal cortex and hippocampus of rats. *Neuroscience Letters, 307*, 33–36.

Chmura, J., Kristztofiak, H., Ziemba, A. W., Nazar, K., & Kaciuba-Uścilko, H. (1998). Psychomotor performance during prolonged exercise above and below the blood lactate threshold. *European Journal of Applied Physiology and Occupational Physiology, 77*, 77–80.

Chmura, J., & Nazar, K. (2010). Parallel changes in the onset of blood lactate accumulation (OBLA) and threshold of psychomotor performance deterioration during incremental exercise after training in athletes. *International Journal of Psychophysiology, 75*, 287–290.

Chmura, J., Nazar, H., & Kaciuba-Uścilko, H. (1994). Choice reaction time during graded exercise in relation to blood lactate and plasma catecholamine thresholds. *International Journal of Sports Medicine, 15*, 172–176.

Coccoz, V., Maldonado, H., & Delorenzi, A. (2011). The enhancement of reconsolidation with a naturalistic mild stressor improves the expression of a declarative memory in humans. *Neuroscience, 185*, 61–72.

Coco, M., Di Corrado, D., Calogero, R. A., Perciavalle, V., & Maci, T. (2009). Attentional processes and blood lactate levels. *Brain Research, 1302*, 205–211.

Collardeau, M., Brisswalter, J., & Audiffren, M. (2001). Effects of a prolonged run on simple reaction time of well trained runners. *Perceptual and Motor Skills, 93*, 679–689.

Cools, R., Barker, R. A., Sahakian, B. J., & Robbins, T. W. (2001). Enhanced or impaired cognitive function in Parkinson's disease as a function of dopaminergic medication and task demands. *Cerebral Cortex, 11*, 1136–1143.

Cooper, C. J. (1973). Anatomical and physiological mechanisms of arousal with specific reference to the effects of exercise. *Ergonomics, 16*, 601–609.

Cornford, E. M., Braun, L. D., Oldendorf, W. H., & Hill, M. A. (1982). Comparison of lipid-related blood-brain barrier penetrability in neonates and adults. *American Journal of Physiology, 243*, C161–C168.

Cotman, C. W., & Berchtold, N. C. (2002). Exercise: a behavioral intervention to enhance brain health and plasticity. *Trends in Neurosciences, 25*, 295–301.

Dalsgaard, M. K., Ott, P., Dela, F., Juul, A., Pedersen, B. K., Warburg, J., et al. (2004). The CSF and arterial to internal jugular venous hormonal differences during exercise in humans. *Experimental Physiology, 89*, 271–277.

Davey, C. P. (1973). Physical exertion and mental performance. *Ergonomics, 16*, 595–599.

Davis, J. M., Alderson, N. L., & Welsh, R. S. (2000). Serotonin and central nervous system fatigue: nutritional considerations. *American Journal of Clinical Nutrition, 72*, 573S–578S.

Davis, H. A., Gass, G. C., & Bassett, J. R. (1981). Serum cortisol response to incremental work in experienced and naive subjects. *Psychosomatic Medicine, 43*, 127–132.

Davranche, K., & Audiffren, M. (2004). Facilitating effects of exercise on information processing. *Journal of Sports Science, 22*, 419–428.

Davranche, K., Audiffren, M., & Denjean, A. (2006). A distributional analysis of physical exercise on a choice reaction time task. *Journal of Sport Science, 24*, 323–329.

Davranche, K., Burle, B., Audiffren, M., & Hasbroucq, T. (2005). Information processing during physical exercise: a chronometric and electromyographic study. *Experimental Brain Research, 165*, 532–540.

Davranche, K., Hall, B., & McMorris, T. (2009). Effect of acute exercise on cognitive control required during an Eriksen flanker task. *Journal of Sport and Exercise Psychology, 31*, 628–639.

Davranche, K., & McMorris, T. (2009). Specific effects of acute moderate exercise on cognitive control. *Brain and Cognition, 69*, 565–570.

De Kloet, E. R., Joëls, M., & Holsboer, F. (2005). Stress and the brain: from adaptation to disease. *Nature Reviews Neuroscience, 6*, 463–475.

De Kloet, E. R., Van Acker, S. A. B. E., Siburg, R. M., Oitzl, M. S., Meijer, O. C., Rahmouni, K., et al. (2000). Aldosterone action in nonepithial cells. *Kidney International, 57*, 1329–1336.

De Vries, W. R., Bernards, N. T. M., De Rooij, M. H., & Koppeschaar, H. P. F. (2000). Dynamic exercise discloses different time-related responses in stress hormones. *Psychosomatic Medicine, 62*, 866–872.

Del Giorno, J. M., Hall, E. E., O'Leary, K. C., Bixby, W. R., & Miller, P. C. (2010). Cognitive function during acute exercise: a test of the transient hypofrontality theory. *Journal of Sport and Exercise Psychology, 32*, 312–323.

Delignières, D., Brisswalter, J., & Legros, P. (1994). Influence of physical exercise on choice reaction time in sports experts: the mediating role of resources allocation. *Journal of Human Movement Studies, 27*, 173–188.

Deuster, P. A., Chrousos, G. P., Luger, A., De Bolt, J. E., Bernier, I. L., Trostman, U. H., et al. (1989). Hormonal and metabolic responses of untrained, moderately trained, and highly trained men to 3 exercise intensities. *Metabolism, 38*, 141–148.

Deutch, A. Y., & Roth, R. H. (1990). The determinants of stress-induced activation of the prefrontal cortical dopamine system. *Progress in Brain Research, 85*, 367–403.

Devoto, P., Flore, G., Saba, P., Fà, M., & Gessa, G. L. (2005). Co-release of noradrenaline and dopamine in the cerebral cortex elicited by single train and repeated train stimulation of the locus coeruleus. *BMC Neuroscience, 6*, 31. http://dx.doi.org/10.1186/1471-2202-6-31.

Di Rocco, A., Bottiglieri, T., Dorfman, D., Werner, P., Morrison, C., & Simpson, D. (2000). Decreased homovanillic acid in cerebrospinal fluid correlates with impaired neuropsychologic function in HIV-1-infected patients. *Clinical Neuropharmacology, 23*, 190–194.

Draper, S., McMorris, T., & Parker, J. K. (2010). Effect of acute exercise of differing intensities on simple and choice reaction and movement times. *Psychology of Sport and Exercise, 11*, 536–541.

Droste, S. K., Chandramohan, Y., Hill, L. E., Linthorst, A. C., & Reul, J. M. (2007). Voluntary exercise impacts on the rat hypothalamic-pituitary-adrenocortical axis mainly at the adrenal level. *Neuroendocrinology, 86*, 26–37.

Droste, S. K., Collins, A., Lightman, S. L., Linthorst, A. C. E., & Reul, J. M. H. M. (2009). Distinct, time-dependent effects of voluntary exercise on circadian and ultradian rhythms and stress responses of free corticosterone in the rat hippocampus. *Endocrinology, 150*, 4170–4179.

Droste, S. K., de Groote, L., Atkinson, H. C., Lightman, S. L., Reul, J. M., & Linthorst, A. C. (2008). Corticosterone levels in the brain show a distinct ultradian rhythm but a delayed response to forced swim stress. *Endocrinology, 149*, 3244–3253.

Droste, S. K., Gesing, A., Ulbricht, S., Müller, M. B., Linthorst, A. C. E., & Reul, J. M. H. M. (2003). Effects of long-term voluntary exercise on the mouse hypothalamic-pituitary-adrenocortical axis. *Endocrinology, 144*, 3012–3023.

Eagle, D. M., Davies, K. R., Towse, B. W., Keeler, J. F., Theobald, D. E., & Robbins, T. W. (2010). Beta-adrenoceptor-mediated action of atomoxetine during behavioral inhibition on the stop-signal task in rats. Society for Neuroscience Abstracts, 508, 510. Cited by Arnsten, A. F. T. (2011). Catecholamine influences on dorsolateral prefrontal cortical networks. *Biological Psychiatry, 69*, e89–e99. http://dx.doi.org/10.1016/j.biopsych.2011.01.027.

Egan, B., Carson, B. P., Garcia-Roves, P. M., Chibalin, A. V., Sarsfield, E. M., Barron, N., et al. (2010). Exercise intensity-dependent regulation of peroxisome proliferator-activated receptor coactivator-1 mRNA abundance is associate with differential activation of upstream signalling kinases in human skeletal muscle. *Journal of Physiology, 588*, 1779–1990.

Ehrlenspiel, F., Wei, K., & Stemad, D. (2010). Open-loop, closed-loop and compensatory control: performance improvement under pressure in a rhythmic task. *Experimental Brain Research, 201*, 729–741.

Eisenhofer, G., Kopin, I. J., & Goldstein, D. S. (2004). Catecholamine metabolism: a contemporary view with implications for physiology and medicine. *Pharmacological Reviews, 56*, 331–348.

El-Ghundi, M., O'Dowd, B. F., & George, S. R. (2007). Insights into the role of dopamine receptor systems in learning and memory. *Reviews Neuroscience, 1*, 37–66.

Endo, K., Matsukawa, K., Liang, N., Nakatsuka, C., Tsuchimochi, H., Okamura, H., et al. (2013). Dynamic exercise improves cognitive function in association with increased prefrontal oxygenation. *Journal of Physiological Sciences, 63*, 287–298.

Etnier, J. L., & Chang, Y.-K. (2009). The effect of physical activity on executive function: a brief commentary on definitions, measurement issues, and the current state of the literature. *Journal of Sport and Exercise Psychology, 31*, 469–483.

Fernstrom, J. D. (2005). Branched-chain amino acids and brain function. *Journal of Nutrition, 135*, 1539S–1546S.

Fernstrom, J. D., & Fernstrom, M. H. (2006). Exercise, serum free tryptophan, and central fatigue. *Journal of Nutrition, 136*, 553S–559S.

Fernstrom, J. D., & Fernstrom, M. H. (2007). Tyrosine, phenylalanine, and catecholamine synthesis and function on the brain. *Journal of Nutrition, 137*, 1539S–1547S.

Ferris, L. T., Williams, J. S., & Shen, C. (2007). The effect of acute exercise on serum brain-derived neurotrophic factor levels and cognitive function. *Medicine and Science in Sports and Exercise, 39*, 728–734.

Féry, Y.-A., Ferry, A., Vom Hofe, A., & Rieu, M. (1997). Effect of physical exhaustion on cognitive functioning. *Perceptual and Motor Skills, 84*, 291–298.

Finlay, J. M., Zigmond, M. J., & Abercrombie, E. D. (1995). Increased dopamine and norepinephrine release in medial prefrontal cortex induced by acute and chronic stress: effects of diazepam. *Neuroscience, 64*, 619–628.

Fontana, F. E., Mazzardo, O., Mokgothu, C., Furtado, O., & Gallagher, J. D. (2009). Influence of exercise intensity on the decision-making performance of experienced and inexperienced soccer players. *Journal of Sport and Exercise Psychology, 31*, 135–151.

Frazer, A., & Hensler, J. G. (1999). Serotonin. In G. J. Siegel, B. W. Agranoff, R. W. Abers, S. K. Fisher, & M. D. Uhler (Eds.), *Basic neurochemistry: Molecular, cellular and medical aspects* (6th ed.) (pp. 263–292). Philadelphia: Lippincott, Williams and Wilkins.

Gelinas, J. N., & Nguyen, P. V. (2005). Beta-adrenergic receptor activation facilitates induction of a protein synthesis-dependent late phase of long-term potentiation. *Journal of Neuroscience, 25*, 3294–3303.

Genuth, S. M. (2004). The endocrine system. In R. M. Berne, M. Levy, N. B. Koepen, & B. A. Stanton (Eds.), *Physiology* (5th ed.) (pp. 719–978). St. Louis, MO: Mosby.

Goekint, M., Bos, I., Heyman, E., Meeusen, R., Michotte, Y., & Sarre, S. (2012). Acute running stimulates hippocampal dopaminergic neurotransmission in rats, but has no impact on brain-derived neurotrophic factor. *Journal of Applied Physiology, 112*, 535–541.

Goekint, M., Heyman, E., Roelands, B., Njemini, R., Bautmans, I., Mets, T., et al. (2008). No influence of noradrenaline manipulation on acute exercise-induced increase of brain derived neurotrophic factor. *Medicine and Science in Sports and Exercise, 40*, 1990–1998.

Gomez-Pinilla, F., Vaynman, S., & Ying, Z. (2008). Brain-derived neurotrophic factor functions as a metabotrophin to mediate the effects of exercise on cognition. *European Journal of Neuroscience, 28*, 2278–2287.

González-Burgos, I., & Feria-Velasco, A. (2008). Serotonin/dopamine interaction in memeory formation. *Progress in Brain Research, 172*, 603–623.

Gordon, R., Spector, S., Sjoerdsma, A., & Udenfriend, S. (1966). Increased synthesis of norepinephrine and epinephrine in the intact rat during exercise and exposure to cold. *Journal of Pharmacology and Experimental Therapeutics, 153*, 440–447.

Green, H. J., Hughson, R. L., Orr, G. W., & Ranney, D. A. (1983). Anaerobic threshold, blood lactate, and muscle metabolites in progressive exercise. *Journal of Applied Physiology, 54*, 1032–1038.

Grego, F., Vallier, J. M., Collardeau, M., Bermon, S., Ferrari, P., Candito, M., et al. (2004). Effects of long duration exercise on cognitive function, blood glucose, and counterregulatory hormones in male cyclists. *Neuroscience Letters, 364*, 76–80.

Grenhoff, J., Nisell, M., Ferré, S., Aston-Jones, G., & Svensson, T. H. (1993). Noradrenergic modulation of dopamine cell firing elicited by stimulation of the locus coeruleus in the rat. *Journal of Neural Transmission. General Section, 93*, 11–25.

Grenhoff, J., & Svensson, T. H. (1993). Prazosin modulates the firing pattern of dopamine neurons in rat ventral tegmental area. *European Journal of Pharmacology, 233*, 79–84.

Griesbach, G. S., Hovda, D. A., & Gomez-Pinilla, F. (2009). Exercise-induced improvement in cognitive performance after traumatic brain-injury in rats is dependent on BDNF activation. *Brain Research, 1288*, 105–115.

Griffin, É. W., Mullally, S., Foley, C., Warmington, S. A., O'Mara, S. M., & Kelly, Á. M. (2011). Aerobic exercise improves hippocampal function and increases BDNF in the serum of young adult males. *Physiology and Behavior, 104*, 934–941.

Guizani, S. M., Bouzaouach, I., Tenenbaum, G., Ben Kheder, A., Feki, Y., & Bouaziz, M. (2006). Simple and choice reaction times under varying levels of physical load in high skilled fencers. *Journal of Sports Medicine and Physical Fitness, 46*, 344–351.

Gullestad, L., Hallén, J., & Sejersted, O. M. (1993). Variable effects of beta-adrenoreceptor blockade on muscle blood flow during exercise. *Acta Physiologica Scandinavica, 149*, 257–271.

Hart, S. G., & Staveland, L. E. (1988). Development of NASA-TLX (Task Load Index): results of empirical and theoretical research (pp. 239–250). In P. A. Hancock, & N. Meshkati (Eds.), *Human mental workload*. Amsterdam: North Holland Press.

Hasegawa, H., Yazawa, T., Yasumatsu, M., Otokawa, M., & Aihara, Y. (2000). Alteration in dopamine metabolism in the thermoregulatory center of exercising rats. *Neuroscience Letters, 289*, 161–164.

Hattori, S., Naoi, M., & Nishino, H. (1994). Striatal dopamine turnover during treadmill running in the rat – relation to the speed of running. *Brain Research Bulletin, 35*, 41–49.

Hawkins, R. A., O'Kane, R. L., Simpson, I. A., & Viña, J. R. (2006). Structure of the blood–brain barrier and its role in the transport of amino acids. *Journal of Nutrition, 136*, 218S–226S.

Herman, J. P., Watson, S. J., Chao, H. M., Coirini, H., & McEwen, B. S. (1993). Diurnal regulation of glucocorticoid receptor and mineralocorticoid receptor mRNAs in rat hippocampus. *Molecular and Cellular Neuroscience, 4*, 181–190.

Hill, E. E., Zack, E., Battaglini, C., Viru, M., Viru, A., & Hackney, A. C. (2008). Exercise and circulating cortisol levels: the intensity threshold effect. *Journal of Endocrinology Investigation, 31*, 587–591.

Hnatowich, M. R., Queen, G., Stein, D., & LaBella, F. S. (1989). ACTH receptors in nervous tissue. High-affinity binding-sequestration of $[^{125}I][Phe^2,Nle^4]ACTH$ 1-24 in homogenates and slices from rat brain. *Canadian Journal of Physiology and Pharmacology, 67*, 568–576.

Hodgetts, V., Coppack, S. W., Frayn, K. N., & Hockaday, T. D. R. (1991). Factors controlling fat mobilization from human subcutaneous adipose-tissue during exercise. *Journal of Applied Physiology, 71*, 445–451.

Hogan, C. L., Matta, J., & Carstensen, L. L. (2013). Exercise holds immediate benefits for affect and cognition in younger and older adults. *Psychology of Aging, 28*, 587–594.

Hogervorst, E., Riedel, W. J., Jeukendrup, A., & Jolies, J. (1996). Cognitive performance after strenuous physical exercise. *Perceptual and Motor Skills, 83*, 479–488.

Höglund, E., Balm, P. H., & Winberg, S. (2000). Skin darkening, a potential social signal in subordinate arctic charr (*Salvelinus alpinus*): the regulatory role of brain monoamines and pro-opiomelanocortin-derived peptides. *Journal of Experimental Biology, 203*, 1711–1720.

Hopkins, W. F., & Johnston, D. (1988). Noradrenergic enhancement of long-term potentiation at mossy fiber synapses in the hippocampus. *Journal of Neurophysiology, 59*, 667–687.

Hu, D., Cao, P., Thiels, E., Chu, C. T., Wu, G.-Y., Oury, T. D., et al. (2007). Hippocampal long-term potentiation, memory, and longevity in mice that overexpress mitochondrial superoxide dismutase. *Neurobiology of Learning and Memory, 87*, 372–384.

Huang, A. M., Jen, C. J., Chen, H. F., Yu, L., Kuo, Y. M., & Chen, H. I. (2006). Compulsive exercise acutely upregulates rat hippocampal brain-derived neurotrophic factor. *Journal of Neural Transmission, 113*, 803–811.

Hung, T.-M., Tsai, C.-L., Chen, F.-T., Wang, C.-C., & Chang, Y.-K. (2013). The immediate and sustained effects of acute exercise on planning aspect of executive function. *Psychology of Sport and Exercise, 14*, 728–736.

Hyodo, K., Dan, I., Suwabe, K., Kyutoku, Y., Yamada, Y., Akahori, M., et al. (2012). Acute moderate exercise enhances compensatory brain activation in older adults. *Neurobiology of Aging, 33*, 2621–2632.

Isaacs, L. D., & Pohlman, R. L. (1991). Effects of exercise intensity on an accompanying timing task. *Journal of Human Movement Studies, 20*, 123–131.

Jiang, Q. Y., Kawashima, H., Iwasaki, Y., Uchida, K., Sugimoto, K., & Itoi, K. (2004). Differential effects of forced swim-stress on the corticotropin-releasing hormone and vasopressin gene transcription in the paravocellular division of the paraventricular nucleus of rat hypothalamus. *Neuroscience Letters, 358*, 201–204.

Jimura, K., Cazalis, F., Stover, E. R. S., & Poldrack, R. A. (2014). The neural basis of task switching changes with skill acquisition. *Frontiers in Human Neuroscience, 8*, 330. http://dx.doi.org/10.3389/fnhum.2014.00339.

Joyce, J., Graydon, J., McMorris, T., & Davranche, K. (2009). The time course effect of moderate intensity exercise on response execution and response inhibition. *Brain and Cognition, 71*, 14–19.

Kamijo, K., Hayashi, Y., Sakai, T., Yahiro, T., Tanaka, K., & Nishihira, Y. (2009). Acute effects of aerobic exercise on cognitive function in older adults. *Journal of Gerontology B-Psychology, 64*, 356–363.

Kamijo, K., Nishihira, Y., Hatta, A., Kaneda, T., Kida, T., Higashiura, T., et al. (2004). Changes in arousal level by differential exercise intensity. *Clinical Neurophysiology, 115*, 2693–2698.

Kamijo, K., Nishihira, Y., Hatta, A., Kaneda, K., Wasaka, T., Kida, T., et al. (2004). Differential influences of exercise intensity on information processing in the central nervous system. *European Journal of Applied Physiology, 92*, 305–311.

Kasamatsu, T. (1970). Maintained and evoked unit activity in the mesencephalic reticular formation of the of the freely behaving cat. *Experimental Neurology, 28*, 450–470.

Kashihara, K., & Nakahara, Y. (2005). Short-term effect of physical exercise at lactate threshold on choice reaction time. *Perceptual and Motor Skills, 100*, 275–291.

Kawashima, H., Saito, T., Yoshizato, H., Fujikawa, T., Sato, Y., McEwen, B. S., et al. (2004). Endurance treadmill training in rats alters CRH activity in the hypothalamic paraventricular nucleus at rest and during acute running according to its period. *Life Sciences, 76*, 763–774.

Ke, Z., Yip, S. P., Li, L., Zheng, X. X., & Tong, K.-Y. (2011). The effects of voluntary, involuntary, and forced exercises on brain-derived neurotrophic factor and motor function recovery: a rat brain ischemia model. *PLoS One, 6*, e16643. http://dx.doi.org/10.1371/journal.pone.0016643.

Kitaoka, R., Fujikawa, G. T., Miyaki, T., Matsumura, S., Fushiki, T., & Inoue, K. (2010). Increased noradrenergic activity in the ventromedial hypothalamus during treadmill running in rats. *Journal of Nutritional Science and Vitaminology, 56*, 185–190.

Knaeppen, K., Goekint, M., Heyman, E. M., & Meeusen, R. (2010). Neuroplasticity – exercise-induced response of peripheral brain-derived neurotrophic factor: a systematic review of experimental studies in human subjects. *Sports Medicine, 40*, 765–801.

Konicki, P. E., Owen, R. R., Litman, R. E., & Pickar, D. E. (1991). The acute effects of central- and peripheral-acting dopamine antagonists on plasma HVA in schizophrenic patients. *Life Sciences, 48*, 1411–1416.

Kopin, I. J., Bankiewicz, K. S., & Harvey-White, J. (1988). Assessment of brain dopamine metabolism from plasma HVA and MHPG during debrisoquine treatment: validation in monkeys treated with MPTP. *Neuropsychopharmacology, 1*, 119–125.

Kudielka, B., Buske-Kirschbaum, A., Hellhammer, D. H., & Kirschbaum, C. (2004). HPA axis response to laboratory psychosocial stress in healthy elderly adults, younger adults, and children: impact of age and gender. *Psychoneuroendocrinology, 29*, 83–98.

Laske, C., Banachbach, S., Stransky, E., Bosch, S., Straten, G., Machann, J., et al. (2010). Exercise-induced normalization of decreased BDNF serum concentration in elderly women with remitted major depression. *International Journal of Neuropsychopharmacology, 13*, 595–602.

Lefebvre, H., Compagnon, P., Contesse, V., Delarue, C., Thuillez, C., Vaudry, H., et al. (2001). Production and metabolism of serotonin (5-HT) by the human adrenal cortex: paracrine stimulation of aldosterone secretion by 5-HT. *Journal of Clinical Endocrinology and Metabolism, 86*, 5001–5007.

Leh, S. E., Petrides, M., & Strafella, A. P. (2010). The neural circuitry of executive functions in healthy subjects and Parkinson's disease. *Neuropsychopharmacology, 35*, 70–85.

Lessmann, V., Gottmann, K., & Malcangio, M. (2003). Neurotrophin secretion: current facts and future prospects. *Progress in Neurobiology, 69*, 341–374.

Liu, Y. F., Chen, H. I., Wu, C. L., Kuo, Y. M., Yu, L., Huang, A. M., et al. (2009). Differential effects of treadmill running and wheel running on spatial or aversive learning and memory: roles of amygdalar brain-derived neurotrophic factor and synaptotagmin 1. *Journal of Physiology, 587*, 3221–3231.

Luciana, M., Collins, P. F., & Depue, R. A. (1998). Opposing roles for dopamine and serotonin in the modulation of human spatial working memory functions. *Cerebral Cortex, 8*, 218–226.

Lupien, S. J., Gillin, C. J., & Hauger, R. L. (1999). Working memory is more sensitive than declarative memory to the acute effects of corticosteroids: a dose-dependent study in humans. *Behavioral Neuroscience, 113*, 420–430.

Lupien, S. J., Maheu, F., Tu, M., Fiocco, A., & Schramek, T. E. (2007). The effects of stress and stress hormones on human cognition: implications for the field of brain and cognition. *Brain and Cognition, 65*, 209–237.

Marin, M.-F., Pilgrim, K., & Lupien, S. J. (2010). Modulatory effects of stress on reactivated emotional memories. *Psychoneuroendocrinology, 35*, 1388–1396.

Mason, J. W. (1975a). A historical view of the stress field. Part I. *Journal of Human Stress, 1*, 6–12.

Mason, J. W. (1975b). A historical view of the stress field. Part II. *Journal of Human Stress, 1*, 22–36.

Mason, J. W., Hartley, L. H., Kotchen, T. A., Mougey, E. H., Ricketts, P. T., & Jones, L. G. (1973). Plasma cortisol and norepinephrine resposnes in anticipation of muscular exercise. *Psychosomatic Medicine, 35*, 406–414.

Matthews, V. B., Aström, M. B., Chan, M. H., Bruce, C. R., Krabbe, K. S., & Prelovsek, O. (2009). Brain-derived neurotrophic factor is produced by skeletal muscle in response to contraction and enhances fat oxidation via activation of AMP-activated protein kinase. *Diabetologia, 52*, 1409–1418.

McGaugh, J. L., Cahill, L., & Roozendaal, B. (1996). Involvement of the amygdala in memory storage: interaction with other brain systems. *Proceedings of the National Academy of Sciences of the United States of America, 93*, 13508–13514.

McMorris, T. (2009). Exercise and decision making in team games. In T. McMorris, P. D. Tomporowski, & M. Audiffren (Eds.), *Exercise and cognitive function* (pp. 180–192). Chichester: Wiley-Blackwell.

McMorris, T., Collard, K., Corbett, J., Dicks, M., & Swain, J. P. (2008). A test of the catecholamines hypothesis for an acute exercise–cognition interaction. *Pharmacology Biochemistry and Behavior, 89*, 106–115.

McMorris, T., Davranche, K., Jones, G., Hall, B., & Minter, C. (2009). Acute incremental exercise, performance of a central executive task, and sympathoadrenal system and hypothalamic-pituitary-adrenal axis activity. *International Journal of Psychophysiology, 73*, 334–340.

McMorris, T., & Graydon, J. (1996a). The effect of exercise on the decision-making performance of experienced and inexperienced soccer players. *Research Quarterly for Exercise and Sport, 67*, 109–114.

McMorris, T., & Graydon, J. (1996b). Effect of exercise on soccer decision-making tasks of differing complexities. *Journal of Human Movement Studies, 30*, 177–193.

McMorris, T., & Graydon, J. (1997). The effect of exercise on cognitive performance in soccer-specific tests. *Journal of Sport Science, 15*, 459–468.

McMorris, T., & Hale, B. J. (2012). Differential effects of differing intensities of acute exercise on speed and accuracy of cognition: a meta-analytical investigation. *Brain and Cognition, 80*, 338–351.

McMorris, T., & Hale, B. J. (2015). Is there an acute exercise-induced physiological/biochemical threshold which triggers increased speed of cognitive functioning? A meta-analytic investigation. *Journal Sport and Health Sciences, 4*, 4–13.

McMorris, T., Hill, C., Sproule, J., Potter, J., Swain, J., Hobson, G., et al. (2005). Supra-maximal effort and reaction and movement times in a non-compatible response time task. *Journal of Sports Medicine and Physical Fitness, 45*, 127–133.

McMorris, T., & Keen, P. (1994). Effect of exercise on simple reaction times of recreational athletes. *Perceptual and Motor Skills, 78*, 123–130.

McMorris, T., Myers, S., MacGillivary, W. W., Sexsmith, J. R., Fallowfield, J., Graydon, J., et al. (1999). Exercise, plasma catecholamine concentration and decision-making performance of soccer players on a soccer-specific test. *Journal of Sport Science, 17*, 667–676.

McMorris, T., Sproule, J., Draper, S., & Child, R. (2000). Performance of a psychomotor skill following rest, exercise at the plasma epinephrine threshold and maximal intensity exercise. *Perceptual and Motor Skills, 91*, 553–562.

McMorris, T., Sproule, J., Turner, A., & Hale, B. J. (2011). Acute, intermediate intensity exercise, and speed and accuracy in working memory tasks: a meta-analytical comparison of effects. *Physiology & Behavior, 102*, 421–428.

McMorris, T., Swain, J., Lauder, M., Smith, N., & Kelly, J. (2006). Warm-up prior to undertaking a dynamic psychomotor task: does it aid performance? *Journal of Sports Medicine and Physical Fitness, 46*, 328–334.

McMorris, T., Tallon, M., Williams, C., Sproule, J., Potter, J., Swain, J., et al. (2003). Incremental exercise, plasma concentrations of catecholamines, reaction time, and motor time during performance of a noncompatible choice response time task. *Perceptual and Motor Skills, 97*, 590–604.

Meeusen, R., & De Meirleir, K. (1995). Exercise and brain neurotransmission. *Sports Medicine, 20*, 160–188.

Meeusen, R., Piacentini, M. F., & De Meirleir, K. (2001). Brain microdialysis in exercise research. *Sports Medicine, 31*, 965–983.

Meeusen, R., Smolders, J., Sarre, S., De Meirleir, K., Keizer, H., Serneels, M., et al. (1997). Endurance training effects on neurotransmitter release in rat striatum: an in vivo microdialysis study. *Acta Physiologica Scandinavica, 159*, 335–341.

Miyake, A., Friedman, N. P., Emerson, M. J., Witzki, A. H., & Howerter, A. (2000). The unity and diversity of executive functions and their contributions to complex "frontal lobe" tasks: a latent variable analysis. *Cognitive Psychology, 41*, 49–100.

Miyake, A., & Shah, P. (1999). Toward unified theories of working memory: emerging general consensus, unresolved theoretical issues, and future research directions. In A. Miyake, & P. Shah (Eds.), *Models of working memory* (pp. 442–481). New York: Cambridge University Press.

Miyashita, T., & Williams, C. L. (2006). Epinephrine administration increases neural impulses propagated along the vagus nerve: role of peripheral beta-adrenergic receptors. *Neurobiology of Learning and Memory, 85*, 116–124.

Mongeau, R., Blier, P., & de Montigny, C. (1997). The serotonergic and noradrenergic systems of the hippocampus: their interactions and the effects of antidepressant treatments. *Brain Research Brain Research Review, 23*, 145–195.

Moore, R. D., Romine, M. W., O'Conner, P. J., & Tomporowski, P. D. (2012). The influence of exercise-induced fatigue on cognitive function. *Journal of Sports Science, 30*, 841–850.

Nanda, B., Balde, J. S., & Manjunatha, S. (2013). The acute effects of a single bout of moderate-intensity aerobic exercise on cognitive functions in healthy adult males. *Journal of Clinical and Diagnostic Research, 7*, 1883–1885.

Neeper, S. A., Gomez-Pinilla, F., Choi, J., & Cotman, C. W. (1995). Exercise and brain neurotrophins. *Nature, 373*, 109.

Olvera-Cortés, M. E., Anguiano-Rodriguez, P., López-Vázquez, M. A., & Alfaro, J. M. (2008). Serotonin/dopamine interaction in learning. *Progress in Brain Research, 172*, 567–602.

Otte, C., Moritz, S., Yassouridis, A., Koop, M., Madrischewski, A. M., Wiedermann, K., et al. (2007). Blockade of the mineralocorticoid receptor in healthy men: effects on experimentally induced panic symptoms, stress hormones and cognition. *Neuropsychopharmacology, 32*, 232–238.

Ozyemisci-Taskiran, O., Gunendi, Z., Bolukbasi, N., & Beyazova, M. (2008). The effect of a single session submaximal aerobic exercise on premotor fraction of reaction time: an electromyographic study. *Clinical Biomechanics, 23*, 231–235.

Pardridge, W. M. (1998). Blood–brain barrier carrier-mediated transport and brain metabolism of amino acids. *Neurochemical Research, 23*, 635–644.

Pesce, C., & Audiffren, M. (2011). Does acute exercise switch off switch costs? A study with younger and older athletes. *Journal of Sport and Exercise Psychology, 33*, 609–626.

Pesce, C., Capranica, L., Tessitore, A., & Figura, F. (2002). Orienting and focusing of visual attention under submaximal physical load. *Journal of Human Movement Studies, 42*, 401–420.

Pesce, C., Capranica, L., Tessitore, A., & Figura, F. (2003). Focusing of visual attention under submaximal physical load. *International Journal of Sport and Exercise Psychology, 1*, 275–292.

Pesce, C., Cereatti, L., Casella, R., Caldari, C., & Capranica, L. (2007). Preservation of visual attention in older expert orienteers at rest and under physical effort. *Journal of Sport and Exercise Psychology, 29*, 78–99.

Pesce, C., Tessitore, A., Casella, R., Pirritano, M., & Capranica, L. (2007). Focusing of visual attention at rest and during physical exercise in soccer players. *Journal of Sports Science, 25*, 1259–1270.

Peyrin, L., Pequignot, J. M., Lacour, J. R., & Fourcade, J. (1987). Relationships between catecholamine or 3-methoxy 4-hydroxy phenylglycol changes and the mental performance under submaximal exercise in man. *Psychopharmacology, 93*, 188–192.

Podolin, D. A., Munger, P. A., & Mazzeo, R. S. (1991). Plasma-catecholamine and lactate response during graded-exercise with varied glycogen conditions. *Journal of Applied Physiology, 71*, 1427–1433.

Podvoll, E. M., & Goodman, S. J. (1967). Averaged neural electrical activity and arousal. *Science, 155*, 223–225.

Poldrack, R. A., & Gabrieli, J. D. E. (2001). Characterizing the neural mechanisms of skill learning and repetition priming: evidence from mirror reading. *Brain, 124*, 67–82.

Poldrack, R. A., Sabb, F. W., Foerde, K., Tom, S. M., Asarnow, R. F., Bookheimer, S. Y., et al. (2005). The neural correlates of motor skill automaticity. *Journal of Neuroscience, 25*, 5356–5364.

Pruessner, J. C., Champagne, F., Meaney, M. J., & Dagher, A. (2004). Dopamine release in response to a psychological stress in humans and its relationship to early life maternal care: a positron emission tomography study using [^{11}C]Raclopride. *Journal of Neuroscience, 24*, 2625–2831.

Rasmussen, P., Brassard, P., Adser, H., Pedersen, M. V., Leick, L., Hart, E., et al. (2009). Evidence for release of brain-derived neurotrophic factor from the brain during exercise. *Experimental Physiology, 94*, 1062–1069.

Reis, D. J., & Fuxe, K. (1968). Depletion of noradrenaline in the brainstem neurons during sham rage behaviour produced by acute brainstem transmission in cat. *Brain Research, 7*, 448–451.

Reis, D. J., & Fuxe, K. (1969). Brain norepinephrine: evidence that neuronal releqase is essential for sham rage behavior following brainstem transection in the cat. *Proceedings of the National Academy of Sciences of the United States of America, 84*, 108–112.

Robbins, T. W., & Roberts, A. C. (2007). Differential regulation of fronto-executive function by the monoamines and acetylcholine. *Cerebral Cortex, 17*(Suppl. 1), i151–i160.

Rojas Vega, S., Strüder, H. K., Vera Wahrmann, B., Schmidt, A., Bloch, W., & Hollmann, W. (2006). Acute BDNF and cortisol response to low intensity exercise and following ramp incremental exercise to exhaustion in humans. *Brain Research, 1121*, 59–65.

Roth, R. H., Tam, S.-Y., Ida, Y., Yang, J.-X., & Deutch, A. Y. (1988). Stress and the mesocorticolimbic dopamine systems. *Annals of the New York Academy of Sciences, 537*, 138–147.

Rothman, S. M., Griffioen, K. J., Wan, R., & Mattson, M. P. (2012). Brain-derived neurotrophic factor as a regulator of systemic and brain energy metabolism and cardiovascular health. *Annals of the New York Academy of Sciences, 1264*, 49–63.

Rushmer, R. F., Smith, O. A., Jr., & Lasher, E. P. (1960). Neural mechanisms of cardiac control during exertion. *Physiological Reviews, 40*(Suppl. 4), 27–34.

Sakaue, M., Somboonthum, P., Nishihara, B., Koyama, Y., Hashimotot, H., Baba, A., et al. (2000). Postsynaptic 5-hydroxytryptamine(1A) receptor activation increases in vivo dopamine release in rat prefrontal cortex. *British Journal of Pharmacology, 129*, 1028–1034.

Samorajaski, T., & Marks, B. H. (1962). Localization of tritiated norepinephrine in mouse brain. *Journal of Histochemistry and Cytochemistry, 10*, 393–399.

Sawada, Y., Nishio, Y., Suzuki, K., Hirayama, K., Takeda, A., Hosokai, Y., et al. (2012). Attentional set-shifting deficit in Parkinson's disease is associated with prefrontal dysfunction: an FDG-PET study. *PLoS One, 7*, e38498. http://dx.doi.org/10.1371/journal.pone.0038498.

Schmidt, E. D., Binnekade, R., Janszen, A. W., & Tilders, F. J. (1996). Short stressor induced long-lasting increases of vasopressin stores in hypothalamic corticotropin-releasing hormone (CRH) neurons in adult rats. *Journal of Neuroendocrinology, 8*, 703–712.

Selye, H. (1956). *The stress of life*. New York: McGraw-Hill.

Shojaei, E. A., Farajov, A., & Jafari, A. (2011). Effect of moderate aerobic cycling on some systemic inflammatory markers in healthy active collegiate men. *International Journal of General Medicine, 4*, 79–84.

Sjöberg, H. (1980). Physical fitness and mental performance during and after work. *Ergonomics, 23*, 977–985.

Sothmann, M. S., Hart, B. A., Horn, T. S., & Gustafson, A. B. (1991). Plasma catecholamines and performance association during psychological stress: evidence for peripheral noradrenergic involvement with an attention-demanding task. *Medicine and Science in Sports and Exercise, 23*, 860–867.

van Stegeren, A. H., Roozenddaal, B., Kindt, M., Wolf, O. T., & Joëls, M. (2010). Interacting noradrenergic and corticosteroid systems shift human brain activation patterns during encoding. *Neurobiology of Learning and Memory, 93*, 56–65.

Straube, T., Korz, V., Balschun, D., & Frey, J. U. (2003). Novelty-exploration induces a protein synthesis-dependent late phase of long-term potentiation: involvement of β-adrenergic receptors. *Journal of Physiology (London), 552*, 953–960.

Ströhle, A., Stoy, M., Graetz, B., Scheel, M., Wittmann, A., Gallinat, J., et al. (2010). Acute exercise ameliorates reduced brain-derived neurotrophic factor in patients with panic disorder. *Psychoneuroendocrinology, 35*, 384–388.

Tang, S. W., Chu, E., Hui, T., Helmeste, D., & Law, C. (2008). Influence of exercise on serum brain-derived neurotrophic factor concentrations in healthy human subjects. *Neuroscience Letters, 431*, 62–65.

Thomson, K., Watt, A., & Liukkonen, J. (2009). Differences in ball sports athletes speed discrimination skills before and after exercise induced fatigue. *Journal of Sports Science and Medicine, 8*, 259–264.

Tomporowski, P. D., & Ganio, M. S. (2006). Short-term effects of aerobic exercise eon executive processing, memory, and emotional reactivity. *International Journal of Sport and Exercise Psychology, 1*, 1–18.

Travlos, A. K. (2009). Effect of submaximal steady-state aerobic exercise and fitness in Random Number Generation test. *Biology of Exercise, 5*, 41–50.

Tsai, C.-L., Chen, F.-C., Pan, C.-Y., Wang, C.-H., Huang, T.-H., & Chen, T.-C. (2014). Impact of acute aerobic exercise and cardiorespiratory fitness on visuospatial attention performance and serum BDNF levels. *Psychoneuroendocrinology, 41*, 121–131.

Urhausen, A., Weiler, B., Coen, B., & Kindermann, W. (1994). Plasma catecholamines during endurance exercise of different intensities as related to the individual anaerobic threshold. *European Journal of Applied Physiology, 69*, 16–20.

Valentino, R. J., Page, M. E., & Curtis, A. L. (1991). Activation of noradrenergic locus coeruleus neurons by hemodynamic stress is due to local release of corticotropin-releasing factor. *Brain Research, 555*, 25–34.

Vale, W., & Rivier, C. (1977). Substances modulating the secretion of ACTH by cultural anterior pituitary cells. *Federation Proceedings, 36*, 2094–2099.

Velásquez-Martinez, M. C., Vázquez-Torres, R., & Jiménez-Riveira, C. A. (2012). Activation of alpha1-adrenoreceptors enhances glutamate release onto ventral tegmental area dopamine cells. *Neuroscience, 216*, 18–30.

Vendsalu, A. (1960). Studies on adrenaline and noradrenaline in human plasma. *Acta Physiologica Scandinavica, 49*(Suppl. 173), 1–123.

Vgontzas, A. N., Pejovic, S., Zoumakis, E., Lin, H. M., Bixier, E. O., Basta, M., et al. (2007). Daytime napping after a night of sleep loss decreases sleepiness, improves performance, and causes beneficial changes in cortisol and interleukin-6 secretion. *American Journal of Physiology: Endocrinology and Metabolism, 292*, E253–E261.

Wager, T. D., Reading, S., & Jonides, J. (2004). Neuroimaging studies of shifting attention: a meta-analysis. *NeuroImage, 22*(4), 1679–1693.

Wand, G. S., Oswald, L. M., McCaul, M. E., Wong, D. F., Johnson, E., Zhou, Y., et al. (2007). Association of amphetamine-induced striatal dopamine release and cortisol responses to psychological stress. *Neuropsychopharmacology, 32*, 2310–2320.

Wang, G.-J., Volkow, N. D., Fowler, J. S., Franchesci, D., Logan, J., Pappas, N. R., et al. (2000). PET studies of the effects of aerobic exercise on human striatal dopamine release. *Journal of Nuclear Medicine, 41*, 1352–1356.

Wann, B. P., Audet, M. C., & Anisman, H. (2010). Impact of acute and chronic stressor experiences on heart atrial and brain natriuretic peptides in response to a subsequent stressor. *Hormones and Behavior, 58*, 907–916.

Waterhouse, B. D., Moises, H. C., & Woodward, D. J. (1980). Noradrenergic modulation of somatosensory cortical neuronal responses to iontophoretically applied putative transmitters. *Experimental Neurology, 69,* 30–49.

Waterhouse, B. D., Moises, H. C., & Woodward, D. J. (1981). Alpha-receptor-mediated facilitation of somatosensory cortical neuronal responses to excitatory synaptic inputs and iontophoretically applied acetylcholine. *Neuropharmacology, 20,* 907–920.

Waterhouse, B., Moises, H., & Woodward, D. J. (1998). Phasic activation of the locus coeruleus enhances responses of primary sensory cortical neurons to peripheral receptive field stimulation. *Brain Research, 790,* 33–44.

Waterhouse, E. G., & Xu, B. (2009). New insights into the role of brain-derived neurotrophic factor in synaptic plasticity. *Molecular and Cellular Neuroscience, 42,* 81–89.

Webb, H. E., Weldy, M. L., Fabianke-Kadue, E. C., Orndorff, G. R., Kamimori, G. H., & Acevedo, E. O. (2008). Psychological stress during exercise: cardiorespiratory and hormonal responses. *European Journal of Applied Physiology, 104,* 973–981.

Weinstein, A. A., Deuster, P. A., Francis, J. L., Bonsall, R. W., Tracy, R. P., & Kop, W. (2010). Neurohormonal and inflammatory hyper-responsiveness to acute mental stress in depression. *Biological Psychology, 84,* 228–234.

Wickens, J. R., Horvitz, J. C., Costa, R. M., & Killcross, S. (2007). Dopaminergic mechanisms in actions and habits. *Journal of Neuroscience, 27,* 8181–8183.

Wieczorek, M., & Dunn, A. (2006). Relationships among the behavioral, noradrenergic, and pituitary-adrenal responses to interleukin-1 and the effects of indomethacin. *Brain, Behavior, and Immunity, 20,* 477–487.

Winter, B., Breitenstein, C., Mooren, F. C., Voelker, K., Fobker, M., Lechtermann, A., et al. (2007). High impact running improves learning. *Neurobiology of Learning and Memory, 87,* 597–609.

Wisse, B. E., & Schwartz, M. W. (2003). The skinny on neurotrophins. *Nature Neuroscience, 6,* 655–656.

Wolf, O. T., Convit, A., McHugh, P. F., Kandil, E., Thorn, E. L., De Santi, S., et al. (2001). Cortisol differentially affects memory in young and elderly men. *Behavioral Neuroscience, 115,* 1002–1011.

Yamamoto, Y., Miyashita, M., Hughson, R. L., Tmura, S., Shiohara, M., & Mutoh, Y. (1991). The ventilatory threshold gives maximal lactate steady state. *European Journal of Applied Physiology, 63,* 55–59.

Yanagisawa, H., Dan, I., Tsuzuki, D., Kato, M., Okamoto, M., Kyutoku, Y., et al. (2010). Acute moderate exercise elicits increased dorsolateral prefrontal activation and improves cognitive performance with Stroop test. *NeuroImage, 50,* 1702–1710.

Yanagita, S., Amemiya, S., Suzuki, S., & Kita, I. (2007). Effects of spontaneous and forced running on activation of hypothalamic corticotropin-releasing hormone neurons in rats. *Life Sciences, 80,* 356–363.

Yang, J., Harte-Hargrove, L. C., Siao, C.-J., Marinic, T., Clarke, R., Ma, Q., et al. (2014). proBDNF negatively regulates neuronal remodeling, synaptic transmission, and synaptic plasticity in hippocampus. *Cell Reports, 7,* 796–806. http://dx.doi.org/10.1016/j.celrep.2014.03.040.

Yerkes, R. M., & Dodson, J. D. (1908). The relation of strength of stimulus to the rapidity of habit formation. *Journal of Comparative Neurology and Psychology, 18,* 459–482.

Zoladz, J. A., Pilc, A., Majerczxak, J., Grandys, M., Zapart-Bukowska, J., & Duda, K. (2008). Endurance training increases plasma brain-derived neurotrophic factor concentration in young healthy men. *Journal of Physiology and Pharmacology, 59*(Suppl. 7), 119–132.

Acute Exercise and Event-Related Potential: Current Status and Future Prospects

Yu-Kai Chang

Graduate Institute of Athletics and Coaching Science, National Taiwan Sport University, Guishan Township, Taoyuan County, Taiwan (R.O.C.)

INTRODUCTION

Regular exercise has been linked to improved physical fitness, reduced chronic disease (Vanhees, De Sutter, et al., 2012; Vanhees, Geladas, et al., 2012), increased positive mood and decreased stress (Yau, Lau, & So, 2011), depression (Silveira et al., 2013), and anxiety (DeBoer, Powers, Utschig, Otto, & Smits, 2012). The beneficial effects of exercise have extended to cognitive function, and research regarding exercise and cognition has been recognized as one of the most prominent issues in exercise psychology (Berger, Pargman, & Weinberg, 2014; Buckworth, Dishamn, O'Connor, & Tomporowski, 2013).

Although the field is relatively new, the effects of acute exercise on cognitive function (i.e., the examination of alterations in cognitive function induced by a single bout of exercise) have been sporadically examined since the 1920s. However, studies between the 1920s and 1980s not only obtained inconsistent results but also had many methodological issues and utilized a non-theoretical parametric approach; thus, definitive conclusions remain elusive (Tomporowski & Ellis, 1986).

Since the review by Tomporowski and Ellis (1986), further progress has been made regarding these methodological and nontheoretical concerns. Although conflicting results were reported in later studies, narrative reviews generally support the positive effect of acute exercise on cognitive function (Brisswalter, Collardeau, & Arcelin, 2002; McMorris & Graydon, 2000; Tomporowski, 2003). For example, based upon the inverted-U hypothesis between incremental exercise intensity and cognitive performance, McMorris and Graydon (2000) claimed that the speed of cognition but not the accuracy is improved when exercising at the level of the individual's plasma adrenaline threshold. Brisswalter et al. (2002) found that the relationship between acute exercise and cognitive function was moderated by different factors such as exercise intensity, physical fitness level, exercise duration, and the nature of the psychological task. When three independent exercise paradigms (i.e., intense anaerobic exercise, short-duration aerobic and

Exercise-Cognition Interaction
http://dx.doi.org/10.1016/B978-0-12-800778-5.00005-0

anaerobic exercise, and steady-state aerobic exercise) were examined, a classic review by Tomporowski (2003) concluded that acute exercise at submaximal aerobic exercise intensity for 20–60 min facilitated specific aspects of information processing.

The positive effect of acute exercise on cognitive function has been further supported by meta-analytic reviews. Etnier et al. (1997) stated that acute exercise has a similar effect (effect size, ES = 0.16) as that obtained from multiple exercise paradigms (ES = 0.25; e.g., acute exercise, chronic exercise, mixed exercise), suggesting that acute exercise has a small but significantly positive effect on cognitive function. Similar small but positive effects of acute exercise on cognitive function were observed in recent meta-analytical reviews that specifically emphasized acute exercise (Chang, Labban, Gapin, & Etnier, 2012; Lambourne & Tomporowski, 2010; McMorris & Hale, 2012; McMorris, Sproule, Turner, & Hale, 2011).

While the majority of studies examining acute exercise and cognitive function assessed cognitive performance using behavioral measures, a growing body of research regarding acute exercise and cognitive function has incorporated neuroelectric approaches, particularly event-related potentials (ERPs), to better understand the intrinsic and specific cognitive processes induced by acute exercise (Hillman, Snook, & Jerome, 2003; Scudder, Drollette, Pontifex, & Hillman, 2012). Specifically, this research approach began in the late 1990s (Nakamura, Nishimoto, Akamatu, Takahashi, & Maruyama, 1999; Yagi, Coburn, Estes, & Arruda, 1999), and it has recently become rapidly developed (Drollette et al., 2014; Hillman et al., 2009; Hillman, Kamijo, & Pontifex, 2012; Hillman, Kamijo, & Scudder, 2011; Hillman, Pontifex, et al., 2012; Kamijo et al., 2009; Pontifex, Saliba, Raine, Picchietti, & Hillman, 2013; Scudder et al., 2012; Stroth et al., 2009).

The purpose of this chapter is to provide an updated review of the effects of acute exercise on ERPs. The relationship between acute exercise and ERPs was analyzed based on two time points following exercise cessation, including the immediate and delayed effects of acute exercise on alterations of ERP components. Specifically, the review consists of four sections. In the first section, selected ERP components are introduced to provide a fundamental knowledge of ERPs. The second section reviews the effects of acute exercise on ERPs at the time point immediately following exercise cessation on a theoretical basis and examines the four primary moderators: the ERP measures, the type of cognition, the participants, and the exercise protocol. The third section reviews the theoretical basis and examines the four moderators at delayed time points. Finally, future directions regarding the moderators underlying acute exercise and ERPs for the exercise paradigms involved in the two time points are discussed.

EVENT-RELATED POTENTIALS

An ERP, a time-locked electroencephalography (EEG) induced by internal or external stimuli or events, reflects neural manifestations of specific psychological functions (Fabiani, Gratton, & Federmeier, 2009). ERP is a noninvasive approach that provides high temporal resolution on the order of milliseconds, which enables the evaluation of covert cognitive processes. In brief, ERP applies an average technique for event-related EEG activity, and with the appropriate amount of time-locked EEG activity, the random EEG activity or the background EEG activity is averaged out and the task-relevant waveform, also known as the component, remains and can be identified. Beyond the overt action, distinct cognitive processes such as stimulus encoding and response execution can be inferred from specific ERP components (Hillman et al., 2011). In general, an ERP component is named based on its polarity (e.g., positive or negative) and latency (i.e., the time since the stimulus). For example, P3 or P300 refers to a positive deflection peaking at approximately 300 ms following the presentation of the stimuli or event onset. Intrinsic cognitive processes can be proposed according to the specific component, amplitude, latency, area, or scale distribution.

ERP components have also been identified and categorized depending on their characteristics (Fabiani et al., 2009). For example, ERP components can be divided into exogenous, endogenous, and mesogenous types. The exogenous type refers to a component that is largely related to the physical parameters of the eliciting stimulus. Examples of exogenous components are the brainstem potential and P1 (Luck, 2005). The endogenous type refers to a component elicited by the internal characteristics of the subject rather than the external physical properties of the eliciting stimulus. Examples of endogenous components are P3 and contingent negative variation (CNV). Lastly, the mesogenous type refers to components that are sensitive to both physical parameters and the internal characteristics of the subject, such as N1. ERP components can also be distinguished by sensory features, attention, memory, and the time point at which it occurred, including those for sensory components (e.g., usually occur at less than 100 ms), early negativities (e.g., usually occur between 100 and 300 ms; e.g., N1, N2), and late cognitive ERPs (e.g., usually occur after 300 ms; e.g., P3, N4). Alternatively, ERP components can be distributed according to the nature of the time-locking events. For example, stimulus-locked components (e.g., P1, N1, N2, P3) are components that occur following the onset of a sensory event (Coles & Rugg, 1995), whereas response-locked components [e.g., error-related negativity (ERN) and error positivity (Pe)] are components that occur following the exact behavioral response (Falkenstein, Hielscher, et al., 2001; Falkenstein, Hoormann, & Hohnsbein, 2001).

Several ERP components are described briefly below; however, the scope of this review is limited to the components that have been applied in studies associated with acute exercise.

P3

P3 has been recognized as the primary ERP component. It was first reported by Sutton, Braren, Zubin, and John (1965) who observed a large positive-going waveform at a latency of approximately 300 ms when an individual performed an auditory simple discrimination task. To elicit P3, an oddball paradigm is usually applied, where P3 robustly occurs at a low-frequency target (known as the deviant) within a high-frequency target (known as the standard), regardless of the modality of the target stimulus (e.g., visual, auditory) (Polich & Kok, 1995). Although P3 can be observed in the frontal lobe, the largest P3 has most often been recorded in the parietal lobe from 300 to 800 ms after the stimulus onset, depending on the task complexity (see Figure 1). Based on its characteristics, P3 is considered to be a late, exogenous, and stimulus-locked component. While the precise meaning of P3 is still arguable, P3 is frequently assumed to be associated with context-updating (Luck, 2005), stimulus evaluation, and antinational allocation (Coles & Rugg, 1995; Polich & Kok, 1995). Specifically, P3 amplitude is believed to reflect the attentional resource

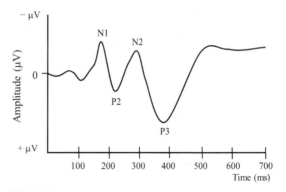

FIGURE 1 Illustration of stimulus-locked ERP components for N1, N2, P2, and P3 components.

allocation devoted to a given task (Polich, 2007; Wickens, Kramer, Vanasse, & Donchin, 1983), whereas P3 latency is associated with the speed of detecting and evaluating the stimulus (Magliero, Bashore, Coles, & Donchin, 1984; Polich, 2007) but is independent of response selection processes and behavioral action (Duncan-Johnson, 1981; Verleger, 1997). In general, a larger P3 amplitude is associated with tasks that require greater amounts of cognitive demand (Hillman et al., 2003), and a shortened P3 latency is related to greater cognitive performance (Polich, 2007).

N1, N2, P2, and N4

N1, P2, and N2 are early, mesogenous, and stimulus-locked ERP components generally observed from 100 to 300 ms after stimuli onset (see Figure 1). N1 refers to a negative-going waveform at a latency of approximately 100 ms. In the classical right and left auditory paradigm, a greater N1 amplitude was elicited on the attended channel (i.e., right or left ear) relative to the unattended channel, suggesting that N1 is associated with selective attention (Knight, Hillyard, Woods, & Neville, 1981; Näätänen, 1992). P2 occurs followed by N1 and is usually observed at the anterior and central lobes, but not the posterior lobe. While P2 was elicited by an infrequent event that was similar to P3, P2 generally occurred in response to a relatively simple stimulus (Luck, 2005); P3 was elicited by a variety of stimuli. N2 is the largest negative-going waveform around the frontal–central area at 150–350 ms post-stimulus (Kopp, Rist, & Mattler, 1996). N2 is generally elicited by the go/no go task paradigm, and a larger N2 is observed in the no go condition compared with the go condition, suggesting that N2 indicates processes of response inhibition and error monitoring (Folstein & Van Petten, 2008).

Unlike N1, N2, and P2, N4 is a late, exogenous, and stimulus-locked component. N4, recorded from 360 to 450 ms following stimulus onset, is related to language comprehension, particularly when a semantically incongruous situation arises (e.g., the pizza was too hot to *cry*) (Kutas & Federmeier, 2000).

Contingent Negative Variation

CNV, which was observed in the 1960s, has been recognized as the first identified component in the modern era of ERP research (Walter, Cooper, Aldridge, McCallum, & Winter, 1964). CNV refers to a steady, slow, negative-going waveform, which is often observed in the central and frontal areas, and is considered a response-locked component. CNV is typically elicited by S1–S2 paradigms in which the participant first experiences a warming single (S1), followed by a certain time period (e.g., 500–1000 ms), and then a response to a latter target stimulus (S2; see Figure 2). A larger CNV was observed when a participant was required to behaviorally respond to the S2, suggesting that CNV reflects expectation and motor preparation (Falkenstein, Hoormann, Hohnsbein, & Kleinsorge, 2003), as well as attention (Rohrbaugh & Gaillard, 1983).

CNV can be further divided into an early orienting wave (O-wave) and a late expectancy wave (E-wave), in which the O-wave is associated with arousal and the orient-response,

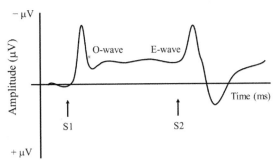

FIGURE 2   Illustration of an S1–S2 paradigm and a contingent negative variation (CNV) component.

whereas the E-wave is related to motor preparation (Bareš, Nestrašil, & Rektor, 2007; Loveless & Sanford, 1974).

Error-Related Negativity and Error Positivity

ERN and Pe are response-locked components and are observed from 50 to 300 ms following the error response; therefore, these components have been linked to action monitoring (see Figure 3). ERN, also known as error negativity (Ne), was observed when the participant made errors during a cognitive task (Falkenstein, Hohnsbein, Hoormann, & Blanke, 1990). The negative-going waveform tends to be larger at the frontocentral areas at a latency of approximately 50–150 ms post-stimulus. ERN is considered an ERP component that reflects the response monitor system (Falkenstein, Hoormann, Christ, & Hohnsbein, 2000) and is most likely generated by the anterior cingulate cortex (Holroyd, Dien, & Coles, 1998).

Pe differs from ERN and is a late and positive-going waveform, which is subsequent to ERN and is larger at the centroparietal areas at approximately 300 ms post-incorrect response. Although both ERN and Pe are related to error response, Pe is associated with post-error possessing (Falkenstein et al., 2000), and the underlying

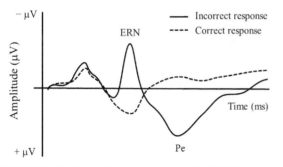

FIGURE 3   Illustration of response-locked ERP components for error-related negativity (ERN) and error positive (Pe).

neural generators between the two components are independent (Herrmann, Römmler, Ehlis, Heidrich, & Fallgatter, 2004).

ERPs FOLLOWING EXERCISE: IMMEDIATE EFFECTS

Previous research has demonstrated a facilitative cognitive effect following exercise cessation. Indeed, recent meta-analytic reviews have consistently observed a small but significant improvement in cognitive performance following a single bout of exercise (Chang, Labban, et al., 2012; Lambourne & Tomporowski, 2010; McMorris & Hale, 2012). It should be noted that Chang, Labban, et al. (2012) categorized the following exercise effects based on two exercise paradigms: immediately following exercise and after a delay following exercise. The researchers found that these two exercise paradigms affect cognitive function differently. Specifically, at the behavioral level, the facilitative effect of acute exercise on cognition is only observed within 15 min of exercise cessation, whereas no difference is observed after 15 min from completion of the exercise. The difference also implies that the two exercise paradigms have a distinct theoretical basis.

The potential mechanism for alterations of cognitive function immediately following exercise has been linked to physiological arousal (Chang & Etnier, 2013). According to the inverted-U hypothesis (Yerkes & Dodson, 1908), there is an inverted-U relationship between arousal and performance. That is, when arousal becomes elevated, performance is affected in a quadratic trend, whereas moderate arousal leads to better performances compared to arousal that is too low and too high (Arent & Landers, 2003). Physiological arousal is believed to increase proportionally with exercise intensity and gradually decrease after exercise cessation. Based upon the hypotheses, exercise-induced physiological arousal, particularly when maintained at a moderate level, would benefit cognitive performance. In contrast, elevated physiological arousal is maintained somewhat transiently, implying that the physiological arousal induced by exercise is insufficient to explain the alteration in cognitive performance after a long delay following exercise. Thus, an alternative interpretation is necessary.

This section emphasizes the influence of ERPs immediately following exercise (within 15 min; see Table 1) as well as the relationship between acute exercise and ERPs based upon four primary moderators.

ERP Measures

The eight studies in Table 1 examined ERP alterations immediately following exercise. The most frequently examined ERP components were P3 (seven studies), CNV and N2 (two studies), P2 (one study), and N1 (one study).

Of the seven studies that examined the acute exercise effects on P3, four studies showed that acute exercise significantly influences P3. Specifically, with the exception of Stroth et al. (2009), acute exercise, particularly an acute exercise program involving moderate exercise for 18–30 min, led to an increase in P3 amplitude (Kamijo et al., 2009; Kamijo, Nishihira, Hatta, Kaneda, Wasaka, et al., 2004; Kamijo, Nishihira, Higashiura, & Kuroiwa, 2007; Nakamura et al., 1999) and shortened P3 latency (Kamijo et al., 2007, 2009). Given that P3 amplitude and P3 latency represent the amount of attentional resource allocation as well as the stimulus evaluation and classification time, respectively, acute exercise may lead to greater attentional resource allocation to a given task and shorten the time of detecting and evaluating the stimulus through the neuroelectric evidence of P3.

Despite three studies that failed to detect a P3 influence following acute exercise (Grego et al., 2004; Stroth et al., 2009; Yagi et al., 1999), the protocols utilized for these studies were different from those employed in the previous studies

mentioned above and involved either a shorter period of time (i.e., 10 min) (Yagi et al., 1999) or a longer period of exercise (i.e., 180 min) (Grego et al., 2004). From the perspective of the inverted-U hypothesis of arousal and performance, it is plausible that an exercise protocol that is NOT within "acute exercise with sub-maximal aerobic exercise intensity for 20–60 min," which was recommended by Tomporowski (2003), would fail to induce moderate physical arousal (i.e., too light or too hard) and would consequently have only limited influence on P3.

The perspective of the inverted-U relationship between exercise-induced arousal and cognition was further supported by studies that examined CNV. The CNV is particularly important because the ERP index has been linked to arousal (Fischer, Langner, Birbaumer, & Brocke, 2008; Higuchi, Watanuki, Yasukouchi, & Sato, 1997). Kamijo and colleagues compared the CNV differences among low, moderate, and high exercise intensity conditions (Kamijo, Nishihira, Hatta, Kaneda, Kida, et al., 2004). The researchers found that the high exercise intensity condition decreased CNV amplitude and that moderate intensity increased CNV amplitude. Thus, acute exercise tends to affect CNV in a curvilinear fashion. Interestingly, moderate exercise simultaneously elevated both the early O-wave and the late E-wave, which are related to arousal and motor preparation, respectively (Bareš et al., 2007; Loveless & Sanford, 1974), suggesting that moderate exercise intensity induced optimal arousal and resulted in improved motor preparation.

In contrast, Stroth et al. (2009) found that a moderate exercise protocol for 20 min influenced neither P3 nor CNV. It should be noted that the researchers examined P3 at the lateral central and occipital electrodes rather than at the midline of the parietal electrodes, where P3 is typically revealed (Polich, 2007), or the midline of the frontal, central, and parietal electrode, where studies of acute exercise and ERP have been investigated (Kamijo et al., 2009; Kamijo, Nishihira, Hatta, Kaneda, Wasaka, et al., 2004;

TABLE 1 Event-related potentials following exercise: immediate effects

Study	Participants	Exercise protocol	Cognitive measure	Time points (following exercise)	ERP measures	Findings
Nakamura et al. (1999)	7 well-trained joggers (34.6 years)	T: jogging; I: self-paced; D: 30 min	Auditory oddball task	10 min	P3 P2 N1, N2	Increased P3 amplitude Increased P2 amplitude No effects for N1, N2
Yagi et al. (1999)	24 college students (20.6 years for female and 19.9 years for male)	T: cycling; I: 130–150 bpm; D: 10 min	Auditory and visual oddball tasks	Immediately	P3	No effect
Grego et al. (2004)	12 well-trained cyclists (29.0 years) with $\dot{V}O_2$max (48.4)	T: cycling; I: 66% $\dot{V}O_2$max; D: 180 min	Auditory oddball task	Immediately 15 min	P3	No effect
Kamijo, Nishihira, Hatta, Kaneda, Kida, et al. (2004)	12 subjects (22–33 years)	T: cycling; I: light = 84.43 bpm; moderate = 118.17 bpm; high = 190.17 bpm; D: 18 min	S1–S2 go/no go reaction time task	3 min	CNV	Decreased in early and late CNV amplitude for high intensity Increased CNV amplitude in moderate intensity
Kamijo, Nishihira, Hatta, Kaneda, Wasaka, et al. (2004)	12 subjects (22–33 years)	T: cycling; I: light = 84.43 bpm; moderate = 118.17 bpm; high = 190.17 bpm; D: 18 min	S1–S2 go/no go reaction time task	3 min	P3	Increased P3 amplitude in moderate intensity for go Increased P3 amplitude in moderate intensity for no go
Kamijo et al. (2007)	12 adults (25.7 years)	T: cycling; I: light RPE = 11; moderate RPE = 13; high RPE = 15; D: 20 min	Modified flanker task	Immediately	P3	Increased P3 in light and moderate intensities Shorted P3 latency in incongruent
Kamijo et al. (2009)	12 older (65.5 years) with $\dot{V}O_2$max (32.4) 12 youngers (21.8 years) with $\dot{V}O_2$max (52.2)	T: treadmill; I: low (30% $\dot{V}O_2$max); Moderate (50% $\dot{V}O_2$max); D: 20 min	Modified flanker task	Pre-test versus immediately	P3	Increased P3 amplitude in moderate intensity in youngers Shorted P3 latency in light and moderate intensities in both age groups
Stroth et al. (2009)	17 high-fit adolescents (14.2 years) with $\dot{V}O_2$max (56.3) 17 lower-fit adolescents (14.2 years) with $\dot{V}O_2$max (38.7) Fitness effect: yes	T: treadmill; I: 60% HR max; D: 20 min	Modified flanker task combined go/no go task	Immediately	P3, N2, CNV	No effects

Notes. $\dot{V}O_2$max: mL/kg/min; PA, physical activity; CNV, contingent negative variation; RPE, rate of perceived exertion; T, exercise type; I, exercise intensity; D, exercise duration.

Kamijo et al., 2007). Similarly, the CNV at the lateral central and occipital electrodes examined by Stroth et al. (2009) was also slightly different from that at the frontal and central areas in which the CNV is normally detected (Pfeuty, Ragot, & Pouthas, 2005; West, & Schwarb, 2006) or at the midline electrode that crossed the frontal to parietal electrodes and was positively induced by acute exercise (Kamijo, Nishihira, Hatta, Kaneda, Kida, et al., 2004). Obviously, only two studies with different methodological designs have been reported, and this is insufficient material from which to draw a conclusion. Furthermore, the cognitive task and the participant's demographic background have been proposed to play a role in interpreting the differences between the studies of Stroth et al. (2009) and others. For a detailed discussion, please refer to the "type of cognition" and "participants" sections below.

Finally, although acute exercise has been shown to increase P2 (Nakamura et al., 1999), other studies did not find that acute exercise influenced N1 and N2 (Nakamura et al., 1999; Stroth et al., 2009), suggesting that acute exercise has a limited influence on the early, mesogenous, and stimulus-locked component ERP immediately after exercise cessation. However, given that only a few studies exist, additional studies that replicate these findings are needed to confirm this conclusion.

Type of Cognition

Two types of cognitive function have been emphasized in the studies associating acute exercise and ERPs: stimulus discrimination (Grego et al., 2004; Nakamura et al., 1999; Yagi et al., 1999) and inhibition (Kamijo, Nishihira, Hatta, Kaneda, Kida, et al., 2004; Kamijo, Nishihira, Hatta, Kaneda, Wasaka, et al., 2004; Kamijo et al., 2007, 2009; Stroth et al., 2009).

Early research generally employed auditory or visual oddball tasks, which are tasks predominantly used to examine ERPs and to investigate the effects of acute exercise on ERPs. These tasks reflect basic information processes, particularly stimulus discrimination. At first glance, the studies examining the stimulus discrimination results found either increased P3 amplitude (Nakamura et al., 1999) or no effect on P3 (Grego et al., 2004; Yagi et al., 1999). However, only Nakamura et al. (1999) applied acute exercise with moderate intensity for 30 min, suggesting that an exercise protocol with an appropriate design would benefit stimulus discrimination. These findings were supported by Kamijo and colleagues, who observed that exercise with moderate intensity led to increased P3 amplitude in the go condition of the go/no go task (Kamijo, Nishihira, Hatta, Kaneda, Wasaka, et al., 2004) and the congruent condition of the flanker task (Kamijo et al., 2007, 2009). Given that both the go condition and the congruent condition are associated with stimulus discrimination, these studies provide evidence of the benefit of acute exercise on stimulus discrimination at the neuroelectric level.

Based on the work of Colcombe and Kramer (2003), who indicated that chronic exercise had a disproportionately enhanced effect on executive function, and Hillman et al. (2003), who first observed that acute exercise had a positive impact on executive function tasks, studies examining the association between acute exercise and ERPs began to focus on executive function. Executive function is a high hierarchical cognitive function that is believed to control, monitor, and regulate several basic levels of cognitive processes (Alvarez & Emory, 2006; Etnier & Chang, 2009). Executive function leads an individual to exhibit goal-directed behavior by suppressing a habitual or automatic response, particularly under novel circumstances (Garon, Bryson, & Smith, 2008), and is recognized as an essential ability for daily life (Vaughan & Giovanello, 2010).

Studies examining the association between acute exercise, ERPs, and executive function have applied executive function-related tasks, such as the go/no go task (Kamijo, Nishihira,

Hatta, Kaneda, Kida, et al., 2004; Kamijo, Nishihira, Hatta, Kaneda, Wasaka, et al., 2004; Stroth et al., 2009) and the flanker task (Kamijo et al., 2007, 2009; Stroth et al., 2009). These two tasks are specifically related to the inhibition aspect of executive function. The go/no go task involves the go and no go conditions, in which the participant is instructed to respond to the go stimulus (e.g., green light) and avoid responding to the no go stimulus (e.g., red light). In general, there are more go stimuli than no go stimuli (or at least similar amounts), which leads to the prepotent response tendency for the go condition. The participant is required to inhibit this tendency to meet the no go requirement. Therefore, the inhibition of motor responses is assessed (Robbins, 2007). With similar designs that compared low, moderate, and high exercise intensity conditions, Kamijo and colleagues found that moderate exercise for 18 min elevated both CNV and P3 amplitude, suggesting that acute exercise induces appropriate arousal and increases the attentional resource allocation for tasks involving executive function (Kamijo, Nishihira, Hatta, Kaneda, Kida, et al., 2004; Kamijo, Nishihira, Hatta, Kaneda, Wasaka, et al., 2004).

On the other hand, the flanker task assesses inhibition using congruent and incongruent conditions. The congruent stimulus is a five-letter or symbol series with the same feature (e.g., HHHHH or >>>>>), and the incongruent stimulus is a five-letter or symbol series with a contrasting symbol in the middle (e.g., HHSHH or >><>>). The participant is instructed to respond to the middle letter or symbol. To perform the incongruent stimulus successfully, the participant must ignore the surrounding distractors and focus on the middle target stimulus. Interestingly, acute exercise led not only to a greater P3 amplitude but also to a shorter P3 latency (Kamijo et al., 2007, 2009), particularly in the incongruent condition (Kamijo et al., 2007), suggesting that acute exercise increases the amount of attentional resources and

facilitates efficient stimulus classification and evaluation in tasks related to executive function. It should be noted that although the go/no go and flanker tasks assess inhibition, they present inhibition from different perspectives. Specifically, go/no go is associated with inhibition regarding execution of the motor level (Aron, 2007), whereas the flanker task is related to inhibition in terms of sensory and attentional processes (Aron, 2007; Robbins, 2007). These studies suggest that acute moderate exercise between 18 and 20 min benefits both perspectives of inhibition.

Although the majority of studies observed positive results in executive function immediately following acute exercise, Stroth et al. (2009) failed to demonstrate the influence of acute exercise on executive function tasks and ERPs. Although Stroth et al. (2009) assessed inhibition, they utilized a task that involved both the go/no go and the flanker tasks with four types of congruent stimuli (i.e., BBBBB, DDDDD, UUUUU, and VVVVV) and four types of incongruent stimuli (i.e., DDBDD, BBDBB, VVUVV, and UUVUU). The participant was required to respond to the target stimulus of B and U (i.e., the go condition), while withholding the stimulus of U and V (i.e., the no go condition). This design greatly enhanced task complexity compared with the traditional version of the go/no go and flanker tasks, particularly for the adolescent children recruited by the researchers; thus, the task may have been too complicated for the participants to perform, which may have resulted in the lack of an observed effect of the acute exercise.

In summary, acute exercise with an appropriate protocol is proposed to increase the stimulus discrimination aspect of basic information processes. Acute exercise may enhance inhibition ability in terms of the motor response level and the sensory and attentional processing levels; however, exercise may have a limited influence when the task is too complex for the participant.

Participants

The majority of studies have focused on adults between the ages of 22 and 35 years (six studies), with one study that targeted older adults (Kamijo et al., 2009) and one study that focused on adolescents (Stroth et al., 2009). Regarding young adults, similar to the previous scenario, an acute exercise protocol with submaximal exercise intensity (Nakamura et al., 1999), particularly moderate exercise intensity, facilitates neuroelectric indices by increasing P3 amplitude (Kamijo et al., 2009; Kamijo, Nishihira, Hatta, Kaneda, Wasaka, et al., 2004; Kamijo et al., 2007) and CNV amplitude (Kamijo, Nishihira, Hatta, Kaneda, Kida, et al., 2004) or shortening P3 latency (Kamijo et al., 2007).

Although the positive effects of acute exercise on ERPs apply to both younger adults and older adults (Kamijo et al., 2007), the underlying mechanism between the two populations might be different. Kamijo et al. (2007) observed that acute exercise with moderate intensity [50% of maximum volume of oxygen uptake ($\dot{V}O_2$max)] increased P3 amplitude in younger adults, which replicated previous findings. However, both light (30% $\dot{V}O_2$max) and moderate exercise intensity decreased P3 latency, regardless of the population age (i.e., younger and older adults). These findings suggested that older adults may benefit from exercise with light intensity. In addition, while acute exercise increases attentional resource allocation and the speed of stimulus classification (i.e., P3 amplitude and latency) for younger adults, acute exercise only increases the efficiency of information processes (i.e., P3 latency) in the given task for older adults, which reflects the neuroelectric differences between younger and older adults. On the other hand, acute exercise has limited effects in adolescents, at least when the task is too complex (Stroth et al., 2009).

Another moderator within the participant's background is fitness level. Five studies examined individuals with a normal level of fitness and have generally shown that acute exercise has a positive effect on ERPs (Kamijo, Nishihira, Hatta, Kaneda, Kida, et al., 2004; Kamijo, Nishihira, Hatta, Kaneda, Wasaka, et al., 2004; Kamijo et al., 2007, 2009; Yagi et al., 1999). However, whether an individual with a higher level of physical fitness receives the same acute exercise benefits as an individual with a normal fitness level is unclear. Stroth et al. (2009) found that although there was no acute exercise effect compared with adolescents with a lower fitness level, individuals with a higher fitness level had greater CNV and P3 amplitudes, suggesting that fitness, but not acute exercise, is positively associated with cognitive function assessed at the neuroelectric level. Two studies recruited participants with high fitness levels, and the results of these studies conflict. Nakamura et al. (1999) recruited seven highly trained joggers and observed that acute exercise with a self-paced intensity for 30 min elevated P3 and P2 amplitudes in a stimulus discrimination task. Interestingly, with 12 highly trained cyclists, Grego et al. (2004) found that acute moderate cycling for 180 min did not influence P3 indices. When conducting longer duration exercise (e.g., more than 60 min), one may expect that individuals experience fatigue and dehydration, which, in turn, negatively impairs cognitive performance (Brisswalter et al., 2002). In addition, longer exercise duration may negatively affect cognitive performance due to the rigorous stress on physiological resources (Tomporowski, 2003). Notably, none of the negative effects were observed in highly trained cyclists (Grego et al., 2004), suggesting that highly trained individuals can counter the cognitive impairment induced by long periods of exercise. Taken together, cognitive function in adolescence has a stronger association with fitness than with acute exercise. For adults, individuals with normal and high levels of physical fitness could show improved cognition, as assessed by neuroelectric levels, immediately after cessation of acute exercise. It is also possible that individuals with high physical fitness could maintain cognitive performance during longer periods of exercise.

Exercise Protocol

Exercise type, intensity, and duration have been considered the important factors of the acute exercise protocol. All studies of acute exercise and ERPs have involved aerobic exercise. Regarding exercise intensity and duration, published studies have taken a variety of approaches that can be categorized into exercise with submaximal intensity for 20–60 min (Nakamura et al., 1999; Stroth et al., 2009) and exercise with submaximal intensity for more than or less than 20–60 min (Grego et al., 2004; Yagi et al., 1999); the dose–response relationship between exercise intensity and ERPs has also been evaluated (Kamijo, Nishihira, Hatta, Kaneda, Kida, et al., 2004; Kamijo, Nishihira, Hatta, Kaneda, Wasaka, et al., 2004; Kamijo et al., 2007, 2009).

In general, facilitative ERPs were observed following acute exercise at submaximal intensity for 18–30 min, and these findings correspond to narrative reviews indicating that exercise at submaximal intensity for 20–60 min benefits cognitive performance (Brisswalter et al., 2002; Tomporowski, 2003). In contrast, when the exercise protocol failed to meet this suggested exercise regimen, particularly when exercise duration was less than 20 min or longer than 60 min, the facilitative effect was no longer observed. For example, an exercise protocol at moderate intensity for both 10 min (Yagi et al., 1999) and 180 min (Grego et al., 2004) failed to influence P3, most likely due to the low arousal induced by the light exercise protocol, and the fatigue and dehydration induced by long exercise protocol.

Studies examining the dose–response relationship provide the basis for identifying the optimal exercise protocol; the dose–response relationship between exercise intensity and cognition has been particularly emphasized in

studies investigating acute exercise and ERPs. Kamijo and colleagues observed that compared with high exercise intensities, moderate exercise for 18 min induced larger CNV and P3 amplitudes; this result suggests that moderate exercise induces an optimal arousal and attentional resource allocation to the given task (Kamijo, Nishihira, Hatta, Kaneda, Kida, et al., 2004; Kamijo, Nishihira, Hatta, Kaneda, Wasaka, et al., 2004). In addition, both light and moderate intensity exercise for 20 min, but not high intensity exercise, are associated with an increased P3 amplitude in tasks related to both basic information processes and executive functions, whereas only moderate exercise is associated with a shortened P3 in tasks involved in executive function. These findings demonstrate that the exercise intensity, the nature of cognition, and the neuroelectric indices are modulated by the relationships between acute exercise and ERPs (Kamijo et al., 2007). It is worth noting that only moderate intensity exercise facilitated P3 amplitude in younger adults, but both light and moderate intensity exercise facilitated P3 latency in older adults, thereby highlighting the different concerns that must be considered when creating an exercise protocol for a specific population. Nonetheless, a submaximal exercise protocol for 30 min that was positively associated with cognitive function in younger and older adults was not observed in adolescents (Stroth et al., 2009). Although the precise explanation is not yet understood, the findings suggest that the acute exercise protocol must be tailored for the target population.

Overall, aerobic exercise at submaximal intensity, particularly moderate intensity, for 18–30 min facilitates ERPs in younger adults, and protocols outside these criteria may have limited effects on ERPs. Furthermore, the optimal exercise protocol in terms of exercise type, intensity, and duration requires slight modifications when considering different populations, including older adults and adolescents.

ERPs FOLLOWING EXERCISE: DELAYED EFFECTS

Another exercise paradigm associated with acute exercise and ERPs is the delayed effects of exercise on ERPs. Specifically, ERPs are examined after the physical arousal (e.g., heart rate, body temperature) induced by acute exercise returns to baseline or close to baseline (e.g., within 10% of baseline heart rate), which normally requires 20–55 min. Because arousal has returned to normal levels, the arousal hypothesis that applies to performance immediately following acute exercise may not be sufficient to explain the effects observed at longer times after acute exercise.

The cognitive–energetic model proposed by Sanders (1983) may provide an alternative viewpoint to address the delayed effects of acute exercise on cognition. According to Sanders' cognitive–energetic model, three levels of mental operations are involved. The first is the information processing level, which is a computational level consisting of four stages, stimulus preprocessing, feature extraction, response selection, and motor adjustment, between the stimuli and the response. The second level is the energetic level, which involves three pools of energy: the arousal pool, the effort pool, and the activation pool. The third is the evaluation or executive control level. These three levels are mutually interactive. For example, arousal is associated with feature extraction of the information processing level, where effort and activation are linked to response selection and motor

adjustment, respectively. On the other hand, the executive control level receives feedback from the arousal and activation pools and guides the allocation of resources, thus having a direct impact on the effort pool and subsequently influencing the arousal and activation pools and activation (see Figure 4).

Based upon the Sanders model involving three energetic mechanisms, acute exercise may facilitate cognitive performance by elevating arousal. Moreover, exercise may also influence cognitive performance through its impact on activation and effort. It is also suspected that acute exercise may be associated with the executive control level, which would consequently alter the energetic levels and lead to a change in the information processing level. Studies examining the association between the exercise paradigm and the delayed effects of exercise on cognition as well as studies examining acute exercise and ERPs may provide evidence that furthers our understanding of the influence of acute exercise on executive function.

This section emphasizes the change in ERPs following a delay after cessation of exercise (see Table 2) and also discusses the relationship between acute exercise and ERPs based on the four moderators.

ERP Measures

The eight studies in Table 2 examined the delayed exercise effect on ERPs. Similar to studies associated with an effect immediately

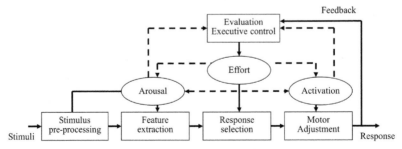

FIGURE 4   Sanders' cognitive–energetic model. *Adapted from Sanders (1983), with permission of Acta Psychologica, Elsevier.*

TABLE 2 Event-related potentials following exercise: delayed effects

Study	Participants	Exercise protocol	Cognitive measure	Time points (following exercise)	ERP measure	Findings
Magnie et al. (2000)	10 cyclists (21.9 years) with $\dot{V}O_2$max (63.8) 10 sedentary (22.9 years) with $\dot{V}O_2$max (47.4) Fitness effect: no	T: cycling I: until volitional exhaustion D: not mentioned	Auditory oddball task	Body temperature and HR back to baseline for cyclist (69 min); for 52 for sedentary	P3 N1, P2, N2, N4	Increased P3 amplitude Shorted P3 latency No effect in N1, P2, N2 Increased N4 amplitude
Hillman et al. (2003)	20 college students (20.5 years) with $\dot{V}O_2$max (48.4)	T: treadmill I:162.4 bpm (83.5% HR max) D: 30 min	Modified Flanker task	HR back to 10% of baseline (48 min)	P3	Increased P3 amplitude Shorted P3 latency for incongruent trails
Duzova et al. (2005)	11 high PA sportsman, 10 moderate PA sportsman, 10 low PA sportsman Age (18–26 years)	T: anaerobic loading coordination test I: maximal exercise (190 bpm) D: 45 s	Auditory oddball task	Body temperature and HR back to baseline	P3 N2	No effect in P3 Deceased in N2 amplitude for high PA sportsman
Themanson and Hillman (2006)	14 higher-fit (20.1 years) with $\dot{V}O_2$max (56.3) 14 lower-fit (20.6 years) with $\dot{V}O_2$max (38.7) Fitness effect: yes	T: treadmill I: 82.8% HR max D: 30 min	Modified flanker task	HR back to 10% of baseline (40.1 min)	N2 ERN, Pe	No effects
Hillman et al. (2009)	20 preadolescent (9.5 years) with $\dot{V}O_2$max (40.1)	T: treadmill I: 60% HR max D: 20 min	Modified flanker task	HR back to 10% of baseline (25.4 min)	P3	Increased P3 amplitude for incongruent Shorted P3 latency for incongruent trails
Scudder et al. (2012)	13 undergraduate students (19.7 years) with $\dot{V}O_2$max (47.2)	T: treadmill I: 60% HR max D: 30 min	AX-continuous performance task	HR back to 10% of baseline (23.5 min)	P3 N2	Increased P3 amplitude
Pontifex et al. (2013)	20 ADHD (9.5 years) 20 healthy (9.8 years)	T: treadmill I: 65–75% HR max D: 20 min	Modified flanker task	HR back to 10% of baseline	P3 ERN	Increased P3 amplitude, shorted P3 latency for both groups Increased ERN amplitude for ADHD
Drollette et al. (2014)	20 higher performers (9.8 years) with $\dot{V}O_2$max (40.1) 20 lower performers (9.6 years) with $\dot{V}O_2$max Inhibitory capacity effect: yes	T: treadmill I: 60–70% HR max D: 20 min	Modified flanker task	HR back to 10% of baseline (22.5 min)	P3 N2	Increased P3 amplitude in lower performers Smaller N2 amplitude, shorter P3 latency for two groups

Notes: $\dot{V}O_2$max: mL/kg/min; PA, physical activity; ADHD, attention deficit hyperactivity disorder; HR, heart rate; T, exercise type; I, exercise intensity; D, exercise. duration.

following exercise, the most examined ERP component in delayed exercise effects was P3 (seven studies). Studies have also examined N2 (five studies), ERN (two studies), N1, P2, and N4 (one study), and Pe (one study).

Regarding P3, with one exception (Duzova, Ozisik, Polat, Emre, & Gullu, 2005), all studies have found that acute exercise increased P3 amplitude (Drollette et al., 2014; Hillman et al., 2003, 2009; Magnie et al., 2000; Pontifex et al., 2013; Scudder et al., 2012), and a few studies also observed shortened P3 latency (Hillman et al., 2003, 2009; Magnie et al., 2000; Pontifex et al., 2013). These findings suggest that acute exercise leads to greater attentional resource allocation and accurate classification and evaluation of the stimulus. The results are interesting because the beneficial effect in the neuroelectric index is observed even when physical arousal returns to or near baseline, reflecting that the beneficial effect from exercise is not completely attributed to arousal. It is possible that exercise-induced activation, effort, and executive function may play roles in improving cognition based on the model proposed by Sanders. In contrast, the lack of consistent findings by Duzova et al. (2005) is possibly a result of the exercise protocol, which involved extremely high intensity for a short period of time (i.e., 45 s).

Acute exercise generally fails to exert an effect on the early ERPs (i.e., N1, P2, and N2) whenever high-intensity (Magnie et al., 2000) or moderate-intensity (Scudder et al., 2012; Themanson & Hillman, 2006) exercise is employed. It should be noted that decreased N2 was observed in athletes involved in high physical activity but not in those involved in moderate or low physical activity (Duzova et al., 2005) and in children irrespective of their level of inhibitory control capacity (Drollette et al., 2014), implying that the alterations in N2 from acute exercise may be moderated by participant characteristics. Interestingly, acute exercise elevates the N4 amplitude (Magnie et al., 2000), in which the ERP component is typically considered an index of semantic priming (Kutas & Federmeier, 2000). Nevertheless, the word presentation that is indexed by N4 is not automatically conducted, but moderated, by attention (McCarthy & Nobre, 1993), suggesting that N4 is associated with attention. Along with the elevated P3 amplitude, the results of N4 have provided additional evidence that acute exercise is positively linked to attention (Magnie et al., 2000).

While the majority of studies have focused on stimulus-locked components, two studies have examined response-locked components, such as ERN (Themanson & Hillman, 2006) and Pe (Pontifex et al., 2013; Themanson & Hillman, 2006). However, in contrast to the stimulus-locked P3 component, acute exercise fails to influence ERN and Pe in healthy populations, such as younger adults (Themanson & Hillman, 2006) and children (Pontifex et al., 2013). This limited influence may be attributed to a low error rate, which is the foundation for the ERN and Pe, and suggests that additional studies are required to examine the issue to appropriately consider the error rate. However, these two studies imply that acute exercise had a limited effect on error response.

These findings of facilitative ERPs, particularly in the P3 component, following acute exercise conflict with findings regarding cognition assessed at the behavioral level. A meta-analytic review conducted by Chang, Labban, et al. (2012) indicated that improved cognitive performance was only found immediately following the cessation of exercise and not at 15 min following exercise. Given that acute exercise is normally shown to positively affect P3, these findings imply that a delayed exercise effect, which has yet to be identified at the behavioral level, exists when examined by more sensitive techniques, as indexed by ERPs.

Type of Cognition

Four types of cognitive function have been emphasized in studies examining the association between acute exercise and ERPs: stimulus discrimination (Duzova et al., 2005; Magnie et al., 2000); inhibition (Drollette et al., 2014; Hillman et al., 2003, 2009; Pontifex et al., 2013); action monitoring (Pontifex et al., 2013); and goal maintenance (Scudder et al., 2012).

Studies examining stimulus discrimination were assessed using a typical auditory oddball task and utilized an exercise protocol with high intensity; however, the results were inconsistent, including an exercise-induced elevation in P3 amplitude and either a shortened P3 latency (Magnie et al., 2000) or no effect on P3 (Duzova et al., 2005). A clear explanation for the conflicting results remains unclear; however, the participants, exercise duration, and modality between these two studies differed, which may account for the disparate findings. Future studies should duplicate these study designs to consider these factors and advance our understanding of these effects.

To date, the flanker task has been extensively applied to measure the inhibition of executive function in studies of acute exercise and ERPs. The research trend began with Hillman et al. (2003) who indicated that there was an increase in P3 amplitude and a shortened P3 latency related to the flanker task following exercise and the return of exercise-induced arousal to 10% of baseline. Interestingly, these facilitative neuroelectric indices were only observed for the incongruent condition, which reflects the inhibition aspect of executive function, but not in the congruent condition, which is associated with stimulus discrimination. These findings suggest that acute exercise had a disproportionate impact on cognition, particularly for cognitive function, which requires a higher cognitive demand. The findings were replicated by later studies (Hillman et al., 2009) and are similar to studies that examined cognition immediately following exercise cessation (Kamijo, Nishihira, Hatta, Kaneda, Wasaka, et al., 2004; Kamijo et al., 2007, 2009). Taken together, acute exercise is positively associated with inhibition, regardless of the time

after exercise termination. According to Sanders' cognitive–energetic model, these results suggest that the beneficial effect of acute exercise is not only associated with exercise-induced arousal but also exercise-induced effort and activation and even the elevation of executive function.

The flanker task also examines action monitoring, another aspect of executive function. Action monitoring refers to an ability that monitors and corrects response error in the environment to regulate a goal-directed behavior. To examine action monitoring, the post-error response slowing is determined from the correct trials following the error trials and the correct trials following the matched-correct trials in the behavioral level (Kerns et al., 2004); ERN and Pe are recorded for action monitoring as the neuroelectric indices (Gehring, Goss, Coles, Meyer, & Donchin, 1993; Mathewson, Dywan, & Segalowitz, 2005). Given that acute exercise is associated with increased attentional resources (i.e., increased P3 amplitude) (Hillman et al., 2003), the increase in top-down control is hypothesized to reduce the response conflict and therefore decrease the ERN amplitude and the influence of Pe (Themanson & Hillman, 2006). However, Themanson and Hillman (2006) observed no relationship between acute exercise on action monitoring at either the behavioral and neuroelectric levels, suggesting that acute exercise is unrelated to action monitoring. Similar results showing no influence on ERN were also replicated in healthy children (Pontifex et al., 2013).

Scudder et al. (2012) examined the effect of acute exercise and ERPs on another aspect of executive function—goal maintenance—using the AX-continuous performance task (AX-CPT). When performing the AX-CPT, an individual is required to respond to a target probe X when preceded by cue "A" (i.e., AX); no response is required for X when it is preceded by "B" (i.e., BX), for Y when it is preceded by "B" (i.e., BY), or for Y when it is preceded by "A" (i.e., AY). Given that the AX trial has a high frequency, which leads to the dominant tendency, the delay observed in other trials between the cue and the target trial represents context representation and goal maintenance (Braver & Barch, 2002). Following acute exercise, Scudder et al. (2012) found that acute exercise not only leads to better accuracy for target trials in the behavioral response but also elevates P3 amplitude for target and nontarget trials. This study presents the first evidence that acute exercise is positively associated with goal maintenance and that attentional resources can be allocated to goal representation and maintenance. This study also illustrates the influence that acute exercise may have on other aspects of executive function.

Participants

With regard to the age of the participants, younger adults have been the focus of most studies on acute exercise and ERPs (Duzova et al., 2005; Hillman et al., 2003; Magnie et al., 2000; Scudder et al., 2012; Themanson & Hillman, 2006); a few later studies have shifted their attention to preadolescent children (Drollette et al., 2014; Hillman et al., 2009; Pontifex et al., 2013). In general, a greater stimulus-locked P3 amplitude was observed following acute exercise in both populations, suggesting that the beneficial effect from acute exercise crosses young adulthood to adolescence.

Notably, certain characteristics of the participants may moderate the relationship between acute exercise and ERPs, such as fitness level (Duzova et al., 2005) and status of inhibitory capacity (Drollette et al., 2014; Pontifex et al., 2013). In term of fitness, three types of results have been observed in acute exercise and ERPs. Magnie et al. (2000) noted that acute exercise elevated P3 amplitude and shortened P3 latency in adults highly trained in cycling and in those with sedentary histories, suggesting that acute exercise affects ERPs irrespective of fitness level. However, Duzova et al. (2005) found that although P3 did not change following acute exercise in sportsmen with low, moderate, and high physical activity, a decreased N2

amplitude was only observed in sportsmen with high physical activity levels, implying that fitness partially modulated the role of acute exercise and ERPs. Interestingly, only a fitness effect but not an acute exercise effect was observed by Themanson and Hillman (2006). Although the exact reason for the conflicting results requires further investigation, the methodological differences with respect to the exercise protocol (e.g., exercise modality and duration) and ERPs (e.g., P3, ERN) are most likely involved.

The level of inhibition capacity may also influence the effect of acute exercise on ERPs. Pontifex et al. (2013) found that although acute exercise increased P3 amplitude and decreased P3 latency in children both with and without attention deficit hyperactivity disorder (ADHD), children with ADHD showed increased ERN amplitude following exercise. ADHD has been linked to dysfunction in sustained attention and executive functions, particularly in inhibitory control ability. Along with ERNs associated with inhibition and conflicting action, these findings suggest that acute exercise may have additional benefits on inhibitory control in children with lower inhibition abilities. This argument corresponds to a later study by Drollette et al. (2014), who assigned healthy children without ADHD into higher and lower inhibitory performance groups. Following acute exercise, a shortened P3 latency and a decreased N2 amplitude were observed in both groups, suggesting that acute exercise led to accurate stimulus classification and improved response conflict. However, increased P3 amplitude was also found in children with a lower inhibitory performance but not in children with a higher inhibitory performance, implying that individuals with a lower inhibitory capacity achieve a greater benefit from the facilitation effect of acute exercise.

Exercise Protocol

Two relatively early studies examined high exercise intensity over different periods of time (e.g., 45 s) (Duzova et al., 2005; Magnie et al., 2000). A consensus was not found in these studies, potentially due to the differences in exercise modality and duration. For example, Magnie et al. (2000) instructed individuals to engage in cycling exercise until reaching volitional exhaustion; in contrast, Duzova et al. (2005) applied anaerobic loading coordination with maximal exercise intensity (e.g., heart rate at 90 bpm).

In contrast, an exercise protocol involving an aerobic exercise modality with moderate exercise intensity for 20–30 min commonly results in beneficial effects in neuroelectric indices, particularly in the endogenous P3 component. (Drollette et al., 2014; Hillman et al., 2003, 2009; Pontifex et al., 2013; Scudder et al., 2012), suggesting that this exercise protocol benefits cognition at the brain neural activity level. In contrast to the exercise paradigm that examined the immediate effects on the dose–response relationship between exercise intensity and ERPs, in which an optimal exercise intensity could not be achieved, these studies examined the delayed effect, which corresponds to the finding that acute exercise benefits cognition and behavioral cognitive performance is enhanced by exercise at submaximal intensity for 20–60 min (Brisswalter et al., 2002; Tomporowski, 2003). In addition, studies examining the association between acute exercise and ERPs extend knowledge regarding specific aspects of basic information processing at the behavioral level and the inhibition aspects of executive function at the neuroelectric level (Chang, Labban, et al., 2012; Lambourne & Tomporowski, 2010).

FUTURE CONSIDERATIONS OF ACUTE EXERCISE AND ERPs

An increasing number of studies have examined the effects of acute exercise on ERPs. With the advantages of high temporal resolution and representation from the neuroelectric technique, research has elucidated the relationship between acute exercise and cognition. It is worth noting that compared to behaviorally assessing acute exercise and cognition, studies of acute exercise and ERPs are relatively new and still in the early stages of investigation. Indeed, studies examining the association between acute exercise and behavioral cognitive function have dramatically developed along a variety of research lines. These issues, which have examined the effect of acute exercise on behavioral cognitive function, may provide the foundation for studies investigating acute exercise and ERPs in the future.

Type of Cognition

Early studies associated with acute exercise and cognition typically examined basic information processing, which was assessed using letter detection, visual search, simple and choice reaction time, and perceptual discrimination (Tomporowski, 2003). Following a study by Hillman et al. (2003), studies began to examine the effect of acute exercise on executive function, which is generally assessed using the go/no go task (Kamijo, Nishihira, Hatta, Kaneda, Kida, et al., 2004; Kamijo, Nishihira, Hatta, Kaneda, Wasaka, et al., 2004; Stroth et al., 2009) and the flanker task (Hillman et al., 2009; Kamijo et al., 2007, 2009; Pontifex et al., 2013; Scudder et al., 2012; Stroth et al., 2009).

It should be noted that executive function is an umbrella term used to describe the meta-level of cognitive function, in which several subconstructs have been proposed involving executive function. For example, through factor analysis, Miyake et al. (2000) argued that there are three primary constructs within executive function: working memory, inhibition, and shifting. Other researchers have indicated that executive function includes distinct subconstructs such as inhibition, scheduling, planning, working memory, coordination, and sequencing (Colcombe & Kramer, 2003; Erickson, 2011). Regarding acute exercise and ERPs, the inhibition aspect of executive function has been widely emphasized, with two studies focused on action monitoring (Pontifex et al., 2013; Themanson & Hillman, 2006) and one study focused on goal maintenance (Scudder et al., 2012). However, an examination of these specific subconstructs was unable to generalize the findings to executive function as a whole. Commentary from Etnier and Chang (2009) argued that exercise may impact specific executive function differently, and future studies examining the specific subconstructs are encouraged. At the behavioral level, many other subconstructs of executive function following acute exercise have been explored including planning (Chang, Ku, et al., 2012; Chang, Tsai, et al., 2011), shifting (Chang, Liu, et al., 2012), working memory (Pontifex, Hillman, Fernhall, Thompson, & Valentini, 2009), switching (Pesce & Audiffren, 2011), and cognitive flexibility (Netz, Argov, & Inbar, 2009), as well as multiple aspects of executive function (Chen, Yan, Yin, Pan, & Chang, 2014). These investigations warrant future studies examining acute exercise and other aspects of executive function using ERP techniques.

Another issue to consider is the cognitive task employed. Etnier and Chang (2009) identified 29 neuropsychological assessments that are frequently used to assess executive function in the neuropsychological field; the top five tasks in order of frequency are the Wisconsin Card Sorting Test (WCST), the Stroop test, the Trail Making Test, verbal fluency, and the Tower of London Task (TOL). Interestingly, of the 128 different cognitive tests that have been used for exercise and cognition research, only 10 tests have been used in the 29 assessments, reflecting that future studies examining the effects of acute exercise on executive function are required to properly select the task applied. Given that many neuropsychological assessments were developed for the purpose of clinical diagnosis, one may argue whether the use of these tests is appropriate in the experimental field. However, these tests have also been extensively applied in experimental studies, suggesting that the usage of these tasks in studies associated with acute exercise and

ERP is applicable. Indeed, the usage of these neuropsychological assessments may stimulate alterative ideas. For example, rather than comparing the Stroop congruent condition (index of basic information processing) and the Stroop incongruent condition (index of executive function), Chang, Tsai, Huang, Wang, and Chu (2014) applied five conditions of the Stroop test (i.e., the Stroop congruent, word, square, neutral, and incongruent conditions) to examine whether the nature of the Stroop test moderates acute exercise and cognition. The results revealed that acute exercise benefits all Stroop conditions but had a larger positive effect on the Stroop incongruent condition, suggesting that acute exercise leads to both general and specific improvements (see Figure 5).

It is interesting that research in cognitive neuroscience and related fields has led to the creation of a modified version of the task that is able to match ERPs and other neuroimaging techniques, such as the WCST (Barceló, 1999; Havelka Mestrović, Palmović, Bojić, Treselj, & Nevajda, 2012), the Stroop test (Badzakova-Trajkov, Barnett, Waldie, & Kirk, 2009; Tillman & Wiens, 2011), and the TOL (Rasser et al., 2005;

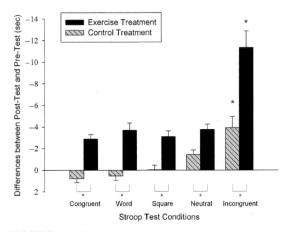

FIGURE 5   The effects of acute resistance exercise on multiple conditions of the Stroop test. *From Chang, Tsai et al. (2014), with permission of Journal of Science and Medicine in Sport, Elsevier.*

Wagner, Koch, Reichenbach, Sauer, & Schlösser, 2006). This development provides the foundation for studies exploring the acute effects of exercise on cognitive performance using these tests, which are frequently used to assess executive function at the neuroelectric level.

Participants

In the early stages, studies examining the association between acute exercise and cognition targeted young adults with high fitness levels (Cian, Barraud, Melin, & Raphel, 2001; McGlynn, Laughlin, & Bender, 1977; Tomporowski, Ellis, & Stephens, 1987). However, after the early 2000s, the target populations shifted to healthy younger adults (Lambourne, Audiffren, & Tomporowski, 2010), then healthy older adults (Barella, Etnier, & Chang, 2010; Chang, Chu, et al., 2011; Chang & Etnier, 2009a; Chang, Ku, et al., 2012; Netz, Tomer, Axelrad, Argov, & Inbar, 2007), and recently children (Cereatti, Casella, Manganelli, & Pesce, 2009; Chen et al., 2014; Pesce, Crova, Cereatti, Casella, & Bellucci, 2009; Tomporowski, Davis, Lambourne, Gregoski, & Tkacz, 2008). Studies examining the association between acute exercise and EPPs show similar trends in targeting younger adults with high fitness levels in the early stages and then healthy younger adults. However, to date, only a few studies have examined older and pre-adolescent populations. Given that older adults experience age-related cognitive decline and children are at stages that are sensitive to brain plasticity, these populations may experience acute exercise effects in a different manner than young adults with relatively mature and stable brain function. Therefore, acute exercise effects on ERPs in these specific populations should be further examined to increase understanding.

In addition to studies focusing on healthy populations, some studies have examined acute exercise effects on cognition in special populations. For example, Chang, Liu, et al. (2012) were the first to demonstrate that the beneficial effects of acute exercise on cognitive function can be extended to children with ADHD. A recent meta-analytic review concluded that the facilitative acute exercise effect on cognition is similar between individuals with healthy versus impaired status; however, it should be noted that the number of the effect size in individuals with impaired status was approximately seven times less than that observed in healthy individuals ($n = 137$ vs 839). These findings suggest that special populations should be explored and assessed in future research regarding acute exercise and ERPs.

Another trend in the study of acute exercise and cognition is examination of the role of fitness status. Although previous studies have indicated that individuals with higher fitness levels receive greater beneficial effects from acute exercise, that perspective is generally presented based on indirect evidence (Brisswalter et al., 2002; Chang, Labban, et al., 2012; Tomporowski, 2003). For example, Chang, Labban, et al. (2012) reported that the effects of acute exercise on cognitive performance were only observed in individuals at moderate and high fitness levels. Recently, Chang and colleagues elucidated the issue by simultaneously examining acute exercise and fitness, and the researchers indicated that acute exercise facilitates cognitive performance as assessed by the Stroop test in older adults, regardless of low or high fitness status. However, older adults with higher fitness levels received larger positive effects relative to those with lower fitness levels, suggesting that fitness moderates the relationship between acute exercise and cognition (Chu, Chen, Hung, Wang, & Chang, in press). Interestingly, when individuals were separated into low, moderate, and "extremely" high fitness groups, individuals with a high fitness level showed the longest response time on the Stroop incongruent condition, suggesting an inverted-U relationship in which the extremely high fitness status did not necessarily increase the benefit (Chang, Chi, et al., 2014). The role of fitness between acute exercise and cognition has only recently been directly explored, and studies applying the ERP technique are needed to elucidate the relationships among fitness, acute exercise, and cognition.

Exercise Protocol

Rather than examining exercise with a high load (e.g., high intensity, longer exercise time) in the early stage, current studies examining the association between acute exercise and cognition have generally studied exercise at submaximal intensity for 18–30 min. This protocol corresponds to the exercise recommendations previously proposed (American College of Sports Medicine, 2013) to promote health outcome (e.g., all-cause mortality) and counter several chronic diseases (e.g., arthritis, cancer, diabetes mellitus). It should be noted that the exercise protocol is complex, and in terms of acute exercise, it requires the consideration of many factors, including modality, intensity, and duration (American College of Sports Medicine, 2013).

In terms of exercise type, treadmill running and cycling in the aerobic exercise modality have been extensively utilized, and both modalities have been found to positively affect ERPs, regardless of the tasks related to stimulus discrimination (Nakamura et al., 1999) or inhibition (Kamijo, Nishihira, Hatta, Kaneda, Kida, et al., 2004; Kamijo, Nishihira, Hatta, Kaneda, Wasaka, et al., 2004; Kamijo et al., 2007, 2009; Stroth et al., 2009). It would be interesting to determine whether the two exercise methods influence ERPs differently, as treadmill running requires more attention and energetic constraint relative to cycling to maintain balance and control whole body coordination. The greater energy demand may cause dual-task attentional allocation during performance of the cognitive task (Brisswalter et al., 2002). Indeed, while facilitative cognition (assessed behaviorally) has been shown following both treadmill running and cycling, the effect of cycling is greater than that of running (Lambourne & Tomporowski, 2010).

Recently, some studies have examined alterations in cognitive performance following different types of exercise, such as resistance exercise. In a series of studies, Chang and colleagues indicated that resistance exercise facilitates cognition in terms of basic stimulus discrimination (Chang & Etnier, 2009b) as well as the inhibition and planning aspects of executive function (Chang, Chu, et al., 2011; Chang & Etnier, 2009a, 2009b, 2013; Chang, Ku, et al., 2012; Chang, Tsai, et al., 2014). Resistance exercise induces arousal proportionally with increased intensity, similar to aerobic exercise, which suggests the two exercise modalities share similar mechanisms of arousal. Nonetheless, the modality may also have its own specific mechanism. For example, aerobic exercise appears to facilitate cognition via elevated brain-derived neurotropic factor (Cotman & Berchtold, 2002), whereas resistance exercise may be related to increased insulin-like growth factor-1 (Kraemer & Ratamess, 2005). Likewise, some studies have applied other acute exercise modalities such as coordinative exercise (Budde, Voelcker-Rehage, Pietrabyk-Kendziorra, Ribeiro, & Tidow, 2008) and yoga (Gothe, Pontifex, Hillman, & McAuley, 2012), in which beneficial effects of the exercise modalities on cognition were also observed. Pesce (2012) stated that future studies should consider examining exercise that involves increased movement task complexity and cognitive demands. These updated research trends and arguments provide future directions for studies examining the association between acute exercise and ERPs.

To determine the optimal level of exercise intensity and duration, research on the dose–response relationship is necessary. This examination also contributes to the establishment of an "exercise prescription." While few studies have examined the dose–response relationship between acute exercise and ERPs (Kamijo, Nishihira, Hatta, Kaneda, Kida, et al., 2004; Kamijo, Nishihira, Hatta, Kaneda, Wasaka, et al., 2004; Kamijo et al., 2007, 2009), a study of acute exercise and behavioral cognition has further explored the dose–response relationship between resistance exercise intensity and cognition. These studies have shown that the type of cognition provides a specific function based on the exercise intensity. For example, there was a linear trend between the intensity and the tasks related to basic information processes (i.e., Stroop congruent) (Chang & Etnier, 2009b), whereas an inverted-U trend was found between the intensity and tasks required for executive control (i.e., Stroop incongruent, paced auditory serial addition task, and TOL) (Chang, Chu, et al., 2011; Chang & Etnier, 2009b). These findings suggest that higher intensity (i.e., 10 repetition maximal) exercise is optimal for tasks with information processes and moderate intensity (40–70% 10 repetitions maximal) exercise is optimal for tasks with executive control.

Remarkably, exercise intensity may differentially impact cognition depending on whether it is immediately following exercise or after a delay. Specifically, Chang, Labban, et al. (2012) concluded that very light to moderate intensities benefit cognition immediately following exercise, whereas hard and very hard, but not maximal, intensities most benefit cognition assessed after a delay (see Figure 6). ERP techniques are recommended to further illuminate

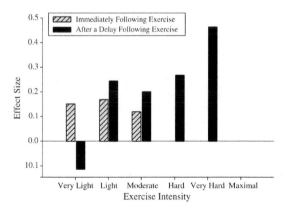

FIGURE 6 The effects of exercise intensity on cognition occur immediately following exercise and after a delay following exercise. *From Chang, Labban, et al. (2012), with permission of Brain Research, Elsevier.*

this argument. Likewise, while exercise durations of 18–30 min show a robust positive impact on cognitive function relatively consistently, only one recent study has specifically examined the dose–response relationship between exercise duration and cognitive function. Chang et al. (2015) observed that 20 min of main exercise with 5-min warm-up and cool-down periods resulted in the best Stroop test performances compared to no exercise, 10 min of main exercise, and 45 min of main exercise, suggesting that the facilitated cognitive performances were moderated by exercise duration. However, no ERP studies have explored the type of dose–response relationship. Because this limited study showed positive results at the behavioral level, future research into the dose–response relationship regarding the intensity and duration of exercise should be considered to explore using ERPs.

CONCLUSIONS

As with exercise and ERPs, it appears reasonable to propose that acute exercise is positively associated with stimulus-locked and endogenous components, such as P3 and N4, and response-related components, such as CNV, regardless of whether the assessment occurs immediately following the exercise or after a delay. However, acute exercise appears to have limited influence on early stimulus-locked components, such as N1 and P2, and response-locked components, such as ERN and Pe. Notably, the beneficial exercise effects on ERPs from these two exercise paradigms may have different theoretical bases.

Studies associated with acute exercise and ERPs have also examined the different natures of cognitive function, particularly the stimulus discrimination and inhibition aspects of executive function. Some recent studies have examined the delayed effects of acute exercise on the action monitoring and goal maintenance aspects of executive function. Healthy younger adults have been primarily emphasized in the study of acute exercise and ERPs, and a few recent studies have examined other populations including older adults, preadolescent children, and children with ADHD, in which acute exercise has generally shown a facilitative effect on cognitive function at the neuroelectric level. Notably, a participant's fitness level and inhibitory capacity may moderate the relationship between acute exercise and ERPs. Finally, although exercise protocols with a high load have shown somewhat conflicting results, which are difficult to interpret based on the different methodological designs these studies applied, an aerobic exercise protocol with submaximal intensity for 18–30 min generally demonstrates positive effects on ERPs.

While it appears plausible that acute exercise is positively associated with cognitive function at the neuroelectric level, substantial work remains for future research. Different types of cognitive functions and tasks to assess the specific cognition should be incorporated in future acute exercise studies associated with ERPs. In addition, factors that are relevant to a participant's demographic background, which may moderate acute exercise and ERPs, should be investigated simultaneously within the experimental design. Finally, the clear "dose" of an exercise protocol, with regard to the exercise modality, intensity, and duration for specific populations and cognition, remains to be determined but will ultimately be used to establish an exercise prescription. Expanded knowledge gained from these recommended directions would provide the foundation for research on acute exercise and ERPs and would lead to the implementation of exercise prescriptions to improve cognitive function.

References

Alvarez, J. A., & Emory, E. (2006). Executive function and the frontal lobes: a meta-analytic review. *Neuropsychology Review, 16,* 17–42.

American College of Sports Medicine. (2013). *ACSM's guidelines for exercise testing and prescription* (9th ed.). New York: Lippincott Williams and Wilkins.

Arent, S. M., & Landers, D. M. (2003). Arousal, anxiety, and performance: a reexamination of the inverted-U hypothesis. *Research Quarterly for Exercise and Sport, 74,* 436–444.

Aron, A. R. (2007). The neural basis of inhibition in cognitive control. *The Neuroscientist, 13,* 214–228.

Badzakova-Trajkov, G., Barnett, K. J., Waldie, K. E., & Kirk, I. J. (2009). An ERP investigation of the Stroop task: the role of the cingulate in attentional allocation and conflict resolution. *Brain Research, 1253,* 139–148.

Barceló, F. (1999). Electrophysiological evidence of two different types of error in the Wisconsin Card Sorting Test. *NeuroReport, 10,* 1299–1303.

Barella, L. A., Etnier, J. L., & Chang, Y. K. (2010). The immediate and delayed effects of an acute bout of exercise on cognitive performance of healthy older adults. *Journal of Aging and Physical Activity, 18,* 87–98.

Bareš, M., Nestrašil, I., & Rektor, I. (2007). The effect of response type (motor output versus mental counting) on the intracerebral distribution of the slow cortical potentials in an externally cued (CNV) paradigm. *Brain Research Bulletin, 71,* 428–435.

Berger, B. G., Pargman, D., & Weinberg, R. S. (2014). *Foundations of exercise psychology* (3rd ed.). Morgantown, WV: Fitness Information Technology.

Braver, T. S., & Barch, D. M. (2002). A theory of cognitive control, aging cognition, and neuromodulation. *Neuroscience and Biobehavioral Reviews, 26,* 809–817.

Brisswalter, J., Collardeau, M., & Arcelin, R. (2002). Effects of acute physical exercise characteristics on cognitive performance. *Sports Medicine, 32,* 555–566.

Buckworth, J., Dishman, R., O'Connor, P. J., & Tomporowski, P. (2013). *Exercise psychology.* Champaign, IL: Human Kinetics.

Budde, H., Voelcker-Rehage, C., Pietrabyk-Kendziorra, S., Ribeiro, P., & Tidow, G. (2008). Acute coordinative exercise improves attentional performance in adolescents. *Neuroscience Letters, 441,* 219–223.

Cereatti, L., Casella, R., Manganelli, M., & Pesce, C. (2009). Visual attention in adolescents: facilitating effects of sport expertise and acute physical exercise. *Psychology of Sport and Exercise, 10,* 136–145.

Chang, Y. K., Chi, L., Etnier, J. L., Wang, C. C., Chu, C. H., & Zhou, C. L. (2014). Effect of acute aerobic exercise on cognitive performance: role of cardiovascular fitness. *Psychology of Sport and Exercise, 15,* 464–470.

Chang, Y. K., Chu, I. H., Chen, F. T., & Wang, C. C. (2011). Dose-response effect of acute resistance exercise on Tower of London in middle-aged adults. *Journal of Sport and Exercise Psychology, 33,* 866–883.

Chang, Y. K., Chu, C. H., Wang, C. C., Wang, Y. C., Song, T. F., Tsai, C. L., et al. (2015). Dose-response relation between exercise duration and cognition. *Medicine and Science in Sports and Exercise, 47*(1), 159–165. http://dx.doi.org/10.1249/MSS.0000000000000383 [E-pub ahead of print].

Chang, Y. K., & Etnier, J. L. (2009a). Effects of an acute bout of localized resistance exercise on cognitive performance in middle-aged adults: a randomized controlled trial study. *Psychology of Sport and Exercise, 10,* 19–24.

Chang, Y. K., & Etnier, J. L. (2009b). Exploring the dose-response relationship between resistance exercise intensity and cognitive function. *Journal of Sport and Exercise Psychology, 31,* 640–656.

Chang, Y. K., & Etnier, J. L. (2013). The dose-response relationship between resistance exercise intensity and cognitive performance: does heart rate mediate this effect? *International Journal of Sport Psychology, 44,* 37–54.

Chang, Y. K., Ku, P. W., Tomporowski, P. D., Chen, F. T., & Huang, C. C. (2012). The effects of acute resistance exercise on late-middle-aged adults' goal planning. *Medicine and Science in Sports and Exercise, 44,* 1773–1779.

Chang, Y. K., Labban, J. D., Gapin, J. I., & Etnier, J. L. (2012). The effects of acute exercise on cognitive performance: a meta-analysis. *Brain Research, 1453,* 87–101.

Chang, Y. K., Liu, S., Yu, H. H., & Lee, Y. H. (2012). Effect of acute exercise on executive function in children with attention deficit hyperactivity disorder. *Archives of Clinical Neuropsychology, 27,* 225–237.

Chang, Y. K., Tsai, C. L., Huang, C. C., Wang, C. C., & Chu, I. H. (2014). Effects of acute resistance exercise on cognition in late middle-aged adults: general or specific cognitive improvement? *Journal of Science and Medicine in Sport, 17,* 51–55.

Chang, Y. K., Tsai, C. L., Hung, T. M., So, E. C., Chen, F. T., & Etnier, J. L. (2011). Effects of acute exercise on executive function: a study with a Tower of London Task. *Journal of Sport and Exercise Psychology, 33,* 847–865.

Chen, A. G., Yan, J., Yin, H. C., Pan, C. Y., & Chang, Y. K. (2014). Effects of acute aerobic exercise on multiple aspects of executive function in preadolescent children. *Psychology of Sport and Exercise, 15,* 627–636.

Chu, C. H., Chen, A. G., Hung, T. M., Wang, C. C., & Chang, Y. K.* (in press). Exercise and fitness modulate cognitive function in older adults. *Psychology and Aging.*

Cian, C., Barraud, P. A., Melin, B., & Raphel, C. (2001). Effects of fluid ingestion on cognitive function after heat stress or exercise-induced dehydration. *International Journal of Psychophysiology, 42,* 243–251.

Colcombe, S. J., & Kramer, A. F. (2003). Fitness effects on the cognitive function of older adults: a meta-analytic study. *Psychological Science, 14,* 125–130.

Coles, M. G. H., & Rugg, M. D. (1995). Event-related potentials: an introduction. In M. D. Rugg, & M. G. H. Coles (Eds.), *Electrophysiology of the mind* (pp. 1–26). New York: Oxford University Press.

Cotman, C. W., & Berchtold, N. C. (2002). Exercise: a behavioral intervention to enhance brain health and plasticity. *Trends in Neurosciences, 25,* 295–301.

DeBoer, L. B., Powers, M. B., Utschig, A. C., Otto, M. W., & Smits, J. A. (2012). Exploring exercise as an avenue for the treatment of anxiety disorders. *Expert Review of Neurotherapeutics, 12,* 1011–1022.

Drollette, E. S., Scudder, M. R., Raine, L. B., Moore, R. D., Saliba, B. J., Pontifex, M. B., et al. (2014). Acute exercise facilitates brain function and cognition in children who need it most: an ERP study of individual differences in inhibitory control capacity. *Developmental Cognitive Neuroscience, 7,* 53–64.

Duncan-Johnson, C. C. (1981). P300 latency: a new metric of information processing. *Psychophysiology, 18,* 207–215.

Duzova, H., Ozisik, H. I., Polat, A., Emre, M. H., & Gullu, E. (2005). Correlations between event-related potential components and nitric oxide in maximal anaerobic exercise among sportsmen trained at various levels. *The International Journal of Neuroscience, 115,* 1353–1373.

Erickson, K. I. (2011). Augmenting brain and cognition by aerobic exercise. *Foundations of Augmented Cognition. Directing the Future of Adaptive Systems, 6780,* 30–38.

Etnier, J. L., & Chang, Y. K. (2009). The effect of physical activity on executive function: a brief commentary on definitions, measurement issues, and the current state of the literature. *Journal of Sport and Exercise Psychology, 31,* 469–483.

Etnier, J. L., Salazar, W., Landers, D. M., Petruzzello, S. J., Han, M., & Nowell, P. (1997). The influence of physical fitness and exercise upon cognitive functioning: a meta-analysis. *Journal of Sport and Exercise Psychology, 19,* 249–277.

Fabiani, M., Gratton, G., & Federmeier, K. D. (2009). Event-related brain potentials: methods, theory, and applications. In J. T. Cacioppo, L. G. Tassinary, & G. G. Berntson (Eds.), *Handbook of psychophysiology* (pp. 85–119). New York: Cambridge University Press.

Falkenstein, M., Hielscher, H., Dziobek, I., Schwarzenau, P., Hoormann, J., Sunderman, B., et al. (2001). Action monitoring, error detection, and the basal ganglia: an ERP study. *NeuroReport, 12,* 157–161.

Falkenstein, M., Hohnsbein, J., Hoormann, J., & Blanke, L. (1990). Effects of errors in choice reaction tasks on the ERP under focused and divided attention. *Psychophysiological Brain Research, 1,* 192–195.

Falkenstein, M., Hoormann, J., Christ, S., & Hohnsbein, J. (2000). ERP components on reaction errors and their functional significance: a tutorial. *Biological Psychology, 51,* 87–107.

Falkenstein, M., Hoormann, J., & Hohnsbein, J. (2001). Changes of error-related ERPs with age. *Experimental Brain Research, 138,* 258–262.

Falkenstein, M., Hoormann, J., Hohnsbein, J., & Kleinsorge, T. (2003). Short-term mobilization of processing resources is revealed in the event-related potential. *Psychophysiology, 40,* 914–923.

Fischer, T., Langner, R., Birbaumer, N., & Brocke, B. (2008). Arousal and attention: self-chosen stimulation optimizes cortical excitability and minimizes compensatory effort. *Journal of Cognitive Neuroscience, 20*, 1443–1453.

Folstein, J. R., & Van Petten, C. (2008). Influence of cognitive control and mismatch on the N2 component of the ERP: a review. *Psychophysiology, 45*, 152–170.

Garon, N., Bryson, S. E., & Smith, I. M. (2008). Executive function in preschoolers: a review using an integrative framework. *Psychological Bulletin, 134*, 31–60.

Gehring, W. J., Goss, B., Coles, M. G., Meyer, D. E., & Donchin, E. (1993). A neural system for error detection and compensation. *Psychological Science, 4*, 385–390.

Gothe, N., Pontifex, M. B., Hillman, C., & McAuley, E. (2012). The acute effects of yoga on executive function. *Journal of Physical Activity and Health, 10*, 488–495.

Grego, F., Vallier, J. M., Collardeau, M., Bermon, S., Ferrari, P., Candito, M., et al. (2004). Effects of long duration exercise on cognitive function, blood glucose, and counterregulatory hormones in male cyclists. *Neuroscience Letters, 364*, 76–80.

Havelka Mestrović, A., Palmović, M., Bojić, M., Treselj, B., & Nevajda, B. (2012). Electrophysiological correlates activated during the Wisconsin Card Sorting Test (WCST). *Collegium Antropologicum, 36*, 513–520.

Herrmann, M. J., Römmler, J., Ehlis, A.-C., Heidrich, A., & Fallgatter, A. J. (2004). Source localization (LORETA) of the error-related-negativity (ERN/Ne) and positivity (Pe). *Cognitive Brain Research, 20*, 294–299.

Higuchi, S., Watanuki, S., Yasukouchi, A., & Sato, M. (1997). Effects of changes in arousal level by continuous light stimulus on contingent negative variation (CNV). *Applied Human Science, 16*, 55–60.

Hillman, C. H., Kamijo, K., & Pontifex, M. B. (2012). The relation of ERP indices of exercise to brain health and cognition. In H. Boecker, C. Hillman, L. Scheef, & H. K. Struder (Eds.), *Functional neuroimaging in exercise and sport sciences* (pp. 419–446). New York: Springer.

Hillman, C. H., Kamijo, K., & Scudder, M. (2011). A review of chronic and acute physical activity participation on neuroelectric measures of brain health and cognition during childhood. *Preventive Medicine, 52*, S21–S28.

Hillman, C. H., Pontifex, M. B., Motl, R. W., O'Leary, K. C., Johnson, C. R., Scudder, M. R., et al. (2012). From ERPs to academics. *Developmental Cognitive Neuroscience, 2*, S90–S98.

Hillman, C. H., Pontifex, M. B., Raine, L. B., Castelli, D. M., Hall, E. E., & Kramer, A. F. (2009). The effect of acute treadmill walking on cognitive control and academic achievement in preadolescent children. *Neuroscience, 159*, 1044–1054.

Hillman, C. H., Snook, E. M., & Jerome, G. J. (2003). Acute cardiovascular exercise and executive control function. *International Journal of Psychophysiology, 48*, 307–314.

Holroyd, C. B., Dien, J., & Coles, M. G. (1998). Error-related scalp potentials elicited by hand and foot movements: evidence for an output-independent error-processing system in humans. *Neuroscience Letters, 242*, 65–68.

Kamijo, K., Hayashi, Y., Sakai, T., Yahiro, T., Tanaka, K., & Nishihira, Y. (2009). Acute effects of aerobic exercise on cognitive function in older adults. *The Journals of Gerontology Series B: Psychological Sciences and Social Sciences, 64*, 356–363.

Kamijo, K., Nishihira, Y., Hatta, A., Kaneda, T., Kida, T., Higashiura, T., et al. (2004). Changes in arousal level by differential exercise intensity. *Clinical Neurophysiology, 115*, 2693–2698.

Kamijo, K., Nishihira, Y., Hatta, A., Kaneda, T., Wasaka, T., Kida, T., et al. (2004). Differential influences of exercise intensity on information processing in the central nervous system. *European Journal of Applied Physiology, 92*, 305–311.

Kamijo, K., Nishihira, Y., Higashiura, T., & Kuroiwa, K. (2007). The interactive effect of exercise intensity and task difficulty on human cognitive processing. *International Journal of Psychophysiology, 65*, 114–121.

Kerns, J. G., Cohen, J. D., MacDonald, A. W., Cho, R. Y., Stenger, V. A., & Carter, C. S. (2004). Anterior cingulate conflict monitoring and adjustments in control. *Science, 303*, 1023–1026.

Knight, R. T., Hillyard, S. A., Woods, D. L., & Neville, H. J. (1981). The effects of frontal cortex lesions on event-related potentials during auditory selective attention. *Electroencephalography and Clinical Neurophysiology, 52*, 571–582.

Kopp, B., Rist, F., & Mattler, U. (1996). N200 in the flanker task as a neurobehavioral tool for investigating executive control. *Psychophysiology, 33*, 282–294.

Kraemer, W. J., & Ratamess, N. A. (2005). Hormonal responses and adaptations to resistance exercise and training. *Sports Medicine, 35*, 339–361.

Kutas, M., & Federmeier, K. D. (2000). Electrophysiology reveals semantic memory use in language comprehension. *Trends in Cognitive Sciences, 4*, 463–470.

Lambourne, K., Audiffren, M., & Tomporowski, P. D. (2010). Effects of acute exercise on sensory and executive processing tasks. *Medicine and Science in Sports and Exercise, 42*, 1396–1402.

Lambourne, K., & Tomporowski, P. D. (2010). The effect of exercise-induced arousal on cognitive task performance: a meta-regression analysis. *Brain Research, 1341*, 12–24.

Loveless, N. E., & Sanford, A. J. (1974). Slow potential correlates of preparatory set. *Biological Psychology, 1*, 303–314.

Luck, S. J. (2005). *An introduction to the event-related potential technique.* Cambridge, MA: MIT Press.

Magliero, A., Bashore, T., Coles, M. G. H., & Donchin, E. (1984). On the dependence of P300 latency on stimulus evaluation processes. *Psychophysiology, 21*, 171–186.

Magnie, M., Bermon, S., Martin, F., Madany-Lounis, M., Suisse, G., Muhammad, W., et al. (2000). P300, N400, aerobic fitness, and maximal aerobic exercise. *Psychophysiology, 37*, 369–377.

Mathewson, K. J., Dywan, J., & Segalowitz, S. J. (2005). Brain bases of error-related ERPs as influenced by age and task. *Biological Psychology, 70*, 88–104.

McCarthy, G., & Nobre, A. C. (1993). Modulation of semantic processing by spatial selective attention. *Electroencephalography and Clinical Neurophysiology, 88*, 210–219.

McGlynn, G. H., Laughlin, N. T., & Bender, V. I. (1977). Effect of strenuous to exhaustive exercise on a discrimination task. *Perceptual and Motor Skills, 44*, 1139–1147.

McMorris, T., & Graydon, J. (2000). The effect of incremental exercise on cognitive performance. *International Journal of Sport Psychology, 31*, 66–81.

McMorris, T., & Hale, B. J. (2012). Differential effects of differing intensities of acute exercise on speed and accuracy of cognition: a meta-analytical investigation. *Brain and Cognition, 80*, 338–351.

McMorris, T., Sproule, J., Turner, A., & Hale, B. J. (2011). Acute, intermediate intensity exercise, and speed and accuracy in working memory tasks: a meta-analytical comparison of effects. *Physiology and Behavior, 102*, 421–428.

Miyake, A., Friedman, N. P., Emerson, M. J., Witzki, A. H., Howerter, A., & Wager, T. D. (2000). The unity and diversity of executive functions and their contributions to complex "frontal lobe" tasks: a latent variable analysis. *Cognitive Psychology, 41*, 49–100.

Nakamura, Y., Nishimoto, K., Akamatu, M., Takahashi, M., & Maruyama, A. (1999). The effect of jogging on P300 event related potentials. *Electromyography and Clinical Neurophysiology, 39*, 71–74.

Näätänen, R. (1992). *Attention and brain function.* Hillsdale, NJ: Lawrence Erlbaum Associates.

Netz, Y., Argov, E., & Inbar, O. (2009). Fitness's moderation of the facilitative effect of acute exercise on cognitive flexibility in older women. *Journal of Aging and Physical Activity, 17*, 154–166.

Netz, Y., Tomer, R., Axelrad, S., Argov, E., & Inbar, O. (2007). The effect of a single aerobic training session on cognitive flexibility in late middle-aged adults. *International Journal of Sports Medicine, 28*, 82–87.

Pesce, C. (2012). Shifting the focus from quantitative to qualitative exercise characteristics in exercise and cognition research. *Journal of Sport and Exercise Psychology, 34*, 766–786.

Pesce, C., & Audiffren, M. (2011). Does acute exercise switch off switch costs? A study with younger and older athletes. *Journal of Sport and Exercise Psychology, 33*, 609–626.

Pesce, C., Crova, C., Cereatti, L., Casella, R., & Bellucci, M. (2009). Physical activity and mental performance in preadolescents: effects of acute exercise on free-recall memory. *Mental Health and Physical Activity, 2*, 16–22.

Pfeuty, M., Ragot, R., & Pouthas, V. (2005). Relationship between CNV and timing of an upcoming event. *Neuroscience Letters, 382*, 106–111.

Polich, J. (2007). Updating P300: an integrative theory of P3a and P3b. *Clinical Neurophysiology, 118*, 2128–2148.

Polich, J., & Kok, A. (1995). Cognitive and biological determinants of P300: an integrative review. *Biological Psychology, 41*, 103–146.

Pontifex, M. B., Hillman, C. H., Fernhall, B., Thompson, K. M., & Valentini, T. A. (2009). The effect of acute aerobic and resistance exercise on working memory. *Medicine and Science in Sports Exercise, 41*, 927–934.

Pontifex, M. B., Saliba, B. J., Raine, L. B., Picchietti, D. L., & Hillman, C. H. (2013). Exercise improves behavioral, neurocognitive, and scholastic performance in children with attention-deficit/hyperactivity disorder. *The Journal of Pediatrics, 162*, 543–551.

Rasser, P. E., Johnston, P., Lagopoulos, J., Ward, P. B., Schall, U., Thienel, R., et al. (2005). Functional MRI BOLD response to Tower of London performance of first-episode schizophrenia patients using cortical pattern matching. *NeuroImage, 26*, 941–951.

Robbins, T. (2007). Shifting and stopping: fronto-striatal substrates, neurochemical modulation and clinical implications. *Philosophical Transactions of the Royal Society of London, Series B, 362*, 917–932.

Rohrbaugh, J. W., & Gaillard, A. W. K. (1983). Sensory and motor aspects of the contingent negative variation. In A. W. K. Gaillard, & W. Ritter (Eds.), *Tutorials in ERP research: Endogenous components* (pp. 269–310). Amsterdam: North-Holland.

Sanders, A. F. (1983). Towards a model of stress and human performance. *Acta Psychologica, 53*, 61–97.

Scudder, M. R., Drollette, E. S., Pontifex, M. B., & Hillman, C. H. (2012). Neuroelectric indices of goal maintenance following a single bout of physical activity. *Biological Psychology, 89*, 528–531.

Silveira, H., Moraes, H., Oliveira, N., Coutinho, E. S., Laks, J., & Deslandes, A. (2013). Physical exercise and clinically depressed patients: a systematic review and meta-analysis. *Neuropsychobiology, 67*, 61–68.

Stroth, S., Kubesch, S., Dieterle, K., Ruchsow, M., Heim, R., & Kiefer, M. (2009). Physical fitness, but not acute exercise modulates event-related potential indices for executive control in healthy adolescents. *Brain Research, 1269*, 114–124.

Sutton, S., Braren, M., Zubin, J., & John, E. R. (1965). Evoked potential correlates of stimulus uncertainty. *Science, 150*, 1187–1188.

Themanson, J. R., & Hillman, C. H. (2006). Cardiorespiratory fitness and acute aerobic exercise effects on neuroelectric and behavioral measures of action monitoring. *Neuroscience, 141*, 757–767.

Tillman, C. M., & Wiens, S. (2011). Behavioral and ERP indices of response conflict in Stroop and flanker tasks. *Psychophysiology*, *48*, 1405–1411.

Tomporowski, P. D. (2003). Effects of acute bouts of exercise on cognition. *Acta Psychologica*, *112*, 297–324.

Tomporowski, P. D., Davis, C. L., Lambourne, K., Gregoski, M., & Tkacz, J. (2008). Task switching in overweight children: effects of acute exercise and age. *Journal of Sport and Exercise Psychology*, *30*, 497–511.

Tomporowski, P. D., & Ellis, N. R. (1986). Effects of exercise on cognitive processes: a review. *Psychological Bulletin*, *99*, 338–346.

Tomporowski, P. D., Ellis, N. R., & Stephens, R. (1987). The immediate effects of strenuous exercise on free recall memory. *Ergonomics*, *30*, 121–129.

Vanhees, L., De Sutter, J., Gelada, S. N., Doyle, F., Prescott, E., Cornelissen, V., et al. (2012). Importance of characteristics and modalities of physical activity and exercise in defining the benefits to cardiovascular health within the general population: recommendations from the EACPR (Part I). *European Journal of Preventive Cardiology*, *19*, 670–686.

Vanhees, L., Geladas, N., Hansen, D., Kouidi, E., Niebauer, J., Reiner, Z., et al. (2012). Importance of characteristics and modalities of physical activity and exercise in the management of cardiovascular health in individuals with cardiovascular risk factors: recommendations from the EACPR. Part II. *European Journal of Preventive Cardiology*, *19*, 1005–1033.

Vaughan, L., & Giovanello, K. (2010). Executive function in daily life: age-related influences of executive processes on instrumental activities of daily living. *Psychology and Aging*, *25*, 343–355.

Verleger, R. (1997). On the utility of P3 latency as an index of mental chronometry. *Psychophysiology*, *34*, 131–156.

Wagner, G., Koch, K., Reichenbach, J. R., Sauer, H., & Schlösser, R. G. (2006). The special involvement of the rostrolateral prefrontal cortex in planning abilities: an event-related fMRI study with the Tower of London paradigm. *Neuropsychologia*, *44*, 2337–2347.

Walter, W. G., Cooper, R., Aldridge, V. J., McCallum, W. C., & Winter, A. L. (1964). Contingent negative variation: an electric sign of sensorimotor association and expectancy in the human brain. *Nature*, *203*, 380–384.

West, R., & Schwarb, H. (2006). The influence of aging and frontal function on the neural correlates of regulative and evaluative aspects of cognitive control. *Neuropsychology*, *20*, 468–481.

Wickens, C., Kramer, A. F., Vanasse, L., & Donchin, E. (1983). The performance of concurrent tasks: a psychophysiological analysis of the reciprocity of information processing resources. *Science*, *221*, 1080–1082.

Yagi, Y., Coburn, K. L., Estes, K. M., & Arruda, J. E. (1999). Effects of aerobic exercise and gender on visual and auditory P300, reaction time, and accuracy. *European Journal of Applied Physiology and Occupational Physiology*, *80*, 402–408.

Yau, S. Y., Lau, B. W., & So, K. F. (2011). Adult hippocampal neurogenesis: a possible way how physical exercise counteracts stress. *Cell Transplantation*, *20*, 99–111.

Yerkes, R. M., & Dodson, J. D. (1908). The relation of strength of stimulus to rapidity of habit formation. *Journal of Comparative Neurology of Psychology*, *18*, 459–482.

6

Acute Exercise and Cognition: Effects of Cerebral Oxygenation and Blood Flow

Soichi Ando

Graduate School of Informatics and Engineering, University of Electro-Communications,
Chofu, Tokyo, Japan

INTRODUCTION

Cognitive function plays an important role in our daily activities, including sports. Because many sports are performed in a dynamic and ever-changing environment, players have to make optimal decisions as quickly as possible under conditions of physiological stress. Hence, it is intriguing to examine how acute exercise alters cognitive function. There is a growing body of evidence to suggest that acute moderate exercise improves cognitive function (Brisswalter, Collardeau, & Rene, 2002; Chang, Labban, Gapin, & Etnier, 2012; Lambourne & Tomporowski, 2010; McMorris, Sproule, Turner, & Hale, 2011). It is of note that these improvements are observed even during a single bout of moderate exercise. These findings suggest that physiological changes induced by acute exercise have the potential to improve cognitive function.

It has been suggested that an exercise-induced increase in arousal to an optimal level leads to improvements in cognitive function (Brisswalter et al., 2002; Tomporowski, 2003), which is known as the Inverted-U theory. However, there are a number of studies that cannot be explained by the Inverted-U theory, suggesting that the exercise–cognition interaction is not so simple. More recently, Dietrich and Audiffren (2011) proposed a reticular-activating hypofrontality model to account for the consequences of acute exercise. This model predicts that, on the one hand, exercise facilitates implicit information by enhanced noradrenergic and dopaminergic systems. On the other hand, extensive activation of motor and sensory systems during strenuous exercise attenuates higher order functions of the prefrontal cortex because the brain has finite metabolic resources. Hence, the effects of acute exercise on cognitive function seem to be determined by the balance between the metabolic demands and beneficial effects of exercise in the brain. According to this model, improvements in cognitive function during moderate exercise suggest that the beneficial effects are predominant during moderate exercise.

Exercise has many physiological effects on the human brain (Ide & Secher, 2000; Meeusen, 2014; Nybo & Secher, 2004; Ogoh & Ainslie, 2009a,b; Secher, Seifert, & Van Lieshout, 2008; Seifert & Secher, 2011). Therefore, it is highly

Exercise-Cognition Interaction
http://dx.doi.org/10.1016/B978-0-12-800778-5.00006-2

likely that the effects of acute exercise on cognitive function are multifaceted and determined by the integration of many physiological, as well as psychological, factors induced by exercise. However, specific mechanisms by which exercise affects cognitive function remain largely unclear. This chapter summarizes recent studies that examined the effects of cerebral oxygenation and cerebral blood flow on cognitive function. Particularly, a focus on how alterations in cerebral oxygenation and cerebral blood flow affect cognitive function during exercise is presented. The findings provided in this chapter help to understand the exercise–cognition interaction under conditions of physiological stress.

CEREBRAL OXYGENATION AND CEREBRAL BLOOD FLOW DURING EXERCISE

Although the human brain represents only about 2% of body weight, it accounts for 15% of total cardiac output and 20% of total body oxygen consumption. Because of a lack of energy stores in the brain, cerebral blood flow needs to supply oxygen to maintain cerebral metabolism. Near-infrared spectroscopy (NIRS) has become a growing method to measure cerebral oxygenation noninvasively during dynamic movement including cycling and running. Cerebral oxygenation represents the balance between oxygen supply and demand, reflecting the balance between oxygen availability and use (Boushel et al., 2001).

There are many reviews that have summarized the principles, techniques, and limitations about NIRS measurements (Ekkekakis, 2009; Hoshi, 2003; Perrey, 2008; Rooks, Thom, McCully, & Dishman, 2010; Villringer & Chance, 1997). In brief, most biological tissue is relatively transparent to near-infrared light between 700 and 1000nm because water and hemoglobin absorption are relatively low within this wavelength

region. Once the brain tissue is irradiated with near-infrared light, the light propagates through the brain tissue. Propagation of near-infrared light through the brain tissue is dependent on absorption and scattering. Near-infrared light is thought to travel through a banana-shaped trajectory from a light source probe to a detector, penetrating the surface of the cortex. The modified Beer–Lambert law, which provides the physical and mathematical basis for NIRS, enables the continuous measurement of concentration changes in oxyhemoglobin (oxy-Hb) and deoxyhemoglobin (deoxy-Hb) by assuming that scattering is constant during the measurement. Total hemoglobin (total-Hb) is calculated as the sum of oxy-Hb and deoxy-Hb. Cerebral oxygenation is expressed as oxy-Hb/total-Hb × 100 (i.e., as a percentage). In this manner, NIRS allows for the measurement of cerebral oxygenation qualitatively during exercise in a noninvasive manner.

However, recent studies have challenged the validity and/or reliability of the measurement using NIRS (Hirasawa et al., 2015; Ogoh et al., 2011; Sorensen et al., 2012; Takahashi et al., 2011). In particular, the biggest concerns raised by recent criticisms are the contamination of extracranial blood flow (e.g., skin blood flow). Some studies attempted to minimize the effects of near-surface blood flow on cerebral oxygenation by subtraction of data from different source-detector distances; however, it might be difficult to exclude the effects of extracranial blood flow completely. Therefore, it was suggested that interpretation of the results obtained by NIRS should be done with caution. In particular, one must take the contamination of skin blood flow into consideration during exercise because skin blood flow substantially increases during exercise as compared with that at a resting condition (Miyazawa et al., 2013; Sato, Ogoh, Hirasawa, Oue, & Sadamoto, 2011).

Despite several shortcomings, NIRS may enable the measurement of cerebral oxygenation during exercise in a noninvasive manner.

Indeed, alterations in response to moderate to strenuous exercise tended to be similar between NIRS-detected cerebral oxygenation and cerebral oxygenation based on arterial to internal jugular venous blood values (Rasmussen et al., 2007; Seifert et al., 2009), which may support the notion that NIRS allows monitoring of cerebral oxygenation qualitatively. However, at the current stage, it is safe to think that there are some inherent limitations when researchers interpret alterations in cerebral oxygenation measured by NIRS during exercise. This chapter discusses the effects of cerebral oxygenation on cognitive function based on the assumption that NIRS is able to measure regional cerebral oxygenation qualitatively, with an aim toward discussion. New algorithms need to be developed for unbiased NIRS detection of cerebral oxygenation (Hirasawa et al., 2015).

A number of researchers have monitored cerebral oxygenation during graded exercise. Rooks et al. (2010) conducted a meta-analysis to quantify the effects of exercise on brain hemodynamics including cerebral oxygenation. The authors reported that prefrontal oxygenation showed a quadratic response to incremental exercise, rising between moderate and strenuous intensities, then falling at very hard intensities. In most studies using NIRS, cerebral oxygenation has been measured over the prefrontal cortex. This makes it difficult to detect regional differences in cerebral oxygenation during exercise. Hence, Subudhi, Miramon, Granger, and Roach (2009) investigated whether hemodynamic changes are different among different brain areas during exercise. They found that overall patterns of hemodynamic changes were similar among prefrontal, premotor, and motor cortices during exercise at maximal intensity despite slight differences in hemodynamic changes among these areas.

There are a couple of methods to measure cerebral blood flow. Among these, transcranial Doppler (TCD) is widely used as a noninvasive method to determine beat-by-beat changes in cerebral blood flow velocity. TCD uses low-frequency (≤2 MHz) ultrasound to insonate cerebral arteries through a relatively thin bone window in the temporal region of the skull. By using spectral analysis of the Doppler frequency shifts from insonated red blood cells moving through a preselected arterial sample volume, TCD calculates and displays cerebral blood flow velocity with a high temporal resolution (Lupetin, Davis, Beckman, & Dash, 1995). The basic assumption with this technique is that changes in cerebral blood flow velocity are directly related to variations in cerebral blood flow. Given that the diameter of the middle cerebral artery remains constant under physiological conditions (Serrador, Picot, Rutt, Shoemaker, & Bondar, 2000), this assumption seems to hold true under physiological conditions including exercise.

During graded exercise, an increase in exercise intensity up to 60% of maximal oxygen uptake elevates cerebral blood flow, after which cerebral blood flow decreases toward baseline levels despite further increases in exercise intensity and brain metabolism (Ide & Secher, 2000; Querido & Sheel, 2007; Secher et al., 2008). These findings indicate that, during exercise, the regulation of cerebral blood flow is affected to a greater extent by other physiological factors rather than neuronal activity and cerebral metabolism (Ogoh & Ainslie, 2009a,b). It is well known that cerebral autoregulation and arterial pressure of CO_2 strongly regulate cerebral blood flow. Given that acute exercise alters ventilation, systemic cardiovascular factors (e.g., cardiac output), cerebral metabolism, and sympathetic nerve activity, these physiological changes affect cerebral blood flow regulation during exercise in an integrative manner (Ogoh & Ainslie, 2009a,b). Interestingly, it was demonstrated that, during graded dynamic exercise, regulation of internal carotid artery blood flow was limited by a large increase in external carotid artery blood flow, which is selectively increased to prioritize thermoregulation (Sato et al., 2011).

The same research group also indicated that cerebral CO_2 reactivity was different among the internal carotid artery, external carotid artery, and vertebral artery. These results may explain different cerebral blood flow responses to physiological stress (Sato et al., 2012).

In this section, alterations in cerebral oxygenation and cerebral blood flow in response to acute exercise, together with methods using NIRS and TCD, have been briefly summarized. Both NIRS and TCD measurements are relatively inexpensive when compared to other neuroimaging techniques. These measurements are repeatable and portable, which offers continuous monitoring during exercise as well as at the bedside. However, up to now, little is known about whether changes in cognitive function are associated with alterations in cerebral oxygenation and cerebral blood flow. In the next section, how alterations in cerebral oxygenation and cerebral blood flow affect cognitive function during exercise are discussed.

COGNITIVE FUNCTION: THE EFFECTS OF CEREBRAL OXYGENATION AND CEREBRAL BLOOD FLOW

In this section, the first question is whether alterations in cerebral oxygenation affect cognitive function. Up to now, a few studies have examined the effects of alterations in cerebral oxygenation on cognitive function under physiological conditions. Ando, Kokubu, Yamada, and Kimura (2011) investigated whether alterations in cerebral oxygenation are associated with cognitive function during exercise (Ando et al., 2011). In this study, subjects performed a modified version of the Eriksen flanker task in which response inhibition and interference suppression are required. Reaction time (RT) and accuracy of response were recorded, and RT was fractionated into premotor and motor components based on surface electromyographic recordings (Ando, Yamada, Tanaka, Oda, & Kokubu, 2009). The premotor component of RT (premotor time) and accuracy of response were used to evaluate the effects of acute exercise on cognitive function. In the exercise condition, subjects performed the cognitive task at rest and while cycling at 40%, 60%, and 80% of peak oxygen uptake ($\dot{V}O_2$). In the control condition, the workload was fixed at 20 W, and cognitive tasks were temporally matched with the tasks in the exercise condition. Cerebral oxygenation was continuously monitored at rest and during exercise using NIRS. Figure 1 illustrates the typical changes in cerebral oxygenation at rest and during exercise. At rest, cerebral oxygenation increased during the cognitive task from the baseline. During exercise at 40% and 60% peak $\dot{V}O_2$, cerebral oxygenation increased relative to the baseline. A further increase in cerebral oxygenation was observed at 40% peak $\dot{V}O_2$ during the cognitive task. In contrast, cerebral oxygenation substantially decreased during exercise at 80% peak $\dot{V}O_2$. It should be noted that the decrease in cerebral oxygenation continued during the cognitive task.

In the exercise condition, premotor time decreased during exercise at 60% peak $\dot{V}O_2$ as compared with that at rest (Figure 2). Accuracy was not affected by exercise at 60% peak $\dot{V}O_2$. In contrast, in the control condition, premotor time (Figure 2) and accuracy were not altered. Cerebral oxygenation during exercise at 60% peak $\dot{V}O_2$ was not different from that at rest (Figure 3). These results suggest that the improvements in cognitive function during exercise at 60% peak $\dot{V}O_2$ were not directly related to alterations in cerebral oxygenation. Furthermore, although cerebral oxygenation slightly, but significantly, increased in the control condition, premotor time was not altered. These results imply that alterations in cerebral oxygenation have negligible effects on cognitive function during exercise. This notion may be corroborated by a study showing that cognitive performance in the Stroop test, which requires attention, response

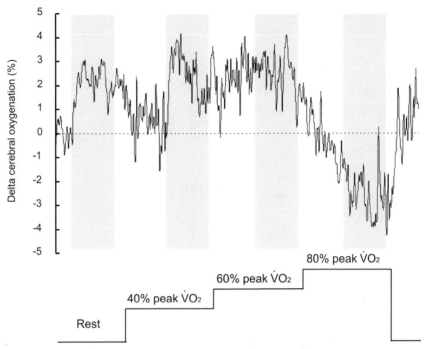

FIGURE 1 Typical example of cerebral oxygenation at rest and during exercise at 40%, 60%, and 80% peak $\dot{V}O_2$. Alterations in cerebral oxygenation were expressed as changes from baseline (horizontal dashed line) that were measured at the beginning of the experiment. Shaded areas show the duration of the cognitive task performed.

inhibition, interference, and behavioral conflict resolution, improved during exercise at 70% of the heart rate range despite a decrease in cerebral oxygenation (Lucas et al., 2012).

When the brain is activated during exercise, an increase in the cerebral oxygen supply is required to match the enhanced level of neuronal metabolism (Ide & Secher, 2000; Ogoh & Ainslie, 2009a,b; Secher et al., 2008). However, hyperventilation induced by strenuous exercise may lead to a decrease in cerebral blood flow (Ogoh et al., 2005) and, thus, cerebral oxygenation (Secher et al., 2008). Accordingly, it was hypothesized that if cerebral oxygenation is associated with cognitive function during exercise, a decrease in cerebral oxygenation may impair cognitive function during strenuous exercise. In a study by Ando et al. (2011), cerebral oxygenation substantially decreased during exercise at 80% peak

$\dot{V}O_2$ (Figure 3). Because the decrease in cerebral oxygenation was accompanied by a decrease in estimated arterial pressure of carbon dioxide, the decrease is at least in part associated with hyperventilation. However, in contrast to the hypothesis, there were no differences in cognitive performance between at rest and during exercise at 80% peak $\dot{V}O_2$ (Figure 2). These results suggest that the effects of reduced cerebral oxygenation during strenuous exercise were not sufficient enough to impair cognitive function. Collectively, cognitive function improved during exercise at moderate intensity, but the improvements during exercise were not directly associated with alterations in cerebral oxygenation during exercise. Furthermore, reduction of cerebral oxygenation during strenuous exercise may not impair cognitive function, at least under this experimental condition.

(A)

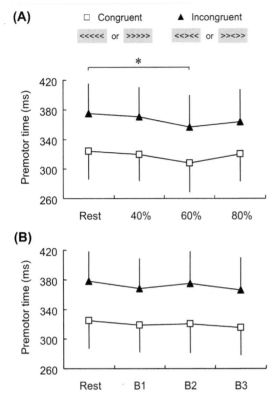

(B)

FIGURE 2　The premotor time in the exercise (A) and control (B) conditions. The subjects responded to the orientation of a central arrow embedded in the array of five arrows. In congruent trials (□), the flanking arrows pointed in the same direction as the central arrow. In incongruent trials (▲), the flanking arrows pointed in the opposite direction as the central arrow. B1, B2, and B3 represent the first, second, and third cognitive tasks during exercise at 20 W in the control condition. Data are expressed as mean ± SD. *$P < 0.05$. *Adopted from Ando et al. (2011). Used with permission.*

(A)

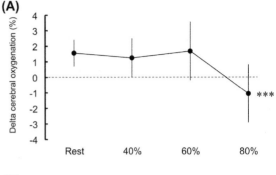

(B)

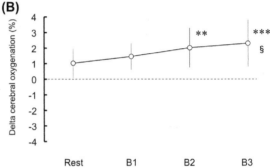

FIGURE 3　Cerebral oxygenation in the exercise (A) and control (B) conditions. Alterations in cerebral oxygenation were expressed as changes from baseline (horizontal dashed line) that were measured at the beginning of the experiment. B1, B2, and B3 represent the first, second, and third cognitive tasks during exercise at 20 W in the control condition. Data are expressed as mean ± SD. (A) ***$P < 0.001$, versus Rest, 40%, and 60%. (B) **$P < 0.01$, ***$P < 0.001$ versus Rest; §$P < 0.05$ versus B1. *Adopted from Ando et al. (2011). Used with permission.*

Endo et al. (2013) investigated how cognitive function is altered after exercise with different exercise intensities and durations. These authors also examined the relationship between changes in both cognitive performance and prefrontal oxy-Hb response. In the study by Endo et al. (2013), subjects performed the Stroop test before and after exercise at 20%, 40%, and 60% of maximum voluntary exercise. The authors indicated that exercise at 40% of maximum voluntary exercise for 15 min improved cognitive function, together with an increase in the prefrontal oxy-Hb response during the Stroop test. Moreover, they reported that the degree of increase in the prefrontal oxy-Hb response tended to be correlated with improved performance in the Stroop test. Similarly, Soya and colleagues examined the effects of acute exercise on cognitive function in young and older subjects using multichannel functional NIRS. In their studies, the Stroop test was conducted before and after exercise. The research group clearly demonstrated that improvements in cognitive function after exercise at mild to moderate intensity were accompanied by the activation in the prefrontal areas

(Byun et al., 2014; Hyodo et al., 2012; Yanagisawa et al., 2010). These findings suggest that improvements in cognitive function are associated with a prefrontal oxy-Hb response measured by NIRS. However, physiological mechanisms underlying enhanced prefrontal activation are yet to be determined.

One may argue that these findings are contradictory to the view that improvement in cognitive function during exercise at moderate intensity was independent of cerebral oxygenation (Ando et al., 2011). However, while cerebral oxygenation was monitored during exercise in the studies by Ando et al. (2011) and Lucas et al. (2012), the authors in other studies measured prefrontal oxy-Hb changes after exercise (Byun et al., 2014; Endo et al., 2013; Hyodo et al., 2012; Yanagisawa et al., 2010). After exercise, prefrontal oxy-Hb response seems to reflect prefrontal neural activation in response to a cognitive task (Byun et al., 2014; Endo et al., 2013; Hyodo et al., 2012; Yanagisawa et al., 2010). In other words, a prefrontal oxy-Hb response is thought to occur as a result of neural activation in the prefrontal cortex. Therefore, the findings from different laboratories are not contradictory and well reconciled. At the current stage, only a few studies examined the relationship between cognitive function and cerebral oxygenation during exercise. Further studies will help us to understand physiological mechanisms underlying changes in cognitive function during exercise at different exercise intensities. The association between cerebral oxygenation and cognitive function during exercise will be further discussed in the following section.

In this section, the second question is whether alterations in cerebral blood flow affect cognitive function. Aging appears to be related to a progressive decrease in cerebral blood flow (Ainslie et al., 2008; Bertsch et al., 2009). Hence, impairments in cognitive function in older people are, at least in part, associated with reduced cerebral blood flow (Bertsch et al., 2009; Heo et al., 2010; Steffener, Brickman, Habeck, Salthouse, & Stern, 2013). Furthermore, Marshall et al. (2001) indicated that transient occlusion of cerebral blood flow in patients with cerebrovascular disease impaired cognitive function, which suggests that cognitive function may be vulnerable to an acute decrease in cerebral blood flow. Taken together, it was suggested that alterations in cerebral blood flow might play a crucial role in changes in cognitive function. However, little is known about the effects of cerebral blood flow on cognitive function under physiological conditions in which cerebral blood flow is altered.

Lucas et al. (2012) were the first to investigate whether an acute increase in cerebral blood flow during exercise is related to an improvement in cognitive function. The authors also examined the effects of aging on changes in cognitive performance induced by acute exercise. In this study, young and older subjects performed the Stroop task at rest and during cycling at 30% and 70% heart rate range simultaneously with cerebral blood flow and cerebral oxygenation measurements. The authors observed that cognitive function improved during exercise, regardless of age. They also found a strong relationship between cognitive function and middle cerebral blood flow velocity at rest. However, the relationship was uncoupled during exercise, suggesting that improvements in cognitive function are not directly related to alterations in cerebral blood flow. More recently, Ogoh et al. (2014) examined whether an increase in cerebral blood flow improves cognitive function during prolonged exercise. The authors also manipulated cerebral blood flow at rest and during exercise using hypercapnic inspired gas (2% CO_2). In this study, the subjects performed the Stroop test at rest and during cycle for 50 min. The authors found that cognitive function improved during prolonged exercise, although cerebral blood flow gradually decreased during prolonged exercise. Furthermore, increase in cerebral blood flow induced by hypercapnia did not affect cognitive function at rest and during exercise. Therefore, the authors suggested that alterations in cerebral blood flow do not affect cognitive function at rest and during exercise, and that changes in cognitive function are attributable to other mechanisms. Taken together, these studies appear to suggest that improvements in cognitive function during exercise are not directly related to alterations in cerebral blood flow. Furthermore, a decrease in cerebral blood flow was not sufficient to impair cognitive function during exercise. In terms of cognitive function, alterations in cerebral blood flow may not be paralleled by oxygen delivery to the brain or by increased cerebral metabolism (Ogoh et al., 2014).

In this section, recent articles that examined the effects of cerebral oxygenation and cerebral blood flow on cognitive function under physiological conditions have been summarized. Collectively, alterations in cerebral oxygenation were not related to improvements in cognitive function during exercise. During strenuous exercise, cognitive function was not impaired despite decreased cerebral oxygenation. These findings suggest that cerebral oxygenation is not directly associated with cognitive function during exercise. By the same token, it was suggested that improvements in cognitive function during exercise were not directly related to alterations in cerebral blood flow. Furthermore, decreased cerebral blood flow did not impair cognitive function during prolonged exercise. These findings suggest that alterations in cerebral oxygenation and cerebral blood flow do not play an essential role in improvement of cognitive function, and that cognitive function is well maintained even when cerebral oxygenation and cerebral blood flow are to some extent compromised during exercise.

Up to now, specific mechanisms by which acute exercise affects cognitive function remain to be elucidated. Future studies are required to clarify how alterations in cerebral oxygenation and cerebral blood flow affect cognitive function in a variety of physiological conditions. Moreover, it is likely that the effects of cerebral oxygenation and/or cerebral blood flow on cognitive function are dependent on task demands.

Therefore, it is important to accumulate empirical evidence to understand how alterations in cerebral oxygenation and cerebral blood flow affect cognitive function.

COGNITIVE FUNCTION UNDER HYPOXIA

Oxygen delivery to the brain tissue may be compromised under hypoxia. Hypoxia is known to have detrimental effects on the central nervous system (Amann & Kayser, 2009; Neubauer & Sunderram, 2004; Verges et al., 2012), which may lead to neurological and physiological deficits as well as structural damage in the brain tissue. It has been suggested that hypoxia has the potential to impair brain function (Hornbein, 2001). Indeed, cognitive function may be impaired under hypoxia at resting conditions (Virues-Ortega, Buela-Casal, Garrido, & Alcazar, 2004; Virues-Ortega, Garrido, Javierre, & Kloezeman, 2006; Yan, 2014). It is of note that impairments of cognitive function were prominent at high altitude (Virues-Ortega et al., 2004, 2006; Yan, 2014). As altitude increases and severity of hypoxia increases, hypoxia decreases arterial pressure of O_2 (PaO_2) and arterial saturation of O_2 (SaO_2) (Kolb, Ainslie, Ide, & Poulin, 2004; Peltonen et al., 2007). As a result, cerebral oxygenation decreases with increases in altitude (Kolb et al., 2004; Peltonen et al., 2007). Moreover, at the cellular level, the turnover of several neurotransmitters appears to be altered under hypoxia despite the preserved state of brain energy stores (Raichle & Hornbein, 2001). Therefore, brain desaturation and resultant biological processes may be responsible for the impairment of cognitive function despite the fact that the underlying mechanisms are not fully understood.

Exercise under hypoxia substantially decreases arterial oxygen saturation and cerebral oxygenation relative to normoxia (Ando, Yamada, & Kokubu, 2010; Subudhi, Dimmen, & Roach, 2007; Subudhi et al., 2009), which suggests that oxygen availability may be compromised in the brain during exercise under hypoxia. Given that brain function and tissue integrity depend on a continuous and sufficient oxygen supply, cognitive function may be impaired during exercise under hypoxia as the severity of hypoxia increases. However, it was unclear how exercise under different levels of hypoxia affects cognitive function.

Ando et al. (2013) examined the effects of exercise under different levels of hypoxia on cognitive function to understand how cognitive function is affected during exercise at different levels of altitude. The degree of decrease in cerebral oxygenation is greater during moderate exercise under hypoxia relative to strenuous exercise under normoxia (Ando et al., 2010). Thus, investigation under hypoxic environment enables the testing of whether a decrease in cerebral oxygenation has detrimental effects on cognitive function during exercise. In the study by Ando et al. (2013), subjects performed cognitive tasks at rest and during exercise at various fractions of inspired oxygen (FIO_2: 0.209, 0.18, and 0.15). Exercise intensity corresponded to 60% of peak $\dot{V}O_2$ under normoxia. The cognitive task used was a go/no go task that requires executive function, including selective attention, response inhibition, and interference control (Chaddock, Hillman, Buck, & Cohen, 2011; Pontifex, Hillman, Fernhall, Thompson, & Valentini, 2009). Cognitive function was evaluated by RT in the go trial, as well as response accuracy. Pulse oximetric saturation (SpO_2) and cerebral oxygenation were continuously monitored to assess oxygen availability during exercise.

At the resting condition, there were no differences in RT in the go trial among different environmental conditions (Figure 4). SpO_2 and cerebral oxygenation gradually decreased as the FIO_2 levels decreased (Figure 5). These results indicate that cognitive function was not altered under hypoxia, suggesting that decreases in cerebral oxygenation did not affect cognitive function, at least under the experimental condition.

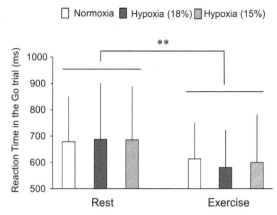

FIGURE 4 Reaction times in the go trial at rest and during exercise under normoxia and hypoxia at 18% and 15% O_2. **$P<0.01$, versus Rest. *From Ando et al. (2013).*

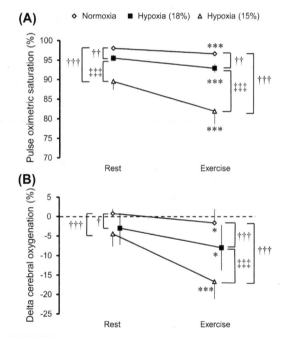

FIGURE 5 SpO_2 and cerebral oxygenation during the cognitive task. (A) SpO_2. (B) Cerebral oxygenation. Alterations in cerebral oxygenation were expressed as the changes from baseline (horizontal dashed line) that were measured under normoxia. †$P<0.05$, ††$P<0.01$, †††$P<0.001$, versus Normoxia; ‡‡‡$P<0.001$, versus Hypoxia at 18% O_2; *$P<0.05$, ***$P<0.001$, versus Rest. *From Ando et al. (2013).*

During exercise, SpO_2 and cerebral oxygenation progressively decreased during exercise as the FIO_2 level decreased (Figure 5), which suggests that oxygen availability might be compromised during exercise under hypoxia. Nevertheless, RT in the go trial decreased during exercise under hypoxia as well as normoxia (Figure 4). The response accuracy was affected by neither exercise nor the difference in FIO_2 levels. These results demonstrate that cognitive function improves during exercise even under moderate hypoxia. Here, it should be noted that improvements in cognitive function were observed during exercise despite the fact that cerebral oxygenation was substantially reduced. These findings support the notion that improvements in cognitive function are not directly associated with alterations in cerebral oxygenation during exercise. Rather, other physiological changes induced by acute exercise would play a crucial role in the improvements in cognitive function during exercise. However, given that physiological responses to exercise are to some extent different between normoxia and hypoxia, further studies are needed to validate the viewpoint.

In a follow-up study, Komiyama and colleagues examined how exercise under moderate hypoxia alters cognitive function when task difficulty was increased (Komiyama et al., 2015). In the study by Komiyama et al., subjects performed cognitive tasks at rest and during exercise under normoxia and moderate hypoxia (FIO_2: 0.15). The authors used a combination of a spatial delayed response (spatial DR) task and go/no go task, where spatial working memory and executive function are required. Working memory was assessed by the accuracy of the spatial DR task, and executive function was assessed by the accuracy and RT in the go/no go task. The subjects cycled an ergometer for 30 min under normoxia and moderate hypoxia while keeping their heart rates at 140 beats/min. Cerebral oxygenation decreased during exercise under moderate hypoxia. However, RT in the go trial decreased during exercise relative to rest under moderate hypoxia as well as normoxia. Exercise and moderate hypoxia did not influence the accuracy of both spatial DR and go/no go tasks. Collectively, from the study by Komiyama et al., exercise under moderate hypoxia did not impair working memory and executive function during exercise even if cerebral oxygenation was substantially reduced. These results are in line with the previous finding, showing that cognitive function improved during exercise despite decreased cerebral oxygenation (Ando et al., 2013), which again reinforces the view that alterations in cerebral oxygenation are not directly associated with cognitive function during exercise.

Endurance performance is known to decrease under hypoxia as compared with normoxia (Amann & Kayser, 2009). It has been suggested that prefrontal cortex oxygenation (Amann, Romer, Subudhi, Pegelow, & Dempsey, 2007; Imray et al., 2005; Subudhi et al., 2007; Subudhi, Lorenz, Fulco, & Roach, 2008; Subudhi et al., 2009) and/or frontal cortex oxygen delivery (Vogiatzis et al., 2011) are limiting factors in maximal exercise performance under severe hypoxia, whereas a decrease in frontal cortex oxygenation is unlikely to limit exercise performance under normoxia. Amann et al. (2007) demonstrated that peripheral fatigue predominantly limits endurance exercise performance under normoxia to moderate hypoxia, whereas central nervous system hypoxia limits endurance exercise performance under severe hypoxic conditions (Amann et al., 2007). The authors proposed that the major determinants of endurance exercise performance might switch from peripheral origin of fatigue to a hypoxia-sensitive central component of fatigue below a level of acutely compromised O_2 transport represented by a range of 70–75% arterial oxygen saturation. This suggests that the effects of exercise on the central nervous system under hypoxia are closely related to the severity of hypoxia. In the studies by Ando and colleagues, the FIO_2 level of 0.15 was equivalent to moderate hypoxia, and SpO_2 was above this level during exercise. Moreover, it was suggested that severe hypoxia substantially reduced cortical voluntary activation during repeated muscle contraction, while the reduction was still less under moderate hypoxia (Goodall, Ross, & Romer, 2010; Millet, Muthalib, Jubeau, Laursen, & Nosaka, 2012). Collectively, although cognitive function is not directly comparable with endurance exercise performance and cortical voluntary activation during muscle contraction, it is likely that the severity of hypoxia was not sufficient enough to impair cognitive function under physiological stress. Further research is required to demonstrate whether cognitive function is impaired during exercise under severe hypoxia.

SUMMARY

In this chapter, the effects of cerebral oxygenation and cerebral blood flow on cognitive function have been discussed. In a series of studies cited in this chapter, response speed (RT) decreased during exercise at moderate intensity. Nevertheless, accuracy was not affected during exercise. These results are generally regarded as improvements in cognitive function, excluding the possibility that a decrease in response speed is ascribed to a speed–accuracy trade-off. Indeed, in the studies that examined the exercise–cognition interaction, decreases in response speed without sacrificing accuracy were frequently observed.

Although definitive and conclusive evidence is still lacking, the literature suggests that alterations in cerebral oxygenation are not directly associated with improvements in cognitive function during exercise. This notion is corroborated by the findings obtained from hypoxic environments in which cognitive function improved during exercise despite substantial decreases in cerebral oxygenation. Furthermore, decreased cerebral oxygenation did not impair cognitive function during strenuous exercise under

normoxic environments. By the same token, recent studies demonstrated that increases in cerebral blood flow were not directly associated with improvements in cognitive function during exercise. Decreased cerebral blood flow during exercise did not impair cognitive function. Taken together, at least under the conditions in which these experiments were performed, alterations in cerebral oxygenation and cerebral blood flow are ruled out as explanatory variables for changes in cognitive performance derived from acute exercise. However, given that oxygen supply is necessary to maintain brain function and tissue integrity, the notion that alterations in cerebral oxygenation and cerebral blood flow are not directly associated with changes in cognitive function does not exclude the possibility that oxygen itself and/or oxygen availability somehow modulate cognitive function during exercise.

Lucas et al. (2012) suggested that there is dissociation between regional cerebral oxygenation and global cerebral blood flow during exercise combined with cognitive task (Lucas et al., 2012). However, despite that, alterations in both cerebral oxygenation and cerebral blood flow appear to have little effect on cognitive function during exercise. In particular, it should be noted that cognitive function was not impaired when cerebral oxygenation and cerebral blood flow were compromised. This implies that humans are able to maintain or improve cognitive function even if cerebral oxygenation and/or cerebral blood flow are compromised to some extent. As Ogoh et al. (2014) suggested, for cognitive function, alterations in cerebral blood flow may not be paralleled by oxygen delivery to the brain or by increased cerebral metabolism. It has been suggested that exercise affects brain circuits involving neurotransmitters including dopamine, noradrenaline, serotonin, adrenocorticotropic hormone, and cortisol (Dietrich & Audiffren, 2011; McMorris et al., 2011; Meeusen & De Meirleir, 1995; Nybo & Secher, 2004). Some of these physiological changes are potential candidates to account for the improvements in cognitive function during exercise (Brisswalter et al., 2002; Chmura, Nazar, & Kaciuba-Uscilko, 1994; McMorris et al., 2011). Therefore, it may be that acute exercise improves cognitive function provided sufficient oxygen and/or nutrients are available and these systems are intact.

The question is open as to what extent humans are able to maintain cognitive function in response to decreased cerebral oxygenation and/or cerebral blood flow. Given that transient occlusion of cerebral blood flow in patients with cerebrovascular disease reversibly impaired cognitive function (Marshall et al., 2001), there may be a threshold below which cognitive function is impaired in response to a decrease in cerebral oxygenation and/or cerebral blood flow. As mentioned above, the effects of cerebral oxygenation and/or cerebral blood flow on cognitive function are likely to depend on task demands. Hence, further studies will be required to elucidate whether there exists a threshold using a variety of cognitive tasks.

Several limitations should be taken into account. First, the exercise–cognition interaction is complex and cognitive function during exercise is influenced by a number of factors including exercise intensity, exercise duration, task difficulty, the fitness level of subjects, aging, and health status. These differences affect the experimental results, suggesting that researchers have to take these factors into consideration in investigations of the exercise–cognition interaction. Second, when subjects perform cognitive tasks, they use a motor response (e.g., button press) in most cases. This means that assessment of cognitive function inevitably involves the motor response. Although a cognitive task is closely associated with higher brain areas such as the prefrontal cortex, many brain areas, including motor and premotor cortices, are presumably activated when a cognitive task is combined with exercise. Thus, the effects of acute exercise on cognitive function (e.g., decrease in RT) also may be derived from altered activation in other brain areas associated with motor response.

These points should be further investigated. Third, many physiological changes simultaneously occur during exercise. Hence, alterations in cerebral oxygenation or cerebral blood flow were not isolated with other physiological changes in response to exercise, which implies that researchers must pay attention to confounding factors. Sophisticated protocols, together with manipulation of physiological parameters, are mandatory to examine physiological mechanisms underlying changes in cognitive function. Finally, as discussed above, there still exists a problem inherent with the NIRS measurement. Technical advancements will help to further examine the relationship between cerebral oxygenation and cognitive function during exercise.

Despite these limitations, up to now, available evidence suggests that alterations in cerebral oxygenation and cerebral blood flow are not directly associated with changes in cognitive function during exercise. Future studies are necessary to clarify how alterations in cerebral oxygenation and cerebral blood flow affect cognitive function during exercise in a variety of experimental conditions.

References

Ainslie, P. N., Cotter, J. D., George, K. P., Lucas, S., Murrell, C., Shave, R., et al. (2008). Elevation in cerebral blood flow velocity with aerobic fitness throughout healthy human ageing. *Journal of Physiology, 586,* 4005–4010.

Amann, M., & Kayser, B. (2009). Nervous system function during exercise in hypoxia. *High Altitude Medicine and Biology, 10,* 149–164.

Amann, M., Romer, L. M., Subudhi, A. W., Pegelow, D. F., & Dempsey, J. A. (2007). Severity of arterial hypoxaemia affects the relative contributions of peripheral muscle fatigue to exercise performance in healthy humans. *Journal of Physiology, 581,* 389–403.

Ando, S., Hatamoto, Y., Sudo, M., Kiyonaga, A., Tanaka, H., & Higaki, Y. (2013). The effects of exercise under hypoxia on cognitive function. *PLoS One, 8,* e63630. http://dx.doi.org/10.1371/journal.pone.0063630.

Ando, S., Kokubu, M., Yamada, Y., & Kimura, M. (2011). Does cerebral oxygenation affect cognitive function during exercise? *European Journal of Applied Physiology, 111,* 1973–1982.

Ando, S., Yamada, Y., & Kokubu, M. (2010). Reaction time to peripheral visual stimuli during exercise under hypoxia. *Journal of Applied Physiology (1985)*, *108*, 1210–1216.

Ando, S., Yamada, Y., Tanaka, T., Oda, S., & Kokubu, M. (2009). Reaction time to peripheral visual stimuli during exercise under normoxia and hyperoxia. *European Journal of Applied Physiology*, *106*, 61–69.

Bertsch, K., Hagemann, D., Hermes, M., Walter, C., Khan, R., & Naumann, E. (2009). Resting cerebral blood flow, attention, and aging. *Brain Research*, *1267*, 77–88.

Boushel, R., Langberg, H., Olesen, J., Gonzales-Alonzo, J., Bulow, J., & Kjaer, M. (2001). Monitoring tissue oxygen availability with near infrared spectroscopy (NIRS) in health and disease. *Scandinavian Journal of Medicine and Science in Sports*, *11*, 213–222.

Brisswalter, J., Collardeau, M., & Rene, A. (2002). Effects of acute physical exercise characteristics on cognitive performance. *Sports Medicine*, *32*, 555–566.

Byun, K., Hyodo, K., Suwabe, K., Ochi, G., Sakairi, Y., Kato, M., et al. (2014). Positive effect of acute mild exercise on executive function via arousal-related prefrontal activations: an fNIRS study. *Neuroimage*, *98*, 336–345.

Chaddock, L., Hillman, C. H., Buck, S. M., & Cohen, N. J. (2011). Aerobic fitness and executive control of relational memory in preadolescent children. *Medicine and Science in Sports and Exercise*, *43*, 344–349.

Chang, Y. K., Labban, J. D., Gapin, J. I., & Etnier, J. L. (2012). The effects of acute exercise on cognitive performance: a meta-analysis. *Brain Research*, *1453*, 87–101.

Chmura, J., Nazar, K., & Kaciuba-Uscilko, H. (1994). Choice reaction time during graded exercise in relation to blood lactate and plasma catecholamine thresholds. *International Journal of Sports Medicine*, *15*, 172–176.

Dietrich, A., & Audiffren, M. (2011). The reticular-activating hypofrontality (RAH) model of acute exercise. *Neuroscience and Biobehavioral Reviews*, *35*, 1305–1325.

Ekkekakis, P. (2009). Illuminating the black box: investigating prefrontal cortical hemodynamics during exercise with near-infrared spectroscopy. *Journal of Sport and Exercise Psychology*, *31*, 505–553.

Endo, K., Matsukawa, K., Liang, N., Nakatsuka, C., Tsuchimochi, H., Okamura, H., et al. (2013). Dynamic exercise improves cognitive function in association with increased prefrontal oxygenation. *Journal of Physiological Sciences*, *63*, 287–298.

Goodall, S., Ross, E. Z., & Romer, L. M. (2010). Effect of graded hypoxia on supraspinal contributions to fatigue with unilateral knee-extensor contractions. *Journal of Applied Physiology*, *109*, 1842–1851.

Heo, S., Prakash, R. S., Voss, M. W., Erickson, K. I., Ouyang, C., Sutton, B. P., et al. (2010). Resting hippocampal blood flow, spatial memory and aging. *Brain Research*, *1315*, 119–127.

Hirasawa, A., Yanagisawa, S., Tanaka, N., Funane, T., Kiguchi, M., Sorensen, H., et al. (2015). Influence of skin blood flow and source-detector distance on near-infrared spectroscopy-determined cerebral oxygenation in humans. *Clinical Physiology and Functional Imaging*, *35*(3), 237–244. http://dx.doi.org/10.1111/cpf.12156.

Hornbein, T. F. (2001). The high-altitude brain. *Journal of Experimental Biology*, *204*, 3129–3132.

Hoshi, Y. (2003). Functional near-infrared optical imaging: utility and limitations in human brain mapping. *Psychophysiology*, *40*, 511–520.

Hyodo, K., Dan, I., Suwabe, K., Kyutoku, Y., Yamada, Y., Akahori, M., et al. (2012). Acute moderate exercise enhances compensatory brain activation in older adults. *Neurobiology of Aging*, *33*, 2621–2632.

Ide, K., & Secher, N. H. (2000). Cerebral blood flow and metabolism during exercise. *Progress in Neurobiology*, *61*, 397–414.

Imray, C. H., Myers, S. D., Pattinson, K. T., Bradwell, A. R., Chan, C. W., Harris, S., et al. (2005). Effect of exercise on cerebral perfusion in humans at high altitude. *Journal of Applied Physiology*, *99*, 699–706.

Kolb, J. C., Ainslie, P. N., Ide, K., & Poulin, M. J. (2004). Protocol to measure acute cerebrovascular and ventilatory responses to isocapnic hypoxia in humans. *Respiratory Physiology and Neurobiology*, *141*, 191–199.

Komiyama, T., Sudo, M., Higaki, Y., Kiyonaga, A., Tanaka, H., & Ando, S. (2015). Does moderate hypoxia alter working memory and executive function during prolonged exercise? *Physiology and Behavior*, *139*, 290–296.

Lambourne, K., & Tomporowski, P. (2010). The effect of exercise-induced arousal on cognitive task performance: a meta-regression analysis. *Brain Research*, *1341*, 12–24.

Lucas, S. J., Ainslie, P. N., Murrell, C. J., Thomas, K. N., Franz, E. A., & Cotter, J. D. (2012). Effect of age on exercise-induced alterations in cognitive executive function: relationship to cerebral perfusion. *Experimental Gerontology*, *47*, 541–551.

Lupetin, A. R., Davis, D. A., Beckman, I., & Dash, N. (1995). Transcranial Doppler sonography. Part 1. Principles, technique, and normal appearances. *Radiographics*, *15*, 179–191.

Marshall, R. S., Lazar, R. M., Pile-Spellman, J., Young, W. L., Duong, D. H., Joshi, S., et al. (2001). Recovery of brain function during induced cerebral hypoperfusion. *Brain*, *124*, 1208–1217.

McMorris, T., Sproule, J., Turner, A., & Hale, B. J. (2011). Acute, intermediate intensity exercise, and speed and accuracy in working memory tasks: a meta-analytical comparison of effects. *Physiology and Behavior*, *102*, 421–428.

Meeusen, R. (2014). Exercise, nutrition and the brain. *Sports Medicine*, *44*(Suppl. 1), S47–S56.

Meeusen, R., & De Meirleir, K. (1995). Exercise and brain neurotransmission. *Sports Medicine*, *20*, 160–188.

Millet, G. Y., Muthalib, M., Jubeau, M., Laursen, P. B., & Nosaka, K. (2012). Severe hypoxia affects exercise performance independently of afferent feedback and peripheral fatigue. *Journal of Applied Physiology, 112,* 1335–1344.

Miyazawa, T., Horiuchi, M., Komine, H., Sugawara, J., Fadel, P. J., & Ogoh, S. (2013). Skin blood flow influences cerebral oxygenation measured by near-infrared spectroscopy during dynamic exercise. *European Journal of Applied Physiology, 113,* 2841–2848.

Neubauer, J. A., & Sunderram, J. (2004). Oxygen-sensing neurons in the central nervous system. *Journal of Applied Physiology, 96,* 367–374.

Nybo, L., & Secher, N. H. (2004). Cerebral perturbations provoked by prolonged exercise. *Progress in Neurobiology, 72,* 223–261.

Ogoh, S., & Ainslie, P. N. (2009). Cerebral blood flow during exercise: mechanisms of regulation. *Journal of Applied Physiology, 107,* 1370–1380.

Ogoh, S., & Ainslie, P. N. (2009). Regulatory mechanisms of cerebral blood flow during exercise: new concepts. *Exercise and Sports Science Review, 37,* 123–129.

Ogoh, S., Dalsgaard, M. K., Yoshiga, C. C., Dawson, E. A., Keller, D. M., Raven, P. B., et al. (2005). Dynamic cerebral autoregulation during exhaustive exercise in humans. *American Journal of Physiology - Heart Circulatory Physiology, 288,* H1461–H1467.

Ogoh, S., Sato, K., Fisher, J. P., Seifert, T., Overgaard, M., & Secher, N. H. (2011). The effect of phenylephrine on arterial and venous cerebral blood flow in healthy subjects. *Clinical Physiology and Functional Imaging, 31,* 445–451.

Ogoh, S., Tsukamoto, H., Hirasawa, A., Hasegawa, H., Hirose, N., & Hashimoto, T. (2014). The effect of changes in cerebral blood flow on cognitive function during exercise. *Physiological Reports, 2.* http://dx.doi.org/10.14814/phy2.12163.

Peltonen, J. E., Kowalchuk, J. M., Paterson, D. H., DeLorey, D. S., duManoir, G. R., Petrella, R. J., et al. (2007). Cerebral and muscle tissue oxygenation in acute hypoxic ventilatory response test. *Respiratory Physiology and Neurobiology, 155,* 71–81.

Perrey, S. (2008). Non-invasive NIR spectroscopy of human brain function during exercise. *Methods, 45,* 289–299.

Pontifex, M. B., Hillman, C. H., Fernhall, B., Thompson, K. M., & Valentini, T. A. (2009). The effect of acute aerobic and resistance exercise on working memory. *Medicine and Science in Sports and Exercise, 41,* 927–934.

Querido, J. S., & Sheel, A. W. (2007). Regulation of cerebral blood flow during exercise. *Sports Medicine, 37,* 765–782.

Raichle, M. E., & Hornbein, T. F. (2001). The high altitude brain. In: Hornbein, T. F., & Schoene, R. B. (Eds.). *High altitude: An exploration of human adaptation.* New York: Marcel Dekker. pp 377–423.

Rasmussen, P., Dawson, E. A., Nybo, L., van Lieshout, J. J., Secher, N. H., & Gjedde, A. (2007). Capillary-oxygenation-level-dependent near-infrared spectrometry in frontal lobe of humans. *Journal of Cerebral Blood Flow and Metabolism, 27,* 1082–1093.

Rooks, C. R., Thom, N. J., McCully, K. K., & Dishman, R. K. (2010). Effects of incremental exercise on cerebral oxygenation measured by near-infrared spectroscopy: a systematic review. *Progress in Neurobiology, 92,* 134–150.

Sato, K., Ogoh, S., Hirasawa, A., Oue, A., & Sadamoto, T. (2011). The distribution of blood flow in the carotid and vertebral arteries during dynamic exercise in humans. *Journal of Physiology, 589,* 2847–2856.

Sato, K., Sadamoto, T., Hirasawa, A., Oue, A., Subudhi, A. W., Miyazawa, T., et al. (2012). Differential blood flow responses to CO(2) in human internal and external carotid and vertebral arteries. *Journal of Physiology, 590,* 3277–3290.

Secher, N. H., Seifert, T., & Van Lieshout, J. J. (2008). Cerebral blood flow and metabolism during exercise: implications for fatigue. *Journal of Applied Physiology, 104,* 306–314.

Seifert, T., Rasmussen, P., Brassard, P., Homann, P. H., Wissenberg, M., Nordby, P., et al. (2009). Cerebral oxygenation and metabolism during exercise following three months of endurance training in healthy overweight males. *American Journal of Physiology - Regulatory, Integrative and Comparative Physiology, 297,* R867–R876.

Seifert, T., & Secher, N. H. (2011). Sympathetic influence on cerebral blood flow and metabolism during exercise in humans. *Progress in Neurobiology, 95,* 406–426.

Serrador, J. M., Picot, P. A., Rutt, B. K., Shoemaker, J. K., & Bondar, R. L. (2000). MRI measures of middle cerebral artery diameter in conscious humans during simulated orthostasis. *Stroke, 31,* 1672–1678.

Sorensen, H., Secher, N. H., Siebenmann, C., Nielsen, H. B., Kohl-Bareis, M., Lundby, C., et al. (2012). Cutaneous vasoconstriction affects near-infrared spectroscopy determined cerebral oxygen saturation during administration of norepinephrine. *Anesthesiology, 117,* 263–270.

Steffener, J., Brickman, A. M., Habeck, C. G., Salthouse, T. A., & Stern, Y. (2013). Cerebral blood flow and gray matter volume covariance patterns of cognition in aging. *Human Brain Mapping, 34,* 3267–3279.

Subudhi, A. W., Dimmen, A. C., & Roach, R. C. (2007). Effects of acute hypoxia on cerebral and muscle oxygenation during incremental exercise. *Journal of Applied Physiology (1985), 103*(1), 177–183. http://dx.doi.org/10.1152/japplphysiol.01460.2006.

Subudhi, A. W., Lorenz, M. C., Fulco, C. S., & Roach, R. C. (2008). Cerebrovascular responses to incremental exercise during hypobaric hypoxia: effect of oxygenation on maximal performance. *American Journal of Physiology - Heart and Circulatory Physiology, 294,* H164–H171.

Subudhi, A. W., Miramon, B. R., Granger, M. E., & Roach, R. C. (2009). Frontal and motor cortex oxygenation during maximal exercise in normoxia and hypoxia. *Journal of Applied Physiology, 106,* 1153–1158.

Takahashi, T., Takikawa, Y., Kawagoe, R., Shibuya, S., Iwano, T., & Kitazawa, S. (2011). Influence of skin blood flow on near-infrared spectroscopy signals measured on the forehead during a verbal fluency task. *Neuroimage, 57,* 991–1002.

Tomporowski, P. D. (2003). Effects of acute bouts of exercise on cognition. *Acta Psychologica, 112,* 297–324.

Verges, S., Rupp, T., Jubeau, M., Wuyam, B., Esteve, F., Levy, P., et al. (2012). Cerebral perturbations during exercise in hypoxia. *American Journal of Physiology - Regulatory, Integrative and Comparative Physiology, 302,* R903–R916.

Villringer, A., & Chance, B. (1997). Non-invasive optical spectroscopy and imaging of human brain function. *Trends in Neuroscience, 20,* 435–442.

Virues-Ortega, J., Buela-Casal, G., Garrido, E., & Alcazar, B. (2004). Neuropsychological functioning associated with high-altitude exposure. *Neuropsychology Review, 14,* 197–224.

Virues-Ortega, J., Garrido, E., Javierre, C., & Kloezeman, K. C. (2006). Human behaviour and development under high-altitude conditions. *Developmental Science, 9,* 400–410.

Vogiatzis, I., Louvaris, Z., Habazettl, H., Athanasopoulos, D., Andrianopoulos, V., Cherouveim, E., et al. (2011). Frontal cerebral cortex blood flow, oxygen delivery and oxygenation during normoxic and hypoxic exercise in athletes. *Journal of Physiology, 589,* 4027–4039.

Yan, X. (2014). Cognitive impairments at high altitudes and adaptation. *High Altitude Medicine and Biology, 15,* 141–145.

Yanagisawa, H., Dan, I., Tsuzuki, D., Kato, M., Okamoto, M., Kyutoku, Y., et al. (2010). Acute moderate exercise elicits increased dorsolateral prefrontal activation and improves cognitive performance with stroop test. *Neuroimage, 50,* 1702–1710.

The Reticular-Activating Hypofrontality (RAH) Model of Acute Exercise: Current Data and Future Perspectives

Michel Audiffren

Research Institute on Cognition and Learning (UMR CNRS 7295), Sport Sciences Faculty, University of Poitiers, Poitiers, France

INTRODUCTION

"How does the brain manage its finite amount of resources when doing two things at once?" is a very old question of cognitive psychology. Traditionally, two approaches were adopted by psychologists to address this question by using dual-task protocols: (1) varying the amount of attention devoted to each task and tracing performance operating characteristics curves (Navon & Gopher, 1979; Norman & Bobrow, 1975); (2) asking participants to prioritize a primary task, while performing a secondary or probe task, and estimating the attentional cost or mental workload of the primary task (Fisk, Derrick, & Schneider, 1986). Cognitive psychologists generally use two cognitive tasks as concurrent tasks and examine the interference in order to study the architecture of the cognitive system such as the central bottleneck (Pashler, 1994) or the central executive (Baddeley, Chincotta, & Adlam, 2001; Baddeley, Della Sala, Papagno, & Spinnler, 1997). Ergonomists and motor control psychologists typically use a sensorimotor task as the primary task and a cognitive task as the secondary task, to assess the level of automaticity of the sensorimotor skill involved in the primary task (Abernethy, 1988). Exercise psychologists are particularly interested in the immediate effect of acute exercise, a motor task, on a concomitant cognitive task (Chang, Labban, Gapin, & Etnier, 2012; Tomporowski, 2003). This chapter will focus on the exercise psychology dual-task approach and present a recent neurocognitive model explaining and predicting two contradictory effects induced by acute exercise on cognitive performance. This model, named the reticular-activating hypofrontality (RAH) model of acute exercise, was first published in 2011 in *Neuroscience and Biobehavioral Reviews* (Dietrich & Audiffren, 2011). It emerges from several debates between two cognitive neuroscientists, with contradictory but complementary ideas, and data on the exercise–cognition relationship: Arne Dietrich, a German researcher from the American University of Beirut who initially formulated the hypofrontality hypothesis in the perspective of altered states of consciousness (Dietrich, 2003, 2004, 2006), and Michel Audiffren, the author of the present chapter, who specializes in exercise psychology and, more particularly, the acute effects of exercise on information processing (Audiffren, Tomporowski, & Zagrodnik, 2008; Davranche & Audiffren, 2004; Davranche, Audiffren, & Denjean, 2006; Lambourne, Audiffren, & Tomporowski, 2010; Pesce & Audiffren, 2011). The RAH model provides a heuristic and falsifiable rationale to investigate detrimental and facilitating effects of cognitive performance observed during acute exercise of moderate to vigorous intensity. The RAH model also makes predictions concerning emotions but this topic will not be addressed in this chapter (for a review of this issue, see Dietrich & Audiffren, 2011).

The chapter is divided into seven sections including this introductive first section. The second section entitled Two Complementary Mechanisms Induced by Exercise includes a short but complete presentation of the RAH model of acute exercise. In the third section entitled Main Predictions of the RAH Model, two main predictions of the RAH model at neurophysiological and behavioral levels are overviewed. Several experimental data supporting these two predictions are presented from section four entitled Arguments for a Facilitating Effect of In-Task Exercise on Implicit Processes to section six entitled Arguments for a Detrimental Effect of In-Task Exercise on tasks Tapping Executive and Explicit Processes. The last section will conclude this chapter by presenting some limitations and future perspectives concerning the RAH model.

TWO COMPLEMENTARY MECHANISMS INDUCED BY EXERCISE

The RAH model considers that two neurophysiological mechanisms start up separately as soon as an individual begins exercise and

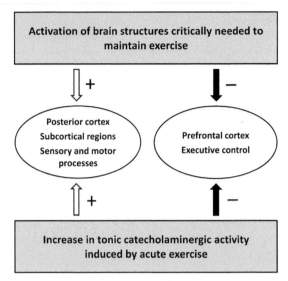

FIGURE 1 Two synergistic mechanisms induced by acute exercise modulate brain activity and cognitive performance: (1) the deactivation of brain structures, not necessary for motor activity, leads to a downregulation of prefrontal areas and executive control; (2) the activation of noradrenergic and dopaminergic tonic systems leads to a facilitation of sensory and motor processes but to a detrimental effect on prefrontal functions.

modulate information processing effectiveness as long as exercise continues. These two mechanisms are (1) the activation of various arousal systems in the brainstem and (2) the deactivation of neural structures whose functions are not critically needed to maintain exercise. Figure 1 illustrates the influence of these two mechanisms on brain areas and related cognitive functions.

The Reticular-Activating Process

The reticular-activating system consists of several distinct but interrelated arousal systems that are differentiated by anatomy, neurotransmitter, and function (Robbins & Everitt, 1995). In this section, I will focus on two arousing and energizing systems: the noradrenergic and the dopaminergic pathways. A large body of evidence shows that acute exercise activates these two monoamine systems and increase the release of noradrenaline (NA) and dopamine (DA) in several brain areas (e.g., Meeusen & De Meirleir, 1995; Meeusen & Piacentini, 2001; Meeusen, Piacentini, & De Meirleir, 2001).

The unique source of NA to hippocampus and neocortex is the locus coeruleus (LC), a brainstem nucleus that widely projects its noradrenergic axons throughout the central nervous system (Berridge & Waterhouse, 2003). NA released by these fibers binds on three families of adrenergic receptors: the α_1, the α_2, and the β_{1-3} receptors (Ramos & Arnsten, 2007). It is important to note that LC neurons may fire in two different activity modes: tonic and phasic (Berridge & Waterhouse, 2003). Tonic LC activity is characterized by a sustained and highly regular pattern above 2 Hz during active waking, such as exercising, but lower rates (<1 Hz) during slow-waves sleep (Foote, Aston-Jones, & Bloom, 1980). Such fluctuations in noradrenergic activity can be detected in cortical electroencephalogram (EEG) patterns and event-related potentials (ERP) (Niewenhuis, Aston-Jones, & Cohen, 2005; Pineda, Foote, & Neville, 1989). Phasic LC activity occurs in response to novel, noxious, stressful, or rewarding events and is characterized by a short-latency and brief burst of two to three action potentials followed by a relatively short period (300–700 ms) of silence (Aston-Jones & Bloom, 1981; Grant, Aston-Jones, & Redmond, 1988; Rasmussen, Morilak, & Jacobs, 1986). Phasic LC responses are associated with overt orienting responses and habituate with repeated stimulus presentation (Aston-Jones, Rajkowski, Kubiak, & Alexinsky, 1994). Extrasynaptic brain levels of NA are linearly related to tonic LC activity (Berridge & Abercrombie, 1999), whereas NA levels within the synaptic cleft are more related to phasic firing of LC presynaptic neurons (Berridge & Waterhouse, 2003). The LC noradrenergic system mediates alertness and appears to be involved in detecting sensory signals and maintaining discrimination processes under high levels of arousal and stress (Berridge & Waterhouse, 2003; Pribram & McGuinness, 1975;

Ramos & Arnsten, 2007; Robbins & Everitt, 1995). NA released at the cortical level improves the signal-to-noise ratio by reducing "noise" and/or facilitating processing of relevant sensory signals (Hurley, Devilbiss, & Waterhouse, 2004; Moxon, Devilbiss, Chapin, & Waterhouse, 2007; Waterhouse & Woodward, 1980). This enhancement of processing of sensory information takes place at both the single neuron and neuronal network levels and leads to improvement of cognitive function under "noisy" conditions, where irrelevant stimuli could impair performance (Berridge & Waterhouse, 2003). The LC noradrenergic system could have played an important role in the survival of many animal species allowing fleeing preys to detect more easily predators in environments rich in irrelevant stimuli. In this situation, typically associated with high arousal level (threat and exercise), it may be necessary for the prey to scan the environment for rapid detection of multiple stimuli. Several arguments for a facilitating effect of exercise on sensory processing will be presented in section 4. The LC noradrenergic system also innervates prefrontal cortex (PFC) and exerts a potent modulatory influence on executive functions such as inhibiting the processing of irrelevant stimuli (Woods & Knight, 1986) or keeping task-relevant information "online" in working memory (Ramos & Arnsten, 2007). PFC processing is strengthened by moderate levels of NA and α_2-receptor stimulation but impaired by higher levels of NA and α_1-receptor stimulation (Arnsten & Robbins, 2002). In this way, NA can be considered as a gradual neurochemical swing from anterior cortical regions to more posterior cortical and subcortical processes. Moreover, moderate to vigorous exercise might lead to a high level of brain NA and consequently a progressive shut off of the PFC. This dysregulation of PFC activity by the LC noradrenergic system under highly stressful conditions could be synergic to the hypofrontality process described later. The role of brain NA in emotional memory consolidation within the amygdala under such high arousal conditions will not be addressed in this chapter. Finally, NA exerts a robust modulatory effect on astrocyte glycogen levels and acts to increase glucose availability, the main energy supply of neuronal activity (Berridge & Waterhouse, 2003). This last action of NA on brain functioning confirms its major role in the energetics of information processing.

The dopaminergic system originates from cell bodies principally located in the substantia nigra pars compacta and from the ventral tegmentum (Grimm, Mueller, Hefti, & Rosenthal, 2004). The nigrostriatal system projects predominantly from the substantia nigra to the corpus striatum, the dorsal putamen, caudate nucleus, and globus pallidus, which, in turn, modulate activity of a large network involving the motor thalamus, supplementary motor area, premotor area, and primary motor cortex (Reeves, Bench, & Howard, 2002). The target sites of the ventral tegmental area are several regions of the limbic system such as the nucleus accumbens, the amygdala, and the anterior cingulate cortex, and widespread regions of the neocortex with higher density of projections to the PFC (Mehta & Riedel, 2006). These two dopaminergic networks have been respectively termed the mesolimbic and the mesocortical systems (Meck, 2006). Microdialysis studies, conducted in animals, showed that acute exercise increases DA level and stays significantly above baseline in the striatum and nucleus accumbens up to 1–2h after running in both trained and untrained animals (Meeusen, Hasegawa, & Piacentini, 2005; Wilson & Marsden, 1995). This elevation of DA level during and after exercise has not yet been replicated in humans with positron emission tomography (PET) technique (Wang et al., 2014). More studies in humans and animals would be necessary to examine the effects of acute exercise on the three dopaminergic systems (nigrostriatal, mesolimbic, and mesocortical) and on DA level in the striatum and the limbic system, as well as the PFC.

Similar to LC noradrenergic neurons, dopaminergic neurons exhibit two distinct modes of spike firing: tonic and phasic (Grace & Bunney, 1984ab). The tonic mode of firing is dependent on the spontaneous tonic spike activity of DA neurons (Goto, Otani, & Grace, 2007). The DA system is tonically activated by excitatory stimuli via sustained increases in DA neuron firing or via presynaptic stimulation of DA terminals by glutamate (Grace, 2000). In that case, DA mainly escapes from the synaptic cleft and enters the extracellular space (Grace, 2000). Bothe et al. (2013) presented experimental arguments for higher tonic levels of extracellular DA induced by acute exercise in humans. Tonic mode of firing controls the responsiveness to phasic activation of DA neurons in such a way that increases in tonic DA levels cause a potent inhibition of phasic, spike-dependent DA release (Grace, 2000). Higher levels of tonic extracellular DA, after acute exercise, could directly inhibit the magnitude of phasic DA release (Bothe et al., 2013). The phasic mode of firing is defined as the spike-dependent release of DA into the synaptic cleft, primarily responsible for the behaviorally relevant actions of DA systems (Grace, 2000). Several arguments from animal studies as well as neuropsychological studies in Parkinson's disease patients suggest a role for the nigrostriatal DA system in response preparation and motor readiness (Robbins & Everitt, 1995). In another respect, the mesocortical DA system plays an important role in working memory and cognitive control (Arnsten, 1998; Floresco & Magyar, 2006). Finally, the mesolimbic DA system is implicated in quantification of reward and incentive motivational processes (Robbins & Everitt, 1995). Concerning the mesocortical system, Cools and D'Esposito (2011) showed that the relationship between cognitive performance and PFC baseline dopamine levels follows an inverted-U-shaped function, where both too little and too much DA impairs performance. It would be very interesting to examine this relationship in animals and humans while manipulating baseline tonic DA levels with exercise intensity. In that way, the impairment of PFC processing and executive control, while exercising, could result from three different and synergistic mechanisms induced by acute exercise: (1) a too high level of NA, induced by an activation of the LC system; (2) a too high level of baseline tonic DA, induced by an activation of the mesocortical DA system; and (3) a deactivation of the PFC according to the hypofrontality mechanism described hereafter.

The Hypofrontality Process

The RAH model considers that when an individual performs a gross motor skill (running, cycling, rowing, and swimming), his/her brain must shift limited metabolic resources (mainly glucose) to neural structures that sustain the movement, which leaves fewer resources for brain regions, such as prefrontal regions whose computing functions are not critically needed at the time, for instance executive functions. Highly automatized motor skills stored in procedural memory are generally performed with maximal efficiency; i.e., low energetic cost and low attentional cost (e.g., Holt, Hamill, & Andres, 1991: Hoyt & Taylor, 1981; Kurosawa, 1994; Brisswalter, Durand, Delignières, & Legros, 1995). They are controlled by the implicit system and do not require executive/explicit control. Explicit interference in the execution of these kinds of motor skills tends to decrease their effectiveness. According to the RAH model, a cognitive task, requiring a complex computation involving the PFC, will suffer from the downregulation of this brain region as long as physical exercise requiring large muscle groups and necessitating a great shift of metabolic resources is performed concomitantly to this cognitive task.

In contrast, cognitive–energetic models, classically used to explain acute effects of exercise on information processing, consider that motor tasks and cognitive tasks share a common capacity-limited reservoir of voluntary attention or mental effort (Audiffren, 2009). When two tasks are performed simultaneously, they have to share available attentional resources. The degree of attentional or executive control required to perform each task is directly related to the amount of practice on each task. Whatever the type of limited resources, in both these theoretical models (RAH model and cognitive–energetic models), the core idea is the same: performing a cognitive task and maintaining exercise simultaneously requires dividing available resources between the two tasks. However, there are several differences between the RAH model and cognitive–energetic models. The first and most important difference rests on the level of explanation used to describe the mechanisms underpinning the interferences between acute exercise and cognition: neurophysiological level in the case of the RAH model and psychological level in the case of cognitive–energetic models. Formalizing hypothetical mechanisms at the neurophysiological level brings a serious advantage for researchers because these mechanisms may be directly observable in animals and humans contrary to psychological mechanisms, which can only be inferred from behavioral data. Another difference directly related to the former lies in the nature of resources that have to be divided between exercise and the cognitive task: mental effort, in the case of cognitive–energetic models, and brain glucose, in the case of the RAH model. It is also important to note that the most recent cognitive–energetic models, such as the Sanders' model (1983), assume multiple resource pools rather than a single pool of metabolic resources as in the RAH model. However, the three energetic mechanisms described by Sanders (arousal, effort, and activation) that allocate resources to stages of information processing can be related to the neurophysiological mechanisms described in the RAH model: arousal and activation are very similar to NA and DA systems (Pribram & McGuinness, 1975) and the effort mechanism would rely on brain glucose availability similarly to the hypofrontality process. A third difference is the way resources are allocated to executive functions and/or exercise. In cognitive–energetic models, the allocation policy is under the control of an attentional supervisor that selects a mode of regulation among several available strategies (Hockey, 1997): either to stop or to decrease intensity of exercise in order to perform the cognitive task without any decrement of cognitive performance, to stop performing the cognitive task in order to maintain the same intensity of exercise, or to maintain both exercising and performing the cognitive task at the risk of impairing both of them (Abernethy, 1988; Huang & Mercer, 2001). In the RAH model, the allocation of metabolic resources to brain regions is not under the control of any attentional supervisor, but is conceived of as a basic tradeoff process. Maintaining bodily motion requires, on the one hand, a substantial allocation of metabolic resources to motor, sensory, and autonomic brain regions that control and underlie the movement and, on the other hand, a simultaneous downregulation of other brain regions like the PFC, which are not necessary for the execution of automatized movements and can decrease their efficiency. The allocation of brain glucose to activate brain regions involved in maintaining exercise follows the biophysical principle of neurovascular coupling (Girouard & Iadecola, 2006). The neural activation of brain structures involved in the execution of exercise leads to an increase of cerebral blood flow (CBF) in these regions. By contrast, a significant decrease in neural activation in other brain regions, not involved in the movement, results in a decrease of CBF in these regions. In other words, neural activation of brain structures involved in the execution of exercise would be intrinsically coupled to a deactivation of the PFC. The RAH model does not deny that each individual can decide to stop exercising, to reduce the exercise load, and/or to stop the cognitive task at any time he/she wants, but it assumes that the downregulation of prefrontal areas, during exercise, is not a voluntary process but an evolutionary prewired mechanism.

MAIN PREDICTIONS OF THE RAH MODEL

In this section, I formulate two main hypotheses directly related to the three mechanisms described in the previous section and propose adequate methodologies to test them. Additional hypotheses may be found in an extensive presentation of the RAH model (Dietrich & Audiffren, 2011). The first hypothesis concerns the reticular-activating process and the relationship between acute exercise, brain catecholamines, and cognition.

H1: The level of extracellular "tonic" brain catecholamines (NA and DA) is a function of intensity of acute exercise in several regions of interest (e.g., striatum and PFC) and explains a significant portion of variance in performance of a concomitant cognitive task. Methodology: in animals, microdialysis during acute exercise in several brain regions; in humans, performing cognitive tasks while running on a treadmill coupled with the use of a PET scan.

It will be very difficult to conduct this complete mediational analysis in animals. The first part of the hypothesis (relationship between catecholamine concentration and exercise intensity) has already been validated for several brain regions (e.g., striatum) but not for other regions such as the PFC and primary sensory cortices. In humans, H1 has never been completely tested and it would be very interesting to ask participants to perform cognitive tasks tapping sensory processes (e.g., signal detection task), motor readiness (e.g., two-choice reaction task, with manipulation of preparatory period duration), or executive functions (e.g., Stroop task) while they exercise. For moderate- to high-intensity exercise, one can expect that the improvement of performance in tasks tapping sensory and motor processes will be explained by an increase in brain NA and DA in sensory and motor brain regions. For high-intensity exercise only, one can expect that the impairment of performance in tasks tapping executive and explicit processes will be correlated with a high level of NA and DA within the PFC. In this type of experiment, the PET tracer should be injected by intravenous administration just before the beginning of exercise and the PET scan carried out just after exercise cessation. Several radioligand tracers, such as [^{11}C]raclopride (Laruelle, 2000) and (S,S)-[^{11}C]O-methyl reboxetine (Ding, Lin, & Logan, 2006), may be used as an index of DA release or NA transporter availability, respectively. At the behavioral level, I will present some arguments for a facilitating effect of acute exercise on sensory and motor processes (see below). Such improvements of performance have already been correlated with plasmatic levels of catecholamines (Peyrin, Pequignot, Lacour, & Fourcade, 1987) but never with brain catecholamines. A lumbar puncture could also be used in humans for the collection of cerebrospinal fluid and then the estimation of extracellular brain catecholamines concentration, but this technique is highly invasive and could be forbidden by local ethical committees.

The second hypothesis concerns the hypofrontality process and the relationship between acute exercise, PFC deactivation, and executive functions. H2: The impairment of tasks tapping executive and explicit processes observed during exercise is explained by a downregulation of the PFC, which is concomitant to exercise and dependent on the exercise workload. Methodology: in humans, performing tasks tapping executive functions while exercising, coupled with the use of EEG and/or NIRS. The hypofrontality is expected to be larger for high workload exercises (e.g., high-intensity exercise involving the whole body) and for low-fit individuals. The workload may be increased by varying the

quantity of muscle tissue involved in the motion and/or the intensity and duration of exercise. The deactivation of prefrontal areas during exercise may be assessed with two presently available techniques: EEG coupled with the ERP technique, and near-infrared spectroscopy (NIRS). Two other less used techniques will be discussed later. On the one hand, cognitive psychologists showed that several brain waves are good indicators of executive functioning during cognitive tasks. For instance, the error negativity or error-related negativity, a sharp negative deflection that occurs 40–100 ms following erroneous response onset at frontocentral electrode positions, is associated with response monitoring and behavioral adaptation after errors (Hoffmann & Falkenstein, 2012). In the same way, the N2/P3 complex, a pronounced frontocentral negativity occurring around 200–300 ms after stimulus onset followed by a frontocentral to centroparietal positivity with a delay of roughly 150 ms, is generally observed in go/no go tasks and considered as a good index of response inhibition (Huster, Enriquez-Geppert, Lavallee, Falkenstein, & Herrmann, 2013). The amplitudes of these two waves should be modulated during high-intensity exercise and reflect poorer response monitoring and response inhibition. To our knowledge, there is only one study that investigated the modulation of N200 amplitude during acute exercise according to the cognitive task conditions (Pontifex & Hillman, 2007). These authors showed a reduction of N2 amplitude and a decrease in interference control that supports the hypofrontality hypothesis (see Table 2 for more details concerning this experiment). On the other hand, exercise scientists showed that NIRS allows one to assess brain oxygenation variations according to the workload of a cognitive task or an acute exercise activity (Albinet, Mandrick, Bernard, Perrey, & Blain, 2014; Moriguchi & Hiraki, 2013; Perrey, 2008). Table 2 presents NIRS studies showing significant decreases in prefrontal oxygenation during high-intensity exercise.

ARGUMENTS FOR A FACILITATING EFFECT OF IN-TASK EXERCISE ON TASKS TAPPING IMPLICIT PROCESSES

In this section, I present some experimental arguments for a facilitating effect of in-task acute exercise on implicit information processing modules that do not require executive control to operate effectively, but whose processing quality may be enhanced by brain catecholamines released during acute exercise. Until now, the improvements in implicit processes induced by exercise have never been directly related to brain level of catecholamines. Some studies showed a significant relationship between cognitive performance and plasmatic level of catecholamines or their metabolites but this approach does not allow the brain catecholamines availability and usage to be accurately assessed (for a review, see McMorris, 2009). For that reason, I made the choice to focus on behavioral studies in humans showing a facilitating effect of acute in-task exercise on performance of cognitive tasks, mainly tapping implicit processes (see Table 1).

Implicit processes are conceived as passive, automatic, not verbalizable, and inaccessible to conscious awareness (Dienes & Perner, 1999). The studies presented in Table 1 mainly focused on early sensory and late motor processes, two stages of processing considered as automatic for the former and requiring little cognitive effort for the latter except in extreme conditions such as sleep deprivation (Sanders, 1983). It would be important in the future to explore the effect of in-task acute exercise on other types of implicit processes such as implicit memory. Table 1 summarizes studies published in journals indexed by the Institute for Scientific Information (ISI) showing a facilitating effect of exercise on implicit processes. "Null effect" studies were not included in the data set because the sample size used in this type of study is generally low and consequently the likelihood of accepting the null hypothesis is high. I also made the choice to select studies using appropriate methodology to tap into and assess accurately implicit processes. For instance, studies using reaction time as a global index of performance in a task including a non-negligible executive component were not taken into account [e.g., visual decision task in Paas and Adam (1991) and Adam, Teeken, Ypelaar, Verstappen, and Paas (1997); visual search task in McMorris and Graydon (1996, 1997) and McMorris et al. (1999); four-choice visuo-manual reaction time task in Davranche, Denjean, and Audiffren (2006); and attentional task in Pesce, Capranica, Tessitore, and Figura (2002), Pesce, Cereatti, Casella, Baldari, and Capranica (2007), Pesce, Tessitore, Casella, Pirritano, and Capranica (2007), Pesce and Audiffren (2011), and Cereatti, Casella, Manganelli, and Pesce (2009)]. All these studies observed a facilitating effect of in-task exercise on reaction time without any speed–accuracy tradeoff but did not localize this effect in the stage structure of information processing. Several methodologies presented elsewhere such as Sternberg's additive factor method and the fractionation of reaction time allow us to highlight a selective effect of exercise on specific information processing stages (for a review, see Audiffren, 2009). Further studies, combining appropriate cognitive tasks and PET scan, are necessary to clarify the locus of this facilitating effect of exercise and its possible brain catecholaminergic origin. Five main pieces of information are displayed in Table 1: (1) the cognitive task and the methodology used in the experiment to show a selective effect of exercise on a specific information processing module, (2) the implicit process facilitated by exercise, (3) the index of performance showing the facilitation, (4) the parameters of the exercise bout leading to the facilitating effect, and (5) the characteristics of the participants relative to age and physical fitness.

TABLE 1   Studies showing a facilitating effect of acute in-task exercise on performance of cognitive tasks mainly tapping implicit processes

References	Task/methodology	Implicit process	Index of performance	Exercise parameters	Characteristics of participants
Arcelin et al. (1998)	Two-choice reaction time task/additive factor method	Motor adjustment stage	Third quartile of reaction time	10 min cycling at 60% MAP	Twelve young adults, $\dot{V}O_{2MAX}=47.7\,mL/min/kg$ for female and 59.9 mL/min/kg for male
Davranche et al. (2005)	Two-choice reaction time task/RT fractionation	Motor adjustment stage	Motor time, alpha angle of EMG burst	15 min cycling at 50% MAP	Twelve young adults, $\dot{V}O_{2MAX}=44\,mL/min/kg$
Davranche et al. (2006)	Simple reaction time task/RT fractionation	Motor adjustment stage	Motor time, alpha angle of EMG burst	15 min cycling at 50% MAP	Twelve young adults, $\dot{V}O_{2MAX}=44\,mL/min/kg$
Audiffren et al. (2008)	Two-choice reaction time task/RT fractionation/ Additive factor method	Motor adjustment stage	Motor time	35 min cycling at 90% VT	Seventeen young adults, $\dot{V}O_{2MAX}=35.44\,mL/min/kg$ for female and 43.10 mL/min/kg for male
Lambourne et al. (2010)	Critical Flicker fusion task	Signal preprocessing stage	Flicker and fusion detection thresholds	35 min cycling at 90% VT	Nineteen young adults, $\dot{V}O_{2MAX}=33.42\,mL/min/kg$ for female and 41.23 mL/min/kg for male

MAP, maximal aerobic power; VT, ventilatory threshold; EMG, electromyogram.

ARGUMENTS FOR A DEACTIVATION OF PREFRONTAL AREAS DURING VIGOROUS EXERCISE

One of the main arguments for the hypofrontality process is the demonstration of a deactivation of PFC during acute exercise. The deactivation of a brain region means a reduction of the electrical activity of the neural network structuring this brain area. A decrease in electrical activity is associated with a reduction in blood flow, oxygenation, and glucose uptake within the brain region of interest. These variations can be detected with several brain imagery techniques: blood flow can be assessed with functional magnetic resonance imagery (fMRI), oxygenation of brain tissue with NIRS, and brain glucose uptake with PET. Very few studies have used fMRI and PET during exercise because these techniques preclude head movements generally associated with cycling and running, and because there was no marketable ergometer adequate to perform exercise while holding the head in the tunnel of the MRI or PET scanners. The rare results obtained with these two techniques will be discussed at the end of this section. By contrast, there are numerous studies using NIRS in order to assess prefrontal oxygenation during acute exercise. Table 2 summarizes NIRS studies showing a decrease in PFC oxygenation during exercise. Three pieces of information are displayed in Table 2: (1) the characteristics of the exercise bout leading to a decrease in PFC oxygenation, (2) the threshold from which hypofrontality is observed, and (3) the characteristics of the participants relative to age and physical fitness. A meta-analysis

TABLE 2   Near-infrared spectroscopy studies showing a decrease in prefrontal cortex oxygenation during acute exercise

References	Exercise parameters	Conditions of occurrence of hypofrontality	Characteristics of participants
Gonzales-Alonzo et al. (2004)	Two maximal 5–10 min cycle ergometer bouts at 360 W separated by 1-h recovery period	Very quickly after the beginning of the maximal exercise	Thirteen trained male young adults, $\dot{V}O_{2MAX}$=4.7 L/min
Shibuya, Tanaka, Kuboyama, and Ogaki (2004)	Seven intermittent bouts of cycling at 150% $\dot{V}O_{2MAX}$ (30 s exercise, 15 s rest)	From the fifth bout of exercise at 150% $\dot{V}O_{2MAX}$	Six male young adults, $\dot{V}O_{2MAX}$=43.0 mL/min/kg
Bhambhani, Malik, and Mookerjee (2007)	Incremental cycling exercise until exhaustion (30 W/2 min)	Above the respiratory compensation threshold	Seventeen male young adults, $\dot{V}O_{2MAX}$=38.8 mL/min/kg
Subudhi, Dimmen, and Roach (2007)	Incremental cycling exercise until exhaustion (25 W/min)	Between 75% and 100% power peak	Thirteen male young adult cyclists, $\dot{V}O_{2MAX}$=42.6 mL/min/kg
Rupp and Perrey (2008)	Incremental cycling exercise until exhaustion (30 W/min)	From the first ventilator threshold to exhaustion	Thirteen male young adult cyclists or triathletes, $\dot{V}O_{2MAX}$=75.0 mL/min/kg
Subudhi, Lorenz, Fulco, and Roach (2008)	Incremental cycling exercise until exhaustion (30 W/2 min)	Between 75% and 100% power peak	Eleven male young adults, $\dot{V}O_{2MAX}$=3.98 L/min
Subudhi, Miramon, Granger, and Roach (2009)	Incremental cycling exercise until exhaustion (25 W/min)	Between 75% and 100% power peak	Twenty-three young adults, $\dot{V}O_{2MAX}$=3.98 L/min
Billaut, Davis, Smith, Marino, and Noakes (2010)	To complete a 5-km running time trial in the shortest time	From 4.5 to 5 km, RPE above 17.5	Eleven well-trained male young adult distance runners
Ando, Kokubu, Yamada, and Kimura (2011)	Cycling 6 min 30 s at three different workloads (40, 60, and 80% VO_{2peak})	80% $\dot{V}O_{2peak}$	Twelve male young adults, $\dot{V}O_{2MAX}$=45.7 mL/kg/min
Oussaidene et al. (2013)	Incremental cycling exercise until exhaustion (20 W/min)	From the respiratory compensation point to the end of exercise	Eight male young adults, $\dot{V}O_{2MAX}$=45.2 mL/kg/min
Tempest, Eston, and Parfitt (2014)	Incremental cycling exercise until exhaustion (20 W/min)	From the respiratory compensation point to the end of exercise in dorsal prefrontal regions	Twenty-five young adults, VO_{2peak}=41.8 mL/kg/min
Oussaidene et al. (2015)	Incremental cycling exercise until exhaustion (20 W/min)	From the respiratory compensation point to the end of exercise in both groups	Eleven untrained male young adults, $\dot{V}O_{2MAX}$=47.3 mL/kg/min and 13 endurance-trained young adult cyclists and triathletes, $\dot{V}O_{2MAX}$=61.2 mL/kg/min

RPE, rating of perceived exertion.

conducted by Rooks, Thom, McCully, and Dishman (2010) quantified more exhaustively the effects of exercise on brain hemodynamics measured by NIRS. To sum up, NIRS studies have consistently shown that prefrontal oxygenation is maintained or increased slightly during light- to moderate-intensity exercise but decreases near maximal exercise intensity.

I used the same bibliographic database as in the previous section and only include studies showing a significant decrease of PFC oxygenation during exercise. NIRS has been shown to be an effective tool for assessing local changes in cerebral oxygenation and hemodynamics during functional brain activation (Colier, Quaresima, Oeseburg, & Ferrari, 1999; Elwell et al., 1994; Hoshi, Kobayashi, & Tamura, 2001; Obrig et al., 1996). NIRS allows us to measure the concentration in brain tissue of two chromophores: oxyhemoglobin (HbO_2) and deoxyhemoglobin (HHb). The hemoglobin difference, i.e., the difference between the concentration of cerebral oxyhemoglobin and deoxyhemoglobin ($[HbO_2] - [HHb]$), is considered a good indicator of cerebral oxygenation when total hemoglobin ($[HbO_2] + [HHb]$) is stable over time (Shibuya et al., 2004). The results displayed in Table 2 support hypofrontality for high-intensity exercise (above 60% $\dot{V}O_{2MAX}$). However, these NIRS results suggest that detrimental effects on executive functions observed for light- and moderate-intensity exercises (up to 60% $\dot{V}O_{2MAX}$) cannot be explained by a deactivation of PFC.

Results obtained with more sophisticated and expensive techniques such as fMRI and PET are also very encouraging. Recently, a Brazilian team constructed a novel cycle ergometer allowing them to measure fMRI brain images during dynamic exercise (Fontes et al., 2013). This new tool is very promising and first results presented by these authors at the 61st annual meeting of the American College of Sport Medicine showed a decrease of PFC activation during exercise (Fontes et al., 2014).

In other respects, several studies used PET and ^{18}F-fluorodeoxyglucose (^{18}F-FDG), a radioligand tracer to assess glucose regional metabolism during exercise, whereas the scan was carried out immediately after exercise (Kemppainen et al., 2005; La Fougère et al., 2010; Shimada et al., 2013; Tashiro et al., 2001). In this protocol, PET scanning is generally initiated 40 min after ^{18}F-FDG injection since the radiotracer uptake in brain tissue reaches the plateau level at around 40–50 min postinjection (Tashiro et al., 2008). Usually, subjects are instructed to exercise for a total of 30–40 min after ^{18}F-FDG injection, with 10–15 min of exercise before injection (Tashiro et al., 2008). In that way, ^{18}F-FDG PET scan allows one to produce a functional index of regional changes in glucose metabolism, of the moving human brain, after the cessation of exercise. Tashiro and coworkers found a decrease in glucose metabolism in basal PFC and temporal lobe while the participants ran at 7.2–9 km/h during 4–5 km (Tashiro et al., 2001), whereas Kemppainen and collaborators found a global (whole brain) decrease in brain glucose metabolism while participants performed a 35-min bicycle exercise at 75% of $\dot{V}O_{2MAX}$ (Kemppainen et al., 2005). Two more recent studies used light-intensity walking as acute exercise and did not show a pattern of hypofrontality while walking (La Fougère et al., 2010; Shimada et al., 2013). The literature reviewed in this section shows that current available brain imagery techniques allow us to test the hypofrontality hypothesis presented earlier. An adequate protocol would require the assessment of brain functioning with NIRS, PET, or fMRI during a cognitive task tapping into executive functions and carried out at rest and while exercising at different intensities (from light to maximal intensities). To our knowledge, only one study used such a protocol but failed to validate the hypofrontality hypothesis because the decrease in cerebral oxygenation observed in PFC at 80% $\dot{V}O_{2peak}$ was not correlated with a higher interference cost in the Eriksen flanker task (Ando et al., 2011). More experiments like the latter are necessary to explore more extensively the hypofrontality hypothesis applied to cognition.

ARGUMENTS FOR A DETRIMENTAL EFFECT OF IN-TASK EXERCISE ON TASKS TAPPING EXECUTIVE AND EXPLICIT PROCESSES

Measuring the smooth running of executive functions is a complex problem because tasks that tap on the executive system generally stress other cognitive systems in addition to the executive (Burgess, 1997; Jurado & Rosselli, 2007). This "task impurity" problem is one of the most challenging obstacles that cognitive psychologists have to address to obtain a satisfying assessment of executive functions. In order to determine whether impairment or improvement of performance strictly affects the executive system, the researcher must be able to identify pertinent performance indicators specifically reflecting the functioning of executive control. In that way, studies proposing a clear rationale for the use of specific performance indicators that accurately reflects the quality of executive processing are a prerequisite of all studies examining the effect of different moderators, such as acute exercise, on executive functioning. Such studies are already available for a variety of well-known cognitive tasks tapping executive functions; for instance, random number generation task (Miyake et al.; 2000; Towse & Neil, 1998) and Wisconsin card sorting task (Greve et al., 2002). For that reason, it is very important to analyze all empirical studies examining the effect of acute exercise on executive functioning according to the cognitive tasks and the indicators of performance used by the researchers to examine the exercise–cognition relationship. In order to show that detrimental effects of acute in-task exercise on executive functions are more frequent than

positive effects, I examined all studies published in journals indexed by ISI, in which the cognitive task was performed simultaneously with acute exercise. "Null effect" studies were not taken into account. After a careful examination of the methodology section of each selected article, I only included studies using appropriate dependent variables to assess executive functions and showing positive or negative effects of exercise on these behavioral indices of performance. Twelve studies satisfied the selection criteria. Three other studies, although included in the review conducted by Dietrich and Audiffren (2011, Table 5), were not selected in the present section because the cognitive tasks performed by the participants did not clearly assess executive functions (Paas & Adam, 1991; Adam et al., 1997; Mahoney, Hirsch, Hasselquist, Lesher, & Lieberman, 2007). As expected, a majority of 9 studies out of 12 showed deleterious effects of in-task acute exercise on executive functions. These nine studies are reported in Table 3. Three main pieces of information are displayed in Table 3: (1) the cognitive task used in the experiment, (2) the executive function(s) tapped by the cognitive task, and (3) the index of performance selected to measure executive functions.

Only 3 studies out of 12 showed positive effects (Pesce & Audiffren, 2011; Lucas et al., 2012; Martins, Kavussanu, Willoughby, & Ring, 2013). The results of these three studies can be explained by the combination of three conditions not favorable to observe hypofrontality: too short exercise duration, too low exercise intensity, and too high level of physical fitness of the participants. This set of behavioral data constitutes a strong argument for a competition of resources between exercise and cognitive tasks tapping executive functions when an individual has to perform these two tasks simultaneously. A complete validation of the hypofrontality hypothesis will require us to show, through a mediational analysis, that the impairment in cognitive performance is significantly explained by a decrease in brain activity in prefrontal brain regions.

TABLE 3   Studies showing a detrimental effect of acute in-task exercise on performance of cognitive tasks tapping executive functions

References	Task	Executive functions	Indices of performance	Exercise parameters	Characteristics of participants
Dietrich and Sparling (2004)—Exp. 1	Wisconsin card sorting task	Switching	Error rate	45 min Pedaling on a cycle ergometer or running on a treadmill at 75% HRmax	Young adults regularly engaged in endurance training
Dietrich and Sparling (2004)—Exp. 2	Paced auditory serial addition task	Inhibition of a verbal response and updating of WM	Error rate	65 min Running on a treadmill at 75% HRmax	Young adults, endurance runners
Pontifex and Hillman (2007)	Ericksen flanker task	Inhibition of a prepotent response	Error rate	6.5 min Pedaling on a cycle ergometer at 60% HRmax	Young adults, 35.8 mL/kg for females and 42.7 mL/min/kg for males
Audiffren, Tomporowski, and Zagrodnik (2009)	Random number generation task	Inhibition of counting	TPI, run	35 min Pedaling on a cycle ergometer at 90% VT	Young adults, 31.39 mL/min/kg for females and 38.67 mL/min/kg for males
Davranche and McMorris (2009)	Simon task	Inhibition of a prepotent response	Interference cost	30 min Pedaling on a cycle ergometer at 50% MAP	Young adults, 42 mL/min/kg for females and 48 mL/kg for males
Del Giorno, Hall, O'Leary, Bixby, and Miller (2010)	Contingent continuous performance task—Wisconsin card sorting task	Inhibition of a prepotent response—Switching	False alarm rate—total errors, perseverative errors, unique errors	25 min Pedaling on a cycle ergometer at 75% VT or 100% VT	Young adults, 41.6 mL/min/kg for females and 50.3 mL/min/kg for males
Labelle, Bosquet, Mekary, and Bherer (2013)	Modified Stroop task	Switching	Error rate	6.5 min Pedaling on a cycle ergometer at 80% PPO	Two groups of older adults, 50.62 and 38.33 mL/min/kg
Wang, Chu, Chu, Chan, and Chang (2013)	Wisconsin card sorting test	Switching	Number of conceptual-level responses, number of categories completed, number of perseverative errors	40 min Pedaling on a cycle ergometer at 80% HRR	Four groups of young adults, 5521.29 METs/week in average
Labelle et al. (2014)	Modified Stroop task	Switching	Error rate	6.5 min Pedaling on a cycle ergometer at 60% and 80% PPO	Two groups of young adults, 50.62 and 38.33 mL/kg, and two groups of older adults, 33.42 and 23.67 mL/min/kg

MAP, maximum aerobic power; HRmax, maximum heart rate; HRR, heart rate reserve; PPO, peak power output; Run, run score; TPI, turning point index; VT, ventilatory threshold; WM, working memory.

LIMITATIONS AND FUTURE PERSPECTIVES OF THE RAH MODEL

The rationale delineated by the RAH model integrates knowledge from cognitive neurosciences and exercise psychology. The synthesis that emerges from this interdisciplinary approach subsumes all acute effects of in-task exercise on cognitive processes into a single, unifying framework. The interest of all integrative models is to formulate new hypotheses that can be tested at different observation levels; in the present case, the neurophysiological level and the behavioral level. However, each model presents some limitations and the RAH model does not depart from this rule. One of the main limitations of the RAH model is related to the principle of neurovascular coupling. The RAH model considers that when an individual performs a gross motor skill, the brain reserves its limited metabolic resources for operations that are critically needed to sustain this motor task, which results in the downregulation of neural structures not involved in this task. However, according to the principle of neurovascular coupling, the voluntary activation of brain structures involved in the execution of a cognitive task performed simultaneously to exercise should lead to an increase of CBF in PFC and other brain regions related to executive control. In that situation, the brain has to manage the performance of two concomitant tasks in spite of its limited metabolic resources. If the amount of available resources exceeds the amount necessary to perform both tasks, the brain has to reduce the amount of energy devoted to one of the two tasks. If the brain prioritizes the motor task and maintains its execution without any decrement in intensity and changes in the movement biomechanics, the CBF in brain regions involved in this task will remain stable. In that case, the brain will have to decrease the amount of resources devoted to the cognitive task up to a level that allows the correct execution of the

motor task. This will lead to a decrease in CBF in brain regions involved in the cognitive task. It is important to note that this regional decrease in CBF should be lower than the decrement in CBF observed in brain regions not critically needed to perform both motor and cognitive tasks. This way of considering how the brain shares its limited metabolic resources is closer to the cognitive–energetic models than to the RAH model. The RAH model predicts a progressive downregulation of neural structures not critically involved in the exercise task from the topmost layers of the functional hierarchy, in a kind of onion-peeling process, toward more basic ones (Dietrich & Audiffren, 2011). The RAH model does not predict that this downregulation fluctuates very subtly according to the involvement of the concerned neural structures in other brain activities such as a concomitant cognitive task. This question needs to be addressed in the future and could result in a modification of the RAH model that would bring it closer to the cognitive–energetic models.

A second main limitation of the RAH model concerns the neural structures supposed to be deactivated during exercise. The RAH model assumes that the PFC would show the earliest and strongest hypoactivity effect during exercise (Dietrich & Audiffren, 2011). However, more and more studies showed that maintaining effortful exercise requires self-regulation, and more particularly the executive function to overcome the urge to stop exercise or to decrease its intensity (for a review, see Audiffren & André, 2015). Neurophysiological studies suggest that the right inferior frontal gyrus, a part of the PFC, is a key component in the neural network that ultimately inhibits behavior, thoughts, and emotion in the service of top-down goals (Aron, Robbins, & Poldrack, 2014; Berkman, Graham, & Fisher, 2012). If high-intensity exercise leads to a general downregulation of the PFC, athletes would drop out of effortful exercise very quickly. For that reason, I think that the downregulation of brain regions, not critically involved in the exercise task, must be conceived as a selective process rather than a general and nonspecific process. In other words, considering the two limitations that have been presented above, it would be more pertinent to consider that downregulated neural networks, in dual-task situations combining acute exercise and cognitive processing, are those that are not specifically involved both in the exercise task and in the cognitive task. To sum up, two principles would guide the automatic downregulation process induced by high-intensity exercise as the brain metabolic resources run out: (1) from the topmost layers (anterior cortex) toward more basic ones (posterior cortex and subcortical structures); (2) from the neural networks not necessary to perform all the tasks required by the situations toward the most critically needed to perform them. In addition to this automatic and dynamic process, it would be interesting to consider a possible action of a voluntary process that would prioritize one task with respect to the other and consequently prioritize downregulation of the neural networks that underpin the execution of the background or secondary task, with respect to neural networks that underlie the execution of the main or primary task.

A third limitation of the RAH model is related to the fact that it does not encompass acute off-task exercise effects and particularly the facilitating effects of acute off-task exercise on executive functions (for a review, see Audiffren & André, 2015). It is somewhat surprising to observe opposite effects of acute exercise on executive functions according to the temporal arrangement between exercising and performing a cognitive task: impairment of executive functions in "concomitance protocols" (in-task exercise) and improvement of executive functions in "sequence protocols" (off-task exercise). A theoretical framework including and explaining these apparently contradictory data will be necessary for our scientific field in the coming years. Baumeister's strength model of self-control is a good candidate for that purpose (Audiffren & André,

2015; Baumeister, Vohs, & Tice, 2007; Hagger, Wood, Stiff, & Chatzisarantis, 2010; Muraven & Baumeister, 2000). Although it considers that self-control resources are dependent on available brain glucose (Beedie & Lane, 2012; Gaillot et al., 2007), this last model suffers from a solid neurophysiological basis. In the near future, it could be helpful for our research community to confront the RAH model and the strength model of self-control and propose a more general model that takes into account the very interesting ideas developed by these two theoretical frameworks and their subsequent revisions.

Acknowledgment

I would like to thank Phillip Tomporowski and Nathalie André for their helpful comments on a previous version of this manuscript.

References

Abernethy, B. (1988). Dual-task methodology and motor skills research: some applications and methodological constraints. *Journal of Human Movement Studies, 14,* 101–132.

Adam, J. J., Teeken, J. C., Ypelaar, P. J. C., Verstappen, F. T. J., & Paas, F. G. W. (1997). Exercise induced arousal and information processing. *International Journal of Sport Psychology, 28,* 217–226.

Albinet, C. T., Mandrick, K., Bernard, P. L., Perrey, S., & Blain, H. (2014). Improved cerebral oxygenation response and executive performance as a function of cardiorespiratory fitness in older women: a fNIRS study. *Frontiers in Aging Neuroscience, 6.* http://dx.doi.org/10.3389/fnagi.2014.00272.

Ando, S., Kokubu, M., Yamada, Y., & Kimura, M. (2011). Does cerebral oxygenation affect cognitive function during exercise? *European Journal of Applied Physiology, 111,* 1973–1982.

Arcelin, R., Delignières, D., & Brisswalter, J. (1998). Selective effects of physical exercise on choice reaction processes. *Perceptual and Motor Skills, 87,* 175–185.

Arnsten, A. F. T. (1998). Catecholamine modulation of prefrontal cortical cognitive function. *Trends in Cognitive Sciences, 2,* 436–446.

Arnsten, A. F. T., & Robbins, T. W. (2002). Neurochemical modulation of prefrontal cortical function in humans and animals. In D. T. Stuss, & R. T. Knight (Eds.), *Principles of frontal lobe function* (pp. 51–84). New York: Oxford University Press.

Aron, A. R., Robbins, T. W., & Poldrack, R. A. (2014). Inhibition and the right inferior frontal cortex: one decade on. *Trends in Cognitive Sciences, 18*, 177–186.

Aston-Jones, G., & Bloom, F. E. (1981). Norepinephrine-containing locus coeruleus neurons in behaving rats exhibit pronounced responses to non-noxious environmental stimuli. *Journal of Neuroscience, 1*, 887–900.

Aston-Jones, G., Rajkowski, J., Kubiak, P., & Alexinsky, T. (1994). Locus coeruleus neurons in monkey are selectively activated by attended cues in a vigilance task. *Journal of Neuroscience, 14*, 4467–4480.

Audiffren, M. (2009). Acute exercise and psychological functions: a cognitive-energetic approach. In T. McMorris, P. D. Tomporowski, & M. Audiffren (Eds.), *Exercise and cognitive function* (pp. 3–39). Chichester: Wiley-Blackwell.

Audiffren, M., & André, N. (2015). The strength model of self-control revisited: Linking acute and chronic effects of exercise on executive functions. *Journal of Sport and Health Science*. http://dx.doi.org/10.1016/j.jshs.2014.09.002 [E-pub ahead of print].

Audiffren, M., Tomporowski, P. D., & Zagrodnik, J. (2008). Acute aerobic exercise and information processing: energizing motor processes during a choice reaction time task. *Acta Psychologica, 129*, 410–419.

Audiffren, M., Tomporowski, P., & Zagrodnik, J. (2009). Acute aerobic exercise and information processing: modulation of executive control in a random number generation task. *Acta Psychologica, 132*, 85–95.

Baddeley, A., Chincotta, D., & Adlam, A. (2001). Working memory and the control of action: evidence from task switching. *Journal of Experimental Psychology: General, 130*, 641–657.

Baddeley, A., Della Sala, S., Papagno, C., & Spinnler, H. (1997). Dual-task performance in dysexecutive and non-dysexecutive patients with a frontal lesion. *Neuropsychology, 11*, 187–194.

Baumeister, R. F., Vohs, K. D., & Tice, D. M. (2007). The strength model of self-control. *Current Directions in Psychological Science, 16*, 351–355.

Beedie, C. J., & Lane, A. M. (2012). The role of glucose in self-control: another look at the evidence and an alternative conceptualization. *Personality and Social Psychology Review, 16*, 143–153.

Berkman, E. T., Graham, A. M., & Fisher, P. A. (2012). Training self-control: a domain-general translational neuroscience approach. *Child Development Perspectives, 6*, 374–384.

Berridge, C. W., & Abercrombie, E. D. (1999). Relationship between locus coeruleus discharge rates and rates of norepinephrine release within neocortex as assessed by in vivo microdialysis. *Neuroscience, 93*, 1263–1270.

Berridge, C. W., & Waterhouse, B. D. (2003). The locus coeruleus-noradrenergic system: modulation of behavioral state and state-dependent cognitive processes. *Brain Research Reviews, 42*, 33–84.

Bhambhani, Y., Malik, R., & Mookerjee, S. (2007). Cerebral oxygenation declines at exercise intensities above the respiratory compensation threshold. *Respiratory Physiology and Neurobiology, 156*, 196–202.

Billaut, F., Davis, J. M., Smith, K. J., Marino, F. E., & Noakes, T. D. (2010). Cerebral oxygenation decreases but does not impair performance during self-paced, strenuous exercise. *Acta Physiologica, 198*, 477–486.

Bothe, N., Zschucke, E., Dimeo, F., Heinz, A., Wüstenberg, T., & Ströhle, A. (2013). Acute exercise influences reward processing in highly trained and untrained men. *Medicine and Science in Sports and Exercise, 45*, 583–591.

Brisswalter, J., Durand, M., Delignières, D., & Legros, P. (1995). Optimal and non-optimal demand in a dual task of pedalling and simple reaction time: effects on energy expenditure and cognitive performance. *Journal of Human Movement Studies, 29*, 15–34.

Burgess, P. (1997). Theory and methodology in executive function research. In P. Rabbitt (Ed.), *Methodology of frontal executive function* (pp. 81–116). Hove: Psychology Press.

Cereatti, L., Casella, R., Manganelli, M., & Pesce, C. (2009). Visual attention in adolescents: facilitating effects of sport expertise and acute physical exercise. *Psychology of Sport and Exercise, 10*, 136–145.

Chang, Y. K., Labban, J. D., Gapin, J. I., & Etnier, J. L. (2012). The effects of acute exercise on cognitive performance: a meta-analysis. *Brain Research, 1453*, 87–101.

Colier, W. N., Quaresima, V., Oeseburg, B., & Ferrari, M. (1999). Human motor-cortex oxygenation changes induced by cyclic coupled movements of hand and foot. *Experimental Brain Research, 129*, 457–461.

Cools, R., & D'Esposito, M. (2011). Inverted-U–shaped dopamine actions on human working memory and cognitive control. *Biological Psychiatry, 69*, 113–125.

Davranche, K., & Audiffren, M. (2004). Facilitating effects of exercise on information processing. *Journal of Sports Sciences, 22*, 419–428.

Davranche, K., Audiffren, M., & Denjean, A. (2006). A distributional analysis of the effect of physical exercise on a choice reaction time task. *Journal of Sports Sciences, 24*(3), 323–329.

Davranche, K., Burle, B., Audiffren, M., & Hasbroucq, T. (2005). Information processing during physical exercise: A chronometric and electromyographic study. *Experimental Brain Research, 165*, 532–540.

Davranche, K., & McMorris, T. (2009). Specific effects of acute moderate exercise on cognitive control. *Brain and Cognition, 69*, 565–570.

Del Giorno, J. M., Hall, E. E., O'Leary, K. C., Bixby, W. R., & Miller, P. C. (2010). Cognitive function during acute exercise: a test of the transient hypofrontality theory. *Journal of Sport and Exercise Psychology, 32*, 312–323.

Dienes, Z., & Perner, J. (1999). A theory of implicit and explicit knowledge. *Behavioural and Brain Sciences, 5*, 735–808.

Dietrich, A. (2003). Functional neuroanatomy of altered states of consciousness: the transient hypofrontality hypothesis. *Consciousness and Cognition, 12*, 231–256.

Dietrich, A. (2004). Neurocognitive mechanisms underlying the experience of flow. *Consciousness and Cognition, 13*, 746–761.

Dietrich, A. (2006). Transient hypofrontality as a mechanism for the psychological effects of exercise. *Psychiatry Research, 145*, 79–83.

Dietrich, A., & Audiffren, M. (2011). The reticular-activating hypofrontality (RAH) model of acute exercise. *Neuroscience and Biobehavioral Reviews, 35*, 1305–1325.

Dietrich, A., & Sparling, P. B. (2004). Endurance exercise selectively impairs prefrontal dependent cognition. *Brain and Cognition, 55*, 516–524.

Ding, Y. S., Lin, K. S., & Logan, J. (2006). PET imaging of norepinephrine transporters. *Current Pharmaceutical Design, 12*, 3831–3845.

Elwell, C. E., Cope, M., Edwards, A. D., Wyatt, J. S., Delpy, D. T., & Reynolds, E. O. (1994). Quantification of adult cerebral hemodynamics by near-infrared spectroscopy. *Journal of Applied Physiology, 77*, 2753–2760.

Fisk, A., Derrick, W. L., & Schneider, W. (1986). A methodological assessment and evaluation of dual-task paradigms. *Current Psychological Research and Reviews, 5*, 315–327.

Floresco, S. B., & Magyar, O. (2006). Mesocortical dopamine modulation of executive functions: beyond working memory. *Psychopharmacology, 188*, 567–585.

Fontes, E. B., Okano, A. H., De Guio, F., Schabort, E. J., Li, L. M., Basset, F. A., et al. (2013). Brain activity and perceived exertion during cycling exercise: an fMRI study. *British Journal of Sports Medicine*. http://dx.doi.org/10.1136/bjsports-2012-091924 [E-pub ahead of print].

Fontes, E. B., Okano, A. H., Gastanho, G. K., Yoshida, H., Campos, B., Schabort, E., et al. (2014). Brain regulation of exercise: effects of perceived exercise intensity on brain activity. *Medicine and Science in Sports and Exercise, 46*(5S), 280–283.

Foote, S. L., Aston-Jones, G., & Bloom, F. E. (1980). Impulse activity of locus coeruleus neurons in awake rats and monkeys is a function of sensory stimulation and arousal. *Proceedings of the National Academy of Sciences of the United States of America: Biological Sciences, 77*, 3033–3037.

Gailliot, M. T., Baumeister, R. F., DeWall, C. N., Maner, J. K., Plant, E. A., Tice, D. M., et al. (2007). Self-control relies on glucose as a limited energy source: willpower is more than a metaphor. *Journal of Personality and Social Psychology, 92*, 325–336.

Girouard, H., & Iadecola, C. (2006). Neurovascular coupling in the normal brain and in hypertension, stroke, and Alzheimer disease. *Journal of Applied Physiology, 100*, 328–335.

González-Alonso, J., Dalsgaard, M. K., Osada, T., Volianitis, S., Dawson, E. A., Yoshiga, C. C., et al. (2004). Brain and central haemodynamics and oxygenation during maximal exercise in humans. *Journal of Physiology, 557*, 331–342.

Goto, Y., Otani, S., & Grace, A. A. (2007). The Yin and Yang of dopamine release: a new perspective. *Neuropharmacology, 53*, 583–587.

Grace, A. A. (2000). The tonic/phasic model of dopamine system regulation and its implications for understanding alcohol and psychostimulant craving. *Addiction, 95*(Suppl. 2), S119–S128.

Grace, A. A., & Bunney, B. S. (1984a). The control of firing pattern in nigral dopamine neurons: single spike firing. *Journal of Neuroscience, 4*, 2866–2876.

Grace, A. A., & Bunney, B. S. (1984b). The control of firing pattern in nigral dopamine neurons: burst firing. *Journal of Neuroscience, 4*, 2877–2890.

Grant, S. J., Aston-Jones, G., & Redmond, D. E. J. (1988). Responses of primate locus coeruleus neurons to simple and complex sensory stimuli. *Brain Research Bulletin, 21*, 401–410.

Greve, K. W., Love, J. M., Sherwin, E., Mathias, C. W., Ramzinski, P., & Levy, J. (2002). Wisconsin Card Sorting Test in chronic severe traumatic brain injury: factor structure and performance subgroups. *Brain Injury, 16*, 29–40.

Grimm, J., Mueller, A., Hefti, F., & Rosenthal, A. (2004). Molecular basis for catecholaminergic neuron diversity. *Proceedings of the National Academy of Sciences of the United States of America, 101*, 13891–13896.

Hagger, M. S., Wood, C., Stiff, C., & Chatzisarantis, N. L. D. (2010). Ego depletion and the strength model of self-control: a meta-analysis. *Psychological Bulletin, 136*, 495–525.

Hockey, G. R. J. (1997). Compensatory control in the regulation of human performance under stress and high workload: a cognitive-energetical framework. *Biological Psychology, 45*, 73–93.

Hoffmann, S., & Falkenstein, M. (2012). Predictive information processing in the brain: errors and response monitoring. *International Journal of Psychophysiology, 83*, 208–212.

Holt, K. G., Hamill, J., & Andres, R. O. (1991). Predicting the minimal energy costs of human walking. *Medicine and Science in Sports and Exercise, 23*, 491–498.

Hoshi, Y., Kobayashi, N., & Tamura, M. (2001). Interpretation of near-infrared spectroscopy signals: a study with a newly developed perfused rat brain model. *Journal of Applied Physiology, 90*, 1657–1662.

Hoyt, D., & Taylor, C. R. (1981). Gait and the energetics of locomotion in horses. *Nature, 292*, 239–240.

Huang, H.-J., & Mercer, V. S. (2001). Dual-task methodology: applications in studies of cognitive and motor performance in adults and children. *Pediatric Physical Therapy, 13*, 133–140.

Hurley, L. M., Devilbiss, D. M., & Waterhouse, B. D. (2004). A matter of focus: monoaminergic modulation of stimulus coding in mammalian sensory networks. *Current Opinion in Neurobiology, 14*, 488–495.

Huster, R. J., Enriquez-Geppert, S., Lavallee, C. F., Falkenstein, M., & Herrmann, C. S. (2013). Electroencephalography of response inhibition tasks: functional networks and cognitive contributions. *International Journal of Psychophysiology, 87*, 217–233.

Jurado, M. B., & Rosselli, M. (2007). The elusive nature of executive functions: a review of our current understanding. *Neuropsychology Review, 17*, 213–233.

Kemppainen, J., Aalto, S., Fujimoto, T., Kalliokoski, K. K., Langsjo, J., Oikonen, V., et al. (2005). High intensity exercise decreases global brain glucose uptake in humans. *Journal of Physiology, 568*, 323–332.

Kurosawa, K. (1994). Effects of various walking speeds on probe reaction time during treadmill walking. *Perceptual and Motor Skills, 78*, 768–770.

La Fougère, C., Zwergal, A., Rominger, A., Förster, S., Fesl, G., Dieterich, M., et al. (2010). Real versus imagined locomotion: a [18F]-FDG PET-fMRI comparison. *NeuroImage, 50*, 1589–1598.

Labelle, V., Bosquet, L., Mekary, S., & Bherer, L. (2013). Decline in executive control during acute bouts of exercise as a function of exercise intensity and fitness level. *Brain and Cognition, 81*, 10–17.

Labelle, V., Bosquet, L., Mekary, S., Minh Vu, T. T., Smilovitch, M., & Bherer, L. (2014). Fitness level moderates executive control disruption during exercise regardless of age. *Journal of Sport and Exercise Psychology, 36*, 258–270.

Lambourne, K., Audiffren, M., & Tomporowski, P. D. (2010). Effects of acute exercise on sensory and executive processing tasks. *Medicine and Science in Sports and Exercise, 42*, 1396–1402.

Laruelle, M. (2000). Imaging synaptic neurotransmission with in vivo binding competition techniques: a critical review. *Journal of Cerebral Blood Flow and Metabolism, 20*, 423–451.

Lucas, S. J., Ainslie, P. N., Murrell, C. J., Thomas, K. N., Franz, E. A., & Cotter, J. D. (2012). Effect of age on exercise-induced alterations in cognitive executive function: relationship to cerebral perfusion. *Experimental Gerontology, 47*, 541–551.

Mahoney, C. R., Hirsch, E., Hasselquist, L., Lesher, L. L., & Lieberman, H. R. (2007). The effects of movement and physical exertion on soldier vigilance. *Aviation, Space, and Environmental Medicine, 78*, B51–B57.

Martins, A. Q., Kavussanu, M., Willoughby, A., & Ring, C. (2013). Moderate intensity exercise facilitates working memory. *Psychology of Sport and Exercise, 14*, 323–328.

McMorris, T. (2009). Exercise and cognitive function: a neuroendocrinological explanation. In T. McMorris, P. D. Tomporowski, & M. Audiffren (Eds.), *Exercise and cognitive function* (pp. 41–68). Chichester: Wiley-Blackwell.

McMorris, T., & Graydon, J. (1996). The effect of exercise on the decision-making performance of experienced and inexperienced soccer players. *Research Quarterly for Exercise & Sport, 67*(1), 109–114.

McMorris, T., & Graydon, J. (1997). The effect of exercise on cognitive performance in soccer-specific tests. *Journal of Sports Sciences, 15*, 459–468.

McMorris, T., & Graydon, J. (2006). The effect of exercise on the decision-making performance of experienced and inexperiences soccer players. *Research Quarterly for Exercise and Sport, 67*(1), 108–114.

McMorris, T., Myers, S., MacGillivary, W. W., Sexsmith, J. R., Fallowfield, J., Graydon, J., et al. (1999). Exercise, plasma catecholamine concentration and decision-making performance of soccer players on a soccer-specific test. *Journal of Sports Sciences, 17*, 667–676.

Meck, W. H. (2006). Neuroanatomical localization of an internal clock: a functional link between mesolimbic, nigrostriatal, and mesocortical dopaminergic systems. *Brain Research, 1109*, 93–107.

Meeusen, R., & De Meirlier, K. (1995). Exercise and brain neurotransmission. *Sports Medicine, 20*, 160–188.

Meeusen, R., Hasegawa, H., & Piacentini, F. M. (2005). Brain microdialysis and its application for the study of neurotransmitter release during exercise. *International Journal of Sport and Exercise Psychology, 3*, 263–284.

Meeusen, R., & Piacentini, M. F. (2001). Exercise and neurotransmission: a window to the future? *European Journal of Sport Science, 1*(1).

Meeusen, R., Piacentini, M. F., & De Meirleir, K. (2001). Brain microdialysis in exercise research. *Sports Medicine, 31*, 965–983.

Mehta, M. A., & Riedel, W. J. (2006). Dopaminergic enhancement of cognitive function. *Current Pharmaceutical Design, 12*, 2487–2500.

Miyake, A., Friedman, N. P., Emerson, M. J., Witzki, A. H., Howerter, A., & Wager, T. D. (2000). The unity and diversity of executive functions and their contributions to complex "frontal lobe" tasks: a latent variable analysis. *Cognitive Psychology, 41*, 49–100.

Moriguchi, Y., & Hiraki, K. (2013). Prefrontal cortex and executive function in young children: a review of NIRS studies. *Frontiers in Human Neuroscience, 7*. http://dx.doi.org/10.3389/fnhum.2013.00867.

Moxon, K. A., Devilbiss, D. M., Chapin, J. K., & Waterhouse, B. D. (2007). Influence of norepinephrine on somatosensory neuronal responses in the rat thalamus: a combined modeling and in vivo multi-channel, multi-neuron recording study. *Brain Research, 1147*, 105–123.

Muraven, M., & Baumeister, R. F. (2000). Self-regulation and depletion of limited resources: does self-control resemble a muscle? *Psychological Bulletin, 126*, 247–259.

Navon, D., & Gopher, D. (1979). On the economy of the human-processing system. *Psychological Review, 86*, 214–255.

Niewenhuis, S., Aston-Jones, G., & Cohen, J. D. (2005). Decision making, the P3, and the locus coeruleus-norepinephrine system. *Psychological Bulletin, 131*, 510–532.

Norman, D. A., & Bobrow, D. G. (1975). On data-limited and resource-limited processes. *Cognitive Psychology, 7*, 44–64.

Obrig, H., Hirth, C., Junge-Hulsing, J. G., Doge, C., Wolf, T., Dirnagl, U., et al. (1996). Cerebral oxygenation changes in response to motor stimulation. *Journal of Applied Physiology, 81*, 1174–1183.

Oussaidene, K., Prieur, F., Bougault, V., Borel, B., Matran, R., & Mucci, P. (2013). Cerebral oxygenation during hyperoxia-induced increase in exercise tolerance for untrained men. *European Journal of Applied Physiology, 113*, 2047–2056.

Oussaidene, K., Prieur, F., Tagougui, S., Abaidia, A., Matran, R., & Mucci, P. (2015). Aerobic fitness influences cerebral oxygenation response to maximal exercise in healthy subjects. *Respiratory Physiology and Neurobiology, 205*, 53–60.

Paas, F. G. W., & Adam, J. J. (1991). Human information processing during physical exercise. *Ergonomics, 34*, 1385–1397.

Pashler, H. (1994). Dual-task interference in simple tasks: data and theory. *Psychological Bulletin, 116*(2), 220–244.

Perrey, S. (2008). Non-invasive NIR spectroscopy of human brain function during exercise. *Methods, 45*, 289–299.

Pesce, C., & Audiffren, M. (2011). Does acute exercise switch off switch costs? A study with younger and older athletes. *Journal of Sport and Exercise Psychology, 33*, 609–626.

Pesce, C., Capranica, L., Tessitore, A., & Figura, F. (2002). Effects of a sub-maximal physical load on the orienting and focusing of visual attention. *Journal of Human Movement Studies, 42*, 401–420.

Pesce, C., Cereatti, L., Casella, R., Baldari, C., & Capranica, L. (2007). Preservation of visual attention in older expert orienteers at rest and under physical effort. *Journal of Sport and Exercise Psychology, 29*, 78–99.

Pesce, C., Tessitore, A., Casella, R., Pirritano, M., & Capranica, L. (2007). Focusing of visual attention at rest and during physical exercise in soccer players. *Journal of Sports Sciences, 25*(11), 1259–1270.

Peyrin, L., Pequignot, J. M., Lacour, J. R., & Fourcade, J. (1987). Relationships between catecholamine or 3-methoxy 4-hydroxy phenylglycol changes and the mental performance under submaximal exercise in man. *Psychopharmacology, 93*, 188–192.

Pineda, J. A., Foote, S. L., & Neville, H. J. (1989). Effects of locus coeruleus lesions on auditory, long latency, event-related potentials in monkey. *Journal of Neuroscience, 9*, 81–93.

Pontifex, M. B., & Hillman, C. H. (2007). Neuroelectric and behavioural indices of interference control during acute cycling. *Clincal Neurophysiology, 118*, 570–580.

Pribram, K. H., & McGuinness, D. (1975). Arousal, activation and effort in the control of attention. *Psychological Review, 82*, 116–149.

Ramos, B. P., & Arnsten, A. F. T. (2007). Adrenergic pharmacology and cognition: focus on the prefrontal cortex. *Pharmacology and Therapeutics, 113*, 523–536.

Rasmussen, K., Morilak, D. A., & Jacobs, B. L. (1986). Single unit activity of locus coeruleus neurons in the freely moving cat I. During naturalistic behaviors and in response to simple and complex stimuli. *Brain Research, 371*, 324–334.

Reeves, S., Bench, C., & Howard, R. (2002). Ageing and the nigrostriatal dopaminergic system. *International Journal of Geriatric Psychiatry, 17*, 359–370.

Robbins, T. W., & Everitt, B. J. (1995). Arousal systems and attention. In M. S. Gazzaniga (Ed.), *The cognitive neurosciences* (pp. 703–720). Cambridge, MA: MIT Press.

Rooks, C. R., Thom, N. J., McCully, K. K., & Dishman, R. K. (2010). Effects of incremental exercise on cerebral oxygenation measured by near-infrared spectroscopy: a systematic review. *Progress in Neurobiology, 92*, 134–150.

Rupp, T., & Perrey, S. (2008). Prefrontal cortex oxygenation and neuromuscular responses to exhaustive exercise. *European Journal of Applied Physiology, 102*, 153–163.

Sanders, A. F. (1983). Towards a model of stress and human performance. *Acta Psychologica, 53*, 61–97.

Shibuya, K.-I., Tanaka, J., Kuboyama, N., & Ogaki, T. (2004). Cerebral oxygenation during intermittent supramaximal exercise. *Respiratory Physiology and Neurobiology, 140*, 165–172.

Shimada, H., Ishii, K., Ishiwata, K., Oda, K., Suzukawa, M., Makizako, H., et al. (2013). Gait adaptability and brain activity during unaccustomed treadmill walking in healthy elderly females. *Gait and Posture, 38*, 203–208.

Subudhi, A. W., Dimmen, A. C., & Roach, R. C. (2007). Effects of acute hypoxia on cerebral and muscle oxygenation during incremental exercise. *Journal of Applied Physiology, 103*, 177–183.

Subudhi, A. W., Lorenz, M. C., Fulco, C. S., & Roach, R. C. (2008). Cerebrovascular responses to incremental exercise during hypobaric hypoxia: effect of oxygenation on maximal performance. *American Journal of Physiology – Heart and Circulatory Physiology, 294*, H164–H171.

Subudhi, A. W., Miramon, B. R., Granger, M. E., & Roach, R. C. (2009). Frontal and motor cortex oxygenation during maximal exercise in normoxia and hypoxia. *Journal of Applied Physiology, 106*, 1153–1158.

Tashiro, M., Itoh, M., Fujimoto, T., Fujiwara, T., Ota, H., Kubota, K., et al. (2001). ^{18}F-FDG PET mapping of regional brain activity in runners. *Journal of Sports Medicine and Physical Fitness, 41*, 11–17.

Tashiro, M., Itoh, M., Fujimoto, T., Masud, M. M., Watanuki, S., & Yanai, K. (2008). Application of positron emission tomography to neuroimaging in sports sciences. *Methods, 45*, 300–306.

Tempest, G. D., Eston, R. G., & Parfitt, G. (2014). Prefrontal cortex haemodynamics and affective responses during exercise: a multi-channel near infrared spectroscopy study. *Plos One, 9*, e95924. http://dx.doi.org/10.1371/journal.pone.0095924.

Tomporowski, P. D. (2003). Effects of acute bouts of exercise on cognition. *Acta Psychologica, 112*, 297–324.

Towse, J. N., & Neil, D. (1998). Analyzing human random generation behavior: a review of methods used and a computer program for describing performance. *Behavior Research Methods, Instruments and Computers, 30*, 582–591.

Wang, C. C., Chu, C. H., Chu, I. H., Chan, K. H., & Chang, Y. K. (2013). Executive function during acute exercise: the role of exercise intensity. *Journal of Sport and Exercise Psychology, 35*, 358–367.

Wang, G.-J., Volkow, N. D., Fowler, J. S., Franceschi, D., Logan, J., Pappas, N. R., et al. (2014). PET studies of the effects of aerobic exercise on human striatal dopamine release. *Journal of Nuclear Medicine, 41*, 1352–1356.

Waterhouse, B. D., & Woodward, D. J. (1980). Interaction of norepinephrine with cerebrocortical activity evoked by stimulation of somatosensory afferent pathways in the rat. *Experimental Neurology, 67*, 11–34.

Wilson, W. M., & Marsden, C. A. (1995). Extracellular dopamine in the nucleus accumbens of the rat during treadmill running. *Acta Physiologica Scandinavica, 155*, 465–466.

Woods, D. L., & Knight, R. T. (1986). Electrophysiologic evidence of increased distractibility after dorsolateral prefrontal lesions. *Neurology, 36*, 212–216.

Chronic Exercise and Cognition in Humans: A Review of the Evidence for a Neurochemical Basis

Terry McMorris

Department of Sport and Exercise Science, University of Chichester, Chichester, West Sussex, UK

INTRODUCTION

Narrative literature reviews provide support for a positive effect of chronic exercise on cognition (e.g., Best, 2010; Colcombe, Kramer, McAuley, Erickson, & Scalf, 2004; Kramer, Colcombe, McAuley, Scalf, & Erickson, 2005; McDonnell, Smith, & Mackintosh, 2011; Voss, Nagamatsu, Liu-Ambrose, & Kramer, 2011), while meta-analyses show significant, low to moderate effect sizes (e.g., Colcombe & Kramer, 2003; Etnier, Nowell, Landers, & Sibley, 2006; Etnier et al., 1997; Fedewa & Ahn, 2011; Hindin & Zelinski, 2012; Smith et al., 2010). Until recently, the underpinnings for such an effect have tended to be somewhat atheoretical. Colcombe and Kramer (2003) listed the first theories as being the speed hypothesis (Dustman et al., 1984), the visuospatial hypothesis (Stones & Kozma, 1989), the controlled-processing hypothesis (Chodzko-Zajko, 1991), and the central executive hypothesis (Kramer et al., 1999), all of which concern the effect of chronic exercise on cognition in the elderly. These hypotheses were based on the argument that tasks requiring these processes are most likely to benefit from chronic exercise. The "hypotheses" are, in fact, more descriptions of the types of tasks that are expected to be affected by chronic exercise rather than being hypotheses based on real theoretical underpinnings, be they psychological, neurological, or neurochemical.

The first to suggest a neurochemical underpinning were van Praag, Christie, Sejnowski, and Gage (1999). They claimed that chronic exercise results in the release of neurotrophins, which aid neurogenesis. Brain-derived neurotrophic factor (BDNF) swiftly became the most studied of the neurotrophins, and BDNF-induced neurogenesis and neuroplasticity are often confidently cited as the cause of chronic exercise-induced improvements in cognition, particularly in the elderly and the young. The purpose of this review was to examine the evidence for the alleged role of BDNF in the chronic exercise–cognition interaction; the possible roles of catecholamines, which have been implicated

Exercise-Cognition Interaction
http://dx.doi.org/10.1016/B978-0-12-800778-5.00008-6

in the acute exercise–cognition interaction in humans (Chmura, Nazar, & Kaciuba-Uścilko, 1994; Cooper, 1973; McMorris et al., 1999; Peyrin, Pequignot, Lacour, & Fourcade, 1987); and possible effects of the hypothalamic–pituitary–adrenal (HPA) axis hormones, which have been studied in animals.

BDNF AND THE CHRONIC EXERCISE–COGNITION INTERACTION

Due to the roles of BDNF in neurogenesis and neuroprotection (Dishman et al., 2006; Knaeppen, Goekint, Heyman, & Meeusen et al., 2010), long-term potentiation (the strengthening, over time, of synaptic connections between neurons (Lømo, 2003)) (Pang et al., 2004), and the fact that rodent studies have shown hippocampal increases in BDNF expression following chronic exercise (e.g., Aguiar et al., 2011; Aguiar, Speck, Prediger, Kapczinski, & Pinho, 2008; Berchtold, Chinn, Chou, Kesslak, & Cotman, 2005; Ferreira, Real, Rodrigues, Alves, & Britto, 2011; Gomez-Pinilla, Vaynman, & Ying, 2008; Vaynman, Ying, & Gomez-Pinilla, 2004), one often sees the BDNF–exercise interaction used to explain chronic exercise-induced improvements in learning and memory (Griesbach, Hovda, & Gomez-Pinilla, 2009; Hopkins & Bucci, 2010; Vaynman et al., 2004). BDNF has particularly been cited as a major player in the positive effects of chronic exercise in the elderly (Erickson et al., 2011; Lafenêtre et al., 2010) and children (Chaddock, Erickson, Prakash, Kim, et al., 2010; Chaddock, Erickson, Prakash, VanPatter, et al., 2010; Chaddock, Erickson, et al., 2012; Chaddock, Hillman, et al., 2012). In this section we examine the theoretical and empirical evidence for these claims in humans.

BDNF is a protein and a member of the neurotrophic family along with nerve growth factor, neurotrophin-3, neurotrophin-4/5,

neurotrophin-6, and neurotrophin-7. It is widely distributed throughout the central nervous system but is particularly well represented in the hippocampus, neocortex, cerebellum, striatum, and amygdala (Binder & Scharfman, 2004; Kawamoto et al., 1996). It is also found peripherally in sensory neurons and glial cells (Knaeppen, Goekint, Heyman, & Meeusen, 2010; Matthews et al., 2009). BDNF is initially encoded by the BDNF gene to pro-BDNF, which is either proteolytically cleaved intracellularly by pro-convertases and secreted as mature BDNF, or secreted as pro-BDNF and then cleaved by extracellular proteases to mature BDNF (Lessmann, Gottmann, & Malcangio, 2003).

The effects of BDNF on neurogenesis and synaptic transmission, and hence learning and memory, are triggered when it binds with one of its receptors, the high-affinity tropomyosin-related kinase-B (Trk-B). Binding to Trk-B results in receptor dimerization and *trans*-autophosphorylation of tyrosine residues in the cytoplasmic domains of the receptor, which initiates a number of intracellular signaling cascades, including calcium/calmodulin kinase II (CaMKII) and mitogen-activated protein kinase (MAPK), resulting in the phosphorylation of cyclic adenosine monophosphate (cAMP)-response element binding protein (CREB) (Binder & Scharfman, 2004; Cunha, Brambilla, & Thomas, 2010; Waterhouse & Xu, 2009). Activation of these signaling pathways is essential for neurogenesis and neuroplasticity, and hence learning and memory. The actual processes are complex, not yet fully understood, and still a matter of some debate (see Cunha et al., 2010; Lessmann et al., 2003; Waterhouse & Xu, 2009). What is not under debate is that BDNF is important in learning and memory even though the actual processes take place downstream of BDNF synthesis and initial release. Rodent studies, using microdialysis and pharmacological interventions with BDNF and/or Trk-B antagonists, provide strong evidence for the interaction between BDNF and learning and memory (Ferreira et al., 2011; Gomez-Pinilla et al., 2008; Vaynman et al., 2004).

BDNF and Exercise in Humans

A number of studies have measured the effect of chronic exercise on serum and/or plasma concentrations of BDNF in humans. Results are somewhat equivocal, although there is a tendency toward there being no significant effect. Several authors found no significant effect (Baker et al., 2010; Erickson et al., 2011; Schiffer, Schulte, Hollmann, Bloch, & Strüder, 2009; Voss et al., 2013). However, Zoladz et al. (2008) demonstrated a significant increase in basal plasma concentrations and increased plasma concentrations of BDNF in response to an acute bout of exercise. On the other hand, Seifert et al. (2010) showed a significant increase in basal concentrations but no change in the response to a bout of acute exercise. Griffin et al. (2011) found that 3 weeks of 60 min cycling at 60% volume of maximal oxygen uptake (VO_2 *max*) blunted the serum BDNF response to a bout of exercise to exhaustion. After 5 weeks of training, participants showed increased post-exercise serum BDNF concentrations compared to pre-training but only when samples were taken 30 min following cessation of the exercise. There were no significant effects of either 3 or 5 weeks of training on basal concentrations. However, Correia et al. (2011) found significantly greater basal plasma concentrations between international athletes and sedentary individuals.

Rodent studies provide very strong evidence that chronic exercise induces increased BDNF and/or BDNF messenger ribonucleic acid (mRNA) expression in the brain, in particular in the hippocampus (e.g., Aguiar et al., 2011, 2008; Berchtold, Castello, & Cotman, 2010; Berchtold et al., 2005; Ding, Ying, & Gómez-Pinilla, 2011; Gomez-Pinilla et al., 2008; Groves-Chapman et al., 2011; Huang et al., 2006; Liu et al., 2009; Neeper, Gomez-Pinilla, Choi, & Cotman, 1995;

Soya et al., 2007; Vaynman et al., 2004). One could argue that these rodent studies strongly support the notion that chronic exercise will induce changes in human BDNF expression in the brain. Gomez-Pinilla et al. (2008) claimed that increased brain BDNF expression is probably due to the fact that the intracellular signaling cascades, which it initiates, CaMKII, MAPK, and CREB, are activated during and following exercise (Calegari et al., 2011; Egan et al., 2010; Kaurstad et al., 2011). Timing of gene induction in response to exercise may vary. Generally, CREB and CaMKII gene expression precede MAPKI and MAPKII gene expression (Molteni, Ying, & Gomez-Pinilla, 2002; Tong, Shen, Perreau, Balazs, & Cotman, 2001).

Another human study providing some insight into the interaction between exercise and brain BDNF is that of Erickson et al. (2011). Participants in the study were elderly individuals, aged 55–80 years. The experimental group undertook a 1-year program exercising at 60–77% maximum heart rate reserve for 40 min per week. Increases in serum BDNF concentrations from pre- to post-treatment were not significant but Δ BDNF concentrations in the exercise group correlated significantly with Δ hippocampal volume as measured by magnetic resonance imaging ($r = 0.36$, $p < 0.01$, for the left hippocampus and $r = 0.37$, $p < 0.01$ for the right). According to Cohen (1988), these are moderate effect sizes; however, they only account for 12.96% and 13.69% of the relationship. Given that BDNF release triggers a whole range of activity involved in neurogenesis, one should not be surprised at the low correlation coefficients.

BDNF, Chronic Exercise, and Cognition Research in Humans

Very few studies have attempted to examine the interaction between chronic exercise, serum and/or plasma BDNF concentrations, and cognition in humans, despite the fact that rodent studies provide strong evidence that such an interaction should occur and that BDNF crosses the blood–brain barrier (Pan, Banks, Fasold, Bluth, & Kastin, 1998; Sartorius et al., 2009). Moreover, many authors simply report the hypothetical interaction as though it were proven. Griffin et al. (2011) demonstrated a significant improvement in memory performance following 5 weeks of training but not after 3 weeks. This improvement coincided with post-exercise increases in serum BDNF concentrations. There were no significant effects on the Stroop color test. Erickson et al. (2011) showed an increase in basal BDNF concentrations after 1 year of training but it did not reach significance. However, there were increases in hippocampal volume, which were related to serum BDNF concentrations. There were improvements in spatial memory, which were related to increased hippocampal volume but not to Δ BDNF concentrations. More recently, Whiteman et al. (2014) showed that a BDNF × fitness interaction was a strong predictor of long-term memory performance. They found that for active participants, serum BDNF concentrations and memory were positively correlated but for sedentary individuals they were negatively correlated. However, BDNF serum concentrations were not correlated with fitness level.

While the theoretical evidence for an interaction between chronic exercise, BDNF, and cognition is very strong, the empirical evidence is weak. The failure of some studies to show any effect of chronic exercise on BDNF serum concentrations or expression in the brain (Baker et al., 2010; Erickson et al., 2011; Schiffer et al., 2009) and the transient nature of increases found in animal studies cast some doubt on claims for a chronic exercise–BDNF–cognition interaction. That increased BDNF serum concentrations or brain expression are transient may not be a major issue as the main role of BDNF is to initiate downstream activity, which is the key to neuroprotection, neurogenesis, and plasticity. Much more research is needed with regard to the effect of acute and chronic exercise on BDNF before any definitive statements concerning its effects on cognition are made. The questions concerning the evidence examined above, with regard to the role of BDNF as a mediator in the chronic exercise–cognition interaction, also mean that we need to examine the possibility of other neurochemicals being involved.

CATECHOLAMINES AND THE CHRONIC EXERCISE–COGNITION INTERACTION

The catecholamines hypothesis for an acute exercise–cognition interaction was first posited by Cooper (1973). Catecholamines play important roles in both cognition and exercise. The importance of the catecholamines, dopamine, noradrenaline (norepinephrine), and adrenaline (epinephrine), with regard to cognition is that noradrenaline and dopamine act as neurotransmitters in the brain. Once synthesized (see Chapter 4) they are held in vesicles in the brain and, when released, innervate the noradrenergic and dopaminergic pathways. The neurons serving the noradrenergic pathway are mainly found in the locus coeruleus and lateral tegmental field. They rely on noradrenaline and, to lesser extent, adrenaline as the neurotransmitters and enervate spinal cord, cerebellum, entire cerebral cortex, hippocampus, brainstem, and hypothalamus. The dopaminergic pathway, which uses dopamine as the neurotransmitter, mainly serves the basal ganglia, frontal cortex, cingulate cortex, septum, nucleus acumbens, and olfactory tubercle (Kuhar, Couceyro, & Lambert, 1999). Thus, between them, noradrenaline and dopamine activate most areas of the brain.

With regard to exercise, during and even immediately before exercise, the hypothalamus and brainstem initiate action of the sympathoadrenal system. This results in the release of catecholamines at the postganglionic cells of those neurons that require activating or inhibiting.

During incremental exercise, once a moderate level (~75% $\dot{V}O_2$ max) is reached, there is a large increase in plasma catecholamines, which are important in the regulation of the cardiovascular system (Podolin, Munger, & Mazzeo, 1991). Lower intensity exercise, but for long duration (>1 h), also leads to increases in plasma noradrenaline and adrenaline concentrations (Hodgetts, Coppack, Frayn, & Hockaday, 1991). Unlike BDNF, however, catecholamines do not readily cross the blood–brain barrier (Cornford, Braun, Oldendorf, & Hill, 1982; Oldendorf, 1977). McMorris et al. (1999) claimed that feedback concerning pain and physiological stress, via the autonomic nervous system to the hypothalamus, might induce increases in the synthesis and release of dopamine and noradrenaline in the brain. However, McMorris and Hale (2012) argued that the most likely factor, in the induction of central changes of catecholamines, was that peripherally circulating adrenaline and noradrenaline activate β-adrenoreceptors on the afferent vagus nerve, which runs from the abdomen through the chest, neck and head, and terminates in the nucleus tractus solitarii (NTS), within the blood–brain barrier. Glutamate mediates synaptic communication between the vagal afferents and the NTS, allowing noradrenergic cells in the NTS, which project into the locus coeruleus, to stimulate noradrenaline synthesis and release to other parts of the brain (Miyashita & Williams, 2006). This may also affect brain dopamine concentrations, as Devoto, Flore, Saba, Fà, and Gessa (2005) showed that electrical stimulation of the rat locus coeruleus resulted in increased concentrations of dopamine and one of its metabolites, 3,4-dihydroxyphenylacetic acid. Also, Grenhoff and associates (Grenhoff, Nisell, Ferré, Aston-Jones, & Svensson, 1993; Grenhoff & Svensson, 1993) have shown that stimulation of the α_1-adrenoreceptor potentiates the firing of dopamine neurons in the ventral tegmental area, probably due to α_1-adrenoreceptor activation inducing enhanced glutamate release, which affects the excitability of dopamine neurons (Velásquez-Martinez, Vázquez-Torres, & Jiménez-Riveira, 2012).

However, these increases are transient. The half-life of catecholamines in the periphery is only ~3 mins, while the half-life of brain catecholamines is in the range of 8–12 h (Eisenhofer, Kopin, & Goldstein, 2004). The half-life of the expression of the tyrosine hydroxylase (TH) gene, TH mRNA, is 14 ± 1 h (Kadzierski, Aguila-Mansilla, Kozlowski, & Porter, 1994). TH is the rate limiter for catecholamines syntheses. Despite this, there is evidence from animal studies to show chronic exercise-induced changes in brain concentrations of noradrenaline and dopamine. Meeusen and colleagues (Meeusen & De Meirleir, 1995; Meeusen, Piacentini, & De Meirleir, 2001) reported that, overall, chronic exercise resulted in increases in whole brain noradrenaline concentrations. They stated that results for dopamine concentrations tended to be region specific with increases in hypothalamus and midbrain but decreases in prefrontal cortex, hippocampus, and striatum. More recently, Marques et al. (2008) showed no significant effect of chronic exercise on extracellular dopamine concentrations.

The most interesting recent research, however, has examined the effect of chronic exercise on TH activity, with some encouraging results. Kim et al. (2011) found increased TH activity in the brains of rodents following training over 28 days, while a number of studies have measured the effect of chronic exercise on TH mRNA expression in animals. Although O'Neal, van Hoomissen, Holmes, and Dishman (2001) showed no significant effect, others (Foley & Fleshner, 2008; Gavrilović et al., 2012; Tümer et al., 2001) found positive results. Tümer et al.'s findings were affected by age and brain region. Young rats (6 months) showed increased brain TH mRNA expression in the locus coeruleus and ventral tegmental areas but not in the substantia nigra, while old rats (2 years) demonstrated increased TH mRNA expression in the substantia nigra only. Foley and Fleshner examined the effect of chronic exercise on TH mRNA expression in the substantia nigra pars compacta (SNpc) and found a significant increase in the mid-SNpc and an increase approaching significance (p = 0.07) in the caudal SNpc. Gavrilović et al. showed increased TH mRNA expression in the stellate ganglia following 12 weeks of 20 min per day running. Related to increases in TH mRNA expression, Higa-Tanaguchi, Silva, Silva, Michelini, and Stern (2007) demonstrated a positive effect of chronic exercise on the density of dopamine-β-hydroxylase (DBH) in the hypothalamic paraventricular nucleus (PVN), while Gavrilović found increased DBH mRNA in the stellate ganglia. DBH is essential for the synthesis of noradrenaline from dopamine (see Chapter 4). Research examining the effect of prolonged exposure to stress on TH and DBH mRNA expressions in the brain has shown increased mRNA coding in the neuronal perikarya (Molinoff & Axelrod, 1971). In normal circumstances, TH synthesis is modulated by end-product inhibition as it competes with free intraneuronal catecholamines (Alousi & Weiner, 1966). It would appear that prolonged activation of TH heightens its affinity for the biopterin cofactor and it becomes less sensitive to end-product inhibition (Zigmond, Schwarzschild, & Rittenhouse, 1989).

Summary

Animal studies show chronic exercise-induced increases in whole brain noradrenaline concentrations but dopamine decreases in the prefrontal cortex, hippocampus, and striatum. While the former would be advantageous to cognitive functioning, the latter would not. Results with regard to TH mRNA expression are exciting. Increased TH activity in the locus coeruleus, ventral tegmental area, and SNpc would have positive consequences. The locus coeruleus contains noradrenergic neurons with endings in the entire cerebral cortex and the hippocampus,

while the SNpc and ventral tegmental area contain dopamine neurons that innervate the frontal and cingulate cortices. These areas are activated during cognitive functioning.

Evidence for a Chronic Exercise–Catecholamines–Cognition Interaction

No study has directly measured the interaction between chronic exercise, catecholamines, and cognition, although a small number of studies provide some insight. Sothmann and colleagues (Sothmann, Gustafson, Garthwaite, Horn, & Hart, 1988; Sothmann, Hart, & Horn, 1992) set out to examine the effect of chronic exercise on catecholamines responses to stress and, as the stressor, they used performance on the Stroop color task. Sothmann et al. (1988) found no effect of fitness on performance of the Stroop test but a small effect on solving anagram problems. However, plasma noradrenaline concentrations in the unfit participants were higher during performance on the Stroop test, which the authors interpreted as showing higher levels of anxiety. It could be interpreted as participants having to work harder to achieve the same success as the fitter individuals. Sothmann et al. (1992) found no significant effects on cognitive performance or adrenaline and noradrenaline plasma concentrations of a 16-week, 3 days per week aerobic training program. Although there were some small improvements in resting heart rate and $\dot{V}O_2$ max, the catecholamines measures would suggest that the training program was not long enough or, possibly, intense enough to elicit changes that might affect cognition, that is, catecholamines concentrations.

Although not actually measuring catecholamines, Stroth et al. (2010) provided some circumstantial evidence for chronic exercise inducing more effective use of dopamine, while undertaking some cognitive tasks. The authors compared the effect of a 17-week running program on performance of central executive tasks (see Chapter 4 for a description of such tasks) by individuals who were homozygote for the valine (Val) allele in the catechol-*O*-methyltransferase (COMT) gene, and those homozygote for the methionine (Met) allele. In normal circumstances, Met carriers are optimal in dopamine signaling in the prefrontal cortex, which would facilitate handling central executive demands, while Val158 carriers are weak. Val158 carriers benefited significantly from training, while Met individuals showed no significant effect. The authors took this as being indicative of increased brain synthesis and usage of dopamine by the Val158 individuals. In the Met carriers this increase would be redundant.

Summary

Despite the findings of Stroth et al. (2010), there would appear to be little direct evidence for catecholamines playing a role in the positive effect of chronic exercise on cognition. However, animal studies show increased brain noradrenaline concentrations and TH mRNA expression. Animal studies also provide evidence to show that noradrenaline plays a role in neurogenesis and neuroplasticity (Jhaveri et al., 2010; Masuda et al., 2011), and long-term potentiation (Gelinas & Nguyen, 2005; Katsuki, Izumi, & Zorumski, 1997).

HPA AXIS HORMONES AND THE CHRONIC EXERCISE–COGNITION INTERACTION

The possibility that exposure to regularly increased HPA axis activity during exercise will lead to the individual developing a decreased sensitivity to HPA hormones, when experiencing other stressors, has been promulgated (Blaney, Sothmann, Raff, Hart, & Horn, 1990; Strüder et al., 1999). Such an effect would be beneficial when executing cognitive tasks, while simultaneously undertaking acute exercise. It would also probably be helpful with cognitive tasks at any time, as these are considered stressors in themselves (Humphreys & Revelle, 1984; Pribram & McGuinness, 1975).

Regardless of the nature of the stressor, stress results in feedback to the hypothalamus from within the brain, if the stress is purely psychological, and/or from the periphery, when the stress is solely physiological or has a physiological component. In response, the hypothalamus initiates the synthesis of corticotropin releasing factor (CRF), often called corticotropin releasing hormone, from the prepro-CRF gene, a process that takes place in the PVN of the hypothalamus. CRF is secreted into the hypophyseal vessels in the median eminence, where it stimulates the synthesis and release by exocytosis of adrenocorticotropin hormone (ACTH) from its precursor preproopiomelanocortin. The nonapeptide, arginine vasopressin, also known as antidiuretic hormone, also acts as a stimulator of ACTH synthesis and release. It is primarily released from its preprohormone in response to feedback concerning osmolality of body fluids, although it is also secreted as the result of other physiological stress. Following synthesis, ACTH passes into the zona fasciculata of the adrenal cortex where it stimulates the synthesis and secretion of cortisol in humans and corticosterone in rodents (Brandenberger et al., 1980; Genuth, 2004).

During exercise, in the periphery, cortisol plays major roles in glucose production from proteins, the facilitation of fat metabolism and muscle function, and the maintenance of blood pressure (Deuster et al., 1989). ACTH, which is synthesized in the gastrointestinal tract as well as in the pituitary, also plays a role in lipolysis (Borer, 2003). Research examining exercise-induced changes in plasma and salivary ACTH and cortisol concentrations strongly suggests that although the HPA axis hormones undergo circadian rhythms, normal concentrations are sufficient for efficient performance unless the exercise is heavy or of moderate intensity but carried out for long periods. Generally speaking exercise needs to be $\geq 80\%$ $\dot{V}O_2$ *max* for it to induce increases in plasma and salivary concentrations of ACTH and cortisol (De Vries, Bernards, De Rooij, & Koppeschaar, 2000; Hill et al., 2008; McMorris, Davranche, Jones, Hall, & Minter, 2009), while exercise of $<80\%$ $\dot{V}O_2$ *max* needs to be at least 45 min in duration (Bridge, Weller, Rayson, & Jones, 2003; Jacks, Sowash, Anning, McGloughlin, & Andres, 2002; Shojaei, Farajov, & Jafari, 2011) to affect plasma and salivary concentrations of ACTH and cortisol.

Chronic Exercise and HPA Axis Hormones

In humans, research has generally shown that chronic exercise does not alter basal plasma ACTH and cortisol concentrations (Chatzitheodorou, Kabitsis, Malliou, & Mougios, 2007; Duclos, Corcuff, Pehourcq, & Tabarin, 2001; Inder, Hellemans, Swanney, Prickett, & Donald, 1998; Strüder et al., 1999; Wittert, Livesey, Espiner, & Donald, 1996). Although, Wittert et al. found athletes to have higher plasma and salivary ACTH concentrations than controls, even though there were no significant differences in cortisol concentrations. Blaney et al. (1990) demonstrated no significant differences in plasma concentrations of ACTH and cortisol between active and sedentary individuals, while undertaking a modified Stroop color test. In a follow-up experiment, a group of sedentary individuals undertook a 4-month training program, which resulted in an 18% improvement in $\dot{V}O_2$ *max*, but again ACTH and cortisol plasma concentrations did not differ from a control group, while undertaking the Stroop color test.

However, these results tell us little. ACTH plasma concentrations provide only very limited information concerning brain concentrations, as ACTH does not cross the blood–cerebrospinal fluid (CSF) barrier and CSF concentrations have

been shown not to correlate with plasma concentrations (Allen, Kendall, McGilvra, & Vancura, 2011; Nappi et al., 1986). Fortunately, brain extracellular corticosterone concentrations and CRF mRNA expression have been studied in rodents. Results concerning CRF mRNA activity are somewhat equivocal. Expression has been shown to be decreased in the hypothalamic PVN following long-term exposure to voluntary exercise (Bi, Scott, Hyun, Ladenheim, & Moran, 2005; Kawashima et al., 2004) but some researchers found no significant effect (Droste, Chandramohan, Hill, Linthorst, & Reul, 2007; Levin & Dunn-Meynell, 2004), while Park et al. (2005) demonstrated an initial increase followed by a return to original levels. Forced exercise regimens have, however, resulted in significant increases (Chennaoui, Gomez Merino, Lesage, Drogou, & Guezennec, 2002; Harbuz & Lightman, 1989).

Examining the concentrations of free corticosterone in the rat brain, Droste, Collins, Lightman, Linthorst, and Reul (2009) found that training needed to be long term before any changes in ultradian or circadian rhythms were shown. Following long-term exercise, they found that exercising rats showed an increased afternoon/evening pulse in hippocampal free corticosterone concentrations, compared to sedentary animals. However, they found no significant differences between exercising and sedentary rats following a forced swim, although both groups demonstrated significant increases in hippocampal free corticosterone concentrations.

Several authors have examined the effect of chronic exercise on brain corticosteroid receptor mRNA gene expressions. Corticosteroid receptors are divided into type I, or mineralocorticoid receptors (MRs), and type II, or glucocorticoid receptors (GRs). Both GR and MR are found in most parts of the brain but in particular in the hippocampus, septum, amygdala, hypothalamus PVN, and brainstem (De Kloet et al., 2000). Activation of MRs and GRs, in the brain, suppress HPA axis activity through inhibition of CRF neurons (Herman, Watson, Chao, Coirini, & McEwen, 1993). Thus, changes in the number of MR and GR receptors will affect HPA axis activity.

There would appear to be little effect of chronic exercise on GR mRNA expression in the hippocampus (Chang et al., 2008; Droste et al., 2003; Fediuc, Campbell, & Riddell, 2006; Zheng et al., 2006), although Park et al. (2005) found a significant decrease in hippocampal region CA4 only, while Droste et al. (2007) found increased GR mRNA levels in hippocampal layers. Reductions in MR mRNA expression have been shown (Chang et al., 2008; Droste et al., 2003) but some authors found no significant effect (Droste et al., 2007; Park et al., 2005). Droste et al. (2007) also demonstrated no significant changes in GR mRNA expression in the hypothalamic PVN, frontal cortex, or anterior pituitary. Park et al. found initial decreases in PVN and anterior pituitary GR mRNA but, as training continued, these returned to pre-training levels. However, with humans, Bonifazi et al. (2009) found that GR-α helices mRNA (which affect ligand selectivity, receptor dimerization, and coactivator recruitment (Lu et al., 2006)) expression, in the peripheral blood mononuclear cells of trained athletes, were significantly repressed compared to those of sedentary individuals matched for age.

HPA Axis Hormones, Chronic Exercise, and Cognition Research

Since Selye's (1956) early work, it has been widely accepted that HPA axis activity can have an effect on all kinds of performance including cognitive. The areas of the brain most likely to be affected by HPA axis hormones are those in which GR, MR, ACTH, and CRF receptors are most widely found. GR and MR receptors are found throughout the brain but are particularly dense in the limbic system (hippocampus, septum, amygdala), hypothalamic PVN, and brainstem (De Kloet, Reul, & Sutanto, 1990; De Kloet et al. 2000). ACTH receptors are also widely spread but are more dense in the hippocampus, hypothalamus, amygdala, and brainstem (Hnatowich, Queen, Stein, & LaBella, 1989; Kapcala Lechan, & Reichlin, 1983; Mountjoy, Mortrud, Low, Simerly, & Cone, 1994). CRF receptors are also widely distributed but found particularly in the PVN, brainstem, locus coeruleus, raphe nuclei, and somatosensory cortex (Austin, Janosky, & Murphy, 2003; Timofeeva, Huang, & Richard, 2003). Given the role of the limbic system in control of arousal and emotions in general, it is not surprising to find that CRF, ACTH, and cortisol have been widely shown to have an effect on attention (Otte et al. 2007) and alertness (Chapotot, Gronfier, Jouny, Muzet, & Brandenberger, 1998; Vgontzas et al., 2007). The most widely studied area has, however, been the hippocampus and several studies have shown negative effects of high concentrations of cortisol on memory consolidation and recall (Abercrombie, Kalin, Thurow, Rosenkranz, & Davidson, 2003; Kirschbaum, Wolf, May, Wippich, & Hellhammer, 1996; Lupien, Gillin, & Hauger, 1999; Newcomer et al., 1999; Wolf et al., 2001).

The two studies examining the effect of chronic exercise on cognition in humans (Blaney et al., 1990; Strüder et al., 1999) found no significant differences in basal ACTH and cortisol plasma concentrations between active and sedentary males. They also failed to show any significant differences in cognitive performance on working memory tasks. Both sets of authors had the sedentary groups undertake training programs but showed no significant changes in ACTH and cortisol profiles or any improvements in cognition. Overall, there is no evidence of changes in plasma cortisol concentrations in humans, and rodent studies also provide only limited support for any changes in brain concentrations of ACTH and corticosterone. Moreover, results concerning corticosteroid receptors tend to be somewhat equivocal, so there is no strong evidence for chronic exercise affecting the individual's hormonal response to stress.

DISCUSSION

Despite the confidence with which some authors state that the chronic exercise–cognition interaction is mediated by BDNF, the evidence examined above raises some questions but also provides promising results. There is little doubt that BDNF, via CaMKII, MAPK, and CREB activity (Binder & Scharfman, 2004; Cunha et al., 2010; Waterhouse & Xu, 2009), aids neurogenesis and neuroplasticity, and hence learning and memory. Human studies, however, do not supply strong evidence for chronic exercise inducing increased plasma or serum concentrations of BDNF, with some authors finding no significant effect (Baker et al., 2010; Erickson et al., 2011; Schiffer et al., 2009), although others found some limited increases (Griffin et al., 2011; Seifert et al., 2010; Zoladz et al., 2008). However, rodent studies provide very strong evidence that chronic exercise induces increased BDNF and/or BDNF mRNA expression in the brain, in particular in the hippocampus (e.g., Berchtold et al., 2010; Cotman & Berchtold, 2002; Gomez-Pinilla et al., 2008; Griesbach et al., 2009; Huang et al., 2006; Liu et al., 2009; Neeper et al., 1995), but these increases were transient and there was evidence of a possible effect of length of time of engaging in physical activity. The transient nature of increased BDNF plasma and serum concentrations is not a major issue as it is the downstream activity induced by increased BDNF concentrations that is the key to neurogenesis and neuroplasticity.

The two studies that examined the interaction between chronic exercise, BDNF, and cognition (Erickson et al., 2011; Griffin et al., 2011) in humans suggest some interaction. Griffin et al. (2011) demonstrated a significant improvement in memory performance but it would appear that there is a minimum length of time for undertaking chronic exercise before any effect is shown. This is not surprising as one would not expect the organism to adapt immediately. However, while long-term memory was aided, working memory was not affected, which suggests that BDNF effects may be limited to specific regions of the brain, for example, hippocampal activity. This would be supported, to some extent, by Erickson et al. (2011), who found improved spatial memory, which was related to increased hippocampal volume. Improved memory was not related to Δ BDNF concentrations but this is hardly surprising as the actions of increased BDNF concentrations occur downstream. However, the increases in hippocampal volume were related to serum BDNF concentrations. Another interesting result of Erickson et al.'s study was that basal BDNF concentrations remained increased for as long as 1 year following training.

Although not directly measuring BDNF concentrations, Hopkins Davis, Vantieghem, Whalen, and Bucci (2012) provided some interesting results. They compared the effect of a 4-week exercise program on recognition memory of participants who were either Val homozygous for the BDNF gene (Val/Val) or were Met carriers (Val/Met or Met/Met). The BDNF Val allele participants exhibited improved recognition memory, but the MET carriers did not. In humans, experience-related neural plasticity (Cheeran et al., 2008; Kleim et al., 2006), and learning and memory are impaired in BDNF Met carriers compared to individuals with the Val allele (Egan et al., 2003; Hajcak et al., 2009). Therefore, the authors concluded that the altered activity-dependent release of BDNF in Met allele carriers may have attenuated the benefits resulting from exercise. Given that the genetic difference between the groups would affect BDNF synthesis and release directly, it would appear safe to say that the results were due to BDNF-initiated activity.

The results outlined above (Erickson et al., 2011; Griffin et al., 2011; Hopkins, Davis, Vantieghem,

Whalen, & Bucci, 2012) demonstrate a prima facie case for a chronic exercise, BDNF, and cognition interaction, and highlight the need for further research. While many animal studies provide evidence for such an interaction, some animal studies question this. Ferreira et al. (2011) showed evidence of neurogenesis in the absence of increased BDNF concentrations or BDNF mRNA expression. They suggested that other growth factors, such as fibroblast growth factor (FGF) and epidermal growth factor, may be, at least partially, responsible for neurogenesis and neuroplasticity. Foster, Rosenblatt, and Kuljiš (2011) similarly suggested FGF but also insulin-like growth factor (IGF-1) and vascular endothelial growth factor (VEGF) as other possible mediators. Fabel et al. (2003) argued that VEGF is the key to exercise-induced hippocampal neurogenesis. However, Whiteman et al. (2014) found that interactions between fitness and IGF-1 and fitness and VEGF did not predict cognitive performance. In the case of VEGF, we must be cautious because VEGF does not cross the blood–brain barrier. However, rodent studies show that exercise induces increased hippocampal VEGF (Cao et al., 2004). Ruiz De Almodovar, Lambrechts, Mazzone, and Carmeliet (2009) claimed that VEGF can affect neurogenesis via effects on brain vasculature.

Observation of the results for human studies shows that growth factors appear to be affective when the cognitive task is a memory task. This is hardly surprising as, although the expression of growth factors is throughout the brain, it would appear that the hippocampus is the main area benefiting from exercise-induced increases in growth factors. However, observations of research examining the effect of chronic exercise on cognition, which did not measure any neurochemicals, shows that tasks other than long-term memory tasks also benefit. In particular, working memory or, to be more precise, central executive tasks have been shown to benefit from chronic exercise (e.g., Chaddock, Erickson, et al., 2012; Chaddock, Hillman, et al., 2012; Stroth et al., 2009; Verstynen et al., 2012; Voss,

Chaddock et al., 2011; Weinstein et al., 2010). Baddeley (1986) described working memory as the interactive functioning of three separate but interdependent parts, the central executive mechanism and two short-term memory systems responsible for the encoding of acoustic and verbal information, and visual and visuospatial information, respectively. The role of the central executive is to oversee and control the whole process. It ensures that integration of perceptual input and comparison of the present situation (held in short-term memory) with recalled information from long-term memory occurs. Positron emission tomography and functional magnetic resonance imaging studies have shown that central executive activity involves large areas of the prefrontal cortex but also includes a great deal of activity from areas outside of the frontal lobe (Leh, Petrides, & Strafella, 2010). Prefrontal cortex activity is served by the dopaminergic and noradrenergic pathways, therefore one would expect to see such activity affected by catecholamines responses to chronic exercise.

The evidence, however, that we examined earlier for the interaction between chronic exercise, catecholamines, and cognition in humans provides no support for such an interaction. However, brain concentrations of catecholamines and TH mRNA have not been measured in humans, therefore we have to rely on animal studies. These do provide evidence of increased brain concentrations of noradrenaline, very limited dopamine increases but strong evidence for increased TH mRNA expression. The latter would undoubtedly facilitate the synthesis of catecholamines in the brain and this may account for some of the effects of chronic exercise and fitness on the performance of central executive tasks. It is also interesting to note that there may be an interaction between increased TH mRNA expression and increased BDNF concentrations. The latter results in the release of CaMKII, which is capable of inducing phosphorylation of TH and thus increased activity of the enzyme (Waymire & Craviso, 1993).

There is also evidence for neurogenesis in the prefrontal cortex as a result of chronic exercise. Weinstein et al. (2010) showed that fit individuals had greater gray matter volume in several regions, including the dorsolateral prefrontal cortex, which is particularly active during the performance of several central executive tasks (Fincham, Carter, van Veen, Stenger, & Anderson, 2002; van Veen, Cohen, Botvinick, Stenger, & Carter, 2001; van Veen, Krug, & Carter, 2008), while Chaddock, Erickson, Prakash, VanPatter et al. (2010) demonstrated greater basal ganglia volumes in fit compared to unfit children. Also, noradrenaline has been shown to increase adult rat dentate–gyrus-derived neural precursor cells via activation of β_2-adrenoreceptors (Masuda et al., 2011). However, as chronic exercise induces increases in concentrations of growth factors, the neurogenesis may be more due to the effect of growth factors or possibly an interaction between growth factors and the sympathoadrenal system.

With regard to the HPA axis hormones, it was thought that increased HPA axis activity might lead to the individual developing a decreased sensitivity to HPA axis activity during exercise. Research in humans examining the effect of chronic exercise on basal plasma cortisol concentrations, however, has shown no significant effects (Blaney et al., 1990; Chatzitheodorou et al., 2007; Duclos et al., 2001; Inder et al., 1998; Strüder et al., 1999; Wittert et al., 1996). Moreover, rodent studies show little effect of chronic exercise on GR mRNA and MR mRNA expression in the brain due to chronic exercise (Chang et al., 2008; Droste et al., 2003, 2007; Fediuc et al., 2006; Park et al., 2005; Zheng et al., 2006).

Before leaving HPA axis hormones, a surprising anomaly arises from animal studies examining the effect of exercise-induced increases in corticosterone on BDNF synthesis. Exogenous corticosterone inhibits BDNF synthesis (Cosi, Spoerri, Comelli, Guidolin, & Skaper, 1993; Gould, Cameron, Daniels, Woolley, & McEwen, 1992) but it appears that endogenous exercise-induced increases in corticosterone do not (Ferreira et al., 2011; Schaaf et al., 1999). Schaaf et al. suggested that during training, the activity of corticosteroid receptors may be repressed by transcription factors activated by membrane signaling pathways.

FUTURE RESEARCH

The prima facie case, outlined above, concerning the role of BDNF as a mediator in the chronic exercise–cognition interaction strongly indicates the need for more research in this area. However, evidence from animal studies also points to the need for inclusion of examination of the possible effects of other growth factors. This could be important if BDNF plasma or serum concentrations were to be used as biomarkers for fitness effects on cognition. The role of BDNF and other growth factors in neurogenesis can also be further examined by using more studies in which both neurochemical and functional magnetic resonance imaging techniques are employed simultaneously. Research is also required to further examine the effects of BDNF gene polymorphisms on the chronic exercise–cognition interaction. Similarly, research looking at the effect of the COMT gene polymorphism and its subsequent effect on catecholamines synthesis following exercise requires attention. Examination of the possible effect of regularly undertaking heavy exercise on cognitive performance during acute bouts of such exercise also requires further research. The possibility that this alters ACTH and cortisol responses would allow for a better understanding of possible effects on GR and MR receptors. Similarly, the use of *a-v* diff studies to measure concentrations of the noradrenaline metabolite 3,4-methoxyhydroxyphenylglycol and the dopamine metabolite 4-hydroxy-3-methoxyphenylacetic acid, also known as homovanillic acid, would provide useful information concerning whether or not chronic exercise does result in greater facilitation of the use of catecholamines during cognition.

CONCLUSION

Human studies provide a prima facie case for BDNF being a mediator in the chronic exercise–cognition interaction. Evidence from animal studies strongly supports this but also points to roles for other growth factors. Although human studies provide no real support for an interaction between chronic exercise, catecholamines, and cognition, results from studies examining the effect of chronic exercise on performance of memory and central executive tasks, which are activated by the noradrenergic and dopaminergic pathways, suggest that such an interaction may be occurring. Animal studies provide strong support for increased whole brain concentrations of noradrenaline and some regional increases in brain dopamine concentrations due to chronic exercise, and perhaps more importantly increased TH mRNA expression in the brain. This would facilitate the synthesis of dopamine and noradrenaline. Evidence for a blunting of HPA axis activity due to undertaking chronic exercise is extremely limited but more research is required in this area.

References

Abercrombie, H. C., Kalin, N. H., Thurow, M. E., Rosenkranz, M. A., & Davidson, R. J. (2003). Cortisol variation in humans affects memory for emotionally laden and neutral information. *Behavioral Neuroscience, 117,* 505–516.

Aguiar, A. S., Jr., Castro, A. A., Moreira, E. L., Glaser, V., Santos, A. R. S., Tasca, C. I., et al. (2011). Short bouts of mild-intensity physical exercise improve spatial learning and memory in aging rats: Involvement of hippocampal plasticity via AKT, CREB and BDNF signaling. *Mechanisms of Ageing and Development, 132,* 560–567.

Aguiar, A. S., Jr., Speck, A. E., Prediger, R. D., Kapczinski, F., & Pinho, R. A. (2008). Downhill training upregulates mice hippocampal and striatal brain-derived neurotrophic factor levels. *Journal of Neural Transmission, 115,* 1251–1255.

Allen, J. P., Kendall, J. W., McGilvra, R., & Vancura, C. (2011). Immunoreactive ACTH in cerebrospinal fluid. *Journal of Clinical Endocrinology Metabolism, 38,* 586–593.

Alousi, A., & Weiner, N. (1966). The regulation of norepinephrine synthesis in sympathetic nerves: effect of nerve stimulation, cocaine and catecholamine-releasing agents. *Proceedings of the National Academy of Sciences of the United States of America, 56,* 1491–1496.

Austin, M. C., Janosky, J. E., & Murphy, H. A. (2003). Increased corticotropin-releasing hormone immunoreactivity in monoamine-containing pontine nuclei of depressed suicide men. *Molecular Psychiatry, 8,* 324–332.

Baddeley, A. D. (1986). *Working memory.* New York: Oxford University Press.

Baker, L. D., Frank, L. L., Foster-Schubert, K., Green, P. S., Wilkinson, C. W., McTiernan, A., et al. (2010). Aerobic exercise improves cognition for older adults with glucose intolerance, a risk factor for Alzheimer's disease. *Journal of Alzheimer's Disease, 22,* 569–579.

Berchtold, N. C., Castello, N., & Cotman, C. W. (2010). Exercise and time-dependent benefits to learning and memory. *Neuroscience, 167,* 588–597.

Berchtold, N. C., Chinn, G., Chou, M., Kesslak, J. P., & Cotman, C. W. (2005). Exercise primes a molecular memory for brain-derived neurotrophic factor protein induction in the rat hippocampus. *Neuroscience, 133,* 853–861.

Best, J. R. (2010). Effects of physical activity on children's executive function: contributions of experimental research on aerobic exercise. *Developmental Review, 30,* 331–551.

Binder, D. K., & Scharfman, H. E. (2004). Brain-derived neurotrophic factor. *Growth Factor, 22,* 123–131.

Bi, S., Scott, K. A., Hyun, J., Ladenheim, E. E., & Moran, T. H. (2005). Running wheel activity prevents hyperphagia and obesity in Otsuka Long-Evans Tokushima fatty rats: role of hypothalamic signaling. *Endocrinology, 148,* 1678–1685.

Blaney, J., Sothmann, M., Raff, H., Hart, B., & Horn, T. (1990). Impact of exercise training on plasma adrenocorticotropin response to a well-learned vigilance task. *Psychoneuroendocrinology, 15,* 453–462.

Bonifazi, M., Mencarelli, M., Fedele, V., Ceccarelli, I., Pecorelli, A., Grasso, G., et al. (2009). Glucocorticoid receptor mRNA expression in peripheral blood mononuclear cells in high trained compared to low trained athletes and untrained subjects. *Journal of Endocrinological Investigations, 32,* 816–820.

Borer, K. T. (2003). *Exercise Endocrinology.* Champaign, IL: Human Kinetics.

Brandenberger, G., Follenius, M., Wittersheim, G., Salame, P., Simeoni, M., & Reinhardt, B. (1980). Plasma-catecholamines and pituitary-adrenal hormones related to mental task demand under quiet and noise conditions. *Biological Psychology, 10,* 239–252.

Bridge, M. W., Weller, A. S., Rayson, M., & Jones, D. A. (2003). Ambient temperature and the pituitary hormone responses to exercise in humans. *Experimental Physiology, 88,* 627–635.

Calegari, V. C., Zoppi, C. C., Bezende, L. F., Silveira, L. R., Carneiro, E. M., & Boschero, B. C. (2011). Endurance training activates AMP-activated protein kinase, increases expression of uncoupling protein 2 and reduces insulin secretion from rat pancreatic islets. *Journal of Endocrinology, 208,* 257–284.

Cao, L., Jiao, X., Zuzga, D. S., Liu, Y., Fong, D. M., Young, D., et al. (2004). VEGF links hippocampal activity with neurogenesis, learning and memory. *Nature Genetics, 36,* 827–835.

Chaddock, L., Erickson, K. I., Prakash, R. S., Kim, J. S., Voss, M. W., VanPatter, M., et al. (2010). A neuroimaging investigation of the association between aerobic fitness, hippocampal volume and memory performance in preadolescent children. *Brain Research, 1358,* 172–183.

Chaddock, L., Erickson, K. I., Prakash, R. S., VanPatter, M., Voss, M. V., Pontifex, M. B., et al. (2010). Basal ganglia volume is associated with aerobic fitness in preadolescent children. *Developmental Neuroscience (Basel, Switz.), 32,* 249–256.

Chaddock, L., Erickson, K. I., Prakash, R. S., Voss, M. W., VanPatter, M., Pontifex, M. B., et al. (2012). A functional MRI investigation of the association between childhood aerobic fitness and neurocognitive control. *Biological Psychology, 89,* 260–268.

Chaddock, L., Hillman, C. H., Pontifex, M. B., Johnson, C. R., Raine, L. B., & Kramer, A. F. (2012). Childhood aerobic fitness predicts cognitive performance one year later. *Journal of Sports Science, 30,* 421–430.

Chang, Y. T., Chen, Y. C., Wu, C. W., Chen, H. I., Jen, C. J., & Kuo, Y. M. (2008). Glucocorticoid signaling an exercise-induced downregulation of the mineralocorticoid receptor in the induction of adult mouse dentate neurogenesis by treadmill running. *Psychoneuroendocrinology, 33,* 1173–1182.

Chapotot, F., Gronfier, J. C., Jouny, C., Muzet, A., & Brandenberger, G. (1998). Cortisol secretion is related to electroencephalographic alertness in human subjects during daytime wakefulness. *Journal of Clinical Endocrinology Metabolism, 83,* 4263–4268.

Chatzitheodorou, D., Kabitsis, C., Malliou, P., & Mougios, V. (2007). A pilot study of the effects of high-intensity aerobic exercise versus passive interventions on pain, disability, psychological strain, and serum cortisol concentrations in people with low back pain. *Physical Therapy, 87,* 304–312.

Cheeran, B., Talelli, P., Mori, F., Koch, G., Suppa, A., Edwards, M., et al. (2008). A common polymorphism in the brain-derived neurotrophic factor gene (BDNF) modulates human cortical plasticity and the response to rTMS. *Journal of Physiology, 586,* 5717–5725.

Chennaoui, M., Gomez Merino, D., Lesage, J., Drogou, C., & Guezennec, C. Y. (2002). Effects of moderate and intensive training on the hypothalamic-pituitary-adrenal axis in rats. *Acta Physiologica Scandinavica, 175,* 113–121.

Chmura, J., Nazar, H., & Kaciuba-Uścilko, H. (1994). Choice reaction time during graded exercise in relation to blood lactate and plasma catecholamine thresholds. *International Journal of Sports Medicine, 15,* 172–176.

Chodzko-Zajko, W. (1991). Physical fitness, cognitive performance, and aging. *Medicine and Science in Sports and Exercise, 23,* 868–872.

Cohen, J. (1988). *Statistical power analysis for the behavioral sciences* (2nd ed.). Hillsdale, NJ: Lawrence Erlbaum Associates.

Colcombe, S., & Kramer, A. F. (2003). Fitness effects on the cognitive function of older adults: a meta-analytic study. *Psychological Science, 14,* 125–130.

Colcombe, S. J., Kramer, A. F., McAuley, E., Erickson, K. I., & Scalf, P. (2004). Neurocognitive aging and cardiovascular fitness: recent findings and future directions. *Journal of Molecular Neuroscience, 24,* 9–14.

Cooper, C. J. (1973). Anatomical and physiological mechanisms of arousal with specific reference to the effects of exercise. *Ergonomics, 16,* 601–609.

Cornford, E. M., Braun, L. D., Oldendorf, W. H., & Hill, M. A. (1982). Comparison of lipid-related blood–brain barrier penetrability in neonates and adults. *American Journal of Physiology, 243,* C161–C168.

Correia, P. R., Scorza, F. A., Gomes da Silva, S., Pansani, A., Toscano-Silva, M., de Almeida, A. C., et al. (2011). Increased basal plasma brain-derived neurotrophic factor levels in sprint runners. *Neuroscience Bulletin, 27,* 325–329.

Cosi, C., Spoerri, P. E., Comelli, M. C., Guidolin, D., & Skaper, S. D. (1993). Glucocorticoids depress activity-dependent expression of BDNF mRNA in hippocampal neurones. *Neuroreport, 4,* 527–530.

Cotman, C. W., & Berchtold, N. C. (2002). Exercise: a behavioral intervention to enhance brain health and plasticity. *Trends in Neuroscience, 25,* 295–301.

Cunha, C., Brambilla, R., & Thomas, K. L. (2010). A simple role for BDNF in learning and memory? *Frontiers in Molecular Neuroscience, 3,* 1. http://dx.doi.org/10.3389/neuro.02.001.2010.

De Kloet, E. R., Reul, J. M., & Sutanto, W. (1990). Corticosteroids and the brain. *Journal of Steroid Biochemistry and Molecular Biology, 20,* 387–394.

De Vries, W. R., Bernards, N. T. M., De Rooij, M. H., & Koppeschaar, H. P. F. (2000). Dynamic exercise discloses different time-related responses in stress hormones. *Psychosomatic Medicine, 62,* 866–872.

De Kloet, E. R., Van Acker, S. A. B.E., Siburg, R. M., Oitzl, M. S., Meijer, O. C., Rahmouni, K., et al. (2000). Aldosterone action in nonepithial cells. *Kidney International, 57,* 1329–1336.

Deuster, P. A., Chrousos, G. P., Luger, A., De Bolt, J. E., Bernier, I. L., Trostman, U. H., et al. (1989). Hormonal and metabolic responses of untrained, moderately trained, and highly trained men to 3 exercise intensities. *Metabolism, 38,* 141–148.

Devoto, P., Flore, G., Saba, P., Fà, M., & Gessa, G. L. (2005). Co-release of noradrenaline and dopamine in the cerebral cortex elicited by single train and repeated train stimulation of the locus coeruleus. *BMC Neuroscience, 6,* 31. http://dx.doi.org/10.1186/1471-2202-6-31.

Ding, Q., Ying, Z., & Gómez-Pinilla, F. (2011). Exercise influences hippocampal plasticity by modulating brain-derived neurotrophic factor processing. *Neuroscience, 192,* 773–780.

Dishman, R. K., Berthoud, H.-R., Booth, F. W., Cotman, C. W., Edgerton, V. R., Fleshner, M. R., et al. (2006). Neurobiology of exercise. *Obesity, 14,* 345–356.

Droste, S. K., Chandramohan, Y., Hill, L. E., Linthorst, A. C., & Reul, J. M. (2007). Voluntary exercise impacts on the rat hypothalamic-pituitary-adrenocortical axis mainly at the adrenal level. *Neuroendocrinology, 86,* 26–37.

Droste, S. K., Collins, A., Lightman, S. L., Linthorst, A. C. E., & Reul, J. M. H.M. (2009). Distinct, time-dependent effects of voluntary exercise on circadian and ultradian rhythms and stress responses of free corticosterone in the rat hippocampus. *Endocrinology, 150,* 4170–4179.

Droste, S. K., Gesing, A., Ulbricht, S., Müller, M. B., Linthorst, A. C. E., & Reul, J. M. H.M. (2003). Effects of long-term voluntary exercise on the mouse hypothalamic-pituitary-adrenocortical axis. *Endocrinology, 144,* 3012–3023.

Duclos, M., Corcuff, J.-B., Pehourcq, F., & Tabarin, A. (2001). Decreased pituitary sensitivity to glucocorticoids in endurance-trained men. *European Journal of Endocrinology, 144,* 363–368.

Dustman, R. E., Ruhkling, R. O., Russell, E. M., Shearer, D. E., Bonekat, W., Shigeoka, J. W., et al. (1984). Aerobic exercise training and improved neurophysiological function of older adults. *Neurobiology of Aging, 5,* 35–42.

Egan, B., Carson, B. P., Garcia-Roves, P. M., Chibalin, A. V., Sarsfield, E. M., Barron, N., et al. (2010). Exercise intensity-dependent regulation of peroxisome proliferator-activated receptor coactivator-1 mRNA abundance is associate with differential activation of upstream signalling kinases in human skeletal muscle. *Journal of Physiology, 588,* 1779–1990.

Egan, M. F., Kojima, M., Callicott, J. H., Goldberg, T. E., Kolachana, B. S., Bertolino, A., et al. (2003). The BDNF val-66met polymorphism affects activity-dependent secretion of BDNF and human memory and hippocampal function. *Cell, 112,* 257–269.

Eisenhofer, G., Kopin, I. J., & Goldstein, D. S. (2004). Catecholamine metabolism: a contemporary view with implications for physiology and medicine. *Pharmacological Reviews, 56,* 331–349.

Erickson, K. I., Voss, M. W., Prakash, R. S., Basak, C., Szabo, A., Chaddock, L., et al. (2011). Exercise training increases size of hippocampus and improves memory. *Proceedings of the National Academy of Sciences of the United States of America, 108,* 3017–3022.

Etnier, J. L., Nowell, P., Landers, D. M., & Sibley, B. A. (2006). A meta-regression to examine the relationship between aerobic fitness and cognitive performance. *Brain Research Reviews, 52,* 119–130.

Etnier, J. L., Salazar, W., Landers, D. M., Petruzzello, S. J., Han, M., & Nowell, P. (1997). The influence of physical fitness and exercise upon cognitive functioning: a meta-analysis. *Journal of Sport and Exercise Psychology, 19,* 249–277.

Fabel, K., Tam, B., Kuafer, D., Barker, A., Simmons, N., Kuo, C. J., et al. (2003). VEGF is necessary for exercise-induced adult hippocampal neurogenesis. *European Journal of Neuroscience, 18,* 2803–2812.

Fedewa, A. L., & Ahn, S. (2011). The effects of physical activity and physical fitness on children's achievement and cognitive outcomes: a meta-analysis. *Research Quarterly for Exercise and Sport, 82,* 521–535.

Fediuc, S., Campbell, J. E., & Riddell, M. C. (2006). Effect of voluntary wheel running on circadian corticosterone release and on HPA axis responsiveness to restraint stress in Sprague-Dawley rats. *Journal of Applied Physiology, 100,* 1867–1875.

Ferreira, A. F. B., Real, C. C., Rodrigues, A. C., Alves, A. S., & Britto, L. R. G. (2011). Short-term, moderate exercise is capable of inducing structural, bdnf-independent hippocampal plasticity. *Brain Research, 1425,* 111–122.

Fincham, J. M., Carter, C. S., van Veen, V., Stenger, V. A., & Anderson, J. R. (2002). Neural mechanisms of planning; a computational analysis using event-related fMRI. *Proceedings of the National Academy of Sciences of the United States of America, 99,* 3346–3351.

Foley, T. E., & Fleshner, M. (2008). Neuroplasticity of dopamine circuits after exercise: implications for central fatigue. *NeuroMolecular Medicine, 10,* 67–80.

Foster, P. P., Rosenblatt, K. P., & Kuljiš, R. O. (2011). Exercise-induced cognitive plasticity, implications for mild cognitive impairment and Alzheimer's disease. *Frontiers in Neurology.* http://dx.doi.org/10.3389/fneur.2011.00028.

Gavrilović, L., Mandusić, V., Stojilković, V., Kasapović, J., Stojiliković, S., Pajović, S. B., et al. (2012). Effect of chronic forced running on gene expression of catecholamine biosynthetic enzymes in stellate ganglia of rats. *Journal of Biological Regulators and Homeostatic Agents, 26,* 367–377.

Gelinas, J. N., & Nguyen, P. V. (2005). Beta-adrenergic receptor activation facilitates induction of a protein synthesis-dependent late phase of long-term potentiation. *Journal of Neuroscience, 25,* 3294–3303.

Genuth, S. M. (2004). The endocrine system. In R. M. Berne, M. Levy, N. B. Koepen, & B. A. Stanton (Eds.), *Physiology* (5th ed.) (pp. 719–978). St. Louis, MO: Mosby.

Gomez-Pinilla, F., Vaynman, S., & Ying, Z. (2008). Brain-derived neurotrophic factor functions as a metabotrophin to mediate the effects of exercise on cognition. *European Journal of Neuroscience, 28,* 2278–2287.

Gould, E., Cameron, H. A., Daniels, D. C., Woolley, C. S., & McEwen, B. S. (1992). Adrenal hormones suppress cell division in the adult rat dentate gyrus. *Journal of Neuroscience, 12,* 3642–3650.

Grenhoff, J., Nisell, M., Ferré, S., Aston-Jones, G., & Svensson, T. H. (1993). Noradrenergic modulation of dopamine cell firing elicited by stimulation of the locus coeruleus in the rat. *Journal of Neural Transmission: General. Section, 93,* 11–25.

Grenhoff, J., & Svensson, T. H. (1993). Prazosin modulates the firing pattern of dopamine neurons in rat ventral tegmental area. *European Journal of Pharmacology, 233,* 79–84.

Griesbach, G. S., Hovda, D. A., & Gomez-Pinilla, F. (2009). Exercise-induced improvement in cognitive performance after traumatic brain-injury in rats is dependent on BDNF activation. *Brain Research, 1288,* 105–115.

Griffin, É. W., Mullally, S., Foley, C., Warmington, S. A., O'Mara, S. M., & Kelly, Á. M. (2011). Aerobic exercise improves hippocampal function and increases BDNF in the serum of young adult males. *Physiology and Behavior, 104,* 934–941.

Groves-Chapman, J. L., Murray, P. S., Stevens, K. L., Monroe, D. C., Koch, L. G., Britton, S. L., et al. (2011). Changes in mRNA levels for brain-derived neurotrophic factor after wheel running in rats selectively bred for high- and low-aerobic capacity. *Brain Research, 1425,* 90–97.

Hajcak, G., Castille, C., Olvet, D. M., Dunning, J. P., Roohi, J., & Hatchwell, E. (2009). Genetic variation in brain-derived neurotrophic factor and human fear conditioning. *Genes, Brain and Behavior, 8,* 80–85.

Harbuz, M. S., & Lightman, S. L. (1989). Responses of hypothalamic and pituitary mRNA to physical and psychological stress in the rat. *Journal of Endocrinology, 122,* 705–711.

Herman, J. P., Watson, S. J., Chao, H. M., Coirini, H., & McEwen, B. S. (1993). Diurnal regulation of glucocorticoid receptor and mineralocorticoid receptor mRNAs in rat hippocampus. *Molecular and Cellular Neuroscience, 4,* 181–190.

Higa-Tanaguchi, K. T., Silva, F. C., Silva, H. M., Michelini, L. C., & Stern, J. E. (2007). Exercise-training induced remodeling of paraventricular nucleus (nor)adrenergic innervation in normotensive and hypertensive rats. *American Journal of Physiology. Regulatory, Integrative Comparative Physiology, 292,* R1717–R1727.

Hill, E. E., Zack, E., Battaglini, C., Viru, M., Viru, A., & Hackney, A. C. (2008). Exercise and circulating cortisol levels: the intensity threshold effect. *Journal of Endocrinology Investigation, 31,* 587–591.

Hindin, S. B., & Zelinski, E. M. (2012). Extended practice and aerobic exercise interventions benefit untrained cognitive outcomes in older adults: a meta-analysis. *Journal of the American Geriatrics Society, 60,* 136–141.

Hnatowich, M. R., Queen, G., Stein, D., & LaBella, F. S. (1989). ACTH receptors in nervous tissue. High-affinity binding-sequestration of [^{125}I] [Phe^2,Nle^4]ACTH 1-24 in homogenates and slices from rat brain. *Canadian Journal of Physiology and Pharmacology, 67,* 568–576.

Hodgetts, V., Coppack, S. W., Frayn, K. N., & Hockaday, T. D. R. (1991). Factors controlling fat mobilization from human subcutaneous adipose-tissue during exercise. *Journal of Applied Physiology, 71,* 445–451.

Hopkins, M. E., & Bucci, D. J. (2010). BDNF expression in perirhinal cortex is associated with exercise-induced improvement in object recognition memory. *Neurobiology of Learning and Memory, 94,* 278–284.

Hopkins, M. E., Davis, F. C., Vantieghem, M. R., Whalen, P. J., & Bucci, D. J. (2012). Differential effects of acute and regular physical exercise on cognition and affect. *Neuroscience, 215,* 59–68.

Huang, A. M., Jen, C. J., Chen, H. F., Yu, L., Kuo, Y. M., & Chen, H. I. (2006). Compulsive exercise acutely upregulates rat hippocampal brain-derived neurotrophic factor. *Journal of Neural Transmission, 113,* 803–811.

Humphreys, M. S., & Revelle, W. (1984). Personality, motivation, and performance. A theory of the relationship between individual differences and information processing. *Psychological Review, 91,* 153–184.

Inder, W. J., Hellemans, J., Swanney, M. P., Prickett, T. C. R., & Donald, R. A. (1998). Prolonged exercise increases peripheral plasma ACTH, CRH, and AVP in male athletes. *Journal of Applied Physiology, 85,* 835–841.

Jacks, D. E., Sowash, J., Anning, J., McGloughlin, T., & Andres, F. (2002). Effect of exercise at three exercise intensities on salivary cortisol. *Journal of Strength and Conditioning Research, 16,* 286–289.

Jhaveri, D. J., Mackay, E. W., Hamlin, A. S., Marathe, S. V. L., Nandam, S., Vaidya, V. A., et al. (2010). Norepinephrine directly activates adult hippocampal precursors via β3 adrenergic receptors. *Journal of Neuroscience, 30,* 2795–2806.

Kadzierski, W., Aguila-Mansilla, N., Kozlowski, G. P., & Porter, J. C. (1994). Expression of tyrosine hydroxylase gene in cultured hypothalamic cells: roles of protein kinase A and C. *Journal of Neurochemistry, 62,* 431–437.

Kapcala, L. P., Lechan, R., & Reichlin, S. (1983). Origin of immunoreactive ACTH in brain sites outside the ventral hypothalamus. *Neuroendocrinology, 37,* 440–445.

Katsuki, H., Izumi, Y., & Zorumski, C. F. (1997). Noradrenergic regulation of synaptic plasticity in the hippocampal CA1 region. *Journal of Neurophysiology, 77,* 3013–3020.

Kaurstad, G., Alves, M. N., Kemi, O. J., Rolim, N., Høydal, M. A., Wisløff, H., et al. (2011). Chronic CaMKII inhibition blunts the cardiac contractile response to exercise training. *European Journal of Applied Physiology, 112,* 579–588.

Kawamoto, Y., Nakamura, S., Nakano, S., Oka, N., Akiguchi, I., & Kimura, J. (1996). Immunohistochemical localization of brain-derived neurotrophic factor in adult rat brain. *Neuroscience, 74*, 1209–1226.

Kawashima, H., Saito, T., Yoshizato, H., Fujikawa, T., Sato, Y., McEwen, B. S., et al. (2004). Endurance treadmill training in rats alters CRH activity in the hypothalamic paraventricular nucleus at rest and during acute running according to its period. *Life Sciences, 76*, 763–774.

Kim, H., Heo, H. I., Kim, D. H., Ko, I. G., Lee, S. S., Kim, S. E., et al. (2011). Treadmill exercise and methylphenidate ameliorate symptoms of attention deficit/hyperactivity disorder through enhancing dopamine synthesis and brain-derived neurotrophic factor expression in spontaneous hypertensive rats. *Neuroscience Letters, 504*, 35–39.

Kirschbaum, C., Wolf, O. T., May, M., Wippich, W., & Hellhammer, D. H. (1996). Stress- and treatment-induced elevations of cortisol levels associated with impaired declarative memory in healthy adults. *Life Sciences, 17*, 1475–1483.

Kleim, J. A., Chan, S., Pringle, E., Schallert, K., Procaccio, V., Jimenez, R., et al. (2006). BDNF val66met polymorphism is associated with modified experience-dependent plasticity in human motor cortex. *Nature Neuroscience, 9*, 735–737.

Knaeppen, K., Goekint, M., Heyman, E. M., & Meeusen, R. (2010). Neuroplasticity – exercise-induced response of peripheral brain-derived neurotrophic factor: a systematic review of experimental studies in human subjects. *Sports Medicine, 40*, 765–801.

Kramer, A. F., Colcombe, A., McAuley, E., Scalf, P. E., & Erickson, K. I. (2005). Fitness, aging and neurocognitive function. *Neurobiology of Aging, 26*(Suppl. 1), 124–127.

Kramer, A. F., Hahn, S., Cohen, N. J., Banich, M. T., McAuley, E., Harrison, C. R., et al. (1999). Ageing, fitness and neurocognitive function. *Nature, 400*, 418–419.

Kuhar, M. J., Couceyro, P. R., & Lambert, P. D. (1999). Catecholamines. In G. J. Siegel, B. W. Agranoff, R. W. Abers, S. K. Fisher, & M. D. Uhler (Eds.), *Basic neurochemistry: Molecular, cellular and medical aspects* (6th ed.) (pp. 243–262). Philadelphia: Lippincott, Williams and Wilkins.

Lafenêtre, P., Leske, O., Ma-Högemeie, Z., Haghikia, A., Bichler, Z., Wahle, P., et al. (2010). Exercise can rescue recognition memory impairment in a model with reduced adult hippocampal neurogenesis. *Frontiers in Behavioral Neuroscience, 3*, 34. http://dx.doi.org/10.3389/neuro.08.034.2009.

Leh, S. E., Petrides, M., & Strafella, A. P. (2010). The neural circuitry of executive functions in healthy subjects and Parkinson's disease. *Neuropsychopharmacology, 35*, 70–85.

Lessmann, V., Gottmann, K., & Malcangio, M. (2003). Neurotrophin secretion: current facts and future prospects. *Progress in Neurobiology, 69*, 341–374.

Levin, B. E., & Dunn-Meynell, A. (2004). Chronic exercise lowers the defended body weight gain and adiposity in diet-induced obese rats. *American Journal of Physiology: Regulatory, Integrative and Comparative Physiology, 286*, R771–R778.

Liu, Y. F., Chen, H. I., Wu, C. L., Kuo, Y. M., Yu, L., Huang, A. M., et al. (2009). Differential effects of treadmill running and wheel running on spatial or aversive learning and memory: roles of amygdalar brain-derived neurotrophic factor and synaptotagmin 1. *Journal of Physiology, 587*, 3221–3231.

Lømo, T. (2003). The discovery of long-term potentiation. *Philosophical Transactions of the Royal Society of London: Series B, Biological Sciences, 358*, 617–620.

Lu, N. Z., Wardell, S. E., Burnstein, K. L., DeFranco, D., Fuller, P. J., Giguere, V., et al. (2006). International Union of Pharmacology. LXV. The pharmacology and classification of the nuclear receptor superfamily: glucocorticoid, mineralocorticoid, progesterone, and androgen receptors. *Pharmacological Reviews, 58*, 782–797.

Lupien, S. J., Gillin, C. J., & Hauger, R. L. (1999). Working memory is more sensitive than declarative memory to the acute effects of corticosteroids: a dose-dependent study in humans. *Behavioral Neuroscience, 113*, 420–430.

Marques, E., Vasconcelos, F., Rolo, M. R., Pereira, F. C., Silva, A. P., Macedo, T. R., et al. (2008). Influence of chronic exercise on the amphetamine-induced dopamine release and neurodegeneration in the striatum of the rat. *Annual of the New York Academy of the Sciences, 1139*, 222–231.

Masuda, T., Nakagawa, S., Boku, S., Nishikawa, H., Takamura, N., Kato, A., et al. (2011). Noradrenaline increases neural precursor cells derived from adult rat dentate gyrus through β2 receptor. *Progress in Neuropsychopharmacology: Biological Psychiatry, 36*, 44–51.

Matthews, V. B., Aström, M. B., Chan, M. H., Bruce, C. R., Krabbe, K. S., & Prelovsek, O. (2009). Brain-derived neurotrophic factor is produced by skeletal muscle in response to contraction and enhances fat oxidation via activation of AMP-activated protein kinase. *Diabetologia, 52*, 1409–1418.

McDonnell, M. N., Smith, A. E., & Mackintosh, S. F. (2011). Aerobic exercise to improve cognitive function in adults with neurological disorders: a systematic review. *Archives of Physical Medicine and Rehabilitation, 92*, 1044–1052.

McMorris, T., Davranche, K., Jones, G., Hall, B., & Minter, C. (2009). Acute incremental exercise, performance of a central executive task, and sympathoadrenal system and hypothalamic-pituitary-adrenal axis activity. *International Journal of Psychophysiology, 73*, 334–340.

McMorris, T., & Hale, B. J. (2012). Differential effects of differing intensities of acute exercise on speed and accuracy of cognition: a meta-analytical investigation. *Brain and Cognition, 2012*(80), 338–351.

McMorris, T., Myers, S., MacGillivary, W. W., Sexsmith, J. R., Fallowfield, J., Graydon, J., et al. (1999). Exercise, plasma catecholamine concentration and decision-making performance of soccer players on a soccer-specific test. *Journal of Sport Science, 17,* 667–676.

Meeusen, R., & De Meirleir, K. (1995). Exercise and brain neurotransmission. *Sports Medicine, 20,* 160–188.

Meeusen, R., Piacentini, M. F., & De Meirleir, K. (2001). Brain microdialysis in exercise research. *Sports Medicine, 31,* 965–983.

Miyashita, T., & Williams, C. L. (2006). Epinephrine administration increases neural impulses propagated along the vagus nerve: role of peripheral beta-adrenergic receptors. *Neurobiology of Learning and Memory, 85,* 116–124.

Molinoff, P. B., & Axelrod, J. (1971). Biochemistry of catecholamines. *Annual Review of Biochemistry, 40,* 465–500.

Molteni, R., Ying, Z., & Gomez-Pinilla, F. (2002). Differential effects of acute and chronic exercise on plasticity-related genes in the rat hippocampus revealed by microarray. *European Journal of Neuroscience, 16,* 1107–1116.

Mountjoy, K. G., Mortrud, M. T., Low, M. J., Simerly, R. B., & Cone, R. D. (1994). Localization of the melanocortin-4 receptor (MC4-R) in neuroendocrine and autonomic control circuits in the brain. *Molecular Endocrinology, 8,* 1298–1308.

Nappi, G., Facchinetti, F., Bono, G., Petraglia, F., Sinforiani, E., & Genezzani, A. R. (1986). CSF and plasma levels pro-opiomelanocortin-related peptides in reversible ischaemic attacks and strokes. *Journal of Neurology, Neurosurgery and Psychiatry, 49,* 17–21.

Neeper, S. A., Gomez-Pinilla, F., Choi, J., & Cotman, C. W. (1995). Exercise and brain neurotrophins. *Nature, 373,* 109.

Newcomer, J. W., Selke, G., Meslon, A. K., Heershey, T., Craft, S., Richards, K., et al. (1999). Decreased memory performance in healthy humans induced by stress-level cortisol treatment. *Archives of General Psychiatry, 56,* 527–533.

Oldendorf, W. H. (1977). The blood–brain barrier. *Experimental Eye Research, 25,* 177–190.

O'Neal, H. A., van Hoomissen, J. D., Holmes, P. V., & Dishman, R. K. (2001). Prepro-galanin messenger RNA levels are increased in rat locus coeruleus after treadmill exercise training. *Neuroscience Letters, 299,* 69–72.

Otte, C., Moritz, S., Yassouridis, A., Koop, M., Madrischewski, A. M., Wiedermann, K., et al. (2007). Blockade of the mineralocorticoid receptor in healthy men: effects on experimentally induced panic symptoms, stress hormones and cognition. *Neuropsychopharmacology, 32,* 232–238.

Pan, W., Banks, W. A., Fasold, M. B., Bluth, J., & Kastin, A. J. (1998). Transport of brain-derived neurotrophic factor across the blood–brain barrier. *Neuropharmacology, 37,* 1553–1561.

Pang, P. T., Teng, H. K., Zaitsev, E., Woo, N. T., Sakata, K., Zhen, S., et al. (2004). Cleavage of proBDNF by tPA/plasmin is essential for long-term hippocampal plasticity. *Science, 306,* 487–491.

Park, E., Chan, O., Li, Q., Kiraly, M., Matthews, S. G., Vranic, M., et al. (2005). Changes in basal hypothalamo-pituitary-adrenal activity during exercise are centrally mediated. *American Journal of Physiology: Regulatory, Integrative and Comparative Physiology, 289,* R1360–R1371.

Peyrin, L., Pequignot, J. M., Lacour, J. R., & Fourcade, J. 1987). Relationships between catecholamine or 3-methoxy 4-hydroxy phenylglycol changes and the mental performance under submaximal exercise in man. *Psychopharmacology, 93,* 188–192.

Podolin, D. A., Munger, P. A., & Mazzeo, R. S. (1991). Plasma-catecholamine and lactate response during graded-exercise with varied glycogen conditions. *Journal of Applied Physiology, 71,* 1427–1433.

van Praag, H., Christie, B. R., Sejnowski, T. J., & Gage, F. H. (1999). Running enhances neurogenesis, learning, and long-term potentiation in mice. *Proceedings of the National Academy of Sciences of the United States of America, 96,* 13427–13431.

Pribram, K. H., & McGuinness, D. (1975). Arousal, activation and effort in the control of attention. *Psychological Review, 82,* 116–149.

Ruiz De Almodovar, C., Lambrechts, D., Mazzone, M., & Carmeliet, P. (2009). Role and therapeutic potential of VEGF in the nervous system. *Physiological Review, 89,* 607–648.

Sartorius, A., Hellweg, R., Litzke, J., Dormann, C., Vollmayr, B., Danker-Hopfe, H., et al. (2009). Correlations and discrepancies between serum and brain levels of neurotrophins after electroconvulsive treatment in rats. *Pharmacopsychiatry, 42,* 270–276.

Schaaf, M. J. M., Sibug, R. M., Duurland, R., Fluttert, M. F., Oitzl, M. S., De Kloet, E. R., et al. (1999). Corticosterone effects on BDNF mRNA expression in the rat hippocampus during Morris Water Maze training. *Stress, 3,* 173–183.

Schiffer, T., Schulte, S., Hollmann, W., Bloch, W., & Strüder, H. K. (2009). Effects of strength and endurance training on brain-derived neurotrophic factor and insulin-like growth factor 1 in humans. *Hormone and Metabolic Research, 41,* 250–254.

Seifert, T., Brassard, P., Wissenberg, M., Rasmussen, P., Nordby, P., Stallknecht, B., et al. (2010). Endurance training enhances BDNF release from the human brain. *American Journal of Physiology: Regulatory, Integrative and Comparative Physiology, 298,* R372–R377.

Selye, H. (1956). *The stress of life.* New York: McGraw-Hill.

Shojaei, E. A., Farajov, A., & Jafari, A. (2011). Effect of moderate aerobic cycling on some systemic inflammatory markers in healthy active collegiate men. *International Journal of General Medicine, 4,* 79–84.

Smith, P. J., Blumenthal, J. A., Hoffman, B. M., Cooper, H., Strauman, T. A., Welsh-Bohmer, K., et al. (2010). Aerobic exercise and neurocognitive performance: a meta-analytic review of randomized controlled trials. *Psychosomatic Medicine, 72*, 239–252.

Sothmann, M. S., Gustafson, A. B., Garthwaite, T. L., Horn, T. S., & Hart, B. A. (1988). Cardiovascular fitness and selected adrenal-hormone responses to cognitive stress. *Endocrine Research, 14*, 59–69.

Sothmann, M. S., Hart, B. A., & Horn, T. S. (1992). Sympathetic nervous-system and behavioral responses to stress following exercise training. *Physiology and Behavior, 51*, 1097–1103.

Soya, H., Nakamura, T., Deocaris, C. C., Kimpara, A., Iimura, M., Fujikawa, T., et al. (2007). BDNF induction with mild exercise in the rat hippocampus. *Biochemical and Biophysical Research Communications, 358*, 961–967.

Stones, M. J., & Kozma, A. (1989). Age, exercise, and coding performance. *Psychology of Aging, 4*, 190–194.

Stroth, S., Kubesch, S., Dieterle, K., Ruchsow, M., Heim, R., & Kiefer, M. (2009). Physical fitness, but not acute exercise modulates event-related potential indices for executive control in healthy adolecents. *Brain Research, 1269*, 114–124.

Stroth, S., Reinhardt, R. K., Thone, J., Hille, K., Schneider, M., Hartel, S., et al. (2010). Impact of aerobic exercise training on cognitive functions and affect associated to the COMT polymorphism in young adults. *Neurobiology of Learning and Memory, 94*, 364–372.

Strüder, H. K., Hollmann, W., Platen, P., Rost, R., Weicker, H., Kirchhof, O., et al. (1999). Neuroendocrine system and mental function in sedentary and endurance-trained elderly males. *International Journal of Sports Medicine, 20*, 159–166.

Timofeeva, E., Huang, Q., & Richard, D. (2003). Effects of treadmill running on brain activation and the corticotropin-releasing hormone system. *Neuroendocrinology, 77*, 388–405.

Tong, L., Shen, H., Perreau, V. M., Balazs, R., & Cotman, C. W. (2001). Effects of exercise on gene-expression profile in the rat hippocampus. *Neurobiology of Disease, 8*, 1046–1056.

Tümer, N., Demirel, H. A., Serova, L., Sabban, E. L., Broxson, C. S., & Powers, S. K. (2001). Gene expression of catecholamine biosynthetic enzymes following exercise: modulation by age. *Neuroscience, 103*, 703–711.

Vaynman, S., Ying, Z., & Gomez-Pinilla, F. (2004). Hippocampal BDNF mediates the efficacy of exercise on synaptic plasticity and cognition. *European Journal of Neuroscience, 20*, 2580–2590.

van Veen, V., Cohen, J. D., Botvinick, M. M., Stenger, V. A., & Carter, C. S. (2001). Anterior cingulate cortex, conflict monitoring, and levels of processing. *NeuroImage, 14*, 1302–1308.

van Veen, V., Krug, M. K., & Carter, C. S. (2008). The neural and computational basis of controlled speed-accuracy tradeoff during task performance. *Journal of Cognitive Neuroscience, 20*, 1952–1965.

Velásquez-Martinez, M. C., Vázquez-Torres, R., & Jiménez-Riveira, C. A. (2012). Activation of alpha1-adrenoreceptors enhances glutamate release onto ventral tegmental area dopamine cells. *Neuroscience, 216*, 18–30.

Verstynen, T. D., Lynch, B., Miller, D. L., Voss, M. W., Prakash, R. S., Chaddock, L., et al. (2012). Caudate nucleus volume mediates the link between cardiorespiratory fitness and cognitive flexibility in older adults. *Journal of Aging Research, 2012*. http://dx.doi.org/10.1155/2012/939285 939285.

Vgontzas, A. N., Pejovic, S., Zoumakis, E., Lin, H. M., Bixier, E. O., Basta, M., et al. (2007). Daytime napping after a night of sleep loss decreases sleepiness, improves performance, and causes beneficial changes in cortisol and interleukin-6 secretion. *American Journal of Physiology: Endocrinology Metabolism, 292*, E253–E261.

Voss, M. W., Chaddock, L., Kim, J. S., VanPatter, M., Pontifex, M. B., Raine, L. B., et al. (2011). Aerobic fitness is associated with greater efficiency of the network underlying cognitive control in preadolescent children. *Neuroscience, 199*, 166–176.

Voss, M. W., Erickson, K. I., Prakash, R. S., Chaddock, L., Kim, J. S., Alves, H., et al. (2013). Neurobiological markers of exercise-related brain plasticity in older adults. *Brain, Behavior, and Immunity, 28*, 90–99.

Voss, M. W., Nagamatsu, L. S., Liu-Ambrose, T., & Kramer, A. F. (2011). Exercise, brain, and cognition across the life span. *Journal of Applied Physiology, 111*, 1505–1513.

Waterhouse, E. G., & Xu, B. (2009). New insights into the role of brain-derived neurotrophic factor in synaptic plasticity. *Molecular and Cellular Neurosciences, 42*, 81–89.

Waymire, J. C., & Craviso, G. L. (1993). Multiple site phosphorylation and activation of tyrosine hydroxylase. *Advances in Protein Phosphotases, 7*, 501–513.

Weinstein, A. A., Deuster, P. A., Francis, J. L., Bonsall, R. W., Tracy, R. P., & Kop, W. (2010). Neurohormonal and inflammatory hyper-responsiveness to acute mental stress in depression. *Biological Psychology, 84*, 228–234.

Whiteman, A. S., Young, D. E., He, X., Chen, T. C., Wagenaar, R. C., Stern, C. E., et al. (2014). Interaction between serum BDNF and aerobic fitness predicts recognition memory in healthy young adults. *Behavioral Brain Research, 259*, 302–312.

Wittert, G. A., Livesey, J. H., Espiner, E. A., & Donald, R. A. (1996). Adaptation of the hypothalamopituitary adrenal axis to chronic exercise in humans. *Medicine and Science in Sports and Exercise, 28*, 1015–1019.

Wolf, O. T., Convit, A., McHugh, P. F., Kandil, E., Thorn, E. L., De Santi, S., et al. (2001). Cortisol differentially affects memory in young and elderly men. *Behavioral Neuroscience, 115*, 1002–1011.

Zheng, H., Liu, Y., Li, W., Yang, B., Chen, D., Wang, X., et al. (2006). Beneficial effects of exercise and its molecular mechanisms on depression in rats. *Behavioral Brain Research, 168*, 47–55.

Zigmond, R. E., Schwarzschild, M. A., & Rittenhouse, A. R. (1989). Acute regulation of tyrosine hydroxylase by nerve activity and by neurotransmitters via phosphorylation. *Annual Review of Neuroscience, 12*, 415–461.

Zoladz, J. A., Pilc, A., Majerczxak, J., Grandys, M., Zapart-Bukowska, J., & Duda, K. (2008). Endurance training increases plasma brain-derived neurotrophic factor concentration in young healthy men. *Journal of Physiology and Pharmacology, 59*(Suppl. 7), 119–132.

Dalsgaard, M. K., Ott, P., Dela, F., Juul, A., Pedersen, B. K., Warburg, J., et al. (2004). The CSF and arterial to internal jugular venous hormonal differences during exercise in humans. *Experimental Physiology, 89*, 271–277.

Goekint, M., Heyman, E., Roelands, B., Njemini, R., Bautmans, I., Mets, T., et al. (2008). No influence of noradrenaline manipulation on acute exercise-induced increase of brain derived neurotrophic factor. *Medicine and Science in Sports and Exercise, 40*, 1990–1998.

Further Reading

Chang, Y.-K., Tsai, C.-L., Hung, T.-M., So, E. C., Chen, F.-T., & Etnier, J. L. (2011). Effects of acute exercise on executive function: a study with a Tower of London task. *Journal of Sport and Exercise Psychology, 33*, 847–865.

The Chronic Exercise–Cognition Interaction: fMRI Research

Michelle W. Voss

Department of Psychological and Brain Sciences, Aging Mind and Brain Initiative (AMBI), The University of Iowa, Iowa City, IA, USA

PHYSICAL ACTIVITY PROMOTES BETTER MENTAL HEALTH BUT HOW REMAINS AN OPEN QUESTION

It may seem like common knowledge that exercise is good for you, and so it may be no surprise that physical activity and exercise are good for your mental health. Indeed, philosophers and physicians have been aware that exercise is good for general health and may reduce age-related "senility" since before the Common Era (Tipton, 2014). These early explanations for the observed benefits circled around the ability for exercise to bring the body into "harmony" with the elements and promote a strong body in stature and function regarding digestive and other regulatory systems in the body.

Today, the most common explanations for the relationship between physical exercise and mental health are that when you exercise you release endorphins that make you feel good, and exercise increases blood flow to the brain.

While these are simplified forms of existing theoretical views about why physical activity affects mental health, even the more extensive theoretical descriptions of these theories cannot explain the numerous observed benefits of physical activity on the brain and mental health. For example, numerous studies have documented that if you block the receptors for a specific molecule called brain-derived neurotrophic factor (BDNF) during exercise, the positive effects of exercise on learning and memory are also blocked (Gomez-Pinilla, Vaynman, & Ying, 2008; Vaynman, Ying, & Gomez-Pinilla, 2004). Since there is no reason to believe that blocking BDNF during exercise would inhibit exercise-induced increases in cerebral blood flow (CBF), these data suggest that an alternative or complementary explanation is needed to explain how exercise improves learning and memory. Furthermore, several studies have demonstrated that the benefits of exercise on BDNF expression can occur after just days of exposure to running (Cotman & Berchtold, 2002), which is too short a time before

Exercise-Cognition Interaction
http://dx.doi.org/10.1016/B978-0-12-800778-5.00009-8

stable changes in cerebral vasculature could be expected to occur.

Other theories have tried to account for these findings, but as of yet no one theory can account for the observed effects of exercise on the brain and cognition. Thus, the field is in need of a more unified and testable theory about how physical activity and exercise affect the brain over the lifespan. This is increasingly important as exercise is being more formally acknowledged as medicine for both preventive and restorative treatment (Lobelo, Stoutenberg, & Hutber, 2014). Yet, for exercise to be effectively prescribed, we must understand how it affects both the central and peripheral nervous systems. There is strong scientific support for the idea that the relationship is bidirectional, and that exercise has direct effects on the brain similar to how it directly affects specific muscles. Together, through investigation with animal models and human neuroscience, we can determine more specifically how these bidirectional pathways work.

With this in mind, the goal of this chapter is to introduce a subset of tools of human neuroscience that have been utilized to study how physical activity and exercise affect the brain and mental health, and to outline their promise and limitations, and outstanding questions for future research. In particular, the chapter focuses on functional magnetic resonance imaging (fMRI) research, and where appropriate it briefly highlights related magnetic resonance (MR) imaging approaches that are complementary to limitations of fMRI.

A BRIEF REVIEW OF THEORETICAL MODELS ON THE MECHANISTIC RELATIONSHIP BETWEEN PHYSICAL ACTIVITY AND MENTAL HEALTH

Before I introduce fMRI research methods that have been used to study the links between physical activity and optimal or improved mental health, I first briefly review several theoretical models that form the basis for hypothesis testing with fMRI and closely related methods. These models are not mutually exclusive (e.g., see Figure 1) but represent the different forms of theoretical models for how physical activity and habitual exercise affect the brain and in turn mental health. Notably, I do not discuss what has been phrased an "endorphin hypothesis" that focuses on the acute effects of exercise on signaling pathways affecting mood and cognitive performance (McMorris, 2009). While the endorphin model may provide insight into the chronic effects of physical activity on mental health, so far there is relatively little research in humans and future research will be needed to generate testable research questions with fMRI.

Cardiovascular Fitness Hypothesis

The cardiovascular fitness hypothesis proposes that cardiovascular (i.e., "aerobic") fitness is the physiological mediator that explains the relationship between physical exercise and improved cognitive performance. Cardiovascular fitness refers to the physical work capacity of an individual, in the form of amount of oxygen capacity per kilogram of body weight over time (mL/kg/min) (ACSM, 2013; Casperson, Powell, & Christenson, 1985). The cardiovascular fitness hypothesis was first proposed in a specific relationship to depression (Morgan, 1969; North, McCullagh, & Tran, 1990) and psychomotor speed (Spirduso, 1980), and the literature has found some support for this hypothesis in nondepressed populations and, for varied cognitive abilities, in preadolescents (Chaddock et al., 2010; Hillman, Castelli, & Buck, 2005; Pontifex et al., 2011), young adults (Åberg et al., 2009), and elderly adults (Erickson et al., 2009; Prakash et al., 2011; Voss et al., 2010). These studies have largely taken the form of examining the cross-sectional correlation between cardiorespiratory fitness (as measured by a graded maximal exercise test)

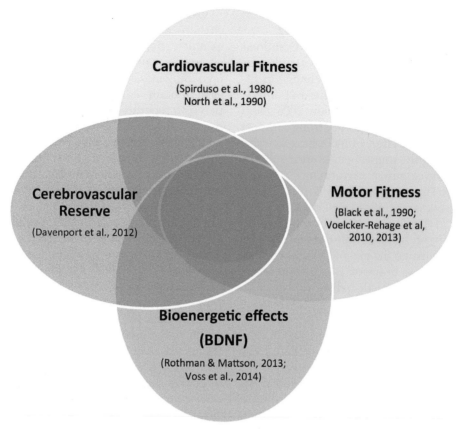

FIGURE 1   Broad theories of mechanistic links between physical activity and optimal mental health.

and a measure of brain structure, a functional biomarker of brain physiology with noninvasive neuroimaging, or cognitive performance. Several training studies have also found support for a correlation between change in fitness and change in brain structure (Erickson et al., 2011; Voss, Heo et al., 2013).

In human studies operating under this hypothesis, it is common for fitness to be used as a manipulation check (Brickman et al., 2014; Dustman et al., 1984), with the implication that gains in cardiovascular fitness are necessary for gains in brain health and cognition to be observed. The proposed sequence of effects would be that increases in cardiovascular fitness are related to improved oxygen transport

and metabolism that would also be realized in the brain, which in turn would support more efficient neurotransmitter function and improve cognitive performance (Dustman et al., 1990, 1984). However, as noted in Dustman et al. (1984), "Since VO_2 max is not specific for brain oxygen consumption and since there is no reason to expect that exercise related increases in oxygen to the brain would closely parallel increases to muscle, a direct relationship between VO_2 max and neuropsychological measures would not be predicted" (pp. 39–40). Thus, while cardiovascular fitness may be a good proxy for a history of moderate and/or vigorous intensity physical activity, the missing link for this hypothesis is exactly how adaptations related to changes in cardiovascular fitness are related to adaptations in the brain.

Moreover, a meta-analysis that examined whether training studies tend to see greater change in cognition with greater change in fitness did not find support for this hypothesis (Etnier, Nowell, Landers, & Sibley, 2006), and animal studies have not found strong support for a dose–response effect of increasing exercise behavior in highly trained endurance rodents and increasing cognitive performance (Rhodes et al., 2003). Thus, overall there is mixed support for the causal significance of cardiorespiratory fitness in the relationship between physical activity and brain health, and future studies are needed to determine the extent to which fitness directly affects the brain or is a physiological correlate of the mechanistic pathway.

Motor Fitness Hypothesis

More recently, a group of researchers have begun to formally distinguish between the metabolic adaptations with cardiovascular fitness training and the motor learning components (Voelcker-Rehage, Godde, & Staudinger, 2010; Voelcker-Rehage & Niemann, 2013). The motor fitness hypothesis proposes that there are unique and overlapping contributions from the perceptual and higher-level cognitive processing demands of motor coordination, needed for perceptual-motor mapping, adaptive motor planning, and postural control. Thus, the hypothesis predicts that activities that increase demand on these motor-learning components will increase an individual's "motor fitness" and that this will be associated with improved cognitive performance, particularly in domains of perceptual speed and executive control. The motor fitness hypothesis mirrors paradigms in animal models that would directly compare the benefits of motor learning with repetitive (automatic) motor activity (Black, Isaacs, Anderson, Alcantara, & Greenough, 1990).

Overall, this type of paradigm led to the conclusion that motor learning may not demand as much energy expenditure but that it is more effective at increasing the density of synapses (synaptogenesis) and blood vessels (angiogenesis) in brain regions involved in learning compared to repetitive motor activity that involved the same limbs as the learning tasks. While there is still very little human intervention research that directly compares motor fitness training to repetitive motor activities like walking, initial results support that they elicit both common and distinct adaptations on the brain and cognition (Niemann, Godde, & Voelcker-Rehage, 2014; Voelcker-Rehage et al., 2010).

It is interesting to note that the motor fitness hypothesis recognizes the multifaceted nature of cardiovascular fitness that Spirduso initially proposed, whereby cardiovascular fitness is a combination of one's physical work capacity and neuromuscular and motor skill integrity (Spirduso, 1980). Thus, the hypothesis can be seen as breaking apart the cardiovascular fitness hypothesis as originally proposed into two distinct components of (1) metabolic capacity for physical work and (2) neuromuscular and motor skill function.

Cerebrovascular Reserve

Cerebrovascular reserve reflects the ability of CBF to increase relative to baseline in response to metabolic demand and its associated chemical, mechanical, or neural stimuli (Davenport, Hogan, Eskes, Longman, & Poulin, 2012). In 1978, Meyer (Meyer, Sakai, Naritomi, & Grant, 1978) characterized cerebrovascular reserve as, "the capacity of regional cerebral blood flow of the brain to increase as a result of induced regional increases of physiologic activity of cerebral neurones by a standard test of brain work. The cerebrovascular functional reserve may be diminished by impaired neuronal function and metabolism or by impaired capacity of diseased blood vessels to dilate or both" (p. 351). Thus, the concept reflects the integrity of the neurovascular unit and signaling mechanisms involved in cerebral autoregulation. In practice, cerebrovascular reserve is typically measured by cerebrovascular reactivity, which measures relative change in blood perfusion following vasoactive stimuli such as inhalation of carbon dioxide (CO_2) or hypoventilation (i.e., breath-holding). In regard to linking the effects of physical activity to improved mental health, the cerebrovascular reserve hypothesis predicts that greater physical activity protects the vascular system from age-related dysfunctions such as increased blood pressure, increased oxidative stress, and increased stiffening, and because these changes in vascular health have been associated with age-related cognitive decline (Brown & Thore, 2011; Iadecola, 2004), it is through this pathway that physical activity is beneficial for the brain and mental health (Davenport et al., 2012). Gauthier and colleagues (Gauthier et al., 2014) recently proposed that cardiorespiratory fitness could be linked with better brain and mental function due to a link between cardiorespiratory fitness and cerebrovascular reserve. However, their results also supported the idea that the links between cardiorespiratory fitness and cognition likely involve factors beyond the effect of fitness on cerebrovascular reserve, which remain to be determined.

Based on the reviewed literature, the cardiovascular fitness and cerebrovascular reserve hypotheses can be considered distinct and complementary proposals. The cardiovascular fitness hypothesis predicts that cardiovascular fitness is an integrated biomarker of the effect of exercise on optimal neuromuscular and neurovascular function, and that the link between cardiovascular fitness and brain health would be present throughout the lifespan. At face value, the hypothesis is not specific to cerebrovascular adaptations from exercise, and the model predicts that any exercise that improves cardiorespiratory fitness should be linked with improved brain health. In contrast, the cerebrovascular reserve hypothesis predicts that physical activity is associated with preserved reactivity of cerebral vasculature. For example, an intervention that would demonstrate improved cerebrovascular reserve without improved fitness, and demonstrate improved cognition that was specifically linked with improved cerebrovascular reserve, would show that improved fitness is not necessary for exercise to positively affect brain health.

While much of the literature supporting the cerebrovascular reserve hypothesis has not made links with cerebrovascular reserve in specific brain regions, recent evidence acknowledges and supports that these effects of exercise on the brain likely vary regionally (Gauthier et al., 2014), and this is precisely where MRI/fMRI shines as a tool to help investigate this hypothesis. Furthermore, as discussed more below, fMRI could be utilized to test predictions of theoretical models by examining the spatial overlap of associations between cardiorespiratory fitness and cerebrovascular reserve in the aging population.

Finally, it is important to note that none of the models discussed so far can fully accounts for the data showing improved learning and memory and markers of hippocampal health following only minutes, days, or just 2 weeks of training (Cotman & Berchtold, 2002). It is also hard to imagine how cerebrovascular reserve could be an explanation for the associations between physical activity and mental health in healthy preadolescent children (Hillman, Erickson, & Kramer, 2008). Thus, another hypothesis is needed to account for how physical activity could affect the brain and cognition independently of or in conjunction with its effects on neuromuscular function and cerebrovascular health.

Bioenergetic Effects

Studies, primarily from animal models, have shown that moderate intensity exercise affects signaling pathways by which the body and the brain communicate about energy homeostasis, which in turn affect systems important for cognition (Rothman & Mattson, 2013; Voss, Carr, Clark, & Weng, 2014). This hypothesis features BDNF transcription and signaling as a critical mediator for how the energetic demands or "challenges" associated with exercise are linked with improved cellular energy metabolism and reduced oxidative stress, which are critical factors for the downstream outcomes of exercise-induced synaptic plasticity and an organism's enhanced ability to learn and remember.

An attractive feature of this model is its potential to bridge across acute and chronic effects of exercise on the brain (Cotman & Berchtold, 2002; Molteni, Ying, & Gomez-Pinilla, 2002) and its integration of exercise into a broader perspective of energy expenditure and homeostatic processes. For instance, Mattson (Mattson, 2014) has proposed that "intermittent energetic challenges" are a fundamental physiological stimulus for regulating and optimizing the health of signaling pathways involved in learning and memory, neuroplasticity, and brain repair. Mattson draws on the example of how intermittent fasting and exercise have similar effects on the brain; in particular, both are associated with increased BDNF expression in the hippocampus. Indeed, a broad literature supports a role for BDNF as a critical mediator for the effects of exercise on learning and memory, and hippocampal structure and function (Voss, Vivar, Kramer, & van Praag, 2013). Another attractive feature of this model is the evidence for dysfunctional energy homeostasis and metabolism in the brain associated with age-related neurodegenerative disorders such as Alzheimer's disease and Parkinson's disease (Mattson, 2014). This means that understanding the central bioenergetic signaling pathways affected by physical activity could elucidate, in part, how physical activity reduces risk for these age-related diseases.

While fMRI cannot test predictions at the molecular level, several studies have tried to make links with this hypothesis using complementary MR imaging approaches. For instance, MR spectroscopy is an imaging technique that allows quantification of biomarkers of neuronal viability, and this has been used to observe regionally specific associations between fitness and brain health in elderly adults (Erickson et al., 2012). Similarly, MR supports a wide spectrum of imaging contrasts and a promising application of MR imaging will be to combine information from both qualitative (e.g., fMRI) and quantitative (e.g., spectroscopy) imaging to break down effects of physical activity on neurons and their signaling pathways in contrast or in conjunction with cerebrovascular integrity and reserve. Another possibility is the combination of measuring biomarkers in the periphery that are proposed to be part of the bidirectional pathways involved in the effects of exercise, and determine the extent to which their modulation is associated with regionally specific modulations in MR imaging biomarkers of neuronal network activity.

Overall, a unified model would likely encompass a combination of these theoretical models, and propose signaling pathways that overlap and/or compete, and their relative contributions for benefits on mental health throughout the lifespan. At the broadest level, a comprehensive model would also appreciate the integrated, bidirectional effects of exercise on the body and the brain (Fiuza-Luces, Garatachea, Berger, & Lucia, 2013). Of course, no one study can test such a comprehensive model; however, the models reviewed here present a start in expanding our theoretical understanding of the effects of physical activity on the brain and identifying gaps in knowledge that we need to address to understand benefits of physical activity at the level of the brain and eventually at an integrated systems level.

INTRODUCTION TO fMRI AS A TOOL IN HUMAN NEUROSCIENCE

Magnetic resonance imaging (MRI) was a breakthrough tool for human neuroscience in the 1980 and 1990s because of its ability to image brain structure and function noninvasively and throughout the brain with relatively good spatial resolution. The ability to image noninvasively is significant because there is no limit to how often successive scans can occur for the purposes of clinical monitoring or research studies that involve experimental manipulations during or between scans. No other noninvasive human imaging technique has the spatial coverage of the whole brain combined with the spatial resolution of millimeters.

Spatial Resolution

The spatial resolution of millimeters may seem too large to capture meaningful signal related to neuronal activity in the brain. Indeed, within a space of several millimeters there are several thousand neurons (or more) in a mesh dense with vasculature and glial cells (Thomas, Dennis, Bandettini, & Johansen-Berg, 2012). However, there are several reasons to believe that fMRI methodology is appropriate for measuring meaningful neural activity. First, fMRI gets the term functional from its ability to measure the hemodynamic response associated with neuronal activity. This blood flow response reflects a well-known relationship between neuronal stimulation and local microvascular changes of blood flow in capillary beds where there is high density of neuronal cell bodies (Iadecola, 2004; Ngai, Ko, Morii, & Winn, 1988). The ability to noninvasively image the blood flow coupled with neuronal activity came from the discovery of an "oxygenation-sensitive contrast [that] could be used to monitor regional oxygen usages in the brain" (Ogawa, Lee, Nayak, & Glynn, 1990, p. 77). This blood-oxygenation-level-dependent (BOLD) contrast in images is the basis of fMRI, measuring intensity variations in MR signal that reflect moment-to-moment changes in primarily venous oxygenation levels. Thus, when imaging for BOLD contrast, the gold standard for spatial resolution is not necessarily the resolution of individual neurons but rather the resolution of the hemodynamic response coupled with the activity of populations of neurons. The unit of spatial resolution in fMR images are 3D (volume) elements of pixels called voxels, and most studies in the last 10 years have had voxels of around 3–4 mm^3 in size. While this size is steadily shrinking with advancements in MR technology, even with this resolution there have been replications of the ability for the BOLD effect to capture local changes in blood flow associated with neuronal activity in animal models and the known organization of sensory systems in humans (Logothetis & Pfeuffer, 2004; Logothetis, 2012). Invasive studies with animals have also shown that the BOLD effect captures more integrative aspects of neuronal activity, such as local field potentials (sum of electrical activity from a population of neurons around a recording site, which reflects inputs and local interactions between neurons of a given population unit), and less so spiking or the outputs (Logothetis & Pfeuffer, 2004). Thus, BOLD fMR imaging is not as much constrained by the spatial constraints of MR imaging but by the spatial specificity of the hemodynamic response coupled with neuronal activity. Despite this limitation, as discussed above, there is good evidence to support the ability to image neuronal activity from populations of neurons that are active together to enable sensory and cognitive processes.

Temporal Resolution of the BOLD Response

Given that fMRI is based on measuring a hemodynamic response following neuronal activity, it follows that the method should have the ability to measure changes in blood flow over time. In general, the hemodynamic response has an overall cycle of about 12 s, and a typical sampling rate of BOLD images in fMRI is 2. Studies have also demonstrated that the shape of the hemodynamic response is unchanged when sampled at a faster sampling rate such as 500 ms. The general, or canonical, shape of the hemodynamic response is shown in Figure 2, for a response to a single short stimulus of neuronal activity. As illustrated, the hemodynamic response often has an initial dip, followed by a rise, peak, and fall, which are followed by an undershoot where the MR signal again dips below baseline. The initial dip is a short (1–2 s) decrease in MR signal, immediately following the onset of neuronal activity, and reflects an initial increase in the proportion of deoxygenated to oxygenated hemoglobin at the site of neuronal activity. Deoxygenated hemoglobin is paramagnetic and disrupts the magnetic field more so than oxygenated blood that is diamagnetic. Therefore, MR signal drops when the ratio of deoxy/oxy increases. Shortly following this local oxygen deficit, there is an inflow of oxygenated blood that supplies more oxygen than is extracted for supporting neuronal activity. This results in a decrease of the deoxy/oxy ratio and an increase in the MR signal that peaks at around 4–6 s following neuronal activity.

When the neuronal stimulation is repetitive or extended over time, the BOLD response also can plateau for up to 20 or 30 s. When neuronal activity ceases, it is believed that blood flow will return to normal while blood volume will remain elevated. This combination could result in a transient increase in the deoxy/oxy ratio reflected in a poststimulus undershoot of the MR signal. Importantly, it is known that the temporal pattern of the hemodynamic response varies slightly for different brain regions and individuals. For example, older adults have a delayed hemodynamic response and in general there is more variability throughout brain regions for older adults (D'Esposito, Deouell, & Gazzaley, 2003) and neurovascular coupling is affected with many age-related neurological diseases (Iadecola, 2004). This is important to keep in mind when using the BOLD effect as a tool to measure effects of physical activity or exercise on functional brain activity in older adults and populations with neurological disease. As

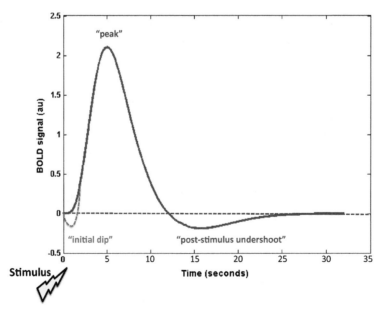

FIGURE 2　Illustration of a common hemodynamic response following a short stimulus that is modeled as a stimulus-evoked BOLD response in task-activation studies examining the links between cardiovascular fitness or physical activity and brain activation during cognitive tasks.

briefly reviewed above, cerebrovascular dynamics play a significant role in the BOLD response and since physical activity and exercise are also related to cerebrovascular health, care must be taken when interpreting the specificity of fMRI effects to neuronal activity. Indeed, some data indicate that cardiovascular fitness is associated with variations in neurovascular coupling in older adults (Fabiani et al., 2014).

Thus, fMR imaging uses the BOLD effect to measure a proxy of neuronal activity that is the relatively local hemodynamic response. Although the hemodynamic response is measured with a spatial resolution of millimeters and is sluggish compared to the timescale of neuronal activity, data support the use of fMRI to noninvasively image brain activity that maps onto the known organization of sensory systems. This leads to the prediction that fMRI may be a tool for discovering new knowledge about how sensory and cognitive processes are implemented in the human brain, and how interventions such as physical activity and exercise programs may improve cognitive performance. There are broadly two approaches to using fMRI to study the functional organization of brain systems: experimental and resting-state fMRI.

Experimental fMRI Approach

In the experimental fMRI approach, researchers experimentally manipulate sensory or psychological processes to systematically evoke perceptual and cognitive processes of interest, and use the BOLD effect to localize where brain activity occurs as a function of the manipulation. The word experimental reflects the importance of the experimental manipulation to the strength of the inferences about the psychological processes that underlie the observed BOLD response. As described above, the BOLD response is a proxy for neuronal activity and the fMRI method is noninvasive. In the majority of cases, fMRI is a correlational technique such that we measure the association between a behavioral manipulation on perceptual and/or psychological processes and the observed change in BOLD contrast. The method does not typically involve manipulation of brain function (e.g., from stimulation or lesion) followed by measurement of the effect on sensory or cognitive performance. Therefore, using fMRI to make links between sensory and psychological processes and how they are implemented in the brain depends on a strong theoretical knowledge of how to experimentally manipulate the sensory or psychological process(es) of interest.

Given a specific manipulation, mathematical models are formed to predict the hemodynamic response of neuronal activity that would be related to the presentation or predicted processing time of each task condition, and a brain map of the statistical relationship between the task model and the data represents which brain regions were most likely active as a function of the manipulation. Critically, since the BOLD signal is not an absolute quantitative measure of blood flow or neuronal activity, all fMRI results with the experimental approach are based on relative changes in BOLD signal between at least two task conditions (Amaro & Barker, 2006). The guiding principle in developing contrasts between task conditions is the pure insertion principle, whereby the goal is to insert the cognitive process of interest into one task condition while leaving the comparison condition the same in every way except the cognitive process of interest. For example, in the classic Stroop task, the control condition often requires responding to the font color of a word when the word is congruent with the color (RED in red font). This is contrasted with an experimental condition where a color word is printed in a color incongruent with its meaning (RED in blue font). In both conditions, participants are attending to color and making a response. Of critical interest is determining where there is a greater relative BOLD signal for the incongruent compared to the congruent condition. In theory, this BOLD signal would reflect brain activity associated with the cognitive process of inhibiting a prepotent response to the word meaning that was isolated based on the pure insertion principle. In practice, the pure insertion principle depends on many assumptions about the psychological demands of the task that may be difficult to empirically test. Therefore, fMRI experimenters must take care in the tasks used, preferably tasks that are well understood from behavioral studies, and experimenters always need to be aware of the possible confounds in their task designs when interpreting their data. Once the contrast(s) of interest are identified, the data can be interrogated to extract properties of the BOLD signal like percent change from baseline for different experimental conditions, strength of fit to the task or psychological model, or time course of the hemodynamic response with respect to the onset of task events. Thus, the experimental fMRI approach is used for questions that depend on examining the patterns and intensities of brain activity while individuals are engaged in specific, experimentally controlled psychological processes.

Within the experimental fMRI approach, there are two broad categories of experimental designs. The simplest approach is a block design, which presents stimuli from at least two conditions in blocks of trials such that within a block trials are typically presented within 0–2 s of each other. Since trials are so close together, the BOLD response to any given trial cannot be recovered. The goal within the block is to present as many trials as possible that all elicit the cognitive process of interest. The BOLD signal takes approximately 10 s to come down following a block so it is optimal to have at least 10 s rest between any two experimental blocks. Optimal block length is between 16 and approximately 30 s, although blocks of 40–50 s could also work (Amaro & Barker, 2006). Since trials are closely spaced, block designs are powerful for detecting the BOLD signal during a cognitive process of interest. However, their drawbacks include not being able to statistically remove error trials from the analysis; possible psychological

confounds of blocked trial presentation, such as expectation and task set or strategies; and, if the blocks are too long, the BOLD signal can become saturated and have a poor fit compared to the statistical model.

Therefore an alternative to the block design is an event-related design, whereby trials of different task conditions are interleaved over time (not clustered together). Algorithms such as optseq2 have been developed to help determine the optimal ordering of trials and timing between trials of different conditions. The basis for these decisions is to insert differential time delays between different trial types in order to minimize the correlation of the evoked BOLD time series between any two conditions. A common range of delays would be between 4 and 10 s, so trials can be spaced relatively close together to avoid participant boredom. Drawbacks of the event-related design include decreased statistical power, increased difficulty in implementation, some psychological processes are hard to turn on and off within a matter of seconds, and interpretation of the relative BOLD signal differences requires assumptions of a linear hemodynamic response system (Dale & Buckner, 1997).

Overall, the design of an experimental fMRI task requires forethought and planning in both the conceptual and methodological issues. Conceptually, the experimenter needs to ask: What is the theoretical background for my question? How was the task designed to measure a cognitive process (or multiple) of interest? Answering these questions often relies on background and expertise in experimental design principles from cognitive psychology. Methodologically, the experimenter needs to ask: What will the BOLD response look like given our schedule of task events? How do we optimize our paradigm to maximize our contrast(s) of interest? Answering these questions often involves a background in basic properties of the BOLD response and statistical models applied to fMRI analysis.

Resting-State fMRI

In contrast to the experimental approach, in the resting-state fMRI approach, individuals are instructed to lie quietly during the acquisition of MR images with BOLD contrast. Participants are told either to close their eyes without going to sleep, or to keep their eyes open and stare at a constant display of a small fixation cross. The rationale for this approach is the discovery that during this "resting state" many of the brain systems that are "evoked" by the experimental fMRI approach are also fluctuating in synchrony during rest (Smith et al., 2009), see Figure 3. Data support that the fluctuations in BOLD signal for these sensory and cognitive systems occur largely in a low frequency range of $0.001 < f < 0.10\,Hz$. The data from animal studies also support the concept that there are low frequency fluctuations in the activity of neuronal populations that are synchronized across spatially remote regions of association cortices, and that the spatial pattern of these fluctuations overlaps with sensory and cognitive systems shown through other animal and human neuroscience imaging methods (Keller et al., 2013; Leopold, Murayama, & Nikos, 2003).

There are numerous benefits of imaging at rest rather than during a task (see Figure 4). These benefits have resulted in a surge of the use of resting-state fMRI in the clinical and cognitive neuroscience fields (Andrews-Hanna, Smallwood,

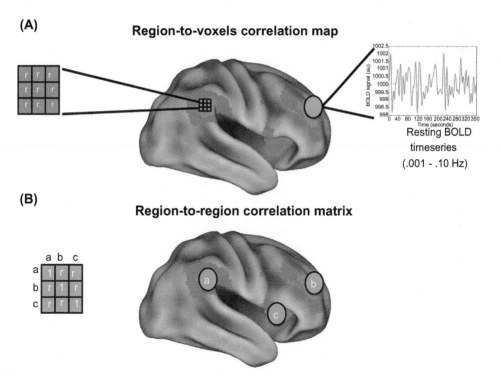

FIGURE 3   Resting-state BOLD signal can be used to examine the synchronous fluctuation of brain regions that form brain networks. Such networks often resemble spatial patterns of evoked BOLD signal during experimental task manipulations. Shown above are two approaches to summarizing synchrony of networks: (A) examine a correlation map for a given brain region of interest or (B) examine the region-to-region correlation of multiple brain regions of interest. The correlations in the correlation map or the region-to-region correlations could be used for further individual differences analyses related to examining the relationships between physical activity, brain function, and cognition.

	Task activation fMRI	Resting State fMRI
Advantages	• Greater experimental control • Examine brain activation during experimental manipulation of specific cognitive process(es) of interest • Behavioral performance measures often collected during scanning so it is possible to examine how brain activation *during* a cognitive process is related to performance • If motion is uncorrelated with the task, it is unlikely to *lead to* activation that may appear of interest	• Generalizable picture of a brain systems • More signal of interest compared to task-based subtractions • Task difficulty not a problem • No practice/re-test effects • Easy to include in a clinical protocol • Easy implementation across multi-site studies (e.g., ADNI) • Summary of mono- and multi-synaptic functional systems that is distinct from structural mapping
Disadvantages	• Measures of task activation depend on model of hemodynamic response and populations may differ in the temporal properties of the function • Interpretation of cognitive relevance depends on strength of task contrast(s) • Some tasks can be difficult to administer to a population diverse in age or clinical status • Task difficulty can be a confound for individual differences analyses • Must consider practice effects in longitudinal studies	• Very little experimental control over what the participant is thinking about • Highly influenced by motion, so individual differences in motion can confound individual differences in functional connectivity • Little agreement on how much data is enough for the most reliable estimates of resting state functional connectivity • Very difficult to examine directionality of region-to-region functional connectivity with resting state fMRI alone

FIGURE 4   Pros and cons of task-activation versus resting-state functional neuroimaging.

& Spreng, 2014). Measures of brain function are derived from different ways to measure the synchrony of known sensory and cognitive systems that are accepted to be present in healthy young individuals (Van Dijk et al., 2010). This approach can also be used to measure the specificity of synchronized BOLD fluctuations by comparing within versus between network fluctuations, inferring about the variability of BOLD fluctuations as a proxy of neuronal variability, or inferring about cerebrovascular reactivity from the amplitude of the BOLD fluctuations in the absence of neuronal "stimulation" from experimental manipulation.

Finally, it is important to recognize that the term "resting" in the phrase resting-state fMRI does not refer to a resting state with the absence of thought. Rather, it refers to an experimentally uncontrolled state. Of course, there are many individual differences associated with personality, attention, and memory that may drive variation in what someone's mind chooses to do during the resting state. This will likely influence the strength of correlation between brain regions in different systems, and is in part the basis of the prediction for why individual differences in the strength of networks derived from the resting BOLD signal would be related to sensory and cognitive abilities. These are important factors to consider when deciding between the experimental and resting-state fMRI approaches, and it is clear that ultimately both approaches can contribute to understanding how physical activity and exercise alter brain function across the lifespan.

THE USE OF fMRI TO TEST THEORIES THAT LINK PHYSICAL ACTIVITY AND MENTAL HEALTH

Now that we have some context for the major theories linking chronic physical activity to improved mental health, and the basics of the fMRI methodology, I briefly review studies that have used fMRI to examine relationships between physical activity and brain function, and provide a synopsis of results and future directions in the context of the theoretical models introduced above. Below is not meant to be an exhaustive review of the literature supporting each hypothesis. Rather the goal of the review is to describe how studies have used fMRI to test their predictions formed by these models.

Cardiovascular Fitness Hypothesis

The majority of studies in the literature that have used fMRI have examined the association between cardiovascular fitness and brain activation using an experimental fMRI approach. The overarching question addressed in these studies is whether brain activation differences between higher- and lower-fit individuals will provide insight into the neural mechanisms of how higher-fit individuals perform better. However, under this broad theme, fMRI provides flexibility in how task contrasts are used to map fitness to brain activation during cognitive processes, and this shapes the nature of the conclusions with regard to the cardiovascular

fitness hypothesis. Therefore, in the following paragraphs, I will highlight several studies that demonstrate distinct approaches in using fMRI to study how cardiovascular fitness is associated with brain activation during a cognitive task, and I will describe one study that applied a variant of resting-state fMRI.

I will first focus on a group of studies that examined the association between cardiovascular fitness and brain activation during a cognitive task designed to manipulate cognitive control. Cognitive control is a construct that represents our ability to control our thoughts and actions in accord with our goals, which includes processes of monitoring performance with respect to intentions, implementing control, and flexibly adapting behavior when expectations of behavior or performance are not met. Behavioral data generally support the idea that higher cardiovascular fitness is associated with faster and more accurate performance on tasks demanding a high degree of cognitive control in children (Hillman et al., 2008) and older adults (Colcombe et al., 2004; Kramer et al., 1999). One approach in determining the mechanism for how this relationship arises is to manipulate cognitive control processes during an fMRI scan in a population of individuals that vary in their cardiovascular fitness. Thus, cardiovascular fitness is the independent variable, with brain activation pattern as the dependent variable, or task performance as the dependent variable and brain activation features acting as a mediator variable.

Two studies that took the first approach examined the cross-sectional association between cardiovascular fitness and brain activation during a cognitive control task in healthy older adults (Colcombe et al., 2004; Prakash et al., 2011). The Colcombe et al. (2004) study examined differences in activation between a lower-fit and higher-fit group of older adults while they performed a modified event-related Eriksen flanker task. The flanker task requires participants to respond to the direction of a central arrow that is flanked by either arrows in a congruent direction with the target (i.e., <<<<<) or arrows incongruent with the target (i.e., <><<). The critical difference inserted on the incongruent condition is the evoked demand of inhibiting the competing response cues to make the correct response. Results showed that higher-fit older adults had greater BOLD signal (i.e., activation) in the incongruent > congruent contrast in the right middle frontal gyrus and bilateral superior parietal lobe, and less activation in the anterior cingulate cortex (ACC), in conjunction with better task performance. The interpretation was that greater fitness was associated with a greater ability for regions involved in cognitive control to physiologically adapt to task demands by invoking control with the prefrontal cortex and more efficiently resolving conflict signals from the ACC. An additional feature of this study was examining the overlap between areas associated with fitness and the areas that showed a change in activation following 6 months of cardiovascular training (walking). While authors did not examine how change in activation was correlated with change in fitness, they examined whether fitness group differences were associated with brain activation in the same regions that would show training-related changes. The authors reported a qualitative overlap in the regions from these two analyses, suggesting the cross-sectional analysis was sensitive to areas that would change with increased fitness. The Colcombe et al. (2004) study illustrates the use of a well-accepted manipulation of a cognitive construct (flanker task) in application to the question of how older adults with greater fitness perform better on the task than those with lower fitness. Only one level of task difficulty was used to manipulate cognitive control, which provides a simple approach to first ask the question of whether brain activity during cognitive control processes is related to fitness.

However, even with only two task conditions, a selective association between fitness and the BOLD signal for one condition supports both an enhanced processing and vascularization

interpretation. That is, if activation during both the congruent and incongruent conditions was associated with fitness, it is possible that the enhanced BOLD signal is related to better vascularization of the tissue. However, when the association is selective (and especially if fitness is related to less activity), then this interpretation is less likely. The ability to hinge interpretations on cognitive processing then depends on the nature of the pure insertion assumptions of the task. If the experimental condition is proposed to activate all the same regions as the control condition, but just more or less, then there is stronger ground for a processing explanation. However, if the experimental condition is proposed to uniquely activate a particular brain region, then it is possible an association with fitness is the result of fitness having an influence on the vascularization of that brain region. This leaves interpretation open to both a neural processing account and a vascularization account of the effects.

An approach that pushes the basic contrast and resulting conclusions further is a parametric manipulation, whereby task conditions are explicitly designed to incrementally increase their demand on a cognitive process of interest. Prakash et al. (2011) used an event-related Stroop task to manipulate cognitive control demand by presenting two versions of the incongruent condition, including an easier incongruent-ineligible condition where the word was a color word but this color was not part of the possible font colors. In the more difficult incongruent-eligible condition, the color word was in a font that directly competed at both a conceptual (color) and response (task set) level. Healthy older adults, who varied on cardiovascular fitness, participated in the study, and higher fitness was associated with faster reaction time and better accuracy on only the most challenging condition (incongruent-eligible). In addition, while across all subjects there were no differences in activation between the two incongruent conditions, cardiovascular fitness was associated with greater activation of the bilateral prefrontal cortex for the eligible compared to the ineligible condition. Similar to the Colcombe et al. (2004) study, the interpretation was that greater fitness was associated with a greater ability for the prefrontal cortex to adaptively respond to increasing task difficulty. The Prakash et al. (2011) study pushed the specificity of the result by using a parametric manipulation of cognitive control in the Stroop task. The overall implication of the two studies is that cardiovascular fitness may be associated with prevention of age-related degradation of prefrontal cortex function. The use of fMRI allowed for the conclusion that the prefrontal cortex is a common region that may be functioning at a higher level for higher-fit older adults, compared to other regions that could also support enhanced cognitive control. Future studies would be needed to test the generalizability of this association beyond cognitive control tasks.

A concern with any study examining individual differences in brain activation as a function of fitness during a cognitive task is whether individual differences in performance, as related to fitness, are driving the activation differences. For example, in both the Colcombe et al. (2004) and Prakash et al. (2011) papers described above, the higher-fit individuals performed better on the task condition where they also showed greater relative BOLD activation. This leads to the possible confound of performance with fitness. For instance, what if it is the number of correct trials that leads to greater BOLD signal and not an inherent difference in physiological BOLD signal per any given trial? Church, Petersen, and Schlaggar (2010) discuss this problem in depth in the context of development. They note that one solution is to match populations (e.g., lower fit and higher fit) on performance before examining group differences in brain activation. This prevents activation differences from being confounded by performance, but could still be related to either task strategy or neurovascular function. We took this approach in a recent study where

we examined the mechanisms underlying the relationship between fitness and cognitive control performance in preadolescent children (Voss et al., 2011). Consistent with the literature, we found that higher-fit children performed more accurately on the most demanding condition of a modified flanker task compared to lower-fit children. We examined the differing activation patterns between groups by comparing performance-matched fitness groups on the Inc > Con contrast. Results showed that lower-fit children showed more activation than higher-fit children in areas associated with attentional control and inhibition, including left and right pre- and postcentral gyri, the supplementary motor area, the left insular cortex, and left middle frontal gyrus. However, there were two important details for interpretation: (1) the interaction was driven by group differences in activation during the congruent condition, such that higher-fit children showed greater activation during congruent trials relative to lower-fit children, and (2) greater activation in the incongruent condition was correlated with better performance. We interpreted these results to illustrate a difference in task strategy between groups, perhaps enabled by the greater flexibility in cognitive control for the higher-fit children. We interpreted the correlation with behavior as a pattern reflective of efficiency. Although the higher-fit group showed less activation, within the lower range of activity there was a positive correlation between activation and performance. Overall, these results illustrate the importance of fully breaking down a group × condition interaction in fMRI results, and examining the correlation between fMRI activation and behavior. Results from both steps are essential for a thorough interpretation of how individual differences in cardiovascular fitness are related to better cognitive performance. Regarding the pattern that higher fit showed lower activation, three factors could account for this: (1) the population was preadolescent children rather than older adults, (2) the groups were matched on performance, or (3) the task design in Voss et al. (2011) was a block design (with neutral trials built in to prevent expectation confounds within blocks) whereas the Colcombe and Prakash studies were event-related trial designs.

Finally, I described an approach called resting-state fMRI, where the goal is to measure the functional synchrony of brain networks that fluctuate together over time. Brain networks are collections of brain regions that have higher correlations with each other relative to other brain regions, and often the spatial patterns of the networks fluctuating at rest overlaps with observed brain activation patterns during experimental fMRI tasks (Smith et al., 2009). The implication of this is that brain networks, as observed in the resting state, may be one way to measure the integrity of brain systems important for cognition, without the constraints of measuring activation during only one representative task, without the task performance confounds described above, and without practice effects on the cognitive task if measuring before and after an exercise intervention. We recently examined the relationship between cardiovascular fitness and functional connectivity in a mediation model, whereby cardiovascular fitness was the independent variable, cognitive performance was the dependent variable, and functional connectivity between different regions in what is known as the "default mode network" or DMN were mediator variables (Voss et al., 2010). The DMN is a potential mediator because studies have linked functional synchrony of this network with better executive function (Andrews-Hanna et al., 2007; Damoiseaux et al., 2008; Hampson, Driesen, Skudlarski, Gore, & Constable, 2006), the network includes the hippocampus, which is well known to benefit from physical activity (Voss, Vivar et al., 2013), and while degradation of the DMN has been described as a predictor of risk for Alzheimer's disease (Greicius & Kimmel, 2012), studies have shown physical activity is protective against risk for cognitive

impairment and Alzheimer's (Sofi et al., 2011). We found that functional connectivity of primarily regions among the temporal and frontal regions of the DMN were associated with fitness and were mediators of the relationship between fitness and performance on executive function tasks. A striking pattern in the data was that all region-to-region pairs in the DMN, with a positive correlation with fitness, included one region from the frontal cortex. These results support the notion that cardiovascular fitness is protective of age-related functional degradation of the prefrontal cortex, and that the positive association between fitness and functional integration of the frontal cortex with the DMN is one explanatory factor in the protective effects of physical activity on AD.

As noted above, the cardiovascular fitness hypothesis suggests that cardiovascular (i.e., "aerobic") fitness is the physiological mediator that explains the relationship between physical exercise and improved cognitive performance. fMRI provides a tool to examine what brain systems operate differently during cognitive performance for individuals who vary in cardiovascular fitness. The ability to examine the spatial pattern of functional activation allows for hypotheses about the regional selectivity of the benefits of cardiovascular fitness, which in turn lends insight into the mechanism for the relationship between fitness and cognition. The data from experimental fMRI and resting-state fMRI overwhelmingly support a regionally selective association for prefrontal cortex function. A possible explanation for this association is that cardiovascular fitness is associated with better oxygen transport and metabolism in the brain, supporting more efficient function of neurotransmitters and neural circuits, and that the effect is most robust in regions with the most vulnerability in development and aging, such as the prefrontal cortex. There have been several reports of greater fitness being associated with less BOLD activation in conjunction with better performance, which suggests the BOLD signal in experimental fMRI tasks is not a measure wholly confounded with regional differences in blood flow or vascularization. However, the largest gap in the cardiovascular fitness theory is the absence of strong data showing that change in fitness is correlated with change in functional activity during a task or functional synchrony of clinically relevant brain networks.

Motor Fitness Hypothesis

The motor fitness hypothesis proposes that part of the benefit of cardiovascular fitness on brain health is derived from the increased experience-dependent plasticity of the motor system, derived from greater history of motor coordination from an active lifestyle. The hypothesis predicts that the plasticity of motor systems involved in exercise will increase an individual's "motor fitness" and this will be associated with improved motor and prefrontal cortex function. Thus the authors predict that both cardiovascular fitness and motor fitness would be related to prefrontal cortex function, whereas activities that specifically train motor fitness should be more selectively associated with functionality of circuits used during motor activities including parietal regions involved in spatial integration and action initiation (Voelcker-Rehage et al., 2010).

In their 2010 study, the authors tested this idea by having participants, who varied in both motor and cardiovascular fitness, complete a modified, blocked-design flanker task during fMRI scanning (Voelcker-Rehage et al., 2010). Unfortunately there were no selective effects for either type of fitness for the contrast of Inc > Con, and BOLD signal findings were only evaluated for all conditions compared to fixation baseline (rest) or for Inc > Rest. Therefore, it is difficult to make conclusions about the specificity of the results for neural processing compared to general benefits on neurovascular function or vascularization. Despite this weakness, it is noteworthy that higher-fit individuals, on both cardiovascular and motor dimensions, showed less prefrontal activation during the task compared to lower-fit individuals. This is intriguing given that this study also used a blocked fMRI design, and may suggest that the fMRI trial design is important in predicting whether higher fitness will be related to lower or higher BOLD signal during cognitive performance, with possible mediating factors being associated with a more proactive strategy of higher-fit individuals or enhanced maintenance of task sets within blocks (more efficiency over blocks). It is also notable that cardiovascular and motor fitness were associated with different regions of greater activation, with motor fitness selectively associated with greater activation in the inferior parietal lobes.

Similar to Colcombe et al. (2004), the authors published a follow-up study, in which they compared the effects of 12 months of cardiovascular training to motor fitness training and a stretching and control intervention (Voelcker-Rehage, Godde, & Staudinger, 2011). Results showed that increases in cardiovascular fitness were associated with activation decreases in the Inc > baseline contrast in several regions of the prefrontal cortex, including the middle frontal gyrus and the ACC, and the left parahippocampal gyrus and right superior and middle temporal gyrus. In contrast, several areas increased activation for the Inc > baseline contrast for the motor fitness training group including the thalamus, caudate nucleus, and the superior parietal lobe. While these results are similar to their cross-sectional findings, they are difficult to interpret in regard to cognitive mechanisms because the contrast is not well-specified to isolate cognitive control processes. Therefore, it will be important for future research to extend these results with more precise contrasts and to further characterize how similarly and differently cardiovascular and motor fitness training affect the aging brain and cognition.

Cerebrovascular Reserve

The cerebrovascular reserve hypothesis predicts that physical activity improves brain health because of its beneficial effect on the ability of CBF to increase in response to metabolic demand and its associated chemical, mechanical, or neural stimuli. Cerebrovascular reserve can be measured with transcranial Doppler measurements on the ascending arteries entering the brain, such as the middle cerebral artery (Brown et al., 2010); however, this method gives limited spatial information about where there are regional associations between cerebrovascular reserve and cardiovascular fitness. Greater spatial specificity can be achieved with MRI based on relative change in cerebral blood perfusion following vasoactive stimuli such as inhalation of carbon dioxide (CO_2) or hypoventilation (i.e., breath-holding).

For example, Gauthier et al. (2014) manipulated CO_2 inhalation using a computer-controlled gas delivery system during MRI scanning. Gas delivery was calibrated based on deviation from target values for end-tidal CO_2 and O_2 during the hypercapnic manipulation and during rest blocks. Regions of interest in the prefrontal cortex were defined based on task-related activation during a modified Stroop task for the contrast of Stroop switching > color naming (control) condition. The task was administered during a scan that simultaneously acquired images with BOLD contrast and a contrast optimized for measuring CBF called arterial spin labeling (ASL). The regions of interest were determined as the overlap of voxels showing activation for the Stroop switching > color naming contrast for both the BOLD and ASL images. In a hierarchical linear model, the authors examined the relative predictive value of age, gender, cardiovascular fitness, and prefrontal cerebrovascular reserve, among other variables capturing brain structure and cardiovascular risk factors, with respect to the dependent variable of reaction time on the most difficult condition of the Stroop task. They also examined regional associations between fitness and cerebrovascular reserve. In this model, only cardiovascular fitness was associated with faster reaction time, suggesting that cerebrovascular reserve in prefrontal regions involved in

the task did not add a significant amount of predictive value for cognitive performance. However, in a model with cerebrovascular reserve as the dependent variable, cardiovascular fitness was negatively associated with prefrontal cerebrovascular reserve. Finally, authors did an exploratory analysis to examine where there was a positive correlation between cardiovascular fitness and cerebrovascular reserve. They found the strongest positive correlation with a right periventricular white matter region, which is an area that typically suffers hypoperfusion with aging (Brown and Thore, 2011). Overall, results suggest that while there was a positive relationship between fitness and cerebrovascular reserve in an area that typically suffers age-related hypoperfusion, the mechanism is more complex than general protection of vascular function in all regions of the brain known to suffer age-related vascular impairments. A negative correlation between fitness and prefrontal cerebrovascular reserve is not generally consistent with the notion that fitness is associated with enhanced executive function due to better cerebrovascular reserve in areas typically associated with age-related decline in vascular function. This study highlights the need for more studies that use MRI and fMRI to examine the spatial specificity of the contribution of cerebrovascular reserve to the relationships between physical activity and mental health.

Bioenergetic Effects

The bioenergetics hypothesis predicts that the effects of exercise on the brain are independent of the specific movements learned or practiced during exercise, but that the causal agent is energy expenditure. BDNF is proposed to be a central mediator in the relationship between energy expenditure and improved mental health. Far fewer studies have examined this possibility with human neuroscience, due to the inability to measure BDNF expression in the brain using MRI. However, one study examined whether exercise training-related change in circulating BDNF protein (in blood) was related to exercise training-related change in functional connectivity of regions in the DMN (Voss, Erickson et al., 2013). We found that exercise training (walking)-associated increases in BDNF, as well as two additional neurotrophic factors (insulin-like growth factor-1 and vascular endothelial growth factor), were related to increases in functional connectivity between the bilateral hippocampus and the lateral middle temporal gyrus; these associations were not statistically significant in a stretching and toning control group. Further, we found greater baseline circulating BDNF was associated with greater change in functional connectivity of the same regions. While we cannot make direct links between circulating and central BDNF, this study represents an example of using fMRI to examine the links between exercise-induced changes in BDNF and spatial specificity of exercise-induced changes in brain function. That the relationship was shown in the hippocampus and temporal cortex is consistent with data from animal models showing that exercise positively affects BDNF expression in hippocampal tissue (Voss et al., 2013), suggesting potential for this approach in future studies.

SUMMARY AND OUTSTANDING QUESTIONS

In this chapter, I have reviewed some of the major theories linking physical activity to improved mental health, the basics of fMRI, and the application of fMRI to testing and advancing the theories. It is apparent that fMRI is a tool that has provided important insights and maintains great promise to advance our understanding of how physical activity improves mental health across the lifespan. Compared to other neuroimaging techniques, it is the only method we have to noninvasively measure brain structure and function with the same modality throughout the brain. The spatial and temporal resolutions combine to provide a functional resolution capable of capturing the functionality of neural circuits important for a wide spectrum of cognitive and affective processes. Furthermore, MR imaging of the BOLD contrast provides a tool for testing the regional specificity of effects on neural processing and cerebrovascular function. Overall, experimental and resting-state fMRI research, applied to understanding the benefits of physical activity on mental health, provides support for positive effects on the efficient engagement of the prefrontal cortex during cognitive control, particularly the superior frontal gyri, the dorsolateral prefrontal cortices, and the ACC. Resting-state fMRI data support the idea that physical activity may exert a positive effect on mental health through enhancement of the organization and synchrony of large-scale brain networks that include the hippocampus and the prefrontal cortex. Future research will be needed to make links between effects on task-evoked and resting-state networks, and to integrate structural MRI methods into fMRI analyses and interpretations.

However, even given the flexibility and array of approaches possible with fMRI, it is important to keep in mind what fMRI is blind to, and which converging measures best complement fMRI to test theories linking physical activity and mental health. Since fMRI is ultimately a hemodynamic indicator of neural activity, electrophysiological measures such as event-related potentials of neural processes are great complements in regard to temporal resolution. Regarding spatial resolution, few in vivo noninvasive imaging techniques offer better spatial resolution than fMRI. However, it is possible that sampling human tissue from biobanks or patients undergoing neurosurgical procedures will offer methods for more basic exercise neuroscience with a human population. An important future direction in the field will be greater adoption of multiple imaging modalities to determine a convergence of results and interpretation across methods and levels of analysis.

Finally, despite the growing body of work in exercise neuroscience, there are still important questions that fMRI will be an important tool for answering. For example, an important outstanding question is the extent to which physical activity and fitness modify neurovascular coupling and in turn the spatial and temporal properties of the BOLD signal. Studies that target neurovascular coupling mechanisms and measurement in humans are needed to advance knowledge on this question. It would be particularly interesting to determine whether animals that vary on wheel running training would show differences in neurovascular coupling as observed with combined electrophysiological stimulation and BOLD signal recordings. Another important outstanding question is the extent to which physical activity affects neural circuits that have a generalizable effect on cognitive constructs. The data support this possibility, but to date no studies have systematically studied this question with fMRI.

References

Åberg, M. A., Pedersen, N. L., Torén, K., Svartengren, M., Bäckstrand, B., Johnsson, T., et al. (2009). Cardiovascular fitness is associated with cognition in young adulthood. *Proceedings of the National Academy of Sciences, 106*(49), 20906–20911.

ACSM. (2013). *ACSM's guidelines for exercise testing and prescription* (9th ed.). Lippincott Williams & Wilkins.

Amaro, E., & Barker, G. J. (2006). Study design in fMRI: basic principles. *Brain and Cognition, 60*(3), 220–232. http://dx.doi.org/10.1016/j.bandc.2005.11.009.

Andrews-Hanna, J. R., Smallwood, J., & Spreng, R. N. (2014). The default network and self-generated thought: component processes, dynamic control, and clinical relevance. *Annals of the New York Academy of Sciences, 1316*(1), 29–52. http://dx.doi.org/10.1111/nyas.12360.

Andrews-Hanna, J. R., Snyder, A. Z., Vincent, J. L., Lustig, C., Head, D., Raichle, M. E., et al. (2007). Disruption of large-scale brain systems in advanced aging. *Neuron, 56*(5), 924–935. http://dx.doi.org/10.1016/j.neuron.2007.10.038.

Black, J. E., Isaacs, K. R., Anderson, B. J., Alcantara, A. A., & Greenough, W. T. (1990). Learning causes synaptogenesis, whereas motor activity causes angiogenesis, in cerebellar cortex of adult rats. *Proceedings of the National Academy of Sciences of the United States of America, 87*(14), 5568–5572. http://dx.doi.org/10.1073/pnas.87.14.5568.

Brickman, A., Khan, U., Provenzano, F., Yeung, L., Suzuki, W., Schroeter, H., et al. (2014). Enhancing dentate gyrus function with dietary flavanols improves cognition in older adults. *Nature Neuroscience.* http://dx.doi.org/10.1038/nn.3850.

Brown, A. D., McMorris, C., Longman, R., Leigh, R., Hill, M., Friedenreich, C., et al. (2010). Effects of cardiorespiratory fitness and cerebral blood flow on cognitive outcomes in older women. *Neurobiology of Aging, 31*(12), 2047–2057. http://dx.doi.org/10.1016/j.neurobiolaging.2008.11.002.

Brown, W. R., & Thore, C. R. (2011). Review: cerebral microvascular pathology in ageing and neurodegeneration. *Neuropathology and Applied Neurobiology, 37*(1), 56–74. http://dx.doi.org/10.1111/j.1365-2990.2010.01139.x.

Casperson, C., Powell, K. E., & Christenson, G. M. (1985). Physical activity, exercise, and physical fitness: definitions and distinctions for health-related research. *Public Health Reports, 100*(2), 126–131.

Chaddock, L., Erickson, K., Prakash, R., Kim, J., Voss, M., Vanpatter, M., et al. (2010). A neuroimaging investigation of the association between aerobic fitness, hippocampal volume, and memory performance in preadolescent children. *Brain Research, 1358,* 172–183. http://dx.doi.org/10.1016/j.brainres.2010.08.049.

Church, J. A., Petersen, S. E., & Schlaggar, B. L. (2010). The "Task B problem" and other considerations in developmental functional neuroimaging. *Human Brain Mapping, 31*(6), 852–862. http://dx.doi.org/10.1002/hbm.21036.

Colcombe, S., Kramer, A., Erickson, K., Scalf, P., McAuley, E., Cohen, N., et al. (2004). Cardiovascular fitness, cortical plasticity, and aging. *Proceedings of the National Academy of Sciences of the United States of America, 101*(9), 3316–3321. http://dx.doi.org/10.1073/pnas.0400266101.

Cotman, C., & Berchtold, N. (2002). Exercise: a behavioral intervention to enhance brain health and plasticity. *Trends in Neurosciences, 25*(6), 295–301.

Dale, A. M., & Buckner, R. L. (1997). Selective averaging of rapidly presented individual trials using fMRI. *Human Brain Mapping, 5*(5), 329–340. http://dx.doi.org/10.1002/(SICI)1097-0193(1997)5:5<329::AID-HBM1>3.0.CO;2-5.

Damoiseaux, J. S., Beckmann, C. F., Arigita, E. J., Barkhof, F., Scheltens, P., Stam, C. J., et al. (2008). Reduced resting-state brain activity in the "default network" in normal aging. *Cerebral Cortex, 18*(8), 1856–1864. http://dx.doi.org/10.1093/cercor/bhm207.

Davenport, M., Hogan, D., Eskes, G., Longman, R., & Poulin, M. (2012). Cerebrovascular reserve: the link between fitness and cognitive function? *Exercise and Sport Sciences Reviews, 40*(3), 153–158. http://dx.doi.org/10.1097/JES.0b013e3182553430.

D'Esposito, M., Deouell, L., & Gazzaley, A. (2003). Alterations in the BOLD fMRI signal with ageing and disease: a challenge for neuroimaging. *Nature Reviews Neuroscience*, 4(11), 863–872. http://dx.doi.org/10.1038/nrn1246.

Dustman, R., Emmerson, R., Ruhling, R., Shearer, D., Steinhaus, L., Johnson, S., et al. (1990). Age and fitness effects on EEG, ERPs, visual sensitivity, and cognition. *Neurobiology of Aging*, 11(3), 193–200.

Dustman, R., Ruhling, R., Russell, E., Shearer, D., Bonekat, H., Shigeoka, J., et al. (1984). Aerobic exercise training and improved neuropsychological function of older individuals. *Neurobiology of Aging*, 5(1), 35–42.

Erickson, K., Prakash, R., Voss, M., Chaddock, L., Hu, L., Morris, K., et al. (2009). Aerobic fitness is associated with hippocampal volume in elderly humans. *Hippocampus*, 19(10), 1030–1039. http://dx.doi.org/10.1002/hipo.20547.

Erickson, K., Voss, M., Prakash, R., Basak, C., Szabo, A., Chaddock, L., et al. (2011). Exercise training increases size of hippocampus and improves memory. *Proceedings of the National Academy of Sciences of the United States of America*, 108(7), 3017–3022. http://dx.doi.org/10.1073/pnas.1015950108.

Erickson, K., Weinstein, A., Sutton, B., Prakash, R., Voss, M., Chaddock, L., et al. (2012). Beyond vascularization: aerobic fitness is associated with N-acetylaspartate and working memory. *Brain and Behavior*, 2(1), 32–41. http://dx.doi.org/10.1002/brb3.30.

Etnier, J., Nowell, P., Landers, D., & Sibley, B. (2006). A meta-regression to examine the relationship between aerobic fitness and cognitive performance. *Brain Research Reviews*, 52(1), 119–130. http://dx.doi.org/10.1016/j.brainresrev.2006.01.002.

Fabiani, M., Gordon, B., Maclin, E., Pearson, M., Brumback-Peltz, C., Low, K., et al. (2014). Neurovascular coupling in normal aging: a combined optical, ERP and fMRI study. *Neuroimage*, 85(Pt 1), 592–607. http://dx.doi.org/10.1016/j.neuroimage.2013.04.113.

Fiuza-Luces, C., Garatachea, N., Berger, N., & Lucia, A. (2013). Exercise is the real polypill. *Physiology (Bethesda)*, 28(5), 330–358. http://dx.doi.org/10.1152/physiol.00019.2013.

Gauthier, C., Lefort, M., Mekary, S., Desjardins-Crepeau, L., Skimminge, A., Iversen, P., et al. (2014). Hearts and minds: linking vascular rigidity and aerobic fitness with cognitive aging. *Neurobiology of Aging*. http://dx.doi.org/10.1016/j.neurobiolaging.2014.08.018.

Gomez-Pinilla, F., Vaynman, S., & Ying, Z. (2008). Brain-derived neurotrophic factor functions as a metabotrophin to mediate the effects of exercise on cognition. *The European journal of neuroscience*, 28(11), 2278–2287. http://dx.doi.org/10.1111/j.1460-9568.2008.06524.x.

Greicius, M., & Kimmel, D. (2012). Neuroimaging insights into network-based neurodegeneration. *Current Opinion in Neurology*, 25(6), 727–734. http://dx.doi.org/10.1097/WCO.0b013e32835a26b3.

Hampson, M., Driesen, N. R., Skudlarski, P., Gore, J. C., & Constable, R. T. (2006). Brain connectivity related to working memory performance. *The Journal of neuroscience : the official journal of the Society for Neuroscience*, 26(51), 13338–13343. http://dx.doi.org/10.1523/JNEUROSCI.3408-06.2006.

Hillman, C., Castelli, D., & Buck, S. (2005). Aerobic fitness and neurocognitive function in healthy preadolescent children. *Medicine and Science in Sports and Exercise*, 37(11), 1967–1974.

Hillman, C., Erickson, K., & Kramer, A. (2008). Be smart, exercise your heart: exercise effects on brain and cognition. *Nature Reviews Neuroscience*, 9(1), 58–65. http://dx.doi.org/10.1038/nrn2298.

Iadecola, C. (2004). Neurovascular regulation in the normal brain and in Alzheimer's disease. *Nature Reviews Neuroscience*, 5(5), 347–360. http://dx.doi.org/10.1038/nrn1387.

Keller, C. J., Bickel, S., Honey, C. J., Groppe, D. M., Entz, L., Craddock, R. C., et al. (2013). Neurophysiological investigation of spontaneous correlated and anticorrelated fluctuations of the BOLD signal. *Journal of Neuroscience*, 33(15), 6333–6342. http://dx.doi.org/10.1523/JNEUROSCI.4837-12.2013.

Kramer, A. F., Hahn, S., Cohen, N. J., Banich, M. T., McAuley, E., Harrison, C. R., et al. (1999). Ageing, fitness and neurocognitive function. *Nature*, 400(6743), 418–419. http://dx.doi.org/10.1038/22682.

Leopold, D. A., Murayama, Y., & Nikos, K. L. (2003). Very slow activity fluctuations in monkey visual cortex: implications for functional brain imaging. *Cerebral Cortex*, 13(4), 422–433. http://dx.doi.org/10.1093/cercor/13.4.422.

Lobelo, F., Stoutenberg, M., & Hutber, A. (2014). The exercise is medicine global health initiative: a 2014 update. *British Journal of Sports Medicine* bjsports-2013–093080.

Logothetis, N. K. (2012). Intracortical recordings and fMRI: an attempt to study operational modules and networks simultaneously. *Neuroimage*, 1–8. http://dx.doi.org/10.1016/j.neuroimage.2012.01.033.

Logothetis, N. K., & Pfeuffer, J. (2004). On the nature of the BOLD fMRI contrast mechanism. *Magnetic Resonance Imaging*, 22(10), 1517–1531. http://dx.doi.org/10.1016/j.mri.2004.10.018.

Mattson, M. (2014). Interventions that improve body and brain bioenergetics for Parkinson's disease risk reduction and therapy. *Jounal of Parkinson's Disease*, 4(1), 1–13. http://dx.doi.org/10.3233/JPD-130335.

McMorris, T. (2009). Exercise and cognitive function: a neuroendocrinological explanation. In *Exercise and cognitive function* (pp. 41–68). Wiley Online Library.

Meyer, J., Sakai, F., Naritomi, H., & Grant, P. (1978). Normal and abnormal patterns of cerebrovascular reserve tested by 133 Xe inhalation. *Archives of Neurology*, 35(6), 350–359.

Molteni, R., Ying, Z., & Gomez-Pinilla, F. (2002). Differential effects of acute and chronic exercise on plasticity-related genes in the rat hippocampus revealed by microarray. *European Journal of Neuroscience*, 16(6), 1107–1116. http://dx.doi.org/10.1046/j.1460-9568.2002.02158.x.

Morgan, W. P. (1969). A pilot investigation of physical working capacity in depressed and non-depressed psychiatric males. *Research Quartely*, 40, 849–861.

Ngai, A. C., Ko, K. R., Morii, S., & Winn, H. R. (1988). Effect of sciatic nerve stimulation on pial arterioles in rats. *American Journal of Physiology*, 254(1 Pt 2), H133–H139.

Niemann, C., Godde, B., & Voelcker-Rehage, C. (2014). Not only cardiovascular, but also coordinative exercise increases hippocampal volume in older adults. *Frontiers in Aging Neuroscience*, 6, 170. http://dx.doi.org/10.3389/fnagi.2014.00170.

North, T. C., McCullagh, P., & Tran, Z. V. (1990). Effect of exercise on depression. *Exercise and Sport Sciences Reviews*, 18(1), 379–416.

Ogawa, S., Lee, T., Nayak, A., & Glynn, P. (1990). Oxygenation-sensitive contrast in magnetic resonance image of rodent brain at high magnetic fields. *Magnetic Resonance in Medicine*, 14(1), 68–78.

Pontifex, M., Raine, L., Johnson, C., Chaddock, L., Voss, M., Cohen, N., et al. (2011). Cardiorespiratory fitness and the flexible modulation of cognitive control in preadolescent children. *Journal of Cognitive Neuroscience*, 23(6), 1332–1345. http://dx.doi.org/10.1162/jocn.2010.21528.

Prakash, R., Voss, M., Erickson, K., Lewis, J., Chaddock, L., Malkowski, E., et al. (2011). Cardiorespiratory fitness and attentional control in the aging brain. *Frontiers in Human Neuroscience*, 4, 229. http://dx.doi.org/10.3389/fnhum.2010.00229.

Rhodes, J., van Praag, H., Jeffrey, S., Girard, I., Mitchell, G., Garland, T. J., et al. (2003). Exercise increases hippocampal neurogenesis to high levels but does not improve spatial learning in mice bred for increased voluntary wheel running. *Behavioral Neuroscience*, 117(5), 1006–1016. http://dx.doi.org/10.1037/0735-7044.117.5.1006.

Rothman, S., & Mattson, M. (2013). Activity-dependent, stress-responsive BDNF signaling and the quest for optimal brain health and resilience throughout the lifespan. *Neuroscience*, 239, 228–240. http://dx.doi.org/10.1016/j.neuroscience.2012.10.014.

Smith, S., Fox, P., Miller, K., Glahn, D., Fox, P., Mackay, C., et al. (2009). Correspondence of the brain's functional architecture during activation and rest. *Proceedings of the National Academy of Sciences of the United States of America*, 106(31), 13040–13045. http://dx.doi.org/10.1073/pnas.0905267106.

Sofi, F., Valecchi, D., Bacci, D., Abbate, R., Gensini, G., Casini, A., et al. (2011). Physical activity and risk of cognitive decline: a meta-analysis of prospective studies. *Journal of Internal Medicine*, 269(1), 107–117. http://dx.doi.org/10.1111/j.1365-2796.2010.02281.x.

Spirduso, W. W. (1980). Physical fitness, aging, and psychomotor speed: a review. *Journal of Gerontology*, 35(6), 850–865. http://dx.doi.org/10.1093/geronj/35.6.850.

Thomas, A. G., Dennis, A., Bandettini, P. A., & Johansen-Berg, H. (2012). The effects of aerobic activity on brain structure. *Frontiers in Psychology*, 3, 86. http://dx.doi.org/10.3389/fpsyg.2012.00086.

Tipton, C. M. (2014). The history of "Exercise Is Medicine" in ancient civilizations. *AJP: Advances in Physiology Education*, 38(2), 109–117. http://dx.doi.org/10.1152/advan.00136.2013.

Van Dijk, K., Hedden, T., Venkataraman, A., Evans, K., Lazar, S., & Buckner, R. (2010). Intrinsic functional connectivity as a tool for human connectomics: theory, properties, and optimization. *Journal of Neurophysiology*, 103(1), 297–321. http://dx.doi.org/10.1152/jn.00783.2009.

Vaynman, S., Ying, Z., & Gomez-Pinilla, F. (2004). Hippocampal BDNF mediates the efficacy of exercise on synaptic plasticity and cognition. *European Journal of Neuroscience*, 20(10), 2580–2590. http://dx.doi.org/10.1111/j.1460-9568.2004.03720.x.

Voelcker-Rehage, C., Godde, B., & Staudinger, U. (2010). Physical and motor fitness are both related to cognition in old age. *European Journal of Neuroscience*, 31(1), 167–176. http://dx.doi.org/10.1111/j.1460-9568.2009.07014.x.

Voelcker-Rehage, C., Godde, B., & Staudinger, U. (2011). Cardiovascular and coordination training differentially improve cognitive performance and neural processing in older adults. *Frontiers in Aging Neuroscience*, 5, 26. http://dx.doi.org/10.3389/fnhum.2011.00026.

Voelcker-Rehage, C., & Niemann, C. (2013). Structural and functional brain changes related to different types of physical activity across the life span. *Neuroscience and Biobehavioral Reviews*, 37(9 Pt B), 2268–2295. http://dx.doi.org/10.1016/j.neubiorev.2013.01.028.

Voss, M. W., Carr, L. J., Clark, R., & Weng, T. (2014). Revenge of the "sit" II: does lifestyle impact neuronal and cognitive health through distinct mechanisms associated with sedentary behavior and physical activity? *Mental Health and Physical Activity*, 7(1), 9–24. http://dx.doi.org/10.1016/j.mhpa.2014.01.001.

Voss, M. W., Chaddock, L., Kim, J., Vanpatter, M., Pontifex, M., Raine, L., et al. (2011). Aerobic fitness is associated with greater efficiency of the network underlying cognitive control in preadolescent children. *Neuroscience*, 199, 166–176. http://dx.doi.org/10.1016/j.neuroscience.2011.10.009.

Voss, M. W., Erickson, K. I., Prakash, R. S., Chaddock, L., Kim, J. S., Alves, H., et al. (2013). Neurobiological markers of exercise-related brain plasticity in older adults. *Brain, Behavior and Immunity*, 28(C), 90–99. http://dx.doi.org/10.1016/j.bbi.2012.10.021.

Voss, M. W., Erickson, K. I., Prakash, R. S., Chaddock, L., Malkowski, E., Alves, H., et al. (2010). Functional connectivity: a source of variance in the association between cardiorespiratory fitness and cognition? *Neuropsychologia*, 48(5), 1394–1406. http://dx.doi.org/10.1016/j.neuropsychologia.2010.01.005.

Voss, M. W., Heo, S., Prakash, R., Erickson, K., Alves, H., Chaddock, L., et al. (2013). The influence of aerobic fitness on cerebral white matter integrity and cognitive function in older adults: results of a one-year exercise intervention. *Human Brain Mapping*, 34(11), 2972–2985. http://dx.doi.org/10.1002/hbm.22119.

Voss, M. W., Vivar, C., Kramer, A. F., & van Praag, H. (2013). Bridging animal and human models of exercise-induced brain plasticity. *Trends in Cognitive Sciences*, 17(10), 525–544. http://dx.doi.org/10.1016/j.tics.2013.08.001.

Physical Activity, Fitness, and Cognition: Insights from Neuroelectric Studies

Keita Kamijo

Faculty of Sport Sciences, Waseda University, Mikajima, Tokorozawa, Saitama, Japan

INTRODUCTION

Many empirical studies support a positive association between physical activity (PA) or physical fitness and cognitive functioning across the human lifespan. Electroencephalogram (EEG) studies, specifically those using event-related brain potentials (ERPs), have played a key role in the development of this research field. This chapter focuses on such neuroelectric studies and updates an earlier review of the subject (Hillman, Kamijo, & Pontifex, 2012).

Given the high temporal resolution (i.e., milliseconds), ERPs can measure a subset of covert cognitive processes occurring between stimulus encoding and response execution, and therefore provide information regarding the mechanisms underlying cognitive functioning above and beyond that provided by overt behavior. For example, when using a Go / Nogo task, in which participants need to respond to Go stimuli and withhold their responses to Nogo stimuli, it is difficult to assess inhibitory processes only on the basis of behavioral data, since no overt response is required for the Nogo trials. The assessment of ERP measures reflecting a subset of inhibitory processes (e.g., Nogo N2 and Nogo P3) along with behavioral task performance (i.e., response accuracy for the Nogo trials) can lead to a deeper understanding of the association between PA/fitness and cognitive function.

Several ERP components have been used to examine the relationship between PA/fitness and cognitive function. As reviewed in Hillman, Kamijo, et al. (2012), the P3 component (also known as the P3b or P300), contingent negative variation (CNV), and error-related negativity (ERN; also known as error negativity: Ne) have often been employed in this area of research. This chapter starts with an overview of such ERP studies, adding some new findings, and then reviews recent neuroelectric studies using other ERP components and EEG techniques.

P3

The P3 (i.e., P3b) is a positive ERP component occurring approximately 300–800 ms after stimulus onset (the timing of P3 occurrence differs depending on such factors as task difficulty and participants' age). This component is believed

Exercise-Cognition Interaction
http://dx.doi.org/10.1016/B978-0-12-800778-5.00010-4

to reflect the neural activity associated with memory updating processes (Donchin, 1981). Its amplitude and latency are considered to reflect the amount of attentional resources deployed during stimulus engagement (Polich, 2007) and stimulus classification speed or stimulus evaluation time (Verleger, 1997), respectively. That is, larger P3 amplitude is assumed to reflect an increased allocation of attentional resources, and shorter P3 latency is thought to represent faster cognitive processing speed.

Earlier P3 Studies

A majority of P3 studies have indicated that higher PA levels or aerobic fitness are associated with larger P3 amplitude and/or shorter P3 latency during stimulus discrimination tasks, such as the oddball and flanker tasks, across the lifespan (Chang, Huang, Chen, & Hung, 2013; Dustman et al., 1990; Hillman, Belopolsky, Snook, Kramer, & McAuley, 2004; Hillman, Buck, Themanson, Pontifex, & Castelli, 2009; Hillman, Castelli, & Buck, 2005; Hillman, Kramer, Belopolsky, & Smith, 2006; Kamijo & Takeda, 2009, 2010; Polich & Lardon, 1997; Pontifex, Hillman, & Polich, 2009; Pontifex et al., 2011). The oddball task requires participants to respond to or count rare target stimuli (e.g., the letter "O" is presented with a probability of 0.2) and ignore frequent nontarget stimuli (e.g., the letter "X" is presented with a probability of 0.8). This task has been widely used in P3 studies, given that a clear P3 component is elicited by the rare target stimuli. The flanker task (arrowhead version) asks participants to press a button corresponding to the direction of a centrally presented target arrowhead. The target arrowhead is flanked by congruent (i.e., <<<<< or >>>>>) or incongruent (i.e., >><>> or <<>><<) distractors. The flanker task has been most often used in this field since several ERP components including P3 and ERN are elicited during this task, and cognitive control

(i.e., higher-order cognitive abilities involved in goal-directed behaviors) demands can be manipulated based on the task conditions. That is, incongruent trials require greater cognitive control demands relative to congruent ones, in order to inhibit incorrect response activation caused by the distractors.

Although some of the above described P3 studies failed to find an association between PA/fitness and task performance measures (i.e., response accuracy and reaction times: RTs), which might be the result of ceiling effects due to the simplicity of the cognitive tasks used, such studies typically indicate that more physically active and aerobically fit individuals exhibit superior task performance relative to their less active/fit counterparts. Thus, the findings from P3 studies suggest that higher PA levels and aerobic fitness are associated with greater recruitment of attentional resources, as reflected by larger P3 amplitude, and faster cognitive processing speed, as reflected by shorter P3 latency, during stimulus discrimination, which should be associated with superior task performance. Further, several of these P3 studies employed cognitive tasks requiring variable cognitive control demands based on task conditions (e.g., flanker task), indicating that the association between PA/fitness and cognitive function is disproportionately larger for task conditions necessitating greater cognitive control demands, such as inhibition, working memory, and cognitive flexibility (Chang et al., 2013; Hillman et al., 2004, 2009, 2006; Kamijo & Takeda, 2009, 2010; Pontifex et al., 2011).

Temporal Dynamics of Visual Attention

Wu and Hillman (2013) provide additional insight into the association between childhood fitness and cognitive function by focusing on the temporal dynamics of visual attention. This study compared lower-fit and higher-fit children's task performance and the associated P3 component during the rapid serial visual presentation (RSVP) task. The RSVP task, in which a series of stimuli are presented quickly in sequence, requires participants to detect two numbers (i.e., the targets, referred to as T1 and T2, respectively) amid the train of letters (i.e., distractors). The processing of T1 impairs detection of T2 if it occurs 200–500 ms after T1, a phenomenon referred to as the attentional blink (Raymond, Shapiro, & Arnell, 1992). Wu and Hillman (2013) employed short (336 ms) and long (672 ms) temporal intervals between T1 and T2, and indicated that higher-fit children exhibited superior task performance on T2 detection for the short interval trials, whereas no such group difference was observed for the long interval trials. This study also showed that both T1- and T2-elicited P3 amplitudes were smaller for higher-fit relative to lower-fit children across both interval trials. These findings suggest that the observed superior task performance for higher-fit children is due to their greater ability to allocate limited resources to meet the time-sensitive nature of the task (i.e., more efficient allocation of attentional resources). Importantly, these data offer a cautionary tale around the interpretation of ERP data: larger P3 amplitude is not necessarily related to superior task performance. It appears that the direction of differences in ERP component amplitude (i.e., larger or smaller) based on PA levels and fitness is task dependent. Accordingly, I would argue that researchers should interpret neuroelectric measure results along with task performance measures and refrain from drawing conclusions on the basis of neuroelectric measures alone.

Randomized Controlled Trial

All of the above-referenced P3 studies employed cross-sectional designs, comparing behavioral and neuroelectric measures of cognition between lower and higher physically active/aerobically fit individuals. That is, these P3 studies did not indicate a causal relationship

between changes in PA levels/fitness and improvements in cognitive function. Recently, a randomized controlled trial investigating the effects of a 9-month PA intervention on cognitive control in preadolescent children has been reported (Hillman et al., 2014). This study compared intervention and waitlist control groups on changes in aerobic fitness, task performance, and the P3 component during cognitive control tasks (i.e., flanker task and task-switching task), which have been used in previous cross-sectional P3 studies (Hillman et al., 2004, 2009, 2006; Kamijo & Takeda, 2010; Pontifex et al., 2011). Results indicated that the PA program improved aerobic fitness and task performance, enhanced P3 amplitude, and shortened P3 latency, suggesting that regular PA leading to increases in aerobic fitness results in improved cognitive control in preadolescent children. It is noteworthy that the findings of this randomized controlled trial are consistent with the findings of many cross-sectional P3 studies (Hillman et al., 2004, 2009, 2006; Kamijo & Takeda, 2010; Pontifex et al., 2011). Thus, although such a longitudinal study design has the advantage of minimizing the effects of potential confounds, cross-sectional designs remain useful in attempts to understand the PA/fitness–cognition relationship, particularly as an initial step.

Types of PA

In the above-mentioned cross-sectional P3 studies, participants were classified according to their overall PA levels or aerobic fitness. A few recent P3 studies examined whether the association between PA and cognitive function differs based on types of PA and sport. Dai, Chang, Huang, and Hung (2013) compared task performance and the P3 component during task-switching among older adults who engaged in open-skill activities (e.g., tennis), closed-skill activities (e.g., jogging), and no regular PA. The participants performed two task-switching conditions. The single-task condition required repeated performance on a single task (i.e., AAAAAA... or BBBBBB...), while the mixed-task condition asked participants to rapidly shift between different tasks (e.g., AABBAA... or ABABAB...). The mixed task condition involves greater cognitive control demands due to working memory-mediated maintenance of multiple task sets and requisite inhibition of a task set on switch trials (Kray & Lindenberger, 2000; Rogers & Monsell, 1995). Dai et al. (2013) found that both physically active groups (i.e., irrespective of PA type) had shorter RTs and larger P3 amplitude relative to the inactive group across task conditions, replicating earlier P3 studies. Similar findings were reported in Fong, Chi, Li, and Chang (2014), in which the same task-switching methodology was used. This study indicated that older adults who engaged in endurance PA (i.e., walking and jogging) or Tai Chi Chuan exhibited shorter RTs and larger P3 amplitudes relative to their physically inactive peers across task conditions. Taken together, these findings imply that the positive association between PA and cognitive control is not type specific.

However, it should be noted that Dai et al. (2013) indicated that the global switch cost (i.e., RT difference between the mixed-task and single-task conditions), which is believed to reflect working memory demands (Kray & Lindenberger, 2000; Rogers & Monsell, 1995), was smaller for the open-skill group relative to the closed-skill and inactive groups. Additionally, Voss, Kramer, Basak, Prakash, and Roberts (2010) conducted a meta-analysis to examine the association between sport expertise and laboratory-based measures of cognition, indicating that the positive association was disproportionately larger for a certain type of sport

(in their terminology, "interceptive sports" such as tennis, fencing, and boxing). Furthermore, a longitudinal, randomized, and controlled intervention study indicated that 12-month resistance training improved cognitive control task performance in older adults (Liu-Ambrose et al., 2010). Taking such findings together, it is plausible that cognitive function can be improved not only by aerobic PA but also by other types of PA. I believe that the public is interested in what types of PA are most beneficial for brain health and cognition. Obviously, further studies are needed to clarify this open question by focusing on various PA types.

CONTINGENT NEGATIVE VARIATION (CNV)

The CNV is a negative slow potential occurring during the period between warning (S1) and imperative (S2) stimuli, such that this slow potential is thought to reflect task preparation processes. It has been well established that the CNV consists of at least two functionally different components, the initial CNV (iCNV), which is associated with stimulus orientation, and the terminal CNV (tCNV), which relates to stimulus anticipation or response preparation (Brunia & van Boxtel, 2001; Loveless & Sanford, 1974; van Boxtel & Brunia, 1994; Weerts & Lang, 1973).

An initial CNV study (Hillman, Weiss, Hagberg, & Hatfield, 2002) indicated that higher-fit young and older adults had smaller tCNV relative to their lower-fit peers during a simple S1–S2 task, in which participants needed to make a decision about their response (i.e., left or right) upon presentation of S1 and to press one of two buttons to subsequently presented S2.[1] Given that task performance measures did not differ based on

---

[1] Indeed, Hillman et al. (2002) used an S1–S2–S3 task. S1 was the word "EASY" or "HARD," which gave participants information about the perceptual task difficulty of the following stimulus discrimination (S2). S2 consisted of two bars differing in height (7.68 cm difference and 0.03 cm difference for the easy and hard conditions, respectively). Participants were required to make a decision regarding which bar is taller (i.e., left or right) but not to respond to S2. S3 was a box, which asked participants to press one of two buttons based on their decision.

participants' fitness levels, the observed smaller CNV for higher-fit individuals is thought to reflect more efficient response preparation.

This finding was replicated in a second CNV study (Kamijo, O'Leary, Pontifex, Themanson, & Hillman, 2010) that used a modified Sternberg task, which is considered to be more cognitively demanding. The Sternberg task requires participants to encode a memory set (S1) containing an array of alphabetical letters (e.g., HBNCW) and to press one of two buttons corresponding to whether a subsequently presented single probe letter (S2) was present or absent from the encoded letter array. In Kamijo et al. (2010), the Sternberg task was performed under two conditions across which task instructions were varied to emphasize either speed (speed instructions) or accuracy (accuracy instructions). It was suggested that the speed instructions should result in increased CNV amplitude relative to accuracy, which is believed to reflect greater allocation of resources (Falkenstein, Hoormann, Hohnsbein, & Kleinsorge, 2003). Kamijo et al. (2010) found that although task performance measures did not differ between fitness groups, higher-fit college students had smaller tCNV amplitude relative to their lower-fit counterparts. Specifically, the group difference in tCNV amplitude was selectively observed for the speed instructions, corroborating P3 studies indicating the selective nature of the relationship between PA/fitness and cognitive function based on task demands (Chang et al., 2013; Hillman et al., 2006; Kamijo & Takeda, 2009, 2010; Pontifex et al., 2011). This group difference was selectively observed at the frontal electrode site. It has been suggested that frontal CNV reflects cognitive preparation processes rather than response preparation processes (Falkenstein et al., 2003; Leynes, Allen, & Marsh, 1998; Lorist et al., 2000; Wild-Wall, Hohnsbein, & Falkenstein, 2007). It is plausible that greater aerobic fitness is associated not only with more efficient response preparation but also with more efficient cognitive preparation in adult populations.

A third CNV study examined the effects of PA intervention on cognitive preparation processes in preadolescent children using a longitudinal randomized controlled design (Kamijo, Pontifex, et al., 2011). This study used the Sternberg task and found that a 9-month PA intervention improved aerobic fitness and task performance and enhanced frontal iCNV. It appears that on the surface, the observed changes in CNV are inconsistent with the above described adult studies indicating that greater fitness is associated with smaller tCNV (Hillman et al., 2002; Kamijo et al., 2010). Based on developmental findings (Jonkman, Lansbergen, & Stauder, 2003; Segalowitz, Unsal, & Dywan, 1992), immature cognitive preparation processes in children are reflected in smaller frontal iCNV rather than tCNV. Accordingly, it is likely that the increased frontal iCNV caused by the PA intervention in Kamijo, Pontifex, et al. (2011) reflects more effective cognitive preparation in children, which in turn might underlie improvements in task performance. I should emphasize again here that, as discussed in the P3 section, the direction of differences in ERP amplitude based on PA levels and fitness is task and age dependent.

ERROR-RELATED NEGATIVITY (ERN)

The ERN is a negative ERP component occurring approximately 50–100 ms after errors of commission. The ERN has been theorized to reflect the detection of conflict in the anterior cingulate cortex (ACC) (Botvinick, Braver, Barch, Carter, & Cohen, 2001; Yeung, Botvinick, & Cohen, 2004) or the transmission of a negative reinforcement learning signal to the ACC (Holroyd & Coles, 2002). Thus, this component is believed to reflect the ACC activity (Carter et al., 1998; Dehaene, Posner, & Tucker, 1994; Miltner et al., 2003) that plays a critical role in action monitoring (Carter et al., 1998; Kerns et al., 2004), which is the ability to monitor performance and adjust goal-directed behavior. That is, this ability is considered to be another aspect of cognitive control.

Conflict Monitoring Theory

Hillman and his colleagues have indicated that higher physically active and aerobically fit individuals exhibit smaller ERN amplitude with superior task performance relative to their less active/fit counterparts, across the lifespan (Hillman et al., 2009; Themanson & Hillman, 2006; Themanson, Hillman, & Curtin, 2006). These results suggest that higher PA levels and aerobic fitness are associated with less ACC activation, which is thought to reflect more efficient action monitoring. This interpretation has been explained in terms of the conflict monitoring theory (Botvinick et al., 2001; Carter & van Veen, 2007). This theory suggests that the ACC monitors response conflict on error trials, which results in increased activation of the dorsolateral prefrontal cortex (PFC) to upregulate cognitive control in support of behavioral adjustments on subsequent trials. Based on this theory, it has been suggested that less ACC activation (as denoted by smaller ERN amplitude) for higher physically active and aerobically fit individuals reflects reductions in response conflict due to increased PFC activation (Hillman et al., 2009; Themanson & Hillman, 2006; Themanson et al., 2006).

Dual Mechanisms of Control Theory

More recently, an alternative possible explanation for the association between PA/fitness and cognitive control, including action monitoring, has been suggested on the basis of child studies (Kamijo, Pontifex, et al., 2011; Pontifex et al., 2011; Voss et al., 2011): dual mechanisms of control (DMC) theory (Braver, 2012; Braver, Gray, & Burgess, 2007). This theory postulates that cognitive control operates on the basis of two different strategies, referred to as proactive control and reactive control. Proactive control is reflected in sustained lateral PFC activation, which is associated with decreased transient ACC activation, in order to actively maintain goal-relevant information and prevent interference before it occurs. Reactive control is reflected in transient activation of the lateral PFC and ACC to reactivate task goals and resolve interference only as needed. Accordingly, proactive control should be reflected in decreased ERN amplitude (i.e., decreased transient ACC activation) and vice versa for reactive control. Based on the DMC theory, it is speculated that smaller ERN amplitude for higher physically active and aerobically fit individuals in the above-cited neuroelectric studies (Hillman et al., 2009; Themanson & Hillman, 2006; Themanson et al., 2006) reflects utilization of a proactive control strategy.

A functional magnetic resonance imaging study (Voss et al., 2011) manipulated the probability of trial types during a modified flanker task and found that higher-fit children exhibited greater ACC activity relative to lower-fit children for the mostly congruent condition (MC) (e.g., 70% of trials were congruent), whereas no such difference was observed for the mostly incongruent condition (MI) (e.g., 70% of trials were incongruent). This study also showed that higher-fit children showed a smaller interference effect on response accuracy (i.e., response accuracy difference between the MI and MC conditions[2]) relative to lower-fit children. De Pisapia and Braver (2006) found that, using the Stroop task, young adult participants exhibited a smaller interference effect on RTs (i.e., RT difference between incongruent and congruent trials) with increased sustained lateral PFC activation and decreased transient ACC activation for the MI condition relative to the MC condition. That is, in contrast with the MI condition, the young adult participants showed decreased sustained PFC activation and increased transient

---

[2] In Voss et al. (2011), the MC and MI condition consisted of 67% congruent and incongruent trials and 33% neutral (e.g., XX < XX, XX > XX) trials, and the neutral trials were not included in their analyses. Although the interference effect is generally calculated within each condition, this effect was calculated between conditions in this study.

ACC activation for the MC condition. From these findings, it seems likely that young adults change cognitive control strategies based on the probability of trial types, from reactive control in the MC condition to proactive control in the MI condition. The pattern of results in Voss et al. (2011) might indicate that greater childhood fitness is associated with a more flexible shift between reactive and proactive modes of cognitive control, in order to adapt to varying task demands. This may be a convenient explanation given that Voss et al. (2011) used a block design, which could not dissociate transient from sustained brain activation. Thus, which account (i.e., conflict monitoring theory or DMC theory) provides a better explanation of the relationship between PA/fitness and action monitoring remains uncertain. Although preliminary, our data suggest that greater childhood fitness is likely to be associated with both superior proactive and reactive control abilities, which is reflected in different changes in ERN amplitude (i.e., transient ACC activation) across MC and MI conditions based on participants' fitness levels (Kamijo, Bae, & Masaki, submitted for publication), thereby supporting both accounts.

Task Demands

It appears that higher physically active and aerobically fit individuals do not necessarily exhibit smaller ERN amplitude relative to their less active/fit peers (Pontifex et al., 2011; Themanson, Pontifex, & Hillman, 2008). In Pontifex et al. (2011), a flanker task was performed under two conditions in which stimulus-response compatibility was manipulated, such that in the compatible stimulus-response condition, participants were required to press a button corresponding to the direction of a centrally presented target stimulus, whereas in the incompatible stimulus-response condition, they were required to press a button that opposed the direction of the target stimulus. The incompatible condition requires greater cognitive control demands to resolve increased conflict due to the need to override prepotent responses (Friedman, Nessler, Cycowicz, & Horton, 2009). Pontifex et al. (2011) found that higher-fit children exhibited comparable response accuracy between the compatible and incompatible conditions, whereas lower-fit children had lower response accuracy for the incompatible condition relative to the compatible condition. Further, neuroelectric data indicated that higher-fit children exhibited smaller ERN amplitude relative to lower-fit children for the compatible condition, replicating previous ERN studies (Hillman et al., 2009; Themanson & Hillman, 2006; Themanson et al., 2006). By contrast, ERN amplitude was comparable between the fitness groups for the incompatible condition. Collectively, these findings suggest that higher-fit children can flexibly upregulate the action monitoring network, which is reflected in increased ERN amplitude, in the incompatible condition that requires greater cognitive control demands to maintain task performance.

Themanson et al. (2008) manipulated task instructions (i.e., speed vs accuracy instructions) during the flanker task, finding that greater aerobic fitness in college students was related to greater post-error accuracy, which is considered to reflect the upregulation of cognitive control, and *larger* ERN amplitude for the accuracy instructions, whereas no such relationship was observed for the speed instructions. It has been noted that accuracy instructions elicit larger ERN relative to speed instructions due to increased error salience (Gehring, Goss, Coles, Meyer, & Donchin, 1993) or increased attentional focus (Yeung et al., 2004). The results of Themanson et al. (2008) suggest that greater aerobic fitness is *positively* associated with ERN amplitude for the task condition requiring extensive amounts of cognitive control (i.e., accuracy instruction), which is in the opposite direction from previous ERN studies using speed instructions (Themanson & Hillman, 2006; Themanson et al., 2006). Further, our preliminary data indicate that higher-fit children exhibit greater post-error accuracy and larger ERN amplitude for the flanker task MC condition, suggesting that higher-fit children can upregulate cognitive control more effectively by recruiting reactive control (Kamijo et al., submitted for publication). It is likely that the direction of differences in ERN amplitude based on PA levels and fitness differs based on task demands and/or the nature of cognitive tasks, in the same manner as the P3 and CNV.

OTHER ERP COMPONENTS AND EEG TECHNIQUES

Academic-Related Cognitive Processes

It has been argued that regular PA and aerobic fitness are positively associated with academic achievement during childhood (Biddle & Asare, 2011; Castelli, Hillman, Buck, & Erwin, 2007). In the context of these findings, a couple of recent ERP studies have focused on academic-related cognitive processes. Scudder et al. (2014) examined the association between childhood fitness and language processing using the N400 and P600 ERPs during a sentence processing task. This task consisted of congruent (e.g., "I like to eat *apples* and bananas."), semantic violation (e.g., "I like to eat *doors* and bananas."), and syntactic violation (e.g., "I like to *apples* eat and bananas.") conditions and required participants to press one of two buttons corresponding to whether the sentence did contain a mistake. The N400 is a negative ERP component occurring approximately 300–500 ms after stimulus onset during the sentence processing task. This component is assumed to reflect semantic integration costs or the ease of accessing information from long-term memory (Kutas & Federmeier, 2011). N400 amplitude is assumed to reflect the richness of the mental lexicon, whereas N400 latency is considered to be a measure of lexical access speed (Scudder et al., 2014). Scudder et al. (2014)

found that higher-fit children had greater reading accuracy, shorter RTs, larger N400 amplitude, and shorter N400 latency relative to lower-fit children across conditions, suggesting that higher-fit children have richer lexico-semantic networks. Furthermore, this study showed that higher-fit children exhibit a larger P600 effect (i.e., difference in amplitude between the syntactic violation and the congruent conditions), which has been considered an index of syntactic reanalysis processing (Friederici, 2002; Kuperberg, 2007). This suggests that greater fitness is also associated with a superior ability to discern and/or correct syntactic errors.

Moore, Drollette, Scudder, Bharij, and Hillman (2014) compared lower-fit and higher-fit children's task performance, P3, and N400 during an arithmetic verification task. This task, which consisted of small (<10) and large (>10) problem solutions, asked participants to press one of two buttons corresponding to whether the presented solution (i.e., $a+b=c$) was correct. Higher-fit children had superior task performance during large but not small problem solutions relative to lower-fit children. Higher-fit children also had smaller P3 amplitude during small problem solutions relative to lower-fit children, whereas no such group difference was observed for large problem solutions. Given that during small problem solutions task performance did not differ between groups, the observed smaller P3 amplitude for higher-fit children is thought to reflect their more efficient allocation of attentional resources, as was the case in the above-mentioned P3 study of Wu and Hillman (2013) that focused on the attentional blink. By contrast, during large problem solutions, higher-fit children appear to recruit a greater amount of attentional resources to meet the increased task demands, which in turn might underlie their superior task performance. Furthermore, this study observed larger N400 amplitude for higher-fit children, replicating Scudder et al. (2014) and suggesting that greater childhood fitness is associated with superior semantic processing not only during sentence reading but also during arithmetic verification. Thus, recent studies have put ERP techniques to more practical use. As I have mentioned, a majority of ERP studies have focused on positive relationships between cognitive control and fitness (Hillman et al., 2009, 2014; Kamijo, Pontifex, et al., 2011; Pontifex et al., 2011), given that this higher-order cognitive function has been heavily implicated in academic achievement (Blair & Razza, 2007; Bull & Scerif, 2001; Hillman, Pontifex et al., 2012; Latzman, Elkovitch, Young, & Clark, 2010). These ERP studies using academic-related tasks (Moore et al., 2014; Scudder et al., 2014) provide further support for a positive relationship between PA/fitness and academic achievement (Biddle & Asare, 2011; Castelli et al., 2007).

Cognitive Variability

As discussed above, it is important to interpret ERP results in conjunction with behavioral task performance. In ERP studies, mean response accuracy and RTs have been generally used as task performance measures. Several studies using cognitive control tasks indicated that the relationship not only between age and mean RTs, but also between age and intraindividual RT variability, show U-shaped curves throughout the entire lifespan (Li et al., 2004; Williams, Hultsch, Strauss, Hunter, & Tannock, 2005). Stated differently, younger children and older adults exhibit longer mean RTs and larger intraindividual RT variability relative to older children and younger adults. Given that longitudinal ERP studies have suggested that regular PA leading to increased aerobic fitness is associated with cognitive development in preadolescent children (Hillman et al., 2014; Kamijo, Pontifex, et al., 2011), it would not be surprising

if childhood fitness is associated not only with task performance but also with intraindividual variability of performance.

Wu et al. (2011) examined mean performance and intraindividual variability (i.e., standard deviation and coefficient of variation) of RTs during a modified flanker task. They found that higher-fit children had greater response accuracy, replicating previous children studies (Hillman et al., 2009; Pontifex et al., 2011), as well as less intraindividual variability. These findings suggest that higher-fit children show more stable task performance relative to their lower-fit peers, such that higher-fit children might be able to maintain optimal levels of cognitive control over the entire course of the flanker task.

Following this study, a further ERP investigation examined the associations between childhood fitness and intraindividual variabilities for RT, P3 amplitude, and P3 latency during the flanker task (Moore et al., 2013). This study demonstrated that greater childhood fitness is associated with smaller intraindividual variability for RTs,[3] replicating Wu et al. (2011), as well as shorter RTs, whereas fitness was not associated with intraindividual variabilities for P3 amplitude and latency. It seems that this ERP finding is inconsistent with previous aging studies showing that smaller intraindividual variabilities for P3 amplitude and P3 latency were associated with better cognitive performance (Fjell, Rosquist, & Walhovd, 2009; Fjell & Walhovd, 2007). One possible source of this discrepancy might be participants' fitness levels in Moore et al. (2013). The mean percentile rank of aerobic fitness for their participants, which was calculated based on age- and sex-specific normative data (Shvartz & Reibold, 1990), was at the 20th percentile. A fairly large portion of this sample considered relatively low-fit children, which in turn should work to blur the fitness–cognition relationship. Although

---

[3] Moore et al. (2013) employed ex-Gaussian parameters (i.e., mu [μ], sigma [σ], and tau [τ]), in addition to standard deviation, to assess intraindividual RT variability, and indicated that greater fitness was associated with both smaller standard deviation and sigma, whereas mu and tau for RTs were not associated with fitness.

further studies are needed to shed light on the association between PA/fitness and intraindividual ERP component variability, these studies (Moore et al., 2013; Wu et al., 2011) suggest that intraindividual variability, at least for RTs, is a useful measure to assess the relationship between fitness and cognitive function.

Lower-Order Cognitive Processes

As described previously, most ERP studies have focused on higher-order cognitive functions. Several ERP studies have instead focused on lower-order cognitive processes using the P3a component, which is also a subcomponent of the P300 but reflects processes distinct from those captured using P3b. One typical cognitive task to elicit the P3a component is a three-stimulus oddball task. This task requires participants to respond to rare target stimuli (e.g., a 55 mm diameter circle is presented with a probability of 0.12) and ignore frequent nontarget stimuli (e.g., a 50 mm diameter circle is presented with a probability of 0.74) and rare distractor stimuli (e.g., a full-screen checkerboard is presented with a probability of 0.12). The rare target stimulus elicits the P3b component, as is the case for the two-stimulus oddball task, and the distractor stimulus elicits the P3a component. The P3a component has shorter peak latency and displays a more frontal topographical distribution relative to the P3b component, and is believed to reflect involuntary allocation of attention to deviant or novel salient stimuli with increased

amplitude related to greater focal attention (Polich, 2007). Pontifex et al. (2009) compared the P3a and P3b components across lower-fit and higher-fit individuals during the three-stimulus oddball task. This study indicated that, although task performance measures did not differ between groups, higher-fit young adults exhibited larger P3b amplitude relative to their lower-fit peers, whereas no such difference was observed for P3a amplitude.[4] That is, aerobic fitness may not be associated with attentional orienting.

Getzmann, Falkenstein, and Gajewski (2013) found the opposite using an auditory duration discrimination task. This task consisted of frequent standard stimuli (1000-Hz tone presented with a probability of 0.8) and rare deviant stimuli (500-Hz and 2000-Hz tones presented with a probability of 0.1), such that half of these stimuli had short durations (200 ms) and the other half had long durations (400 ms). This task asked participants to press one of two buttons corresponding to the duration of the tones irrespective of the tone pitch. Difference waves (i.e., deviant minus standard) were calculated to analyze P3a, and indicated that higher-fit older adults showed a smaller RT difference between the deviant and standard stimuli and smaller P3a amplitude relative to their lower-fit counterparts. These findings suggest that higher-fit older adults can conserve limited resources for suppressing task-irrelevant information associated with deviant stimuli (i.e., tone pitch) to adequately detect target stimuli or focus on task-relevant information

---

[4] Pontifex et al. (2009) employed a two-stimulus easy discrimination oddball task (target = 55 mm diameter circle, nontarget = 30 mm diameter circle) and a three-stimulus difficult discrimination oddball task (target = 55 mm diameter circle, nontarget = 50 mm diameter circle). Results indicated that greater aerobic fitness was associated with shorter RTs and larger P3b amplitude during the easy two-stimulus oddball task for both young and older adults. By contrast, during the difficult three-stimulus oddball task, RT did not differ between fitness groups irrespective of age, likely due to the increased perceptual task difficulty. Furthermore, the fitness group difference in P3b amplitude was observed for young but not for older adult participants, suggesting that aerobic fitness may not be sufficient to overcome age-related cognitive decline if task difficulty is too high. P3a amplitude during the three-stimulus oddball task did not differ between fitness groups irrespective of age.

(i.e., tone duration). Although merely speculation, I believe that one possible source of this inconsistency concerns differences in the nature of cognitive tasks used to elicit the P3a component across these neuroelectric studies. Thus, it is still controversial whether fitness is associated with attentional orienting. Our preliminary data indicate that higher-fit children have smaller P3a amplitude relative to lower-fit children, corroborating the findings of Getzmann et al. (2013). Obviously, further studies are needed to clarify the association between fitness and attentional orienting, but it appears that fitness is not only associated with higher-order cognitive control but also with lower-order cognitive processes.

Our study focusing on face processing, which serves as an example of lower-order cognitive processes, supports this assertion (Kamijo & Takeda, 2014). This study employed a hybrid face recognition/oddball task, in which participants were asked to respond to rarely presented famous faces (with a probability of 0.17) and ignore frequently presented unfamiliar faces (with a probability of 0.83). It is well known that the occipito-temporal cortex plays an important role in face processing (Kanwisher, McDermott, & Chun, 1997), and several occipito-temporal ERPs that reflect face processing stages from perceptual encoding (N170) to recognition (N250 and face-N400), as well as the P3 component, are elicited during the hybrid face recognition/oddball task. Physically active young adults had shorter RTs (although this result was marginally statistically significant) and larger P3 amplitude relative to their physically inactive peers, replicating P3 studies using a two-stimulus oddball task (Hillman et al., 2005; Polich & Lardon, 1997; Pontifex et al., 2009). Furthermore, although N170 amplitude did not differ between groups, time courses of N250/face-N400 did show such a difference. Specifically, although both groups exhibited larger face-N400 amplitude for famous faces relative to unfamiliar faces, the active group had larger N250 amplitude for famous faces relative to unfamiliar faces, with no such effect for

the inactive group. These findings suggest that PA levels are not associated with efficacy of the early perceptual encoding stage of face processing as indicated by a lack of group differences in N170 amplitude (Bentin, Allison, Puce, Perez, & McCarthy, 1996; Bentin & Deouell, 2000; Eimer, 2000), but are associated with the early stage of occipito-temporal face recognition as reflected by the group difference in N250 amplitude (Gosling & Eimer, 2011). Given that a majority of ERP studies have focused on the association between PA/fitness and higher-order processes, I believe that further studies focusing on different aspects of cognitive function are needed to get a more complete picture of the PA/fitness–cognition association.

Functional Connectivity between Brain Regions

My colleagues and I have examined the association between PA and functional connectivity between brain regions using phase-locking values (PLVs), to examine one possible mechanism underlying the PA–cognition relationship (Kamijo & Takeda, 2013; Kamijo, Takeda, & Hillman, 2011). PLVs are an index of phase synchronization between EEG signals measured from two electrodes across trials. Higher PLVs indicate that a phase difference between EEG signals from two electrodes is consonant across trials, suggesting a long-distance functional connectivity between brain regions near these electrodes (Lachaux, Rodriguez, Martinerie, & Varela, 1999). That is, in contrast to ERPs, which predominantly reflect oscillatory neural activity in a local brain region phase-locked to the onset of events, PLVs reflect information transfer from one brain region to other regions. It has been suggested that top-down and bottom-up cognitive control are reflected in neural synchrony at lower frequency bands (22–34 Hz; i.e., beta) and higher frequency bands (36–56 Hz; i.e., gamma), respectively (Buschman & Miller, 2007; Phillips & Takeda, 2009).

Kamijo, Takeda, et al. (2011) compared task performance and PLVs during a spatial priming task across physically active and inactive young adults. The spatial priming task, in which the letters "O" and "X" were presented at two of four possible locations simultaneously, requires participants to press one of four buttons corresponding to the position of the letter "O" (i.e., target) and ignore the location of the letter "X" (i.e., distractor). RTs become longer when the probe (trial n) target appears at the location of the prime (trial $n-1$) distractor, a phenomenon referred to as negative priming (Tipper, Brehaut, & Driver, 1990). The negative priming effect is assumed to reflect inhibitory control to prevent interference from distractors in working memory, with larger negative priming effects being associated with superior inhibitory control (Kamijo & Takeda, 2009). Kamijo, Takeda, et al. (2011) found that physically active young adults had larger negative priming effects relative to their physically inactive peers, suggesting that higher PA levels are associated with superior inhibitory control. Further, the active group exhibited larger beta band PLV for the negative priming condition relative to the control condition, whereas no such difference was observed for the inactive group or for the gamma band PLV. These findings suggest that higher PA levels are selectively associated with greater functional connectivity between brain regions during task conditions requiring greater amounts of top-down cognitive control. This finding is consistent with ERP studies that highlight the selective nature of the relationship between PA/fitness and cognitive function based on cognitive control demands (Hillman et al., 2006; Kamijo & Takeda, 2009, 2010; Pontifex et al., 2011).

Kamijo and Takeda (2013) investigated the association between PA and conflict adaptation using PLVs during a perceptual conflict task (i.e., Navon task). The Navon task, which involves presentation of a global letter made up of local letters of either the same kind (i.e., congruent trials) or a different kind (i.e., incongruent trials), requires participants to press a button corresponding to the local letters and to ignore the global letter. Kamijo and Takeda (2013) compared task performance and PLVs on incongruent trials that were preceded by either congruent trials (cI) or incongruent trials (iI) across physically active and inactive young adults. It has been found that greater trial-by-trial adjustments (i.e., more accurate and faster responses) are observed for the iI trials relative to the cI trials (Botvinick, Nystrom, Fissell, Carter, & Cohen, 1999; Gratton, Coles, & Donchin, 1992). This greater trial-by-trial adjustment on iI trials has been accounted for in terms of conflict monitoring theory as well as post-error adjustments (Botvinick et al., 2001; Kerns et al., 2004): the ACC monitors response conflict on trial $n-1$ and activates the dorsolateral PFC to upregulate cognitive control in support of trial n. Kamijo and Takeda (2013) indicated that active individuals exhibited greater trial-by-trial adjustments relative to their inactive counterparts. Furthermore, active individuals had larger beta band PLV on the iI trials relative to the cI trials, whereas inactive individuals did not show such a difference. These results suggest that the observed greater trial-by-trial adjustments for the active individuals can be attributed to upregulation of top-down cognitive control. This finding is consonant with previous ERN studies suggesting greater upregulation of cognitive control for higher physically active and aerobically fit individuals (Hillman et al., 2009; Themanson & Hillman, 2006; Themanson et al., 2006). Although PLVs and ERPs represent different aspects of neural processing, PLVs are also useful to assess the PA/fitness–cognition association and may be able to explain one of the possible mechanisms underlying this association (i.e., functional connectivity between brain regions).

CONCLUSIONS

Earlier neuroelectric studies of the P3, CNV, and ERN ERPs focused on overall PA levels, aerobic fitness, and higher-order cognitive control, and indicated that higher physically active and aerobically fit individuals exhibit superior cognitive control relative to their less active/fit peers across the lifespan. Newer neuroelectric studies have provided additional insights into the PA/fitness–cognition association by focusing on different types of PA and different aspects of cognitive processes, and by using more practical cognitive tasks, other ERP components, and other analysis techniques. In addition, a few recent ERP studies employed a longitudinal, randomized, and controlled design (Hillman et al., 2014; Kamijo, Pontifex, et al., 2011) and demonstrated a causal relationship between changes in fitness and cognitive function, which is generally consistent with the findings of cross-sectional studies. These neuroelectric studies have played a critical role in this area of research, and I would conclude that neuroelectric measures, coupled with behavioral task performance, can lead to a deeper understanding of the PA/fitness–cognition association.

References

Bentin, S., Allison, T., Puce, A., Perez, E., & McCarthy, G. (1996). Electrophysiological studies of face perception in humans. *Journal of Cognitive Neuroscience, 8*, 551–565.

Bentin, S., & Deouell, L. Y. (2000). Structural encoding and identification in face processing: ERP evidence for separate mechanisms. *Cognitive Neuropsychology, 17*, 35–55.

Biddle, S. J., & Asare, M. (2011). Physical activity and mental health in children and adolescents: a review of reviews. *British Journal of Sports Medicine, 45*, 886–895.

Blair, C., & Razza, R. P. (2007). Relating effortful control, executive function, and false belief understanding to emerging math and literacy ability in kindergarten. *Child Development, 78*, 647–663.

Botvinick, M. M., Braver, T. S., Barch, D. M., Carter, C. S., & Cohen, J. D. (2001). Conflict monitoring and cognitive control. *Psychological Review, 108*, 624–652.

Botvinick, M., Nystrom, L. E., Fissell, K., Carter, C. S., & Cohen, J. D. (1999). Conflict monitoring versus selection-for-action in anterior cingulate cortex. *Nature, 402*, 179–181.

van Boxtel, G. J., & Brunia, C. H. (1994). Motor and non-motor aspects of slow brain potentials. *Biological Psychology, 38*, 37–51.

Braver, T. S. (2012). The variable nature of cognitive control: a dual mechanisms framework. *Trends in Cognitive Sciences, 16*, 106–113.

Braver, T. S., Gray, J. R., & Burgess, G. C. (2007). Explaining the many varieties of working memory variation: dual mechanisms of cognitive control. In A. R. A. Conway, C. Jarrold, M. J. Kane, A. Miyake, & J. N. Towse (Eds.), *Variation in working memory* (pp. 76–106). New York: Oxford University Press.

Brunia, C. H., & van Boxtel, G. J. (2001). Wait and see. *International Journal of Psychophysiology, 43*, 59–75.

Bull, R., & Scerif, G. (2001). Executive functioning as a predictor of children's mathematics ability: inhibition, switching, and working memory. *Developmental Neuropsychology, 19*, 273–293.

Buschman, T. J., & Miller, E. K. (2007). Top-down versus bottom-up control of attention in the prefrontal and posterior parietal cortices. *Science, 315*, 1860–1862.

Carter, C. S., Braver, T. S., Barch, D. M., Botvinick, M. M., Noll, D., & Cohen, J. D. (1998). Anterior cingulate cortex, error detection, and the online monitoring of performance. *Science, 280*, 747–749.

Carter, C. S., & van Veen, V. (2007). Anterior cingulate cortex and conflict detection: an update of theory and data. *Cognitive, Affective, and Behavioral Neuroscience, 7*, 367–379.

Castelli, D. M., Hillman, C. H., Buck, S. M., & Erwin, H. E. (2007). Physical fitness and academic achievement in third- and fifth-grade students. *Journal of Sport and Exercise Psychology, 29*, 239–252.

Chang, Y. K., Huang, C. J., Chen, K. F., & Hung, T. M. (2013). Physical activity and working memory in healthy older adults: an ERP study. *Psychophysiology, 50*, 1174–1182.

Dai, C. T., Chang, Y. K., Huang, C. J., & Hung, T. M. (2013). Exercise mode and executive function in older adults: an ERP study of task-switching. *Brain and Cognition, 83*, 153–162.

De Pisapia, N., & Braver, T. S. (2006). A model of dual control mechanisms through anterior cingulate and prefrontal cortex interactions. *Neurocomputing, 69*, 1322–1326.

Dehaene, S., Posner, M. I., & Tucker, D. M. (1994). Localization of a neural system for error detection and compensation. *Psychological Science, 5*, 303–305.

Donchin, E. (1981). Surprise!...Surprise? *Psychophysiology, 18*, 493–513.

Dustman, R. E., Emmerson, R. Y., Ruhling, R. O., Shearer, D. E., Steinhaus, L. A., Johnson, S. C., et al. (1990). Age and fitness effects on EEG, ERPs, visual sensitivity, and cognition. *Neurobiology of Aging, 11*, 193–200.

Eimer, M. (2000). Effects of face inversion on the structural encoding and recognition of faces. Evidence from event-related brain potentials. *Brain Research: Cognitive Brain Research, 10*, 145–158.

Falkenstein, M., Hoormann, J., Hohnsbein, J., & Kleinsorge, T. (2003). Short-term mobilization of processing resources is revealed in the event-related potential. *Psychophysiology, 40*, 914–923.

Fjell, A. M., Rosquist, H., & Walhovd, K. B. (2009). Instability in the latency of P3a/P3b brain potentials and cognitive function in aging. *Neurobiology of Aging, 30*, 2065–2079.

Fjell, A. M., & Walhovd, K. B. (2007). Stability of brain potentials, mental abilities, and cortical thickness. *NeuroReport*, *18*, 725–728.

Fong, D. Y., Chi, L. K., Li, F., & Chang, Y. K. (2014). The benefits of endurance exercise and Tai Chi Chuan for the task-switching aspect of executive function in older adults: an ERP study. *Frontiers in Aging Neuroscience*, *6*, 295. http://dx.doi.org/10.3389/fnagi.2014.00295.

Friederici, A. D. (2002). Towards a neural basis of auditory sentence processing. *Trends in Cognitive Sciences*, *6*, 78–84.

Friedman, D., Nessler, D., Cycowicz, Y. M., & Horton, C. (2009). Development of and change in cognitive control: a comparison of children, young adults, and older adults. *Cognitive, Affective and Behavioral Neuroscience*, *9*, 91–102.

Gehring, W. J., Goss, B., Coles, M. G. H., Meyer, D. E., & Donchin, E. (1993). A neural system for error detection and compensation. *Psychological Science*, *4*, 385–390.

Getzmann, S., Falkenstein, M., & Gajewski, P. D. (2013). Long-term cardiovascular fitness is associated with auditory attentional control in old adults: neuro-behavioral evidence. *PLoS One*, *8*, e74539. http://dx.doi.org/10.1371/journal.pone.0074539.

Gosling, A., & Eimer, M. (2011). An event-related brain potential study of explicit face recognition. *Neuropsychologia*, *49*, 2736–2745.

Gratton, G., Coles, M. G., & Donchin, E. (1992). Optimizing the use of information: strategic control of activation of responses. *Journal of Experimental Psychology: General*, *121*, 480–506.

Hillman, C. H., Belopolsky, A. V., Snook, E. M., Kramer, A. F., & McAuley, E. (2004). Physical activity and executive control: implications for increased cognitive health during older adulthood. *Research Quarterly for Exercise and Sport*, *75*, 176–185.

Hillman, C. H., Buck, S. M., Themanson, J. R., Pontifex, M. B., & Castelli, D. M. (2009). Aerobic fitness and cognitive development: event-related brain potential and task performance indices of executive control in preadolescent children. *Developmental Psychology*, *45*, 114–129.

Hillman, C. H., Castelli, D. M., & Buck, S. M. (2005). Aerobic fitness and neurocognitive function in healthy preadolescent children. *Medicine and Science in Sports and Exercise*, *37*, 1967–1974.

Hillman, C. H., Kamijo, K., & Pontifex, M. B. (2012). The relation of ERP indices of exercise to brain health and cognition. In H. Boecker, C. H. Hillman, L. Scheef, & H. K. Strüder (Eds.), *Functional neuroimaging in exercise and sport sciences* (pp. 419–446). New York: Springer.

Hillman, C. H., Kramer, A. F., Belopolsky, A. V., & Smith, D. P. (2006). A cross-sectional examination of age and physical activity on performance and event-related brain potentials in a task switching paradigm. *International Journal of Psychophysiology*, *59*, 30–39.

Hillman, C. H., Pontifex, M. B., Castelli, D. M., Khan, N. A., Raine, L. B., Scudder, M. R., et al. (2014). Effects of the FITKids randomized controlled trial on executive control and brain function. *Pediatrics*, *134*, e1063–1071. http://dx.doi.org/10.1542/peds.2013-3219.

Hillman, C. H., Pontifex, M. B., Motl, R. W., O'Leary, K. C., Johnson, C. R., Scudder, M. R., et al. (2012). From ERPs to academics. *Developmental Cognitive Neuroscience*, *2*(Suppl. 1), S90–S98.

Hillman, C. H., Weiss, E. P., Hagberg, J. M., & Hatfield, B. D. (2002). The relationship of age and cardiovascular fitness to cognitive and motor processes. *Psychophysiology*, *39*, 303–312.

Holroyd, C. B., & Coles, M. G. (2002). The neural basis of human error processing: reinforcement learning, dopamine, and the error-related negativity. *Psychological Review*, *109*, 679–709.

Jonkman, L. M., Lansbergen, M., & Stauder, J. E. (2003). Developmental differences in behavioral and event-related brain responses associated with response preparation and inhibition in a go/nogo task. *Psychophysiology*, *40*(5), 752–761.

Kamijo, K., Bae, S., & Masaki, H. *The association of childhood fitness to proactive and reactive action monitoring* manuscript submitted for publication.

Kamijo, K., O'Leary, K. C., Pontifex, M. B., Themanson, J. R., & Hillman, C. H. (2010). The relation of aerobic fitness to neuroelectric indices of cognitive and motor task preparation. *Psychophysiology*, *47*, 814–821.

Kamijo, K., Pontifex, M. B., O'Leary, K. C., Scudder, M. R., Wu, C. T., Castelli, D. M., et al. (2011). The effects of an afterschool physical activity program on working memory in preadolescent children. *Developmental Science*, *14*, 1046–1058.

Kamijo, K., & Takeda, Y. (2009). General physical activity levels influence positive and negative priming effects in young adults. *Clinical Neurophysiology*, *120*, 511–519.

Kamijo, K., & Takeda, Y. (2010). Regular physical activity improves executive function during task switching in young adults. *International Journal of Psychophysiology*, *75*, 304–311.

Kamijo, K., & Takeda, Y. (2013). Physical activity and trial-by-trial adjustments of response conflict. *Journal of Sport and Exercise Psychology*, *35*, 398–407.

Kamijo, K., & Takeda, Y. (2014). The association of physical activity to occipito-temporal processing during face recognition. *Psychology of Sport and Exercise*, *15*, 255–259.

Kamijo, K., Takeda, Y., & Hillman, C. H. (2011). The relation of physical activity to functional connectivity between brain regions. *Clinical Neurophysiology*, *122*, 81–89.

Kanwisher, N., McDermott, J., & Chun, M. M. (1997). The fusiform face area: a module in human extrastriate cortex specialized for face perception. *Journal of Neuroscience*, *17*, 4302–4311.

Kerns, J. G., Cohen, J. D., MacDonald, A. W., 3rd, Cho, R. Y., Stenger, V. A., & Carter, C. S. (2004). Anterior cingulate conflict monitoring and adjustments in control. *Science, 303,* 1023–1026.

Kray, J., & Lindenberger, U. (2000). Adult age differences in task switching. *Psychology of Aging, 15,* 126–147.

Kuperberg, G. R. (2007). Neural mechanisms of language comprehension: challenges to syntax. *Brain Research, 1146,* 23–49.

Kutas, M., & Federmeier, K. D. (2011). Thirty years and counting: finding meaning in the N400 component of the event-related brain potential (ERP). *Annual Review of Psychology, 62,* 621–647.

Lachaux, J. P., Rodriguez, E., Martinerie, J., & Varela, F. J. (1999). Measuring phase synchrony in brain signals. *Human Brain Mapping, 8,* 194–208.

Latzman, R. D., Elkovitch, N., Young, J., & Clark, L. A. (2010). The contribution of executive functioning to academic achievement among male adolescents. *Journal of Clinical and Experimental Neuropsychology, 32,* 455–462.

Leynes, P. A., Allen, J. D., & Marsh, R. L. (1998). Topographic differences in CNV amplitude reflect different preparatory processes. *International Journal of Psychophysiology, 31,* 33–44.

Li, S. C., Lindenberger, U., Hommel, B., Aschersleben, G., Prinz, W., & Baltes, P. B. (2004). Transformations in the couplings among intellectual abilities and constituent cognitive processes across the life span. *Psychological Science, 15,* 155–163.

Liu-Ambrose, T., Nagamatsu, L. S., Graf, P., Beattie, B. L., Ashe, M. C., & Handy, T. C. (2010). Resistance training and executive functions: a 12-month randomized controlled trial. *Archives of Internal Medicine, 170,* 170–178.

Lorist, M. M., Klein, M., Nieuwenhuis, S., De Jong, R., Mulder, G., & Meijman, T. F. (2000). Mental fatigue and task control: planning and preparation. *Psychophysiology, 37,* 614–625.

Loveless, N. E., & Sanford, A. J. (1974). Slow potential correlates of preparatory set. *Biological Psychology, 1,* 303–314.

Miltner, W. H., Lemke, U., Weiss, T., Holroyd, C., Scheffers, M. K., & Coles, M. G. (2003). Implementation of error-processing in the human anterior cingulate cortex: a source analysis of the magnetic equivalent of the error-related negativity. *Biological Psychology, 64,* 157–166.

Moore, R. D., Drollette, E. S., Scudder, M. R., Bharij, A., & Hillman, C. H. (2014). The influence of cardiorespiratory fitness on strategic, behavioral, and electrophysiological indices of arithmetic cognition in preadolescent children. *Frontiers in Human Neuroscience, 8,* 258. http://dx.doi.org/10.3389/fnhum.2014.00258.

Moore, R. D., Wu, C. T., Pontifex, M. B., O'Leary, K. C., Scudder, M. R., Raine, L. B., et al. (2013). Aerobic fitness and intra-individual variability of neurocognition in preadolescent children. *Brain and Cognition, 82,* 43–57.

Phillips, S., & Takeda, Y. (2009). Greater frontal-parietal synchrony at low gamma-band frequencies for inefficient than efficient visual search in human EEG. *International Journal of Psychophysiology, 73,* 350–354.

Polich, J. (2007). Updating P300: an integrative theory of P3a and P3b. *Clinical Neurophysiology, 118,* 2128–2148.

Polich, J., & Lardon, M. T. (1997). P300 and long-term physical exercise. *Electroencephalography Clinical Neurophysiology, 103,* 493–498.

Pontifex, M. B., Hillman, C. H., & Polich, J. (2009). Age, physical fitness, and attention: P3a and P3b. *Psychophysiology, 46,* 379–387.

Pontifex, M. B., Raine, L. B., Johnson, C. R., Chaddock, L., Voss, M. W., Cohen, N. J., et al. (2011). Cardiorespiratory fitness and the flexible modulation of cognitive control in preadolescent children. *Journal of Cognitive Neuroscience, 23,* 1332–1345.

Raymond, J. E., Shapiro, K. L., & Arnell, K. M. (1992). Temporary suppression of visual processing in an RSVP task: an attentional blink? *Journal of Experimental Psychology: Human Perception and Performance, 18,* 849–860.

Rogers, R. D., & Monsell, S. (1995). Costs of a predictable switch between simple cognitive tasks. *Journal of Experimental Psychology: General, 124,* 207.

Scudder, M. R., Federmeier, K. D., Raine, L. B., Direito, A., Boyd, J. K., & Hillman, C. H. (2014). The association between aerobic fitness and language processing in children: Implications for academic achievement. *Brain and Cognition, 87,* 140–152.

Segalowitz, S. J., Unsal, A., & Dywan, J. (1992). Cleverness and wisdom in 12-year-olds: electrophysiological evidence for late maturation of the frontal lobe. *Developmental Neuropsychology, 8,* 279–298.

Shvartz, E., & Reibold, R. C. (1990). Aerobic fitness norms for males and females aged 6 to 75 years: A review. *Aviation, Space, and Environmental Medicine, 61,* 3–11.

Themanson, J. R., & Hillman, C. H. (2006). Cardiorespiratory fitness and acute aerobic exercise effects on neuroelectric and behavioral measures of action monitoring. *Neuroscience, 141,* 757–767.

Themanson, J. R., Hillman, C. H., & Curtin, J. J. (2006). Age and physical activity influences on action monitoring during task switching. *Neurobiology of Aging, 27,* 1335–1345.

Themanson, J. R., Pontifex, M. B., & Hillman, C. H. (2008). Fitness and action monitoring: evidence for improved cognitive flexibility in young adults. *Neuroscience, 157,* 319–328.

Tipper, S. P., Brehaut, J. C., & Driver, J. (1990). Selection of moving and static objects for the control of spatially directed action. *Journal of Experimental Psychology: Human Perception and Performance, 16,* 492–504.

Verleger, R. (1997). On the utility of P3 latency as an index of mental chronometry. *Psychophysiology, 34,* 131–156.

Voss, M. W., Chaddock, L., Kim, J. S., Vanpatter, M., Pontifex, M. B., Raine, L. B., et al. (2011). Aerobic fitness is associated with greater efficiency of the network underlying cognitive control in preadolescent children. *Neuroscience, 199*, 166–176.

Voss, M. W., Kramer, A. F., Basak, C., Prakash, R. S., & Roberts, B. (2010). Are expert athletes "expert" in the cognitive laboratory? A meta-analytic review of cognition and sport expertise. *Applied Cognitive Psychology, 24*, 812–826.

Weerts, T. C., & Lang, P. J. (1973). The effects of eye fixation and stimulus and response location on the contingent negative variation (CNV). *Biological Psychology, 1*, 1–19.

Wild-Wall, N., Hohnsbein, J., & Falkenstein, M. (2007). Effects of ageing on cognitive task preparation as reflected by event-related potentials. *Clinical Neurophysiology, 118*, 558–569.

Williams, B. R., Hultsch, D. F., Strauss, E. H., Hunter, M. A., & Tannock, R. (2005). Inconsistency in reaction time across the life span. *Neuropsychology, 19*, 88–96.

Wu, C. T., & Hillman, C. H. (2013). Aerobic fitness and the attentional blink in preadolescent children. *Neuropsychology, 27*, 642–653. http://dx.doi.org/10.1037/a0034025.

Wu, C. T., Pontifex, M. B., Raine, L. B., Chaddock, L., Voss, M. W., Kramer, A. F., et al. (2011). Aerobic fitness and response variability in preadolescent children performing a cognitive control task. *Neuropsychology, 25*, 333–341.

Yeung, N., Botvinick, M. M., & Cohen, J. D. (2004). The neural basis of error detection: conflict monitoring and the error-related negativity. *Psychological Review, 111*, 931–959.

Effects of Athletic Fitness on the Exercise–Cognition Interaction

Terry McMorris[1], Jo Corbett[2]

[1] Department of Sport and Exercise Science, University of Chichester, Chichester, West Sussex, UK;
[2] Department of Sport and Exercise Science, Faculty of Science, University of Portsmouth, Portsmouth, UK

INTRODUCTION

Most of the chapters in this book, and indeed most of the chronic exercise–cognition interaction literature, look at effects of an active lifestyle on cognitive functioning. In this chapter, we examine the effects of fitness per se, rather than simply the effects of having an active lifestyle or, in other words, being fitter than someone who is sedentary. We are interested in comparisons between individuals of different "above average" fitness levels and whether getting fitter is advantageous for cognitive functioning of individuals who are already "above average." Of particular interest to us is the effect of fitness levels on cognitive performance during exercise, as one finds with sports performers, the military, firefighters, and individuals working in similar occupations. We begin by examining what exactly we mean by fitness, from a physiological perspective, and how its effects might interact with cognition. Changes in brain neurochemistry as the result of long-duration, high-intensity training are also discussed. With

regard to undertaking cognition during exercise, especially heavy exercise, a key issue would appear to be how these physiological and neurochemical changes interact with perceptions of stress and, from a neuroscience perspective, with hypothalamic–pituitary–adrenal (HPA) axis activity. In the later parts of the chapter, we discuss the empirical evidence for fitness effects.

DEFINING FITNESS

Fitness can be defined as the ability to meet the physical demands of a given task and can be viewed as a multifaceted construct incorporating various components such as: agility; balance; cardiorespiratory endurance; coordination; flexibility; local muscular endurance; power; and strength. However, in the context of the exercise–cognition interaction, fitness is typically expressed in terms of cardiorespiratory fitness, that is, the rate at which the circulatory and respiratory systems are able to take up oxygen and transport oxygen to the working muscles

Exercise-Cognition Interaction
http://dx.doi.org/10.1016/B978-0-12-800778-5.00011-6

and subsequently the ability of the working muscles to utilize that oxygen to provide the energy to power muscular contractions. More specifically, cardiorespiratory fitness is determined by an individual's ability to ventilate the lungs with ambient air and to transport the oxygen contained within the air across the lung's alveolar membrane into the capillary network perfusing the lung, where it will bind to hemoglobin within the blood. Thereafter, the oxygen-rich blood must be pumped by the heart, through the vasculature, to the capillaries perfusing the working muscles where the oxygen will bind to myoglobin and be transported to the mitochondria contained within the muscle cells. Inside the mitochondria, the oxygen acts as the final acceptor in the electron transport chain. This process serves to liberate the energy contained within the food stuffs (predominantly fats and carbohydrates) that we consume and produces the bulk of the aerobically derived (with oxygen) adenosine triphosphate, a high-energy phosphate molecule, which is broken down to provide the energy used to power muscular contraction, as well as other energy requiring processes.

As work rate, and therefore energy demand, increases, the rate of oxygen uptake will increase in proportion, in an approximately linear manner. However, with continual increases in work rate a point may eventually be reached whereby there is no further increase in oxygen uptake despite further increases in work rate, that is, a plateau is reached in the work rate–oxygen uptake relationship. This point signifies the individual's maximum rate of oxygen uptake, or $\dot{V}O_{2MAX}$, that is, the maximum rate at which they are able to take up and utilize oxygen to produce energy during exercise involving a significant muscle mass. The $\dot{V}O_{2MAX}$ is usually expressed as the amount of oxygen (in liters) consumed per minute ($L\,min^{-1}$), termed the *absolute* $\dot{V}O_{2MAX}$, or as the amount of oxygen consumed (in milliliters) per unit of body weight (kg) per minute ($mL\,kg^{-1}\,min^{-1}$), termed the *relative* $\dot{V}O_{2MAX}$; the relative $\dot{V}O_{2MAX}$ is typically used when comparing individuals of substantially different size or when studying modes of exercise where the individual must carry their own body mass, for example, walking, running, etc. However, the use of this "ratio-standard" approach has been criticized because it typically fails to satisfy a condition known as Tanner's law and it has been suggested that the surface law exponent of 0.67 should be used to more satisfactorily scale for differences in body mass ($mL\,kg^{-067}\,min^{-1}$) (Winter, 2007), but in practice this is less common.

Most lines of evidence suggest that under most circumstances, the $\dot{V}O_{2MAX}$ is limited by the supply of oxygen-rich blood to the working muscles, as determined by the oxygen carrying capacity of the blood and the ability of the heart to pump that blood to the muscles (cardiac output), rather than the uptake of oxygen across the lung or the utilization of oxygen within the working muscles (Bassett & Howley, 2007). $\dot{V}O_{2MAX}$ is considered the primary marker of cardiorespiratory fitness and athletes excelling in sports requiring high levels of endurance, or cardiorespiratory fitness, will typically have the highest $\dot{V}O_{2MAX}$; values in the region of $95\,mL\,kg^{-1}\,min^{-1}$ have been reported for some elite endurance athletes, which is approximately double that of an active, healthy, nonelite athlete (Wilmore & Costill, 2004). Consequently, $\dot{V}O_{2MAX}$ is typically used as the criterion measure for defining "fitness" in exercise science research. However, it should be noted that while $\dot{V}O_{2MAX}$ is often regarded as being synonymous with both "training-status" and "performance" in endurance sports, this is not entirely accurate. There is a substantial genetic component to $\dot{V}O_{2MAX}$ and each individual will have their own, genetically influenced, baseline (untrained) values, and ceiling for trainability (Bouchard et al., 1999). Some individuals who are not highly trained may naturally possess a $\dot{V}O_{2MAX}$ in excess of some highly trained (but less fortunate) individuals, whereas other factors such as the ability to sustain a high percentage of the $\dot{V}O_{2MAX}$ for a prolonged time and the ability to efficiently convert the energy from aerobic metabolism into movement are also important determinants of endurance performance (Joyner & Coyle, 2008).

STANDARDIZING EXERCISE STRESS

Once we have defined fitness, we may be presented with a quandary; unless we very carefully select our participants, we will encounter a range of fitness levels within a given population sample. Thus, if we are conducting a study looking at an aspect of cognition during exercise and ask all participants to exercise at the same *absolute exercise intensity*, for instance cycle ergometer exercise at an external work rate of 100 W, the physiological responses (which may influence cognition) and the degree of physiological stress will differ between the participants; it is likely that the physiological stress will be lower for the fitter individuals and higher for the less fit participants. Moreover, there is evidence to suggest that the exercise–cognition interaction effect may be influenced by the level of relative physiological stress (Chang, Labban, Gapin, & Etnier, 2012; McMorris & Hale, 2012). Thus, a common approach is to standardize the *relative exercise intensity* to try to ensure a more uniform physiological response and more homogeneous degree of physiological stress between participants. To achieve the same relative exercise intensity, it is necessary to adjust the absolute external work rate of the participants on an individual basis in order to induce the same, or a very similar, response in a given physiological parameter.

Given that $\dot{V}O_{2MAX}$ is typically regarded as being the primary index of cardiorespiratory fitness, one of the most common approaches to standardizing exercise intensity is to adjust the absolute external work rate to ensure that participants are working at the same percentage of their $\dot{V}O_{2MAX}$, for example, 75% $\dot{V}O_{2MAX}$. Depending on the level of precision required,

this can be achieved through a trial and error approach, through using various formulas (e.g., American College of Sports Medicine, 2010), or by establishing the individual work rate: $\dot{V}O_{2MAX}$ relationship across a range of submaximal exercise intensities and $\dot{V}O_{2MAX}$, and using linear interpolation. However, direct measurement of $\dot{V}O_{2MAX}$ requires relatively expensive equipment and $\dot{V}O_{2MAX}$ necessitates maximal exercise, which may not be appropriate for certain populations; various submaximal (e.g., Åstrand & Rhyming, 1954; Maritz, Morrison, Peter, & Strydom, 1961) and maximal (e.g., Cooper, 1968; Léger & Lambert, 1982) predicative tests for $\dot{V}O_{2MAX}$ are available and overcome these issues, although they afford reduced accuracy. It should also be noted that under certain conditions, $\dot{V}O_{2MAX}$ may change over time, even when the external work rate is fixed; this may be particularly evident with very prolonged exercise durations, very cold or hot ambient conditions, or high intensities of exercise. Moreover, it has been shown that the VO_2 reserve (VO_2R), which represents the achievable VO_2 range for a given participant, that is, the difference between VO_{2REST} and $\dot{V}O_{2MAX}$, more accurately reflects energy expenditure than percent $\dot{V}O_{2MAX}$ (Swain & Leutholtz, 1997). However, measurement of "true" resting VO_2 in a laboratory setting can often be practically difficult and a standard value of $3.5\,mL\,kg^{-1}\,min^{-1}$ is often assumed. Exercise intensity can be standardized based upon a target percent of VO_2R (percent expressed as a decimal, e.g., 50% = 0.5), as follows: target $VO_2R = [(\dot{V}O_{2MAX} - VO_{2REST}) \times$ percent intensity required] + VO_{2REST}. On occasion, exercise intensity is standardized with reference to the same absolute VO_2, for example, all participants exercise at the individual external work rate eliciting an absolute VO_2 of $2\,L\,min^{-1}$. While this approach may be appropriate when addressing certain research questions, in the main it suffers from the same limitations as standardizing exercise intensity based upon a fixed absolute external work rate.

Another popular approach to standardizing the relative exercise intensity is to use a given target heart rate for all participants, for example, $150 \text{ beats min}^{-1}$, particularly as there is an approximately linear relationship between heart rate and VO_2 during exercise of increasing intensity and because equipment for measuring heart rate is much cheaper than equipment for measuring VO_2. However, given that maximum heart rate (HR_{MAX}) varies between individuals and declines with age, it is more common to use a standardized percentage of the HR_{MAX}, for example, 75% HR_{MAX}, and individuals with different HR_{MAX} would therefore be exercising at different absolute heart rates according to this approach. The HR_{MAX} rate can be estimated using a variety of formula taking into account the individual's age (Fox, Naughton, & Haskell, 1971; Tanaka, Monahan, & Seals, 2001), but these can be imprecise and if greater accuracy is required, and the population being studied is suitable for undertaking maximal exercise, then some form of intense exercise test to elicit maximum heart rate may be appropriate. It should be noted that even when the external work rate is fixed, heart rate will often increase over time, particularly at higher exercise intensities. Heart rate is also influenced by the participant's hydration status, the temperature of the participant and the environment, and substances such as caffeine and certain medications. These factors need to be controlled in an experimental setting. Pertinently, when considering the study of exercise–cognition interaction effects, heart rate may also be influenced by mental stress (Hjortskov et al., 2004). Moreover, it has been noted that considerable interindividual variation also exists in the individual resting heart rate (HR_{REST}); the heart rate reserve (HRR) method has been developed as a way of taking the interindividual variations in HR_{REST} and HR_{MAX} into account (Karvonen & Vuorimaa, 1988), and is conceptually similar to the VO_2R method. Determining the HRR requires that, in addition to HR_{MAX}, the HR_{REST} of the participant must also be measured, although this can be difficult under laboratory conditions and may

be subject to small daily variations. Thereafter, the HRR can be calculated as: $HR_{MAX} - HR_{REST}$. To determine a target percent HRR value, the appropriate percentage of HRR (as a decimal, e.g., 50% = 0.5) is added to the HR_{REST}, for example, target percent $HRR = HR_{REST} + (HRR \times percent$ intensity required). In many circumstances HRR is preferred instead of percent HR_{MAX} as the method of standardizing exercise intensity, because it more accurately reflects the rate of energy expenditure than percent maximum heart rate and is related to VO_2 reserve (Swain & Leutholtz, 1997).

Although VO_2 and heart rate increase in an approximately linear fashion with increasing work rate, the kinetics of blood lactate accumulation display "threshold" behavior with an increasing work rate. This means that there may be a range of exercise intensities across which blood lactate is relatively unchanging (or may even decrease slightly), before a work rate is reached beyond which blood lactate concentration begins to increase in an approximately exponential fashion. Traditional dogma pertains that the *lactate threshold* (LT) is caused by the development of anaerobic conditions within the exercising muscle. This explanation has now been largely discredited and it is now believed that this phenomenon is underpinned by a combination of factors such as increased recruitment of the type II muscle fibers, which have a greater reliance on carbohydrate metabolism, and a reduced lactate clearance, which together tip the balance between lactate production and lactate clearance in favor of lactate accumulation. Nevertheless, although the physiological significance of the LT has been questioned, it is one of the most powerful physiological predictors of endurance performance (Yoshida, Udo, Iwai, & Yamaguchi, 1993) and there is considerable interindividual variation in the LT. Practically, this is relevant because a situation can arise where two participants may be exercising at the same percent $\dot{V}O_{2MAX}$, VO_2R, HR_{MAX}, or HRR, yet one of the participants may be exercising below their LT, while the other may be exercising above their LT. Therefore, this marker of physiological "stress" may differ between participants, to a significant extent, even when attempts have been made to standardize the relative exercise intensity according to some of the most commonly used approaches previously outlined. It should be noted that at fixed external work rates just in excess of the individual LT, the blood lactate concentration will be elevated but stable, or even slightly decreasing, over time. However, with further increases in external work rate, a point will be reached where, even when work rate is fixed, blood lactate concentration will increase as a function of time. The highest work rate where stable (albeit elevated relative to exercise below LT) blood lactate concentrations can be achieved is termed the *maximal lactate steady state* (MLSS). Given that this point represents a transition from steady-state to non-steady-state metabolic conditions, the MLSS may be of greater significance than the LT in terms of standardizing the exercise "stress," but is practically much more difficult to determine, requiring multiple laboratory visits at increasing work rates to identify the highest external work rate where lactate can be stabilized over a given exercise period (usually 30 min).

Ventilation also exhibits threshold behavior, with the *ventilatory threshold* (VT) typically occurring at approximately the same work rate as the LT (Beaver, Wassermann, & Whipp, 1986). This is because buffering of the protons that dissociate from lactic acid by the bicarbonate buffering system results in the production of carbon dioxide, which stimulates an increase in ventilation to blow off this "excess" carbon dioxide at the lung. Thus, the VT is often used as a surrogate measure of the LT, and is therefore also used as a means of standardizing the relative level of exercise stress. Indeed, the VT may be preferable under certain circumstances, particularly where blood lactate sampling is not possible. However, the physiological basis of the VT has been questioned for a variety of reasons, including the observation that a VT may also

be evident in individuals with McArdle's disease (Hagberg et al., 1982), despite the fact that these individuals have no discernible LT. Moreover, there may often be some small difference in the absolute work rate at which the LT and VT occur (Simon et al., 1986); this may have a physiological basis or could be caused by methodological factors. Typically, both the LT and VT are measured using an incremental exercise test, but it is common to employ relatively long stage duration (>5 min) for an LT test in order to enable sufficient time for the slower kinetics of blood lactate to achieve a stable blood lactate concentration, whereas shorter stage durations (~1 min) are more often used in the determination of the VT.

Although the LT and VT concepts are relatively well documented within exercise physiology, the existence of thresholds for adrenaline and noradrenaline are, perhaps, less often acknowledged. Adrenaline and noradrenaline have both been shown to increase in an approximately exponential manner with increasing intensities of exercise (Beaver et al., 1986; Chmura, Nazar, & Kaciuba-Uścilko, 1994) and while the absolute concentration of noradrenaline is typically at least ~4–5 times higher than that of adrenaline, their thresholds appear to occur at approximately the same absolute external work rate (Weltman et al., 1994) and they are often collectively referred to as the *catecholamine threshold* (T_{CATS}). Moreover, the release of adrenaline may play an important role in the accelerated rates of glycolysis that contribute to the LT and VT (Febbraio, Lambert, Starkie, Proietto, & Hargreaves, 1998; Richter, Ruderman, Gavras, Belur, & Galbo, 1982), although others have argued that accelerated lactate production and the associated decrease in pH in contracting muscle might increase sympathetic outflow resulting in the increased plasma catecholamine concentrations (Kjaer, Secher, Bach, Sheikh, & Galbo, 1989). Regardless, strong correlations have been reported between the T_{CATS} and LT (Chwalbinska-Moneta, Krysztofiak, Ziemba,

Nazar, & Kaciuba-Uściłko, 1996; Mazzeo & Marshall, 1989), with each occurring at a similar work rate (Chwalbinska-Moneta et al., 1996; Mazzeo & Marshall, 1989), but it should be noted that these findings are not universal (Dickhuth et al., 1999; McMorris et al., 2000; Schneider, McGuiggin, & Kamimori, 1992; Weltman et al., 1994), although the various threshold determination methods employed may have influenced these findings (McMorris et al., 2000). Importantly, with regard to exercise–cognition interaction research, the T_{CATS} is likely to represent a more relevant metabolic threshold than the LT or VT because, from such research, the LT and VT are only important in that they correlate with T_{CATS} and it is the effect of T_{CATS} on brain concentrations of dopamine and noradrenaline that is the key factor in the exercise–cognition interaction. Accordingly, accounting for the individual variations in the T_{CATS} is potentially of paramount importance when studying cognitive performance in exercising individuals.

An important physiological concept that has seldom been considered in the exercise–cognition literature is *critical power* (CP). The basis of the CP concept is that there is a hyperbolic relationship between external work rate and the time that the external work rate can be sustained. The work rate asymptote of this relationship is termed the CP, and this external work rate can theoretically be sustained without fatigue. Physiologically, the CP represents the highest external work rate that can be sustained without invoking a contribution from the finite anaerobic energy stores, that is, solely aerobic metabolism, and signifies the transition point from steady-state conditions to nonsteady-state exercise. Beyond the CP both VO_2 and blood lactate (i.e., MLSS) will increase as a function of time, even when the external work rate is fixed. Accordingly this point may be important in standardizing the exercise "stress" between participants and may have relevance for the study of exercise–cognition interaction effects. Practically it can be physically demanding and time-consuming to determine CP. The external work rate versus time asymptote can

be described based on the results of a series of three to seven or more timed all-out predicting trials, completed on separate days and at work rates eliciting volitional exhaustion between 2 and 15 min (Vanhatalo, Jones, & Burnley, 2011). An alternative, single 3 min test has been proposed, which requires participants to exercise in an all-out manner from the onset of exercise to rapidly exhaust their anaerobic energy capacity (Vanhatalo, Doust, & Burnley, 2008), with the assumption that once the anaerobic energy reserves are exhausted (toward the end of the exercise bout) the external work rate that can be elicited will be derived entirely from aerobic energy sources and therefore represents the CP. This test may be difficult to complete unless participants are highly motivated.

Taken together the key physiological events occurring with increasing intensities of exercise have been used to define discrete exercise intensity domains (Whipp & Rossiter, 2005), which may be conceptually useful for standardizing exercise stress between participants. The *moderate* intensity exercise domain encompasses all work rates below the LT (and/or VT or T_{CATS}). The LT defines the lower boundary of the *heavy* intensity exercise domain, with the upper boundary delineated by the MLSS, which broadly corresponds to CP. *Very heavy* intensity exercise is represented by all work rates in excess of MLSS/CP up until $\dot{V}O_{2MAX}$, whereas *severe* intensity exercise is represented by all work rates in excess of $\dot{V}O_{2MAX}$. However, it should be noted that there may be small differences in the terminology employed by different authors (Vanhatalo et al., 2011), for example, in most of the exercise–cognition interaction research, descriptions of intensities tend to be similar to those of Borer (2003), which are based on neuroendocrinological measures. Most researchers have limited their terminology to those similar to Borer's, that is, moderate (she used the word "intermediate") and heavy. Moderate would include postthreshold exercise and ranges from 50% to 79% $\dot{V}O_{2MAX}$ and exercise above 80% $\dot{V}O_{2MAX}$ would be described as heavy (see Chapters 1 and 4).

So far, all of the approaches presented for standardizing exercise stress have been based on physiological criteria. An alternative approach, which may prove fruitful in the study of the exercise–cognition interaction, is the *Rating of Perceived Exertion* [RPE (Borg, 1982)]. The perception of exertion has been described as the subjective sense of effort strain discomfort and/ or fatigue that is experienced during physical exercise (Robertson & Noble, 1997). It has been suggested that RPE represents the single best measure for determining physiological strain because it represents an integration of information from the peripheral working muscles and joints, from the central cardiovascular and respiratory systems, and from the central nervous system (Borg, 1982); RPE is well correlated with other indices of relative exercise intensity such as lactate concentration, heart rate, and % $\dot{V}O_{2MAX}$ (Edwards, Melcher, Hesser, Wigertz, & Ekelund, 1972; Faulkner & Eston, 2007). To measure the RPE, participants are simply required to report a number on a scale (most commonly a 6–20 category scale with verbal descriptors to guide the participant in their choice) having received a standardized set of instructions and ideally with some prior exercise performed across a range of intensities in order to familiarize the participant with the scale and to "anchor" the scale. RPE can be used in estimation mode, where the external work rate may be set and participants rate the resulting RPE, or in production mode, which is an "active" process where the participant will be free to vary their external work rate to elicit the required RPE. The ability to freely regulate external work rate is important, because it has been suggested that the variation in external work rate, that is, pacing, is an important task that humans will undertake during spontaneous exercise and is in itself a cognitively demanding task (Noakes, 2008), but is often disregarded in laboratory studies of exercise–cognition interaction because the external work rate is typically fixed in order to standardize the absolute or relative work rate between participants. Presently, it

is unclear if removing this cognitively demanding task confounds the results of exercise–cognition studies where external work rate is clamped, and may limit their ecological validity for many nonlaboratory situations. Future exercise–cognition studies should consider the use of RPE as a potential approach for standardizing exercise stress and studying exercise–cognition interactions.

NEUROCHEMICAL AND MORPHOLOGICAL RESPONSES TO TRAINING

Catecholamines

Training Effects and Responses to Undertaking Acute Exercise

Before examining the effects of training on brain and plasma catecholamines concentrations, it is necessary to look at responses to acute exercise. As these effects are covered in some detail in Chapter 4, here we will simply outline the process. During and even immediately before exercise, the hypothalamus and brainstem initiate action of the sympathoadrenal system. This results in the release of catecholamines at the postganglionic cells of those neurons that require activating or inhibiting. As we saw in the previous section, if exercise intensity continues to be increased, T_{CATS} will eventually be reached; this normally occurs at ~75% $\dot{V}O_{2MAX}$ (Podolin, Munger, & Mazzeo, 1991), but there are large interindividual variations (McMorris et al., 2000; Urhausen, Weiler, Coen, & Kindermann, 1994). McMorris and Hale (2012) claimed that reaching this threshold will result in peripherally circulating adrenaline and noradrenaline activating β-adrenoreceptors on the afferent vagus nerve, which terminates in the nucleus tractus solitarii (NTS) within the blood–brain barrier. Noradrenergic cells in the NTS, which project into the locus coeruleus, stimulate noradrenaline synthesis and release to other parts of the brain

(Miyashita & Williams, 2006). There is also evidence that vagal/NTS pathway activity results in increased synthesis and release of brain dopamine via stimulation of α_1-adrenoreceptor potentiated firing of dopamine neurons in the ventral tegmental area (Grenhoff, Nisell, Ferré, Aston-Jones, & Svensson, 1993; Grenhoff & Svensson, 1993). If exercise intensity increases beyond T_{CATS}, plasma catecholamines concentrations continue to rise and soon reach very high levels. Given that catecholamines have been shown to affect cognition in an inverted-U manner (Arnsten, 2009, 2011), one would expect exercise of moderate intensity to induce optimal cognitive functioning, and low and high intensities to inhibit performance. To some extent this has been shown to be the case (McMorris & Hale, 2012, 2015), but we have some reservations (see Chapter 4).

As we can see from the above, peripheral, plasma concentrations of adrenaline and noradrenaline play major roles, via activation of the vagal/NTS pathways, in the effect of acute exercise on cognition. However, fitness affects catecholamines responses to acute exercise. Following training, plasma concentrations of noradrenaline, at any absolute workload, are lower than at the same workload pre-exercise (Ehsani, Heath, Martin, Hagberg, & Holloszy, 1984; Greiwe, Hickner, Shah, Cryer, & Holloszy, 1999; Hagberg et al., 1984). However, the evidence concerning concentrations at relative workloads, that is, a percentage of $\dot{V}O_{2MAX}$ or maximum power output (W_{MAX}), is contradictory. Some authors have shown no significant effect (Péronnet et al., 1981; Winder, Hickson, Hagberg, Ehsani, & McLane, 1979), others a significant lowering (Hartley et al., 1972), yet others have shown an increase (Greiwe et al., 1999; Hagberg et al., 1984; Winder, Hagberg, Hickson, Ehsani, & McLane, 1978). Results for the effects of training on adrenaline concentrations during exercise are fairly unequivocal. At submaximal intensities, adrenaline concentrations are not affected by training; however, at maximal intensity, concentrations are higher, reflecting the increased absolute workload (Greiwe et al., 1999; Rogers et al., 1991). Given that since Tomporowski and Ellis' (1986) seminal paper research into the effects of exercise on cognition has tended to be undertaken at relative intensities, one would not expect fit and unfit individuals to differ in their responses to undertaking a cognitive task during exercise, except possibly at maximal intensity. At this intensity, increased activation of α_1- and β-adrenoreceptors might inhibit working memory tasks but facilitate perceptual tasks more in athletes than in unfit individuals (see Chapter 4 for more detail). This, however, is comparing fit athletes to sedentary individuals; the extent to which different levels of fitness would be affected cannot be ascertained from the research literature.

Training Effects on Brain Concentrations

In Chapter 4, we reported that animal studies had demonstrated significant evidence to show that chronic exercise induces increased brain concentrations of noradrenaline but mixed results for dopamine (Meeusen & De Meirleir, 1995; Meeusen, Piacentini, & De Meirleir, 2001). Overall, chronic exercise resulted in increases in whole brain noradrenaline concentrations, while results for dopamine concentrations tended to be region specific. Increases were found in the hypothalamus and midbrain but decreases in prefrontal cortex, hippocampus, and striatum. More recently, Marques et al. (2008) showed no significant effect of chronic exercise on extracellular dopamine concentrations. While these results suggest possible mixed effects, results concerning tyrosine hydroxylase (TH) messenger ribonucleic acid (mRNA) gene expression suggest very positive effects. TH is the rate limiter for catecholamines synthesis (Fernstrom & Fernstrom, 2007).

Increased TH mRNA expression has been shown in several animal studies (Foley & Fleshner, 2008; Gavrilović et al., 2012; Kim et al., 2011; Tümer et al., 2001), although O'Neal, van Hoomissen, Holmes, and Dishman (2001) showed no significant effect. Moreover, Higa-Tanaguchi, Silva, Silva, Michelini, and Stern (2007) demonstrated a positive effect of chronic exercise on the density of dopamine-β-hydroxylase (DBH) in the hypothalamic para-ventricular nucleus (PVN), while Gavrilović et al. found increased DBH mRNA in stellate ganglia. DBH is essential for the synthesis of noradrenaline from dopamine (see Chapter 4). These changes may have positive effects on cognition even at rest.

HPA Axis Hormones

Training Effects and Responses to Undertaking Acute Exercise

In Chapter 4, we saw that, during exercise, intensity needs to exceed 80% $\dot{V}O_{2MAX}$ for it to induce increases in plasma and salivary concentrations of adrenocorticotropin hormone (ACTH) and cortisol (Hill et al., 2008; De Vries, Bernards, Rooij, & Koppeschaar, 2000). Evidence from studies with trained athletes (Grasso, Lodi, Lupo, & Muscettola, 1997; Mastorakos, Pavlatou, Diamanti-Kandarakis, & Chrousos, 2005) suggests no change with training but obviously the fitter athletes will reach 80% $\dot{V}O_{2MAX}$ at a later absolute workload than will untrained or lower trained individuals. Similarly, in Chapter 4, we found that exercise of <80% $\dot{V}O_{2MAX}$ has to be of at least 45 min duration (Bridge, Weller, Rayson, & Jones, 2003; Shojaei, Farajov, & Jafari, 2011) to affect plasma and salivary concentrations of ACTH and cortisol. It is logical to expect fitter athletes to last for longer lengths of time without increases in peripheral HPA axis hormones.

Training Effects on Brain Concentrations

Research with humans comparing physically active people with sedentary individuals, or examining the effects of training programs on previously sedentary persons, has generally shown that chronic exercise does not alter basal plasma ACTH or cortisol concentrations (Blaney, Sothmann, Raff, Hart, & Horn, 1990; Chatzitheodorou, Kabitsis, Malliou, & Mougios, 2007; Duclos, Corcuff, Pehourcq, & Tabarin, 2001; Inder, Hellemans, Swanney, Prickett, & Donald, 1998; Strüder et al., 1999; Wittert, Livesey, Espiner, & Donald, 1996). As we saw in Chapter 8, plasma ACTH concentrations may tell us very little about central values as ACTH does not cross the blood–cerebrospinal fluid (CSF) barrier and CSF concentrations have been shown not to correlate with plasma concentrations (Allen, Kendall, McGilvra, & Vancura, 2011; Nappi et al., 1986). Changes in cortisol concentrations, or rather the lack of them, should be indicative of a lack of change in the brain but we need also to examine animal studies as these allow for direct examination of brain concentrations and gene expressions.

Research measuring the effects of chronic exercise on brain corticosterone concentrations in rodents has shown different results between forced and voluntary exercise. Forced exercise tends to result in increased corticosterone concentrations (Chennaoui, Gomez Merino, Lesage, Drogou, & Guezennec, 2002; Harbuz & Lightman, 1989), while voluntary exercise appears to have no significant effect (Droste et al., 2003; Ke, Yip, Li, Zheng, & Tong, 2011; Yanagita, Amemiya, Suzuki, & Kita, 2007). This is, of course, probably due to the stress involved in forced exercise. Moreover, apart from the fact that Campbell et al. (2010) showed increased corticotropin releasing factor (CRF) expression in the hypothalamus, studies examining chronic exercise-induced changes in CRF mRNA expression also supply support for no significant effect of chronic exercise on HPA axis activity. Some authors found CRF mRNA expression to be decreased in the hypothalamic PVN (Bi, Scott, Hyun, Ladenheim, & Moran, 2005; Kawashima et al., 2004), others no significant effect (Droste, Chandramohan, Hill, Linthorst, & Reul, 2007; Levin & Dunn-Meynell, 2004), while Campbell, Rakhshani, Fediuc, Bruni, and Riddell (2009) and Park et al. (2005) demonstrated initial increases followed by a return to original levels. Before leaving training studies with rodents, we should examine the effects on brain mRNA gene expressions of corticosteroid receptors, as these are vital in regulating corticosterone concentrations in rodents and cortisol concentrations in humans. Activation of mineralocorticoid receptors (MR) and glucocorticoid receptors (GR) in the brain suppresses HPA axis activity through inhibition of CRF neurons (Herman, Watson, Chao, Coirini, & McEwen, 1993). Thus, changes in the number of MR and GR receptors will affect HPA axis activity.

As we saw in Chapter 8, there would appear to be little effect of chronic exercise on GR mRNA expression in the hippocampus (Campbell et al., 2010; Chang et al., 2008; Droste et al., 2003; Fediuc, Campbell, & Riddell, 2006; Zheng et al., 2006), although Park et al. (2005) found a significant decrease in hippocampal region CA4 only, while Droste et al. (2007) found increased GR mRNA levels in hippocampal layers. Reductions in MR mRNA expression have been shown (Chang et al., 2008; Droste et al., 2003) but some authors found no significant effect (Droste et al., 2007; Park et al., 2005). Droste et al. (2007) also demonstrated no significant changes in GR mRNA expression in the hypothalamic PVN, frontal cortex, or anterior pituitary. Park et al. found initial decreases in PVN and anterior pituitary GR mRNA but as training continued these returned to pre-training levels.

Trained "Athletes"

It would appear from the above that training and/or regularly exercising has little or no effect on HPA axis activity, but we need to look at effects on trained "athletes" as these go beyond the levels of physical activity that we have so far examined. We have put the word "athletes" in inverted commas because we include individuals who train physically for working in the military or firefighting or any occupation or hobby that requires above-moderate levels of fitness. Despite the claims of some authors (e.g., Mastorakos et al., 2005) that athletes demonstrate hypercortisolism at baseline, there appears to be little evidence for this with the vast majority of studies showing no significant differences between well-trained athletes and sedentary individuals (Duclos, Corcuff, Rashedi, Fougere, & Manier, 1997; Duclos et al., 2001; Kern, Perras, Wodick, Fehm, & Born, 1995; Neary, Wheeler, Maclean, Cumming, & Quinney, 1994; Wittert et al., 1996). Some authors have shown increased plasma ACTH but without the expected, resultant increase in cortisol synthesis and release (Inder et al., 1995; Lehmann et al., 1993) (see the final paragraph of this subsection for a possible explanation for this).

Grasso et al. (1997) claimed that although there is little evidence of reduced GR mRNA in trained athletes, high-intensity exercise may result in decreased GR binding capacity. As the measurement of GR in the brain in humans is not possible, they decided to measure GR mRNA expression in the peripheral blood mononuclear cells. They argued that circulating lymphocyte GR reflect brain GR regulation, particularly hippocampal activity, as there is simultaneous downregulation of hippocampal and lymphocyte GR (Lowy, 1991). They found significantly lower GR binding capacity in young soccer players compared even to elderly individuals. They also found hypercortisolism in the soccer players but lower concentrations of testosterone. Similarly, Bonifazi et al. (2009) compared GR-α helices mRNA in the peripheral blood mononuclear cells of highly trained athletes to those of "low" trained athletes and sedentary individuals. GR-α helices are crucial to ligand binding in GR (Lu et al., 2006). GR-α mRNA were significantly lower in the highly fit athletes compared to both the sedentary group and "low" trained athletes, although the difference was far less with the latter group.

With regard to the effect of high-intensity training on HPA responses to acute exercise, several authors have shown that there is a smaller effect at the same absolute intensity

(Bouno, Yeager, & Sucec, 1987; Lehmann et al., 1993; Luger et al., 1987). This is most likely due to increased fitness lowering the relative intensity (Luger et al., 1987). However, Duclos et al. (1997) found that athletes demonstrated greater increases in ACTH release than sedentary individuals immediately following exercise but not in cortisol concentrations. In later studies, Duclos and colleagues (Duclos et al., 1998, 2001) claimed that this was probably due to decreased pituitary sensitivity to cortisol negative feedback.

To summarize, it is fair to say that although there is some evidence for fit athletes to demonstrate significantly higher plasma concentrations of ACTH, these do not result in increased cortisol concentrations, due to adaptations probably in the pituitary. Apart from the research of Grasso and colleagues (Grasso et al., 1997; Bonifazi et al., 2009), there is a consensus of opinion that GR and MR mRNA expression are not altered by high-intensity, long-duration training. Therefore, we would expect to see no advantage or disadvantage for athletes from an interaction between training, HPA axis hormones activity, and cognition.

Brain-Derived Neurotrophic Factor

Brain-derived neurotrophic factor (BDNF) is a protein and a member of the neurotrophic family. It is widely distributed throughout the brain but is particularly well represented in the hippocampus, neocortex, cerebellum, striatum, and amygdala (Binder & Scharfman, 2004; Kawamoto et al., 1996). BDNF plays major roles in neurogenesis and neuroprotection (Dishman et al., 2006; Knaeppen, Goekint, Heyman, & Meeusen et al., 2010), and long-term potentiation (Pang et al., 2004), which is the strengthening, over time, of synaptic connections between neurons (Lømo, 2003). These effects of BDNF on neurogenesis and synaptic transmission are triggered when it binds with one of its receptors, the high-affinity tropomyosin-related kinase-B

(Trk-B), which initiates a number of intracellular signaling cascades, including calcium/calmodulin kinase II (CaMKII) and mitogen-activated protein kinase (MAPK), resulting in the phosphorylation of cyclic adenosine monophosphate (cAMP)-response element binding protein (CREB) (Binder & Scharfman, 2004; Cunha, Brambilla, & Thomas, 2010; Waterhouse & Xu, 2009).

Serum and Plasma BDNF Concentrations in Physically Active Nonathletes

As the effects of chronic exercise on BDNF in nonathletes, who are physically active, are covered in some detail in Chapter 8, here we will simply outline the research results. Research examining the effect of chronic exercise on serum and/or plasma concentrations of BDNF in humans shows a tendency toward there being no significant effect on basal levels. Most authors have found no significant effect (Baker et al., 2010; Erickson et al., 2011; Griffin et al., 2011; Schiffer, Schulte, Hollmann, Bloch, & Strüder, 2009; Voss et al., 2013). On the other hand, Seifert et al. (2010) and Zoladz et al. (2008) showed significant increases in basal concentrations. However, rodent studies provide very strong evidence that chronic exercise induces increased BDNF concentrations and/or BDNF mRNA expression in the brain, in particular in the hippocampus (e.g., Aguiar, Speck, Prediger, Kapczinski, & Pinho, 2008; Aguiar et al., 2011; Berchtold, Castello, & Cotman, 2010; Berchtold, Chinn, Chou, Kesslak, & Cotman, 2005; Ding, Ying, & Gómez-Pinilla, 2011; Ferreira, Real, Rodrigues, Alves, & Britto, 2011; Gomez-Pinilla, Vaynman, & Ying, 2008; Groves-Chapman et al., 2011; Huang et al., 2006; Liu et al., 2009; Neeper, Gomez-Pinilla, Choi, & Cotman, 1995; Soya et al., 2007; Vaynman, Ying, & Gomez-Pinilla, 2004). In humans, the situation with regard to the effects of chronic exercise on serum and plasma concentrations of BDNF in response to an acute bout of exercise appears more complex. Seifert et al. (2010) demonstrated no significant effect but Zoladz et al. (2008) showed increased plasma concentrations. Griffin et al. (2011) found that 3 weeks of 60 min cycling at 60% $\dot{V}O_{2MAX}$ blunted the serum BDNF response to a bout of exercise to exhaustion. After 5 weeks' training, participants showed increased post-exercise serum BDNF concentrations compared to pre-training but only when samples were taken 30 min following cessation of the exercise.

Serum and Plasma BDNF Concentrations in Athletes

The research examined in the previous subsection would suggest that training has little effect on serum and plasma concentrations of BDNF. In this subsection, we specifically examine research into athletes rather than moderately fit individuals. Unfortunately, few studies have measured effects in athletes. Correia et al. (2011) found significantly greater basal plasma concentrations in international sprinters compared to sedentary individuals, and Brazilian "domestic level" (p. 325) sprinters. Pareja-Galeano et al. (2013) found that basal BDNF plasma concentrations were significantly higher in athletically trained adolescents than in sedentary individuals. They also found higher concentrations of serum insulin-like growth factor-1 (IGF-1) in the trained athletes. To the contrary, lower resting serum BDNF concentrations have been shown by other researchers (Babaei, Damirchi, Mehdipoor, & Tehrani, 2014; Lee et al., 2014; Nofuji et al., 2008). Kraus, Stallings, Yeager, and Gavin (2004) found no significant effect of exercise on another member of the growth factor family, vascular endothelial growth factor (VEGF). Moreover, in the two studies where correlations between serum BDNF concentrations and a measure of cardiorespiratory fitness were undertaken, negative correlations were demonstrated (Babaei et al., 2014; Lee et al., 2014). When BDNF concentrations were measured post-acute exercise, Heyman et al. (2012) showed that fit young athletes had significantly higher concentrations of BDNF than sedentary individuals. However,

Babaei et al. (2014) found that both athletes and sedentary individuals demonstrated significantly elevated serum BDNF concentrations, with no between group differences. It should be noted that Babaei et al.'s participants were masters athletes and much older than Heyman et al.'s. The difference in findings between basal concentrations and post-acute exercise are highlighted by Lee et al. (2014), who found that the relationship between the cardiorespiratory fitness and BDNF was positive when BDNF was measured immediately after exercise, the opposite to that for basal concentrations.

Although we expected to see that athletes had greater basal and post-exercise concentrations of BDNF than sedentary individuals and possibly even physically active nonathletes, we thought that this might be compromised by the intensity × duration of the training undertaken by the athletes. Long-term, high-intensity training results in generation of reactive oxygen species (ROS) (Krüger & Mooren, 2014), which in turn induces oxidative stress. High oxidative stress levels result in a decrease in BDNF levels (Gomez-Pinilla, 2011) and BDNF-mediated synaptic neuroplasticity (Wu, Ying, & Gómez-Pinilla, 2004). Examination of the intensity and duration of training of the athletes in the studies in which athletes showed significantly higher BDNF levels than nonathletes (Correia et al., 2011; Pareja-Galeano et al., 2013) and those where athletes' levels were lower (Babaei et al., 2014; Lee et al., 2014; Nofuji et al., 2008) do not suggest that this has been a factor in these results. We should note that individual differences due to genetic polymorphisms can affect results (Gomez-Pinilla, 2011).

Brain Morphology

As we saw in Chapter 8, there is strong evidence that nonathlete individuals undertaking exercise show enhanced gray matter volume in several regions, including the dorsolateral prefrontal cortex (Weinstein et al., 2012), increased basal ganglia and hippocampus volumes in children (Chaddock, Erickson, Prakash, Kim et al., 2010; Chaddock Erickson, Prakash, VanPatter et al., 2010), and larger hippocampus volume in the elderly (Erickson et al., 2011). Research into the effects of exercise on brain morphology of athletes is also very recent. Several authors (Hänggi, Koeneke, Bezzola, & Jäncke, 2010; Hüfner et al., 2011; Jacini et al., 2009; Jäncke, Koeneke, Hoppe, Rominger, & Hänggi, 2009; Wei, Zhang, Jiang, & Luo, 2011) have looked at athletes to examine effects of skill acquisition to an expert level on brain morphology and their findings could be relevant to effects of exercise, but it is impossible to say what effects are due to expertise training and what are due to exercise per se. Schlaffke et al. (2014) attempted to differentiate between exercise effects and skill effects by comparing martial artists and endurance athletes to one another and to a group of sedentary men. They found higher gray matter volumes in the supplementary motor area/dorsal premotor cortex in both athlete groups compared to the control group. Interestingly, endurance athletes showed significantly higher gray matter volume in the medial temporal lobe, specifically in the hippocampus and parahippocampal gyrus compared to both the martial arts and sedentary groups. This latter result is, of course, relevant to declarative memory performance. Interestingly, the supplementary motor area/dorsal premotor cortex areas affected included the presupplementary motor area. Despite its name, this region has only sparse connections to the primary motor cortex and spinal cord, but is extensively connected to prefrontal areas. It plays a role in cognitive control, response selection, and response inhibition (Dum & Strick, 1991; Lehéricy et al., 2004), all of which are central executive activities (Miyake, Friedman, Emerson, Witzki, & Howerter, 2000).

The second recent study (Tseng et al., 2013) compared the brain morphology of elderly masters athletes (mean age 72.4, SD 5.6 years) and elderly sedentary individuals (mean age 74.6, SD 4.3 years). Masters athletes had higher gray and white matter tissue concentrations mainly in the right parietal and occipital lobes when compared to their sedentary counterparts. These are brain regions heavily involved in visuospatial processing and motor control (Indovina & Macaluso, 2004), which suggests a possible interaction with motor skill levels.

SUMMARY

Results for the effects of athletic level training on basal catecholamines, HPA axis hormones, and BDNF concentrations tend toward it having no significant effect. The situation with regard to concentrations of catecholamines and HPA axis hormones following bouts of acute exercise also tends toward no significant effect. This is similar to effects of undertaking lower level training as in physically active nonathletes. With regard to post-acute exercise BDNF concentrations, the very limited amount of research makes it impossible to draw any conclusions. Physically active nonathletes tend to show no significant effect (Baker et al., 2010; Erickson et al., 2011; Schiffer et al., 2009; Voss et al., 2013), but not unequivocally (Griffin et al., 2011; Seifert et al., 2010; Zoladz et al., 2008). However, the fact that brain morphology studies show a trend toward a positive, significant effect of training confuses the picture. The reasons why this apparent contradiction should exist are discussed below.

EXERCISE EFFECTS ON COGNITION IN ATHLETES

Very few studies have been carried out that compare athletes' cognitive functioning to sedentary individuals or between athletes of different levels of fitness. Even fewer have included neurochemical or psychophysiological measures. Two recent studies have examined the interaction between exercise, BDNF, and cognition. Babaei et al. (2014) tested former Iranian national league soccer players, who had continued exercising since retiring from soccer. They were aged between 45 and 65 years, mean ~51.33 years (unfortunately it is not clear from the article what the exact mean was). Participants undertook a test of long-term memory, at rest. Also, two subgroups took the test following either a single bout of acute aerobic or anaerobic exercise. Their performances were compared to that of a control group of sedentary individuals of similar age. The mean $\dot{V}O_{2MAX}$ of the soccer players was ~44 mL kg^{-1} min^{-1}. This is slightly higher than that shown by Saltin and Grimby (1968) for similarly aged ex-athletes who no longer trained, and slightly lower than for ex-athletes who had continued to train. The athletes in that study were mostly runners or cross-country skiers, who normally show higher $\dot{V}O_{2MAX}$ than soccer players (see Freeman, Williams, & Nute, 1990; for runners; Hoff, 2005; for soccer players; Losnegard, Myklebust, Spencer, & Hallén, 2013; for cross-country skiing). In the at-rest condition, recall memory was better in the athlete group compared to the control group. There were no significant differences between groups after either aerobic or anaerobic exercise. Unfortunately the authors did not carry out a two-way comparison using at-rest scores as baseline scores, nor were any correlational statistics carried out between BDNF concentrations and cognitive performance.

In the other study, Lee et al. (2014) examined a group of elite runners, swimmers, rowers, and triathletes, mean age 16.49 (SD = 2.04), on the Stroop Color-Word Test (Stuss, Floden, Alexander, Levine, & Katz, 2001), the Wisconsin Card Sorting Task (WCST) (Stuss et al., 2000), Baddeley, Della Sala, Papagno, and Spinner's (1997) dual task, and tasks of spatial memory and spatial associative learning (Howard, Mrigankka, Fotedar, Datey, & Hasselmo, 2005). Their performances were compared to an age-matched control group. The athletes were significantly better on the Stroop, WCST, and spatial associative learning tasks. However, the athletes demonstrated negative correlations between BDNF

and VEGF serum concentrations, and cognitive performance.

Tseng et al. (2013) compared masters athletes (mean age 72.4, SD 5.6 years), an age equivalent sedentary group (mean age 74.6, SD 4.3 years) and a group of young nonactive individuals (mean age 27.2, SD 3.6 years) on a battery of cognitive tests, as well as examining differences in brain morphology. Unfortunately no correlational or regression analyses were undertaken between morphological factors and cognition. The masters athletes demonstrated significantly better cognitive performance than the sedentary groups on the Wechsler Test of Adult Reading and two tests of working memory, Letter Fluency and Category Fluency. They also recorded significantly better performance than the young control group in the latter test. However, they performed no better than either of the other groups on several other working memory and perceptual tests.

Pontifex, Hillman, and Polich (2009) compared the performance of young athletes (mean age 20.3, SD 1.1 years), young sedentary individuals (mean age 20.1, SD 1.5 years), highly fit older people (mean age 66.2, SD 3.5 years), and an older sedentary group (mean age 67.4, SD 3.2 years) on the auditory oddball test and the three-stimulus oddball task (Hagen, Gatherwright, Lopez, & Polich, 2006). The two fit groups showed well-above average $\dot{V}O_{2MAX}$ levels for their ages, 56.7 (SD 8.0) mL kg^{-1} min^{-1} and 36.6 (SD 3.5) mL kg^{-1} min^{-1}, for the younger and older groups, respectively (Saltin & Grimby, 1968). There were no significant differences in accuracy for either task but the higher-fit participants were significantly faster than the sedentary ones. As well as comparing behavioral data, the authors examined N2 amplitude and latency and P3a and P3b amplitude and latency. There was no effect of fitness on any N2 measure or on P3a or P3b latency. While there was no fitness effect on P3a amplitude, the younger fit group showed a significantly greater P3b amplitude than the younger age sedentary group. P3b amplitude is a measure of neuronal activity associated with allocation of attention during a working memory task (Donchin & Coles, 1988).

Although not measuring any neurochemical or psychophysiological factors, Guizani et al. (2006) compared the simple and choice reaction times of professional fencers to those of a sedentary control group at rest and while exercising at 40%, 60%, and 80% maximum power output (W_{MAX}). The fencers demonstrated significantly faster choice reaction times during exercise at all intensities. Moreover, there were main effects of both simple and choice reaction times with the fencers being the faster. Two other studies examined the effect of exercise on cognitive performance of athletes without comparison to nonathlete groups. Davranche, Paleresompoulle, Pernaud, Labarelle, and Hasbroucq (2009) examined performance of French national-level kayakers on a Simon task while paddling at 75% HR_{MAX} and at 40% HR_{MAX}. There was a significant improvement in speed of performance during the heavier load but no effect on accuracy. Thomson, Watt, and Liukkonen (2009) tested the ability of Estonian national-level soccer, basketball, and volleyball players, to judge the velocity of stimuli presented on a computer, at rest, and following exercise to exhaustion. Their speed of decision increased but accuracy decreased. This strongly suggests that a speed–accuracy tradeoff may have been a factor.

To summarize, these results suggest positive effects of exercise on the cognitive performance of athletes both at baseline and following bouts of acute exercise. However, results are not unequivocal and the sample is very small. Moreover, the results of the Guizani et al. (2006) study may well be due to the type of expertise needed by fencers rather than fitness levels. This is supported by observation of the mean $\dot{V}O_{2MAX}$ of the fencers, 50.7 mL kg^{-1} min^{-1}, which is only slightly above that regarded the norm for young males [~47 mL kg^{-1} min^{-1} (Shvartz & Reibold, 1990)]. Moreover, the standard deviation, 5.61 mL kg^{-1} min^{-1}, shows that some individuals

would be well below average. Therefore, it would be unlikely that fitness per se was the key factor affecting these results.

Implications for Neuroscience

From a neuroscience perspective, the results of the research outlined above are somewhat puzzling. Cognition appears to be better in athletes than nonathletes but there is little in the research examining effects of athletic training on catecholamines, HPA axis hormones, or BDNF levels to suggest why athletes should benefit cognitively from such training. There is evidence that athletic training induces increased gray and white matter (Schlaffke et al., 2014; Tseng et al., 2013), which would support improved cognitive functioning. From a theoretical perspective, such changes would most likely occur as a result of chronic exercise-induced increases in brain concentrations of BDNF, BDNF mRNA expression, and possibly other growth factors. However, research examining peripheral, basal BDNF plasma/serum concentrations in athletes provides somewhat equivocal results. Positive, significant effects have been shown by some (Correia et al., 2011; Pareja-Galeano et al., 2013), but lower concentrations by others (Babaei et al., 2014; Lee et al., 2014; Nofuji et al., 2008). Rodent research, however, has shown significant chronic exercise-induced increases in brain concentrations of BDNF and BDNF mRNA expression (e.g., Aguiar et al., 2008, 2011; Berchtold et al., 2010, 2005; Ding et al., 2011). There is no reason to think that similar changes do not occur in the human brain but the extent to which the intensity and duration of exercise undertaken by the rodents compares to that undertaken by athletes is questionable.

A possible explanation for a failure of peripheral concentrations of BDNF to show training-induced increases could be based on the claims of Carro, Nuñez, Busiguina, and Torres-Aleman (2000). These authors examined IGF-1 concentrations in the brain and periphery of rats following 1 h of treadmill running. They demonstrated significant increases in the brain but not in the periphery, as measured by serum concentrations. They argued that because brain IGF-I mRNA levels do not change, the most likely explanation for the brain–periphery differences is that increased brain levels are caused by increased uptake of IGF-I from circulating serum. Thus, peripheral serum IGF-I levels remain unaltered but brain concentrations increase due to uptake of circulating IGF-I by the brain. They also claimed that other target organs such as muscles will also take up IGF-1. Although brain BDNF mRNA levels do alter, increased uptake of circulating BDNF during exercise may, at least to some extent, mean that peripheral serum/plasma concentrations are not significantly affected by exercise.

As well as expecting to find training-induced changes in basal BDNF concentrations, we also expected to see significant effects on basal catecholamines and cortisol plasma concentrations. No such effects were demonstrated. Given that catecholamines do not readily cross the blood–brain barrier, we can only hypothesize that there are, in fact, similar effects to those found in rodent studies, that is, increased brain noradrenaline and dopamine concentrations (Meeusen & De Meirleir, 1995; Meeusen et al., 2001) and TH mRNA expression (Foley & Fleshner, 2008; Gavrilović et al., 2012; Kim et al., 2011; Tümer et al., 2001). If this is the case, we would expect some positive effect on cognitive performance at baseline.

Cortisol does cross the blood–brain barrier and there are claims that athletes demonstrate hypercortisolism (Mastorakos et al., 2005) at rest, therefore we expected some effect of athletic training on baseline plasma cortisol concentrations. However, we found that evidence for any significant effect of athletic participation on athletes' baseline plasma concentrations of cortisol is almost zero (Duclos et al., 1997, 2001; Kern et al., 1995; Neary et al., 1994; Wittert et al., 1996). This is a little surprising. One might expect that

repeated high-intensity training would have a negative effect on basal cortisol concentrations. In fact, there is evidence that ACTH shows increased activity but there is reduced sensitivity to negative cortisol feedback in the pituitary (Duclos et al., 1998, 2001), thus cortisol concentrations remain stable.

The logical conclusion from the brain morphology findings outlined above, the probability that chronic exercise-induced changes in brain neurochemistry found in rodent studies are demonstrative of similar changes in humans and evidence that athletes have outperformed sedentary individuals on cognitive tests, albeit in a small sample of studies, is that athletes should be smarter than other people. As Fabel and Kempermann (2008) stated, "everyday experience" (p. 59) shows us that this is not the case. They argued that the extrapolation from rodent studies is, in fact, flawed. Fabel and Kempermann claim that for rodents "cognition is almost inseparable from locomotion" (p. 59). While this may be true when exercise involves such tasks as the Morris water maze, it is not true of wheel running or treadmill running. Regardless of this, Fabel and Kempermann are undoubtedly correct; athletes are no cleverer than any other group of healthy people. All training can do is help the individual to reach his/her full potential.

Interestingly, there were no signs of a negative effect of high-intensity, long-duration training on cognition, and/or on HPA axis hormones and BDNF protein. We do not see lowering of BDNF levels due to oxidative stress or hypercortisolism due to GR and MR depletion. Given that only a few studies have been undertaken with trained athletes it may be that these have not trained at very high intensities. This appears to be unlikely. It could well be that high-intensity exercise, even for many years, does not have the same effects as many other stressors. Heavy exercise is undoubtedly stressing but it is not life threatening like the stress of fighting in a war, as experienced by the military. Mason (1975a, 1975b) would see the fact that the athletes know what they are doing and that it is not beyond their capabilities, which makes it a low stressor from a psychological perspective. Research examining the effect of overtraining on cognition would be interesting in this context.

CONCLUSIONS

When drawing conclusions from the literature reviewed, we need to keep in mind the fact that there have been very few experiments on athletes, therefore caution is required. It would appear that the effects of training on athletes' cognitive functioning are very similar to those experienced by physically active nonathletes. There is evidence of a positive effect when compared to sedentary persons. However, we cannot say whether or not athletes have any advantage over physically active nonathletes. Observation of research examining differences between the brain morphologies of athletes and sedentary individuals show some positive effects of athletic training but research looking at peripheral concentrations of BDNF does not support this. Given that BDNF and other growth hormones are essential for changes in brain morphology, we can only assume that changes in the periphery are not indicative of changes in the brain, which have been shown in rodent studies. This could be due to a number of factors such as increased uptake of the growth factors by target cells in the brain resulting in peripheral concentrations remaining constant. That BDNF mRNA expression in the brain may be increased in athletes, as studies with trained rodents would suggest, cannot be ruled out. Interestingly, there is no evidence of exercise-induced ROS having negative effects on athletes' BDNF levels. However, this may be the case with overtrained athletes.

As with physically active nonathletes, athletes show no significant advantages over sedentary individuals with regard to plasma catecholamines and HPA axis hormones concentrations. Again, however, we need to consider the possibility that the picture within the brain is not the same as that peripherally. Rodent studies would suggest that this is particularly the case with regard to TH mRNA. With regard to the HPA axis hormones, repeated high-intensity exercise could have been expected to induce negative effects. That no negative effects on basal cortisol concentrations were demonstrated may appear a little strange, given that there does seem to be training-induced increases in ACTH concentrations. However, rodent studies demonstrated desensitization to negative cortisol feedback in the pituitary (Duclos et al., 1998, 2001), which would explain why hypercortisolism is not shown by athletes.

References

Aguiar, A. S., Jr., Speck, A. E., Prediger, R. D., Kapczinski, F., & Pinho, R. A. (2008). Downhill training upregulates mice hippocampal and striatal brain-derived neurotrophic factor levels. *Journal of Neural Transmission, 115*, 1251–1255.

Aguiar, A. S., Jr., Castro, A. A., Moreira, E. L., Glaser, V., Santos, A. R. S., Tasca, C. I., et al. (2011). Short bouts of mild-intensity physical exercise improve spatial learning and memory in aging rats: involvement of hippocampal plasticity via AKT, CREB and BDNF signaling. *Mechanism of Ageing and Development, 132*, 560–567.

Allen, J. P., Kendall, J. W., McGilvra, R., & Vancura, C. (2011). Immunoreactive ACTH in cerebrospinal fluid. *The Journal of Clinical Endocrinology & Metabolism, 38*, 586–593.

American College of Sports Medicine. (2010). *ACSM's guidelines for exercise testing and prescription* (8th ed.). Philadelphia, PA: Lippincott Williams and Wilkins.

Arnsten, A. F. T. (2009). Stress signalling pathways that impair prefrontal cortex structure and function. *Nature Reviews Neuroscience, 10*, 410–422.

Arnsten, A. F. T. (2011). Catecholamine influences on dorsolateral prefrontal cortical networks. *Biological Psychiatry, 69*, e89–e99. http://dx.doi.org/10.1016/j.biopsych.2011.01.027.

Åstrand, P. O., & Rhyming, I. A. (1954). A nomogram for calculation of aerobic capacity (physical fitness) from pulse rate during sub-maximal work. *Journal of Applied Physiology, 7*, 218–221.

Babaei, P., Damirchi, A., Mehdipoor, M., & Tehrani, B. S. (2014). Long term habitual exercise is associated with lower resting level of serum BDNF. *Neuroscience Letters, 566*, 304–308.

Baddeley, A., Della Sala, S., Papagno, C., & Spinnler, H. (1997). Dual-task performance in dysexecutive and non-dysexecutive patients with a frontal lesion. *Neuropsychology*, *11*, 187–194.

Baker, L. D., Frank, L. L., Foster-Schubert, K., Green, P. S., Wilkinson, C. W., McTiernan, A., et al. (2010). Aerobic exercise improves cognition for older adults with glucose intolerance, a risk factor for Alzheimer's disease. *Journal of Alzheimer's Disease*, *22*, 569–579.

Bassett, D. R., & Howley, E. T. (2000). Limiting factors for maximum oxygen uptake and determinants of endurance performance. *Medicine & Science in Sports & Exercise*, *32*, 70–84.

Beaver, W. L., Wasserman, K., & Whipp, B. J. (1986). A new method for detecting anaerobic threshold by gas exchange. *Journal of Applied Physiology*, *60*, 2020–2027.

Berchtold, N. C., Chinn, G., Chou, M., Kesslak, J. P., & Cotman, C. W. (2005). Exercise primes a molecular memory for brain-derived neurotrophic factor protein induction in the rat hippocampus. *Neuroscience*, *133*, 853–861.

Berchtold, N. C., Castello, N., & Cotman, C. W. (2010). Exercise and time-dependent benefits to learning and memory. *Neuroscience*, *167*, 588–597.

Bi, S., Scott, K. A., Hyun, J., Ladenheim, E. E., & Moran, T. H. (2005). Running wheel activity prevents hyperphagia and obesity in Otsuka long-evans Tokushima fatty rats: role of hypothalamic signaling. *Endocrinology*, *148*, 1678–1685.

Binder, D. K., & Scharfman, H. E. (2004). Brain-derived neurotrophic factor. *Growth Factor*, *22*, 123–131.

Blaney, J., Sothmann, M., Raff, H., Hart, B., & Horn, T. (1990). Impact of exercise training on plasma adrenocorticotropin response to a well-learned vigilance task. *Psychoneuroendocrinology*, *15*, 453–462.

Bonifazi, M., Mencarelli, M., Fedele, V., Ceccarelli, I., Pecorelli, A., Grasso, G., et al. (2009). Glucocorticoid receptor mRNA expression in peripheral blood mononuclear cells in high trained compared to low trained athletes and untrained subjects. *Journal of Endocrinological Investigation*, *32*, 816–820.

Borer, K. T. (2003). *Exercise endocrinology*. Champaign, IL: Human Kinetics.

Borg, G. A. (1982). Psychophysical bases of perceived exertion. *Medicine & Science in Sports & Exercise*, *14*, 377–381.

Bouchard, C., An, P., Rice, T., Skinner, J. S., Wilmore, J. H., Gagnon, J., et al. (1999). Familial aggregation of VO2 max response to exercise training: results from the HERITAGE Family Study. *Journal of Applied Physiology*, *87*, 1003–1008.

Bouno, M. I., Yeager, J. E., & Sucec, A. A. (1987). Effect of aerobic training on the plasma ACTH response to exercise. *Journal of Applied Physiology*, *63*, 2499–2501.

Bridge, M. W., Weller, A. S., Rayson, M., & Jones, D. A. (2003). Ambient temperature and the pituitary hormone responses to exercise in humans. *Experimental Physiology*, *88*, 627–635.

Campbell, J. E., Rakhshani, N., Fediuc, S., Bruni, S., & Riddell, M. C. (2009). Voluntary wheel running initially increases adrenal sensitivity to adrenocorticotrophic hormone, which is attenuated with long-term training. *Journal of Applied Physiology*, *106*, 66–72.

Campbell, J. E., Király, M. A., Atkinson, D. J., D'souza, A. M., Vranic, M., & Riddell, M. C. (2010). Regular exercise prevents the development of hyperglucocorticoidemia via adaptations in the brain and adrenal glands in male Zucker diabetic fatty rats. *American Journal of Physiology. Regulatory Integrative and Comparative Physiology*, *299*, R168–R176.

Carro, E., Nuñez, A., Busiguina, S., & Torres-Aleman, I. (2000). Circulating insulin-like growth factor I mediates effects of exercise on the brain. *Journal of Neuroscience*, *20*, 2926–2933.

Chaddock, L., Erickson, K. I., Prakash, R. S., Kim, J. S., Voss, M. W., VanPatter, M., et al. (2010). A neuroimaging investigation of the association between aerobic fitness, hippocampal volume and memory performance in pre-adolescent children. *Brain Research*, *1358*, 172–183.

Chaddock, L., Erickson, K. I., Prakash, R. S., VanPatter, M., Voss, M. V., Pontifex, M. B., et al. (2010). Basal ganglia volume is associated with aerobic fitness in preadolescent children. *Developmental Neuroscience (Basel, Switzerland)*, *32*, 249–256.

Chang, Y. T., Chen, Y. C., Wu, C. W., Chen, H. I., Jen, C. J., & Kuo, Y. M. (2008). Glucocorticoid signaling an exercise-induced downregulation of the mineralocorticoid receptor in the induction of adult mouse dentate neurogenesis by treadmill running. *Psychoneuroendocrinology*, *33*, 1173–1182.

Chang, Y. K., Labban, J. D., Gapin, J. I., & Etnier, J. L. (2012). The effects of acute exercise on cognitive performance: a meta-analysis. *Brain Research*, *1453*, 87–101.

Chatzitheodorou, D., Kabitsis, C., Malliou, P., & Mougios, V. (2007). A pilot study of the effects of high-intensity aerobic exercise versus passive interventions on pain, disability, psychological strain, and serum cortisol concentrations in people with low back pain. *Physical Therapy*, *87*, 304–312.

Chennaoui, M., Gomez Merino, D., Lesage, J., Drogou, C., & Guezennec, C. Y. (2002). Effects of moderate and intensive training on the hypothalamic-pituitary-adrenal axis in rats. *Acta Physiologica Scandinavica*, *175*, 113–121.

Chmura, J., Nazar, H., & Kaciuba-Uścilko, H. (1994). Choice reaction time during graded exercise in relation to blood lactate and plasma catecholamine thresholds. *International Journal of Sports Medicine*, *15*, 172–176.

Chwalbinska-Moneta, J., Krysztofiak, H., Ziemba, A., Nazar, K., & Kaciuba-Uścikło, H. (1996). Threshold increases in plasma growth hormone in relation to plasma catecholamine and blood lactate concentrations during progressive exercise in endurance-trained athletes. *European Journal of Applied Physiology. Occupational Physiology*, *73*, 117–120.

Cooper, K. H. (1968). A means of assessing maximal oxygen intake: correlation between field and treadmill testing. *Journal of the American Medical Association, 203*, 201–204.

Correia, P. R., Scorza, F. A., Gomes da Silva, S., Pansani, A., Toscano-Silva, M., de Almeida, A. C., et al. (2011). Increased basal plasma brain-derived neurotrophic factor levels in sprint runners. *Neuroscience Bulletin, 27*, 325–329.

Cunha, C., Brambilla, R., & Thomas, K. L. (2010). A simple role for BDNF in learning and memory? *Frontiers in Molecular Neuroscience, 3*, 1. http://dx.doi.org/10.3389/neuro.02.001.2010.

Davranche, K., Paleresompoulle, D., Pernaud, R., Labarelle, J., & Hasbroucq, T. (2009). Decision making in elite whitewater athletes paddling on a kayak ergometer. *Journal of Sport Exercise Psychology, 31*, 554–565.

Dickhuth, H. H., Yin, L., Niess, A., Röcker, K., Mayer, F., et al. (1999). Ventilatory, lactate-derived and catecholamine thresholds during incremental treadmill running: relationship and reproducibility. *International Journal of Sports Medicine, 20*, 122–127.

Ding, Q., Ying, Z., & Gómez-Pinilla, F. (2011). Exercise influences hippocampal plasticity by modulating brain-derived neurotrophic factor processing. *Neuroscience, 192*, 773–780.

Dishman, R. K., Berthoud, H.-R., Booth, F. W., Cotman, C. W., Edgerton, V. R., Fleshner, M. R., et al. (2006). Neurobiology of exercise. *Obesity, 14*, 345–356.

Donchin, E., & Coles, M. G. H. (1988). Is the P300 component a manifestation of context updating? *Behavioural Brain Science, 11*, 355–372.

Droste, S. K., Gesing, A., Ulbricht, S., Müller, M. B., Linthorst, A. C. E., & Reul, J. M. H. M. (2003). Effects of long-term voluntary exercise on the mouse hypothalamic-pituitary-adrenocortical axis. *Endocrinology, 144*, 3012–3023.

Droste, S. K., Chandramohan, Y., Hill, L. E., Linthorst, A. C., & Reul, J. M. (2007). Voluntary exercise impacts on the rat hypothalamic-pituitary-adrenocortical axis mainly at the adrenal level. *Neuroendocrinology, 86*, 26–37.

Duclos, M., Corcuff, J. B., Rashedi, M., Fougere, V., & Manier, G. (1997). Trained versus untrained men: different immediate post-exercise responses of pituitary-adrenal axis. *European Journal of Applied Physiology, 75*, 343–350.

Duclos, M., Corcuff, J. B., Arsac, L., Moreau-Gaudry, F., Rashedi, M., Roger, P., et al. (1998). Corticotroph axis sensitivity after exercise in endurance-trained athletes. *Clinical Endocrinology, 48*, 493–501.

Duclos, M., Corcuff, J.-B., Pehourcq, F., & Tabarin, A. (2001). Decreased pituitary sensitivity to glucocorticoids in endurance-trained men. *European Journal of Endocrinology, 144*, 363–368.

Dum, R. P., & Strick, P. L. (1991). The origin of corticospinal the frontal lobe projections from the premotor areas in the frontal lobe. *Journal of Neuroscience, 11*, 667–689.

Edwards, R. H. T., Melcher, A., Hesser, C. M., Wigertz, O., & Ekelund, L. G. (1972). Physiological correlates of perceived exertion in continuous and intermittent exercise with the same average power output. *European Journal of Clinical Investigation, 2*, 108–114.

Ehsani, A. A., Heath, G. W., Martin, W. H., Hagberg, J. M., & Holloszy, J. O. (1984). Effects of intense exercise training on plasma catecholamines in coronary patients. *Journal of Applied Physiology, 57*, 154–159.

Erickson, K. I., Voss, M. W., Prakash, R. S., Basak, C., Szabo, A., Chaddock, L., et al. (2011). Exercise training increases size of hippocampus and improves memory. *Proceedings of the National Academy of Science USA, 108*, 3017–3022.

Fabel, K., & Kempermann, G. (2008). Physical activity and the regulation of neurogenesis in the adult and aging brain. *NeuroMolecular Medicine, 10*, 59–66.

Faulkner, J., & Eston, R. (2007). Overall and peripheral ratings of perceived exertion during a graded exercise test to volitional exhaustion in individuals of high and low fitness. *European Journal of Applied Physiology, 101*, 613–620.

Febbraio, M. A., Lambert, D. L., Starkie, R. L., Proietto, J., & Hargreaves, M. (1998). Effect of epinephrine on muscle glycogenolysis during exercise in trained men. *Journal of Applied Physiology, 84*, 465–470.

Fediuc, S., Campbell, J. E., & Riddell, M. C. (2006). Effect of voluntary wheel running on circadian corticosterone release and on HPA axis responsiveness to restraint stress in Sprague-Dawley rats. *Journal of Applied Physiology, 100*, 1867–1875.

Fernstrom, J. D., & Fernstrom, M. H. (2007). Tyrosine, phenylalanine, and catecholamine synthesis and function on the brain. *Journal of Nutrition, 137*, 1539S–1547S.

Ferreira, A. F. B., Real, C. C., Rodrigues, A. C., Alves, A. S., & Britto, L. R. G. (2011). Short-term, moderate exercise is capable of inducing structural, bdnf-independent hippocampal plasticity. *Brain Research, 1425*, 111–122.

Foley, T. E., & Fleshner, M. (2008). Neuroplasticity of dopamine circuits after exercise: implications for central fatigue. *NeuroMolecular Medicine, 10*, 67–80.

Fox, S. M., 3rd, Naughton, J. P., & Haskell, W. L. (1971). Physical activity and the prevention of coronary heart disease. *Annals of Clinical Research, 3*, 404–432.

Freeman, W., Williams, C., & Nute, M. G. (1990). Endurance running performance in athletes with asthma. *Journal of Sports Science, 8*, 103–117.

Gavrilović, L., Mandusić, V., Stojiliković, V., Kasapović, J., Stojiliković, S., Pajović, S. B., et al. (2012). Effect of chronic forced running on gene expression of catecholamine biosynthetic enzymes in stellate ganglia of rats. *Journal of Biological Regulators & Homeostatic Agents, 26*, 367–377.

Gomez-Pinilla, F. (2011). The influences of diet and exercise on mental health through hormesis. *Ageing Research Review, 7*, 49–62.

Gomez-Pinilla, F., Vaynman, S., & Ying, Z. (2008). Brain-derived neurotrophic factor functions as a metabotrophin to mediate the effects of exercise on cognition. *European Journal of Neuroscience, 28,* 2278–2287.

Grasso, G., Lodi, L., Lupo, C., & Muscettola, M. (1997). Glucocorticoid receptors in human peripheral blood mononuclear cells in relation to age and to sport activity. *Life Sciences, 61,* 301–333.

Greiwe, J. S., Hickner, R. C., Shah, S. D., Cryer, P. E., & Holloszy, J. O. (1999). Norepinephrine response to exercise at the same relative intensity before and after endurance exercise training. *Journal of Applied Physiology, 86,* 531–535.

Grenhoff, J., & Svensson, T. H. (1993). Prazosin modulates the firing pattern of dopamine neurons in rat ventral tegmental area. *European Journal of Pharmacology, 233,* 79–84.

Grenhoff, J., Nisell, M., Ferré, S., Aston-Jones, G., & Svensson, T. H. (1993). Noradrenergic modulation of dopamine cell firing elicited by stimulation of the locus coeruleus in the rat. *Journal of Neural Transmission General Section, 93,* 11–25.

Groves-Chapman, J. L., Murray, P. S., Stevens, K. L., Monroe, D. C., Koch, L. G., Britton, S. L., et al. (2011). Changes in mRNA levels for brain-derived neurotrophic factor after wheel running in rats selectively bred for high- and low-aerobic capacity. *Brain Research, 1425,* 90–97.

Guizani, S. M., Bouzaouach, I., Tenenbaum, G., Ben Kheder, A., Feki, Y., & Bouaziz, M. (2006). Simple and choice reaction times under varying levels of physical load in high skilled fencers. *Journal of Sports Medicine and Physical Fitness, 46,* 344–351.

Hagberg, J. M., Coyle, E. F., Carroll, J. E., Miller, J. M., Martin, W. H., & Brooke, M. H. (1982). Exercise hyperventilation in patients with McArdle's disease. *Journal of Applied Physiology, 52,* 991–994.

Hagberg, J. M., Goldring, D., Heath, G. W., Ehsani, A. A., Hernandez, A., & Holloszy, J. O. (1984). Effects of exercise-training on plasma catecholamines and haemodynamics of adolescent hypertensives during rest, submaximal exercise and orthostatic stress. *Clinical Physiology, 4,* 117–124.

Hagen, G. F., Gatherwright, J. R., Lopez, B. A., & Polich, J. (2006). P3a from visual stimuli: primary task difficulty effects. *International Journal of Psychophysiology, 59,* 8–14.

Hänggi, J., Koeneke, S., Bezzola, L., & Jäncke, L. (2010). Structural neuroplasticity in the sensorimotor network of professional female ballet dancers. *Human Brain Mapping, 31,* 1196–1206.

Harbuz, M. S., & Lightman, S. L. (1989). Responses of hypothalamic and pituitary mRNA to physical and psychological stress in the rat. *Journal of Endocrinology, 122,* 705–711.

Hartley, H. L., Mason, J. W., Hogan, R. P., Jones, L. G., Kitchen, T. A., Mougey, E. H., et al. (1972). Multiple hormonal responses to prolonged exercise in relation to physical training. *Journal of Applied Physiology, 33,* 602–606.

Herman, J. P., Watson, S. J., Chao, H. M., Coirini, H., & McEwen, B. S. (1993). Diurnal regulation of glucocorticoid receptor and mineralocorticoid receptor mRNAs in rat hippocampus. *Molecullar and Cellular Neuroscience, 4,* 181–190.

Heyman, E., Gamelin, F. X., Goekint, M., Piscitelli, F., Roelands, B., Leclair, E. et al. (2012). Intense exercise increases circulating endocannabinoid and BDNF levels in humans—possible implications for reward and depression. *Psychoneuroendocrinology, 37,* 844–851.

Higa-Tanaguchi, K. T., Silva, F. C., Silva, H. M., Michelini, L. C., & Stern, J. E. (2007). Exercise-training induced remodeling of paraventricular nucleus (nor)adrenergic innervation in normotensive and hypertensive rats. *American Journal of Physiology. Regulatory Integrative and Comparative Physiology, 292,* R1717–R1727.

Hill, E. E., Zack, E., Battaglini, C., Viru, M., Viru, A., & Hackney, A. C. (2008). Exercise and circulating cortisol levels: the intensity threshold effect. *Journal of Endocrinological Investigation, 31,* 587–591.

Hjortskov, N., Rissén, D., Blangsted, A. K., Fallentin, N., Lundberg, U., & Søgaard, K. (2004). The effect of mental stress on heart rate variability and blood pressure during computer work. *European Journal of Applied Physiology, 92,* 84–89.

Hoff, J. (2005). Training and testing physical capacities for elite soccer players. *Journal of Sports Science, 23,* 573–582.

Howard, M. W., Mrigankka, Fotedar, M. S., Datey, A. V., & Hasselmo, M. E. (2005). The temporal context model in spatial navigation and relational learning: toward a common explanation of medial temporal lobe function across domains. *Psychological Review, 112,* 75–116.

Huang, A. M., Jen, C. J., Chen, H. F., Yu, L., Kuo, Y. M., & Chen, H. I. (2006). Compulsive exercise acutely upregulates rat hippocampal brain-derived neurotrophic factor. *Journal of Neural Transmission, 113,* 803–811.

Hüfner, K., Binetti, C., Hamilton, D. A., Stephan, T., Flanagin, V. L., Linn, J., et al. (2011). Structural and functional plasticity of the hippocampal formation in professional dancers and slackliners. *Hippocampus, 21,* 855–865.

Inder, W. J., Hellemans, J., Ellis, M. J., Evans, M. J., Livesey, J. H., & Donald, R. A. (1995). Elevated basal adrenocorticotropin and evidence for increased central opioid tone in highly trained male athletes. *Journal of Clinical Endocrinology & Metabolism, 80,* 244–248.

Inder, W. J., Hellemans, J., Swanney, M. P., Prickett, T. C. R., & Donald, R. A. (1998). Prolonged exercise increases peripheral plasma ACTH, CRH, and AVP in male athletes. *Journal of Applied Physiology, 85,* 835–841.

Indovina, I., & Macaluso, E. (2004). Occipital-parietal interactions during shifts of exogenous visuospatial attention: trial-dependent changes of effective connectivity. *Magnetic Resonance Imaging, 22,* 1477–1486.

Jacini, W. F. S., Gianna, C., Cannonieri, P. T., Fernandes, L. B., Cendes, F., & Li, L. M. (2009). Can exercise shape your brain? Cortical differences associated with judo practice. *Journal of Science and Medicine in Sport, 12*, 688–690.

Jäncke, L., Koeneke, S., Hoppe, A., Rominger, C., & Hänggi, J. (2009). The architecture of the Golfer's brain. *PLoS One, 4*, e4785. http://dx.doi.org/10.1371/journal.pone.0004785.

Joyner, M. J., & Coyle, E. F. (2008). Endurance exercise performance: the physiology of champions. *Journal of Physiology, 586*, 35–44.

Karvonen, J., & Vuorimaa, T. (1988). Heart rate and exercise intensity during sports activities. *Sports Medicine, 5*, 303–311.

Kawamoto, Y., Nakamura, S., Nakano, S., Oka, N., Akiguchi, I., & Kimura, J. (1996). Immunohistòchemical localization of brain-derived neurotrophic factor in adult rat brain. *Neuroscience, 74*, 1209–1226.

Kawashima, H., Saito, T., Yoshizato, H., Fujikawa, T., Sato, Y., McEwen, B. S., et al. (2004). Endurance treadmill training in rats alters CRH activity in the hypothalamic paraventricular nucleus at rest and during acute running according to its period. *Life Sciences, 76*, 763–774.

Ke, Z., Yip, S. P., Li, L., Zheng, X. X., & Tong, K.-Y. (2011). The effects of voluntary, involuntary, and forced exercises on brain-derived neurotrophic factor and motor function recovery: a rat brain ischemia model. *PLoS One, 6*, e16643. http://dx.doi.org/10.1371/journal.pone.0016643.

Kern, W., Perras, B., Wodick, R., Fehm, H. L., & Born, J. (1995). Hormonal secretion during night-time sleep indicating stress of daytime exercise. *Journal of Applied Physiology, 79*, 1461–1468.

Kim, H., Heo, H. I., Kim, D. H., Ko, I. G., Lee, S. S., Kim, S. E., et al. (2011). Treadmill exercise and methylphenidate ameliorate symptoms of attention deficit/hyperactivity disorder through enhancing dopamine synthesis and brain-derived neurotrophic factor expression in spontaneous hypertensive rats. *Neuroscience Letters, 504*, 35–39.

Kjaer, M., Secher, N. H., Bach, F. W., Sheikh, S., & Galbo, H. (1989). Hormonal and metabolic responses to exercise in humans: effect of sensory nervous blockade. *American Journal of Physiology, 257*, E95–E101.

Knaeppen, K., Goekint, M., Heyman, E. M., & Meeusen, R. (2010). Neuroplasticity – exercise-induced response of peripheral brain-derived neurotrophic factor: a systematic review of experimental studies in human subjects. *Sports Medicine, 40*, 765–801.

Kraus, R. M., Stallings, H. W., Yeager, R. C., & Gavin, T. P. (2004). Circulating plasma VEGF response to exercise in sedentary and endurance trained men. *Journal of Applied Physiology, 96*, 1445–1450.

Krüger, K., & Mooren, F. C. (2014). Exercise-induced leukocyte apoptosis. *Exercise Immunology Review, 20*, 117–134.

Lee, T. M. C., Wong, M. L., Lau, B. W. -M., Lee, J. C. -D., Yau, S.-Y., & So, K.-F. (2014). Aerobic exercise interacts with neurotrophic factors to predict cognitive functioning in adolescents. *Psychoneuroendocrinology, 39*, 214–224.

Léger, L. A., & Lambert, J. (1982). A maximal multistage 20-m shuttle run test to predict VO2max. *European Journal of Applied Physiology. Occupational Physiology, 49*, 1–12.

Lehéricy, S., Ducros, M., Krainik, A., Francois, C., Van de Moortele, P.-F., Ugurbil, K., et al. (2004). 3-D diffusion tensor axonal tracking shows distinct SMA and pre-SMA projections to the human striatum. *Cerebral Cortex, 14*, 1302–1309.

Lehmann, M., Knizia, K., Gastmann, U., Petersen, K. G., Khalaf, A. N., Bauer, S., et al. (1993). Influence of 6-week, 6 days per week, training on pituitary function in recreational athletes. *British Journal of Sports Medicine, 27*, 186–192.

Levin, B. E., & Dunn-Meynell, A. (2004). Chronic exercise lowers the defended body weight gain and adiposity in diet-induced obese rats. *American Journal of Physiology. Regulatory Integrative and Comparative Physiology, 286*, R771–R778.

Liu, Y. F., Chen, H. I., Wu, C. L., Kuo, Y. M., Yu, L., Huang, A. M., et al. (2009). Differential effects of treadmill running and wheel running on spatial or aversive learning and memory: roles of amygdalar brain-derived neurotrophic factor and synaptotagmin 1. *Journal of Physiology, 587*, 3221–3231.

Lømo, T. (2003). The discovery of long-term potentiation. *Philosophical Transactions of the Royal Society B, 358*, 617–620.

Losnegard, T., Myklebust, H., Spencer, M., & Hallén, J. (2013). Seasonal variations in VO2max, O-2 cost, O-2 deficit, and performance in elite cross-country skiers. *Journal of Strength & Conditioning Research, 27*, 1780–1790.

Lowy, M. T. (1991). Corticosterone regulation of brain and lymphoid corticosteroid receptors. *Journal of Steroid Biochemistry Molecular Biology, 39*, 147–154.

Lu, N. Z., Wardell, S. E., Burnstein, K. L., DeFranco, D., Fuller, P. J., Giguere, V., et al. (2006). International Union of Pharmacology. LXV. The pharmacology and classification of the nuclear receptor superfamily: glucocorticoid, mineralocorticoid, progesterone, and androgen receptors. *Pharmacological Review, 58*, 782–797.

Luger, A., Deuster, P. A., Kyle, S. B., Gallucci, W. T., Montgomery, L. C., Gold, P. W., et al. (1987). Acute hypothalamic-pituitary-adrenal responses to the stress of treadmill exercise. Physiologic adaptations to physical training. *New England Journal of Medicine, 316*, 1309–1315.

Maritz, J. S., Morrison, J. F., Peter, J., & Strydom, N. B. (1961). A practical method of estimating an individual's maximal oxygen intake. *Ergonomics, 4*, 97–122.

Marques, E., Vasconcelos, F., Rolo, M. R., Pereira, F. C., Silva, A. P., Macedo, T. R., et al. (2008). Influence of chronic exercise on the amphetamine-induced dopamine release and neurodegeneration in the striatum of the rat. *Annals of the New York Academy of Sciences, 1139*, 222–231.

Mason, J. W. (1975a). A historical view of the stress field. Part I. *Journal of Human Stress, 1*, 6–12.

Mason, J. W. (1975b). A historical view of the stress field. Part II. *Journal of Human Stress, 1*, 22–36.

Mastorakos, G., Pavlatou, M., Diamanti-Kandarakis, E., & Chrousos, G. P. (2005). Exercise and the stress system. *Hormones, 4*, 73–89.

Mazzeo, R. S., & Marshall, P. (1989). Influence of plasma catecholamines on the lactate threshold during graded exercise. *Journal of Applied Physiology, 67*(4), 1319–1322.

McMorris, T., & Hale, B. J. (2012). Differential effects of differing intensities of acute exercise on speed and accuracy of cognition: a meta-analytical investigation. *Brain and Cognition, 80*, 338–351.

McMorris, T., & Hale, B. J. (2015). Is there an acute exercise-induced physiological/biochemical threshold which triggers increased speed of cognitive functioning? A meta-analytic investigation. *Journal of Sport and Health Science, 4*, 4–13.

McMorris, T., Sproule, J., Draper, S., Child, R., Sexsmith, J. R., Forster, C. D., et al. (2000). The measurement of plasma catecholamine and lactate thresholds: a comparison of methods. *European Journal of Applied Physiology, 82*, 262–267.

Meeusen, R., & De Meirleir, K. (1995). Exercise and brain neurotransmission. *Sports Medicine, 20*, 160–188.

Meeusen, R., Piacentini, M. F., & De Meirleir, K. (2001). Brain microdialysis in exercise research. *Sports Medicine, 31*, 965–983.

Miyake, A., Friedman, N. P., Emerson, M. J., Witzki, A. H., & Howerter, A. (2000). The unity and diversity of executive functions and their contributions to complex "frontal lobe" tasks: a latent variable analysis. *Cognitive Psychology, 41*, 49–100.

Miyashita, T., & Williams, C. L. (2006). Epinephrine administration increases neural impulses propagated along the vagus nerve: role of peripheral beta-adrenergic receptors. *Neurobiology of Learning and Memory, 85*, 116–124.

Griffin, É. W., Mullally, S., Foley, C., Warmington, S. A., O'Mara, S. M., & Kelly, Á. M. (2011). Aerobic exercise improves hippocampal function and increases BDNF in the serum of young adult males. *Physiology & Behavior, 104*, 934–941.

Nappi, G., Facchinetti, F., Bono, G., Petraglia, F., Sinforiani, E., & Genezzani, A. R. (1986). CSF and plasma levels pro-opiomelanocortin-related peptides in reversible ischaemic attacks and strokes. *Journal of Neurology, Neurosurgery, & Psychiatry, 49*, 17–21.

Neary, J. P., Wheeler, G. D., Maclean, I., Cumming, S. C., & Quinney, H. A. (1994). Urinary free cortisol as an indicator of exercise training stress. *Clinical Journal of Sports Medicine, 4*, 160–165.

Neeper, S. A., Gomez-Pinilla, F., Choi, J., & Cotman, C. W. (1995). Exercise and brain neurotrophins. *Nature, 373*, 109.

Noakes, T. D. (2008). Testing for maximum oxygen consumption has produced a brainless model of human exercise performance. *British Journal of Sports Medicine, 42*, 551–555.

Nofuji, Y., Suwa, M., Moriyama, Y., Nakano, H., Ichimiya, A., Nishichi, R., et al. (2008). Decreased serum brain derived neurotrophic factor intrained men. *Neuroscience Letters, 437*, 29–32.

O'Neal, H. A., van Hoomissen, J. D., Holmes, P. V., & Dishman, R. K. (2001). Prepro-galanin messenger RNA levels are increased in rat locus coeruleus after treadmill exercise training. *Neuroscience Letters, 299*, 69–72.

Pang, P. T., Teng, H. K., Zaitsev, E., Woo, N. T., Sakata, K., Zhen, S., et al. (2004). Cleavage of proBDNF by tPA/plasmin is essential for long-term hippocampal plasticity. *Science, 306*, 487–491.

Pareja-Galeano, H., Brioche, T., Sanchis-Gomar, F., Montal, A., Jovaní, C., et al. (2013). Impact of exercise training on neuroplasticity-related growth factors in adolescents. *Journal of Musculoskeletal & Neuronal Interaction, 13*, 368–371.

Park, E., Chan, O., Li, Q., Kiraly, M., Matthews, S. G., Vranic, M., et al. (2005). Changes in basal hypalamo-pituitary-adrenal activity during exercise are centrally mediated. *American Journal of Physiology. Regulatory Integrative and Comparative Physiology, 289*, R1360–R1371.

Péronnet, F., Cleroux, J., Perrault, H., Cousineau, D., Champlain, J., & Nadeau, B. (1981). Plasma norepinephrine response to exercise before and after training in humans. *Journal of Applied Physiology, 51*, 812–815.

Podolin, D. A., Munger, P. A., & Mazzeo, R. S. (1991). Plasma-catecholamine and lactate response during graded-exercise with varied glycogen conditions. *Journal of Applied Physiology, 71*, 1427–1433.

Pontifex, M. B., Hillman, C. H., & Polich, J. (2009). Age, physical fitness, and attention: P3a and P3b. *PsychoPhysiology, 46*, 379–387.

Richter, E. A., Ruderman, N. B., Gavras, H., Belur, E. R., & Galbo, H. (1982). Muscle glycogenolysis during exercise: dual control by epinephrine and contractions. *American Journal of Physiology, 242*, E25–E32.

Robertson, R. J., & Noble, B. J. (1997). Perception of physical exertion: methods, mediators, and applications. *Exercise & Sport Sciences Reviews, 25*, 407–452.

Rogers, P. J., Tyce, G. M., Weinshilboum, R. M., O'Connor, D. T., Bailey, K. R., & Bove, A. A. (1991). Catecholamine metabolic pathways and exercise training. Plasma and urine catecholamines, metabolic enzymes, and chromogranin-A. *Circulation, 84*, 2346–2356.

Saltin, B., & Grimby, G. (1968). Physiological analysis of middle-aged and old former athletes: comparison with still active athletes of the same ages. *Circulation, 38*, 1104–1115.

Schiffer, T., Schulte, S., Hollmann, W., Bloch, W., & Strüder, H. K. (2009). Effects of strength and endurance training on brain-derived neurotrophic factor and insulin-like growth factor 1 in humans. *Hormone and Metabolic Research, 41*, 250–254.

Schlaffke, L., Lissek, S., Lenz, M., Brüne, G., Juckel, G., Hinrichs, T., et al. (2014). Sports and brain morphology – a voxel-based morphometry study with endurance athletes and martial artists. *Neuroscience, 259*, 35–42.

Schneider, D. A., McGuiggin, M. E., & Kamimori, G. H. (1992). A comparison of the blood lactate and plasma catecholamine thresholds in untrained male subjects. *International Journal of Sports Medicine, 13*, 562–566.

Seifert, T., Brassard, P., Wissenberg, M., Rasmussen, P., Nordby, P., Stallknecht, B., et al. (2010). Endurance training enhances BDNF release from the human brain. *American Journal of Physiology. Regulatory Integrative and Comparative Physiology, 298*, R372–R377.

Shojaei, E. A., Farajov, A., & Jafari, A. (2011). Effect of moderate aerobic cycling on some systemic inflammatory markers in healthy active collegiate men. *International Journal of Genetic Medicine, 4*, 79–84.

Shvartz, E., & Reibold, R. C. (1990). Aerobic fitness norms for males and females aged 6 years to 75 years—a review. *Aviation, Space, and Environmental Medicine, 61*, 3–11.

Simon, J., Young, J. L., Blood, D. K., Segal, K. R., Case, R. B., & Gutin, B. (1986). Plasma lactate and ventilation thresholds in trained and untrained cyclists. *Journal of Applied Physiology, 60*, 777–781.

Soya, H., Nakamura, T., Deocaris, C. C., Kimpara, A., Iimura, M., Fujikawa, T., et al. (2007). BDNF induction with mild exercise in the rat hippocampus. *Biochemical & Biophysical Research Communication, 358*, 961–967.

Strüder, H. K., Hollmann, W., Platen, P., Rost, R., Weicker, H., Kirchhof, O., et al. (1999). Neuroendocrine system and mental function in sedentary and endurance-trained elderly males. *International Journal of Sports Medicine, 20*, 159–166.

Stuss, D. T., Levine, B., Alexander, M. P., Hong, J., Palumbo, C., Hamer, L., et al. (2000). Wisconsin card sorting test performance in patients with focal frontal and posterior brain damage: effects of lesion location and test structure on separable cognitive processes. *Neuropsychologia, 38*, 388–402.

Stuss, D. T., Floden, D., Alexander, M. P., Levine, B., & Katz, D. (2001). Stroop performance in focal lesion patients: dissociation of processes and frontal lobe lesion location. *Neuropsychologia, 39*, 771–786.

Swain, D. P., & Leutholtz, B. C. (1997). Heart rate reserve is equivalent to %VO2 reserve, not to %VO2max. *Medicine & Science in Sports & Exercise, 29*, 410–414.

Tanaka, H., Monahan, K. D., & Seals, D. R. (2001). Age-predicted maximal heart rate revisited. *Journal of the American College of Cardiology, 37*, 153–156.

Thomson, K., Watt, A., & Liukkonen, J. (2009). Differences in ball sports athletes speed discrimination skills before and after exercise induced fatigue. *Journal of Sports Science and Medicine, 8*, 259–264.

Tomporowski, P. D., & Ellis, N. R. (1986). Effects of exercise on cognitive processes: a review. *Psychological Bulletin, 99*, 338–346.

Tseng, B. Y., Uh, J., Rossetti, H. C., Cullum, M. C., Diaz-Arrastia, R. F., Levine, B. D., et al. (2013). Masters athletes exhibit larger regional brain volume and better cognitive performance than sedentary older adults. *Journal of Magnetic Resonance Imaging, 38*, 1169–1176.

Tümer, N., Demirel, H. A., Serova, L., Sabban, E. L., Broxson, C. S., & Powers, S. K. (2001). Gene expression of catecholamine biosynthetic enzymes following exercise: modulation by age. *Neuroscience, 103*, 703–711.

Urhausen, A., Weiler, B., Coen, B., & Kindermann, W. (1994). Plasma catecholamines during endurance exercise of different intensities as related to the individual anaerobic threshold. *European Journal of Applied Physiology, 69*, 16–20.

Vanhatalo, A., Doust, J. H., & Burnley, M. (2008). A 3-min all-out cycling test is sensitive to a change in critical power. *Medicine & Science in Sports & Exercise, 40*, 1693–1699.

Vanhatalo, A., Jones, A. M., & Burnley, M. (2011). Application of critical power in sport. *International Journal of Sports Physiology Performance, 6*, 128–136.

Vaynman, S., Ying, Z., & Gomez-Pinilla, F. (2004). Hippocampal BDNF mediates the efficacy of exercise on synaptic plasticity and cognition. *European Journal of Neuroscience, 20*, 2580–2590.

Voss, M. W., Erickson, K. I., Prakash, R. S., Chaddock, L., Kim, J. S., Alves, H., et al. (2013). Neurobiological markers of exercise-related brain plasticity in older adults. *Brain, Behavior, and Immunity, 28*, 90–99.

De Vries, W. R., Bernards, N. T. M., De Rooij, M. H., & Koppeschaar, H. P. F. (2000). Dynamic exercise discloses different time-related responses in stress hormones. *Psychosomatic Medicine, 62*, 866–872.

Waterhouse, E. G., & Xu, B. (2009). New insights into the role of brain-derived neurotrophic factor in synaptic plasticity. *Molecular and Cellular Neuroscience, 42*, 81–89.

Wei, G., Zhang, Y., Jiang, T., & Luo, J. (2011). Increased cortical thickness in sports experts: a comparison of diving players with the controls. *PLoS One, 6*, e17112. http://dx.doi.org/10.1371/journal.pone.0017112.

Weinstein, A. M., Voss, M. W., Prakash, R. S., Chaddock, L., Szabo, A., Siobhan, M., et al. (2012). The association between aerobic fitness and executive function is mediated by prefrontal cortex volume. *Brain, Behavior, and Immunity, 26*, 811–819.

Weltman, A., Wood, C. M., Womack, C. J., Davis, S. E., Blumer, J. L., Alvarez, J., et al. (1994). Catecholamine and blood lactate responses to incremental rowing and running exercise. *Journal of Applied Physiology, 76*, 1144.

Whipp, B. J., & Rossiter, H. B. (2005). The kinetics of oxygen uptake: physiological inferences from the parameters. In A. M. Jones & D. C. Poole (Eds.), *Oxygen uptake kinetics in sport, exercise and medicine* (pp. 62–94). London: Routledge.

Wilmore, J. H., & Costill, D. L. (2004). *Physiology of sport and exercise* (3rd ed.). Champaign, IL: Human Kinetics.

Winder, W. W., Hagberg, J. M., Hickson, R. C., Ehsani, A. A., & McLane, J. A. (1978). Time course of sympathoadrenal adaptation to endurance exercise training in man. *Journal of Applied Physiology, 45*, 370–374.

Winder, W. W., Hickson, R. C., Hagberg, J. M., Ehsani, A. A., & McLane, J. A. (1979). Training-induced changes in hormonal and metabolic responses to submaximal exercise. *Journal of Applied Physiology Respiratory Environmental and Exercise Physiology, 46*, 766–771.

Winter, E. M. (2007). Scaling: adjusting physiological and performance measures for differences in body size. In E. M. Winter, A. M. Jones, R. C. Davison, P. D. Bromley, & T. H. Mercer (Eds.), *Sport exercise physiology test guide l Sport testing: Volume one.* (pp. 49–53). London: Routledge.

Wittert, G. A., Livesey, J. H., Espiner, E. A., & Donald, R. A. (1996). Adaptation of the hypothalamo-pituitary adrenal axis to chronic exercise in humans. *Medicine & Science in Sports & Exercise, 28*, 1015–1019.

Wu, A., Ying, Z., & Gómez-Pinilla, F. (2004). The interplay between oxidative stress and brain-derived neurotrophic factor modulates the outcome of a saturated fat diet on synaptic plasticity and cognition. *European Journal of Neuroscience, 19*, 1699–1707.

Yanagita, S., Amemiya, S., Suzuki, S., & Kita, I. (2007). Effects of spontaneous and forced running on activation of hypothalamic corticotropin-releasing hormone neurons in rats. *Life Sciences, 80*, 356–363.

Yoshida, T., Udo, M., Iwai, K., & Yamaguchi, T. (1993). Physiological characteristics related to endurance running performance in female distance runners. *Journal of Sports Science, 11*, 57–62.

Zheng, H., Liu, Y., Li, W., Yang, B., Chen, D., Wang, X., et al. (2006). Beneficial effects of exercise and its molecular mechanisms on depression in rats. *Behavioral Brain Research, 168*, 47–55.

Zoladz, J. A., Pilc, A., Majerczxak, J., Grandys, M., Zapart-Bukowska, J., & Duda, K. (2008). Endurance training increases plasma brain-derived neurotrophic factor concentration in young healthy men. *Journal of Physiology Pharmacology, 59*(Suppl. 7), 119–132.

"Cogito ergo sum" or "ambulo ergo sum"? New Perspectives in Developmental Exercise and Cognition Research

Caterina Pesce[1], Tal Dotan Ben-Soussan[2,3]

[1]Department of Movement, Human and Health Sciences, Italian University Sport and Movement "Foro Italico", Rome, Italy; [2]Research Institute for Neuroscience, Education and Didactics, Patrizio Paoletti Foundation for Development and Communication, Assisi, Italy; [3]Bar-Ilan University, Ramat-Gan, Israel

INTRODUCTION

The philosophical proposition "I think, therefore I am" by René Descartes rose to fame much more than the objection of his coeval Pierre Gassendi: "I walk, therefore I am." This testifies the dominating prioritization of cognition over movement. Several decades of research have highlighted the relevant associations between physical exercise and cognitive functioning, between motor and cognitive development. Advancements in psychophysiological, neurostructural, and neurochemical investigation have strengthened the neuroscience rationale for the beneficial effect of physical exercise and exercise-related fitness on brain development and cognitive functioning in children and adolescents.

Let us take a look back on the pathway through which the neuroscience perspective has been applied to the study of the effects of physical activity and sport participation on cognition

at developmental age. Sport and sport-related neurosciences have something in common: they were both *adult born*: youth sport came to life as an age-appropriate translation of adult athletic training (Wiggins, 2013); the application of neurosciences to sport and exercise research started by studying the brain correlates of cognitive expertise of high-level adult athletes (Zani & Rossi, 1991). The health and wellness movement in the 1980s, along with the extension of sport psychology toward exercise psychology (Tomporowski, Davis, Miller, & Naglieri, 2008), led to seminal neuroscientific works on the exercise–cognition interaction in older individuals and, finally, in children and adolescents (see Hillman, Erickson, & Kramer, 2008, for a review). These represent the ascending and descending phases of the parabola of life where the benefits of exercise on the brain mean the most.

In the following paragraphs we show selected evidence of chronic and acute exercise effects on children and adolescents' cognition, focusing on

Exercise-Cognition Interaction
http://dx.doi.org/10.1016/B978-0-12-800778-5.00012-8

251

the functional, structural, and neurobiological mechanisms of the brain, which act on this relationship. Even though intriguing evidence from adult studies suggests that some neurobiological changes supporting structural brain development in the long term also underlie the transient benefits for cognitive performance induced by acute exercise (Winter et al., 2007), neuroscience research on chronic and acute exercise effects in children or adolescents have been developed on separate tracks with few exceptions (see Stroth et al., 2009 for a coupled acute–chronic exercise investigation and Nieman et al., 2013 for an integrated acute–chronic research design). Therefore, we present selected evidence on acute and chronic exercise research in separate paragraphs, but looking for both common and differentiated neural correlates or mediators.

THE CHRONIC EXERCISE– COGNITION INTERACTION IN CHILDREN AND ADOLESCENTS

Juvenal's ancient sentence: "a healthy mind in a healthy body" ("mens sana in corpore sano") is commonly cited in its wrong interpretation that to be mentally healthy, you have to have a healthy body. While this linkage did not exist in Juvenal's context of discourse, which was simply aimed at encouraging people to prioritize both physical and mental health in the prayers that human beings turn to the gods, almost 2000 years later, there is actually strong neuroscientific evidence that already with children as young as preadolescent age, we can actively contribute to "catch both those birds with one stone": physical activity. This evidence is summarized in Table 1.

Brain Correlates of Physical Activity and Fitness Effects on Cognition and Academics

In the last decade, there has been a flourishing of research on how chronic physical exercise impacts preadolescent children's brains, mainly performed in the Neurocognitive Kinesiology Laboratory directed by Charles Hillman at the University of Illinois at Urbana–Champaign. The majority of those studies are cross-sectional in nature and have consistently demonstrated the benefits, for children's brains and cognition, of being physically fit. Similar to aging research, developmental studies have mainly focused on cardiovascular fitness and its brain structural and functional correlates (see Chaddock, Pontifex, Hillman, & Kramer, 2011; Hillman et al., 2008; Hillman, Kamijo, & Scudder, 2011; Khan & Hillman, 2014, for reviews).

At a functional level, studies using event-related brain potentials (ERPs) have highlighted the "added value" of complementing overt behavioral measures of children's cognitive functioning with neuroelectric measures of brain activity (Berchicchi et al., 2015; Hillman, Buck, Themanson, Pontifex, & Castelli, 2009; Hillman, Castelli, & Buck, 2005; Pontifex et al., 2011). ERPs, being characterized by high temporal resolution, allow insight into discrete cognitive processes occurring prior to and after the occurrence of task relevant stimuli. Hillman et al. (2005) started with a stimulus discrimination task (oddball paradigm) and found first evidence that the benefit of being fit, revealed by behavioral indices of cognitive performance, was paralleled by a larger amplitude of the P3, a positive-going ERP wave occurring between 300 and 500 ms after stimulus onset, whose amplitude is considered an index of the allocation of attentional resources during stimulus engagement.

In line with the increasing interest for the selective and disproportionately larger benefits of exercise and exercise-related fitness for higher-level cognitive function, the executive (Etnier & Chang, 2009), Hillman, Buck et al. (2009) furthered their line of research employing a task that challenges executive control at a higher degree (flanker task). They found a higher behavioral accuracy in higher-fit children

TABLE 1 Summary of findings, from a neuroscience perspective, of studies performed to assess the chronic effects of exercise on cognition

Author(s), PY	N	Age (weight)	Design	Intervention type, duration	Physical assessment	Cognitive assessment	Neuroscience approach	Results
Hillman et al. (2005)	51	9.6 vs 19.3 years	Chronic cross-sectional	/	Fitnessgram (PACER)	Oddball paradigm	ERPs[a]	Fitness-related benefit
Hillman, Buck et al., 2009	38	9.4 years	Chronic cross-sectional	/	Fitnessgram (PACER)	Eriksen flanker task	ERPs[a]	Fitness-related benefit
Pontifex et al., 2011	48	10 years	Chronic cross-sectional	/	Modified Balke protocol	Modified flanker task	ERPs[a]	Fitness-related benefit
Berchicchi et al., 2015	41	10 years	Chronic cross-sectional	/	Modified Balke protocol	Modified flanker task	ERPs[a]	Fitness-related benefit
Moore et al., 2014	40	9–10	Chronic cross-sectional	/	Modified Balke protocol	KTEA-2[b], arithmetic task	ERPs[a]	Fitness-related benefit
Scudder et al., 2014	46	9–10 years	Chronic cross-sectional	/	Modified Balke protocol	WRAT3[c], sentence processing task	ERPs[a]	Fitness-related benefit
Lee et al., 2014	91	Teens	Chronic cross-sectional	/	IPAQ[d]	Stroop test, WCST[e], dual task, SMT[f], SALT[g]	BDNF, IGF-1, VEGF	PA[h] level-related benefit
Hillman et al., 2014	221	7–9 years	Chronic interventional RCT[i]	"FIT Kids" MVPA[j] training, 9 months	VO$_2$ max test	Modified flanker task, switch task	ERPs[a]	PA-related improvement
Kamijo et al., 2011	36	9 years	Chronic interventional RCT[i]	Aerobic and strength training, 9 months	Modified Balke protocol	Modified flanker task	ERPs[a]	PA-related improvement
Chang et al., 2013	26	6–7.5	Chronic interventional RCT[i]	Coordinative exercise of low vs moderate intensity, 2 months	60-s curl up, long jump, 1-leg standing eyes closed, sit-and-reach	Eriksen flanker task	ERPs[a]	PA-related improvement, No dose–response
Davis et al., 2011	171	7–11 years (overweight)	Chronic interventional RCT[i]	Aerobic training, 13 weeks, 20 vs 40min/day	/	CAS[k], Achievement tests, antisaccade	fMRI[l]	PA-related improvement, dose–response

Continued

TABLE 1 Summary of findings, from a neuroscience perspective, of studies performed to assess the chronic effects of exercise on cognition—cont'd

Author(s), PY	N	Age (weight)	Design	Intervention type, duration	Physical assessment	Cognitive assessment	Neuroscience approach	Results
Chaddock-Heyman, Erickson, Voss, Knecht, et al., 2013	32	8–9 years	Chronic interventional RCT[i]	"FIT Kids" MVPA[j] training, 9 months	VO2 max test	Modified flanker task	fMRI[l]	PA-related improvement
Krafft et al., 2014	43	8–11 years (overweight)	Chronic interventional RCT[i]	Aerobic training, 8 months	Modified Balke protocol	Antisaccade, flanker task	fMRI[l]	No PA effect on cognitive control, but neural changes
Chaddock, Erickson, Prakash, VanPatter, et al., 2010	55	9–10 years	Chronic cross-sectional	/	Modified Balke protocol	Flanker task	fMRI[l] sMRI[m]	Fitness-related cognitive and neurostructural enhancement
Chaddock, Erickson, Prakash, Kim, et al., 2010	49	9–10 years	Chronic cross-sectional	/	VO2 max test	Item and relational memory task	fMRI[l] sMRI[m]	Fitness-related memory and neurostructural enhancement
Herting & Nagel, 2012	34	15–18 years	Chronic cross-sectional	/	Youth Adolescent Activity Questionaire, VO2 peak	vMWT[n], RAVLT[o]	sMRI[m]	Fitness-related memory and neurostructural enhancement
Herting & Nagel, 2013	34	15–18 years	Chronic cross-sectional	/	Youth Adolescent Activity Questionaire, VO2 peak	Verbal associative memory encoding task	fMRI[l]	No fitness effect on memory, but changes in connectivity
Chaddock-Heyman et al., 2014	24	9–10	Chronic cross-sectional	/	Modified Balke protocol	/	DTI[p]	Fitness-related white matter microstructural enhancement
Chaddock-Heyman, Erickson, Voss, Powers, et al., 2013	61	7–9	Chronic cross-sectional	/	Modified Balke protocol	/	DTI[p]	Fitness-related white matter microstructural enhancement

Herting et al., 2014	34	15–18 years	Chronic cross-sectional	/	Youth Adololescent Activity Questionaire, VO$_2$ peak	/	DTI[p]	Fitness-related white matter connectivity enhancement
Stroth et al., 2009	35	13–14 years	Chronic cross-sectional parallel to acute off-task	20min stationary bike cycling at 60% HRmax[q]	Graded maximal exercise test	Modified flanker task	ERPs[a]	Fitness-related benefit, no acute after-effect of PA[h]
Niemann et al., 2013	42	9.7 years	Chronic cross-sectional integrated with acute off-task	12min running at individual target HR of 180–190 bpm	MoMo[i]	d2-test of attention	Testosterone	Beneficial acute after-effect, no individual differences

[a] ERPs: event-related brain potentials.
[b] KTEA-2: Kaufman Test of Academic and Educational Achievement 2.
[c] WRAT3: Wide Range Achievement Test 3.
[d] IPAQ: international physical activity questionnaire.
[e] WCST: Winsconsin card sorting test.
[f] SMT: spatial memory task.
[g] SALT: spatial associative learning task.
[h] PA: physical activity.
[i] RCT: randomized controlled trials.
[j] MVPA: moderate-to-vigorous physical activity.
[k] CAS: cognitive assessment system.
[l] fMRI: functional magnetic resonance imaging.
[m] sMRI: structural magnetic resonance imaging.
[n] vMWT: virtual Morris water task.
[o] RAVLT: Rey Auditory Verbal Learning Test.
[p] DTI: diffusion tensor imaging.
[q] HRmax: estimated maximal heart rate.

that was paralleled again by larger P3 amplitude. In that and a further study (Hillman, Buck, et al., 2009; Pontifex et al., 2011), the authors also extended their search for fitness effects to response-locked components of ERPs that reflect error processing (error-related negativity, ERN) and attention allocation toward error commission [error-related positivity (Pe)]. Higher-fit children, as compared to lower-fit ones, had smaller ERN and larger Pe, suggesting a more proficient action monitoring.

A further step forward in the comprehension of the neural correlates of children's cardiovascular fitness was to identify whether being higher fit translates into a generally larger allocation of neural resources across task conditions, or also into a shift in cognitive strategy when the task becomes more challenging. To this aim, Pontifex et al. (2011) included in the flanker task incompatible stimulus-response conditions. In contrast to lower-fit children, higher-fit ones showed no loss of accuracy and a greater modulation of P3 amplitude and ERN from the compatible to the incompatible condition. Taken together, these results indicated that more efficient cognitive strategies, as reflected in the modulation of the P3 and ERN components, subtend the higher performance accuracy of higher-fit children in tasks that require effortful cognitive control and flexibility.

Neural correlates of the overt behavioral benefit, for children, of being aerobically fit were also found at prestimulus and early poststimulus processing stages, as indicated by larger negativity over the prefrontal cortex [(pN) that starts more than 1 s before movement onset] and modulation of an ERP component at an early stage of poststimulus processing over the posterior cortex (P1) (Berchicchi et al., 2015). This suggests that the fitness effect comes online soon in children's brains, as early as the stages of cognitive preparation of the response and early discrimination of task-relevant visual stimuli.

The only ERP study addressing the fitness effect at adolescent age (Stroth et al., 2009) showed a modulation of a further prestimulus

ERP component, the contingent negative variation (CNV) that reflects anticipation processes elicited in the interval between the onset of a warning stimulus and that of following response stimuli. Higher-fit adolescents showed larger CNV amplitude, reflecting enhanced task preparation processes.

Another cross-sectional investigation of chronic exercise effects on cognition of adolescents was performed with behavioral and neurochemical assessments (Lee et al., 2014). Chronic exercise was positively associated with executive function and spatial memory performance. However, participants' physical activity level interacted with the concentration of brain-derived neurotrophic factor (BDNF): better executive function was associated with low BDNF levels in active adolescents, but with high BDNF levels in their sedentary counterparts. This result, which is in disagreement with evidence of a generally positive relationship between exercise and neurotrophins concentration, might be due to methodological discrepancies. In individuals with high cardiorespiratory fitness, neurotrophins concentration is affected by time of measurement (Cho et al., 2012). Moreover, Lee et al. (2014) have used a measurement method that does not allow differentiating between precursor and mature neurotrophin. Concentration of the former seems to be associated with cognitive decline, while the latter has a role in exercise-related improvement (see Venditti et al., 2015 discussed later in this chapter). Regardless of this, in their conclusions, Lee et al. (2014) stated that their findings could not explain the mechanisms underlying these interaction effects between neurotrophic factor concentration and fitness status in predicting cognitive performance of adolescents.

Further developmental studies are needed to determine whether and how exercise effects on neurochemical factors mediate the effects of physical activity on cognition in childhood. To date, there are intriguing hypotheses, derived from adult studies, on the aptitude of aerobic exercise or resistance training to have a bio-chemical influence on synaptic function under-lying cognitive function, learning, and memory in children (Chaddock et al., 2011; Gomez-Pinilla & Hillman, 2013).

To investigate if a causal relationship between chronic exercise and cognition underlies the observed association between cardiovascular fitness (or physical activity level) and cognitive efficiency, afterschool physical activity interventions (RCT) aimed at enhancing cardiovascular fitness were performed and children were tested at cognitive–behavioral and functional–neural level. After the intervention, the children showed an increment in P3 amplitude as a neural correlate of more pronounced improvement in cognitive control and flexibility compared to children in the control group (Hillman et al., 2014). Kamijo et al. (2011) showed that fitness improvements in the intervention group also benefited working memory performance, with this benefit being greater under more demanding task conditions, and paralleled by larger CNV especially over frontal areas, indicating enhanced cognitive control of working memory. Also, a parallelism between increased task-evoked prefrontal activation and cognitive control performance was observed after a physical activity intervention by means of functional magnetic resonance imaging (fMRI) (Chaddock-Heyman, Erickson, Voss, Knecht et al., 2013) also in overweight children (Davis et al., 2011). Davis et al. (2011) also found decreased posterior parietal activity that was confirmed in a further intervention with overweight children (Krafft et al., 2014).

MRI has also been used to demonstrate that participation in physical activity and increased cardiovascular fitness enhance brain structure. The first structural MRI studies with children were those conducted by Chaddock and colleagues, which focused on fitness effects on basal ganglia and hippocampus. Chaddock, Erickson, Prakash, VanPatter et al. (2010) demonstrated that there are fitness-related differences in volume of specific regions of the basal ganglia implicated

in controlled processes of action selection and execution and that such structural differences are related to behavioral differences in cognitive control performance. Chaddock, Erickson, Prakash, Kim et al. (2010), in children, and Herting and Nagel (2012), in adolescents, found an analogous relationship of cardiovascular fitness with the volume of the hippocampus, which is a subcortical brain region implicated in both spatial and relational memory. Higher-fit children or adolescents had larger hippocampal volumes compared to their lower-fit counterparts and this difference partially mediated fitness-related differences in relational memory performance in children and paralleled enhanced visuospatial memory learning in adolescents. Even though some specific aspects of memory performance such as item memory (Chaddock, Erickson, Prakash, Kim et al., 2010) or associative memory encoding (Herting & Nagel, 2013) seem not to be affected by aerobic fitness, during adolescence fitness seems to impact functional connectivity of the hippocampus and memory-related neural circuitry.

Also, as assessed using diffusion tensor imaging (DTI), children's cardiovascular fitness seems related to greater white matter integrity of structures, such as the corpus callosum, that are responsible for communication between and integration of regions into networks (Chaddock-Heyman et al., 2014) and this brain structural advantage translates into more efficient cognitive control (Chaddock-Heyman, Erickson, Voss, Powers et al., 2013). A similar fitness-related advantage in terms of white matter connectivity and microstructure of regions that connect frontal and motor fibers seems to extend into adolescent age (Herting, Colby, Sowell, & Nagel, 2014).

Collectively, the above-reviewed studies further our understanding of the neural underpinnings of cognitive enhancement through physical activity and increased cardiovascular fitness during development. The applied take-home message is the value of physical activity for early promotion of brain health.

At a behavioral level, there is increasing evidence of the relationship between physical activity or fitness and academic achievement (e.g., Howie & Pate, 2012). Neuroscientific studies have added to this issue, showing that the modulation of specific ERP components and the activation of specific brain areas are the neural correlates both of academic achievement skills and of their relation to children's fitness. The amplitude of the P3 component of stimulus-locked ERPs, which is the mostly studied neural correlate of cognitive efficiency in higher-fit children, is a predictor of arithmetic and reading aptitude independently of IQ and school grade (Hillman et al., 2012). Also, its modulation seems to be a marker of fitness-related differences in arithmetic task performance during conditions in which problem solving is more challenging (Moore, Drollette, Scudder, Bharij, & Hillman, 2014). Other ERP components with later onset, involved in the processing of semantic information (the N400) and the analysis of language structure (the P600) underlying reading skills, showed a differential amplitude as a function of fitness level during a reading task (Scudder et al., 2014). Also an interventional fMRI study (Davis et al., 2011) showed a causal relationship between a fitness-enhancing program of high-dose physical activity and math achievement that had a neural correlate in the increment of prefrontal activation and decrement of parietal activation. However, in their conclusions, the authors also wondered whether cardiovascular fitness gains or other metabolic, neurophysiological, and neurotrophic mechanisms, influencing the integrity of the neural "hardware," may not be the only mediators of physical exercise effects on cognitive functioning.

Looking for New Pathways of Chronic Exercise–Cognition Interaction

In a recent review, Pesce (2012) claimed that if we merely focus on dose–response relations and dose-related fitness outcomes of physical

exercise, we neglect relevant aspects of physical activity that may render physical activity a unique means to promote cognitive development. Promoting cognitive development through movement is not only an issue of the "right dose" of physical activity, as exercise-related cognitive benefits may be also due to neural stimulation by movement, which influences the efficiency of the brain "software" (Tomporowski, Lambourne, & Okumura, 2011). A review of animal and human studies (Curlik & Shors, 2013) convincingly suggests that while physical activity—especially aerobic exercise—increases the number of new neurons that are produced in the hippocampus, mental training increases the number of those that survive. On the one side, Curlik and Shor's (2013) review is in line with the human developmental evidence on the benefits of fitness and fitness-enhancing exercise training for brain and cognitive health (e.g., Khan & Hillman, 2014), thus justifying the call for ensuring the right "dose" of activity as early as childhood. On the other side, the above review also supports the complementary role of physical and mental training for promoting brain health. Pesce (2012) and Moreau and Conway (2013) moved a step forward, proposing not simply to complement, but to integrate physical and mental training, and highlighting the potential of physical activity and sports to pursue this aim.

From this integrative perspective, Pesce (2012) coined the umbrella term "gross-motor cognitive training" as a potential means to capitalize on the cognitive benefits of joining physical effort and mental engagement, and called for shifting the focus from dose–response to quality–response relations in exercise and cognition research. Moreau and Conway (2013), after performing a comparative review of the cognitive benefits of physical and mental training practices, highlighted an emerging third approach: "designed sports training," which is addressed later in this chapter. The challenge related to this integrative view is to define and operational-ize what are the qualitative facets of cognitively challenging physical activity and sport tasks, and the pathways by which they may promote cognitive development. Apart from the biophys-iological changes induced in the brain by the metabolic demands of aerobic physical activity, Best (2010) proposed that there may be further pathways of brain stimulation elicited by the coordinative and cognitive complexity of the movement tasks.

To date, only one developmental ERP study (Chang, Tsai, Chen, & Hung, 2013) has addressed the impact of coordinative exer-cise on children's cognition with the joint manipulation of a quantitative exercise param-eter (exercise intensity). The study outcomes show that as early as preschool age, a short (2 months) intervention of low to moderate inten-sity coordinative exercise twice a week posi-tively impacted children's cognitive control, as assessed with a flanker task, and its neural correlate, as reflected in the modulation of P3 amplitude and latency. This is promising evi-dence suggesting that coordinative exercise, which builds on complex sensory-motor learning processes, may specifically benefit prefrontal-dependent cognitive control as early as child-hood by enhancing the allocation of attentional resources on task relevant stimuli and the pro-cessing speed of these stimuli.

Moreau and Conway (2013) argued that sen-sorimotor learning in sport tasks designed to challenge cognition is a potential mechanism that mediates the beneficial effects of sport practice on cognitive efficiency. The possibility to capitalize on the linkage between cognitive and motor demands in physical activity and sport experiences that emphasize motor learn-ing is supported by evidence that sequential cognitive and motor task learning share the same underlying mechanisms and substrates as the presupplementary motor area (pre-SMA) (Hardwick, Rottschy, Miall, & Eickhoff, 2013; Leek & Johnston, 2009).

THE ACUTE EXERCISE–COGNITION INTERACTION IN CHILDREN AND ADOLESCENTS

Neurosciences have provided compelling evidence that regular physical activity and enhanced aerobic fitness may improve cognitive function and brain health during development, thus supporting the widely acknowledged notion that physical activity is an investment that may benefit children in motor and non-motor domains (National Association for Sport and Physical Education, 2011). However, from a translational perspective to inform educational policy development, it is also relevant to under-stand to what extent acute bouts of exercise may benefit learning and academic performance. This kind of evidence, summarized in Table 2, may be important for educators, being pertinent to the organization of learning-supportive envi-ronments: acute bouts of physical activity inter-spersed between intellectual learning phases may act as a contextual factor facilitating execu-tive function, attention, memory, and learning at ages ranging from preschool to adolescence (e.g., Budde, Voelcker-Rehage, Pietraßyk-Kendziorra, Ribeiro, & Tidow, 2008; Chen, Yan, Yin, Pan, & Chang, 2014; Pesce, Crova, Cereatti, Casella, & Bellucci, 2009).

Brain Correlates of Acute Exercise Effects on Cognition during Development

As compared to the growing body of research on the neural correlates of the relationship between chronic exercise, cardiovascular fitness, and cognition in preadolescent children, the neural correlates of acute exercise effects on cog-nition have been rarely investigated in children (Drollette et al., 2014; Hillman, Pontifex et al., 2009, Pontifex, Saliba, Raine, Picchietti, & Hillman 2013) and adolescents (Stroth et al., 2009) and few further studies have examined the acute exercise–cognition interaction from a biochemi-cal perspective in children (Budde, Windisch,

TABLE 2   Summary of findings, from a neuroscience perspective, of studies performed to assess the acute effects of exercise on cognition

Author(s), PY	N	Age (special needs)	Design	Intervention Type, Duration	Physical Assessment	Cognitive Assessment	Neuroscience Approach	Results
Hillman, Pontifex et al., 2009	20	9.5 years	Acute off-task	20 min treadmill walking at 60% HRmax[a]	Modified Balke protocol and RPE[b]	Modified flanker task, WRAT3[c]	ERPs[d]	Beneficial after-effect of PA[e]
Pontifex et al., 2013	40	8–10 years (ADHD[f])	Acute off-task	20 min treadmill walking at 60–75% HRmax[a]	PARQ[g]	Modified flanker task, WRAT3[c]	ERPs[d]	Beneficial after-effect of PA[e]
Drollette et al., 2014	40	9.7 years	Acute off-task	20 min treadmill walking at 60–70% HRmax[a]	Modified Balke protocol	Modified flanker task	ERPs[d]	Beneficial after-effect of PA[e] with individual differences
Stroth et al., 2009	35	13–14 years	Chronic cross-sectional parallel to acute off-task	/ 20 min stationary bike cycling at 60% HRmax[a]	Graded maximal exercise test	Modified flanker task	ERPs[d]	Fitness-related benefit, no acute after-effect of PA[e]
Budde, Voelcker-Rehage, et al., 2010	60	15–16 years	Acute off-task	12 min running at 50–65% vs 70–85% HRmax[a]	Shuttle run test	LDS[h] working memory task	Testosterone, cortisol	Intensity-dependent increase of T and C, individual differences
Niemann et al., 2013	42	9.7 years	Chronic cross-sectional integrated with acute off-task	12 min running at indival target HR of 180–190 bpm	MoMo[i]	d2-test of attention	Testosterone	Beneficial acute after-effect, no individual differences

[a] HR max: estimated maximal heart rate.
[b] RPE: ratings of perceived exertion.
[c] WRAT: Wide Range Achievement Test 3.
[d] ERPs: event-related brain potentials.
[e] PA: physical activity.
[f] ADHD: attention-deficit hyperactivity disorder.
[g] PARQ: Physical Activity Readiness Questionnaire.
[h] LDS: Letter Digit Span.
[i] MoMo: "Motorik-Modul" activity questionnaire.

Kudielka, & Voelcker-Rehage, 2010) and adolescents (Budde, Voelcker-Rehage et al., 2010; Nieman et al., 2013). Given the applied relevance of the beneficial cognitive outcomes of acute exercise for attentive behavior and successful learning in the school setting, all acute exercise studies mentioned above belong to off-task exercise research that investigates the after-effects of single bouts of acute exercise performed before cognitive testing.

The first evidence by Hillman, Pontifex et al. (2009) was that a 20 min bout of moderately intense aerobic exercise transiently affects children's cognition in the same way that chronic aerobic exercise and exercise-related fitness do: after exercising, children exhibited larger P3 amplitude, were more accurate in flanker task performance, and performed better on an academic achievement test. To extend the generalizability of such kinds of results, the researchers at the Neuroscience and Kinesiology Laboratory (Pontifex et al., 2013) performed a further study with children affected by attention-deficit hyperactivity disorder (ADHD). Similar to typically developing children, also children with ADHD exhibited, after acute exercise, larger P3 amplitude, higher response accuracy in the flanker task, and better academic skill performance. Moreover, they exhibited selective enhancements in regulatory processes, as reflected in the ERN component of response-locked ERPs: their lower ERN amplitude as compared to healthy match controls, observed after a seated resting period, was evened out after the exercise bout. Finally, Drollette et al. (2014) demonstrated that acute exercise has a differential effect on children who have lower or higher capability to exert cognitive control. In fact, only lower performers showed enhanced P3 amplitude and flanker test performance accuracy following the exercise bout. The only ERP study that investigated acute exercise effects in adolescents showed no modulation of prestimulus (CNV) and poststimulus (N1 and P3) ERP components after

the exercise bout (Stroth et al., 2009). Taken together, those results support the use of moderate acute exercise as a contributing factor for increasing cognitive control and academic performance at preadolescent age and for supporting the provision of children's right to equal learning opportunity.

Holding in mind the aim to provide evidence for the educational system, it is also appropriate to test children directly in the school context after acute bouts of physical exercise that fit into that setting, choosing exercise type and duration that can be performed within a regular school break. Studies with this kind of ecological validity are those performed by Budde and colleagues (Budde, Voelcker-Rehage et al., 2010; Nieman et al., 2013), who used biochemical markers of neuroendocrine activation after acute exercise in the school context. In the first studies with preadolescents (Budde, Windish et al., 2010) and adolescents (Budde, Pietrassyk-Kendziorra, Bohm, & Voelcker-Rehage, 2010), the authors found that 12 min high-intensity exercise at school activated the hypothalamic–pituitary–gonadal (HPG) and hypothalamic–pituitary–adrenal (HPA) axis in adolescents, as revealed by increased testosterone and cortisol concentration in the saliva after exercise, but no significant exercise-related changes in cortisol in preadolescent children.

Further studies extended this type of research including cognitive testing to investigate if exercise-induced changes in hormonal concentrations are associated with an impact of exercise on cognitive performance. Budde, Voelcker-Rehage et al. (2010) confirmed that a bout of high-intensity exercise leads to an increase in testosterone concentration in adolescents, but this had proven detrimental to (i.e., negatively correlated with) working memory performance. The authors argued that testosterone concentration might modify the function of the prefrontal cortex, which belongs to the neural substrate of working memory. Instead in preadolescent children, acute high-intensity exercise benefited attentional performance and this effect was not paralleled by incremental changes in testosterone concentration (Nieman et al., 2013).

Interestingly in the above study, the authors also aimed at analyzing the potential interplay between acute and chronic exercise effects on cognition, which has received limited consideration in exercise and cognition research (Pesce, 2009). They provided cross-sectional evidence for the role of chronic exercise on the acute exercise–cognition relation by dividing their children into lower and higher fit. After exercise, lower-active children exhibited decreased testosterone levels and a less pronounced improvement in attention than higher-fit children. Thus, habitual physical activity levels seem to influence the reactivity of the HPG to intensive exercise, with a disruption of this axis in children who are less physically active. This result has neuroscientific relevance, as testosterone has a neuroprotective role in the central nervous system (see Bialek, Zaremba, Borowicz, & Czuczwar, 2004, for a review) and the hippocampus is a target of steroid modulation (Beyenburg et al., 2000). To explain the discrepancy between the studies performed with children and adolescents, the authors also referred to the potential confounding by cohort effects: since physical fitness is not the only outcome of chronic physical activity participation, it may not be an independent moderator acting on the acute exercise–cognition relationship (Pesce, 2009).

Further moderators that seem to act on the relationship of interest are the characteristics of the physical activity task: intensity (Budde, Volecker-Rehage et al., 2010), cognitive or social interaction demands (Best, 2012; Pesce et al., 2009), and motor coordination demands (Budde et al., 2008; Gallotta et al., 2011). This highlights the need, also in developmental acute exercise research, to complement the view on quantitative exercise parameters with a novel view on the qualitative characteristics of the movement tasks composing any physical activity bout (Pesce, 2012).

Bringing Cognition into the Gym and Movement into the Classroom

To date, few acute exercise studies with children or adolescents have focused on the effects of qualitatively different exercise bouts while controlling for exercise intensity and duration. Budde et al. (2008) compared the effects, on executive attention of adolescents, of aerobic exercise bouts performed in the school setting that differed in the level of coordinative complexity. The authors found that attention performance benefited from the exercise bout with enhanced motor coordination challenges. Gallotta et al. (2011) tried to extend this finding to preadolescent children, but failed to find an attention benefit of coordinatively enriched physical education lessons as compared to traditional physical education. Pesce et al. (2009) found that an acute bout of physical education at school benefited following memory recall performance in the classroom, with additional memory benefits when the antecedent physical activity bout consisted of a cognitively and socially engaging team game as compared to less challenging circuit training. In contrast, Best (2012) could not find evidence of larger cognitive benefits after a cognitively challenging physical activity bout (i.e., physical exercise coupled with an interactive video game) as compared to a similarly intense exercise bout that did not involve mental effort (i.e., physical exercise coupled with a repetitive video game).

In the light of these inconsistent results, the interpretations on the role of the amount of cognitive engagement by movement are divergent. While Gallotta et al. (2011) referred to older theories of exercise as a stressor, arguing that the enriched physical education environment elicited excessive increases in arousal that worsened children's attention, the other authors made tentative conclusions in terms of more recent theories on the relationship between exercise and higher-order cognition (Etnier & Chang, 2009). Budde et al. (2008) interpreted their results suggesting that motor coordination tasks facilitate neural circuitries that are recruited in complex motor coordination and associated with cognitive executive function (Serrien, Ivry, & Swinnen, 2007). Pesce et al. (2009) argued that while the general effect of physical exercise on memory is mediated by an increment in arousal that translates into enhanced memory recall and metamemory (Salas, Minakata, & Kelemen, 2011), the specific effect of a cognitively engaging physical activity as a team game may be mediated by the activation of cognitive functions involved in decision making and action selection under situational uncertainty and time pressure. To reconcile Pesce et al.'s (2009) finding with his own results showing absence of any cognitive effort effect, Best (2012) argued that the key issue was not the cognitive effort, but that the social interaction demands inherent in a team game may activate executive function and therefore ameliorate memory performance that relies on executive function. In fact, the ability to interact with opponents in order to anticipate their ongoing actions depends on the development of the "theory of mind," which in turn is linked to the development of executive function (Perner & Lang, 1999).

None of the above studies, however, have been performed with neuroelectric or biochemical measures of neural or neuroendocrine activation. Thus, these interpretations remain speculative and a neuroscience approach to the study of the role played by the coordinative, cognitive, and social interaction demands of physical activity may further our understanding of this issue.

To exploit the potential of physical activity to impact on cognitive development in the formal education context, rendering physical education tasks cognitively challenging is only one side of the coin. Getting classroom learning "moved" represents the other side. There are two types of classroom-based physical activity: active breaks and integrated physical activity. The first, also labeled energizers, consists of movement activities unrelated to subject content, while the second incorporates academic content of various subject areas into movement actions.

There is evidence, broadly ranging from preschool to elementary school age, that classroom-based physical activity is an effective means not only for enhancing children's physical activity levels and fitness, but also for enhancing cognitive function and attention, and for improving on-task, learning-appropriate behavior and academic achievement skills in both the short and medium term (e.g., Erwin, Abel, Beighle, & Beets, 2011; Hill et al., 2010; Kibbe et al., 2011; Mahar et al., 2006; Palmer, Miller, & Robinson, 2013). The general conclusion is that introducing in the classroom physical activities that take a minimum amount of time to implement and require little or no training is feasible and may help schools achieve both physical and mental health policies (Mahar et al., 2006). To contribute designing physical activities for the classroom that jointly aid physical fitness and cognitive development, it is essential to perform comparative research on classroom-based physical activities that differ quantitatively and/or qualitatively, ranging from active breaks that involve minimum cognitive engagement to integrated physical activities that challenge cognition and metacognition (Vazou & Smiley-Oyen, 2014).

A neuroscience approach to this issue is still lacking; it would considerably strengthen the evidence base of those organizations, which have begun to advocate acute activity breaks in the classroom (National Association for Sport and Physical Education, 2008). Biochemical markers, such as neurotrophins concentration in the saliva, would be the most feasible way, in the ecological school context, to shed light onto the mechanisms that may account for changes in cognitive performance following classroom-based physical activity (Venditti et al., 2015). Indeed, among the multiple mechanisms proposed to mediate the changes in cognitive performance induced by acute exercise, adult studies indicate a modulation of circulating neurotrophins that interacts with the individual cardiovascular fitness level (Cho et al., 2012).

THE CHICKEN-AND-EGG PROBLEM IN MOTOR AND COGNITIVE DEVELOPMENTAL TRAJECTORIES

It is claimed that Marcus Cicero stated that "it is exercise alone that supports the spirits and keeps the mind in vigor." With the advances in neuroscience it is possible to understand the underlying mechanism of motor and cognitive development, which can uplift mind and emotion, thus enhancing well-being. However, cognitive neuroscience has mostly focused on exercise-induced frontal neuroplasticity (Dietrich, 2006) and less on other subcortical areas that are related to movement, such as the cerebellum. Instead, developmental neuroscientists highlight the potential of moving from the research focusing solely on corticocortical connections to an integrated view on the close interrelation also with subcortical regions, particularly on frontocerebellar connections (Diamond, 2000; Vandervert, Schimpf, & Liu, 2007). Recent studies emphasize the importance of investigating the connection between exercise-induced cerebellar changes and cognitive development.

Consequently in this section, we focus on the pivotal role of the cerebellum and its connections with the prefrontal cortex for providing a grounding in the neuroscience for the qualitative view on exercise and cognition interaction that we propose as a new developmental perspective. The study of the neural correlates of motor behavior suggests that neural regions typically considered responsible for cognitive operations may also be recruited during the performance of new complex motor skills, with the frontal lobe being considered the primary locus of overlap between cognition and action monitoring

(Serrien et al., 2007). The cerebellum in turn, which reaches maturity as late as the prefrontal cortex, seems to be important for motor, but also for cognitive, functions (Iacoboni, 2001). In fact, on the one side, the cerebellum is involved in motor learning that occurs by performing novel movement patterns in physical activity (Hardwick et al., 2013). On the other side, it is also considered a computational system contributing to cognitive and metacognitive functions by modeling iterative processes of working memory that, when fed back to the cerebral cortex as learnt cognitive control models, increase the efficiency and adaptability of the original cerebral functions (Vandervert et al., 2007).

Joint Role of the Frontal Lobe and the Cerebellum

Cognitive and motor development are fundamentally interrelated, displaying equally extended developmental timetables (Diamond, 2000). However, studies investigating whole-body training-induced changes in executive functions have almost exclusively concentrated on frontal changes and generally reported increased frontal alpha synchronization following training (see Dietrich, 2004, 2006, for reviews). However, also long distance connections are crucial for cognitive development (Sporns, Chialvo, Kaiser, & Hilgetag, 2004).

Functional connectivity has been generally ignored in the context of the exercise–cognition interaction, while either local ERP measures or MRI and DTI assessments of brain activation and health at structural and microstructural levels have received attention limited to the examination of aerobic fitness effects (e.g., Chaddock-Heyman et al., 2014; Herting et al., 2014; Krafft et al., 2014; see Khan & Hillman, 2014, for a review). However, a recent study found that Quadrato motor training (QMT), a specifically structured sensorimotor training in response to verbal instruction, enhances interhemispheric and intrahemispheric alpha coherence, an important measure of functional connectivity; also, QMT-induced cognitive flexibility was found to be correlated to increased frontal coherence (Ben-Soussan, Glicksohn, Goldstein, Berkovich-Ohana, & Donchin, 2013). These findings emphasize the need of expanding the research from local ERP and power measures toward including functional connectivity and of extending the focus from fitness effects toward the effects of cognitively challenging sensorimotor training. These results are well in line with a considerable body of literature demonstrating that in parallel to cognitive enhancement, functional connectivity can be empowered by mental training of attention (Lutz, Slagter, Dunne, & Davidson, 2008). For example, a positive relationship has been reported following transcendental meditation training, where practitioners exhibit both higher frontal alpha power and coherence as compared to controls (Travis, 2001; Travis, Tecce, Arenander, & Wallace, 2002).

In addition to frontal networks, the fronto-cerebellar network has been shown to be crucial for the development of attention functions (Bonnet et al., 2009; Diamond, 2000). In this context, it is important to note that children with ADHD have been shown to have reduced functional connectivity in the fronto-cerebellar network as well as in other motor-related areas relative to healthy control subjects (Cao et al., 2006; Zang et al., 2007). Children with ADHD further have reduced prefrontal and cerebellar activity during attentional and temporal processes, including tasks of motor timing, time discrimination, and temporal foresight (Rubia, Halari, Christakou, & Taylor, 2009; Rubia et al., 2001; Smith, Taylor, Brammer, Halari, & Rubia, 2008). Together, these findings suggest that dysfunctions in ADHD do not solely affect isolated brain regions, but also functional interregional connectivity between affected regions (Rubia, 2011).

The cerebellar deficits in development may well explain the fact that in a range of developmental disorders, such as ADHD, dyslexia, and autism, in parallel to the cognitive deficits,

children suffer from deficient motor function and sensorimotor symptoms (see Levit-Binnun, Davidovitch, & Golland, 2013, for a review). The appearance of these symptoms in a child may indicate that his brain is less resilient, and thus he/she has a higher probability of developing psychopathology following unfavorable circumstances. This further emphasizes the importance of efficient training paradigms.

Many cognitive functions, such as verbal fluency and memory, which require prefrontal cortex activation, also require cerebellum activation. Importantly, both the cerebellum and the prefrontal cortex play a crucial role in the neural network, which is activated when attention and attention shifting are required, especially during challenging and/or new tasks (Diamond, 2000; Rubia, 2011). The cerebellum is thought to serve as a general timing mechanism for both sensorimotor and cognitive processes (Ivry, 1996; Tesche & Karhu, 2000; Tesche et al., 2007). This may be mediated by the cerebellum's role in regulating the rate, force, rhythm, and accuracy of movements, which are crucial for controlling the speed, capacity, consistency, and appropriateness of cognitive processes (Buckner, 2013; Hölzel et al., 2011; Schmahmann, 2004). In fact, motor learning studies have long been aware of the cerebellum's oscillatory importance in neuroplasticity and its role in learning, such as bimanual skill acquisition (Andres et al., 1999; De Zeeuw et al., 2011; Swinnen, 2002).

Since sensorimotor deficits are often observed in different developmental disorders, some researchers attributed their cognitive and motor deficiencies to abnormal development and functioning of the cerebellum (Nicolson, Fawcett, & Dean, 2001; Piek & Dyck, 2004). In order to examine this hypothesis and test whether training-induced improvements in cerebellar function can in fact ameliorate dyslexia, Ben-Soussan, Avirame et al. (2014) have recently measured changes in cerebellar alpha power and reading performance in dyslexic adults following 4 weeks of daily QMT. While baseline cerebellar alpha was lower in the dyslexic group, following 1 month of intensive training it significantly increased in parallel to improved reading capacity. Their results support the hypothesis that the cerebellum plays a role in skilled reading and begin to unravel the underlying mechanisms that mediate cerebellar contribution in cognitive and neuronal augmentation following training.

In addition, 12-week daily QMT was found to induce structural changes in the cerebellum, including cerebellar gray matter volume increment (Ben-Soussan et al., 2015). The increase in cerebellar volume was further positively correlated with increased BDNF, an important neurotrophin closely linked to cerebellar development and neuroplasticity (Morrison & Mason, 1998). We thus suggest that increased cerebellar size and cognitive development could be related to the important role of cerebellar alpha oscillations in voluntary actions (Ivry, Spencer, Zelaznik, & Diedrichsen, 2002; Tesche & Karhu, 2000).

Joint Development of Executive Functions and Fundamental Motor Skills

The functional and structural connectivity between specific brain areas, particularly between frontal and cerebellar areas, translates into intersections and reciprocal influences between the developmental trajectories of executive functions and children's ability to perform coordinated movements, and efficient and adaptable goal-directed actions (Best, 2010; Diamond, 2000). The neural basis of adaptive variability, that is the ability to select the one most appropriate movement solution from the individually available repertoire, is cerebral connectivity (Hadders-Algra, 2010).

The general idea of action–cognition coupling, that is the effect of doing on knowing, was already formulated in the past century by Jean Piaget, who proposed that cognitive development originates from children's hands-on engagement with their environment (Piaget, 1952). This embodied cognition perspective has received large support in recent years. The coupling between action and cognition already emerges within the first few weeks of life and continues through infancy and childhood (Best, 2010). The movement–attention coupling in early infancy has been proven to be predictive of later attention and cognitive development (Friedman, Watamura, & Robertson, 2005).

Cognitive development seems to be intertwined with the development of both object control and locomotor skills. Infants may better learn discerning object boundaries if they are more active in exploring objects as compared to less active infants (Needham, 2000). By the end of the first year of life, the onset of locomotion and exploration are linked to major transitions in early development characterized by the emergence of adaptability and flexibility, as they involve a wide set of changes in perception, spatial cognition, and social and emotional development (Campos et al., 2000). In early childhood, the aspect of physical activity that seems to be most clearly associated to cognitive and especially executive function development is represented by the motor coordination demands (Chang et al., 2013; Planinsec, 2002).

Also studies conducted with children with intellectual disabilities confirm that motor coordination and executive function appear to be closely related, as those children experience problems with qualitative motor performance, especially in object control skills, and this results in poorer executive function and vice versa (Hartman, Houwen, Scherder, & Visscher, 2010). This pattern of reciprocal negative influence seems to extend to adulthood with impairments to qualitative motor skills being paralleled by impaired executive functioning, as assessed with dual tasks (Horvat, Croce, Tomporowski, & Barna, 2013).

Potential nonmetabolic mechanisms relating action to cognition are supposed to be an action-induced employment of new attentional strategies or proprioceptive input from action that impacts perception and cognition (Rakison & Woodward, 2008). A further mediating mechanism proposed by Serrien et al. (2007) refers to motor coordination and executive function: the pattern of recruitment of executive function circuitries elicited by complex movements would broadly transfer to subsequent goal-directed cognitive operations and behaviors.

The linkage between motor coordination and cognition during development is also supported by emerging evidence at preschool and elementary school age that not only children's physical fitness, but also motor proficiency may be a correlate and a predictor of brain efficiency and academic achievement later in life. Two studies examined this linkage cross-sectionally (Haapala et al., 2014; Lopes, Santos, Pereira, & Lopes, 2013), while another two also applied a longitudinal noninterventional design to test if motor skills are relevant for cognition and academic skills in the phase of transition to school (Niederer et al., 2011; Roebers et al., 2014). Mathematics and language skills were associated with both gross-motor skills (Lopes et al., 2012) and fine-motor skills (Haapala et al., 2014) and prospectively predicted by fine motor skills (Roebers et al., 2014). Also prospectively, fitness and motor proficiency seem to have differential effects on cognitive function: whereas cardiovascular fitness predicted children's later attention performance, dynamic balance predicted later working memory performance. In general, motor skill proficiency was associated with academic achievement independently of fitness and body mass (Lopes et al., 2012) and its relation to later academic skills is largely accounted for by the mediating role of executive function. Thus, motor and cognitive developmental trajectories seem interrelated and motor development seems to have a longer-lasting predictive value for cognitive efficiency.

TOWARD AN INTEGRATED VIEW ON COGNITION AND "E-MOTION" IN PHYSICAL ACTIVITY

The generation of movement, volition, and cognition are deeply related. In fact, it has been suggested that the nervous system has evolved to allow active movement and provide a goal-oriented plan, in which motivation and emotion represent facets of a common phenomenon. That commonality is the motivational–emotional system, which interacts with learning and higher-order cognition (Buck, 1999; Llinás, 2002). Thus, motivation can be defined as the internal drive of the organism, whereas emotions can be considered as the readout of this internal drive (Buck, 1999; Llinás, 2002). In this section, we highlight the potential of moving from a single focus on cognition to an integrated view on cognition and "e-motion," underlining the interconnectedness of neuronal systems related to emotional regulation, volition, and cognitive function and possible implications in normal and abnormal development. Indeed, child-appropriate interventions aiding executive function development are considered those in which cognitive challenges are embedded into emotionally adequate and socially engaging playful activities (Diamond & Lee, 2011).

A Neuroscience Perspective on "E-motion" in Children

Emotional development and emotion regulation both influence and are being influenced by the development of executive functions, including working memory, inhibitory control, and mental flexibility. Most noted problems with regulation, particularly problems with following directions and controlling attention, are thought to be the main cause of children's lack of school readiness. In addition to preschool expulsion and poor school readiness, there is a rapid and troubling increase in prescriptions of psychotropic medications, stimulants, and antidepressants to children (Zuvekas, Vitiello, & Norquist, 2006).

While the cerebellum has largely been excluded from scientific enquiry beyond motor function, the intimate afferent and efferent connections to the midbrain and limbic system provide for the neuroanatomical foundation of cerebellar involvement in emotion and emotional regulation. In addition, an increasing body of empirical evidence indicates that the cerebellum may be involved in emotion disorders (Schutter & Van Honk, 2005, p. 290). Schmahmann was one of the first to examine the functional role of the cerebellum into the domain of cognition and emotion, and investigate the cerebellar cognitive–affective syndrome (CCAS), characterized by both emotional and cognitive impairments, which are similar in many ways to those of patients with frontal damage (Schmahmann & Sherman, 1998). Children in CCAS suffer from deficits in emotional regulation (Levisohn, Cronin-Golomb, & Schmahmann, 2000). Interestingly, depression is also associated with volumetric reduction of both frontal lobes and the cerebellum (Beyer & Krishnan, 2002; Soares & Mann, 1997). It is thus no coincidence that depression is associated with psychomotor disturbances involving coordination of movements (Schutter & Van Honk, 2005).

Taking into account that the cerebellum serves as a general timing mechanism for both sensorimotor and cognitive processes (Hölzel et al., 2011; Schmahmann, 2004), it should be kept in mind that all these functions are crucially important for emotional regulation and communication. Thus, it is not surprising that serious developmental disorders such as autism, which are reported to be associated with delayed maturation of or decreased cerebellar volume, are characterized by attentional deficits that are paralleled by emotional and communicational deficits. Decreased cerebellar volume in autistic children and cerebellar maldevelopment are thus claimed to contribute to an inability to execute rapid attention shifts, which in turn undermines cognitive, emotional, and social development (Courchesne et al., 2001, 1994). These, together with the alarming rate of increased diagnosis of autism and autistic spectrum disorders, may emphasize the need to investigate the effectiveness of motor-based intervention paradigms to ameliorate these deficits and help children be more physically active.

Although here we have mostly focused on the cerebellum in relation to cognitive and emotional development, other parts of the motor system are also closely related, such as the basal ganglia, and specifically the caudiate nuclus, the main generator of dopamine. The dopamine system has been shown to regulate motor behavior, as well as motivation and reward behavior. Dopamine plays an important role in both cognitive and emotional development (Diamond, 1996), and is also closely linked to motivational control of both movement and reward (Kawagoe, Takikawa, & Hikosaka, 2004). It has been reported that different interventions resulting in stress-alleviating effects are accompanied by increased dopamine and decreased cortisol level (Field, Hernandez-Reif, Diego, Schanberg, & Kuhn, 2005), thus emphasizing the importance of tailoring specific training for children.

Physical activity, in turn, causes changes in neuronal signaling in the dopaminergic system, possibly representing a reinforcing behavioral mechanism, which is especially crucial during development (Knab & Lightfoot, 2010). Importantly, dopamine has been recently reported to be modulated by both physical and mental attentional training (Kjaer et al., 2002; Knab & Lightfoot, 2010). Thus, in order to foster child development and learning abilities that enable the child to be physically and emotionally dynamic and flexible, and cognitively engaged, we should invest in creating training paradigms that involve the child's interest, optimizing the physical and cognitive challenges embedded in the exercise according to the child's developmental status. In addition to nurturing self-efficacy and well-being, this strategy, if integrated from a young age, may perhaps serve in the prevention of eventual psychopathology in predisposed children (Levit-Binnun et al., 2013).

Aiding Executive Function Development by Motion with "E-motion"

Emotion regulation is considered a critical developmental acquisition. Yet, there has been very little research on the neural underpinnings of training-induced enhancement of emotion regulation across childhood and adolescence. Emotion regulation is closely related to attention, and training attention through mental practice and verbal labeling may call upon emotion regulation processes instantiated in the prefrontal cortex (Wadlinger & Isaacowitz, 2011, http://www.ncbi.nlm.nih.gov/pmc/articles/PMC2970710/). Consequently, it may disrupt or inhibit automatic affective responses, diminishing their intensity and duration (Hayes & Feldman, 2004; Lutz et al., 2008).

Noteworthy in this context is the fact that studies report improved emotional regulation (Arch & Craske, 2006) following different mental attention training regimens, in parallel to activation in areas closely linked to motor learning, including the basal ganglia and cerebellum (Hölzel et al., 2011; Pagnoni & Cekic, 2007; Vestergaard-Poulsen et al., 2009). As stated above, when the cerebellar timing function is disrupted, the information processing stream becomes desynchronized, providing the ground for a range of psychopathological conditions (Schutter & van Honk, 2005). Thus, we suggest that enabling or actively stimulating cerebellar oscillations through specifically structured sensorimotor training can normalize its activity and therefore emotional and cognitive functions.

While several "noninvasive" attempts have been made in this direction to electrically stimulate the cerebellum by transcranial magnetic stimulation (Schutter & Van Honk, 2009), why not use our body's inherent ability to move in order to stimulate cerebellar and consequently frontal synchronization, which may enhance emotional and cognitive development? Posner and Petersen (1990) have defined attention as a complex, cognitive system containing three independent, but related, network stages of alerting, orienting, and executive control. The alerting network heightens internal awareness and maintains sufficient neural activation enabling the attention system to make a fast response. The orienting network guides our focus toward selective and salient inputs, thereby augmenting attentional processing. The executive control network resolves conflict among different neural systems competing for control, facilitates the deconstruction of habitual responses, and directs planning, error detection, decision making, and novel-response formation functions. The cerebellum and the prefrontal cortex are especially activated during difficult and/or novel tasks, which require our full attention, and less in tasks in which the "automatic pilot" is sufficient (Diamond, 2000; Rubia, 2011).

Keeping this in mind and using Posner and Petersen's (1990) model of attention as a foundation, we suggest that it is worthwhile to add attention control and attention shifting with an optimal level of difficulty to physical training paradigms. In turn, optimal level of cognitive and emotional engagement could allow the child to be more "bodily-centered" in a state of flow enabling increased creativity, motivation, and enjoyment (Ben-Soussan et al., 2013; Dietrich, 2004). Training paradigms with these characteristics can be relatively easily practiced with limited space requirements. Further scientific exploration is warranted to the aim of implementation in different educational setups. This is especially true when taking into consideration longer-term adverse developmental consequences resulting from psychotropic interventions in children (http://www.ncbi.nlm.nih.gov/pmc/articles/PMC2593474/Stanwood & Levitt, 2004). Together, this suggests that alternative strategies, such as mental and motor training modes, are needed to address what appear to be a growing problem of poorly regulated behavior in children and the related need among caregivers and teachers for assistance in managing children's problem behavior (Blair & Diamond, 2008).

On the one side, exercise has been acknowledged as having beneficial outcomes for mental health and emotional well-being in children (see Biddle & Aasare, 2011, for a review); on the other side, mindfulness training and meditation seem to benefit emotional regulation by enhancing attentional monitoring systems in the brain (Farb, Anderson, & Segal, 2012). Nevertheless, training that combines movement with meditative focus is often ignored, especially in children. A few examples do exist in adults and have generally been termed as *meditative movement*. Meditative movement has been defined as a practice involving movement, a meditative state of mind, attention, and deep relaxation (Larkey, Jahnke, Etnier, & Gonzalez, 2009). Different sensorimotor attentional practices and meditative movement practices such as Qigong and Tai Chi, multimodal mind–body exercise regimens joining fitness, motor coordination, social interaction, and meditation, have been shown to improve general quality of life and self-efficacy as well as alleviate anxiety and depression (see Jahnke, Larkey, Rogers, Etnier, & Lin, 2010; Payne & Crane-Godreau, 2013, for reviews). Recently, Chang and colleagues have provided an overview of potential mediators of Tai Chi effects on cognition from a neuroscience perspective (Chang, Nien, Chen, & Yan, 2014) and ERP evidence that participation in Tai Chi Chuan is equivalently beneficial to cognitive flexibility as endurance exercise at both the behavioral and neuroelectric levels (Fong, Chi, Li, & Chang, 2014).

In conclusion, specifically tailored mindful movement training can be of service for cognitive and emotional development in children, aiding the harmonious development of attentive, emotionally-regulated, motivated minds in healthy, self-efficient, and happy children. This is an essential requirement for personal and social well-being.

BRIDGING THEORY AND PRACTICE: FROM NEUROSCIENCE TO TRANSLATIONAL RESEARCH

In the previous sections, we have introduced the notion of brain plasticity, mentioning the enormous increase in volume that the developing brain undergoes from birth to adolescence and the modifications of synapses that underlie functional connectivity and continue beyond adolescence across the lifespan (Lenroot, 2006). Overproduced synapses that are not used are eliminated or pruned, suggesting that neuronal networks in the immature brain may be guided by environmental factors, particularly in sensitive periods of brain development that have been identified in the transitions from childhood to adolescence and to adulthood (Andersen, 2003; Thomas & Johnson, 2008). The synaptic density in the prefrontal cortex slightly declines from 3 years to over 20 years of age (Bourgeois, Goldman-Rakic, & Rakic, 1994). Therefore, there is a large time window during which the prefrontal cortex and its primary functions, the executive, are modeled to match the emerging needs of the environment.

It has been hypothesized that exposure to both positive and negative environmental elements before adolescence can strongly imprint on the final adult "brain topography" (Andersen, 2003). Indeed, "The very nature of executive functions that makes them vulnerable is also a source of untapped opportunities..." (Garon, Bryson, & Smith, 2008, p. 52). Physical exercise may be conceived as a unique form of enrichment that impinges on lifelong brain sculpturing and executive function development (Hertzog, Kramer, Wilson, & Lindenberger, 2008; Sale, Berardi, & Maffei, 2014). As we have seen, major putative mechanisms by which physical activity may affect brain function and health are the selective sensitivity to physical exercise of the prefrontal cortex during its protracted development and the neurogenic capacity of the hippocampus across the lifespan (Khan & Hillman, 2014). In their concluding remarks on open questions, Sale et al. (2014) stated that while there is robust evidence that physical exercise benefits cognition from youth to elderly, it still is less known to what extent mentally engaging activities may contribute to the effects of environmental enrichment. The gains derived via specific types of quality physical activity interventions that are physically, mentally, and emotionally engaging may be of particular importance for children. In this section we address this issue, focusing on the little available evidence in ecological learning and sport training contexts.

Promoting Brain Development by Challenging Movement and Sport Experiences

As reviewed previously in this chapter, chronic exercise studies performed with a neuroscience approach have been mainly cross-sectional in nature with focus on cardiovascular fitness effects on the children's brain. Few RCT studies have been performed and, with only one exception (Chang et al., 2013), they focus on aerobic training in order to obtain interventional evidence that cardiovascular fitness gains are associated with enhanced brain efficiency and better cognitive (particularly executive function) performance in both lean and overweight children (Davis et al., 2011; Hillman et al., 2014; Kamijo et al., 2011; Krafft et al., 2014). Davis et al. (2011) also manipulated the duration of training sessions and found evidence of dose–response relations in overweight children. Thus, their concluding recommendation for educators was to implement vigorous physical activity.

Conversely, in a behavioral study, Crova et al. (2014) could demonstrate that practicing a cognitively engaging ball sport, even though with a weekly frequency and duration that corresponded to the "low" dose in Davis et al.'s (2011) study, enhanced executive function in overweight children. The authors concluded that even though embedded in a low-dose physical training program, cognitively challenging movement actions may help enhance executive functioning of those children who are at risk of poor cognition (Reinert, Po'e, & Barkin, 2013). On the other side, given the limited impact of low-dose exercise on physical health, the authors recommended an integration of high-dose physical activity with an appropriate level of cognitive challenge by movement. The study by Chang et al. (2013) added to this issue, as it was the first to investigate the neural correlates of the exercise–cognition interaction using coordinative exercise. However, the authors did not manipulate the coordinative demands of the physical tasks, but only its intensity. Since children's executive functions similarly benefited from coordinative exercise interventions of low or moderate exercise intensity, it may be argued that the benefit was at least partially due to the mental engagement needed to realize coordinated movements.

It is fair to assume that coordinative exercise, if it is not highly repetitive and automatized, involves motor skill learning to some extent. As introduced previously, mental training via skill learning increases the number of hippocampal neurons that survive, particularly when the training tasks are challenging (Curlik & Shors, 2013). Also, Diamond (2013), from a developmental neuroscience perspective, has clearly underlined the relevance of the level of engagement for executive function development. Cognitive engagement or effort may be conceived as the allocation of limited resources to an ongoing task determined by executive processes that draw on such resources, such as when individuals perform novel or complex tasks (Tomporowski, McCullick, & Horvat, 2010). Children who do not experience challenge because there are no increments in task difficulty, do not improve in executive functioning (Diamond & Lee, 2011).

Also, a step forward in the comprehension of the role of task complexity in the exercise–cognition interaction is to consider cognitive engagement in physical activity not as a unitary construct. Indeed, physical activity games may be tailored to elicit a specific engagement of individual executive functions by matching the principles of neuropsychological executive function tasks (Garon et al., 2008; Huizinga, Dolan, & van der Molen, 2006). We consider this approach to the exercise–cognition interaction as a novel way to capitalize on quality physical activity (Tomporowski, McCullick, & Pesce, 2015).

Therefore similar to the established notion of optimal challenge point in motor learning research (Guadagnoli & Lee, 2004), Pesce et al. (2013) performed an intervention study with preschool and school children to understand what "dose" and "type" of coordinative and cognitive demands of physical tasks is appropriate to reach the optimal challenge point and gain the largest cognitive benefits according to age and individual skill level. To this aim, the authors operationalized and manipulated task complexity of physical activity games while providing the same duration and frequency of exercise and controlling for intensity. Classes differed on the complexity of physical activity games performed. Differential intervention outcomes were observed as a function of motor developmental status. Typically developing children reaped the largest benefits for executive attention from the "enriched" program. Instead, children with coordinative problems/impairment could better profit from the less challenging games to enhance their attention, probably because of their need for tonic allocation of executive control resources to deal with movement coordination difficulties and/or worse control over the attentional processes underlying visuomotor control (Pesce et al., 2013).

Also, the relevance of the concept of optimal challenge point in motor learning for the study of the qualitative facets of the exercise–cognition interaction emerges from neuroscience studies of effortful learning. One condition that seems to strongly impact on the neuroplastic changes proven to subserve skillful motor performance is the complexity of tasks during motor training (Carey, Bhatt, & Nagpal, 2005). Also, the type of skills that keep new hippocampal cells alive is not domain specific, but broadly includes all those that are acquired in learning experiences that are new, effortful, and successful. Animal studies on gross-motor skill training have demonstrated that training on a simple, effortless, and repetitive version of the task does not keep the new hippocampal neurons alive. However, if the task becomes more effortful and difficult to master, significantly more new neurons are retained (Shors, 2014). From a human model of age-related changes in learning, it has been suggested that implicit learning of fundamentally new skills that cannot profit from transfer from skills already possessed is most effective before adolescence (Janacsek, Fiser, & Nemeth, 2012). This is in line with everyone's experience that an early start in learning some sports, second language, or other skills often allows higher levels of competence to be attained.

Moreover, sports activities may have qualitative characteristics that render them cognitively challenging. We have previously mentioned that Moreau and Conway (2013) have claimed that designed sports training may be an optimal way to combine the benefits of cognitive training and physical exercise. A step forward on this path is to consider the potential of given sports and sport training programs to aid the development of metacognition. Tomporowski, McCullick, Pendleton, and Pesce (2015) have, for the first time, indicated a new line of exercise and cognition research that, moving from Pesce's (2009, 2012) conceptual model of qualitative task factors acting on the exercise–cognition interaction and Howie and Pate's (2012) model of the relationship of physical activity, executive function and academic achievement, proposes to add the process of metacognition.

Metacognition reflects the understanding and conscious and thoughtful use of strategies to solve problems and self-regulate behavior. Such abilities as planning and creativity that have also been labeled "higher-level" executive functions (Diamond, 2013) to distinguish them from core executive functions (inhibition, updating, shifting) may be trained through sport. For instance, Memmert and colleagues have demonstrated that actual sport-specific creative thinking is positively associated with the time that athletes have spent in diversified, unstructured play activities in early youth (Memmert, Baker, & Bertsch, 2010) and that "ad hoc" sport enrichment programs lead to the development of sport-relevant creative thinking (Memmert, 2006). The thoughtfulness that is central to the concept of metacognition is complementary to the mechanism of implicit learning, mentioned above, which lies at the opposite end of the continuum. Thoughtfulness is an essential element of two areas of interventional research that connect sport activities with metacognition. The first area is that of life skill training interventions in sport (Hodge, Danish, & Martin, 2012; Goudas, 2010) that are tailored to teach, through thoughtful reflection on action, skills as goal-setting, monitoring of goal-directed behaviors, and self-regulation that rely on executive function and metacognition. The second area regards self-regulated learning in physical activity, where a recent development considers the role of metacognition (Goudas, Dermitzaki, & Kolovelonis, in press).

Moreover, physical activity games and youth sports have emotional and social characteristics that may maximize the effect of physical and mental engagement on executive function. We recall that to improve executive functions, cognitive stimulation is most effective when the environment is also emotionally and socially enriched (Diamond & Lee, 2011). This is not surprising, since adjacent areas of the anterior cingulate are involved in regulation of cognition and emotion. Therefore, attention training might also be important for establishing better regulation of emotion (Posner & Rothbart, 2005; Wadlinger & Isaacowitz, 2011). Sensorimotor attentional practices have the advantage of requiring the child to be constantly embodied in comparison to other attention training practices; adding body awareness and consciousness into the equation is also recommended (Mehling et al., 2009).

Future studies should examine effectiveness in improving cognitive, emotional, and physical functions longitudinally by comparing the effects of different sensorimotor attentional practices, such as QMT, Tai Chi, Qigong, and other training regimes. To date, the practices that have been proven effective in promoting attention development and self-regulation are mindfulness and integrative body–mind training and exposure to nature (Tang & Posner, 2009). The question that remains open is to identify the optimal "dosage" of challenges at different stages of development of typically and atypically developing children to aid cognitive and emotional development. This may represent a key element for an evidence-based model of quality physical activity for children and adolescents to inform policy development.

Outlook: What Does Quality Physical Activity Mean for the Child's Emerging Mind?

Most of the reviewed chronic exercise studies start off with the growing public health concern of the pandemic of physical inactivity as early as the pediatric age and conclude claiming that neuroscientific evidence of exercise effects on children's brain health has broad relevance for the public health and educational systems. While contrasting the severe consequences of inactivity is a priority for societies, devoting attention also to the qualitative characteristics of physical activity entails the potential to obtain much broader benefits for a healthy development. This kind of evidence is needed if we want to go beyond a discourse about getting children moved narrowly linked to the inactivity and overweight epidemic.

In line with the call for "whole child" initiatives (National Association for Sport and Physical Education, 2009), broader theoretical frameworks are emerging from a holistic view on physical activity promotion for children. There are efforts to include in a comprehensive frame all physical, psychosocial, and health factors that are considered mediators or moderators of the exercise–cognition interaction in children as in older adults (Tomporowski et al., 2011). Also, a recent proposal of "human capital" growth through physical activity (Bailey, Hillman, Arent, & Petitpas, 2013) frames the outcomes of physical activity as multiple domain-specific "capitals" in the physical, emotional, individual, social, intellectual, and financial domains.

However, there still are barriers to effective translation of evidence into practice that may render implementation unsuccessful despite the existence of comprehensive models and the adoption of physical activity promotion guidelines (Leone & Pesce, submitted). Leone et al. (2015) have recently proposed a holistic perspective on healthy child development that links the advocacy of physical activity promotion for children to the right to play and be physically active (United Nations, 2013). Specifically, the authors discuss how the two fields of human rights and public health ethics may jointly contribute to recognize the protection of human rights as a health determinant itself and to identify how synergies between public and private actors from different policy sectors may be exploited.

To transition theory into practice, we need to design a process that moves from an idea to sustainable actions. Paoletti (2009) has proposed a general model that moves from philosophy (the idea) through arts (the creative product) and science (the evidence) to economy (the sustainable action). We have indicated the philosophical root in the title, reflecting on the propositions by Descartes (Cartesius) and Gassendi. The need to go beyond the philosophical proposition that prioritizes cognition over movement ("I think, therefore I am") has found renewed attention in recent neurophilosophical educational approaches (Thompson, 2007) that "shift from a Cartesian notion of cognition as consisting of a homunculus-like, little person in the head, isolated phenomenon that occurs in brains, to a phenomenon that spans multiple scales across brain, body, and environment" (Favela, 2014, p. 2).

The theoretical framework of radical embodied cognitive neuroscience emphasizes a body-centric, nonbrain-centric treatment of cognition that encompasses the entire brain–body–environment system. From this perspective, an ecological approach is needed not only in the final step of translation of research into health promotion practice (Dzewaltowski, Estabrooks, & Glasgow, 2004), but also in the step of designing innovative mind–body interventions for children that build on embodied cognition and dynamical systems theory. "Back to the future": following the intuitions of Nikolai Bernstein (1940, in Latash & Turvey, 1995) that are milestones for dynamical systems theorists, a dexterous action is defined as an action that displays outstanding features of switchability, resourcefulness, and maneuverability. These are characteristics that we actually recognize to belong to the domain of prefrontal cognition and, in the light of what we discussed earlier in this chapter, to prefrontal–cerebellar circuitries.

Thus, capitalizing on neuroscience as an educational tool rather than a cutting edge of basic research, we propose a neuroscientific expansion of Paoletti's (2008) educational model (Ben-Soussan & Paoletti, 2014).

The model in Figure 1 conjoins the three trajectories of bodily motion, cognition, and emotion, to indicate their interdependent contribution to the whole and the related opportunity to investigate them utilizing a multidisciplinary approach. We recommend a joint consideration of bodily motion, emotion, and cognition when performing research on cost-efficient integrative training of cognition and e-motion, as well as longitudinal studies utilizing multidisciplinary noninvasive examinations of new and traditional mindful movement paradigms.

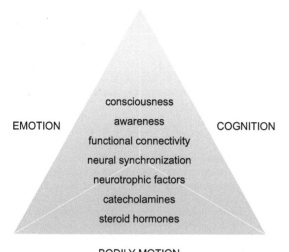

consciousness
awareness
functional connectivity
neural synchronization
neurotrophic factors
catecholamines
steroid hormones

EMOTION   COGNITION

BODILY MOTION

FIGURE 1 Interconnected relationship between bodily motion, emotion, and cognition and their neurobiological effects on self-awareness through increased neuronal synchronization (Ben-Soussan, T. D., & Paoletti, P., 2014, In J-Y. Béziau, & K. Gan-Krzywoszyńska (Eds), World Congress on the square of oppositions (pp. 21–22). Vatican: Pontifical Lateran University). This perspective emphasizes the need to design integrated training paradigms, which involve these three trajectories.

Nevertheless, in the past each trajectory has been usually examined separately, for example: the connection between enhanced neuronal synchronization and cognitive change (Ben-Soussan et al., 2013) and consciousness (Ben-Soussan, Berkovich-Ohana, Glicksohn, & Goldstein, 2014; Varela, Lachaux, Rodriguez, & Martinerie, 2001); the connection between increased neuronal synchronization, consciousness, and dopamine secretion following mental training (Kjaer et al., 2002), as well as between neuroplasticity and BDNF level following training (Ben-Soussan, Piervincenzi et al., in press); and last but not least, the importance of awareness and being embodied in order to awaken consciousness (Thompson & Varela, 2001).

The new perspective we suggest to apply in the context of developmental exercise–cognition interactions is to take into consideration these three trajectories of training-induced changes in bodily motion, emotion, and cognition—toward a greater understanding of how children can achieve self-awareness in an embodied way. Toward the final common path of embodied emotion and cognition: "I am."

References

Andersen, S. L. (2003). Trajectories of brain development: point of vulnerability or window of opportunity? *Neuroscience Biobehavior Review, 27*, 3–18.

Andres, F. G., Mima, T., Schulman, A. E., Dichgans, J., Hallett, M., & Gerloff, C. (1999). Functional coupling of human cortical sensorimotor areas during bimanual skill acquisition. *Brain, 122*, 855–870.

Arch, J. J., & Craske, M. G. (2006). Mechanisms of mindfulness: emotion regulation following a focused breathing induction. *Behaviour Research and Therapy, 44*, 1849–1858.

Bailey, R., Hillman, C., Arent, S., & Petitpas, A. (2013). Physical activity: an underestimated investment in human capital? *Journal of Physical Activity and Health, 10*, 289–308.

Ben-Soussan, T. D., Avirame, K., Glicksohn, J., Goldstein, A., Harpaz, Y., & Ben-Shachar, M. (2014). Changes in cerebellar activity and inter-hemispheric coherence accompany improved reading performance following Quadrato Motor Training. *Frontiers in Systems Neuroscience, 8.* http://dx.doi.org/10.3389/fnsys.2014.00081.

Ben-Soussan, T. D., Berkovich-Ohana, A., Glicksohn, J., & Goldstein, A. (2014). A suspended act: increased reflectivity and gender-dependent electrophysiological change following Quadrato Motor Training. *Frontiers in Psychology, 3.* http://dx.doi.org/10.3389/fpsyg.2014.00055.

Ben-Soussan, T. D., Glicksohn, J., Goldstein, A., Berkovich-Ohana, A., & Donchin, O. (2013). Into the square and out of the box: the effects of Quadrato Motor Training on creativity and alpha coherence. *PLoS One, 8*, e55023. http://dx.doi.org/10.1371/journal.pone.0055023.

Ben-Soussan, T. D., & Paoletti, P. (2014). Plasticity in the square–from a philosophical model to neurocognitive applications. In J.-Y. Béziau, & K. Gan-Krzywoszyńska (Eds.), *World Congress on the square of oppositions* (pp. 21–22). Vatican City: Pontifical Lateran University.

Ben-Soussan, T. D., Piervincenzi, C., Venditti, S., Verdone, L., Caserta, M., & Carducci, F. (2015). Increased cerebellar volume and BDNF level following quadrato motor training. *Synapse, 6*, 1–6. http://dx.doi.org/10.1002/syn.21787.

Berchicci, M., Pontifex, M. B., Drollette, E. S., Pesce, C., Hillman, C. H., & Di Russo, F. (2015). From cognitive motor preparation to visual processing: the benefits of childhood fitness to brain health. *Neuroscience.* http://dx.doi.org/10.1016/j.neuroscience.2015.04.028. Epub April 20, 2015.

Best, J. (2010). Effects of physical activity on children's executive function: contributions of experimental research on aerobic exercise. *Developmental Review, 30*, 331–351.

Best, J. (2012). Exergaming immediately enhances children's executive function. *Developmental Psychology, 48*, 1501–1510.

Beyenburg, S., Watzka, M., Clusmann, H., Blumcke, I., Bidlingmaier, F., Elger, C. E., et al. (2000). Androgen receptor mRNA expression in the human hippocampus. *Neuroscience Letters, 294*, 25–28.

Beyer, J. L., & Krishnan, K. R. R. (2002). Volumetric brain imaging findings in mood disorders. *Bipolar Disorders, 4*, 89–104.

Bialek, M., Zaremba, P., Borowicz, K. K., & Czuczwar, S. J. (2004). Neuroprotective role of testosterone in the nervous system. *Poland Journal of Pharmacology, 56*, 509–518.

Biddle, S. J. H., & Asare, M. (2011). Physical activity and mental health in children and adolescents: a review of reviews. *British Journal of Sports Medicine, 45*, 886–895.

Blair, C., & Diamond, A. (2008). Biological processes in prevention and intervention: the promotion of self-regulation as a means of preventing school failure. *Developmental Psychopathology, 20*, 899–911.

Bonnet, M. C., Dilharreguy, B., Allard, M., Deloire, M. S., Petry, K. G., & Brochet, B. (2009). Differential cerebellar and cortical involvement according to various attentional load: role of educational level. *Human Brain Mapping, 30*, 1133–1143.

Bourgeois, J. P., Goldman-Rakic, P. S., & Rakic, P. (1994). Synaptogenesis in the prefrontal cortex of rhesus monkeys. *Cerebral Cortex, 4*, 78–96.

Buck, R. (1999). The biological affects: a typology. *Psychological Review, 106*, 301–336.

Buckner, R. L. (2013). The cerebellum and cognitive function: 25 years of insight from anatomy and neuroimaging. *Neuron, 80*, 807–815.

Budde, H., Pietrassyk-Kendziorra, S., Bohm, S., & Voelcker-Rehage, C. (2010). Hormonal responses to physical and cognitive stress in a school setting. *Neuroscience Letters, 474*, 131–134.

Budde, H., Voelcker-Rehage, C., Pietrassyk-Kendziorra, S., Machado, S., Ribeiro, P., & Arafat, A. M. (2010). Steroid hormones in the saliva of adolescents after different exercise intensities and their influence on working memory in a school setting. *Psychoneuroendocrinology, 35*, 382–391.

Budde, H., Voelcker-Rehage, C., Pietraßyk-Kendziorra, S., Ribeiro, P., & Tidow, G. (2008). Acute coordinative exercise improves attentional performance in adolescents. *Neuroscience Letters, 441*, 219–223.

Budde, H., Windisch, C., Kudielka, B. M., & Voelcker-Rehage, C. (2010). Saliva cortisol in school children after acute physical exercise. *Neuroscience Letters, 483*, 16–19.

Campos, J. J., Anderson, D. I., Barbu-Roth, M. A., Hubbard, E. M., Hertenstein, M. J., & Witherington, D. (2000). Travel broadens the mind. *Infancy, 1*, 149–219.

Cao, Q., Zang, Y., Sun, L., Sui, M., Long, X., Zou, Q., et al. (2006). Abnormal neural activity in children with attention deficit hyperactivity disorder: a resting-state functional magnetic resonance imaging study. *Neuroreport, 17*, 1033–1036.

Carey, J. R., Bhatt, E., & Nagpal, A. (2005). Neuroplasticity promoted by task complexity. *Exercise and Sport Science Reviews, 33*, 24–31.

Chaddock-Heyman, L., Erickson, K. I., Holtrop, J. L., Voss, M. W., Pontifex, M. B., Raine, L. B., et al. (2014). Aerobic fitness is associated with greater white matter integrity in children. *Frontiers in Human Neuroscience, 8*(587), 1–7. http://dx.doi.org/10.3389/fnhum.2014.00584.

Chaddock-Heyman, L., Erickson, K. I., Voss, M. W., Knecht, A. M., Pontifex, M. B., Castelli, D. M., et al. (2013). The effects of physical activity on functional MRI activation associated with cognitive control in children: a randomized controlled intervention. *Frontiers in Human Neuroscience, 7*(72), 1–13. http://dx.doi.org/10.3389/fnhum.2013.000727.

Chaddock-Heyman, L., Erickson, K. I., Voss, M. W., Powers, J. P., Knecht, A. M., Pontifex, M. B., et al. (2013). White matter microstructure is associated with cognitive control in children. *Biological Psychology, 94*, 109–115.

Chaddock, L., Erickson, K. I., Prakash, R. S., Kim, J. S., Voss, M. W., Vanpatter, M., et al. (2010). A neuroimaging investigation of the association between aerobic fitness, hippocampal volume, and memory performance in preadolescent children. *Brain Research, 28*, 172–183.

Chaddock, L., Erickson, K. I., Prakash, R. S., VanPatter, M., Voss, M. W., Pontifex, M. B., et al. (2010). Basal ganglia volume is associated with aerobic fitness in preadolescent children. *Developmental Neuroscience, 32*, 249–256.

Chaddock, L., Pontifex, M. B., Hillman, C. H., & Kramer, A. F. (2011). A review of the relation of aerobic fitness and physical activity to brain structure and function in children. *Journal of the International Neuropsychology Society, 17*, 1–11.

Chang, Y. K., Nien, Y. H., Chen, A. G., & Yan, J. (2014). Tai Ji Quan, the brain, and cognition in older adults. *Journal of Sport and Health Science, 3*, 36–42.

Chang, Y.-K., Tsai, Y.-J., Chen, T.-T., & Hung, T.-M. (2013). The impacts of coordinative exercise on executive function in kindergarten children: an ERP study. *Experimental Brain Research, 225*, 187–196.

Chen, A.-G., Yan, J., Yin, H.-C., Pan, C.-Y., & Chang, Y.-K. (2014). Effects of acute aerobic exercise on multiple aspects of executive function in preadolescent children. *Psychology of Sport and Exercise, 15*, 627–636.

Cho, H.-C., Kim, J., Kim, S., Son, Y. H., Lee, N., & Jung, S. H. (2012). The concentrations of serum, plasma and platelet BDNF are all increased by treadmill VO2max performance in healthy college man. *Neuroscience Letters, 529*, 78–83.

Courchesne, E., Karns, C. M., Davis, H. R., Ziccardi, R., Carper, R. A., Tigue, Z. D., et al. (2001). Unusual brain growth patterns in early life in patients with autistic disorder an MRI study. *Neurology, 57*, 245–254.

Courchesne, E., Townsend, J., Akshoomoff, N. A., Saitoh, O., Yeung-Courchesne, R., Lincoln, A. J., et al. (1994). Impairment in shifting attention in autistic and cerebellar patients. *Behavior Neuroscience, 108,* 848–865.

Crova, C., Struzzolino, I., Marchetti, R., Masci, I., Vannozzi, G., Forte, R., et al. (2014). Benefits of cognitively challenging physical activity in overweight children. *Journal of Sports Science, 32,* 201–211.

Curlik, D. M., & Shors, T. J. (2013). Training your brain: do mental and physical (MAP) training enhance cognition through the process of neurogenesis in the hippocampus? *Neuropharmacology, 64,* 506–514.

Davis, C. L., Tomporowski, P. D., McDowell, J. E., Austin, B. P., Miller, P. H., Yanasak, N. E., et al. (2011). Exercise improves executive function and achievement and alters brain activation in overweight children: a randomized, controlled trial. *Health Psychology, 30,* 91–98.

De Zeeuw, C. I., Hoebeek, F. E., Bosman, L. W., Schonewille, M., Witter, L., & Koekkoek, S. K. (2011). Spatiotemporal firing patterns in the cerebellum. *Nature Reviews Neuroscience, 12,* 327–344.

Diamond, A. (1996). Evidence for the importance of dopamine for prefrontal cortex functions early in life [and discussion]. *Philosophical Transaction of the Royal Society B, 351,* 1483–1494.

Diamond, A. (2000). Close interrelation of motor development and cognitive development and of the cerebellum and prefrontal cortex. *Child Development, 71,* 44–56.

Diamond, A. (2013). Executive functions. *Annual Review of Psychology, 64,* 135–168.

Diamond, A., & Lee, K. (2011). Interventions shown to aid executive function development in children 4 to 12 years old. *Science, 333,* 954–969.

Dietrich, A. (2004). Neurocognitive mechanisms underlying the experience of flow. *Consciousness and Cognition, 13,* 746–761.

Dietrich, A. (2006). Transient hypofrontality as a mechanism for the psychological effects of exercise. *Psychiatry Research, 145,* 79–83.

Drollette, E. S., Scudder, M. R., Raine, L. B., Moore, R. D., Saliba, B. J., Pontifex, M. B., et al. (2014). Acute exercise facilitates brain function and cognition in children who need it most: an ERP study of individual differences in inhibitory control capacity. *Developmental Cognitive Neuroscience, 7,* 53–64.

Dzewaltowski, D. A., Estabrooks, P. A., & Glasgow, R. E. (2004). The future of physical activity behavior change research: what is needed to improve translation of research into health promotion practice? *Exercise and Sport Science Reviews, 32,* 57–63.

Erwin, H. E., Abel, M., Beighle, A., & Beets, M. W. (2011). Promoting children's health through physically active math classes: a pilot study. *Health Promotion and Practice, 12,* 244–251.

Etnier, J. L., & Chang, Y. K. (2009). The effect of physical activity on executive function: a brief commentary on definitions, measurement issues, and the current state of the literature. *Journal of Sport and Exercise Psycholology, 31,* 469–483.

Farb, N. A. S., Anderson, A. K., & Segal, Z. V. (2012). The mindful brain and emotion regulation in mood disorders. *Canadian Journal of Psychiatry, 57,* 70–77.

Favela, L. H. (2014). Radical embodied cognitive neuroscience: addressing "grand challenges" of the mind sciences. *Frontiers in Human Neuroscience, 8,* 796. http://dx.doi.org/10.3389/fnhum.2014.00796.

Field, T., Hernandez-Reif, M., Diego, M., Schanberg, S., & Kuhn, C. (2005). Cortisol decreases and serotonin and dopamine increase following massage therapy. *International Journal of Neuroscience, 115,* 1397–1413.

Fong, D., Chi, L., Li, F., & Chang, Y. (2014). The benefits of endurance exercise and Tai Chi Chuan for the task-switching aspect of executive function in older adults: an ERP study. *Frontiers in Aging Neuroscience, 6,* 295. http://dx.doi.org/10.3389/fnagi.2014.00295.

Friedman, A. H., Watamura, S. E., & Robertson, S. S. (2005). Movement–attention coupling in infancy and attention problems in childhood. *Developmental Medicine and Child Neurology, 47,* 660–665.

Gallotta, M. C., Guidetti, L., Franciosi, E., Emerenziani, G. P., Bonavolontà, V., & Baldari, C. (2011). Effects of varying type of exertion on children's attention capacity. *Medicine & Science in Sports & Exercise, 44,* 550–555. http://dx.doi.org/10.1249/MSS.0b013e3182305552.

Garon, N., Bryson, S., & Smith, I. M. (2008). Executive function in preschoolers: a review using an integrative framework. *Psychological Bulletin, 134,* 31–60.

Gomez-Pinilla, F., & Hillman, C. H. (2013). The influence of exercise on cognitive abilities. *Comparative Physiology, 1,* 403–428.

Goudas, M. (2010). Prologue: a review of life skills teaching in sport and physical education. *Hellenic Journal of Psychology, 7,* 241–258.

Goudas, M., Dermitzaki, I., & Kolovelonis, A. Self-regulated learning and student's metacognitive feelings in physical education. *International Journal of Sport and Exercise Psychology,* in press.

Guadagnoli, M. A., & Lee, T. D. (2004). Challenge point: a framework for conceptualizing the effects of various practice conditions in motor learning. *Journal of Motor Behavior, 36,* 212–224.

Haapala, E. A., Poikkeus, A. M., Tompuri, T., Kukkonen-Harjula, K., Leppänen, P. H., Lindi, V., & Lakka, T. A. (2014). Associations of motor and cardiovascular performance with academic skills in children. *Medicine & Science in Sports & Exercise, 46,* 1016–1024. http://dx.doi.org/10.1249/MSS.0000000000000186.

Hadders-Algra, M. (2010). Variation and variability: key words in human motor development. *Physical Therapy, 90,* 1823–1837.

Hardwick, R. M., Rottschy, C., Miall, R. C., & Eickhoff, S. B. (2013). A quantitative meta-analysis and review of motor learning in the human brain. *NeuroImage, 67*, 283–297.

Hartman, E., Houwen, S., Scherder, E., & Visscher, C. (2010). On the relationship between motor performance and executive functioning in children with intellectual disabilities. *Journal of Intellectual Disability Research, 54*, 468–477.

Hayes, A. M., & Feldman, G. (2004). Clarifying the construct of mindfulness in the context of emotion regulation and the process of change in therapy. *Clinical Psychology Science and Practice, 11*, 255–262.

Herting, M. M., Colby, J. B., Sowell, E. R., & Nagel, B. J. (2014). White matter connectivity and aerobic fitness in male adolescents. *Developmental Cognitive Neuroscience, 7*, 65–75.

Herting, M. M., & Nagel, B. J. (2012). Aerobic fitness relates to learning on a virtual Morris water task and hippocampal volume in adolescents. *Behavioral Brain Resesearch, 233*, 517–525.

Herting, M. M., & Nagel, B. J. (2013). Differences in brain activity during a verbal associative memory encoding task in high- and low-fit adolescents. *Journal of Cognitive Neuroscience, 25*, 595–612.

Hertzog, C., Kramer, A. F., Wilson, R. S., & Lindenberger, U. (2008). Enrichment effects on adult cognitive development. *Psychological Science in the Public Interest, 9*, 1–65.

Hill, E. L. (2004). Evaluating the theory of executive dysfunction in autism. *Developmental Review, 24*, 189–233.

Hill, L., Williams, J. H. G., Aucott, L., Milne, J., Thomson, J., Greig, J., et al. (2010). Exercising attention within the classroom. *Developmental Medicine and Child Neurology, 52*, 929–934.

Hillman, C. H., Buck, S. M., Themanson, J. R., Pontifex, M. B., & Castelli, D. M. (2009). Aerobic fitness and cognitive development: event-related brain potential and task performance indices of executive control in preadolescent children. *Developmental Psychology, 45*, 114–129.

Hillman, C. H., Castelli, D. M., & Buck, S. M. (2005). Aerobic fitness and neurocognitive function in healthy preadolescent children. *Medicine & Science in Sports & Exercise, 37*, 1967–1974.

Hillman, C. H., Erickson, K. I., & Kramer, A. F. (2008). Be smart, exercise your heart: exercise effects on brain and cognition. *Nature Reviews Neuroscience, 8*, 58–65.

Hillman, C. H., Kamijo, K., & Scudder, M. R. (2011). A review of chronic and acute physical activity participation on neuroelectric measures of brain health and cognition during childhood. *Preventive Medicine, 52*, 21–28.

Hillman, C. H., Pontifex, M. B., Castelli, D. M., Khan, N. A., Raine, N. B., Scudder, M. R., et al. (2014). Effects of the FITKids randomized controlled trial on executive control and brain function. *Pediatrics, 134*, e1063. http://dx.doi.org/10.1542/peds.2013-3219.

Hillman, C. H., Pontifex, M. B., Motl, R. W., O'Leary, K. C., Johnson, C. R., Scudder, M. R., et al. (2012). From ERPs to academics. *Developmental Cognitive Neuroscience, 2*, 90–98.

Hillman, C. H., Pontifex, M. B., Raine, L. B., Castelli, D. M., Hall, E. E., & Kramer, A. F. (2009). The effect of acute treadmill walking on cognitive control and academic achievement in preadolescent children. *Neuroscience, 159*, 1044–1054.

Hodge, K., Danish, S., & Martin, J. (2012). Developing a conceptual framework for life skills interventions. *The Counseling Psychologist, 20*, 1–28.

Hölzel, B. K., Carmody, J., Vangel, M., Congleton, C., Yerramsetti, S. M., Gard, T., et al. (2011). Mindfulness practice leads to increases in regional brain gray matter density. *Psychiatry Research, 191*, 36–43.

Horvat, M., Croce, R., Tomporowski, P., & Barna, M. C. (2013). The influence of dual-task conditions on movement in young adults with and without Down syndrome. *Research in Developmental Disabilities, 34*, 3517–3525.

Howie, E. K., & Pate, R. R. (2012). Physical activity and academic achievement in children: a historical perspective. *Journal of Sport and Health Science, 1*, 160–169.

Huizinga, M., Dolan, C. V., & van der Molen, M. W. (2006). Age-related change in executive function: developmental trends and a latent variable analysis. *Neuropsychologia, 44*, 2017–2036.

Iacoboni, M. (2001). Playing tennis with the cerebellum. *Nature Neuroscience, 4*, 555–556.

Ivry, R. (1996). Cerebellar timing systems. *International Review in Neurobiology, 41*, 555–573.

Ivry, R. B., Spencer, R. M., Zelaznik, H. N., & Diedrichsen, J. (2002). The cerebellum and event timing. *Annals of the New York Academy of Sciences, 978*, 302–317.

Jahnke, R., Larkey, L., Rogers, C., Etnier, J., & Lin, F. (2010). A comprehensive review of health benefits of qigong and tai chi. *American Journal of Health Promotion, 24*, 1–25.

Janacsek, K., Fiser, J., & Nemeth, D. (2012). The best time to acquire new skills: age-related differences in implicit sequence learning across the human lifespan. *Developmental Science, 15*, 496–505.

Kamijo, K., Pontifex, M. B., O'Leary, K. C., Scudder, M. R., Wu, C.-T., Castelli, D. M., et al. (2011). The effects of an afterschool physical activity program on working memory in preadolescent children. *Developmental Science, 14*, 1046–1058.

Kawagoe, R., Takikawa, Y., & Hikosaka, O. (2004). Reward-predicting activity of dopamine and caudate neurons—a possible mechanism of motivational control of saccadic eye movement. *Journal of Neurophysiology, 91*, 1013–1024.

Khan, N. A., & Hillman, C. H. (2014). The relation of childhood physical activity and aerobic fitness to brain function and cognition: a review. *Pediatric Exercise Science, 26*, 138–146.

Kibbe, D. L., Hackett, J., Hurley, M., McFarland, A., Schubert, K. G., Schultz, A., et al. (2011). Ten years of TAKE 10!: integrating physical activity with academic concepts in elementary school classrooms. *Preventive Medicine, 52,* 43–50.

Kjaer, T. W., Bertelsen, C., Piccini, P., Brooks, D., Alving, J., & Lou, H. C. (2002). Increased dopamine tone during meditation-induced consciousness. *Brain Research Cognitive Brain Research, 13,* 255–259.

Knab, A. M., & Lightfoot, J. T. (2010). Does the difference between physically active and couch potato lie in the dopamine system? *International Journal of Biological Science, 6,* 133.

Krafft, C. E., Schwarz, N. F., Chi, L., Weinberger, A. L., Schaeffer, D. J., Pierce, J. E., et al. (2014). An 8-month randomized controlled exercise trial alters brain activation during cognitive tasks in overweight children. *Obesity, 22,* 232–242.

Larkey, L., Jahnke, R., Etnier, J., & Gonzalez, J. (2009). Meditative movement as a category of exercise: implications for research. *Journal of Physical Activity and Health, 6,* 230–238.

Latash, M. L., & Turvey, M. T. (1995). *Dexterity and its development – With on dexterity and its development by Nicholai A. Bernstein.* Mahwah, NJ: Lawrence Erlbaum.

Leek, E. C., & Johnston, S. J. (2009). Functional specialization in the supplementary motor complex. *Nature Review Neuroscience, 10,* 79. http://dx.doi.org/10.1038/nrn2478-c1.

Lee, T. M. C., Wong, M. L., Lau, B. W., Lee, J. C., Yau, S. Y., et al. (2014). Aerobic exercise interacts with neurotrophic factors to predict cognitive functioning in adolescents. *Psychoneuroendocrinology, 39,* 214–224.

Lenroot, R. K. (2006). Brain development in children and adolescents: insights from anatomical magnetic resonance imaging. *Neuroscience & Biobehavioral Review, 30,* 718–729.

Leone, L., Ling, T., Baldassarre, L., Barnett, L., Capranica, L., & Pesce, C. (2015). Corporate responsibility for childhood physical activity promotion in the UK. *Health Promotion International* pii: dav051. [Epub ahead of print]

Leone, L., & Pesce, C. A realist synthesis of physical-activity promotion guidelines: methodological issues. *Health Promotion International* (submitted).

Levisohn, L., Cronin-Golomb, A., & Schmahmann, J. D. (2000). Neuropsychological consequences of cerebellar tumour resection in children: cerebellar cognitive affective syndrome in a paediatric population. *Brain, 123,* 1041–1050.

Levit-Binnun, N., Davidovitch, M., & Golland, Y. (2013). Sensory and motor secondary symptoms as indicators of brain vulnerability. *Journal of Neurodevelopmental Disorders, 5,* 5–26.

Llinás, R. R. (2002). *I of the vortex: From neurons to self.* Cambridge, MA: MIT Press.

Lopes, L., Santos, R., Pereira, B., & Lopes, V. P. (2013). Associations between gross motor coordination and academic achievement in elementary school children. *Human Movement Science, 32,* 9–20. http://dx.doi.org/10.1016/j.humov.2012.05.005.

Lutz, A., Slagter, H. A., Dunne, J. D., & Davidson, R. J. (2008). Attention regulation and monitoring in meditation. *Trends in Cognitive Science, 12,* 163–169.

Mahar, M. T., Murphy, S. K., Rowe, D. A., Golden, J., Shields, A. T., & Raedeke, T. D. (2006). Effects of a classroom-based program on physical activity and on-task behavior. *Medicine & Science and Sport & Exercise, 38,* 2086–2094.

Mehling, W. E., Gopisetty, V., Daubenmier, J., Price, C. J., Hecht, F. M., & Stewart, A. (2009). Body awareness: construct and self-report measures. *PloS One, 4,* e5614. http://dx.doi.org/10.1371/journal.pone.0005614.

Memmert, D. (2006). Developing creative thinking in a gifted sport enrichment program and the crucial role of attention processes. *High Ability Studies, 17,* 101–115.

Memmert, D., Baker, J., & Bertsch, C. (2010). Play and practice in the development of sport-specific creativity in team ball sports. *High Ability Studies, 21,* 3–18.

Moreau, D., & Conway, A. R. A. (2013). Cognitive enhancement: a comparative review of computerized and athletic training programs. *International Review of Sport and Exercise Psychology, 6,* 155–183.

Moore, R. D., Drollette, E. S., Scudder, M. R., Bharij, A., & Hillman, C. H. (2014). The influence of cardiorespiratory fitness on strategic, behavioral, and electrophysiological indices of arithmetic cognition in preadolescent children. *Frontiers in Human Neuroscience, 8,* 258. http://dx.doi.org/10.3389/fnhum.2014.00258.

Morrison, M. E., & Mason, C. A. (1998). Granule neuron regulation of Purkinje cell development: striking a balance between neurotrophin and glutamate signaling. *Journal of Neuroscience, 18,* 3563–3573.

National Association for Sport and Physical Education. (2008). *Comprehensive school physical activity programs [Position statement].* Reston, VA: Author.

National Association for Sport and Physical Education. (2009). *Physical education position statements.* Available at: www.psahperd.org/Resources/Documents/Advocacy/Physical-Education-Is-Critical-to-Educating-the-Whole-Child-Final-5-19-2011.pdf.

National Association for Sport and Physical Education. (2011). *Physical education is critical to educating the whole child [Position statement].* Reston, VA: Author.

Needham, A. (2000). Improvements in object exploration skills may facilitate the development of object segregation in early infancy. *Journal of Cognitive Development, 1,* 131–156.

Nicolson, R. I., Fawcett, A. J., & Dean, P. (2001). Developmental dyslexia: the cerebellar deficit hypothesis. *Trends Neuroscience, 24,* 508–511.

Niederer, I., Kriemler, S., Gu, J., Hartmann, T., Schindler, C., Barra, J., & Puder, J. J. (2011). Relationship of aerobic fitness and motor skills with memory and attention in preschoolers (Ballabeina): A cross-sectional and longitudinal study. *BMC Pediatrics*, *11*, 34. http://dx.doi.org/10.1186/1471-2431-11-34.

Niemann, C., Wegner, M., Voelcker-Rehage, C., Holzweg, M., Arafat, A. M., & Budde, H. (2013). Influence of acute and chronic physical activity on cognitive performance and saliva testosterone in preadolescent school children. *Mental Health and Physical Activity*, *6*, 197–204.

Pagnoni, G., & Cekic, M. (2007). Age effects on gray matter volume and attentional performance in Zen meditation. *Neurobiological Aging*, *28*, 1623–1627.

Palmer, K. K., Miller, M. W., & Robinson, L. E. (2013). Acute exercise enhances preschoolers' ability to sustain attention. *Journal of Sport and Exercise Psychology*, *35*, 433–437.

Paoletti, P. (2008). *Crescere nell'eccellenza. [Growing in excellence].* Rome: Armando Publishing.

Paoletti, P. (2009). *21minuti – I saperi dell'eccellenza: Educational training per condividere modelli di eccellenza e sostenibilità [21 minutes – Knowledge of eccellence: Educational training to share excellence and sustainability models].* http://www.21min.org/21min/images/stories/brochure_21min_next_2013.pdf.

Payne, P., & Crane-Godreau, M. A. (2013). Meditative movement for depression and anxiety. *Frontiers in Psychiatry*, *4*, 71. http://dx.doi.org/10.3389/fpsyt.2013.00071.

Perner, J., & Lang, B. (1999). Development of theory of mind and executive control. *Trends in Cognitive Sciences*, *3*, 337–344.

Pesce, C. (2009). An integrated approach to the effect of acute and chronic exercise on cognition: the linked role of individual and task constraints. In T. McMorris, P. D. Tomporowski, & M. Audiffren (Eds.), *Exercise and cognitive function* (pp. 213–226). Chichester: Wiley-Blackwell.

Pesce, C. (2012). Shifting the focus from quantitative to qualitative exercise characteristics in exercise and cognition research. *Journal of Sport and Exercise Psychology*, *34*, 766–786.

Pesce, C., Crova, C., Cereatti, L., Casella, R., & Bellucci, M. (2009). Physical activity and mental performance in preadolescents: effects of acute exercise on free-recall memory. *Mental Health and Physical Activity*, *2*, 16–22.

Pesce, C., Crova, C., Marchetti, M., Struzzolino, I., Masci, I., Vannozzi, G., et al. (2013). Searching for cognitively optimal challenge point in physical activity for children with typical and atypical motor development. *Mental Health and Physical Activity*, *6*, 172–180.

Piaget, J. (1952). *The origins of intelligence in children.* New York: International Universities Press.

Piek, J. P., & Dyck, M. J. (2004). Sensory-motor deficits in children with developmental coordination disorder, attention deficit hyperactivity disorder and autistic disorder. *Human Movement Science*, *23*, 475–488.

Planinsec, J. (2002). Relations between the motor and cognitive dimensions of preschool girls and boys. *Perceptual and Motor Skills*, *94*, 415–423.

Pontifex, M. B., Raine, L. B., Johnson, C. R., Chaddock, L., Voss, M. W., Cohen, N. J., et al. (2011). Cardiorespiratory fitness and the flexible modulation of cognitive control in preadolescent children. *Journal of Cognitive Neuroscience*, *23*, 1332–1345.

Pontifex, M. B., Saliba, B. J., Raine, L. B., Picchietti, D. L., & Hillman, C. H. (2013). Exercise improves behavioral, neurocognitive, and scholastic performance in children with attention-deficit/hyperactivity disorder. *Journal of Pediatrics*, *162*, 543–551.

Posner, M. I., & Petersen, S. E. (1990). The attention systems in the human brain. *Annual Review Neuroscience*, *13*, 25–42.

Posner, M. I., & Rothbart, M. K. (2005). Influencing brain networks: implications for education. *Trends in Cognitive Sciences*, *9*, 99–103.

Rakison, D. H., & Woodward, A. L. (2008). New perspectives on the effects of action on perceptual and cognitive development. *Developmental Psychology*, *44*, 1209–1213.

Reinert, K. R., Po'e, E. K., & Barkin, S. L. (2013). The relationship between executive function and obesity in children and adolescents: a systematic literature review. 820956 *Journal of Obesity.* http://dx.doi.org/10.1155/2013/820956.

Roebers, C. M., Röthlisberger, M., Neuenschwander, R., Cimeli, P., Michel, E., & Jäger, K. (2014). The relation between cognitive and motor performance and their relevance for children's transition to school: a latent variable approach. *Human Movement Science*, 284–297. http://dx.doi.org/10.1016/j.humov.2013.08.011.

Rubia, K. (2011). "Cool" inferior frontostriatal dysfunction in attention-deficit/hyperactivity disorder versus "hot" ventromedial orbitofrontal-limbic dysfunction in conduct disorder: a review. *Biological Psychiatry*, *69*, 69–87.

Rubia, K., Halari, R., Christakou, A., & Taylor, E. (2009). Impulsiveness as a timing disturbance: neurocognitive abnormalities in attention-deficit hyperactivity disorder during temporal processes and normalization with methylphenidate. *Philosophical Transactions of the Royal Society B*, *364*, 1919–1931.

Rubia, K., Taylor, E., Smith, A. B., Oksannen, H., Overmeyer, S., & Newman, S. (2001). Neuropsychological analyses of impulsiveness in childhood hyperactivity. *British Journal of Psychiatry*, *179*, 138–143.

Salas, C. R., Minakata, K., & Kelemen, W. L. (2011). Walking before study enhances free recall but not judgement-of-learning magnitude. *Journal of Cognitive Psychology*, *23*, 507–513.

Sale, A., Berardi, N., & Maffei, L. (2014). Environment and brain plasticity: towards an endogenous pharmacotherapy. *Physiological Review*, *94*, 189–234.

Schmahmann, J. D. (2004). Disorders of the cerebellum: ataxia, dysmetria of thought, and the cerebellar cognitive affective syndrome. *Journal of Neuropsychiatry & Clinical Neuroscience, 16,* 367–378.

Schmahmann, J. D., & Sherman, J. C. (1998). The cerebellar cognitive affective syndrome. *Brain, 121,* 561–579.

Schutter, D. J., & Van Honk, J. (2005). The cerebellum on the rise in human emotion. *Cerebellum, 4,* 290–294.

Schutter, D. J., & Van Honk, J. (2009). The cerebellum in emotion regulation: a repetitive transcranial magnetic stimulation study. *Cerebellum, 8,* 28–34.

Scudder, M. R., Federmeier, K. D., Raine, L. B., Direito, A., Boyd, J. K., & Hillman, C. H. (2014). The association between aerobic fitness and language processing in children: implications for academic achievement. *Brain and Cognition, 87,* 140–152.

Serrien, D. J., Ivry, R. B., & Swinnen, S. P. (2007). The missing link between action and cognition. *Progress in Neurobiology, 82,* 95–107.

Shors, T. J. (2014). The adult brain makes new neurons, and effortful learning keeps them alive. *Current Directions in Psychological Science, 23,* 311–318.

Smith, A. B., Taylor, E., Brammer, M., Halari, R., & Rubia, K. (2008). Reduced activation in right lateral prefrontal cortex and anterior cingulate gyrus in medication–naïve adolescents with attention deficit hyperactivity disorder during time discrimination. *Journal of Child Psychology and Psychiatry, 49,* 977–985.

Soares, J. C., & Mann, J. J. (1997). The anatomy of mood disorders—review of structural neuroimaging studies. *Biological Psychiatry, 41,* 86–106.

Sporns, O., Chialvo, D. R., Kaiser, M., & Hilgetag, C. C. (2004). Organization, development and function of complex brain networks. *Trends in Cognitive Science, 8,* 418–425.

Stanwood, G. D., & Levitt, P. (2004). Drug exposure early in life: functional repercussions of changing neuropharmacology during sensitive periods of brain development. *Current Opinion in Pharmacology, 4,* 65–71.

Stroth, S., Kubesch, S., Dieterle, K., Ruchsowd, M., Heim, R., & Kiefer, M. (2009). Physical fitness, but not acute exercise modulates event-related potential indices for executive control in healthy adolescents. *Brain Research, 1269,* 114–124.

Swinnen, S. P. (2002). Intermanual coordination: from behavioural principles to neural-network interactions. *Nature Reviews Neuroscience, 3,* 348–359.

Tang, Y.-Y., & Posner, M. I. (2009). Attention training and attention state training. *Trends in Cognitive Science, 13,* 222–227.

Tesche, C. D., & Karhu, J. J. (2000). Anticipatory cerebellar responses during somatosensory omission in man. *Human Brain Mapping, 9,* 119–142.

Tesche, C. D., Moses, S. N., Houck, J. M., Martin, T., Hanlon, F. M., Jackson, G., et al. (2007). Dynamics of frontal and cerebellar activation during aversive conditioning: an MEG study. *International Congress Series, 1300,* 437–440.

Thomas, M. S. C., & Johnson, M. H. (2008). New advances in understanding sensitive periods in brain development. *Current Directions in Psychological Science, 17,* 1–5.

Thompson, E. (2007). *Mind in life: Biology, phenomenology, and the sciences of the mind.* Cambridge, MA: Belknap Press of Harvard University Press.

Thompson, E., & Varela, F. J. (2001). Radical embodiment: neural dynamics and consciousness. *Trends in Cognitive Science, 5,* 418–425.

Tomporowski, P. D., Davis, C. L., Miller, P. H., & Naglieri, J. A. (2008). Exercise and children's intelligence, cognition, and academic performance. *Educational Psychology Review, 20,* 111–131.

Tomporowski, P. D., Lambourne, K., & Okumura, M. S. (2011). Physical activity interventions and children's mental function: an introduction and overview. *Preventative Medicine, 52,* 3–9.

Tomporowski, P. D., McCullick, B. A., & Horvat, M. (2010). The role of contextual interference and mental engagement on learning. In F. Edvardsen, & H. Kulle (Eds.), *Educational games: Design, learning, and applications* (pp. 127–155). Hauppauge, NY: Nova Science Publishers.

Tomporowski, P. D., McCullick, B., Pendleton, D. M., & Pesce, C. (2015). Exercise and children's cognition: the role of exercise characteristics and a place for metacognition. *Journal of Sport and Health Science, 4,* 47–55.

Tomporowski, P. D., McCullick, B., & Pesce, C. (2015). *Enhancing children's cognition with physical activity games.* Champaign, IL: Human Kinetics.

Travis, F. (2001). Autonomic and EEG patterns distinguish transcending from other experiences during Transcendental Meditation practice. *International Journal of Psychophysiology, 42,* 1–9.

Travis, F., Tecce, J., Arenander, A., & Wallace, R. K. (2002). Patterns of EEG coherence, power, and contingent negative variation characterize the integration of transcendental and waking states. *Biological Psychology, 61,* 293–319.

United Nations. (2013). *Committee on the Rights of the Child, General Comment No. 17. The right of the child to rest, leisure, play, recreational activities, cultural life and the arts (Article 31).* CRC/C/GC/17, 18 March http://www2.ohchr.org/english/bodies/crc/docs/GC/CRC-C-GC-17_en.doc.

Vandervert, L. R., Schimpf, P. H., & Liu, H. (2007). How working memory and the cerebellum collaborate to produce creativity and innovation. *Creativity Research Journal, 19,* 1–18.

Varela, F., Lachaux, J. P., Rodriguez, E., & Martinerie, J. (2001). The brainweb: phase synchronization and large-scale integration. *Nature Reviews Neuroscience, 2,* 229–239.

Vazou, S., & Smiley-Oyen, A. (2014). Moving and academic learning are not antagonists: acute effects on executive function and enjoyment. *Journal of Sport and Exercise Psychology, 36,* 474–485.

Venditti, S., Verdone, L., Pesce, C., Caserta, M., Tocci, N., & Dotan Ben-Soussan, T. Creating well-being: increased creativity and proNGF decrease following Quadrato Motor Training. *Biomedical Research*, Article ID 275062, in press.

Vestergaard-Poulsen, P., van Beek, M., Skewes, J., Bjarkam, C. R., Stubberup, M., Bertelsen, J., et al. (2009). Long-term meditation is associated with increased gray matter density in the brain stem. *NeuroReport*, *20*, 170–174.

Wadlinger, H. A., & Isaacowitz, D. M. (2011). Fixing our focus: Training attention to regulate emotion. http://www.ncbi.nlm.nih.gov/entrez/eutils/elink.fcgi?dbfrom=pubmed&retmode=ref&cmd=prlinks&id=20435804\tpmc_ext. Pers *Soc Psychological Review*, *15*, 75–102. http://dx.doi.org/10.1177%2F1088868310365565\tpmc_ext10.1177/1088868310365565.

Wiggins, D. K. (2013). A worthwhile effort? History of organized youth sport in the United States. *Kinesiology Review*, *2*, 65–75.

Winter, B., Breitenstein, C., Mooren, F. C., Voelker, K., Fobker, M., Lechtermann, A., et al. (2007). High impact running improves learning. *Neurobiology of Learning & Memory*, *87*, 597–609.

Zang, Z., Yong, H., Chao-Zhe, Z., Qing-Jiu, C., Man-Qiu, S., Meng, L., et al. (2007). Altered baseline brain activity in children with ADHD revealed by resting-state functional MRI. *Brain Development*, *29*, 83–91.

Zani, A., & Rossi, B. (1991). Cognitive psychophysiology as an interface between cognitive and sport psychology. *International Journal of Sport Psychology*, *22*, 376–398.

Zuvekas, S., Vitiello, B., & Norquist, G. (2006). Recent trends in stimulant medication use among US children. *American Journal of Psychiatry*, *163*, 579–585.

Acute Exercise and Cognition in Children and Adolescents: The Roles of Testosterone and Cortisol

Flora Koutsandréou[1,3], Claudia Niemann[2], Mirko Wegner[3], Henning Budde[1,4]

[1]Medical School Hamburg, Faculty of Human Sciences, Department of Pedagogy, Hamburg, Germany; [2]Jacobs Center on Lifelong Learning and Institutional Development, Jacobs University, Bremen, Germany; [3]University of Bern, Institute of Sport Science, Bern, Switzerland; [4]Reykjavik University, School of Science and Engineering, Department of Sport Science, Reykjavik, Iceland

INTRODUCTION

In adults, numerous studies have shown that acute bouts of exercise of a moderate intensity lead to better performance in subsequent cognitive tasks (Brisswalter, Collardeau, & Rene, 2002; Hillman, Snook, & Jerome, 2003; Pontifex, Hillman, Fernhall, Thompson, & Valentini, 2009; Tomporowski, 2003). Fewer studies have shown a positive effect of exercise on children's and adolescents' cognitive performances (Budde, Voelcker-Rehage et al., 2010; Chang, Labban, Gapin, & Etnier, 2012). For all ages, the underlying physiological mechanisms of acute exercise that influence subsequent cognitive performance are still unclear. One possible factor might be exercise-induced altered levels of the steroid hormones cortisol and testosterone. This assumption is supported by research that revealed cortisol (see Lupien et al., 2005, for review) and testosterone in young adults (see Hampson, 1995, for review) and adolescents (Budde, Voelcker-Rehage et al., 2010) influence cognitive performance. Thus, the central thesis of this chapter is that acute physical exercise improves cognitive performance and at the same time changes the secretion of the steroid hormones cortisol and testosterone, and that these changes in hormone concentration may be responsible for the cognitive changes.

THE HPA AND HPG AXES IN RESPONSE TO STRESS

Describing physiological processes in response to stress might contribute to understanding the fundamentals of the proposed assumption. In response to stress (e.g., an acute bout of at least moderate exercise, but also psychological stressors), the hypothalamic–pituitary–adrenal (HPA) as well as the hypothalamic–pituitary–gonadal (HPG) axes are activated: first, the hypothalamus releases the corticotropin-releasing hormone (CRH) and arginine vasopressin (AVP) (both HPA axis) into the portal blood vessel system and gonadotropin-releasing hormone (GnRH) (HPG axis) to the anterior pituitary (see Figure 1). In the anterior pituitary, CRH and AVP stimulate the production and secretion of adrenocorticotropic hormone (ACTH) (HPA axis), whereas GnRH causes the secretion of gonadotropins such as luteinizing hormone (LH) and follicle-stimulating hormone (FSH) (HPG axis). In the adrenal gland, ACTH results in increasing levels of glucocorticoids (cortisol in humans, corticosterone in rodents), which can easily cross the blood–brain barrier. The steroid hormone cortisol then is the final product of the HPA axis activation. LH and FSH, in turn, activate the gonads to synthesize the steroid hormones estrogen and testosterone, as the final products of the HPG axis. The reactivity of the HPA and HPG differs between individuals. Research identified some individuals to show elevations of cortisol or testosterone in response to stressors (responders), while others do not (nonresponders) (Salvador, Suay, Gonzalez-Bono, & Serrano, 2003).

Hormonal Assessment

The concentration of both cortisol and testosterone can be assessed in blood as well as in saliva samples. Salivary cortisol measurement has been accepted as a good index of HPA functioning and reflects the unbound, biologically active hormone fraction (Kirschbaum & Hellhammer, 1994). Assessing steroid hormones in saliva has several advantages to measurements in serum and urine (Windisch, Wegner, & Budde, 2012). This measurement method is noninvasive and does not lead to additional stress as caused by venipuncture (Lac, Lac, & Robert, 1993) and thus might be especially suitable for studies in children and adolescents. Similarly, testosterone can be obtained in saliva, serum, and urine. As the saliva hormone measurements are easily obtained, research on the effects of steroid hormones has increased. Studies on steroid hormones, as one underlying factor of the exercise-induced physiological stress response, might help to further narrow down the dose characteristics (e.g., intensity and duration) of an acute bout of exercise that potentially lead to cognitive benefits in children and adolescents and to investigate whether there are differences between age groups.

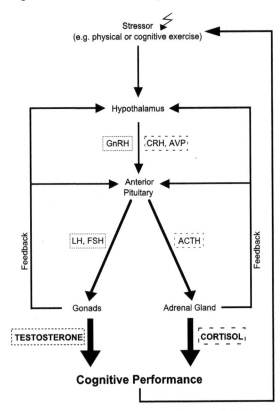

FIGURE 1   Activation pathways for cortisol (HPA axis) and testosterone (HPG axis) in response to physical stress and its hypothesized effects on cognition. *Modified from Wegner, Windisch, and Budde (2012).*

Effects of Cortisol on Cognition

Typically, research on human cognitive performance employs executive functions. Executive functions can be described as "higher-level cognitive functions," like problem solving and reasoning (Alvarez & Emory, 2006; Diamond, 2013), and are separated from "lower-level" cognitive processes. Typical executive functions found in the research are inhibition, working memory, and cognitive flexibility (for a review see Diamond, 2013). Executive functions are critical for school and job success, and for mental and physical health (Diamond, 2012). Therefore, they can be seen as highly relevant to children and adolescents. In this chapter, many of the introduced studies refer to the performance of one or more of these executive functions.

A possible link between cortisol release and a change in cognitive performance is supported by the fact that many cortisol receptors are located in brain regions that are crucial for cognitive processing, like the neocortex, the cerebellum, and the hippocampus (Heffelfinger & Newcomer, 2001). There are two glucocorticoid receptors: mineralocorticoid and glucocorticoid receptors. In the brain glucocorticoids bind to both receptors with different affinities (Gunnar & Quevedo, 2007). The physiological mechanism induced by this binding leads to an inverted-U shape in studies on the relationship between cortisol and cognitive performance in young adults (Lupien et al., 2005). Glucocorticoid receptors bind cortisol with less affinity than do mineralocorticoid receptors and therefore remain unoccupied at low levels of stimulation. With moderate cortisol increase, glucocorticoid receptor occupation increases, supporting synaptic long-term potentiation important for executive function, learning, and memory consolidation (Erickson, Drevets, & Schulkin, 2003; de Kloet, Oitzl, & Joels, 1999). However, increases beyond a moderate level, indicating increasingly high glucocorticoid receptor occupation, are associated with synaptic long-term depression rather than long-term potentiation (Blair, Granger, & Razza, 2005). Accordingly, it has been shown that very low and high cortisol levels affected memory performance negatively (Oei, Everaerd, Elzinga, van Well, & Bermond, 2006; Wolf et al., 2001), whereas medium levels of cortisol enhanced working memory performance (Schoofs, Preuß, & Wolf, 2008). Regarding neuronal changes by the catabolic hormone cortisol, studies found that very low, but also very high, levels of cortisol suppress neuronal activity and change synaptic plasticity (Heffelfinger & Newcomer, 2001).

Studies in humans and animals alike point to the fact that a certain level of adrenergic arousal, induced by nonhabituated testing procedure, is crucial for the effect of corticosterone on working memory performance (see Roozendaal, 2000, for a review). Accordingly, it might be assumed that the underlying mechanism for cognitive performance is due to changes in the cortisol level. However, there are still many open questions concerning the mechanisms underlying the relationship of cortisol and cognitive performance.

Effects of Testosterone on Cognition

For testosterone, moderate increases have been previously associated with improved cognitive performance whereas high and low levels of testosterone have been particularly associated with low spatial ability (see Hampson, 1995, for review; Wolf & Kirschbaum, 2002). However, other studies failed to find any relationship between levels of testosterone and cognitive performance (Gordon & Lee, 1986; McKeever & Deyo, 1990) or reported a linear relationship (Schattmann & Sherwin, 2007; Silverman, Kastuk, Choi, & Phillips, 1999). With regard to the heterogeneous results on the inverted-U shape relationship between testosterone and spatial cognition, Budde, Voelcker-Rehage et al. (2010) concluded that an inverted nonlinear function might be best used to describe this relationship. However, until now one can only speculate about the underlying mechanisms of testosterone changes on cognitive performance.

Testosterone binds to androgen receptors in the cytoplasm, e.g., in the brain. The neurophysiological explanation of better cognitive performance, due to increased testosterone levels, is that androgen receptors mainly exist in brain regions affecting learning and memory, including the prefrontal cortex and the hippocampus (Janowsky, 2006). When the androgen receptor binds to testosterone, it is activated, resulting in up- or downregulation of specific gene transcription (Heemers & Tindall, 2007). Upregulation or activation of transcription results in increased synthesis of messenger RNA, which, in turn, is translated by ribosomes to produce specific proteins, e.g., for synaptogenesis (Frye, Edinger, Seliga, & Wawrzycki, 2004). In addition, animal models found that testosterone increases the number of dendritic spines in the CA1 field of the hippocampus (Leranth, Petnehazy, & MacLusky, 2003) as well as in the prefrontal cortex (Hajszan, MacLusky, Johansen, Jordan, & Leranth, 2007).

Research suggests that cognitive performance is not only mediated by testosterone itself but also by its metabolically active derivatives, estradiol or dihydrotestosterone (Moffat, 2005). The enzyme aromatase, which is also found in the hippocampus, can convert testosterone to estradiol (Roselli, Klosterman, & Resko, 2001), which then binds to estradiol receptors. Estradiol also acts on the striatal dopamine system and effects prefrontal functions (Janowsky, Chavez, & Orwoll, 2000).

Effects of Acute Bouts of Exercise on Cortisol

With regard to the intensity and duration of an acute bout of exercise, research in adults showed that the workload necessary to affect the cortisol level must exceed a specific threshold for both intensity and duration (Brownlee, Moore, & Hackney, 2005; Gatti & De Palo, 2011; Hill et al., 2008; Kirschbaum & Hellhammer, 1994).

Consistently it has been shown that intensity should exceed 60% of the individual's maximal oxygen uptake ($VO_{2\,max}$) to induce cortisol release above resting levels in adults. A minimum duration of 10–15 min may result in increased cortisol levels with peak concentrations 20–30 min after the cessation of the exercise bout (Kirschbaum & Hellhammer, 1994). In agreement with findings in studies examining adults, adolescents in Tanner stages 4 and 5 (on average at 14–15 years) show a similar reactivity of the HPA resulting in cortisol increases in response to acute bouts of exercise (Hackney et al., 2011). For 15- to 16-year-old adolescents, a 12-min exercise bout with an intensity of 70–85% HR_{max} led to an increase in cortisol levels compared to a group exercising at moderate intensity (50–65% HR_{max}) (Budde, Voelcker-Rehage et al., 2010). These results confirm the threshold phenomenon for adults and also in adolescents of late puberty stages, and indicate that the concentration of cortisol after acute bouts of exercise is intensity dependent.

A study by Di Luigi et al. (2006) investigated salivary cortisol in adolescent male soccer players after 90 min of medium- to high-intensity exercise compared to pre-exercise. A subsample of boys in Tanner stages 4 and 5 (mean age 15.2 years) showed a significant cortisol increase. These findings are in accordance with the results of Budde, Pietrassyk-Kendziorra, Bohm and Voelcker-Rehage (2010), who studied 40 adolescents, aged 15–16 years. They found that a 12-min exercise bout of 70–85% HR_{max} led to an increase of salivary cortisol.

A recent study (Wegner, Müller-Alcarzar et al., 2014) investigated how cortisol levels of adolescents at the age of 14 react to different types of stressors. Exercise as a stressor to elevate saliva cortisol was induced by running 15 min at a medium intensity level of 65–75% HR_{max}. In the control condition, adolescents attended a teacher-centered lecture for the same amount of time. The acute bout of physical exercise was not able to significantly increase cortisol levels. It was suggested that medium exercise intensity, like that applied in the study, is not able to significantly elevate cortisol levels of adolescents.

Although results of the HPA reactivity to acute exercise are consistent for adults and adolescents in late puberty stages, in most of the studies there seem to be differences within the earlier Tanner stages. Studies revealed that HPA function in response to acute exercise differs in young adolescents and adults. In the previously mentioned study by Di Luigi et al. (2006), children and adolescents in early to mid-puberty stages (Tanner stages 1–3, mean age 12.7 years) showed higher cortisol increases than adolescents in the 4th and 5th Tanner stages, after 90 min of physical exercise. This result is in accordance with a study by Viru, Laaneots, Karelson, Smirnova, and Viru (1998), who reported that the cortisol level, in response to 20 min of acute exercise at 60% $VO_{2\,max}$ in girls, was highest during mid-puberty (Tanner stages 2 and 3) in comparison to late puberty (stages 4 and 5). Another study compared the cortisol levels of 38 prepubescent boys in Tanner stage 1 with that of 32 pubescent boys in stages 3 and 4 after an intense exercise bout (induced by a shuttle-run test). According to the results of the shuttle-run test, the boys were split into "high fit" and "average fit." All pubescent as well as the prepubescent "high-fit" boys showed increased cortisol levels after the physical exercise, whereas the prepubescent "average fit" did not (Benitez-Sillero et al., 2009). These findings may suggest that the level of fitness interacts with the exercise-induced stress response and thereby explains diverging results for cortisol levels after an acute bout of exercise in different samples. Furthermore, duration and intensity differed completely in the studies reviewed: Di Luigi et al. (2006) investigated an acute bout of 90 min comprised a mixture of warm-up followed by coordination, strength, and flexibility training, game simulation as well as cool down. This workload might not be comparable to the shuttle-run test in the study by Benitez-Sillero et al. (2009) in regard to effects on cortisol levels and thus results may not conform to one another.

In 2010, Budde, Windisch, Kudielka, and Voelcker-Rehage observed no changes in the cortisol concentration of 9- to 10-year-old children (probably Tanner stages 1 and 2) after a 12 min high intensity (85–90% HR_{max}) exercise bout. These findings are in line with the previously mentioned prepubescent "average-fit" boys: they also did not show an increase in cortisol after exercise (Benitez-Sillero et al., 2009). Taken together, the reported data support the argument that there might be a marked age-related development in the regulation of stress from children to adolescents (Gunnar, Wewerka, Frenn, Long, & Griggs, 2009).

The reviewed data indicate that the different HPA reactivity of children and adolescents, in comparison to adults' HPA reactivity, are due to major developmental differences between early and late puberty stages. Moreover, there are several factors that need consideration, among them fitness level, increased cortisol levels in anticipation of the measurement, gender, daytime nutrition, and the experimental environment (leisure vs. school setting). Moreover, results from a recent study suggest that personality variables like the implicit affiliation motive (need for affiliation) can also moderate the cortisol response in adolescents (Wegner, Schüler, & Budde, 2014).

Effects of Acute Bouts of Exercise on Testosterone

The level of the sex hormone testosterone in response to an acute bout of exercise depends on the intensity and duration of the performed activity. The concentration of testosterone, similarly to levels of cortisol, increases after an acute bout of exercise once a specific intensity threshold is reached (Budde, Voelcker-Rehage et al., 2010). This threshold seems to be at approximately 50% $VO_{2\,max}$ (which represents a lower intensity than for cortisol) (Gatti & De Palo, 2011; Maresh, Cook, Cohen, Graham, & Gunn, 1988). Peak concentrations in adults occur after 20 min (Wilkerson, Horvath, & Gutin, 1980). In addition, the duration of exercise seems to play an important role for the effect on testosterone levels. A short exercise duration, of 12 min in combination with an intensity of 50–65% of the maximum heart rate, failed to increase testosterone levels in 15- to 16-year-old adolescents (Budde, Voelcker-Rehage et al., 2010), whereas in adults a 40-min exercise bout, with a similar moderate intensity of 50–55% $VO_{2\,max}$, induced increased testosterone levels (Tremblay, Copeland, & van Helder, 2004). According to Viru (1985), the total load of exercise that is the product of intensity and duration seems to be an important determinant of the magnitude of the steroid hormone response. Thus, if low-intensity exercise is prolonged enough in duration, it might result in significant elevations in testosterone (Tremblay et al., 2004).

In children and adolescents, the production of steroid hormones increases over all puberty stages in both sexes, while boys' testosterone levels on average do not rise before the age of 12. For girls, testosterone levels do not start to increase before the age of 10 (Courant et al., 2010). However, by measuring pre- to postchanges of testosterone, acute exercise studies in adolescents did not find gender differences (Budde, Pietrassyk-Kendziorra et al., 2010; Viru, 1985). Furthermore, the activity, or rather the fitness status, influences the reactivity of the HPG axis. The reactivity of the HPG axis, in response to 12 min of intensive exercise, seems to emerge only in active children. A low activity status led to decreased testosterone levels after exercising and was interpreted as a disturbance of the anabolic/catabolic balance (Niemann et al., 2013). The assumption was supported by previous results in trained adults. Kraemer et al. (1992) found that the testosterone levels of adult participants, who had exercised regularly over a long period of time, increased following bouts of acute exercise.

For adolescents at the age of 15–16 years, testosterone levels increased after a 12-min exercise bout at 70–85% HR_{max} (Budde, Voelcker-Rehage et al., 2010). Furthermore, Di Luigi et al. (2006), with 10- to 11-year-olds, demonstrated an increase in testosterone of approximately 30% above the baseline levels, after 90 min of exercise. These result are contradicted by results from 9- to 10-year-old children, who were exercising with 180–190 bpm for 12 min (Niemann et al., 2013) as well as from 15-year-old adolescents, who were exercising with 65–75% HR_{max} for 15 min (Wegner, Koedijker, & Budde, 2014). These heterogeneous results could either be due to the different exercise durations or participants' age differences. Different pre-exercise testosterone concentrations were found for different age groups (9/10 and 15/16 years) in two studies with similar designs. Before exercising, the young boys' and girls' testosterone level was around 3 pg/ml (Niemann et al., 2013), whereas for participants in the older group it was around 40 pg/ml (Budde, Voelcker-Rehage et al., 2010). This indicates a massive increase in the HPG axis activity between these age groups.

In general, during middle childhood (between the ages of 6 and 10), the hormones axes seem to be less reactive in comparison to adolescents' hormonal axes (between ages 11 and 18) (Marceau, Dorn, & Susman, 2012). Accordingly, Di Luigi et al. (2006) reported a significant higher testosterone increase after a football exercise bout for late puberty stages (Tanner 3–5) compared to early stages (Tanner 1 and 2).

EFFECTS OF ACUTE BOUTS OF EXERCISE ON COGNITION

Many reviews have investigated the relationship between acute exercise and cognitive performance. They have generally reported a positive effect of acute exercise on cognition (particularly immediately following the exercise), with small to large effect sizes (from 0.10 to 1.41) (for reviews see Chen, Yan, Yin, Pan, & Chang, 2014; Lambourne & Tomporowski, 2010; McMorris, Sproule, Turner, & Hale, 2011; Verburgh, Konigs, Scherder, & Oosterlaan, 2013). The wide ranges of effect sizes indicate that certain factors like physical activity status (Budde et al., 2012), intensity (Budde et al., 2012), duration (Hillman, Kamijo, & Scudder, 2011), and type of exercise (Budde, Voelcker-Rehage, Pietrassyk-Kendziorra, Ribeiro, & Tidow, 2008), as well as the investigated aspect of cognition (Tomporowski, 2003), may moderate the relationship between acute exercise and cognition. With regard to exercise intensity, cognitive performance (with certain constraints) seems to be affected by acute exercise in an inverted-U function. Moderate-intensity exercise in the range of 40–85% of $VO_{2\,max}$ results in improved performance (Tomporowski, 2003). Exercise below and above that intensity range is assumed to result in a deterioration of performance (Lambourne & Tomporowski, 2010; Tomporowski, 2003). Another study revealed that the impact of acute exercise on cognition is not uniform across all individuals and that it is only beneficial for those who performed suboptimally in cognitive testing (Sibley & Beilock, 2007). This was supported by results of Budde, Voelcker-Rehage et al. (2010) showing that exercise improves working memory especially in low-performing adolescents, whereas there was no improvement for high performers.

While the majority of research focuses on young adults (e.g., Budde et al., 2012), middle-aged adults (e.g., Chang, Tsai, Huang, Wang, & Chu, 2014), or old adults (e.g., Pesce & Audiffren, 2011), less research has been conducted focusing on adolescents and preadolescent children. Hillman et al. (2011) reported a positive effect of acute exercise on cognition in children, but noted that it was difficult to draw conclusions across multiple studies due to the use of different cognitive tasks, age groups, and types and intensities of exercise, for example.

A meta-analysis carried out by Sibley and Etnier (2003) reported a small positive relationship with an effect size of 0.32 between exercise and cognition for children and adolescents. Another meta-analysis investigated this relationship across the lifespan but the revealed overall effect size was smaller (0.25) (Etnier

et al., 1997). A recent meta-analysis carried out by Verburgh et al. (2013) investigated 19 empirical studies with regard to the effects of physical exercise on executive functions in preadolescent children, adolescents, and young adults. They reported a significant overall effect (d = 0.52) of acute exercise on executive functions and no differences between the three age groups.

Is the Effect of Acute Exercise on Cognition Mediated by Steroid Hormones?

So far, only a small number of studies exist investigating the link between exercise-related steroid hormone changes and improved cognitive performance due to acute bouts of exercise in children and adolescents. Thus, in this paragraph, we also present research studies investigating psychosocial stressors to activate the HPA and HPG axes and to impact cognition. The first study investigating the impact of acute exercise on cognitive performance and on steroid hormones, with 15- to 16-year-old adolescents, failed to show a relationship between cortisol levels and cognitive performance in a working memory task (Budde, Voelcker-Rehage et al., 2010). Salivary cortisol was increased after a high-intensity exercise bout (70–85% $VO_{2\,max}$), whereas the performance in a working memory task mainly benefited from exercising with moderate intensity (65–70% $VO_{2\,max}$). Thus, the enhanced working memory performance could not be attributed to the increased cortisol concentration. On the basis of studies by Budde, Voelcker-Rehage et al. (2010) and Niemann et al. (2013), a recent study tested the effects of 20 min of cognitively engaging, playful exercise on executive functions and on cortisol levels in 6- to 8-year-old children (Jäger, Schmidt, Conzelmann, & Roebers, 2014). Children in the experimental group improved their performance significantly on the inhibition task compared to the control group. Cortisol elevation in the experimental group did not reach significance from pre-to posttest, confirming the results of Budde, Voelcker-Rehage et al. (2010); nonetheless, in the experimental group cortisol increased significantly between posttest and after 40 min and the authors were able to correlate this cortisol change with the performance in the inhibition task. Unfortunately, this study has a lack of standardized testing concerning the exercise intensity.

Studies with different kinds of stressors, especially psychosocial stressors, partly failed (but under certain conditions were able) to demonstrate a relationship between cortisol increases after stress and working memory. In one study, cortisol elevation was induced by psychological as well as highly intensive physical stress (Hoffman & al'Absi, 2004). However, the following neuropsychological tests did not result in working memory improvements. On the other hand, a study by Elzinga and Roelofs (2005), using a psychological stress protocol, did show a link between stress-induced cortisol increases and working memory performance. They divided participants into cortisol responders and nonresponders, after a psychological stress phase, and found working memory impairments during the psychosocial stress phase but only for the cortisol responders. In addition, one study found that psychosocial stress impaired working memory performance at high, but not low, working memory loads (Oei et al., 2006). The previously mentioned results need further explorations. This is also true for the link between exercise-induced cognitive changes and testosterone.

In adults many findings point to testosterone as a possible mediator for the effect of exercise on cognition. A study by Moffat and Hampson (1996) demonstrated that intermediate levels of testosterone were linked to better spatial functioning. In another study, men with lower testosterone levels showed an increased performance in cognitive tests (Wolf & Kirschbaum, 2002). Furthermore, a high dose of injected testosterone in elderly men was associated with a decreased performance in a verbal fluency task (Wolf et al., 2000).

For adolescents it also has been shown that exercise-induced changes in testosterone concentrations are correlated with changes in cognitive performance. A study with adolescents, at the age of 15–16 years, found high-intensity exercise induced increased testosterone levels, which were negatively related to changes in working memory performance (Budde, Voelcker-Rehage et al., 2010). Testosterone levels have also been found to be positively related to changes in fine motor skills (Wegner, Koedijker et al., 2014), an interesting finding, because cognition and motor skills seem to be fundamentally interrelated behaviorally and with regard to the underlying brain structures (Pangelinan et al., 2011).

A possible explanation for exercise and stress-induced testosterone changes being, to some extent, responsible for enhanced cognitive performance is testosterone-induced synaptogenesis. Testosterone was found to have a neuroprotective function and preserves neurons and synapses (Kurth et al., 2014). In addition, research with animals revealed that testosterone treatment resulted in increased synaptogenesis, which was associated with improved synaptic function (Ziehn et al., 2012). These structural changes of synapses and their associated dendritic spines can appear as fast as minutes to hours after exercise training (Johansen-Berg, Baptista, & Thomas, 2012). Synaptic functioning is a well-established electrophysiological biomarker for cognitive function in rodents. Taken together, this illustrated physiological process can be seen as a further explanation for testosterone as mediating the link between acute exercise and cognitive performance (see Figure 2).

For preadolescent children, aged 9–10 years, this effect of testosterone on attention could not be confirmed (Niemann et al., 2013). Exercising intensively at a heart rate of 180–190 bpm resulted in larger improvement in selective attention performance (d2-test) compared to a control group, but no increase in testosterone concentration was found. Instead, the habitually low-active children showed a significant decrease in testosterone, which was interpreted as a possible disruption of the HPG

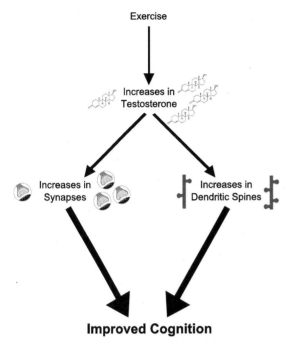

Improved Cognition

FIGURE 2 Testosterone as a possible mediator for the link between acute exercise and cognitive performance.

axis in these children. As outlined above, the HPG axis activity and reactivity are still developing in this age group.

CONCLUSION

In sum, this chapter presents a short overview on the current state of the research focusing on the relationship between acute exercise, steroid hormones, and cognitive performance of children and adolescents. It can be concluded that acute exercise induces increased testosterone and cortisol levels in adolescents if the intensity exceeds a specific threshold, which seems to be lower for testosterone. As the influence of acute bouts of exercise on cognition still follows similar kinetics, it is reasonable to speculate about the link between exercise-related steroid hormones changes and improved cognitive performance due to acute bouts of exercise. We assume

that the underlying mechanisms of a change in cognitive functions after acute exercise, at least in older adolescents whose HPA and HPG axis are already reactive like those in adults, are due to an alteration in these steroid hormones. The connection between acute bouts of exercise and cognition might be explained by a change in testosterone, whereas the effect of cortisol so far has mainly been illustrated in nonphysical stressors.

There are still many questions related to the association between acute exercise, cognitive performance, and the mediating effects of steroid hormones, which need to be answered. Future studies may investigate the relationship between exercise and cognition with regard to a possible mediation effect of other steroid hormones (e.g., estradiol) and should control factors such as age, gender, physical activity status, exercise intensity, and psychological variables. Together, the research suggests a positive association between acute exercise bouts and cognitive performance during childhood and adolescence. Therefore, there should be more short bouts of exercise, which could be included very easily in a school setting. The exercise duration needed to enhance cognitive performance can be performed within a normal school break of 15 min. Even moderate -intensity exercise, for example fast walking, is able to enhance cognitive performance, which can be easily implemented in various settings because neither sports clothes nor sports facilities are necessary for this type of exercise.

References

Alvarez, J. A., & Emory, E. (2006). Executive function and the frontal lobes: a meta-analytic review. *Neuropsychology Review, 16*, 17–42.

Benitez-Sillero, J. D., Perez-Navero, J. L., Tasset, I., Guillen-Del Castillo, M., Gil-Campos, M., & Tunez, I. (2009). Influence of intense exercise on saliva glutathione in prepubescent and pubescent boys. *European Journal of Applied Physiology, 106*, 181–186.

Blair, C., Granger, D., & Razza, R. P. (2005). Cortisol reactivity is positively related to executive function in preschool children attending head start. *Child Development, 76*, 554–567.

Brisswalter, J., Collardeau, M., & Rene, A. (2002). Effects of acute physical exercise characteristics on cognitive performance. *Sports Medicine, 32*, 555–566.

Brownlee, K. K., Moore, A. W., & Hackney, A. C. (2005). Relationship between circulating cortisol and testosterone: influence of physical exercise. *Journal of Sports Science and Medicine, 4*, 76–83.

Budde, H., Brunelli, A., Machado, S., Velasques, B., Ribeiro, P., Arias-Carrión, O., et al. (2012). Intermittent maximal exercise improves attentional performance only in physically active students. *Archives of Medical Research, 2*, 43.

Budde, H., Pietrassyk-Kendziorra, S., Bohm, S., & Voelcker-Rehage, C. (2010). Hormonal responses to physical and cognitive stress in a school setting. *Neuroscience Letters, 474*, 131–134.

Budde, H., Voelcker-Rehage, C., Pietrassyk-Kendziorra, S., Machado, S., Ribeiro, P., & Arafat, A. M. (2010). Steroid hormones in the saliva of adolescents after different exercise intensities and their influence on working memory in a school setting. *Psychoneuroendocrinology, 35*, 382–391.

Budde, H., Voelcker-Rehage, C., Pietrassyk-Kendziorra, S., Ribeiro, P., & Tidow, G. (2008). Acute coordinative exercise improves attentional performance in adolescents. *Neuroscience Letters, 441*, 219–223.

Budde, H., Windisch, C., Kudielka, B. M., & Voelcker-Rehage, C. (2010). Saliva cortisol in school children after acute physical exercise. *Neuroscience Letters, 483*, 16–19.

Chang, Y. K., Labban, J. D., Gapin, J. I., & Etnier, J. L. (2012). The effects of acute exercise on cognitive performance: a meta-analysis. *Brain Research, 1453*, 87–101.

Chang, Y. K., Tsai, C. L., Huang, C. C., Wang, C. C., & Chu, I. H. (2014). Effects of acute resistance exercise on cognition in late middle-aged adults: general or specific cognitive improvement? *Journal of Science and Medicine in Sport, 17*, 51–55.

Chen, A. G., Yan, J., Yin, H. C., Pan, C. Y., & Chang, Y. K. (2014). Effects of acute aerobic exercise on multiple aspects of executive function in preadolescent children. *Psychology of Sport and Exercise, 15*, 627–636.

Courant, F., Aksglaede, L., Antignac, J. P., Monteau, F., Sorensen, K., Andersson, A. M., et al. (2010). Assessment of circulating sex steroid levels in prepubertal and pubertal boys and girls by a novel ultrasensitive gas chromatography-tandem mass spectrometry method. *Journal of Clinical Endocrinology and Metabolism, 95*, 82–92.

Di Luigi, L., Baldari, C., Gallotta, M. C., Perroni, F., Romanelli, F., Lenzi, A., et al. (2006). Salivary steroids at rest and after a training load in young male athletes: relationship with chronological age and pubertal development. *International Journal of Sports Medicine, 27*, 709–717.

Diamond, A. (2012). Activities and programs that improve children's executive functions. *Current Directions in Psychological Science, 21*, 335–341.

Diamond, A. (2013). Executive functions. *Annual Review of Psychology, 64*, 135–168.

Elzinga, B. M., & Roelofs, K. (2005). Cortisol-induced impairments of working memory require acute sympathetic activation. *Behavioral Neuroscience, 119*, 98–103.

Erickson, K., Drevets, W., & Schulkin, J. (2003). Glucocorticoid regulation of diverse cognitive functions in normal and pathological emotional states. *Neuroscience & Biobehavioral Reviews, 27*, 233–246.

Etnier, J. L., Salazar, W., Landers, D. M., Petruzzello, S. J., Han, M., & Nowell, P. M. (1997). The influence of physical fitness and exercise upon cognitive functioning: a meta-analysis. *Journal of Sport and Exercise Psychology, 19*, 249–277.

Frye, C. A., Edinger, K. L., Seliga, A. M., & Wawrzycki, J. M. (2004). 5α-reduced androgens may have actions in the hippocampus to enhance cognitive performance of male rats. *Psychoneuroendocrinology, 29*, 1019–1027.

Gatti, R., & De Palo, E. F. (2011). An update: salivary hormones and physical exercise. *Scandinavian Journal of Medicine & Science in Sports, 21*, 157–169.

Gordon, H. W., & Lee, P. A. (1986). A relationship between gonadotropins and visuospatial function. *Neuropsychologia, 24*, 563–576.

Gunnar, M. R., & Quevedo, K. (2007). The neurobiology of stress and development. *Annual Review of Psychology, 58*, 145–173.

Gunnar, M. R., Wewerka, S., Frenn, K., Long, J. D., & Griggs, C. (2009). Developmental changes in hypothalamus-pituitary-adrenal activity over the transition to adolescence: normative changes and associations with puberty. *Development and Psychopathology, 21*, 69–85.

Hackney, A. C., Viru, M., VanBruggen, M., Janson, T., Karelson, K., & Viru, A. (2011). Comparison of the hormonal responses to exhaustive incremental exercise in adolescent and young adult males. *Arquivos Brasileiros de Endocrinologia e Metabologia, 55*, 213–218.

Hajszan, T., MacLusky, N. J., Johansen, J. A., Jordan, C. L., & Leranth, C. (2007). Effects of androgens and estradiol on spine synapse formation in the prefrontal cortex of normal and testicular feminization mutant male rats. *Endocrinology, 148*, 1963–1967.

Hampson, E. (1995). Spatial cognition in humans: possible modulation by androgens and estrogens. *Journal of Psychiatry & Neuroscience, 20*, 397–404.

Heemers, H. V., & Tindall, D. J. (2007). Androgen receptor (AR) coregulators: a diversity of functions converging on and regulating the AR transcriptional complex. *Endocrine Reviews, 28*, 778–808.

Heffelfinger, A. K., & Newcomer, J. W. (2001). Glucocorticoid effects on memory function over the human life span. *Development and Psychopathology, 13*, 491–513.

Hillman, C. H., Kamijo, K., & Scudder, M. (2011). A review of chronic and acute physical activity participation on neuroelectric measures of brain health and cognition during childhood. *Preventive Medicine, 52*(Suppl.), S21–S28.

Hillman, C. H., Snook, E. M., & Jerome, G. J. (2003). Acute cardiovascular exercise and executive control function. *International Journal of Psychophysiology, 48*, 307–314.

Hill, E. E., Zack, E., Battaglini, C., Viru, M., Viru, A., & Hackney, A. C. (2008). Exercise and circulating cortisol levels: the intensity threshold effect. *Journal of Endocrinological Investigation, 31*, 587–591.

Hoffman, R., & al'Absi, M. (2004). The effect of acute stress on subsequent neuropsychological test performance. *Archives of Clinical Neuropsychology, 19*, 497–506.

Jäger, K., Schmidt, M., Conzelmann, A., & Roebers, C. M. (2014). Cognitive and physiological effects of an acute physical activity intervention in elementary school children. *Frontiers in Psychology, 5*, 1473.

Janowsky, J. S. (2006). Thinking with your gonads: testosterone and cognition. *Trends in Cognitive Sciences, 10*, 77–82.

Janowsky, J. S., Chavez, B., & Orwoll, E. (2000). Sex steroids modify working memory. *Journal of Cognitive Neuroscience, 12*, 407–414.

Johansen-Berg, H., Baptista, C. S., & Thomas, A. G. (2012). Human structural plasticity at record speed. *Neuron, 73*, 1058–1060.

Kirschbaum, C., & Hellhammer, D. H. (1994). Salivary cortisol in psychoneuroendocrine research: recent developments and applications. *Psychoneuroendocrinology, 19*, 313–333.

de Kloet, E. R., Oitzl, M. S., & Joels, M. (1999). Stress and cognition: are corticosteroids good or bad guys? *Trends in Neurosciences, 22*, 422–426.

Kraemer, W. J., Fry, A. C., Warren, B. J., Stone, M. H., Fleck, S. J., Kearney, J. T., et al. (1992). Acute hormonal responses in elite junior weightlifters. *International Journal of Sports Medicine, 13*, 103–109.

Kurth, F., Luders, E., Sicotte, N. L., Gaser, C., Giesser, B. S., Swerdloff, R. S., et al. (2014). Neuroprotective effects of testosterone treatment in men with multiple sclerosis. *NeuroImage: Clinical, 4*, 454–460.

Lac, G., Lac, N., & Robert, A. (1993). Steroid assays in saliva: a method to detect plasmatic contaminations. *Archives Internationales de Physiologie de Biochimie et de Biophysique, 101*, 257–262.

Lambourne, K., & Tomporowski, P. (2010). The effect of exercise-induced arousal on cognitive task performance: a meta-regression analysis. *Brain Research, 1341*, 12–24.

Leranth, C., Petnehazy, O., & MacLusky, N. J. (2003). Gonadal hormones affect spine synaptic density in the CA1 hippocampal subfield of male rats. *Journal of Neuroscience, 23*, 1588–1592.

Lupien, S. J., Fiocco, A., Wan, N., Maheu, F., Lord, C., Schramek, T., et al. (2005). Stress hormones and human memory function across the lifespan. *Psychoneuroendocrinology, 30*, 225–242.

Marceau, K., Dorn, L. D., & Susman, E. J. (2012). Stress and puberty-related hormone reactivity, negative emotionality, and parent–adolescent relationships. *Psychoneuroendocrinology, 37*, 1286–1298.

Maresh, C. M., Cook, M. R., Cohen, H. D., Graham, C., & Gunn, W. S. (1988). Exercise testing in the evaluation of human responses to powerline frequency fields. *Aviation, Space, and Environmental Medicine, 59*, 1139–1145.

McKeever, W. F., & Deyo, R. A. (1990). Testosterone, dihydrotestosterone, and spatial task perforrgances of males. *Bulletin of the Psychonomic Society, 28*, 305–308.

McMorris, T., Sproule, J., Turner, A., & Hale, B. J. (2011). Acute, intermediate intensity exercise, and speed and accuracy in working memory tasks: a meta-analytical comparison of effects. *Physiology & Behavior, 102*, 421–428.

Moffat, S. D. (2005). Effects of testosterone on cognitive and brain aging in elderly men. *Annals of the New York Academy of Sciences, 1055*, 80–92.

Moffat, S. D., & Hampson, E. (1996). A curvilinear relationship between testosterone and spatial cognition in humans: possible influence of hand preference. *Psychoneuroendocrinology, 21*, 323–337.

Niemann, C., Wegner, M., Voelcker-Rehage, C., Holzweg, M., Arafat, A. M., & Budde, H. (2013). Influence of acute and chronic physical activity on cognitive performance and saliva testosterone in preadolescent school children. *Mental Health and Physical Activity, 6*, 197–204.

Oei, N. Y., Everaerd, W. T., Elzinga, B. M., van Well, S., & Bermond, B. (2006). Psychosocial stress impairs working memory at high loads: an association with cortisol levels and memory retrieval. *Stress, 9*, 133–141.

Pangelinan, M. M., Zhang, G., VanMeter, J. W., Clark, J. E., Hatfield, B. D., & Haufler, A. J. (2011). Beyond age and gender: relationships between cortical and subcortical brain volume and cognitive-motor abilities in school-age children. *NeuroImage, 54*, 3093–3100.

Pesce, C., & Audiffren, M. (2011). Does acute exercise switch off switch costs? A study with younger and older athletes. *Journal of Sport & Exercise Psychology, 33*, 609–626.

Pontifex, M. B., Hillman, C. H., Fernhall, B., Thompson, K. M., & Valentini, T. A. (2009). The effect of acute aerobic and resistance exercise on working memory. *Medicine and Science in Sports and Exercise, 41*, 927–934.

Roozendaal, B. (2000). Glucocorticoids and the regulation of memory consolidation. *Psychoneuroendocrinology, 25*, 213–238.

Roselli, C. E., Klosterman, S., & Resko, J. A. (2001). Anatomic relationships between aromatase and androgen receptor mRNA expression in the hypothalamus and amygdala of adult male cynomolgus monkeys. *Journal of Comparative Neurology, 439*, 208–223.

Salvador, A., Suay, F., Gonzalez-Bono, E., & Serrano, M. A. (2003). Anticipatory cortisol, testosterone and psychological responses to judo competition in young men. *Psychoneuroendocrinology, 28*, 364–375.

Schattmann, L., & Sherwin, B. B. (2007). Testosterone levels and cognitive functioning in women with polycystic ovary syndrome and in healthy young women. *Hormones and Behavior, 51*, 587–596.

Schoofs, D., Preuß, D., & Wolf, O. T. (2008). Psychosocial stress induces working memory impairments in an n-back paradigm. *Psychoneuroendocrinology, 33*, 643–653.

Sibley, B. A., & Beilock, S. L. (2007). Exercise and working memory: an individual differences investigation. *Journal of Sport and Exercise Psychology, 29*, 783–791.

Sibley, B. A., & Etnier, J. L. (2003). The relationship between physical activity and cognition in children: a meta analysis. *Pediatric Exercise Science, 15*, 243–256.

Silverman, I., Kastuk, D., Choi, J., & Phillips, K. (1999). Testosterone levels and spatial ability in men. *Psychoneuroendocrinology, 24*, 813–822.

Tomporowski, P. D. (2003). Effects of acute bouts of exercise on cognition. *Acta Psychologica, 112*, 297–324.

Tremblay, M. S., Copeland, J. L., & van Helder, W. (2004). Effect of training status and exercise mode on endogenous steroid hormones in men. *Journal of Applied Physiology, 96*, 531–539.

Verburgh, L., Konigs, M., Scherder, E. J., & Oosterlaan, J. (2013). Physical exercise and executive functions in preadolescent children, adolescents and young adults: a meta-analysis. *British Journal of Sports Medicine, 48*, 973–979.

Viru, A. (1985). The pituitary-adrenocortical system. In A. Viru (Ed.), *Hormones in muscular activity* (pp. 25–60). Boca Raton: CRC Press.

Viru, A., Laaneots, L., Karelson, K., Smirnova, T., & Viru, M. (1998). Exercise-induced hormone responses in girls at different stages of sexual maturation. *European Journal of Applied Physiology and Occupational Physiology, 77*, 401–408.

Wegner, M., Koedijker, J. M., & Budde, H. (2014). The effect of acute exercise and psychosocial stress on fine motor skills and testosterone concentration in the saliva of high school students. *PLoS One, 9*, e92953.

Wegner, M., Müller-Alcarzar, A., Jäger, A., Machado, S., Arias-Carrión, O., & Budde, H. (2014). Psychosocial stress but not exercise increases cortisol and reduces state anxiety levels in school classes – results from a stressor applicable in large group settings. *CNS & Neurological Disorders - Drug Targets, 13*.

Wegner, M., Schüler, J., & Budde, H. (2014). The implicit affiliation motive moderates cortisol responses to acute psychosocial stress in high school students. *Psychoneuroendocrinology, 48*, 162–168.

Wegner, M., Windisch, C., & Budde, H. (2012). Psychophysische Auswirkungen von akuter körperlicher Belastung im Kontext Schule. *Zeitschrift für Sportpsychologie, 19*, 37–47.

Wilkerson, J. E., Horvath, S. M., & Gutin, B. (1980). Plasma testosterone during treadmill exercise. *Journal of Applied Physiology, 49*, 249–253.

Windisch, C., Wegner, M., & Budde, H. (2012). Testosterone. In F. Ehrlenspiel, & K. Strahler (Eds.), *Psychoneuroendocrinology of sport and exercise: Foundations, markers, trends* (pp. 61–85). London: Routledge.

Wolf, O. T., Convit, A., McHugh, P. F., Kandil, E., Thorn, E. L., De Santi, S., et al. (2001). Cortisol differentially affects memory in young and elderly men. *Behavioral Neuroscience, 115*, 1002–1011.

Wolf, O. T., & Kirschbaum, C. (2002). Endogenous estradiol and testosterone levels are associated with cognitive performance in older women and men. *Hormones and Behavior, 41*, 259–266.

Wolf, O. T., Preut, R., Hellhammer, D. H., Kudielka, B. M., Schurmeyer, T. H., & Kirschbaum, C. (2000). Testosterone and cognition in elderly men: a single testosterone injection blocks the practice effect in verbal fluency, but has no effect on spatial or verbal memory. *Biological Psychiatry, 47*, 650–654.

Ziehn, M. O., Avedisian, A. A., Dervin, S. M., Umeda, E. A., O'Dell, T. J., & Voskuhl, R. R. (2012). Therapeutic testosterone administration preserves excitatory synaptic transmission in the hippocampus during autoimmune demyelinating disease. *Journal of Neuroscience, 32*, 12312–12324.

The Chronic Exercise–Cognition Interaction in Older Adults

Claudia Voelcker-Rehage[1,2], Claudia Niemann[1,2], Ben Godde[2]

[1]Institute of Human Movement Science and Health, Technische Universitaet Chemnitz, Chemnitz, Germany; [2]Jacobs Center on Lifelong Learning and Institutional Development, Jacobs University, Bremen, Germany

INTRODUCTION TO EXERCISE AND COGNITION IN OLDER ADULTS

Recent aging research has investigated the influence of physical activity on health, psychological well-being, cognitive performance, and brain structure and function (e.g., Hillman, Erickson, & Kramer, 2008). In this chapter, we review in detail how physical activity, physical fitness, and fitness interventions are related to and influence cognitive performance and brain health in older adults. To lay the ground for the understanding of differential exercise effects on cognitive and brain function, we will start with an overview of age-related cognitive and brain changes in normal aging, including evidence for the plasticity of brain and behavior. After introducing methodological approaches for the investigation of the exercise–cognition interaction, we will review effects and associations of different types of physical activity and exercise on, and with, cognition and brain structure and function. This section will be followed by a summary of biological and physiological mechanisms that

might link physical activity and exercise to brain function and biological processes, and by a section on dose–response relationships. We will conclude with the discussion of some limitations of the current research and an outlook to potential future research approaches.

NORMAL AGING OF COGNITIVE FUNCTIONS AND THE BRAIN

Cognitive Changes

Cognitive aging is characterized by high variability of developmental trajectories (Lövdén, Bäckman, Lindenberger, Schaefer, & Schmiedek, 2010; Rönnlund, Nyberg, Bäckman, & Nilsson, 2005), between individuals as well as within individuals, for different cognitive functions. On average, so-called "cognitive mechanics" or "fluid intelligence," i.e., those functions that strongly depend on the integrity of the underlying neural hardware and physiological processes, peak at early adulthood and start to decline continuously very early in life (from 25 to 30 years of age) (for a review of the two-component theory of intelligence, cf. Baltes, Dittmann-Kohli, & Dixon, 1984). This includes, for example, the speed and accuracy of perceptual processes, working memory, and inhibitory control functions. Similarly, for episodic memory and the recall of information from long-term memory, cross-sectional data indicate a linear age-related decline from middle adulthood onwards. Some of these cognitive functions seem to be particularly vulnerable to performance loss and accelerated decline in late adulthood (cf. Hedden & Gabrieli, 2004; Hommel, Li, & Li, 2004; Park et al., 2002) and it is those that have been mainly targeted by exercise studies. Interestingly, some longitudinal data point to a beginning in performance loss not before the age of 60 implicating strong cohort, particularly education and other lifestyle or social factors' effects, on age trajectories (Hedden & Gabrieli, 2004; Rönnlund et al., 2005). On the other hand, "cognitive pragmatics" or "crystallized intelligence" as knowledge- and wisdom-based abilities, comprise verbal knowledge and comprehension, autobiographical memory, emotional processes, strategies of processing and learning, and learned skills such as reading, writing, or occupational skills. These abilities remain not only stable but may be improved even until or into old age and are often able to compensate for a decline in cognitive mechanics. As a consequence of these compensatory potentials, in normal aging cognitive impairment has only a small impact on activities of daily living. Nevertheless, particularly under laboratory settings, with high demands on speed and accuracy, or in which subjects have to perform two or more tasks simultaneously, or in stressful situations, differences in performance levels between young and old subjects increase with task difficulty and/or complexity.

Contemporary Theories on Cognitive Aging

There exist different theories about the causes of cognitive impairment during aging and

the debate is still going on. General factors or common cause theories favor single biological factors to cause decline in most cognitive abilities. White matter (WM) integrity deficits or decreased signal-to-noise ratios might be responsible for a general slowing of cortical processing as indicated by increased reaction times for various cognitive tasks (general slowing hypothesis (Salthouse, 1996)). The frontal lobe hypothesis (West, 1996) states that neuronal decline in the frontal lobe, particularly the prefrontal cortex (PFC), has a major impact on cognitive impairment since functions controlled by the PFC, such as selective attention, response inhibition, and working memory, seem to be more affected by aging than functions that rely on activity in other cortical or even subcortical regions. One of the most recent theories argues that deficient modulation of neural activity by the neurotransmitter dopamine due to a decline in the frontostriatal network is a promising correlate of cognitive impairment during aging (Bäckman et al., 2000). Reduced signal-to-noise ratios due to a loss of dopamine support of the PFC may explain age effects in working memory, selective attention, inhibitory control, and other cognitive functions. More and more evidence, however, reveal that however, revealed that common causes cannot easily explain all facets of cognitive impairment during aging and that age-effects vary considerably across tasks. These task-dependent age-effects indicate that one factor is not sufficient to explain cognitive impairment during normal aging but that both common and specific factors have to be regarded.

Evidence from Functional Neuroimaging

Functional neuroimaging data reveal over- and underactivation, as compared to younger adults, in the aging cortex as well as changed activity patterns. Underactivation of the PFC is often observed in older adults with difficulties in working memory and executive control (Hedden & Gabrieli, 2004) and may be conceived as the equivalent of reduced integrity of cortical areas and neuronal circuitries. Less activity in the hippocampal formation of the mediotemporal lobe could be related to impaired recognition memory and attentional orienting, and to impaired novelty detection processes (Cabeza et al., 2004). Underactivation has also been shown for sensory cortical networks like the occipitotemporal (ventral) and visual pathway (Cabeza et al., 2004).

On the other hand, cognitive aging is also paralleled by overactivation of certain brain regions, which is particularly the case for those regions representing executive functions, motor control, and episodic, autobiographical, and working memory (Reuter-Lorenz & Lustig, 2005; Seidler et al., 2010). It has been suggested that increased activity in the PFC of older adults, as shown for a variety of tasks like face matching, lexical decision, word-pair encoding and retrieval, temporal-order memory, verbal working memory, and movement control, represents a posterior-to-anterior shift in activation (PASA) (Davis, Dennis, Daselaar, Fleck, & Cabeza, 2008) and compensates for processing deficits in the sensory or other domains of functioning. Compensatory overactivation, however, comes with costs. As described by the CRUNCH hypothesis (compensation-related utilization of neural circuits hypothesis (Reuter-Lorenz & Lustig, 2005)), the engagement of more neural circuitry at lower levels of task demands in older adults suggests that they recruit more "cognitive reserve" (Scarmeas et al., 2003) and thus are more likely to reach a limit of available resources to perform the task (DiGirolamo et al., 2001). The costs of such compensatory overactivation might be a reduction of cognitive resources available for high-demanding and more complex tasks (Grady, 2012).

Further task-specific age-effects include a decreased lateralization in activation of the PFC. For example, in young adults the left PFC is activated primarily in working memory tasks and the right PFC in visual attention tasks, whereas in older subjects increased activity in the contralateral homolog regions of the PFC can be found.

This hemispheric asymmetry reduction in older adults (HAROLD (Cabeza et al., 2004)) might be the consequence of compensation processes to enable normal cognitive functioning by recruiting contralateral resources. This view is supported by findings that asymmetry reduction mostly occurs in high-performing versus low-performing older adults or in successful versus unsuccessful trials.

On the other hand, decreased lateralization can be conceived as decreased specialization of brain processes reflecting difficulties in recruiting specialized neuronal processes (Dedifferentiation hypothesis (Li et al., 2004)). Thus, overactivation might mirror decreased inhibition and inefficient processing. Supporting evidence comes from human imaging studies, which show increased activations in perceptual areas and the anterior cingulate in tasks with conflicting conditions, and from animal experiments revealing reduced tuning strength of neurons in the visual and somatosensory cortex (Dinse, 2006). Various findings suggest, however, that changed processing strategies, in well-performing older adults, may lead to youth-like activation patterns. Based on these findings, behaviorally derived theories suggest that along with aging, a failure in top-down (self-initiated) control and regulation of activation of task-specific brain regions, such as the occipital and mediotemporal cortices, occurs (Reuter-Lorenz & Lustig, 2005).

More recently, functional connectivity data, obtained in resting state, emerge to be a valuable addition to task-related functional data, since they have the potential to reveal deeper insight in terms of the quantity/quality of the collaboration of different brain regions (Voss, Erickson et al., 2010). The analysis of the default mode network (DMN) has gained popularity within the domain of functional connectivity research. DMN describes a set of brain regions that show activity at rest and a decrease in activity during task processing (Raichle et al., 2001). It includes sites across frontal, parietal, (medial-)temporal, and visual areas such as the posterior cingulate cortex, middle frontal cortex, the lateral parietal region, and the lingual gyrus (Raichle et al., 2001). Older adults seem to have difficulties in downregulating the DMN resulting in less efficiency and smaller dynamic range of task-related processing.

Morphological Changes of the Brain

During aging, the average brain volume decreases from about 1300 g at the age of 20 to about 1150 g at the age of 80 (Brizzee, 1975; Hedman, van Haren, Schnack, Kahn, & Hulshoff, 2012). This finding suggests that the number of cortical neurons declines with age and that this process is related to cognitive impairment. However, during normal aging there is—if at all—only a modest reduction in cell number of about 10%, and it is now common sense that this decline is not significant for functional loss (Morrison & Hof, 1997). This is in contrast to patients suffering from Alzheimer's disease who, in fact, show cell loss rates of between 30% and 50% (Morrison & Hof, 1997). Accordingly, gray matter (GM) volume decrease with age has been related to a decrease in the quality and quantity of connections between neurons (Peters, 2002). Particularly, dendritic branches and spines show age-related decline. Further, a reduction of blood capillaries and glial cells contributes to brain volume decline. The latter provide a protective and supportive structure for the neurons and connect them to the blood capillaries. Besides changes in GM, also the microstructure of the WM changes with age. Density and integrity of axons, as well as their myelinization, are impaired. Axonal fibers split or show local thickening. These changes can be observed as so-called WM hyperintensities (WMH) with magnetic resonance imaging (MRI) (Raz & Rodrigue, 2006). WMH are often regarded as bases for slowed and less efficient processing of cognitive, motor, and sensory information. Even though WM and GM volume is reduced with age, there is also no general reduction of axonal extent and dendritic branching, as well as synaptic density. Thus, not the total number of neurons and their connections but the specificity of neurons and connections affected seem to be crucial for cognitive functioning.

Strongest brain volume decline is observed in the caudate nucleus (as part of the basal ganglia), the cerebellum, the hippocampus, and the PFC, and these changes are strongly correlated to deficits in executive control and memory processes. Spatial memory seems to be particularly sensitive to a loss of axodendritic synapses in the dentate gyrus. On the contrary, there is much less decline in the limbic system and occipital (visual) cortex (Park & Reuter-Lorenz, 2009; Raz & Rodrigue, 2006). Such posterior–anterior gradient in age-related structural decline has also been described for WM integrity.

Age effects also include the frontostriatal system resulting in decreased levels of the neurotransmitters dopamine, norepinephrine, and serotonin, which in turn negatively influence the functional integrity of the PFC as supposed by the dopamine theory of aging (Bäckman et al., 2000). Also, reduced neurogenesis in the hippocampus (cf. below on mechanisms) is associated with deficits in spatial cognition and memory formation (van Praag, Shubert, Zhao, & Gage, 2005). Other age-related changes on the brain include alterations in the brain hemodynamics and microvasculature. With aging, a reduction of both the general cerebral blood flow (CBF) and the increase of local CBF as correlate of brain activation, can be found. The resulting reduced hemodynamic response strength in functional brain imaging may be one cause for the cortical underactivation as measured by functional brain imaging. Interestingly, morphological changes do not inevitably and necessarily correlate with alterations in neuronal activity as measured with brain imaging methods (Raz & Lindenberger, 2011).

Cognitive and Neuronal Plasticity

The described age-related changes in brain and cognition show remarkable individual differences (interindividual variability) but also differences within a person between different functions and structures (intraindividual variability). Aging trajectories may be delayed or reveal changes in slope in both a positive and a negative direction, and reveal the plasticity of the aging process. Plasticity denotes an individual's potential for modifications, in his or her developmental trajectory, throughout the lifespan. Cognitive plasticity refers to the potential for the modifiability of the trajectory of cognitive development within one individual (Baltes, Lindenberger, & Staudinger, 1998). Brain plasticity denotes the fact that the brain shows structural and/or functional changes when people are faced with new or altering demands (Lövdén et al., 2010; Staudinger, 2012) or as a reaction to a loss of neural resources as a consequence of lesions, diseases, or even aging. The latter type of neural plasticity is strongly linked to compensational mechanisms in the aging brain. The degree of plasticity depends on the available individual (physiological, psychological) or contextual (social, cultural) developmental resources (cf. Staudinger, Marsiske, & Baltes, 1993). The high inter- and intraindividual variability of cognitive impairment during aging indicates that besides genetic predisposition, individual lifestyle is a crucial factor. Cognitive training programs and active social involvement may stimulate functional plasticity and therefore compensation for cortical atrophy, WM damage, and neurotransmitter dysfunction (Reuter-Lorenz & Lustig, 2005). Recently, there has been public debate between groups of leading neuroscientists, psychologists, and other experts on the effectiveness of cognitive training interventions (Stanford Center on Longevity, consensus paper, 2014; open letter by more than 100 neuroscientists and psychologists in response to this consensus paper, 2014). At least, there seems to be a consensus that physical activity is another—probably even more—important and successful possibility to stimulate cognitive plasticity. In the scaffolding theory of cognitive aging (STAC), Park and Reuter-Lorenz (2009) integrated most recent

theories on cognitive aging and compensatory plasticity into one model. Within this model, aging-related neural changes have three main effects: (1) functional deterioration of neural systems, as a consequence, (2) cognitive functions, and (3) these changes introduce compensatory scaffolding mechanisms on the neural level with positive effects on cognitive function. This scaffolding may be enhanced by learning and training, engagement, or exercise (Park & Reuter-Lorenz, 2009; Reuter-Lorenz & Park, 2014).

METHODOLOGICAL APPROACHES TO INVESTIGATE THE EXERCISE–COGNITION RELATIONSHIP

The importance of physical activity for improvement and preservation of cognitive abilities in healthy older adults has repeatedly been examined since the mid-twentieth century. However, the studies differ noticeably in their measurement instruments, their study designs (e.g., problems of sample selectivity due to lack of random assignment), and the type of exercise.

Study Designs

Different methodological approaches exist to investigate the chronic exercise–cognition relationship in older adults. Cross-sectional studies assess fitness levels without a training intervention and compare either different fitness or age groups. The disadvantage of cross-sectional studies is that the conclusion of a causal relationship is questionable, since the correlation can be driven in both directions (e.g., better physical fitness leads to larger brain volume, or higher cognitive and brain function enables physical activity and better fitness). To find out more about causal relationships between two or more variables, randomized controlled trials (RCT) or controlled interventional study designs are necessary. In these studies, (controlled) fitness interventions over several weeks or months are performed in an experimental-control group design, and changes in cognition and eventually brain or other parameters are assessed. A third approach is the longitudinal or epidemiological study in which participation in exercise sessions or the physical activity behavior is assessed by questionnaires and related to outcomes in brain and cognition over an even longer period of time. Here the prospective approach attempts, for example, to assess lifestyle behaviors like physical activity over many years and to determine how these behaviors might affect rates of cognitive and brain decline. This approach allows assessment of behavior over a long period of time but, similar to the cross-sectional analysis, the conclusion of a causal relationship is questionable. Further, in this design physical activity is often assessed with rather unspecific questionnaires.

Types and Assessment of Exercise

Fitness and physical activity can be assessed by subjective and objective measures. Subjective measures of physical fitness and exercise are mainly standardized questionnaires. Questionnaires further differ in length and information acquired, and range between one-item (e.g., "How many hours do you spend on physical activities in a typical week?") and many-item questionnaires. From these questionnaires, activity levels can be quantified in terms of calories or metabolic equivalents, or as the number, frequency, and duration of performed activities. A variety of objective measures also exist. Cardiovascular, also referred to as aerobic or cardiorespiratory, fitness usually is assessed in terms of maximum volume of oxygen uptake ($\dot{V}O_2\ max$) or peak oxygen uptake ($\dot{V}O_2\ peak$) values (Wasserman, Sue, Stringer, & Whipp, 2005), or by lactate-step tests by (spiro-)ergometry, or by walking tests protocol (e.g., Rockport 1-Mile Walk Test), where highly automated movements like walking or cycling are performed. Even strength or coordinative motor

fitness can easily and objectively be assessed in laboratory settings by use of, for example, motor tests like the chair-stand test or one-leg stance, respectively (Rikli & Jones, 2001; Ekdahl, Jarnlo, & Andersson, 1989).

THE PHYSICAL ACTIVITY–BRAIN AND COGNITION–RELATIONSHIP

Since the 1990s, four meta-analyses (Angevaren, Aufdemkampe, Verhaar, Aleman, & Vanhees, 2008; Colcombe & Kramer, 2003; Heyn, Johnson, & Kramer, 2008; Hindin & Zelinski, 2012), as well as a number of review articles (e.g., Hillman et al., 2008; Voelcker-Rehage & Niemann, 2013), concerning the influence of physical activity on cognitive functions in healthy older adults have been published. For example, Colcombe and Kramer (2003) analyzed 18 intervention studies (1966–2001) on the influence of physical activity on cognition in adults, 55 years of age and older. They found the highest benefit of physical activity on executive control functions. Independent of cognitive task assessed, training parameters like session duration or scheduling, and sample characteristics, physical activity enhanced cognitive performance by 0.5 standard deviations. The effect of physical activity was influenced by the length, extent, and type of intervention. In this section, we will detail the differential effects of different types of exercise and fitness on brain and cognitive function. Interestingly, systematic fitness training leads to improved cognitive functioning even in seniors who have been rather inactive previously.

Cardiovascular Exercise and Fitness

Most exercise paradigms have utilized cardiovascular exercise, also referred to as aerobic or cardiorespiratory exercise, where highly automated movements like walking or cycling are performed. In a longitudinal study, Zhu et al. (2014) investigated whether greater cardiorespiratory fitness was associated with better cognitive function in a sample of 2747 participants between 18 and 30 years at recruitment in 1985–1986 (Community-based Coronary Artery Risk Development in Young Adults Study). Better verbal memory and faster psychomotor speed at ages 43–55 years were clearly associated with better cardiorespiratory fitness 25 years earlier. Data were controlled for race, sex, age, education, and clinical center. Similarly, large-scale prospective studies have shown cardiovascular fitness to be positively related to cognitive performance. Barnes, Yaffe, Satariano, and Tager (2003) revealed that cardiorespiratory fitness assessed at baseline predicted cognitive performance 6 years later in a variety of cognitive domains (working memory, processing speed, attention, and general mental functioning).

The great progress in neurophysiological methods, electrophysiology, and especially brain imaging led to an extensive popularity of brain research during the last decade. Colcombe et al. (2004) first conducted a MRI study suggesting that after cardiovascular training, older adults applied cognitive resources more effectively and cognition was improved. Using a modified flanker task (where irrelevant stimuli have to be inhibited in order to respond to a relevant target stimulus) they showed significantly higher brain activation, for physically active as compared to inactive older participants, in different frontal and parietal regions, and significantly lower activity in the anterior cingulate cortex (ACC). The same was true for older adults participating in a 6-month aerobic exercise intervention (walking training) as compared to a stretching and toning control group (Colcombe et al., 2004). Higher frontal activation may contribute to better performance in a range of high-level cognitive functions including attentional selection (Casey et al., 2000), working memory (Lie, Specht, Marshall, & Fink, 2006), task switching (Kim, Cilles, Johnson, & Gold, 2012), and inhibitory control (Botvinick, Braver, Barch, Carter, & Cohen, 2001; Casey et al., 2000). Parietal

structures that revealed higher activation in this study are mainly associated with visuospatial processing, but also with language and tactile processing. Less activation in the ACC, on the contrary, indicates reduced response conflict (Botvinick et al., 2001).

Other studies have confirmed the findings by Colcombe et al. (2004). Interestingly, some studies also revealed differential activation patterns. Following a 12-month aerobic exercise intervention, Voelcker-Rehage and coauthors (Voelcker-Rehage, Godde, & Staudinger, 2010, 2011) found lower activation in the PFC but higher activation in temporal regions during performance of the incongruent flanker trials in high- compared to low-fit older adults. Similarly, cognitive training studies revealed reduced frontal activation after training in at least some regions that had been activated prior to training (for a review, see Lustig, Shah, Seidler, & Reuter-Lorenz, 2009). As introduced above, in the cognitive aging literature these contradictory findings are explained twofold: on the one hand, increasing task load is associated with increased recruitment (until a critical point after which a decrease occurs) and training may serve to increase the engagement of task-relevant regions. On the other hand, increased efficiency in the processes subserved by these regions might lead to reduced activations, i.e., less need for resources. Moreover, higher activation in frontal brain areas, in older as compared to young adults, has often been interpreted as compensation for age-related changes (for a review, see Reuter-Lorenz & Lustig, 2005). Thus, reduced activation after training might indicate a more youth-like or efficient brain and in turn less need for compensation. Thus, over-activation might be reduced in high-fit (Prakash et al., 2011) or trained (Liu-Ambrose, Nagamatsu, Voss, Khan, & Handy, 2012) older adults for less demanding, but also for challenging (Voelcker-Rehage et al., 2010, 2011), tasks. Lustig et al. (2009) stated that the association of extra activation (reflecting compensatory processes) with good performance in older adults often occurs in single-session studies before the task is well practiced. They predicted that this pattern of activation changes over the course of training in a way that older adults' processing would become more youth-like, such that reliance on additional processes would decrease. Differences in activation patterns in high- and low-fit participants or following a training intervention may derive from task differences in cognitive load, practice across the course of the flanker task execution, and sample characteristics. Another explanation for differences in activation patterns seen in high- versus low-fit participants is the use of different strategies while completing cognitive tasks (less optimal reactive control strategy in low-fit individuals and proactive strategy in high-fit persons; see Voss et al., 2011). Thus, both increased and decreased activation patterns may turn out to reflect physical activity-induced executive control improvement in older adults. Overall, physical activity seems to interact with brain activation during performance of executive control tasks; particularly in frontal and parietal areas (cf. Figure 1). Depending on sample and type of task, physical activity may free up cognitive resources, to increase the engagement of task-relevant regions or to change performance strategies leading either to increased or to reduced, but more efficient, activations in task-relevant areas.

Other studies focused on memory performance. Here higher physical activity levels were paralleled by higher brain activation in the hippocampus and parahippocampal gyrus as well as with activity in the frontal lobe during spatial learning or memory tasks, in high-fit participants (Holzschneider, Wolbers, Röder, & Hötting, 2012; Smith et al., 2011). As both the frontal lobe and hippocampus are especially vulnerable to age-related functional changes (e.g., Grady, Springer, Hongwanishkul, McIntosh, & Winocur, 2006), one might assume that higher cardiovascular fitness or aerobic training are associated with better functioning of these regions.

Connectivity data provide the potential to reveal task-independent measures of brain function. Findings suggest that higher cognitive performance in high-fit older adults, or after an aerobic intervention, might be based on a higher functional connectivity within and between task-relevant brain regions at rest. Voss and colleagues (Voss, Prakash et al., 2010) could indeed demonstrate that higher functional connectivity of the DMN was related to better executive control function. Whether other cognitive domains would also benefit from exercise-induced higher functional connectivity is currently not clear. As functional connectivity of the hippocampus with several other brain regions (Burdette et al., 2010) also seems to be enhanced through cardiovascular activity, memory function may also be positively influenced. To confirm this suggestion additional research is needed.

On the level of brain anatomy, again, Colcombe et al. (2003) were the first to examine the association between brain volume and cardiovascular fitness. They found that age-related decline in brain volume in frontal, parietal, and temporal cortices was attenuated as a function of cardiovascular fitness (Colcombe et al., 2003).

So far, brain regions that are associated with cardiovascular fitness and/or training differ between studies. A positive relationship has been found between cardiovascular training and frontal areas (e.g., ACC) (Bugg & Head, 2011; Colcombe et al., 2003, 2006; Flöel et al., 2010; Ruscheweyh et al., 2011; Weinstein et al., 2012), the temporal lobe (Colcombe et al., 2006) or hippocampus (Erickson et al., 2011; Niemann, Godde, & Voelcker-Rehage, 2014). However, there are also studies that did not find any relationship between GM volume and a physical activity parameter (Rosano et al., 2010; Smith et al., 2011).

In comparison to GM volume, less research has been done on physical activity and WM. Some research on WM changes revealed a positive association with physical activity (Colcombe et al., 2003, 2006; Ho et al., 2011). The hypothesis that aerobic fitness is significantly

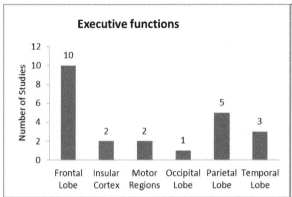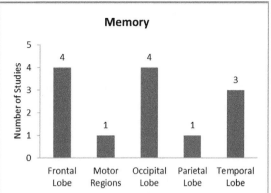

FIGURE 1   Number of studies per associated brain area that found associations between metabolic exercise (cardiovascular exercise and resistance training) and brain activity during execution of an executive control task (left, 10 studies in total) and a memory task (right, 5 studies in total) in children and adults (cf. Voelcker-Rehage & Niemann, 2013).

related to specific prefrontal regions of the brain is also partly supported by fiber tracking results of Johnson, Kim, Clasey, Bailey, and Gold (2012), longitudinal data of Voss et al. (2012), and findings by Marks, Katz, Styner, and Smith (2011). However, the majority of studies did not find a relationship between WM volume and physical activity (Erickson et al., 2010; Flöel et al., 2010; Gordon et al., 2008; Peters et al., 2009, for young adults; Ruscheweyh et al., 2011; Smith et al., 2011). An association between WM volume and cognitive performance is also not established so far, although a positive association with information processing speed is highly likely (Jacobs et al., 2011). The first studies on WM integrity suggest that a high aerobic fitness level may attenuate age-related decline in myelination of axons in portions of the corpus callosum (Johnson et al., 2012) and cingulum (Marks et al., 2007, 2011). However, in terms of WM lesions and hyperintensities, physical activity does not seem to influence age-related changes positively (for an exception in men, see Sen et al., 2012).

There is also increasing evidence for fitness-related modulations of cognitive event-related potentials (ERPs). Age-related amplitude reduction and slowing of the P3 component may be attenuated by physical activity (Fong, Chi, Li, &

Chang, 2014; Hillman, Weiss, Hagberg, & Hatfield, 2002; Kamijo et al., 2009). According to Daffner et al. (2011), the usually observed reduction in P3 amplitude with aging is associated with fewer available resources due to preceding processing steps that share a common pool of resources. A cross-sectional study confirmed that in older adults participating in light and moderate aerobic exercise, at least three times per week within the past 6 months, the early (sensory processing-related) N1 amplitudes were increased as compared to a control group (Chang, Huang, Chen, & Hung, 2013). The authors interpreted their data as showing that the exercise group was able to engage more attentional resources for the early stimulus encoding processes. Further, several studies reported a latency reduction of the P3 (Kamijo, Nishihira, Higashiura, & Kuroiwa, 2007), and N2 and P2 (attention-related ERP components) (Ozkaya et al., 2005) ERP components following only 9–12 weeks of aerobic exercise in older adults, suggesting an improvement in processing speed. Given the diversity of experimental designs and testing parameters together with the small number of studies, particularly in older adults, the effects of exercise interventions on ERP components, as markers of cognitive functioning and attentional control, require further investigation.

In order to understand the potential role of brain-derived neurotrophic factor (BDNF) in exercise-induced improvement in brain function, some studies with older adults examined the effects of cardiovascular exercise on cognitive function and BDNF concentrations. Despite using different cognitive measurements, most of the studies showed that cognitive functioning was improved and serum BDNF concentration increased after chronic aerobic exercise (Erickson et al., 2011; Griffin et al., 2011; Ruscheweyh et al., 2011). These studies provide some evidence that peripheral BDNF is associated with exercise-induced enhancement in brain function (cf. Huang, Larsen, Ried-Larsen, Moller, & Andersen, 2014, for a review).

Effects of Other Types of Exercise and Fitness

Fewer studies have investigated other types of exercise, such as coordination or resistance exercise. Similar to cardiovascular fitness, resistance exercise (resistance training) affects metabolic and energetic processes (Bogdanis, 2012) and to some extent intramuscular coordination (Young, 2006). Unlike metabolic exercise, coordination training comprises exercises for fine and gross motor body coordination such as balance, eye–hand coordination, and leg–arm coordination, as well as spatial orientation and reaction to moving objects/persons (Voelcker-Rehage et al., 2011). Coordination training induces less change in energy metabolism than cardiovascular and resistance exercise. Instead, coordinative movements require perceptual and higher-level cognitive processes, such as attention, that are essential for mapping sensation to action and ensuring anticipatory and adaptive aspects of coordination. Thus, changes induced by coordination exercise are likely to be related to changes in information processing (Monno, Temprado, Zanone, & Laurent, 2002) and cognitive tasks that demand, besides attention, the ability to handle visual and spatial information (Smith & Baltes, 1999).

By contrast, perceptual and higher-level cognitive processes are less relevant in highly automated movements, such as walking or cycling, as used in cardiovascular exercise. Recently, dancing has come into focus as an attractive leisure activity among older adults. Dancing is a multimodal type of physical activity that addresses cardiovascular as well as coordinative and cognitive demands, and it is difficult to disentangle effects of cardiovascular from other fitness effects in these studies. Below, however, we will combine dancing and coordination training and contrast them to studies on resistance training.

Resistance Training

Although some studies have reported conflicting findings on the role of resistance training in preventing cognitive decline with age, other studies have demonstrated a beneficial effect of such training on specific cognitive measures. A recent review of studies, with healthy older adults (Chang, Pan, Chen, Tsai, & Huang, 2012), revealed overall positive effects of resistance training on cognitive functions including information-processing speed, attention, memory formation, and specific types of executive function. In comparing resistance-exercise training with other types of exercise, such as flexibility, toning, relaxation, calisthenics, and even endurance exercises (Brown, Liu-Ambrose, Tate, & Lord, 2009; Cancela Carral & Ayan Perez, 2007; Ozkaya et al., 2005), some studies have shown that resistance training produces equivalent or even higher performance increases in specific cognitive functions. Chang et al. (2012) noted, however, that studies of higher quality (e.g., single-blinded RCT, larger sample sizes, etc.) yielded inconsistent findings and that some of the results only concerned within-group differences. Further, resistance training seems to show clear dose–response effects (cf. below on dose–response effects of fitness interventions).

The beneficial effects of resistance training were supported by functional MRI and ERP data. Liu-Ambrose et al. (2012) showed that 12 months of resistance training, twice a week (once a week revealed no effect), led to higher activation in the left middle temporal gyrus and the left anterior insula extending into the lateral orbitofrontal cortex during incongruent flanker trials. No correlation of change in brain activation with change in flanker performance was found. Nagamatsu, Handy, Hsu, Voss, and Liu-Ambrose (2012) found that a resistance training program, twice a week over 26 weeks, improved memory performance (associative memory task) and led to higher activation of the right lingual and occipital-fusiform gyri and frontal areas, probably indicating changes in (visual) processing strategy. Ozkaya et al. (2005) investigated the effect of a 9-week (three times per week) moderate resistance training program on ERP components in older adults. After training, the latencies of early (sensory) and late (cognitive) frontocentral ERP components decreased and their amplitudes increased as compared to control groups doing endurance or no training. These data suggest that resistance training might facilitate early sensory processing and cognitive functioning in older individuals.

Motor Coordinative Fitness and Related Exercises

A recent study investigated the impact of different types of motor activity training (contemporary dance, fall prevention, and Tai Chi) on attentional control in older adults (Coubard, Duretz, Lefebvre, Lapalus, & Ferrufino, 2011). Six months of contemporary dance training (60 min, once per week) was able to improve cognitive flexibility in 59- to 89-year-olds (Coubard et al., 2011). As the low-intensity intervention (Tai Chi) has not shown to facilitate cognitive function, one could argue that the more aerobic character of contemporary dance led to cognitive benefits in the older participants. However, another study has shown better cognitive performances in participants (mean age 79 years) after 2 months (40 min, once per week) of Tai Chi coordination training (Kwok et al., 2011). Furthermore, an ERP study on task-switching revealed that P3 amplitudes were increased and reaction times reduced in older adults with a history of regularly participating in Tai Chi as compared to sedentary older adults (Fong et al., 2014). The limited behavioral findings in Coubard's study (only for contemporary dance) may be explained by the quite selective cognitive measurements. Coubard and coworkers only assessed executive functions and did not include a task for visual–spatial performance, which has been shown to be facilitated by coordinative fitness and training by Voelcker-Rehage et al. (2010, 2011). Here motor fitness was related to more efficient cognitive processing, indicated by less cortical activation in the superior and middle frontal cortex. In addition, motor fitness was also related to higher activation of the right inferior frontal–posterior parietal network indicative of improved processing and integration of visuospatial information (Voelcker-Rehage et al., 2010, 2011). They also revealed that after a 12-month coordination training (60 min, three times per week) brain activation levels during a flanker task increased particularly in the right inferior frontal gyrus and the superior parietal cortex, which form part of the so-called visuospatial attention network (Corbetta & Shulman, 2002; De Graaf, Roebroeck, Goebel, & Sack, 2009), as well as in the thalamus and caudate body. These latter subcortical structures are more important for process automation without conscious control (Aron et al., 2003). This fits well with other findings showing that high-fit older adults need fewer dorsolateral prefrontal (cognitive) resources for movement control than low-fit participants (Godde & Voelcker-Rehage, 2010).

Furthermore, structural brain data revealed older adults with higher levels of motor fitness, or participating in a 12-month coordination training program, revealed larger volumes of the hippocampus (Niemann, Godde, & Voelcker-Rehage, 2014) and the basal ganglia nuclei caudate, putamen, and globus pallidus (Niemann, Godde, Staudinger, & Voelcker-Rehage, 2014). Larger volume of the basal ganglia, in addition, moderated the relationship between higher motor fitness levels and executive control performance. Also, episodic memory was improved after stretching and coordination training (Hötting et al., 2012). These authors investigated middle-aged adults between 40 and 56 years of age, participating either in aerobic endurance training (cycling) or stretching and coordination training twice a week for 6 months (third group: control group).

With regard to dancing, a first prospective study, by Verghese et al. (2003), showed leisure dancing to be associated with a reduced risk of developing dementia. A few years later, however, a cross-sectional study did not confirm this result. Adults aged 80 years, who had engaged in many years of nonprofessional dancing activity, did not demonstrate better cognitive performance in the domains of memory and executive control in comparison to nondancers (Verghese, 2006). Similarly, a pilot study with 13 healthy, older women did not reveal improvements in cognitive performance measured by the Mini Mental Status Examination, after a 12-week jazz dance intervention (Alpert et al., 2009). Recent studies, again, show more positive results. Older adults, with long-term dancing experience, showed better cognitive performance in the domains of fluid intelligence and attention in comparison to age-matched inactive controls (Kattenstroth, Kolankowska, Kalisch, & Dinse, 2010). Furthermore, the same research group observed increasing performance in an overall index of cognition (comprised of concentration, attention, and nonverbal learning) in older adults participating in a 6-month dancing intervention (Kattenstroth, Kalisch, Holt, Tegenthoff, & Dinse, 2013). A first neuroimaging study revealed only small effects, of long-term senior dance experience, in frontal GM volume in the right medial frontal gyrus and the left middle frontal gyrus (Niemann, Godde, & Voelcker-Rehage, under review).

Physical Activity Behavior

Several, particularly longitudinal and cross-sectional, studies do not differentiate between different types of exercise, but investigate physical activity behavior in general. Also these studies demonstrated a positive association between exercise on cognition. In nationally representative samples of noninstitutionalized persons aged 50 years and older, across 11 European countries (Austria, Germany, Sweden, Denmark, Switzerland, the Netherlands, Belgium, France, Spain, Italy, and Greece), Aichberger et al. (2010) reported that individuals who participated in any type of regular physical activity showed less cognitive decline after 2.5 years, especially when they engaged in vigorous activities more than once a week. Other prospective longitudinal studies across the lifespan revealed that being more physically active, especially as a teenager, is beneficial for cognitive performance in late adulthood (Jedrziewski, Lee, & Trojanowski, 2007, for a revision; Middleton, Barnes, Lui, & Yaffe, 2010). Similarly, Yaffe, Barnes, Nevitt, Lui, and Covinsky (2001) showed physical activity in late adulthood (blocks walked per week) to be positively related to cognitive performance in older ages. Hillman and colleagues (Hillman, Belopolsky, Snook, Kramer, & McAuley, 2004) conducted an ERP study to look at the relationship between physical activity and attentional control in older and younger adults. Physical activity status did not influence behavioral (flanker) performance. P3 amplitude measures, however, revealed a more frontally distributed brain activation in highly and moderately active older adults during the incongruent condition of the flanker task, as compared to sedentary older adults. Thus, physically active older adults may compensate for sensory and cognitive deficits by recruiting frontal areas relevant for attentional control (Polich, 1997). In a sample of middle-aged adults an association between higher physical activity levels and improved attentional control, as well as increased N2 amplitudes, were shown (Winneke, Godde, Reuter, Vieluf, & Voelcker-Rehage, 2012). This increase in N2 amplitude can be interpreted as improved conflict monitoring (Yeung, Botvinick, & Cohen, 2004).

CELLULAR AND MOLECULAR CORRELATES OF EXERCISE–COGNITION INTERACTION IN OLDER ADULTS

Different mechanisms are discussed to underlie the chronic exercise–cognition relationship on the cellular level (e.g., increased neurogenesis and synaptogenesis as well as increased neuronal survival, and facilitation of angiogenesis in the capillary system and thus improved blood supply) and on the molecular level (e.g., facilitation of gene expression and thus production of growth factors such as BDNF and IGF-1, increased neurotransmitter (e.g., dopamine) production and effectivity, decreased corticol levels as indicator of stress resistance and reactivity). However, studies on older adults, particularly on humans, are rare and most evidence today comes from animal experiments. Nevertheless, it is thought that the mechanisms identified in animals apply to the human system as well. The general results of animal research on the exercise–cognition interaction were summarized earlier. Here we focus, in particular, on results and mechanisms either specific for older individuals or gained with older samples, where available.

Cellular Level

Research regarding the underlying mechanisms of physical activity on cognitive performance and brain function, and anatomy also focus on the investigation of cardiovascular activity. One mechanism thought to be responsible for cognitive benefits after cardiovascular training is the generation of new neurons (neurogenesis) in the dentate gyrus, which is a part of the hippocampus (van Praag, Kempermann, & Gage, 1999). The hippocampus is crucial for learning and memory, and displays one of only two brain regions (the other is the olfactory bulb) that until now have been revealed to show neurogenesis across the whole lifespan. Generally, voluntary cardiovascular activity has been a very robust stimulus for adult hippocampal neurogenesis in rodents from birth to oldest age (Kannangara et al., 2011; Kronenberg et al., 2003; van Praag et al., 1999, 2005). Running can, at least in part, reverse the massive decrease in neurogenesis observed in aged animals (Kronenberg et al., 2006). In old animals, the usually observed age-related decline in hippocampal neurogenesis was halved after 1 month of cardiovascular training and associated with better spatial learning abilities, indicating beneficial effects of cardiovascular activity even in late adulthood (Kronenberg et al., 2006; van Praag et al., 2005).

In more detail, cardiovascular activity in adult rodents was shown to promote the proliferation of new neurons in the dentate gyrus (van Praag et al., 1999; for a review, see also Fabel & Kempermann, 2008). Moreover, physical activity at a young age seems to promote changes in neurogenesis that persist over the long term, which is important for our understanding of the modulation of neurogenesis by exercise with older age. Merkley, Jian, Mosa, Tan, and Wojtowicz (2014) were able to demonstrate that the number of proliferating and differentiating neuronal precursors is stable beyond the initial weeks postrunning, and that the rate of neuronal maturation and survival during a 4-week period after cell division was enhanced up to 11 months of age (the end of the study period). It could be concluded that high chronic cardiovascular exercise levels, across the lifespan, provide higher neuron numbers in the hippocampus later in life and thus might buffer usual age-related decline. Evidence for this hypothesis is still missing, however.

Studies focusing on neurogenesis in the hippocampus also indicate that different types of activity stimulate the generation of new neurons in different ways (van Praag et al., 1999). As described above, cardiovascular activity induces the proliferation of newborn cells in the hippocampus to a large extent. In contrast, an "enriched environment" which, with its highly varied and appealing cage arrangement (e.g., tubes, ropes, and obstacles), promotes increased sensory, cognitive, and motor experiences and might be termed an animal homolog of human coordinative exercise. It also facilitated the proliferation of newborn cells (approx. 50% of cardiovascular training effects) but led to a higher degree to the integration and survival of the neurons (van Praag et al., 1999). Thus, for the integration and the survival of newly generated neurons, additional stimuli seem to be crucial (for a review, see also Kempermann et al., 2010). Kempermann, Kuhn, and Gage (1997) reported that mice living in an enriched environment had more new hippocampal granule cells than controls. This pro-neurogenic effect of environmental enrichment was even maintained into old age. Even though at old age the activity-induced proliferation of precursor cells was much greater than at young age, the overall absolute level was much lower (Kempermann, 2002). Continued environmental stimulation and motor activity beginning early, in contrast, maintained the potential but is obviously dependent on the level of precursor cell proliferation (and the number of precursor cells) at the time when training starts. The consequence from this observation is that a lack of activity early in life can only be partly compensated for later (van Praag et al., 2005). Thus, not only cardiovascular exercise but also other forms of interventions induce neuronal plasticity.

Additional plastic changes after activity-induced motor learning and environmental enrichment include synaptogenesis, dendritic and glial cell hypertrophy, and myelinization (for a review, see Markham & Greenough, 2004). Black and colleagues (Anderson et al., 1994; Black, Isaacs, Anderson, Alcantara, & Greenough, 1990) provided evidence that acrobatic training induces the generation of new synapses and new glia cells in the cerebellar cortex. Their findings are confirmed by Kleim, Lussnig, Schwarz, Comery, and Greenough (1996) who also found acrobatic training to increase synaptogenesis and dendritic hypertrophy in motor cortex and cerebellar regions (Kleim et al., 1996). With respect to glia changes, Thomas, Dennis, Bandettini, and Johansen-Berg (2012) argued that growth of astrocytes and other glial cells (important part of the neuropil) strongly depends on motor learning. Because of their role in giving metabolic support to the neurons, they are also affected by cardiovascular exercise, but to a smaller extent. A study by Anderson et al. (1994) indeed revealed different effects of cardiovascular and motor exercise in the adult rat cerebellum. While overall density of glia cells was similar between groups, glia volume per Purkinje cell was increased for the motor learning group only (Anderson et al., 1994). Furthermore, the motor activity-based components of the morphological brain changes seem to be more stable than the cardiovascular activity-induced ones (Markham & Greenough, 2004), an indicator of the different maintenance periods for both types of physical activity.

Angiogenesis, after cardiovascular activity, has been shown in adult rodents, for example in the motor cortex (Kleim, Cooper, & VandenBerg, 2002), the cerebellum (Black et al., 1990), the basal ganglia (Ding et al., 2004), and the hippocampus (Cotman & Berchtold, 2002). Higher density of cerebral microvessels were found also for older rats and associated with upregulation of angiogenic mRNA expression (Ding, Vaynman, Akhavan, Ying, & Gomez-Pinilla, 2006). Induction of angiogenesis seems to start after only 3 days of repeated cardiovascular exercise. Black and colleagues (Anderson et al., 1994; Black et al., 1990) provided evidence that while cardiovascular training increases capillary density (see above), the motor-based training initiated blood vessel growth only to maintain the diffusion distance. Shear stress on the walls of the capillaries and hypoxia has been shown to play a key role in angiogenesis (Makanya, Hlushchuk, & Djonov, 2009). This might explain why angiogenesis is observed mainly with cardiovascular rather than motor-related exercise.

Potential associations between increased angiogenesis and better brain function after physical exercise might be based on different mechanisms. In humans, decreased functional brain activations after cardiovascular training might be caused by better oxygen supply, probably via a higher density of capillaries and/or shorter diffusion distances for the oxygen, and are associated with a higher $\dot{V}O_2$ max (Colcombe et al., 2004; Voelcker-Rehage et al., 2011). In the same vein, after a 3-month cardiovascular training program, cerebral blood volume (CBV) in the hippocampus of middle-aged adults was enhanced, pointing to a better vascularization of the tissue, and was in line with better memory performance of the participants (Pereira et al., 2007). In line with these findings, after a stretching and relaxation intervention, a decreased $\dot{V}O_2$ max was associated with increased brain activation (Voelcker-Rehage et al., 2011).

Changes in the vascular pattern, like the occlusion of small cerebral vessels, local ischemic changes, and leakage of ventricular and blood plasma fluid into the WM, might underlie age-related WMH associated with impaired function (Burzynska et al., 2014). Here, as a secondary effect, angiogenesis, induced by physical activity, might act in a protective or rehabilitative manner. Studies with aging rats using the calcium antagonist nimodipine confirmed a strong association between the regulation of brain vascular patterns and hemodynamics (De Jong, Nyakas,

Schuurman, & Luiten, 1993) with motor activity, maintenance of synaptic contacts in the dentate gyrus, and sensorimotor brain aging and plasticity (Dinse, 2005). A recent study demonstrated the superior role of angiogenesis, in comparison with neurogenesis, for learning and memory performance in exercising animals (Kerr, Steuer, Pochtarev, & Swain, 2010), and revealed findings that point to the fact that neurogenesis alone is not critical for better memory performances.

Although most of the effects described above are found in young adult animal models and have so far not been much investigated in older samples, it is plausible that similar or the same mechanisms apply to aging humans and underlie the alterations in GM and WM found after physical activity interventions (Voelcker-Rehage & Niemann, 2013). A recent study using a small sample of macaques replicated the increase in vascular volume fraction in the motor cortex, with 5 months of daily treadmill exercise. Interestingly, this effect was found only in older animals (15–17 years old), while middle-aged animals (10–12 years old) showed no change in vascular volume fraction (Thomas et al., 2012).

In addition to enhancing motor activity and motor learning, enriched environments also provide cognitive stimulation and animals are usually kept in small groups to cultivate social contact. The role of social interaction, as additional stimuli for facilitation of neurogenesis following cardiovascular or other types of motor activity, is still debated (Kannangara et al., 2011). In a study with adult marmosets, Kozorovitskiy et al., (2005) revealed that although a month-long stay in a complex environment enhanced the length and complexity of the dendritic tree and increased dendritic spine density and synaptic protein levels in the hippocampus and PFC, no differences were detected between the brains of marmosets living alone or as pairs in the complex environments. Thus, perhaps the enhanced sensory, cognitive, and motor experience (in other terms coordinative motor activity) plays the crucial role as additional stimuli.

Pereira et al. (2007) performed one of the first studies combining animal and human experiments and exposed rodents to a similar cardiovascular training regime as humans. In both animals and humans, the cardiovascular training induced the same enhancement of CBV in the dentate gyrus and better learning performance. After a 3-month cardiovascular training with middle-aged adults, CBV in the dentate gyrus of the hippocampus was enhanced and coupled with improved $\dot{V}O_2$ max, suggesting better vascularization of this tissue. CBV was in line with better declarative memory performance of the participants (Pereira et al., 2007). In young rats, enhanced CBV in the dentate gyrus and better learning performance were also associated with neurogenesis (Pereira et al., 2007) and it might be assumed that similar beneficial mechanisms are at work in the brains of older adults.

Importantly, what we know about activity-dependent changes from animal experiments is about effects on the microscopic level, whereas human imaging methods reveal effects on the more macroscopic level of GM and WM structure and volume. Although, based on the fact that more than 50% of GM are composed by the neuropil (axons, dendrites, and glia cells) and 20% by cell bodies, it is plausible that neural changes described above contribute to GM volume changes associated with physical activity. It is not easily possible to draw conclusions on which microscopic structural changes within GM cause an increase or decrease in volume (Thomas et al., 2012).

Molecular Level

Very promising factors on the molecular level that could mediate the activity-induced changes on the microscopic morphological (cell) level and related improvements in cognitive functioning are neurotrophins such as BDNF, vascular endothelial growth factor (VEGF), nerve growth factor (NGF), and insulin-like growth factor (IGF-1). These neurotrophins and growth factors promote the regeneration of blood vessels (angiogenesis), neurons (neurogenesis), and synapses (synaptogenesis) as well as the formation of dendrites and neuron body growth and thus have an impact on brain structure and cognitive functioning.

After only a few days (2–7 days) of cardiovascular activity the release of BDNF (Cotman & Berchtold, 2002; Ding et al., 2006; Gomez-Pinilla, Vaynman, & Ying, 2008; Neeper, Gomez-Pinilla, Choi, & Cotman, 1996), VEGF (Lou, Liu, Chang, & Chen, 2008), NGF (Neeper et al., 1996), and IGF-1 (Cotman & Berchtold, 2002; Ding et al., 2006) is enhanced across brain regions (e.g., hippocampus, cerebellum, cortex, and basal ganglia) in rodents (Gomez-Pinilla et al., 2008). BDNF is age dependent and less pronounced in older individuals (Adlard, Perreau, & Cotman, 2005; see also Mora, Segovia, & del Arco, 2007 for a review). After cardiovascular training interventions, in older humans, higher basal levels of BDNF are measured (Erickson et al., 2011; Ruscheweyeh et al., 2011). Similarly, in young adults, BDNF release is a response to an acute bout of cardiovascular activity and is higher in more cardiovascular fit individuals than in less-trained ones (Zoladz et al., 2008). This could also account for the positive effects of regular physical activity on cognitive performances in older persons. Also, resistance exercise training results in an increase of IGF-1 or BDNF levels (Ahlskog, Geda, Graff-Radford, & Petersen, 2011). Long-term resistance training elevated serum IGF-1 concentrations in two prospective, controlled trials (Borst et al., 2001; Cassilhas et al., 2007), but not in another (Borst, Vincent, Lowenthal, & Braith, 2002). Results for BDNF are also mixed for older adults and mostly nonsignificant for young adults. Coelho et al. (2012) performed an uncontrolled trial with 20 older women, 71 years of age, undertaking resistance training of knee extensors and flexors, 3 times per week for 10 weeks, and revealed increased plasma BDNF after the training program. In contrast, Levinger et al. (2008) performed an RCT, with 49 untrained men and women with a mean age of 50.1 years, at 40–50% of 1 repetition maximum (RM) (week 1), 50–85% of 1 RM (weeks 2–10), 3 times per week for 10 weeks, with no effect on plasma BDNF. It remains open if the age differences between the participants in these two studies are causal for the different results. Combined, increasing evidence suggests that the release of neurochemical factors, which are supposed to be crucial for brain structure and cognitive performance and which show age-related decline, is modifiable by physical activity.

Also neurotransmitters (e.g., dopamine; DA) are assumed to influence the association between physical activity and improved cognitive functioning. In animal studies, regular physical exercise suggests an increase in the DA concentration (Hattori, Naoi, & Nishino, 1994; Sutoo & Akiyama, 2003). After 6 months of physical training, older adults revealed increased plasma concentrations of DA (Ruscheweyh et al., 2011), although no mediation effect on better memory performance could be demonstrated. DA is a central player in cognition in healthy and pathological brains (Bäckman et al., 2000; Dash, Moore, Kobori, & Runyan, 2007; Rieckmann et al., 2011). Large concentrations of DA receptors are found in the PFC, a key region for executive control (Dash et al., 2007) but also in striatal regions (Mukherjee et al., 2002), which support tasks that involve cognitive flexibility (Erickson et al., 2010). DA losses with increasing age have repeatedly been shown for D2 (Bäckman et al., 2000; Mukherjee et al., 2002) and D1 receptors (Rieckmann et al., 2011). These changes mediate age-related cognitive decline (Erixon-Lindroth et al., 2005). Li, Lindenberger, & Bäckman et al. (2010) proposes an inverted-U curve with regards to lifespan development of DA functioning and cognition, with a peak in early and middle adulthood. Interestingly, Asghar, George, and Lokhandwala (2007) reported that exercise facilitates antioxidant defense in old rats and therefore is able to reduce D1 receptor dysfunction induced

by oxidative stress, inflammation, and proteinuria. To sum up, DA is relevant for cognitive performance and is age sensitive (the release decreases and receptor density declines). However, DA levels seem to be modifiable by physical activity (the release increases). One could speculate that physical activity might shift older adults leftwards on the inverted-U curve toward the peak of DA functioning.

Currently, few studies have investigated the cross-link between lifestyle factors such as physical activity, cognitive performance, and the catechol-O-methyltransferase (COMT) polymorphisms. Stroth et al. (2010) revealed that in a sample of healthy adults (17–47 years of age), COMT val homozygotes improved their cognitive performance (Stroop task, dots-mixed task) after 17 weeks of running training, to a greater extent compared to met allele carriers. Similarly, investigating the effect of a 6-month multicomponent training program (cognitive, aerobic, and activities of daily living), in healthy older adults, Pieramico et al. (2012) revealed the greatest exercise benefits in COMT val/val and val/met allele carriers (and DRD3 ser9gly carriers) (for other lifestyle factors and the relation to cognitive performance and COMT, cf. Loughhead et al. (2009) for smoking and Witte, Jansen, Schirmacher, Young, and Flöel (2010) for dietary interventions). Voelcker-Rehage, Jeltsch, Godde, Becker, and Staudinger (2015) revealed a positive influence of overall fitness, and an interactive effect of fitness and COMT polymorphisms on flanker accuracy performance. Val/val carriers revealed the highest positive correlation between fitness and cognition suggesting that particularly val/val allele carriers benefit from exercise by improved cognitive functioning whereas met/met carriers already perform closer at their optimum level.

Endocrinological changes (especially glucocorticoids) have also been established as a factor that facilitates the positive effects of acute and/or chronic exercise on cognitive functioning.

Similar to DA, cortisol seems to have an impact on cognitive performance, but with a different pattern; high levels of cortisol impair cognitive functioning. An inverted-U-shaped relation has been reported between acutely measured cortisol and executive functioning for young subjects (Lupien, Gillin, & Hauger, 1999). Thus, negative effects of a high cortisol level or stress treatment have been described (Schoofs, Preuss, & Wolf, 2008; Wolf, Schommer, Hellhammer, McEwen, & Kirschbaum, 2001), while mild stress or an intermediate cortisol level are supposed to result in enhanced executive functioning (Schoofs et al., 2008). Age is accompanied by increasing basal cortisol concentrations and flatter circadian profiles (Kudielka, Schmidt-Reinwald, Hellhammer, Schurmeyer, & Kirschbaum, 2000 for contradictory results; cf. Tortosa-Martinez & Clow, 2012, for a review). Over a 3- to 6-year-long period, Lupien et al. (1996) observed increasing cortisol levels in approximately 80% of their older adults sample (24 h measure), with 23.5% revealing high and 56.8% demonstrating moderate increases. HPA axis reactivity in response to a stressor also showed a positive relationship with age that was stronger for women than for men (cf. Otte et al., 2005 for a meta-analysis). In addition, higher basal levels of cortisol in older adults are associated with neurostructural changes and cognitive impairment (Csernansky et al., 2006; Lupien et al., 1998). Positive effects of higher physical fitness (due to chronic exercise) were seen in a lower acute release of cortisol in response to an acute stressor (Puterman et al., 2011 for older adults) as well as in decreased levels of basal cortisol (Nabkasorn et al., 2006, after 12 weeks cardiovascular training in young women). Baker et al. (2010) revealed increased concentrations of cortisol in older adults, with mild cognitive impairment, after 6 months of physical training. Also Korkushko, Frolkis, and Shatilo (1995) showed lower HPA axis reactivity in response to acute exercise for trained older individuals in comparison to their less-fit counterparts. On the contrary, Heaney, Carroll, and Phillips (2013) revealed

that acute exercise performed on a regular basis over years does not appear to influence resting hormone levels. However, they also did not find differences among older adults in relation to their exercise training status. Also, Traustadottir, Bosch, and Matt (2005) reported no differences in cortisol levels between high- and average-fit older women. Again, missing effects might be due to too low exercise intensities or durations. A chronic exercise-dependent hormonal link to cognition has still not been tested but is highly suggested (Tortosa-Martinez & Clow, 2012).

DOSE–RESPONSE RELATIONS

Less is known about the optimal amount, length, and intensity of physical activity sessions to improve cognitive functioning in older adults. Moderate physical activity, 2–3 times per week of a minimum of 30 min, has been proven to show positive effects, and after only a few weeks of exercise. Furthermore, older adults reveal almost linear changes across 12 months of cardiovascular or coordinative exercise training on brain functioning, indicating that long-term training might lead to even more positive effects (Voelcker-Rehage et al., 2011). When examining the dose–response relationship, focusing on intensity and frequency of resistance training, intervention designs in loads of 60–80% 1RM with approximately 7 movements in 2 sets separated by 2 min of rest at least twice per week for 2–12 months (usually 6 months), could positively affect cognition.

LIMITATIONS IN STUDIES INVESTIGATING THE EXERCISE–COGNITION RELATIONSHIP IN OLDER ADULTS

A limitation of studies on age-related differences that use a young–old comparison is that the age comparison is based on a mixed cross-sectional design. Although performance changes due to practice are measured longitudinally in a pre-/posttest design, the age comparisons are limited to age-related averages and evidence about long-term changes at the individual level is not available. Particularly in older age, individuals vary considerably in their individual performance level and probably also in their performance gains due to exercise. In addition, cross-sectional studies that cover a wide age span—whether it be a young–old comparison, or a comparison of multiple age groups across the lifespan—may not only represent age-related differences but also reflect cohort effects.

A further limitation of aging studies is the sample selectivity. In the case of aging populations, the generalizability of results can be impaired in the ways that the average level of functional competence and/or learning is overestimated as individuals with lower levels of functioning are less likely to participate in a study than individuals with higher levels of functioning. Furthermore, it is undeniable that the incidence of disability in older groups progressively increases. One of the ways other than age that two or more age groups in cross-sectional research could be different is the incidence of disabilities that could impact performance. In general, one can assume that all studies described above appoint comprehensive screenings prior to the start of the study in order to eliminate participants with health-related or cognitive impairments that could potentially influence the outcome of the study.

If we focus on the exercise–cognition relationship in older age, we need to take into consideration that this is a very broad age range covering about 30 years. Cognitive change in the very old, the so-called fourth age, provides special features and constraints: sensory and motor limitations, increasing multimorbidity, and limits to independence are common characteristics of people at the end of their lives, and might also affect their cognitive abilities. However, chronic physical activity seems to have the potential not only to improve health and abilities in general but also to ameliorate age-related changes in brain and cognition, and thus might help older adults to prolong an independent lifestyle.

References

Adlard, P. A., Perreau, V. M., & Cotman, C. W. (2005). The exercise-induced expression of BDNF within the hippocampus varies across life-span. *Neurobiology of Aging, 26,* 511–520.

Ahlskog, J. E., Geda, Y. E., Graff-Radford, N. R., & Petersen, R. C. (2011). Physical exercise as a preventive or disease-modifying treatment of dementia and brain aging. *Mayo Clinic Proceedings, 86,* 876–884.

Aichberger, M. C., Busch, M. A., Reischies, F. M., Ströhle, A., Heinz, A., & Rapp, M. A. (2010). Effect of physical inactivity on cognitive performance after 2.5 years of follow-up: longitudinal results from the Survey of Health, Ageing, and Retirement (SHARE). *GeroPsych: The Journal of Gerontopsychology and Geriatric Psychiatry, 23,* 7–15.

Alpert, P. T., Miller, S. K., Wallmann, H., Havey, R., Cross, C., Chevalia, T., et al. (2009). The effect of modified jazz dance on balance, cognition, and mood in older adults. *Journal of the American Academy of Nurse Practitioners, 21,* 108–115.

Anderson, B. J., Li, X., Alcantara, A. A., Isaacs, K. R., Black, J. E., & Greenough, W. T. (1994). Glial hypertrophy is associated with synaptogenesis following motor-skill learning, but not with angiogenesis following exercise. *Glia, 11,* 73–80.

Angevaren, M., Aufdemkampe, G., Verhaar, H. J., Aleman, A., & Vanhees, L. (2008). Physical activity and enhanced fitness to improve cognitive function in older people without known cognitive impairment. *Cochrane Database Systematic Reviews, 3,* CD005381. http://dx.doi.org/10.1002/14651858.

Aron, A. R., Schlaghecken, F., Fletcher, P. C., Bullmore, E. T., Eimer, M., Barker, R., et al. (2003). Inhibition of subliminally primed responses is mediated by the caudate and thalamus: evidence from functional MRI and Huntington's disease. *Brain, 126,* 713–723.

Asghar, M., George, L., & Lokhandwala, M. F. (2007). Exercise decreases oxidative stress and inflammation and restores renal dopamine D1 receptor function in old rats. *American Journal of Physiology, 293,* F914–F919.

Bäckman, L., Ginovart, N., Dixon, R. A., Robins-Wahlin, T.-B., Wahlin, A., Halldin, C., et al. (2000). Age-related cognitive deficits mediated by changes in the striatal dopamine system. *American Journal of Psychiatry, 157,* 635–637.

Baker, L. D., Frank, L. L., Foster-Schubert, K., Green, P. S., Wilkinson, C. W., McTiernan, A., et al. (2010). Effects of aerobic exercise on mild cognitive impairment: a controlled trial. *Archives of Neurology, 67,* 71–79.

Baltes, P. B., Dittmann-Kohli, F., & Dixon, R. A. (1984). New perspectives on the development of intelligence in adulthood: toward a dual-process conception and a model of selective optimization with compensation. In P. B. Baltes, & O. G. Brim, Jr. (Eds.), *Life-span development and behavior* (Vol. 6) (pp. 33–76). New York: Academic Press.

Baltes, P. B., Lindenberger, U., & Staudinger, U. M. (1998). Life-span theory in developmental psychology. In R. M. Lerner (Ed.), *Handbook of child development Theoretical models of human development: Vol. 1.* (pp. 1029–1143). New York: Wiley & Sons.

Barnes, D. E., Yaffe, K., Satariano, W. A., & Tager, I. B. (2003). A longitudinal study of cardiorespiratory fitness and cognitive function in healthy older adults. *Journal of American Geriatrics Society, 51,* 459–465.

Black, J. E., Isaacs, K. R., Anderson, B. J., Alcantara, A. A., & Greenough, W. T. (1990). Learning causes synaptogenesis, whereas motor activity causes angiogenesis, in cerebellar cortex of adult rats. *Proceedings of the National Academy of Sciences of the United States of America, 87,* 5568–5572.

Bogdanis, G. C. (2012). Effects of physical activity and inactivity on muscle fatigue. *Frontiers in Physiology, 3,* 142. http://dx.doi.org/10.3389/fphys.2012.00142.

Borst, S. E., De Hoyos, D. V., Garzarella, L., Vincent, K., Pollock, B. H., Lowenthal, D. T., et al. (2001). Effects of resistance training on insulin-like growth factor-I and IGF binding proteins. *Medicine and Science in Sports and Exercise, 33,* 648–653.

Borst, S. E., Vincent, K. R., Lowenthal, D. T., & Braith, R. W. (2002). Effects of resistance training on insulin-like growth factor and its binding proteins in men and women aged 60 to 85. *Journal of American Geriatrics Society, 50,* 884–888.

Botvinick, M., Braver, T., Barch, D., Carter, C., & Cohen, J. (2001). Conflict monitoring and cognitive control. *Psychological Review, 108,* 624–652.

Brizzee, K. R. (1975). Gross morphometric analyses and quantitative histology of the aging brain. *Neurobiology of Aging, 16,* 401–423.

Brown, A. K., Liu-Ambrose, T., Tate, R., & Lord, S. R. (2009). The effect of group-based exercise on cognitive performance and mood in seniors residing in intermediate care and self-care retirement facilities: a randomised controlled trial. *British Journal of Sports Medicine, 43,* 608–614.

Bugg, J. M., & Head, D. (2011). Exercise moderates age-related atrophy of the medial temporal lobe. *Neurobiology of Aging, 32,* 506–514.

Burdette, J. H., Laurienti, P. J., Espeland, M. A., Morgan, A., Telesford, Q., Vechlekar, C. D., et al. (2010). Using network science to evaluate exercise-associated brain changes in older adults. *Frontiers in Aging Neuroscience, 2,* 23. http://dx.doi.org/10.3389/fnagi.2010.00023.

Burzynska, A. Z., Chaddock-Heyman, L., Voss, M. W., Wong, C. N., Gothe, N. P., Olson, E. A., et al. (2014). Physical activity and cardiorespiratory fitness are beneficial for white matter in low-fit older adults. *PLoS One, 9,* e107413.

Cabeza, R., Daselaar, S. M., Dolcos, F., Prince, S. E., Budde, M., & Nyberg, L. (2004). Task-independent and task-specific age effects on brain activity during working memory, visual attention and episodic retrieval. *Cerebral Cortex, 14,* 364–375.

Cancela Carral, J. M., & Ayan Perez, C. (2007). Effects of high-intensity combined training on women over 65. *Gerontology, 53,* 340–346.

Casey, B., Thomas, K., Welsh, T., Badgaiyan, R., Eccard, C., Jennings, J., et al. (2000). Dissociation of response conflict, attentional selection, and expectancy with functional magnetic resonance imaging. *Proceedings of the National Academy of Sciences of the United States of America, 97,* 8728–8733.

Cassilhas, R. C., Viana, V. A., Grassmann, V., Santos, R. T., Santos, R. F., Tufik, S., et al. (2007). The impact of resistance exercise on the cognitive function of the elderly. *Medicine and Science in Sports and Exercise, 39,* 1401–1407.

Chang, Y. K., Huang, C. J., Chen, K. F., & Hung, T. M. (2013). Physical activity and working memory in healthy older adults: an ERP study. *Psychophysiology, 50,* 1174–1182.

Chang, Y. K., Pan, C. Y., Chen, F. T., Tsai, C. L., & Huang, C. C. (2012). Effect of resistance-exercise training on cognitive function in healthy older adults: a review. *Journal of Aging and Physical Activity, 20,* 497–517.

Coelho, F. M., Pereira, D. S., Lustosa, L. P., Silva, J. P., Dias, J. M., Dias, R. C., et al. (2012). Physical therapy intervention (PTI) increases plasma brain-derived neurotrophic factor (BDNF) levels in non-frail and pre-frail elderly women. *Archives of Gerontology and Geriatrics, 54,* 415–420.

Colcombe, S. J., Erickson, K. I., Raz, N., Webb, A. G., Cohen, N. J., McAuley, E., et al. (2003). Aerobic fitness reduces brain tissue loss in aging humans. *Journals of Gerontology, Series A: Biological Sciences and Medical Sciences, 58,* 176–180.

Colcombe, S. J., Erickson, K. I., Scalf, P. E., Kim, J. S., Prakash, R., McAuley, E., et al. (2006). Aerobic exercise training increases brain volume in aging humans. *Journals of Gerontology, Series A: Biological Sciences and Medical Sciences, 61,* 1166–1170.

Colcombe, S., & Kramer, A. F. (2003). Fitness effects on the cognitive function of older adults: a meta-analytic study. *Psychological Science, 14,* 125–130.

Colcombe, S. J., Kramer, A. F., Erickson, K. I., Scalf, P., McAuley, E., Cohen, N. J., et al. (2004). Cardiovascular fitness, cortical plasticity, and aging. *Proceedings of the National Academy of Sciences of the United States of America, 101,* 3316–3321.

Corbetta, M., & Shulman, G. L. (2002). Corbetta and Shulman (2002). Control of goal-directed and stimulus-driven attention in the brain. *Nature Reviews Neurosciences, 3,* 201–215.

Cotman, C. W., & Berchtold, N. C. (2002). Exercise: a behavioral intervention to enhance brain health and plasticity. *Trends in Neurosciences, 25,* 295–301.

Coubard, O. A., Duretz, S., Lefebvre, V., Lapalus, P., & Ferrufino, L. (2011). Practice of contemporary dance improves cognitive flexibility in aging. *Frontiers in Aging Neuroscience, 3,* 13.

Csernansky, J. G., Dong, H., Fagan, A. M., Wang, L., Xiong, C., Holtzman, D. M., et al. (2006). Plasma cortisol and progression of dementia in subjects with alzheimer-type dementia. *American Journal of Psychiatry, 163,* 2164–2169.

Daffner, K. R., Chong, H., Sun, X., Tarbi, E. C., Riis, J. L., McGinnis, S. M., et al. (2011). Mechanisms underlying age- and performance-related differences in working memory. *Journal of Cognitive Neuroscience, 23,* 1298–1314.

Dash, P. K., Moore, A. N., Kobori, N., & Runyan, J. D. (2007). Molecular activity underlying working memory. *Learning and Memory, 14,* 554–563.

Davis, S. W., Dennis, N. A., Daselaar, S. M., Fleck, M. S., & Cabeza, R. (2008). Que PASA? the posterior-anterior shift in aging. *Cerebral Cortex, 18,* 1201–1209.

De Graaf, T. A., Roebroeck, A., Goebel, R., & Sack, A. T. (2009). Brain network dynamics underlying visuospatial judgment: an fMRI connectivity study. *Journal of Cognitive Neuroscience, 22,* 2012–2026.

De Jong, G. I., Nyakas, C., Schuurman, T., & Luiten, P. G. M. (1993). Aging-related alterations in behavioral activation and cerebrovascular integrity in rats are dose-dependently influenced by nimodipine. *Neurosciences Research Communications, 12,* 1–8.

DiGirolamo, G., Kramer, A., Barad, V., Cepeda, N., Weissman, D., Milham, M., et al. (2001). General and task-specific frontal lobe recruitment in older adults during executive processes: a fMRI investigation of task-switching. *NeuroReport, 12,* 2065–2071.

Ding, Y., Li, J., Luan, X., Ding, Y. H., Lai, Q., Rafols, J. A., et al. (2004). Exercise pre-conditioning reduces brain damage in ischemic rats that may be associated with regional angiogenesis and cellular overexpression of neurotrophin. *Neuroscience, 124,* 583–591.

Ding, Q., Vaynman, S., Akhavan, M., Ying, Z., & Gomez-Pinilla, F. (2006). Insulin-like growth factor I interfaces with brain-derived neurotrophic factor-mediated synaptic plasticity to modulate aspects of exercise-induced cognitive function. *Neuroscience, 140,* 823–833.

Dinse, H. R. (2005). Treating the aging brain: cortical reorganization and behavior. *Acta Neurochirurgica, 93*(Suppl.), 79–84.

Dinse, H. R. (2006). Cortical reorganization in the aging brain. *Progress in Brain Research, 157,* 57–80.

Ekdahl, C., Jarnlo, G. B., & Andersson, S. I. (1989). Standing balance in healthy subjects. evaluation of a quantitative test battery on a force platform. Scandinavian Journal of Rehabilitation Medicine, 21(4), 187–195.

Erickson, K. I., Raji, C. A., Lopez, O. L., Becker, J. T., Rosano, C., Newman, A. B., et al. (2010). Physical activity predicts gray matter volume in late adulthood: the Cardiovascular Health Study. *Neurology, 75,* 1415–1422.

Erickson, K. I., Voss, M. W., Prakash, R. S., Basak, C., Szabo, A., Chaddock, L., et al. (2011). Exercise training increases size of hippocampus and improves memory. *Proceedings of the National Academy of Sciences of the United States of America, 108,* 3017–3022.

Erixon-Lindroth, N., Farde, L., Wahlin, T. B., Sovago, J., Halldin, C., & Bäckman, L. (2005). The role of the striatal dopamine transporter in cognitive aging. *Psychiatry Research, 138,* 1–12.

Fabel, K., & Kempermann, G. (2008). Physical activity and the regulation of neurogenesis in the adult and aging brain. *NeuroMolecular Medicine, 10,* 59–66.

Flöel, A., Ruscheweyh, R., Kruger, K., Willemer, C., Winter, B., Volker, K., et al. (2010). Physical activity and memory functions: are neurotrophins and cerebral gray matter volume the missing link? *NeuroImage, 49,* 2756–2763.

Fong, D. Y., Chi, L. K., Li, F., & Chang, Y. K. (2014). The benefits of endurance exercise and Tai Chi Chuan for the task-switching aspect of executive function in older adults: an ERP study. *Frontiers in Aging Neuroscience, 6,* 295. http://dx.doi.org/10.3389/fnagi.2014.00295.

Godde, B., & Voelcker-Rehage, C. (2010). More automation and less cognitive control of imagined walking movements in high versus low fit older adults. *Frontiers in Aging Neuroscience, 2,* 139. http://dx.doi.org/10.3389/fnagi.2010.00139.

Gomez-Pinilla, F., Vaynman, S., & Ying, Z. (2008). Brain-derived neurotrophic factor functions as a metabotrophin to mediate the effects of exercise on cognition. *European Journal of Neuroscience, 28,* 2278–2287.

Gordon, B. A., Rykhlevskaia, E. I., Brumback, C. R., Lee, Y., Elavsky, S., Konopack, J. F., et al. (2008). Neuroanatomical correlates of aging, cardiopulmonary fitness level, and education. *Psychophysiology, 45,* 825–838.

Grady, C. (2012). The cognitive neuroscience of ageing. *Nature Reviews Neurosciences, 13,* 491–505.

Grady, C., Springer, M., Hongwanishkul, D., McIntosh, A., & Winocur, G. (2006). Age related changes in brain activity across the adult lifespan. *Journal of Cognitive Neuroscience, 18,* 227–241.

Griffin, É. W., Mullally, S., Foley, C., Warmington, S. A., O'Mara, S. M., & Kelly, A. M. (2011). Aerobic exercise improves hippocampal function and increases BDNF in the serum of young adult males. *Physiology and Behavior, 104,* 934–941.

Hattori, S., Naoi, M., & Nishino, H. (1994). Striatal dopamine turnover during treadmill running in the rat: relation to the speed of running. *Brain Research Bulletin, 35,* 41–49.

Heaney, J. L., Carroll, D., & Phillips, A. C. (2013). DHEA, DHEA-S and cortisol responses to acute exercise in older adults in relation to exercise training status and sex. *Age, 35,* 395–405.

Hedden, T., & Gabrieli, J. D. (2004). Insights into the ageing mind: a view from cognitive neuroscience. *Nature Reviews Neurosciences, 5*, 87–96.

Hedman, A. M., van Haren, N. E., Schnack, H. G., Kahn, R. S., & Hulshoff, P. H. (2012). Human brain changes across the life span: a review of 56 longitudinal magnetic resonance imaging studies. *Human Brain Mapping, 33*(8), 1987–2002.

Heyn, P. C., Johnson, K. E., & Kramer, A. F. (2008). Endurance and strength training outcomes on cognitively impaired and cognitively intact older adults: a meta-analysis. *Journal of Nutrition, Health and Aging, 12*, 401–409.

Hillman, C. H., Belopolsky, A. V., Snook, E. M., Kramer, A. F., & McAuley, E. (2004). Physical activity and executive control: implications for increased cognitive health during older adulthood. *Research Quarterly for Exercise and Sport, 75*, 176–185.

Hillman, C. H., Erickson, K. I., & Kramer, A. F. (2008). Be smart, exercise your heart: exercise effects on brain and cognition. *Nature Reviews Neurosciences, 9*, 58–65.

Hillman, C. H., Weiss, E. P., Hagberg, J. M., & Hatfield, B. D. (2002). The relationship of age and cardiovascular fitness to cognitive and motor processes. *Psychophysiology, 39*, 303–312.

Hindin, S. B., & Zelinski, E. M. (2012). Extended practice and aerobic exercise interventions benefit untrained cognitive outcomes in older adults: a meta-analysis. *Journal of American Geriatrics Society, 60*, 136–141.

Ho, A. J., Raji, C. A., Becker, J. T., Lopez, O. L., Kuller, L. H., Hua, X., et al. (2011). The effects of physical activity, education, and body mass index on the aging brain. *Human Brain Mapping, 32*, 1371–1382.

Holzschneider, K., Wolbers, T., Röder, B., & Hötting, K. (2012). Cardiovascular fitness modulates brain activation associated with spatial learning. *NeuroImage, 59*, 3003–3014.

Hommel, B., Li, K. Z., & Li, S. C. (2004). Visual search across the life span. *Developmental Psychology, 40*, 545–558.

Hötting, K., Reich, B., Holzschneider, K., Kauschke, K., Schmidt, T., Reer, R., et al. (2012). Differential cognitive effects of cycling versus stretching/coordination training in middle-aged adults. *Health Psychology, 31*, 145–155.

Huang, T., Larsen, K. T., Ried-Larsen, M., Moller, N. C., & Andersen, L. B. (2014). The effects of physical activity and exercise on brain-derived neurotrophic factor in healthy humans: a review. *Scandinavian Journal of Medicine and Science in Sports, 24*, 1–10.

Jacobs, H. I., Leritz, E. C., Williams, V. J., Van Boxtel, M. P., Elst, W. V., Jolles, J., et al. (2011). Association between white matter microstructure, executive functions, and processing speed in older adults: the impact of vascular health. *Human Brain Mapping, 34*, 77–95.

Jedrziewski, M. K., Lee, V. M., & Trojanowski, J. Q. (2007). Physical activity and cognitive health. *Alzheimer's Dementia, 3*, 98–108.

Johnson, N. F., Kim, C., Clasey, J. L., Bailey, A., & Gold, B. T. (2012). Cardiorespiratory fitness is positively correlated with cerebral white matter integrity in healthy seniors. *NeuroImage, 59*, 1514–1523.

Kamijo, K., Hayashi, Y., Sakai, T., Yahiro, T., Tanaka, K., & Nishihira, Y. (2009). Acute effects of aerobic exercise on cognitive function in older adults. *Journals of Gerontology, Series B: Psychological Sciences and Social Sciences, 64*, 356–363.

Kamijo, K., Nishihira, Y., Higashiura, T., & Kuroiwa, K. (2007). The interactive effect of exercise intensity and task difficulty on human cognitive processing. *International Journal of Psychophysiology, 65*, 114–121.

Kannangara, T. S., Lucero, M. J., Gil-Mohapel, J., Drapala, R. J., Simpson, J. M., Christie, B. R., et al. (2011). Running reduces stress and enhances cell genesis in aged mice. *Neurobiology of Aging, 32*, 2279–2286.

Kattenstroth, J. C., Kalisch, T., Holt, S., Tegenthoff, M., & Dinse, H. R. (2013). Six months of dance intervention enhances postural, sensorimotor, and cognitive performance in elderly without affecting cardio-respiratory functions. *Frontiers in Aging Neuroscience, 5*, 5. http://dx.doi.org/10.3389/fnagi.2013.00005.

Kattenstroth, J. C., Kolankowska, I., Kalisch, T., & Dinse, H. R. (2010). Superior sensory, motor, and cognitive performance in elderly individuals with multi-year dancing activities. *Frontiers in Aging Neuroscience, 2*, 31. http://dx.doi.org/10.3389/fnagi.2010.00031.

Kempermann, G. (2002). Why new neurons? Possible functions for adult hippocampal neurogenesis. *Journal of Neurosciences, 22*, 635–638.

Kempermann, G., Fabel, K., Ehninger, D., Babu, H., Leal-Galicia, P., Garthe, A., et al. (2010). Why and how physical activity promotes experience-induced brain plasticity. *Frontiers in Neuroscience, 4*, 189. http://dx.doi.org/10.3389/fnins.2010.00189.

Kempermann, G., Kuhn, H. G., & Gage, F. H. (1997). More hippocampal neurons in adult mice living in an enriched environment. *Nature, 386*, 493–495.

Kerr, A. L., Steuer, E. L., Pochtarev, V., & Swain, R. A. (2010). Angiogenesis but not neurogenesis is critical for normal learning and memory acquisition. *Neuroscience, 171*, 214–226.

Kim, C., Cilles, S. E., Johnson, N. F., & Gold, B. T. (2012). Domain general and domain preferential brain regions associated with different types of task switching: a meta-analysis. *Human Brain Mapping, 33*, 130–142.

Kleim, J. A., Cooper, N. R., & VandenBerg, P. M. (2002). Exercise induces angiogenesis but does not alter movement representations within rat motor cortex. *Brain Research, 934*, 1–6.

Kleim, J. A., Lussnig, E., Schwarz, E. R., Comery, T. A., & Greenough, W. T. (1996). Synaptogenesis and Fos expression in the motor cortex of the adult rat after motor skill learning. *Journal of Neuroscience, 16*, 4529–4535.

Korkushko, O. V., Frolkis, M. V., & Shatilo, V. B. (1995). Reaction of pituitary-adrenal and autonomic nervous systems to stress in trained and untrained elderly people. *Journal of the Autonomic Nervous System, 54,* 27–32.

Kozorovitskiy, Y., Gross, C. G., Kopil, C., Battaglia, L., McBreen, M., Stranahan, A. M., et al. (2005). Experience induces structural and biochemical changes in the adult primate brain. *Proceedings of the National Academy of Sciences of the United States of America, 102*(48), 17478–17482.

Kronenberg, G., Bick-Sander, A., Bunk, E., Wolf, C., Ehninger, D., & Kempermann, G. (2006). Physical exercise prevents age-related decline in precursor cell activity in the mouse dentate gyrus. *Neurobiology of Aging, 27,* 1505–1513.

Kronenberg, G., Reuter, K., Steiner, B., Brandt, M. D., Jessberger, S., Yamaguchi, M., et al. (2003). Subpopulations of proliferating cells of the adult hippocampus respond differently to physiologic neurogenic stimuli. *Journal of Comparative Neurology, 467,* 455–463.

Kudielka, B. M., Schmidt-Reinwald, A. K., Hellhammer, D. H., Schurmeyer, T., & Kirschbaum, C. (2000). Psychosocial stress and HPA functioning: no evidence for a reduced resilience in healthy elderly men. *Stress, 3,* 229–240.

Kwok, T. C., Lam, K. C., Wong, P. S., Chau, W. W., Yuen, K. S., Ting, K. T., et al. (2011). Effectiveness of coordination exercise in improving cognitive function in older adults: a prospective study. *Clinical Interventions in Aging, 6,* 261–267.

Levinger, I., Goodman, C., Matthews, V., Hare, D. L., Jerums, G., Garnham, A., et al. (2008). BDNF, metabolic risk factors, and resistance training in middle-aged individuals. *Medicine and Science in Sports and Exercise, 40,* 535–541.

Li, S. C., Lindenberger, U., & Bäckman, L. (2010). Dopaminergic modulation of cognition across the life span. *Neuroscience and Biobehavioral Reviews, 34,* 625–630.

Li, S. C., Lindenberger, U., Hommel, B., Aschersleben, G., Prinz, W., & Baltes, P. B. (2004). Transformations in the couplings among intellectual abilities and constituent cognitive processes across the life span. *Psychological Science, 15,* 155–163.

Lie, C., Specht, K., Marshall, J., & Fink, G. (2006). Using fMRI to decompose the neural processes underlying the Wisconsin Card Sorting Test. *NeuroImage, 30,* 1038–1049.

Liu-Ambrose, T., Nagamatsu, L. S., Voss, M. W., Khan, K. M., & Handy, T. C. (2012). Resistance training and functional plasticity of the aging brain: a 12-month randomized controlled trial. *Neurobiology of Aging, 33,* 1690–1698.

Lou, S. J., Liu, J. Y., Chang, H., & Chen, P. J. (2008). Hippocampal neurogenesis and gene expression depend on exercise intensity in juvenile rats. *Brain Research, 1210,* 48–55.

Loughead, J., Wileyto, E. P., Valdez, J. N., Sanborn, P., Tang, K., Strasser, A. A., et al. (2009). Effect of abstinence challenge on brain function and cognition in smokers differs by COMT genotype. *Molecular Psychiatry, 14,* 820–826.

Lövdén, M., Bäckman, L., Lindenberger, U., Schaefer, S., & Schmiedek, F. (2010). A theoretical framework for the study of adult cognitive plasticity. *Psychological Bulletin, 136,* 659–676.

Lupien, S., Lecours, A. R., Schwartz, G., Sharma, S., Hauger, R. L., Meaney, M. J., et al. (1996). Longitudinal study of basal cortisol levels in healthy elderly subjects: evidence for subgroups. *Neurobiology of Aging, 17,* 95–105.

Lupien, S. J., Gillin, C. J., & Hauger, R. L. (1999). Working memory is more sensitive than declarative memory to the acute effects of corticosteroids: a dose-response study in humans. *Behavioral Neuroscience, 113,* 420–430.

Lupien, S. J., de Leon, M., de Santi, S., Convit, A., Tarshish, C., Nair, N. P., et al. (1998). Cortisol levels during human aging predict hippocampal atrophy and memory deficits. *Nature Neuroscience, 1,* 69–73.

Lustig, C., Shah, P., Seidler, R., & Reuter-Lorenz, P. A. (2009). Aging, training, and the brain: a review and future directions. *Neuropsychology Review, 19,* 504–522.

Makanya, A. N., Hlushchuk, R., & Djonov, V. G. (2009). Intussusceptive angiogenesis and its role in vascular morphogenesis, patterning, and remodeling. *Angiogenesis, 12,* 113–123.

Markham, J. A., & Greenough, W. T. (2004). Experience-driven brain plasticity: beyond the synapse. *Neuron Glia Biology, 1,* 351–363.

Marks, B. L., Katz, L. M., Styner, M., & Smith, J. K. (2011). Aerobic fitness and obesity: relationship to cerebral white matter integrity in the brain of active and sedentary older adults. *British Journal of Sports Medicine, 45,* 1208–1215.

Marks, B. L., Madden, D. J., Bucur, B., Provenzale, J. M., White, L. E., Cabeza, R., et al. (2007). Role of aerobic fitness and aging on cerebral white matter integrity. *Annals of the New York Academy of Sciences, 1097,* 171–174.

Merkley, C. M., Jian, C., Mosa, A., Tan, Y. F., & Wojtowicz, J. M. (2014). Homeostatic regulation of adult hippocampal neurogenesis in aging rats: long-term effects of early exercise. *Frontiers in Neuroscience, 8,* 174. http://dx.doi.org/10.3389/fnins.2014.00174.

Middleton, L. E., Barnes, D. E., Lui, L. Y., & Yaffe, K. (2010). Physical activity over the life course and its association with cognitive performance and impairment in old age. *Journal of American Geriatrics Society, 58,* 1322–1326.

Monno, A., Temprado, J. J., Zanone, P. G., & Laurent, M. (2002). The interplay of attention and bimanual coordination dynamics. *Acta Psychologica, 110,* 187–211.

Mora, F., Segovia, G., & del Arco, A. (2007). Aging, plasticity and environmental enrichment: structural changes and neurotransmitter dynamics in several areas of the brain. *Brain Research Reviews, 55,* 78–88.

Morrison, J. H., & Hof, P. R. (1997). Life and death of neurons in the aging brain. *Science, 278,* 412–419.

Mukherjee, J., Christian, B. T., Dunigan, K. A., Shi, B., Narayanan, T. K., Satter, M., et al. (2002). Brain imaging of 18F-fallypride in normal volunteers: blood analysis, distribution, test-retest studies, and preliminary assessment of sensitivity to aging effects on dopamine D-2/D-3 receptors. *Synapse, 46*, 170–188.

Nabkasorn, C., Miyai, N., Sootmongkol, A., Junprasert, S., Yamamoto, H., Arita, M., et al. (2006). Effects of physical exercise on depression, neuroendocrine stress hormones and physiological fitness in adolescent females with depressive symptoms. *European Journal of Public Health, 16*, 179–184.

Nagamatsu, L. S., Handy, T. C., Hsu, C. L., Voss, M., & Liu-Ambrose, T. (2012). Resistance training promotes cognitive and functional brain plasticity in seniors with probable mild cognitive impairment. *Archives of Internal Medicine, 172*, 666–668.

Neeper, S. A., Gomez-Pinilla, F., Choi, J., & Cotman, C. W. (1996). Physical activity increases mRNA for brain-derived neurotrophic factor and nerve growth factor in rat brain. *Brain Research, 726*, 49–56.

Niemann, C., Godde, B., Staudinger, U. M., & Voelcker-Rehage, C. (2014). Exercise-induced changes in basal ganglia volume and cognition in older adults. *Neuroscience, 281C*, 147–163.

Niemann, C., Godde, B., & Voelcker-Rehage, C. (2014). Not only cardiovascular, but also coordinative exercise increases hippocampal volume in older adults. *Frontiers in Aging Neuroscience, 6*, 170. http://dx.doi.org/10.3389/fnagi.2014.00170.

Niemann, C., Godde, B., & Voelcker-Rehage, C. Senior dance experience, cognitive performance and brain volume in older females, under review.

Open Letter to the Stanford Center on Longevity. (2014). http://www.cognitivetrainingdata.org/.

Otte, C., Hart, S., Neylan, T. C., Marmar, C. R., Yaffe, K., & Mohr, D. C. (2005). A meta-analysis of cortisol response to challenge in human aging: importance of gender. *Psychoneuroendocrinology, 30*, 80–91.

Ozkaya, G. Y., Aydin, H., Toraman, F. N., Kizilay, F., Ozdemir, O., & Cetinkaya, V. (2005). Effect of strength and endurance training on cognition in older people. *Journal of Sports Science and Medicine, 4*, 300–313.

Park, D. C., Lautenschlager, G., Hedden, T., Davidson, N. S., Smith, A. D., & Smith, P. K. (2002). Models of visuospatial and verbal memory across the adult life span. *Psychology of Aging, 17*, 299–320.

Park, D. C., & Reuter-Lorenz, P. A. (2009). The adaptive brain: aging and neurocognitive scaffolding. *Annual Review of Psychology, 60*, 173–196.

Pereira, A. C., Huddleston, D. E., Brickman, A. M., Sosunov, A. A., Hen, R., McKhann, G. M., et al. (2007). An in vivo correlate of exercise-induced neurogenesis in the adult dentate gyrus. *Proceedings of the National Academy of Sciences of the United States of America, 104*, 5638–5643.

Peters, A. (2002). Structural changes in the normally aging cerebral cortex of primates. *Progress in Brain Research, 136*, 455–465.

Peters, J., Dauvermann, M., Mette, C., Platen, P., Franke, J., Hinrichs, T., et al. (2009). Voxel-based morphometry reveals an association between aerobic capacity and grey matter density in the right anterior insula. *Neuroscience, 163*, 1102–1108.

Pieramico, V., Esposito, R., Sensi, F., Cilli, F., Mantini, D., Mattei, P. A., et al. (2012). Combination training in aging individuals modifies functional connectivity and cognition, and is potentially affected by dopamine-related genes. *PLoS One, 7*. http://dx.doi.org/10.1371/journal.pone.0043901.

Polich, J. (1997). On the relationship between EEG and P300: individual differences, aging, and ultradian rhythms. *International Journal of Psychophysiology, 26*, 299–317.

van Praag, H., Kempermann, G., & Gage, F. H. (1999). Running increases cell proliferation and neurogenesis in the adult mouse dentate gyrus. *Nature Neuroscience, 2*, 266–270.

van Praag, H., Shubert, T., Zhao, C., & Gage, F. H. (2005). Exercise enhances learning and hippocampal neurogenesis in aged mice. *Journal of Neuroscience, 25*, 8680–8685.

Prakash, R. S., Voss, M. W., Erickson, K. I., Lewis, J. M., Chaddock, L., Malkowski, E., et al. (2011). Cardiorespiratory fitness and attentional control in the aging brain. *Frontiers in Human Neuroscience, 4*, 229. http://dx.doi.org/10.3389/fnhum.2010.00229.

Puterman, E., O'Donovan, A., Adler, N. E., Tomiyama, A. J., Kemeny, M., Wolkowitz, O. M., et al. (2011). Physical activity moderates effects of stressor-induced rumination on cortisol reactivity. *Psychosomatic Medicine, 73*, 604–611.

Raichle, M. E., MacLeod, A. M., Snyder, A. Z., Powers, W. J., Gusnard, D. A., & Shulman, G. L. (2001). A default mode of brain function. *Proceedings of the National Academy of Sciences of the United States of America, 98*, 676–682.

Raz, N., & Lindenberger, U. (2011). Only time will tell: cross-sectional studies offer no solution to the age-brain-cognition triangle: comment on Salthouse (2011). *Psychological Bulletin, 137*, 790–795.

Raz, N., & Rodrigue, K. M. (2006). Differential aging of the brain: patterns, cognitive correlates and modifiers. *Neuroscience and Biobehavioral Reviews, 30*, 730–748.

Reuter-Lorenz, P. A., & Lustig, C. (2005). Brain aging: reorganizing discoveries about the aging mind. *Current Opinion in Neurobiology, 15*, 245–251.

Reuter-Lorenz, P. A. & Park, D. C. (2014). How Does it STAC Up? Revisiting the Scaffolding Theory of Aging and Cognition. Neuropsychology Review, 24, 355–370.

Rieckmann, A., Karlsson, S., Karlsson, P., Brehmer, Y., Fischer, H., Farde, L., et al. (2011). Dopamine D1 receptor associations within and between dopaminergic pathways in younger and elderly adults: links to cognitive performance. *Cerebral Cortex, 21*, 2023–2032.

Rikli, R. E., & Jones, C. J. (2001). Senior fitness test manual. Development and validation of a functional fitness test for community-residing older adults. Champaign, IL: Human Kinetics.

Rönnlund, M., Nyberg, L., Bäckman, L., & Nilsson, L. G. (2005). Stability, growth, and decline in adult life span development of declarative memory: cross-sectional and longitudinal data from a population-based study. *Psychology of Aging, 20*, 3–18.

Rosano, C., Venkatraman, V. K., Guralnik, J., Newman, A. B., Glynn, N. W., Launer, L., et al. (2010). Psychomotor speed and functional brain MRI 2 years after completing a physical activity treatment. *Journals of Gerontology, Series A: Biological Sciences and Medical Sciences, 65A*, 639–647.

Ruscheweyh, R., Willemer, C., Kruger, K., Duning, T., Warnecke, T., Sommer, J., et al. (2011). Physical activity and memory functions: an interventional study. *Neurobiology of Aging, 32*, 1304–1319.

Salthouse, T. A. (1996). The processing-speed theory of adult age differences in cognition. *Psychological Review, 103*, 403–428.

Scarmeas, N., Zarahn, E., Anderson, K., Hilton, J., Flynn, J., Van Heertum, R., et al. (2003). Cognitive reserve modulates functional brain responses during memory tasks: a PET study in healthy young and elderly subjects. *NeuroImage, 19*, 1215–1227.

Schoofs, D., Preuss, D., & Wolf, O. T. (2008). Psychosocial stress induces working memory impairments in an n-back paradigm. *Psychoneuroendocrinology, 33*, 643–653.

Seidler, R. D., Bernard, J. A., Burutolu, T. B., Fling, B. W., Gordon, M. T., Gwin, J. T., et al. (2010). Motor control and aging: links to age-related brain structural, functional, and biochemical effects. *Neuroscience and Biobehavioral Reviews, 34*, 721–733.

Sen, A., Gider, P., Cavalieri, M., Freudenberger, P., Farzi, A., Schallert, M., et al. (2012). Association of cardiorespiratory fitness and morphological brain changes in the elderly: results of the Austrian Stroke Prevention Study. *Neurodegenerative Disease, 10*, 135–137.

Smith, J., & Baltes, P. B. (1999). Trends and profiles of psychological functioning in very old age. In P. B. Baltes, & K. U. Mayer (Eds.), *The Berlin aging study* (pp. 197–226). New York: Cambridge University Press.

Smith, J. C., Nielson, K. A., Woodard, J. L., Seidenberg, M., Durgerian, S., Antuono, P., et al. (2011). Interactive effects of physical activity and APOE-epsilon 4 on BOLD semantic memory activation in healthy elders. *NeuroImage, 54*, 635–644.

Stanford Center on Longevity. (2014). *A consensus on the brain training industry from the scientific community.* http://longevity3.stanford.edu/blog/2014/10/15/the-consensus-on-the-brain-training-industry-from-the-scientific-community-2/.

Staudinger, U. M. (2012). Möglichkeiten und Grenzen menschlicher Entwicklungen über die Lebensspanne (Opportunities and limits of human development across the lifespan). In J. Hacker, & M. Hecker (Eds.), *Was ist Leben? (What is life?)* (pp. 255–266). Stuttgart: Wissenschaftliche Verlagsgesellschaft.

Staudinger, U. M., Marsiske, M., & Baltes, P. B. (1993). Resilience and levels of reserve capacity in later adulthood: perspectives from life-span theory. *Development and Psychopathology, 5*, 541–566.

Stroth, S., Reinhardt, R. K., Thone, J., Hille, K., Schneider, M., Hartel, S., et al. (2010). Impact of aerobic exercise training on cognitive functions and affect associated to the COMT polymorphism in young adults. *Neurobiology of Learning Memory, 94*, 364–372.

Sutoo, D., & Akiyama, K. (2003). Regulation of brain function by exercise. *Neurobiology of Disease, 13*, 1–14.

Thomas, A. G., Dennis, A., Bandettini, P. A., & Johansen-Berg, H. (2012). The effects of aerobic activity on brain structure. *Frontiers in Psychology, 3*, 86. http://dx.doi.org/10.3389/fpsyg.2012.00086.

Tortosa-Martinez, J., & Clow, A. (2012). Does physical activity reduce risk for Alzheimer's disease through interaction with the stress neuroendocrine system? *Stress, 15*, 243–261.

Traustadottir, T., Bosch, P. R., & Matt, K. S. (2005). The HPA axis response to stress in women: effects of aging and fitness. *Psychoneuroendocrinology, 30*, 392–402.

Verghese, J. (2006). Cognitive and mobility profile of older social dancers. *Journal of American Geriatrics Society, 54*, 1241–1244.

Verghese, J., Lipton, R. B., Katz, M. J., Hall, C. B., Derby, C. A., Kuslansky, G., et al. (2003). Leisure activities and the risk of dementia in the elderly. *New England Journal of Medicine, 348*, 2508–2516.

Voelcker-Rehage, C., Godde, B., & Staudinger, U. M. (2010). Physical and motor fitness are both related to cognition in old age. *European Journal of Neuroscience, 31*, 167–176.

Voelcker-Rehage, C., Godde, B., & Staudinger, U. M. (2011). Cardiovascular and coordination training differentially improve cognitive performance and neural processing in older adults. *Frontiers in Human Neuroscience, 5*, 26.

Voelcker-Rehage, C., Jeltsch, A., Godde, B., Becker, S. & Staudinger U.M. (2015). COMT gene polymorphisms, cognitive performance, and physical fitness in older adults. Psychology of Sport and exercise, 20, 20–28.

Voelcker-Rehage, C., & Niemann, C. (2013). Structural and functional brain changes related to different types of physical activity across the life span. *Neuroscience and Biobehavioral Reviews, 37*, 2268–2295.

Voss, M. W., Chaddock, L., Kim, J. S., Vanpatter, M., Pontifex, M. B., Raine, L. B., et al. (2011). Aerobic fitness is associated with greater efficiency of the network underlying cognitive control in preadolescent children. *Neuroscience, 199*, 166–176.

Voss, M. W., Erickson, K. I., Prakash, R. S., Chaddock, L., Malkowski, E., Alves, H., et al. (2010). Functional connectivity: a source of variance in the association between cardiorespiratory fitness and cognition? *Neuropsychologia, 48,* 1394–1406.

Voss, M. W., Heo, S., Prakash, R. S., Erickson, K. I., Alves, H., Chaddock, L., et al. (2012). The influence of aerobic fitness on cerebral white matter integrity and cognitive function in older adults: results of a one-year exercise intervention. *Human Brain Mapping, 34,* 2972–2985.

Voss, M. W., Prakash, R. S., Erickson, K. I., Basak, C., Chaddock, L., Kim, J. S., et al. (2010). Plasticity of brain networks in a randomized intervention trial of exercise training in older adults. *Frontiers in Aging Neuroscience, 2,* 32. http://dx.doi.org/10.3389/fnagi.2010.00032.

Wasserman, K. E. H.J., Sue, D. Y., Stringer, W. W., & Whipp, B. J. (2005). *Principles of exercise testing and interpretation.* Philadelphia, PA: Lippincott Williams & Wilkins.

Weinstein, A. M., Voss, M. W., Prakash, R. S., Chaddock, L., Szabo, A., White, S. M., et al. (2012). The association between aerobic fitness and executive function is mediated by prefrontal cortex volume. *Brain, Behavior, and Immunity, 26,* 811–819.

West, R. L. (1996). An application of prefrontal cortex function theory to cognitive aging. *Psychological Bulletin, 120,* 272–292.

Winneke, A. H., Godde, B., Reuter, E.-M., Vieluf, S., & Voelcker-Rehage, C. (2012). The association between physical activity and attentional control in younger and older middle-aged adults: an ERP study. *Journal of Gerontopsychology and Geriatric Psychiatry, 25,* 207–221.

Witte, A. V., Jansen, S., Schirmacher, A., Young, P., & Floel, A. (2010). COMT Val158Met polymorphism modulates cognitive effects of dietary intervention. *Frontiers in Aging Neuroscience, 2,* 146. http://dx.doi.org/10.3389/fnagi.2010.00146.

Wolf, O. T., Schommer, N. C., Hellhammer, D. H., McEwen, B. S., & Kirschbaum, C. (2001). The relationship between stress induced cortisol levels and memory differs between men and women. *Psychoneuroendocrinology, 26,* 711–720.

Yaffe, K., Barnes, D., Nevitt, M., Lui, L. Y., & Covinsky, K. (2001). A prospective study of physical activity and cognitive decline in elderly women: women who walk. *Archives of Internal Medicine, 161,* 1703–1708.

Yeung, N., Botvinick, M. M., & Cohen, J. D. (2004). The neural basis of error detection: conflict monitoring and the error-related negativity. *Psychological Review, 111,* 931–959.

Young, W. B. (2006). Transfer of strength and power training to sports performance. *International Journal of Sports Physiology and Performance, 1,* 74–83.

Zhu, N., Jacobs, D. R., Jr., Schreiner, P. J., Yaffe, K., Bryan, N., Launer, L. J., et al. (2014). Cardiorespiratory fitness and cognitive function in middle age: the CARDIA study. *Neurology, 82,* 1339–1346.

Zoladz, J. A., Pilc, A., Majerczak, J., Grandys, M., Zapart-Bukowska, J., & Duda, K. (2008). Endurance training increases plasma brain-derived neurotrophic factor concentration in young healthy men. *Journal of Physiology and Pharmacology, 59*(Suppl. 7), 119–132.

The Chronic Exercise–Cognition Interaction and Parkinson Disease

Madeleine E. Hackney[1], Joe R. Nocera[2], Dawn Bowers[3], Lori J.P. Altmann[4], Chris J. Hass[5]

[1]Atlanta VA Center for Visual and Neurocognitive Rehabilitation, Division of General Medicine and Geriatrics, Department of Medicine, Emory University School of Medicine, Decatur, GA, USA; [2]Atlanta VA Center for Visual and Neurocognitive Rehabilitation, Department of Neurology, Emory University School of Medicine, Decatur, GA, USA; [3]Department of Clinical & Health Psychology, University of Florida, Gainesville, FL, USA; [4]Department of Speech, Language and Hearing Sciences, University of Florida, Gainesville, FL, USA; [5]Department of Applied Physiology and Kinesiology, University of Florida, Gainesville, FL, USA

CAUSES AND SYMPTOMS OF PARKINSON DISEASE

Parkinson disease (PD) is the second most common neurodegenerative disorder of later life and is related to lost dopamine cells in the substantia nigra of the basal ganglia, a collection of subcortical nuclei. PD results from a synucleinopathy that results in the formation of alpha-synuclein aggregates (a.k.a. Lewy bodies). When the synucleinopathy affects substantia nigra, dopamine loss gives rise to classic motor symptoms of PD, which affects approximately one million adults in the United States. By 2030, the number of people living with PD is expected to double (Dorsey et al., 2007). Due to progressive worsening of PD-related symptoms,

management and treatment of this disease can be costly. The costs of PD are formidable (>$34 billion/year) and increasing (Noyes, Liu, Li, Holloway, & Dick, 2006). The dopamine depletion in the basal ganglia contributes to the cardinal features of the disease including bradykinesia (i.e., extreme slowness of moving), tremor, rigidity, and gait/postural instability. These cardinal features manifest into altered neuromuscular control of the upper extremities and poor lower extremity function, leading to reduced independence and decreased health-related quality of life (QOL). Difficulty turning and dual-tasking, postural instability, and gait impairment rob individuals with PD of their QOL (Muslimovic, Post, Speelman, Schmand, & de Haan, 2008), leading to falls, fear of falling, and withdrawal from society (Bloem, Hausdorff, Visser, & Giladi, 2004; Bloem, van Vugt, & Beckley, 2001). One study demonstrated that 70% of patients fell within a 1-year period, and 50% fell again the following year (Bloem et al., 2004). Notably, individuals with PD are 3.2 times more likely to sustain a hip fracture than people of similar age without PD (Melton et al., 2006). Adverse changes to gait while dual-tasking are greater in those with PD than those without (Hackney & Earhart, 2009; O'Shea, Morris, & Iansek, 2002). Shorter stride length and slower gait speed, while performing a cognitive dual task, may result from an underlying cognitive impairment, which is common in PD (Leroi, Collins, & Marsh, 2006).

The basal ganglia, the brain area best characterized in PD, are components of a family of functionally segregated, cortico-subcortical reentrant pathways (Albin, Young, & Penney, 1989; Alexander, Crutcher, & DeLong, 1990; DeLong et al., 1984; DeLong & Wichmann, 1993; Wichmann & DeLong, 1996, 1998). The motor circuit of the basal ganglia is strongly implicated in the pathophysiology of PD and other movement disorders (Alexander & Crutcher, 1990; Alexander et al., 1990; DeLong, 1983, 1990; DeLong, Alexander, Mitchell, & Richardson, 1986; DeLong & Wichmann, 1993). Activity in the basal ganglia portion of the motor circuit in animal models of parkinsonism has been studied directly by recording neuronal activity (Bergman, Wichmann, Karmon, & DeLong, 1994; Elder & Vitek, 2001; Filion, Tremblay, & Bedard, 1988; Miller & DeLong, 1988; Vitek, Ashe, DeLong, & Alexander, 1990) and with indirect anatomic techniques (Sidibe & Smith, 1996; Smith, Wichmann, & DeLong, 1994; Wise, Murray, & Gerfen, 1996). In parkinsonian animals, the discharge rate of neurons is decreased in globus pallidus externus (GPe) (Thigpen, Light, Creel, & Flynn, 2000) and increased in subthalamic nucleus (STN) and globus pallidus pars internus (GPi) (Miller & DeLong, 1988; Wichmann, Bergman, & DeLong, 1994). The lower GPe → STN (inhibitory) output

leads to disinhibition of the STN, which in turn results in increased excitation of GPi, inhibition of thalamocortical activity, and the development of parkinsonian motor signs.

An involuntary muscular response called the automatic postural response (APR) (Torres-Oviedo & Ting, 2007; Welch & Ting, 2009) might shed more light on the story of postural instability in PD. The APR is generated by brainstem and spinal mechanisms (Honeycutt, Gottschall, & Nichols, 2009) that may be downstream targets of focused inhibition from the basal ganglia output nuclei to brainstem nuclei, e.g., the pedunculopontine nucleus (PPN) (Pahapill & Lozano, 2000). PD may lead to impaired focused inhibition by the basal ganglia (Mink, 1996) as well as to degeneration in the PPN (Pahapill & Lozano, 2000). In individuals with PD, studies of APR onset latency have allowed researchers to note inappropriate cocontraction between agonists and antagonists (Carpenter, Allum, Honegger, Adkin, & Bloem, 2004; Dimitrova, Horak, & Nutt, 2004). Individuals with PD also exhibit increased total displacement of the center of mass during responses to support-surface translation perturbations (Dimitrova, Nutt, & Horak, 2004; Horak, Dimitrova, & Nutt, 2005). Abnormally elevated levels of agonist–antagonist muscle coactivation have been reported in individuals with PD in various activities involving both the upper and the lower limbs (Carpenter et al., 2004; Dimitrova, Horak et al., 2004; Kelly & Bastian, 2005).

PD can severely impact psychological and cognitive aspects of well-being (Schrag, Jahanshahi, & Quinn, 2000), which may precede PD diagnosis by several years (Palacios, Gao, Schwarzschild, & Ascherio, 2012). QOL is affected early in PD by multiple nonmotor symptoms (Tolosa, Compta, & Gaig, 2007). As the disease progresses, this collage of motor, affective, and behavioral symptoms often leads to considerably reduced QOL for many with PD (Duncan et al., 2014). Mood disorders, impaired cognition, and sleep patterns worsen, which contributes to increased stress and social isolation over time (McNamara, Durso, & Harris, 2006; Suzukamo, Ohbu, Kondo, Kohmoto, & Fukuhara, 2006). QOL is particularly affected by depression and anxiety, which is comorbid with PD in nearly half of those affected. Psychopathology, found in many individuals with PD, results from the underlying physiology of the disease (Jones et al., 2014; Zurowski, McDonald, Fox, & Marsh, 2013). Neurotransmitter systems that are typically degraded in PD, for example, dopamine and serotonin, also contribute to depression (Lagopoulos, Malhi, Ivanovski, Cahill, & Morris, 2005). Decreased availability of the dopamine transporter in the anterior putamen correlates with depressive symptoms and anxiety (Weintraub et al., 2005).

While PD has traditionally been considered a "movement" disorder, it is a multisystem disorder affecting multiple neurotransmitter systems and encompassing cognitive, mood, and motivational systems. In fact, nearly 80% of individuals with PD develop cognitive impairment (Aarsland, Andersen, Larsen, & Lolk, 2003). Individuals with PD commonly experience impairment in domains of spatial cognition (Possin, Filoteo, Song, & Salmon, 2008) and executive function (EF) (Hausdorff et al., 2006). These cognitive deficits can interact with motor difficulties, impairing mobility, and increasing fall risk (Camicioli & Majumdar, 2010). Further, a simultaneous cognitive task in a dual-task paradigm can exacerbate PD motor symptoms (Leroi et al., 2006); and axial impairment and postural instability in PD are associated with increased risk of dementia (Taylor et al., 2008). Likely, these problems stem from the impairment of overlapping neural systems serving both cognitive and motor function (Domellof, Elgh, & Forsgren, 2011).

THE EFFECTS OF PD ON COGNITION

At the time of diagnosis, 5–20% of individuals with PD show signs of cognitive impairment (Aarsland et al., 2004). Cross-sectional studies indicate 25–30% of individuals with PD are demented, whereas longitudinal studies show that 80% of patients have become demented after 15–18 years (Hely, Reid, Adena, Halliday, & Morris, 2008). Cognitive changes can occur early in the disease course, worsen with disease progression, and have detrimental effects on survival, QOL, and occurrence of nursing home placement (Aarsland et al., 2001; Buter et al., 2008; Schrag et al., 2000).

The typical cognitive decline in PD involves difficulty with psychomotor and cognitive slowing, set-shifting and multitasking, working memory, and forgetfulness. From a neural systems perspective, PD-related cognitive decline has been attributed to deregulation of dopamine-mediated frontostriatal circuitry and further exacerbated by associated cholinergic and serotonergic deficits affecting cortical systems (Dubois & Pillon, 1997; Williams-Gray, Foltynie, Lewis, & Barker, 2006). Thus, executive cognitive impairments have been attributed to dopamine deficiency in frontostriatal circuitry; however, dopamine therapy helps and hinders cognitive function in many (Ray & Strafella, 2012). Forgetfulness and memory difficulties in PD have been attributed to frontostriatal dysfunction, but growing evidence also points to involvement of mesial temporal lobe systems based on neuroimaging.

Over the past decade, it has become apparent that there may be multiple cognitive subtypes of PD with different trajectories of cognitive decline (Troster, 2011). While most individuals with PD show executive difficulties, others have co-occurring, distinct memory difficulties. The underlying neuropathophysiology of PD cognitive impairment is also variable but approximately 60% of individuals with PD show Lewy bodies and Alzheimer's disease pathology. In individuals with PD, before the onset of dementia, neuroimaging has revealed decreased cortical volume, increased white matter (WM) diffusion changes, and decreased resting metabolic activity (Silbert & Kaye, 2010). Therefore, the neuropathophysiology of cognitive impairment in PD remains to be clarified; however, the behavioral impact on cognitive and motor–cognitive function is relatively well characterized.

Motor–Cognition Interaction

Historically, distinct human behaviors such as movement and cognition were thought to be directed by isolated, proprietary, cortical regions. However, overlapping neural systems likely serve both cognitive and motor function (Domellof et al., 2011). In PD the link between motor and cognitive function is especially clear. Motor learning is slower and likely uses more brain activity in individuals with PD than those without (Nieuwboer, Rochester, Muncks, & Swinnen, 2009). Increased bradykinesia—a reliable clinical measure of the nigrostriatal lesion in PD—is associated with the presence of mild cognitive impairment (MCI) and impaired executive performance (Poletti et al., 2012). With careful concentration on critical movement aspects, those with PD can achieve nearly normal movement amplitudes (Baker, Rochester, & Nieuwboer, 2007; Morris, Huxham, McGinley, & Iansek, 2001). For example, by focusing on external auditory cues, individuals with PD have improved movement initiation and cadence (Baker, Rochester, & Nieuwboer, 2008). During externally cued movements, people with PD might be able to bypass the malfunctioning basal ganglia (Freedland et al., 2002) and activate the cerebellar-thalamo-cortical neural network, in a manner similar to that noted in age-matched controls (Lewis et al., 2007). There are also well-known facilitating effects of cues for alleviating freezing of gait (Jiang & Norman, 2006).

The advent of functional neuroimaging techniques has graphically demonstrated that there is considerable overlap in brain regions for many disparate behaviors. Two primary regions have been identified that are activated by both cognitive

and motor tasks: the sensorimotor cortex and the dorsolateral prefrontal cortex (dlPFC).

Sensorimotor Cortex Involvement in Cognition

While it is axiomatic that motor tasks will activate sensorimotor cortices and their association cortices, recent studies have found that action words, both verbs and nouns, can activate somatotopically appropriate locations within sensorimotor cortices (Pulvermuller, 2001) and the supplementary motor cortex (Kemmerer, Castillo, Talavage, Patterson, & Wiley, 2008; Raposo, Moss, Stamatakis, & Tyler, 2009). Researchers have concluded that the cortical representation of action word meaning includes the cortex used for *enacting* a particular verb (e.g., writing and painting) or *using* an action-related noun (e.g., pencil and paintbrush) (Grossi, Maitra, & Rice, 2007). From a behavioral standpoint, processing hand action-related words can impact finger and hand movements but not foot movement (Scorolli, & Borghi, 2007). Conversely, hand and arm movements also impact processing of hand-related words (Rodriguez, 2010). However, the literature documents both facilitation and inhibition of movement following action word processing (Dalla Volta, Gianelli, Campione, & Gentilucci, 2009), and currently, it is impossible to predict whether an action-priming experiment will elicit faster or slower responses. Nevertheless, these findings present an interesting example of interactions between motor tasks and cognitive processing.

Dorsolateral Prefrontal Cortex Involvement in Cognition and Movement

The dlPFC comprises the heteromodal cortex (the region receiving input from multiple sensory and multimodal areas) with projections to and from occipital, temporal, and parietal lobes, as well as sensorimotor cortices. This region is assumed to provide "processing resources" (i.e., computational resources for calculating complex behaviors) for resource-demanding tasks of all types that involve controlled processing, including nonautomatic movement, EF, working memory, and language. DlPFC is vulnerable to age-related declines in function due to loss of synapses (Raz, 2000). In PD, declines in dlPFC functional connectivity are more pronounced than in age-matched peers (Rowe et al., 2002), resulting in fewer resources available for calculating complex behaviors.

Because the dlPFC supports processing in multiple domains (Cabeza, 2001), there is often competition for processing resources during concurrent tasks. Robust evidence from dual-task literature demonstrates that simultaneous walking and talking (Plummer-D'Amato, Altmann, & Reilly, 2011; Verghese et al., 2007) or walking while doing a cognitive task (Hackney & Earhart, 2010a; Nocera, Roemmich, Elrod, Altmann, & Hass, 2013; Woollacott & Shumway-Cook, 2002) can negatively impact either walking or concurrent cognitive task, or both in older adults with and without PD. These effects are greater in older adults than in young people due to reduced processing resources (Lindenberger, Marsiske, & Baltes, 2000). Considering that dlPFC degradation is more pronounced in PD than in healthy aging, it is not surprising that people with PD often experience exaggerated dual task impairments relative to their age-matched peers (O'Shea et al., 2002). The magnitude of dual task effects, or decrement in performance during concurrent tasks, is highly dependent on the task difficulty: as the secondary cognitive task increases in difficulty, so does the impairment in the primary motor task (Al-Yahya et al., 2011). Findings from the dual task literature are consistent with the idea that motor and cognitive processing share cortical processing resources.

Cognitive Impairments in PD

Many individuals with PD exhibit deficiencies in planning and executing complex, goal-directed behavior (Plotnik, Giladi, Dagan, & Hausdorff, 2011), secondary to EF deficits. Speed of cognitive processing, working memory, language, visual–spatial processing, and emotional cognition are also impaired in many of those with PD (Taylor & Saint-Cyr, 1995).

Speed of Processing

The neural instantiation of speed of processing is likely to be multifactorial, depending on the extent of cortical interconnectivity (dependent on experience and speed of neural encoding), pathology (e.g., availability of neurotransmitters), and minimally on the speed of neural encoding, which is likely genetically determined. Pathologically slow speed of processing (bradyphrenia) is characteristic of early PD (McKinlay, Grace, Dalrymple-Alford, & Roger, 2010; Rogers, Lees, Smith, Trimble, & Stern, 1987). Further, cognitive processing continues slowing over the individual time course of PD (de Frias, Dixon, Fisher, & Camicioli, 2007). Cognitive slowing may contribute to (but not be wholly responsible for) deficits in a range of other abilities, including category fluency (McDowd et al., 2011; McKinlay et al., 2010), EFs (McKinlay et al., 2010), e.g., inhibition, set-shifting, problem solving, working memory (Lanni et al., 2014), and motor performance (Stegemoller, Wilson, et al., 2014).

Executive Function

While simpler forms of attention, such as alerting, orienting, selective attention, and vigilance, are relatively preserved in PD, more complex attentional processing, often known as supervisory attention or executive attention, is frequently impaired in PD (McKinlay et al., 2010). Depending on the task, executive attention is supported by cortical association cortices in the cingulate gyrus, posterior parietal lobe, and dlPFC (Zgaljardic et al., 2006). Executive attention is required for a number of complex, multicomponent cognitive processes known as EFs.

EFs comprise a collection of intentional, controlled cognitive processes that supervise or coordinate other lower-order processes (Lezak, Howieson, Loring, Hannay, & Fischer, 2004; Spreen & Strauss, 1998). When a task is effortful and novel, EFs are required. Some common types of EFs are planning and prioritizing, problem solving, goal selection, as well as changing goals, updating knowledge representations, and inhibition of inappropriate actions. Due to the degradation of frontal lobe networks, PD leads to impairments in many EFs. The most commonly described impairments involve planning and problem solving, set switching, inhibition, and verbal fluency (McKinlay et al., 2010; Taylor & Saint-Cyr, 1995).

Planning and problem solving refer to the ability to analyze and organize the steps needed to achieve a goal or solve a problem (Dirnberger & Jahanshahi, 2013; Kostering, McKinlay, Stahl, & Kaller, 2012). Planning and problem solving are often assessed with the Tower of London or Tower of Hanoi tasks (Lezak et al., 2004) or tasks like the Key Search or Zoo Map tasks from the Behavioral Assessment of Dysexecutive Syndromes (BADS) (Wilson et al., 1998). However, reports of impaired planning and problem solving in PD are variable. Several studies report impaired performance in people with PD on tower tasks (Lewis, Dove, Robbins, Barker, & Owen, 2003; McKinlay et al., 2010; Muslimovic, Post, Speelman, & Schmand, 2005). Yet, McKinley and colleagues report preserved performance on the planning tasks from the BADS. The differential findings across tasks may be due to task difficulty. McKinley and colleagues (McKinlay et al., 2010, 2008) suggest that people with PD are only impaired at more difficult levels of towers tasks.

Set-shifting, the ability to change one's behavior quickly in response to task requirements, is often referred to as a measure of cognitive flexibility (e.g., Kostering et al., 2012),

and assessed using the Wisconsin Card Sorting Task (Nelson, 1976) or the Trail Making Test (Lezak et al., 2004). Frequently set-shifting has been found to be impaired in PD (Dirnberger & Jahanshahi, 2013; Richards, Cote, & Stern, 1993). Imaging studies suggest that set-shifting is supported not only by the lateral prefrontal cortex and the ventromedial frontal lobe, but also by the striatum; therefore, set-shifting impairments in PD may be directly related to degeneration of the striatum due to disease processes (Monchi et al., 2004).

Inhibition, the ability to suppress attention to irrelevant stimulus variables, often refers to the suppression of a prepotent response, i.e., a response for which immediate reinforcement (positive or negative) is available or has been previously associated with that response. Inhibition deficits are common in PD (Henik, Singh, Beckley, & Rafal, 1993; Koerts, Leenders, & Brouwer, 2009). Inhibitory deficits are frequently assessed with the Stroop or flanker tasks, in which the natural tendency to do something, e.g., read a word, must be suppressed, in favor of doing something less typical, e.g., saying the color the word is printed in. People with PD are particularly impaired at suppressing their first impulse to read the word in a Stroop task instead of stating the color it is printed in, leading to greater error rates on the task than their healthy peers without PD (Henik et al., 1993). Interestingly, inhibition tasks, such as the auditory Stroop task, have been found to interact with motor performance, particularly gait (McFadyen, Hegeman, & Duysens, 2009; Plummer-D'Amato et al., 2011).

Verbal fluency tasks are complex tasks requiring the development of strategies for searching either semantic memory, in the case of category fluency, or phonemic memory, in the case of letter fluency. Participants are given 1 min to generate as many exemplars as possible fitting a particular criterion, such as "animals" or "words starting with F." People with PD often produce fewer exemplars than healthy peers for both phonemic and category fluency (Flowers, Robertson, & Sheridan, 1995; Henry & Crawford, 2004; Jaywant, Musto, Neargarder, Stavitsky Gilbert, & Cronin-Golomb, 2014). People with PD show even more pronounced impairments on action fluency (e.g., "tell me all the things you can do with an egg," "things you can do with your hands") (McDowd et al., 2011; Peran et al., 2003; Piatt, Fields, Paolo, Koller, & Tröster, 1999), consistent with other findings of impaired verb access in PD (Martin, Wetzel, Blossom-Stach, & Feher, 1989; Peran, Goutines, Demonet, Rascol, & Cardebat, 2006; Peran et al., 2003). Verbal fluency task performance has been found to be predictive of QOL in PD (Stegemoller, Nocera, et al., 2014). Controversy exists over whether verbal fluency should be classified as a language or EF task. Current evidence suggests classifying it as an EF task may be more appropriate (McDowd et al., 2011).

Memory

Memory complaints are common in individuals with PD, although the nature of the "memory disturbance" typically involves difficulties with use of effortful learning and retrieval strategies (i.e., frontally mediated), rather than frank difficulties with retention (i.e., hippocampally based). Supporting this view are observations that individuals with PD exhibit a dissociation in their performance on word list versus story memory tasks, with word list learning typically being impaired relative to normal memory recall of stories (Hartikainen, Helkala, Soininen, & Riekkinen, 1993; Zahodne et al., 2011). While both types of memory tasks require rapid processing of a constant stream of information, word list tasks require one to *self-generate* organizational and retrieval strategies. By contrast, performance on story memory tasks benefits from intrinsic semantic organization of the material (Helmstaedter, Wietzke, & Lutz, 2009; Wicklund, Johnson, Rademaker, Weitner, & Weintraub, 2006). Of relevance to PD, the latter

(memory for word lists, compared to stories) has been associated with cognitive measures of EF (Tremont, Halpert, Javorsky, & Stern, 2000) and dysfunction of frontal lobe systems (Kopelman & Stanhope, 1998).

Other types of memory frequently impaired in PD are temporal (i.e., time tagging), prospective, and working memory (Hoppe, Muller, Werheid, Thone, & von Cramon, 2000; Werheid et al., 2002; Zgaljardic et al., 2006). All have been associated with integrity of frontal lobe systems. Prospective memory requires remembering to do a planned action at an appointed time or in response to a prespecified cue. Noncued prospective memory, in which a person must remember to do something at an appointed time, is particularly impaired in PD, while cued prospective memory is relatively intact (Costa, Peppe, Caltagirone, & Carlesimo, 2008; Foster, McDaniel, Repovš, & Hershey, 2009). Working memory, often considered one of the EFs, refers to the ability to flexibly encode or store information such that information can be manipulated and is impervious to distraction. Thus, working memory tasks require both storage and manipulation of information and are essentially divided attention tasks.

Language

Language use is arguably the most complex cognitive task in which people engage on a regular basis. Learning to understand and produce language has direct effects on the brain's organization and efficiency. From a behavioral standpoint, language provides an organizing template for experiences and knowledge, and also facilitates abstract thought about the past, present, and future. Language consists of meaning representations, i.e., words, rules for combining these representations, grammar, and syntax. Together these elements allow for the communication of vastly complicated ideas. Using language, either understanding or producing it, requires the activation of stored meaning representations and the manipulation of these according to the rules of the grammar of the language. Thus, language use success will be necessarily constrained by the efficiency and capacity of the cognitive abilities discussed above (i.e., attention, EFs, working memory, and speed of processing), each of which contributes to different aspects of language use (Kemper & Sumner, 2001; Troche & Altmann, 2012). For the purposes of this chapter, we have included verbal fluency as an EF task, and picture naming as a semantic memory task. The discussion of language will focus on actual language use, understanding and producing sentences and discourse-level language, both of which are impaired in PD (Murray, 2008).

Although not debilitating, several studies have reported deficits in sentence comprehension in people with PD (Grossman, 1999; Grossman, Lee, Morris, Stern, & Hurtig, 2002; Grossman, Zurif, et al., 2002; Lieberman et al., 1992; Murray, 2008). Errors in comprehension are typically limited to sentences with complex syntax, such as those with passive verbs (Hochstadt, 2009) or center-embedded relative clauses (Grossman, Zurif, et al., 2002; Hochstadt, 2009). Many of these studies have found that sentence comprehension performance of people with PD correlates with performance on tasks measuring set-shifting (Grossman, Lee, et al., 2002; Grossman, Zurif, et al., 2002; Hochstadt, 2009; Lees & Smith, 1983), inhibition (Grossman, Zurif, et al., 2002), semantic fluency (Lee, Grossman, Morris, Stern, & Hurtig, 2003), and sequencing ability (Lieberman et al., 1992), as well as processing speed and working memory (Grossman, Zurif, et al., 2002).

Language production at the sentence and discourse level also shows subtle impairments relative to that of age- and education-matched peers (for a review, see Altmann & Troche, 2011). Research suggests that PD has a broad range of effects on language production, including reduced information content, impaired grammaticality, disrupted fluency, and reduced grammatical complexity. Many studies have documented that cognitive abilities account for

significant variance in these aspects of language production (e.g., Lieberman et al., 1992; Murray, 2008; Troche & Altmann, 2012). However, evidence demonstrates that cognitive impairments cannot fully account for the range of language production impairments found in PD (Troche & Altmann, 2012), suggesting that PD may affect cortical circuits used for language that are not tapped by common EF and working memory tasks.

Visuospatial Processing

Although PD executive and working memory impairments are relatively well documented, visuocognitive dysfunction in PD is described more variably in the literature. Because spatial cognition is supported by brain structures particularly vulnerable to normal cerebral aging (Klencklen, Despres, & Dufour, 2012), some researchers assert that it is especially vulnerable to the neurodegenerative processes occurring in PD (Possin, 2010). Some, but not all studies examining visuoperceptual abilities in PD have revealed impairments in visual form discrimination, face recognition, and speed of visual object recognition (Meppelink et al., 2009; Pereira et al., 2009). Studies assessing visuospatial abilities demonstrated that PD patients are impaired on tasks requiring space-based attention, memory for spatial location, perception of flow and egocentric reference, and line orientation (Davidsdottir, Cronin-Golomb, & Lee, 2005; Montse, Pere, Carme, Francesc, & Eduardo, 2001; Possin, 2010).

The mechanisms underlying visuocognitive changes are not well understood. Recent observations have implicated structural gray matter (GM) reductions in temporoparietal cortical regions in the development of visuoperceptual and visuospatial impairments in PD (Pereira et al., 2009). Moreover, these changes occurred in different patterns, such that GM reductions in ventral occipitotemporal cortex correlate with visuoperceptual task performance, and GM reductions in dorsal–parietal areas correlate with visuospatial performance. These findings, which mirror the distinction between dorsal and ventral stream visual processing outlined by Mishkin and Ungerleider (1982), suggest that individuals with PD may be distinguished by visuocognitive task performance. One important implication of this approach pertains to the importance of spatial cognition in forming cognitive maps of spatial relationships used in successful navigation of dynamic environments. Therefore, spatial cognition deficits may interact with mobility and orientation impairments (Klencklen et al., 2012).

THE EFFECTS OF EXERCISE ON COGNITION

Over the last few decades abundant data have demonstrated that higher levels of habitual exercise can delay cognitive decline associated with aging and neurological disease. Further, higher levels of habitual exercise enhance functioning in specific cognitive domains in aging and age-related disease. Here, we highlight and review the purported neurobiological mechanisms responsible for protecting and enhancing brain health and related outcomes. We focus on neuroplasticity-related changes attributed to physical activity, the specific mechanisms accounting for exercise benefits on cognitive function.

Neuroplasticity is changes or adaptations in structure or function of the nervous system on the basis of experience/exposure/practice. Plastic changes can occur on anatomical, molecular, genetic, structural, and functional levels within the nervous system. A possible neurobiological mechanism underlying the positive effects of exercise is the increased synthesis and release of neurotransmitters and neurotrophins, which could enhance neurogenesis, angiogenesis, and thus neuroplasticity (Voss, Erickson, et al., 2013). In addition, reorganization of cortical representations, synaptogenesis, and synaptic potentiation likely play a role.

Changes in the horizontal spread of cortical representations of a particular body segment or movement in response to a change in stimulus lead to reorganization of cortical maps. The somatosensory cortex has a sophisticated, somatotopic organizational structure, characterized by an intricate interconnection of neural structures. Typically, increased usage of or skill acquisition by one body part is followed by increased spread in the cortical map for that body part. Some changes have been attributed to competitive plasticity, referring to competition between body parts for limited cortical space, while others attribute the changes to the unmasking of previously silent or inactive neural connections. Changes in map representations have been clearly demonstrated in both animal and human models of injury as well as demonstrating plastic changes associated with training and experience (Buonomano & Merzenich, 1998; Merzenich et al., 1984).

Synaptogenesis, the creation of new synaptic connections, may be an important neural substrate for plasticity. Evidence of synaptogenesis can be observed via increased density of dendritic spines or the branching of dendritic arbors within neurons. Specifically, with training dendritic spine density increases. Conversely, a loss in dendritic spines has been associated with injury or loss of sensory/motor experience (Comery et al., 1997). Synaptic potentiation [a.k.a. long-term potentiation (LTP)] is a process by which the strength of synaptic transmission between two neurons is enhanced. This improved signal transmission allows for improved communication between the neurons. Synaptic potentiation, i.e., strengthening of synapses, occurs according to Hebb's principle (paraphrased): "When an axon of cell A excites cell B and repeatedly and persistently takes part in firing it, some growth process or metabolic change takes place in one or both of the cells so that A's efficiency as one of the cells firing B is increased" (Hebb, 1949).

As per Hebb's principle, if pre- and postsynaptic cells are firing simultaneously, the likelihood they will again fire simultaneously is strengthened, i.e., the synapse is strengthened. Conversely, if a postsynaptic cell is firing in the absence of one of its presynaptic cell's firing, the likelihood that the two cells will fire simultaneously is weakened, i.e., the synapse is weakened. Synaptic plasticity induced by LTP may be one of the cellular mechanisms that underlie learning and memory formation (including for motor processes). Although LTP is not well understood, current theory suggests there is increased postsynaptic neuron sensitivity to neurotransmitter release from the presynaptic neuron. Increased postsynaptic sensitivity can occur via increased activity of already-existing neurotransmitter receptors or via generation of new neurotransmitter receptor sites on the postsynaptic membrane. The mechanisms that underlie these changes in neurotransmitter receptors are still debated, but many suggest that N-methyl-D-aspartate receptors play a large part in LTP. Another contributor to neuroplasticity may be angiogenesis, the development of new blood vessels, which increases blood flow to the brain and has been shown to stimulate neurogenesis and synaptogenesis, while also contributing to synaptic and neuronal plasticity (Ergul, Alhusban, & Fagan, 2012). Below we highlight the effects of habitual exercise with respect to these mechanisms.

Exercise, Neuroplasticity, and Cognition

Significant progress has been made in understanding how neuroplasticity mechanisms primed through physical activity exert an effect on the brain. Exercise effects on hippocampal neuronal regeneration are especially well documented in populations including stroke, PD, and normal aging (Klaus & Amrein, 2011; Lau, Patki, Das-Panja, Le, & Ahmad, 2011; McCrate & Kaspar, 2008; Sahay et al., 2011). Erickson and colleagues longitudinally demonstrated 1–2% increases in hippocampal volume following a

year-long aerobic exercise intervention in older adults. Significantly, a nonaerobic exercise control group experienced a 1–2% degradation of hippocampal volume over that same time course (Erickson et al., 2011). Similarly, 6 months of aerobic training significantly increased total hippocampal volume compared with a balance training group in persons with MCI. In this study, both left and right hippocampal volumes improved significantly over the intervention in the aerobic group, whereas hippocampal volumes in the balance and tone training group declined and resistance training did not significantly improve volume (Ten Brinke et al., 2014). A related study showed that a 6-month aerobic exercise intervention demonstrated increased GM density in the anterior cingulate cortex, the supplementary motor area, superior frontal gyrus and increased WM in the anterior corpus callosum in older adults (Colcombe et al., 2006). Further, researchers have examined associations between cardiovascular fitness levels and the density of GM and WM in adults aged 55–79. Older adults with greater levels of cardiovascular fitness had significantly less atrophy of GM in the frontal cortex as well as significantly less loss of tissues in both the anterior and posterior WM tracts (Colcombe et al., 2003).

Alterations in structure may indeed correlate to improved behavioral and functional outcomes. Neuronal regeneration in the hippocampus is critical because of its vital role in memory formation and spatial navigation. In the Erickson study (2011), the increase in hippocampal volume following exercise was associated with more accurate performance on a spatial memory task. However, Ten Brinke and colleagues demonstrated that increased left hippocampal volume was significantly associated with greater loss in word recollection after interference. In the same sample, aerobic training significantly improved word recall after a delay as measured by the Rey Auditory Verbal Learning Test (Ten Brinke et al., 2014). These findings may be explained by hypothesized hemispheric differences in hippocampal contributions to memory, i.e., for spatial memory, left hippocampal activity is associated with an egocentric, sequential representation of space but right hippocampal activity is associated with an allocentric representation (Igloi, Doeller, Berthoz, Rondi-Reig, & Burgess, 2010). Other factors, such as WM degeneration, may significantly moderate the association between brain volume and cognitive performance. For example, the connectivity between the hippocampus and other brain areas may be greatly disrupted by WM abnormalities, which is likely the case in MCI (Rowley et al., 2013). Thus, increasing hippocampal volume alone, through aerobic, other exercise, or other means, in older populations may not always result in improved memory performance.

Similarly, demonstrated enhancement in frontal connectivity associated with aerobic fitness is correlated with improvements in frontally mediated EFs. For example, aerobic exercise is associated with improvements in attention and processing speed, EF, and memory in healthy and impaired individuals, including aged individuals (Voss, Heo, et al., 2013). Seminal work demonstrated that 124 older adults randomly assigned to receive aerobic training experienced substantial improvement in performance of tasks dependent on executive control processes and the integrity of the prefrontal and frontal cortex (Kramer et al., 1999). A recent study assigned older individuals (65 years and over) to ride stationary bicycles for 3 "spin" sessions per week for 12 weeks in comparison to a control group. The exercise group demonstrated significantly higher category verbal fluency after the intervention. Further, follow-up analysis demonstrated significant correlations between increase in cardiovascular fitness and improvements in verbal fluency (Nocera, McGregor, Hass, & Crosson, 2014). In another study, 6 months of thrice-weekly moderate- or high-intensity resistance training improved cognitive performance of memory and verbal

concept formation among senior men (Cassilhas et al., 2007). Similarly, 12 months of progressive resistance training once or twice weekly improved selective attention and conflict resolution relative to twice-weekly balance and toning exercises in community-dwelling women aged 65–75 years (Liu-Ambrose et al., 2010). Most notably, these results report that the effects of resistance training on executive cognitive functions are selective, i.e., resistance training enhanced selective attention and conflict resolution in older women, but cognitive abilities associated with manipulating verbal information in working memory and shifting between task sets or instructions were unaffected. In follow-up evaluations of this cohort, Best et al. reported that women who made greater improvements in EF during the training period showed better adherence to physical activity during the 1-year follow-up period (Best, Nagamatsu, & Liu-Ambrose, 2014). The mechanism for these changes comes from cross-sectional studies that indicate that exercise may mitigate decreases in vital cortical inhibitory mechanisms in older adults (McGregor et al., 2012, 2013). As noted above, semantic fluency output following an aerobic exercise intervention in previously sedentary older adults has been observed.

Although the body of evidence supporting the effect of aerobic exercise on brain health has grown considerably, other studies have failed to observe such a relationship (Madden, Blumenthal, Allen, & Emery, 1989; Niemann, Godde, Staudinger, & Voelcker-Rehage, 2014; Okumiya et al., 1996). It must be acknowledged that the cardiovascular fitness assessment has differed between studies [e.g., resting heart rate vs. the benchmark maximum volume of oxygen uptake ($\dot{V}O_2$max)]. In addition, some studies have employed cognitive tasks that may fall outside the capacity of hypothesized exercise-related improvements (e.g., measures of "crystalized" intelligence). Finally, the age, health, sex, and fitness level of the participants have differed between studies. However, collectively, recent research demonstrates that the relationship between aerobic fitness and cognitive health is encouraging. Aerobic exercise can protect the brain from age-related atrophy and aerobic interventions increase activity and mitigate loss of inhibition during tasks requiring executive control. Further, structural and functional improvements are consistent with behavioral studies demonstrating improvements in executive control processes reliant on the frontal cortex and hippocampus.

Not all of the effects of exercise are mediated by plastic changes in the neocortex. Exercise has effects in other central nervous system structures particularly implicated in PD including substantia nigra and the rest of basal ganglia (Smith, Goldberg, & Meshul, 2011; Vucckovic et al., 2010; Wu et al., 2011), corticostriatal synapses (Cepeda et al., 2010), and cerebellum (Ben-Ari et al., 2012).

The Effects of Exercise on PD

Exercise has been shown to improve motor function both in animal models of PD (Tajiri et al., 2010) and in humans with PD (Fisher et al., 2008). Goodwin and colleagues conducted a systematic review of the literature related to exercise interventions and functional improvements in people with PD (Goodwin, Richards, Taylor, Taylor, & Campbell, 2008). Of the 14 studies reviewed, 5 demonstrated exercise-related improvements in balance, 4 showed exercise-related improvements in strength, and 4 showed improved QOL related to exercise. In a 2011 review, it was suggested that vigorous, ongoing exercise, which increases the heart rate and oxygen uptake, could be neuroprotective; therefore, it should be encouraged and emphasized as a potential strategy for a more favorable disease course (Ahlskog, 2011).

THE EFFECTS OF EXERCISE ON COGNITION IN PD

In the last decade there has been a significant increase in research and clinical interest in using exercise as a treatment for mobility problems in people with PD. During this time, the number of publications addressing exercise for PD has more than tripled (van der Kolk & King, 2013). A 2012 study looked at a 10-month community-based exercise program for people with PD (Steffen, Petersen, & Dvorak, 2012) and found that the group exercise program resulted in improved endurance with maintained walking speed and balance. Another 16-month community exercise program investigated three exercise approaches: functional exercise addressing flexibility and balance, supervised aerobic exercises, and home-based exercises (Schenkman et al., 2012). At 4 months, the functional exercise program improved overall function. The aerobic program was superior for improving walking specifically. Similarly, the efficacy of resistance training for improving Parkinsonian motor signs has been demonstrated in participants with PD who exercised for 2 years (Corcos et al., 2013). More recently, interest in investigating the effects of exercise upon cognitive abilities has grown, based upon the neuroplasticity principles outlined in the previous section.

A recent review considered six preclinical studies in rodent models of PD (Murray, Sacheli, Eng, & Stoessl, 2014). The results were mixed but revealed some positive effects of exercise on cognition in these rodents, specifically improving long-term memory, motor learning, and short-term social memory. Along with these behavioral changes were neurobiological changes including upregulation of the neurotrophic factors, brain-derived neurotrophic factor (BDNF), and glial cell-derived neurotrophic factor (GDNF) in striatum and increased dopamine in the striatum. These findings are in line with three proposed mechanisms of improved cognition via exercise specifically for individuals with PD: enhanced availability of dopamine projections to the dorsal and/or ventral striatum; increased neurotrophic factor availability; and/or decreased neuroinflammation in the basal ganglia. The same review also covered recent human studies and found eight studies that demonstrated improved cognitive function as a result of exercise. Notably, the four studies with stronger evidence had measured specific aspects of cognitive function, whereas those measuring nonspecific aspects of cognition had weaker findings (Murray et al., 2014).

Probably the strongest evidence to suggest the benefits of exercise for cognition in PD was produced by Uc et al. (2014), who demonstrated that 6 months (thrice weekly) of an aerobic walking program in 60 independently ambulatory individuals with PD led to improvements in gait speed, Unified Parkinson's Disease Rating Scale (UPDRS)-III scores, and one aspect of EF, resistance to interference, as measured by the flanker task (Uc et al., 2014). However, the lack of a control group tempers some of the power of these findings.

Other researchers have demonstrated the motor and cognitive effects of dance exercise. Tango instruction has led to improvement in PD mobility and QOL versus other partnered dances (Hackney & Earhart, 2009), nonpartnered dance (Hackney & Earhart, 2010b), and generalized exercise (Hackney, Kantorovich, Levin, & Earhart, 2007). McKee and Hackney (2013) demonstrated that, in addition to expected motor improvements, 30 h of adapted tango over 12 weeks improved spatial cognition (as measured with the mental imagery, Brooks task) in individuals with mild–moderate PD (McKee & Hackney, 2013). Tango could be considered light–moderate exercise. Participants are stepping at 60–120 beats/minute (tempo of tango music) and expending at least three metabolic equivalent of tasks (METs) per minute (Heyward, 2010). Importantly, the exercise dose in this study—30 h over 10–12 weeks—exceeds weekly exercise dosage recommendations for deconditioned older adults with chronic illness (Chodzko-Zajko et al., 2009), which may have contributed to cognitive and motor improvements. Thus, the possibility exists that cognitive gains noted in the adapted tango group occurred because aerobic exercise has beneficial effects upon cognition (Kraft, 2012; Ratey & Loehr, 2011). Notably, the researchers in this study ruled out partnered/social learning and interaction as being responsible for gains. Thus, adapted tango elements, including structured motor components that engage memory of steps and directions while encouraging keen awareness of spatial relationships, could have contributed to cognitive gains. A within-group improvement of tango participants in global/EF, as measured by the Montreal Cognitive Assessment, represented only a small absolute change, but this change in the adapted tango group's scores represented moving from a diagnosis of MCI (<26 points) to normal cognition (>26 points) (Nasreddine et al., 2005).

Several small studies have examined the benefits of exercise for those with PD on various aspects of cognition. Six months of generalized moderate-intensity, multimodal physical training (consisting of aerobic, resistance, coordination, and balance elements) led to improvements in the capacity for abstraction and mental flexibility (aspects of EF) as measured by the Wisconsin Card Sorting Task in 10 older individuals with PD in comparison to a nonexercising control group (Tanaka et al., 2009). Fifteen individuals with PD, who participated in programs of anabolic and aerobic exercise twice weekly for 12 weeks, showed improvements in verbal fluency (Cruise et al., 2011). Low-intensity passive cycling on a tandem bike, in a "forced exercise" situation once per week over 4 weeks has led to improvements by 19 people with PD on the Trails Making Test A & B, an EF measure (Ridgel, Kim, Fickes, Muller, & Alberts, 2011). dos Santos Mendes et al. (2012) assigned 16 individuals with early PD to Wii Fit training, to evaluate the motor and cognitive demands of the games on people with PD, in comparison to 11 healthy older adults. Compared to healthy controls, those with PD had no deficit in motor learning or retention on 7 of the 10 games, but had marked learning deficits on 3 games. However, the PD cohort was able to transfer motor ability gained from the games to a similar, but untrained task (dos Santos Mendes et al., 2012). Muller and Muhlack (2010) investigated the effects of a single bout (rather than an intervention) of high-intensity endurance aerobic exercise (heart rate-targeted cycling) or rest following 3,4-dihydroxy–L-phenylalanine (L-dopa) administration on reaction time, and complex movement sequence ability in 22 individuals with PD in a crossover design. Participants improved on reaction time, tapping rate, and peg insertion interval time after exercise, whereas they gave fewer correct answers after rest, and reaction time increased after rest (Muller & Muhlack, 2010).

These recent studies are encouraging and provide preliminary evidence that supports the effects of exercise on a variety of aspects of cognition for those with PD. The findings by Uc et al. (2014) are encouraging because they agree with research supporting the beneficial effects of aerobic exercise on cognition in older adults; however, these findings must be replicated in Phase III clinical trials. Further, all of these studies employed a range of cognitive outcome tasks, and improvements were limited to one or two EF measures. The exception are the improvements noted by McKee and Hackney, which provide novel evidence that supports further study into application of complex exercise programs, like adapted tango, for improving cognition. Such study is warranted and definitely needed (Hindle, Petrelli, Clare, & Kalbe, 2013) given the prevalence of MCI in PD, which affects the spectrum of mental function.

However, the number and size of the published studies of exercise effects in PD are limited making it difficult to reach a definitive conclusion. Based on evidence presented here, evaluating the effects of exercise on the particular aspects of cognitive function that are implicated in PD is recommended. Studies also need to examine the effects of exercise over both longer and shorter intervals and doses, and more randomized clinical trials are necessary to highlight

which symptoms of PD are amenable to change. In particular, to examine neural mechanisms of plasticity and improvement, it will be necessary to observe cognitive and motor changes in a group of PD participants over 6-month or, better, 12-month intervals, on a range of cognitive and motor abilities, in order to bring the research on exercise in PD in line with previous research in older adults.

FUTURE RESEARCH AND PRACTICAL APPLICATION

Exercise, which may benefit cognition, may also prove economic because group exercise classes are comparatively inexpensive to administer (Frick, Kung, Parrish, & Narrett, 2010; Liu & Frank, 2010). However, engaging in exercise habitually remains overwhelmingly poor in even the general older adult population. An epidemiologic study reported only one in eight older adults engage in strength or balance-challenging activities (Merom et al., 2012). Individuals with PD are less active than their age-matched peers without PD (Toth, Fishman, & Poehlman, 1997). Future research should include retention measures and delineate ideal frequency, duration, and intensity of exercise to obtain and retain gains in cognition.

To address the needs of those with PD, motor symptom treatment cannot be the sole concern in care. As pharmacological and surgical methods remain only partially effective in treating symptoms of those with PD, and fall risk and related injury are prevalent among older adults, additional, nonpharmacological approaches that address cognitive, motor, and motor–cognitive impairments are necessary. Exercise has shown much promise recently; however, activities that engage older individuals and sustain interest are mandated, as approximately 60% of Americans older than 65 do not achieve the recommended daily amount of physical activity (Macera et al., 2005). Given that activity levels in individuals with PD have been estimated to be between 15% lower (Toth et al., 1997) and, in a study with 699 people with PD and 1959 controls, 29% lower (van Nimwegen et al., 2011) than age-matched controls, the task ahead may be challenging.

Dose is a matter of great relevance in exercise research. Voss et al. (2010) demonstrated that behaviorally relevant changes in functional connectivity were correlated to improvements in EF in older adults who participated in 12 months of a walking program. This cohort was also examined at 6 months but there were only nonsignificant trends toward improvement (Voss et al., 2010). Therefore, ongoing exercise over a substantial period of time is likely necessary to benefit significantly from neuroplastic mechanisms of improvement.

Many studies do not ensure that all participants receive the same amount of treatment, which makes inference difficult about the effects of one dose versus another. Better monitoring of studies' success with exercise compliance and actual dosing achieved per participant would be helpful. Beyond laboratory, controlled experiments investigating dose-responsiveness and attrition rates, comparative effectiveness studies evaluating the potential of real-life exercise interventions with community participants with PD are necessary. Such studies would shed light on the practicality of disseminating and implementing evidence-based exercise programs and further expose challenges to adherence within this difficult to treat population with an intractable condition.

In addition, future work is needed to evaluate the importance of regular exercise versus increases in leisure time physical activity. Exercise trials with doses ranging from 20 to 40 min, 2–3 times per week provide activity times that are overcompensated by the increasing habit of being sedentary. In this example, this typical dose of exercise produces 2 h of sustained physical activity per week, which is less than 2% of waking hours. In contrast, almost 60% of older

adults reported sitting for more than 4 h per day (28 h per week), 65% sit in front of a television or computer screen for more than 3 h daily. Individuals with PD report even higher rates of inactivity. Thus, neuroprotective and neuroplastic effects of exercise may be blunted in these small doses in the face of overwhelming inactivity. Interventions that increase standing time throughout the day or physical activity even at low-intensity levels may help tip the scales leading to more positive improvements in cognitive performance.

Going forward, uncovering mechanisms may be the most important area of discovery for enhancing nonpharmacological interventions that address cognitive issues in PD. The knowledge and principles gained could impact not only exercise disciplines but also pharmacological, surgical, physical, and occupational therapy for older adults with PD and related neurological disorders. Investigating mechanisms of mediating variables, e.g., mood capability to accomplish activities of daily living, to impact cognition via exercise must be examined. The neuroprotection and neurorestoration that may be derived from consistent, task specific and frequent aerobic exercise may extend into improved mood and functional activity performance, thereby impacting cognition. Obviously, further work related to neurobiological mechanisms will be crucial to informing rehabilitative interventions as well as pharmacological and surgical treatments. Imaging with positron emission tomography, functional magnetic resonance imaging, and *transcranial magnetic stimulation* hold promise as well, given that lower limb neural pathways, implicated in exercise, are virtually unexplored in connection with rehabilitative efforts in PD.

Rehabilitation to restore and/or improve cognition in people with PD must be efficient and effective, because adherence to an exercise regimen is critical. Thus, identifying aspects of exercise, which are most responsible for benefits to cognition-mediating symptoms, e.g., axial impairment and depression, will impact adherence to exercise. Understanding these crucial aspects will help determine foundational principles of exercise training to evince cognitive maintenance and/or gains. Creating sustained behavioral change through targeted exercise programs may be most effective at addressing cognitive issues in PD. With improved and/or maintained independence via enhanced mobility, and targeted application of neuroplasticity principles, the overall goal of improving cognition in those with PD can be reached.

References

Aarsland, D., Andersen, K., Larsen, J. P., & Lolk, A. (2003). Prevalence and characteristics of dementia in Parkinson disease: an 8-year prospective study. *Archives of Neurology*, *60*, 387–392.

Aarsland, D., Andersen, K., Larsen, J. P., Lolk, A., Nielsen, H., & Kragh-Sorensen, P. (2001). Risk of dementia in Parkinson's disease: a community-based, prospective study. *Neurology*, *56*, 730–736.

Aarsland, D., Andersen, K., Larsen, J. P., Perry, R., Wentzel-Larsen, T., Lolk, A., et al. (2004). The rate of cognitive decline in Parkinson disease. *Archives of Neurology*, *61*, 1906–1911.

Ahlskog, J. E. (2011). Does vigorous exercise have a neuroprotective effect in Parkinson disease? *Neurology*, *77*, 288–294.

Albin, R. L., Young, A. B., & Penney, J. B. (1989). The functional anatomy of basal ganglia disorders. *Trends in Neuroscience*, *12*, 366–375.

Alexander, G. E., & Crutcher, M. D. (1990). Functional architecture of basal ganglia circuits: neural substrates of parallel processing [see comments]. *Trends in Neuroscience*, *13*, 266–271.

Alexander, G. E., Crutcher, M. D., & DeLong, M. R. (1990). Basal ganglia-thalamocortical circuits: parallel substrates for motor, oculomotor, "prefrontal" and "limbic" functions. *Progress in Brain Research*, *85*, 119–146.

Altmann, L. J. P., & Troche, M. S. (2011). High-level language production in Parkinson's disease: a review. *Parkinsons Disease*. http://dx.doi.org/10.4061/2011/238956.

Al-Yahya, E., Dawes, H., Smith, L., Dennis, A., Howells, K., & Cockburn, J. (2011). Cognitive motor interference while walking: a systematic review and meta-analysis. *Neuroscience and Biobehavioral Reviews*, *35*, 715–728.

Baker, K., Rochester, L., & Nieuwboer, A. (2007). The immediate effect of attentional, auditory, and a combined cue strategy on gait during single and dual tasks in Parkinson's disease. *Archives of Physical Medicine and Rehabilitation*, *88*, 1593–1600.

Baker, K., Rochester, L., & Nieuwboer, A. (2008). The effect of cues on gait variability–reducing the attentional cost of walking in people with Parkinson's disease. *Parkinsonism and Related Disorders*, *14*, 314–320.

Ben-Ari, S., Ofek, K., Barbash, S., Meiri, H., Kovalev, E., Greenberg, D. S., et al. (2012). Similar cation channels mediate protection from cerebellar exitotoxicity by exercise and inheritance. *Journal of Cellular and Molecular Medicine*, *16*, 555–568.

Bergman, H., Wichmann, T., Karmon, B., & DeLong, M. R. (1994). The primate subthalamic nucleus. II. Neuronal activity in the MPTP model of parkinsonism. *Journal of Neurophysiology*, *72*, 507–520.

Best, J. R., Nagamatsu, L. S., & Liu-Ambrose, T. (2014). Improvements to executive function during exercise training predict maintenance of physical activity over the following year. *Frontiers in Human Neuroscience*, *8*, 353. http://dx.doi.org/10.3389/fnhum.2014.00353.

Bloem, B. R., Hausdorff, J. M., Visser, J. E., & Giladi, N. (2004). Falls and freezing of gait in Parkinson's disease: a review of two interconnected, episodic phenomena. *Movement Disorders*, *19*, 871–884.

Bloem, B. R., van Vugt, J. P., & Beckley, D. J. (2001). Postural instability and falls in Parkinson's disease. *Advances in Neurology*, *87*, 209–223.

Buonomano, D. V., & Merzenich, M. M. (1998). Cortical plasticity: from synapses to maps. *Annual Review of Neuroscience*, *21*, 149–186.

Buter, T. C., van den Hout, A., Matthews, F. E., Larsen, J. P., Brayne, C., & Aarsland, D. (2008). Dementia and survival in Parkinson disease: a 12-year population study. *Neurology*, *70*, 1017–1022.

Cabeza, R. (2001). Functional neuroimaging of cognitive aging. In R. Cabeza, & A. Kingstone (Eds.), *Handbook of functional neuroimaging of cognition* (pp. 331–377). Cambridge, MA: MIT Press.

Camicioli, R., & Majumdar, S. R. (2010). Relationship between mild cognitive impairment and falls in older people with and without Parkinson's disease: 1-year prospective cohort study. *Gait and Posture*, *32*, 87–91.

Carpenter, M. G., Allum, J. H., Honegger, F., Adkin, A. L., & Bloem, B. R. (2004). Postural abnormalities to multidirectional stance perturbations in Parkinson's disease. *Journal of Neurology, Neurosurgery and Psychiatry*, *75*, 1245–1254.

Cassilhas, R. C., Viana, V. A., Grassmann, V., Santos, R. T., Santos, R. F., Tufik, S., et al. (2007). The impact of resistance exercise on the cognitive function of the elderly. *Medicine and Science in Sports and Exercise*, *39*, 1401–1407.

Cepeda, C., Cummings, D. M., Hickey, M. A., Kleiman-Weiner, M., Chen, J. Y., Watson, J. B., et al. (2010). Rescuing the corticostriatal synaptic disconnection in the R6/2 mouse model of Huntington's disease: exercise, adenosine receptors and ampakines. *PLoS Currents, 2.* http://dx.doi.org/10.1371/currents.RRN1182.

Chodzko-Zajko, W. J., Proctor, D. N., Fiatarone Singh, M. A., Minson, C. T., Nigg, C. R., Salem, G. J., et al. (2009). American College of Sports Medicine position stand. Exercise and physical activity for older adults. *Medicine and Science in Sports and Exercise, 41,* 1510–1530.

Colcombe, S. J., Erickson, K. I., Raz, N., Webb, A. G., Cohen, N. J., McAuley, E., et al. (2003). Aerobic fitness reduces brain tissue loss in aging humans. *Journal of Gerontology, Series A, 58,* 176–180.

Colcombe, S. J., Erickson, K. I., Scalf, P. E., Kim, J. S., Prakash, R., McAuley, E., et al. (2006). Aerobic exercise training increases brain volume in aging humans. *Journal of Gerontology, Series A, 61,* 1166–1170.

Comery, T. A., Harris, J. B., Willems, P. J., Oostra, B. A., Irwin, S. A., Weiler, I. J., et al. (1997). Abnormal dendritic spines in fragile X knockout mice: maturation and pruning deficits. *Proceedings of the National Academy of Sciences of the United States of America, 94,* 5401–5404.

Corcos, D. M., Robichaud, J. A., David, F. J., Leurgans, S. E., Vaillancourt, D. E., Poon, C., et al. (2013). A two-year randomized controlled trial of progressive resistance exercise for Parkinson's disease. *Movement Disorders, 28,* 1230–1240.

Costa, A., Peppe, A., Caltagirone, C., & Carlesimo, G. A. (2008). Prospective memory impairment in individuals with Parkinson's disease. *Neuropsychology, 22,* 283–292.

Cruise, K. E., Bucks, R. S., Loftus, A. M., Newton, R. U., Pegoraro, R., & Thomas, M. G. (2011). Exercise and Parkinson's: benefits for cognition and quality of life. *Acta Neurologica Scandinavica, 123,* 13–19.

Dalla Volta, R., Gianelli, C., Campione, G. C., & Gentilucci, M. (2009). Action word understanding and overt motor behavior. *Experimental Brain Research, 196,* 403–412.

Davidsdottir, S., Cronin-Golomb, A., & Lee, A. (2005). Visual and spatial symptoms in Parkinson's disease. *Vision Research, 45,* 1285–1296.

DeLong, M. R. (1983). The neurophysiologic basis of abnormal movements in basal ganglia disorders. *Neurobehavioral Toxicology and Teratology, 5,* 611–616.

DeLong, M. R. (1990). Primate models of movement disorders of basal ganglia origin. *Trends in Neuroscience, 13,* 281–285.

DeLong, M. R., Alexander, G. E., Mitchell, S. J., & Richardson, R. T. (1986). The contribution of basal ganglia to limb control. *Progress in Brain Research, 64,* 161–174.

DeLong, M. R., Georgopoulos, A. P., Crutcher, M. D., Mitchell, S. J., Richardson, R. T., & Alexander, G. E. (1984). Functional organization of the basal ganglia: contributions of single-cell recording studies. *Ciba Foundation Symposium, 107,* 64–82.

DeLong, M. R., & Wichmann, T. (1993). Basal ganglithalamocortical circuits in parkinsonian signs. *Clinical Neuroscience, 1,* 18–26.

Dimitrova, D., Horak, F. B., & Nutt, J. G. (2004). Postural muscle responses to multidirectional translations in patients with Parkinson's disease. *Journal of Neurophysiology, 91,* 489–501.

Dimitrova, D., Nutt, J., & Horak, F. B. (2004). Abnormal force patterns for multidirectional postural responses in patients with Parkinson's disease. *Experimental Brain Research, 156,* 183–195.

Dirnberger, G., & Jahanshahi, M. (2013). Executive dysfunction in Parkinson's disease: a review. *Journal of Neuropsychology, 7,* 193–224.

Domellof, M. E., Elgh, E., & Forsgren, L. (2011). The relation between cognition and motor dysfunction in drug-naive newly diagnosed patients with Parkinson's disease. *Movement Disorders, 26,* 2183–2189.

Dorsey, E. R., Constantinescu, R., Thompson, J. P., Biglan, K. M., Holloway, R. G., Kieburtz, K., et al. (2007). Projected number of people with Parkinson disease in the most populous nations, 2005 through 2030. *Neurology, 68,* 384–386.

Dubois, B., & Pillon, B. (1997). Cognitive deficits in Parkinson's disease. *Journal of Neurology, 244*(1), 2–8.

Duncan, G. W., Khoo, T. K., Yarnall, A. J., O'Brien, J. T., Coleman, S. Y., Brooks, D. J., et al. (2014). Health-related quality of life in early Parkinson's disease: the impact of nonmotor symptoms. *Movement Disorders, 29,* 195–202.

Elder, C., & Vitek, J. (2001). The motor thalamus: alteration of neuronal activity in the parkinsonian state. In K. Kultas-Ilinsky, & I. Ilinsky (Eds.), *Basal ganglia and thalamus in health and movement disorders* (pp. 257–265). New York: Kluwer Academic/Plenum Publishers.

Ergul, A., Alhusban, A., & Fagan, S. C. (2012). Angiogenesis: a harmonized target for recovery after stroke. *Stroke, 43,* 2270–2274.

Erickson, K. I., Voss, M. W., Prakash, R. S., Basak, C., Szabo, A., Chaddock, L., et al. (2011). Exercise training increases size of hippocampus and improves memory. *Proceedings of the National Academy of Sciences of the United States of America, 108,* 3017–3022.

Filion, M., Tremblay, L., & Bedard, P. J. (1988). Abnormal influences of passive limb movement on the activity of globus pallidus neurons in parkinsonian monkeys. *Brain Research, 444,* 165–176.

Fisher, B. E., Wu, A. D., Salem, G. J., Song, J., Lin, C. H., Yip, J., et al. (2008). The effect of exercise training in improving motor performance and corticomotor excitability in people with early Parkinson's disease. *Archives of Physical Medicine and Rehabilitation, 89,* 1221–1229.

Flowers, K. A., Robertson, C., & Sheridan, M. R. (1995). Some characteristics of word fluency in Parkinson's disease. *Journal of Neurolinguistics, 9,* 33–46.

Foster, E. R., McDaniel, M. A., Repovš, G., & Hershey, T. (2009). Prospective memory in Parkinson disease across laboratory and self-reported everyday performance. *Neuropsychology, 23,* 347–358.

Freedland, R. L., Festa, C., Sealy, M., McBean, A., Elghazaly, P., Capan, A., et al. (2002). The effects of pulsed auditory stimulation on various gait measurements in persons with Parkinson's Disease. *NeuroRehabilitation, 17*, 81–87.

de Frias, C. M., Dixon, R. A., Fisher, N., & Camicioli, R. (2007). Intraindividual variability in neurocognitive speed: a comparison of Parkinson's disease and normal older adults. *Neuropsychologia, 45*, 2499–2507.

Frick, K. D., Kung, J. Y., Parrish, J. M., & Narrett, M. J. (2010). Evaluating the cost-effectiveness of fall prevention programs that reduce fall-related hip fractures in older adults. *Journal of the American Geriatrics Society, 58*, 136–141.

Goodwin, V. A., Richards, S. H., Taylor, R. S., Taylor, A. H., & Campbell, J. L. (2008). The effectiveness of exercise interventions for people with Parkinson's disease: a systematic review and meta-analysis. *Movement Disorders, 23*, 631–640.

Grossi, J. A., Maitra, K. K., & Rice, M. S. (2007). Semantic priming of motor task performance in young adults: implications for occupational therapy. *American Journal of Occupational Therapy, 61*, 311–320.

Grossman, M. (1999). Sentence processing in Parkinson's disease. *Brain and Cognition, 40*, 387–413.

Grossman, M., Lee, C., Morris, J., Stern, M. B., & Hurtig, H. I. (2002). Assessing resource demands during sentence processing in Parkinson's disease. *Brain and Language, 80*, 603–616.

Grossman, M., Zurif, E., Lee, C., Prather, P., Kalmanson, J., Stern, M. B., et al. (2002). Information processing speed and sentence comprehension in Parkinson's disease. *Neuropsychology, 16*, 174–181.

Hackney, M. E., & Earhart, G. M. (2009). Effects of dance on movement control in Parkinson's disease: a comparison of Argentine tango and American ballroom. *Journal of Rehabilitation Medicine, 41*, 475–481.

Hackney, M. E., & Earhart, G. M. (2010a). The effects of a secondary task on forward and backward walking in Parkinson's disease. *Neurorehabilitation and Neural Repair, 24*, 384–392.

Hackney, M. E., & Earhart, G. M. (2010b). Effects of dance on gait and balance in Parkinson's disease: a comparison of partnered and nonpartnered dance movement. *Neurorehabilitation and Neural Repair, 24*, 384–392.

Hackney, M. E., Kantorovich, S., Levin, R., & Earhart, G. M. (2007). Effects of tango on functional mobility in Parkinson's disease: a preliminary study. *Journal of Neurologic Physical Therapy, 31*, 173–179.

Hartikainen, P., Helkala, E. L., Soininen, H., & Riekkinen, P., Sr. (1993). Cognitive and memory deficits in untreated Parkinson's disease and amyotrophic lateral sclerosis patients: a comparative study. *Journal of Neural Transmission. Parkinson's Disease and Dementia Section, 6*, 127–137.

Hausdorff, J. M., Doniger, G. M., Springer, S., Yogev, G., Simon, E. S., & Giladi, N. (2006). A common cognitive profile in elderly fallers and in patients with Parkinson's disease: the prominence of impaired executive function and attention. *Experimental Aging Research, 32*, 411–429.

Hebb, D. O. (1949). *The organization of behavior; a neuropsychological theory.* New York: Wiley.

Helmstaedter, C., Wietzke, J., & Lutz, M. T. (2009). Unique and shared validity of the "Wechsler logical memory test", the "California verbal learning test", and the "verbal learning and memory test" in patients with epilepsy. *Epilepsy Research, 87*, 203–212.

Hely, M. A., Reid, W. G., Adena, M. A., Halliday, G. M., & Morris, J. G. (2008). The Sydney multicenter study of Parkinson's disease: the inevitability of dementia at 20 years. *Movement Disorders, 23*, 837–844.

Henik, A., Singh, J., Beckley, D. J., & Rafal, R. D. (1993). Disinhibition of atomatic word reading in Parkinson's disease. *Cortex, 29*, 589–599.

Henry, J. D., & Crawford, J. R. (2004). Verbal fluency deficits in Parkinson's disease: a meta-analysis. *Journal of the International Neuropsychological Society, 10*, 608–622.

Heyward, V. H. (2010). *Advanced fitness assessment and exercise prescription* (6th ed.). Champaign, IL: Human Kinetics.

Hindle, J. V., Petrelli, A., Clare, L., & Kalbe, E. (2013). Nonpharmacological enhancement of cognitive function in Parkinson's disease: a systematic review. *Movement Disorders, 28*, 1034–1049.

Hochstadt, J. (2009). Set-shifting and the on-line processing of relative clauses in Parkinson's disease: results from a novel eye-tracking method. *Cortex, 45*, 991–1011.

Honeycutt, C. F., Gottschall, J. S., & Nichols, T. R. (2009). Electromyographic responses from the hindlimb muscles of the decerebrate cat to horizontal support surface perturbations. *Journal of Neurophysiology, 101*, 2751–2761.

Hoppe, C. D., Muller, U. D., Werheid, K. D., Thone, A. D., & von Cramon, Y. D. (2000). Digit Ordering Test: clinical, psychometric, and experimental evaluation of a verbal working memory test. *Clinical Neuropsychologist, 14*, 38–55.

Horak, F. B., Dimitrova, D., & Nutt, J. G. (2005). Direction-specific postural instability in subjects with Parkinson's disease. *Experimental Neurology, 193*, 504–521.

Igloi, K., Doeller, C. F., Berthoz, A., Rondi-Reig, L., & Burgess, N. (2010). Lateralized human hippocampal activity predicts navigation based on sequence or place memory. *Proceedings of the National Academy of Sciences of the United States of America, 107*, 14466–14471.

Jaywant, A., Musto, G., Neargarder, S., Stavitsky Gilbert, K., & Cronin-Golomb, A. (2014). The effect of Parkinson's disease subgroups on verbal and nonverbal fluency. *Journal of Clinical and Experimental Neuropsychology, 36*, 278–289.

Jiang, Y., & Norman, K. E. (2006). Effects of visual and auditory cues on gait initiation in people with Parkinson's disease. *Clinical Rehabilitation, 20*, 36–45.

Jones, J. D., Butterfield, L. C., Song, W., Lafo, J., Mangal, P., Okun, M. S., et al. (2014). Anxiety and depression are better correlates of Parkinson's disease quality of life than apathy. *Journal of Neuropsychiatry and Clinical Neuroscience.* http://dx.doi.org/10.1176/appi.neuropsych.13120380.

Kelly, V. E., & Bastian, A. J. (2005). Antiparkinson medications improve agonist activation but not antagonist inhibition during sequential reaching movements. *Movement Disorders, 20*, 694–704.

Kemmerer, D., Castillo, J. G., Talavage, T., Patterson, S., & Wiley, C. (2008). Neuroanatomical distribution of five semantic components of verbs: evidence from fMRI. *Brain and Language, 107*, 16–43.

Kemper, S., & Sumner, A. (2001). The structure of verbal abilities in young and older adults. *Psychology and Aging, 16*, 312–322.

Klaus, F., & Amrein, I. (2011). Running in laboratory and wild rodents: differences in context sensitivity and plasticity of hippocampal neurogenesis. *Behavioural Brain Research, 227*, 363–370.

Klencklen, G., Despres, O., & Dufour, A. (2012). What do we know about aging and spatial cognition? Reviews and perspectives. *Ageing Research Reviews, 11*, 123–135.

Koerts, J., Leenders, K. L., & Brouwer, W. H. (2009). Cognitive dysfunction in non-demented Parkinson's disease patients: controlled and automatic behavior. *Cortex, 45*, 922–929.

van der Kolk, N. M., & King, L. A. (2013). Effects of exercise on mobility in people with Parkinson's disease. *Movement Disorders, 28*, 1587–1596.

Kopelman, M. D., & Stanhope, N. (1998). Recall and recognition memory in patients with focal frontal, temporal lobe and diencephalic lesions. *Neuropsychologia, 36*, 785–795.

Kostering, L., McKinlay, A., Stahl, C., & Kaller, C. P. (2012). Differential patterns of planning impairments in Parkinson's disease and sub-clinical signs of dementia? A latent-class model-based approach. *PLoS One, 7*(6), e38855. http://dx.doi.org/10.1371/journal.pone.0038855.

Kraft, E. (2012). Cognitive function, physical activity, and aging: possible biological links and implications for multimodal interventions. *Neuropsychology, Development, and Cognition. Section B: Aging, Neuropsychology and Cognition, 19*, 248–263.

Kramer, A. F., Hahn, S., Cohen, N. J., Banich, M. T., McAuley, E., Harrison, C. R., et al. (1999). Ageing, fitness and neurocognitive function. *Nature, 400*, 418–419.

Lagopoulos, J., Malhi, G. S., Ivanovski, B., Cahill, C. M., & Morris, J. G. (2005). A matter of motion or an emotional matter? Management of depression in Parkinson's disease. *Expert Review of Neurotherapeutics, 5*, 803–810.

Lanni, K. E., Ross, J. M., Higginson, C. I., Dressler, E. M., Sigvardt, K. A., Zhang, L., et al. (2014). Perceived and performance-based executive dysfunction in Parkinson's disease. *Journal of Clinical and Experimental Neuropsychology, 36*, 342–355.

Lau, Y. S., Patki, G., Das-Panja, K., Le, W. D., & Ahmad, S. O. (2011). Neuroprotective effects and mechanisms of exercise in a chronic mouse model of Parkinson's disease with moderate neurodegeneration. *European Journal of Neuroscience, 33*, 1264–1274.

Lee, C., Grossman, M., Morris, J., Stern, M. B., & Hurtig, H. I. (2003). Attentional resource and processing speed limitations during sentence processing in Parkinson's disease. *Brain and Language, 85*, 347–356.

Lees, A. J., & Smith, E. (1983). Cognitive deficits in the early stages of Parkinson's disease. *Brain, 106*, 257–270.

Leroi, I., Collins, D., & Marsh, L. (2006). Non-dopaminergic treatment of cognitive impairment and dementia in Parkinson's disease: a review. *Journal of Neurological Sciences, 248*, 104–114.

Lewis, S. J. G., Dove, A., Robbins, T. W., Barker, R. A., & Owen, A. M. (2003). Cognitive impairments in early Parkinson's disease are accompanied by reductions in activity in frontostriatal neural circuitry. *Journal of Neuroscience, 23*, 6351–6356.

Lewis, M. M., Slagle, C. G., Smith, A. B., Truong, Y., Bai, P., McKeown, M. J., et al. (2007). Task specific influences of Parkinson's disease on the striato-thalamo-cortical and cerebello-thalamo-cortical motor circuitries. *Neuroscience, 147*, 224–235.

Lezak, M. D., Howieson, D. B., Loring, D. W., Hannay, H. J., & Fischer, J. S. (2004). *Neuropsychological assessment* (4th ed.). New York: Oxford University Press.

Lieberman, P., Kako, E., Friedman, J., Tajchman, G., Feldman, L. S., & Jiminez, E. B. (1992). Speech production, syntax comprehension, and cognitive deficits in Parkinson's disease. *Brain and Language, 43*, 169–189.

Lindenberger, U., Marsiske, M., & Baltes, P. B. (2000). Memorizing while walking: increase in dual-task costs from young adulthood to old age. *Psychology and Aging, 15*, 417–436.

Liu-Ambrose, T., Nagamatsu, L. S., Graf, P., Beattie, B. L., Ashe, M. C., & Handy, T. C. (2010). Resistance training and executive functions: a 12-month randomized controlled trial. *Archives of Internal Medicine, 170*, 170–178.

Liu, H., & Frank, A. (2010). Tai chi as a balance improvement exercise for older adults: a systematic review. *Journal of Geriatric Physical Therapy, 33*, 103–109.

Macera, C. A., Ham, S. A., Yore, M. M., Jones, D. A., Ainsworth, B. E., Kimsey, C. D., et al. (2005). Prevalence of physical activity in the United States: behavioral risk factor surveillance system, 2001. *Prevention of Chronic Disease, 2*, A17.

Madden, D. J., Blumenthal, J. A., Allen, P. A., & Emery, C. F. (1989). Improving aerobic capacity in healthy older adults does not necessarily lead to improved cognitive performance. *Psychology and Aging, 4*, 307–320.

Martin, R. C., Wetzel, W. F., Blossom-Stach, C., & Feher, E. (1989). Syntactic loss versus processing deficit: an assessment of two theories of agrammatism and syntactic comprehension deficits. *Cognition, 32*, 157–191.

McCrate, M. E., & Kaspar, B. K. (2008). Physical activity and neuroprotection in amyotrophic lateral sclerosis. *Neuro-Molecular Medicine, 10*, 108–117.

McDowd, J. M., Hoffman, L., Rozek, E., Lyons, K., Pahwa, R., Burns, J., et al. (2011). Understanding verbal fluency in healthy aging, Alzheimer's disease, and Parkinson's disease. *Neuropsychology, 25*, 210–225.

McFadyen, B. J., Hegeman, J., & Duysens, J. (2009). Dual task effects for asymmetric stepping on a split-belt treadmill. *Gait and Posture, 30*, 340–344.

McGregor, K. M., Heilman, K. M., Nocera, J. R., Patten, C., Manini, T. M., Crosson, B., et al. (2012). Aging, aerobic activity and interhemispheric communication. *Brain Science, 2*, 634–648.

McGregor, K. M., Nocera, J. R., Sudhyadhom, A., Patten, C., Manini, T. M., Kleim, J. A., et al. (2013). Effects of aerobic fitness on aging-related changes of interhemispheric inhibition and motor performance. *Frontiers in Aging Neuroscience, 5*, 66. http://dx.doi.org/10.3389/fnagi.2013.00066.

McKee, K. E., & Hackney, M. E. (2013). The effects of adapted tango on spatial cognition and disease severity in Parkinson's disease. *Journal of Motor Behavior, 45*, 519–529.

McKinlay, A., Grace, R. C., Dalrymple-Alford, J. C., & Roger, D. (2010). Characteristics of executive function impairment in Parkinson's disease patients without dementia. *Journal of the International Neuropsychological Society, 16*, 268–277.

McKinlay, A., Kaller, C. P., Grace, R. C., Dalrymple-Alford, J. C., Anderson, T. J., Fink, J., et al. (2008). Planning in Parkinson's disease: a matter of problem structure? *Neuropsychologia, 46*, 384–389.

McNamara, P., Durso, R., & Harris, E. (2006). Life goals of patients with Parkinson's disease: a pilot study on correlations with mood and cognitive functions. *Clinical Rehabilitation, 20*, 818–826.

Melton, L. J., III, Leibson, C. L., Achenbach, S. J., Bower, J. H., Maraganore, D. M., Oberg, A. L., et al. (2006). Fracture risk after the diagnosis of Parkinson's disease: influence of concomitant dementia. *Movement Disorders, 21*, 1361–1367.

Meppelink, A. M., de Jong, B. M., Renken, R., Leenders, K. L., Cornelissen, F. W., & van Laar, T. (2009). Impaired visual processing preceding image recognition in Parkinson's disease patients with visual hallucinations. *Brain, 132*, 2980–2993.

Merom, D., Pye, V., Macniven, R., van der Ploeg, H., Milat, A., Sherrington, C., et al. (2012). Prevalence and correlates of participation in fall prevention exercise/physical activity by older adults. *Preventive Medicine, 55*, 613–617.

Merzenich, M. M., Nelson, R. J., Stryker, M. P., Cynader, M. S., Schoppmann, A., & Zook, J. M. (1984). Somatosensory cortical map changes following digit amputation in adult monkeys. *Journal of Comparative Neurology, 224*, 591–605.

Miller, W. C., & DeLong, M. R. (1988). Parkinsonian symptomatology. An anatomical and physiological analysis. *Annals of the New York Academy of Sciences, 515*, 287–302.

Mink, J. W. (1996). The basal ganglia: focused selection and inhibition of competing motor programs. *Progress in Neurobiology, 50*, 381–425.

Mishkin, M., & Ungerleider, L. G. (1982). Contribution of striate inputs to the visuospatial functions of parieto-preoccipital cortex in monkeys. *Behavioural Brain Research, 6*, 57–77.

Monchi, O., Petrides, M., Doyon, J., Postuma, R. B., Worsley, K., & Dagher, A. (2004). Neural bases of set-shifting deficits in Parkinson's disease. *Journal of Neuroscience, 24*, 702–710.

Montse, A., Pere, V., Carme, J., Francesc, V., & Eduardo, T. (2001). Visuospatial deficits in Parkinson's disease assessed by judgment of line orientation test: error analyses and practice effects. *Journal of Clinical and Experimental Neuropsychololology, 23*, 592–598.

Morris, M. E., Huxham, F. E., McGinley, J., & Iansek, R. (2001). Gait disorders and gait rehabilitation in Parkinson's disease. *Advances in Neurology, 87*, 347–361.

Muller, T., & Muhlack, S. (2010). Effect of exercise on reactivity and motor behaviour in patients with Parkinson's disease. *Journal of Neurology, Neurosurgery and Psychiatry, 81*, 747–753.

Murray, L. L. (2008). Language and Parkinson's disease. *Annual Review of Applied Linguistics, 28*, 113–127.

Murray, D. K., Sacheli, M. A., Eng, J. J., & Stoessl, A. J. (2014). The effects of exercise on cognition in Parkinson's disease: a systematic review. *Translational Neurodegeneration, 3*, 5. http://dx.doi.org/10.1186/2047-9158-3-5.

Muslimovic, D., Post, B., Speelman, J. D., & Schmand, B. (2005). Cognitive profile of patients with newly diagnosed Parkinson disease. *Neurology, 65*, 1239–1245.

Muslimovic, D., Post, B., Speelman, J. D., Schmand, B., & de Haan, R. J. (2008). Determinants of disability and quality of life in mild to moderate Parkinson disease. *Neurology, 70*, 2241–2247.

Nasreddine, Z. S., Phillips, N. A., Bedirian, V., Charbonneau, S., Whitehead, V., Collin, I., et al. (2005). The Montreal Cognitive Assessment, MoCA: a brief screening tool for mild cognitive impairment. *Journal of the American Geriatrics Society, 53*, 695–699.

Nelson, H. E. (1976). A modified card sorting test sensitive to frontal lobe defects. *Cortex, 12*, 313–324.

Niemann, C., Godde, B., Staudinger, U. M., & Voelcker-Rehage, C. (2014). Exercise-induced changes in basal ganglia volume and cognition in older adults. *Neuroscience.* http://dx.doi.org/10.1016/j.neuroscience.2014.09.033.

Nieuwboer, A., Rochester, L., Muncks, L., & Swinnen, S. P. (2009). Motor learning in Parkinson's disease: limitations and potential for rehabilitation. *Parkinsonism and Related Disorders, 15*(Suppl. 3), S53–S58.

van Nimwegen, M., Speelman, A. D., Hofman-van Rossum, E. J., Overeem, S., Deeg, D. J., Borm, G. F., et al. (2011). Physical inactivity in Parkinson's disease. *Journal of Neurology, 258*, 2214–2221.

Nocera, J., McGregor, K. M., Hass, C., & Crosson, B. (2014). 'Spin' exercise improves semantic fluency in previously sedentary older adults. *Journal of Aging and Physical Activity*. http://dx.doi.org/10.1123/japa.2013-0107.

Nocera, J. R., Roemmich, R., Elrod, J., Altmann, L. J., & Hass, C. J. (2013). Effects of cognitive task on gait initiation in Parkinson disease: evidence of motor prioritization? *Journal of Rehabilitation Research and Development, 50*, 699–708.

Noyes, K., Liu, H., Li, Y., Holloway, R., & Dick, A. W. (2006). Economic burden associated with Parkinson's disease on elderly Medicare beneficiaries. *Movement Disorders, 21*, 362–372.

Okumiya, K., Matsubayashi, K., Wada, T., Kimura, S., Doi, Y., & Ozawa, T. (1996). Effects of exercise on neurobehavioral function in community-dwelling older people more than 75 years of age. *Journal of the American Geriatrics Society, 44*, 569–572.

O'Shea, S., Morris, M. E., & Iansek, R. (2002). Dual task interference during gait in people with Parkinson disease: effects of motor versus cognitive secondary tasks. *Physical Therapy, 82*, 888–897.

Pahapill, P. A., & Lozano, A. M. (2000). The pedunculopontine nucleus and Parkinson's disease. *Brain, 123*, 1767–1783.

Palacios, N., Gao, X., Schwarzschild, M., & Ascherio, A. (2012). Declining quality of life in Parkinson disease before and after diagnosis. *Journal of Parkinson's Disease, 2*, 153–160.

Peran, P., Goutines, E., Demonet, J. F., Rascol, O., & Cardebat, D. (2006). Verb processing in Parkinson's disease and Huntington's disease. *Journal of Neurological Sciences, 248*, 282–283.

Peran, P., Rascol, O., Demonet, J. F., Celsis, P., Nespoulous, J. L., Dubois, B., et al. (2003). Deficit of verb generation in nondemented patients with Parkinson's disease. *Movement Disorders, 18*, 150–156.

Pereira, J. B., Junque, C., Marti, M. J., Ramirez-Ruiz, B., Bargallo, N., & Tolosa, E. (2009). Neuroanatomical substrate of visuospatial and visuoperceptual impairment in Parkinson's disease. *Movement Disorders, 24*, 1193–1199.

Piatt, A., Fields, J. A., Paolo, A. M., Koller, W. C., & Tröster, A. (1999). Lexial, semantic, and action verbal fluency in Parkinson's disease with and without dementia. *Journal of Clinical and Experimental Neuropsychology, 21*, 435–443.

Plotnik, M., Giladi, N., Dagan, Y., & Hausdorff, J. M. (2011). Postural instability and fall risk in Parkinson's disease: impaired dual tasking, pacing, and bilateral coordination of gait during the "ON" medication state. *Experimental Brain Research, 210*, 529–538.

Plummer-D'Amato, P., Altmann, L. J. P., & Reilly, K. (2011). Dual-task effects of spontaneous speech and executive function on gait in aging: exaggerated effects in slow walkers. *Gait and Posture, 33*, 233–237.

Poletti, M., Frosini, D., Pagni, C., Baldacci, F., Nicoletti, V., Tognoni, G., et al. (2012). Mild cognitive impairment and cognitive-motor relationships in newly diagnosed drug-naive patients with Parkinson's disease. *Journal of Neurology, Neurosurgery and Psychiatry, 83*, 601–606.

Possin, K. L. (2010). Visual spatial cognition in neurodegenerative disease. *Neurocase, 16*, 466–487.

Possin, K. L., Filoteo, J. V., Song, D. D., & Salmon, D. P. (2008). Spatial and object working memory deficits in Parkinson's disease are due to impairment in different underlying processes. *Neuropsychology, 22*, 585–595.

Pulvermuller, F. (2001). Brain reflections of words and their meaning. *Trends in Cognitive Sciences, 5*, 517–524.

Raposo, A., Moss, H. E., Stamatakis, E. A., & Tyler, L. K. (2009). Modulation of motor and premotor cortices by actions, action words and action sentences. *Neuropsychologia, 47*, 388–396.

Ratey, J. J., & Loehr, J. E. (2011). The positive impact of physical activity on cognition during adulthood: a review of underlying mechanisms, evidence and recommendations. *Reviews in the Neurosciences, 22*, 171–185.

Ray, N. J., & Strafella, A. P. (2012). The neurobiology and neural circuitry of cognitive changes in Parkinson's disease revealed by functional neuroimaging. *Movement Disorders, 27*, 1484–1492.

Raz, N. (2000). Aging of the brain and its impact on cognitive performance: integration of structural and functional findings. In F. I. M. Craik, & T. A. Salthouse (Eds.), *The handbook of aging and cognition* (2nd ed.) (pp. 1–90). Mahwah, N.J.: Lawrence Erlbaum.

Richards, M., Cote, L. J., & Stern, Y. (1993). Executive function in Parkinson's disease: set-shifting or set-maintenance? *Journal of Clinical and Experimental Neuropsychology, 15*, 266–279.

Ridgel, A. L., Kim, C. H., Fickes, E. J., Muller, M. D., & Alberts, J. L. (2011). Changes in executive function after acute bouts of passive cycling in Parkinson's disease. *Journal of Aging and Physical Activity, 19*, 87–98.

Rodriguez, A. D. (2010). *Semantic-motor representations: Effects on language and motor production* (71). US: ProQuest Information & Learning. Retrieved from https://search.ebscohost.com/login.aspx?direct=true&db=psyh&AN=2011-99040-217&site=ehost-live.

Rogers, D., Lees, A. J., Smith, E., Trimble, M., & Stern, G. M. (1987). Bradyphrenia in Parkinson's disease and psychomotor retardation in depressive illness. An experimental study. *Brain, 110*, 761–776.

Rowe, J., Stephan, K. E., Friston, K., Frackowiak, R., Lees, A., & Passingham, R. (2002). Attention to action in Parkinson's disease: impaired effective connectivity among frontal cortical regions. *Brain, 125*, 276–289.

Rowley, J., Fonov, V., Wu, O., Eskildsen, S. F., Schoemaker, D., Wu, L., et al. (2013). White matter abnormalities and structural hippocampal disconnections in amnestic mild cognitive impairment and Alzheimer's disease. *PLoS One, 8*, e74776. http://dx.doi.org/10.1371/journal.pone.0074776.

Sahay, A., Scobie, K. N., Hill, A. S., O'Carroll, C. M., Kheirbek, M. A., Burghardt, N. S., et al. (2011). Increasing adult hippocampal neurogenesis is sufficient to improve pattern separation. *Nature, 472*, 466–470.

dos Santos Mendes, F. A., Pompeu, J. E., Modenesi Lobo, A., Guedes da Silva, K., Oliveira Tde, P., Peterson Zomignani, A., et al. (2012). Motor learning, retention and transfer after virtual-reality-based training in Parkinson's disease–effect of motor and cognitive demands of games: a longitudinal, controlled clinical study. *Physiotherapy, 98*, 217–223.

Schenkman, M., Hall, D. A., Baron, A. E., Schwartz, R. S., Mettler, P., & Kohrt, W. M. (2012). Exercise for people in early- or mid-stage Parkinson disease: a 16-month randomized controlled trial. *Physical Therapy, 92*, 1395–1410.

Schrag, A., Jahanshahi, M., & Quinn, N. (2000). How does Parkinson's disease affect quality of life? A comparison with quality of life in the general population. *Movement Disorders, 15*, 1112–1118.

Scorolli, C., Borghi, A. M. (2007). Sentence comprehension and action: effector specific modulation of the motor system. *Brain Res, 1130*(1), 119–124 Epub 2006 Dec 15. PMID: 17174278.

Sidibe, M., & Smith, Y. (1996). Differential synaptic innervation of striatofugal neurones projecting to the internal or external segments of the globus pallidus by thalamic afferents in the squirrel monkey. *Journal of Comparative Neurology, 365*, 445–465.

Silbert, L. C., & Kaye, J. (2010). Neuroimaging and cognition in Parkinson's disease dementia. *Brain Pathology, 20*, 646–653.

Smith, B. A., Goldberg, N. R., & Meshul, C. K. (2011). Effects of treadmill exercise on behavioral recovery and neural changes in the substantia nigra and striatum of the 1-methyl-4-phenyl-1,2,3,6-tetrahydropyridine-lesioned mouse. *Brain Research, 1386*, 70–80.

Smith, Y., Wichmann, T., & DeLong, M. R. (1994). The external pallidum and the subthalamic nucleus send convergent inputs onto single neurons in the internal pallidal segment in the monkey: anatomical organization and functional significance. In G. Percheron, F. S. McKenzie, & J. Feger (Eds.), *The basal ganglia IV – new ideas and data on structure and function* (pp. 51–61). New York: Plenum Press.

Spreen, O., & Strauss, E. (1998). *A compendium of neuropsychological tests: Administration, norms and commentary* (2nd ed.). New York: Oxford University Press.

Steffen, T., Petersen, C., & Dvorak, L. (2012). Community-based exercise and wellness program for people diagnosed with Parkinson disease: experiences from a 10-month trial. *Journal of Geriatric Physical Therapy, 35*, 173–180.

Stegemoller, E. L., Nocera, J., Malaty, I., Shelley, M., Okun, M. S., Hass, C. J., et al. (2014). Timed up and go, cognitive, and quality-of-life correlates in Parkinson's disease. *Archives of Physical Medicine and Rehabilitation, 95*, 649–655.

Stegemoller, E. L., Wilson, J. P., Hazamy, A., Shelley, M. C., Okun, M. S., Altmann, L. J., et al. (2014). Associations between cognitive and gait performance during single- and dual-task walking in people with Parkinson disease. *Physical Therapy, 94*, 757–766.

Suzukamo, Y., Ohbu, S., Kondo, T., Kohmoto, J., & Fukuhara, S. (2006). Psychological adjustment has a greater effect on health-related quality of life than on severity of disease in Parkinson's disease. *Movement Disorders, 21*, 761–766.

Tajiri, N., Yasuhara, T., Shingo, T., Kondo, A., Yuan, W., Kadota, T., et al. (2010). Exercise exerts neuroprotective effects on Parkinson's disease model of rats. *Brain Research, 1310*, 200–207.

Tanaka, K., Quadros, A. C., Jr., Santos, R. F., Stella, F., Gobbi, L. T., & Gobbi, S. (2009). Benefits of physical exercise on executive functions in older people with Parkinson's disease. *Brain and Cognition, 69*, 435–441.

Taylor, J. P., Rowan, E. N., Lett, D., O'Brien, J. T., McKeith, I. G., & Burn, D. J. (2008). Poor attentional function predicts cognitive decline in patients with non-demented Parkinson's disease independent of motor phenotype. *Journal of Neurology, Neurosurgery and Psychiatry, 79*, 1318–1323.

Taylor, A. E., & Saint-Cyr, J. A. (1995). The neuropsychology of Parkinson's disease. *Brain and Cognition, 28*, 281–296.

Ten Brinke, L. F., Bolandzadeh, N., Nagamatsu, L. S., Hsu, C. L., Davis, J. C., Miran-Khan, K., et al. (2014). Aerobic exercise increases hippocampal volume in older women with probable mild cognitive impairment: a 6-month randomised controlled trial. *British Journal of Sports Medicine*. http://dx.doi.org/10.1136/bjsports-2013-093184.

Thigpen, M. T., Light, K. E., Creel, G. L., & Flynn, S. M. (2000). Turning difficulty characteristics of adults aged 65 years or older. *Physical Therapy, 80*, 1174–1187.

Tolosa, E., Compta, Y., & Gaig, C. (2007). The premotor phase of Parkinson's disease. *Parkinsonism and Related Disorders, 13*(Suppl.), S2–S7.

Torres-Oviedo, G., & Ting, L. H. (2007). Muscle synergies characterizing human postural responses. *Journal of Neurophysiology, 98*, 2144–2156.

Toth, M. J., Fishman, P. S., & Poehlman, E. T. (1997). Free-living daily energy expenditure in patients with Parkinson's disease. *Neurology, 48*, 88–91.

Tremont, G., Halpert, S., Javorsky, D. J., & Stern, R. A. (2000). Differential impact of executive dysfunction on verbal list learning and story recall. *Clinical Neuropsychology, 14*, 295–302.

Troche, M. S., & Altmann, L. J. P. (2012). Sentence production in Parkinson disease: effects of conceptual and task complexity. *Applied Psycholinguistics, 33*, 225–251.

Troster, A. I. (2011). A precis of recent advances in the neuropsychology of mild cognitive impairment(s) in Parkinson's disease and a proposal of preliminary research criteria. *Journal of the International Neuropsychological Society, 17,* 393–406.

Uc, E. Y., Doerschug, K. C., Magnotta, V., Dawson, J. D., Thomsen, T. R., Kline, J. N., et al. (2014). Phase I/II randomized trial of aerobic exercise in Parkinson disease in a community setting. *Neurology, 83,* 413–425.

Verghese, J., Kuslansky, G., Holtzer, R., Katz, M., Xue, X., Buschke, H., et al. (2007). Walking while talking: effect of task prioritization in the elderly. *Archives of Physical Medicine and Rehabilitation, 88,* 50–53.

Vitek, J. L., Ashe, J., DeLong, M. R., & Alexander, G. E. (1990). Altered somatosensory response properties of neurons in the 'motor' thalamus of MPTP treated parkinsonian monkeys. *Society for Neuroscience Abstracts, 16,* 425.

Voss, M. W., Erickson, K. I., Prakash, R. S., Chaddock, L., Kim, J. S., Alves, H., et al. (2013). Neurobiological markers of exercise-related brain plasticity in older adults. *Brain, Behavior, and Immunity, 28,* 90–99.

Voss, M. W., Heo, S., Prakash, R. S., Erickson, K. I., Alves, H., Chaddock, L., et al. (2013). The influence of aerobic fitness on cerebral white matter integrity and cognitive function in older adults: results of a one-year exercise intervention. *Human Brain Mapping, 34,* 2972–2985.

Voss, M. W., Prakash, R. S., Erickson, K. I., Basak, C., Chaddock, L., Kim, J. S., et al. (2010). Plasticity of brain networks in a randomized intervention trial of exercise training in older adults. *Frontiers in Aging Neuroscience, 2.* http://dx.doi.org/10.3389/fnagi.2010.00032.

Vucckovic, M. G., Li, Q., Fisher, B., Nacca, A., Leahy, R. M., Walsh, J. P., et al. (2010). Exercise elevates dopamine D2 receptor in a mouse model of Parkinson's disease: in vivo imaging with [^{18}F]fallypride. *Movement Disorders, 25,* 2777–2784.

Weintraub, D., Newberg, A. B., Cary, M. S., Siderowf, A. D., Moberg, P. J., Kleiner-Fisman, G., et al. (2005). Striatal dopamine transporter imaging correlates with anxiety and depression symptoms in Parkinson's disease. *Journal of Nuclear Medicine, 46,* 227–232.

Welch, T. D. J., & Ting, L. H. (2009). A feedback model explains the differential scaling of human postural responses to perturbation acceleration and velocity. *Journal of Neurophysiology, 101,* 3294–3309.

Werheid, K. D., Hoppe, C. D., Thone, A. D., Muller, U., Mungersdorf, M., & von Cramon, D. Y. (2002). The adaptive digit ordering test: clinical application, reliability, and validity of a verbal working memory test. *Archives of Clinical Neuropsychology, 17,* 547–565.

Wichmann, T., Bergman, H., & DeLong, M. R. (1994). The primate subthalamic nucleus. III. Changes in motor behavior and neuronal activity in the internal pallidum induced by subthalamic inactivation in the MPTP model of parkinsonism. *Journal of Neurophysiology, 72,* 521–530.

Wichmann, T., & DeLong, M. R. (1996). Functional and pathophysiological models of the basal ganglia. *Current Opinions in Neurobiology, 6,* 751–758.

Wichmann, T., & DeLong, M. R. (1998). Models of basal ganglia function and pathophysiology of movement disorders. *Neurosurgery Clinics of North America, 9,* 223–236.

Wicklund, A. H., Johnson, N., Rademaker, A., Weitner, B. B., & Weintraub, S. (2006). Word list versus story memory in Alzheimer disease and frontotemporal dementia. *Alzheimer Disease and Associated Disorders, 20,* 86–92.

Williams-Gray, C. H., Foltynie, T., Lewis, S. J., & Barker, R. A. (2006). Cognitive deficits and psychosis in Parkinson's disease: a review of pathophysiology and therapeutic options. *CNS Drugs, 20,* 477–505.

Wilson, B. A., Evans, J. J., Emslie, H., Alderman, N., Burgess, P. (1998). The Development of an Ecologically Valid Test for Assessing Patients with a Dysexecutive Syndrome. *Neuropsychological Rehabilitation: an International Journal, 8*(3), 213–228.

Wise, S. P., Murray, E. A., & Gerfen, C. R. (1996). The frontal cortex-basal ganglia system in primates. *Critical Reviews in Neurobiology, 10,* 317–356.

Woollacott, M., & Shumway-Cook, A. (2002). Attention and the control of posture and gait: a review of an emerging area of research. *Gait and Posture, 16,* 1–14.

Wu, S. Y., Wang, T. F., Yu, L., Jen, C. J., Chuang, J. I., Wu, F. S., et al. (2011). Running exercise protects the substantia nigra dopaminergic neurons against inflammation-induced degeneration via the activation of BDNF signaling pathway. *Brain, Behavior, and Immunity, 25,* 135–146.

Zahodne, L. B., Bowers, D., Price, C. C., Bauer, R. M., Nisenzon, A., Foote, K. D., et al. (2011). The case for testing memory with both stories and word lists prior to dbs surgery for Parkinson's Disease. *Clinical Neuropsychology, 25,* 348–358.

Zgaljardic, D. J., Borod, J. C., Foldi, N. S., Mattis, P. J., Gordon, M. F., Feigin, A., et al. (2006). An examination of executive dysfunction associated with frontostriatal circuitry in Parkinson's disease. *Journal of Clinical and Experimental Neuropsychology, 28,* 1127–1144.

Zurowski, M., McDonald, W. M., Fox, S., & Marsh, L. (2013). Psychiatric comorbidities in dystonia: emerging concepts. *Movement Disorders, 28,* 914–920.

The Chronic Exercise–Cognition Interaction and Dementia and Alzheimer's Disease

Flávia Gomes de Melo Coelho[1,2], Thays Martins Vital[1,4], Ruth Ferreira Santos-Galduróz[1,3], Sebastião Gobbi[1]

[1]Institute of Biosciences, UNESP, Univ. Estadual Paulista, Physical Activity and Aging Lab (LAFE), Rio Claro, São Paulo, Brazil; [2]Department of Sports Sciences, UFTM, Univ. Federal do Triângulo Mineiro, Uberaba, Minas Gerais, Brazil; [3]Center of Mathematics, Computing and Cognition, UFABC, Univ. Federal of ABC, Santo André, São Paulo, Brazil; [4]Instituto Federal Goiano - Campus Morrinhos, Morrinhos, GO, Brazil

INTRODUCTION

As life expectancy increases, so also does the increase in the number of dementia cases all over the world. Prince et al. (2013) investigated the global prevalence of dementia and verified that in 2010, 35 million people presented clinical diagnoses of dementia. The study also showed that this number will double every 20 years, with an expected 65.7 and 115.4 millions of people suffering from dementia in 2030 and 2050, respectively. Among the most common types of dementia, Alzheimer's disease (AD) is responsible for 60–80% of cases (Alzheimer's Association, 2014). In the United States, 4% of individuals who are less than 65 years old have AD; between 65 and 74 years old, the prevalence is 15%; and for those who are between 75 and

84 years old, it can reach 44% (Hebert, Weuve, Scherr, & Evans, 2013). Dementia is characterized by loss of memory and ability to perform daily living activities, as well as possible changes in behavior and motor functionality (Alzheimer's Association, 2014).

Physical inactivity has been indicated as an important risk factor for AD development; 13% of AD cases in the world can be attributed to this factor (Barnes & Yaffe, 2011). The same authors reviewed 24 studies of which 20 indicated an association between physical inactivity and cognitive decline. Besides this, many other studies showed that remaining physically active decreases cognitive decline (Barnes & Yaffe, 2011; Lista & Sorrentino, 2009). Prince et al. (2013) argued that in order to decrease the number of dementia cases in the next few years, it will be

Exercise-Cognition Interaction
http://dx.doi.org/10.1016/B978-0-12-800778-5.00016-5

necessary to implement strategies of prevention or even the use of interventions that can modify the course and the progression of this pathology. Among these strategies of prevention and treatment, we can emphasize the regular practice of physical exercise as an important, nonpharmacological tool for this population. The relation between physical exercise and mental health has gained much significance in the last few years, and many studies have indicated that physical exercise promotes benefits for mental health, including for the elderly who already present with mild cognitive impairment or dementia (Deslandes et al., 2009; Heyn, Abreu, & Ottenbacher, 2004; Lista & Sorrentino, 2009).

The aim of physical exercise, when practiced by the elderly with dementia, rather than being the restoration of levels of cognitive function already lost, is the improvement of residual cognitive abilities in order to maintain the highest possible level of independency. In addition, physical exercise can modify the course of the disease. Lautenschlager, Cox, and Cyarto (2012), in a review, emphasized that the benefits of physical exercise to improve cognitive performance need to be investigated at three levels of intervention, primary, secondary, and tertiary. According to Leavell and Clark (1976), primary intervention aims to protect health, thus avoiding the appearance of diseases; the secondary level refers to early identification of the pathology, when the disease is still asymptomatic, and treating it, thus trying to establish the normal state again; tertiary level has the aim of avoiding the progression of the disease, which is already installed, and also treating its symptoms. In the context of mental health and aging, these levels would respectively benefit the following populations: the elderly without cognitive decline; the elderly with cognitive decline; and the elderly with dementia (Lautenschlager et al., 2012). Although the number of elderly people with dementia, involved in programs of physical exercise, has increased, the evidence shows that numbers are still low (Lima, Freitas,

Smethurst, Santos, & Barros, 2010; Vital et al., 2012). On the positive side, Heyn et al. (2004), in a meta-analysis, indicated that many studies demonstrate improvement in global cognitive performance by elderly individuals with mild cognitive decline or with dementia, and who participate in a program of physical exercise.

In this chapter, we will discuss the interaction between cognitive functioning and physical exercise as a protective or therapeutic factor on dementia in general and on AD in particular [in this chapter the term "dementia" is used to refer to dementia in general, since several studies, which include the elderly with dementia, do not specify the type of dementia nor do they state heterogeneous samples (i.e., different pathologies such as vascular dementia, mixed dementia, AD, and other dementias)]. Further, potential mechanisms through physical exercise that can benefit cognition will be discussed.

THE CHRONIC PHYSICAL EXERCISE–COGNITION INTERACTION IN DEMENTIA

In relation to physical exercise as a kind of nonpharmacological therapy (tertiary level), review studies demonstrated that it promotes benefits for the elderly with dementia, such as improvement in physical capacity, improvement, or maintenance of cognitive functions, decrease of depressive symptoms, and others (Bowes, Dawson, Jepson, & McCabe, 2013; Forbes, Thiessen, Blake, Forbes, & Forbes, 2013; Heyn et al., 2004). Although there are many studies that have investigated the relationship between physical exercise and cognitive functions in elderly people with dementia, there are still many gaps in our knowledge that need to be clarified. Deslandes (2014) claimed that researchers in the field of physical exercise and mental health need to develop a more adequate prescription of physical exercise for each neurodegenerative disease, because many different protocols have been used, making it difficult to determine the best exercise prescription for these populations. In order to explain the types of training applied and the findings, we have separated the studies by the type of intervention used (i.e., aerobic exercise and multimodal exercise).

Aerobic Exercise

Many studies have demonstrated that the regular practice of physical exercise may prevent brain atrophy and, consequently, avoid the appearance of neurodegenerative diseases, such as dementia (Colcombe et al., 2003, 2006; Yuki et al., 2012). Among the different types of physical exercise, aerobic has become known for promoting benefits on cognitive functions in elderly people without dementia (Erickson & Kramer, 2009; Kramer & Erickson, 2007). However, in elderly individuals who have already presented with some type of diagnosed dementia, the question is what would be the relationship between aerobic physical exercise and cognitive functions?

Eggermont, Swaab, Hol, and Scherder (2009) investigated elderly people with moderate dementia who lived in a long-stay institution. They divided the participants into intervention and control groups. The intervention group completed a walking protocol for 6 months, 5 times a week, with a duration of 30 min per session, at a self-selected speed. The control group received social visits with the same frequency and duration of the intervention group's physical exercise protocol. After 6 months' intervention and a follow-up test, there were no significant improvements in cognitive functions. The authors attributed the lack of effect of physical exercise to the short intervention period and the fact that most of the individuals from both groups also had cardiovascular diseases, which may have interfered with the results. Miu, Szeto, and Mak (2008) also examined community-dwelling elderly people with dementia of different types (AD, vascular dementia, mixed dementia, and dementia plus Parkinson's disease). They divided participants into training and control groups. The training group exercised aerobically on a treadmill and a cycle ergometer, and undertook arm and flexibility exercises. The training had a total duration of 3 months and was conducted twice a week, 45–60 min per session. The control group remained with their normal daily routine. Both groups were evaluated before the intervention and at 3, 6, 9, and 12 months postintervention. There were no improvements in cognitive functions.

While many studies emphasize aerobic exercise as an important intervention for the improvement or maintenance of cognitive functions in the elderly (e.g., Erickson & Kramer, 2009; Kramer & Erickson, 2007), regarding the elderly with dementia, results are still inconsistent, because few studies have investigated only the effects of aerobic exercise on cognition of elderly individuals with dementia, which makes it harder to determine the best prescription of physical exercise for this population. Another important limitation was highlighted by Ohman, Savikko, Strandberg, and Pitkala (2014) in a literature review. They found that most studies that investigated the effects of physical exercise on cognition in the elderly with dementia showed weak methodological quality, which questions the credibility of the results. It is important also to emphasize that most studies that observed a relationship between physical exercise and dementia were undertaken with elderly individuals who presented AD diagnosis, due to the fact that it is the most frequent type of dementia.

Multimodal Exercise

There is no consensus yet, with regard to the frequency and intensity of physical exercise, in order to improve cognitive functions in elderly individuals with dementia. Blankevoort et al. (2010) recommended that in order to improve the motor functionality of this population, it is necessary to make multimodal interventions, with a minimal period of 12 weeks, at least 3 times a week, with duration from 45 to 60 min per session. Recently, Bossers et al. (2014) carried out a nonrandomized study in elderly people with dementia who lived in a nursing home. The training intervention consisted of 6 weeks: walking 3 times a week at a moderate intensity, and resistance training for the lower limbs twice a week, for 3 series of 8–12 repetitions. The control group received individualized visits with the same duration and frequency of the training group's physical activity. There were no significant improvements in cognitive functions.

In another study, Eggermont, Knol, Hol, Swaab, and Scherder (2009) had patients from a nursing home undertake 6 weeks of exercise. Elderly individuals with AD, vascular dementia, and mixed dementia were randomly divided into exercise and control groups. Exercises involved movements for hands, 5 times a week, for 30 min a session. The control group undertook group conversation sessions with the same duration and frequency that experimental group exercised. After 6 weeks of interventions, there were no significant improvements in cognitive functions for either group. The absence of benefits may be due to the fact that the protocol required only movement with hands, thus possibly providing insufficient stimuli, or due to the fact that the individuals were already at the moderate stage of the disease. Stevens and Killeen (2006) also investigated the effects of a program of exercise on cognitive functions in elderly people with dementia at the mild and moderate stages, and who were living in a nursing home. Participants were divided into three groups: Group 1, which did not receive any intervention; Group 2, which received social visits with discussions about health themes; and Group 3, who practiced physical exercise that consisted of movements to music. The interventions of Groups 2 and 3 lasted 12 weeks, with, at least, 30 min duration per session. Group 2 demonstrated a decline in cognitive functions while

Group 3 maintained performance levels. Van de Winckel, Feys, and Weerdt (2004) divided elderly participants with dementia by multi-infarct or AD, who were hospitalized, into an exercise group and a control group. The exercise group carried out a dance program with trunk movements, development of strength in lower and upper limbs, balance and flexibility, for 30 min every day for 12 weeks. The control group undertook talking activities for the same period, frequency, and duration. The exercise group demonstrated improved cognitive functioning.

Most of the studies described above were developed with populations living in a nursing home, which highlights the lack of studies with the community-dwelling elderly with dementia. The interventions of Bossers et al. (2014) and Eggermont, Swaab et al. (2009) covered a period of 6 weeks, and did not show significant improvements in cognitive function. Nevertheless, protocols developed for 12 weeks, such as those by Stevens and Killeen (2006) and Van de Winckel et al. (2004), demonstrated improvements in cognitive function due to the physical exercise. These results with elderly individuals with dementia living in nursing homes indicate that 6 weeks may be insufficient to promote benefits in cognitive functioning for this population. We must also take into account the fact that the elderly with dementia, and who live in long-stay institutions, may present high levels of functional inability and high rates of depressive symptoms, making them more dependent (Beland & Zunzunnegui, 1999; Plati, Covre, Lukasova, & Macedo, 2006). These factors could influence the application of results of a motor intervention, with the aim of improving cognitive functions.

Burgener, Yang, Gilbert, and Marsh-Yant (2008) examined individuals with differing types of mild dementia (e.g., Alzheimer, Lewy body, vascular, frontal lobe, or mixed dementia), who were living in the community. In a controlled and randomized study, participants were divided into two groups. The intervention group participated in a program of multimodal activities, which included Taiji, 3 times a week for 60 min a session; cognitive behavioral therapy (Teri & Gallagher-Thompson, 1991), biweekly for 90 min a session; and support, i.e., sharing experiences of dementia, biweekly for 90 min a session, alternated with cognitive behavioral therapy. All activities were undertaken for 40 weeks. The control group participated in educational programs during the same period. After 20 weeks the intervention group demonstrated significant improvements in cognitive functions. From 20 to 40 weeks there were no further improvements.

As stated above, there are, as yet, no recommendations as to the best prescription of physical exercise in order to benefit cognitive functions in the elderly with dementia. So far there is insufficient evidence from which to establish some kind of recommendation. Therefore, new studies are suggested in order to know, in the deepest way, the effective dose–response for the application of physical exercise programs to benefit cognitive functions of elderly individuals with dementia. In this regard, Blankevoort et al. (2010), in a review, highlighted some directions for future research. They suggested that motor interventions should be compatible with the cognitive level of the patients, which means that the intervention may be altered according to dementia state. In addition to that, Lautenschlager et al. (2012) indicated that when we work with the elderly, it is necessary not only to worry about variables related to training prescription but also to seek strategies that motivate participants, through psychological and social stimuli, thus increasing the physical activity level on this population.

THE CHRONIC PHYSICAL EXERCISE–COGNITION INTERACTION IN ALZHEIMER'S DISEASE

Today, many studies demonstrate that regular practice of physical exercise is a factor with regard to neuroprotection, which may slow down or even stop the appearance of neurodegenerative diseases, such as AD (Laurin, Verreault, Lindsay, MacPherson, & Rockwood, 2001; Lautenschlager et al., 2009). Also, physical exercise is considered a nonpharmacological alternative that may positively affect the cognitive, motor, and behavioral symptoms of AD. In general, research concerning the effects of physical exercise on cognition in the elderly with AD has shown positive results. In a systematic review, Coelho, Santos-Galduroz, Gobbi, and Stella (2009) emphasized that the practice of systematized physical activity, with or without adding cognitive tasks, resulted in improvement and/or maintenance of cognitive domains, such as executive functions, language, and attention. Recently, Farina, Rusted, and Tabet (2014), also through a systematic review on the effect of physical activity in the elderly with AD, reported that physical activity may have a protective effect against cognitive deterioration in AD. A series of physical exercise interventions with different durations, frequencies, and intensities may, potentially, promote benefits to cognition in the elderly with AD. Each one of these interventions is described in some detail below.

Aerobic Exercise

Increasingly, there is much evidence to indicate an association between cardiorespiratory fitness and cerebral atrophy at the first clinical stage of AD. Burns, Cronk, and Anderson (2008) demonstrated that higher levels of cardiorespiratory fitness in the elderly with mild AD were associated with cerebral volume, while Vidoni, Honea, Billinger, Swerdlow, and Burns (2012) indicated that a decrease in cardiorespiratory fitness over 2 years was associated with cerebral atrophy in the elderly with mild AD. However, aerobic exercise may increase the volume of gray matter in the frontal and temporal cortices, in a similar way to increased white matter in the anterior regions of the brain, which results in an improvement in cognitive functions in old people (Colcombe et al., 2006). Rolland et al. (2000) evaluated elderly individuals with moderate and severe AD, and with a mean score of 16 on the mini-mental state examination (MMSE). A program of aerobic exercises, consisting of walking and cycling for 35 min, was undertaken by the participants. The study demonstrated that 7 weeks of training improved global cognitive performance as measured by the MMSE. However, this study did not have a control group and weekly training frequency and intensity were not reported.

Venturelli, Scarsini, and Schena (2011) randomly divided elderly individuals with severe AD into training and control groups. The training group completed a walking protocol, 4 times a week, with maximal duration of 30 min per session. After 6 months of training, they showed less decline in performance on the MMSE than the control group. This study suggests that it is possible to reduce the decline in AD through a walking program. However, they did not report the exercise intensity (walking). Similarly, Winchester et al. (2013) also had elderly people with mild and moderate AD undertake a walking program. The participants walked for more than 2 h per week over a year and showed a significant improvement in MMSE scores. This study reinforces the finding that walking is a strategy of intervention that may be useful for AD individuals, and further supports the claims that more clinical trials are necessary in order to investigate the effective dose of exercise necessary to induce improved cognition.

The use of measures of intensity of aerobic training, such as percent of maximal heart rate (HRmax) and maximal oxygen consumption ($\dot{V}O_2$max), in order to control training with elderly AD individuals, is still rare in the literature. It is known that the dose–response effect of aerobic exercise on cognition in the elderly with AD is important for the right training prescription. Accordingly, Yu et al. (2015) had elderly people, with low and moderate AD, undertake a 6-month program of aerobic training on a cycle ergometer. Training intensity was moderate, 65–75% heart rate reserve; session duration started with 15 min, gradually increasing to 45 min; and frequency was 3 times a week. Cognitive functions were evaluated using the Alzheimer's Disease Assessment Scale-Cognition (ADAS-Cog). Scores on the cognitive tests did not alter after 3 and 6 months of aerobic training, therefore the authors suggested that aerobic exercise of moderate intensity was important in order to attenuate cognitive decline in AD patients.

Arcoverde et al. (2014), in a randomized and controlled study, evaluated the effect of aerobic exercise of moderate intensity on cognitive functions in the elderly with AD. The training was undertaken on a treadmill. After familiarization sessions on the treadmill, the participants were subjected to 30 min walking, twice a week, for 3 months. Aerobic training was divided into two stages: (1) warm-up exercises on the treadmill for 10 min at an intensity of 40% of $\dot{V}O_2$max; and (2) running for 20 min at an intensity of 60% of $\dot{V}O_2$max. Cognitive function was evaluated by the Cambridge Cognitive Examination (CAMCOG), and other specific instruments were also applied to evaluate attention and executive functions. After 16 weeks of aerobic training on the treadmill, it was found that participants had improved their cognitive performance, as evaluated by the CAMCOG, while a control group demonstrated a decline in performance.

Although these studies show positive results related to cognitive functions, such as maintenance or improvement of these variables, it is necessary to have more controlled and randomized studies in order to control intensity of training and to analyze the dose–response effect of aerobic training on cognitive symptoms of the elderly with AD.

Resistance Exercise

Few studies have investigated the effect of resistance training on cognitive functions.

Cassilhas et al. (2007) demonstrated positive effects of training with weights on memory in elderly individuals without dementia, while Busse, Jacob-Filho, Magaldi, and Coelho (2008) found that resistance training undertaken by elderly people with memory impairment resulted in a significant improvement in episodic memory. Only one study (Vital et al., 2012) has examined the effects of resistance training in elderly individuals with AD. They compared the cognitive performance of a training group and a control group, which had a social interaction intervention. Protocols were performed 3 times a week, with a duration of 60 min, for 16 weeks. Resistance training was of low intensity (20 repetitions of 85% maximum resistance) and consisted of developing 5 exercises (Peck Deck, Pull Down, Leg Press, Barbell Curls, and Triceps Pulley), with 3 series of 20 repetitions and 2 min of rest between series and between exercises. There were no significant improvements in executive functions, attention, or language. The authors felt that the intensity of the resistance training was not enough to generate a satisfactory response in the cognitive functioning of elderly individuals with AD.

Further studies with resistance exercises and with different training intensities are needed in order to verify their effects on cognitive functions in the elderly with AD.

Multimodal Exercise

Farina et al. (2014), in a systematic review, indicated that the six controlled and randomized studies that they examined all demonstrated benefits on cognitive functions. The authors concluded that involvement in multimodal exercises by the elderly with AD may be more effective than any single exercise type alone. Studies that have applied multimodal training have utilized different protocols, i.e., duration of sessions, weekly frequencies, and training durations, as well as different cognitive evaluations. Yágüez Shaw, Morris, and Matthews (2010), in

a controlled and randomized study, divided elderly participants with AD into two groups: an exercise group, which received 6 weeks of training, and a control group, which undertook memory exercises and psychological support in the same time period. Cognitive functions were evaluated using six computerized tests from the CANTAB Cambridge Neuropsychological Test Automated Battery. The training protocol was based on the "Brain Gym" protocol (Dennison, 2010), which consisted of exercises that involved stretching, circular motions of the extremities, and isometric tension of muscle groups. The exercises applied required fine motor coordination and balance. Sessions had 2 h of duration, with a break of 30 min, and were undertaken once a week. After 6 weeks, the exercise group demonstrated a significant improvement in sustained attention and visual memory in comparison to the control group.

Kemoun et al. (2010), also in a controlled and randomized study, divided elderly participants with AD into training and control groups. The training group performed multimodal exercises for 15 weeks, with 3 sessions per week, and a duration of 1 h each session. The program involved gait, balance, and resistance exercises. Every week, a session was designed that improved gait parameters (e.g., stride walking, climbing steps, and zigzag walking). After that, the second weekly session was undertaken, which was exercising on a cycle ergometer with an intensity of 60–70% of heart rate reserve. The third and last weekly session involved dance and step activities that combined resistance and balance. The control group did not participate in any physical activity program. After 15 weeks, the training group improved their cognition compared to the control group, which actually demonstrated a reduced score on the Rapid Evaluation of Cognitive Function test.

Steinberg, Leoutsakos, Podewils, and Lyketsos (2009) divided 27 elderly individuals with AD into an exercise group and a control group. The training of the exercise group consisted of three parts: (1) aerobic capacity, fast walking; (2) strength training, exercises for large muscle groups, using resistive bands and leggings; and (3) balance training and flexibility, exercises aiming to move the center of gravity, such as walking forward, backward, and to the side; sitting down; and standing up. Exercises were performed daily for 12 weeks. In order to evaluate cognitive functions, the MMSE, the Boston Naming Test, and the Hopkins Verbal Learning Test were administered. After the intervention there were no significant differences between groups for cognitive functions. The authors did not report if there were improvements or maintenance of cognitive functions in the trained elderly.

Vreugdenhil, Cannell, Davies, and Razay (2012), in a randomized clinical trial, evaluated 40 elderly people with AD. The elderly were randomly divided into a training group (physical exercise and usual treatment) or control group (usual treatment). The exercise program was performed daily and consisted of many exercises involving muscle strength of lower and upper limbs, balance exercises, and 30 min of walking. Volunteers were evaluated at the baseline and after 4 months of intervention, using the MMSE and ADAS-Cog. After 4 months, the trained volunteers, in comparison to the control group, showed improvement in cognitive abilities, verified by an improved score of 2.6 on the MMSE and a lower score of 7.1 on the ADAS-Cog (the lower score represents better cognitive functioning in this test).

Several studies have utilized multimodal physical exercises, while simultaneously carrying out cognitive tasks. Andrade et al. (2013), Coelho, Andrade et al. (2013), and Pedroso et al. (2012) investigated the effect of physical exercise, performed simultaneously with cognitive tasks, in elderly people with mild and moderate AD. The multimodal intervention program consisted of aerobic exercises, exercises with weights, balance exercises, agility, motor coordination, and flexibility. The cognitive tasks tested attention, language, and executive functions, such as

judgment, abstraction, mental flexibility, and behavior self-control. For example, participants had to perform a motor task (bounce ball, walking, and exercises with weights), and, at the same time, execute a cognitive task, such as generate words according to semantic criteria (e.g., say people's names, name fruits, name animals, and name flowers and numbers), or react against sensorial stimuli (whistle and music) and verbal commands. Interventions in this protocol were made three times a week, on nonconsecutive days, during 60-min sessions. For each day of the week, a different functional component was developed: on the first day of the week, agility and coordination were emphasized; on the second, flexibility; and on the third, balance. During the training, there were cognitive and motor overloads. Cognitive overload was achieved by increasing the difficulty level of the task. For example, the number of pictures for the patient to nominate was increased at the same time they climbed up and down steps. In the weights training exercises, the weight of dumbbells and ankle weights was increased. Intensity of the aerobic training was maintained between 65% and 75% of heart rate maximum.

Andrade et al. (2013) observed that after 4 months of multimodal training, improvement on global cognitive functions (Montreal Cognitive Assessment), on executive functions (Frontal Assessment Battery), and on language (Verbal Fluency Test—category animals) were shown by the training group compared to the control group, who demonstrated reductions in these functions. Coelho, Andrade et al. (2013) observed improvement on executive functions (Clock Drawing Test and Frontal Assessment Battery) and on attention (Symbol Search Subtest) after 4 months of multimodal training. The control group showed poorer performance, in comparison to their baseline scores, on cognitive functions evaluated by the Clock Drawing Test. Pedroso et al. (2012) observed significant improvement on global cognitive functions (evaluated by MMSE) in the elderly with AD, who participated in the multimodal exercise program, compared to the control group, who demonstrated decrements in cognitive functions.

Hernandez, Coelho, Gobbi, and Stella (2010) divided 16 elderly individuals into two groups: an intervention group and a control group. Sessions of multimodal physical exercise were performed 3 times a week, each session lasting 60 min, over 6 months and carried out as a group activity. Exercises were structured to promote motor and cognitive stimulation, simultaneously or separately. Physical activities included stretching, weight training, dance sequences, ludic activities, circuit training, and relaxation. The aim was to develop components of functional capacity of coordination, agility, balance, flexibility, strength, and aerobic capacity. Heart rate was maintained at 60–80% of heart rate maximum. After 6 months, there was a positive effect of multimodal exercise on the maintenance of global cognitive functions (MMSE), while the control group demonstrated a reduction in cognitive performance.

Arkin (2007) included 24 elderly people with AD in a program of multimodal exercises, which involved flexibility, balance, weight training, and aerobic activities (treadmill and stationary bike), for 3 sessions per week, over 10 weeks. In each week, one session was designed for activities that stimulate language and memory. In order to analyze cognitive functions, participants were tested on the Consortium for the Establishment of a Registry for Alzheimer's Disease test, Wechsler Adult Intelligence Test-Revised (WAIS-R), Arizona Battery for Communication Disorders of Dementia test, and the Clinical Dementia Rating (CDR). The study period extended for 4 years. After 1 year of the multimodal exercises program, there was no cognitive decrease on the Verbal Fluency test and on the Similarity factor of the WAIS-R in all 24 elderly with AD. After 2 years, the 13 elderly that remained in the program did not suffer any decline on scores of the CDR scale, Verbal Fluency, the Boston Naming Test, and WAIS-R Similarity. After 3 years, the 8 elderly who remained in the program demonstrated significant improvements on tests of Verbal Fluency, Boston Naming, WAIS-R Similarity, and WAIS-R comprehension, as well as maintaining scores on the MMSE and CDR scale. This study demonstrated the importance of physical exercise as a therapy for a possible stabilization of cognitive decline in AD over 4 years. However, there are some limitations, such as no inclusion of a control group, and the reduced number of elderly that participated in the program over the whole study.

When studying the effect of multimodal physical exercise in the elderly with AD, resident in a nursing home, Heyn (2003) used a program of aerobic physical exercises, resistance exercises, and flexibility simultaneously with cognitive (attention) and sensorial stimulation (touch, hearing, and vision). Thirteen elderly (12 women and 1 man) individuals, with clinical diagnoses of AD, were included. Cognitive functions were measured by the Brief Cognitive Rating Scale. After 8 weeks of multimodal exercises, 3 times a week, cognitive functions in institutionalized elderly with AD were maintained. Arcoverde et al. (2008) also included sessions of cognitive stimulation in a program of multimodal exercises. Sessions were performed twice a week, over 6 months, and included respiratory exercises, training of static and dynamic balance, gait circuits with and without obstacles, stimuli of daily activities, motor coordination, and balance. There were also sessions of cognitive stimulation, which included exercises to improve attention, verbal fluency, and general recognition. In this study, there was a reduction on global cognitive decline (MMSE) in patients who trained compared to a sedentary group. Heyn (2003), Arkin (2007), and Arcoverde et al. (2008) did not describe the intensity of training; moreover, only Arcoverde et al. (2008) included a control group.

Based on these studies, it is possible to conclude that multimodal exercise along with cognitive tasks (single or simultaneous) promote benefits to cognitive functioning in the elderly with AD. Results suggest that multimodal physical exercise may have a positive effect on cognitive functions in elderly people with AD. Nevertheless, variations between methods of study and the lack of reports of exercise intensities limit the ability to recommend the best type of multimodal protocol, as well as the optimal weekly frequency, duration of session, and adequate intensity in order to achieve benefits in cognitive functions.

NEUROBIOLOGICAL MECHANISMS OF PHYSICAL EXERCISE RELATED TO COGNITION AND MENTAL HEALTH

An increase in metabolic demands, associated with our ancestors' need to hunt and search for food, may have developed human genomes to deal with such demands, and, thus, probably the need for physical activity is programmed as an evolution in our genes (Booth, Chakravarthy, Gordon, & Spangenburg, 2002; Ratey & Loehr, 2011). Commonly, exercised animals (runners) activate genes associated with inhibitory neurotransmission, while sedentary animals fail in upregulating the expression of such genes. This may indicate that improvements in learning and memory induced by exercise involve changes in gene transcription in the central nervous system, which improves and protects cerebral functions through the preservation of inhibitory neurotransmission (for review, see Stranahan, Martin, & Maudsley, 2012). Therefore, physical exercise is not only the foundation for physical fitness, but it can contribute as an important factor in cognitive fitness, which was conceptualized by Gilkey and Kilts (2007) as "a state of optimized ability to reason, remember, learn, plan, and adapt that is enhanced by certain attitudes, lifestyle choices, and exercises." While still in the early stages of study, there is evidence

to support physical activity as a factor in the prevention of neuronal loss or preservation of its function and prevention of cognitive decline (Barber, Clegg, & Young, 2012). Great improvements have been shown, but of course there is still a lot to be done (McAuley, Mullen, & Hillman, 2013). Potential mechanisms responsible for the interaction between regular exercise and mental health are still a matter of discussion and seem to result from a complex interrelation between physiological, biochemical, and psychosocial factors (Crone, Smith, & Gough, 2006).

Psychosocial mechanisms include the hypothesis of distraction, self-efficacy theory, mastery (i.e., when overcoming a challenging task related to exercise, there is an increase of independence, success, and sense of control), and social interaction (Crone et al., 2006). However, discussion of such mechanisms is not the aim of the present approach. Unlike Crone et al. (2006), Ratey and Loehr (2011) pointed to biologic mechanisms, which they classified at three levels (systemic, molecular, and cellular). Systemic mechanisms are the result of increased neuroelectrical activity, cerebral volume, and cerebral blood flow; molecular mechanisms are due to the availability of neurotrophins and growth factors in the brain [brain-derived neurotrophic factor (BDNF), fibroblast growth factor (FGF-2), insulin growth factor (IGF-1), vascular endothelial growth factor (VEGF)]; while cellular mechanisms result from the effects of signaling cascades, induced by neurotrophins and growth factors, which support synaptic plasticity, neurogenesis, and angiogenesis.

Biochemical Mechanisms

Growth factors and neurotrophins appear to be vital with regard to biochemical mechanisms. A large number of studies, with animals, have shown positive interactions between exercise/physical fitness, cognition, and BDNF-, IGF-1-, VEGF-stimulated neurogenesis. BDNF is important for synaptic plasticity, learning, and memory.

Studies with animals show that physical exercise increases performance in tasks involving learning and spatial memory. On the other hand, blocking BDNF activity eliminates such benefits. In elderly women, poor cognitive performance has been associated with lower levels of BDNF, while in young adults, acute exercise has induced increased serum BDNF (for a review, see Ratey & Loehr, 2011). In animals, it has been shown that physical activity increases neurogenesis, associated with an increase in BDNF concentrations, and also improved performance in an object recognition task (for a review, see Lafenêtre et al., 2011); while estrogen, in women may modulate BDNF expression through physical activity (for review see Gligoroska & Manchevska, 2012). Chronic physical exercise increases peripheral levels of BDNF in healthy elderly individuals with different pathologies (for a review, see Coelho, Gobbi, et al., 2013). Such benefits seem, also, to occur in the elderly with dementia, as demonstrated by a recent study, which found that the elderly with AD increased their plasma concentrations of BDNF after acute aerobic exercise of moderate intensity (Coelho et al., 2014).

In a review, Ratey and Loehr (2011) indicated that exercise-induced increases in brain growth factors and neurotrophins had several major effects due to their many properties: e.g., IGF-1 can be synthesized in specific tissues in the brain or transported, from the liver, to the brain in serum because it crosses the blood–brain barrier; BDNF and IGF-1 may act together in order to increase the effects of exercise in the brain, particularly in the hippocampus; in animals, an increase of VEGF in the hippocampus can enhance neurogenesis and this is associated with improvement in cognitive performance, also VEGF may act together with IGF-1 to induce vascular alterations in the brain; and, in animals, FGF-2 has been shown to increases neurogenesis in the hippocampus, in a similar way to IGF-1, VEGF, and BDNF. However, it should be noted that the results of the effects of physical exercises on VEGF concentrations, in cognitively

preserved elderly individuals, are still controversial, as it is not possible to establish the dose–response or type of exercise in order to produce such effect (for a review, see Vital et al., 2014).

Increases in neurotransmitters, such as serotonin, dopamine, acetylcholine, and norepinephrine, as well as the activity of certain subtypes of receptors, changing cortical/subcortical activity, including association with learning and memory, have also been proposed as mechanism for an exercise–cognition interaction (for review see Deslandes et al., 2009). Physical training can also improve gene expressions that regulate production of antioxidant enzymes (superoxide dismutase, catalase, and glutathione peroxidase) that can reduce damage caused to neurons by free radical and neurodegenerative diseases (for review see Barber et al., 2012). A further need for the investigation of biochemical mechanisms is necessary due to preliminary evidence suggesting that physical exercise has a beneficial effect on the genetic polymorphisms of apolipoprotein E (APOE), which is important for growth and regeneration of neural tissues. However, presence of allele ε4 of APOE has been considered a risk marker of late onset AD. Association between physical exercise and risk reduction can be independent of the genetic polymorphism, APOE, or exercise may stimulate a better response on carriers of the ε4 allele, since sedentary individuals with this allele may show increased risk of cognitive decline (for a review, see Foster, Rosenblatt, & Kuljis, 2011). Potential mechanisms mediating such a response may be related to BDNF increase, restoration of the levels of tyrosine kinase, and synaptophysin increase, which is a synaptic function marker (Nichol, Deeny, Seif, Camaclang, & Cotman, 2009).

Structural Mechanisms

From the previous subsection, it is obvious that biochemical changes affect structural mechanisms. Following their review, Ratey and Loehr (2011) claimed that physical fitness or physical exercise is related to: (1) preservation or even increase of cerebral volume in several areas; (2) increased production of new neurons in the dentate gyrus of the hippocampus; (3) neurogenesis through proliferation, survival, functional maturation, and cellular incorporation in hippocampus circuitry; and (4) growth of new microvessels or the increase of already existing vessels in the cerebral net (angiogenesis is linked to neurogenesis because it facilitates transportation of growth factors, contributors of proliferation, and survival of new cells). These claims are supported by the fact that low levels of IGF-1 are associated with deficiencies in angiogenesis and neurogenesis. In summary, exercise promotes vessel growth through VEGF and IGF-1, and angiogenesis is linked to neurogenesis. Increases in dendritic densities of the hippocampus, as well as increases of neuronal mitochondria, which improves metabolism and energy supply to the brain, also have a positive effect (for a review, see Barber et al., 2012).

Regarding aging, exercise may protect against the loss of cerebral volume that is associated with this process. Erickson et al. (2010), in a longitudinal study with the elderly, concluded that large amounts of walking were related to high volumes of gray matter, which reduce risk of cognitive impairment. Erickson et al. (2011) found, also in the elderly, that increases of hippocampal volume, in response to physical training, were associated with increases in BDNF concentrations and with improvements in memory.

Physiological Mechanisms

Finally, biochemical and structural mechanisms interact to affect physiological mechanisms, which could be described as the underlying mechanisms determining outcome. One way of assessing these mechanisms is by the measurement of event-related potentials (ERPs). One of the most measured components of brain ERPs is P3. Its amplitude is relative to the amount of action needed, while its latency reflects speed

of stimulus evaluation, and exercise/physical fitness appear to increase amplitude and reduce latency of P3 (for a review, see Ratey & Loehr, 2011). In two groups of preadolescents (approximate mean age 10 years old) classified as high or low performers on the flanker task, Drollette et al. (2014) analyzed the P3 and N2 components of ERPs and found that in response to exercise, low performers improved their accuracy, with an increase in P3 amplitude. In both groups, N2 amplitude, which monitors response conflict, increased and P3 latency decreased, which suggests general facilitation in response conflict and speed of stimulus classification.

Stranahan et al. (2012), based on animal studies, suggested that the positive effects of exercise on physiological mechanisms may be due to exercise-induced reductions in proinflammatory interleukin-1β and tumor necrosis factor-α (TNF-α) in the hippocampus of exercising individuals with AD. The authors highlighted research that had shown that when transgenic mice models of AD, who were previously sedentary, were given an exercise protocol, interleukin-1β and TNF-α were reduced to similar levels as those found in wild-type mice. They also showed a reduction in interferon-γ and chemokine (C–C motif) ligand 3 (Ccl3, also known as MIP-1α). Together, such results indicate that exercise (running) may modulate the posttranslational target of beta-amyloid in the transgenic model of AD, promoting a neuroprotective effect, possibly through alterations in the profile of inflammatory response in the hippocampus. Similarly, exercising transgenic mice showed reduced amyloidal precursor protein mRNA, attenuated alterations in beta-amyloidal processing, and reduced phosphorylation of tau protein, indicating that exercise can be neuroprotective in animal models of AD. Recent research in humans (Nascimento et al., 2014) has supported this argument by showing that training with multimodal exercise benefited elderly individuals with mild cognitive impairment. Moreover, this improvement was related to decreases in

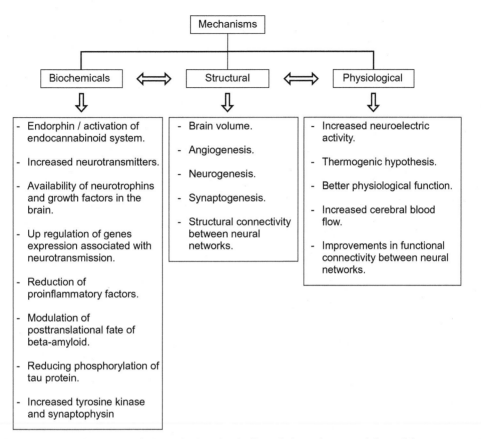

FIGURE 1 Potential mechanisms underlying the beneficial effect of physical exercise/physical fitness on cognition and mental health.

interleukin-6 and TNF-α, along with increases in BDNF concentrations and improvements in cognitive functions.

In other research examining the effects of physiological mechanisms, Voss et al. (2010) showed that physical training improved functional connectivity, as in default mode network (DMN), in the brain frontal executive network (aerobic) or frontal parietal network (nonaerobic) in exercising elderly people. DMN involves brain regions, being activated during "rest" (nonconcentration in the outside world/introspection). In addition, they found that increased functional connectivity was associated with higher improvements on executive function.

In order to illustrate this, Figure 1 summarizes the potential mechanisms underlying the beneficial effect of physical exercise/physical fitness on cognition and mental health covered in this review.

FINAL CONSIDERATIONS

The literature presented in this chapter suggests that the interaction between physical exercise and cognition in individuals with dementia in general and with AD in particular is positive. There is much scientific evidence that demonstrates that physical activity, when practiced in a systematized and regular way, promotes improvement or maintenance of cognitive functions in this population. The protocols of physical exercise, which were most commonly undertaken by this population, were multimodal exercises and aerobic exercises. For the elderly with AD, multimodal physical exercise seems to have a greater effect on cognitive function than other types of exercise. On the other hand, for the elderly with dementia, it is not possible to recommend any specific exercise protocols as much more research is required with these individuals.

If we are to control increases in the number of dementia cases in the world, it is necessary to stimulate the development of new public policies for this population and to create nonpharmacological strategies that can help treatment, and to promote a better quality of life for these people. Thus, a directed program of physical exercises for the elderly with dementia must be devised by universities and other organs and applied in day care centers, health units, and nursing homes.

References

Alzheimer's Association. (2014). Alzheimer's disease facts and figures. *Alzheimer's & Dementia, 10,* e47–e92. http://dx.doi.org/10.1016/j.jalz.2014.02.001.

Andrade, L., Gobbi, L. T. B., Coelho, F. G. M., Christofoletti, G., Costa, J. L., & Stella, F. (2013). Benefits of multimodal exercise intervention on postural control and frontal cognitive functions in patients with Alzheimer's disease: a controlled trial. *Journal of the American Geriatrics Society, 61,* 1919–1926.

Arcoverde, C., Deslandes, A., Moraes, H., Almeida, C., Araujo, N. B., Vasques, P. E., et al. (2014). Treadmill training as an augmentation treatment for Alzheimer's disease: a pilot randomized controlled study. *Archives of Neuropsychiatry, 72,* 190–196.

Arcoverde, C., Deslandes, A., Rangel, A., Rangel, A., Pavão, R., Nigri, F., et al. (2008). Role of physical activity on the maintenance of cognition and activities of daily living in elderly with Alzheimer's disease. *Arquivos de Neuropsiquiatria, 66,* 323–327.

Arkin, S. (2007). Language - enriched plus socialization slows cognitive decline in Alzheimer's Disease. *American Journal of Alzheimer's Disease and Other Dementias, 22,* 62–77.

Barber, S. E., Clegg, A. P., & Young, J. B. (2012). Is there a role for physical activity in preventing cognitive decline in people with mild cognitive impairment? *Age and Ageing, 41,* 5–8.

Barnes, D. E., & Yaffe, K. (2011). The projected effect of risk factor reduction on Alzheimer's disease prevalence. *Lancet Neurology, 10,* 819–828.

Beland, F., & Zumzunegui, M. V. (1999). Predictor of functional status in older people living at home. *Age and Ageing, 28,* 153–159.

Blankevoort, C. G., Heuvelen, M. J. G., Boersma, F., Luning, H., Jong, J., & Scherder, E. J. A. (2010). Review of effects of physical activity on strength, balance, mobility and ADL performance in elderly subjects with dementia. *Dementia and Geriatric Cognitive Disorders, 30,* 392–402.

Booth, F. W., Chakravarthy, M. V., Gordon, S. E., & Spangenburg, E. E. (2002). Waging war on physical inactivity: using modern molecular ammunition against an ancient enemy. *Journal of Applied Physiology, 93,* 3–30.

Bossers, W. J. R., Scherder, E. J. A., Boersma, F., Hortobágyi, T., Woude, L. H. V., & Heuvelen, M. J. G. (2014). Feasibility of a combined aerobic and strength training program and its effects on cognitive and physical function in institutionalized dementia patients. A pilot study. *PLoS One, 9,* 1–10.

Bowes, A., Dawson, A., Jepson, R., & McCabe, L. (2013). Physical activity for people with dementia: a scoping study. *BMC Geriatrics, 13,* 129.

Burgener, S. C., Yang, Y., Gilbert, R., & Marsh-Yant, S. (2008). the effects of a multimodal intervention on outcomes of persons with early-stage dementia. *American Journal of Alzheimers Disease and Other Dementia, 23,* 382–394.

Burns, J. M., Cronk, B. B., & Anderson, H. S. (2008). Cardiorespiratory fitness and brain atrophy in early Alzheimer disease. *Neurology, 71,* 210–216.

Busse, A. L., Jacob-Filho, W., Magaldi, R. M., & Coelho, V. A. (2008). Effects of resistance training exercise on cognitive performance in elderly individuals with memory impairment: results of a controlled trial. *Einstein, 6,* 402–407.

Cassilhas, R. C., Viana, V. A., Grassmann, V., Santos, R. T., Santos, R. F., Tufik, S., et al. (2007). The impact of resistance exercise on the cognitive function of the elderly. *Medicine and Science in Sports and Exercise, 39,* 1401–1407.

Coelho, F. G. M., Andrade, L. P., Pedroso, R. V., Santos-Galduroz, R. F., Gobbi, S., Costa, J. L., et al. (2013). Multimodal exercise intervention improves frontal cognitive functions and gait in Alzheimer's disease: a controlled trial. *Geriatrics and Gerontology International, 13,* 198–203.

Coelho, F. G. M., Gobbi, S., Andreatto, C. A., Corazza, D. I., Pedroso, R. V., & Santos-Galduróz, R. F. (2013). Physical exercise modulates peripheral levels of brain derived neurotrophic factor (BDNF): a systematic review of experimental studies in the elderly. *Archives of Gerontology and Geriatrics, 54,* 348–351.

Coelho, F. G. M., Santos-Galduroz, R. F., Gobbi, S., & Stella, F. (2009). Atividade física sistematizada e desempenho cognitivo em idosos com demência de Alzheimer: uma revisão sistemática (Systematized physical activity and cognitive performance in elderly with Alzheimer's disease: a systematic review). *Revista Brasileira de Psiquiatria*, *31*, 163–170.

Coelho, F. G. M., Vital, T. M., Stein, A. M., Arantes, F. J., Rueda, A. V., Camarini, R., et al. (2014). Acute aerobic exercise increases brain derived neurotrophic factor levels in elderly with Alzheimer's disease. *Journal of Alzheimer's Disease*, *39*, 401–408.

Colcombe, S. J., Erickson, K. I., Raz, N., Webb, A. G., Cohen, N. J., McAuley, E., et al. (2003). Aerobic fitness reduces brain tissue loss in aging humans. *Journal of Gerontology Series A*, *58*, 176–180.

Colcombe, S. J., Erickson, K. I., Scalf, P. E., Kim, J. S., Prakash, R., McAuley, E., et al. (2006). Aerobic exercise training increases brain volume in aging humans. *Journal of Gerontology Series A*, *61*, 1166–1170.

Crone, D., Smith, A., & Gough, B. (2006). The physical activity and mental health relationship – a contemporary perspective from qualitative research. *Acta Universitatis Palackianae Olomucensis Gymnica*, *36*, 29–35.

Dennison, P. E. (2010). *Brain gym: Teacher's edition*. Ventura, CA: Edu-Kinesthetic Inc.

Deslandes, A. C. (2014). Exercise and mental health: what did we learn in the last 20 years? *Frontiers in Psychiatry*, *5*. http://dx.doi.org/10.3389/fpsyt.2014.00066.

Deslandes, A., Moraes, H., Ferreira, C., Veiga, H., Silveira, H., Mouta, R., et al. (2009). Exercise and mental health: many reasons to move. *Neuropsychobiology*, *59*, 191–198.

Drollette, E. S., Scudde, M. R., Raine, L. B., Moor, R. D., Saliba, B. J., Pontifex, M. B., et al. (2014). Acute exercise facilitates brain function and cognition in children who need it most: an ERP study of individual differences in inhibitory control capacity. *Developmental Cognitive Neuroscience*, *7*, 53–64.

Eggermont, L. H. P., Knol, D. L., Hol, E. M., Swaab, D. F., & Scherder, E. J. A. (2009). Hand motor activity, cognition, mood, and the rest–activity rhythm in dementia: a clustered RCT. *Behavioural Brain Research*, *196*, 271–278.

Eggermont, L. H. P., Swaab, D. F., Hol, E. M., & Scherder, E. J. A. (2009). Walking the line: a randomised trial on the effects of a short term walking programme on cognition in dementia. *Journal of Neurology, Neurosurgery and Psychiatry*, *80*, 802–804.

Erickson, K. I., & Kramer, A. F. (2009). Aerobic exercise effects on cognitive and neural plasticity in older adults. *British Journal of Sports Medicine*, *43*, 22–24.

Erickson, K. I., Raji, C. A., Lopez, O. L., Becker, J. T., Rosano, C., Newman, A. B., et al. (2010). Physical activity predicts gray matter volume in late adulthood: the Cardiovascular Health Study. *Neurology*, *75*, 1415–1422.

Erickson, K. I., Voss, M. W., Prakash, R. S., Basak, C., Szabo, A., Chaddock, L., et al. (2011). Exercise training increases size of hippocampus and improves memory. *Proceedings of the National Academy of Sciences of the United States of America*, *108*, 3017–3022.

Farina, N., Rusted, J., & Tabet, N. (2014). The effect of exercise interventions on cognitive outcome in Alzheimer's disease: a systematic review. *International Psychogeriatrics*, *26*, 9–18.

Forbes, D., Thiessen, E. J., Blake, C. M., Forbes, S. C., & Forbes, S. (2013). Exercise programs for people with dementia. *Cochrane Database Systematic Reviews*, *12*. http://dx.doi.org/10.1002/14651858.pub3.

Foster, P. P., Rosenblatt, K. P., & Kuljis, R. O. (2011). Exercise-induced cognitive impairment plasticity implications for mild cognitive impairment and Alzheimer's disease. *Frontiers in Neurology*, *2*. http://dx.doi.org/10.3389/fneur.2011.00028.

Gilkey, R., & Kilts, C. (2007). Cognitive fitness. *Harvard Business Review*, *85*, 53–54.

Gligoroska, J. P., & Manchevska, S. (2012). The effect of physical activity on cognition – physiological mechanisms. *Materia Socio Medica*, *24*, 198–202.

Hebert, L. E., Weuve, J., Scherr, P. A., & Evans, D. A. (2013). Alzheimer disease in the United States (2010-2050) estimated using the 2010 Census. *Neurology*, *80*, 1778–1783.

Hernandez, S. S. S., Coelho, F. G. M., Gobbi, S., & Stella, F. (2010). Efeitos de um programa de atividade física nas funções cognitivas, equilíbrio e risco de quedas em idosos com demência de Alzheimer (Effects of physical activity on cognitive functions, balance and risk of falls in elderly patients with Alzheimer's disease). *Revista Brasileira de Fisioterapia*, *14*, 68–74.

Heyn, P. (2003). The effect of a multisensory exercise program on engagement, behavior, nd selected physiological indexes in persons with dementia. *American Journal of Alzheimer's Disease and Other Dementias*, *18*, 247–251.

Heyn, P., Abreu, B. C., & Ottenbacher, K. J. (2004). The effects of exercise training on elderly persons with cognitive impairment and dementia: a meta-analysis. *Archives of Physical Medicine and Rehabilitation*, *85*, 1694–1704.

Kemoun, G., Thibaud, M., Roumagne, N., Carette, P., Albinet, C., Toussaint, L., et al. (2010). Effects of a physical training programme on cognitive function and walking efficiency in elderly persons with dementia. *Dementia and Geriatrics Cognitive Disorders*, *29*, 109–114.

Kramer, A. F., & Erickson, K. I. (2007). Effects of physical activity on cognition, well-being, and brain: human interventions. *Alzheimer's and Dementia*, *3*, S45–S51.

Lafenêtre, P., Leske, O., Wahle, P., & Heumann, R. A. (2011). The beneficial effects of physical activity on impaired adult neurogenesis and cognitive performance. *Frontiers in Neuroscience*, *12*, 1–8.

Laurin, D., Verreault, R., Lindsay, J., MacPherson, K., & Rockwood, K. (2001). Physical activity and risk of cognitive impairment and dementia in elderly persons. *Archives Neurology, 58*, 498–504.

Lautenschlager, N. T., Cox, K., & Cyarto, E. V. (2012). The influence of exercise on brain aging and dementia. *Biochimica et Biophysica Acta, 1822*, 474–481.

Lautenschlager, N. T., Cox, K. L., Flicker, L., Foster, J. K., Van Bockxmeer, F. M., Xiao, J., et al. (2009). Effect of physical activity on cognitive function in older adults at risk for Alzheimer Disease: a randomized trial. *JAMA, Journal of American Medical Association, 300*, 1027–1037.

Leavell, H., & Clark, E. G. (1976). *Medicina preventiva*. São Paulo: McGraw-Hill do Brasil.

Lima, R. A., Freitas, C. M. S.M., Smethurst, W. S., Santos, C. M., & Barros, M. V. G. (2010). Nível de atividade física em idosos com doença de Alzheimer mediante aplicação do IPAQ e de pedômetros (Physical activity level among elderly with Alzheimer disease by using the IPAQ questionnaire and pedometers). *Revista Brasileira de Atividade Física e Saúde, 15*, 180–185.

Lista, I., & Sorrentino, G. (2009). Biological mechanisms of physical activity in preventing cognitive decline. *Cellular and Molecular Neurobiology, 30*, 493–503.

McAuley, E., Mullen, S. P., & Hillman, C. H. (2013). Physical activity, cardiorespiratory fitness, and cognition across the lifespan. In P. A. Hall (Ed.), *Social neuroscience and public health: Foundations for the science of chronic disease prevention*. New York: Springer Science & Business Media pp. 235–252.

Miu, D. K. Y., Szeto, S. L., & Mak, Y. F. (2008). A randomized controlled trial on the effect of exercise on physical, cognitive and affective function in dementia subjects. *Asian Journal of Gerontology & Geriatrics, 3*, 8–16.

Nascimento, C. M., Pereira, J. R., Andrade, L. P., Garuffi, M., Talib, L. L., Forlenza, O., et al. (2014). Physical exercise in MCI elderly promotes reduction of pro-inflammatory cytokines and improvements on cognition and BDNF peripheral levels. *Current Alzheimer Research, 11*, 799–805.

Nichol, K., Deeny, S. P., Seif, J., Camaclang, K., & Cotman, C. W. (2009). Exercise improves cognition and hippocampal plasticity in APOE epsilon 4 mice. *Alzheimer's & Dementia, 5*, 287–294.

Ohman, H., Savikko, N., Strandberg, T. E., & Pitkala, K. H. (2014). Effect of physical exercise on cognitive performance in older adults with mild cognitive impairment or dementia: a systematic review. *Dementia and Geriatrics Cognitive Disorders, 38*, 347–365.

Pedroso, R. G., Coelho, F. G. ., Santos-Galduróz, R. F., Costa, J. L., Gobbi, S., & Stella, F. (2012). Balance, executive functions and falls in elderly with Alzheimer's disease (AD): a longitudinal study. *Archives of Gerontology and Geriatrics, 54*, 348–351.

Plati, M. C. F., Covre, P., Lukasova, K., & Macedo, E. C. (2006). Depressive symptoms and cognitive performance of the elderly: relationship between institutionalization and activity programs. *Revista Brasileira de Psiquiatria, 28*, 118–121.

Prince, M., Bryce, R., Albanese, E., Wimo, A., Ribeiro, W., & Ferri, C. P. (2013). The global prevalence of dementia: a systematic review and metaanalysis. *Alzheimer's & Dementia, 9*, 63–75.

Ratey, J. J., & Loehr, J. E. (2011). The positive impact of physical activity on cognition during adulthood: a review of underlying mechanisms, evidence and recommendations. *Reviews in the Neurosciences, 22*, 171–185.

Rolland, Y., Rival, L., Pillard, F., Lafont, C. H., Riviere, D., Albarede, J. L., et al. (2000). Feasibility of regular physical exercise for patients with moderate to severe Alzheimer disease. *Journal of Nutrition, Health and Aging, 4*, 109–113.

Steinberg, M., Leoutsakos, J.-M. S., Podewils, L. J., & Lyketsos, C. G. (2009). Evaluation of a home-based exercise program in the treatment of Alzheimer's disease: the maximizing independence in dementia (MIND) study. *International Journal of Geriatric Psychiatry, 24*, 680–685.

Stevens, J., & Kileen, M. (2006). A randomised controlled trial testing the impact of exercise on cognitive symptoms and disability of residents with dementia. *Contemporary Nurse, 21*, 32–40.

Stranahan, A. M., Martin, B., & Maudsley, S. (2012). Anti-inflammatory effects of physical activity in relationship to improved cognitive status in humans and mouse models of Alzheimer's disease. *Current Alzheimer Research, 9*, 86–92.

Teri, L., & Gallagher-Thompson, D. (1991). Cognitive-behavioral interventions for treatment of depression in Alzheimer's patients. *Gerontologist, 31*, 413–416.

Van de Winckel, A., Feys, H., & Weerdt, W. (2004). Cognitive and behavioral effects of music-based exercises in patients with dementia. *Clinical Rehabilitation, 18*, 253–260.

Venturelli, M., Scarsini, R., & Schena, F. (2011). Six-month walking program changes cognitive and ADL performance in patients with Alzheimer. *American Journal of Alzheimers Disease & Other Dementias, 26*, 381–388.

Vidoni, E. D., Honea, R. A., Billinger, S. A., Swerdlow, R. H., & Burns, J. M. (2012). Cardiorespiratory fitness is associated with atrophy in Alzheimer's and aging over 2 years. *Neurobiology of Aging, 33*, 1624–1632.

Vital, T. M., Hernandez, S. S. S., Stein, A. M., Garuffi, M., Corazza, D. I., Andrade, L. P., et al. (2012). Depressive symptoms and level of physical activity in patients with Alzheimer's disease. *Geriatrics and Gerontology International, 12*, 637–642.

Vital, T. M., Stein, A. M., Coelho, F. G. M., Arantes, F. J., Teodorov, E., & Santos-Galduroz, R. F. (2014). Physical exercise and vascular endothelial growth factor (VEGF) in elderly: a systematic review. *Archives of Geriatrics and Gerontology, 59*, 234–239.

Voss, M. W., Prakash, R. S., Erickson, K. I., Basak, C., Chaddock, L., Kim, J. S., et al. (2010). Plasticity of brain networks in a randomized intervention trial of exercise training in older adults. *Frontiers in Aging Neuroscience*, 2, 1–17.

Vreugdenhil, A., Cannell, J., Davies, A., & Razay, G. (2012). A community-based exercise programme to improve functional ability in people with Alzheimer's disease: a randomized controlled trial. *Scandinavian Journal of Caring Sciences*, 26, 12–19.

Winchester, J., Dick, M. B., Gillen, D., Reed, B., Miller, B., Tinklenberg, J., et al. (2013). Walking stabilizes cognitive functioning in Alzheimer's disease (AD) across one year. *Archives of Gerontology and Geriatrics*, 56, 96–103.

Yágüez, L., Shaw, K. N. K., Morris, R., & Matthews, D. (2010). The effects on cognitive functions of a movement-based intervention in patients with Alzheimer's type dementia: a pilot study. *International Journal of Geriatric Psychiatry*, 26, 173–181.

Yuki, A., Lee, S., Kim, H., Kozakai, R., Ando, F., & Shimokata, H. (2012). Relationship between physical activity and brain atrophy progression. *Medicine and Science in Sports and Exercise*, 44, 2362–2368.

Yu, F., Thomas, W., Nelson, N. W., Bronas, U. G., Dysken, M., & Wyman, J. F. (2015). Impact of 6-month aerobic exercise on Alzheimer's symptoms. *Journal of Applied Gerontology*, 34, 484–500.

The Chronic Exercise–Cognition Interaction and Diabetes

Maria Pedersen[1], Jesper Krogh[2]

[1]Department of Clinical Physiology and Nuclear Medicine, Copenhagen University Hospital Herlev, Herlev, Denmark; [2]Department of Medicine, Center of Endocrinology and Metabolism, Copenhagen University Hospital Herlev, Herlev, Denmark

INTRODUCTION

Long-lasting metabolic disturbances may contribute to cognitive decline in patients with diabetes mellitus. A relationship between cognitive impairment and diabetes mellitus was demonstrated as early as 90 years ago (Miles & Root, 1922), although the causal relationship has been difficult to unravel. Type 2 diabetes and dementia are part of a disease network and share risk factors such as physical inactivity (Kramer et al., 1999; Pedersen, 2009), inflammation (Strachan, Reynolds, Marioni, & Price, 2011), and obesity (Lyssenko et al., 2005; Pradhan, 2007; Whitmer et al., 2008). The cause of decreased cognitive ability in elderly patients with type 2 diabetes is probably multifactorial. Identifying potentially modifiable risk factors for cognitive impairment in patients with type 2 diabetes is therefore of major importance for future diabetes health-care strategies. It is hypothesized that regular physical exercise may reduce the deleterious effect of metabolic dysregulation on cognitive function. In this chapter, the interaction between type 2 diabetes and cognitive dysfunction will be discussed with emphasis on/highlighting the effect of physical activity (Figure 1).

DIABETES MELLITUS AND METABOLIC DETERIORATION

Type 2 Diabetes

Type 2 diabetes represents a global health problem approaching epidemic proportions. By 2030, the number of patients with diabetes, estimated at 285 million in 2010, is expected to rise to an alarming level of 439 million (Chen, Magliano, & Zimmet, 2011). In addition, even greater numbers of individuals are expected to be in a prediabetic state. To understand the possible pathophysiological mechanism leading to cognitive dysfunction in the diabetic brain, we have to understand the mechanism of diabetes mellitus and metabolic deterioration. Type 2 diabetes is a complex metabolic disorder that affects several organs including heart, kidneys, vascular system, nervous system, and brain.

Exercise-Cognition Interaction
http://dx.doi.org/10.1016/B978-0-12-800778-5.00017-7

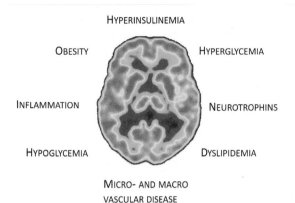

FIGURE 1 Factors related to cognitive impairment and diabetes mellitus. The figure illustrates metabolic activity in a healthy brain and conditions known to influence cognitive function. Several of the conditions are modifiable by physical activity.

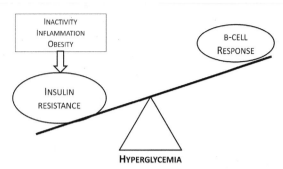

FIGURE 2 Pathogenesis of type 2 diabetes. In healthy humans, there is a balance between insulin resistance and the beta-cell response/function leading to a well-controlled blood glucose level. Physical inactivity, inflammation, and obesity increase insulin resistance. With severe type 2 diabetes, the beta-cell function is impaired and the balance is disturbed to a hyperglycemic state.

Type 2 diabetes is characterized by insulin resistance in liver, skeletal muscle, and adipose tissue in combination with pancreatic beta-cell failure (Lyssenko et al., 2005). With decreased insulin sensitivity in the skeletal muscles in the early stage of type 2 diabetes, a compensatory elevated pancreatic insulin secretion occurs leading to *hyperinsulinemia*. In more severe phases, lower beta-cell function results in lower insulin secretion and therefore chronic *hyperglycemia* appears (Figure 2). Type 2 diabetes is defined by World Health Organization as a condition with a "level of hyperglycemia giving rise to risk of microvascular damage" (WHO/IDF Consultation, 2006).

Diabetes Mellitus and Obesity

Obesity and physical inactivity are known to play a crucial role in the development of type 2 diabetes. It has been demonstrated that adipose tissue is vulnerable to immune cell infiltration and inflammation (Odegaard & Chawla, 2013). Even 60 years ago, it was suggested that adipose tissue could work as a secretory organ to control food intake. But for many years the primary task for adipocytes were thought to be energy storage. Adipose tissue expresses and releases inflammatory mediators known to induce metabolic

disturbances and type 2 diabetes. These days several "adipocytokines" have been identified, defined as cytokines produced and released from adipose tissues. For example, leptin and adiponectin are released to regulate food intake; also various proinflammatory cytokines including tumor necrosis factor (TNF)-α, interleukin (IL)-1β, and IL-6 are released resulting in local and systemic inflammation (Kwon & Pessin, 2013). Not only the amount but also the location of adipose tissue is important. Especially, central abdominal fat accumulation is related to an increased risk of type 2 diabetes (Lyssenko et al., 2005). It is hypothesized that visceral adipose tissue is more inflamed than subcutaneous tissue. In addition, the anatomical location close to the portal vein results in higher levels of mediators (e.g., free fatty acids and proinflammatory cytokines) inhibiting pancreatic insulin release (Kashyap et al., 2003; Yudkin, 2007) and decreasing insulin signaling in the periphery. Consequently, insulin resistance escalates (Bajaj et al., 2002; Krogh-Madsen et al., 2008; Shoelson, Herrero, & Naaz, 2007).

Diabetes Mellitus and Physical Activity

The development of type 2 diabetes is multifactorial but it is believed that a lack of regular physical exercise plays a fundamental role in its development. This hypothesis is supported by epidemiological evidence suggesting that physical inactivity plays a role in the development of type 2 diabetes, whereas regular physical activity significantly lowers risk of type 2 diabetes (Bassuk & Manson, 2005; Katzmarzyk, Gledhill, & Shephard, 2000).

To investigate the causal relationship between physical activity level and type 2 diabetes, different human and animal models have been reported. Several studies have investigated the effect of training on sedentary humans with type 2 diabetes, and focused on the metabolic and cardiovascular effects. Other models are developed, where physically active humans are exposed to a sedentary lifestyle for a predefined period. Some of these studies, including increased sitting time, decreased physical activity in athletes as well as "bed rest" studies, have been conducted. One of the first bed rest studies was described by Saltin et al. in 1968, known as "the Dallas bed rest study" (Saltin et al., 1968). Five young healthy athletes were placed in a supine position for 3 weeks. The study focused on the effect of bed rest and training on submaximal and maximal performance, but did not report metabolic changes.

Krogh-Madsen and colleagues investigated 2 weeks of sedentary lifestyle and focused on metabolic changes. Participants were told to live as inactively as possible, and not exceed 1500 steps/day. The study demonstrated that even a short period of physical inactivity was associated with metabolic changes, including development of insulin resistance, loss of muscle mass, and accumulation of visceral fat (Krogh-Madsen et al., 2010, 2014; Figure 3).

The molecular link between inactivity and metabolic deterioration has been closely investigated. Skeletal muscles are responsible for the majority of glucose disposal in humans, and therefore skeletal muscles are considered as the primary site of whole body insulin resistance. Contracting skeletal muscles increase glucose uptake and thereby lower the blood glucose level in a direct manner, and several studies

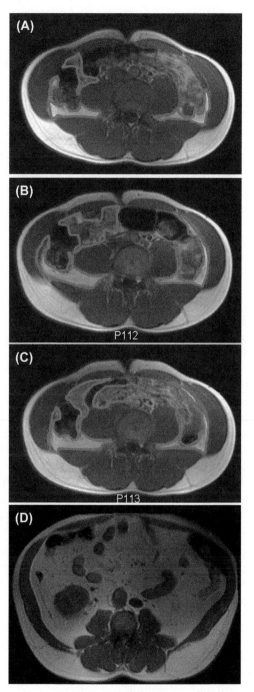

FIGURE 3 Visceral fat accumulation with sedentary lifestyle. Magnetic resonance image of an abdomen demonstrates fat area at baseline (A), after 1 week (B), and after 2 weeks (C) of sedentary lifestyle. Picture (D) illustrates visceral fat accumulation in a middle-aged inactive male with impaired glucose tolerance.

have found an acute effect of exercise on insulin sensitivity (Sigal et al., 2007; Wood & O'Neill, 2012), but more importantly skeletal muscle produces and secretes cytokines and other biomarkers in response to contraction. During the past 30 years, it has been well documented that exercise has a profound effect on the immune system. With the discovery that exercise provokes an increase in a number of cytokines and peptides—the so-called "humoral factor"—a possible link between skeletal muscle activity and immune changes was established. The biomarkers released from contracting skeletal muscles are many, thus it has been demonstrated that skeletal muscle secretes, for example, brain-derived neurotropic factor (BDNF) (Matthews et al., 2009), IL-6 (Steensberg et al., 2000), IL-15 (Nielsen et al., 2007), and leukemia-inhibiting factor (Broholm & Pedersen, 2010). Such factors might also act in a hormone-like fashion and communicate in an endocrine manner with other organs, such as adipose tissue, liver, and brain, and protect against lifestyle-related diseases such as type 2 diabetes, cardiovascular diseases, and degeneration in the brain. In contrast, with physical inactivity for a longer period, the endocrine function in the muscle fails, affecting several other tissues and organs and eventually increased risk of morbidity, including type 2 diabetes. Today, there are no doubts that the positive effects of exercise are exerted through multiple pathways, including anti-inflammatory mechanisms and enhanced insulin-dependent energy metabolism (Cholerton, Baker, & Craft, 2011).

THE DIABETIC BRAIN

Patients with diabetes have increased risk of stroke, dementia, and Alzheimer's disease. The major focus of diabetes research and health care primarily concerns adequate blood sugar control and prevention of end-organ disease in kidneys, eyes, and the peripheral nervous system. However, an increasing awareness of the interaction between diabetes and the brain has become apparent. It is now being recognized that patients with diabetes have not only cognitive deficits but also structural brain changes compared to healthy controls.

Structural Cerebral Changes in Patients with Diabetes

Structural cerebral changes have been reported in both patients with type 1 and type 2 diabetes. Imaging studies have reported lower gray matter density (Musen et al., 2006), lower gray matter volume (Jongen et al., 2007; Northam et al., 2009), white matter volume (Northam et al., 2009), and brain atrophy (van Elderen et al., 2010; Kumar, Anstey, Cherbuin, Wen, & Sachdev, 2008), while other studies did not find any significant differences between diabetic patients and healthy controls (Lobnig, Kromeke, Optenhostert-Porst, & Wolf, 2006; Perantie et al., 2007; Weinger et al., 2008). These inconsistent results can be explained by differences in patient populations (e.g., age and psychiatric comorbidity) and imaging techniques. Furthermore, low-grade inflammation, obesity, and metabolic syndrome have been associated with reduced brain volume (Lu, Nagappan, & Lu, 2014; Onyewuenyi, Muldoon, Christie, Erickson, & Gianaros, 2014) offering several explanations for structural brain changes in patients with diabetes.

Neurotrophins and Diabetes

Neurotrophins are characterized by their ability to induce differentiation of progenitor cells to form new neurons. This process is termed neurogenesis and takes place in the dentate gyrus of the hippocampus and the subventricular zone in the lateral ventricles of the brain. In addition, they induce development and function of neurons. The classic neurotrophins are nerve growth factor, BDNF, neurotrophic factor 3, and neurotrophic factor 4. In a diabetes context, BDNF has been the main neurotrophic factor of interest to researchers. BDNF is expressed throughout the adult mammalian brain as well as in muscle and adipose tissue. In the brain, BDNF is involved in proliferation, differentiation, synaptic plasticity, and cognitive function (Lu et al., 2014). However, recent findings also suggest that BDNF is involved in food intake, glucose metabolism, and energy balance (Lebrun, Bariohay, Moyse, & Jean, 2006; Nakagawa et al., 2002). Peripheral treatment with BDNF has reduced hyperphagia and hyperglycemia in obese diabetic rodents supporting a casual association between BDNF and glycemic regulation (Lebrun et al., 2006).

A number of studies have found lower plasma and serum levels of BDNF in patients with type 2 diabetes (Krabbe et al., 2007; He & Wang, 2014) while others were unable to confirm this (Suwa et al., 2006). In the study by Krabbe et al. (2007), including 233 subjects, they investigated the association between plasma BDNF and obesity and plasma BDNF and diabetes. The study found an inverse relation between plasma BDNF and obesity and lower BNDF levels in diabetic subjects. These results are supported by the study by He and Wang, who showed reduced serum BDNF levels in 74 patients with type 2 diabetes. However, another study of 31 participants, including newly diagnosed female patients with type 2 diabetes, found increased levels of serum BDNF and increased BDNF in obese individuals—the opposite of previously cited studies. However, the latter study was small and restricted inclusion to female subjects. In conclusion, the majority of available studies in rodents and humans suggest an inverse association between peripheral levels of BDNF and diabetes and obesity.

Inflammation in the Diabetic Brain

Inflammatory biomarkers increase with age and levels of IL-6 and TNF-α are found to be increased in healthy elderly individuals, although at a much lower level than seen with acute infections (Bruunsgaard, Pedersen, & Pedersen, 2001). Case–control studies have demonstrated that high concentrations of inflammatory biomarkers are found in patients with Alzheimer's disease and in lower amounts in the aging brain without dementia (Duong, Nikolaeva, & Acton, 1997; Grammas & Ovase, 2001). A longitudinal study by Schmidt et al. (2002) demonstrated, in a group of 1050 Asian men, a higher prevalence of dementia in the individuals with the highest level of C-reactive protein (CRP) as early as midlife and independent of cardiovascular risk factors. Inflammatory biomarkers can penetrate the blood–brain barrier directly or act indirectly via vagal nerve stimulation. There is evidence that inflammatory mechanisms within the central nervous system contribute to cognitive impairment via cytokine-mediated interactions between neurons and glial cells. Therefore, inflammatory markers are suggested as a reliable explanation for the age-related decline in cognitive function. It is not clear whether increased circulating levels of inflammatory biomarkers cause neuroinflammation directly or via inflammation-mediated atherosclerosis causing vascular dementia.

With regard to diabetes, mutual dependence between systemic inflammation and dysregulated glucose metabolism are evident. In patients with type 2 diabetes, levels of inflammatory biomarkers are increased compared to age-matched healthy individuals (Pedersen et al., 2003; Pradhan, 2007). Therefore, it is tempting to suggest that the cognitive impairment seen in patients with type 2 diabetes is to some degree caused by systemic inflammation seen with metabolic deterioration. A cross-sectional study demonstrated that elevated levels of circulating inflammatory biomarkers such as IL-6, TNF-α, and CRP were associated with poorer cognitive ability in patients with type 2 diabetes (Marioni et al., 2010). Other studies have not been able to demonstrate any association, probably due to the huge amount of patients needed and the relatively long follow-up time required to demonstrate an association, as well as the multifactorial pathogenesis.

Blood Glucose Level Influences the Diabetic Brain

Not only may chronic inflammation contribute to an accelerated cognitive decline but also other factors modifiable by physical activity can affect cognitive function. A higher risk of poor cognition among diabetic patients with poorer glycemic control is demonstrated, and acute changes in glucose concentration are known to affect cognitive ability. Hypoglycemia is a potential adverse effect of type 2 diabetes, resulting in decreased delivery of glucose to the brain, followed by downregulation of biomarkers of neuroplasticity and increased levels of neurotoxic glutamate in brain. A large-scale longitudinal cohort study from 1980 to 2007, including 16,667 elderly patients with type 2 diabetes, demonstrated the prevalence of dementia was 11% during a follow-up period, but more interestingly it was demonstrated that episodes of hypoglycemia, severe enough to require hospitalization, were associated with higher risk of dementia compared to patients with no episodes of hypoglycemia (Whitmer, Karter, Yaffe, Quesenberry, & Selby, 2009), even after adjustment for glycemic control, treatment, and comorbidity. In addition, repetitive episodes of moderate to severe hypoglycemia are involved in the development and progression of cognitive dysfunction seen in diabetes (Diaz-Gerevini et al., 2014).

Also hyperglycemia seems to affect cognitive ability in patients with type 2 diabetes. In elderly patients with type 2 diabetes, working memory and attention deficits were observed during a glucose clamp in the hyperglycemic state but not in the euglycemic state (Sommerfield, Deary, & Frier, 2004). In cross-sectional studies, associations between high HbA1c, a measure of plasma glucose concentration during the past 3 months, and cognitive dysfunction are demonstrated in elderly (Cukierman-Yaffe et al., 2009) and middle-aged individuals (Ryan & Geckle, 2000). In addition, Yaffe and coworkers (Yaffe, Blackwell, Whitmer, Krueger, & Barrett, 2006) demonstrated, in a prospective study, that hyperglycemia defined as HbA1c above 7.0% was associated with a fourfold increased risk of mild cognitive impairment. Rizzo et al. (2010) reported a relationship between glucose fluctuations during the day and impairment of cognitive function in older patients with type 2 diabetes. Accordingly, an interventional case–control study demonstrated that middle-aged patients with type 2 diabetes improved cognitive function if they were subjected to intensified glycemic control, involving optimization of the drug treatment, close monitoring of blood glucose level, and instruction in diet and physical activity (Cooray et al., 2011). The above results indicated that glucose fluctuations in patients with type 2 diabetes may affect their cognitive abilities and a possible reversibility in cognitive impairment with improved glucose control.

Insulin Level in the Diabetic Brain

Disturbances in peripheral insulin signaling in skeletal muscles and adipose tissue play a crucial role in development of type 2 diabetes. Recently, it has been demonstrated that insulin also acts in the brain. Two main functions have been described; first, insulin acts in the hypothalamus to modulate food intake, glucose homeostasis, and body weight (Porte & Woods, 1981). Second, the presence and expression of insulin receptors in the hippocampus and cerebral cortex emphasize a major role of insulin in the cognitive process (Wickelgren, 1998) especially in memory processing in humans (Benedict, Kern, Schultes, Born, & Hallschmid, 2008; Kern et al., 2001; Marfaing et al., 1990). Increased levels of insulin in the brain (Guthoff et al., 2010) and cerebrospinal fluid (Wallum et al., 1987) are seen upon administration of insulin in a peripheral vein or after intranasal administration. When insulin is administered to the brain, a positive effect on memory function occurs in healthy humans

(Ott, Benedict, Schultes, Born, & Hallschmid, 2011) as well as in patients with mild cognitive impairments (e.g., due to Alzheimer's disease) (Reger et al., 2008). A pronounced beneficial effect on hippocampus-dependent memory function, after intranasal insulin administration, has been demonstrated in women compared to men (Benedict et al., 2008).

In contrast, long-lasting hyperinsulinemia, as is the case in individuals with type 2 diabetes, is followed by downregulation of insulin receptors on the blood–brain barrier and reduced insulin transport into the brain (Cholerton et al., 2011). A cross-sectional study in individuals representing a broad spectrum of glucose tolerance, from normal glucose tolerance to type 2 diabetes, demonstrated that low scores in executive functions were related to several measures of glucose tolerance, such as low insulin sensitivity as well as high fasting insulin levels (Pedersen et al., 2012). In conclusion, it is hypothesized that chronic hyperinsulinemia will result in a reduced insulin level in the brain, due to decreased insulin transport into the brain (Banks, Jaspan, Huang, & Kastin, 1997) followed by reduced cognitive function.

CAN PHYSICAL ACTIVITY AFFECT THE DIABETIC BRAIN?

In the previous sections we have reported evidence for a causal relationship between cognitive impairment and type 2 diabetes, and discussed their mutual risk factors, all of which are modifiable by physical activity. The question is whether physical activity can serve as a therapeutic tool to prevent cognitive impairment in patients with type 2 diabetes. In humans, physical activity during midlife may protect against cognitive impairment and improve cognitive performance in older adults with impaired memory function (Andel et al., 2008; Best, Nagamatsu, & Liu-Ambrose, 2014; Rovio et al., 2005).

Physical Activity and BDNF

Peripheral BDNF increases in response to acute exercise in humans, while the response to exercise training is less clear with some studies showing an increased BDNF level and others not (Huang, Larsen, Ried-Larsen, Moller, & Andersen, 2013). In rodents, the increase in hippocampal volume is thought to be mediated by BDNF (Vaynman, Ying, & Gomez-Pinilla, 2004). In humans, the effect of exercise training on hippocampal volume/neurogenesis is more controversial. Randomized clinical trials suggest that exercise leads to an increased hippocampal volume in healthy old adults (Erickson et al., 2011), while the evidence for schizophrenia and depression is conflicting (Krogh et al., 2014; Pajonk et al., 2010; Scheewe et al., 2013). Furthermore, in two of these trials the increase in hippocampal volume was positively associated with increased maximal oxygen uptake, BDNF, and spatial and verbal memory (Erickson et al., 2011; Pajonk et al., 2010). The effect of exercise on hippocampal volume remains to be investigated in patients with type 1 or type 2 diabetes. However, in diabetic animal models several studies suggest that exercise leads to increased neurogenesis (Hwang et al., 2014; Stranahan et al., 2009).

Studies on rodents have found that the exercise-related increases in memory and learning are mediated through an upregulation of BDNF, which has the ability to stimulate synaptic plasticity (Tapia-Arancibia, Rage, Givalois, & Arancibia, 2004). The exercise-induced cell proliferation is inhibited by peripheral blockade of either insulin growth factor 1 (IGF-1) or vascular endothelial growth factor (VEGF) (Fabel et al., 2003; Trejo, Llorens-Martin, & Torres-Aleman, 2008), which indicates that the exercise-induced neurogenesis is dependent on not only BDNF but also peripheral IGF-1 and VEGF.

Exercise as an Anti-Inflammatory Mediator

Regular physical exercise protects against conditions known to be associated with chronic inflammation. Contracting skeletal muscles release cytokines and other peptides acting in a paracrine or endocrine manner—the so-called "myokines" (Pedersen, 2009). Several studies show that markers of inflammation are reduced following longer-term behavioral changes involving both reduced energy intake and increased physical activity (see Petersen & Pedersen, 2005, for a review). It is suggested that the anti-inflammatory effect of physical activity may be primarily mediated by the exercise effect on decreased inflammation in visceral fat and other ectopic fat deposits, via specific anti-inflammatory effects of myokines.

Nevertheless, large-scale studies finding causal relationships between anti-inflammatory biomarkers and exercise-induced improved cognitive ability are still missing. Whether exercise protects against cognitive decline by altering brain cytokine levels has been reviewed by Packer, Pervaiz, and Hoffman-Goetz (2010), based only on 10 studies, of which only 2 involved humans. The authors suggested that exercise training reduces cerebral levels of proinflammatory cytokines, decreased proapoptotic protein, and improved cognitive abilities in behavioral tests.

Glycemic Control

Exercise has repeatedly been shown to improve glycemic control, primarily monitored by HbA1c. If blood glucose is monitored by continuous glucose monitoring, it is concluded in a recently published meta-analysis that exercise reduces average glucose concentrations and time spent in hyperglycemia despite not significantly affecting outcomes such as fasting glucose and hypoglycemia in patients with type 2 diabetes (MacLeod, Terada, Chahal, & Boule, 2013). In a setup with 2 weeks of step reduction to 1500 steps/day, the participants developed a poorer glycemic control, increased endogenous glucose production, and decreased hepatic insulin extraction. In addition, participants developed decreased cognitive function with regard to capacity of attention (Krogh-Madsen et al., 2014).

CONCLUSION

The metabolic changes observed in patients with diabetes are partly responsible for cognitive impairment in later life. These metabolic changes can be modified by physical activity. Observational studies have demonstrated that exercise can improve the metabolic state as well as the cognitive function in humans and rodents, and hypotheses involving obesity, inflammation, and neurotrophins are established. However, firm evidence of a causal relationship between exercise and cognitive function in patients with diabetes needs to be confirmed in adequately powered, randomized clinical trials.

References

Andel, R., Crowe, M., Pedersen, N. L., Fratiglioni, L., Johansson, B., & Gatz, M. (2008). Physical exercise at midlife and risk of dementia three decades later: a population-based study of Swedish twins. *Journal of Gerontology Series A, 63,* 62–66.

Bajaj, M., Pratipanawatr, T., Berria, R., Pratipanawatr, W., Kashyap, S., Cusi, K., et al. (2002). Free fatty acids reduce splanchnic and peripheral glucose uptake in patients with type 2 diabetes. *Diabetes, 51,* 3043–3048.

Banks, W. A., Jaspan, J. B., Huang, W., & Kastin, A. J. (1997). Transport of insulin across the blood–brain barrier: saturability at euglycemic doses of insulin. *Peptides, 18,* 1423–1429.

Bassuk, S. S., & Manson, J. E. (2005). Epidemiological evidence for the role of physical activity in reducing risk of type 2 diabetes and cardiovascular disease. *Journal of Applied Physiology, 99,* 1193–1204.

Benedict, C., Kern, W., Schultes, B., Born, J., & Hallschmid, M. (2008). Differential sensitivity of men and women to anorexigenic and memory-improving effects of intranasal insulin. *Journal of Clinical Endocrinology and Metabolism, 93,* 1339–1344.

Best, J. R., Nagamatsu, L. S., & Liu-Ambrose, T. (2014). Improvements to executive function during exercise training predict maintenance of physical activity over the following year. *Frontiers in Human Neuroscience, 8,* 353. http://dx.doi.org/10.3389/fnhum.2014.00353.

Broholm, C., & Pedersen, B. K. (2010). Leukaemia inhibitory factor–an exercise-induced myokine. *Exercise Immunology Review, 16*, 77–85.

Bruunsgaard, H., Pedersen, M., & Pedersen, B. K. (2001). Aging and proinflammatory cytokines. *Current Opinion in Hematology, 8*, 131–136.

Chen, L., Magliano, D. J., & Zimmet, P. Z. (2011). The worldwide epidemiology of type 2 diabetes mellitus–present and future perspectives. *Nature Reviews Endocrinology, 8*, 228–236.

Cholerton, B., Baker, L. D., & Craft, S. (2011). Insulin resistance and pathological brain ageing. *Diabetic Medicine, 28*, 1463–1475.

Cooray, G., Nilsson, E., Wahlin, A., Laukka, E. J., Brismar, K., & Brismar, T. (2011). Effects of intensified metabolic control on CNS function in type 2 diabetes. *Psychoneuroendocrinology, 36*, 77–86.

Cukierman-Yaffe, T., Gerstein, H. C., Williamson, J. D., Lazar, R. M., Lovato, L., Miller, M. E., et al. (2009). Relationship between baseline glycemic control and cognitive function in individuals with type 2 diabetes and other cardiovascular risk factors: the action to control cardiovascular risk in diabetes-memory in diabetes (ACCORD-MIND) trial. *Diabetes Care, 32*, 221–226.

Diaz-Gerevini, G. T., Repossi, G., Dain, A., Tarres, M. C., Das, U. N., & Eynard, A. R. (2014). Cognitive and motor perturbations in elderly with longstanding diabetes mellitus. *Nutrition, 30*, 628–635.

Duong, T., Nikolaeva, M., & Acton, P. J. (1997). C-reactive protein-like immunoreactivity in the neurofibrillary tangles of Alzheimer's disease. *Brain Research, 749*, 152–156.

van Elderen, S. G., de, R. A., de Craen, A. J., Westendorp, R. G., Blauw, G. J., Jukema, J. W., et al. (2010). Progression of brain atrophy and cognitive decline in diabetes mellitus: a 3-year follow-up. *Neurology, 75*, 997–1002.

Erickson, K. I., Voss, M. W., Prakash, R. S., Basak, C., Szabo, A., Chaddock, L., et al. (February 15, 2011). Exercise training increases size of hippocampus and improves memory. *Proceedings of National Academy of Sciences, 108*, 3017–3022.

Fabel, K., Fabel, K., Tab, B., Kaufer, D., Baiker, A., Simmons, N., et al. (2003). VEGF is necessary for exercise-induced adult hippocampal neurogenesis. *European Journal of Neuroscience, 18*, 2803–2812.

Grammas, P., & Ovase, R. (2001). Inflammatory factors are elevated in brain microvessels in Alzheimer's disease. *Neurobiology of Aging, 22*, 837–842.

Guthoff, M., Grichisch, Y., Canova, C., Tschritter, O., Veit, R., Hallschmid, M., et al. (2010). Insulin modulates food-related activity in the central nervous system. *Journal of Clinical Endocrinology and Metabolism, 95*, 748–755.

He, M., & Wang, J. (2014). Decreased serum brain-derived neurotrophic factor in Chinese patients with type 2 diabetes mellitus. *Acta Biochimica et Biophysica Sinica (Shanghai), 46*, 426–427.

Huang, T., Larsen, K. T., Ried-Larsen, M., Moller, N. C., & Andersen, L. B. (2013). The effects of physical activity and exercise on brain-derived neurotrophic factor in healthy humans: a review. *Scandinavian Journal of Medicine and Science in Sports, 24*, 1–10.

Hwang, I. K., Choi, J. H., Nam, S. M., Park, O. K., Yoo, D. Y., Kim, W., et al. (2014). Activation of microglia and induction of pro-inflammatory cytokines in the hippocampus of type 2 diabetic rats. *Neurological Research, 36*, 824–832.

Jongen, C., van der, G. J., Kappelle, L. J., Biessels, G. J., Viergever, M. A., & Pluim, J. P. (2007). Automated measurement of brain and white matter lesion volume in type 2 diabetes mellitus. *Diabetologia, 50*, 1509–1516.

Kashyap, S., Belfort, R., Gastaldelli, A., Pratipanawatr, T., Berria, R., Pratipanawatr, W., et al. (2003). A sustained increase in plasma free fatty acids impairs insulin secretion in nondiabetic subjects genetically predisposed to develop type 2 diabetes. *Diabetes, 52*, 2461–2474.

Katzmarzyk, P. T., Gledhill, N., & Shephard, R. J. (2000). The economic burden of physical inactivity in Canada. *Canadian Medical Association Journal, 163*, 1435–1440.

Kern, W., Peters, A., Fruehwald-Schultes, B., Deininger, E., Born, J., & Fehm, H. L. (2001). Improving influence of insulin on cognitive functions in humans. *Neuroendocrinology, 74*, 270–280.

Krabbe, K. S., Nielsen, A. R., Krogh-Madsen, R., Plomgaard, P., Rasmussen, P., Erikstrup, C., et al. (2007). Brain-derived neurotrophic factor (BDNF) and type 2 diabetes. *Diabetologia, 50*, 431–438.

Kramer, A. F., Hahn, S., Cohen, N. J., Banich, M. T., McAuley, E., Harrison, C. R., et al. (1999). Ageing, fitness and neurocognitive function. *Nature, 400*, 418–419.

Krogh-Madsen, R., Pedersen, M., Solomon, T. P., Knudsen, S. H., Hansen, L. S., Karstoft, K., et al. (2014). Normal physical activity obliterates the deleterious effects of a high-caloric intake. *Journal of Applied Physiology, 116*, 231–239.

Krogh-Madsen, R., Plomgaard, P., Akerstrom, T., Moller, K., Schmitz, O., & Pedersen, B. K. (2008). Effect of short-term intralipid infusion on the immune response during low-dose endotoxemia in humans. *American Journal of Physiology, Endocrinology and Metabolism, 294*, E371–E379.

Krogh-Madsen, R., Thyfault, J. P., Broholm, C., Mortensen, O. H., Olsen, R. H., Mounier, R., et al. (2010). A 2-wk reduction of ambulatory activity attenuates peripheral insulin sensitivity. *Journal of Applied Physiology, 108*, 1034–1040.

Krogh, J., Rostrup, E., Thomsen, C., Elfving, B., Videbech, P., & Nordentoft, M. (2014). The effect of exercise on hippocampal volume and neurotrophines in patients with major depression–a randomized clinical trial. *Journal of Affective Disorders, 165*, 24–30.

Kumar, R., Anstey, K. J., Cherbuin, N., Wen, W., & Sachdev, P. S. (2008). Association of type 2 diabetes with depression, brain atrophy, and reduced fine motor speed in a 60- to 64-year-old community sample. *American Journal of Geriatric Psychiatry, 16*, 989–998.

Kwon, H., & Pessin, J. E. (2013). Adipokines mediate inflammation and insulin resistance. *Frontiers in Endocrinology*, 4, 71. http://dx.doi.org/10.3389/fendo.2013.00071.

Lebrun, B., Bariohay, B., Moyse, E., & Jean, A. (2006). Brain-derived neurotrophic factor (BDNF) and food intake regulation: a minireview. *Autonomic Neuroscience*, 126-127, 30–38.

Lobnig, B. M., Kromeke, O., Optenhostert-Porst, C., & Wolf, O. T. (2006). Hippocampal volume and cognitive performance in long-standing type 1 diabetic patients without macrovascular complications. *Diabetic Medicine*, 23, 32–39.

Lu, B., Nagappan, G., & Lu, Y. (2014). BDNF and synaptic plasticity, cognitive function, and dysfunction. *Handbook of Experimental Pharmacology*, 220, 223–250.

Lyssenko, V., Almgren, P., Anevski, D., Perfekt, R., Lahti, K., Nissen, M., et al. (2005). Predictors of and longitudinal changes in insulin sensitivity and secretion preceding onset of type 2 diabetes. *Diabetes*, 54, 166–174.

MacLeod, S. F., Terada, T., Chahal, B. S., & Boule, N. G. (2013). Exercise lowers postprandial glucose but not fasting glucose in type 2 diabetes: a meta-analysis of studies using continuous glucose monitoring. *Diabetes Metabolism Research and Reviews*, 29, 593–603.

Marfaing, P., Penicaud, L., Broer, Y., Mraovitch, S., Calando, Y., & Picon, L. (1990). Effects of hyperinsulinemia on local cerebral insulin binding and glucose utilization in normoglycemic awake rats. *Neuroscience Letters*, 115, 279–285.

Marioni, R. E., Strachan, M. W., Reynolds, R. M., Lowe, G. D., Mitchell, R. J., Fowkes, F. G., et al. (2010). Association between raised inflammatory markers and cognitive decline in elderly people with type 2 diabetes: the Edinburgh type 2 diabetes study. *Diabetes*, 59, 710–713.

Matthews, V. B., Astrom, M. B., Chan, M. H., Bruce, C. R., Krabbe, K. S., Prelovsek, O., et al. (2009). Brain-derived neurotrophic factor is produced by skeletal muscle cells in response to contraction and enhances fat oxidation via activation of AMP-activated protein kinase. *Diabetologia*, 52, 1409–1418.

Miles, W. R., & Root, H. F. (1922). Psychologic tests applied to diabetic patients. *Archives of Internal Medicine*, 30, 767–777.

Musen, G., Lyoo, I. K., Sparks, C. R., Weinger, K., Hwang, J., Ryan, C. M., et al. (2006). Effects of type 1 diabetes on gray matter density as measured by voxel-based morphometry. *Diabetes*, 55, 326–333.

Nakagawa, T., Ono-Kishino, M., Sugaru, E., Yamanaka, M., Taiji, M., & Noguchi, H. (2002). Brain-derived neurotrophic factor (BDNF) regulates glucose and energy metabolism in diabetic mice. *Diabetes Metabolism Research and Reviews*, 18, 185–191.

Nielsen, A. R., Mounier, R., Plomgaard, P., Mortensen, O. H., Penkowa, M., Speerschneider, T., et al. (2007). Expression of interleukin-15 in human skeletal muscle effect of exercise and muscle fibre type composition. *Journal of Physiology*, 584, 305–312.

Northam, E. A., Rankins, D., Lin, A., Wellard, R. M., Pell, G. S., Finch, S. J., et al. (2009). Central nervous system function in youth with type 1 diabetes 12 years after disease onset. *Diabetes Care*, 32, 445–450.

Odegaard, J. I., & Chawla, A. (2013). Pleiotropic actions of insulin resistance and inflammation in metabolic homeostasis. *Science*, 339, 172–177.

Onyewuenyi, I. C., Muldoon, M. F., Christie, I. C., Erickson, K. I., & Gianaros, P. J. (2014). Basal ganglia morphology links the metabolic syndrome and depressive symptoms. *Physiology and Behavior*, 123, 214–222.

Ott, V., Benedict, C., Schultes, B., Born, J., & Hallschmid, M. (2011). Intranasal administration of insulin to the brain impacts cognitive function and peripheral metabolism. *Diabetes, Obesity and Metabolism*, 14, 214–221.

Packer, N., Pervaiz, N., & Hoffman-Goetz, L. (2010). Does exercise protect from cognitive decline by altering brain cytokine and apoptotic protein levels? A systematic review of the literature. *Exercise Immunology Review*, 16, 138–162.

Pajonk, F. G., Wobrock, T., Gruber, O., Scherk, H., Berner, D., Kaizl, I., et al. (2010). Hippocampal plasticity in response to exercise in schizophrenia. *Archives of General Psychiatry*, 67, 133–143.

Pedersen, B. K. (2009). The diseasome of physical inactivity–and the role of myokines in muscle–fat cross talk. *Journal of Physiology*, 587, 5559–5568.

Pedersen, M., Bruunsgaard, H., Weis, N., Hendel, H. W., Andreassen, B. U., Eldrup, E., et al. (2003). Circulating levels of TNF-alpha and IL-6-relation to truncal fat mass and muscle mass in healthy elderly individuals and in patients with type-2 diabetes. *Mechanisms of Ageing and Development*, 124, 495–502.

Pedersen, M., Pedersen, K. K., Bruunsgaard, H., Krabbe, K. S., Thomsen, C., Faerch, K., et al. (2012). Cognitive functions in middle aged individuals are related to metabolic disturbances and aerobic capacity: a cross-sectional study. *PLoS One*, 7, e51132.

Perantie, D. C., Wu, J., Koller, J. M., Lim, A., Warren, S. L., Black, K. J., et al. (2007). Regional brain volume differences associated with hyperglycemia and severe hypoglycemia in youth with type 1 diabetes. *Diabetes Care*, 30, 2331–2337.

Petersen, A. M., & Pedersen, B. K. (2005). The anti-inflammatory effect of exercise. *Journal of Applied Physiology*, 98, 1154–1162.

Porte, D., Jr., & Woods, S. C. (1981). Regulation of food intake and body weight in insulin. *Diabetologia*, 20(Suppl.), 274–280.

Pradhan, A. (2007). Obesity, metabolic syndrome, and type 2 diabetes: inflammatory basis of glucose metabolic disorders. *Nutrition Reviews*, 65, S152–S156.

Reger, M. A., Watson, G. S., Green, P. S., Wilkinson, C. W., Baker, L. D., Cholerton, B., et al. (2008). Intranasal insulin improves cognition and modulates beta-amyloid in early AD. *Neurology*, 70, 440–448.

Rizzo, M. R., Marfella, R., Barbieri, M., Boccardi, V., Vestini, F., Lettieri, B., et al. (2010). Relationships between daily acute glucose fluctuations and cognitive performance among aged type 2 diabetic patients. *Diabetes Care, 33,* 2169–2174.

Rovio, S., Kareholt, I., Helkala, E. L., Viitanen, M., Winblad, B., Tuomilehto, J., et al. (2005). Leisure-time physical activity at midlife and the risk of dementia and Alzheimer's disease. *Lancet Neurology, 4,* 705–711.

Ryan, C. M., & Geckle, M. O. (2000). Circumscribed cognitive dysfunction in middle-aged adults with type 2 diabetes. *Diabetes Care, 23,* 1486–1493.

Saltin, B., Blomqvist, G., Mitchell, J. H., Johnson, R. L., Jr., Wildenthal, K., & Chapman, C. B. (1968). Response to exercise after bed rest and after training. *Circulation, 38,* 71–78.

Scheewe, T. W., van Haren, N. E., Sarkisyan, G., Schnack, H. G., Brouwer, R. M., de Glint, M., et al. (2013). Exercise therapy, cardiorespiratory fitness and their effect on brain volumes: a randomised controlled trial in patients with schizophrenia and healthy controls. *European Neuropsychopharmacol, 23,* 675–685.

Schmidt, R., Schmidt, H., Curb, J. D., Masaki, K., White, L. R., & Launer, L. J. (2002). Early inflammation and dementia: a 25-year follow-up of the Honolulu-Asia aging study. *Annals of Neurology, 52,* 168–174.

Shoelson, S. E., Herrero, L., & Naaz, A. (2007). Obesity, inflammation, and insulin resistance. *Gastroenterology, 132,* 2169–2180.

Sigal, R. J., Kenny, G. P., Boule, N. G., Wells, G. A., Prud'homme, D., Fortier, M., et al. (2007). Effects of aerobic training, resistance training, or both on glycemic control in type 2 diabetes: a randomized trial. *Annals of Internal Medicine, 147,* 357–369.

Sommerfield, A. J., Deary, I. J., & Frier, B. M. (2004). Acute hyperglycemia alters mood state and impairs cognitive performance in people with type 2 diabetes. *Diabetes Care, 27,* 2335–2340.

Steensberg, A., van, H. G., Osada, T., Sacchetti, M., Saltin, B., & Pedersen, B. K. (2000). Production of interleukin-6 in contracting human skeletal muscles can account for the exercise-induced increase in plasma interleukin-6. *Journal of Physiology, 529,* 237–242.

Strachan, M. W., Reynolds, R. M., Marioni, R. E., & Price, J. F. (2011). Cognitive function, dementia and type 2 diabetes mellitus in the elderly. *Nature Reviews Endocrinology, 7,* 108–114.

Stranahan, A. M., Lee, K., Martin, B., Maudsley, S., Golden, E., Cutler, R. G., et al. (2009). Voluntary exercise and caloric restriction enhance hippocampal dendritic spine density and BDNF levels in diabetic mice. *Hippocampus, 19,* 951–961.

Suwa, M., Kishimoto, H., Nofuji, Y., Nakano, H., Sasaki, H., Radak, Z., et al. (2006). Serum brain-derived neurotrophic factor level is increased and associated with obesity in newly diagnosed female patients with type 2 diabetes mellitus. *Metabolism, 55,* 852–857.

Tapia-Arancibia, L., Rage, F., Givalois, L., & Arancibia, S. (2004). Physiology of BDNF: focus on hypothalamic function. *Frontiers in Neuroendocrinology, 25,* 77–107.

Trejo, J. L., Llorens-Martin, M. V., & Torres-Aleman, I. (2008). The effects of exercise on spatial learning and anxiety-like behavior are mediated by an IGF-I-dependent mechanism related to hippocampal neurogenesis. *Molecular and Cellular Neuroscience, 37,* 402–411.

Vaynman, S., Ying, Z., & Gomez-Pinilla, F. (2004). Hippocampal BDNF mediates the efficacy of exercise on synaptic plasticity and cognition. *European Journal of Neuroscience, 20,* 2580–2590.

Wallum, B. J., Taborsky, G. J., Jr., Porte, D., Jr., Figlewicz, D. P., Jacobson, L., Beard, J. C., et al. (1987). Cerebrospinal fluid insulin levels increase during intravenous insulin infusions in man. *Journal of Clinical Endocrinology and Metabolism, 64,* 190–194.

Weinger, K., Jacobson, A. M., Musen, G., Lyoo, I. K., Ryan, C. M., Jimerson, D. C., et al. (2008). The effects of type 1 diabetes on cerebral white matter. *Diabetologia, 51,* 417–425.

Whitmer, R. A., Gustafson, D. R., Barrett-Connor, E., Haan, M. N., Gunderson, E. P., & Yaffe, K. (2008). Central obesity and increased risk of dementia more than three decades later. *Neurology, 71,* 1057–1064.

Whitmer, R. A., Karter, A. J., Yaffe, K., Quesenberry, C. P., Jr., & Selby, J. V. (2009). Hypoglycemic episodes and risk of dementia in older patients with type 2 diabetes mellitus. *Journal of American Medical Association, 301,* 1565–1572.

WHO/IDF. (2006). *Definition and diagnosis of diabetes mellitus and intermediate hyperglycaemia.* Geneva: WHO Document Production Services.

Wickelgren, I. (1998). Tracking insulin to the mind. *Science, 280,* 517–519.

Wood, R. J., & O'Neill, E. C. (2012). Resistance training in type ii diabetes mellitus: impact on areas of metabolic dysfunction in skeletal muscle and potential impact on bone. *Journal of Nutrition and Metabolism, 2012,* 268197. http://dx.doi.org/10.1155/2012/268197.

Yaffe, K., Blackwell, T., Whitmer, R. A., Krueger, K., & Barrett, C. E. (2006). Glycosylated hemoglobin level and development of mild cognitive impairment or dementia in older women. *Journal of Nutrition Health and Aging, 10,* 293–295.

Yudkin, J. S. (2007). Inflammation, obesity, and the metabolic syndrome. *Hormone and Metabolic Research, 39,* 707–709.

The Exercise–Cognition Interaction and ADHD

Sarah C. O'Neill[1,2], Olga G. Berwid[3], Anne-Claude V. Bédard[4]

[1]Department of Psychology, City College of the City University of New York, New York, NY, USA;
[2]Department of Psychology, Graduate Center of the City University of New York, New York, NY,
USA; [3]Department of Behavioral Sciences, York College of the City University of New York, Jamaica,
NY, USA; [4]Department of Applied Psychology and Human Development, Ontario Institute for Studies
in Education, University of Toronto, Toronto, Ontario, Canada

WHAT IS ATTENTION-DEFICIT/ HYPERACTIVITY DISORDER?

Attention deficit/hyperactivity disorder (ADHD) is an early-emerging neurodevelopmental disorder characterized by elevated levels of inattention, hyperactivity, and/or impulsivity. Under the current Diagnostic and Statistical Manual of Mental Disorders (DSM-5) (American Psychiatric Association; APA, 2013), individuals may be ascribed one of the following presentations: Inattentive, Hyperactive/Impulsive, or Combined Inattentive and Hyperactive/Impulsive. These "presentations" reflect the relative number of inattentive and hyperactive-impulsive symptoms present at the time of assessment, consistent with data showing that ADHD symptom severity falls along a continuum. Accordingly, ADHD presentations are not fixed and may change over the course of development (Willcutt et al., 2012).

Recent estimates suggest that 11% of 4–17-year-old American children and adolescents have received a diagnosis of ADHD (Visser et al., 2014). Worldwide, the prevalence of ADHD is estimated at 5% (Polanczyk, Willcutt, Salum, Kieling, & Rohde, 2014). For most individuals, symptoms of inattention and, more commonly, hyperactivity/impulsivity emerge during early childhood. Over development, overt hyperactivity declines, although children and adolescents report subjective feelings of restlessness. Inattention becomes more prominent and problematic for youngsters as they try to manage the academic and social demands of school. A significant proportion—but certainly not all children—continue to meet criteria for ADHD in adolescence/early adulthood, with rates of persistence varying from approximately 15% to 65% (e.g., Halperin, Trampush, Miller, Marks, & Newcorn, 2008; Mannuzza, Klein, Bessler, Malloy, & LaPadula, 1993; Shaw et al., 2013).

ADHD is associated with impairment across multiple domains. Individuals are at greater risk for academic and occupational difficulties, psychiatric comorbidity, obesity, relationship difficulties, substance use, and criminality (e.g., Cortese, Ramos Olazagasti, et al., 2013; Mannuzza, Klein, Bessler, Malloy, & Hynes, 1997; Mrug et al., 2012; Sibley et al., 2014).

Although these behaviors and developmental progression of symptoms are typical at the group level, individual-based trajectories of ADHD symptoms and their associated impairments are highly variable. Thus, ADHD is characterized by heterogeneity in behavioral phenotype and clinical course. It is therefore critical to learn not only about etiological risk and resilience factors but also about the features that predict which trajectory children will follow.

ETIOLOGY OF ADHD

Identifying "the cause" of ADHD has been an enormous challenge to the field, which is perhaps not surprising in light of its heterogeneity. To explain this heterogeneity, it has been proposed that ADHD is the result of a dynamic interaction among genes, prenatal, perinatal, and postnatal environmental factors. Risk or resilience factors may present at any point in development, which in turn will impact on risk or protective factors already present to alter behavior and possible clinical course of the disorder (Halperin, Bedard, & Curchack-Lichtin, 2012; Sonuga-Barke & Halperin, 2010).

Neurobiological Factors

Genetics

The heritability estimate for ADHD has been measured at 0.76 (Faraone et al., 2005), with many risk genes exerting a small effect on susceptibility for the disorder. Several candidate genes conferring risk for ADHD have been identified, including those involved in dopaminergic transmission (e.g., *DAT1*, *DRD4*, and *DRD5*); serotonergic transmission (e.g., *5HTT* and *HT1RB*); and nervous system development (e.g., *SNAP-25*) (see the meta-analytic review by Gizer, Ficks,

& Waldman, 2009). There is, however, significant variability in observed effect sizes between ADHD and the above genes, as well as for several other genes involved in monoamine synthesis or metabolism (e.g., *DBH*, *ADRA2A*, *TPH2*, *MAOA* (Gizer et al., 2009)). There may be many variables that moderate the relation between these genes and ADHD, thereby reducing or amplifying risk for the disorder (Gizer et al., 2009).

Neuroanatomy and Neurochemistry

Neuroimaging data provide evidence that children, adolescents, and adults with ADHD differ from non-ADHD peers on functional and structural measures derived from multiple brain regions associated with a wide range of cognitive tasks (see review by Cortese et al., 2012). In a recent review of magnetic resonance imaging (MRI) data, Rubia, Alegria, and Brinson (2014) summarize that individuals with ADHD have alterations in frontostriatal, frontoparietotemporal, frontocerebellar, and frontolimbic networks. Also implicated are abnormalities in the anterior cingulate, thought to be involved in the detection of errors and processing of conflict (Amico, Stauber, Koutsouleris, & Frodl, 2011; Cherkasova & Hechtman, 2009). Finally, longitudinal structural imaging research has shown that children and adolescents with ADHD have smaller total cerebral and cerebellar volumes when compared to age- and sex-matched controls (Castellanos et al., 2002). As such, it is likely that alterations in brain development play a central role in the emergence and persistence of the disorder.

Underlying these structural and functional brain differences are alterations in catecholamine neurotransmission. Studies have demonstrated that individuals with ADHD have reduced levels of dopamine (DA) and norepinephrine (NE), likely due to abnormal functioning of relevant transporter systems (as reviewed by Prince, 2008). In addition, current effective medications for ADHD act via these neurotransmitter systems, reinforcing the idea that the catecholamines play a central role in the neurobiology of ADHD (see review by Minzenberg, 2012).

Environmental Factors

A multitude of pre- and perinatal risk factors have been associated with ADHD. Some of these include: parental smoking during the prenatal period, particularly maternal nicotine consumption (e.g., Nomura, Marks, & Halperin, 2010; Zhu et al., 2014); maternal stress, obesity, and alcohol use during pregnancy (Buss et al., 2012; Mick, Biederman, Faraone, Sayer, & Kleinman, 2002; Motlagh et al., 2010); and fetal exposure to lead and low birth weight (Sioen et al., 2013; Szatmari, Saigal, Rosenbaum, & Campbell, 1993). Complex relations are observed among these risk factors (e.g., Nomura et al., 2012), thus careful examination of interactions among risks, gene × environment interactions, and epigenetic mechanisms is needed to further elucidate the ways in which these factors confer risk.

In the postnatal environmental, lower socioeconomic status, exposure to organophosphates and other metals, and a more harsh parenting style are all risk factors for ADHD (Bouchard, Bellinger, Wright, & Weisskopf, 2010; Johnston & Mash, 2001). Extreme deprivation that extends beyond the first 6 months of life is associated with later inattention and hyperactivity (Stevens et al., 2008). Television viewing has also been associated with greater attentional problems (e.g., Swing, Gentile, Anderson, & Walsh, 2010), which is also of concern because sedentary behavior (commonly assessed as television viewing) is associated with lower levels of physical activity (Mansoubi, Pearson, Biddle, & Clemes, 2014).

Neuropsychological Dysfunction

Traditionally, ADHD had been conceptualized as primarily driven by executive dysfunction. Barkley's (1997) model posits that ADHD stems from a primary deficit in behavioral inhibition. Indeed, there is a robust literature indicating that individuals with ADHD show significantly poorer performance on tasks that purportedly measure inhibitory control, such as the stop-signal task (Lijffijt, Kenemans, Verbaten, & van Engeland, 2005) and the go/no go task (Rubia, Smith, & Taylor, 2007). In contrast, Rapport and colleagues (2008) consider working memory problems to be the primary deficit in ADHD. Working memory is critical for reducing distraction and controlling attention during complex cognitive activities, with deficits in working memory linked to academic difficulties (Gathercole, Pickering, Knight, & Stegmann, 2004; Gathercole, Tiffany, Briscoe, Thorn, & ALSPAC team, 2005).

As well as showing deficits in inhibitory control and working memory, individuals with ADHD also show poorer performance on tasks measuring other executive functions, such as set-shifting and planning (Coghill, Seth, & Matthews, 2014; Hervey, Epstein, & Curry, 2004; Sjowall, Roth, Lindqvist, & Thorell, 2013). There are, however, limits to these neuropsychological findings. First, the magnitude of group differences in performance on these tasks is moderate (Willcutt, Doyle, Nigg, Faraone, & Pennington, 2005). Second, there is no common area of impaired functioning across all individuals with ADHD. For example, most studies show that only a small proportion of individuals with ADHD have a deficit in each domain of executive functioning. Third, deficits in one domain do not necessarily portend risk for poor performance on a second cognitive domain and many individuals with ADHD show no cognitive dysfunction at all (Coghill, Seth, et al., 2014).

These findings challenge the notion that executive dysfunction is the primary etiological pathway to ADHD. Alternate models suggest that "lower-order" deficits such as arousal, alerting, and basic motor control processes may be critical to the development and expression of ADHD. Halperin and Schulz (2006) propose that ADHD is the result of subcortical deficits, which arise early in development and remain fairly stable across the lifespan. Other researchers have proposed that individuals with ADHD show altered motivational states (Sagvolden, Aase, Zeiner, & Berger, 1998; Sonuga-Barke, 2003).

In support of these models, there is an abundance of research showing that children with ADHD show impaired performance in nonexecutive domains (Carte, Nigg, & Hinshaw, 1996; Coghill, Seth, et al., 2014; Johnson et al., 2001), which may account for some, or all, of individuals' poor performance on higher-order executive tasks (Marks et al., 2005; Rommelse et al., 2007). Several recent studies that have utilized diffusion modeling (Ratcliff & McKoon, 2008) suggest that individuals with ADHD exhibit less efficient information processing, reflected by slower *drift rate*, than their non-ADHD peers. After accounting for drift rate, executive functioning deficits are significantly attenuated or are no longer observed (Huang-Pollock, Karalunas, Tam, & Moore, 2012; Metin et al., 2013).

Researchers now consider that there are likely multiple, independent pathways to ADHD (Nigg, Willcutt, Doyle, & Sonuga-Barke, 2005; Sonuga-Barke, 2005). Castellanos and Tannock (2002) have proposed four candidate endophenotypes (i.e., shortened delayed gradient, temporal processing, working memory, and response inhibition), which may mediate the link between neurobiological risk and the downstream behavioral expression of the disorder. Nigg et al. (2005) have questioned whether there is value in considering neuropsychologically based subtypes of ADHD. Future work is needed to determine if these neuropsychological subtypes predict clinical outcomes. Finding such relationships would undoubtedly help to inform the design of novel interventions and to whom specific treatments are targeted.

DETERMINANTS OF ADHD TRAJECTORIES

Much recent work has examined the extent to which neural factors may predict trajectories of symptoms and impairment. Recently, Rajendran et al. (2013) showed that in a sample of preschoolers considered "at risk" for ADHD, those who made the greatest gains in neuropsychological function over time showed the greatest decline in ADHD severity and impairment. This suggests that interventions that affect growth of neuropsychological function may confer long-term benefits to young children with elevated inattention and hyperactivity/impulsivity. However, which neuropsychological functions should be targeted cannot be ascertained from Rajendran et al.'s study.

Halperin and Schulz (2006) hypothesized a specific role for the development of the prefrontal cortex (PFC) and the executive functions it mediates in driving the recovery from ADHD. However, whereas some studies have demonstrated specific protective effects of executive functions on symptom severity (Bedard, Trampush, Newcorn, & Halperin, 2010; Halperin et al., 2008) others have found no such association. For example, a review of 18 longitudinal studies showed that ADHD Persisters and Remitters could not be differentiated based on performance of higher-level or lower-level cognitive tasks, and both groups performed more poorly on all types of cognitive tasks than never-ADHD controls. Furthermore, cognitive functioning (irrespective of whether this was higher or lower level) predicted ADHD over time (van Lieshout, Luman, Buitelaar, Rommelse, & Oosterlaan, 2013). Most recently, Coghill, Hayward, Rhodes, Grimmer and Matthews (2014) administered tests with high and low executive demands to a small sample of boys with and without ADHD at age 10 and again at age 14 years. Of all of the domains assessed, only change in short-term memory performance over time was associated with change in clinical presentation.

Taken together, neurocognitive functioning appears to be a correlate of later ADHD severity. Whether interventions should be focused on higher-order executive functions or lower-order processes remains an empirical question. Findings do, however, align with those of Shaw and colleagues (Shaw, De Rossi, et al., 2014; Shaw et al., 2006, 2013; Shaw, Sudre, et al., 2014), whose elegant studies have revealed variability in cortical and subcortical development in individuals with ADHD, which maps onto trajectories of ADHD severity.

Shaw and colleagues recruited a sample of ADHD probands and typically developing controls and carried out repeated MRI scans over subsequent years. The median age at which children with ADHD had reached peak thickness in 50% of cortical points was 10.5 years compared to 7.5 years for controls, with lags most prominent in superior and dorsolateral prefrontal areas (Shaw et al., 2007). Across the follow-up period, there was no difference in the rate of change of cortical thickness between Persisters and Controls; however, Remitters showed normalization of cortical thickness in right parietal cortex (Shaw et al., 2006). During adulthood, greater inattention was associated with cortical thinning of medial cortical and dorsolateral prefrontal regions. Whereas the trajectory of cortical development for Persisters largely paralleled that of Controls, Remitters showed normalization of medial/cingulate cortical thickness from childhood through early adulthood (Shaw et al., 2013). Together, findings suggest that cortical thickness of key anatomical regions associated with the posterior attentional system, inhibitory control, and resistance to interference are associated with better clinical outcomes.

Shaw and colleagues (Shaw, De Rossi, et al., 2014; Shaw, Sudre, et al., 2014) also suggest that variability in development of basal ganglia and white matter integrity may also be implicated in determining outcome. For example, a gradual reduction in the volume of the ventral striatum in ADHD probands from age 4 through 19 years was reported, in marked contrast to the growth seen in their non-ADHD counterparts (Shaw, De Rossi, et al., 2014). In light of the role that ventral striatum plays in reward processing, these findings lend support to Sonuga-Barke (2003) and Castellanos and Tannock (2002), who have implicated deficits in reward processing in the onset of ADHD.

Greater structural integrity of white matter tracts (seemingly related to differences in myelination) involved in attentional control and reward processing were related to better clinical outcomes in adults diagnosed with ADHD in childhood (Shaw, Sudre, et al., 2014). Thus, interventions that affect white matter tract integrity may have some utility for treating ADHD. In contrast, Cortese, Imperati, et al. (2013) found that reduced integrity of white matter tracts involved in both higher-order and lower-order sensorimotor processing were seen in adults diagnosed with ADHD in childhood, irrespective of current ADHD severity. Given this variability in findings, more research is needed to determine which fiber tracts are implicated in the pathophysiology, and potentially recovery, from ADHD.

CURRENT EVIDENCE-BASED TREATMENTS FOR ADHD

Numerous reviews, meta-analyses, and practice parameters have identified treatments that provide benefits for individuals with ADHD (e.g., Daley et al., 2014; Holtmann, Sonuga-Barke, Cortese, & Brandeis, 2014; Sonuga-Barke, Brandeis, Holtmann, & Cortese, 2014). Pharmacological interventions, such as stimulant and nonstimulant medications, act by directly or indirectly increasing DA and NE neurotransmission (Reddy, 2013), whereas behavioral interventions include parent training and contingency management in the classroom (Pelham & Fabiano, 2008). Both stimulant and nonstimulant pharmacotherapy have been shown to significantly benefit functioning across multiple domains, including medication-related improvements in core symptoms, compliance, aggression, and academic productivity (e.g., Conners, 2002; Greenhill, Halperin, & Abikoff, 1999; Spencer et al., 1996). Similarly, behavioral parent training has been shown to reduce ADHD symptoms and oppositional behaviors in children, as well as improve parental functioning including reducing stress and increasing competence (e.g., Cunningham, Bremner, & Boyle, 1995; Sonuga-Barke, Daley, Thompson, Laver-Bradbury, & Weeks, 2001). School-based behavior contingency management has been shown to promote academic productivity and children's classroom-based functioning (e.g., Abramowitz, O'Leary, & Rosen, 1987; Hoffman & DuPaul, 2000).

Despite these benefits, limitations of current evidence-based interventions for ADHD necessitate development of novel treatment paradigms. Pharmacological interventions are easy to implement, but unpalatable to many parents (Charach, Yeung, Volpe, Goodale, & Dosreis, 2014). Moreover, a large proportion of individuals treated with stimulant medication report side effects and poor tolerability (Charach, Ickowicz, & Schachar, 2004). Recently, concerns have been voiced about the possible abuse potential of stimulant medications, as well as problematic interactive effects of stimulant medication with underlying cardiac conditions (Dalsgaard, Mortensen, Frydenberg, & Thomsen, 2014; Knight, 2007). Compared to pharmacological treatment, behavioral interventions may be less effective, more challenging to implement, and generally quite costly (MTA Cooperative Group, 1999). Furthermore, finding trained clinicians with the requisite skills to implement these behavioral interventions can be challenging.

There are several additional limitations that are common to both classes of intervention. First, the effects of pharmacological and behavioral interventions do not seem to persist past the point of active implementation/dosing (Martens, Peterson, Witt, & Cirone, 1986; Weiss, Gadow, & Wasdell, 2006). That is, symptoms of ADHD and everyday impairments can return when active treatment is discontinued. In addition, long-term adherence with these interventions is problematic (Sanchez, Crismon, Barner, Bettinger, & Wilson, 2005) and only a subgroup of those receiving behavioral or pharmacological interventions achieves a response that approximates normal functioning (Swanson et al., 2001).

In light of the above limitations, there has been an increasing interest in the development and use of interventions that are both biologically plausible and supported by basic cognitive neuroscience. For example, cognitive training approaches, such as working memory training, are being increasingly used to target both the symptoms and the underlying neuropsychological deficits in individuals with ADHD. However, a recent meta-analytic review of working memory training highlighted the inconsistency of findings among studies and across outcome measures (Sonuga-Barke et al., 2014). Alternative treatment approaches for inattention/hyperactivity such as neurofeedback and dietary-based interventions, including restricted elimination diets, artificial food color elimination, and supplementation with free fatty acids, have gained some promising empirical support from controlled studies (Holtmann et al., 2014; Stevenson et al., 2014). More research is required, however, before definitive conclusions can be reached. Physical exercise also offers potential as a new treatment approach for ADHD.

WHY MIGHT EXERCISE BENEFIT INDIVIDUALS WITH ADHD?

Cognition

Given the proposed role of neuropsychological dysfunction in the pathophysiology and recovery of ADHD (Bedard et al., 2010; Halperin & Schulz, 2006; Rajendran et al., 2013; Sonuga-Barke, 2003), exercise may lead to long-term improvement in symptoms via its beneficial impact on the development of neurocognitive functioning. In humans, acute and longer-term exercise appear to enhance effortful neurocognitive functions (e.g., inhibitory and interference control, working memory) as well as more basic cognitive processes (e.g., response speed) across all developmental levels (Barenberg, Berse, & Dutke, 2011; Bothe et al., 2013; Chang, Labban, Gapin, & Etnier, 2012; Lambourne, Audiffren, &

Tomporowski, 2010; Verburgh, Konigs, Scherder, & Oosterlaan, 2014). Moreover, exercise seems to disproportionately benefit those who experience greater deficits in these areas (Drollette et al., 2014; Sibley & Beilock, 2007).

Recent imaging studies in non-ADHD children have also associated exercise with macroscopic alterations in brain structure and function. For example, Chaddock and colleagues have shown that 9–10-year-old children with higher fitness levels have greater basal ganglia volume, particularly the dorsal striatum, and bilateral hippocampal volume. In turn, these structural differences were associated with better response inhibition and relational memory performance, respectively (Chaddock, Erickson, Prakash, Kim, et al., 2010; Chaddock, Erickson, Prakash, VanPatter, et al., 2010). Although causal interpretations cannot be made from these correlational studies, Schaeffer et al. (2014) showed that an 8-month exercise intervention for overweight 8–11-year-olds led to enhanced integrity of the uncinate fasiculus, connecting temporal and frontal cortices. Taken together, these studies support the positive impact of physical activity on the brain.

The beneficial impact of physical exercise on neurocognitive functioning is likely mediated by a number of different neurobiological mechanisms that underlie enhanced brain plasticity, including increased neurogenesis, synaptogenesis, myelination, angiogenesis; upregulation of glutamate receptors and neurotrophic factors, including brain-derived neurotrophic factor (BDNF), insulin-like growth factor 1 (IGF-1), and vascular endothelial growth factor (VEGF); and increased catecholaminergic neurotransmission (for reviews, see Lin & Kuo, 2013; Voss, Vivar, Kramer, & van Praag, 2013).

Modulation of Catecholaminergic Neurotransmission

The PFC plays a vital role in regulation of attention, behavior, motivation, and emotion, and its functioning is known to be disrupted in ADHD. The PFC is highly sensitive to alterations in levels of the catecholaminergic neuromodulators DA and NE, which are released in the PFC in accordance with arousal state (as reviewed by Arnsten & Pliszka, 2011). At optimal levels, DA decreases PFC neuronal activity in response to irrelevant stimuli. Conversely, suboptimal levels of both NE and DA have been associated with impaired cognitive functioning. In humans, lower activity of dopamine β-hydroxylase, the enzyme that synthesizes NE, is associated with poor sustained attention and executive functioning, and elevated levels of impulsivity. Excessive NE release is associated with impaired working memory. Thus, optimal levels of both NE and DA are both required for optimal PFC functioning (as reviewed by Arnsten & Pliszka, 2011).

Most medications used to treat ADHD (including stimulants, atomoxetine, and guanfacine) are believed to exert some of their therapeutic influence by increasing catecholamine transmission in the PFC, which in turn enhances PFC-regulated cognitive control (Arnsten & Pliszka, 2011; Reddy, 2013). It is possible that nonpharmacologic interventions acting via similar mechanisms would confer comparable therapeutic effects. Postexercise, enhanced release of NE and DA has been observed in animals centrally (Hattori, Naoi, & Nishino, 1994; Lin & Kuo, 2013; Meeusen & De Meirleir, 1995; Sutoo & Akiyama, 2003) and in humans peripherally (Kochanska-Dziurowicz et al., 2013; Skriver et al., 2014; Winter et al., 2007). In humans, this peripheral increase in DA and NE has been correlated with improved memory and learning (Skriver et al., 2014; Winter et al., 2007).

Neurogenesis/Angiogenesis via Neurotrophic Factors

Neurotrophic factors, such as BDNF, IGF-1, and VEGF, play a role in both neurogenesis and angiogenesis. A robust animal literature suggests that chronic aerobic exercise is positively associated with levels of these neurotrophic factors, which in turn are associated with improved cognitive functions (e.g., Li et al., 2013; Petzinger et al., 2007; Ratey & Loehr, 2011; Samorajski et al., 1985). These relations appear to be more pronounced at younger ages (Adlard, Perreau, & Cotman, 2005; Kim et al., 2004).

In humans, acute exercise-related changes in neurotrophic factors have been measured peripherally with findings generally mirroring those in animals (Hotting & Roder, 2013). There is greater inconsistency in the relationships among longer-term physical activity in humans, neurotrophin concentrations, and cognitive performance. This may be due to complex interactions among premorbid fitness and levels of various neurotrophic factors, as well as differences between central levels of a particular substrate and its peripheral biomarkers (Hotting & Roder, 2013). Nevertheless, several studies in young adults have shown links between exercise-related increases in peripheral neurotrophic factors and improvements in learning and memory (Griffin et al., 2011; Whiteman et al., 2014; Winter et al., 2007), visuospatial attention (Tsai et al., 2014), and motor memory (Skriver et al., 2014).

It may be, therefore, that the beneficial effects of exercise on cognition are mediated by neurobiological changes, including enhanced catecholaminergic neurotransmission and increased neurotrophin levels. If further evidence supports such a model, this offers a potential mechanism by which exercise may alter the neurodevelopmental trajectory of ADHD.

THE IMPACT OF EXERCISE ON ADHD

An Animal Model of ADHD: Spontaneously Hypertensive Rats

Exercise has been shown to have a positive effect on cognitive and physiological outcomes in the spontaneously hypertensive rat (SHR) model of ADHD. The SHR is the most frequently used animal model of ADHD because these rats are inattentive, overactive, and impulsive, and exhibit cognitive impairments in sustained attention and working memory similar to that of ADHD children (Sagvolden, 2000). In addition, SHRs have some of the same neurobiological abnormalities thought to underlie ADHD, including catecholamine dysfunction (Russell, 2002).

The physiological and cognitive impacts of exercise in SHRs appear to be widely distributed throughout the brain. For example, chronic treadmill exercise blunted the developmental rise of blood pressure while increasing glutamic acid decarboxylase mRNA in the caudal hypothalamus (Little, Kramer, Beatty, & Waldrop, 2001). It also reduced hyperactivity while increasing DA synthesis and BDNF expression, similar to treatment with methylphenidate, a common stimulant medication used to treat ADHD (Hattori et al., 1994; Kim et al., 2011). Treadmill exercise reduced hyperactivity and increased tyrosine hydroxylase activity in the striatum and substantia nigra. Additionally, treadmill exercise reduced Purkinje cell loss and astrocytic reaction in the cerebellum, which is critical for motor learning and coordination, balance, and control (Yun et al., 2014). Swimming exercise decreased ADHD-like behaviors as well as improved short-term memory by upregulating the expression of DA and downregulating the expression of the DA D2 receptor (Ko et al., 2013). Finally, treadmill exercise-related improvements in ADHD-like orienting and hypersocial behavior were similar to improvements seen in SHRs treated with either methylphenidate or atomoxetine, an NE reuptake inhibitor (Robinson, Eggleston, & Bucci, 2012).

Finally, there is preliminary evidence for heterogeneity in response to exercise in SHRs. For instance, Ji, Kim, Park, and Bahn (2014) showed duration-dependent effects of treadmill exercise. Specifically, 30 min of daily exercise over 28 days reduced hyperactivity and increased tyrosine hydroxylase activity in striatum and substantia nigra, whereas no effect was seen in those exercising for 10 min daily. Gender- and age-dependent effects are also suggested in that running wheel access significantly reduced hyperorienting behavior in both male and female adolescent SHRs (Robinson, Hopkins, & Bucci, 2011), whereas others have found that only female rats show such improvement in behavior (Hopkins, Sharma, Evans, & Bucci, 2009).

The Impact of Exercise on Individuals with ADHD

Since approximately 1980, around a dozen studies have been published that examine the effect of exercise on cognition and symptoms in individuals (mainly children) with ADHD. Below, we review the literature investigating the acute impact of physical exercise on individuals with ADHD, as well as the few studies that have employed more chronic interventions. All studies are in school-aged children unless otherwise noted.

Acute Effects of Physical Exercise

Studies employing acute aerobic, physical exercise have typically focused on its effects on cognitive functions, most notably executive functions, probably because acute changes in behavior are difficult to measure. One study has also looked at whether exercise benefits academic functioning, and two studies have investigated changes in DA following acute bouts of physical exercise.

Executive Functions

Four experimental trials have found modest benefits of acute bouts of moderate-to-vigorous aerobic physical exercise on executive functioning measures. Using a mixed-factorial design, Chang, Liu, Yu, and Lee (2012) investigated the impact of 30 min of moderate-intensity treadmill running on medicated and unmedicated children with ADHD, relative to controls with ADHD who did not run. Runners showed greater pre- to post-improvements in interference control on the Color-Word condition of

the Stroop task and on some components of a set-shifting task (i.e., the Wisconsin Card Sort Task categories completed and nonperseverative errors), with no differential improvement on perseverative responses and total errors.

Also using a mixed-factorial design, Pontifex, Saliba, Raine, Picchietti, and Hillman (2013) showed significantly better accuracy on a flanker task in unmedicated children with ADHD after 20 min of moderate-intensity treadmill walking compared to performance on a reading control condition. Findings suggest some benefit of acute physical exercise on inhibitory control. In addition, they found increased EEG-measured P3 amplitude and decreased latency (suggestive of greater allocation of attentional resources and faster processing speed, respectively) during the incongruent trials of the flanker task. Post-error slowing was enhanced during flanker task performance after exercise such that, when compared to typically developing controls, the responses of children with ADHD appeared to normalize.

In a within-subjects design, Medina et al. (2010) found a significant reduction in anticipatory responses (reaction times (RTs) < 100 ms) during a go/no go task (i.e., the Conners' Continuous Performance Test II (CPT-II)) after 30 min of high-intensity interval running on a treadmill, relative to a 1-min stretching control session, in a sample of both medicated and unmedicated preadolescent and adolescent boys. While these anticipatory responses are typically considered indications of impulsive responding on the CPT-II, they can also be attributed to recovery from lapses in sustained attention (i.e., abnormally slow responses to a previous trial). Improvement in rate of commission errors, which is typically regarded as a measure of inhibitory control, however, was not found.

Nonexecutive Functions

Two studies have found an acute impact of moderate-to-vigorous intensity aerobic exercise on nonexecutive cognitive functions in children with ADHD. The study by Medina et al. (2010) showed significant postexercise improvement in response speed (i.e., Hit RT) and RT variability on the CPT-II. Employing a within-subjects design, Tantillo, Kesick, Hynd, and Dishman (2002) found improvement in motor persistence (i.e., the ability to sustain simple motor behaviors, such as tongue protrusion, keeping eyelids closed) in a sample of medicated children with ADHD after a graded exercise test to peak exertion (5–25 min in duration). Similar gains were not seen after either moderate-intensity aerobic exercise of the same duration or a rest condition. Of note, this positive effect of maximal exertion was only observed in boys.

Academic Functioning

The study by Pontifex et al. (2013) evaluated academic achievement using the Wide Range Achievement Test-3. Gains in reading comprehension and arithmetic performance were observed in children with ADHD and typically developing controls after 20 min of moderate-intensity physical activity relative to a reading control condition.

Dopamine Assays

Given the proposed role of catecholaminergic functioning in ADHD pathophysiology, two investigations have examined the acute impact of aerobic activity on measures thought to reflect dopaminergic functioning. Tantillo et al. (2002) found changes in several DA probes (i.e., rates of spontaneous eye blinks; acoustic startle eye blink response (ASER) amplitude and latency) after either maximal or submaximal exercise. There were differences across sex in terms of the specific effects, but in general greater effects (i.e., increased ASER amplitude, decreased latency) were seen in girls after submaximal exercise relative to maximal exercise. The pattern was reversed for boys, who exhibited decreased ASER latency and faster spontaneous blink rate. Despite these sex differences, however, the authors concluded that exercise

may enhance DA response to environmental stimuli.

On the other hand, Wigal et al. (2003) concluded that it was not clear whether the lack of a DA response in the periphery in ADHD is related to a systemic "DA deficit" or, alternatively, simply to less stimulation of the adrenals in response to exercise. The authors assayed the peripheral response of catecholaminergic biomarkers (i.e., radiolabeled metabolites of epinephrine, NE, DA, and plasma lactate in blood) following 30 min of moderate-intensity aerobic interval training interspersed with rest in a small sample of medication-naïve preadolescent children with and without ADHD. At baseline, only NE was significantly lower in the ADHD group. While exercise resulted in increases in all metabolites in controls, increases in all metabolites *except* DA were seen in children with ADHD. Although quite different from Tantillo et al. (2002), differences in methods of assessment, medication status, and sample size render the results across studies difficult to integrate.

Taken together, preliminary evidence suggests that exercise acutely enhances some neurocognitive and academic functions in individuals with ADHD. In addition, there is some suggestion of exercise-related acute alterations in catecholaminergic functioning, although these have not been linked to changes in neurocognitive functioning. Despite being limited in quality and quantity, findings are generally consistent with the extant literature in typically developing populations.

Of note, the amount of time spent exercising may be an important variable in determining whether effects of physical exercise will be seen acutely. Using a parametric within-subjects design, Craft (1983) found no pre- to post-exercise changes on tasks measuring verbal or nonverbal short-term information maintenance, working memory, or processing speed after brief (i.e., 1-, 5-, and 10-min) bouts of vigorous-intensity cycling sessions compared to rest in either hyperactive children or nonhyperactive controls. Although null results are always difficult to interpret, they are consistent with findings from SHR studies (e.g., Ji et al., 2014) and Lambourne and Tomporowski's (2010) meta-analysis in typically developing individuals indicating that a minimum duration of approximately 20 min of aerobic physical exercise is necessary to see acute effects.

Chronic Physical Activity: Correlational Studies

Several correlational studies provide evidence that ongoing physical exercise may benefit cognitive and psychological functioning in individuals with ADHD. One study (Gapin & Etnier, 2010) indicated that for 8–12-year-old medicated boys with ADHD, time spent in moderate-to-vigorous physical exercise was positively related to performance on a measure of planning, but not on other executive (i.e., working memory and set-shifting) or nonexecutive functions (i.e., immediate span of attention and processing speed).

Others have examined the relationship between physical exercise and either ADHD behavioral symptoms or comorbid anxiety/depression symptoms. In a large community-based sample of kindergarten children, Bernard-Brak, Davis, Sulak, and Brak (2011) found that physical education within the school curriculum was related to decreased levels of ADHD symptoms during first grade. Furthermore, inverse correlations between physical exercise levels and anxiety and depression symptoms were seen in children (Kiluk, Weden, & Culotta, 2009) and adults (Abramovitch, Goldzweig, & Schweiger, 2013). Abramovitch et al. (2013) also found a negative relationship between physical exercise and self-rated levels of impulsivity in adults. Despite the limitations inherent in correlational studies, these findings provide an impetus for experimental trials examining the impact of physical exercise on ADHD-related psychopathology as well as on neurocognitive functioning.

Chronic Physical Activity: Experimental Studies

Most studies examining longer-term interventions (Chang, Hung, Huang, Hatfield, & Hung, 2014; Hoza et al., 2014; Pan et al., 2014; Smith et al., 2013; Verret, Guay, Berthiaume, Gardiner, & Beliveau, 2012) have been multifaceted, including coordinated motor activity training (coordinative exercise), aerobic activity, and strength and/or muscular endurance training. Below we describe key findings related to the impact of these interventions on the cognitive functioning, motor skills, and severity of inattention and hyperactivity/impulsivity of children with ADHD.

Cognitive Functioning

Three studies examined changes in measures of inhibitory control after chronic exercise programs. Smith et al. (2013) employed an 8-week before-school moderate-to-vigorous intensity physical exercise program consisting of 5 weekly 26-min sessions in 14, 5–8-year-old medication-naïve children identified as symptomatic for ADHD. They found pre- to post-intervention improvement on some measures of inhibitory control (i.e., Shape School Condition B; Red Light-Green Light proportion of inhibition failures) but not on others (i.e., Shape School Conditions C and D, Simon Says proportion of inhibition failures).

Chang, Hung, et al. (2014) employed a 9-week after-school aerobic/coordinative aquatic exercise program (90 min, twice weekly) for 5–10-year-old children with a DSM-IV diagnosis of ADHD. Outcomes were compared to a wait-list control group. Of note, half of the children in each group were medicated. They also found fairly large pre- to post-improvements in correct inhibitions on a go/no go task (Cohen's $d = 0.9$) following exercise compared to controls (Cohen's $d = -0.04$).

Finally, Verret et al. (2012) failed to find significant improvements on a measure of inhibitory control (Walk Don't Walk subtest of Test of Everyday Attention (Tea-Ch)) in a sample of 9, 7–12-year-old children with ADHD relative to 9 nonexercising children with ADHD after a 10-week program consisting of 3 weekly 45-min sessions of combined aerobic, muscular, and motor skills training. Thus, there is mixed evidence suggesting that longer-term interventions combining aerobic and coordinative exercise may exert some impact on measures of inhibitory control.

Two studies examined the impact of chronic physical exercise on measures of sustained attention. The study by Verret et al. (2012) found significant post-program improvements on a measure of auditory sustained attention (Tea-Ch Score Pondered). Another study examined the impact of twice weekly moderate-intensity aerobic and coordinative exercise in addition to methylphenidate treatment over the course of 6 weeks in pre-adolescent boys with ADHD (Kang, Choi, Kang, & Han, 2011). They found greater pre-/post-improvement on the Digit–Symbol Test and time to complete Trails B (without the contrast from Trails A) in the medicine plus chronic physical exercise group compared to a medicine plus education control group. While these two neuropsychological measures are classically interpreted as reflecting processing speed and set-shifting, respectively, without appropriate control conditions to determine some degree of process specificity the contribution of possible improvements in sustained attention cannot be ruled out.

Two of these studies included measures of divided attention (Sky Search DT subtest of Test of Everyday Attention (Verret et al., 2012)) and working memory (Finger Windows task or Woodcock-Johnson-III Numbers Reversed task (Smith et al., 2013)). No significant effect of exercise was found on these executive measures. Finally, only the study by Smith et al. (2013) examined the impact of long-term physical exercise on the nonexecutive construct of visual selective attention (Sky Search subtest of the Test of Everyday Attention), but found no significant effect.

Motor Skills

Four studies have examined the impact of longer-term physical exercise interventions on motor skills including gross motor coordination and manual dexterity. Ahmed and Mohamed (2011) randomly assigned 48, 11–16-year-old children with ADHD to either a 10-week aerobic exercise program, which consisted of 3–4 weekly sessions of 30–50 min, or a no intervention control group. They found significant improvement in teacher-reported motor skills (translated into ratings on a modified version of Conners' Behavior Rating Scale by an interviewer) for the exercise group, but not for the controls. Using more objective measures, the studies by Smith et al. (2013) and Verret et al. (2012) found exercise-related improvements in motor skills. Smith et al. (2013) found improvement of a large effect size (Cohen's $d = 0.96$) on the abbreviated version of the Bruininks–Oseretsky Test of Motor Proficiency (BOT-2 Short Form). Verret et al. (2012) found significant improvements in two of three measures (Locomotor and Total Motor Skills) on the Test of Gross-Motor Development-2. Chang, Hung, et al. (2014) also reported improvements in hand–eye coordination (target throwing subtest of Basic Motor Ability Test (BMAT)) and bilateral hand–eye coordination and dexterity (Bead Moving subtest of the BMAT).

Finally, using an intriguing intervention, Pan et al. (2014) administered 12 weekly 90-min sessions of a comprehensive aerobic and muscular endurance, strength, and coordination training program to a group of 12, 7–15-year-old boys with ADHD. Each session included 45 min on an oscillating horse-back-riding simulator during which children participated in complex coordinative activity (e.g., catching and throwing balls to one another, performing various upper body movements with and without equipment), as well as a social interaction component (playing competitive team games). They compared these boys to a group of 12 non-exercising children with ADHD matched on age, IQ, and ADHD subtype, as well as 24 typically developing nonexercising children on the BOT-2 and various measures of physical fitness. While the intervention did not completely normalize motor functioning in boys with ADHD, who were initially quite impaired relative to non-training, non-ADHD children, large post-training improvements were seen in the Total Motor Composite of the BOT-2 (Cohen's $d = 2.51$) in the context of significant improvement on several measures of fitness of medium-to-large size.

Behavior

Parent, teacher, and self-reports of behavior and functional impairment are standard in assessing severity of psychopathology and behavioral impact of interventions. However, informants' symptom severity ratings may be biased by expected effects of treatment (Kirsch, 1985). Accurate assessment of intervention-related changes on behavior requires raters to be blind to treatment status. In fact, a recent meta-analysis of nonpharmacological treatments for ADHD indicated that treatment-related effect sizes vary systematically as a function of proximity to the patient; those informants least likely to be blind to treatment status typically report greater effects (Sonuga-Barke et al., 2013). Blinding of informants to treatment condition is relatively straightforward in medication studies, where a placebo condition is typically used to keep raters blind (at least initially). However, this requirement presents logistic issues when assessing the efficacy of behavioral interventions. Unfortunately, in studies of nonpharmacological interventions in children, it is extremely difficult to maintain blind status of raters, and investigators are often left with the inferior option of blinding raters to study hypotheses rather than to treatment condition.

A number of trials have assessed the impact of longer-term physical exercise interventions in children with ADHD, but no blind ratings of behavior were obtained in any of these studies. Furthermore, while some studies have employed random assignment to exercise and control conditions, others have used simple repeated-measures (pre-/post-change) designs without adequate between-subjects (nonexercising and/or typically developing) controls, and the vast majority of studies have used small samples. Thus, with few exceptions, the majority of these studies should be viewed as pilot investigations and interpreted with due caution.

Several pilot studies (Ahmed & Mohamed, 2011; Kang et al., 2011; Lufi & Parish-Plass, 2011; McKune, Pautz, & Lombard, 2003; Smith et al., 2013) and one randomized controlled trial (RCT) (Hoza et al., 2014) have assessed the impact of chronic physical exercise interventions on parent-, teacher-, and self-rated symptoms of ADHD, as well as comorbid conditions. Children in these studies ranged in age from 5 to 16 years and were either diagnosed with ADHD or exhibited levels of symptoms high enough to be "at risk" for ADHD. Using various commonly used symptom checklists, two studies found significant improvement in inattentive symptoms (Ahmed & Mohamed, 2011; Kang et al., 2011), while three studies found overall improvement in severity of ADHD symptoms spanning both hyperactive/impulsive and inattentive symptom domains (Hoza et al., 2014; Lufi & Parish-Plass, 2011; Smith et al., 2013). Hoza et al. (2014) found improvements in parent- (but not teacher-) rated inattention after the exercise intervention that were significantly greater than those observed in a sedentary control condition, which included aspects of empirically supported behavioral treatments for ADHD (i.e., behavior modification).

Three studies found exercise-related improvements in disruptive/externalizing behaviors and/or aggression (Hoza et al., 2014; Lufi & Parish-Plass, 2011; Smith et al., 2013). Two studies found improvements in symptoms indicative of anxiety and depression (Hoza et al., 2014; Lufi & Parish-Plass, 2011), while another did not (Ahmed & Mohamed, 2011).

Finally, three studies found improvements in social skills and peer relations after exercising (Hoza et al., 2014; Kang et al., 2011; Lufi & Parish-Plass, 2011). Of note, one study (McKune et al., 2003) failed to find exercise-induced improvements in parent ratings of attention, emotion, motor skills, task orientation, and oppositional behavior in children taking medication for ADHD.

Taken together, these studies provide preliminary evidence that for children with ADHD, physical activity, in the form of aerobic plus coordinative exercise, has a positive impact on several executive domains and on motor functioning. Children who engage in exercise are rated as showing improvement in core ADHD symptoms and in social functioning. There is mixed support for physical activity reducing the severity of comorbid behavioral and emotional dysregulation.

WHERE TO FROM HERE?

Multiple reviews have been published on the utility of exercise as a treatment for ADHD, indicating a keen interest among the research community in this area (e.g., Berwid & Halperin, 2012; Gapin, Labban, & Etnier, 2011; Halperin, Berwid, & O'Neill, 2014). This interest is warranted, as preliminary findings are certainly encouraging. However, the extant literature is limited by several factors including widely varying methodologies; very small sample sizes; absence of adequate control conditions; and a lack of studies using randomized assignment of individuals to experimental groups. Thus, very few published investigations to date can be characterized as RCTs—the Hoza et al. (2014) study being an exception. The following sections outline critical issues for the research community to address so we can improve our understanding of, and our confidence in findings related to, the impact of exercise on the cognition and behavior of children and adults with ADHD.

Exercise is for Everybody

The question of who will obtain greatest benefit from an exercise intervention remains. Individual differences are observed in response to medication (e.g., Polanczyk et al., 2008) and nonpharmacological interventions for ADHD (e.g., Rucklidge, Johnstone, Gorman, Boggis, & Frampton, 2014). Thus, it is reasonable to expect that in an ADHD population some individuals will respond better to physical exercise than others. Both Sibley and Beilock (2007) and Drollette et al. (2014) showed that in healthy adults and children, moderate-intensity aerobic exercise was most beneficial for those individuals with poorer executive skills. In light of the heterogeneity in neuropsychological functioning of individuals with ADHD, it is quite possible that similar moderating effects of cognitive functioning will be seen in individuals with ADHD who engage in exercise.

Nevertheless, we propose that all individuals with ADHD should be encouraged to exercise. We cannot yet pinpoint exactly which children will show remitting versus persisting trajectories of ADHD. It does seem, however, that degree of positive change in neuropsychological functioning over time predicts severity of symptoms (Coghill, Hayward, et al. 2014; Rajendran et al., 2013). Given that physical activity has a highly favorable risk:benefit ratio, it seems reasonable to promote the idea that exercise may be beneficial and is unlikely to do harm (see Halperin et al., 2014 for instances where extra care is likely warranted).

Encouraging everyone to engage in physical activity also seems appropriate in light of the potential for exercise to protect against internalizing problems (Strohle, 2009) and to directly promote physical health. This is particularly relevant to children with ADHD, as they appear to be at increased risk of later overweight/obesity relative to non-ADHD peers (Cortese & Angriman, 2008; Khalife et al., 2014). This phenomenon is even observed in adults whose childhood ADHD symptoms have remitted (Cortese, Ramos Olazagasti, et al., 2013). Although the underlying mechanism driving the relation between ADHD and overweight/obesity is not yet known, it has been speculated that inattention, executive dysfunction, and/or altered reward signaling play a role (Cortese et al., 2008). Changing children's lifestyles at an early age, when the behaviors are more likely to become lifetime habits, is of critical importance (Telama et al., 2005).

"Ain't What You Do (It's the Way that You Do It)"

Coordination and Resistance Training

Physical activity recommendations provided by the Centers for Disease Control state that children and adolescents should get at least 60 min of exercise per day (Centers for Disease Control and Prevention, 2011). Over the course of a week, adults should engage in moderate–vigorous physical activity for at least 150 min and muscle strengthening activities on at least 2 days (Centers for Disease Control and Prevention, 2014). Critically, it does not matter if this activity is carried out in a single session or in shorter bursts (e.g., 3 × 10-min sessions). Children and adults are also encouraged to vary the type of exercise they do. Thus, individuals are afforded a lot of flexibility in how and when they work out. At present, the issue of whether type or duration of physical exercise moderates its impact on cognition is less well known; this is particularly true for ADHD populations.

Studies employing longer-term interventions for ADHD populations have tended to utilize multimodal treatment programs. Given that these programs comprise variations of cardiovascular *and* coordination training, resistance training, and social–motivational components, identifying which specific aspect of training is most beneficial is difficult. In older human populations, both resistance and coordination training have been associated with improved performance on executive functioning tasks (Fallah et al., 2013; Forte et al., 2013). Similarly, selectively greater gains in interference control relative to gains in more basic skills (such as word reading) have been seen in older populations after just one session of resistance training (Chang, Tsai, Huang, Wang, & Chu, 2014). It is also possible that the impact of a specific type of exercise on cognition is moderated by age, as Pontifex, Hillman, Fernhall, Thompson, and Valentini (2009) found that an acute aerobic exercise session was superior to an acute resistance exercise session on young adults' working memory capacity. Alternatively, this relationship may be even more complex, with interactions observed among age, type of exercise, and duration of exercise intervention. Whether coordination training (e.g., balance, agility) or resistance training offer unique benefits for individuals with ADHD over and above aerobic exercise is unclear and needs to be addressed empirically.

Exercise as Part of a Multicomponent Intervention

One major question for the field to address is whether physical activity can boost the effectiveness of interventions in which an individual is already engaged. That is, does exercise offer "added value" to pharmacotherapy, cognitive remediation, or behavior management? At present, there is very limited research evaluating this question.

Preliminary work suggests physical activity *may* bolster the effects of medication. Recall that Kang et al. (2011) found that compared to children in an education control group, children in sports therapy seemed to show improvements in executive functioning, teacher ratings of cooperativeness, and parent ratings of attention over and above methylphenidate. Replication is clearly needed, however, to verify this pattern of findings.

Two recent pilot studies have examined the effectiveness of noncomputerized cognitive training for very young children with ADHD (Halperin et al., 2013; Healey & Halperin, 2014). Both included physical activity in a larger treatment regimen focused primarily on using games to target and strengthen neuropsychological function and self-regulation. Consequently, it is impossible to determine the specific contribution of physical activity to children's outcomes in these studies. To our knowledge, no study has systematically investigated the impact of cognitive remediation with and without exercise in individuals with ADHD. Based on studies of typically developing children and adolescents, Best (2010) suggested that the benefits of exercise on executive functions might be moderated by the cognitive and movement demands of the activity. That is, exercises that require greater coordination and/or strategy should be more effective for improving cognition compared to simpler, repetitive motor activity.

Peer Modeling, Reward, and Motivation

Many individuals fail to meet the recommended daily "dose" of physical activity (Carson, Staiano, & Katzmarzyk, 2014; Johnson, Hayes, Brown, Hoo, & Ethier, 2014). For individuals with ADHD, it is possible that reward-signaling deficits contribute to this phenomenon such that the more immediate reward is chosen (e.g., continued television watching or video game playing) over a more delayed reward that is consequent to physical exercise (e.g., fitness and health gains). Although speculative, adding rewards to an exercise intervention may improve adherence among individuals with ADHD—at least at the beginning of a program until exercising becomes intrinsically rewarding. Finally, designing interventions around social media platforms may be a way to target more individuals, and offer a novel, palatable technique to change physical activity behavior (Wojcicki, Grigsby-Toussaint, Hillman, Huhman, & McAuley, 2014). These are all avenues for future research in ADHD populations specifically.

Begin Exercising when Young and Don't Stop

"Sooner rather than later" is most likely the best time to begin regular physical activity. The English National Health Service advises that all ambulatory preschoolers engage in at least 180 min of unstructured (e.g., skipping) or more highly structured (e.g., riding a bicycle) physical activity per day (National Health Service, 2013). Furthermore, sedentary activity should be limited. Similarly, the US Department of Health and Human Services advises early childcare providers to provide toddlers and preschoolers with 60–90 min of outdoor or indoor play that promotes moderate-to-vigorous physical activity (National Resource Center for Health and Safety in Child Care and Early Education, n.d.).

The primary impetus for these recommendations is the importance of exercise for physical health and the development of motor skills. However, researchers have stressed that early intervention may also be critical for changing the trajectory of ADHD, in part because any neural changes may be multiplicative (Halperin et al., 2012; Sonuga-Barke & Halperin, 2010). The concept of *multifinality*—individuals with similar risk factors may have manifestly different outcomes—seems particularly relevant given that such heterogeneity in clinical course of symptoms and impairment is observed in children with ADHD. Opportunities to promote resilience are crucial and youngsters who exercise may be considered to be developing in an enriched environment, which is a potent stimulus for brain development. Few studies have been carried out with preschoolers (with or without ADHD); one study by Palmer, Miller, and Robinson (2013) showed that a half-hour of exercise led to improved sustained attention in typically developing preschoolers. To our knowledge, no one has followed preschoolers over time.

One of the greatest challenges facing almost anybody who has tried to increase the amount of exercise they get in a given week is how to maintain behavior change over the long term. We do not believe that a 12-week intervention will lead to sustained changes in behavior or cognition. Rather, we consider that regular exercise must become part of an everyday routine, along with school, work, and other commitments facing families. It has been proposed that gains in executive functions achieved following an exercise intervention actually drive (or at least increase the probability of) the continuation of regular physical activity during a 12-month follow-up period in older women (Best, Nagamatsu, & Liu-Ambrose, 2014; as reviewed by Buckley, Cohen, Kramer, McAuley, & Mullen, 2014). Whether similar findings hold for younger typically developing individuals or for ADHD populations remains to be seen. However, the cascading impact of exercise benefiting cognition, which in turn promotes long-term behavior change, is another example of how the gains of an exercise intervention may be multiplicative.

SUMMARY AND CONCLUSIONS

ADHD is one of the most prevalent disorders of childhood, which for many will continue through to adulthood. Current evidence-based interventions for ADHD appear to attenuate symptoms and some areas of impaired functioning in the short term, but do not substantively alter long-term outcome. Given the high disease burden of ADHD, novel yet efficacious interventions are urgently needed.

Theoretically, physical activity seems to offer a viable approach to treating ADHD, given its effects on a host of neural factors that are also implicated in the pathophysiology of the disorder. Pilot studies in ADHD populations suggest that acutely, aerobic physical activity promotes gains in executive functions (most consistently inhibitory control), processing speed, motor persistence, and academic achievement. Whether single bouts of moderate–vigorous aerobic exercise

also enhance catecholaminergic function is still unclear, although this suggestion has been made. Similarly, multimodal chronic physical activity interventions seem to benefit some areas of executive (inhibitory control, sustained attention, set-shifting) and nonexecutive (processing speed, motor skills) functioning. Children's behavior also seems to improve, although the lack of blinding of raters is a significant problem in interpreting these results. Taken together, however, there is a growing body of literature arguing that physical activity is of benefit to individuals with ADHD. RCTs, such as that recently carried out by Hoza et al. (2014), are essential for overcoming limitations of these studies. Additionally, future work is needed to determine the contexts in which these findings are observed. Type of exercise, duration of exercise, age of participants, and gender may all influence results. Exercise may also confer benefits independent of other treatment approaches. This knowledge is critical for clinicians who are responsible for treatment planning.

Finally, ADHD researchers need to follow the lead of colleagues who work with typically developing populations and begin to integrate behavioral, neuropsychological, and neuroscience methods to study the impact of exercise on cognition. Within the context of RCTs, if we can show that physical exercise impacts brain structure and function, and then relate those changes to reductions in severity of inattention, hyperactivity/impulsivity, and associated impairment, we can make a strong case that physical activity is an efficacious approach for treating ADHD.

References

Abramovitch, A., Goldzweig, G., & Schweiger, A. (2013). Correlates of physical activity with intrusive thoughts, worry and impulsivity in adults with attention deficit/hyperactivity disorder: a cross-sectional pilot study. *Israel Journal of Psychiatry and Related Sciences, 50*, 47–54.

Abramowitz, A. J., O'Leary, S. G., & Rosen, L. A. (1987). Reducing off-task behavior in the classroom: a comparison of encouragement and reprimands. *Journal of Abnormal Child Psychology, 15*, 153–163.

Adlard, P. A., Perreau, V. M., & Cotman, C. W. (2005). The exercise-induced expression of BDNF within the hippocampus varies across life-span. *Neurobiology of Aging, 26*, 511–520.

Ahmed, G. M., & Mohamed, S. (2011). Effect of regular aerobic exercises on behavioral, cognitive and psychological response in patients with attention deficit-hyperactivity disorder. *Life Science Journal, 8*, 366–371.

Amico, F., Stauber, J., Koutsouleris, N., & Frodl, T. (2011). Anterior cingulate cortex gray matter abnormalities in adults with attention deficit hyperactivity disorder: a voxel-based morphometry study. *Psychiatry Research, 191*, 31–35.

APA. (2013). *Diagnostic and statistical manual of mental disorders* (5th ed.). Arlington, VA: American Psychiatric Publishing.

Arnsten, A. F., & Pliszka, S. R. (2011). Catecholamine influences on prefrontal cortical function: relevance to treatment of attention deficit/hyperactivity disorder and related disorders. *Pharmacology, Biochemistry and Behavior, 99*, 211–216.

Barenberg, J., Berse, T., & Dutke, S. (2011). Executive functions in learning processes: do they benefit from physical activity? *Educational Research Review, 6*, 208–222.

Barkley, R. A. (1997). Behavioral inhibition, sustained attention, and executive functions: constructing a unifying theory of ADHD. *Psychological Bulletin, 121*, 65–94.

Bedard, A. C., Trampush, J. W., Newcorn, J. H., & Halperin, J. M. (2010). Perceptual and motor inhibition in adolescents/young adults with childhood-diagnosed ADHD. *Neuropsychology, 24*, 424–434.

Bernard-Brak, L., Davis, T., Sulak, T., & Brak, V. (2011). The association between physical education and symptoms of attention deficit hyperactivity disorder. *Journal of Physical Activity and Health, 8*, 964–970.

Berwid, O. G., & Halperin, J. M. (2012). Emerging support for a role of exercise in attention-deficit/hyperactivity disorder intervention planning. *Current Psychiatry Reports, 14*, 543–551.

Best, J. R. (2010). Effects of physical activity on Children's executive function: contributions of experimental research on aerobic exercise. *Developmental Review, 30*, 331–551.

Best, J. R., Nagamatsu, L. S., & Liu-Ambrose, T. (2014). Improvements to executive function during exercise training predict maintenance of physical activity over the following year. *Frontiers in Human Neuroscience, 8*, 353. http://dx.doi.org/10.3389/fnhum.2014.00353.

Bothe, N., Zschucke, E., Dimeo, F., Heinz, A., Wustenberg, T., & Strohle, A. (2013). Acute exercise influences reward processing in highly trained and untrained men. *Medicine and Science in Sports and Exercise, 45*, 583–591.

Bouchard, M. F., Bellinger, D. C., Wright, R. O., & Weisskopf, M. G. (2010). Attention-deficit/hyperactivity disorder and urinary metabolites of organophosphate pesticides. *Pediatrics, 125*, e1270–e1277. http://dx.doi.org/10.1542/peds.2009-3058.

Buckley, J., Cohen, J. D., Kramer, A. F., McAuley, E., & Mullen, S. P. (2014). Cognitive control in the self-regulation of physical activity and sedentary behavior. *Frontiers in Human Neuroscience, 8*, 747. http://dx.doi.org/10.3389/fnhum.2014.00747.

Buss, C., Entringer, S., Davis, E. P., Hobel, C. J., Swanson, J. M., Wadhwa, P. D., et al. (2012). Impaired executive function mediates the association between maternal pre-pregnancy body mass index and child ADHD symptoms. *PLoS One, 7*, e37758. http://dx.doi.org/10.1371/journal.pone.0037758.

Carson, V., Staiano, A., & Katzmarzyk, P. (2014). Physical activity, screen time, and sitting among US adolescents. *Pediatric Exercise Science*. http://dx.doi.org/10.1123/pes.2014-0022.

Carte, E. T., Nigg, J. T., & Hinshaw, S. P. (1996). Neuropsychological functioning, motor speed, and language processing in boys with and without ADHD. *Journal of Abnormal Child Psychology, 24*, 481–498.

Castellanos, F. X., Lee, P. P., Sharp, W., Jeffries, N. O., Greenstein, D. K., Clasen, L. S., et al. (2002). Developmental trajectories of brain volume abnormalities in children and adolescents with attention-deficit/hyperactivity disorder. *JAMA, 288*, 1740–1748.

Castellanos, F. X., & Tannock, R. (2002). Neuroscience of attention-deficit/hyperactivity disorder: the search for endophenotypes. *Nature Reviews Neuroscience, 3*, 617–628.

Centers for Disease Control and Prevention. (2011). *How much physical activity do children need?* Retrieved November 17, 2014, from http://www.cdc.gov/physicalactivity/everyone/guidelines/children.html.

Centers for Disease Control and Prevention. (2014). *How much physical activity do adults need?* Retrieved November 17, 2014, from http://www.cdc.gov/physicalactivity/everyone/guidelines/adults.html.

Chaddock, L., Erickson, K. I., Prakash, R. S., Kim, J. S., Voss, M. W., VanPatter, M., et al. (2010). A neuroimaging investigation of the association between aerobic fitness, hippocampal volume, and memory performance in preadolescent children. *Brain Research, 1358*, 172–183.

Chaddock, L., Erickson, K. I., Prakash, R. S., VanPatter, M., Voss, M. W., Pontifex, M. B., et al. (2010). Basal ganglia volume is associated with aerobic fitness in preadolescent children. *Developmental Neuroscience, 32*, 249–256.

Chang, Y. K., Hung, C. L., Huang, C. J., Hatfield, B. D., & Hung, T. M. (2014a). Effects of an aquatic exercise program on inhibitory control in children with ADHD: a preliminary study. *Archives of Clinical Neuropsychology, 29*, 217–223.

Chang, Y. K., Labban, J. D., Gapin, J. I., & Etnier, J. L. (2012). The effects of acute exercise on cognitive performance: a meta-analysis. *Brain Research, 1453*, 87–101.

Chang, Y. K., Liu, S., Yu, H. H., & Lee, Y. H. (2012). Effect of acute exercise on executive function in children with attention deficit hyperactivity disorder. *Archives of Clinical Neuropsychology, 27*, 225–237.

Chang, Y. K., Tsai, C. L., Huang, C. C., Wang, C. C., & Chu, I. H. (2014b). Effects of acute resistance exercise on cognition in late middle-aged adults: general or specific cognitive improvement? *Journal of Science and Medicine in Sport*, *17*, 51–55.

Charach, A., Ickowicz, A., & Schachar, R. (2004). Stimulant treatment over five years: adherence, effectiveness, and adverse effects. *Journal of the American Academy of Child and Adolescent Psychiatry*, *43*, 559–567.

Charach, A., Yeung, E., Volpe, T., Goodale, T., & Dosreis, S. (2014). Exploring stimulant treatment in ADHD: narratives of young adolescents and their parents. *BMC Psychiatry*, *14*, 110. http://dx.doi.org/10.1186/1471-244X-14-110.

Cherkasova, M. V., & Hechtman, L. (2009). Neuroimaging in attention-deficit hyperactivity disorder: beyond the frontostriatal circuitry. *Canadian Journal of Psychiatry*, *54*, 651–664.

Coghill, D. R., Hayward, D., Rhodes, S. M., Grimmer, C., & Matthews, K. (2014). A longitudinal examination of neuropsychological and clinical functioning in boys with attention deficit hyperactivity disorder (ADHD): improvements in executive functioning do not explain clinical improvement. *Psychological Medicine*, *44*, 1087–1099.

Coghill, D. R., Seth, S., & Matthews, K. (2014). A comprehensive assessment of memory, delay aversion, timing, inhibition, decision making and variability in attention deficit hyperactivity disorder: advancing beyond the three-pathway models. *Psychological Medicine*, *44*, 1989–2001.

Conners, C. K. (2002). Forty years of methylphenidate treatment in Attention-Deficit/Hyperactivity Disorder. *Journal of Attention Disorders*, *6*(Suppl. 1), S17–S30.

Cortese, S., & Angriman, M. (2008). Attention-deficit/hyperactivity disorder and obesity: moving to the next research generation. *Pediatrics*, *122*, 1155, author reply 1155–1156.

Cortese, S., Angriman, M., Maffeis, C., Isnard, P., Konofal, E., Lecendreux, M., et al. (2008). Attention-deficit/hyperactivity disorder (ADHD) and obesity: a systematic review of the literature. *Critical Review of Food Science and Nutrition*, *48*, 524–537.

Cortese, S., Imperati, D., Zhou, J., Proal, E., Klein, R. G., Mannuzza, S., et al. (2013). White matter alterations at 33-year follow-up in adults with childhood attention-deficit/hyperactivity disorder. *Biological Psychiatry*, *74*, 591–598.

Cortese, S., Kelly, C., Chabernaud, C., Proal, E., Di Martino, A., Milham, M. P., et al. (2012). Toward systems neuroscience of ADHD: a meta-analysis of 55 fMRI studies. *American Journal of Psychiatry*, *169*, 1038–1055.

Cortese, S., Ramos Olazagasti, M. A., Klein, R. G., Castellanos, F. X., Proal, E., & Mannuzza, S. (2013). Obesity in men with childhood ADHD: a 33-year controlled, prospective, follow-up study. *Pediatrics*, *131*, e1731–e1738. http://dx.doi.org/10.1542/peds.2012-0540.

Craft, D. H. (1983). Effect of prior exercise on cognitive performance tasks by hyperactive and normal young boys. *Perceptual and Motor Skills*, *56*, 979–982.

Cunningham, C. E., Bremner, R., & Boyle, M. (1995). Large group community-based parenting programs for families of preschoolers at risk for disruptive behaviour disorders: utilization, cost effectiveness, and outcome. *Journal of Child Psychology and Psychiatry*, *36*, 1141–1159.

Daley, D., van der Oord, S., Ferrin, M., Danckaerts, M., Doepfner, M., Cortese, S., et al. (2014). Behavioral interventions in attention-deficit/hyperactivity disorder: a meta-analysis of randomized controlled trials across multiple outcome domains. *Journal of the American Academy of Child and Adolescent Psychiatry*, *53*, 835–847.

Dalsgaard, S., Mortensen, P. B., Frydenberg, M., & Thomsen, P. H. (2014). ADHD, stimulant treatment in childhood and subsequent substance abuse in adulthood - a naturalistic long-term follow-up study. *Addictive Behaviors*, *39*, 325–328.

Drollette, E. S., Scudder, M. R., Raine, L. B., Moore, R. D., Saliba, B. J., Pontifex, M. B., et al. (2014). Acute exercise facilitates brain function and cognition in children who need it most: an ERP study of individual differences in inhibitory control capacity. *Developmental Cognitive Neurosciencve*, *7*, 53–64.

Fallah, N., Hsu, C. L., Bolandzadeh, N., Davis, J., Beattie, B. L., Graf, P., et al. (2013). A multistate model of cognitive dynamics in relation to resistance training: the contribution of baseline function. *Annals of Epidemiology*, *23*, 463–468.

Faraone, S. V., Perlis, R. H., Doyle, A. E., Smoller, J. W., Goralnick, J. J., Holmgren, M. A., et al. (2005). Molecular genetics of attention-deficit/hyperactivity disorder. *Biological Psychiatry*, *57*, 1313–1323.

Forte, R., Boreham, C. A., Leite, J. C., De Vito, G., Brennan, L., Gibney, E. R., et al. (2013). Enhancing cognitive functioning in the elderly: multicomponent vs resistance training. *Clinical Interventions in Aging*, *8*, 19–27.

Gapin, J., & Etnier, J. L. (2010). The relationship between physical activity and executive function performance in children with attention-deficit hyperactivity disorder. *Journal of Sport and Exercise Psychology*, *32*, 753–763.

Gapin, J. I., Labban, J. D., & Etnier, J. L. (2011). The effects of physical activity on attention deficit hyperactivity disorder symptoms: the evidence. *Preventive Medicine*, *52*(Suppl. 1), S70–S74.

Gathercole, S. E., Pickering, S. J., Knight, C., & Stegmann, Z. (2004). Working memory skills and educational attainment: evidence from national curriculum assessment at 7 and 14 years of age. *Applied Cognitive Psychology*, *18*, 1–16.

Gathercole, S. E., Tiffany, C., Briscoe, J., Thorn, A., & ALSPAC team (2005). Developmental consequences of poor phonological short-term memory function in childhood: a longitudinal study. *Journal of Child Psychology and Psychiatry*, *46*, 598–611.

Gizer, I. R., Ficks, C., & Waldman, I. D. (2009). Candidate gene studies of ADHD: a meta-analytic review. *Human Genetics, 126*, 51–90.

Greenhill, L. L., Halperin, J. M., & Abikoff, H. (1999). Stimulant medications. *Journal of the American Academy of Child and Adolescent Psychiatry, 38*, 503–512.

Griffin, E. W., Mullally, S., Foley, C., Warmington, S. A., O'Mara, S. M., & Kelly, A. M. (2011). Aerobic exercise improves hippocampal function and increases BDNF in the serum of young adult males. *Physiology and Behavior, 104*, 934–941.

Halperin, J. M., Bedard, A. C., & Curchack-Lichtin, J. T. (2012). Preventive interventions for ADHD: a neurodevelopmental perspective. *Neurotherapeutics, 9*, 531–541.

Halperin, J. M., Berwid, O. G., & O'Neill, S. (2014). Healthy body, healthy mind?: the effectiveness of physical activity to treat ADHD in children. *Child and Adolescent Psychiatry Clinics of North America, 23*, 899–936.

Halperin, J. M., Marks, D. J., Bedard, A. C., Chacko, A., Curchack, J. T., Yoon, C. A., et al. (2013). Training executive, attention, and motor skills: a proof-of-concept study in preschool children with ADHD. *Journal of Attenrion Disorders, 17*, 711–721.

Halperin, J. M., & Schulz, K. P. (2006). Revisiting the role of the prefrontal cortex in the pathophysiology of attention-deficit/hyperactivity disorder. *Psychological Bulletin, 132*, 560–581.

Halperin, J. M., Trampush, J. W., Miller, C. J., Marks, D. J., & Newcorn, J. H. (2008). Neuropsychological outcome in adolescents/young adults with childhood ADHD: profiles of persisters, remitters and controls. *Journal of Child Psychology and Psychiatry, 49*, 958–966.

Hattori, S., Naoi, M., & Nishino, H. (1994). Striatal dopamine turnover during treadmill running in the rat: relation to the speed of running. *Brain Research Bulletin, 35*, 41–49.

Healey, D. M., & Halperin, J. M. (2014). Enhancing Neurobehavioral Gains with the Aid of Games and Exercise (ENGAGE): initial open trial of a novel early intervention fostering the development of preschoolers' self-regulation. *Child Neuropsychology*, 1–16. http://dx.doi.org/10.1080/09297049.2014.906567 [E-pub ahead of print].

Hervey, A. S., Epstein, J. N., & Curry, J. F. (2004). Neuropsychology of adults with attention-deficit/hyperactivity disorder: a meta-analytic review. *Neuropsychology, 18*, 485–503.

Hoffman, J. B., & DuPaul, G. J. (2000). Psychoeducational interventions for children and adolescents with attention-deficit/hyperactivity disorder. *Child and Adolescent Psychiatr Clinics of North America, 9*, 647–661, ix.

Holtmann, M., Sonuga-Barke, E., Cortese, S., & Brandeis, D. (2014). Neurofeedback for ADHD: a review of current evidence. *Child and Adolescent Psychiatric Clinics of North America, 23*, 789–806.

Hopkins, M. E., Sharma, M., Evans, G. C., & Bucci, D. J. (2009). Voluntary physical exercise alters attentional orienting and social behavior in a rat model of attention-deficit/hyperactivity disorder. *Behavioral Neuroscience, 123*, 599–606.

Hotting, K., & Roder, B. (2013). Beneficial effects of physical exercise on neuroplasticity and cognition. *Neuroscience and Biobehavioral Reviews, 37*, 2243–2257.

Hoza, B., Smith, A. L., Shoulberg, E. K., Linnea, K. S., Dorsch, T. E., Blazo, J. A., et al. (2014). A randomized trial examining the effects of aerobic physical activity on attention-deficit/hyperactivity disorder symptoms in young children. *Journal of Abnormal Child Psychology*. http://dx.doi.org/10.1007/s10802-014-9929-y [E-pub ahead of print].

Huang-Pollock, C. L., Karalunas, S. L., Tam, H., & Moore, A. N. (2012). Evaluating vigilance deficits in ADHD: a meta-analysis of CPT performance. *Journal of Abnormal Psychology, 121*, 360–371.

Ji, E. S., Kim, C. J., Park, J. H., & Bahn, G. H. (2014). Duration-dependence of the effect of treadmill exercise on hyperactivity in attention deficit hyperactivity disorder rats. *Journal of Exercise Rehabilitation, 10*, 75–80.

Johnson, D. E., Epstein, J. N., Waid, L. R., Latham, P. K., Voronin, K. E., & Anton, R. F. (2001). Neuropsychological performance deficits in adults with attention deficit/hyperactivity disorder. *Archives of Clinical Neuropsychology, 16*, 587–604.

Johnson, N. B., Hayes, L. D., Brown, K., Hoo, E. C., & Ethier, K. A. (2014). CDC national health report: leading causes of morbidity and mortality and associated behavioral risk and protective factors-United States, 2005–2013. *MMWR Surveillance Summaries, 63*, 3–27.

Johnston, C., & Mash, E. J. (2001). Families of children with attention-deficit/hyperactivity disorder: review and recommendations for future research. *Clinical Child and Family Psychology Review, 4*, 183–207.

Kang, K. D., Choi, J. W., Kang, S. G., & Han, D. H. (2011). Sports therapy for attention, cognitions and sociality. *International Journal of Sports Medicine, 32*, 953–959.

Khalife, N., Kantomaa, M., Glover, V., Tammelin, T., Laitinen, J., Ebeling, H., et al. (2014). Childhood attention-deficit/hyperactivity disorder symptoms are risk factors for obesity and physical inactivity in adolescence. *Journal of the American Academy of Child and Adolescent Psychiatry, 53*, 425–436.

Kiluk, B. D., Weden, S., & Culotta, V. P. (2009). Sport participation and anxiety in children with ADHD. *Journal of Attention Disorders, 12*, 499–506.

Kim, H., Heo, H. I., Kim, D. H., Ko, I. G., Lee, S. S., Kim, S. E., et al. (2011). Treadmill exercise and methylphenidate ameliorate symptoms of attention deficit/hyperactivity disorder through enhancing dopamine synthesis and brain-derived neurotrophic factor expression in spontaneous hypertensive rats. *Neuroscience Letters, 504*, 35–39.

Kim, Y. P., Kim, H., Shin, M. S., Chang, H. K., Jang, M. H., Shin, M. C., et al. (2004). Age-dependence of the effect of treadmill exercise on cell proliferation in the dentate gyrus of rats. *Neuroscience Letters, 355,* 152–154.

Kirsch, I. (1985). Response expectancy as a determinant of experience and bheavior. *American Psychologist, 40,* 1189–1202.

Knight, M. (2007). Stimulant-drug therapy for attention-deficit disorder (with or without hyperactivity) and sudden cardiac death. *Pediatrics, 119,* 154–155.

Kochanska-Dziurowicz, A. A., Janikowska, G., Bogacz, A., Bijak, A., Stanjek-Cichoracka, A., Mazurek, U., et al. (2013). Catecholamines and beta2-adrenoceptor gene expression before and after maximal incremental cycle test in young ice hockey players: relation to work performed. *Biology of Sport, 30,* 85–90.

Ko, I. G., Kim, S. E., Kim, T. W., Ji, E. S., Shin, M. S., Kim, C. J., et al. (2013). Swimming exercise alleviates the symptoms of attention-deficit hyperactivity disorder in spontaneous hypertensive rats. *Molecular Medicine Report, 8,* 393–400.

Lambourne, K., Audiffren, M., & Tomporowski, P. D. (2010). Effects of acute exercise on sensory and executive processing tasks. *Medicine and Science in Sports and Exercise, 42,* 1396–1402.

Lambourne, K., & Tomporowski, P. (2010). The effect of exercise-induced arousal on cognitive task performance: a meta-regression analysis. *Brain Research, 1341,* 12–24.

van Lieshout, M., Luman, M., Buitelaar, J., Rommelse, N. N., & Oosterlaan, J. (2013). Does neurocognitive functioning predict future or persistence of ADHD? A systematic review. *Clinical Psychology Review, 33,* 539–560.

Lijffijt, M., Kenemans, J. L., Verbaten, M. N., & van Engeland, H. (2005). A meta-analytic review of stopping performance in attention-deficit/hyperactivity disorder: deficient inhibitory motor control? *Journal of Abnormal Psychology, 114,* 216–222.

Li, H., Liang, A., Guan, F., Fan, R., Chi, L., & Yang, B. (2013). Regular treadmill running improves spatial learning and memory performance in young mice through increased hippocampal neurogenesis and decreased stress. *Brain Research, 1531,* 1–8.

Lin, T. W., & Kuo, Y. M. (2013). Exercise benefits brain function: the monoamine connection. *Brain Sciences, 3,* 39–53.

Little, H. R., Kramer, J. M., Beatty, J. A., & Waldrop, T. G. (2001). Chronic exercise increases GAD gene expression in the caudal hypothalamus of spontaneously hypertensive rats. *Brain Research Molecular Brain Research, 95,* 48–54.

Lufi, D., & Parish-Plass, J. (2011). Sport-based group therapy program for boys with ADHD or with other behavioral disorders. *Child and Family Behavior Therapy, 33,* 217–230.

Mannuzza, S., Klein, R. G., Bessler, A., Malloy, P., & Hynes, M. E. (1997). Educational and occupational outcome of hyperactive boys grown up. *Journal of the American Academy of Child and Adolescent Psychiatry, 36,* 1222–1227.

Mannuzza, S., Klein, R. G., Bessler, A., Malloy, P., & LaPadula, M. (1993). Adult outcome of hyperactive boys. Educational achievement, occupational rank, and psychiatric status. *Archives of General Psychiatry, 50,* 565–576.

Mansoubi, M., Pearson, N., Biddle, S. J., & Clemes, S. (2014). The relationship between sedentary behaviour and physical activity in adults: a systematic review. *Preventive Medicine, 69C,* 28–35.

Marks, D. J., Berwid, O. G., Santra, A., Kera, E. C., Cyrulnik, S. E., & Halperin, J. M. (2005). Neuropsychological correlates of ADHD symptoms in preschoolers. *Neuropsychology, 19,* 446–455.

Martens, B. K., Peterson, R. L., Witt, J. C., & Cirone, S. (1986). Teacher perceptions of school-based interventions. *Exceptional Child, 53,* 213–223.

McKune, A. J., Pautz, J., & Lombard, J. (2003). Behavioural response to exercise in children with attention-deficit/hyperactivity disorder. *South African Journal of Sports Medicine, 15,* 17–21.

Medina, J. A., Netto, T. L., Muszkat, M., Medina, A. C., Botter, D., Orbetelli, R., et al. (2010). Exercise impact on sustained attention of ADHD children, methylphenidate effects. *Attention Deficit Hyperactactivity Disorders, 2,* 49–58.

Meeusen, R., & De Meirleir, K. (1995). Exercise and brain neurotransmission. *Sports Medicine, 20,* 160–188.

Metin, B., Roeyers, H., Wiersema, J. R., van der Meere, J. J., Thompson, M., & Sonuga-Barke, E. (2013). ADHD performance reflects inefficient but not impulsive information processing: a diffusion model analysis. *Neuropsychology, 27,* 193–200.

Mick, E., Biederman, J., Faraone, S. V., Sayer, J., & Kleinman, S. (2002). Case-control study of attention-deficit hyperactivity disorder and maternal smoking, alcohol use, and drug use during pregnancy. *Journal of the American Academy of Child and Adolescent Psychiatry, 41,* 378–385.

Minzenberg, M. J. (2012). Pharmacotherapy for attention-deficit/hyperactivity disorder: from cells to circuits. *Neurotherapeutics, 9,* 610–621.

Motlagh, M. G., Katsovich, L., Thompson, N., Lin, H., Kim, Y. S., Scahill, L., et al. (2010). Severe psychosocial stress and heavy cigarette smoking during pregnancy: an examination of the pre- and perinatal risk factors associated with ADHD and Tourette syndrome. *European Child and Adolescent Psychiatry, 19,* 755–764.

Mrug, S., Molina, B. S., Hoza, B., Gerdes, A. C., Hinshaw, S. P., Hechtman, L., et al. (2012). Peer rejection and friendships in children with attention-deficit/hyperactivity Disorder: contributions to long-term outcomes. *Journal of Abnormal Child Psychology, 40,* 1013–1026.

MTA Cooperative Group. (1999). A 14-month randomized clinical trial of treatment strategies for ADHD. *Archives of General Psychiatry, 56*, 1073–1086.

National Health Service. (2013). *Physical activity guidelines for children (under 5 years)*. Retrieved November 17, 2014, from http://www.nhs.uk/Livewell/fitness/Pages/physical-activity-guidelines-for-children.aspx.

National Resource Center for Health and Safety in Child Care and Early Education. (n.d.). *Caring for our children: National health and safety performance standards: Guideline for early care and education programs* (3rd ed.). (Chapter 3: Health Promotion and Protection). Retrieved November 17, 2014, from http://cfoc.nrckids.org/StandardView/3.1.3.1

Nigg, J. T., Willcutt, E. G., Doyle, A. E., & Sonuga-Barke, E. J. (2005). Causal heterogeneity in attention-deficit/hyperactivity disorder: do we need neuropsychologically impaired subtypes? *Biological Psychiatry, 57*, 1224–1230.

Nomura, Y., Marks, D. J., Grossman, B., Yoon, M., Loudon, H., Stone, J., et al. (2012). Exposure to gestational diabetes mellitus and low socioeconomic status: effects on neurocognitive development and risk of attention-deficit/hyperactivity disorder in offspring. *Archives of Pediatric and Adolescent Medicine, 166*, 337–343.

Nomura, Y., Marks, D. J., & Halperin, J. M. (2010). Prenatal exposure to maternal and paternal smoking on attention deficit hyperactivity disorders symptoms and diagnosis in offspring. *Journal of Nervous and Mental Disease, 198*, 672–678.

Palmer, K. K., Miller, M. W., & Robinson, L. E. (2013). Acute exercise enhances preschoolers' ability to sustain attention. *Journal of Sport and Exercise Psychology, 35*, 433–437.

Pan, C. Y., Chang, Y. K., Tsai, C. L., Chu, C. H., Cheng, Y. W., & Sung, M. C. (2014). Effects of physical activity intervention on motor proficiency and physical fitness in children with ADHD: an exploratory study. *Journal of Attention Disorders*. http://dx.doi.org/10.1177/1087054714533192.

Pelham, W. E. & Fabiano, G. A. (2008). Evidence-based psychosocial treatments for attention-deficit/hyperactivity disorder. *Journal of Clinical Child and Adolescent Psychology, 37*(1), 184–214. http://dx.doi.org/10.1080/15374410701818681.

Petzinger, G. M., Walsh, J. P., Akopian, G., Hogg, E., Abernathy, A., Arevalo, P., et al. (2007). Effects of treadmill exercise on dopaminergic transmission in the 1-methyl-4-phenyl-1,2,3,6-tetrahydropyridine-lesioned mouse model of basal ganglia injury. *Journal of Neuroscience, 27*, 5291–5300.

Polanczyk, G., Faraone, S. V., Bau, C. H., Victor, M. M., Becker, K., Pelz, R., et al. (2008). The impact of individual and methodological factors in the variability of response to methylphenidate in ADHD pharmacogenetic studies from four different continents. *American Journal of Medical Genetics, Part B, 147B*, 1419–1424.

Polanczyk, G. V., Willcutt, E. G., Salum, G. A., Kieling, C., & Rohde, L. A. (2014). ADHD prevalence estimates across three decades: an updated systematic review and meta-regression analysis. *International Journal of Epidemiology, 43*, 434–442.

Pontifex, M. B., Hillman, C. H., Fernhall, B., Thompson, K. M., & Valentini, T. A. (2009). The effect of acute aerobic and resistance exercise on working memory. *Medicine and Science in Sports and Exercise, 41*, 927–934.

Pontifex, M. B., Saliba, B. J., Raine, L. B., Picchietti, D. L., & Hillman, C. H. (2013). Exercise improves behavioral, neurocognitive, and scholastic performance in children with attention-deficit/hyperactivity disorder. *Journal of Pediatrics, 162*, 543–551.

Prince, J. (2008). Catecholamine dysfunction in attention-deficit/hyperactivity disorder: an update. *Journal of Clinical Psychopharmacology, 28*(Suppl. 2), S39–S45.

Rajendran, K., Trampush, J. W., Rindskopf, D., Marks, D. J., O'Neill, S., & Halperin, J. M. (2013). Association between variation in neuropsychological development and trajectory of ADHD severity in early childhood. *American Journal of Psychiatry, 170*, 1205–1211.

Rapport, M. D., Alderson, R. M., Kofler, M. J., Sarver, D. E., Bolden, J., & Sims, V. (2008). Working memory deficits in boys with attention-deficit/hyperactivity disorder (ADHD): the contribution of central executive and subsystem processes. *Journal of Abnormal Child Psychology, 36*, 825–837.

Ratcliff, R., & McKoon, G. (2008). The diffusion decision model: theory and data for two-choice decision tasks. *Neural Computation, 20*, 873–922.

Ratey, J. J., & Loehr, J. E. (2011). The positive impact of physical activity on cognition during adulthood: a review of underlying mechanisms, evidence and recommendations. *Reviews of Neuroscience, 22*, 171–185.

Reddy, D. S. (2013). Current pharmacotherapy of attention deficit hyperactivity disorder. *Drugs Today, 49*, 647–665.

Robinson, A. M., Eggleston, R. L., & Bucci, D. J. (2012). Physical exercise and catecholamine reuptake inhibitors affect orienting behavior and social interaction in a rat model of attention-deficit/hyperactivity disorder. *Behavioral Neuroscience, 126*, 762–771.

Robinson, A. M., Hopkins, M. E., & Bucci, D. J. (2011). Effects of physical exercise on ADHD-like behavior in male and female adolescent spontaneously hypertensive rats. *Developmental Psychobiology, 53*, 383–390.

Rommelse, N. N., Altink, M. E., de Sonneville, L. M., Buschgens, C. J., Buitelaar, J., Oosterlaan, J., et al. (2007). Are motor inhibition and cognitive flexibility dead ends in ADHD? *Journal of Abnormal Child Psychology, 35*, 957–967.

Rubia, K., Alegria, A., & Brinson, H. (2014). Imaging the ADHD brain: disorder-specificity, medication effects and clinical translation. *Expert Review of Neurotherapy, 14*, 519–538.

Rubia, K., Smith, A., & Taylor, E. (2007). Performance of children with attention deficit hyperactivity disorder (ADHD) on a test battery of impulsiveness. *Child Neuropsychology, 13*, 276–304.

Rucklidge, J. J., Johnstone, J., Gorman, B., Boggis, A., & Frampton, C. M. (2014). Moderators of treatment response in adults with ADHD treated with a vitamin-mineral supplement. *Progress in Neuropsychopharmacology and Biological Psychiatry, 50*, 163–171.

Russell, V. A. (2002). Hypodopaminergic and hypernoradrenergic activity in prefrontal cortex slices of an animal model for attention-deficit hyperactivity disorder–the spontaneously hypertensive rat. *Behavioural Brain Research, 130*, 191–196.

Sagvolden, T. (2000). Behavioral validation of the spontaneously hypertensive rat (SHR) as an animal model of attention-deficit/hyperactivity disorder (AD/HD). *Neuroscience and Biobehavioral Reviews, 24*, 31–39.

Sagvolden, T., Aase, H., Zeiner, P., & Berger, D. (1998). Altered reinforcement mechanisms in attention-deficit/hyperactivity disorder. *Behavioural Brain Research, 94*, 61–71.

Samorajski, T., Delaney, C., Durham, L., Ordy, J. M., Johnson, J. A., & Dunlap, W. P. (1985). Effect of exercise on longevity, body weight, locomotor performance, and passive-avoidance memory of C57BL/6J mice. *Neurobiology of Aging, 6*, 17–24.

Sanchez, R. J., Crismon, M. L., Barner, J. C., Bettinger, T., & Wilson, J. P. (2005). Assessment of adherence measures with different stimulants among children and adolescents. *Pharmacotherapy, 25*, 909–917.

Schaeffer, D. J., Krafft, C. E., Schwarz, N. F., Chi, L., Rodrigue, A. L., Pierce, J. E., et al. (2014). An 8-month exercise intervention alters frontotemporal white matter integrity in overweight children. *Psychophysiology, 51*, 728–733.

Shaw, P., De Rossi, P., Watson, B., Wharton, A., Greenstein, D., Raznahan, A., et al. (2014). Mapping the development of the basal ganglia in children with attention-deficit/hyperactivity disorder. *Journal of the American Academy of Child and Adolescent Psychiatry, 53*, 780–789.

Shaw, P., Eckstrand, K., Sharp, W., Blumenthal, J., Lerch, J. P., Greenstein, D., et al. (2007). Attention-deficit/hyperactivity disorder is characterized by a delay in cortical maturation. *Proceedings of the National Academy of Sciences of the United States of America, 104*, 19649–19654.

Shaw, P., Lerch, J., Greenstein, D., Sharp, W., Clasen, L., Evans, A., et al. (2006). Longitudinal mapping of cortical thickness and clinical outcome in children and adolescents with attention-deficit/hyperactivity disorder. *Archives of General Psychiatry, 63*, 540–549.

Shaw, P., Malek, M., Watson, B., Greenstein, D., de Rossi, P., & Sharp, W. (2013). Trajectories of cerebral cortical development in childhood and adolescence and adult attention-deficit/hyperactivity disorder. *Biological Psychiatry, 74*, 599–606.

Shaw, P., Sudre, G., Wharton, A., Weingart, D., Sharp, W., & Sarlls, J. (2014). White matter microstructure and the variable adult outcome of childhood attention deficit hyperactivity disorder. *Neuropsychopharmacology*. http://dx.doi.org/10.1038/npp.2014.241.

Sibley, B. A., & Beilock, S. L. (2007). Exercise and working memory: an individual differences investigation. *Journal of Sport and Exercise Psychology, 29*, 783–791.

Sibley, M. H., Pelham, W. E., Molina, B. S., Coxe, S., Kipp, H., Gnagy, E. M., et al. (2014). The role of early childhood ADHD and subsequent CD in the initiation and escalation of adolescent cigarette, alcohol, and marijuana use. *Journal of Abnormal Psychology, 123*, 362–374.

Sioen, I., Den Hond, E., Nelen, V., Van de Mieroop, E., Croes, K., Van Larebeke, N., et al. (2013). Prenatal exposure to environmental contaminants and behavioural problems at age 7–8 years. *Environment International, 59*, 225–231.

Sjowall, D., Roth, L., Lindqvist, S., & Thorell, L. B. (2013). Multiple deficits in ADHD: executive dysfunction, delay aversion, reaction time variability, and emotional deficits. *Journal of Child Psychology and Psychiatry, 54*, 619–627.

Skriver, K., Roig, M., Lundbye-Jensen, J., Pingel, J., Helge, J. W., Kiens, B., et al. (2014). Acute exercise improves motor memory: exploring potential biomarkers. *Neurobiology of Learning and Memory, 116C*, 46–58.

Smith, A. L., Hoza, B., Linnea, K., McQuade, J. D., Tomb, M., Vaughn, A. J., et al. (2013). Pilot physical activity intervention reduces severity of ADHD symptoms in young children. *Journal of Attention Disorders, 17*, 70–82.

Sonuga-Barke, E. J. (2003). The dual pathway model of AD/HD: an elaboration of neuro-developmental characteristics. Neurosci. *Biobehavioral Reviews, 27*, 593–604.

Sonuga-Barke, E. J. (2005). Causal models of attention-deficit/hyperactivity disorder: from common simple deficits to multiple developmental pathways. *Biological Psychiatry, 57*, 1231–1238.

Sonuga-Barke, E. J., Brandeis, D., Cortese, S., Daley, D., Ferrin, M., Holtmann, M., et al. (2013). Nonpharmacological interventions for ADHD: systematic review and meta-analyses of randomized controlled trials of dietary and psychological treatments. *American Journal of Psychiatry, 170*, 275–289.

Sonuga-Barke, E., Brandeis, D., Holtmann, M., & Cortese, S. (2014). Computer-based cognitive training for ADHD: a review of current evidence. *Child and Adolescent Psychiatry Clinics of North America, 23*, 807–824.

Sonuga-Barke, E. J., Daley, D., Thompson, M., Laver-Bradbury, C., & Weeks, A. (2001). Parent-based therapies for preschool attention-deficit/hyperactivity disorder: a randomized, controlled trial with a community sample. *Journal of the American Academy of Child and Adolescent Psychiatry, 40*, 402–408.

Sonuga-Barke, E. J., & Halperin, J. M. (2010). Developmental phenotypes and causal pathways in attention deficit/hyperactivity disorder: potential targets for early intervention? *Journal of Child Psychology and Psychiatry*, 51, 368–389.

Spencer, T., Biederman, J., Wilens, T., Harding, M., O'Donnell, D., & Griffin, S. (1996). Pharmacotherapy of attention-deficit hyperactivity disorder across the life cycle. *Journal of the American Academy of Child and Adolescent Psychiatry*, 35, 409–432.

Stevenson, J., Buitelaar, J., Cortese, S., Ferrin, M., Konofal, E., Lecendreux, M., et al. (2014). Research review: the role of diet in the treatment of attention-deficit/hyperactivity disorder–an appraisal of the evidence on efficacy and recommendations on the design of future studies. *Journal of Child Psychology and Psychiatry*, 55, 416–427.

Stevens, S. E., Sonuga-Barke, E. J., Kreppner, J. M., Beckett, C., Castle, J., Colvert, E., et al. (2008). Inattention/overactivity following early severe institutional deprivation: presentation and associations in early adolescence. *Journal of Abnormal Child Psychology*, 36, 385–398.

Strohle, A. (2009). Physical activity, exercise, depression and anxiety disorders. *Journal of Neural Transmission*, 116, 777–784.

Sutoo, D., & Akiyama, K. (2003). Regulation of brain function by exercise. *Neurobiology of Disease*, 13, 1–14.

Swanson, J. M., Kraemer, H. C., Hinshaw, S. P., Arnold, L. E., Conners, C. K., Abikoff, H. B., et al. (2001). Clinical relevance of the primary findings of the MTA: success rates based on severity of ADHD and ODD symptoms at the end of treatment. *Journal of the American Academy of Child and Adolescent Psychiatry*, 40, 168–179.

Swing, E. L., Gentile, D. A., Anderson, C. A., & Walsh, D. A. (2010). Television and video game exposure and the development of attention problems. *Pediatrics*, 126, 214–221.

Szatmari, P., Saigal, S., Rosenbaum, P., & Campbell, D. (1993). Psychopathology and adaptive functioning among extremely low birthweight children at eight years of age. *Development and Psychopathology*, 5, 345–357.

Tantillo, M., Kesick, C. M., Hynd, G. W., & Dishman, R. K. (2002). The effects of exercise on children with attention-deficit hyperactivity disorder. *Medicine and Science in Sports and Exercise*, 34, 203–212.

Telama, R., Yang, X., Viikari, J., Valimaki, I., Wanne, O., & Raitakari, O. (2005). Physical activity from childhood to adulthood: a 21-year tracking study. *American Journal of Preventive Medicine*, 28, 267–273.

Tsai, C. L., Chen, F. C., Pan, C. Y., Wang, C. H., Huang, T. H., & Chen, T. C. (2014). Impact of acute aerobic exercise and cardiorespiratory fitness on visuospatial attention performance and serum BDNF levels. *Psychoneuroendocrinology*, 41, 121–131.

Verburgh, L., Konigs, M., Scherder, E. J., & Oosterlaan, J. (2014). Physical exercise and executive functions in preadolescent children, adolescents and young adults: a meta-analysis. *British Journal of Sports Medicine*, 48, 973–979.

Verret, C., Guay, M. C., Berthiaume, C., Gardiner, P., & Beliveau, L. (2012). A physical activity program improves behavior and cognitive functions in children with ADHD: an exploratory study. *Journal of Attention Disorders*, 16, 71–80.

Visser, S. N., Danielson, M. L., Bitsko, R. H., Holbrook, J. R., Kogan, M. D., Ghandour, R. M., et al. (2014). Trends in the parent-report of health care provider-diagnosed and medicated attention-deficit/hyperactivity disorder: United States, 2003–2011. *Journal of the American Academy of Child and Adolescent Psychiatry*, 53, 34–46.

Voss, M. W., Vivar, C., Kramer, A. F., & van Praag, H. (2013). Bridging animal and human models of exercise-induced brain plasticity. *Trends in Cognitive Science*, 17, 525–544.

Weiss, M. D., Gadow, K., & Wasdell, M. B. (2006). Effectiveness outcomes in attention-deficit/hyperactivity disorder. *Journal of Clincal Psychiatry*, 67(Suppl. 8), 38–45.

Whiteman, A. S., Young, D. E., He, X., Chen, T. C., Wagenaar, R. C., Stern, C. E., et al. (2014). Interaction between serum BDNF and aerobic fitness predicts recognition memory in healthy young adults. *Behavioural Brain Research*, 259, 302–312.

Wigal, S. B., Nemet, D., Swanson, J. M., Regino, R., Trampush, J., Ziegler, M. G., et al. (2003). Catecholamine response to exercise in children with attention deficit hyperactivity disorder. *Pediatric Research*, 53, 756–761.

Willcutt, E. G., Doyle, A. E., Nigg, J. T., Faraone, S. V., & Pennington, B. F. (2005). Validity of the executive function theory of attention-deficit/hyperactivity disorder: a meta-analytic review. *Biological Psychiatry*, 57, 1336–1346.

Willcutt, E. G., Nigg, J. T., Pennington, B. F., Solanto, M. V., Rohde, L. A., Tannock, R., et al. (2012). Validity of DSM-IV attention deficit/hyperactivity disorder symptom dimensions and subtypes. *Journal of Abnormal Psychology*, 121, 991–1010.

Winter, B., Breitenstein, C., Mooren, F. C., Voelker, K., Fobker, M., Lechtermann, A., et al. (2007). High impact running improves learning. *Neurobiology of Learning and Memory*, 87, 597–609.

Wojcicki, T. R., Grigsby-Toussaint, D., Hillman, C. H., Huhman, M., & McAuley, E. (2014). Promoting physical activity in low-active adolescents via Facebook: a pilot randomized controlled trial to test feasibility. *JMIR Research Protocols*, 3, e56. http://dx.doi.org/10.2196/resprot.3013.

Yun, H. S., Park, M. S., Ji, E. S., Kim, T. W., Ko, I. G., Kim, H. B., et al. (2014). Treadmill exercise ameliorates symptoms of attention deficit/hyperactivity disorder through reducing Purkinje cell loss and astrocytic reaction in spontaneous hypertensive rats. *Journal of Exercise Rehabilitation*, 10, 22–30.

Zhu, J. L., Olsen, J., Liew, Z., Li, J., Niclasen, J., & Obel, C. (2014). Parental smoking during pregnancy and ADHD in children: the Danish national birth cohort. *Pediatrics*, 134, e382–e388. http://dx.doi.org/10.1542/peds.2014-0213.

Cognitive Impairment in Breast Cancer Survivors: The Protective Role of Physical Activity, Cardiorespiratory Fitness, and Exercise Training

Michael J. Mackenzie[1], Krystle E. Zuniga[2], Edward McAuley[3]

[1]Department of Behavioral Health & Nutrition, University of Delaware, Newark, DE, USA;
[2]Nutrition & Foods, Texas State University, San Marcos, TX, USA; [3]Department of Kinesiology &
Community Health, University of Illinois at Urbana-Champaign, Urbana, IL, USA

INTRODUCTION

Breast cancer is the most common type of cancer in women in the United States, and is expected to account for 29% of all new cancers among women (Siegel, Ma, Zou, & Jemal, 2014). It is estimated that one in eight women will be diagnosed with breast cancer in their lifetime (DeSantis, Ma, Bryan, & Jemal, 2014). Due to advances in the detection and treatment of cancer, mortality rates for breast cancer are down from peak rates by 34% and the 5-year survival rate of breast cancer has risen to 89% (DeSantis et al., 2014; Siegel et al., 2014), resulting in an increasingly larger population of breast cancer survivors. In the present chapter, we focus on an important health outcome associated with breast cancer and its treatment, cancer-related cognitive impairment (CRCI). We describe the prevalence of this condition, the effects of treatment on brain health, and explore the potential underlying mechanisms of CRCI. Using the aging literature as a model, we consider the roles that physical activity, cardiorespiratory fitness, and exercise training may play as protective agents against CRCI, as well as factors that may serve to restore declines in cognitive function from breast cancer treatment. Careful attention is paid to the measurement of CRCI and these physical activity-related factors. Finally, we conclude with recommendations for future research in this area and some clinical recommendations.

Exercise-Cognition Interaction
http://dx.doi.org/10.1016/B978-0-12-800778-5.00019-0

PREVALENCE OF COGNITIVE IMPAIRMENT IN BREAST CANCER SURVIVORS

This burgeoning population of cancer patients and survivors is living with treatment-related side effects affecting their health and quality of life. A growing body of evidence suggests that consequences of breast cancer and treatment also include cognitive dysfunction (Janelsins, Kesler, Ahles, & Morrow, 2014). In 1998, the President's Cancer Panel and the National Coalition for Cancer Survivorship formally recognized CRCI as a quality of life issue that deserved higher priority in clinical research (Ahles & Saykin, 2001; United States President's Cancer Panel, 1998). CRCI, colloquially termed "chemobrain," is the loss of mental acuity associated with cancer and cancer treatment. The clinical prevalence of CRCI across breast cancer diagnoses is estimated to range from 17% to 75% (Argyriou, Assimakopoulos, Iconomou, Giannakopoulou, & Kalofonos, 2011; Jean-Pierre, 2010; Wefel & Schagen, 2012). Evidence suggests cognitive impairment can be detected in up to 33% of patients prior to treatment, whereas approximately 75% of breast cancer survivors report some impact on cognitive functioning during treatment (Janelsins et al., 2014). Additionally, cognitive impairment can persist in up to 35% of cancer survivors many years following treatment completion (Koppelmans et al., 2012; Yamada, Denburg, Beglinger, & Schultz, 2010). Given the breadth in reported incidence of cognitive deficits, it has been suggested that CRCI is relatively common but largely underdiagnosed and often left untreated in cancer patients (Argyriou et al., 2011).

BREAST CANCER TREATMENT AND BRAIN HEALTH

Despite the heterogeneity of neuropsychological tests used in cognitive assessments, numerous studies have identified cognitive dysfunction in breast cancer survivors. Multiple domains of cognitive function are thought to be influenced in CRCI including memory, learning, concentration, reasoning, executive function, attention, and visual–spatial skills (Argyriou et al., 2011). The most commonly identified cognitive deficits are suggestive of disruption of the frontal–subcortical network systems (Janelsins et al., 2014). These cognitive changes may occur both before and after treatment and, in some instances, may affect cancer survivors up to 20 years after completion of cancer treatment (Koppelmans et al., 2012; Yamada et al., 2010). However, additional longitudinal studies in cancer survivors are needed to determine whether cognitive changes are transient or permanent. Meta-analyses of chemotherapy effects on cognitive functioning in breast cancer survivors have concluded the magnitude of cognitive impairment is generally small and subtle (Falleti, Sanfilippo, Maruff, Weih, & Phillips, 2005; Jim et al., 2012). Subjective cognitive dysfunction is a frequent complaint of breast cancer survivors both during and after treatment (Pullens, De Vries, & Roukema, 2010), and typical concerns reported by cancer survivors include memory lapses, difficulty concentrating, trouble with word retrieval and remembering details, slower processing speeds, difficulty following directions, as well as gait and dexterity disturbances (Asher, 2011; Evens & Eschiti, 2009). Breast cancer survivors experiencing cognitive declines report greater difficulty working (Wefel, Lenzi, Theriault, Davis, & Meyers, 2004) and describe CRCI as frustrating and at times harmful to their self-confidence and social relationships (Von Ah, Habermann, Carpenter, & Schneider, 2013).

Neuroimaging studies have reported smaller total brain volume and volume of brain structures important for executive function (i.e., frontal and prefrontal cortex) in chemotherapy-treated individuals compared to healthy controls (Koppelmans et al., 2014). Additionally, a number of reports have shown decreased gray matter density in breast cancer survivors compared to healthy controls (Conroy et al., 2013; Koppelmans et al., 2014). Although there are limited longitudinal studies, over the course of chemotherapy decreases in frontal, parietal, and occipital white matter (Deprez et al., 2012) and reductions in gray matter volume of frontal and temporal brain regions have been reported (McDonald, Conroy, Ahles, West, & Saykin, 2010). These changes in both brain structure and function suggest a relationship with cognitive decline (Wigmore, 2013). Functional magnetic resonance imaging (fMRI) studies have identified alterations in brain network efficiency and brain activation in breast cancer survivors. In resting state fMRI, chemotherapy-treated breast cancer survivors displayed altered global and regional network organization compared to healthy controls, including networks that are implicated in executive control, memory, and emotion regulation (Bruno, Hosseini, & Kesler, 2012). The authors noted the disruption of large-scale functional brain networks in breast cancer survivors were similar to those reported in normal aging and is suggestive of a decrease in processing efficiency. Task-specific and generalized brain hypoactivation and decreased cerebral blood flow and metabolism have been identified in breast cancer survivors up to 10 years posttreatment (Conroy et al., 2013; de Ruiter et al., 2011). Interestingly, some studies have also revealed altered cerebral blood flow and metabolism, hyperactivation, and hyperconnectivity in breast cancer survivors during cognitive tasks, providing evidence of compensatory mechanisms that help these individuals preserve cognitive performance, potentially masking impairments (Hosseini & Kesler, 2014; Silverman et al., 2007). Different patterns of brain activation may also be suggestive of cognitive impairments that only manifest behaviorally when the difficulty of the task increases. It has been noted that hyperactivation diminishes with increasing task difficulty, and hypoactivation has primarily been identified in long-term survivors, suggesting

that compensatory processes are not sufficient to overcome impairments during greater task demands and may diminish with age (Reuter-Lorenz & Cimprich, 2013).

Potential Underlying Mechanisms of CRCI

An array of biological and psychological mechanisms that contribute to cognitive dysfunction has been proposed. The current literature suggests a complex constellation of mechanisms for CRCI that includes neurotoxicity due to treatments (e.g., radiation, chemotherapy, hormone therapy), patient characteristics (e.g., genetic predisposition, age, cognitive reserve), oxidative stress (e.g., telomere shortening, estrogen-mediated effects), psychological factors (e.g., fatigue, anxiety, depression, perceived stress), and immune dysregulation (e.g., irregular cytokine production) (Ahles, 2012; Walker, Drew, Antoon, Kalueff, & Beckman, 2012).

Although most chemotherapy agents do not readily cross the blood–brain barrier, the presence of cisplatin and paclitaxel in the brain shortly after intravenous administration of chemotherapy has been identified (Ginos et al., 1987). Even small amounts of chemotherapy are neurotoxic, and hormonal changes secondary to neurotoxicity may also affect cognition (Argyriou et al., 2011; Walker et al., 2012). Furthermore, there is evidence of a dose–response relationship, in that breast cancer survivors treated with high-dose chemotherapy have more compromised cognitive function than those treated with standard-dose chemotherapy (van Dam et al., 1998). Many chemotherapy agents achieve their therapeutic efficacy, in part, through DNA damage, reflecting another potential mechanism for cognitive decline. DNA damage is implicated in neural degeneration and the development of neurodegenerative disorders such as Alzheimer's disease and mild cognitive impairment. Higher oxidative DNA damage has been identified in breast cancer survivors compared to healthy controls both before and after chemotherapy, and higher levels were inversely associated with cognitive function and gray matter density in several brain regions (Conroy et al., 2013).

Cytokines produced in the periphery can cross the blood–brain barrier, increasing oxidative stress and neuronal damage in the brain. Elevated cytokine levels have been identified in women with breast cancer both before and during chemotherapy (Janelsins et al., 2012; Kesler et al., 2013). Changes in cognitive function due to elevated cytokine levels have been well documented, and immune dysregulation, particularly in the form of higher circulating cytokine levels, is thought to be associated with poorer executive function, spatial ability, and reaction time (Argyriou et al., 2011; Fardell, Vardy, Johnston, & Winocur, 2011; Walker et al., 2012). In women with breast cancer, higher cytokine levels were associated with reduced cognitive performance, changes in perceived cognitive function, and smaller hippocampal volume (Janelsins et al., 2012; Kesler et al., 2013). Collectively this suggests that tumor associated and/or treatment-related increases in inflammation may have neurotoxic effects.

Some evidence exists to suggest a genetic pathway to CRCI. The APOEe4 genotype is implicated in both Alzheimer's disease and cognitive impairment in healthy aging and may also predispose patients to cognitive changes as part of their cancer diagnosis and treatment (Ahles et al., 2003). Two polymorphisms in the catechol-O-methyltransferase gene, an enzyme crucial for the metabolism of catecholamine, have been identified (methionine [Met] and valine [Val]), with the Val allele resulting in greater degradation and less availability of dopamine. A recent study in breast cancer survivors and healthy controls revealed individuals with the Val allele had poorer performance on measures of attention, verbal fluency, and motor speed than those with the Met allele. Furthermore, compared to healthy controls,

chemotherapy-treated breast cancer survivors with the Val allele performed more poorly on measures of attention, suggesting those with the Val allele may be more susceptible to CRCI (Small et al., 2011). Additionally, polymorphisms have been identified in various genes involved in the function of drug transporters at the blood–brain barrier, DNA repair, cytokines, and neurotransmitters. Consequently, there are numerous potential genetic polymorphisms that may influence an individual's response to cancer treatment and subsequent risk of cognitive impairment.

Breast cancer therapies can block or lower hormonal levels and have implications for cognitive function. Over 70% of premenopausal women who receive chemotherapy experience chemotherapy-induced amenorrhea (Reyno, Levine, Skingley, Arnold, & Abu Zahra, 1993), and current guidelines recommend that all women with hormone receptor positive breast cancer should receive at least 5 years of endocrine therapy after primary treatment (Buwalda & Schagen, 2013). Estradiol is locally produced in the brain and reduces oxidative stress, attenuates telomere shortening, stimulates the production of neurotrophic factors, and enhances hippocampal neurogenesis. Ahles et al. (2010) reported that patients treated with tamoxifen performed worse on measures of processing speed, verbal memory, and verbal ability than healthy controls, but patients not treated with tamoxifen did not significantly differ from controls. Additionally, 5–10 years after chemotherapy, women who were also treated with tamoxifen had lower basal ganglia activity than those who had only received chemotherapy, suggesting endocrine therapy may decrease metabolism in certain parts of the brain (Silverman et al., 2007). Thus, women who have undergone endocrine therapy may experience a more accelerated and persistent decline in cognitive function related to the loss of many of the neuroprotective actions of estrogen.

In addition to these neurobiological mechanisms, participant baseline characteristics including age, education, and other cancer-related comorbidities such as psychological distress, fatigue, anxiety, and depression have been identified as correlates of CRCI. Many breast cancer survivors report cognitive impairment prior to any adjunctive treatment (Asher, 2011; Wefel et al., 2004). This could partially be due to any number of emotional states including anxiety, depression, stress, and potential sleep disturbance after a devastating diagnosis (Asher, 2011). Fatigue may also mediate the relationship between cancer survivorship and memory impairment; however, few studies have examined the relationship between cancer-related fatigue and neuropsychological outcomes (Asher, 2011). In addition, many cancer survivors report sustained psychophysiological stress as part of cancer diagnosis, treatment, and recovery.

There is limited understanding of the pathophysiology of CRCI; however, given emerging evidence, it is safe to assume the etiology is multifactorial and should be examined from a variety of perspectives. To develop preventive and treatment interventions, the mechanisms behind the effects of cancer treatment on cognition must be further clarified.

MEASURING COGNITIVE FUNCTION IN BREAST CANCER SURVIVORS

It has been suggested that clinical- and community-based cancer care without a focus on developing clear methods to assess and treat rehabilitation concerns (i.e., physical, cognitive, and psychosocial) in cancer survivors limits cancer recovery and quality of life (Silver, Baima, & Mayer, 2013). Despite the prevalence of CRCI and its influence on all aspects of cancer survivorship, effective treatments lag far behind. This lack of effective treatment is partially due to difficulties understanding the underlying mechanisms of CRCI and limited methods to

diagnose the presence and severity of cognitive dysfunction in cancer survivors (Jean-Pierre, Johnson-Greene, & Burish, 2014). The interaction of pre-existing physical, cognitive, and psychosocial factors with cancer and its treatment necessitates careful assessment to better identify these moderating conditions and likely trajectories of cognitive change. Such assessments can and should include screening at baseline and the measurement of physical, cognitive, and emotional function. This ensures cancer survivors have both the appropriate assessments of global cognitive function and the development of interventions to improve these functional components across the disease–treatment continuum.

The choice of appropriate neuropsychological tests is essential in evaluating presence, severity, and locus of cognitive impairments in cancer survivors, as well as how CRCI impacts global functioning and quality of life (Cheung, Tan, & Chan, 2012). These tests can also be used to monitor the clinical course of CRCI over time, develop prescriptive rehabilitation goals and interventions, and evaluate the efficacy of CRCI treatments (Jean-Pierre et al., 2014) and active assessment tools to characterize cognitive functioning in cancer survivors. Recent reviews recommend neuropsychological assessment of cognitive function in the following domains: attention, processing speed, memory, and executive function (Cheung et al., 2012; Hodgson, Hutchinson, Wilson, & Nettelbeck, 2013; Jean-Pierre, 2010). The International Cognition and Cancer Task Force recommend the use of the following neuropsychological instruments at a minimum in the assessment of cognitive function in cancer survivors: the Hopkins Verbal Learning Test-Revised, the Trail Making Test, and the Controlled Oral Word Association of the Multilingual Aphasia Examination (Wefel, Vardy, Ahles, & Schagen, 2011). The Task Force also suggests cognitive testing using instruments such as the Wechsler Adult Intelligence Scale and Stroop Color and Word Test warrant further investigation. In screening for initial cognitive impairment, it has been advised that use of the Mini-Mental State Examination be precluded due to the measure's low sensitivity in detecting cognitive impairment in cancer survivors (Meyers & Wefel, 2003). Instead, the Montreal Cognitive Assessment has been recommended for cancer survivors (Olson et al., 2011).

Instruments like the Functional Assessment of Cancer Therapy Cognitive Function scale may also be of utility in gauging cancer survivors' subjective perception of cognitive impairment (Wagner, Sweet, Butt, Lai, & Cella, 2009). However, self-report measures of cognitive function may be more often related to self-reported depression, anxiety, and fatigue than objective cognitive function (Pullens et al., 2010). Research evidence linking the subjective experience of cognitive impairment and objective measures of the phenomenon, including objective cognitive testing and neuroimaging, remain equivocal (Cheung et al., 2012; Pullens et al., 2010). Indeed, a recent meta-analysis (Crumley, Stetler, & Horhota, 2014) suggests the relationship between measures of subjective and objective measures of cognitive function, although reliably different from zero, is very small (r = 0.062). However, Ganz et al. suggest about one in five postadjuvant treatment breast cancer survivors had subjective memory and/or executive function complaints, which are significantly associated with both domain-specific neuropsychological test performances and depressive symptoms (Ganz et al., 2013). In addition, combined chemotherapy and radiation treatments were also significantly associated with subjective memory complaints. These results suggest subjective cognitive complaints in part reflect objective cognitive performance.

At present, there are no "gold standard" measures of CRCI. However, both neuropsychological assessments and self-reported indices of cognitive impairment provide important, independent information relative to CRCI. Nelson and Suls (2013) suggest objective neuropsychological measures and subjective participant-reported measures of cognitive function be used in combination, plus the inclusion of functional measurements. Edelstein and Bernstein (2014) recommend that a thorough cognitive evaluation should include, "an interview documenting change in functional status, self-report and family rating measures, and tests of performance that emphasize attention, memory, processing speed, and executive functions" (Edelstein & Bernstein, 2014, p. 353). This combined assessment approach can be used to identify risk factors that contribute to CRCI, the functional implications of these impairments, and treatments that may prevent or alleviate these cognitive symptoms in cancer survivors throughout the treatment and recovery continuum.

In addition to objective neuropsychological testing and patient-reported outcomes, there is an emerging role for the translational addition of structural and functional imaging for the assessment of CRCI, inclusive of the neural circuitry underlying cognitive problems related to breast cancer (de Ruiter & Schagen, 2013). This includes: "a) delineating components of cognitive function and underlying neural processes most affected by cancer and its treatment, b) uncovering compensatory processes and their limits, c) identifying altered resting state networks that may relate to subjective complaints and longer term outcomes, and d) clarifying relationships between pre-treatment alterations in brain activity and longer term neural and behavioral outcomes" (Reuter-Lorenz, & Cimprich, 2013, p. 33). The use of these modalities will allow for better understanding of the neurocognitive effects of breast cancer, its treatment, and associated comorbidities.

The Intersection Between Cancer, Aging, and Physical Function

Approximately 40% of all new breast cancer cases are diagnosed in women aged 65 and older (DeSantis et al., 2014). Physiological functioning deteriorates with age, though this rate of decline varies significantly based on genetic, lifestyle, and environmental factors (Leon, 2012). In this capacity, it has been hypothesized that cancer and aging are linked via common underlying biological pathways and that cancer and its treatment may accelerate physical and cognitive aging (Ahles, 2012; Edelstein & Bernstein, 2014; Mandelblatt et al., 2013; Schwartz & Winters-Stone, 2013). Specifically, changes in cognition associated with cancer treatment may parallel age-related cognitive declines, but occur significantly earlier for cancer survivors than for healthy individuals of a similar age (Merriman, Von Ah, Miaskowski, & Aouizerat, 2013). For example, similar brain structure and function changes in women with breast cancer have been demonstrated in studies of healthy older adults, including decreases in total brain volume, gray matter, white matter connectivity, and hippocampal volume. In one study, total gray matter volume difference between chemotherapy-treated breast cancer survivors (mean years posttreatment = 21) and age-matched controls was similar to losses seen in 4 years of aging (Koppelmans et al., 2014). Additionally, there is evidence of changes in cognitive function and brain function in cancer patients before any treatment. Brain activation patterns in middle-aged breast cancer survivors prior to chemotherapy were similar to activation patterns seen in healthy, older (65–75 years) individuals (Cimprich et al., 2010). Together, these findings may reflect underlying common etiologies for both cancer occurrence and cognitive function not attributable to cancer treatment alone.

Relative to the intersection of CRCI and aging, three interrelated hypotheses have been proposed (Mandelblatt et al., 2013). The first suggests that cancer therapy-induced dysfunction parallels normal aging (i.e., the phase shift hypothesis). The second proposes this trajectory is more pronounced than normal aging (i.e., accelerated aging). Finally, the depletion of cognitive reserve leads to frailty in those who have had a cancer experience (i.e., reliability theory of aging). Frailty is an age-related syndrome described as a net impairment in functioning across multiple physiological systems, leading to the decreased ability of an organism to respond to stressors and an accompanying increased susceptibility to allostatic load and adverse health outcomes (Bherer, Erickson, & Liu-Ambrose, 2013; Mandelblatt et al., 2013; Merriman et al., 2013; Robertson, Savva, & Kenny, 2013). Relations among age and physical and cognitive function lead to a matrix in which those who are younger, fitter, and have higher cognitive reserve may experience greater preservation of cognitive function than those who are older, less fit, and have limited cognitive reserve. Thus, a similar change in brain resources can have a minimal effect on cognitive performance in a young adult, a moderate effect in an older adult with high cognitive reserve, and a greater effect on an older adult with low cognitive reserve. Indeed, older breast cancer survivors with lower baseline cognitive reserve were at higher risk of decline in processing speed from chemotherapy (Ahles et al., 2010). For older cancer survivors, this leads to a "double jeopardy," as they are already at risk for age-related cognitive impairment (McDougall, Oliver, & Scogin, 2014).

Of particular interest is whether declines in physical function mediate changes in cognitive function. Older cancer survivors experience a higher prevalence of functional limitations, frailty, and geriatric syndromes including dementia, depression, osteoporosis, and falls than older adults without cancer (Mohile et al., 2011). Cancer and cancer treatment may accelerate declines in aspects of physical condition that have established relationships with cognitive function such as physical activity and cardiorespiratory fitness. Sweeney et al. (2006) reported that elderly, female, 5-year cancer survivors had greater prevalence of self-reported physical function limitations than age-matched controls, suggesting the long-term effects of cancer treatment can result in long-term functional limitations. Additionally, these limitations were reported in the ability to do heavy housework, walk up and down stairs, and walk half a mile (Sweeney et al., 2006). Thus, cancer-related functional limitations may impact an individual's ability to remain physically active. Indeed, significant reductions in physical activity after breast cancer diagnosis have been reported (Irwin et al., 2003; Kwan et al., 2012). Littman, Tang, and Rossing (2010) have demonstrated that physical activity levels decrease by almost 50% in the first 12 months postdiagnosis and remain below prediagnosis levels 19–30 months postdiagnosis. Chemotherapeutic agents are associated with short- and long-term cardiac complications; radiotherapy can result in cardiopulmonary damage, and HER-2-directed therapies (e.g., Herceptin) are associated with cardiac toxicity and risk of heart failure. Subsequently, cancer management can be responsible for multiple insults to cardiovascular function (Jones, Haykowsky, Swartz, Douglas, & Mackey, 2007). Jones et al. (2012) identified significant impairments in cardiopulmonary function of breast cancer survivors over the continuum of the disease (Jones et al., 2012). Across the breast cancer trajectory (i.e., before, during, and after treatment), peak volume of oxygen uptake ($\dot{V}O_2$ peak) averaged 27% lower than that of age-matched, sedentary women with no history of breast cancer, suggesting that cancer and cancer therapy may significantly accelerate age-related declines in cardiopulmonary function (Jones et al., 2012).

Frailty and cognitive impairment share associated risk factors in breast cancer survivors and can include impaired cardiovascular health and other physiological insults and treatment-related behavioral changes. These include reduced physical activity, which may result in further frailty and potentially resultant cognitive impairment. Importantly, there is some evidence that frailty may be an early indicator of cognitive decline, independent of baseline cognitive function (Robertson et al., 2013), and a clinically useful marker of risk for cognitive decline after cancer and its treatments (Mandelblatt et al., 2013).

PHYSICAL ACTIVITY AND COGNITIVE FUNCTION IN BREAST CANCER SURVIVORS

Physical activity can be defined as any movement of the body resulting in increased energy expenditure and encompasses all bodily movements, from sports to activities of daily living (American College of Sports Medicine, 2013; Caspersen, Powell, & Christenson, 1985). The American College of Sports Medicine (ACSM) suggests cancer survivors, regardless of where they are in the treatment continuum, should avoid inactivity and that any level of physical activity carries with it some benefit. The sooner cancer survivors maintain, re-establish, or improve upon prediagnosis physical activity within their cancer experience, the more likely they are to report improved treatment and health outcomes (Schmitz et al., 2010). However, the majority of breast cancer survivors do not meet physical activity recommendations, either prediagnosis or throughout the survivorship continuum (Courneya, Katzmarzyk, & Bacon, 2008; Mason et al., 2013). Some findings have suggested breast cancer survivors spend less than 2% of their day engaged in moderate-to-vigorous physical activity and almost 80% of their time engaged in sedentary activity (Sabiston, Brunet, Vallance, & Meterissian, 2014). Importantly, both pre- and postdiagnosis higher physical activity are associated with better prognosis and reduced breast cancer-specific and all-cause mortality (Irwin et al., 2003; Zhong et al., 2014).

A recent study reported fatigued breast cancer survivors to experience greater cognitive dysfunction, less total daytime physical activity, and lower subjective mood and quality of life than their nonfatigued counterparts (Minton & Stone, 2012).

Bherer et al. (2013) suggest sedentary behavior is a major risk factor for frailty in older adults and that physical activity is a significant moderator of age-related cognitive decline (Bherer et al., 2013). Specifically, older adults who participate in more physical activity over time are less likely to become frail and show less cognitive decline, suggesting physical activity may be protective against the deleterious effects of age on health and cognition. In older adult cancer survivors who were undergoing or had completed chemotherapy, those who increased physical activity also reported improved cognitive health and quality of life over time (Fitzpatrick, Edgar, & Holcroft, 2012). In older adults, objectively- measured total daily physical activity has been positively associated with global measures of cognition (Buchman, Wilson, & Bennett, 2008) and shorter response times during a working memory task in comparison with older adults with lower physical activity levels (Chang, Huang, Chen, & Hung, 2013). A cross-sectional study by Hillman et al. (2006) also suggests that across the aging continuum those with higher physical activity had faster reaction times in general and better accuracy during inhibition task with greater cognitive load (Hillman et al., 2006). In a sample of older Latinos, higher light, moderate–vigorous, and total daily physical activity counts were associated with higher levels of verbal fluency (Wilbur et al., 2012). Other findings suggest a dose–response association between moderate-to-vigorous physical activity intensity and cognitive functioning in older adults. Specifically, moderate-to-vigorous physical activity was associated with 20% greater processing speed during executive function tasks and reduced age-related decline in processing during a cognitive flexibility task (Kerr et al., 2013; Kimura, Yasunaga, & Wang, 2013). These effects appear to be stronger for tasks that require extensive amounts of executive control (McAuley, Mullen, & Hillman, 2013). In sum, in addition to the physical health benefits of engaging in regular physical activity for cancer survivors, the emerging literature at the intersection between cancer and aging highlight these benefits on cognitive function.

CARDIORESPIRATORY FITNESS AND COGNITIVE FUNCTION

One of the most important moderators of CRCI in breast cancer survivors may be cardiorespiratory fitness. Clinical research suggests cancer diagnosis and treatment are associated with cardiovascular injury and decreased cardiorespiratory fitness across the survivorship continuum. This course of events accelerates the aging process among breast cancer survivors resulting in many women with fitness levels equivalent to women 10–30 years older without a history of breast cancer (Jones et al., 2012; Lakoski et al., 2013; Peel, Thomas, Dittus, Jones, & Lakoski, 2014). In turn, cardiorespiratory fitness is a key predictor of cardiovascular disease risk and premature morbidity and mortality in breast cancer survivors in comparison with the general population (Jones et al., 2012). These associations between cancer, cardiorespiratory fitness impairment, and premature age-related declines has been labeled the "multiple-hit" hypothesis by Jones et al. (2007) and point to an accelerated aging process among breast cancer survivors that can negatively affect cardiorespiratory fitness and potentially prognosis (Jones et al., 2007; Peel et al., 2014).

There is evidence to support cardiorespiratory fitness as both a moderator of age-related cognitive function and supportive brain structures (Colcombe, Kramer, McAuley, Erickson, & Scalf, 2004) and a potential mediating mechanism of exercise training effects on cognition and brain health (e.g., Erickson et al., 2011). Cardiorespiratory fitness has been associated with preservation of cognitive function in older adults, and improving cardiorespiratory fitness helps to improve age-related effects on brain structure and cognitive function. Higher fitness levels in older adults have been associated with preventing age-related brain tissue loss, more efficient brain processing, and better behavioral performance during cognitive tasks that involve higher-level executive control (Gomez-Pinilla & Hillman, 2013; Prakash et al., 2011; Szabo et al., 2011). These improvements in executive control processes may be further related to increased fitness-related functioning of the attentional network in the brain, including the prefrontal, parietal, and anterior cingulate cortices involved in spatial selection, inhibitory functioning, and conflict monitoring (Colcombe, Kramer, Erickson, et al., 2004). Higher levels of aerobic fitness are also associated with greater hippocampal volume, which is related to better spatial working memory function (Erickson et al., 2009, 2011; Szabo et al., 2011). In addition, significant age-related deficits in functional connectivity in the default mode network can be partially mitigated by aerobic fitness level (Voss et al., 2010).

As noted earlier, understanding the effects of breast cancer treatment on cognitive impairment may best be done from the perspective of accelerated aging in breast cancer survivors due to treatment. Jones et al. (2012) provide compelling data to suggest the effects of normal aging on cardiorespiratory fitness in breast cancer survivors are exacerbated by cancer treatments. Such a process has considerable implications for this population in terms of cardiovascular disease (Jones, 2010) and all-cause mortality (Jones, Eves, Haykowsky, Joy, & Douglas, 2008). In their secondary analysis of data, they compared four groups of women (N=248): prior to, during, and after adjuvant therapy for nonmetastatic disease, and a group during therapy for advanced metastatic disease. Maximal graded exercise testing indicated that, as a whole, the sample had cardiorespiratory fitness levels 27% below age and sex predicted values. In 32% of the sample, $\dot{V}O_2$ peak was below the minimal aerobic capacity for functional independence (Paterson, Cunningham, Koval, & St Croix, 1999). Fitness values were significantly lower in the metastatic

group and adjuvant therapy group relative to the after therapy group. Comparison of the breast cancer survivors with age-matched controls revealed an interesting pattern of decline in cardiorespiratory fitness. There were large and significant differences between these two groups at each age category: 34% less at age 40; 30% less at age 50; 25% less at age 60; and 17% less at age 70. Examination of overall mean level data suggested a 40-year-old breast cancer survivor to have similar levels of fitness as a 70-year-old healthy, sedentary woman. Although cross-sectional, these data are suggestive of the importance of cardiorespiratory fitness testing in this population. Additionally, if fitness is associated with cognitive declines and brain structure independent of normal aging, then exercise training interventions represent lifestyle mechanisms for the enhancement of fitness and remediation of cancer-related cognitive dysfunction and degradations to brain structure.

An emerging area of interest in measuring cardiovascular fitness in breast cancer survivors is heart rate variability (HRV). Briefly, the autonomic nervous system is the most prominent physiological factor in determining heart functions and is comprised of both parasympathetic and sympathetic input (Thayer, Åhs, Fredrikson, Sollers, & Wager, 2012). The amount of input received from each is examined through the study of HRV, the complex beat-to-beat variation in heart rate produced by the interplay of sympathetic and parasympathetic neural activity (Task Force of the European Society of Cardiology and the North American Society of Pacing and Electrophysiology, 1996). In general, the heart is under tonic inhibitory control by parasympathetic dominance over sympathetic influences, and higher resting HRV, characterized by parasympathetic predominance, is associated with positive health outcomes (Acharya, Joseph, Kannathal, Lim, & Suri, 2006; Thayer et al., 2012).

HRV declines as people age (De Meersman & Stein, 2007), and in cancer settings, decrements in autonomic nervous system function have been associated with both short- and long-term cardiovascular complications (Hansen, Rosenberg, & Gögenur, 2013; Scott et al., 2014). In addition, lower HRV has been implicated in an increased risk of depression in metastatic breast cancer patients (Giese-Davis et al., 2006), cancer-related fatigue in breast cancer survivors (Crosswell, Lockwood, Ganz, & Bower, 2014; Fagundes et al., 2011), increased nausea postchemotherapy (Morrow, Hickok, DuBeshter, & Lipshultz, 1999), increased cancer cachexia (Chauhan et al., 2012), and shortened survival time in cancer patients with advanced cancer (Stone, Kenny, Nolan, & Lawlor, 2012). Conversely, higher HRV is associated with higher levels of cardiorespiratory fitness, which is protective against the decline in parasympathetic control of heart rate associated with normal aging (De Meersman & Stein, 2007). Exercise has been associated with higher HRV in cancer survivors, and improved autonomic function and quality of life have been implicated in longer survival times (Niederer et al., 2012). Physically fit individuals who have higher levels of cardiorespiratory fitness and HRV also exhibit better performance on sustained attention and executive function tasks (Hansen, Johnsen, Sollers, Stenvik, & Thayer, 2004; Luque-Casado, Zabala, Morales, Mateo-March, & Sanabria, 2013). In older adults, a 12-week aerobic exercise intervention increased HRV parameters and improved performance on an executive function task (Albinet, Boucard, Bouquet, & Audiffren, 2010). The use of HRV as a clinical marker of cardiac-related autonomic activity provides an additional tool to investigate cardiovascular fitness in cancer survivors and its relation to cognitive function.

Further related to HRV is heart rate recovery, the rate at which the heart rate decreases following exercise completion. The ability of the heart to recover post-exercise serves as an additional indicator of cardiac autonomic activity and involves a complex interaction between initial parasympathetic reactivation and subsequent sympathetic withdrawal (Borresen & Lambert, 2008; Peçanha, Silva-Júnior, & Forjaz, 2014). Although optimal heart rate recovery declines with aging, impaired heart rate recovery has been related to increased morbidity and mortality risk (Carnethon et al., 2012; Peçanha et al., 2014) and impaired cognitive function in older adults (Keary et al., 2012). In contrast, older adults with higher cardiorespiratory fitness had faster heart rate recovery postexercise and performed significantly better on a memory task than those with poor heart rate recovery (Pearman & Lachman, 2010). Improving cardiorespiratory fitness via exercise training leads to improved heart rate recovery and improved all-cause mortality (Jolly, Brennan, & Cho, 2011).

EXERCISE TRAINING EFFECTS ON COGNITIVE FUNCTION AND BRAIN HEALTH

In cancer survivors, many age-related physical and functional declines can be mitigated with exercise training (Schwartz & Winters-Stone, 2013), and there is a growing interest in developing exercise interventions specifically to ameliorate cancer's destructive role in patient's overall quality of life. In general, exercise engenders a multitude of health benefits for breast cancer survivors (Schmitz et al., 2010), including improvements in cardiorespiratory function, body composition, strength, and patient-reported outcomes (Battaglini et al., 2014). In intervention studies, regardless of intervention specifics, exercise has been shown to improve a variety of quality of life, psychosocial, and health outcomes in various cancer survivor groups both during and after cancer treatment, and may also help to manage long-term effects of treatment (Spence, Heesch, & Brown, 2010). Evidence suggests exercise may also speed recovery, reduce the risk of cancer recurrence and the development of other chronic illnesses, and increase overall survival as compared to survivors who are physically inactive (Barbaric, Brooks, Moore, & Cheifetz, 2010; Speed-Andrews & Courneya, 2009).

A growing body of research suggests exercise training is an effective way to maintain and enhance cognition and slow age-related cognitive declines in older adults, and that starting an exercise training regimen, even later in life, enhances cognitive performance (Chan, Yan, & Payne, 2013; Erickson & Kramer, 2009; Erickson et al., 2011). Exercise training may improve cognition both directly and indirectly by influencing structural and functional aspects of brain activity, reducing distress, improving health behaviors, and lessening symptoms of age-related and chronic disease (Bherer et al., 2013). Exercise training increases the number of new cells in the hippocampus (i.e., neurogenesis), increases the amount of capillaries (i.e., angiogenesis), and changes the production and secretion of several neurotrophic factors and neurotransmitters (i.e., neuroplasticity). Cognitive benefits derived from exercise training may be a function of enhanced connectivity between brain regions and improved efficiency of preparatory states (Erickson, Miller, Weinstein, Akl, & Banducci, 2012). Additional hypothesized mechanisms include enhanced blood flow and oxygenation to the brain and reduced oxidative stress and cytokine levels (Evens & Eschiti, 2009).

Importantly, the effects of aerobic exercise might even be greater in cognitively impaired populations, such as those with CRCI (Erickson et al., 2012). Exercise training may improve neurophysiological mechanisms affected by cancer and its treatment, including cell proliferation and survival in the hippocampus, white matter integrity, blood flow and neurotransmitter regulation, neuro- and cardiac toxicities, bone loss, fatigue, sleep disruption, anxiety and depression, as well as improving overall physiological function and body composition (Gehring, Roukema, & Sitskoorn, 2012; Janelsins et al., 2011). If, as hypothesized, cancer treatment leads to accelerated aging and frailty, inclusive of cognitive impairment, then interventions to reduce frailty in cancer survivors may be targeted with the goal of preventing or even reversing further cognitive decline (Robertson et al., 2013). For example, Langlois et al. investigated the benefits of exercise training on cognition and quality of life in frail older adults (Langlois et al., 2013). Compared with controls, the exercise training group showed significant improvement in physical capacity, cognitive performance, and quality of life and these benefits were equivalent between both frail and nonfrail participants.

Whereas the body of research indicating beneficial effects of exercise training on cognitive function in older adults has continued to emerge over the past decade, equivalent research in the area of CRCI lags behind. However, preliminary findings are promising. For example, in a longitudinal study, patients on chemotherapy or having completed chemotherapy who increased their exercise activities had improved cognitive health and quality of life over 6 weeks (Fitzpatrick et al., 2012). Cancer patients who exercised during treatment reported less memory loss, fatigue, and better self-rated health (Sprod et al., 2012), and described returning to exercise following cancer treatment as beneficial to cognitive function (Myers, 2012). Other findings suggest participation in a 10-week taijiquan program resulted in improved neuropsychological and physical functioning in a sample of female cancer survivors (Reid-Arndt, Matsuda, & Cox, 2012). Breast cancer survivors enrolled in a 12-week yoga intervention also demonstrated improvements in varying domains of cognition through chemotherapy treatment and at 1- and 3-month follow-ups (Galantino et al., 2012). Patients who participated in a medical qigong program reported improved cognitive function and quality of life and exhibited reduced inflammation levels, as measured by C-reactive protein, compared to controls (Oh et al., 2012). In addition, significant cognitive improvements were evident in breast cancer survivors after participating in 12 weeks of resistance training (Baumann et al., 2011). Despite these reported benefits, a recent study by Crowgey et al. (2013) suggested that while breast cancer survivors engaged in significantly less objectively- measured weekly physical activity and had lower cardiorespiratory fitness than noncancer controls, both groups demonstrated comparable cognitive performance on a standardized cognitive testing battery, and physical activity and cardiorespiratory fitness were weakly to moderately correlated to the majority of cognitive scores (Crowgey et al., 2013).

FUTURE DIRECTIONS

There is currently no recognized physical activity or exercise training regimen designed specifically for the amelioration of CRCI in breast cancer survivors. The dose–response relationship between physical activity, exercise training, cardiorespiratory fitness, and cognitive functioning needs to be further explored and public health recommendations established (Albinet et al., 2010; Bherer et al., 2013; Colcombe & Kramer, 2003; DeFina et al., 2013). In addition, more comprehensive studies inclusive of objective measures of physical activity, cardiorespiratory fitness, brain structure and function, and cognitive performance are warranted to determine underlying mechanisms for the protective effects of physical activity and fitness on cognitive function in breast cancer survivors and to explore the potential for therapeutic improvement (Keary et al., 2012). Although recommendations suggest cardiorespiratory fitness be assessed via standardized maximal exercise testing and norms developed (Peel et al., 2014), additional indices of cardiac autonomic tone, including resting HRV and heart rate recovery, will also be of importance in determining whether cardiac autonomic improvements moderate both physical health and cognitive function in addition to and independent of physical activity and cardiorespiratory fitness. However, as with assessment of cardiorespiratory fitness, these indices also need to be standardized in their assessment, and normative values and clinical cut-points established. As noted earlier, the adoption and standardization of neuropsychological measures sensitive to CRCI in breast cancer survivors is an important endeavor essential to both effective screening and monitoring of the cognitive effects of cancer and its treatment (Jean-Pierre et al., 2014).

As the breast cancer population is heterogeneous in terms of age, cancer stage, treatment, and a host of genetic, lifestyle, and environmental covariates, large sample sizes or more targeted research is required that examines the independent effects of these factors (Scherling, Collins, Mackenzie, Bielajew, & Smith, 2011). Understanding these individual and treatment-related associations will increase insight into risks for differential age-related cognitive declines. Given changes in cognitive function across the survivorship continuum, when possible, baseline fitness and cognitive assessments are essential in determining when physical and cognitive impairments occur above and beyond baseline functioning. For example, it will be important to determine whether chemotherapy or other adjuvant treatments independently predict CRCI or whether cancer and its treatment merely exacerbate existing cognitive deficits. In addition, given the breadth of constituent elements that comprise cognitive function, further studies are required to deconstruct which elements of cognitive function are most affected in breast cancer survivors and how physical activity and exercise training may differentially affect these constituent elements (McDonald, Conroy, Ahles, West, & Saykin, 2012; Szabo et al., 2011). Research in the area of accelerated aging, frailty and the multiple-hit hypothesis suggest commonalities in the associations between cancer treatment, physiological decrements, and the aging process.

More work on the predictive value of these theories is warranted and will be useful in identifying those at risk of preventable cognitive decline (Ahles, 2012; Jones et al., 2007; Maccormick, 2006; Mandelblatt et al., 2013; Robertson et al., 2013). If these interrelated mechanisms are shown to lead to cognitive impairment, then interventions can be targeted toward vulnerable breast cancer survivors with the aim of preventing or even reversing further physical and cognitive decline.

In sum, CRCI is a recognizable syndrome with potentially long-term consequences that can effect multiple elements of function in cancer survivors, including overall health-related quality of life. Very little is known about this condition, its mechanisms, and assessment. Subsequently, CRCI has proven difficult to treat due to a lack of understanding of the precise etiology of the syndrome, as well as a lack of consensus on appropriate neuropsychological assessment protocols (Jean-Pierre, 2010). Research recommendations from the International Cognition and Cancer Task Force include: utilization of disease-specific and healthy control groups, broad study inclusion criteria, use of clinical significance indices, longitudinal and intervention studies that incorporate prechemotherapy assessments; a brief standardized test battery shown to be sensitive to cognitive changes after chemotherapy; control variables that account for physical and psychosocial factors; multilevel modeling approaches; and multidisciplinary collaborative studies given the complex etiology and therefore treatment of CRCI (Wefel et al., 2011). These recommendations are aimed at improving research designs to allow more accurate estimates of incidence, severity, risk factors, causes, and treatment of cognitive impairment in cancer survivors. Studies utilizing these recommendations are required not only to examine the interconnected mechanisms by which cancer affects cognition but also the development and evaluation of comprehensive, multidisciplinary, empirically- based, and theoretically-driven interventions that will serve to treat CRCI as an important sequelae of cancer and its treatment.

CLINICAL RECOMMENDATIONS

Whereas exercise training benefits cognitive health in breast cancer survivors and older adults, a preferred modality has yet to be endorsed by the scientific community. The majority of exercise training interventions have focused on aerobic activity. Other exercise modalities (e.g., strength training, yoga) have proven to be well tolerated by older adults, and may improve cognitive functioning (Gregory, Gill, & Petrella, 2013; Gothe, Kramer, & McAuley, 2014). In addition, more general exercise guidelines for cancer survivors (Schmitz et al., 2010) concluded exercise is safe both during and after cancer treatments, and leads to improvements in quality of life, physical functioning, and cancer-related fatigue in several cancer survivor groups. In older adults, exercise comprising both aerobic and resistance components is generally recommended as a means of improving physical health while ameliorating cognitive declines (Chan et al., 2013). Additionally, randomized controlled trials have found moderate-intensity, twice-weekly resistance training can significantly improve cognitive function and brain plasticity in both healthy older adults and those with mild cognitive impairments (Liu-Ambrose & Nagamatsu, 2013). These findings reinforce ACSM Guidelines for Cancer Survivors (Schmitz et al., 2010), which suggest an overall weekly activity volume of 150 min of moderate-intensity exercise, or 75 min of vigorous-intensity exercise, or an equivalent combination. An acceptable strength training prescription is to perform two to three weekly resistance training sessions including exercises for all major muscle groups. Flexibility guidelines suggest stretching on days other exercises are performed. These recommendations are not dissimilar from general population guidelines and have been shown to be associated with a variety of health outcomes (Garber et al., 2011). Thus, clinicians should consider encouraging breast cancer survivors to undertake both aerobic and resistance exercise training for both physical and cognitive health.

It is clear that one size of exercise prescription does not fit all and cancer-specific exercise guidelines acknowledge that exercise programs must be adapted for individual patient needs on the basis of their health status, treatments, and anticipated disease trajectory (Hudis & Jones, 2014; Schmitz et al., 2010). As such, individual needs must be clearly defined in order for appropriate goals to be formulated, taking into account the individual's current abilities, past exercise experience, and comorbid conditions to best tailor the exercise intervention program (Hacker, 2009). Reaching this level of complexity in exercise prescription will be contingent on state-of-science knowledge of cancer etiology and treatment as well as clinical exercise physiology and behavioral health interventions. Until the optimal dosage of physical activity for breast cancer survivors experiencing CRCI can be identified, the ACSM recommendations serve as a strong basis for the prescription of physical activity and exercise training. In maintaining any physical activity and exercise training regimen, the "by-product" will always be reduced frailty, inclusive of improved physical and cognitive function, regardless of intervention specifics. Developing these training guidelines are especially important given the rate at which our population is aging, the increased rate of breast cancer diagnosis as one ages, the accompanying risks for other comorbid conditions, and the chronicity of the breast cancer experience as a whole (Mandelblatt et al., 2013; Schwartz & Winters-Stone, 2013).

In conclusion, the current review suggests a subset of breast cancer survivors experience CRCI, that the associations between cognition and aging in this population may be exacerbated by cancer and its treatment leading to accelerated aging and age-related cognitive decline.

Additionally, being physically active with higher cardiorespiratory fitness may serve a protective function for cognitive and physical function over time. Similarly, beginning or increasing physical activity and exercise training could be protective for lowering both physical degradation and cognitive decline in breast cancer survivors.

References

Acharya, U. R., Joseph, K. P., Kannathal, N., Lim, C. M., & Suri, J. S. (2006). Heart rate variability: a review. *Medical and Biological Engineering and Computing, 44*, 1031–1051.

Ahles, T. A. (2012). Brain vulnerability to chemotherapy toxicities. *Psycho-Oncology, 21*, 1141–1148.

Ahles, T. A., & Saykin, A. (2001). Cognitive effects of standard-dose chemotherapy in patients with cancer. *Cancer Investigation, 19*, 812–820.

Ahles, T. A., Saykin, A. J., McDonald, B. C., Li, Y., Furstenberg, C. T., Hanscom, B. S., et al. (2010). Longitudinal assessment of cognitive changes associated with adjuvant treatment for breast cancer: impact of age and cognitive reserve. *Journal of Clinical Oncology, 28*, 4434–4440.

Ahles, T. A., Saykin, A. J., Noll, W. W., Furstenberg, C. T., Guerin, S., Cole, B., et al. (2003). The relationship of APOE genotype to neuropsychological performance in long–term cancer survivors treated with standard dose chemotherapy. *Psycho-Oncology, 12*, 612–619.

Albinet, C. T., Boucard, G., Bouquet, C. A., & Audiffren, M. (2010). Increased heart rate variability and executive performance after aerobic training in the elderly. *European Journal of Applied Physiology, 109*, 617–624.

American College of Sports Medicine. (2013). *ACSM's guidelines for exercise testing and prescription*. Philadelphia: Lippincott, Williams & Wilkins.

Argyriou, A. A., Assimakopoulos, K., Iconomou, G., Giannakopoulou, F., & Kalofonos, H. P. (2011). Either called "chemobrain" or "chemofog," the long-term chemotherapy-induced cognitive decline in cancer survivors is real. *Journal of Pain and Symptom Management, 41*, 126–139.

Asher, A. (2011). Cognitive dysfunction among cancer survivors. *American Journal of Physical Medicine and Rehabilitation/Association of Academic Physiatrists, 90*, S16–S26.

Barbaric, M., Brooks, E., Moore, L., & Cheifetz, O. (2010). Effects of physical activity on cancer survival: a systematic review. *Physiotherapy Canada, 62*, 25–34.

Battaglini, C. L., Mills, R. C., Phillips, B. L., Lee, J. T., Story, C. E., Nascimento, M. G., et al. (2014). Twenty-five years of research on the effects of exercise training in breast cancer survivors: a systematic review of the literature. *World Journal of Clinical Oncology, 5*, 177.

Baumann, F. T., Drosselmeyer, N., Leskaroski, A., Knicker, A., Krakowski-Roosen, H., Zopf, E. M., et al. (2011). 12-week resistance training with breast cancer patients during chemotherapy: effects on cognitive abilities. *Breast Care, 6*, 142–143.

Bherer, L., Erickson, K. I., & Liu-Ambrose, T. (2013). A review of the effects of physical activity and exercise on cognitive and brain functions in older adults. *Journal of Aging Research, 2013*, 657508.

Borresen, J., & Lambert, M. I. (2008). Autonomic control of heart rate during and after exercise. *Sports Medicine, 38*, 633–646.

Bruno, J., Hosseini, S., & Kesler, S. (2012). Altered resting state functional brain network topology in chemotherapy-treated breast cancer survivors. *Neurobiology of Disease, 48*, 329–338.

Buchman, A. S., Wilson, R. S., & Bennett, D. A. (2008). Total daily activity is associated with cognition in older persons. *The American Journal of Geriatric Psychiatry, 16*, 697–701.

Buwalda, B., & Schagen, S. B. (2013). Is basic research providing answers if adjuvant anti-estrogen treatment of breast cancer can induce cognitive impairment? *Life Sciences, 93*, 581–588.

Carnethon, M. R., Sternfeld, B., Liu, K., Jacobs, D. R., Jr., Schreiner, P. J., Williams, O. D., et al. (2012). Correlates of heart rate recovery over 20 years in a healthy population sample. *Medicine and Science in Sports and Exercise, 44*, 273–279.

Caspersen, C. J., Powell, K. E., & Christenson, G. M. (1985). Physical activity, exercise, and physical fitness: definitions and distinctions for health-related research. *Public Health Reports (Washington, D.C.: 1974), 100*, 126–131.

Chang, Y., Huang, C., Chen, K., & Hung, T. (2013). Physical activity and working memory in healthy older adults: an ERP study. *Psychophysiology, 50*, 1174–1182.

Chan, J. S., Yan, J. H., & Payne, V. G. (2013). The impact of obesity and exercise on cognitive aging. *Frontiers in Aging Neuroscience, 5*. http://dx.doi.org/10.3389/fnagi.2013.00097.

Chauhan, A., Sequeria, A., Manderson, C., Maddocks, M., Wasley, D., & Wilcock, A. (2012). Exploring autonomic nervous system dysfunction in patients with cancer cachexia: a pilot study. *Autonomic Neuroscience, 166*, 93–95.

Cheung, Y. T., Tan, E. H., & Chan, A. (2012). An evaluation on the neuropsychological tests used in the assessment of postchemotherapy cognitive changes in breast cancer survivors. *Supportive Care in Cancer, 20*, 1361–1375.

Cimprich, B., Reuter-Lorenz, P., Nelson, J., Clark, P. M., Therrien, B., Normolle, D., et al. (2010). Prechemotherapy alterations in brain function in women with breast cancer. *Journal of Clinical and Experimental Neuropsychology, 32*, 324–331.

Colcombe, S., & Kramer, A. F. (2003). Fitness effects on the cognitive function of older adults: a meta-analytic study. *Psychological Science, 14*, 125–130.

Colcombe, S. J., Kramer, A. F., Erickson, K. I., Scalf, P., McAuley, E., Cohen, N. J., et al. (2004). Cardiovascular fitness, cortical plasticity, and aging. *Proceedings of the National Academy of Sciences of the United States of America, 101*, 3316–3321.

Colcombe, S. J., Kramer, A. F., McAuley, E., Erickson, K. I., & Scalf, P. (2004). Neurocognitive aging and cardiovascular fitness. *Journal of Molecular Neuroscience, 24*, 9–14.

Conroy, S. K., McDonald, B. C., Smith, D. J., Moser, L. R., West, J. D., Kamendulis, L. M., et al. (2013). Alterations in brain structure and function in breast cancer survivors: effect of post-chemotherapy interval and relation to oxidative DNA damage. *Breast Cancer Research and Treatment, 137*, 493–502.

Courneya, K. S., Katzmarzyk, P. T., & Bacon, E. (2008). Physical activity and obesity in Canadian cancer survivors. *Cancer, 112*, 2475–2482.

Crosswell, A. D., Lockwood, K. G., Ganz, P. A., & Bower, J. E. (2014). Low heart rate variability and cancer-related fatigue in breast cancer survivors. *Psychoneuroendocrinology, 45*, 58–66.

Crowgey, T., Peters, K. B., Hornsby, W. E., Lane, A., McSherry, F., Herndon, J. E., et al. (2013). Relationship between exercise behavior, cardiorespiratory fitness, and cognitive function in early breast cancer patients treated with doxorubicin-containing chemotherapy: a pilot study 1. *Applied Physiology, Nutrition, Metabolism, 39*, 724–729.

Crumley, J. J., Stetler, C. A., & Horhota, M. (2014). Examining the relationship between subjective and objective memory performance in older adults: a meta-analysis. *Psychology and Aging, 29*, 250.

van Dam, F. S., Schagen, S. B., Muller, M. J., Boogerd, W., vd Wall, E., Droogleever Fortuyn, M. E., et al. (1998). Impairment of cognitive function in women receiving adjuvant treatment for high-risk breast cancer: high-dose versus standard-dose chemotherapy. *Journal of National Cancer Institute, 90*, 210–218.

De Meersman, R. E., & Stein, P. K. (2007). Vagal modulation and aging. *Biological Psychology, 74*, 165–173.

DeFina, L. F., Willis, B. L., Radford, N. B., Gao, A., Leonard, D., Haskell, W. L., et al. (2013). The association between midlife cardiorespiratory fitness levels and later-life DementiaA cohort study. *Annals of Internal Medicine, 158*, 162–168.

Deprez, S., Amant, F., Smeets, A., Peeters, R., Leemans, A., Van Hecke, W., et al. (2012). Longitudinal assessment of chemotherapy-induced structural changes in cerebral white matter and its correlation with impaired cognitive functioning. *Journal of Clinical Oncology, 30*, 274–281.

DeSantis, C., Ma, J., Bryan, L., & Jemal, A. (2014). Breast cancer statistics, 2013. *CA: A Cancer Journal for Clinicians, 64,* 52–62.

Edelstein, K., & Bernstein, L. J. (2014). Cognitive dysfunction after chemotherapy for breast cancer. *Journal of the International Neuropsychological Society, 20,* 351–356.

Erickson, K. I., & Kramer, A. F. (2009). Aerobic exercise effects on cognitive and neural plasticity in older adults. *British Journal of Sports Medicine, 43,* 22–24.

Erickson, K. I., Miller, D. L., Weinstein, A. M., Akl, S. L., & Banducci, S. (2012). Physical activity and brain plasticity in late adulthood: a conceptual and comprehensive review. *Ageing Research, 4,* e6.

Erickson, K. I., Prakash, R. S., Voss, M. W., Chaddock, L., Hu, L., Morris, K. S., et al. (2009). Aerobic fitness is associated with hippocampal volume in elderly humans. *Hippocampus, 19,* 1030–1039.

Erickson, K. I., Voss, M. W., Prakash, R. S., Basak, C., Szabo, A., Chaddock, L., et al. (2011). Exercise training increases size of hippocampus and improves memory. *Proceedings of the National Academy of Sciences of the United States of America, 108,* 3017–3022.

Evens, K., & Eschiti, V. S. (2009). Cognitive effects of cancer treatment: "chemo brain" explained. *Clinical Journal of Oncology Nursing, 13,* 661–666.

Fagundes, C. P., Murray, D. M., Hwang, B. S., Gouin, J., Thayer, J. F., Sollers, J. J., III, et al. (2011). Sympathetic and parasympathetic activity in cancer-related fatigue: more evidence for a physiological substrate in cancer survivors. *Psychoneuroendocrinology, 36,* 1137–1147.

Falleti, M. G., Sanfilippo, A., Maruff, P., Weih, L., & Phillips, K. (2005). The nature and severity of cognitive impairment associated with adjuvant chemotherapy in women with breast cancer: a meta-analysis of the current literature. *Brain and Cognition, 59,* 60–70.

Fardell, J., Vardy, J., Johnston, I., & Winocur, G. (2011). Chemotherapy and cognitive impairment: treatment options. *Clinical Pharmacology and Therapeutics, 90,* 366–376.

Fitzpatrick, T. R., Edgar, L., & Holcroft, C. (2012). Assessing the relationship between physical fitness activities, cognitive health, and quality of life among older cancer survivors. *Journal of Psychosocial Oncology, 30,* 556–572.

Galantino, M. L., Greene, L., Daniels, L., Dooley, B., Muscatello, L., & O'Donnell, L. (2012). Longitudinal impact of yoga on chemotherapy-related cognitive impairment and quality of life in women with early stage breast cancer: a case series. *Explore: The Journal of Science and Healing, 8,* 127–135.

Ganz, P. A., Kwan, L., Castellon, S. A., Oppenheim, A., Bower, J. E., Silverman, D. H., et al. (2013). Cognitive complaints after breast cancer treatments: examining the relationship with neuropsychological test performance. *Journal of National Cancer Institute, 105,* 791–801.

Garber, C. E., Blissmer, B., Deschenes, M. R., Franklin, B. A., Lamonte, M. J., Lee, I. M., et al. (2011). American college of sports medicine position stand. Quantity and quality of exercise for developing and maintaining cardiorespiratory, musculoskeletal, and neuromotor fitness in apparently healthy adults: guidance for prescribing exercise. *Medicine and Science in Sports and Exercise, 43*(7), 1334–1359.

Gehring, K., Roukema, J. A., & Sitskoorn, M. M. (2012). Review of recent studies on interventions for cognitive deficits in patients with cancer. *Expert Review of Anticancer Therapy, 12,* 255–269.

Giese-Davis, J., Wilhelm, F. H., Conrad, A., Abercrombie, H. C., Sephton, S., Yutsis, M., et al. (2006). Depression and stress reactivity in metastatic breast cancer. *Psychosomatic Medicine, 68,* 675–683.

Ginos, J. Z., Cooper, A. J., Dhawan, V., Lai, J. C., Strother, S. C., Alcock, N., et al. (1987). [^{13}N]Cisplatin PET to assess pharmacokinetics of intra-arterial versus intravenous chemotherapy for malignant brain tumors. *Journal of Nuclear Medicine, 28,* 1844–1852.

Gomez-Pinilla, F., & Hillman, C. (2013). The influence of exercise on cognitive abilities. *Comprehensive Physiology, 3,* 403–428.

Gothe, N. P., Kramer, A. F., & McAuley, E. (2014). The effects of an 8-week Hatha yoga intervention on executive function in older adults. *Journals of Gerontology, Series A: Biological Sciences and Medical Sciences, 69,* 1109–1116.

Gregory, M. A., Gill, D. P., & Petrella, R. J. (2013). Brain health and exercise in older adults. *Current Sports Medicine Reports, 12,* 256–271.

Hacker, E. (2009). Exercise and quality of life: strengthening the connections. *Clinical Journal of Oncology Nursing, 13,* 31–39.

Hansen, A. L., Johnsen, B. H., Sollers, J. J., III, Stenvik, K., & Thayer, J. F. (2004). Heart rate variability and its relation to prefrontal cognitive function: the effects of training and detraining. *European Journal of Applied Physiology, 93,* 263–272.

Hansen, M. V., Rosenberg, J., & Gögenur, I. (2013). Lack of circadian variation and reduction of heart rate variability in women with breast cancer undergoing lumpectomy: a descriptive study. *Breast Cancer Research and Treatment, 140,* 317–322.

Hillman, C. H., Motl, R. W., Pontifex, M. B., Posthuma, D., Stubbe, J. H., Boomsma, D. I., et al. (2006). Physical activity and cognitive function in a cross-section of younger and older community-dwelling individuals. *Health Psychology, 25,* 678.

Hodgson, K. D., Hutchinson, A. D., Wilson, C. J., & Nettelbeck, T. (2013). A meta-analysis of the effects of chemotherapy on cognition in patients with cancer. *Cancer Treatment Reviews, 39,* 297–304.

Hosseini, S., & Kesler, S. R. (2014). Multivariate pattern analysis of fMRI in breast cancer survivors and healthy women. *Journal of the International Neuropsychological Society, 20,* 391–401.

Hudis, C. A., & Jones, L. (2014). Promoting exercise after a cancer diagnosis: easier said than done. *British Journal of Cancer, 110,* 829–830.

Irwin, M. L., Crumley, D., McTiernan, A., Bernstein, L., Baumgartner, R., Gilliland, F. D., et al. (2003). Physical activity levels before and after a diagnosis of breast carcinoma. *Cancer, 97,* 1746–1757.

Janelsins, M. C., Kesler, S. R., Ahles, T. A., & Morrow, G. R. (2014). Prevalence, mechanisms, and management of cancer-related cognitive impairment. *International Review of Psychiatry, 26,* 102–113.

Janelsins, M. C., Mustian, K. M., Palesh, O. G., Mohile, S. G., Peppone, L. J., Sprod, L. K., et al. (2012). Differential expression of cytokines in breast cancer patients receiving different chemotherapies: implications for cognitive impairment research. *Supportive Care in Cancer, 20,* 831–839.

Janelsins, M. C., Mustian, K. M., Peppone, L. J., Sprod, L. K., Shayne, M., Mohile, S., et al. (2011). Interventions to alleviate symptoms related to breast cancer treatments and areas of needed research. *Journal of Cancer Science and Therapy, S2,* 1–21.

Jean-Pierre, P. (2010). Management of cancer-related cognitive dysfunction-conceptualization challenges and implications for clinical research and practice. *US Oncological Review, 6,* 9–12.

Jean-Pierre, P., Johnson-Greene, D., & Burish, T. G. (2014). Neuropsychological care and rehabilitation of cancer patients with chemobrain: strategies for evaluation and intervention development. *Supportive Care in Cancer, 22,* 2251–2260.

Jim, H. S., Phillips, K. M., Chait, S., Faul, L. A., Popa, M. A., Lee, Y. H., et al. (2012). Meta-analysis of cognitive functioning in breast cancer survivors previously treated with standard-dose chemotherapy. *Journal of Clinical Oncology, 30,* 3578–3587.

Jolly, M. A., Brennan, D. M., & Cho, L. (2011). Impact of exercise on heart rate recovery. *Circulation, 124,* 1520–1526.

Jones, L. W. (2010). Cardiorespiratory exercise testing in adult cancer patients. In M. Irwin (Ed.), *ACSMs guide to exercise and cancer survivorship* (pp. 223–236). Champaign, IL: Human Kinetics.

Jones, L. W., Courneya, K. S., Mackey, J. R., Muss, H. B., Pituskin, E. N., Scott, J. M., et al. (2012). Cardiopulmonary function and age-related decline across the breast cancer survivorship continuum. *Journal of Clinical Oncology, 30,* 2530–2537.

Jones, L. W., Eves, N. D., Haykowsky, M., Joy, A. A., & Douglas, P. S. (2008). Cardiorespiratory exercise testing in clinical oncology research: systematic review and practice recommendations. *The Lancet Oncology, 9,* 757–765.

Jones, L. W., Haykowsky, M. J., Swartz, J. J., Douglas, P. S., & Mackey, J. R. (2007). Early breast cancer therapy and cardiovascular injury. *Journal of the American College of Cardiology, 50,* 1435–1441.

Keary, T. A., Galioto, R., Hughes, J., Waechter, D., Spitznagel, M. B., Rosneck, J., et al. (2012). Reduced heart rate recovery is associated with poorer cognitive function in older adults with cardiovascular disease. *Cardiovascular Psychiatry and Neurology.* http://dx.doi.org/10.1155/2012/392490.

Kerr, J., Marshall, S. J., Patterson, R. E., Marinac, C. R., Natarajan, L., Rosenberg, D., et al. (2013). Objectively measured physical activity is related to cognitive function in older adults. *Journal of American Geriatrics Society, 61,* 1927–1931.

Kesler, S., Janelsins, M., Koovakkattu, D., Palesh, O., Mustian, K., Morrow, G., et al. (2013). Reduced hippocampal volume and verbal memory performance associated with interleukin-6 and tumor necrosis factor-alpha levels in chemotherapy-treated breast cancer survivors. *Brain, Behavior, and Immunity, 30,* S109–S116.

Kimura, K., Yasunaga, A., & Wang, L. (2013). Correlation between moderate daily physical activity and neurocognitive variability in healthy elderly people. *Archives of Gerontology Geriatrics, 56,* 109–117.

Koppelmans, V., Breteler, M. M., Boogerd, W., Seynaeve, C., Gundy, C., & Schagen, S. B. (2012). Neuropsychological performance in survivors of breast cancer more than 20 years after adjuvant chemotherapy. *Journal of Clinical Oncology, 30,* 1080–1086.

Koppelmans, V., Groot, M. D., de Ruiter, M. B., Boogerd, W., Seynaeve, C., Vernooij, M. W., et al. (2014). Global and focal white matter integrity in breast cancer survivors 20 years after adjuvant chemotherapy. *Human Brain Mapping, 35,* 889–899.

Kwan, M. L., Sternfeld, B., Ergas, I. J., Timperi, A. W., Roh, J. M., Hong, C., et al. (2012). Change in physical activity during active treatment in a prospective study of breast cancer survivors. *Breast Cancer Research and Treatment, 131,* 679–690.

Lakoski, S. G., Barlow, C. E., Koelwyn, G. J., Hornsby, W. E., Hernandez, J., DeFina, L. F., et al. (2013). The influence of adjuvant therapy on cardiorespiratory fitness in early-stage breast cancer seven years after diagnosis: the cooper center longitudinal study. *Breast Cancer Research and Treatment, 138,* 909–916.

Langlois, F., Vu, T. T., Chasse, K., Dupuis, G., Kergoat, M. J., & Bherer, L. (2013). Benefits of physical exercise training on cognition and quality of life in frail older adults. *Journal of Gerontology Series B: Psychological Sciences and Social Sciences, 68,* 400–404.

Leon, A. S. (2012). Interaction of aging and exercise on the cardiovascular system of healthy adults. *American Journal of Lifestyle Medicine, 6,* 368–375.

Littman, A. J., Tang, M., & Rossing, M. A. (2010). Longitudinal study of recreational physical activity in breast cancer survivors. *Journal of Cancer Survivorship, 4,* 119–127.

Liu-Ambrose, T., & Nagamatsu, L. S. (2013). Resistance training and cognitive and cortical plasticity in older adults. In P. A. Hall (Ed.), *Social neuroscience and public health* (pp. 265–273). New York: Springer.

Luque-Casado, A., Zabala, M., Morales, E., Mateo-March, M., & Sanabria, D. (2013). Cognitive performance and heart rate variability: the influence of fitness level. *PLoS One, 8*, e56935.

Maccormick, R. E. (2006). Possible acceleration of aging by adjuvant chemotherapy: a cause of early onset frailty? *Medical Hypotheses, 67*, 212–215.

Mandelblatt, J. S., Hurria, A., McDonald, B. C., Saykin, A. J., Stern, R. A., VanMeter, J. W., et al. (2013). Cognitive effects of cancer and its treatments at the intersection of aging: what do we know; what do we need to know? *Seminars in Oncology, 40*, 709–725.

Mason, C., Alfano, C. M., Smith, A. W., Wang, C. Y., Neuhouser, M. L., Duggan, C., et al. (2013). Long-term physical activity trends in breast cancer survivors. *Cancer Epidemiology, Biomarkers, and Prevention, 22*, 1153–1161.

McAuley, E., Mullen, S. P., & Hillman, C. H. (2013). Physical activity, cardiorespiratory fitness, and cognition across the lifespan. In P. A. Hall (Ed.), *Social neuroscience and public health* (pp. 235–252). New York: Springer.

McDonald, B. C., Conroy, S. K., Ahles, T. A., West, J. D., & Saykin, A. J. (2010). Gray matter reduction associated with systemic chemotherapy for breast cancer: a prospective MRI study. *Breast Cancer Research and Treatment, 123*, 819–828.

McDonald, B. C., Conroy, S. K., Ahles, T. A., West, J. D., & Saykin, A. J. (2012). Alterations in brain activation during working memory processing associated with breast cancer and treatment: a prospective functional magnetic resonance imaging study. *Journal of Clinical Oncology, 30*, 2500–2508.

McDougall, G. J., Jr., Oliver, J. S., & Scogin, F. (2014). Memory and cancer: a review of the literature. *Archives of Psychiatric Nursing, 28*, 180–186.

Merriman, J. D., Von Ah, D., Miaskowski, C., & Aouizerat, B. E. (2013). Proposed mechanisms for cancer-and treatment-related cognitive changes. *Seminars in Oncology Nursing, 29*, 260–269.

Meyers, C. A., & Wefel, J. S. (2003). The use of the mini-mental state examination to assess cognitive functioning in cancer trials: no ifs, ands, buts, or sensitivity. *Journal of Clinical Oncology, 21*, 3557–3558.

Minton, O., & Stone, P. C. (2012). A comparison of cognitive function, sleep and activity levels in disease-free breast cancer patients with or without cancer-related fatigue syndrome. *BMJ Supportive and Palliative Care, 2*, 231–238.

Mohile, S. G., Fan, L., Reeve, E., Jean-Pierre, P., Mustian, K., Peppone, L., et al. (2011). Association of cancer with geriatric syndromes in older medicare beneficiaries. *Journal of Clinical Oncology, 29*, 1458–1464.

Morrow, G. R., Hickok, J. T., DuBeshter, B., & Lipshultz, S. E. (1999). Changes in clinical measures of autonomic nervous system function related to cancer chemotherapy-induced nausea. *Journal of the Autonomic Nervous System, 78*, 57–63.

Myers, J. S. (2012). Chemotherapy-related cognitive impairment: the breast cancer experience. *Oncology Nursing Forum, 39*, E31–E40.

Nelson, W. L., & Suls, J. (2013). New approaches to understand cognitive changes associated with chemotherapy for non-central nervous system tumors. *Journal of Pain Symptom Management, 46*, 707–721.

Niederer, D., Vogt, L., Thiel, C., Schmidt, K., Bernhörster, M., Lungwitz, A., et al. (2012). Exercise effects on HRV in cancer patients. *International Journal of Sports Medicine, 34*, 68–73.

Oh, B., Butow, P. N., Mullan, B. A., Clarke, S. J., Beale, P. J., Pavlakis, N., et al. (2012). Effect of medical qigong on cognitive function, quality of life, and a biomarker of inflammation in cancer patients: a randomized controlled trial. *Supportive Care in Cancer, 20*, 1235–1242.

Olson, R., Tyldesley, S., Carolan, H., Parkinson, M., Chhanabhai, T., & McKenzie, M. (2011). Prospective comparison of the prognostic utility of the mini mental state examination and the montreal cognitive assessment in patients with brain metastases. *Supportive Care in Cancer, 19*, 1849–1855.

Paterson, D. H., Cunningham, D. A., Koval, J. J., & St Croix, C. M. (1999). Aerobic fitness in a population of independently living men and women aged 55–86 years. *Medicine and Science in Sports and Exercise, 31*, 1813–1820.

Pearman, A., & Lachman, M. E. (2010). Heart rate recovery predicts memory performance in older adults. *Applied Psychophysiology and Biofeedback, 35*, 107–114.

Peçanha, T., Silva-Júnior, N. D., & Forjaz, C. L. (2014). Heart rate recovery: autonomic determinants, methods of assessment and association with mortality and cardiovascular diseases. *Clinical Physiology and Function Imaging, 34*, 327–339.

Peel, A. B., Thomas, S. M., Dittus, K., Jones, L. W., & Lakoski, S. G. (2014). Cardiorespiratory fitness in breast cancer patients: a call for normative values. *Journal of the American Heart Association, 3*, 1–9.

Prakash, R. S., Voss, M. W., Erickson, K. I., Lewis, J. M., Chaddock, L., Malkowski, E., et al. (2011). Cardiorespiratory fitness and attentional control in the aging brain. *Frontiers in Human Neuroscience, 4*, 229. http://dx.doi.org/10.3389/fnhum.2010.00229.

Pullens, M. J., De Vries, J., & Roukema, J. A. (2010). Subjective cognitive dysfunction in breast cancer patients: a systematic review. *Psycho-Oncology, 19*(11), 1127–1138.

Reid-Arndt, S. A., Matsuda, S., & Cox, C. R. (2012). Tai chi effects on neuropsychological, emotional, and physical functioning following cancer treatment: a pilot study. *Complementary Therapies in Clinical Practice, 18*, 26–30.

Reuter-Lorenz, P. A., & Cimprich, B. (2013). Cognitive function and breast cancer: promise and potential insights from functional brain imaging. *Breast Cancer Research and Treatment, 137*, 33–43.

Reyno, L. M., Levine, M. N., Skingley, P., Arnold, A., & Abu Zahra, H. (1993). Chemotherapy induced amenorrhoea in a randomised trial of adjuvant chemotherapy duration in breast cancer. *European Journal of Cancer, 29*, 21–23.

Robertson, D. A., Savva, G. M., & Kenny, R. A. (2013). Frailty and cognitive impairment—a review of the evidence and causal mechanisms. *Ageing Research Reviews, 12*, 840–851.

de Ruiter, M. B., Reneman, L., Boogerd, W., Veltman, D. J., van Dam, F. S., Nederveen, A. J., et al. (2011). Cerebral hyporesponsiveness and cognitive impairment 10 years after chemotherapy for breast cancer. *Human Brain Mapping, 32*, 1206–1219.

de Ruiter, M. B., & Schagen, S. B. (2013). Functional MRI studies in non-CNS cancers. *Brain Imaging and Behavior, 7*, 388–408.

Sabiston, C. M., Brunet, J., Vallance, J. K., & Meterissian, S. (2014). Prospective examination of objectively assessed physical activity and sedentary time after breast cancer treatment: sitting on the crest of the teachable moment. *Cancer Epidemiology, Biomarkers and Prevention, 23*, 1324–1330.

Scherling, C., Collins, B., Mackenzie, J., Bielajew, C., & Smith, A. (2011). Pre-chemotherapy differences in visuospatial working memory in breast cancer patients compared to controls: an FMRI study. *Frontiers in Human Neuroscience, 5*, 122. http://dx.doi.org/10.3389/fnhum/2011.00122.

Schmitz, K. H., Courneya, K. S., Matthews, C., Demark-Wahnefried, W., Galvao, D. A., Pinto, B. M., et al. (2010). American college of sports medicine roundtable on exercise guidelines for cancer survivors. *Medicine and Science in Sports and Exercise, 42*, 1409–1426.

Schwartz, A. L., & Winters-Stone, K. (2013). Exercise in elderly cancer survivors. In C. M. Ulrich, K. Steindorf, & N. A. Berger (Eds.), *Exercise, energy balance, and cancer* (pp. 181–198). New York: Springer.

Scott, J. M., Jones, L. W., Hornsby, W. E., Koelwyn, G. J., Khouri, M. G., Joy, A. A., et al. (2014). Cancer therapy-induced autonomic dysfunction in early breast cancer: implications for aerobic exercise training. *International Journal of Cardiology, 171*, e50–e51.

Siegel, R., Ma, J., Zou, Z., & Jemal, A. (2014). Cancer statistics, 2014. *CA: A Cancer Journal for Clinicians, 64*, 9–29.

Silver, J. K., Baima, J., & Mayer, R. S. (2013). Impairment-driven cancer rehabilitation: an essential component of quality care and survivorship. *CA: A Cancer Journal for Clinicians, 63*, 295–317.

Silverman, D. H., Dy, C. J., Castellon, S. A., Lai, J., Pio, B. S., Abraham, L., et al. (2007). Altered frontocortical, cerebellar, and basal ganglia activity in adjuvant-treated breast cancer survivors 5–10 years after chemotherapy. *Breast Cancer Research and Treatment, 103*, 303–311.

Small, B. J., Rawson, K. S., Walsh, E., Jim, H. S., Hughes, T. F., Iser, L., et al. (2011). Catechol-O-methyltransferase genotype modulates cancer treatment–related cognitive deficits in breast cancer survivors. *Cancer, 117*, 1369–1376.

Speed-Andrews, A. E., & Courneya, K. S. (2009). Effects of exercise on quality of life and prognosis in cancer survivors. *Current Sports Medicine Reports, 8*(4), 176–181.

Spence, R. R., Heesch, K. C., & Brown, W. J. (2010). Exercise and cancer rehabilitation: a systematic review. *Cancer Treatment Reviews, 36*(2), 185–194.

Sprod, L. K., Mohile, S. G., Demark-Wahnefried, W., Janelsins, M. C., Peppone, L. J., Morrow, G. R., et al. (2012). Exercise and cancer treatment symptoms in 408 newly diagnosed older cancer patients. *Journal of Geriatric Oncology, 3*, 90–97.

Stone, C. A., Kenny, R. A., Nolan, B., & Lawlor, P. G. (2012). Autonomic dysfunction in patients with advanced cancer; prevalence, clinical correlates and challenges in assessment. *BMC Palliative Care, 11*, 3. http://dx.doi.org/10.1186/1472-684X-11-3.

Sweeney, C., Schmitz, K. H., Lazovich, D., Virnig, B. A., Wallace, R. B., & Folsom, A. R. (2006). Functional limitations in elderly female cancer survivors. *Journal of National Cancer Institute, 98*, 521–529.

Szabo, A. N., McAuley, E., Erickson, K. I., Voss, M., Prakash, R. S., Mailey, E. L., et al. (2011). Cardiorespiratory fitness, hippocampal volume, and frequency of forgetting in older adults. *Neuropsychology, 25*(5), 545.

Task Force of the European Society of Cardiology and the North American Society of Pacing and Electrophysiology. (1996). Heart rate variability: standards of measurement, physiological interpretation, and clinical use. *European Heart Journal, 17*, 354–381.

Thayer, J. F., Åhs, F., Fredrikson, M., Sollers, J. J., III, & Wager, T. D. (2012). A meta-analysis of heart rate variability and neuroimaging studies: implications for heart rate variability as a marker of stress and health. *Neuroscience and Biobehavioral Reviews, 36*, 747–756.

United States. President's Cancer Panel. (1998). *Cancer care issues in the United States: Quality of care, quality of life.* National Cancer Program. National Cancer Institute.

Von Ah, D., Habermann, B., Carpenter, J. S., & Schneider, B. L. (2013). Impact of perceived cognitive impairment in breast cancer survivors. *European Journal of Oncology Nursing, 17*, 236–241.

Voss, M. W., Erickson, K. I., Prakash, R. S., Chaddock, L., Malkowski, E., Alves, H., et al. (2010). Functional connectivity: a source of variance in the association between cardiorespiratory fitness and cognition? *Neuropsychologia, 48*, 1394–1406.

Wagner, L., Sweet, J., Butt, Z., Lai, J., & Cella, D. (2009). Measuring patient self-reported cognitive function: development of the functional assessment of cancer therapy-cognitive function instrument. *Journal of Supportive Oncology, 7*, W32–W39.

Walker, C. H., Drew, B. A., Antoon, J. W., Kalueff, A. V., & Beckman, B. S. (2012). Neurocognitive effects of chemotherapy and endocrine therapies in the treatment of breast cancer: recent perspectives. *Cancer Investigation, 30*, 135–148.

Wefel, J. S., Lenzi, R., Theriault, R. L., Davis, R. N., & Meyers, C. A. (2004). The cognitive sequelae of standard-dose adjuvant chemotherapy in women with breast carcinoma. *Cancer, 100*, 2292–2299.

Wefel, J. S., & Schagen, S. B. (2012). Chemotherapy-related cognitive dysfunction. *Current Neurology and Neuroscience Reports, 12*, 267–275.

Wefel, J. S., Vardy, J., Ahles, T., & Schagen, S. B. (2011). International cognition and cancer task force recommendations to harmonise studies of cognitive function in patients with cancer. *The Lancet Oncology, 12*, 703–708.

Wigmore, P. (2013). The effect of systemic chemotherapy on neurogenesis, plasticity and memory. In C. Belzung, & P. Wigmore (Eds.), *Neurogenesis and neural plasticity* (pp. 211–240). New York: Springer.

Wilbur, J., Marquez, D. X., Fogg, L., Wilson, R. S., Staffileno, B. A., Hoyem, R. L., et al. (2012). The relationship between physical activity and cognition in older latinos. *Journal of Gerontology Series B: Psychological Sciences and Social Sciences, 67*, 525–534.

Yamada, T., Denburg, N., Beglinger, L., & Schultz, S. (2010). Neuropsychological outcomes of older breast cancer survivors: cognitive features ten or more years after chemotherapy. *Journal of Neuropsychiatry and Clinical Neuroscience, 22*, 48–54.

Zhong, S., Jiang, T., Ma, T., Zhang, X., Tang, J., Chen, W., et al. (2014). Association between physical activity and mortality in breast cancer: a meta-analysis of cohort studies. *European Journal of Epidemiology, 29*, 391–404.

20

Physical Activity and Cognition in Older Adults with Heart Failure

Lindsay Miller[1], John Gunstad[2]

[1]Department of Psychiatry and Human Behavior, Warren Alpert Medical School of Brown University, Providence, RI, USA; [2]Department of Psychological Sciences, Kent State University, Kent, OH, USA

INTRODUCTION

Within the United States, more than 5 million individuals have heart failure (HF) and an estimated 670,000 new cases are reported each year. With the increasing age of the American population, HF has become more prevalent and it is estimated that by 2030, the prevalence of HF will increase by 25% (American Heart Association, 2013). In addition to being of clinical concern, HF also produces a significant economic burden, costing an estimated $32 billion annually, with this cost projected to increase to $70 billion by 2030 (American Heart Association, 2013).

In contrast to normal cardiovascular aging, HF is a complex clinical syndrome associated with structural and functional damage such that the heart is unable to pump blood sufficiently enough to meet the body's metabolic needs. The condition of HF usually evolves over time and progresses as the body tries to compensate for the work the damaged heart can no longer perform (Francis, Sonnenblick, Wilson Tang, & Poole-Wilson, 2008). For example, left ventricular dysfunction is a common abnormality in HF and results in a decrease of cardiac output.

In response, activation of neurohormonal compensatory mechanisms, such as sympathetic nervous system activation (e.g., increase in heart rate, peripheral vasoconstriction), occur in an attempt to maintain cardiac output. While this initially maintains cardiac output, chronic sympathetic nervous system activation ultimately leads to further weakening of the heart and cardiac muscle cell death, hypertrophy, and focal myocardial necrosis (Jackson, Gibbs, Davies, & Lip, 2000). The compensatory mechanisms recruited ultimately prove to be insufficient and have additional negative effects on the heart, and these initially adaptive responses contribute to the progression of HF (Francis et al., 2008; Jackson et al., 2000).

In addition to a host of physical symptoms, cognitive dysfunction is common in HF and has been documented in 25–80% of individuals (e.g., Bennett & Sauvé, 2003; Dodson, Truong, Towle, Kerins, & Chaudhry, 2013; Miller et al., 2012; Vogels, Oosterman et al., 2007; Vogels Scheltens, Schroeder-Tanka, & Weinstein, 2007). The risk for impairment increases with HF severity (Pressler et al., 2010; Vogels, Scheltens et al., 2007) and is four times that of matched controls with mild cardiovascular disease, but without HF (Sauvé, Lewis, Blankenbiller, Rickabaugh, & Pressler, 2009). Deficits are found in multiple domains including memory, attention, executive function, psychomotor speed, and language (e.g., Almeida & Flicker, 2001; Bennett & Sauvé, 2003; Pressler et al., 2010; Vogels, Scheltens et al., 2007), and the pattern of deficits has been found to be heterogeneous (Miller et al., 2012). Such impairment is also associated with adverse outcomes, including a fivefold increase in risk of mortality (Zuccala et al., 2003) and a sixfold increase in disability (Zuccala et al., 2001).

The etiology of cognitive dysfunction in HF is still being elucidated, though several contributors have been identified, including functional and structural brain changes and the presence of comorbid conditions such as hypertension, type 2 diabetes mellitus (T2DM), obstructive sleep apnea, and depression. Although each of these factors is associated with adverse neurocognitive outcomes in non-HF populations, the work in addressing their relationship to cognition in HF is limited, and the available findings are often inconsistent (e.g., Alosco, Brickman et al., 2012; Beer et al., 2009; Garcia et al., 2011; Knecht et al. 2012; Vogels et al., 2008). This argues for consideration of additional contributors. One likely risk factor that has received limited attention is reduced physical activity. Further examination of the role of physical activity on cognition in HF is warranted, as physical inactivity is not only a risk factor for the development of HF (He et al., 2001) but also implicated in disease progression (Conraads et al., 2012). A greater understanding of the relationship between physical activity and cognition is warranted as it may not only aid in the early identification of those at risk for cognitive dysfunction, but could also attenuate the degree of decline, or possibly even delay its onset. Importantly, reduced physical activity is a modifiable risk factor. While some damage cannot be undone (e.g., atrophy and white matter hyperintensities), increasing physical activity may reduce the risk of further damage

and/or the impact of the other proposed mechanisms on cognition, as each of these factors has been found to share a common link—namely, positive outcomes are associated with increased levels of physical activity.

REDUCED PHYSICAL ACTIVITY AS A MODIFIABLE RISK FACTOR FOR COGNITIVE DYSFUNCTION IN HF

The Capacity for Physical Activity is Reduced in HF

The progression of HF is associated with a decreasing capacity for physical activity and the New York Heart Association (NYHA) functional class system subjectively quantifies this reduction. Higher NYHA classification is indicative of a greater inability to carry out physical activities and the experience of more severe symptoms associated with activity. As HF progresses even minimally exerting activities can result in the experience of significant physical symptoms (Swedberg et al., 2005).

Given the physical symptoms individuals with HF experience during exertion, it is not surprising that many patients would intentionally avoid physical activity, particularly exercise. In fact, exercise was once thought to be a contraindication in HF, and that it actually contributed to the progression of the disease. This has been invalidated though, and exercise is now considered a safe, viable, nonpharmacological treatment option (Boudreau & Genovese, 2007). However, despite the recommendation to remain physically active, many individuals with HF do not adhere to this (Evangilista, Berg, & Dracup, 2001; van der Wal et al., 2006).

The Benefits of Physical Activity in HF

Functional capacity (i.e., the ability to engage in physical activity) is an important prognostic marker in HF, with greater impairment in capacity being related to poorer prognosis. For example, lower peak oxygen consumption has been found to be a significant predictor of mortality in HF (Lund & Mancini, 2008; Myers et al., 2008). Given that exercise can readily improve functional capacity, a growing number of studies have shown that increased physical activity has significant benefits in persons with HF.

Exercise Interventions in HF

Numerous studies have been conducted examining the impact of exercise interventions on outcomes among individuals with HF. Findings indicate that participation in such programs increases peak oxygen consumption by an average of nearly 17% and is associated with a lower risk of adverse events including hospitalizations and mortality (Smart & Marwick, 2004, for a review; Boudreau & Genovese, 2007). Closer examination shows that aerobic-only interventions produce the largest gains, with peak oxygen consumption increasing by an average of 16.5%, followed by combined aerobic and strength training (15%) and strength training alone (3%); interestingly, other intervention characteristics (e.g., duration and intensity) were not related to outcomes (Smart & Marwick, 2004). Involvement in an exercise training program has also been shown to result in significant improvements in NYHA classification in HF individuals with preserved ejection fraction. Specifically, nearly 16% moved from NYHA class II to class I and 6% from class III to class II (Edelmann et al., 2011), indicating a subjective reduction in the experience of physical symptoms associated with physical activity.

To determine if the benefits of participation in a formal exercise intervention persist over time, Mueller et al. (2007) examined outcomes among HF patients 6 years after completion of an exercise program. In the original study, peak oxygen consumption was increased by 21.4% in the exercise group 1 month after completing the intervention. In contrast, no change was observed in the HF controls that received "usual care" treatment

and were encouraged to remain active and provided with education regarding exercising at home. At the 6-year follow-up, however, current peak oxygen consumption did not significantly differ from baseline levels among groups. Although statistically nonsignificant, those who completed the exercise program demonstrated an average increase in peak oxygen consumption of 7% from baseline, which may still be clinically meaningful. It is also important to note that prior to the onset of the intervention, both groups demonstrated approximately normal levels of peak oxygen consumption, suggesting that HF severity was likely minimal. Interestingly, at the 6-year follow-up both groups reported high levels of involvement in recreational activities that were associated with levels of energy expenditure that exceeded minimum recommendations; those who had completed the exercise program reported significantly greater levels of current energy expenditure. The authors note that those patients who completed the exercise intervention could not have been expected to maintain the level of exercise involved during the intervention period (i.e., 2 h/day). However, the fact that at a 6-year follow-up functional capacity was similar to that of baseline levels, and that these individuals continued to remain meaningfully active in other ways, suggests some longstanding benefit of exercise interventions in maintaining a lesser degree of HF severity. In addition, that those in the control group demonstrated similar stability suggests some benefit of simply encouraging individuals with HF to stay active. While consideration must be given to the makeup of the sample and replication in additional work is needed, these findings underscore not only the immediate benefits of an exercise intervention but also the importance of informal daily activities in maintaining functional capacity (i.e., attenuating disease progression) in HF (Mueller et al., 2007).

In a systematic review of studies examining home-based exercise interventions, Chien, Lee, Wu, Chen, and Wu (2008) found a benefit of such exercise regimens on exercise capacity in HF (NYHA classes II and III). Studies included ranged from 2 weeks to 6 months in duration, consisted of aerobic and aerobic with resistance training regimens, and were mixed regarding the extent of researcher involvement (i.e., no home visits, home visits, or phone calls). When compared to control groups that maintained their normal levels of activity, those completing a home-based exercise program significantly increased peak oxygen consumption and distance walked on the 6-Minute Walk Test (6MWT), a measure of cardiovascular fitness. The pooled increase in peak oxygen consumption was 2.7 mL/kg/min, a value equivalent to that seen in past hospital-based interventions. Importantly, participation in home-based exercise did not elevate risk of hospitalization (Chien et al., 2008).

Self-Reported Levels of Physical Activity in HF

Self-reported levels of greater physical activity have also been found to be associated with favorable outcomes in HF. In one study examining the relationship between self-reported physical activity and outcomes following hospitalization due to HF or coronary heart disease, greater levels of activity were related to better outcomes. Based on their reported activities during the previous 6 months, individuals were characterized as sedentary or nonsedentary. Those who were considered sedentary demonstrated a near fourfold increased risk for mortality compared to those who were active. When examining just those with HF, only 25% of the sedentary patients were alive 2.5 years following hospitalization, whereas 75% of the active patients remained alive (Oerkild, Frederiksen, Hansen, & Prescott, 2011).

Impact of Physical Activity on Comorbid Conditions of HF

Physical activity has also been found to reduce the incidence of conditions that are frequently comorbid with HF and are associated with adverse neurocognitive outcomes, including hypertension (Whelton, Chin, Xin, & He, 2002), T2DM (Sigal, Kenny, Wasserman, & Castaneda-Sceppa, 2004), sleep-disordered breathing (Awad, Malhotra, Barnet, Quan, & Peppard, 2012), and depression (Teychenne, Ball, & Salmon, 2008). Moreover, a recent meta-analysis of 33 large prospective cohort studies found that physical activity, formally measured or self-reported, was associated with a 35% risk reduction for cardiovascular mortality and a 33% reduction in risk for all-cause mortality (Nocon et al., 2008). Physical activity has also been found to impact disease severity/symptoms when these conditions are already present. Specifically, aerobic exercise lowers blood pressure in hypertensive individuals (Whelton et al., 2002); a brief exercise program improves glycemic control prior to changes in fitness and adiposity in T2DM (Mikus, Oberlin, Boyle, & Thyfault, 2011); decreased exercise is associated with worsening of sleep-disordered breathing symptoms (Awad et al., 2012); and depressive symptoms are reduced with physical activity and the extent of the effect is comparable to that of antidepressant medication (Dinas, Koutedakis, & Flouris, 2011). Given the independent relationship that has been observed between these comorbidities and cognition (e.g., van den Berg, Kloppenborg, Kessels, Kappelle, & Biessels, 2009; Duron & Hanon, 2008; Kohler et al., 2010; Sforza & Roche, 2012) it is possible that reducing the incidence of these conditions in HF may have implications for attenuating cognitive dysfunction.

Adherence to Physical Activity Recommendations

Exercise is considered safe for HF patients who are clinically stable and when regimens are made on an individual basis with consideration given to the individual's HF status, comorbid conditions, and exercise tolerance (Vanhees et al., 2012). Despite recommendations to remain physically active, however, many individuals with HF fail to do so. For example, although 80% of HF patients acknowledged that it was important to engage in physical activity, only 39% actually did (van der Wal et al., 2006). In another study, only 53% of HF patients adhered to exercise recommendations. Follow-up analyses showed that 61% reported that it was more difficult to adhere to exercise recommendations than it was to adhere to other recommendations, including smoking cessation (Evangilista et al., 2001).

Summary of the Benefits of Physical Activity in HF

Taken together, there is evidence to suggest that physical activity is associated with favorable outcomes in HF, including a significant increase in peak oxygen consumption and the ability to tolerate exercise, potential attenuation of comorbidities, as well as a reduced risk of hospitalization and mortality. Physical activity is considered a safe treatment option in HF, though despite the recommendations to do so, many individuals with HF do not engage in regular physical activity. Increasing HF severity is associated with a decrease in the ability to carry out physical activity (Swedberg et al., 2005), as well as an increased risk of cognitive dysfunction (e.g., Pressler et al., 2010; Vogels, Scheltens et al., 2007). Taken together, this argues for a link between the physical inactivity and the cognitive dysfunction seen in HF.

BENEFITS OF PHYSICAL ACTIVITY ON NEUROCOGNITIVE OUTCOMES IN NON-HF POPULATIONS

Exercise Interventions in Healthy Older Adults

There is growing evidence from both cross-sectional and prospective studies that physical activity is associated with better neurocognitive outcomes in older adults. An early meta-analysis concluded that exercise interventions produced medium-sized effects on cognitive function in healthy older adults ($d = 0.48$), with the largest effects found in persons aged 66–70 years (Colcombe & Kramer, 2003). In a larger, more recent meta-analysis, Smith et al. (2010) reviewed 29 randomized clinical trials, totaling over 2000 participants, on the impact of exercise interventions on cognition. This review examined the impact of exercise by cognitive domain and potential moderating factors were also examined (e.g., intervention characteristics and study sample characteristics). Interventions ranged from 6 weeks to 18 months and the most frequent type of intervention was aerobic. The effects of aerobic exercise were associated with consistent, modest improvements in attention and processing speed, executive function, and memory when compared to control groups. Interventions combining aerobic exercise with other interventions (e.g., strength training) incrementally improved only attention and processing speed tasks. For all domains, intervention duration or intensity did not moderate the relationship and the findings were independent of the mean age of study participants (Smith et al., 2010).

Exercise Interventions in Older Adults with Cardiovascular Disease

Work has extended the findings from healthy older adults to older adults with cardiovascular disease (CVD) and similarly found that participation in a cardiac rehabilitation program was associated with improvements in cognitive function. For example, one study examined the effects of a 12-week cardiac rehabilitation program among individuals with heterogeneous forms of CVD, including HF. The intervention included 75 min of monitored aerobic exercise three times per week, with cognitive testing focusing on attention/psychomotor speed completed pre- and postintervention. Participation in the program was found not only to be associated with improved cardiovascular fitness, but cognitive improvement was demonstrated on a task of visual attention/psychomotor speed and information processing speed. Moreover, the changes in cognitive performance were related to the observed fitness gains. No separate analyses were conducted to examine any specific impact on cognition in those with HF (Gunstad et al., 2005).

A more recent study sought to extend these findings by examining performance in additional cognitive domains among older adults with heterogeneous forms of CVD, including HF, completing cardiac rehabilitation. The intervention included 3, 40-min sessions of aerobic and strength training exercises per week. Following the 12-week intervention, improvements were noted in global cognition and in aspects of attention/executive function/psychomotor speed and memory. Specifically, participants improved on tasks of complex attention, motor function, and verbal learning and memory. While an overall improvement was demonstrated in cardiovascular fitness, this was only related to gains made in verbal memory (Stanek et al., 2011).

Self-Reported Levels of Physical Activity and Cognition in Older Adults

Prospective studies have found that physical activity reduces risk of dementia. A meta-analysis of 16 longitudinal studies examined the relationship between primarily self-reported levels of activity and incidence of dementia among initially intact older adults. After controlling for important confounds (e.g., vascular risk factors), physical activity reduced the risk of dementia in general by 28%, and more specifically the risk for Alzheimer's disease (AD) by 45% (Hamer & Chida, 2009).

In a recent cross-sectional study, a relationship was found between self-reported physical activity and cognition among 331 cognitively intact older adults. Older adults reported the number of light (e.g., walking) and hard (e.g.,

running) exercises they engage in for at least 30 min per week. Based on their report, individuals were classified into four categories of activity (i.e., very low, low, medium, and high). A positive association between increasing levels of physical activity and performance on tasks of executive function, semantic verbal fluency, and global cognition was demonstrated. When additional variables known to impact cognition were controlled for (e.g., glucose levels, blood pressure, and education), these associations remained significant, with the exception of global cognitive performance (Benedict et al., 2013).

A recent meta-analysis examined the impact of self-reported physical activity on the risk of cognitive decline in nondemented adults. Studies included were prospective in nature and followed individuals for at least 1 year, though some were followed for up to 12 years. Participants in these studies completed questionnaires regarding the amount and type of physical activity they engaged in (e.g., walking and leisure sports). Cognition was most frequently measured with a brief global screen of cognitive function, though some studies implemented more comprehensive measurements. A total of 15 studies from 2001 to 2010 were included, all of which examined older adults with the exception of one study that included middle-aged adults. Pooled results demonstrated that physically active individuals at baseline had significantly lower risk of cognitive decline at follow-up. Among those who engaged in high levels of physical activity, a 38% reduction in risk for cognitive decline was found when compared to sedentary adults. In addition, even low to moderate levels of physical activity reduced the risk of cognitive decline by 35%. Taken together, these findings suggest that the effect of physical activity on cognition is not necessarily dose dependent and argues that any level of physical activity can serve as a protective factor (Sofi et al., 2011).

Vercambre, Grodstein, Manson, Stampfer, and Kang (2011) have extended past work by prospectively examining cognitively intact women aged 40 and above with CVD or vascular risk factors. Similar to previous work, the level of physical activity was determined by self-reported participation in various physical/recreational activities, daily flights of stairs walked, and usual pace of walking; cognition was assessed with a brief telephone screen of global cognitive function as well as memory and semantic verbal fluency tasks. Consistent with past findings, results indicated that greater levels of physical activity were associated with a slower rate of cognitive decline from baseline to follow-up (mean of 5.4 years). Specifically, physical activity was associated with a slower decline in global cognitive performance and memory, but not semantic fluency. Moreover, the association was not limited to women engaging in more vigorous levels of activity (e.g., tennis and running), as less cognitive decline was also found in women who simply engaged in more walking. In fact, based on the rates of decline between different levels of physical activity, the authors found that engagement in physical activity that was equivalent to briskly walking 30 min per day was comparable to being 5–7 years younger cognitively (Vercambre et al., 2011).

BENEFITS OF PHYSICAL ACTIVITY ON BRAIN HEALTH

Objective Measures of Fitness and Brain Health

Age-related structural brain changes are common (e.g., Caserta et al., 2009; Raz & Rodrigue, 2006), though fitness has been shown to play an important moderating role in these changes. Greater levels of fitness have been found to be associated with decreased atrophy, particularly in the gray matter of the prefrontal, superior parietal, and temporal cortices, as well as in the anterior white matter tracts. This association remained significant even after controlling for potential confounds such as hypertension and education (Colcombe et al., 2003). Erickson et al. (2009) similarly found that higher levels of aerobic fitness were associated with greater hippocampal volumes. In addition, hippocampal volume partially mediated the relationship between higher levels of aerobic fitness and better performance on a spatial memory task (Erickson et al., 2009).

Self-Reported Levels of Physical Activity and Brain Health in Older Adults

Self-reported levels of physical activity have also been found to be associated with gray matter volume and associated risk of cognitive impairment in older adults. For example, Erickson et al. (2010) longitudinally followed 299 older adults who were cognitively intact at baseline. Reported walking distance was positively associated with greater volume in the frontal, temporal, and occipital lobes, as well as in the entorhinal cortex and hippocampus. In follow-up analyses 13 years from baseline, 39% of this sample demonstrated significant cognitive decline (i.e., diagnosis of mild cognitive impairment or dementia) and increased gray matter volume that was associated with walking was found to reduce the risk of cognitive decline twofold. In particular, greater volume of the inferior frontal gyrus, hippocampal formation, and supplementary motor area were related to a lower risk for developing cognitive impairment (Erickson et al., 2010).

Work by Benedict et al. (2013) was previously discussed in terms of the positive relationship between higher levels of reported physical activity and better cognitive performance. The authors also employed neuroimaging and found greater levels of physical activity were positively related to total brain and white matter volumes. Moreover, gray matter volume in the precuneus, a region implicated in early AD, was also positively associated with physical activity (Benedict et al., 2013).

Exercise Interventions in Older Adults

Exercise interventions have also been shown to positively impact brain volume. For example, to examine the impact of a 6-month training program Colcombe et al. (2006) randomized cognitively intact, but sedentary, older adults into a cardiovascular exercise group or a nonaerobic (i.e., stretching/toning) control group. Following the intervention, those in the aerobic exercise group demonstrated a significant increase in peak oxygen consumption and participation in the aerobic exercise program resulted in significant gray and white matter volumetric gains, particularly in the prefrontal and temporal cortex (Colcombe et al., 2006).

Erickson et al. (2011) examined the impact of a 1-year aerobic exercise program on hippocampal volume in older adults without dementia. Following the intervention, a 2% increase in anterior hippocampal volume was seen among those in the aerobic exercise group, while those in the stretching control group demonstrated a nearly 1.5% decline in hippocampal volume (Erickson et al., 2011). These findings are of particular interest as the hippocampus can begin to shrink in early adulthood, and annual volumetric losses of 0.3–2.1% have been documented (Miller & O'Callaghan, 2005). The 2% increase in hippocampal volume associated with the exercise intervention suggests delaying hippocampal deterioration is possible. This clearly has implications for cognition, and memory in particular. Moreover, greater increases in hippocampal volume were associated with greater aerobic fitness gains (i.e., greater improvement in fitness from pre- to postintervention; Erickson et al., 2011).

Summary of the Beneficial Impact of Physical Activity on Neurocognitive Outcomes

There is clear evidence that engagement in physical activity serves as a neuroprotective factor against cognitive decline in healthy aging,

as well as in CVD. The evidence for observed cognitive improvement, particularly with CVD populations, suggests that a similar benefit might be appreciated in HF populations. Although cognitive dysfunction is common in HF and is associated with increased risk for dementia (e.g., Bennett & Sauvé, 2003; Roman, 2005) there is evidence to suggest that cognition in this population may be modifiable. One study found that over a 12-month period, individuals with HF demonstrated improvements on a measure of global cognitive function, while their peers with non-HF CVD remained stable. More specifically, improvements were noted in aspects of attention and executive function. While this was not an intervention study, follow-up analyses identified improved blood pressure control as a possible contributor to cognitive gains. Although this sample was relatively intact and likely comprised of individuals whose HF was well maintained, the results are encouraging (Stanek et al., 2009). More recently, additional work has similarly shown stability and improvement in cognitive functioning among older adults with stable HF. Over the course of 12 months, attention/executive functioning was found to remain stable, while memory performance improved (Alosco, Garcia et al., 2014). These findings suggest that continued cognitive decline in HF is not necessarily imminent or indicative of dementia, as such impairments may be modifiable. Such findings not only underscore the importance of adhering to treatment recommendations for HF as well as its associated comorbidities, but also suggest that persons with HF may also be receptive to the benefits physical activity has on cognition.

BENEFITS OF PHYSICAL ACTIVITY ON COGNITIVE OUTCOMES IN HF POPULATIONS

Although reduced levels of functional capacity have consistently been linked to poorer cognitive outcomes in HF (Alosco, Spitznagel et al., 2012;

Baldasseroni et al., 2010; Garcia et al., 2013; Miller et al., 2012), there is limited work examining the potentially beneficial effect of increased physical activity on cognitive outcomes in HF. While intervention studies on the impact of cardiac rehabilitation on cognition in CVD have included individuals with HF in their sample (Gunstad et al., 2005; Stanek et al., 2011), literature on the specific impact of exercise interventions on cognition in HF is scarce. However, existing studies provide promising results that cognitive dysfunction in HF is, in part, associated with physical activity and warrants further investigation.

Tanne et al. (2005) examined the impact of an 18-week exercise-training program on physical fitness parameters and cognition in individuals with moderate–severe HF (NYHA class III). Similar to other interventions, this training program included 50 min of aerobic exercise, 2 times per week. Following the intervention, participants demonstrated significant improvement on performance on the 6MWT, as well as on a stress test, indicating gains in functional capacity. Cognitive improvements were also noted on tasks of attention/psychomotor speed and executive function. In line with previous findings (e.g., Colcombe & Kramer, 2003), the most marked improvement was on a well-established task of executive function. A small HF control group who did not complete the intervention was also included in the study and did not demonstrate any change in cognitive performance. Although further analyses were not conducted to determine to what extent functional capacity gains were related to the cognitive improvements, the fact that the controls did not improve argues for the existence of a relationship (Tanne et al., 2005). Moreover, evidence from other populations relating functional gains to cognitive gains (e.g., Gunstad et al., 2005; Stanek et al., 2011) further supports this notion.

More recently, Alosco et al. (2014) examined the acute and lasting cognitive benefits of a 12-week cardiac rehabilitation program in a sample of 52 older adults with HF. Participants completed 3, 40-min sessions of circuit training per week and underwent neuropsychological testing at baseline, following completion of cardiac rehabilitation (i.e., 12 weeks), and at 12-month follow-up. Following the intervention, improvements in attention/executive function and memory were observed. Specifically, attention/executive function improved from baseline to 12 weeks, and this improvement persisted at the 12-month follow-up. Memory also improved from baseline to 12 months. There was a multivariate trend ($p = 0.08$) for improvement in functional capacity (i.e., 2-min step test [2MST]), with a significant increase noted from baseline to 12 weeks. However, the improvement in functional capacity was not predictive of cognitive performance, though performance on the 2MST was correlated with cognitive performance (Alosco, Spitznagel et al., 2014).

While encouraging, the findings from these studies need to be viewed in light of a number of limitations including the lack of direct comparison control groups, generally intact cognitive functioning at baseline, and small sample sizes. Additional prospective work that addresses these limitations is needed to more fully elucidate the relationship between exercise interventions and cognition in HF.

SUMMARY AND FUTURE DIRECTIONS

HF represents a significant clinical and economic burden, and with the increasing proportion of older adults, the number of individuals with HF and the associated costs of care can only be expected to grow (American Heart Association, 2013). Cognitive dysfunction is common in this population (Bennett & Sauvé, 2003; Dodson et al., 2013; Miller et al., 2012; Vogels, Scheltens et al., 2007) and recent evidence indicates that the pattern of cognitive deficits is heterogeneous (Miller et al., 2012), suggesting a variable degree of limitations in daily activities. Not surprisingly, cognitive dysfunction in this population is associated with adverse outcomes, including increased disability and mortality risks (Zuccala et al., 2001; 2003). These patterns highlight the urgent need to develop interventions aimed at attenuating the progression of HF as well as preventing/stabilizing cognitive decline, as such interventions ultimately impact activities of daily living and quality of life.

There is strong evidence to suggest that reduced physical activity is a significant risk factor for cognitive dysfunction in HF. The capacity for physical activity is substantially reduced as HF progresses, with the most severe stage of the disease associated with discomfort even when at rest (Swedberg et al., 2005). It is therefore not surprising that HF patients become increasingly sedentary with disease progression and do not adhere to the recommendation to remain physically active (Evangilista et al., 2001). The benefits of physical activity on neurocognitive outcomes in healthy populations are well established, including cognitive improvements and fewer pathological brain changes (e.g., Colcombe et al., 2006; Colcombe & Kramer, 2003; Erickson et al., 2011; Smith et al., 2010). Cognitive improvements have also been demonstrated in CVD populations engaging in exercise interventions (Gunstad et al., 2005; Stanek et al., 2011), and this suggests that individuals with HF might similarly benefit. Although the relationship between physical activity and cognition in HF is an emerging topic in the field, encouraging findings have been documented (i.e., Alosco, Garcia et al., 2014; Alosco, Spitznagel et al., 2014; Tanne et al., 2005). Additional work is much needed to further elucidate the relationship between physical activity and cognition in HF, including prospective intervention studies.

Future Directions

An important direction for future work involves examination of the possible cognitive benefits of high-intensity exercise in older adults with and without HF. Although past work has shown that the cognitive benefits of physical activity are not influenced by exercise type (e.g., Smith et al., 2010; Vercambre et al., 2011), there is rapidly growing evidence that intensity may play a key role. For example, more intense physical activity has been shown to be independently associated with better cognitive performance after controlling for demographic and medical (e.g., CVD) characteristics in healthy older adults (Brown et al., 2012) and a recent review also identified exercise intensity as an important factor for cognitive outcomes in older adults (Kirk-Sanchez & McGough, 2014).

Similar work has recently been extended into the HF population and has found that improvements in cardiorespiratory fitness correspond to the intensity of exercise, with higher intensity associated with greater functional improvement (Ismail, McFarlane, Nojoumian, Dieberg, & Smart, 2013). Specifically, high-intensity interval training (i.e., repetitions of brief, intense exercise followed by a rest period) has been shown to produce greater improvements in functional capacity than traditional aerobic exercise (Freyssin et al., 2012), and combination programs are associated with greater benefits on functional capacity in HF when compared to interval training alone (Smart, Dieberg, & Giallauria, 2013). Given that higher-intensity exercise programs have recently been linked to better cognitive outcomes in healthy adults, a similar relationship may exist within the HF population, and this possibility warrants further investigation. Importantly, vigorous to high levels of physical activity do not appear to be associated with an increased risk for adverse events in HF (Ismail et al., 2013). Given the potential benefits, from both a clinical and economic perspective, it will be important for future work to understand how these aspects of exercise may influence cognitive outcomes in HF.

References

Almeida, O. P., & Flicker, L. (2001). The mind of a failing heart: a systematic review of the association between congestive heart failure and cognitive functioning. *Internal Medicine Journal, 31*, 290–295.

Alosco, M. L., Brickman, A. M., Spitznagel, M. B., van Dulmen, M., Raz, N., Cohen, R., et al. (2012). The independent association of hypertension with cognitive function among older adults with heart failure. *Journal of Neurological Science, 323*, 216–220.

Alosco, M. L., Garcia, S., Spitznagel, M. B., van Dulmen, M., Cohen, R., Sweet, L. H., et al. (2014). Cognitive performance in older adults with stable heart failure: longitudinal evidence for stability and improvement. *Aging, Neuropsychology, and Cognition, 21*, 239–256.

Alosco, M. L., Spitznagel, M. B., Cohen, R., Sweet, L. H., Josephson, R., Hughes, J., et al. (2014). Cardiac rehabilitation is associated with lasting improvements in cognitive function in older adults with heart failure. *Acta Cardiologica, 69*, 407–414.

Alosco, M. L., Spitznagel, M. B., Raz, N., Cohen, R., Sweet, L. H., Colbert, L. H., et al. (2012). The 2-minute step test is independently associated with cognitive function in older adults with heart failure. *Aging Clinical and Experimental Research, 24*, 468–474.

American Heart Association. (2013). Heart disease and stroke statistics 2013 update: a report from the American Heart Association. *Circulation, 127*, e6–e245.

Awad, K. M., Malhotra, A., Barnet, J. H., Quan, S. F., & Peppard, P. E. (2012). Exercise is associated with a reduced incidence of sleep-disordered breathing. *The American Journal of Medicine, 125*, 485–490.

Baldasseroni, S., Mossello, E., Romboli, B., Orso, F., Colombi, C., Fumagalli, S., et al. (2010). Relationship between cognitive function and 6-minute walking test in older outpatients with chronic heart failure. *Aging Clinical and Experimental Research, 22*, 308–313.

Beer, C., Ebenezer, E., Fenner, S., Lautenschlager, N. T., Arnolda, L., Flicker, L., et al. (2009). Contributors to cognitive impairment in congestive heart failure: a pilot case-control study. *Internal Medicine Journal, 39*, 600–605.

Benedict, C., Brooks, S. J., Kullberg, J., Nordenskjold, R., Burgos, J., Le Greves, M., et al. (2013). Association between physical activity and brain health in older adults. *Neurobiology of Aging, 34*, 83–90.

Bennett, S. J., & Sauvé, M. J. (2003). Cognitive deficits in patients with heart failure: a review of the literature. *Journal of Cardiovascular Nursing, 18*, 219–242.

van den Berg, E., Kloppenborg, R. P., Kessels, R. P., Kappelle, L. J., & Biessels, G. J. (2009). Type 2 diabetes mellitus, hypertension, dyslipidemia and obesity: a systematic comparison of their impact on cognition. *Biochimica et Biophysica Acta, 1792*, 470–481.

Boudreau, M., & Genovese, J. (2007). Cardiac rehabilitation: a comprehensive program for the management of heart failure. *Progress in Cardiovascular Nursing, 22*, 88–92.

Brown, B. M., Peiffer, J. J., Sohrabi, H. R., Mondal, A., Gupta, V. B., Rainey-Smith, S. R., et al. (2012). Intense physical activity is associated with cognitive performance in the elderly. *Translational Psychiatry, 2*, e191.

Caserta, M. T., Bannon, Y., Fernandez, F., Giunta, B., Schoenberg, M. R., & Tan, J. (2009). Normal brain aging: clinical, immunological, neuropsychological, and neuroimaging features. *International Review of Neurobiology, 84*, 1–19.

Chien, C. L., Lee, C. M., Wu, Y. W., Chen, T. A., & Wu, Y. T. (2008). Home-based exercise increases exercise capacity but not quality of life in people with chronic heart failure: a systematic review. *Australian Journal of Physiotherapy, 54*, 87–93.

Colcombe, S. J., Erickson, K. I., Raz, N., Webb, A. G., Cohen, N. J., McAuley, E., et al. (2003). Aerobic fitness reduces brain tissue loss in aging humans. *Journal of Gerontology Series A, 58*, 176–180.

Colcombe, S. J., Erickson, K. I., Scalf, P. E., Kim, J. S., Prakash, R., McAuley, E., et al. (2006). Aerobic exercise training increases brain volume in aging humans. *Journal of Gerontology Series A, 61*, 1166–1170.

Colcombe, S., & Kramer, A. F. (2003). Fitness effects on the cognitive function of older adults: a meta-analytic study. *Psychological Science, 14*, 125–130.

Conraads, V. M., Craenenbroeck, E. M., De Maeyer, C., Berendoncks, A. M., Beckers, P. J., & Vrints, C. J. (2012). Unraveling new mechanisms of exercise intolerance in chronic heart failure: role of exercise training. *Heart Failure Reviews, 18*, 65–77.

Dinas, P. C., Koutedakis, Y., & Flouris, A. D. (2011). Effects of exercise and physical activity on depression. *Irish Journal of Medical Science, 180*, 319–325.

Dodson, J. A., Truong, T. T., Towle, V. R., Kerins, G., & Chaudhry, S. I. (2013). Cognitive impairment in older adults with heart failure: prevalence, documentation, and impact on outcomes. *American Journal of Medicine, 126*, 120–126.

Duron, E., & Hanon, O. (2008). Hypertension, cognitive decline, and dementia. *Archives of Cardiovascular Disease, 101*, 181–190.

Edelmann, F., Gelbrich, G., Dungen, H. D., Frohling, S., Wachter, R., Stahrenberg, R., et al. (2011). Exercise training improves exercise capacity and diastolic function in patients with heart failure with preserved ejection fraction. *Journal of American College of Cardiology, 58*, 1781–1791.

Erickson, K. I., Prakash, R. S., Voss, M. W., Chaddock, L., Hu, L., Morris, K. S., et al. (2009). Aerobic fitness is associated with hippocampal volume in elderly humans. *Hippocampus, 19,* 1030–1039.

Erickson, K. I., Raji, C. A., Lopez, O. L., Becker, J. T., Rosano, C., Newmna, A. B., et al. (2010). Physical activity predicts gray matter volume in late adulthood. *Neurology, 75,* 1415–1422.

Erickson, K. I., Voss, M. W., Prakash, R. S., Basak, C., Szabo, A., Chaddock, L., et al. (2011). Exercise training increases size of hippocampus and improves memory. *Proceedings of National Academy of Sciences United States of America, 108,* 3017–3022.

Evangilista, L. S., Berg, J., & Dracup, K. (2001). Relationship between psychosocial variables and compliance in patients with heart failure. *Heart Lung, 30,* 294–301.

Francis, G. S., Sonnenblick, E. H., Wilson Tang, W. H., & Poole-Wilson, P. (2008). In V. Fuster, R. A. O'Rourke, R. Walsh, & P. Poole-Wilson (Eds.), *Hurst's the heart* (12th ed.) (pp. 691–712). New York: McGraw Hill.

Freyssin, C., Verkindt, C., Prieur, F., Benaich, P., Maunier, S., & Blanc, P. (2012). Cardiac rehabilitation in chronic heart failure: effect of an 8-week, high-intensity interval training versus continuous training. *Archives of Physical Medicine and Rehabilitation, 93,* 1359–1364.

Garcia, S., Alosco, M. L., Spitznagel, M. B., Cohen, R., Raz, N., Sweet, L., et al. (2013). Cardiovascular fitness associated with cognitive performance in heart failure patients enrolled in cardiac rehabilitation. *BMC Cardiovascular Disorders, 13,* 29. http://dx.doi.org/10.1186/1471-2261-13-29.

Garcia, S., Spitznagel, M. B., Cohen, R., Raz, N., Sweet, L., Colbert, L., et al. (2011). Depression is associated with cognitive dysfunction in older adults with heart failure. *Cardiovascular Psychiatry and Neurology.* http://dx.doi.org/10.1155/2011/368324.

Gunstad, J., MacGreggor, K. L., Paul, R. H., Poppas, A., Jefferson, A. L., Todaro, J. F., et al. (2005). Cardiac rehabilitation improves cognitive function in older adults with cardiovascular disease. *Journal of Cardiopulmonary Research, 25,* 173–176.

Hamer, M., & Chida, Y. (2009). Physical activity and risk of neurodegenerative disease: a systematic review of prospective evidence. *Psychological Medicine, 39,* 3–11.

He, J., Ogden, L. G., Bazzano, L. A., Vupputuri, S., Loria, C., & Whelton, P. K. (2001). Risk factors for congestive heart failure in US men and women: NHANES I epidemiologic follow-up study. *Archives of Internal Medicine, 161,* 996–1002.

Ismail, H., McFarlane, J. R., Nojoumian, H., Dieberg, G., & Smart, N. A. (2013). Clinical outcomes and cardiovascular response to different exercise training intensities in patients with heart failure. *Journal of the American College of Cardiology: Heart Failure, 1,* 514–522.

Jackson, G., Gibbs, C. R., Davies, M. K., & Lip, G. Y. H. (2000). ABC of heart failure pathophysiology. *British Medical Journal, 320,* 167–170.

Kirk-Sanchez, N. J., & McGough, E. L. (2014). Physical exercise and cognitive performance in the elderly: current perspectives. *Clinical Interventions in Aging, 9,* 51–62.

Knecht, K. M., Alosco, M. L., Spitznagel, M. B., Cohen, R., Raz, N., Sweet, L., et al. (2012). Sleep apnea and cognitive function in heart failure. *Cardiovascular Psychiatry and Neurology.* http://dx.doi.org/10.1155/2012/402079.

Kohler, S., Thomas, A. J., Lloyd, A., Barber, R., Almeida, O. P., & O'Brien, J. T. (2010). White matter hyperintensities, cortisol levels, brain atrophy, and continuing cognitive deficits in late-life depression. *The British Journal of Psychiatry, 196,* 143–149.

Lund, L. H., & Mancini, D. M. (2008). Peak VO$_2$ in patients with heart failure. *International Journal of Cardiology, 125,* 166–171.

Miller, D. B., & O'Callaghan, J. P. (2005). Aging, stress, and the hippocampus. *Ageing Research Reviews, 4,* 123–140.

Miller, L. A., Spitznagel, L. A., Alosco, M. L., Cohen, R. A., Raz, N., Sweet, L. H., et al. (2012). Cognitive profiles in heart failure: a cluster analytic approach. *Journal of Clinical and Experimental Neuropsychology, 34,* 509–520.

Mikus, C. R., Oberlin, D. J., Libla, J., Boyle, L. J., & Thyfault, J. P. (2011). Glycaemic control is improved by 7 days of aerobic exercise training in patients with type 2 diabetes. *Diabetologia, 55,* 1417–1423.

Mueller, L., Myers, J., Kottman, W., Oswald, U., Boesch, C., Arbol, N., et al. (2007). Exercise capacity, physical activity patterns and outcomes six years after cardiac rehabilitation in patients with heart failure. *Clinical Rehabilitation, 21,* 923–931.

Myers, J., Arena, R., Dewey, F., Bensimhon, D., Abella, J., Hsu, L., et al. (2008). A cardiopulmonary exercise testing score for predicting outcomes in patients with heartfailure. *American Heart Journal, 156,* 1177–1183.

Nocon, M., Hiemann, T., Muller-Riemenschneider, F., Thalau, F., Roll, S., & Willich, S. N. (2008). Association of physical activity with all-cause and cardiovascular mortality: a systematic review and meta-analysis. *European Journal of Cardiovascular Prevention and Rehabilitation, 15,* 239–246.

Oerkild, B., Frederiksen, M., Hansen, J. F., & Prescott, E. (2011). Self-reported physical inactivity predicts survival after hospitalization for heart disease. *European Journal of Preventive Cardiology, 18,* 475–480.

Pressler, S. J., Subramanian, U., Kareken, D., Perkins, S. M., Gradus-Pizlo, I., Sauvé, J., et al. (2010). Cognitive deficits in chronic heart failure. *Nursing Research, 59,* 127–139.

Raz, N., & Rodrigue, K. M. (2006). Differential aging of the brain: patterns, cognitive correlates, and modifiers. *Neuroscience and Biobehavioral Reviews, 30,* 730–748.

Roman, G. C. (2005). Vascular dementia prevention: a risk factor analysis. *Cerebrovascular Diseases, 20,* 91–100.

Sauvé, M. J., Lewis, W. R., Blankenbiller, M., Rickabaugh, B., & Pressler, S. J. (2009). Cognitive impairments in chronic heart failure: a case controlled study. *Journal of Cardiac Failure, 15*, 1–10.

Sforza, E., & Roche, F. (2012). Sleep apnea syndrome and cognition. *Frontiers in Neurology, 3*, 87. http://dx.doi.org/10.3389/fneur.2012/00087.

Sigal, R. J., Kenny, G. P., Wasserman, D. H., & Castaneda-Sceppa, C. (2004). Physical activity/exercise and type 2 diabetes. *Diabetes Care, 27*, 2518–2539.

Smart, N. A., Dieberg, G., & Giallauria, F. (2013). Intermittent versus continuous exercise training in chronic heart failure: a meta-analysis. *International Journal of Cardiology, 166*, 352–358.

Smart, N., & Marwick, T. H. (2004). Exercise training for patients with heart failure: a systematic review of factors that improve mortality and morbidity. *American Journal of Medicine, 116*, 693–706.

Smith, P. J., Blumenthal, J. A., Hoffman, B. M., Cooper, H., Strauman, T. A., Welsh-Bohmer, K., et al. (2010). Aerobic exercise and neurocognitive performance: a meta analytic review of randomized control trials. *Psychosomatic Medicine, 72*, 239–252.

Sofi, F., Valecchi, D., Bacci, D., Abbate, R., Gensini, G. F., Casini, A., et al. (2011). .Physical activity and risk of cognitive decline: a meta-analysis of prospective studies. *Journal of Internal Medicine, 269*, 107–117.

Stanek, K. M., Gunstad, J., Spitznagel, M. B., Waechter, D., Hughes, J. W., Luyster, F., et al. (2011). Improvements in cognitive function following cardiac rehabilitation for older adults with cardiovascular disease. *International Journal of Neuroscience, 121*, 86–93.

Stanek, K. M., Gunstad, J., Paul, R. H., Poppas, A., Jefferson, A. L., Sweet, L. H., et al. (2009). Longitudinal cognitive performance in older adults with cardiovascular disease: evidence for improvement in heart failure. *Journal of Cardiovascular Nursing, 24*, 192–197.

Swedberg, K., Cleland, J., Dargie, H., Drexler, H., Follath, F., Komajda, M., et al. (2005). Guidelines for the diagnosis and treatment of chronic heart failure: executive summary (update 2005): the task force for the diagnosis and treatment of chronic heart failure of the European Society of Cardiology. *European Heart Journal, 26*, 1115–1140.

Tanne, D., Freimark, D., Poreh, A., Merzeliak, O., Bruck, B., Schwammenthal, Y., et al. (2005). Cognitive functions in severe congestive heart failure before and after an exercise training program. *International Journal of Cardiology, 103*, 145–149.

Teychenne, M., Ball, K., & Salmon, J. (2008). Physical activity and likelihood of depression in adults: a review. *Preventive Medicine, 46*, 397–411.

Vanhees, L., Rauch, B., Piepoli, M., van Buuren, F., Takken, T., Borjesson, M., et al. (2012). Importance of characteristics and modalities of physical activity and exercise in the management of cardiovascular health in individuals with cardiovascular disease (part III). *Preventive Cardiology, 19*, 1333–1356.

Vercambre, M. N., Grodstein, F., Manson, J. E., Stampfer, M. J., & Kang, J. H. (2011). Physical activity and cognition in women with vascular conditions. *Archives of Internal Medicine, 171*, 1244–1250.

Vogels, R. L. C., Oosterman, J. M., Laman, D. M., Gouw, A. A., Schroeder-Tanka, J. M., Scheltens, P., et al. (2008). Transcranial doppler blood flow assessment in patients with mild heart failure: correlates with neuroimaging and cognitive performance. *Congestive Heart Failure, 14*, 61–65.

Vogels, R. L. C., Oosterman, J. M., van Harten, B., Scheltens, P., van der Flier, W. M., Schroeder-Tanka, J. M., et al. (2007). Profile of cognitive impairment in chronic heart failure. *Journal of American Geriatrics Society, 55*, 1764–1770.

Vogels, R. L. C., Scheltens, P., Schroeder-Tanka, J. M., & Weinstein, H. C. (2007). Cognitive impairment in heart failure: a systematic review of the literature. *European Journal of Heart Failure, 9*, 440–449.

van der Wal, M. H. L., Jaarsma, T., Moser, D. K., Veeger, N. J., van Gilst, W. H., & van Veldhuisen, D. J. (2006). Compliance in heart failure patients: the importance of knowledge and beliefs. *European Journal of Heart Failure, 27*, 434–440.

Whelton, S. P., Chin, A., Xin, X., & He, J. (2002). Effects of aerobic exercise on blood pressure: a meta-analysis of randomized, controlled trials. *Annals of Internal Medicine, 136*, 493–503.

Zuccala, G., Onder, G., Pedone, C., Cocchi, A., Carosella, L., Cattel, C., et al. (2001). Cognitive dysfunction as a major determinant of disability with heart failure: results from a multicentre survey. *Journal of Neurology, Neurosurgery and Psychiatry, 70*, 109–112.

Zuccala, G., Pedone, C., Cesari, M., Onder, G., Pahor, M., Marzetti, E., et al. (2003). The effects of cognitive impairment on mortality among hospitalized patients with heart failure. *American Journal of Medicine, 115*, 97–103.

The Effect of Regular Exercise on Cognition in Special Populations of Children: Overweight and Attention-Deficit Hyperactivity Disorder

Eduardo E. Bustamante[1], Cynthia E. Krafft[2], David J. Schaeffer[3], Jennifer E. McDowell[3], Catherine L. Davis[1]

[1]Georgia Prevention Institute, Medical College of Georgia, Department of Pediatrics, Georgia Regents University, Augusta, GA, USA; [2]MIND Institute, Department of Psychiatry and Behavioral Sciences, University of California Davis, Sacramento, CA, USA; [3]Department of Neuroscience, University of Georgia, Athens, GA, USA

INTRODUCTION

In the United States, 18% of children and adolescents are obese, and one-third of students are already overweight or obese in elementary school (Ogden, Carroll, Kit, & Flegal, 2014). About 13–20% of US children and adolescents experience a mental health disorder each year, with attention-deficit hyperactivity disorder (ADHD) the most common at 7–8% prevalence (Perou et al., 2013). Unfortunately, high rates are compounded by disparities in prevalence, severity, and recurrence along racial, ethnic, and socioeconomic lines (Ogden et al., 2014; Perou et al., 2013), and the inadequacy of our current preventive and treatment approaches to address

the challenges they present (Kazdin & Rabbitt, 2013; Yancey & Sallis, 2009). These common childhood conditions and their disparities present a moral imperative and practical challenge for our nation. High-quality research can guide our efforts by providing evidence to inform policy. This applies indirectly through identifying mechanisms that may be useful to refine interventions, and more directly through the development of evidence for interventions that result in meaningful improvement on outcomes valued by decision makers, and which are suitable for broad dissemination (Baker, McFall, & Shoham, 2008). Policy implementation research can inform our approaches to changing the status quo (Howie & Stevick, 2014).

Exercise-Cognition Interaction
http://dx.doi.org/10.1016/B978-0-12-800778-5.00021-9

As a nation we face interrelated challenges of unwavering chronic disease and obesity epidemics (Ogden et al., 2014); ubiquitous and affordable fast and processed foods (Kearney, 2010); increasing rates of physical inactivity, such as screen time (Anderson, Economos, & Must, 2008); and decreases in global academic standing (Organization for Economic Cooperation and Development, 2014, p. 173). Programs and policies that promote physical activity may be helpful, because physical activity is critical to physical health across the lifespan ("Physical Activity Guidelines for Americans," 2008) and preliminary evidence suggests that it promotes cognition, brain function, and achievement across the lifespan (Hillman, Erickson, & Kramer, 2008). In this chapter we will focus on such findings specific to special populations of children: those that are overweight or obese, and those with ADHD.

Research in these populations is of particular interest for two main reasons: (1) these are populations in which researchers are most likely to observe the impact of exercise training on children's cognition due to low levels of the dependent variable (i.e., aspects of cognitive function are impaired in children with ADHD (Qian, Shuai, Cao, Chan, & Wang, 2010) and those that are overweight or obese (Davis & Cooper, 2011) relative to children without these conditions) and low exposure to the independent variable of interest (i.e., physical activity and fitness levels are lower in children with ADHD (Cortese & Morcillo, 2010) and those that are overweight or obese Must, & Tybor, 2005; Ness et al. 2007, in a large cohort (N = 5500) with excellent measurement of fat and PA (Davis & Cooper, 2011) relative to children without these conditions); and (2) evidence specific to these populations is of high relevance to practitioners, parents, educators, and policy makers struggling to meet the growing needs presented by these disorders.

Importantly, obesity and ADHD appear to be comorbid (Cortese & Morcillo, 2010), with similar demographic disparities (Adler & Rehkopf, 2008; Nolan, Gadow, & Sprafkin, 2001). Over half of children and adolescents hospitalized for obesity in one study met criteria for ADHD (Agranat–Meged et al., 2005). In another study, boys with ADHD had twice the obesity rate of normal weight peers (Holtkamp et al., 2004). This situation highlights the potential of physical activity as a tool to impact multiple health challenges simultaneously, and the need for research to elucidate the magnitude of physical activity's impact on brain function, cognition, and academic performance, and the means by which such impacts are achieved in order to optimize health intervention strategies.

In this chapter, we will focus on regular (also known as chronic, or habitual) exercise. This term refers to physical activity undertaken over an extended period of time (i.e., weeks, months, or years) in order to achieve health benefits. This is distinct from acute (i.e., single) bouts of exercise, which last only a few minutes or hours. Acute bouts of exercise result in neurobiological, cognitive, and affective changes that are transient, dissipating in a few hours. The literature on acute bouts is especially promising in children with ADHD (Pontifex, Saliba, Raine, Picchietti, & Hillman, 2013) and typically developing children in classroom settings (Howie, Beets, & Pate, 2014; Mahar et al., 2006). With proper planning, transient effects of single bouts of exercise (e.g., increased focus and alertness) can potentially be harnessed to increase daily functioning and lower medication doses in children with ADHD, or perhaps could be scheduled prior to academic classes that typically developing children find boring or difficult (Piepmeier et al., 2015; Ratey & Hagerman, 2008).

Regular exercise or exercise training (a program of regular exercise designed to improve fitness) seems to promise a more ambitious yet enigmatic benefit than the transient increases in concentration deriving from acute bouts. Regular aerobic exercise has been shown to alter the development of brain structure and function during childhood, when circuitry and performance are rapidly changing. It is theorized that these changes might result in improved developmental trajectories, with positive long-term consequences lasting months, years, or over the lifespan (Diamond, 2000; Hillman et al., 2008). Below, we provide an overview of what is known with regard to the long-term exercise–cognition effect in these special populations of children, what is not known, and what to do next.

Executive Function

Kramer and colleagues first presented the "executive control hypothesis," which states that executive function processes and the brain areas that support them are disproportionately influenced by aerobic physical activity (Kramer et al., 1999). The executive control hypothesis was based on evidence that aerobic exercise selectively improves older adults' performance on executive function tasks, and supported by a meta-analysis and a clinical trial showing improved cognitive performance and corresponding changes in brain activation (Colcombe & Kramer, 2003; Colcombe et al., 2004; Kramer et al., 1999). The cognitive benefits of exercise may be greater for children's developing brains than for adults', and therefore might influence long-term trajectories of cognitive development and social functioning (Asato, Terwilliger, Woo, & Luna, 2010; Kolb & Whishaw, 1998).

Executive function (also known as cognitive control or executive control) is a broad construct encompassing higher order cognitive functions necessary for reasoning, problem-solving, planning, organization, and behavioral execution (Diamond, 2013). Planning and carrying out action sequences that make up goal directed behavior requires allocation of attention and memory, response selection and inhibition, goal setting, self-control, self-monitoring, and skillful and flexible use of strategies (Eslinger, 1996). Effortful control is a related concept in developmental psychology, referring to an emotional control aspect of temperament (Diamond, 2013; Rueda, Posner, & Rothbart, 2005).

Miyake identified core elements of executive function: inhibition, working memory (updating), and cognitive flexibility (shifting) (Diamond, 2013; Miyake et al., 2000). Inhibition is defined as controlling one's attention, behavior, thoughts, and/or emotions to override a strong internal predisposition or external lure. Closely related terms include self-control, selective attention, and executive attention. Self-control (e.g., selecting a healthful portion size rather than an excessive portion of tempting food, waiting without interrupting), self-discipline (e.g., persisting at a task even though you would rather stop, delay of gratification), and paying attention while ignoring distractions (selective attention) all require inhibition (Mischel, Shoda, & Rodriguez, 1989; Rachlin, Raineri, & Cross, 1991). Antisaccade, flanker, and go/no go tasks rely on inhibition (Eriksen & Eriksen, 1974; Goldstein et al., 2007; McDowell et al., 2002; Rueda et al., 2004). Working memory refers to holding information in mind and mentally working with it. Working memory is distinct from short-term memory in that short-term memory only requires one to hold in mind information (e.g., remember a telephone number), whereas working memory requires one to hold the numbers in mind while simultaneously manipulating them (e.g., remembering a telephone number and considering the location implications of the area code). The ability to remember a point one wishes to make in a conversation while listening and waiting for one's turn to speak is a manifestation of working memory and inhibition. Working memory tasks include random number generation, backward digit span, and N-back (Diamond, 2013; Miyake et al., 2000). Finally, cognitive flexibility is the most demanding of the core executive functions and refers to creativity, changing perspectives or approaches to a problem, and flexibly adjusting to new demands, rules, or priorities. Examples include, putting asides one's personal views on an issue to considering another's perspective, and changing strategies in a game of chess.

Tasks such as set-shifting and switching tasks are designed to tap cognitive flexibility (Berg, 1948; Reitan, 1971). Together, these three core elements work together to generate more complex executive functions (i.e., reasoning, problem-solving, planning, and fluid intelligence) (Diamond, 2013).

All three executive functions are highly related and interdependent; no task relies exclusively on one core executive function (Davidson, Amso, Anderson, & Diamond, 2006). One cannot perform on an inhibitory task without using memory to retain the rules of the task while executing it. Working memory cannot function without inhibiting unwanted thoughts to clear space for the desired content. Cognitive flexibility cannot be effective without working memory because one cannot switch between approaches to a problem without holding in mind the various options and determining which is correct. Like all processes utilizing mental effort, executive functions are fatigable and trainable (Muraven & Baumeister, 2000; Muraven, Baumeister, & Tice, 1999). Thinking before you act requires all three core functions (inhibition to prevent acting too quickly, working memory to think through possible alternatives and consequences, and cognitive flexibility to consider alternative perspectives and actions). Executive function development begins in early childhood; however, the variability in task performance among children tends to be in accuracy (proportion of correct responses), while in adults it is reaction times (Davidson et al., 2006; Luna, Velanova, & Geier, 2008).

Measures of executive function have typically relied on single neuropsychological tasks with limited reliability and normative information (Rabbitt, 1997). More complex psychometric assessments, such as intelligence tests and academic achievement tests used together to determine eligibility for special education services, have better reliability (in part because they incorporate a number of individual tasks). These tests are scored with reference to a child's age peers. Standard scores (population mean = 100, standard deviation = 15) are used for scales (i.e., composite scores) from such tests; scaled scores (population mean = 10, standard deviation = 3) for the individual subtests comprising those scales. Percentiles can also be used to describe a child's performance. Because performance increases dramatically with development, these tests are preferred for clinical evaluation of children. A few examples include the traditional Wechsler tests of intelligence, the more neuropsychologically oriented Cognitive Assessment System (CAS) and the NEuroPSYchological Assessment test, and academic achievement tests such as the Woodcock-Johnson (Korkman, Kirk, & Kemp, 2007; McGrew & Woodcock, 2001; Naglieri & Das, 1997; Wechsler, 2004).

Three main methods have been used to interrogate neurological processes underlying executive function: (1) functional magnetic resonance imaging (fMRI), (2) electroencephalogram (EEG), and (3) diffusion tensor imaging (DTI).

fMRI: It measures the hemodynamic response of a brain area in real time [termed blood oxygen level dependent (BOLD) activity]. Increases in the BOLD signal indicate the activation of a population of neurons in close proximity to a blood vessel. Increase in oxygenated blood delivery is a signal of resource consumption in a given area. With fMRI, researchers are able to take a snapshot of brain activity at rest and compare it to activity during tasks, demonstrating which areas are active during different cognitive tasks. On occasions that alterations in brain activity resulting from an intervention do not correspond with concomitant changes in cognitive performance in children, it can be unclear whether greater activity in a region is adaptive or maladaptive as both increased resource allocation (greater BOLD activity) and greater efficiency (less BOLD activity) have been interpreted as adaptive in different studies (Chaddock-Heyman et al., 2013; Davis et al., 2011; Krafft, Schwarz et al., 2014). Over the course of development, children first increase in diffuse brain activation in response to a given task; then as they master the task with less mental effort required, their activation becomes more focal (Casey, Giedd, & Thomas, 2000; Tamm, Menon, & Reiss, 2002). Because the BOLD signal depends on hemodynamic function, the temporal resolution of fMRI is relatively slow (on the order of seconds). However, spatial resolution depends largely on the strength (Tesla rating) of the magnet and can be as small as 1 mm per voxel. Clustering of adjacent voxels is a way to limit Type 1 error; there is a balance between false positives and precise locations of brain activation (Ward, 1997). Resting-state fMRI is a variant of this method that measures brain activation at rest, when no task is being undertaken. The best-known feature of the resting-state fMRI literature is the default mode network, which activates during rest and deactivates during task performance; altered connectivity, in particular excessive connectivity between the default mode and cognitive control networks, characterizes ADHD and may explain attentional lapses (Posner, Park, & Wang, 2014).

EEG: It uses electrodes placed on the scalp to measure the brain's spontaneous electrical activity. Electrical potentials arising from different areas of the brain can be decomposed into their component frequencies, and changes in the relative contribution of activity at different frequencies have been linked to different cognitive states. The P300 event-related potential amplitude is used to assess attentional resource allocation in response to a stimulus, including attention and working memory processes (Polich, 2007). EEG signals reflect the local field potential in a population of neurons and thus allow researchers to examine the amount of synchrony in neural firing. EEG has a quicker temporal resolution than fMRI (milliseconds), because it depends on electrical rather than hemodynamic changes. However, spatial resolution is limited. Thus, EEG is a complementary method to fMRI (Mulert, 2013).

DTI: Structural MRI allows researchers to discern neural anatomy including gray matter, which is comprised of unmyelinated neurons associated with local processing, and white matter, comprised of myelinated axons, which provide the means for communication across brain regions. DTI, a form of structural MRI, characterizes the degree of white matter coherence by measuring the anisotropy (directional dependence) of water diffusion within the tissue. As an interconnecting neural tract is myelinated as a child matures, water diffuses more rapidly in the direction aligned with the white matter tract and more slowly perpendicular to the tract. Higher levels of anisotropic diffusion (in the direction of the tract) correspond to a greater extent of microstructural integrity of white matter (i.e., axonal membrane structure and myelination) and are often indexed by fractional anisotropy, a scalar measure from 0 to 1 where 0 = equal movement of water in all directions (isotropic) and 1 = movement along the direction of the tract, termed fully anisotropic diffusion (Beaulieu, 2002). A complementary measure of white matter structural integrity is radial diffusivity (RD); lower values of RD primarily reflect a greater degree of myelination (Johansen-Berg & Behrens, 2009; Song et al., 2002). Unlike fMRI and EEG, DTI is a measure of structure rather than function so it does not change across tasks. Moreover, DTI results are more straightforward to interpret than fMRI and EEG. Greater white matter integrity is considered adaptive, and less white matter integrity is maladaptive or immature.

Exercise Training Improves Executive Function in Typically Developing Children

Substantial evidence demonstrates that executive function benefits from aerobic exercise across the lifespan, including in typically developing children (Hillman et al., 2008, 2014). Mechanisms have been described that may explain these changes (Dishman et al., 2006). A randomized controlled trial in 221 typically developing children demonstrated greater improvements on a cognitive flexibility task, and alterations in EEG activity in a 9 month after-school physical activity program relative to a wait-list control group (Hillman et al., 2014).

EXERCISE TRAINING AND COGNITION IN OVERWEIGHT AND OBESE CHILDREN

Observational Studies of Fitness, Fatness, and Children's Neurocognitive Function

Childhood obesity has more than doubled in children and tripled in adolescents since 1980 (US. Department of Health and Human Services, 2012; Ogden et al., 2014). Driven by environmental shifts, this unwavering epidemic has troubling implications for physical and mental health, including children's cognition and academic performance (Adler & Rehkopf, 2008). Cross-sectional studies demonstrate that children who are overweight or obese are low on both the independent variables (physical activity and fitness) (Must & Tybor, 2005) and the dependent variables (brain function, cognition, and academic performance) (Davis & Cooper, 2011). An important limitation to studies examining relationships between physical activity, weight status, physical fitness, and cognition is that they are unable to disentangle the independent effects of these factors on cognition, since the outcomes are so highly related. For example, Davis and Cooper found that measures of lower fatness and better fitness (relative body mass index, waist girth, body fat, and aerobic fitness) were each associated with better cognition, achievement, and behavior ratings. But were the differences in functioning due to weight status and adiposity, or were they due to some other factor? For example, overweight children are typically less physically active and watch more TV (Eisenmann, Bartee, & Wang, 2002), are more

likely to have sleep disorders than normal weight children (Redline et al., 1999), and are likely to have poorer fitness (Cottrell, Northrup, & Wittberg, 2007; Ortega, Ruiz, Castillo, & Sjostrom, 2008) and diet quality. Each of these factors has been related to children's cognitive capacity and academic functioning (Bourke et al., 2011; Hillman et al., 2008; Jennings, Welch, van Sluijs, Griffin, & Cassidy, 2011; Roberts, Freed, & McCarthy, 2010; Sigfúsdóttir, Kristjánsson, & Allegrante, 2007; Stevenson & Prescott, 2014; van der Niet et al., 2014; Zimmerman & Christakis, 2005); therefore, any combination of these may have driven the relationships identified in a cross-sectional analysis.

Recent observational studies have taken preliminary steps toward disentangling the effects of fitness, fatness, and physical activity on children's cognition. To assess the independent effects of regular physical activity and weight status, Davis and colleagues compared cognitive scores between groups of normal weight active, normal weight sedentary, and overweight or obese sedentary children, matched for each comparison on demographic characteristics, including socioeconomic status indicators (Davis, Tkacz, Tomporowski, & Bustamante, in press). Physical activity status was based on enrollment in an organized extra-curricular physical activity program. Normal weight active children had higher CAS Planning and Attention scores than overweight or obese sedentary children. This contrast reflects the combined impact of weight status and physical activity level. A contrast isolating the impact of physical activity on normal weight children found higher Planning scores, a measure of complex executive function, in the regularly active children. The contrast isolating weight status among sedentary children showed higher Attention scores in the normal weight children. Thus, weight status may independently influence selective attention, while physical activity may independently influence children's more complex executive function.

Pontifex et al. (2014) approached a related research question, focusing on fitness rather than physical activity behavior, using statistical modeling methods in preadolescent children. They identified unique independent relationships of both adiposity and physical fitness with performance on inhibition and cognitive flexibility tasks. Findings reinforce that fitness and adiposity appear to be separable factors, as fitness was independently associated with both inhibition and cognitive flexibility whereas adiposity was only independently associated with cognitive flexibility.

These cross-sectional data present a strong starting point but cannot address the causal direction of the relationships between physical health factors and cognition in children. For example, it is reasonable to speculate that lower executive function, particularly inhibition, could manifest in overindulgence in unhealthy lifestyles, which might in turn lead to obesity. What's more, even in a longitudinal study where one can establish temporal precedence, there is still no confidence that increases in one factor caused improvements in another; for this, randomized clinical trials are necessary (Davis & Cooper, 2011; Keeley & Fox, 2009).

Randomized Controlled Trials of Exercise Training in Children Who are Overweight or Obese

To date, two randomized controlled trials of exercise training on cognition in overweight or obese children have been conducted. Both have focused on executive functions and the brain areas that support them, especially the prefrontal cortex, a brain region that is crucial for executive function tasks and is highly connected to other brain regions. The first, entitled the "PLAY project" Davis et al. (2011), randomized a community sample of overweight or obese children (N = 222) into three groups: high dose (40 min of exercise training per day

after school), low dose (20 min of exercise training per day after school), or a no-intervention group for 12 weeks. The exercise treatments reduced fatness, improved fitness, and reduced diabetes risk (Davis et al., 2012). Prior to and following the intervention, measures of cognitive processes (CAS), brain function (fMRI), mental health (depressive symptoms and self-worth), and academic achievement were obtained (Davis et al., 2011). This research design is unique because it tested a dose–response relationship (i.e., 0 min vs 20 min vs 40 min per day of vigorous physical activity) using an experimental design rather than *post hoc* association. Experimental data and dose–response relationships are important forms of evidence to establish causality (Hill, 1965). Both exercise training groups were well attended (M = 85%, SD = 13%), with high daily average heart rates showing vigorous exertion (M = 166, SD = 8 beats per minute in physical activity groups). Aerobic fitness tests confirmed the training effect of both exercise groups versus the no-intervention control condition; however, effects were similar between the exercise groups, suggesting that exercise intensity is more influential than volume (i.e., intensity X time, energy expenditure) in determining fitness effects. Findings from this trial provide strong evidence for a causal impact of an exercise program on overweight children's brain function, cognition, mental health, and academic performance, as described below.

Results from the Planning Scale of the CAS (Naglieri & Das, 1997) demonstrated a linear dose–response trend across the three conditions (N = 171) such that a higher dose of (i.e., more time in) the exercise training program resulted in greater benefits in executive function (i.e., the Planning Scale of the CAS) across the intervention period. A concomitant dose–response trend was observed for math achievement between groups over the intervention period, despite no math instruction in the exercise program. No other CAS scales, including

Attention, responded to the program, supporting the selective effect of exercise training on more complex executive functions. Figure 1 presents findings on Planning and Math across groups (Davis et al., 2011).

A dose–response benefit of exercise on depressive symptoms was also observed in the PLAY project (Petty, Davis, Tkacz, Young-Hyman, & Waller, 2009). This finding concurs with the best-documented finding in the physical activity and mental health literature, antidepressive effects (Penedo & Dahn, 2005). A dose–response effect of exercise was found on global self-worth among White, but not Black participants in the PLAY project (Petty et al., 2009). The reason for the disparate findings between White and Black children on self-worth is unclear, but the authors hypothesized

that it may be due to differing cultural values related to body size (Smith, Thompson, Raczynski, & Hilner, 1999).

Concomitant group × time differences in brain activation patterns during an antisaccade (inhibition) task were found in a subsample from the PLAY project (Davis et al., 2011). Findings demonstrated greater increases in BOLD activity in the prefrontal cortex, and greater decreases in BOLD activity in the posterior parietal cortex, in the exercise training groups relative to children randomized to the no-intervention control condition. Figure 2 presents fMRI results in an image format while Figure 3 presents them in boxplot form.

In the context of improvements in executive function seen in the exercise conditions versus no-intervention control group, the findings

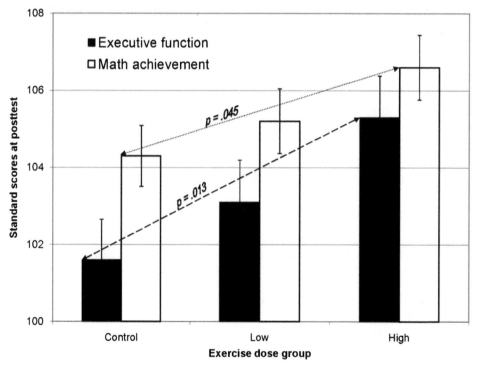

FIGURE 1   Executive function (planning) at posttest, adjusted for sex, parent education, and baseline score; and math achievement means (SE) at posttest, adjusted for race, parent education, and baseline score, showing dose–response effects of the aerobic exercise program. *Reprinted on May 8, 2015 with permission of the American Psychological Association from article: Davis et al. (2011).*

of altered BOLD activity in the prefrontal and parietal cortex were posited to be a potential mechanism underlying the cognitive benefits of regular exercise. The authors suggest that as the prefrontal cortex picks up a greater share of the cognitive demands of the inhibition task, that the posterior parietal cortex may be relieved of its burden, or alternatively that the prefrontal cortex may actively suppress the posterior parietal cortex in order to complete the task more effectively (Davis et al., 2011).

The PLAY project was a landmark study in that it demonstrated dose–response effects of a physical activity program on cognitive and mental health outcomes (Davis et al., 2011; Petty et al., 2009). However, the design was unable to disentangle the extent to which the benefit was due to exposure to additional physical activity, or exposure to other important program features such as engaging and structured activities, attention from adult staff, social interaction, rules, and behavioral incentives. Thus, the SMART

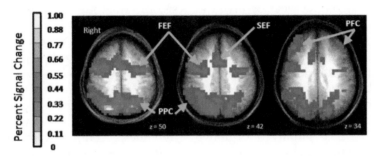

FIGURE 2 Axial views displaying blood oxygenation level-dependent percent signal change associated with antisaccade performance from one-sample analysis. Data from 39 sessions (20 children at baseline, 19 at posttest) are shown radiologically oriented (right hemisphere on left side). Colors from pink to yellow indicate increasing percent signal change. The background is an anatomical image averaged over 20 participants. FEF, frontal eye field; SEF, supplementary eye field; PFC, prefrontal cortex; PPC, posterior parietal cortex. *Reprinted on May 8, 2015 with permission of the American Psychological Association from article: Davis et al. (2011).*

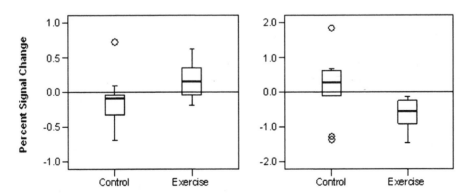

FIGURE 3 Boxplots by experimental condition showing change in activation from baseline to posttest. Left panel: prefrontal cortex. Right panel: posterior parietal cortex. *Adapted on May 8, 2015 with permission of the American Psychological Association from article: Davis et al. (2011).*

study utilized a sedentary attention control comparison group to isolate the impact of the aerobic exercise *per se* from other program elements (Krafft, Pierce et al., 2014; Krafft, Schaeffer et al., 2014; Krafft, Schwarz et al., 2014; Schaeffer et al., 2014). The study also implemented a longer intervention (8 months vs 3 months), and added DTI measures of white matter integrity. Primary outcomes were cognition and fMRI activation.

The white matter integrity measures focused on the superior longitudinal fasciculus, the main white matter tract connecting the prefrontal and posterior parietal cortices where differences in activation due to exercise were observed in the PLAY project. The development of executive function capacity from childhood through young adulthood parallels the progression of myelination of white matter during this period. Better functional connectivity supported by improved myelination, particularly in long-range tracts such as the superior longitudinal fasciculus, may underlie improved cognitive capacity by connecting the prefrontal cortex to other regions (Asato et al., 2010; Lebel et al., 2012). Executive function is associated with the superior longitudinal fasciculus (Klarborg et al., 2013; Vestergaard et al., 2011). Therefore, greater exercise-induced improvement in white matter integrity in the superior longitudinal fasciculus was predicted.

The study examined another white matter tract, the uncinate fasciculus, a frontotemporal white matter fiber tract with projections between the hippocampal area and dorsolateral prefrontal cortex (Schmahmann et al., 2007). White matter integrity in the uncinate fasciculus has been related to verbal memory in children (Mabbott, Rovet, Noseworthy, Smith, & Rockel, 2009), and physical fitness is related to brain activation during verbal memory tasks (Herting & Nagel, 2013), hippocampal volume (Chaddock et al., 2010), and uncinate fasciculus integrity (Marks et al., 2007). Thus, the authors hypothesized that the exercise training program would show greater gains in uncinate fasciculus integrity and

verbal memory relative to the sedentary attention control program.

The SMART study randomized 175 children to the exercise training program or a comparable, but sedentary, attention control program. Each met every school day, for approximately an academic year (~8 months). To date, four papers have been published from these data reporting neurobiological benefits of exercise (Krafft, Pierce et al., 2014; Krafft, Schaeffer et al., 2014; Krafft, Schwarz et al., 2014; Schaeffer et al., 2014); results on cognitive and achievement outcomes are forthcoming. Krafft, Schwarz et al. found significant group × time changes in fMRI BOLD activity. Consistent with the results of the PLAY project, alterations were found in prefrontal and posterior parietal cortices in BOLD activity during cognitive tasks (i.e., antisaccade and flanker tasks), but the behavioral performance on the tasks did not differ by group. It is possible that the more stringent test of the exercise–cognition hypothesis, controlling for other program elements, is responsible for this null finding. However, the neuroimaging assays may simply be more sensitive than cognitive tests to the effects of exercise intervention. Improved resting-state fMRI results were also detected: the default mode, cognitive control, and motor networks showed more spatial refinement over time in the exercise group compared to controls, consistent with quicker brain maturation in the exercise group (Krafft, Pierce et al., 2014).

Krafft et al. reported a group × time × attendance interaction on superior longitudinal fasciculus white matter integrity, such that attendance to the exercise training program was related to greater gains, while attendance to the attendance control program was unrelated (Krafft, Schaeffer et al., 2014). Moreover, when participants were split between those that demonstrated an increase in white matter integrity in the superior longitudinal fasciculus and those that did not (regardless of randomization), the groups differed in improvements on both teacher ratings and neuropsychological tests of executive function, a rare and meaningful example of a relationship between neurobiological and behavioral changes in the exercise–cognition literature (Krafft, Schaeffer et al., 2014). Findings in the other white matter tract investigated in the SMART trial, the uncinate fasciculus, were even more robust. A group × time interaction emerged such that participants in the exercise training program demonstrated greater gains in white matter integrity in the uncinate fasciculus relative to those in the attention control condition (Schaeffer et al., 2014). The results from the full sample (forthcoming) will lend important insights into the influence of regular exercise *per se* on children's cognitive function and academic achievement.

EXERCISE TRAINING AND COGNITION IN CHILDREN WITH ATTENTION-DEFICIT HYPERACTIVITY DISORDER

ADHD is characterized by developmentally excessive inattention, hyperactivity, and/or impulsivity that disrupts functioning in multiple settings (American Psychiatric Association, 1994). National prevalence of ADHD in children and adolescents is estimated to be about 7–9% (Perou et al., 2013; Froehlich et al., 2007), but teachers report rates as high as 16% among students overall (Nolan et al., 2001), and as high as 44% among African-American students (Nolan et al., 2001). If untreated, children with ADHD are likely to suffer impairments in socialization and academic performance that persist into adulthood and impact educational, employment, driving, sexual, reproductive, and relationship outcomes (Barkley, 2002).

Thus far, there are evidence-based psychopharmacological and psychosocial interventions for ADHD. Medication is effective in reducing symptoms, but 20% of children experience side effects, such as insomnia, social stigma, mood disturbance, high blood pressure, or appetite suppression (Barkley, 1998). Psychosocial interventions are also effective but require extensive time and effort by teachers and other caregivers. Seventy to 80% of psychosocial services are provided in schools; however, in low-income schools, limited resources, deteriorating conditions, high staff stress, and pressure to improve standardized test scores make time and resources associated with intervention implementation challenging (Atkins, Frazier, Adil, & Talbott, 2003; Boyd & Shouse, 1997). Consequently, an analysis of three national surveys indicated that nearly 80% of low-income youth, and 90% of uninsured youth, in need of mental health services had not received any within the preceding 12 months (Kataoka, Zhang, & Wells, 2002). Thus, there is a need for additional, perhaps adjunct treatments with broad reach to address this unmet need. Physical activity programs might help fill this gap.

ADHD is Characterized by Deficits in Executive Function

Barkley (1997, 2001) first argued that ADHD is the behavioral manifestation of impairments in the development of executive function. Indeed, the literature has borne this out, with parents and teachers reporting higher levels of behaviors consistent with executive dysfunction in everyday life in ADHD versus typically developing children (Qian et al., 2010). Children with ADHD perform significantly worse on neuropsychological tasks of executive function than typically developing peers (Wodka et al., 2008).

Neurobiological Underpinnings of ADHD

Findings from studies using fMRI, DTI, and EEG suggest that functional and structural abnormalities (e.g., catecholamine dysregulation (Casey et al., 1997; Filipek et al., 1997; Heilman, Voeller, & Nadeau, 1991; Hynd et al., 1993a; Hynd,

Semrudclikeman, Lorys, Novey, & Eliopulos, 1990; Prince, 2008; Sagvolden, Johansen, Aase, & Russell, 2005) and blood flow or volume asymmetries (Castellanos et al., 1996; Filipek et al., 1997; Hynd et al., 1993) in the frontal lobes) form the fundamental pathophysiology of ADHD. Diamond (2007, 2011) has shown that the ADHD inattentive subtype is distinct from ADHD with hyperactivity, in pathophysiology as well as symptoms. When ADHD symptoms include hyperactivity, a striatal abnormality in a prefrontal–striatal circuit seems to be at fault. For children with the inattentive type of ADHD, the striatum is not involved; it is prefrontal cortex activity that is suboptimal. The prefrontal–striatal circuitry of interest in ADHD hyperactive–impulsive subtype is pictured in Figure 4. Genetic polymorphisms relate to the two subtypes

differently. Polymorphisms in the DAT1 gene, which codes for dopamine active transporter (DAT), a protein that clears dopamine from synapses. DAT occurs abundantly in the striatum but less so in the prefrontal cortex, is correlated with hyperactive–impulsive symptoms but not inattentive symptoms, while polymorphisms in the DRD4 gene, a dopamine receptor present in the prefrontal cortex but not the striatum, is related to attention but not hyperactivity (Diamond, 2007, 2011). Furthermore, children with the inattentive-only type are not as responsive as hyperactive–impulsive children to methylphenidate, a drug that blocks DAT-mediated reuptake of dopamine (Diamond, 2007).

Our research team recently conducted a pilot study of brain imaging in which 11 children with

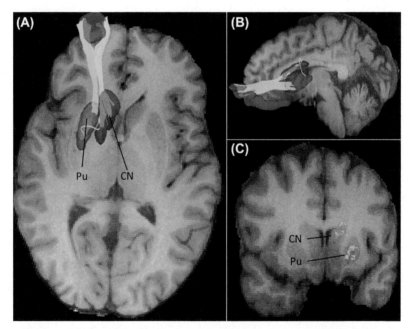

FIGURE 4   Prefrontal–striatal white matter fiber connectivity. Fibers were traced from regions transformed from the Automated Anatomical Labeling (AAL) atlas1 to the DTI native space of a representative subject. (A) shows fibers seeded in left orbitofrontal cortex (red) that connect to putamen (Pu; green) and caudate nucleus (CN; blue) on an axial T1 weighted slice. Fibers connecting orbitofrontal cortex to Pu are shown in light green; fibers connecting orbitofrontal cortex to CN are shown in cyan. (B) shows the same regions and fibers as panel a, but overlaid on a sagittal T1 weighted slice. (C) shows the endpoint distributions of the fibers in CN (cyan) and Pu (light green) on a coronal T1 slice.

ADHD (10 medicated, 10 Black) were matched to 11 Black children without ADHD. Results indicated significantly greater brain activation during a cognitive task in two right-lateralized regions located mainly in the dorsolateral prefrontal cortex and caudate nucleus in children with ADHD compared to children in the control group. Although comparable on behavioral measures, the groups differed in the recruitment of neural circuitry in support of task performance, suggesting that medication increased activation enough in the prefrontal–striatal circuits to normalize performance (Schwarz et al., in review).

Exercise–Cognition Potential in Children with ADHD

A conceptual model for how exercise training may benefit children with ADHD is presented in Figure 5.

Exercise training might permit reduction of the medication dose and provide reprieve to children unresponsive to medication, those that do not have access to medication, those for whom medication does not provide sufficient symptom relief, and those for whom the side effects

disrupt their daily functioning via sleep, mood, and appetite changes. Implications also extend to the management of children with ADHD by clinicians, parents, teachers, and schools such that physical activity might be considered as an adjunct to broader treatment plans.

A promising but methodologically weak literature specific to ADHD and physical activity has emerged in recent years dominated by acute bout studies (Gapin & Etnier, 2010; Medina et al., 2010; Piepmeier et al., 2015; Pontifex et al., 2013; Tantillo, Kesick, Hynd, & Dishman, 2002) and single group (Halperin et al., 2012; Smith et al., 2013) and nonrandomized trials (Chang, Hung, Huang, Hatfield, & Hung, 2014; McKune, Pautz, & Lomjbard, 2004; Verret, Guay, Berthiaume, Gardiner, & Beliveau, 2012).

Halperin et al. (2012) and Smith et al. (2013) demonstrated moderate–large within-group effects on inattention/hyperactivity, inhibition, impairment, and interrupting, but absence of comparison groups in these studies makes it difficult to draw conclusions about the unique contributions of the interventions. The quasi-experimental studies (nonrandomized trials) have shown equivocal results. Two nonrandomized trials showed greater improvements in

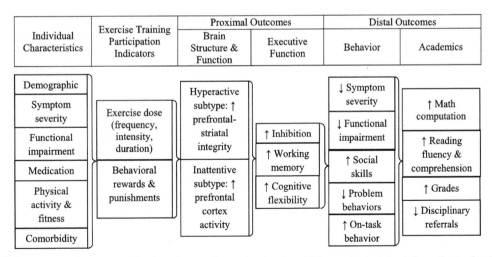

FIGURE 5 Aspects of neurocognitive function are the mechanism by which exercise training is hypothesized to influence behavior, which in turn is hypothesized to influence academic performance. Individual characteristics and participation indicators are hypothesized to moderate the impact of exercise training.

physical activity than no-intervention controls on inhibition, information processing, sustained attention, and social, thought, attentional, and total problems (Chang et al., 2014; Verret et al., 2012), while a third showed no differences between groups over time (McKune et al., 2004). This literature provides only preliminary evidence of a transient impact of acute physical activity on cognition, and associations between regular physical activity and cognition in children with ADHD. Rigorous randomized controlled trials, however, are necessary to establish causal impacts of regular physical activity on ADHD outcomes. To date, one large and two smaller trials have been published investigating the impact of multi-week physical activity interventions on children with ADHD (Choi, Han, Kang, Jung, & Renshaw, 2015; Hoza et al., 2014; Kang, Choi, Kang, & Han, 2011).

Kang et al. (2011) employed a random assignment of 32 children with ADHD and demonstrated greater gains (N=28) on inattention, cooperativeness, working memory, and cognitive flexibility in 6 weeks of "medication and education for behavior control" (N=15, 50 min, biweekly, 2 staff) versus "medication and sports therapy" (N=13, 90 min, biweekly, 4 staff) (Kang et al., 2011). In 2015, this same group published results of a trial randomizing 35 adolescent males with ADHD to the same conditions. Per protocol analyses (N=30) (24% of those initially randomized to sports therapy were excluded from analyses for nonadherence) suggested greater improvements in brain function, especially the dorsolateral prefrontal cortex, and ADHD symptom severity in sports therapy (N=13, 90 min, 3 days/week, 6 staff, 6 weeks) compared to education (N=17, 50 min, biweekly, 2 staff, 6 weeks) (Choi et al., 2015). In both of these studies, differences between groups in format (active vs passive), staffing, behavior management strategies, and intervention duration result in multiple confounds that preclude isolation of physical activity's impact on outcomes. In addition, per protocol analyses

(i.e., excluding children who did not adhere to the assigned conditions) result in potentially biased findings in both studies. The CONSORT guidance considers a per protocol analysis to be a "non-randomised, observational comparison," because it compromises randomization by introducing bias (Moher et al., 2010).

The largest and most rigorous trial of regular physical activity on ADHD to date was Hoza et al. (2014), who randomized predominantly middle class K-2nd grade students at risk for ADHD (N=94) and typically developing children (N=108) to a before-school physical activity program or a structured sedentary attention control program of equal duration (5 days per week, 30 min per day, 12 weeks). Both programs used similar behavior management strategies (e.g., praise, effective instruction, and token economy), effectively isolating the impact of physical activity. They did not describe who generated the random allocation sequence, how it was generated, nor the concealment of this sequence from the investigators enrolling participants. While intent-to-treat analyses were a strength of the study, last observation carried forward was used to impute missing posttest measures; this process has been widely criticized for introducing bias (Moher et al., 2010). The study yielded similar within-group improvements in the physical activity program as studies described above on symptom severity and social functioning (neurological and cognitive measures were not reported), but participants in the arts and crafts focused attention control group demonstrated similar gains. Consequently, the physical activity group demonstrated greater gains than attention control participants on only 1 of 12 measures (parent-reported inattentive symptoms). There was no evidence of differential effects of physical activity for ADHD versus typically developing children (Hoza et al., 2014).

Thus, in contrast to the findings from the two smaller trials (Choi et al., 2015; Kang et al., 2011), findings from this trial were null. Moreover, though this trial was more rigorous than its predecessors, the study used an unorthodox randomization process (switching group assignment for some children after randomization to rebalance groups, rather than stratifying randomization on relevant factors), and neither this study nor the two smaller trials reported adherence measures (e.g., heart rate), provided sufficient levels of activity to meet current guidelines (U.S. Department of Health and Human Services, 2008), excluded sibling pairs from analyses (sibling pairs are not independent observations), or met CONSORT criteria for reporting of clinical trials (i.e., blind, randomization, power analysis, allocation concealment, and specification of primary outcome) (Moher et al., 2010).

A fourth randomized controlled trial of exercise training for ADHD was distinct from the previous trials in several ways (Bustamante et al., in review). (1) Sample (exclusion of siblings and typically developing children from analyses, inclusion of children with disruptive behavior disorders (DBD) as well as ADHD, and recruitment of an African-American sample living in an urban poor community with limited access to safe, structured activities, high rates of childhood behavioral disorders, and few available mental health services resources), (2) intervention delivery (provision of a physical activity dose sufficient to meet current guidelines, which was larger (50 h of structured and 25 h of unstructured physical activity vs 18 h (Kang et al., 2011), 27 h (Choi et al., 2015), and 30 h (Hoza et al., 2014)) and more vigorous than previous trials (75% of maximum heart rate during structured activity vs 60% in previous trials (Choi et al., 2015; Kang et al., 2011)), (3) measurement and analytic design (randomization, intent-to-treat analysis, adherence measures, comparison to a sedentary attention control program with staff rotated across conditions and behavior management systems held constant to avoid bias and isolate the impact of physical activity, exclusion of sibling pairs from analyses, inclusion of novel outcomes, blinding of data collectors, and specification of primary and secondary outcomes),

and (4) reporting (adherence to CONSORT reporting standards) (Moher et al., 2010).

This study randomized 35 children with ADHD and/or DBD (i.e., oppositional defiant disorder and conduct disorder) living in an urban poor African-American community to either a 10-week after-school physical activity program, which provided 60 min of structured and 30 min of unstructured physical activity per day, 5 days per week, or a sedentary attention control program focused on arts and crafts activities (Bustamante et al., in review). While the program met its feasibility goals, no group × time interactions were significant in mixed models. Small to moderate group × time effect sizes (Cohen's d, a measure of the magnitude of an effect) (Cohen, 1988) were hypothesized to favor the physical activity group on secondary outcomes of cognition and behavior. A moderate effect size favored physical activity on hyperactive symptom severity, and a small effect size favored controls on visuospatial working memory. In each group, within-group effect sizes were moderate to large on most outcomes. In more clinically relevant terms, ADHD symptom severity dropped by one-third, while impairment and school disciplinary referrals dropped by more than half. The small effect size on visuospatial working memory favoring controls was further buoyed by a group × time × attendance interaction on that outcome, such that attendance to the control program was related to greater improvements in visuospatial working memory while attendance to the exercise program was not.

These results suggest some potentially unique benefits of physically active versus sedentary extracurricular programs on children's cognition and behavior. For example, the moderate effect size on hyperactive symptom severity favoring physical activity over the sedentary attention control condition suggests a potentially unique benefit of regular aerobic activity on hyperactive symptoms above and beyond other program features, while the small effect size and attendance interaction favoring controls on visuospatial working memory suggest a training specificity effect of the arts and crafts-based control program. In a review of the executive function intervention literature, Diamond (2011) suggested that diverse activities, both active and sedentary, generate executive function adaptations specific to the dimension that is stressed (Diamond & Lee, 2011); thus, different activities (e.g., physical activity, art, and music) may have differential effects on cognition. In the case of visuospatial working memory, the outcome measure was similar to the arts and craft activities in that it required participants to remember the position and orientation of materials.

Overall, however, the similar pattern of results between Bustamante and colleagues (Bustamante et al., in review) and Hoza and colleagues (Hoza et al., 2014) (moderate to large effect sizes over time within physical activity and sedentary groups, but largely small non-significant effects between groups over time) underscore the importance of features of quality programs generally, such as consistent routines, engaging activities, prosocial interaction, adult attention, homework support, and behavior management strategies for improving cognition and behavior in children with ADHD (Frazier, Chacko, Van Gessel, O'Boyle, & Pelham, 2012; Posner & Vandell, 1994).

The evidence for a regular exercise effect on cognition in children with ADHD is compelling but insufficient. Acute bout, cross-sectional, and quasi-experimental evidence is promising but only three published studies utilized randomized controlled designs, and each suffered from methodological shortcomings. Preliminary results suggest that physical activity programs outperform no-intervention and education comparison groups, but not quality sedentary attention control programs. Unfortunately, to date, no three-arm study has compared a physical activity program versus a sedentary attention control program versus a no-intervention comparison group. Without the third arm, neither Hoza et al.

(2014) nor Bustamante et al. (in review) can state definitively that the within-group improvements identified in those studies were due to the interventions and not confounding factors (e.g., practice, expectancy, maturation, and history). Some might erroneously contend that significant findings from such a trial are a foregone conclusion, but children with ADHD present with a unique neurocognitive etiology, and while it is possible that they may derive a greater benefit from exercise training than other populations due to lower baseline functioning, it is also possible that the same neurological dysfunctions that impair their cognition could also impair their responsivity to exercise training. Moreover, it is critical that scientists demonstrate the efficacy of interventions before investing substantial societal resources in treatment strategies such as physical activity (Moher et al., 2010). On the other hand, the broadly health promoting nature of physical activity (Strong et al., 2005) and absence of negative side effects argue for implementing vigorous physical activity programs for children with ADHD before overwhelming experimental evidence is available (Hill, 1965). Once efficacy is established, questions about the neurobiological mechanism and active program ingredients may remain. To date, no studies of regular exercise in preadolescent children with ADHD have utilized brain imaging. Figure 5 hypothesized some candidate mediation pathways, but these are yet to be tested. Once neurobiological mechanisms are identified, it remains for researchers to discern how best to harness this knowledge to maximize program benefits.

CONCLUSIONS AND FUTURE DIRECTIONS

Research on the impact of regular physical activity on cognition in special populations of children largely supports the broader literature on regular exercise and cognition in that preliminary data suggest that physical activity programs benefit cognitive function. Perhaps more than anything else, what the research on special populations of children adds is that much of this benefit may derive from features of these programs other than their physical activity. Three trials from this literature, Hoza et al. (2014), Bustamante et al. (in review), and Krafft et al. (2014) each compared physical activity programs to equivalent but sedentary attention control programs. Each found some differences favoring physical activity (e.g., brain activation (Krafft, Schwarz et al., 2014), white matter integrity (Krafft, Schaeffer et al., 2014), parent-reported inattention (Hoza et al., 2014), and hyperactive–impulsive symptom severity (Bustamante et al., in review)), however, overall results reported have been null on cognitive tasks and behavioral outcomes. The results of these studies diverge from studies in which physical activity programs were compared to no-intervention controls (Chaddock-Heyman et al., 2013; Davis et al., 2011; Hillman et al., 2014; Kamijo et al., 2011) or education (Choi et al., 2015; Kang et al., 2011) and results decisively favored physical activity programs across domains. This divergence reflects the substantially more stringent comparison presented by a quality sedentary attention-control program.

The 2008 Federal Physical Activity Guidelines Committee report (U.S. Department of Health and Human Services, 2008) presented a series of questions for each mental health benefit of physical activity. Questions specific to cognitive function included:

1. "Do the effects of physical activity on cognitive function differ according to genetics, age, sex, race/ethnicity, or medical condition?"
2. "Do the effects of physical activity vary according to features of physical activity, including type, intensity, or timing (i.e., session duration, weekly frequency, and length of participation)?"

Seven years later, we remain unable to answer these questions and more information has yielded more questions. The PLAY study found that among overweight or obese children, program impacts did not vary by gender or race (Davis et al., 2011); however, genetic differences and medical conditions have yet to be explored. Genetic differences are especially intriguing for identifying neurobiological mechanisms of impact, as several genome-wide association studies have revealed single nucleotide polymorphisms that are related to both child obesity and specific brain processes.

For example, a polymorphism affects the activity of catechol-O-methyltransferase (COMT), an enzyme that degrades dopamine and is present throughout the central nervous system, including cerebral cortex, numerous subcortical brain regions, and the spinal cord (Hong, Shu-Leong, Tao, & Lap-Ping, 1998; Matsumoto et al., 2003). Evidence indicates that COMT is particularly important in the prefrontal cortex, a brain region crucial for cognitive control, due to the fact that it is the prefrontal cortex's major clearing step for synaptic dopamine (Tunbridge, Bannerman, Sharp, & Harrison, 2004) because unlike other brain regions (e.g., striatum), DAT is relatively scarce in the prefrontal cortex. In studies of adults, individuals homozygous for the valine (Val) allele have greater COMT activity and thus less synaptic dopamine and lower cognitive performance compared to those homozygous for the methionine (Met) allele (MM carriers) (Chen et al., 2004). Among individuals with ADHD, the COMT genotype has been related to both hyperactive–impulsive symptom severity (Halleland, Lundervold, Halmøy, Haavik, & Johansson, 2009) and responsivity to ADHD medication (Mattay et al., 2003). Thus, investigation of variation of physical activity impact by the COMT genotype would have interesting implications for the role of catecholamine regulation in the prefrontal cortex in regular exercise's impact on cognition. Explorations of genetic and epigenetic mechanisms of impact have grown exponentially in recent years and may have tremendous implications for our understanding of the relationships between physical activity and mental health broadly (Ekkekakis, 2008).

The literature on special populations of children includes only moderate–vigorous aerobic activity programs. Variation by mode remains unknown. In the PLAY project, a linear trend showed that more activity led to greater gains in executive function and math achievement in overweight and obese children, and the low dose group in that study outperformed no-intervention controls. New questions about how physical activity might improve cognitive function have come up since the PLAY project was designed, focused on traditional physical activity dimensions of frequency, intensity, and duration. It is being increasingly acknowledged that the active ingredients in these programs could include cognitive challenge associated with activity (Pesce, 2012), learning new motor skills (Diamond & Lee, 2011), setting (indoor vs outdoor) (Kuo & Taylor, 2004), social interaction (group vs alone) (Stranahan, Khalil, & Gould, 2006), emotional arousal, structure (rules and regulations), behavior management strategies (incentives, consequences), and mastery experiences (Frazier et al., 2012). Elucidation of mechanisms and active ingredients will contribute to designing physical activity interventions that maximize impact and efficiency in a society with limited resources, and burdened by concurrent obesity, mental health, and academic failure epidemics.

References

American Psychiatric Association. (1994). *Diagnostic and statistical manual of mental disorders* (4th ed.). Washington, DC: American Psychiatric Association.

Adler, N. E., & Rehkopf, D. H. (2008). US disparities in health: descriptions, causes, and mechanisms. *Annual Review of Public Health*, 29, 235–252.

Agranat-Meged, A. N., Deitcher, C., Goldzweig, G., Leibenson, L., Stein, M., & Galili–Weisstub, E. (2005). Childhood obesity and attention deficit/hyperactivity disorder: a newly described comorbidity in obese hospitalized children. *International Journal of Eating Disorders*, 37, 357–359.

Anderson, S. E., Economos, C. D., & Must, A. (2008). Active play and screen time in US children aged 4 to 11 years in relation to sociodemographic and weight status characteristics: a nationally representative cross-sectional analysis. *BMC Public Health*, 8, 366. http://dx.doi.org/10.1186/1471-2458-8-366.

Asato, M. R., Terwilliger, R., Woo, J., & Luna, B. (2010). White matter development in adolescence: a DTI study. *Cerebral Cortex*, 20, 2122–2131.

Atkins, M. S., Frazier, S. L., Adil, J., & Talbott, E. (2003). School mental health in urban communities. In M. Weist, S. Evans, & N. Lever (Eds.), *School mental health handbook* (pp. 165–178). New York: Kluwer.

Baker, T. B., McFall, R. M., & Shoham, V. (2008). Current status and future prospects of clinical psychology toward a scientifically principled approach to mental and behavioral health care. *Psychological Science in the Public Interest*, 9, 68–103.

Barkley, R. A. (1997). Behavioral inhibition, sustained attention, and executive functions: constructing a unifying theory of ADHD. *Psychological Bulletin*, 121, 65–94.

Barkley, R. (1998). *Attention deficit hyperactivity disorder: A handbook for diagnosis and treatment* (2nd ed.). New York: Guilford Press.

Barkley, R. A. (2001). The executive functions and self-regulation: an evolutionary neuropsychological perspective. *Neuropsychology Review*, 11, 1–29.

Barkley, R. (2002). Major life activity and health outcomes associated with attention-deficit/hyperactivity disorder. *Journal of Clinical Psychiatry*, 63, 10–15.

Beaulieu, C. (2002). The basis of anisotropic water diffusion in the nervous system—a technical review. *NMR in Biomedicine*, 15, 435–455.

Berg, E. A. (1948). A simple objective technique for measuring flexibility in thinking. *Journal of General Psychology*, 39, 15–22.

Bourke, R., Anderson, V., Yang, J. S., Jackman, A. R., Killedar, A., Nixon, G. M., et al. (2011). Cognitive and academic functions are impaired in children with all severities of sleep-disordered breathing. *Sleep Medicine*, 12, 489–496.

Boyd, W. L., & Shouse, R. C. (1997). The problems and promise of urban schools. In H. J. Walber, O. Reyes, & R. P. Weissberg (Eds.), *Children and youth: Interdisciplinary perspectives*. Thousand Oaks, CA: Sage.

Bustamante, E. E., Davis, C. L., Frazier, S. L., Rusch, D., Fogg, L. F., Atkins, M. S., et al. (in review). Randomized controlled trial of exercise for ADHD and Disruptive Behavior Disorders.

Casey, B. J., Castellanos, F. X., Giedd, J. N., Marsh, W. L., Hamburger, S. D., Schubert, A. B., et al. (1997). Implication of right frontostriatal circuitry in response inhibition and attention-deficit/hyperactivity disorder. *Journal of the American Academy of Child & Adolescent Psychiatry*, 36, 374–383.

Casey, B. J., Giedd, J. N., & Thomas, K. M. (2000). Structural and functional brain development and its relation to cognitive development. *Biological Psychology, 54,* 241–257.

Castellanos, F. X., Giedd, J. N., Marsh, W. L., Hamburger, S. D., Vaituzis, A. C., Dickstein, D. P., et al. (1996). Quantitative brain magnetic resonance imaging in attention-deficit hyperactivity disorder. *Archives of General Psychiatry, 53,* 607–616.

Chaddock-Heyman, L., Erickson, K. I., Voss, M. W., Knecht, A. M., Pontifex, M. B., Castelli, D. M., et al. (2013). The effects of physical activity on functional MRI activation associated with cognitive control in children: a randomized controlled intervention. *Frontiers in Human Neuroscience, 7,* 72. http://dx.doi.org/10.3389/fnhum.2013.00072.

Chaddock, L., Erickson, K. I., Prakash, R. S., Kim, J. S., Voss, M. W., Vanpatter, M., et al. (2010). A neuroimaging investigation of the association between aerobic fitness, hippocampal volume, and memory performance in preadolescent children. *Brain Research, 1358,* 172–183.

Chang, Y.-K., Hung, C.-L., Huang, C.-J., Hatfield, B. D., & Hung, T.-M. (2014). Effects of an aquatic exercise program on inhibitory control in children with ADHD: a preliminary study. *Archives of Clinical Neuropsychology, 29,* 217–223.

Chen, J., Lipska, B. K., Halim, N., Ma, Q. D., Matsumoto, M., Melhem, S., et al. (2004). Functional analysis of genetic variation in catechol-O-methyltransferase (COMT): effects on mRNA, protein, and enzyme activity in postmortem human brain. *American Journal of Human Genetics, 75,* 807–821.

Choi, J. W., Han, D. H., Kang, K. D., Jung, H. Y., & Renshaw, P. F. (2015). Aerobic exercise and attention deficit hyperactivity disorder: brain research. *Medicine and Science in Sports and Exercise, 47,* 33–39.

Cohen, J. (1988). *Statistical power for the behavioral sciences.* Hillsdale, NJ: Lawrence Erlbaum Associates.

Colcombe, S., & Kramer, A. F. (2003). Fitness effects on the cognitive function of older adults: a meta-analytic study. *Psychological Science, 14,* 125–130.

Colcombe, S. J., Kramer, A. F., Erickson, K. I., Scalf, P., McAuley, E., Cohen, N. J., et al. (2004). Cardiovascular fitness, cortical plasticity, and aging. *Proceedings of the National Academy of Sciences of the United States of America, 101,* 3316–3321.

Cortese, S., & Morcillo, P. C. (2010). Comorbidity between ADHD and obesity: exploring shared mechanisms and clinical implications. *Postgraduate Medicine, 122,* 88–96.

Cottrell, L. A., Northrup, K., & Wittberg, R. (2007). The extended relationship between child cardiovascular risks and academic performance measures. *Obesity, 15,* 3170–3177.

Davidson, M. C., Amso, D., Anderson, L. C., & Diamond, A. (2006). Development of cognitive control and executive functions from 4 to 13 years: evidence from manipulations of memory, inhibition, and task switching. *Neuropsychologia, 44,* 2037–2078.

Davis, C. L., & Cooper, S. (2011). Fitness, fatness, cognition, behavior, and academic achievement among overweight children: do cross-sectional associations correspond to exercise trial outcomes? *Preventive Medicine, 52,* S65–S69.

Davis, C. L., Pollock, N. K., Waller, J. L., Allison, J. D., Dennis, B. A., Bassali, R., et al. (2012). Exercise dose and diabetes risk in overweight and obese children: a randomized controlled trial. *Journal of the American Medical Association, 308,* 1103–1112.

Davis, C. L., Tkacz, J. P., Tomporowski, P. D., & Bustamante, E. E. (in press). Independent associations of organized physical activity and weight status with children's cognitive functioning: A matched-pairs design *Pediatric Exercise Science, 27*(4).

Davis, C. L., Tomporowski, P. D., McDowell, J. E., Austin, B. P., Miller, P. H., Yanasak, N. E., et al. (2011). Exercise improves executive function and achievement and alters brain activation in overweight children: a randomized, controlled trial. *Health Psychology, 30,* 91–98.

Diamond, A. (2000). Close interrelation of motor development and cognitive development and of the cerebellum and prefrontal cortex. *Child Development, 71,* 44–56.

Diamond, A. (2007). Consequences of variations in genes that affect dopamine in prefrontal cortex. *Cerebral Cortex, 17*(Suppl.1), i161–i170.

Diamond, A. (2011). Biological and social influences on cognitive control processes dependent on prefrontal cortex. *Progress in Brain Research, 189,* 319–339.

Diamond, A. (2013). Executive functions. *Annual Review of Psychology, 64,* 135–168.

Diamond, A., & Lee, K. (2011). Interventions shown to aid executive function development in children 4 to 12 years old. *Science, 333,* 959–964.

Dishman, R. K., Berthoud, H. R., Booth, F. W., Cotman, C. W., Edgerton, V. R., Fleshner, M. R., et al. (2006). Neurobiology of exercise. *Obesity, 14,* 345–356.

Eisenmann, J. C., Bartee, R. T., & Wang, M. Q. (2002). Physical activity, TV viewing, and weight in US youth: 1999 Youth Risk Behavior Survey. *Obesity Research, 10,* 379–385.

Ekkekakis, P. (2008). The genetic tidal wave finally reached our shores: will it be the catalyst for a critical overhaul of the way we think and do science? *Mental Health and Physical Activity, 1,* 47–52.

Eriksen, B. A., & Eriksen, C. W. (1974). Effects of noise letters upon the identification of a target letter in a nonsearch task. *Perception and Psychophysics, 16,* 143–149.

Eslinger, P. J. (1996). Conceptualizing, describing, and measuring components of executive function: a summary. In G. R. Lyon, & N. A. Krasnegor (Eds.), *Attention, memory, and executive function* (pp. 367–395). Baltimore, MD: Paul H Brookes Publishing.

Filipek, P. A., Semrud-Clikeman, M., Steingard, R. J., Renshaw, P. F., Kennedy, D. N., & Biederman, J. (1997). Volumetric MRI analysis comparing subjects having attention-deficit hyperactivity disorder with normal controls. *Neurology*, *48*, 589–601.

Frazier, S. L., Chacko, A., Van Gessel, C., O'Boyle, C., & Pelham, W. E. (2012). The summer treatment program meets the south side of Chicago: bridging science and service in urban after-school programs. *Child & Adolescent Mental Health*, *17*, 86–92.

Froehlich, T. E., Lanphear, B. P., Epstein, J. N., Barbaresi, W. J., Katusic, S. K., & Kahn, R. S. (2007). Prevalence, recognition, and treatment of attention-deficit/hyperactivity disorder in a national sample of US children. *Archives of Pediatrics & Adolescent Medicine*, *161*, 857–864.

Gapin, J., & Etnier, J. L. (2010). The relationship between physical activity and executive function performance in children with attention-deficit hyperactivity disorder. *Journal of Sport & Exercise Psychology*, *32*, 753–763.

Goldstein, M., Brendel, G., Tuescher, O., Pan, H., Epstein, J., Beutel, M., et al. (2007). Neural substrates of the interaction of emotional stimulus processing and motor inhibitory control: an emotional linguistic go/no-go fMRI study. *NeuroImage*, *36*, 1026–1040.

Halleland, H., Lundervold, A., Halmøy, A., Haavik, J., & Johansson, S. (2009). Association between catechol O–methyltransferase (COMT) haplotypes and severity of hyperactivity symptoms in adults. *American Journal of Medical Genetics Part B: Neuropsychiatric Genetics*, *150*, 403–410.

Halperin, J. M., Marks, D. J., Bedard, A. C., Chacko, A., Curchack, J. T., Yoon, C. A., et al. (2012). Training executive, attention, and motor skills: a proof-of-concept study in preschool children with ADHD. *Journal of Attention Disorders*, *17*, 711–721.

Heilman, K. M., Voeller, K. K., & Nadeau, S. E. (1991). A possible pathophysiologic substrate of attention deficit hyperactivity disorder. *Journal of Child Neurology*, *6*(Suppl), S76–S81.

Herting, M. M., & Nagel, B. J. (2013). Differences in brain activity during a verbal associative memory encoding task in high-and low-fit adolescents. *Journal of Cognitive Neuroscience*, *25*, 595–612.

Hill, A. B. (1965). The environment and disease: association or causation? *Proceedings of the Royal Society of Medicine*, *58*, 295.

Hillman, C. H., Erickson, K. I., & Kramer, A. F. (2008). Be smart, exercise your heart: exercise effects on brain and cognition. *Nature Reviews Neuroscience*, *9*, 58–65.

Hillman, C. H., Pontifex, M. B., Castelli, D. M., Khan, N. A., Raine, L. B., Scudder, M. R., et al. (2014). Effects of the FITKids randomized controlled trial on executive control and brain function. *Pediatrics*, *134*, e1063–e1071.

Holtkamp, K., Konrad, K., Müller, B., Heussen, N., Herpertz, S., Herpertz-Dahlmann, B., et al. (2004). Overweight and obesity in children with attention-deficit/hyperactivity disorder. *International Journal of Obesity*, *28*, 685–689.

Hong, J., Shu-Leong, H., Tao, X., & Lap-Ping, Y. (1998). Distribution of catechol-O-methyltransferase expression in human central nervous system. *Neuroreport*, *9*, 2861–2864.

Howie, E. K., Beets, M. W., & Pate, R. R. (2014). Acute classroom exercise breaks improve on-task behavior in 4th and 5th grade students: a dose-response. *Mental Health and Physical Activity*, *7*, 65–71.

Howie, E. K., & Stevick, E. D. (2014). The "ins" and "outs" of physical activity policy implementation: inadequate capacity, inappropriate outcome measures, and insufficient funds. *Journal of School Health*, *84*, 581–585.

Hoza, B., Smith, A. L., Shoulberg, E. K., Linnea, K. S., Dorsch, T. E., Blazo, J. A., et al. (2014). A randomized trial examining the effects of aerobic physical activity on attention-deficit/hyperactivity disorder symptoms in young children. *Journal of Abnormal Child Psychology*, *43*, 655–667.

Hynd, G. W., Hern, K. L., Novey, E. S., Eliopulos, D., Marshall, R., Gonzalez, J. J., et al. (1993). Attention-deficit hyperactivity disorder and asymmetry of the caudate-nucleus. *Journal of Child Neurology*, *8*, 339–347.

Hynd, G. W., Semrudclikeman, M., Lorys, A., Novey, E. S., & Eliopulos, D. (1990). Brain morphology in developmental dyslexia and attention deficit disorder hyperactivity. *Journal of Clinical and Experimental Neuropsychology*, *12*, 62–63.

Jennings, A., Welch, A., van Sluijs, E. M., Griffin, S. J., & Cassidy, A. (2011). Diet quality is independently associated with weight status in children aged 9–10 years. *Journal of Nutrition*, *141*, 453–459.

Johansen-Berg, H., & Behrens, T. E. (2009). *Diffusion MRI: From quantitative measurement to in-vivo neuroanatomy.* New York: Academic Press.

Kamijo, K., Pontifex, M. B., O'Leary, K. C., Scudder, M. R., Wu, C. T., Castelli, D. M., et al. (2011). The effects of an afterschool physical activity program on working memory in preadolescent children. *Developmental Science*, *14*, 1046–1058.

Kang, K. D., Choi, J. W., Kang, S. G., & Han, D. H. (2011). Sports therapy for attention, cognitions and sociality. *International Journal of Sports Medicine*, *32*, 953–959.

Kataoka, S. H., Zhang, L., & Wells, K. B. (2002). Unmet need for mental health care among US children: variation by ethnicity and insurance status. *American Journal of Psychiatry*, *159*, 1548–1555.

Kazdin, A. E., & Rabbitt, S. M. (2013). Novel models for delivering mental health services and reducing the burdens of mental illness. *Clinical Psychological Science.* http://dx.doi.org/10.1177/2167702612463566.

Kearney, J. (2010). Food consumption trends and drivers. *Philosophical Transactions of the Royal Society B, 365,* 2793–2807.

Keeley, T. J., & Fox, K. R. (2009). The impact of physical activity and fitness on academic achievement and cognitive performance in children. *International Review of Sport and Exercise Psychology, 2,* 198–214.

Klarborg, B., Skak Madsen, K., Vestergaard, M., Skimminge, A., Jernigan, T. L., & Baare, W. F. (2013). Sustained attention is associated with right superior longitudinal fasciculus and superior parietal white matter microstructure in children. *Human Brain Mapping, 34,* 3216–3232.

Kolb, B., & Whishaw, I. Q. (1998). Brain plasticity and behavior. *Annual Review of Psychology, 49,* 43–64.

Korkman, M., Kirk, U., & Kemp, S. L. (2007). *NEPSY II. Clinical and interpretative manual.* San Antonio, Texas: Psychological Corporation.

Krafft, C. E., Pierce, J. E., Schwarz, N. F., Chi, L., Weinberger, A. L., Schaeffer, D. J., et al. (2014). An eight month randomized controlled exercise intervention alters resting state synchrony in overweight children. *Neuroscience, 256,* 445–455.

Krafft, C. E., Schaeffer, D. J., Schwarz, N. F., Chi, L., Weinberger, A. L., Pierce, J. E., et al. (2014). Improved frontoparietal white matter integrity in overweight children is associated with attendance at an after-school exercise program. *Developmental Neuroscience, 36,* 1–9.

Krafft, C. E., Schwarz, N. F., Chi, L., Weinberger, A. L., Schaeffer, D. J., Pierce, J. E., et al. (2014). An 8–month randomized controlled exercise trial alters brain activation during cognitive tasks in overweight children. *Obesity, 22,* 232–242.

Kramer, A. F., Hahn, S., Cohen, N. J., Banich, M. T., McAuley, E., Harrison, C. R., et al. (1999). Ageing, fitness and neurocognitive function. *Nature, 400,* 418–419.

Kuo, F. E., & Taylor, A. F. (2004). A potential natural treatment for attention-deficit/hyperactivity disorder: evidence from a national study. *American Journal of Public Health, 94,* 1580–1586.

Lebel, C., Gee, M., Camicioli, R., Wieler, M., Martin, W., & Beaulieu, C. (2012). Diffusion tensor imaging of white matter tract evolution over the lifespan. *NeuroImage, 60,* 340.

Luna, B., Velanova, K., & Geier, C. F. (2008). Development of eye-movement control. *Brain and Cognition, 68,* 293–308.

Mabbott, D. J., Rovet, J., Noseworthy, M. D., Smith, M. L., & Rockel, C. (2009). The relations between white matter and declarative memory in older children and adolescents. *Brain Research, 1294,* 80–90.

Mahar, M. T., Murphy, S. K., Rowe, D. A., Golden, J., Shields, A. T., & Raedeke, T. D. (2006). Effects of a classroom-based program on physical activity and on-task behavior. *Medicine & Science in Sports & Exercise, 38,* 2086.

Marks, B. L., Madden, D. J., Bucur, B., Provenzale, J. M., White, L. E., Cabeza, R., et al. (2007). Role of aerobic fitness and aging on cerebral white matter integrity. *Annals of the New York Academy of Sciences, 1097,* 171–174.

Matsumoto, M., Weickert, C. S., Akil, M., Lipska, B. K., Hyde, T. M., Herman, M. M., et al. (2003). Catechol O-methyltransferase mRNA expression in human and rat brain: evidence for a role in cortical neuronal function. *Neuroscience, 116,* 127–137.

Mattay, V. S., Goldberg, T. E., Fera, F., Hariri, A. R., Tessitore, A., Egan, M. F., et al. (2003). Catechol O-methyltransferase val158-met genotype and individual variation in the brain response to amphetamine. *Proceedings of the National Academy of Sciences, 100,* 6186–6191.

McDowell, J. E., Brown, G. G., Paulus, M., Martinez, A., Stewart, S. E., Dubowitz, D. J., et al. (2002). Neural correlates of refixation saccades and antisaccades in normal and schizophrenia subjects. *Biological Psychiatry, 51,* 216–223.

McGrew, K. S., & Woodcock, R. W. (2001). *Woodcock-Johnson III: Technical manual.* Itasca, IL: Riverside Publishing.

McKune, A., Pautz, J., & Lomjbard, J. (2004). Behavioural response to exercise in children with attention-deficit/hyperactivity disorder. *South African Journal of Sports Medicine, 15,* 17–21.

Medina, J. A., Netto, T. L., Muszkat, M., Medina, A. C., Botter, D., Orbetelli, R., et al. (2010). Exercise impact on sustained attention of ADHD children, methylphenidate effects. *Attention Deficit Hyperactivity Disorder, 2,* 49–58.

Mischel, W., Shoda, Y., & Rodriguez, M. I. (1989). Delay of gratification in children. *Science, 244,* 933–938.

Miyake, A., Friedman, N. P., Emerson, M. J., Witzki, A. H., Howerter, A., & Wager, T. D. (2000). The unity and diversity of executive functions and their contributions to complex "Frontal Lobe" tasks: a latent variable analysis. *Cognitive Psychology, 41,* 49–100.

Moher, D., Hopewell, S., Schulz, K. F., Montori, V., Gøtzsche, P. C., Devereaux, P., et al. (2010). CONSORT 2010 explanation and elaboration: updated guidelines for reporting parallel group randomised trials. *Journal of Clinical Epidemiology, 63,* e1–e37.

Mulert, C. (2013). Simultaneous EEG and fMRI: towards the characterization of structure and dynamics of brain networks. *Dialogues in Clinical Neuroscience, 15,* 381–386.

Muraven, M., & Baumeister, R. F. (2000). Self-regulation and depletion of limited resources: does self-control resemble a muscle? *Psychological Bulletin, 126,* 247–259.

Muraven, M., Baumeister, R. F., & Tice, D. M. (1999). Longitudinal improvement of self-regulation through practice: building self-control strength through repeated exercise. *Journal of Social Psychology, 139*, 446–457.

Must, A., & Tybor, D. (2005). Physical activity and sedentary behavior: a review of longitudinal studies of weight and adiposity in youth. *International Journal of Obesity, 29*, S84–S96.

Naglieri, J. A., & Das, J. P. (1997). *Cognitive assessment system: Interpretive handbook.* Itasca, IL: Riverside Publishing.

van der Niet, A. G., Smith, J., Scherder, E. J., Oosterlaan, J., Hartman, E., & Visscher, C. (2014). Associations between daily physical activity and executive functioning in primary school-aged children. *Journal of Science and Medicine in Sport.* http://dx.doi.org/10.1016/j.jsams.2014.09.006.

Ness, A. R., Leary, S. D., Mattocks, C., Blair, S. N., Reilly, J. J., Wells, J., Ingle, S., Tilling, K., Smith, G. D., Riddoch, C. (2007). Objectively measured physical activity and fat mass in a large cohort of children. *PLoS Med, 14*(3), e97. http://www.ncbi.nlm.nih.gov/pubmed/17388663.

Nolan, E. E., Gadow, K. D., & Sprafkin, J. (2001). Teacher reports of DSM-IV ADHD, ODD, and CD symptoms in school children. *Journal of the American Academy of Child & Adolescent Psychiatry, 40*, 241–249.

Ogden, C. L., Carroll, M. D., Kit, B. K., & Flegal, K. M. (2014). Prevalence of childhood and adult obesity in the United States, 2011–2012. *Journal of the American Medical Association, 311*, 806–814.

Organization for Economic Cooperation and Development. (2014). *PISA 2012 results in focus: What 15-year-olds know and what they can do with what they know.* Paris, France: Organisation for Economic Co-operation and Development.

Ortega, F. B., Ruiz, J. R., Castillo, M. J., & Sjostrom, M. (2008). Physical fitness in childhood and adolescence: a powerful marker of health. *International Journal of Obesity, 32*, 1–11.

Penedo, F. J., & Dahn, J. R. (2005). Exercise and well-being: a review of mental and physical health benefits associated with physical activity. *Current Opinion in Psychiatry, 18*, 189–193.

Perou, R., Bitsko, R. H., Blumberg, S. J., Pastor, P., Ghandour, R. M., Gfroerer, J. C., et al. (2013). Mental health surveillance among children-United States, 2005–2011. *MMWR Surveillance Summary, 62*(Suppl. 2), 1–35.

Pesce, C. (2012). Shifting the focus from quantitative to qualitative exercise characteristics in exercise and cognition research. *Journal of Sport and Exercise Psychology, 34*, 766.

Petty, K. H., Davis, C. L., Tkacz, J., Young-Hyman, D., & Waller, J. L. (2009). *Exercise effects on depressive symptoms and self-worth in overweight children: A randomized controlled.*

Piepmeier, A. T., Shih, C.-H., Whedon, M., Williams, L., Davis, M., Henning, D., et al. (2015). The effect of acute exercise on cognitive performance in children with and without ADHD. *Journal of Sport and Health Science, 4*, 97–104.

Polich, J. (2007). Updating P300: an integrative theory of P3a and P3b. *Clinical Neurophysiology, 118*, 2128–2148.

Pontifex, M. B., Kamijo, K., Scudder, M. R., Raine, L. B., Khan, N. A., Hemrick, B., et al. (2014). V. The differential association of adiposity and fitness with cognitive control in preadolescent children. *Monographs of the Society for Research in Child Development, 79*, 72–92.

Pontifex, M. B., Saliba, B. J., Raine, L. B., Picchietti, D. L., & Hillman, C. H. (2013). Exercise improves behavioral, neurocognitive, and scholastic performance in children with attention-deficit/hyperactivity disorder. [Research Support, N.I.H., Extramural] *Journal of Pediatrics, 162*, 543–551.

Posner, J., Park, C., & Wang, Z. (2014). Connecting the dots: a review of resting connectivity MRI studies in attention-deficit/hyperactivity disorder. *Neuropsychology Review, 24*, 3–15.

Posner, J. K., & Vandell, D. L. (1994). Low-income children's after-school care: are there beneficial effects of after-school programs? *Child Development, 65*, 440–456.

Prince, J. (2008). Catecholamine dysfunction in attention-deficit/hyperactivity disorder–an update. *Journal of Clinical Psychopharmacology, 28*, S39–S45.

Qian, Y., Shuai, L., Cao, Q., Chan, R. C., & Wang, Y. (2010). Do executive function deficits differentiate between children with attention deficit hyperactivity disorder (ADHD) and ADHD comorbid with oppositional defiant disorder? A cross-cultural study using performance-based tests and the behavior rating inventory of executive function. *Clinical Neuropsychologist, 24*, 793–810.

Rabbitt, P. (1997). Introduction: methodologies and models in the study of executive function. In P. Rabbit (Ed.), *Methodology of frontal and executive function* (pp. 1–38). Hove, East Sussex: Psychology Press Ltd.

Rachlin, H., Raineri, A., & Cross, D. (1991). Subjective probability and delay. *Journal of the Experimental Analysis of Behavior, 55*, 233–244.

Ratey, J., & Hagerman, E. (2008). *Spark: The revolutionary new science of exercise and the brain.* New York, NY: Little, Brown and Company.

Redline, S., Tishler, P. V., Schluchter, M., Aylor, J., Clark, K., & Graham, G. (1999). Risk factors for sleep-disordered breathing in children: associations with obesity, race, and respiratory problems. *American Journal of Respiratory and Critical Care Medicine, 159*, 1527–1532.

Reitan, R. M. (1971). Trail making test results for normal and brain-damaged children. *Perceptual and Motor Skills, 33*, 575–581.

Roberts, C. K., Freed, B., & McCarthy, W. J. (2010). Low aerobic fitness and obesity are associated with lower standardized test scores in children. *Journal of Pediatrics, 156*, 711–718.

Rueda, M. R., Fan, J., McCandliss, B. D., Halparin, J. D., Gruber, D. B., Lercari, L. P., et al. (2004). Development of attentional networks in childhood. *Neuropsychologia, 42,* 1029–1040.

Rueda, M. R., Posner, M. I., & Rothbart, M. K. (2005). The development of executive attention: contributions to the emergence of self-regulation. *Developmental Neuropsychology, 28,* 573–594.

Sagvolden, T., Johansen, E. B., Aase, H., & Russell, V. A. (2005). A dynamic developmental theory of attention-deficit/hyperactivity disorder (ADHD) predominantly hyperactive/impulsive and combined subtypes. *Behavioral Brain Science, 28,* 397–419 discussion 419–368.

Schaeffer, D. J., Krafft, C. E., Schwarz, N. F., Chi, L., Rodrigue, A. L., Pierce, J. E., et al. (2014). An 8–month exercise intervention alters frontotemporal white matter integrity in overweight children. *Psychophysiology, 51,* 728–733.

Schmahmann, J. D., Pandya, D. N., Wang, R., Dai, G., D'Arceuil, H. E., de Crespigny, A. J., et al. (2007). Association fibre pathways of the brain: parallel observations from diffusion spectrum imaging and autoradiography. *Brain, 130,* 630–653.

Schwarz, N. F., Krafft, C. E., Chi, L., Weinberger, A. L., Schaeffer, D. J., Pierce, J. E., et al. (in press). Brain activation associated with antisaccade performance in children with ADHD: A functional MRI study. *Psychiatry Research: Neuroimaging.*

Sigfúsdóttir, I. D., Kristjánsson, Á. L., & Allegrante, J. P. (2007). Health behaviour and academic achievement in Icelandic school children. *Health Education Research, 22,* 70–80.

Smith, A. L., Hoza, B., Linnea, K., McQuade, J. D., Tomb, M., Vaughn, A. J., et al. (2013). Pilot physical activity intervention reduces severity of ADHD symptoms in young children. *Journal of Attention Disorders, 17,* 70–82.

Smith, D. E., Thompson, J. K., Raczynski, J. M., & Hilner, J. E. (1999). Body image among men and women in a biracial cohort: the CARDIA Study. *International Journal of Eating Disorders, 25,* 71–82.

Song, S.-K., Sun, S.-W., Ramsbottom, M. J., Chang, C., Russell, J., & Cross, A. H. (2002). Dysmyelination revealed through MRI as increased radial (but unchanged axial) diffusion of water. *NeuroImage, 17,* 1429–1436.

Stevenson, R. J., & Prescott, J. (2014). Human diet and cognition. *Wiley Interdisciplinary Reviews: Cognitive Science, 5,* 463–475.

Stranahan, A. M., Khalil, D., & Gould, E. (2006). Social isolation delays the positive effects of running on adult neurogenesis. *Nature Neuroscience, 9,* 526–533.

Strong, W. B., Malina, R. M., Blimkie, C. J., Daniels, S. R., Dishman, R. K., Gutin, B., et al. (2005). Evidence based physical activity for school-age youth. *Journal of Pediatrics, 146,* 732–737.

Tamm, L., Menon, V., & Reiss, A. L. (2002). Maturation of brain function associated with response inhibition. *Journal of the American Academy of Child & Adolescent Psychiatry, 41,* 1231–1238.

Tantillo, M., Kesick, C. M., Hynd, G. W., & Dishman, R. K. (2002). The effects of exercise on children with attention-deficit hyperactivity disorder. *Medicine & Science in Sports & Exercise, 34,* 203–212.

Tunbridge, E. M., Bannerman, D. M., Sharp, T., & Harrison, P. J. (2004). Catechol-O-methyltransferase inhibition improves set-shifting performance and elevates stimulated dopamine release in the rat prefrontal cortex. *Journal of Neuroscience, 24,* 5331–5335.

U.S. Department of Health and Human Services. (2008). *Physical activity guidelines for Americans.* Washington, DC: U.S. Department of Health and Human Services.

U.S. Department of Health and Human Services. (2012). *Health, United States, 2011: With special feature on socioeconomic status and health.* Washington, DC: U.S. Department of Health and Human Services.

Verret, C., Guay, M. C., Berthiaume, C., Gardiner, P., & Beliveau, L. (2012). A physical activity program improves behavior and cognitive functions in children with ADHD: an exploratory study. *Journal of Attention Disorders, 16*(1), 71–80. http://dx.doi.org/10.1177/1087054710379735.

Vestergaard, M., Madsen, K. S., Baare, W. F., Skimminge, A., Ejersbo, L. R., Ramsoy, T. Z., et al. (2011). White matter microstructure in superior longitudinal fasciculus associated with spatial working memory performance in children. *Journal of Cognitive Neuroscience, 23,* 2135–2146.

Ward, B. (1997). *Simultaneous inference for FMRI data.* Milwaukee, WI: Biophysics Research Institute, Medical College of Wisconsin.

Wechsler, D. (2004). *The Wechsler intelligence scale for children* (4th ed.). London: Pearson Assesssment.

Wodka, E. L., Mostofsky, S. H., Prahme, C., Larson, J. C. G., Loftis, C., Denckla, M. B., et al. (2008). Process examination of executive function in ADHD: sex and subtype effects. *Clinical Neuropsychologist, 22,* 826–841.

Yancey, A. K. T., & Sallis, J. F. (2009). Physical activity: Cinderella or Rodney Dangerfield? *Preventive Medicine, 49,* 277–279.

Zimmerman, F. J., & Christakis, D. A. (2005). Children's television viewing and cognitive outcomes: a longitudinal analysis of national data. *Archives of Pediatrics & Adolescent Medicine, 159,* 619–625.

Exercise–Cognition Interaction: State of the Art and Future Research

Terry McMorris

Department of Sport and Exercise Science, University of Chichester, Chichester, West Sussex, UK

INTRODUCTION

In this chapter, I will outline the research findings for both acute and chronic exercise effects on cognition. There will also be a critique of research designs and protocols, and suggestions for future research. Also of great importance is an examination of the extent to which neuroscience can explain the exercise–cognition interaction. In the penultimate section, I will discuss transactional issues, with particular reference to the use of exercise in fostering healthy aging, in aiding cognition in individuals suffering from neurological diseases and as an aid to learning by children.

ACUTE EXERCISE

Research Findings

Research results for behavioral dependent variables are not unequivocal. There appears to be differences when accuracy and speed are the measures. Accuracy results show a tendency toward no significant effect, while speed findings are dependent on the exercise intensity

and possibly duration. McMorris and Hale (2012) claimed that the accuracy results were almost certainly due to the fact that the majority of tasks used in the research, e.g., the flanker task (Eriksen & Eriksen, 1974), the Simon task (Simon, 1969), and the Stroop color test (1935), were designed to measure performance through speed of processing rather than accuracy. As a result, when accuracy is the dependent variable, there is a ceiling effect. In general, the speed tests show facilitation during and following moderate intensity exercise (≥40% maximum of volume of oxygen uptake ($\dot{V}O_{2MAX}$) but <80% $\dot{V}O_{2MAX}$) of moderate duration (10–20 min) (see McMorris & Hale, 2012; McMorris, Turner, Hale, & Sproule, Chapter 4, this text, for reviews). Exercise of this intensity for >60 min can lead to a deterioration in performance (e.g., Grego et al., 2004; Moore, Romine, O'Conner, & Tomporowski, 2012). On the other hand, heavy exercise (≥80% $\dot{V}O_{2MAX}$) appears to affect tasks in different ways depending on their complexity and type. Autonomous tasks (e.g., Fontana, Mazzardo, Mokgothu, Furtado, & Gallagher, 2009; McMorris & Graydon, 1996a,b, 1997) and learning tasks (Griffin et al., 2011; Winter et al., 2007) benefit from heavy exercise, while results for attention/perception tasks are somewhat equivocal (see McMorris et al., this text). The limited amount of research examining working memory tasks during heavy exercise (Griffin et al., 2011; Kamijo et al., 2004; McMorris, Davranche, Jones, Hall, & Minter, 2009) is too small to detect a trend.

Support for Neuroscientific Explanations of the Acute Exercise–Cognition Interaction

Neurochemical Explanations

Animal studies provide a great deal of support for the claims of neurochemists that acute exercise induces increases in brain concentrations of dopamine, noradrenaline (norepinephrine), corticotropin-releasing factor (CRF), adrenocorticotropin hormone (ACTH), and cortisol (corticosterone in animals). Increases in noradrenaline are probably due to activation of the vagal/nucleus tractus solitarii (NTS) pathway, which stimulates the synthesis and release of noradrenaline in the locus coeruleus (McGaugh, Cahill, & Roozendaal, 1996; Miyashita & Williams, 2006) and dopamine via stimulation of α_1-adrenoreceptors by the noradrenaline released from the locus coeruleus, which potentiates the firing of dopamine neurons in the ventral tegmental area (Grenhoff & Svensson, 1993; Grenhoff, Nisell, Ferré, Aston-Jones, & Svensson, 1993). The initial increase in peripheral catecholamines, including adrenaline (epinephrine), during exercise, is due to their roles in the periphery when the person is exercising. A similar need for ACTH and cortisol activity in the periphery leads to increased concentrations of these hypothalamic–pituitary–adrenal cortex (HPA) axis hormones. Increased brain concentrations occur because cortisol readily crosses the blood–brain barrier and interactions between CRF, ACTH, and cortisol, and the saturation status of their receptors, lead to changes in brain concentrations, although brain concentrations may also be altered due to perceptions of stress.

Given that moderate intensity, moderate duration exercise induces moderate increases in peripheral catecholamines concentrations, and that dopamine and noradrenaline are major neurotransmitters in the brain, it is not surprising to see that exercise of this duration and intensity tends to induce facilitation, certainly in speed of performance (e.g., Joyce, Graydon, McMorris, & Davranche, 2009; Pesce, Capranica, Tessitore, & Figura, 2003; Yanagisawa et al., 2010). This is in line with research into the effects of increased peripheral and brain concentrations of catecholamines due to other stressors in humans (e.g., Cools, Barker, Sahakian, & Robbins, 2001). Exercise of this intensity does not result in increased HPA axis hormones concentrations in the periphery (Hill et al., 2008) but long duration, moderate intensity exercise does (Grego et al., 2004), hence we find that this latter type of exercise can have a detrimental effect on cognitive performance, as CRF, ACTH, and cortisol can induce increased dopamine and noradrenaline synthesis and release beyond the optimal, which has a negative effect on cognition (Abercrombie, Kalin, Thurow, Rosenkranz, & Davidson, 2003; Lupien, Gillin, & Hauger, 1999). Moreover, during heavy exercise, very high peripheral concentrations of the catecholamines themselves lead to very high concentrations of dopamine and noradrenaline centrally and hence negative effects on cognition (Arnsten, 2009, 2011). However, this is not true of all types of task (Arnsten, 2011; Robbins & Roberts, 2007).

Arnsten (2009, 2011) provides evidence for the claim that tasks, like working, memory tasks, which are highly dependent on prefrontal cortex activation, benefit from increased activations of α_{2A}-adrenoreceptors and D_1-receptors, which strengthen the signal to "noise" ratio. This occurs during moderate levels of stress. However, during high levels of stress, activation of α_1- and β-adrenoreceptors dampens all neuronal activity, thus weakening the signal to "noise" ratio (Roth, Tam, Ida, Yang, & Deutch, 1988). This has a negative effect on tasks heavily dependent on prefrontal cortex activation. However, attention/perception and autonomous tasks appear to benefit from α_1- and/or β-adrenoreceptors activation. While activation of α_1- and β-adrenoreceptors dampens neuronal activity in the prefrontal cortex, high concentrations of noradrenaline activating α_1- and β-adrenoreceptors actually increase the signal to "noise" ratio in the primary sensory cortices (Waterhouse, Moises, & Woodward, 1980, 1981). Moreover, Waterhouse, Moises, and Woodward (1998) have shown that increased noradrenaline concentrations in sensory neurons enable greater precision of the encoding of sensory information. Learning/long-term memory tasks are also enhanced by heavy exercise due to activation of β-adrenoreceptors in the hippocampus (Hopkins & Johnston, 1988; Hu et al., 2007) and the induction of long-term potentiation (Gelinas & Nguyen, 2005; Straube, Korz, Balschun, & Frey, 2003). Moreover, Wickens, Horvitz, Costa, and Killcross (2007) have shown that high concentrations of dopamine aid the promotion of habit formation in the basal ganglia. Some working memory tasks, if they significantly require sensory cortices activation for successful performance, may also be positively affected by α_1- and/or β-adrenoreceptor activation (e.g., Bondi, Jett, & Morilak, 2010; Robbins & Roberts, 2007).

The results for research into the effects of heavy exercise, outlined in the previous subsection, are not in full agreement with findings for other stressors, nor do they fully support the neurochemical explanations for the acute exercise–cognition interaction effect. Autonomous tasks, with a large dependency on sensory cortical activity, do show improved performance but attention/perception tasks results are somewhat equivocal between no significant effect and facilitation. Far more research is needed before we can make any definitive statement on these tasks. Working memory tasks are also surprisingly somewhat equivocal and again more research is required as there is so little research to draw on. Learning/memory tasks results are

the same as for other stressors but again there are very few such studies.

The neurochemical explanations outlined above do have some support from the empirical literature. Moreover, when taken together with the psychophysiological explanations, a better understanding of the interaction is provided. It is far from simple, certainly not as simple as taking the cognitive–energetic theories and applying them to the research.

Reticular Activation Hypofrontality Theory

The research provides only partial support for reticular activation hypofrontality (RAH) theory (Audiffren, Chapter 7, this text; Dietrich & Audiffren, 2011). According to RAH theory, moderate intensity exercise will have a beneficial effect on performance of simple and well-learned tasks due to excitation of the reticular activation formation. It will not affect complex tasks, such as working memory tasks, as these are too complex to simply benefit from increased attention. While the former has been supported by the empirical research, the latter has not. Working memory tasks are enhanced by moderate intensity exercise, in fact probably more so than other tasks (McMorris & Hale, 2012). RAH theory also predicts a deterioration in working memory tasks during heavy exercise, as Dietrich and Audiffren argued that competition between the prefrontal cortex, for cognitive performance, and the motor cortex, for motor activity, results in the prefrontal cortex being taken off line, hence poor cognitive performance.

Interestingly, RAH theory and neurochemical and psychophysiological explanations are in agreement concerning activation of the reticular activation formation during moderate intensity exercise. With regard to heavy exercise, they also tend to agree to some extent but the agreement is not obvious, at first. There is, as yet, no research using psychophysiological measures on heavy exercise in acute exercise–cognition research, but neurochemical theory and research using other stressors (Arnsten, 2009, 2011) suggests some similarities between RAH theory and the cat-echolamines hypothesis for an acute exercise–cognition interaction effect during heavy exercise (Cooper, 1973; Chmura, Nazar, & Kaciuba-Uścilko, 1994; McMorris et al., 2009). According to Arnsten, during high levels of stress, working memory tasks are disrupted by excessive concentrations of the neurotransmitter noradrenaline activating α_1- and β-adrenoreceptors, which leads to a dampening of neural activity in the prefrontal cortex, thus a deterioration in cognitive functioning. Moreover, if the stress is high enough a shutting down of the prefrontal cortex will occur, thus allowing more resources for the sensory and motor cortices, which are essential for survival when under high levels of stress. It is unlikely that exercise in a controlled laboratory situation will have such an extreme effect but in real life situations, such as military and adventurous activity expeditions, it is more than possible.

Psychophysiological Explanations

Almost all psychophysiological research into the effects of acute exercise on cognition has utilized measures of event-related potential (ERP) using electroencephalography (EEG) (see Chang, Chapter 5, this text; Kamijo, Chapter 10, this text). Measures of ERP allow the researchers to infer the cognitive processes being undertaken by the participant, based on specific ERP components (Hillman, Kamijo, & Scudder, 2011). The components that have been most commonly measured are P3 (or P300), N2, contingent negative variation (CNV), and error-related negativity (ERN). P3 latency refers to the speed of detecting and evaluating the stimulus, while P3 amplitude is a measure of attentional resource allocation (Polich, 2007). N2 has been used to indicate processes of response inhibition and error monitoring (Folstein & Van Petten, 2008) and has been identified as representing ACC activation, which plays an important role in inhibition of prepotent responses (Barbas, 2000). However,

this has been challenged (Donkers & van Boxtel, 2004). CNV indicates expectation of a stimulus, motor preparation for a response (Falkenstein, Hoormann, Hohnsbein, & Kleinsorge, 2003), and attention (Rohrbaugh & Gaillard, 1983). ERN is thought of as being an ERP component, which demonstrates activation of the response monitor system (Falkenstein, Hoormann, Christ, & Hohnsbein, 2000) and is most likely generated by the ACC (Holroyd, Dien, & Coles, 1998).

ERP measures are taken either immediately following exercise or after a delay. Results for research testing cognition immediately following exercise do not present an unequivocal picture but they do show a trend toward moderate intensity having a facilitative effect on P3 latency, N2, CNV, and, to a lesser extent, P3 amplitude. Research using delayed measures also fails to demonstrate unequivocal results but strongly demonstrates facilitative effects of moderate intensity exercise on both P3 latency and amplitude. N2 shows very limited effects and there is limited research examining CNV and ERN. It should be noted that most of this research has been undertaken with central executive tasks.

Functional anatomy research. Although there have not been any functional anatomy studies using neuroimaging methods, such as functional magnetic resonance imaging (fMRI) or positron emission tomography, Yanagisawa et al. (2010) carried out a study using functional near-infrared spectroscopy (fNIRS). They found that acute moderate intensity exercise (50% $\dot{V}O_{2MAX}$) induced improved speed of performance on the Stroop color test. They also showed that there was increased activation of the left dorsolateral prefrontal cortex (DLPFC). Using the McNemar test (1947), they demonstrated that changes in speed of performance coincided with changes in oxygenated hemoglobin concentrations in the left DLPFC. In a later study (Hyodo et al., 2012) from the same laboratory but this time with elderly participants rather than young adults, they failed to replicate the results. In this study they found that activation of the right frontopolar area was enhanced while undertaking the Stroop test following exercise.

Cerebral blood flow. The Yanagisawa et al. (2010) and Hyodo et al. (2012) studies also, of course, measure regional cerebral blood flow (rCBF). Although they demonstrated changes in rCBF, Ando (Chapter 6, this text) points out that there is little evidence to support an interaction between acute exercise-induced changes in rCBF and cognition, at least when blood flow is measured during exercise. Studies in which blood flow has been measured postexercise (Byun et al., 2014; Hyodo et al., 2012; Yanagisawa et al., 2010) did demonstrate significant effects on rCBF when undertaking a cognitive task. However, authors (Ando, this text; Lucas et al., 2012; Rooks, Thom, McCully, & Dishman, 2010) have pointed out that cerebral blood flow during exercise is affected by several factors other than the need for oxygen delivery to the brain or by increased cerebral metabolism during cognition (Ogoh et al., 2014) and this affects the interaction between acute exercise, rCBF, and cognition.

Research Design Issues

Measuring Exercise Intensity

Despite the exhortations of Tomporowski (2003, 2009) and Tomporowski and Ellis (1986), with regard to research designs, issues remain. It is now very rare to see studies in which the workload is absolute rather than relative but there are often weaknesses in how intensity is measured. While many studies use percent of $\dot{V}O_{2MAX}$ or maximum power output ($\dot{W}_{MAX}$), many opt for percentage of estimated maximum heart rate (HR_{MAX}) based on the formula, $HR_{MAX} = 220 - age$ (see Fox , Naughton, & Haskell, 1971). Robergs and Landwehr (2005) showed that the method used to determine this formula was greatly flawed and one can have little confidence in it. Some authors prefer to use the formula of Tanaka, Monahan, and Seals (2001), $HR_{MAX} = 208 - (0.7 \times age)$. This receives

some support from Robergs and Landwehr but they concluded "Currently, there is no acceptable method to estimate HRmax" (p. 7). While use of estimated HR_{MAX} saves a lot of time, it may also be leading to inaccurate results.

Another measure that is sometimes used is rate of perceived exertion (Borg, 1982). The scale has its supporters and its detractors, but my main concern is that it does not supply information concerning the individual's physiological or biochemical status, i.e., their sensory state, but rather an affective state, which depends on many factors other than the physical. As such, I see it as providing very useful information with regard to responses by the limbic system to perceptions of stress, which Mason (1975a,b) saw as being so important with regard to catecholamines responses to exercise. With regard to physiological and sensory responses, however, it tells us nothing. Some authors use it to say that "this" activity is harder than "that" activity, which may have some use in physical education contexts, but provides no realistic information for the exercise scientist or neuroscientist.

Cognitive Task Issues

In general, authors tend to utilize tests that are commonly used in cognitive research. These tests have normally been validated and have undergone tests for reliability. However, I have issues with the lack of control over habituation trials in many experiments. Rarely does one see any attempt to determine the point at which there is plateauing of performance pretesting. Indeed it is not uncommon to see researchers simply allow the participants to practice "until they feel comfortable." Counterbalancing does, to some extent, offset this. Interestingly, McMorris and Hale (2012) showed that counterbalanced designs led to higher effect sizes than when testing always took place in the same order, i.e., "at rest" followed by moderate intensity exercise. In these latter experiments, the "at rest" condition normally occurred immediately pre-exercise, therefore the participant was probably in a state of some stress due to anticipation of the task to come. In the counterbalanced design, the "at rest" condition took place on a day without any exercise, therefore the person's stress levels were more likely to be normal. McMorris and Hale pointed to the findings of Mason et al. (1973) that showed increased plasma catecholamines concentrations pre-exercise, while McMorris, Collard, Corbett, Dicks, and Swain (2008) found plasma cortisol concentrations to be elevated pre-exercise.

An issue, which concerns me, is the categorization of short-term memory tasks as being working memory tasks. Miyake and Shah (1999) pointed out that short-term memory is only part of working memory when the information to be recalled is for use in a task that requires central executive control. Although Baddeley (1986) does not explicitly state this, it is definitely implied in his descriptions of the phonological loop and visuospatial sketchpad. Despite this, one often sees short-term memory, recall tasks described as being working memory tasks. This is confusing and leads to inaccurate conclusions being made. Miyake and Shah and Miyake, Friedman, Emerson, Witzki, and Howerter (2000) also raised the issue of authors claiming that tasks are working memory tasks based on rather flimsy evidence. In fact, often there is no evidence at all. Personally, I am not happy with a task being called a working memory task, or certainly being called a central executive task, if there is no psychophysiological evidence of high levels of prefrontal cortex activation.

It is also very common to simply perceive working memory tasks as being complex just because they are working memory tasks. The opposite is generally concluded about attention/perception tasks. Generally speaking, this is the case but one needs to be careful. Some perpetual tasks can require a great deal of prefrontal cortex activity, when organizing and interpreting information received from the sensory cortices and sensory association areas is demanding, while sometimes the working memory task is so easy that prefrontal activation is limited.

Neuroscience Measures

Neurochemical measures. With regard to neurochemical measures, there are a few issues. Given that the main hypothesis is the catecholamines hypothesis, the most obvious measures are the catecholamines themselves. However, as catecholamines do not cross the blood–brain barrier, this raises an issue. While the interaction between the circulating peripheral catecholamines, or rather noradrenaline and adrenaline, and the vagal/NTS pathway is crucial in determining central synthesis and release of noradrenaline and dopamine, it may not be the best measure of what is happening in the brain. Peyrin, Pequignot, Lacour, and Fourcade (1987) claimed that measures of the noradrenaline metabolite 3,4-methoxyhydroxyphenylglycol (MHPG) was a much better indicator of central noradrenergic activity than plasma concentrations of noradrenaline. McMorris et al. (2008) included the dopamine metabolite 4-hydroxyl-3-methoxyphenylacetic acid, also known as homovanillic acid (HVA). Both sets of authors argued that these were better indicators of brain turnover of noradrenaline and dopamine, respectively, than are peripheral measures of the catecholamines themselves. Indeed, dopamine, synthesized and released in the brain, remains in the brain and peripheral dopamine is synthesized and released from the renal system. Thus, peripheral measures of dopamine bear no relationship to central measures (Eisenhofer, Kopin, & Goldstein, 2004).

Although Peyrin et al. (1987) and McMorris et al. (2008) both used measures of MHPG, and the latter also used HVA, there was in fact a major difference between their measures. Peyrin et al. measured urinary MHPG, while McMorris et al. measured plasma concentrations. There is controversy about which is the better measure to use, urine or plasma. Tulen et al. (1992), in a pharmacological study, found urinary MHPG was a better indicator of central activity than plasma MHPG. However, Tsuji et al. (1986) claimed that plasma concentrations of MHPG are better indicators of the turnover of noradrenaline in the brain than are urinary concentrations. More recently, Eisenhofer et al. (2004) argued that neither urine nor plasma concentrations of MHPG were good indicators of brain noradrenaline activity. They claimed that contributions from brain activity could be as low as 3% and no higher than 20%.

With regard to HVA, several authors have demonstrated significant correlations between plasma concentrations and cognitive performance (e.g., Di Rocco et al., 2000; Kahn et al., 1994) and plasma concentrations have been shown to change in accordance with pharmacologically and surgically induced changes in brain concentrations in animals (Bacopoulos, Hattox, & Roth, 1979; Konicki, Owen, Litman, & Pickar, 1991). Kopin, Bankiewicz, and Harvey-White (1988) showed that ~25% of plasma HVA was from central dopamine turnover while Amin et al. (1995) demonstrated figures of ~30%. Eisenhofer et al. (2004), however, claimed that only 12% of plasma concentrations of HVA were from brain activity. The situation with regard to peripheral measures of HVA, however, is complicated by the fact that in dopaminergic neurons, dopamine is stored or metabolized into HVA. However, in noradrenergic neurons not all of the dopamine is converted to noradrenaline, the remainder is metabolized to HVA. Thus, plasma HVA concentrations are indicative of peripheral noradrenaline turnover as well as central and peripheral dopamine activity (Amin et al., 1995; Kopin et al., 1988). As a result, Amin et al. (1995, 1998) claimed that changes, particularly small ones, in plasma HVA concentrations due to brain activity may be masked by peripheral activity, particularly peripheral noradrenaline activity. Thus, the situation is far from clear. Peyrin et al.'s (1987) method of measuring both metabolites and actual catecholamines may be the best, but it is obviously financially more

demanding. However, this does not answer the questions of whether to take plasma or urine measures. In our experiment (McMorris et al., 2008), we chose plasma measures because we wanted to see effects at very specific times and did not wish to wait for urine samples when the participant could oblige. Peyrin et al.'s design allowed for such a wait. No matter which way one goes there are limitations and at best peripheral measures can only be indicative of central ones.

Another issue that has arisen in the literature with regard to neurochemical measures is the use of the lactate and ventilatory thresholds, instead of the catecholamines thresholds (T_{CATS}), to indicate a threshold point at which there will be increased brain concentrations of dopamine and noradrenaline. Several authors have drawn on the fact that the adrenaline, noradrenaline, lactate, and ventilatory thresholds are all fairly highly correlated (McMorris, Sproule, Child, Draper, & Sexsmith, 2000; Yamamoto et al., 1991) and that it is at T_{CATS} that changes in circulating concentrations of adrenaline and noradrenaline are thought to be most likely to induce activation of the vagal/NTS pathway (McMorris & Hale, 2012, 2015; McMorris, Turner, Hale, & Sproule, 2011) and hence increased brain catecholamines concentrations. Given that taking venous blood samples, which are necessary for plasma catecholamines measures, is more difficult than taking finger prick measures of lactate, this latter method has been preferred, while ventilatory threshold is also noninvasive. The fact that peripheral measures of catecholamines are only indicative of central concentrations probably means that these measures are acceptable even though they are not the best measures.

Psychophysiological measures. Great developments in the technology of EEG and fNIRS have added to the efficiency of these measures. The technological developments are ongoing and will help us to move forward in the use of psychophysiological measures. Generally speaking, psychophysiologists are well aware of the limitations of both EEG and fNIRS, which results in a healthy cautiousness with regard to conclusions drawn from the studies.

Sample Size and Statistical Power

An issue that was highlighted to me, when undertaking meta-analyses on acute exercise–cognition interaction studies, was the effect of sample size on probability. Time and time again, nonsignificant ($p > 0.05$) studies were throwing up moderate to high effect sizes. Hence, the effect sizes produced by meta-analyses tend to be greater than one might expect from narrative reviews. In a previous review (McMorris, 2009), I pointed out that sample sizes in the studies examined ranged from 17 to 6. In the studies reviewed by McMorris et al. (this text), the range was from 163 to 6, the mean was 33.26 (SD 55.82) but the mode was only 12. Using tables based on Cohen (1988) (see Clark-Carter, 2002), with $N = 12$, for a one-tailed t-test to achieve a power > 0.80 (generally regarded as being the acceptable cut-off point), the effect size would need to reach $d = 1.1$ (p. 607). McMorris et al. (2011) showed a mean effect size greater than this for response times in working memory tasks but no other meta-analysis has shown anything anywhere near that size (Chang, Labban, Gapin, & Etnier, 2012; Etnier et al., 1997; Lambourne & Tomporowski, 2010). Until higher sample sizes are utilized, we are going to continue to see Type II errors galore. I fully understand and empathize with researchers, as I have the same problems myself, but we would be better off doing fewer experiments and using fewer independent variables, but using larger sample sizes, if we wish to answer the issues that continually arise from the research.

Future Research

Future research needs to begin by clearing up the many untidy conclusions that reviewers find themselves having to make. The position concerning the differing effects found between accuracy and speed-dependent variables needs to be cleared. Studies with lager sample sizes examining the effect of moderate intensity exercise on performance of cognitive tests in which accuracy is the only, or at least the major, dependent variable are required. This will tell us whether or not the different effects on speed of response and accuracy are due to ceiling effects on the accuracy-dependent variable, as argued by McMorris and Hale (2012). We also need more experiments where the effects of acute exercise on the more complex central executive tasks, e.g., planning, problem solving, and decision making, are investigated.

With regard to exercise intensity, the position concerning moderate intensity exercise, at first sight, appears to be clear—it has a positive effect. However, closer inspection opens up some interesting issues. The question of the role of T_{CATS} is unclear. More research is required comparing performance pre- and post-T_{CATS} exercise. Similarly, we need to examine whether or not a threshold exists concerning the time at which long duration, moderate intensity exercise begins to induce a deterioration in performance. This should be examined with regard to both catecholamines and HPA axis hormones concentrations. Similar research should examine the effect of heavy exercise on cognition.

The effects of heavy exercise are underresearched. Interactions with task types require clarification. Does acute exercise have the same effects as acute stress, i.e., working memory tasks are inhibited, while autonomous, attention/perception, and learning/memory tasks are facilitated? Effects of catecholamines and HPA axis hormones should be examined in this research. The question of when exercise should be undertaken in learning/memory tasks is also worthwhile investigating. Is it better to exercise during or prior to encoding and/or consolidation?

Much more research is also required with respect to the types of exercise. The vast majority of studies have utilized aerobic exercise and mainly running but recently authors have begun to examine the effects of resistance exercise (e.g., Chang & Etnier, 2009a,b) and yoga (Gothe, Pontifex, Hillman, & McAuley, 2012). This can only add to our understanding.

From a neurochemical perspective, the roles of 5-hydroxytryptamine (5-HT) and glutamate should also be investigated. Both are affected by acute exercise (Chaouloff, 1997; Dietrich et al., 2005), and play roles in cognition and attention (Mattson, 2008; Meneses, 1999), therefore their omission from all but a few papers is surprising. The effects of genetics also require attention and some work has been undertaken in this area (Hopkins, Davis, Van Tieghem, Whalen, & Bucci, 2012; Stroth et al., 2010). This research does suggest that there are some important interactions with genetic polymorphisms, which could have major medical considerations.

CHRONIC EXERCISE

Research Findings

Age

Young and middle-aged healthy adults. Although most of the acute exercise research has been with young or middle-aged healthy adults, very little research has been undertaken examining the effect of chronic exercise on this particular group (Etnier, Chapter 2, this text). Voelcker-Rehage, Niemann, and Godde (Chapter 14, this text) point out that there is evidence to suggest that exercise undertaken at this stage of life appears to have a beneficial effect on cognitive functioning during aging. The Community-based Coronary Artery Risk Development in Young Adults Study of Zhu et al. (2014) provides huge support for this claim, from a sample of 2747 participants between 18 and 30 years at recruitment in 1985–1986. This is an area that requires more research.

Childhood. Etnier (Chapter 2, this text) and Bustamante, Krafft, Schaeffer, McDowell, and

Davis (Chapter 21, this text) urge caution in interpreting the results for studies with children, as few have been randomized controlled trials (RCTs). Results of cross-sectional studies have, however, generally demonstrated significant, positive effects. Fitness also appears to be beneficial for children (see Voelcker-Rehage et al., this text; Voss, Chapter 9, this text). Recent research with children has also shown a tendency for exercise, plus simultaneously undertaking a cognitive task, having a beneficial effect on children's cognitive functioning including learning (see Pesce & Ben Soussan, Chapter 12, this text).

The elderly. While Etnier (this text) recommends caution in interpreting results for childhood studies due to the lack of RCTs, she points out that this is not an issue in studies with the elderly. The general consensus of the authors in this text (Etnier; Voelcker-Rehage et al.; Voss) is that research shows that chronic exercise, undertaken by the elderly, has beneficial effects on cognition in both healthy participants and those with clinical impairments. As with children, fitness also appears to be beneficial for the elderly (see Colcombe & Kramer, 2003; Voss, this text).

Special Populations

Athletes. As with other individuals, the fitness levels of athletes has a beneficial effect on cognition. However, it does not appear that being athletically fit is of any more advantage than simply being moderately fit (McMorris & Corbett, Chapter 11, this text).

Participants with clinical impairments. Chronic exercise appears to be beneficial for cognition in most clinically impaired groups. Positive effects have been shown for individuals with Parkinson's disease (Hackney, Nocera, Bowers, Altmann, & Hass, Chapter 15, this text), dementia and Alzheimer's disease (Coelho, Vital, Santos-Galduróz, & Gobbi, Chapter 16, this text), attention-deficit hyperactivity disorder (ADHD) (Bustamente et al., Chapter 21, this text; O'Neill, Berwid, & Bédard, Chapter 17, this text), diabetes (Pedersen & Krogh, Chapter 18, this text), breast cancer (Mackenzie, Zuniga, & McAuley, Chapter 19, this text), heart failure (Miller & Gunstad, Chapter 20, this text), schizophrenia (Malchow et al., 2015), and multiple sclerosis (Sandroff, Hillman, Benedict, & Motl, 2015).

Support for Neuroscientific Explanations of the Chronic Exercise–Cognition Interaction

Neurochemical Explanations

Brain-derived neurotrophic factor. Pioneering research by Henriette van Praag (e.g., van Praag, Christie, Sejnowski, & Gage, 1999) led to brain-derived neurotrophic factor (BDNF) being identified as the most likely neurochemical involved in the positive effects of chronic exercise on cognition. van Praag saw that exercise induces increases in BDNF and that when BDNF binds with one of its receptors, the high-affinity tropomyosin-related kinase-B, a number of intracellular signaling cascades, including calcium/calmodulin kinase II and mitogen-activated protein kinase, are initiated, resulting in the phosphorylation of cAMP-response element-binding protein (Binder & Scharfman, 2004; Cunha, Brambilla, & Thomas, 2010; Waterhouse & Xu, 2009). Activation of these signaling pathways is essential for neurogenesis and neuroplasticity, and hence learning and memory (Cunha et al., 2010; Lessmann, Gottmann, & Malcangio, 2003; Waterhouse & Xu, 2009). Moreover, several authors (e.g., Berchtold, Castello, & Cotman, 2010; Cotman & Berchtold, 2002; Gomez-Pinilla, Vaynman, & Ying, 2008; Griesbach, Hovda, & Gomez-Pinilla, 2009; Huang et al., 2006; Liu et al., 2009; Neeper, Gomez-Pinilla, Choi, & Cotman, 1995) have shown that, in rodents, chronic exercise induces increased expression of the BDNF messenger ribonucleic acid (mRNA) gene in the brain, in particular in the hippocampus. More recently, it has been argued that several growth factors are involved in chronic exercise-induced neurogenesis and neuroplasticity, e.g., fibroblast growth factor, epidermal growth factor, insulin-like growth factor, and vascular endothelial growth factor (Cao et al., 2004; Fabel et al., 2003; Ferreira, Real, Rodrigues, Alves, & Britto, 2011; Foster, Rosenblatt, & Kuljiš, 2011).

The few human studies that have directly examined the interaction between chronic exercise, BDNF, and cognition (Erickson et al., 2011; Griffin et al., 2011; Whiteman et al., 2014) provide some support for an interaction actually taking place. More research is required but it is difficult to prove that it is exercise-induced increases in BDNF concentrations that are causing neurogenesis and neuroplasticity. The actions of BDNF occur downstream of synthesis and release, so it is difficult to know when to measure BDNF concentrations in relation to cognitive performance.

Catecholamines. Despite the great interest in the role of catecholamines in the acute exercise–cognition interaction, little research has attempted to examine an interaction with chronic exercise. Animal studies have shown, however, that chronic exercise induces increased tyrosine hydroxylase (TH) mRNA gene expression in the brain (Foley & Fleshner, 2008; Gavrilović et al., 2012; Tümer et al., 2001). As TH is the rate limiter for catecholamines synthesis, one would expect this to have a positive effect on cognition. Moreover, animal studies have shown that noradrenaline plays a role in neurogenesis, neuroplasticity (Jhaveri et al., 2010; Masuda et al., 2011), and long-term potentiation (Gelinas & Nguyen, 2005; Katsuki, Izumi, & Zorumski, 1997). It would appear that this deserves further research.

HPA axis hormones. It is logical to expect that repeated exposure to heavy exercise, which is a stressor, would lead to some desensitization to the HPA axis hormones and probably a decrease in glucocorticoid (GR) and mineralocorticoid (MR) receptor mRNA expression in the brain. However, in humans, research has generally shown that chronic exercise does not alter basal plasma ACTH and cortisol concentrations (Chatzitheodorou, Kabitsis, Malliou, & Mougios, 2007; Duclos, Corcuff, Pehourcq, & Tabarin, 2001; Inder, Hellemans, Swanney, Prickett, & Donald, 1998; Strüder et al., 1999; Wittert, Livesey, Espiner, & Donald, 1996). In rodents, research generally shows very limited effects of chronic exercise on GR mRNA expression in the hippocampus (Chang et al., 2008; Droste et al., 2003; Fediuc, Campbell, & Riddell, 2006; Zheng et al., 2006), although Park et al. (2005) found a significant decrease in hippocampal region CA4 only, while Droste, Chandramohan, Hill, Linthorst, and Reul (2007) found increased GR mRNA levels in hippocampal layers. Reductions in MR mRNA expression have been shown (Chang et al., 2008; Droste et al., 2003) but some authors found no significant effect (Droste et al., 2007; Park et al., 2005). Thus, it would appear that HPA axis hormones are not involved in the chronic exercise–cognition interaction.

Psychophysiological Explanations

Electroencephalography. The vast majority of ERP studies have been cross-sectional and mostly comparing fit individuals with unfit ones. Fit people have generally shown larger P3 amplitude and/or shorter P3 latency during working memory tasks. Interestingly, despite this, differences in the behavioral measure, reaction time, was not always demonstrated. Other ERP measures have tended not to show any advantage for fit participants (Kamijo, this text). It should be noted that most studies have utilized working memory tasks and there is a need for research into attention/perception tasks. Moreover, RCTs are needed. A recent RCT (Hillman et al., 2014) provided results consistent with the findings of many cross-sectional P3 studies.

The fact that research has shown decreased P3 latency and increased P3 amplitude, however, tells us little about what is actually causing these changes. Recently, Kamijo and colleagues (Kamijo & Takeda, 2013; Kamijo, Takeda, & Hillman, 2011) have attempted to shed some

light on the underlying processes. They examined the interaction between fitness and functional connectivity between brain regions, using phase-locking values (PLVs). PLVs allow the researcher to determine the functional connectivity between brain regions during task conditions, which require large amounts of top-down cognitive control (Lachaux, Rodriguez, Martinerie, & Varela, 1999). Fit individuals demonstrated greater functional connectivity than unfit participants, hence allowing one to conclude that functional connectivity between brain regions is an underlying mechanism in the chronic exercise–cognition interaction (see Kamijo, this text, for more detail).

Functional magnetic resonance imaging. Most of the fMRI studies are cross-sectional and have examined the effect of cardiovascular fitness on brain activation (Voelcker-Rehage et al., this text; Voss, this text). The literature reviewed by these authors supports the conclusions reached by Hillman, Erickson, and Kramer (2008) with all ages, and Colcombe, Kramer, McAuley, Erickson, and Scalf (2004) and Kramer et al. (1999) with older adults. During inhibition tasks, fit older adults show greater activation in the right middle frontal gyrus and bilateral superior parietal lobe, and less activation in the anterior cingulate cortex (ACC) than the unfit elderly. They also demonstrate superior task performance. Research examining the effects of chronic exercise on the elderly has also shown increased activation in the hippocampus (Erickson et al., 2011; Niemann, Godde, & Voelcker-Rehage, 2014). This has also been shown with children (Chaddock et al., 2010). As Voelcker-Rehage et al. (this text) point out, however, there are studies that did not find any relationship between gray matter volume and physical activity parameters (Rosano et al., 2010; Smith et al., 2011), while the majority of studies did not find a relationship between white matter volume and physical activity (Erickson et al., 2010; Flöel et al., 2010; Gordon et al., 2008; Ruscheweyh et al., 2011; Smith et al., 2011), even in young adults (Peters et al., 2009).

These results supply strong support from the positive effects of BDNF and growth factors with regard to neurogenesis and neuroprotection. Moreover, given that fit individuals tend to show more activation in areas vital to central executive performance, I would argue that they supply circumstantial evidence for more efficient synthesis and release of dopamine and noradrenaline in the brain, a possible result of increased TH mRNA expression due to chronic exercise.

Research Design Issues and Future Research

Although several chronic exercise–cognition interaction, empirical studies have small sample sizes, the situation is nowhere near as problematic as with acute exercise studies. The research design issues found in the chronic exercise research are somewhat different to those found in acute exercise studies. Etnier (this text), Kamijo (this text), and Bustamente et al. (this text) all highlight the use of cross-sectional designs rather than RCTs. However, this is mainly in research using EEG. fMRI research appears to have utilized RCTs more readily, especially in more recent studies. Although the lack of RCTs is seen by many as leaving research findings open to question, it was probably unavoidable in the early research comparing those who had led active lifestyles with those who had been sedentary or between fit and unfit children. The fact that similar findings have been shown when RCTs have been conducted shows that cross-sectional studies can be useful.

Perhaps the greatest problem with cross-sectional studies is the use of questionnaires to assess the amount and intensity of the physical activity undertaken by individuals. These can be especially problematic when they are retrospective, as many were with elderly participants. However, another problem with questionnaires is the fact that often the researcher and, probably more so, the participant tend to focus on recreational physical activity forgetting work-related physical activity. When questionnaires are more concerned with present day activity, the use of log books can be helpful, while pedometers and similar devices can provide some empirical data, although, we should be aware of the limitations of these devices. Certainly the limitations of measuring physical activity have led to the lack of real knowledge concerning the effects of intensity and frequency of physical activity necessary to induce better cognitive functioning. This is something that needs to be examined.

The fit versus unfit comparisons seen in much of the literature, especially that with children, also lead to issues concerning the ways in which researchers have determined fitness levels. Laboratory-based $\dot{V}O_{2MAX}$ tests are often used and this is sensible but time-consuming, particularly when sample sizes are high. As a result, sometimes field tests of estimated $\dot{V}O_{2MAX}$, such as the bleep test, are used. These have lots of practical advantages in that they can be administered to many individuals at the same time, cost very little, and provide a quick result. However, they are not particularly accurate. Researchers using such protocols should make sure that accurate measures of fitness are not vital to their hypotheses or research questions.

The fairly common use of $\dot{V}O_{2MAX}$ tests reminds one that most of the research has examined the use of aerobic exercise, or aerobic-type activities, on cognition. There is, without a doubt, a need for examination of the effects of other types of physical activity. Resistance training is an obvious example. It is undertaken by many, yet we know little about its long-term effects, indeed even its acute effects, on cognition. It is good to see that some researchers are beginning to undertake such research (Chang, Pan, Chen, Tsai, & Huang, 2012; Tsai, Wang, Pan, & Chen, 2015). However, other activities need to be examined, e.g., swimming, tennis, yoga, dance, golf, lawn bowls, and even popular team games like soccer, basketball, field hockey, and ice hockey.

Cognitive task issues. Several authors in this text (Etnier; Kamijo; Voelcker-Rehage et al.; Voss) have pointed out that the research has been undertaken with working memory tasks, especially central executive tasks, long-term memory, and learning. There is a lack of interest in perception/attention tasks. This is particularly surprising given that chronic exercise effects on such tasks must be of interest to the military, firefighters, police, and sports people. This is a real weakness in the research.

Atheoretical Nature of Much of the Research

Early research into the effect of chronic exercise on cognition was atheoretical, even the early EEG and fMRI studies tended to simply report the activation of specific areas of the brain (see Etnier, this text). It is good to see authors beginning to test theoretically driven hypotheses. Kamijo's (Kamijo & Takeda, 2013; Kamijo et al., 2011) examination of the hypothesis that physical activity induces increased functional connectivity, between task-relevant regions of the brain, is very promising in EEG research. Voss (this text) outlines fMRI research that has examined several theories concerning the interaction between biomarkers of fitness and cognition. The most popular of the theoretically driven research has been studies examining the interaction between chronic exercise, BDNF concentrations, and cognition. It is good to see such research but blind belief in the BDNF hypothesis is leading to researchers ignoring the effects of neurochemicals such as growth factors and catecholamines.

TRANSLATIONAL ISSUES

Exercise as an Aid to Healthy Aging

A great deal of research has been carried out into the effect of chronic exercise on aging in healthy individuals. It would appear fair to say that the evidence that regular exercise aids healthy aging is overwhelming (Hayes, Alosco, & Forman, 2014; van Praag, Fleshner, Schwartz, & Mattson, 2014). Moreover, it would appear that exercising in young adulthood can have a lasting effect and aid cognitive performance even into old age (Zhu et al., 2014). This does not mean that the elderly have to join gym clubs. Any type of exercise appears to be helpful. This could simply be walking (Dehi, Aghajari, Shahshahani, Takfallah, & Jahangiri, 2014) but other types of popular exercise like dancing have been shown to be effective (Kattenstroth, Kalisch, Holt, Tegenthoff, & Dinse, 2013). Indeed, even housework can qualify as exercise, depending on the intensity and duration. Unfortunately, there is, as far as I can tell, no research examining the effects of games popular with the elderly, such as golf or lawn bowls, but it would appear logical to expect these to have positive effects. The message to the elderly is loud and clear: keep exercising as long as you can.

Exercise as a Preventive Medicine

In this book, we have focused on the exercise–cognition interaction, even in the chapters covering cognitive performance in individuals with a variety of diseases, but we should not forget that chronic exercise has been shown to be useful as a preventive medicine and/or alleviator of symptoms for several of these diseases, e.g., multiple sclerosis (Sandroff et al., 2015), schizophrenia (Malchow et al., 2015), Parkinson's disease (Dashtipour et al., 2015), dementia (Bossers et al., 2015), diabetes (Juraschek et al., 2015), and ADHD (Halperin, Berwid, & O'Neill, 2014). As with the elderly, the range of exercise types used is being increased with promising results. However, people suffering from these diseases may well find it more difficult to exercise than healthy individuals, even elderly ones. The use of activities like aquatic aerobics would appear to have some possibilities with these individuals. With younger individuals there are many activities including games that have the potential to provide exercise opportunities. Moreover, the possibility that exercising, while simultaneously undertaking cognitive tasks, should not be dismissed for these groups of people. The mechanics of this are covered in the next subsection.

Studies have shown the possibilities of the use of exercise with individuals with certain genetic polymorphisms. In humans, Stroth et al. (2010) examined the effect of a 17-week running program on a variety of central executive functions in individuals who were homozygote for the valine (Val) 158 variant in the catechol-O-methyltransferase gene and those homozygote for the methionine (Met) allele. In normal circumstances, Met carriers are optimal in dopamine signaling in the prefrontal cortex, which would facilitate handling central executive demands, while Val carriers are low. The Val carriers benefited significantly from training while Met individuals showed no significant effect. The authors took this as being indicative of increased brain synthesis and usage of dopamine by the Val individuals. In the Met carriers this increase would be redundant. This needs far more research but appears to have great potential.

Exercise as an Aid to Children's Learning

As with the elderly, it would appear that, for children, the benefits of chronic exercise on learning, academic success, and working memory are overwhelming. However, getting children to exercise is not as easy as one might think. Children being taken to school by car, even when living well within walking distance, is endemic in the developed world. Overweight and obesity have thus become a problem (see Bustamente et al., this text). In some countries, physical education is given an important place in schools, but in others it is not. One hopes that the evidence that exercise can aid learning and academic achievement will help persuade governments, educators, and parents of the need for regular exercise. As with the groups dealt with in the two previous subsections, one would expect all types of physical activity to have positive effects. Moreover, there is strong evidence that both chronic and acute exercise have beneficial effects on cognitive performance in children. This has implications for the school timetable. Cooper, Bandelow, Nute, Morris, and Nevill (2015) found positive effects of acute exercise on cognition as long as 1h following cessation of the activity. While this appears a long time, it should be remembered that although the half-life of catecholamines in the periphery is only ~3min (Genuth, 2004), Eisenhofer et al. (2004) reported the half-life of brain catecholamines as being in the range of 8–12h, while Kadzierski, Aguila-Mansilla, Kozlowski, and Porter (1994) stated that the half-life of TH mRNA was 14 ± 1h. So daily physical education would have the positive effects of both acute and chronic exercise.

Recent research with children has shown that exercising, while simultaneously undertaking cognitively demanding tasks, is beneficial. Central executive tasks have been shown to particularly benefit (Pesce, 2009). As a result, Pesce (2012) advocated integrated exercise–cognition training, what she termed "gross-motor cognitive training." Pesce and Ben Soussan (this text) argue convincingly that acute exercise and cognition both activate similar neural regions. They particularly focus on the roles of the cerebellum and its connections with the prefrontal cortex. While I agree with their comments, I think that we might go a little further and develop the use of exercise/cognitive games, which directly tap factors involved in central executive functioning. The children's game "Simon says" does, in fact, do that. The children must respond to instructions when the teacher uses the phrase "Simon says," but not respond when the teacher does not use that phrase. This is similar to the go/no go task and requires inhibition of prepotent responses.

It can be added to by having the children make an alternative response when the words "Simon says" are not spoken; this would be an incongruent response. This task demands activation of the ACC, the DLPFC, and presupplementary motor area (pre-SMA) (Nieuwenhuis, Yeung, van den Wildenburg, & Ridderinkhof, 2003; Simmonds, Pekara, & Mostofsky, 2008). Increased demand for the neurotransmitters dopamine and noradrenaline, which activate the ACC, DLPFC, and pre-SMA, should be met by the exercise-induced increases in dopamine and noradrenaline. Other similar games could easily be developed. A chronic effect of undertaking such activities could be neurogenesis and long-term potentiation in these regions due to the effects of BDNF and growth factors. This may have potential with prevention and treatment of ADHD in children and, in adults, possibly even other diseases such as schizophrenia. Other games could easily be developed, which would require the use of other central executive functions and hence activate different brain regions.

Effects on Occupations Involving Heavy Exercise

The effects of heavy exercise on cognitive performance are important to the military, firefighters, and sports performers, on a regular basis, but also to other occupations occasionally. The concern for these people is undertaking heavy exercise and/or long-duration moderate intensity exercise, while having to make decisions and/or perceive the presence/absence of stimuli, particularly visual stimuli. Performance of the attention/perception tasks might actually benefit from heavy exercise or, at worst, not be negatively affected, but working memory, especially central executive, tasks are negatively affected (see McMorris et al., this text), However, McMorris and colleagues point out that well-learned, automatic tasks tend to benefit from heavy exercise. There is, therefore,

a great deal of sense in practicing the tasks to be undertaken, so that they become automatic. It may be more beneficial to actually practice while simultaneously undertaking heavy exercise or immediately following such exercise. Improving fitness levels will also have an effect, as cognitive performance post-training, at any given absolute level of fitness, will be better than it was pre-training. However, at the same relative level there will probably be no significant effect.

When discussing automaticity in the previous paragraph, I suggested that training should be task specific, i.e., ecologically valid. Whether there is transfer, from nonecologically valid tasks to ecologically valid ones, is debatable. Dahlin, Neely, Larsson, Bäckman, and Nyberg (2008) demonstrated transfer between central executive tasks but only when identical striatal regions where activated in both tasks. In a literature review, Klingberg (2010) came to a similar conclusion for working memory tasks, arguing that cognitive "training-induced plasticity in an intraparietal–prefrontal network that is common for WM [working memory]" (p. 322) is responsible for the transfer. However, Klingberg also pointed out that there is a limited amount of research and one must be cautious when drawing conclusions from the research. Trying to be ecologically valid appears to be the safest method to use.

Exercise as an Aid to Performance of Workers in Sedentary Occupations

If exercise has a positive effect on cognition, it is logical to expect sedentary workers to benefit from undertaking physical activity at some time during the working day. This is especially so in the modern era when most individuals arrive at work in cars rather than by cycling or walking. It is good to see that many employers are now encouraging workers to exercise in their lunch break, some even have gymnasia and personal trainers. Others are utilizing work stations that allow the worker to exercise while simultaneously carrying out their work. Much more research is needed in this area. The research examined in this book would suggest improved employee output, which should interest all employers.

Warm-Up for Sports Performers

Until recently, most sports performers saw warm-up as something that helped prevent injuries. In recent years, sports people, who must make decisions during physical activity, have become aware of the fact that warm-up can aid technical performance and decision making. Hence, warm-up has become longer and more sophisticated. Based on the catecholamines hypothesis, elsewhere I have suggested that optimal warm-up would require exercise at an intensity equal to that needed to induce T_{CATS} (McMorris et al., 1999). Recent research (McMorris & Hale, 2015), however, suggests that it can be lower than that as long as it is of sufficient duration, probably ~30 min. Moreover, a recent meta-analysis, examining the effect of exercise on psychomotor performance (McMorris, Hale, Corbett, Robertson, & Hodgson, 2015), suggested that effects were different when tasks required both a motor and cognitive response.

CONCLUSION

Acute exercise appears to affect speed of responses but has limited effect on accuracy. However, this is probably due to a ceiling effect on the accuracy dependent variables of the cognitive tasks rather than a real lack of effect. When speed is the dependent variable, moderate intensity exercise ($\geq 40\%$ $\dot{V}O_{2MAX}$ but $<80\%$ $\dot{V}O_{2MAX}$) of moderate duration (10–20 min) facilitates cognitive performance. However, exercise of this intensity for >60 min can lead to a deterioration in performance. Heavy exercise ($\geq 80\%$ $\dot{V}O_{2MAX}$) appears to facilitate autonomous tasks and learning tasks, but results for attention/perception tasks show equivocal results. The limited amount of research examining working memory tasks, during heavy exercise, is too small to detect a trend.

The literature, from animal and human studies, suggests that during exercise, activation of the vagal/NTS pathway by adrenaline and noradrenaline stimulates the synthesis and release of noradrenaline in the locus coeruleus and dopamine via stimulation of α_1-adrenoreceptors by the noradrenaline released from the locus coeruleus, which potentiates the firing of dopamine neurons in the ventral tegmental area. Research has shown that these brain neurotransmitters have beneficial effects when concentrations are moderate. When concentrations are high, most, but not all, working memory tasks are disrupted, while tasks activating the sensory cortices can be facilitated. The psychophysiological research provides some support for this. When cognition takes place following acute exercise of moderate intensity, facilitative effects on both P3 latency and amplitude are shown almost unequivocally.

Chronic exercise would appear to have positive effects for everyone but especially the elderly and children. It has also been shown to be effective in alleviating the negative effects on cognition of several clinical impairments. Chronic exercise-induced increases in BDNF brain concentrations and BDNF mRNA expression would appear to play a major role in neuroprotection and long-term potentiation. Increased brain expression of TH mRNA may also be a key factor. The translational possibilities with the elderly, children, and those with clinical issues are wide ranging and require much more research. The positive effects of daily physical education in schools and the provision of opportunities for physical activity in the workplace should not be ruled out.

References

Abercrombie, H. C., Kalin, N. H., Thurow, M. E., Rosenkranz, M. A., & Davidson, R. J. (2003). Cortisol variation in humans affects memory for emotionally laden and neutral information. *Behavioral Neuroscience, 117*, 505–516.

Amin, F., Davidson, M., Kahn, R. S., Schmeidler, J., Stern, R., Knott, P. J., et al. (1995). Assessment of the central dopaminergic index of plasma HVA in schizophrenia. *Schizophrenia Bulletin, 21*, 53–66.

Amin, F., Stroe, A. E., Kahn, T., Knott, P. J., Kahn, R. S., & Davidson, M. (1998). Control of renal factors in plasma homovanillic acid measurements. *Neuropsychopharmacology, 18*, 317–320.

Arnsten, A. F. T. (2009). Stress signalling pathways that impair prefrontal cortex structure and function. *Nature Reviews Neuroscience, 10*, 410–422.

Arnsten, A. F. T. (2011). Catecholamine influences on dorsolateral prefrontal cortical networks. *Biological Psychiatry, 69*, e89–e99. http://dx.doi.org/10.1016/j.biopsych.2011.01.027.

Bacopoulos, N. G., Hattox, S. E., & Roth, R. H. (1979). 3,4-Dihydroxyphenylacetic acid and homovanillic acid in rat plasma: possible indicators of central dopaminergic activity. *European Journal Pharmacology, 56*, 225–236.

Baddeley, A. D. (1986). *Working memory*. New York: Oxford University Press.

Barbas, H. (2000). Connections underlying the synthesis of cognition, memory, and emotion in primate prefrontal cortices. *Brain Research Bulletin, 52*, 319–330.

Berchtold, N. C., Castello, N., & Cotman, C. W. (2010). Exercise and time-dependent benefits to learning and memory. *Neuroscience, 167*, 588–597.

Binder, D. K., & Scharfman, H. E. (2004). Brain-derived neurotrophic factor. *Growth Factors, 22*, 123–131.

Bondi, C. O., Jett, J. D., & Morilak, D. A. (2010). Beneficial effects of desipramine on cognitive function of chronically stressed rats are mediated by alpha1-adrenergic receptors in medial prefrontal cortex. *Progress in Neuropsychopharmacology Biological Psychiatry, 34*, 913–923.

Borg, G. A. V. (1982). Psychophysical bases of perceived exertion. *Medicine and Science in Sports and Exercise, 14*, 377–381.

Bossers, W. J., van der Woude, L. H., Boersma, F., Hortobágyi, T., Scherder, E. J., & van Heuvelen, M. J. (2015). A 9-week aerobic and strength training program improves cognitive and motor function in patients with dementia: a randomized, controlled trial. *American Journal of Geriatric Psychiatry*. http://dx.doi.org/10.1016/j.jagp.2014.12.191 [Epub ahead of print].

Byun, K., Hyodo, K., Suwabe, K., Ochi, G., Sakairi, Y., Kato, M., et al. (2014). Positive effect of acute mild exercise on executive function via arousal-related prefrontal activations: an fNIRS study. *NeuroImage, 98*, 336–345.

Cao, L., Jiao, X., Zuzga, D. S., Liu, Y., Fong, D. M., Young, D., et al. (2004). VEGF links hippocampal activity with neurogenesis, learning and memory. *Nature Genetics, 36*, 827–835.

Chaddock, L., Erickson, K. I., Prakash, R. S., Kim, J. S., Voss, M. W., VanPatter, M., et al. (2010). A neuroimaging investigation of the association between aerobic fitness, hippocampal volume and memory performance in preadolescent children. *Brain Research, 1358*, 172–183.

Chang, Y. T., Chen, Y. C., Wu, C. W., Chen, H. I., Jen, C. J., & Kuo, Y. M. (2008). Glucocorticoid signaling an exercise-induced downregulation of the mineralocorticoid receptor in the induction of adult mouse dentate neurogenesis by treadmill running. *Psychoneuroendocrinology, 33*, 1173–1182.

Chang, Y. K., & Etnier, J. L. (2009a). Effects of an acute bout of localized resistance exercise on cognitive performance in middle-aged adults: a randomized controlled trial study. *Psychology of Sport and Exercise, 10*, 19–24.

Chang, Y. K., & Etnier, J. L. (2009b). Exploring the dose-response relationship between resistance exercise intensity and cognitive function. *Journal of Sport and Exercise Psychology, 31*, 640–656.

Chang, Y. K., Labban, J. D., Gapin, J. I., & Etnier, J. L. (2012). The effects of acute exercise on cognitive performance: a meta-analysis. *Brain Research, 1453*, 87–101.

Chang, Y. K., Pan, C. Y., Chen, F. T., Tsai, C. L., & Huang, C. C. (2012). Effect of resistance-exercise training on cognitive function in healthy older adults: a review. *Journal of Aging and Physical Activity, 20*, 497–517.

Chaouloff, F. (1997). Effects of acute physical exercise on central serotonergic systems. *Medicine and Science in Sports and Exercise, 29*, 58–62.

Chatzitheodorou, D., Kabitsis, C., Malliou, P., & Mougios, V. (2007). A pilot study of the effects of high-intensity aerobic exercise versus passive interventions on pain, disability, psychological strain, and serum cortisol concentrations in people with low back pain. *Physical Therapy, 87*, 304–312.

Chmura, J., Nazar, H., & Kaciuba-Uścilko, H. (1994). Choice reaction time during graded exercise in relation to blood lactate and plasma catecholamine thresholds. *International Journal of Sports Medicine, 15*, 172–176.

Clark-Carter, D. (2002). *Doing quantitative psychological research*. Hove: Psychology Press.

Cohen, J. (1988). *Statistical power analysis for the behavioral sciences* (2nd ed.). Hillsdale, NJ: Lawrence Erlbaum Associates.

Colcombe, S., & Kramer, A. F. (2003). Fitness effects on the cognitive function of older adults: a meta-analytic study. *Psychological Science, 14*, 125–130.

Colcombe, S. J., Kramer, A. F., McAuley, E., Erickson, K. I., & Scalf, P. (2004). Neurocognitive aging and cardiovascular fitness: recent findings and future directions. *Journal of Molecular Neuroscience, 24*, 9–14.

Cools, R., Barker, R. A., Sahakian, B. J., & Robbins, T. W. (2001). Enhanced or impaired cognitive function in Parkinson's disease as a function of dopaminergic medication and task demands. *Cerebral Cortex, 11*, 1136–1143.

Cooper, C. J. (1973). Anatomical and physiological mechanisms of arousal with specific reference to the effects of exercise. *Ergonomics, 16*, 601–609.

Cooper, S. B., Bandelow, S., Nute, M. L., Morris, J. G., & Nevill, M. E. (2015). Breakfast glycaemic index and exercise: combined effects on adolescents' cognition. *Physiology and Behavior, 139*, 104–111.

Cotman, C. W., & Berchtold, N. C. (2002). Exercise: a behavioral intervention to enhance brain health and plasticity. *Trends in Neurosciences, 25*, 295–301.

Cunha, C., Brambilla, R., & Thomas, K. L. (2010). A simple role for BDNF in learning and memory? *Frontiers in Molecular Neuroscience, 3*, 1. http://dx.doi.org/10.3389/neuro.02.001.2010.

Dahlin, E., Neely, A. S., Larsson, A., Bäckman, L., & Nyberg, L. (2008). Transfer of learning after updating training mediated by the striatum. *Science, 320*, 1510–1512.

Dashtipour, K., Johnson, E., Kani, C., Kani, K., Hadi, E., Ghamsary, M., et al. (2015). Effect of exercise on motor and nonmotor symptoms of Parkinson's disease. *Parkinson's Disease.* http://dx.doi.org/10.1155/2015/586378.

Dehi, M., Aghajari, P., Shahshahani, M., Takfallah, L., & Jahangiri, L. (2014). The effect of stationary walking on the quality of life of the elderly women: a randomized controlled trial. *Journal of Caring Sciences, 3*, 103–111.

Di Rocco, A., Bottiglieri, T., Dorfman, D., Werner, P., Morrison, C., & Simpson, D. (2000). Decreased homovanillic acid in cerebrospinal fluid correlates with impaired neuropsychologic function in HIV-1-infected patients. *Clinical in Neuropharmacology, 23*, 190–194.

Dietrich, A., & Audiffren, M. (2011). The reticular-activating hypofrontality (RAH) model of acute exercise. *Neuroscience and Biobehavioral Reviews, 35*, 1305–1325.

Dietrich, M. O., Mantese, C. E., Porciuncula, L. O., Ghisleni, G., Vinade, L., Souza, D. O., et al. (2005). Exercise affects glutamate receptors in postsynaptic densities from cortical mice brain. *Brain Research, 1065*, 20–25.

Donkers, F. C., & van Boxtel, G. J. (2004). The N2 in go/no-go tasks reflects conflict monitoring not response inhibition. *Brain and Cognition, 56*, 165–176.

Droste, S. K., Chandramohan, Y., Hill, L. E., Linthorst, A. C., & Reul, J. M. (2007). Voluntary exercise impacts on the rat hypothalamic-pituitary-adrenocortical axis mainly at the adrenal level. *Neuroendocrinology, 86*, 26–37.

Droste, S. K., Gesing, A., Ulbricht, S., Müller, M. B., Linthorst, A. C. E., & Reul, J. M. H.M. (2003). Effects of long-term voluntary exercise on the mouse hypothalamic-pituitary-adrenocortical axis. *Endocrinology, 144*, 3012–3023.

Duclos, M., Corcuff, J.-B., Pehourcq, F., & Tabarin, A. (2001). Decreased pituitary sensitivity to glucocorticoids in endurance-trained men. *European Journal of Endocrinology, 144*, 363–368.

Eisenhofer, G., Kopin, I. J., & Goldstein, D. S. (2004). Catecholamine metabolism: a contemporary view with implications for physiology and medicine. *Pharmacological Reviews, 56*, 331–348.

Erickson, K. I., Raji, C. A., Lopez, O. L., Becker, J. T., Rosano, C., Newman, A. B., et al. (2010). Physical activity predicts gray matter volume in late adulthood: the Cardiovascular Health Study. *Neurology, 75*, 1415–1422.

Erickson, K. I., Voss, M. W., Prakash, R. S., Basak, C., Szabo, A., Chaddock, L., et al. (2011). Exercise training increases size of hippocampus and improves memory. *Proceedings of the National Academy of Sciences of the United States of America, 108*, 3017–3022.

Eriksen, B. A., & Eriksen, C. W. (1974). Effects of noise letters upon the identification of a target letter in a nonsearch task. *Perception and Psychophysics, 16*, 143–149.

Etnier, J. L., Salazar, W., Landers, D. M., Petruzzello, S. J., Han, M., & Nowell, P. (1997). The influence of physical fitness and exercise upon cognitive functioning: a meta-analysis. *Journal of Sport and Exercise Psychology, 19*, 249–277.

Fabel, K., Tam, B., Kuafer, D., Barker, A., Simmons, N., Kuo, C. J., et al. (2003). VEGF is necessary for exercise-induced adult hippocampal neurogenesis. *European Journal of Neuroscience, 18*, 2803–2812.

Falkenstein, M., Hoormann, J., Christ, S., & Hohnsbein, J. (2000). ERP components on reaction errors and their functional significance: a tutorial. *Biological Psychology, 51*, 87–107.

Falkenstein, M., Hoormann, J., Hohnsbein, J., & Kleinsorge, T. (2003). Short-term mobilization of processing resources is revealed in the event-related potential. *Psychophysiology, 40*, 914–923.

Fediuc, S., Campbell, J. E., & Riddell, M. C. (2006). Effect of voluntary wheel running on circadian corticosterone release and on HPA axis responsiveness to restraint stress in Sprague-Dawley rats. *Journal of Applied Physiology, 100*, 1867–1875.

Ferreira, A. F. B., Real, C. C., Rodrigues, A. C., Alves, A. S., & Britto, L. R. G. (2011). Short-term, moderate exercise is capable of inducing structural, bdnf-independent hippocampal plasticity. *Brain Research, 1425*, 111–122.

Flöel, A., Ruscheweyh, R., Kruger, K., Willemer, C., Winter, B., Volker, K., et al. (2010). Physical activity and memory functions: are neurotrophins and cerebral gray matter volume the missing link? *NeuroImage, 49*, 2756–2763.

Foley, T. E., & Fleshner, M. (2008). Neuroplasticity of dopamine circuits after exercise: implications for central fatigue. *NeuroMolecular Medicine, 10*, 67–80.

Folstein, J. R., & Van Petten, C. (2008). Influence of cognitive control and mismatch on the N2 component of the ERP: a review. *Psychophysiology, 45*, 152–170.

Fontana, F. E., Mazzardo, O., Mokgothu, C., Furtado, O., & Gallagher, J. D. (2009). Influence of exercise intensity on the decision-making performance of experienced and inexperienced soccer players. *Journal of Sport and Exercise Psychology, 31*, 135–151.

Foster, P. P., Rosenblatt, K. P., & Kuljiš, R. O. (2011). Exercise-induced cognitive plasticity, implications for mild cognitive impairment and Alzheimer's disease. *Frontiers in Neurology.* http://dx.doi.org/10.3389/fneur.2011.00028.

Fox, S. M., III, Naughton, J. P., & Haskell, W. L. (1971). Physical activity and the prevention of coronary heart disease. *Annals of Clinical Research, 3*, 404–432.

Gavrilović, L., Mandusić, V., Stojiliković, V., Kasapović, J., Stojiliković, S., Pajović, S. B., et al. (2012). Effect of chronic forced running on gene expression of catecholamine biosynthetic enzymes in stellate ganglia of rats. *Journal of Biological Regulators and Homeostatic Agents, 26*, 367–377.

Gelinas, J. N., & Nguyen, P. V. (2005). Beta-adrenergic receptor activation facilitates induction of a protein synthesis-dependent late phase of long-term potentiation. *Jounal of Neuroscience, 25*, 3294–3303.

Genuth, S. M. (2004). The endocrine system. In R. M. Berne, M. Levy, N. B. Koepen, & B. A. Stanton (Eds.), *Physiology* (5th ed.) (pp. 719–978). St. Louis, MO: Mosby.

Gomez-Pinilla, F., Vaynman, S., & Ying, Z. (2008). Brain-derived neurotrophic factor functions as a metabotrophin to mediate the effects of exercise on cognition. *European Journal of Neuroscience, 28*, 2278–2287.

Gordon, B. A., Rykhlevskaia, E. I., Brumback, C. R., Lee, Y., Elavsky, S., Konopack, J. F., et al. (2008). Neuroanatomical correlates of aging, cardiopulmonary fitness level, and education. *Psychophysiology, 45*, 825–838.

Gothe, N., Pontifex, M. B., Hillman, C., & McAuley, E. (2012). The acute effects of yoga on executive function. *Journal of Physical Activity and Health, 10*, 488–495.

Grego, F., Vallier, J. M., Collardeau, M., Bermon, S., Ferrari, P., Candito, M., et al. (2004). Effects of long duration exercise on cognitive function, blood glucose, and counterregulatory hormones in male cyclists. *Neuroscience Letters, 364*, 76–80.

Grenhoff, J., Nisell, M., Ferré, S., Aston-Jones, G., & Svensson, T. H. (1993). Noradrenergic modulation of dopamine cell firing elicited by stimulation of the locus coeruleus in the rat. *Journal of Neural Transmission: General Section, 93*, 11–25.

Grenhoff, J., & Svensson, T. H. (1993). Prazosin modulates the firing pattern of dopamine neurons in rat ventral tegmental area. *European Journal of Pharmacology, 233*, 79–84.

Griesbach, G. S., Hovda, D. A., & Gomez-Pinilla, F. (2009). Exercise-induced improvement in cognitive performance after traumatic brain-injury in rats is dependent on BDNF activation. *Brain Research, 1288*, 105–115.

Griffin, É. W., Mullally, S., Foley, C., Warmington, S. A., O'Mara, S. M., & Kelly, Á. M. (2011). Aerobic exercise improves hippocampal function and increases BDNF in the serum of young adult males. *Physiology and Behavior, 104*, 934–941.

Halperin, J. M., Berwid, O. G., & O'Neill, S. (2014). Healthy body, healthy mind?: the effectiveness of physical activity to treat ADHD in children. *Child and Adolescent Psychiatry Clinics of North America, 23*, 899–936.

Hayes, S. M., Alosco, M. L., & Forman, D. E. (2014). The effects of aerobic exercise on cognitive and neural decline in aging and cardiovascular disease. *Current Geriatrics Reports, 3*, 282–290.

Hillman, C., Erickson, K., & Kramer, A. (2008). Be smart, exercise your heart: exercise effects on brain and cognition. *Nature Reviews Neuroscience, 9*, 58–65.

Hillman, C. H., Kamijo, K., & Scudder, M. (2011). A review of chronic and acute physical activity participation on neuroelectric measures of brain health and cognition during childhood. *Preventive Medicine, 52*, S21–S28.

Hillman, C. H., Pontifex, M. B., Castelli, D. M., Khan, N. A., Raine, L. B., Scudder, M. R., et al. (2014). Effects of the FITKids randomized controlled trial on executive control and brain function. *Pediatrics, 134*(4), e1063–1071.

Hill, E. E., Zack, E., Battaglini, C., Viru, M., Viru, A., & Hackney, A. C. (2008). Exercise and circulating cortisol levels: the intensity threshold effect. *Journal of Endocrinology Investigation, 31*, 587–591.

Holroyd, C. B., Dien, J., & Coles, M. G. (1998). Error-related scalp potentials elicited by hand and foot movements: evidence for an output-independent error-processing system in humans. *Neuroscience Letters, 242*, 65–68.

Hopkins, M. E., Davis, F. C., Van Tieghem, M. R., Whalen, P. J., & Bucci, D. J. (2012). Differential effects of acute and regular physical exercise on cognition and affect. *Neuroscience, 215*, 59–68.

Hopkins, W. F., & Johnston, D. (1988). Noradrenergic enhancement of long-term potentiation at mossy fiber synapses in the hippocampus. *Journal of Neurophysiology, 59*, 667–687.

Huang, A. M., Jen, C. J., Chen, H. F., Yu, L., Kuo, Y. M., & Chen, H. I. (2006). Compulsive exercise acutely upregulates rat hippocampal brain-derived neurotrophic factor. *Journal of Neural Transmission, 113*, 803–811.

Hu, D., Cao, P., Thiels, E., Chu, C. T., Wu, G.-Y., Oury, T. D., et al. (2007). Hippocampal long-term potentiation, memory, and longevity in mice that overexpress mitochondrial superoxide dismutase. *Neurobiology of Learning and Memory, 87*, 372–384.

Hyodo, K., Dan, I., Suwabe, K., Kyutoku, Y., Yamada, Y., Akahori, M., et al. (2012). Acute moderate exercise enhances compensatory brain activation in older adults. *Neurobiology of Aging, 33*, 2621–2632.

Inder, W. J., Hellemans, J., Swanney, M. P., Prickett, T. C. R., & Donald, R. A. (1998). Prolonged exercise increases peripheral plasma ACTH, CRH, and AVP in male athletes. *Journal of Applied Physiology, 85*, 835–841.

Jhaveri, D. J., Mackay, E. W., Hamlin, A. S., Marathe, S. V. L., Nandam, S., Vaidya, V. A., et al. (2010). Norepinephrine directly activates adult hippocampal precursors via β3 adrenergic receptors. *Journal of Neuroscience, 30*, 2795–2806.

Joyce, J., Graydon, J., McMorris, T., & Davranche, K. (2009). The time course effect of moderate intensity exercise on response execution and response inhibition. *Brain and Cognition, 71*, 14–19.

Juraschek, S. P., Blaha, M. J., Blumenthal, R. S., Brawner, C., Qureshi, W., Keteyian, S. J., et al. (2015). Cardiorespiratory fitness and incident diabetes: the fit (Henry Ford exercise testing) project. *Diabetes Care* pii: dc142714. [Epub ahead of print].

Kadzierski, W., Aguila-Mansilla, N., Kozlowski, G. P., & Porter, J. C. (1994). Expression of tyrosine hydroxylase gene in cultured hypothalamic cells: roles of protein kinase A and C. *Journal of Neurochemistry, 62*, 431–437.

Kahn, R. S., Harvey, P. D., Davidson, M., Keefe, R. S., Apter, S., Neale, J. M., et al. (1994). Neuropsychological correlates of central monoamine function in chronic schizophrenia: relationship between CSF metabolites and cognitive function. *Schizophrenia Research, 11*, 217–224.

Kamijo, K., Nishihira, Y., Hatta, A., Kaneda, K., Wasaka, T., Kida, T., et al. (2004). Differential influences of exercise intensity on information processing in the central nervous system. *European Journal of Applied Physiology, 92*, 305–311.

Kamijo, K., & Takeda, Y. (2013). Physical activity and trial-by-trial adjustments of response conflict. *Journal of Sport and Exercise Psychology, 35*, 398–407.

Kamijo, K., Takeda, Y., & Hillman, C. H. (2011). The relation of physical activity to functional connectivity between brain regions. *Clincal Neurophysiology, 122*, 81–89.

Katsuki, H., Izumi, Y., & Zorumski, C. F. (1997). Noradrenergic regulation of synaptic plasticity in the hippocampal CA1 region. *Jounal of Neurophysiology, 77*, 3013–3020.

Kattenstroth, J. C., Kalisch, T., Holt, S., Tegenthoff, M., & Dinse, H. R. (2013). Six months of dance intervention enhances postural, sensorimotor, and cognitive performance in elderly without affecting cardio-respiratory functions. *Frontiers in Aging Neuroscience.* http://dx.doi.org/10.3389/fnagi.2013.00005.

Klingberg, T. (2010). Training and plasticity of working memory. *Trends in Cognitive Science, 14*, 317–324.

Konicki, P. E., Owen, R. R., Litman, R. E., & Pickar, D. E. (1991). The acute effects of central- and peripheral-acting dopamine antagonists on plasma HVA in schizophrenic patients. *Life Sciences, 48*, 1411–1416.

Kopin, I. J., Bankiewicz, K. S., & Harvey-White, J. (1988). Assessment of brain dopamine metabolism from plasma HVA and MHPG during debrisoquine treatment: validation in monkeys treated with MPTP. *Neuropsychopharmacology, 1*, 119–125.

Kramer, A. F., Hahn, S., Cohen, N. J., Banich, M. T., McAuley, E., Harrison, C. R., et al. (1999). Ageing, fitness and neurocognitive function. *Nature, 400*, 418–419.

Lachaux, J. P., Rodriguez, E., Martinerie, J., & Varela, F. J. (1999). Measuring phase synchrony in brain signals. *Human Brain Mapping, 8*, 194–208.

Lambourne, K., & Tomporowski, P. D. (2010). The effect of acute exercise on cognitive task performance: a meta-regression analysis. *Brain Research, 1341*, 12–24.

Lessmann, V., Gottmann, K., & Malcangio, M. (2003). Neurotrophin secretion: current facts and future prospects. *Progress in Neurobiology, 69*, 341–374.

Liu, Y. F., Chen, H. I., Wu, C. L., Kuo, Y. M., Yu, L., Huang, A. M., et al. (2009). Differential effects of treadmill running and wheel running on spatial or aversive learning and memory: roles of amygdalar brain-derived neurotrophic factor and synaptotagmin 1. *Journal of Physiology, 587*, 3221–3231.

Lucas, S. J., Ainslie, P. N., Murrell, C. J., Thomas, K. N., Franz, E. A., & Cotter, J. D. (2012). Effect of age on exercise-induced alterations in cognitive executive function: relationship to cerebral perfusion. *Experimental Gerontology, 47*, 541–551.

Lupien, S. J., Gillin, C. J., & Hauger, R. L. (1999). Working memory is more sensitive than declarative memory to the acute effects of corticosteroids: a dose-dependent study in humans. *Behavioral Neuroscience, 113*, 420–430.

Malchow, B., Keller, K., Hasan, A., Dörfler, S., Schneider-Axmann, T., Hillmer-Vogel, U., et al. (2015). Effects of endurance training combined with cognitive remediation on everyday functioning, symptoms, and cognition in multiepisode schizophrenia patients. *Schizophrenia Bulletin* pii: sbv020. [Epub ahead of print].

Mason, J. W. (1975a). A historical view of the stress field. Part I. *Journal of Human Stress, 1*, 6–12.

Mason, J. W. (1975b). A historical view of the stress field. Part II. *Journal of Human Stress, 1*, 22–36.

Mason, J. W., Hartley, L. H., Kotchen, T. A., Mougey, E. H., Ricketts, P. T., & Jones, L. G. (1973). Plasma cortisol and norepinephrine resposnes in anticipation of muscular exercise. *Psychosomatic Medicine, 35*, 406–414.

Masuda, T., Nakagawa, S., Boku, S., Nishikawa, H., Takamura, N., Kato, A., et al. (2011). Noradrenaline increases neural precursor cells derived from adult rat dentate gyrus through β2 receptor. *Progress in Neuropsychopharmacology: Biological Psychiatry, 36*, 44–51.

Mattson, M. P. (2008). Glutamate and neurotrophic factors in neuronal plasticity and disease. *Annals of the New York Academy of Sciences, 1144*, 97–112.

McGaugh, J. L., Cahill, L., & Roozendaal, B. (1996). Involvement of the amygdala in memory storage: interaction with other brain systems. *Proceedings of the National Academy of Sciences of the United States of America, 93*, 13508–13514.

McMorris, T. (2009). Exercise and cognitive function: a neuroendocrinological explanation. In T. McMorris, P. D. Tomporowski, & M. Audiffren (Eds.), *Exercise and cognitive function* (pp. 54–98). Chichester: Wiley-Blackwell.

McMorris, T., Collard, K., Corbett, J., Dicks, M., & Swain, J. P. (2008). A test of the catecholamines hypothesis for an acute exercise–cognition interaction. *Pharmacology, Biochemistry and Behavior, 89*, 106–115.

McMorris, T., Davranche, K., Jones, G., Hall, B., & Minter, C. (2009). Acute incremental exercise, performance of a central executive task, and sympathoadrenal system and hypothalamic-pituitary-adrenal axis activity. *International Journal of Psychophysiology, 73*, 334–340.

McMorris, T., & Graydon, J. (1996a). The effect of exercise on the decision-making performance of experienced and inexperienced soccer players. *Research Quarterly for Exercise and Sport, 67*, 109–114.

McMorris, T., & Graydon, J. (1996b). Effect of exercise on soccer decision-making tasks of differing complexities. *Journal of Human Movement Studies, 30*, 177–193.

McMorris, T., & Graydon, J. (1997). The effect of exercise on cognitive performance in soccer-specific tests. *Journal of Sports Science, 15*, 459–468.

McMorris, T., & Hale, B. J. (2012). Differential effects of differing intensities of acute exercise on speed and accuracy of cognition: a meta-analytical investigation. *Brain and Cognition, 80*, 338–351.

McMorris, T., & Hale, B. J. (2015). Is there an acute exercise-induced physiological/biochemical threshold which triggers increased speed of cognitive functioning? A meta-analytic investigation. *Journal of Sports and Health Sciences, 4*, 4–13.

McMorris, T., Hale, B. J., Corbett, J., Robertson, K., & Hodgson, C. L. (2015). Does acute exercise affect the performance of whole-body, psychomotor skills in an inverted-U fashion? A meta-analytic investigation. *Physiology and Behavior, 141C*, 180–189.

McMorris, T., Myers, S., MacGillivary, W. W., Sexsmith, J. R., Fallowfield, J., Graydon, J., et al. (1999). Exercise, plasma catecholamine concentration and decision-making performance of soccer players on a soccer-specific test. *Journal of Sports Science, 17*, 667–676.

McMorris, T., Sproule, J., Child, R., Draper, S., & Sexsmith, J. R. (2000). The measurement of plasma lactate and catecholamine thresholds: a comparison of methods. *European Journal of Applied Physiology and Occupational Physiology, 82*, 262–267.

McMorris, T., Sproule, J., Turner, A., & Hale, B. J. (2011). Acute, intermediate intensity exercise, and speed and accuracy in working memory tasks: a meta-analytical comparison of effects. *Physiology and Behavior, 102*, 421–428.

McNemar, Q. (1947). Note on the sampling error of the difference between correlated proportions or percentages. *Psychometrika, 12*, 153–157.

Meneses, A. (1999). 5-HT system and cognition. *Neuroscience and Biobehavioral Reviews, 23*, 1111–1125.

Miyake, A., Friedman, N. P., Emerson, M. J., Witzki, A. H., & Howerter, A. (2000). The unity and diversity of executive functions and their contributions to complex "frontal lobe" tasks: a latent variable analysis. *Cognitive Psychology, 41*, 49–100.

Miyake, A., & Shah, P. (1999). Toward unified theories of working memory: emerging general consensus, unresolved theoretical issues, and future research directions. In A. Miyake, & P. Shah (Eds.), *Models of working memory* (pp. 442–481). New York: Cambridge University Press.

Miyashita, T., & Williams, C. L. (2006). Epinephrine administration increases neural impulses propagated along the vagus nerve: role of peripheral beta-adrenergic receptors. *Neurobiology of Learning and Memory, 85*, 116–124.

Moore, R. D., Romine, M. W., O'Conner, P. J., & Tomporowski, P. D. (2012). The influence of exercise-induced fatigue on cognitive function. *Journal of Sports Science, 30*, 841–850.

Neeper, S. A., Gomez-Pinilla, F., Choi, J., & Cotman, C. W. (1995). Exercise and brain neurotrophins. *Nature, 373*, 109.

Niemann, C., Godde, B., & Voelcker-Rehage, C. (2014). Not only cardiovascular, but also coordinative exercise increases hippocampal volume in older adults. *Frontiers in Aging Neuroscience, 6*, 170. http://dx.doi.org/10.3389/fnagi.2014.00170.

Nieuwenhuis, S., Yeung, N., van den Wildenburg, W., & Ridderinkhof, K. R. (2003). Electrophysiological correlates of anterior cingulate function in a go/no-go task: effects of response conflict and trial type frequency. *Cognitive, Affective, and Behavioral Neuroscience, 3*, 17–26.

Ogoh, S., Tsukamoto, H., Hirasawa, A., Hasegawa, H., Hirose, N., & Hashimoto, T. (2014). The effect of changes in cerebral blood flow on cognitive function during exercise. *Physiological Reports, 2*. http://dx.doi.org/10.14814/phy2.12163.

Park, E., Chan, O., Li, Q., Kiraly, M., Matthews, S. G., Vranic, M., et al. (2005). Changes in basal hypalamo-pituitary-adrenal activity during exercise are centrally mediated. *American Journal of Physiology: Regulatory, Integrative and Comparative Physiology, 289*, R1360–R1371.

Pesce, C. (2009). An integrated approach to the effect of acute and chronic exercise on cognition: the linked role of individual and task constraints. In T. McMorris, P. D. Tomporowski, & M. Audiffren (Eds.), *Exercise and cognitive function* (pp. 213–226). Chichester: Wiley-Blackwell.

Pesce, C. (2012). Shifting the focus from quantitative to qualitative exercise characteristics in exercise and cognition research. *Journal of Sport and Exercise Psychology, 34*, 766–786.

Pesce, C., Capranica, L., Tessitore, A., & Figura, F. (2003). Focusing of visual attention under submaximal physical load. *International Journal of Sport and Exercise Psychology*, 1, 275–292.

Peters, J., Dauvermann, M., Mette, C., Platen, P., Franke, J., Hinrichs, T., et al. (2009). Voxel-based morphometry reveals an association between aerobic capacity and grey matter density in the right anterior insula. *Neuroscience, 163*, 1102–1108.

Peyrin, L., Pequignot, J. M., Lacour, J. R., & Fourcade, J. (1987). Relationships between catecholamine or 3-methoxy 4-hydroxy phenylglycol changes and the mental performance under submaximal exercise in man. *Psychopharmacology, 93*, 188–192.

Polich, J. (2007). Updating P300: an integrative theory of P3a and P3b. *Clinical Neurophysiology, 118*, 2128–2148.

van Praag, H., Christie, B. R., Sejnowski, T. J., & Gage, F. H. (1999). Running enhances neurogenesis, learning, and long-term potentiation in mice. *Proceedings of the National Academy of Sciences of the United States of America, 96*, 13427–13431.

van Praag, H., Fleshner, M., Schwartz, M. W., & Mattson, M. P. (2014). Exercise, energy intake, glucose homeostasis, and the brain. *Journal of Neuroscience, 34*, 15139–15149.

Robbins, T. W., & Roberts, A. C. (2007). Differential regulation of fronto-executive function by the monoamines and acetylcholine. *Cerebral Cortex, 17*(Suppl. 1), i151–i160.

Robergs, R. A., & Landwehr, R. (2005). The surprising history of the "HRmax=220-age" equation. *Journal of Exercise Physiology Online, 5*, 1–10.

Rohrbaugh, J. W., & Gaillard, A. W. K. (1983). Sensory and motor aspects of the contingent negative variation. In A. W. K. Gaillard, & W. Ritter (Eds.), *Tutorials in ERP research: Endogenous components* (pp. 269–310). Amsterdam: North-Holland.

Rooks, C. R., Thom, N. J., McCully, K. K., & Dishman, R. K. (2010). Effects of incremental exercise on cerebral oxygenation measured by near-infrared spectroscopy: a systematic review. *Progress in Neurobiology, 92*, 134–150.

Rosano, C., Venkatraman, V. K., Guralnik, J., Newman, A. B., Glynn, N. W., Launer, L., et al. (2010). Psychomotor speed and functional brain MRI 2 years after completing a physical activity treatment. *Journals of Gerontology, Series A, 65A*, 639–647.

Roth, R. H., Tam, S.-Y., Ida, Y., Yang, J.-X., & Deutch, A. Y. (1988). Stress and the mesocorticolimbic dopamine systems. *Annals of the New York Academy of Sciences, 537*, 138–147.

Ruscheweyh, R., Willemer, C., Kruger, K., Duning, T., Warnecke, T., Sommer, J., et al. (2011). Physical activity and memory functions: an interventional study. *Neurobiology of Aging, 32*, 1304–1319.

Sandroff, B. M., Hillman, C. H., Benedict, R. M., & Motl, R. W. (2015). Acute effects of walking, cycling, and yoga exercise on cognition in persons with relapsing-remitting multiple sclerosis without impaired cognitive processing speed. *Journal of Clinical and Experimental Neuropsychology, 37*, 209–219.

Simmonds, D. J., Pekara, J. J., & Mostofsky, S. H. (2008). Meta-analysis of Go/No-go tasks demonstrating that fMRI activation associated with response inhibition is task-dependent. *Neuropsychologia, 46*, 224–232.

Simon, J. R. (1969). Reactions towards the source of stimulation. *Journal of Experimental Psychology, 81*, 174–176.

Smith, J. C., Nielson, K. A., Woodard, J. L., Seidenberg, M., Durgerian, S., Antuono, P., et al. (2011). Interactive effects of physical activity and APOE-epsilon 4 on BOLD semantic memory activation in healthy elders. *NeuroImage, 54*, 635–644.

Straube, T., Korz, V., Balschun, D., & Frey, J. U. (2003). Requirement of β-adrenergic receptor activation and protein synthesis for LTP-reinforcement by novelty in rat dentate gyrus. *Journal of Physiology (Lond), 552*, 953–960.

Stroop, J. R. (1935). Studies of interference in serial verbal reactions. *Journal of Experimental Psychology, 18*, 643–662.

Stroth, S., Reinhardt, R. K., Thone, J., Hille, K., Schneider, M., Hartel, S., et al. (2010). Impact of aerobic exercise training on cognitive functions and affect associated to the COMT polymorphism in young adults. *Neurobiology of Learning and Memory, 94*, 364–372.

Strüder, H. K., Hollmann, W., Platen, P., Rost, R., Weicker, H., Kirchhof, O., et al. (1999). Neuroendocrine system and mental function in sedentary and endurance-trained elderly males. *International Journal of Sports Medicine, 20*, 159–166.

Tanaka, H., Monahan, K. D., & Seals, D. R. (2001). Age-predicted maximal heart rate revisited. *Journal of the American College of Cardiology, 37*, 153–156.

Tomporowski, P. D. (2003). Effects of acute bouts of exercise on cognition. *Acta Psychologica, 112*, 297–324.

Tomporowski, P. D. (2009). Methodological issues: research approaches, research design and task selection. In T. McMorris, P. D. Tomporowski, & M. Audiffren (Eds.), *Exercise and cognitive function* (pp. 139–177). Chichester: Wiley-Blackwell.

Tomporowski, P. D., & Ellis, N. R. (1986). Effects of exercise on cognitive processes: a review. *Psychological Bulletin, 99*, 338–346.

Tsai, C.-L., Wang, C.-H., Pan, C.-Y., & Chen, F.-C. (2015). The effects of long-term resistance exercise on the relationship between neurocognitive performance and GH, IGF-1, and homocysteine levels in the elderly. *Frontiers in Behavioral Neuroscience*. http://dx.doi.org/10.3389/fnbeh.2015.00023.

Tsuji, M., Yamane, H., Yamada, N., Iida, H., Taga, C., & Myojin, T. (1986). Studies on 3-methoxy-4-hydroxyphenylglycol (MHPG) and 3: 4-dihydroxyphenylglycol (DHPG) levels in human urine, plasma and cerebrospinal fluids, and their significance in studies of depression. *Japanese Journal of Psychiatry and Neurology, 40*, 47–56.

Tulen, J. H. M., van de Wetering, B. J. M., Kruijk, M. P. C.W., von Saher, R. A., Moleman, P., Boomsma, F., et al. (1992). Cardiovascular, neuroendocrine, and sedative responses to four graded doses of clonidine in a placebo-controlled study. *Biological Psychiatry, 32*, 485–500.

Tümer, N., Demirel, H. A., Serova, L., Sabban, E. L., Broxson, C. S., & Powers, S. K. (2001). Gene expression of catecholamine biosynthetic enzymes following exercise: modulation by age. *Neuroscience, 103*, 703–711.

Waterhouse, B. D., Moises, H. C., & Woodward, D. J. (1980). Noradrenergic modulation of somatosensory cortical neuronal responses to iontophoretically applied putative transmitters. *Experimental Neurology, 69*, 30–49.

Waterhouse, B. D., Moises, H. C., & Woodward, D. J. (1981). Alpha-receptor-mediated facilitation of somatosensory cortical neuronal responses to excitatory synaptic inputs and iontophoretically applied acetylcholine. *Neuropharmacology, 20*, 907–920.

Waterhouse, B., Moises, H., & Woodward, D. J. (1998). Phasic activation of the locus coeruleus enhances responses of primary sensory cortical neurons to peripheral receptive field stimulation. *Brain Research, 790*, 33–44.

Waterhouse, E. G., & Xu, B. (2009). New insights into the role of brain-derived neurotrophic factor in synaptic plasticity. *Molecular and Cellular Neurscience, 42*, 81–89.

Whiteman, A. S., Young, D. E., He, X., Chen, T. C., Wagenaar, R. C., Stern, C. E., et al. (2014). Interaction between serum BDNF and aerobic fitness predicts recognition memory in healthy young adults. *Behavioral Brain Research, 259*, 302–312.

Wickens, J. R., Horvitz, J. C., Costa, R. M., & Killcross, S. (2007). Dopaminergic mechanisms in actions and habits. *Journal of Neuroscience, 27*, 8181–8183.

Winter, B., Breitenstein, C., Mooren, F. C., Voelker, K., Fobker, M., Lechtermann, A., et al. (2007). High impact running improves learning. *Neurobiology of Learning and Memory, 87*, 597–609.

Wittert, G. A., Livesey, J. H., Espiner, E. A., & Donald, R. A. (1996). Adaptation of the hypothalamopituitary adrenal axis to chronic exercise in humans. *Medicine and Science in Sports and Exercise, 28*, 1015–1019.

Yamamoto, Y., Miyashita, M., Hughson, R. L., Tmura, S., Shiohara, M., & Mutoh, Y. (1991). The ventilatory threshold gives maximal lactate steady state. *European Journal of Applied Physiology, 63*, 55–59.

Yanagisawa, H., Dan, I., Tsuzuki, D., Kato, M., Okamoto, M., Kyutoku, Y., et al. (2010). Acute moderate exercise elicits increased dorsolateral prefrontal activation and improves cognitive performance with Stroop test. *NeuroImage, 50*, 1702–1710.

Zheng, H., Liu, Y., Li, W., Yang, B., Chen, D., Wang, X., et al. (2006). Beneficial effects of exercise and its molecular mechanisms on depression in rats. *Behavioral Brain Research, 168*, 47–55.

Zhu, N., Jacobs, D. R., Jr., Schreiner, P. J., Yaffe, K., Bryan, N., Launer, L. J., et al. (2014). Cardiorespiratory fitness and cognitive function in middle age: the CARDIA study. *Neurology, 82*, 1339–1346.

Index

Note: Page numbers followed by "f" or "t" indicate figures and tables respectively.